T0142356

Lecture Notes in Computer Science 11208

Commenced Publication in 1973
Founding and Former Series Editors:
Gerhard Goos, Juris Hartmanis, and Jan van Leeuwen

More information about this series at http://www.springer.com/series/7412

Vittorio Ferrari · Martial Hebert
Cristian Sminchisescu · Yair Weiss (Eds.)

Computer Vision – ECCV 2018

15th European Conference
Munich, Germany, September 8–14, 2018
Proceedings, Part IV

Springer

Editors
Vittorio Ferrari
Google Research
Zurich
Switzerland

Cristian Sminchisescu
Google Research
Zurich
Switzerland

Martial Hebert
Carnegie Mellon University
Pittsburgh, PA
USA

Yair Weiss
Hebrew University of Jerusalem
Jerusalem
Israel

ISSN 0302-9743   ISSN 1611-3349   (electronic)
Lecture Notes in Computer Science
ISBN 978-3-030-01224-3   ISBN 978-3-030-01225-0   (eBook)
https://doi.org/10.1007/978-3-030-01225-0

Library of Congress Control Number: 2018955489

LNCS Sublibrary: SL6 – Image Processing, Computer Vision, Pattern Recognition, and Graphics

This Springer imprint is published by the registered company Springer Nature Switzerland AG
The registered company address is: Gewerbestrasse 11, 6330 Cham, Switzerland

Foreword

It was our great pleasure to host the European Conference on Computer Vision 2018 in Munich, Germany. This constituted by far the largest ECCV event ever. With close to 2,900 registered participants and another 600 on the waiting list one month before the conference, participation more than doubled since the last ECCV in Amsterdam. We believe that this is due to a dramatic growth of the computer vision community combined with the popularity of Munich as a major European hub of culture, science, and industry. The conference took place in the heart of Munich in the concert hall Gasteig with workshops and tutorials held at the downtown campus of the Technical University of Munich.

One of the major innovations for ECCV 2018 was the free perpetual availability of all conference and workshop papers, which is often referred to as open access. We note that this is not precisely the same use of the term as in the Budapest declaration. Since 2013, CVPR and ICCV have had their papers hosted by the Computer Vision Foundation (CVF), in parallel with the IEEE Xplore version. This has proved highly beneficial to the computer vision community.

We are delighted to announce that for ECCV 2018 a very similar arrangement was put in place with the cooperation of Springer. In particular, the author's final version will be freely available in perpetuity on a CVF page, while SpringerLink will continue to host a version with further improvements, such as activating reference links and including video. We believe that this will give readers the best of both worlds; researchers who are focused on the technical content will have a freely available version in an easily accessible place, while subscribers to SpringerLink will continue to have the additional benefits that this provides. We thank Alfred Hofmann from Springer for helping to negotiate this agreement, which we expect will continue for future versions of ECCV.

September 2018

Horst Bischof
Daniel Cremers
Bernt Schiele
Ramin Zabih

Preface

Welcome to the proceedings of the 2018 European Conference on Computer Vision (ECCV 2018) held in Munich, Germany. We are delighted to present this volume reflecting a strong and exciting program, the result of an extensive review process. In total, we received 2,439 valid paper submissions. Of these, 776 were accepted (31.8%): 717 as posters (29.4%) and 59 as oral presentations (2.4%). All oral presentations were presented as posters as well. The program selection process was complicated this year by the large increase in the number of submitted papers, +65% over ECCV 2016, and the use of CMT3 for the first time for a computer vision conference. The program selection process was supported by four program co-chairs (PCs), 126 area chairs (ACs), and 1,199 reviewers with reviews assigned.

We were primarily responsible for the design and execution of the review process. Beyond administrative rejections, we were involved in acceptance decisions only in the very few cases where the ACs were not able to agree on a decision. As PCs, and as is customary in the field, we were not allowed to co-author a submission. General co-chairs and other co-organizers who played no role in the review process were permitted to submit papers, and were treated as any other author is.

Acceptance decisions were made by two independent ACs. The ACs also made a joint recommendation for promoting papers to oral status. We decided on the final selection of oral presentations based on the ACs' recommendations. There were 126 ACs, selected according to their technical expertise, experience, and geographical diversity (63 from European, nine from Asian/Australian, and 54 from North American institutions). Indeed, 126 ACs is a substantial increase in the number of ACs due to the natural increase in the number of papers and to our desire to maintain the number of papers assigned to each AC to a manageable number so as to ensure quality. The ACs were aided by the 1,199 reviewers to whom papers were assigned for reviewing. The Program Committee was selected from committees of previous ECCV, ICCV, and CVPR conferences and was extended on the basis of suggestions from the ACs. Having a large pool of Program Committee members for reviewing allowed us to match expertise while reducing reviewer loads. No more than eight papers were assigned to a reviewer, maintaining the reviewers' load at the same level as ECCV 2016 despite the increase in the number of submitted papers.

Conflicts of interest between ACs, Program Committee members, and papers were identified based on the home institutions, and on previous collaborations of all researchers involved. To find institutional conflicts, all authors, Program Committee members, and ACs were asked to list the Internet domains of their current institutions. We assigned on average approximately 18 papers to each AC. The papers were assigned using the affinity scores from the Toronto Paper Matching System (TPMS) and additional data from the OpenReview system, managed by a UMass group. OpenReview used additional information from ACs' and authors' records to identify collaborations and to generate matches. OpenReview was invaluable in refining conflict definitions and in generating quality matches. The only glitch is that, once the matches were generated, a small percentage of papers were unassigned because of discrepancies between the OpenReview conflicts and the conflicts entered in CMT3. We manually assigned these papers. This glitch is revealing of the challenge of using multiple systems at once (CMT3 and OpenReview in this case), which needs to be addressed in future.

After assignment of papers to ACs, the ACs suggested seven reviewers per paper from the Program Committee pool. The selection and rank ordering were facilitated by the TPMS affinity scores visible to the ACs for each paper/reviewer pair. The final assignment of papers to reviewers was generated again through OpenReview in order to account for refined conflict definitions. This required new features in the OpenReview matching system to accommodate the ECCV workflow, in particular to incorporate selection ranking, and maximum reviewer load. Very few papers received fewer than three reviewers after matching and were handled through manual assignment. Reviewers were then asked to comment on the merit of each paper and to make an initial recommendation ranging from definitely reject to definitely accept, including a borderline rating. The reviewers were also asked to suggest explicit questions they wanted to see answered in the authors' rebuttal. The initial review period was five weeks. Because of the delay in getting all the reviews in, we had to delay the final release of the reviews by four days. However, because of the slack included at the tail end of the schedule, we were able to maintain the decision target date with sufficient time for all the phases. We reassigned over 100 reviews from 40 reviewers during the review period. Unfortunately, the main reason for these reassignments was reviewers declining to review, after having accepted to do so. Other reasons included technical relevance and occasional unidentified conflicts. We express our thanks to the emergency reviewers who generously accepted to perform these reviews under short notice. In addition, a substantial number of manual corrections had to do with reviewers using a different email address than the one that was used at the time of the reviewer invitation. This is revealing of a broader issue with identifying users by email addresses that change frequently enough to cause significant problems during the timespan of the conference process.

The authors were then given the opportunity to rebut the reviews, to identify factual errors, and to address the specific questions raised by the reviewers over a seven-day rebuttal period. The exact format of the rebuttal was the object of considerable debate among the organizers, as well as with prior organizers. At issue is to balance giving the author the opportunity to respond completely and precisely to the reviewers, e.g., by including graphs of experiments, while avoiding requests for completely new material or experimental results not included in the original paper. In the end, we decided on the two-page PDF document in conference format. Following this rebuttal period, reviewers and ACs discussed papers at length, after which reviewers finalized their evaluation and gave a final recommendation to the ACs. A significant percentage of the reviewers did enter their final recommendation if it did not differ from their initial recommendation. Given the tight schedule, we did not wait until all were entered.

After this discussion period, each paper was assigned to a second AC. The AC/paper matching was again run through OpenReview. Again, the OpenReview team worked quickly to implement the features specific to this process, in this case accounting for the existing AC assignment, as well as minimizing the fragmentation across ACs, so that each AC had on average only 5.5 buddy ACs to communicate with. The largest number was 11. Given the complexity of the conflicts, this was a very efficient set of assignments from OpenReview. Each paper was then evaluated by its assigned pair of ACs. For each paper, we required each of the two ACs assigned to certify both the final recommendation and the metareview (aka consolidation report). In all cases, after extensive discussions, the two ACs arrived at a common acceptance decision. We maintained these decisions, with the caveat that we did evaluate, sometimes going back to the ACs, a few papers for which the final acceptance decision substantially deviated from the consensus from the reviewers, amending three decisions in the process.

We want to thank everyone involved in making ECCV 2018 possible. The success of ECCV 2018 depended on the quality of papers submitted by the authors, and on the very hard work of the ACs and the Program Committee members. We are particularly grateful to the OpenReview team (Melisa Bok, Ari Kobren, Andrew McCallum, Michael Spector) for their support, in particular their willingness to implement new features, often on a tight schedule, to Laurent Charlin for the use of the Toronto Paper Matching System, to the CMT3 team, in particular in dealing with all the issues that arise when using a new system, to Friedrich Fraundorfer and Quirin Lohr for maintaining the online version of the program, and to the CMU staff (Keyla Cook, Lynnetta Miller, Ashley Song, Nora Kazour) for assisting with data entry/editing in CMT3. Finally, the preparation of these proceedings would not have been possible without the diligent effort of the publication chairs, Albert Ali Salah and Hamdi Dibeklioğlu, and of Anna Kramer and Alfred Hofmann from Springer.

September 2018   Vittorio Ferrari
                                                     Martial Hebert
                                             Cristian Sminchisescu
                                                        Yair Weiss

Organization

General Chairs

Horst Bischof	Graz University of Technology, Austria
Daniel Cremers	Technical University of Munich, Germany
Bernt Schiele	Saarland University, Max Planck Institute for Informatics, Germany
Ramin Zabih	CornellNYCTech, USA

Program Committee Co-chairs

Vittorio Ferrari	University of Edinburgh, UK
Martial Hebert	Carnegie Mellon University, USA
Cristian Sminchisescu	Lund University, Sweden
Yair Weiss	Hebrew University, Israel

Local Arrangements Chairs

Björn Menze	Technical University of Munich, Germany
Matthias Niessner	Technical University of Munich, Germany

Workshop Chairs

Stefan Roth	TU Darmstadt, Germany
Laura Leal-Taixé	Technical University of Munich, Germany

Tutorial Chairs

Michael Bronstein	Università della Svizzera Italiana, Switzerland
Laura Leal-Taixé	Technical University of Munich, Germany

Website Chair

Friedrich Fraundorfer	Graz University of Technology, Austria

Demo Chairs

Federico Tombari	Technical University of Munich, Germany
Joerg Stueckler	Technical University of Munich, Germany

Publicity Chair

Giovanni Maria   University of Catania, Italy
  Farinella

Industrial Liaison Chairs

Florent Perronnin   Naver Labs, France
Yunchao Gong   Snap, USA
Helmut Grabner   Logitech, Switzerland

Finance Chair

Gerard Medioni   Amazon, University of Southern California, USA

Publication Chairs

Albert Ali Salah   Boğaziçi University, Turkey
Hamdi Dibeklioğlu   Bilkent University, Turkey

Area Chairs

Kalle Åström   Lund University, Sweden
Zeynep Akata   University of Amsterdam, The Netherlands
Joao Barreto   University of Coimbra, Portugal
Ronen Basri   Weizmann Institute of Science, Israel
Dhruv Batra   Georgia Tech and Facebook AI Research, USA
Serge Belongie   Cornell University, USA
Rodrigo Benenson   Google, Switzerland
Hakan Bilen   University of Edinburgh, UK
Matthew Blaschko   KU Leuven, Belgium
Edmond Boyer   Inria, France
Gabriel Brostow   University College London, UK
Thomas Brox   University of Freiburg, Germany
Marcus Brubaker   York University, Canada
Barbara Caputo   Politecnico di Torino and the Italian Institute
                           of Technology, Italy
Tim Cootes   University of Manchester, UK
Trevor Darrell   University of California, Berkeley, USA
Larry Davis   University of Maryland at College Park, USA
Andrew Davison   Imperial College London, UK
Fernando de la Torre   Carnegie Mellon University, USA
Irfan Essa   GeorgiaTech, USA
Ali Farhadi   University of Washington, USA
Paolo Favaro   University of Bern, Switzerland
Michael Felsberg   Linköping University, Sweden

Yasuyuki Matsushita	Osaka University, Japan
Dimitris Metaxas	Rutgers University, USA
Greg Mori	Simon Fraser University, Canada
Vittorio Murino	Istituto Italiano di Tecnologia, Italy
Richard Newcombe	Oculus Research, USA
Minh Hoai Nguyen	Stony Brook University, USA
Sebastian Nowozin	Microsoft Research Cambridge, UK
Aude Oliva	MIT, USA
Bjorn Ommer	Heidelberg University, Germany
Tomas Pajdla	Czech Technical University in Prague, Czechia
Maja Pantic	Imperial College London and Samsung AI Research Centre Cambridge, UK
Caroline Pantofaru	Google, USA
Devi Parikh	Georgia Tech and Facebook AI Research, USA
Sylvain Paris	Adobe Research, USA
Vladimir Pavlovic	Rutgers University, USA
Marcello Pelillo	University of Venice, Italy
Patrick Pérez	Valeo, France
Robert Pless	George Washington University, USA
Thomas Pock	Graz University of Technology, Austria
Jean Ponce	Inria, France
Gerard Pons-Moll	MPII, Saarland Informatics Campus, Germany
Long Quan	Hong Kong University of Science and Technology, SAR China
Stefan Roth	TU Darmstadt, Germany
Carsten Rother	University of Heidelberg, Germany
Bryan Russell	Adobe Research, USA
Kate Saenko	Boston University, USA
Mathieu Salzmann	EPFL, Switzerland
Dimitris Samaras	Stony Brook University, USA
Yoichi Sato	University of Tokyo, Japan
Silvio Savarese	Stanford University, USA
Konrad Schindler	ETH Zurich, Switzerland
Cordelia Schmid	Inria, France and Google, France
Nicu Sebe	University of Trento, Italy
Fei Sha	University of Southern California, USA
Greg Shakhnarovich	TTI Chicago, USA
Jianbo Shi	University of Pennsylvania, USA
Abhinav Shrivastava	UMD and Google, USA
Yan Shuicheng	National University of Singapore, Singapore
Leonid Sigal	University of British Columbia, Canada
Josef Sivic	Czech Technical University in Prague, Czechia
Arnold Smeulders	University of Amsterdam, The Netherlands
Deqing Sun	NVIDIA, USA
Antonio Torralba	MIT, USA
Zhuowen Tu	University of California, San Diego, USA

Tinne Tuytelaars   KU Leuven, Belgium
Jasper Uijlings   Google, Switzerland
Joost van de Weijer   Computer Vision Center, Spain
Nuno Vasconcelos   University of California, San Diego, USA
Andrea Vedaldi   University of Oxford, UK
Olga Veksler   University of Western Ontario, Canada
Jakob Verbeek   Inria, France
Rene Vidal   Johns Hopkins University, USA
Daphna Weinshall   Hebrew University, Israel
Chris Williams   University of Edinburgh, UK
Lior Wolf   Tel Aviv University, Israel
Ming-Hsuan Yang   University of California at Merced, USA
Todd Zickler   Harvard University, USA
Andrew Zisserman   University of Oxford, UK

Technical Program Committee

Hassan Abu Alhaija	Peter Anderson	Arunava Banerjee
Radhakrishna Achanta	Juan Andrade-Cetto	Atsuhiko Banno
Hanno Ackermann	Mykhaylo Andriluka	Aayush Bansal
Ehsan Adeli	Anelia Angelova	Yingze Bao
Lourdes Agapito	Michel Antunes	Md Jawadul Bappy
Aishwarya Agrawal	Pablo Arbelaez	Pierre Baqué
Antonio Agudo	Vasileios Argyriou	Dániel Baráth
Eirikur Agustsson	Chetan Arora	Adrian Barbu
Karim Ahmed	Federica Arrigoni	Kobus Barnard
Byeongjoo Ahn	Vassilis Athitsos	Nick Barnes
Unaiza Ahsan	Mathieu Aubry	Francisco Barranco
Emre Akbaş	Shai Avidan	Adrien Bartoli
Eren Aksoy	Yannis Avrithis	E. Bayro-Corrochano
Yağız Aksoy	Samaneh Azadi	Paul Beardlsey
Alexandre Alahi	Hossein Azizpour	Vasileios Belagiannis
Jean-Baptiste Alayrac	Artem Babenko	Sean Bell
Samuel Albanie	Timur Bagautdinov	Ismail Ben
Cenek Albl	Andrew Bagdanov	Boulbaba Ben Amor
Saad Ali	Hessam Bagherinezhad	Gil Ben-Artzi
Rahaf Aljundi	Yuval Bahat	Ohad Ben-Shahar
Jose M. Alvarez	Min Bai	Abhijit Bendale
Humam Alwassel	Qinxun Bai	Rodrigo Benenson
Toshiyuki Amano	Song Bai	Fabian Benitez-Quiroz
Mitsuru Ambai	Xiang Bai	Fethallah Benmansour
Mohamed Amer	Peter Bajcsy	Ryad Benosman
Senjian An	Amr Bakry	Filippo Bergamasco
Cosmin Ancuti	Kavita Bala	David Bermudez

Jesus Bermudez-Cameo
Leonard Berrada
Gedas Bertasius
Ross Beveridge
Lucas Beyer
Bir Bhanu
S. Bhattacharya
Binod Bhattarai
Arnav Bhavsar
Simone Bianco
Adel Bibi
Pia Bideau
Josef Bigun
Arijit Biswas
Soma Biswas
Marten Bjoerkman
Volker Blanz
Vishnu Boddeti
Piotr Bojanowski
Terrance Boult
Yuri Boykov
Hakan Boyraz
Eric Brachmann
Samarth Brahmbhatt
Mathieu Bredif
Francois Bremond
Michael Brown
Luc Brun
Shyamal Buch
Pradeep Buddharaju
Aurelie Bugeau
Rudy Bunel
Xavier Burgos Artizzu
Darius Burschka
Andrei Bursuc
Zoya Bylinskii
Fabian Caba
Daniel Cabrini Hauagge
Cesar Cadena Lerma
Holger Caesar
Jianfei Cai
Junjie Cai
Zhaowei Cai
Simone Calderara
Neill Campbell
Octavia Camps

Xun Cao
Yanshuai Cao
Joao Carreira
Dan Casas
Daniel Castro
Jan Cech
M. Emre Celebi
Duygu Ceylan
Menglei Chai
Ayan Chakrabarti
Rudrasis Chakraborty
Shayok Chakraborty
Tat-Jen Cham
Antonin Chambolle
Antoni Chan
Sharat Chandran
Hyun Sung Chang
Ju Yong Chang
Xiaojun Chang
Soravit Changpinyo
Wei-Lun Chao
Yu-Wei Chao
Visesh Chari
Rizwan Chaudhry
Siddhartha Chaudhuri
Rama Chellappa
Chao Chen
Chen Chen
Cheng Chen
Chu-Song Chen
Guang Chen
Hsin-I Chen
Hwann-Tzong Chen
Kai Chen
Kan Chen
Kevin Chen
Liang-Chieh Chen
Lin Chen
Qifeng Chen
Ting Chen
Wei Chen
Xi Chen
Xilin Chen
Xinlei Chen
Yingcong Chen
Yixin Chen

Erkang Cheng
Jingchun Cheng
Ming-Ming Cheng
Wen-Huang Cheng
Yuan Cheng
Anoop Cherian
Liang-Tien Chia
Naoki Chiba
Shao-Yi Chien
Han-Pang Chiu
Wei-Chen Chiu
Nam Ik Cho
Sunghyun Cho
TaeEun Choe
Jongmoo Choi
Christopher Choy
Wen-Sheng Chu
Yung-Yu Chuang
Ondrej Chum
Joon Son Chung
Gökberk Cinbis
James Clark
Andrea Cohen
Forrester Cole
Toby Collins
John Collomosse
Camille Couprie
David Crandall
Marco Cristani
Canton Cristian
James Crowley
Yin Cui
Zhaopeng Cui
Bo Dai
Jifeng Dai
Qieyun Dai
Shengyang Dai
Yuchao Dai
Carlo Dal Mutto
Dima Damen
Zachary Daniels
Kostas Daniilidis
Donald Dansereau
Mohamed Daoudi
Abhishek Das
Samyak Datta

Achal Dave
Shalini De Mello
Teofilo deCampos
Joseph DeGol
Koichiro Deguchi
Alessio Del Bue
Stefanie Demirci
Jia Deng
Zhiwei Deng
Joachim Denzler
Konstantinos Derpanis
Aditya Deshpande
Alban Desmaison
Frédéric Devernay
Abhinav Dhall
Michel Dhome
Hamdi Dibeklioğlu
Mert Dikmen
Cosimo Distante
Ajay Divakaran
Mandar Dixit
Carl Doersch
Piotr Dollar
Bo Dong
Chao Dong
Huang Dong
Jian Dong
Jiangxin Dong
Weisheng Dong
Simon Donné
Gianfranco Doretto
Alexey Dosovitskiy
Matthijs Douze
Bruce Draper
Bertram Drost
Liang Du
Shichuan Du
Gregory Dudek
Zoran Duric
Pınar Duygulu
Hazım Ekenel
Tarek El-Gaaly
Ehsan Elhamifar
Mohamed Elhoseiny
Sabu Emmanuel
Ian Endres

Aykut Erdem
Erkut Erdem
Hugo Jair Escalante
Sergio Escalera
Victor Escorcia
Francisco Estrada
Davide Eynard
Bin Fan
Jialue Fan
Quanfu Fan
Chen Fang
Tian Fang
Yi Fang
Hany Farid
Giovanni Farinella
Ryan Farrell
Alireza Fathi
Christoph Feichtenhofer
Wenxin Feng
Martin Fergie
Cornelia Fermuller
Basura Fernando
Michael Firman
Bob Fisher
John Fisher
Mathew Fisher
Boris Flach
Matt Flagg
Francois Fleuret
David Fofi
Ruth Fong
Gian Luca Foresti
Per-Erik Forssén
David Fouhey
Katerina Fragkiadaki
Victor Fragoso
Jan-Michael Frahm
Jean-Sebastien Franco
Ohad Fried
Simone Frintrop
Huazhu Fu
Yun Fu
Olac Fuentes
Christopher Funk
Thomas Funkhouser
Brian Funt

Ryo Furukawa
Yasutaka Furukawa
Andrea Fusiello
Fatma Güney
Raghudeep Gadde
Silvano Galliani
Orazio Gallo
Chuang Gan
Bin-Bin Gao
Jin Gao
Junbin Gao
Ruohan Gao
Shenghua Gao
Animesh Garg
Ravi Garg
Erik Gartner
Simone Gasparin
Jochen Gast
Leon A. Gatys
Stratis Gavves
Liuhao Ge
Timnit Gebru
James Gee
Peter Gehler
Xin Geng
Guido Gerig
David Geronimo
Bernard Ghanem
Michael Gharbi
Golnaz Ghiasi
Spyros Gidaris
Andrew Gilbert
Rohit Girdhar
Ioannis Gkioulekas
Georgia Gkioxari
Guy Godin
Roland Goecke
Michael Goesele
Nuno Goncalves
Boqing Gong
Minglun Gong
Yunchao Gong
Abel Gonzalez-Garcia
Daniel Gordon
Paulo Gotardo
Stephen Gould

Venu Govindu
Helmut Grabner
Petr Gronat
Steve Gu
Josechu Guerrero
Anupam Guha
Jean-Yves Guillemaut
Alp Güler
Erhan Gündoğdu
Guodong Guo
Xinqing Guo
Ankush Gupta
Mohit Gupta
Saurabh Gupta
Tanmay Gupta
Abner Guzman Rivera
Timo Hackel
Sunil Hadap
Christian Haene
Ralf Haeusler
Levente Hajder
David Hall
Peter Hall
Stefan Haller
Ghassan Hamarneh
Fred Hamprecht
Onur Hamsici
Bohyung Han
Junwei Han
Xufeng Han
Yahong Han
Ankur Handa
Albert Haque
Tatsuya Harada
Mehrtash Harandi
Bharath Hariharan
Mahmudul Hasan
Tal Hassner
Kenji Hata
Soren Hauberg
Michal Havlena
Zeeshan Hayder
Junfeng He
Lei He
Varsha Hedau
Felix Heide

Wolfgang Heidrich
Janne Heikkila
Jared Heinly
Mattias Heinrich
Lisa Anne Hendricks
Dan Hendrycks
Stephane Herbin
Alexander Hermans
Luis Herranz
Aaron Hertzmann
Adrian Hilton
Michael Hirsch
Steven Hoi
Seunghoon Hong
Wei Hong
Anthony Hoogs
Radu Horaud
Yedid Hoshen
Omid Hosseini Jafari
Kuang-Jui Hsu
Winston Hsu
Yinlin Hu
Zhe Hu
Gang Hua
Chen Huang
De-An Huang
Dong Huang
Gary Huang
Heng Huang
Jia-Bin Huang
Qixing Huang
Rui Huang
Sheng Huang
Weilin Huang
Xiaolei Huang
Xinyu Huang
Zhiwu Huang
Tak-Wai Hui
Wei-Chih Hung
Junhwa Hur
Mohamed Hussein
Wonjun Hwang
Anders Hyden
Satoshi Ikehata
Nazlı Ikizler-Cinbis
Viorela Ila

Evren Imre
Eldar Insafutdinov
Go Irie
Hossam Isack
Ahmet Işcen
Daisuke Iwai
Hamid Izadinia
Nathan Jacobs
Suyog Jain
Varun Jampani
C. V. Jawahar
Dinesh Jayaraman
Sadeep Jayasumana
Laszlo Jeni
Hueihan Jhuang
Dinghuang Ji
Hui Ji
Qiang Ji
Fan Jia
Kui Jia
Xu Jia
Huaizu Jiang
Jiayan Jiang
Nianjuan Jiang
Tingting Jiang
Xiaoyi Jiang
Yu-Gang Jiang
Long Jin
Suo Jinli
Justin Johnson
Nebojsa Jojic
Michael Jones
Hanbyul Joo
Jungseock Joo
Ajjen Joshi
Amin Jourabloo
Frederic Jurie
Achuta Kadambi
Samuel Kadoury
Ioannis Kakadiaris
Zdenek Kalal
Yannis Kalantidis
Sinan Kalkan
Vicky Kalogeiton
Sunkavalli Kalyan
J.-K. Kamarainen

Martin Kampel
Kenichi Kanatani
Angjoo Kanazawa
Melih Kandemir
Sing Bing Kang
Zhuoliang Kang
Mohan Kankanhalli
Juho Kannala
Abhishek Kar
Amlan Kar
Svebor Karaman
Leonid Karlinsky
Zoltan Kato
Parneet Kaur
Hiroshi Kawasaki
Misha Kazhdan
Margret Keuper
Sameh Khamis
Naeemullah Khan
Salman Khan
Hadi Kiapour
Joe Kileel
Chanho Kim
Gunhee Kim
Hansung Kim
Junmo Kim
Junsik Kim
Kihwan Kim
Minyoung Kim
Tae Hyun Kim
Tae-Kyun Kim
Akisato Kimura
Zsolt Kira
Alexander Kirillov
Kris Kitani
Maria Klodt
Patrick Knöbelreiter
Jan Knopp
Reinhard Koch
Alexander Kolesnikov
Chen Kong
Naejin Kong
Shu Kong
Piotr Koniusz
Simon Korman
Andreas Koschan

Dimitrios Kosmopoulos
Satwik Kottur
Balazs Kovacs
Adarsh Kowdle
Mike Krainin
Gregory Kramida
Ranjay Krishna
Ravi Krishnan
Matej Kristan
Pavel Krsek
Volker Krueger
Alexander Krull
Hilde Kuehne
Andreas Kuhn
Arjan Kuijper
Zuzana Kukelova
Kuldeep Kulkarni
Shiro Kumano
Avinash Kumar
Vijay Kumar
Abhijit Kundu
Sebastian Kurtek
Junseok Kwon
Jan Kybic
Alexander Ladikos
Shang-Hong Lai
Wei-Sheng Lai
Jean-Francois Lalonde
John Lambert
Zhenzhong Lan
Charis Lanaras
Oswald Lanz
Dong Lao
Longin Jan Latecki
Justin Lazarow
Huu Le
Chen-Yu Lee
Gim Hee Lee
Honglak Lee
Hsin-Ying Lee
Joon-Young Lee
Seungyong Lee
Stefan Lee
Yong Jae Lee
Zhen Lei
Ido Leichter

Victor Lempitsky
Spyridon Leonardos
Marius Leordeanu
Matt Leotta
Thomas Leung
Stefan Leutenegger
Gil Levi
Aviad Levis
Jose Lezama
Ang Li
Dingzeyu Li
Dong Li
Haoxiang Li
Hongdong Li
Hongsheng Li
Hongyang Li
Jianguo Li
Kai Li
Ruiyu Li
Wei Li
Wen Li
Xi Li
Xiaoxiao Li
Xin Li
Xirong Li
Xuelong Li
Xueting Li
Yeqing Li
Yijun Li
Yin Li
Yingwei Li
Yining Li
Yongjie Li
Yu-Feng Li
Zechao Li
Zhengqi Li
Zhenyang Li
Zhizhong Li
Xiaodan Liang
Renjie Liao
Zicheng Liao
Bee Lim
Jongwoo Lim
Joseph Lim
Ser-Nam Lim
Chen-Hsuan Lin

Shih-Yao Lin
Tsung-Yi Lin
Weiyao Lin
Yen-Yu Lin
Haibin Ling
Or Litany
Roee Litman
Anan Liu
Changsong Liu
Chen Liu
Ding Liu
Dong Liu
Feng Liu
Guangcan Liu
Luoqi Liu
Miaomiao Liu
Nian Liu
Risheng Liu
Shu Liu
Shuaicheng Liu
Sifei Liu
Tyng-Luh Liu
Wanquan Liu
Weiwei Liu
Xialei Liu
Xiaoming Liu
Yebin Liu
Yiming Liu
Ziwei Liu
Zongyi Liu
Liliana Lo Presti
Edgar Lobaton
Chengjiang Long
Mingsheng Long
Roberto Lopez-Sastre
Amy Loufti
Brian Lovell
Canyi Lu
Cewu Lu
Feng Lu
Huchuan Lu
Jiajun Lu
Jiasen Lu
Jiwen Lu
Yang Lu
Yujuan Lu

Simon Lucey
Jian-Hao Luo
Jiebo Luo
Pablo Márquez-Neila
Matthias Müller
Chao Ma
Chih-Yao Ma
Lin Ma
Shugao Ma
Wei-Chiu Ma
Zhanyu Ma
Oisin Mac Aodha
Will Maddern
Ludovic Magerand
Marcus Magnor
Vijay Mahadevan
Mohammad Mahoor
Michael Maire
Subhransu Maji
Ameesh Makadia
Atsuto Maki
Yasushi Makihara
Mateusz Malinowski
Tomasz Malisiewicz
Arun Mallya
Roberto Manduchi
Junhua Mao
Dmitrii Marin
Joe Marino
Kenneth Marino
Elisabeta Marinoiu
Ricardo Martin
Aleix Martinez
Julieta Martinez
Aaron Maschinot
Jonathan Masci
Bogdan Matei
Diana Mateus
Stefan Mathe
Kevin Matzen
Bruce Maxwell
Steve Maybank
Walterio Mayol-Cuevas
Mason McGill
Stephen Mckenna
Roey Mechrez

Christopher Mei
Heydi Mendez-Vazquez
Deyu Meng
Thomas Mensink
Bjoern Menze
Domingo Mery
Qiguang Miao
Tomer Michaeli
Antoine Miech
Ondrej Miksik
Anton Milan
Gregor Miller
Cai Minjie
Majid Mirmehdi
Ishan Misra
Niloy Mitra
Anurag Mittal
Nirbhay Modhe
Davide Modolo
Pritish Mohapatra
Pascal Monasse
Mathew Monfort
Taesup Moon
Sandino Morales
Vlad Morariu
Philippos Mordohai
Francesc Moreno
Henrique Morimitsu
Yael Moses
Ben-Ezra Moshe
Roozbeh Mottaghi
Yadong Mu
Lopamudra Mukherjee
Mario Munich
Ana Murillo
Damien Muselet
Armin Mustafa
Siva Karthik Mustikovela
Moin Nabi
Sobhan Naderi
Hajime Nagahara
Varun Nagaraja
Tushar Nagarajan
Arsha Nagrani
Nikhil Naik
Atsushi Nakazawa

P. J. Narayanan
Charlie Nash
Lakshmanan Nataraj
Fabian Nater
Lukáš Neumann
Natalia Neverova
Alejandro Newell
Phuc Nguyen
Xiaohan Nie
David Nilsson
Ko Nishino
Zhenxing Niu
Shohei Nobuhara
Klas Nordberg
Mohammed Norouzi
David Novotny
Ifeoma Nwogu
Matthew O'Toole
Guillaume Obozinski
Jean-Marc Odobez
Eyal Ofek
Ferda Ofli
Tae-Hyun Oh
Iason Oikonomidis
Takeshi Oishi
Takahiro Okabe
Takayuki Okatani
Vlad Olaru
Michael Opitz
Jose Oramas
Vicente Ordonez
Ivan Oseledets
Aljosa Osep
Magnus Oskarsson
Martin R. Oswald
Wanli Ouyang
Andrew Owens
Mustafa Özuysal
Jinshan Pan
Xingang Pan
Rameswar Panda
Sharath Pankanti
Julien Pansiot
Nicolas Papadakis
George Papandreou
N. Papanikolopoulos

Hyun Soo Park
In Kyu Park
Jaesik Park
Omkar Parkhi
Alvaro Parra Bustos
C. Alejandro Parraga
Vishal Patel
Deepak Pathak
Ioannis Patras
Viorica Patraucean
Genevieve Patterson
Kim Pedersen
Robert Peharz
Selen Pehlivan
Xi Peng
Bojan Pepik
Talita Perciano
Federico Pernici
Adrian Peter
Stavros Petridis
Vladimir Petrovic
Henning Petzka
Tomas Pfister
Trung Pham
Justus Piater
Massimo Piccardi
Sudeep Pillai
Pedro Pinheiro
Lerrel Pinto
Bernardo Pires
Aleksis Pirinen
Fiora Pirri
Leonid Pischulin
Tobias Ploetz
Bryan Plummer
Yair Poleg
Jean Ponce
Gerard Pons-Moll
Jordi Pont-Tuset
Alin Popa
Fatih Porikli
Horst Possegger
Viraj Prabhu
Andrea Prati
Maria Priisalu
Véronique Prinet

Victor Prisacariu
Jan Prokaj
Nicolas Pugeault
Luis Puig
Ali Punjani
Senthil Purushwalkam
Guido Pusiol
Guo-Jun Qi
Xiaojuan Qi
Hongwei Qin
Shi Qiu
Faisal Qureshi
Matthias Rüther
Petia Radeva
Umer Rafi
Rahul Raguram
Swaminathan Rahul
Varun Ramakrishna
Kandan Ramakrishnan
Ravi Ramamoorthi
Vignesh Ramanathan
Vasili Ramanishka
R. Ramasamy Selvaraju
Rene Ranftl
Carolina Raposo
Nikhil Rasiwasia
Nalini Ratha
Sai Ravela
Avinash Ravichandran
Ramin Raziperchikolaei
Sylvestre-Alvise Rebuffi
Adria Recasens
Joe Redmon
Timo Rehfeld
Michal Reinstein
Konstantinos Rematas
Haibing Ren
Shaoqing Ren
Wenqi Ren
Zhile Ren
Hamid Rezatofighi
Nicholas Rhinehart
Helge Rhodin
Elisa Ricci
Eitan Richardson
Stephan Richter

Gernot Riegler
Hayko Riemenschneider
Tammy Riklin Raviv
Ergys Ristani
Tobias Ritschel
Mariano Rivera
Samuel Rivera
Antonio Robles-Kelly
Ignacio Rocco
Jason Rock
Emanuele Rodola
Mikel Rodriguez
Gregory Rogez
Marcus Rohrbach
Gemma Roig
Javier Romero
Olaf Ronneberger
Amir Rosenfeld
Bodo Rosenhahn
Guy Rosman
Arun Ross
Samuel Rota Bulò
Peter Roth
Constantin Rothkopf
Sebastien Roy
Amit Roy-Chowdhury
Ognjen Rudovic
Adria Ruiz
Javier Ruiz-del-Solar
Christian Rupprecht
Olga Russakovsky
Chris Russell
Alexandre Sablayrolles
Fereshteh Sadeghi
Ryusuke Sagawa
Hideo Saito
Elham Sakhaee
Albert Ali Salah
Conrad Sanderson
Koppal Sanjeev
Aswin Sankaranarayanan
Elham Saraee
Jason Saragih
Sudeep Sarkar
Imari Sato
Shin'ichi Satoh

Torsten Sattler
Bogdan Savchynskyy
Johannes Schönberger
Hanno Scharr
Walter Scheirer
Bernt Schiele
Frank Schmidt
Tanner Schmidt
Dirk Schnieders
Samuel Schulter
William Schwartz
Alexander Schwing
Ozan Sener
Soumyadip Sengupta
Laura Sevilla-Lara
Mubarak Shah
Shishir Shah
Fahad Shahbaz Khan
Amir Shahroudy
Jing Shao
Xiaowei Shao
Roman Shapovalov
Nataliya Shapovalova
Ali Sharif Razavian
Gaurav Sharma
Mohit Sharma
Pramod Sharma
Viktoriia Sharmanska
Eli Shechtman
Mark Sheinin
Evan Shelhamer
Chunhua Shen
Li Shen
Wei Shen
Xiaohui Shen
Xiaoyong Shen
Ziyi Shen
Lu Sheng
Baoguang Shi
Boxin Shi
Kevin Shih
Hyunjung Shim
Ilan Shimshoni
Young Min Shin
Koichi Shinoda
Matthew Shreve

Tianmin Shu
Zhixin Shu
Kaleem Siddiqi
Gunnar Sigurdsson
Nathan Silberman
Tomas Simon
Abhishek Singh
Gautam Singh
Maneesh Singh
Praveer Singh
Richa Singh
Saurabh Singh
Sudipta Sinha
Vladimir Smutny
Noah Snavely
Cees Snoek
Kihyuk Sohn
Eric Sommerlade
Sanghyun Son
Bi Song
Shiyu Song
Shuran Song
Xuan Song
Yale Song
Yang Song
Yibing Song
Lorenzo Sorgi
Humberto Sossa
Pratul Srinivasan
Michael Stark
Bjorn Stenger
Rainer Stiefelhagen
Joerg Stueckler
Jan Stuehmer
Hang Su
Hao Su
Shuochen Su
R. Subramanian
Yusuke Sugano
Akihiro Sugimoto
Baochen Sun
Chen Sun
Jian Sun
Jin Sun
Lin Sun
Min Sun

Qing Sun
Zhaohui Sun
David Suter
Eran Swears
Raza Syed Hussain
T. Syeda-Mahmood
Christian Szegedy
Duy-Nguyen Ta
Tolga Taşdizen
Hemant Tagare
Yuichi Taguchi
Ying Tai
Yu-Wing Tai
Jun Takamatsu
Hugues Talbot
Toru Tamak
Robert Tamburo
Chaowei Tan
Meng Tang
Peng Tang
Siyu Tang
Wei Tang
Junli Tao
Ran Tao
Xin Tao
Makarand Tapaswi
Jean-Philippe Tarel
Maxim Tatarchenko
Bugra Tekin
Demetri Terzopoulos
Christian Theobalt
Diego Thomas
Rajat Thomas
Qi Tian
Xinmei Tian
YingLi Tian
Yonghong Tian
Yonglong Tian
Joseph Tighe
Radu Timofte
Massimo Tistarelli
Sinisa Todorovic
Pavel Tokmakov
Giorgos Tolias
Federico Tombari
Tatiana Tommasi

Chetan Tonde
Xin Tong
Akihiko Torii
Andrea Torsello
Florian Trammer
Du Tran
Quoc-Huy Tran
Rudolph Triebel
Alejandro Troccoli
Leonardo Trujillo
Tomasz Trzcinski
Sam Tsai
Yi-Hsuan Tsai
Hung-Yu Tseng
Vagia Tsiminaki
Aggeliki Tsoli
Wei-Chih Tu
Shubham Tulsiani
Fred Tung
Tony Tung
Matt Turek
Oncel Tuzel
Georgios Tzimiropoulos
Ilkay Ulusoy
Osman Ulusoy
Dmitry Ulyanov
Paul Upchurch
Ben Usman
Evgeniya Ustinova
Himanshu Vajaria
Alexander Vakhitov
Jack Valmadre
Ernest Valveny
Jan van Gemert
Grant Van Horn
Jagannadan Varadarajan
Gul Varol
Sebastiano Vascon
Francisco Vasconcelos
Mayank Vatsa
Javier Vazquez-Corral
Ramakrishna Vedantam
Ashok Veeraraghavan
Andreas Veit
Raviteja Vemulapalli
Jonathan Ventura

Matthias Vestner
Minh Vo
Christoph Vogel
Michele Volpi
Carl Vondrick
Sven Wachsmuth
Toshikazu Wada
Michael Waechter
Catherine Wah
Jacob Walker
Jun Wan
Boyu Wang
Chen Wang
Chunyu Wang
De Wang
Fang Wang
Hongxing Wang
Hua Wang
Jiang Wang
Jingdong Wang
Jinglu Wang
Jue Wang
Le Wang
Lei Wang
Lezi Wang
Liang Wang
Lichao Wang
Lijun Wang
Limin Wang
Liwei Wang
Naiyan Wang
Oliver Wang
Qi Wang
Ruiping Wang
Shenlong Wang
Shu Wang
Song Wang
Tao Wang
Xiaofang Wang
Xiaolong Wang
Xinchao Wang
Xinggang Wang
Xintao Wang
Yang Wang
Yu-Chiang Frank Wang
Yu-Xiong Wang

Yang Yu
Zhiding Yu
Ganzhao Yuan
Jing Yuan
Junsong Yuan
Lu Yuan
Stefanos Zafeiriou
Sergey Zagoruyko
Amir Zamir
K. Zampogiannis
Andrei Zanfir
Mihai Zanfir
Pablo Zegers
Eyasu Zemene
Andy Zeng
Xingyu Zeng
Yun Zeng
De-Chuan Zhan
Cheng Zhang
Dong Zhang
Guofeng Zhang
Han Zhang
Hang Zhang
Hanwang Zhang
Jian Zhang
Jianguo Zhang
Jianming Zhang
Jiawei Zhang
Junping Zhang
Lei Zhang
Linguang Zhang
Ning Zhang
Qing Zhang

Quanshi Zhang
Richard Zhang
Runze Zhang
Shanshan Zhang
Shiliang Zhang
Shu Zhang
Ting Zhang
Xiangyu Zhang
Xiaofan Zhang
Xu Zhang
Yimin Zhang
Yinda Zhang
Yongqiang Zhang
Yuting Zhang
Zhanpeng Zhang
Ziyu Zhang
Bin Zhao
Chen Zhao
Hang Zhao
Hengshuang Zhao
Qijun Zhao
Rui Zhao
Yue Zhao
Enliang Zheng
Liang Zheng
Stephan Zheng
Wei-Shi Zheng
Wenming Zheng
Yin Zheng
Yinqiang Zheng
Yuanjie Zheng
Guangyu Zhong
Bolei Zhou

Guang-Tong Zhou
Huiyu Zhou
Jiahuan Zhou
S. Kevin Zhou
Tinghui Zhou
Wengang Zhou
Xiaowei Zhou
Xingyi Zhou
Yin Zhou
Zihan Zhou
Fan Zhu
Guangming Zhu
Ji Zhu
Jiejie Zhu
Jun-Yan Zhu
Shizhan Zhu
Siyu Zhu
Xiangxin Zhu
Xiatian Zhu
Yan Zhu
Yingying Zhu
Yixin Zhu
Yuke Zhu
Zhenyao Zhu
Liansheng Zhuang
Zeeshan Zia
Karel Zimmermann
Daniel Zoran
Danping Zou
Qi Zou
Silvia Zuffi
Wangmeng Zuo
Xinxin Zuo

Contents – Part IV

Video

Humans Analysis

Poster Session

BSN: Boundary Sensitive Network for Temporal Action Proposal Generation

Tianwei Lin[1], Xu Zhao[1(✉)], Haisheng Su[1], Chongjing Wang[2], and Ming Yang[1]

[1] Department of Automation, Shanghai Jiao Tong University, Shanghai, China
{wzmsltw,zhaoxu,suhaisheng,mingyang}@sjtu.edu.cn
[2] China Academy of Information and Communications Technology, Beijing, China
wangchongjing@caict.ac.cn

Abstract. Temporal action proposal generation is an important yet challenging problem, since temporal proposals with rich action content are indispensable for analysing real-world videos with long duration and high proportion irrelevant content. This problem requires methods not only generating proposals with precise temporal boundaries, but also retrieving proposals to cover truth action instances with high recall and high overlap using relatively fewer proposals. To address these difficulties, we introduce an effective proposal generation method, named Boundary-Sensitive Network (BSN), which adopts *"local to global"* fashion. *Locally*, BSN first locates temporal boundaries with high probabilities, then directly combines these boundaries as proposals. *Globally*, with Boundary-Sensitive Proposal feature, BSN retrieves proposals by evaluating the confidence of whether a proposal contains an action within its region. We conduct experiments on two challenging datasets: ActivityNet-1.3 and THUMOS14, where BSN outperforms other state-of-the-art temporal action proposal generation methods with high recall and high temporal precision. Finally, further experiments demonstrate that by combining existing action classifiers, our method significantly improves the state-of-the-art temporal action detection performance.

Keywords: Temporal action proposal generation
Temporal action detection · Temporal convolution · Untrimmed video

1 Introduction

Nowadays, with fast development of digital cameras and Internet, the number of videos is continuously booming, making automatic video content analysis methods widely required. One major branch of video analysis is action recognition, which aims to classify manually trimmed video clips containing only one action instance. However, videos in real scenarios are usually long, untrimmed

---

This research has been supported by the funding from NSFC (61673269, 61273285) and the Cooperative Medianet Innovation Center (CMIC).

V. Ferrari et al. (Eds.): ECCV 2018, LNCS 11208, pp. 3–21, 2018.
https://doi.org/10.1007/978-3-030-01225-0_1

and contain multiple action instances along with irrelevant contents. This problem requires algorithms for another challenging task: temporal action detection, which aims to detect action instances in untrimmed video including both temporal boundaries and action classes. It can be applied in many areas such as video recommendation and smart surveillance.

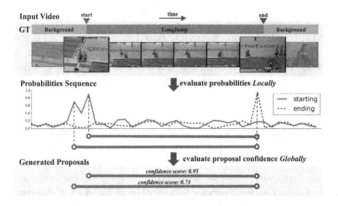

Fig. 1. Overview of our approach. Given an untrimmed video, (1) we evaluate boundaries and actionness probabilities of each temporal location and generate proposals based on boundary probabilities, and (2) we evaluate the confidence scores of proposals with proposal-level feature to get retrieved proposals.

Similar with object detection in spatial domain, temporal action detection task can be divided into two stages: proposal and classification. Proposal generation stage aims to generate temporal video regions which may contain action instances, and classification stage aims to classify classes of candidate proposals. Although classification methods have reached convincing performance, the detection precision is still low in many benchmarks [6,22]. Thus recently temporal action proposal generation has received much attention [4,5,9,13], aiming to improve the detection performance by improving the quality of proposals. High quality proposals should come up with two key properties: (1) proposals can cover truth action regions with both high recall and high temporal overlap, (2) proposals are retrieved so that high recall and high overlap can be achieved using fewer proposals to reduce the computation cost of succeeding steps.

To achieve high proposal quality, a proposal generation method should generate proposals with flexible temporal durations and precise temporal boundaries, then retrieve proposals with reliable confidence scores, which indicate the probability of a proposal containing an action instance. Most recently proposal generation methods [4,5,9,32] generate proposals via sliding temporal windows of multiple durations in video with regular interval, then train a model to evaluate the confidence scores of generated proposals for proposals retrieving, while there is also method [13] making external boundaries regression. However, proposals generated with pre-defined durations and intervals may have some major drawbacks: (1) usually not temporally precise; (2) not flexible enough to cover variable temporal durations of ground truth action instances, especially when the range of temporal durations is large.

To address these issues and generate high quality proposals, we propose the Boundary-Sensitive Network (BSN), which adopts *"local to global"* fashion to locally combine high probability boundaries as proposals and globally retrieve candidate proposals using proposal-level feature as shown in Fig. 1. In detail, BSN generates proposals in three steps. **First**, BSN evaluates the probabilities of each temporal location in video whether it is inside or outside, at or not at the boundaries of ground truth action instances, to generate starting, ending and actionness probabilities sequences as local information. **Second**, BSN generates proposals via directly combining temporal locations with high starting and ending probabilities separately. Using this bottom-up fashion, BSN can generate proposals with flexible durations and precise boundaries. **Finally**, using features composed by actionness scores within and around proposal, BSN retrieves proposals by evaluating the confidence of whether a proposal contains an action. These proposal-level features offer global information for better evaluation.

In summary, the main contributions of our work are three-folds:

(1) We introduce a new architecture (BSN) based on *"local to global"* fashion to generate high quality temporal action proposals, which *locally* locates high boundary probability locations to achieve precise proposal boundaries and *globally* evaluates proposal-level feature to achieve reliable proposal confidence scores for retrieving.
(2) Extensive experiments demonstrate that our method achieves significantly better proposal quality than other state-of-the-art proposal generation methods, and can generate proposals in unseen action classes with comparative quality.
(3) Integrating our method with existing action classifier into detection framework leads to significantly improved performance on temporal action detection task.

2   Related Work

Action Recognition. Action recognition is an important branch of video related research areas and has been extensively studied. Earlier methods such as improved Dense Trajectory (iDT) [38,39] mainly adopt hand-crafted features such as HOF, HOG and MBH. In recent years, convolutional networks are widely adopted in many works [10,33,35,41] and have achieved great performance. Typically, two-stream network [10,33,41] learns appearance and motion features based on RGB frame and optical flow field separately. C3D network [35] adopts 3D convolutional layers to directly capture both appearance and motion features from raw frames volume. Action recognition models can be used for extracting frame or snippet level visual features in long and untrimmed videos.

Object Detection and Proposals. Recent years, the performance of object detection has been significantly improved with deep learning methods. R-CNN

[17] and its variations [16,30] construct an important branch of object detection methods, which adopt "detection by classifying proposals" framework. For proposal generation stage, besides sliding windows [11], earlier works also attempt to generate proposals by exploiting low-level cues such as HOG and Canny edge [37,50]. Recently some methods [25,28,30] adopt deep learning model to generate proposals with faster speed and stronger modelling capacity. In this work, we combine the properties of these methods via evaluating boundaries and actionness probabilities of each location using neural network and adopting "*local to global*" fashion to generate proposals with high recall and accuracy.

Boundary probabilities are also adopted in LocNet [15] for revising the horizontal and vertical boundaries of existing proposals. Our method differs in (1) BSN aims to generate while LocNet aims to revise proposals and (2) boundary probabilities are calculated repeatedly for all boxes in LocNet but only once for a video in BSN.

Temporal Action Detection and Proposals. Temporal action detection task aims to detect action instances in untrimmed videos including temporal boundaries and action classes, and can be divided into proposal and classification stages. Most detection methods [32,34,49] take these two stages separately, while there is also method [3,26] taking these two stages jointly. For proposal generation, earlier works [23,29,40] directly use sliding windows as proposals. Recently some methods [4,5,9,13,32] generate proposals with pre-defined temporal durations and intervals, and use multiple methods to evaluate the confidence score of proposals, such as dictionary learning [5] and recurrent neural network [9]. TAG method [49] adopts watershed algorithm to generate proposals with flexible boundaries and durations in *local* fashion, but without *global* proposal-level confidence evaluation for retrieving. In our work, BSN can generate proposals with flexible boundaries meanwhile reliable confidence scores for retrieving.

Recently temporal action detection method [48] detects action instances based on class-wise start, middle and end probabilities of each location. Our method is superior than [48] in two aspects: (1) BSN evaluates probabilities score using temporal convolution to better capture temporal information and (2) "*local to global*" fashion adopted in BSN brings more precise boundaries and better retrieving quality.

3   Our Approach

3.1   Problem Definition

An untrimmed video sequence can be denoted as $X = \{x_n\}_{n=1}^{l_v}$ with l_v frames, where x_n is the n-th frame in X. Annotation of video X is composed by a set of action instances $\Psi_g = \{\varphi_n = (t_{s,n}, t_{e,n})\}_{n=1}^{N_g}$, where N_g is the number of truth action instances in video X, and $t_{s,n}$, $t_{e,n}$ are starting and ending time of action instance φ_n separately. Unlike detection task, classes of action instances are not considered in temporal action proposal generation. Annotation set Ψ_g is used during training. During prediction, generated proposals set Ψ_p should cover Ψ_g with high recall and high temporal overlap.

3.2 Video Features Encoding

To generate proposals of input video, first we need to extract feature to encode visual content of video. In our framework, we adopt two-stream network [33] as visual encoder, since this architecture has shown great performance in action recognition task [42] and has been widely adopted in temporal action detection and proposal generation tasks [12,26,49]. Two-stream network contains two branches: spatial network operates on single RGB frame to capture appearance feature, and temporal network operates on stacked optical flow field to capture motion information.

To extract two-stream features, as shown in Fig. 2(a), first we compose a snippets sequence $S = \{s_n\}_{n=1}^{l_s}$ from video X, where l_s is the length of snippets sequence. A snippet $s_n = (x_{t_n}, o_{t_n})$ includes two parts: x_{t_n} is the t_n-th RGB frame in X and o_{t_n} is stacked optical flow field derived around center frame x_{t_n}. To reduce the computation cost, we extract snippets with a regular frame interval σ, therefore $l_s = l_v/\sigma$. Given a snippet s_n, we concatenate output scores in top layer of both spatial and temporal networks to form the encoded feature vector $f_{t_n} = (f_{S,t_n}, f_{T,t_n})$, where f_{S,t_n}, f_{T,t_n} are output scores from spatial and temporal networks separately. Thus given a snippets sequence S with length l_s, we can extract a feature sequence $F = \{f_{t_n}\}_{n=1}^{l_s}$. These two-stream feature sequences are used as the input of BSN.

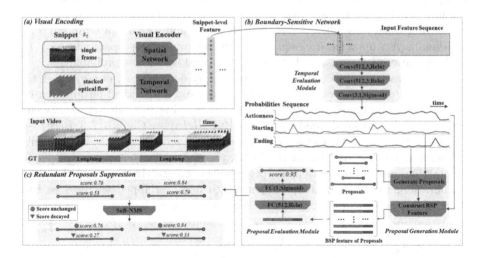

Fig. 2. The framework of our approach. (a) Two-stream network is used for encoding visual features in snippet-level. (b) The architecture of Boundary-Sensitive Network: *temporal evaluation module* handles the input feature sequence, and evaluates starting, ending and actionness probabilities of each temporal location; *proposal generation module* generates proposals with high starting and ending probabilities, and construct Boundary-Sensitive Proposal (BSP) feature for each proposal; *proposal evaluation module* evaluates confidence score of each proposal using BSP feature. (c) Finally, we use Soft-NMS algorithm to suppress redundant proposals by decaying their scores.

3.3   Boundary-Sensitive Network

To achieve high proposal quality with both precise temporal boundaries and reliable confidence scores, we adopt *"local to global"* fashion to generate proposals. In BSN, we first generate candidate boundary locations, then combine these locations as proposals and evaluate confidence score of each proposal with proposal-level feature.

Network Architecture. The architecture of BSN is presented in Fig. 2(b), which contains three modules: temporal evaluation, proposal generation and proposal evaluation. *Temporal evaluation module* is a three layers temporal convolutional neural network, which takes the two-stream feature sequences as input, and evaluates probabilities of each temporal location in video whether it is inside or outside, at or not at boundaries of ground truth action instances, to generate sequences of starting, ending and actionness probabilities respectively. *Proposal generation module* first combines the temporal locations with separately high starting and ending probabilities as candidate proposals, then constructs Boundary-Sensitive Proposal (BSP) feature for each candidate proposal based on actionness probabilities sequence. Finally, *proposal evaluation module*, a multilayer perceptron model with one hidden layer, evaluates the confidence score of each candidate proposal based on BSP feature. Confidence score and boundary probabilities of each proposal are fused as the final confidence score for retrieving.

Temporal Evaluation Module. The goal of temporal evaluation module is to evaluate starting, ending and actionness probabilities of each temporal location, where three binary classifiers are needed. In this module, we adopt temporal convolutional layers upon feature sequence, with good modelling capacity to capture local semantic information such as boundaries and actionness probabilities.

A temporal convolutional layer can be simply denoted as $Conv(c_f, c_k, Act)$, where c_f, c_k and Act are filter numbers, kernel size and activation function of temporal convolutional layer separately. As shown in Fig. 2(b), the temporal evaluation module can be defined as $Conv(512, 3, Relu) \rightarrow Conv(512, 3, Relu) \rightarrow Conv(3, 1, Sigmoid)$, where the three layers have same stride size 1. Three filters with sigmoid activation in the last layer are used as classifiers to generate starting, ending and actionness probabilities separately. For convenience of computation, we divide feature sequence into non-overlapped windows as the input of temporal evaluation module. Given a feature sequence F, temporal evaluation module can generate three probability sequences $P_S = \left\{ p_{t_n}^s \right\}_{n=1}^{l_s}$, $P_E = \left\{ p_{t_n}^e \right\}_{n=1}^{l_s}$ and $P_A = \left\{ p_{t_n}^a \right\}_{n=1}^{l_s}$, where $p_{t_n}^s$, $p_{t_n}^e$ and $p_{t_n}^a$ are respectively starting, ending and actionness probabilities in time t_n.

Proposal Generation Module. The goal of proposal generation module is to generate candidate proposals and construct corresponding proposal-level feature. We achieve this goal in two steps. First we locate temporal locations with high boundary probabilities, and combine these locations to form proposals. Then for each proposal, we construct Boundary-Sensitive Proposal (BSP) feature.

As shown in Fig. 3(a), to locate where an action likely to start, for starting probabilities sequence P_S, we record all temporal location t_n where $p_{t_n}^s$ (1) has

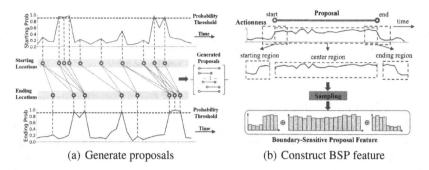

(a) Generate proposals	(b) Construct BSP feature

Fig. 3. Details of proposal generation module. (a) Generate proposals. First, to generate candidate boundary locations, we choose temporal locations with high boundary probability or being a probability peak. Then, we combine candidate starting and ending locations as proposals when their duration satisfying condition. (b) Construct BSP feature. Given a proposal and actionness probabilities sequence, we can sample actionness sequence in starting, center and ending regions of proposal to construct BSP feature.

high score: $p_{t_n}^s > 0.9$ or (2) is a probability peak: $p_{t_n}^s > p_{t_{n-1}}^s$ and $p_{t_n}^s > p_{t_{n+1}}^s$. These locations are grouped into candidate starting locations set $B_S = \{t_{s,i}\}_{i=1}^{N_S}$, where N_S is the number of candidate starting locations. Using same rules, we can generate candidate ending locations set B_E from ending probabilities sequence P_E. Then, we generate temporal regions via combing each starting location t_s from B_S and each ending location t_e from B_E. Any temporal region $[t_s, t_e]$ satisfying $d = t_e - t_s \in [d_{min}, d_{max}]$ is denoted as a candidate proposal φ, where d_{min} and d_{max} are minimum and maximum durations of ground truth action instances in dataset. Thus we can get candidate proposals set $\Psi_p = \{\varphi_i\}_{i=1}^{N_p}$, where N_p is the number of proposals.

To construct proposal-level feature as shown in Fig. 3(b), for a candidate proposal φ, we denote its center region as $r_C = [t_s, t_e]$ and its starting and ending region as $r_S = [t_s - d/5, t_s + d/5]$ and $r_E = [t_e - d/5, t_e + d/5]$ separately. Then, we sample the actionness sequence P_A within r_c as f_c^A by linear interpolation with 16 points. In starting and ending regions, we also sample actionness sequence with 8 linear interpolation points and get f_s^A and f_e^A separately. Concatenating these vectors, we can get Boundary-Sensitive Proposal (BSP) feature $f_{BSP} = (f_s^A, f_c^A, f_e^A)$ of proposal φ. BSP feature is highly compact and contains rich semantic information about corresponding proposal. Then we can represent a proposal as $\varphi = (t_s, t_e, f_{BSP})$.

Proposal Evaluation Module. The goal of proposal evaluation module is to evaluate the confidence score of each proposal whether it contains an action instance within its duration using BSP feature. We adopt a simple multilayer perceptron model with one hidden layer as shown in Fig. 2(b). Hidden layer with 512 units handles the input of BSP feature f_{BSP} with Relu activation. The output layer outputs confidence score p_{conf} with sigmoid activation, which estimates the overlap extent between candidate proposal and ground truth action instances. Thus, a generated proposal can be denoted as $\varphi = (t_s, t_e, p_{conf}, p_{t_s}^s, p_{t_e}^e)$, where $p_{t_s}^s$ and $p_{t_e}^e$ are starting and ending probabilities in t_s and t_e separately. These scores are fused to generate final score during prediction.

3.4   Training of BSN

In BSN, temporal evaluation module is trained to learn local boundary and actionness probabilities from video features simultaneously. Then based on probabilities sequence generated by trained temporal evaluation module, we can generate proposals and corresponding BSP features and train the proposal evaluation module to learn the confidence score of proposals. The training details are introduced in this section.

Temporal Evaluation Module. Given a video X, we compose a snippets sequence S with length l_s and extract feature sequence F from it. Then we slide windows with length $l_w = 100$ in feature sequence without overlap. A window is denoted as $\omega = \{F_\omega, \Psi_\omega\}$, where F_ω and Ψ_ω are feature sequence and annotations within the window separately. For ground truth action instance $\varphi_g = (t_s, t_e)$ in Ψ_ω, we denote its region as action region r_g^a and its starting and ending region as $r_g^s = [t_s - d_g/10, t_s + d_g/10]$ and $r_g^e = [t_e - d_g/10, t_e + d_g/10]$ separately, where $d_g = t_e - t_s$.

Taking F_ω as input, temporal evaluation module generates probabilities sequence $P_{S,\omega}$, $P_{E,\omega}$ and $P_{A,\omega}$ with same length l_w. For each temporal location t_n within F_ω, we denote its region as $r_{t_n} = [t_n - d_s/2, t_n + d_s/2]$ and get corresponding probability scores $p_{t_n}^s$, $p_{t_n}^e$ and $p_{t_n}^a$ from $P_{S,\omega}$, $P_{E,\omega}$ and $P_{A,\omega}$ separately, where $d_s = t_n - t_{n-1}$ is temporal interval between two snippets. Then for each r_{t_n}, we calculate its IoP ratio with r_g^a, r_g^s and r_g^e of all φ_g in Ψ_ω separately, where IoP is defined as the overlap ratio with groundtruth proportional to the duration of this proposal. Thus we can represent information of t_n as $\phi_n = (p_{t_n}^a, p_{t_n}^s, p_{t_n}^e, g_{t_n}^a, g_{t_n}^s, g_{t_n}^e)$, where $g_{t_n}^a$, $g_{t_n}^s$, $g_{t_n}^e$ are maximum matching overlap IoP of action, starting and ending regions separately.

Given a window of matching information as $\Phi_\omega = \{\phi_n\}_{n=1}^{l_s}$, we can define training objective of this module as a three-task loss function. The overall loss function consists of actionness loss, starting loss and ending loss:

$$L_{TEM} = \lambda \cdot L_{bl}^{action} + L_{bl}^{start} + L_{bl}^{end}, \tag{1}$$

where λ is the weight term and is set to 2 in BSN. We adopt the sum of binary logistic regression loss function L_{bl} for all three tasks, which can be denoted as:

$$L_{bl} = \frac{1}{l_w} \sum_{i=1}^{l_w} \left(\alpha^+ \cdot b_i \cdot log(p_i) + \alpha^- \cdot (1 - b_i) \cdot log(1 - p_i) \right), \tag{2}$$

where $b_i = sign(g_i - \theta_{IoP})$ is a two-values function for converting matching score g_i to $\{0, 1\}$ based on threshold θ_{IoP}, which is set to 0.5 in BSN. Let $l^+ = \sum g_i$ and $l^- = l_w - l^+$, we can set $\alpha^+ = \frac{l_w}{l^+}$ and $\alpha^- = \frac{l_w}{l^-}$, which are used for balancing the effect of positive and negative samples during training.

Proposal Evaluation Module. Using probabilities sequences generated by trained temporal evaluation module, we can generate proposals using proposal generation module: $\Psi_p = \{\varphi_n = (t_s, t_e, f_{BSP})\}_{n=1}^{N_p}$. Taking f_{BSP} as input, for a proposal φ, confidence score p_{conf} is generated by proposal evaluation module. Then we calculate its Intersection-over-Union (IoU) with all φ_g in Ψ_g, and denote the maximum overlap score as g_{iou}. Thus we can represent proposals set as $\Psi_p = \{\varphi_n = \{t_s, t_e, p_{conf}, g_{iou}\}\}_{n=1}^{N_p}$. We split Ψ_p into two parts based on g_{iou}: Ψ_p^{pos} for $g_{iou} > 0.7$ and Ψ_p^{neg} for $g_{iou} < 0.3$. For data balancing, we take all proposals in Ψ_p^{pos} and randomly sample the proposals in Ψ_p^{neg} to insure the ratio between two sets be nearly 1:2.

The training objective of this module is a simple regression loss, which is used to train a precise confidence score prediction based on IoU overlap. We can define it as:

$$L_{PEM} = \frac{1}{N_{train}} \sum_{i=1}^{N_{train}} (p_{conf,i} - g_{iou,i})^2, \qquad (3)$$

where N_{train} is the number of proposals used for training.

3.5   Prediction and Post-processing

During prediction, we use BSN with same procedures described in training to generate proposals set $\Psi_p = \{\varphi_n = (t_s, t_e, p_{conf}, p_{t_s}^s, p_{t_e}^e)\}_{n=1}^{N_p}$, where N_p is the number of proposals. To get final proposals set, we need to make score fusion to get final confidence score, then suppress redundant proposals based on these score.

Score Fusion for Retrieving. To achieve better retrieving performance, for each candidate proposal φ, we fuse its confidence score with its boundary probabilities by multiplication to get the final confidence score p_f:

$$p_f = p_{conf} \cdot p_{t_s}^s \cdot p_{t_e}^e. \qquad (4)$$

After score fusion, we can get generated proposals set $\Psi_p = \{\varphi_n = (t_s, t_e, p_f)\}_{n=1}^{N_p}$, where p_f is used for proposals retrieving. In Sect. 4.2, we explore the recall performance with and without confidence score generated by proposal evaluation module.

Redundant Proposals Suppression. Around a ground truth action instance, we may generate multiple proposals with different temporal overlap. Thus we need to suppress redundant proposals to obtain higher recall with fewer proposals.

Soft-NMS [2] is a recently proposed non-maximum suppression (NMS) algorithm which suppresses redundant results using a score decaying function. First all proposals are sorted by their scores. Then proposal φ_m with maximum score is used for calculating overlap IoU with other proposals, where scores of highly overlapped proposals is decayed. This step is recursively applied to the remaining proposals to generate re-scored proposals set. The Gaussian decaying function of Soft-NMS can be denoted as:

$$p'_{f,i} = \begin{cases} p_{f,i}, & iou(\varphi_m, \varphi_i) < \theta \\ p_{f,i} \cdot e^{-\frac{iou(\varphi_m, \varphi_i)^2}{\epsilon}}, & iou(\varphi_m, \varphi_i) \geq \theta \end{cases} \qquad (5)$$

where ε is parameter of Gaussian function and θ is pre-fixed threshold. After suppression, we get the final proposals set $\Psi'_p = \left\{ \varphi_n = (t_s, t_e, p'_f) \right\}_{n=1}^{N_p}$.

4   Experiments

4.1   Dataset and Setup

Dataset. ActivityNet-1.3 [6] is a large dataset for general temporal action proposal generation and detection, which contains 19994 videos with 200 action classes annotated and was used in the ActivityNet Challenge 2016 and 2017. ActivityNet-1.3 is divided into training, validation and testing sets by ratio of 2:1:1. **THUMOS14** [22] dataset contains 200 and 213 temporal annotated untrimmed videos with 20 action classes in validation and testing sets separately. In this section, we compare our method with state-of-the-art methods on both ActivityNet-1.3 and THUMOS14.

Evaluation Metrics. In temporal action proposal generation task, Average Recall (AR) calculated with multiple IoU thresholds is usually used as evaluation metrics. Following conventions, we use IoU thresholds set [0.5 : 0.05 : 0.95] in ActivityNet-1.3 and [0.5 : 0.05 : 1.0] in THUMOS14. To evaluate the relation between recall and proposals number, we evaluate AR with Average Number of proposals (AN) on both datasets, which is denoted as AR@AN. On ActivityNet-1.3, area under the AR vs. AN curve (AUC) is also used as metrics, where AN varies from 0 to 100.

In temporal action detection task, mean Average Precision (mAP) is used as evaluation metric, where Average Precision (AP) is calculated on each action class respectively. On ActivityNet-1.3, mAP with IoU thresholds {0.5, 0.75, 0.95} and average mAP with IoU thresholds set [0.5 : 0.05 : 0.95] are used. On THU-MOS14, mAP with IoU thresholds {0.3, 0.4, 0.5, 0.6, 0.7} is used.

Implementation Details. For visual feature encoding, we use the two-stream network [33] with architecture described in [45], where BN-Inception network [20] is used as temporal network and ResNet network [18] is used as spatial network. Two-stream network is implemented using Caffe [21] and pre-trained on ActivityNet-1.3 training set. During feature extraction, the interval σ of snippets is set to 16 on ActivityNet-1.3 and is set to 5 on THUMOS14.

On ActivityNet-1.3, since the duration of videos are limited, we follow [27] to rescale the feature sequence of each video to new length $l_w = 100$ by linear interpolation, and the duration of corresponding annotations to range [0, 1]. In BSN, temporal evaluation module and proposal evaluation module are both implemented using Tensorflow [1]. On both datasets, temporal evaluation module is trained with batch size 16 and learning rate 0.001 for 10 epochs, then 0.0001 for another 10 epochs, and proposal evaluation module is trained with batch size 256 and same learning rate. For Soft-NMS, we set the threshold θ to 0.8 on ActivityNet-1.3 and 0.65 on THUMOS14 by empirical validation, while ε in Gaussian function is set to 0.75 on both datasets.

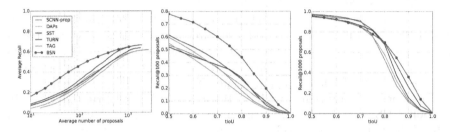

Fig. 4. Comparison of our proposal generation method with other state-of-the-art methods in THUMOS14 dataset. **(left)** BSN can achieve significant performance gains with relatively few proposals. **(center)** Recall with 100 proposals vs tIoU figure shows that with few proposals, BSN gets performance improvements in both low and high tIoU. **(right)** Recall with 1000 proposals vs tIoU figure shows that with large number of proposals, BSN achieves improvements mainly while tIoU >0.8.

4.2   Temporal Proposal Generation

Taking a video as input, proposal generation method aims to generate temporal proposals where action instances likely to occur. In this section, we compare our method with state-of-the-art methods and make external experiments to verify effectiveness of BSN.

Comparison with State-of-the-Art Methods. As aforementioned, a good proposal generation method should generate and retrieve proposals to cover ground truth action instances with *high recall* and *high temporal overlap* using relatively few proposals. We evaluate these methods in two aspects.

First we evaluate the ability of our method to generate and retrieve proposals with high recall, which is measured by average recall with different number of proposals (AR@AN) and area under AR-AN curve (AUC). We list the comparison results of ActivityNet-1.3 and THUMOS14 in Tables 1 and 2 respectively, and plot the average recall against average number of proposals curve of THUMOS14 in Fig. 4 (left). On THUMOS14, our method outperforms other state-of-the-art proposal methods when proposal number varies from 10 to 1000. Especially, when average number of proposals is 50, our method significantly improves average recall from 21.86% to 37.46% by 15.60%. On ActivityNet-1.3, our method outperforms other state-of-the-art proposal generation methods on both validation and testing set.

Second, we evaluate the ability of our method to generate and retrieve proposals with high temporal overlap, which is measured by recall of multiple IoU thresholds. We plot the recall against IoU thresholds curve with 100 and 1000 proposals in Fig. 4 (center) and (right) separately. Figure 4 (center) suggests that our method achieves significant higher recall than other methods with 100 proposals when IoU threshold varied from 0.5 to 1.0. And Fig. 4 (right) suggests that with 1000 proposals, our method obtains the largest recall improvements when IoU threshold is higher than 0.8.

Furthermore, we make some controlled experiments to confirm the contribution of BSN itself in Table 2. For video feature encoding, except for two-stream network, C3D network [35] is also adopted in some works [4,9,13,32]. For NMS method, most previous work adopt Greedy-NMS [8] for redundant proposals suppression. Thus, for fair comparison, we train BSN with feature extracted by C3D network [35] pre-trained on UCF-101 dataset, then perform Greedy-NMS and Soft-NMS on C3D-BSN and original 2Stream-BSN respectively. Results in Table 2 show that (1) C3D-BSN still outperforms other C3D-based methods especially with small proposals number, (2) Soft-NMS only brings small performance promotion than Greedy-NMS, while Greedy-NMS also works well with BSN. These results suggest that the architecture of BSN itself is the main reason for performance promotion rather than input feature and NMS method.

Table 1. Comparison between our method with other state-of-the-art proposal generation methods on validation set of ActivityNet-1.3 in terms of AR@AN and AUC.

Method	Zhao et al. [49]	Dai et al. [7]	Yao et al. [14]	Lin et al. [27]	BSN
AR@100 (val)	63.52	-	-	73.01	**74.16**
AUC (val)	53.02	59.58	63.12	64.40	**66.17**
AUC (test)	-	61.56	64.18	64.80	**66.26**

These results suggest the effectiveness of BSN. And BSN achieves the salient performance since it can generate proposals with (1) *flexible temporal duration* to cover ground truth action instances with various durations; (2) *precise temporal boundary* via learning starting and ending probability using temporal convolutional network, which brings high overlap between generated proposals and ground truth action instances; (3) *reliable confidence score* using BSP feature, which retrieves proposals properly so that high recall and high overlap can be achieved using relatively few proposals. Qualitative examples on THUMOS14 and ActivityNet-1.3 datasets are shown in Fig. 5.

Generalizability of Proposals. Another key property of a proposal generation method is the ability to generate proposals for unseen action classes. To evaluate this property, we choose two semantically different action subsets on ActivityNet-1.3: "Sports, Exercise, and Recreation" and "Socializing, Relaxing, and Leisure" as *seen* and *unseen* subsets separately. *Seen* subset contains 87 action classes with 4455 training and 2198 validation videos, and *unseen* subset contains 38 action classes with 1903 training and 896 validation videos. To guarantee the experiment effectiveness, instead of two-stream network, here we adopt C3D network [36] trained on Sports-1M dataset [24] for video features encoding. Using C3D feature, we train BSN with *seen* and *seen+unseen* videos on training set separately, then evaluate both models on *seen* and *unseen* validation videos separately. As shown in Table 3, there is only slight performance drop in unseen classes, which demonstrates that BSN has great generalizability and can learn a generic concept of temporal action proposal even in semantically different unseen actions.

Table 2. Comparison between our method with other state-of-the-art proposal generation methods on THUMOS14 in terms of AR@AN.

Feature	Method	@50	@100	@200	@500	@1000
C3D	DAPs [9]	13.56	23.83	33.96	49.29	57.64
C3D	SCNN-prop [32]	17.22	26.17	37.01	51.57	58.20
C3D	SST [4]	19.90	28.36	37.90	51.58	60.27
C3D	TURN [13]	19.63	27.96	38.34	53.52	**60.75**
C3D	BSN + Greedy-NMS	27.19	35.38	43.61	53.77	59.50
C3D	BSN + Soft-NMS	**29.58**	**37.38**	**45.55**	**54.67**	59.48
2-Stream	TAG [49]	18.55	29.00	39.61	-	-
Flow	TURN [13]	21.86	31.89	43.02	57.63	64.17
2-Stream	BSN + Greedy-NMS	35.41	43.55	52.23	**61.35**	**65.10**
2-Stream	BSN + Soft-NMS	**37.46**	**46.06**	**53.21**	60.64	64.52

Table 3. Generalization evaluation of BSN on ActivityNet-1.3. *Seen* subset: "Sports, Exercise, and Recreation"; *Unseen* subset: "Socializing, Relaxing, and Leisure".

	Seen (validation)		*Unseen* (validation)	
	AR@100	AUC	AR@100	AUC
BSN trained with *Seen + Unseen* (training)	72.40	63.80	71.84	63.99
BSN trained with *Seen* (training)	72.42	64.02	**71.32**	**63.38**

Effectiveness of Modules in BSN. To evaluate the effectiveness of temporal evaluation module (TEM) and proposal evaluation module (PEM) in BSN, we demonstrate experiment results of BSN with and without PEM in Table 4, where TEM is used in both results. These results show that: (1) using only TEM without PEM, BSN can also reach considerable recall performance over state-of-the-art methods; (2) PEM can bring considerable further performance promotion in BSN. These observations suggest that TEM and PEM are both effective and indispensable in BSN.

Boundary-Sensitive Proposal Feature. BSP feature is used in proposal evaluation module to evaluate the confidence scores of proposals. In Table 4, we also make ablation studies of the contribution of each component in BSP. These results suggest that although BSP feature constructed from boundary regions contributes less improvements than center region, best recall performance is achieved while PEM is trained with BSP constructed from both boundary and center region.

4.3   Action Detection with Our Proposals

To further evaluate the quality of proposals generated by BSN, we put BSN proposals into "detection by classifying proposals" temporal action detection framework with state-of-the-art action classifier, where temporal boundaries of detection results are provided by our proposals. On ActivityNet-1.3, we use top-1 video-level class generated by classification model [44] for all proposals in a video and keep BSN confidence scores of proposals for retrieving. On THUMOS14, we use top-2 video-level classes generated by UntrimmedNet [43] for proposals generated by BSN and other methods, where multiplication of confidence score and class score is used for retrieving detections. Following previous works, on THUMOS14, we also implement SCNN-classifier on BSN proposals for proposal-level classification and adopt Greedy NMS as [32]. We use 100 and 200 proposals per video on ActivityNet-1.3 and THUMOS14 datasets separately.

Table 4. Study of effectiveness of modules in BSN and contribution of components in BSP feature on THUMOS14, where PEM is trained with BSP feature constructed by *Boundary* region (f_s^A, f_e^A) and *Center* region (f_c^A) independently and jointly.

	Boundary	Center	@50	@100	@200	@500	@1000
BSN without PEM			30.72	40.52	48.63	57.78	63.04
	✓		35.61	44.86	52.46	60.00	64.17
BSN with PEM		✓	36.80	45.65	52.63	60.18	64.22
	✓	✓	**37.46**	**46.06**	**53.21**	**60.64**	**64.52**

The comparison results of ActivityNet-1.3 shown in Table 5 suggest that detection framework based on our proposals outperforms other state-of-the-art methods. The comparison results of THUMOS14 shown in Table 6 suggest that (1) using same action classifier, our method achieves significantly better performance than other proposal generation methods; (2) comparing with proposal-level classifier [32], video-level classifier [43] achieves better performance on BSN proposals and worse performance on [4,13] proposals, which indicates that confidence scores generated by BSN are more reliable than scores generated by proposal-level classifier, and are reliable enough for retrieving detection results in action detection task; (3) detection framework based on our proposals significantly outperforms state-of-the-art action detection methods, especially when the overlap threshold is high. These results confirm that proposals generated by BSN have high quality and work generally well in detection frameworks.

Table 5. Action detection results on validation and testing set of ActivityNet-1.3 in terms of mAP@$tIoU$ and average mAP, where our proposals are combined with video-level classification results generated by [44].

Method	Validation				Testing
	0.5	0.75	0.95	Average	Average
Wang et al. [44]	42.28	3.76	0.05	14.85	14.62
SCC [19]	40.00	17.90	4.70	21.70	19.30
CDC [31]	43.83	25.88	0.21	22.77	22.90
TCN [7]	-	-	-	-	23.58
SSN [46]	39.12	23.48	5.49	23.98	28.28
Lin et al. [27]	48.99	32.91	7.87	32.26	33.40
BSN + [44]	**52.50**	**33.53**	**8.85**	**33.72**	**34.42**

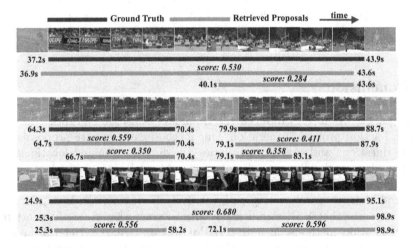

Fig. 5. Qualitative examples of proposals generated by BSN on THUMOS14 (top and middle) and ActivityNet-1.3 (bottom), where proposals are retrieved using post-processed confidence score.

Table 6. Action detection results on testing set of THUMOS14 in terms of mAP@$tIoU$, where classification results generated by UntrimmedNet [43] and SCNN-classifier [32] are combined with proposals generated by BSN and other methods.

Action detection methods						
Detection method		0.7	0.6	0.5	0.4	0.3
SCNN [32]		5.3	10.3	19.0	28.7	36.3
SMS [48]		-	-	17.8	27.8	36.5
CDC [31]		8.8	14.3	24.7	30.7	41.3
SSAD [26]		7.7	15.3	24.6	35.0	43.0
TCN [7]		9.0	15.9	25.6	33.3	-
R-C3D [47]		9.3	19.1	28.9	35.6	44.8
SS-TAD [3]		9.6	-	29.2	-	45.7
SSN [46]		-	-	29.1	40.8	50.6
CBR [12]		9.9	19.1	31.0	41.3	50.1
Proposal generation methods + Action classifier						
Proposal method	Classifier	0.7	0.6	0.5	0.4	0.3
SST [4]	SCNN-cls	-	-	23.0	-	-
TURN [13]	SCNN-cls	7.7	14.6	25.6	33.2	44.1
SST [4]	UNet	4.7	10.9	20.0	31.5	41.2
TURN [13]	UNet	6.3	14.1	24.5	35.3	46.3
BSN	SCNN-cls	15.0	22.4	29.4	36.6	43.1
BSN	UNet	**20.0**	**28.4**	**36.9**	**45.0**	**53.5**

5   Conclusion

In this paper, we have introduced the Boundary-Sensitive Network (BSN) for temporal action proposal generation. Our method can generate proposals with flexible durations and precise boundaries via directly combing locations with high boundary probabilities, and make accurate retrieving via evaluating proposal confidence score with proposal-level features. Thus BSN can achieve high recall and high temporal overlap with relatively few proposals. In experiments, we demonstrate that BSN significantly outperforms other state-of-the-art proposal generation methods on both THUMOS14 and ActivityNet-1.3 datasets. And BSN can significantly improve the detection performance when used as the proposal stage of a full detection framework. Codes are available in https:// github.com/wzmsltw/BSN-boundary-sensitive-network.

References

1. Abadi, M., Agarwal, A., Barham, P., et al.: TensorFlow: large-scale machine learning on heterogeneous distributed systems. arXiv preprint arXiv:1603.04467 (2016)
2. Bodla, N., Singh, B., Chellappa, R., Davis, L.S.: Improving object detection with one line of code. arXiv preprint arXiv:1704.04503 (2017)
3. Buch, S., Escorcia, V., Ghanem, B., Fei-Fei, L., Niebles, J.C.: End-to-end, single-stream temporal action detection in untrimmed videos. In: Proceedings of the British Machine Vision Conference (2017)
4. Buch, S., Escorcia, V., Shen, C., Ghanem, B., Niebles, J.C.: SST: single-stream temporal action proposals. In: IEEE International Conference on Computer Vision (2017)
5. Caba Heilbron, F., Carlos Niebles, J., Ghanem, B.: Fast temporal activity proposals for efficient detection of human actions in untrimmed videos. In: Proceedings of the IEEE Conference on Computer Vision and Pattern Recognition, pp. 1914–1923 (2016)
6. Caba Heilbron, F., Escorcia, V., Ghanem, B., Carlos Niebles, J.: ActivityNet: a large-scale video benchmark for human activity understanding. In: Proceedings of the IEEE Conference on Computer Vision and Pattern Recognition, pp. 961–970 (2015)
7. Dai, X., Singh, B., Zhang, G., Davis, L.S., Chen, Y.Q.: Temporal context network for activity localization in videos. In: 2017 IEEE International Conference on Computer Vision (ICCV), pp. 5727–5736. IEEE (2017)
8. Dalal, N., Triggs, B.: Histograms of oriented gradients for human detection. In: IEEE Conference on Computer Vision and Pattern Recognition, pp. 886–893 (2005)
9. Escorcia, V., Caba Heilbron, F., Niebles, J.C., Ghanem, B.: DAPs: deep action proposals for action understanding. In: Leibe, B., Matas, J., Sebe, N., Welling, M. (eds.) ECCV 2016. LNCS, vol. 9907, pp. 768–784. Springer, Cham (2016). https://doi.org/10.1007/978-3-319-46487-9_47
10. Feichtenhofer, C., Pinz, A., Zisserman, A.: Convolutional two-stream network fusion for video action recognition. In: Proceedings of the IEEE Conference on Computer Vision and Pattern Recognition, pp. 1933–1941 (2016)
11. Felzenszwalb, P.F., Girshick, R.B., McAllester, D., Ramanan, D.: Object detection with discriminatively trained part-based models. IEEE Trans. Pattern Anal. Mach. Intell. **32**(9), 1627–1645 (2010)
12. Gao, J., Yang, Z., Nevatia, R.: Cascaded boundary regression for temporal action detection. arXiv preprint arXiv:1705.01180 (2017)
13. Gao, J., Yang, Z., Sun, C., Chen, K., Nevatia, R.: Turn tap: temporal unit regression network for temporal action proposals. arXiv preprint arXiv:1703.06189 (2017)
14. Ghanem, B., et al.: ActivityNet challenge 2017 summary. arXiv preprint arXiv:1710.08011 (2017)
15. Gidaris, S., Komodakis, N.: LocNet: improving localization accuracy for object detection. In: Proceedings of the IEEE Conference on Computer Vision and Pattern Recognition, pp. 789–798 (2016)
16. Girshick, R.: Fast R-CNN. In: Proceedings of the IEEE International Conference on Computer Vision, pp. 1440–1448 (2015)
17. Girshick, R., Donahue, J., Darrell, T., Malik, J.: Rich feature hierarchies for accurate object detection and semantic segmentation. In: Proceedings of the IEEE Conference on Computer Vision and Pattern Recognition, pp. 580–587 (2014)

18. He, K., Zhang, X., Ren, S., Sun, J.: Deep residual learning for image recognition. In: Proceedings of the IEEE Conference on Computer Vision and Pattern Recognition, pp. 770–778 (2016)
19. Heilbron, F.C., Barrios, W., Escorcia, V., Ghanem, B.: SCC: semantic context cascade for efficient action detection. In: IEEE Conference on Computer Vision and Pattern Recognition (CVPR), vol. 2 (2017)
20. Ioffe, S., Szegedy, C.: Batch normalization: accelerating deep network training by reducing internal covariate shift. In: International Conference on Machine Learning, pp. 448–456 (2015)
21. Jia, Y., et al.: Caffe: convolutional architecture for fast feature embedding. In: Proceedings of the 22nd ACM International conference on Multimedia, pp. 675–678. ACM (2014)
22. Jiang, Y.G., et al.: THUMOS challenge: action recognition with a large number of classes. In: ECCV Workshop (2014)
23. Karaman, S., Seidenari, L., Del Bimbo, A.: Fast saliency based pooling of fisher encoded dense trajectories. In: ECCV THUMOS Workshop (2014)
24. Karpathy, A., Toderici, G., Shetty, S., Leung, T., Sukthankar, R., Fei-Fei, L.: Large-scale video classification with convolutional neural networks. In: Proceedings of the IEEE Conference on Computer Vision and Pattern Recognition, pp. 1725–1732 (2014)
25. Kuo, W., Hariharan, B., Malik, J.: DeepBox: learning objectness with convolutional networks. In: Proceedings of the IEEE International Conference on Computer Vision, pp. 2479–2487 (2015)
26. Lin, T., Zhao, X., Shou, Z.: Single shot temporal action detection. In: Proceedings of the 25nd ACM International Conference on Multimedia (2017)
27. Lin, T., Zhao, X., Shou, Z.: Temporal convolution based action proposal: submission to ActivityNet 2017. arXiv preprint arXiv:1707.06750 (2017)
28. Lin, T.Y., Dollár, P., Girshick, R., He, K., Hariharan, B., Belongie, S.: Feature pyramid networks for object detection. arXiv preprint arXiv:1612.03144 (2016)
29. Oneata, D., Verbeek, J., Schmid, C.: The LEAR submission at Thumos 2014. In: ECCV THUMOS Workshop (2014)
30. Ren, S., He, K., Girshick, R., Sun, J.: Faster R-CNN: towards real-time object detection with region proposal networks. In: Advances in Neural Information Processing Systems, pp. 91–99 (2015)
31. Shou, Z., Chan, J., Zareian, A., Miyazawa, K., Chang, S.F.: CDC: convolutional-de-convolutional networks for precise temporal action localization in untrimmed videos. arXiv preprint arXiv:1703.01515 (2017)
32. Shou, Z., Wang, D., Chang, S.F.: Temporal action localization in untrimmed videos via multi-stage CNNS. In: Proceedings of the IEEE Conference on Computer Vision and Pattern Recognition, pp. 1049–1058 (2016)
33. Simonyan, K., Zisserman, A.: Two-stream convolutional networks for action recognition in videos. In: Advances in Neural Information Processing Systems, pp. 568–576 (2014)
34. Singh, G., Cuzzolin, F.: Untrimmed video classification for activity detection: submission to ActivityNet challenge. arXiv preprint arXiv:1607.01979 (2016)
35. Tran, D., Bourdev, L., Fergus, R., Torresani, L., Paluri, M.: Learning spatiotemporal features with 3d convolutional networks. In: Proceedings of the IEEE International Conference on Computer Vision, pp. 4489–4497 (2015)
36. Tran, D., Ray, J., Shou, Z., Chang, S.F., Paluri, M.: ConvNet architecture search for spatiotemporal feature learning. arXiv preprint arXiv:1708.05038 (2017)

37. Uijlings, J.R., van de Sande, K.E., Gevers, T., Smeulders, A.W.: Selective search for object recognition. Int. J. Comput. Vis. **104**(2), 154–171 (2013)
38. Wang, H., Kläser, A., Schmid, C., Liu, C.L.: Action recognition by dense trajectories. In: 2011 IEEE Conference on Computer Vision and Pattern Recognition (CVPR), pp. 3169–3176. IEEE (2011)
39. Wang, H., Schmid, C.: Action recognition with improved trajectories. In: Proceedings of the IEEE International Conference on Computer Vision, pp. 3551–3558 (2013)
40. Wang, L., Qiao, Y., Tang, X.: Action recognition and detection by combining motion and appearance features. THUMOS14 Action Recognit. Challenge **1**, 2 (2014)
41. Wang, L., Xiong, Y., Wang, Z., Qiao, Y.: Towards good practices for very deep two-stream ConvNets. arXiv preprint arXiv:1507.02159 (2015)
42. Wang, L., et al.: Temporal segment networks: towards good practices for deep action recognition. In: Leibe, B., Matas, J., Sebe, N., Welling, M. (eds.) ECCV 2016. LNCS, vol. 9912, pp. 20–36. Springer, Cham (2016). https://doi.org/10.1007/978-3-319-46484-8_2
43. Wang, L., Xiong, Y., Lin, D., Van Gool, L.: UntrimmedNets for weakly supervised action recognition and detection. arXiv preprint arXiv:1703.03329 (2017)
44. Wang, R., Tao, D.: UTS at ActivityNet 2016. AcitivityNet Large Scale Act. Recognit. Challenge **2016**, 8 (2016)
45. Xiong, Y., et al.: CUHK & ETHZ & SIAT submission to ActivityNet challenge 2016. arXiv preprint arXiv:1608.00797 (2016)
46. Xiong, Y., Zhao, Y., Wang, L., Lin, D., Tang, X.: A pursuit of temporal accuracy in general activity detection. arXiv preprint arXiv:1703.02716 (2017)
47. Xu, H., Das, A., Saenko, K.: R-c3d: region convolutional 3d network for temporal activity detection. arXiv preprint arXiv:1703.07814 (2017)
48. Yuan, Z., Stroud, J.C., Lu, T., Deng, J.: Temporal action localization by structured maximal sums. arXiv preprint arXiv:1704.04671 (2017)
49. Zhao, Y., Xiong, Y., Wang, L., Wu, Z., Lin, D., Tang, X.: Temporal action detection with structured segment networks. arXiv preprint arXiv:1704.06228 (2017)
50. Zitnick, C.L., Dollár, P.: Edge Boxes: locating object proposals from edges. In: Fleet, D., Pajdla, T., Schiele, B., Tuytelaars, T. (eds.) ECCV 2014. LNCS, vol. 8693, pp. 391–405. Springer, Cham (2014). https://doi.org/10.1007/978-3-319-10602-1_26

Progressive Structure from Motion

Alex Locher[1]([✉]), Michal Havlena[2]([✉]), and Luc Van Gool[1,3]([✉])

[1] Computer Vision Laboratory, ETH Zurich, Zürich, Switzerland
{alocher,vangool}@vision.ee.ethz.ch
[2] Vuforia, PTC, Vienna, Austria
mhavlena@ptc.com
[3] VISICS, KU Leuven, Leuven, Belgium

Abstract. Structure from Motion or the sparse 3D reconstruction out of individual photos is a long studied topic in computer vision. Yet none of the existing reconstruction pipelines fully addresses a progressive scenario where images are only getting available during the reconstruction process and intermediate results are delivered to the user. Incremental pipelines are capable of growing a 3D model but often get stuck in local minima due to wrong (binding) decisions taken based on incomplete information. Global pipelines on the other hand need the access to the complete viewgraph and are not capable of delivering intermediate results. In this paper we propose a new reconstruction pipeline working in a progressive manner rather than in a batch processing scheme. The pipeline is able to recover from failed reconstructions in early stages, avoids to take binding decisions, delivers a progressive output and yet maintains the capabilities of existing pipelines. We demonstrate and evaluate our method on diverse challenging public and dedicated datasets including those with highly symmetric structures and compare to the state of the art.

1 Introduction

3D reconstruction from individual photographs is a long studied topic in computer vision [1,12,31]. The field of Structure from Motion (SfM) deals with the intrinsic and extrinsic calibration of sets of images and recovers a sparse 3D structure of the scene at the same time. Traditional methods are usually designed as batch processing algorithms, where image acquisition and image processing are separated into two independent steps. This contrasts with current demand, when one would like to be able to convert an object or a scene into a 3D model anytime and anywhere, just by using the mobile phone one is carrying in her pocket. Recent developments in mobile technology and the availability of 3D printers raised the need for 3D content even more and underlay the importance of 3D modeling. In a user-centric scenario, images are taken on the spot and processed by a 3D modeling pipeline on-the-fly [16,19]. Any feedback which gets available to the user helps to guide her acquisition and, even more importantly, assures that the 3D model represents the real-world object in the

V. Ferrari et al. (Eds.): ECCV 2018, LNCS 11208, pp. 22–38, 2018.
https://doi.org/10.1007/978-3-030-01225-0_2

desired quality. In a collaborative scenario, multiple users acquire pictures of the same object and images are gathered on the reconstruction server in the cloud. The 3D model is progressively built and intermediate reconstruction results are shown to the user. Images are getting available as they are taken and the SfM pipeline has never access to the complete set of information in the dataset. Moreover, the whole reconstruction process might have a starting, but no predefined end point. Users might always decide to add more images to an existing model.

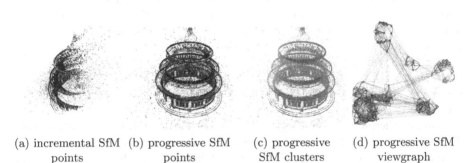

(a) incremental SfM   (b) progressive SfM   (c) progressive   (d) progressive SfM
    points   points   SfM clusters   viewgraph

Fig. 1. Opposed to existing methods, a favorable image order is not crucial for the proposed progressive SfM pipeline. While the baseline method (a) fails to recover the structure of the scene our method successfully reconstructs the temple (b). Individual clusters are identified in the viewgraph (d) and merged (c) based on a lightweight optimization.

In this work we therefore propose a progressive SfM pipeline which avoids taking (potentially fatal) binding decisions and therefore is as independent of the input image order as possible. Moreover, the proposed pipeline reuses already computed intermediate results in later steps and is suited for delivering progressive modeling results back to the user within seconds.

1.1   Related Work

Classical SfM pipelines are typically not suited to be used in such a progressive – multiuser-centric scenario. Global pipelines [22,29] start by estimating poses of all cameras in the dataset and estimate the structure in a second step. Evidently, this relies on the access to the complete dataset which contradicts the idea of progressive 3D modeling. Sequential SfM pipelines, sometimes termed SLAM [7,23], are inherently suitable for processing (potentially infinite) streams of images. Nevertheless, the underlying assumption often is that images neighboring in the sequence are spatially close in the scene, which is easily violated when streams from multiple users are combined together. Incremental SfM pipelines [28,31,36] build a 3D model by initializing the structure from a small seed and gradually growing it by adding additional cameras. This scheme is closer to the requested progressive scenario but, unfortunately, is strongly dependent on the order in which images are added to the model [21, 27]. View selection algorithms [34] carefully determine the image order usually by employing the global matching information which is not available in the progressive case. Hierarchical SfM pipelines [8, 10] try to overcome the problem of improper seed selection by starting from several seed locations at the same time and eventually merging the partial 3D models into a single global model in later stages. Sweeney et al. [33] group multiple individual cameras and optimize them jointly as a distributed camera. However all hierarchical methods require the knowledge of all images in advance. Our proposed method is partially inspired by these approaches but in order to provide the progressive capability, the hierarchy is not fixed but rather re-defined every time new images are added to the reconstruction process.

Due to the lack of global information, an incremental pipeline would connect new images to the existing model based on incomplete information which often causes corrupted 3D models [11, 14, 15, 26, 37]. Even more importantly, incremental pipelines cannot recover from wrong decisions taken based on missing information and therefore can easily get stuck in only locally optimal reconstructions. The only reliable solution would be re-running an incremental or global pipeline from scratch when new images become available which leads to an impractical algorithm runtime. Heinly et al. [11] detected erroneous reconstructions of scenes with duplicate structure in a post processing step by evaluating different splits of the model into submodels and potentially merge them in the correct configuration by leveraging conflicting observations. Our method in contrary is a full fledged SfM pipeline which avoids getting trapped in a local minima in the first place. Faulty configurations are detected and corrected on-the-fly and not in a post processing step.

Our work bases on a lightweight representation of the complete scene as a viewgraph. Many existing approaches investigated robustification of the global view-graph by filtering out bad epipolar geometries [6, 34] and enforcing loop constraints [38]. Wilson and Snavely [35] are able to reconstruct scenes with repetitive structures by scoring repetitive features using local clustering. Recent work of Cui [5] takes a similar approach to our pipeline. The Hybrid SfM pipeline estimates all rotations of the viewgraph in a community based global algorithm. The estimated orientations are leveraged in the second phase of the pipeline by estimating the translations and structure of the scene in an incremental scheme with reduced dimensionality. While sharing the idea of combining global and incremental schemes, HSfM is a pure batch processing algorithm. The global rotation averaging needs access to the complete view graph in advance which is not available in a progressive scheme. In our work we combine a dynamic global view graph with a local clustering based on a connectivity score and combine the advantages of incremental and global structure from motion. In order to accommodate for the demands of a progressive pipeline, we allow for flexibility in already reconstructed parts of the model and constantly verify the local reconstructions against the globally optimized viewgraph.

1.2 Contributions

We propose a novel progressive SfM pipeline which enables 3D reconstruction in an anytime anywhere multiuser-centric scenario. Unlike traditional pipelines, the proposed approach avoids taking binding decisions, does not depend on the order of incoming images and is able to recover from wrong decisions taken due to the lack of information. Moreover, the computed intermediate results are propagated along the reconstruction process resulting in an efficient use of computational resources. A C++ implementation of the proposed progressive pipeline is publicly available under: https://github.com/alexlocher/progsfm.

2 Progressive Reconstruction

In the following section we give an overview of our progressive SfM pipeline and detail individual components and key aspects later on.

2.1 Overview

Our progressive SfM pipeline takes an ordered sequence of images with its geometrically verified correspondences as the input and delivers a sparse pointcloud and calibrated camera poses as the output (see Fig. 2). The resulting sparse configuration is updated with every image added to the scene. A viewgraph with nodes being images and edges connecting pairs of matched images is gradually built and serves as the global knowledge throughout the whole reconstruction. On every iteration of the algorithm, the viewgraph is clustered based on local connectivity and individual clusters are processed locally. In each of the local clusters a robust rotation averaging scheme filters out wrong two-view geometries and the 3D structure is estimated using either an incremental or a global SfM pipeline. The cluster configuration between two time steps is tracked and the already estimated parts of the 3D model are passed to the next stage. The global configuration of individual clusters is estimated in the last stage by robustly estimating 7 DoF similarity transforms between them using the remaining inter-cluster constraints. Generally, the local incremental method enables robust and efficient reconstructions while the viewgraph combined with the robust rotation averaging injects the global knowledge and allows for correction of corrupted 3D models.

2.2 Progressive Viewgraph

The algorithm takes a (randomly) ordered sequence of images $\mathbf{I} = (I_0, I_1, I_2, \dots)$ as the input. Every incoming image is matched against the most relevant images already present in the scene and geometrically verified pairwise correspondences are obtained. A viewgraph $\mathcal{G}(\mathcal{V}_t, \mathcal{E}_t)$ with images as vertices $\mathcal{V}_t = \{I_i | i \leq t\}$ is maintained at every time step t. Two vertices (V_i, V_j) are connected by an undirected edge $\mathcal{E}_{ij}$ iff there exists a minimum amount of correspondences

$(\mathbf{M}_{ij} > \eta \land i < j \le t)$ between them where $\mathbf{M} \in \mathbb{R}^{t \times t}$ is the matching matrix. Every edge $\mathcal{E}_{ij}$ has an associated relative rotation $\mathbf{R}_{ij}$ and translation direction t_{ij} which is obtained by decomposing either the estimated essential matrix in the calibrated case or the fundamental matrix when the focal length is not known.

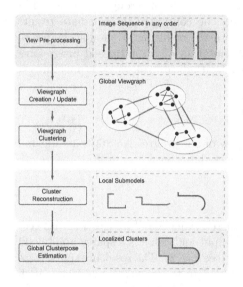

Fig. 2. An overview of the main steps of the progressive SfM pipeline and its involved components.

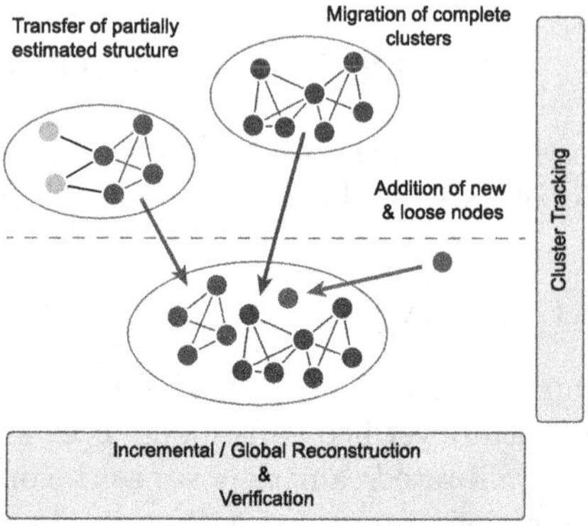

Fig. 3. Depending on the status of an individual cluster, its structure is estimated with different methods.

The order in which images are fed to a reconstruction pipeline plays an important role and every snapshot of the viewgraph only captures the past information of the reconstruction process. This is why filtering of supposedly wrong two-view geometries at this stage can be very dangerous. It might happen that a geometry is inconsistent with other local geometries in the neighborhood[1] at the current time-step but connecting images added in later steps may show that the two-view geometry was actually correct. As a wrong decision in the global viewgraph could lead to a local minimum in the reconstruction, i.e. a corrupted 3D model, we do not conduct any outlier rejection and defer robustification to a later stage.

2.3   Clustering

Motivated by the general observation that densely connected regions of the viewgraph are likely to form a 3D model worth reconstruction, the viewgraph is clustered in a second step. The distance d_{ij} between two vertices V_{ij} is based

---

[1] This can, e.g., be checked by computing the cumulative rotation of loops in which the edge is participating [38].

on the weighted Jaccard distance of the adjacent edges where connections to neighboring vertices are weighted by the number of verified correspondences.

$$d_{ij} = 1 - \left| \frac{\sum\limits_{n \in \mathcal{N}} \mathbf{M}_{in} + \mathbf{M}_{nj}}{\sum\limits_{n=0}^{t} \mathbf{M}_{in} + \mathbf{M}_{nj}} \right| \quad \mathcal{N} = \{k | \mathbf{M}_{ik} \cdot \mathbf{M}_{kj} > 0\} \tag{1}$$

A set of clusters $\mathcal{C}_t$ is hierarchically grown by single-linkage clustering until no single edge with $d_{ij} < \eta$ between two clusters exists. Single-linkage clustering tends to generate clusters with a chain-like topology where the two ending nodes might have a distance way larger than the defined threshold. While this might be a disadvantage in other applications it is actually beneficial in our application as local (incremental) reconstruction pipeline performs well for such graph structures.

Incremental Clustering. Due to the single-linkage hierarchical clustering, a simplified incremental scheme can be used to update an existing cluster topology with a new node. While generally a single extra node can cause a complete change in topology of the clustered graph, the changes are limited to clusters which are connected to the new node. As a result only clusters with an edge connecting to the new node have to be re-clustered which leads to an efficient and scalable implementation. Note that in worst case the whole graph still might be updated – but in most cases a new image only connects to few clusters and therefore most of the existing clusters remain untouched.

2.4   Cluster Tracking and Recycling

Between the transition of two timesteps t_b and $t_a = t_b + 1$ the topology of clusters can undergo large changes but mostly will either stay the same or be extended by the new image. All changes in the clusters have to be propagated to the eventually estimated 3D structure. We therefore keep track of the nodes changing cluster between the two timesteps and add or remove the corresponding images in the local reconstruction. The recycling of intermediate (partial) 3D reconstructions can be realized by a merge and split scheme. If a group of interconnected nodes transfer together from one cluster to another, the corresponding cameras in the 3D model can be separated from the rest and merged into the potentially existing structure of the new cluster.

2.5   Cluster Reconstruction

Once individual clusters $\mathcal{C}_i$ have been identified by the hierarchical clustering, the 3D structure of the images and correspondences of every cluster C is estimated. The cluster reconstruction process is only triggered if its topology has changed meaning either some nodes were added or some nodes were removed from the cluster. If the topology of the cluster is unchanged between the two time steps t_b and t_a, the reconstruction step is skipped as a whole.

A sub-graph $\mathcal{V}_C$ capturing all vertices and edges of the cluster C is extracted in a first step. All following operations are restricted to the scope of the extracted graph $\mathcal{V}_C$.

Robust Rotation Averaging. The unfiltered viewgraph is potentially corrupted by outliers and has to be cleaned up for further usage. As this step is performed in every iteration it is safe to reject outlier two-view geometries. As a result of the repetitive execution of the filtering stage, it is important to use a computationally efficient filtering scheme. As proposed by Chatterjee et al. [3] we estimate the global rotations of the subgraph with a robust ℓ_1 optimization. Global Rotations $\bar{\mathbf{R}}$ are initialized by concatenating the relative rotations of a Maximum Spanning Tree (MST) extracted from the viewgraph $\mathcal{V}_C$ using the number of verified inliers $\mathbf{M}_{ij}$ as edge weights. The global rotations are then optimized by minimizing the relative rotation errors ρ_{ij}.

$$\arg\min_{\bar{\mathbf{R}}} \sum_{(i,j) \in \mathcal{E}_C} \rho_{ij} \left(\mathbf{R}_{ij}, \bar{\mathbf{R}}_j \bar{\mathbf{R}}_i^{-1} \right) \tag{2}$$

By using the Lie-algebraic approximation of the relative rotation, the error can be expressed as a difference of the corresponding rotations ω. Where $\omega = \Theta\mathbf{n} \in \mathfrak{so}(3)$ denotes a rotation by angle Θ around the unit axis $\mathbf{n}$.

$$\omega_{ij} \approx \omega_j - \omega_i \tag{3}$$

The relative rotations can be encoded in a sparse matrix $\mathbf{A}$ where each row only has two nonzero $-1, +1$ entries. The robust ℓ_1 norm combined with an edge weighting ρ depending on the number of verified correspondences allows us to obtain the global rotations of the cluster C in an iterative scheme by optimizing Eq. 4 in every step. For more details we refer the reader to the original publication [3].

$$\arg\min_{\omega_g} \| \mathbf{A} \, \Delta\omega_g - \rho\omega_{rel} \|_{\ell_1} \tag{4}$$

The obtained global rotations can optionally be refined by Iteratively Reweighted Least Squares (IRLS) method using a robustified ℓ_2 norm. As we are primarily interested in rejecting outliers, the results of the ℓ_1 optimization is accurate enough and we omit the refinement step.

Finally edges with a relative error above $\rho_{g\,\max}$ are removed from the local viewgraph.

Reconstruction. Using the global rotations and the pairwise matches as the input, the structure of the individual clusters is estimated with different methods depending on the current status (Fig. 3).

New: If we could not recover any structure from t_b and the cluster contains at least μ_{min} nodes but less than μ_{max} images a new reconstruction is starting using an incremental SfM pipeline similar to [31,36]. If the number of images in the cluster is larger than μ_{max}, incremental pipelines get inefficient and a global pipeline is more suited. We therefore refine the global rotations and estimate global position using the 1DSfM method [35]. The structure is then obtained by triangulating consistent feature-tracks and the configuration is refined by a bundle adjustment step.

Extend: In most cases an existing local reconstruction can be extended by one or multiple images which are either new or transferred from another cluster. In order to extend an existing 3D reconstruction with a new image we extend existing feature tracks by the new correspondences and estimate the 3D position of the camera by the P3P algorithm [17]. New tracks are added and potential conflicting tracks are split up. A local bundle adjustment refines the structure and calibration of the newly added cameras. If the model has grown by more than η_{grow} percent, a bundle adjustment step over the local reconstruction refines the whole structure.

Transfer: If a large part (more than μ_{min} nodes) of an already estimated local model is transferred to another cluster, its already estimated structure is kept and transferred to the new cluster. Commonly estimated tracks are fused and a bundle adjustment step refines the structure. Potentially unestimated cameras are then added in an incremental scheme as described before.

Detection of Bad Configurations. Due to the incremental reconstruction scheme for cluster reconstruction we can reuse most of the intermediate results from an earlier stage and propagate them to later stages. The incremental scheme is highly dependent on the actual image ordering and therefore some unfortunate decisions taken in early stages (e.g. wrongly connecting an image due to missing information) cannot be recovered in later stages. Global clustering usually solves this problem for us as the wrongly connected image or sub-model is likely to be transferred to another cluster at a later stage. But it might also happen that the image actually belongs to the same cluster and yet is wrongly connected. Without any additional counter measurements, we would end up with a corrupted reconstruction in such cases.

By using the relative global rotations of the local viewgraph (which is independent of the image order) we can evaluate an error measure between the rotations of the current local reconstruction $\hat{\mathbf{R}}$ and the global rotations $\bar{\mathbf{R}}$.

$$\rho_l = \left\| \left\{ \bar{\mathbf{R}}_{ij}\,\hat{\mathbf{R}}_{ij}^{-1} \middle| (i,j) \in \mathcal{E}_C \right\} \right\|_\infty \tag{5}$$

If the rotation error ρ_l is above a certain limit $\rho_{l\,max}$ the reconstruction is likely to be erroneous. Hence it is reset and re-estimated in the next phase of the reconstruction.

2.6   Cluster Pose Estimation

The output of the pipeline so far are multiple locally highly consistent but disconnected model parts. In order to merge them to a final representation we make use of the remaining inter-cluster connections. As this step of merging multiple models is often rather fragile and can easily go wrong, several methods employed a rather conservative merging criteria as multiple cameras of overlap [10] or a high amount of common points [36]. Instead, we are estimating pairwise similarity transforms $\mathcal{T}_{ab} \in Sim(3)$ between clusters C_a and C_b and optimize the global positions of the cluster centers. For robustification, we use a two stage verification scheme for individual inter-cluster constraints.

In the first stage, a similarity transform based on 3D-to-3D correspondences from every single edge $\mathcal{E}_{ij}$ between clusters C_a and C_b is estimated in a RANSAC scheme [9,13]. The vertices (camera centers) of C_a are afterwards transformed using the estimated transformation and the camera configuration of the obtained combined model is compared to the individual configuration before. A neighborhood similarity measure $\mathfrak{s}$ evaluates how many of the cameras $\mathbf{p}_k$ in the merged cluster would retain their closest neighbors $\mathrm{NN}_a(\mathbf{p}_k)$ and $\mathrm{NN}_b(\mathbf{p}_k)$ for the cameras from clusters C_a and C_b, respectively. $\mathbf{p}_k$ denotes the camera center of the node k and the operator $\mathcal{T}_{ij} \circ \mathbf{p}_k$ transforms a point by the similarity transform.

$$\mathcal{T}_{ij} \ \forall \ i \in C_a \wedge j \in C_b \wedge (i,j) \in \mathcal{E}_C \tag{6}$$

$$\mathbf{P}_a = \mathbf{p}_k | k \in C_a \tag{7}$$
$$\mathbf{P}_b = \mathbf{p}_k | k \in C_b \tag{8}$$
$$\mathbf{P}_c = \mathbf{P}_b \cup \mathcal{T}_{ij} \circ \mathbf{p}_k | k \in C_a \tag{9}$$

$$\mathfrak{s} = \frac{1}{|\mathbf{P}_c|} \sum_{\mathbf{p}_k \in \mathbf{P}_c} s_k \tag{10}$$

$$s_k = \begin{cases} 1 & k \in C_a \wedge \mathcal{T}_{ij} \circ \mathrm{NN}_a(\mathbf{p}_k) = \mathrm{NN}_c(\mathcal{T}_{ij} \circ \mathbf{p}_k) \\ 1 & k \in C_b \wedge \mathrm{NN}_b(\mathbf{p}_k) = \mathrm{NN}_c(\mathbf{p}_k) \\ 0 & \text{otherwise} \end{cases} \tag{11}$$

Edges with the neighborhood similarity measure below λ_c are rejected as outliers for the final constraint estimation. The measure is motivated by the observation that nearby cameras should already be clustered by the original algorithm and prevents merged models where the cameras are extensively interleaved.

In the second stage, a final transformation $\mathcal{T}_{ij}$ between the clusters is estimated using all correspondences of edges that survived the first filtering stage. All relative constraints are gathered and a cluster graph $\mathcal{G}_C$ with local reconstructions as nodes and pairwise inter-cluster constraints as edges is created.

$$\arg\min_{\mathcal{P}_C} \sum_{(a,b) \in \mathcal{G}_C} \left\| \delta \left(\mathcal{T}_{ab} \mathcal{P}_b \mathcal{P}_a^{-1} \right) \right\|^2 \tag{12}$$

The global poses $\mathcal{P}_C$ of the clusters are afterwards obtained by iteratively minimizing the pairwise relative pose constraints $\mathcal{T}_{ab}$, where $\delta(.)$ denotes the robust Huber error function.

While this in the optimal case leads to a single 3D model, the flexibility and efficiency of the global optimization allows us to choose a much less conservative threshold for cluster merging. In addition to its efficiency, the cluster graph representation can easily incorporate additional extrinsic constraints, e.g., the gravity vector for orientation with respect to the ground plane or coarse cluster-wise GPS locations for geo-referencing. Such additional constraints can help to put individual models in relative perspective even if pure vision based inter-cluster constraints are not (yet) available.

3   Experiments and Results

In the following section, we first give some implementation details of the proposed solution and introduce the conducted experiments.

3.1   Implementation

We implemented the proposed pipeline as a C++ software. SIFT [20] features are detected on all images and described with the RootSift descriptor [2]. The pipeline is setup for stream processing dedicated by the progressive reconstruction scheme. Every incoming image is indexed by a 1M word vocabulary trained on the independent Oxford5k [24] dataset and the top 100 nearest neighbors are retrieved using a fast tf-idf scoring [30]. Matches are geometrically verified by estimating the fundamental or essential matrix (depending on the availability of the focal length) as well as a homography matrix in a RANSAC scheme using the general USAC framework [25]. The relative rotation and translation direction are obtained by decomposing the fundamental, essential, or homography matrix (depending on the amount of inliers). The incremental and global reconstruction of cluster centers bases on the publicly available Theia library [32] and the final clustergraph optimization is realized in the g2o [18] framework. The following parameters were used within all the conducted experiments: $\mu_{min} = 5$, $\mu_{max} = 50$, $\lambda_s = 0.9$, $\rho_{l\,max} = \rho_{g\,max} = 10°$, $\eta = 0.2$, $\eta_{grow} = 0.15$.

3.2   Baselines

Throughout our experiments we compare the proposed progressive pipeline against two linear pipelines (VisualSFM [36] and incremental Theia [32]) as well as to the recently published hybrid pipeline HSfM [5]. For an unbiased comparision, all geometrically verified matches were precomputed and imported into the various pipelines. The streaming part of the pipeline was skipped and matches directly loaded from disk.

Within the experiments we run the pipelines in different modes:

batch mode. All images are added to the pipeline at once and the model is reconstructed without intermediate results. This is the classical SfM operation mode.

progressive mode. Images are fed to the pipeline in a certain order and intermediate reconstructions are enforced. In VisualSFM this is realized by the "Add Image" option and in Theia we dictated the order in which views are added to an ongoing reconstruction by a slight code modification.

3.3   Randomized Image Order

One of the key contributions of the proposed pipeline is the ability of recovering from wrong connections between image pairs made in previous reconstruction cycles. Wrong connections often occur in symmetric environments which is why we chose the publicly available TempleOfHeaven dataset [15] with a rotationaly symmetric structure for the first experiment. The dataset consists of 341 images taken in a regular spacing and perfectly demonstrates problems arising from unpleasant orderings. As a reference model, we reconstructed the scene using VisualSFM and restricted the matches to sequential matching in the original order. Figure 5 shows the development of the model as a function of the timestep t. We report the number of clusters before and after global cluster position estimation as well as the number of outlier cameras. A camera is considered to be an outlier if the position error is larger than half the minimum distance between two cameras in the reference model.

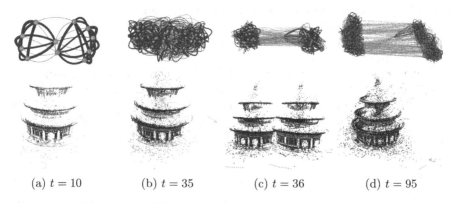

(a) $t = 10$ (b) $t = 35$ (c) $t = 36$ (d) $t = 95$

Fig. 4. Individual snapshots showing the viewgraph *(top)* and the sparse structure *(bottom)* of a reconstruction of the temple scene using a very unfortunate image ordering document the algorithm's recovery ability. Two separate parts of the temple are initially wrongly reconstructed in a single model (a-b) and are later successfully separated (c) and the real structure is recovered (d).

As expected both methods perform well in the "linear" case, where the images are fed to the pipeline in the original ordering. A single cluster is reconstructed and maximum of 8 cameras are classified as outliers. In a second experiment we randomly shuffled the order of images. After an initial set of 20 images, the baseline merges all clusters to a single one and as a result the number of outlier cameras increases linearly. The final 3D model is highly corrupted and only covers about a third of the temple (Fig. 1a).

In contrast, the proposed pipeline creates up to 6 individual but locally consistent clusters. After 84 out of the 341 images the clusters are correctly localized into a single effective cluster by the cluster positioning (dashed line). Figure 1 shows the resulting reconstruction after 100 images as well as the corresponding clustered viewgraph.

3.4   Very Unfortunate Image Order

In order to demonstrate the recovery capabilities of our proposed pipeline we conducted an additional experiment on the TempleOfHeaven dataset. The temple has a strong rotational symmetry which repeats with 60°. One of the worst conditions for an algorithm would be if the image ordering had exactly this 60° periodicity. To test the algorithm, we created an artificial image sequence by feeding the images alternatively in the following order: $(I_0, I_{60}, I_1, I_{61}, ...)$. Figure 6 shows the number of clusters, images, and outliers in every timestep. Due to the high amount of matches between the symmetric part and the lack of images in between, the clustering algorithm sees enough evidence for putting

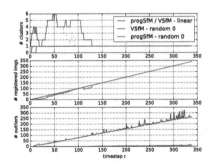

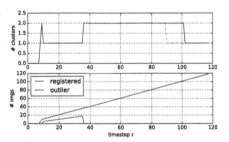

Fig. 5. Behavior of the incremental and progressive SfM pipelines on the TempleOfHeaven dataset. In the well behaving "linear" case *(blue)*, both pipelines reconstruct the temple. If the input order is shuffled the incremental pipeline gets stuck in a local minimum *(green)* whereas the proposed pipeline recovers and reconstructs the whole scene *(red)*. (Color figure online)

Fig. 6. Evolution of the clusters and images in a very unfortunately ordered image sequence. Despite the heavy rotational symmetry of the temple dataset, the pipeline is able to recover from a wrong configuration (timestep 36).

all images into a single cluster (Fig. 4a) and roughly every second image is an outlier. After the addition of the 36th image, the connectivity has sufficiently changed so that the two clusters are recognized and the 3D models are separated.

Due to the highly interleaved configuration the structure of the individual models cannot be recycled in this case and both clusters are reconstructed from scratch. At this stage there are no inter-cluster constraints available yet, which is why the global cluster positioning does not succeed and the models are displayed as independent sub-models (Fig. 4c). On the 95th image enough intra-cluster evidence is available s.t. the models can be placed into a common coordinate system (Fig. 4d) and with the 101st image a single cluster is formed (this time the structure of the individual sub-models can be recovered and a simple merging is needed). The experiment shows that the proposed pipeline can recover from a wrong local minimum of the reconstruction.

Fig. 7. Comparison of the proposed progressive pipeline *(left, center)* to the incremental SfM pipeline *(right)* on the Stanford dataset.

3.5   Realworld Progressive Reconstruction

While the experiments so far demonstrated the capabilities of the progressive pipeline for unfortunate image orderings, its behavior in real world applications remains to be shown. Therefore we collected a series of 4516 images with three different mobile devices (*HTC Nexus 9*, *LG Nexus 5x*, and *Google Pixel*) consisting of 29 sequences on the main quad of the Stanford University. The sequences were then progressively reconstructed in an interleaved order (simulating multiple users collaboratively acquiring the pictures) as well as in the batch-processing mode. An additional similar experiment was conducted using the publicly available Quad dataset [4] consisting of 6514 images, mainly taken by *iPhone 3G*. Images were shuffled randomly and pushed to the reconstruction algorithms.

Table 1 shows the proposed pipeline compared to the incremental Theia [32] pipeline in batch and progressive modes. In addition we compare against the HSfM [5] pipeline purely in batch-processing mode. The proposed algorithm as the only pipeline can deal with the progressive scheme while the other get stuck in a local minimum and only reconstruct a very small subpart of the scene[2]. In the case of the progressive pipeline, we also report the number of failure recoveries during the whole reconstruction (the number of resets with a local

---

[2] Experiments were repeated using multiple random orderings.

cluster due to major topological changes). Figure 7 illustrates the final result of the proposed pipeline versus the local minimum of the incremental pipeline. The compute times of the proposed pipeline are comparable to existing pipelines despite the continuous flow of intermediate results. This is due to the fact that our pipeline practically never operates on the whole image sets, but only on the local clusters. This allows significantly faster execution times of the bundle adjustment.

We furthermore run our method on several of the datasets presented by [11]. We used random ordering of the crowd sourced data and pushed them to the progressive pipeline as done in the Quad [4] experiment. Figure 8 shows a sample result on the Radcliffe scene. While both HSfM and the incremental baseline method got confused by the duplicate structure, our pipeline successfully separated the front and rear views of Radcliffe. The two clusters were merged successfully into the correct configuration by the global cluster pose optimization. In contrary to [11], this is not done in a post processing step but erroneous connections are detected on-the-fly during the reconstruction. Table 1 shows the results on the resulting numbers on the dataset equally to the experiment before. Our method was able to separate duplicate structure in all datasets. As the reconstruction backbone of the presented pipeline bases on the well known incremental [32] and global [35] pipelines, the accuracy of the resulting structure is equals the accuracy of these pipelines.

Fig. 8. Result on the Radcliffe dataset with HSfM (*left*), Theia (incr.) (*right*) and the proposed method (*right*).

Table 1. Evaluation of our pipeline versus the incremental Theia pipeline and HSfM. Only the proposed pipeline can successfully handle the progressive scenario.

			Stanford	Quad [4]	BigBen	Radcliffe Camera	Alexander Nevsky Cathedral	Branden-burg Gate	Arc De Triomphe
	total imgs	[#]	4516	6514	402	282	448	175	434
batch	HSfM [5] imgs	[#]	2,140	4,832	375	272	430	173	441
	time	[s]	11,490	23,570	1,932	1,654	1,900	389	2,131
	Theia (incr.) [32] imgs	[#]	3,298	5,462	394	278	443	173	410
	time	[s]	34,749	158,853	2,385	1,307	3,687	1,018	3,348
progressive	Theia (incr.) [32] imgs	[#]	51	527	394	280	418	173	416
	time	[s]	7,605	215,064	2,026	1,473	2,268	1,141	3,516
	proposed imgs	[#]	3,165	3,894	285	279	427	173	405
	time	[s]	13,276	25,713	552	1,121	2,163	627	377
	clusters	[#]	76	92	5	2	4	2	5
	recoveries	[#]	14	29	1	0	5	1	1

4   Conclusions

We proposed a novel progressive SfM pipeline which addresses a multiuser-centric scenario, where a 3D model is simultaneously reconstructed from multiple image streams handled by a cloud-based reconstruction service. In contrary to existing work, our pipeline does not depend on the image order and does not require any a-priori global knowledge about image connectivity. The progressive pipeline avoids taking any binding decisions and is able to recover for erroneous configurations. A global viewgraph is incrementally built and maintained. The graph is clustered based on the local connectivity of cameras and individual clusters are reconstructed using either an incremental or a global reconstruction pipeline. In the last step, individual models are merged using a lightweight posegraph optimization just on the cluster centers. We demonstrated the effectiveness and efficiency of our pipeline on multiple dataset and compared it to existing solutions.

References

1. Agarwal, S., et al.: Building rome in a day. Commun. ACM **54**, 105–112 (2011)
2. Arandjelovic, R., Zisserman, A.: Three things everyone should know to improve object retrieval C. In: CVPR, pp. 2911–2918 (2012)
3. Chatterjee, A., Govindu, V.M.: Efficient and robust large-scale rotation averaging. In: ICCV, pp. 521–528 (2013)
4. Crandall, D., Owens, A., Snavely, N., Huttenlocher, D.: SfM with MRFs: discrete-continuous optimization for large-scale structure from motion. PAMI **35**(12), 2841–2853 (2013)
5. Cui, H., Gao, X., Shen, S., Hu, Z.: HSFM: hybrid structure-from-motion. In: CVPR. pp, 1212–1221 (2017)
6. Cui, Z., Tan, P.: Global structure-from-motion by similarity averaging. In: CVPR, pp. 864–872 (2015)
7. Davison, A.J.: Real-time simultaneous localisation and mapping with a single camera. In: ICCV, pp. 1403–1410 (2003)
8. Farenzena, M., Fusiello, A., Gherardi, R.: Structure-and-motion pipeline on a hierarchical cluster tree. In: ICCV Work, pp. 1489–1496 (2009)
9. Fischler, M.A., Bolles, R.C.: Random sample consensus: a paradigm for model fitting with applications to image analysis and automated cartography. Commun. ACM **24**(6), 381–395 (1981)
10. Havlena, M., Torii, A., Pajdla, T.: Efficient Structure from Motion by Graph Optimization. In: ECCV, pp. 1–14 (2010)
11. Heinly, J., Dunn, E., Frahm, J.-M.: Correcting for duplicate scene structure in sparse 3D reconstruction. In: Fleet, D., Pajdla, T., Schiele, B., Tuytelaars, T. (eds.) ECCV 2014. LNCS, vol. 8692, pp. 780–795. Springer, Cham (2014). https://doi.org/10.1007/978-3-319-10593-2_51
12. Heinly, J., Schönenberger, J.L., Dunn, E., Frahm, J.M.: Reconstructing the World * in Six Days. In: CVPR (2015)

13. Horn, B.K.P.: Closed-form solution of absolute orientation using unit quaternions. J. Opt. Soc. Am. A **4**(4), 629 (1987)
14. Irschara, A., Zach, C., Bischof, H.: Towards wiki-based dense city modeling. In: ICCV (2007)
15. Jiang, N., Tan, P., Cheong, L.F.: Seeing double without confusion: Structure-from-motion in highly ambiguous scenes. In: CVPR, pp. 1458–1465 (2012)
16. Kang, Z., Medioni, G.: Progressive 3D model acquisition with a commodity hand-held camera. In: WACV, pp. 270–277 (2015)
17. Kneip, L., Scaramuzza, D., Siegwart, R.: A novel parametrization of the perspective-three-point problem for a direct computation of absolute camera position and orientation. In: CVPR (2011)
18. Kummerle, R., Grisetti, G., Strasdat, H., Konolige, K., Burgard, W.: G2o: a general framework for graph optimization. In: ICRA, pp. 3607–3613, May 2011
19. Locher, A., Perdoch, M., Van Gool, L.: Progressive prioritized multi-view stereo. In: CVPR, pp. 3244–3252 (2016)
20. Lowe, D.G.: Distinctive image features from scale-invariant keypoints. Int. J. Comput. Vis. **60**(2), 91–110 (2004)
21. Martinec, D., Pajdla, T.: Robust rotation and translation estimation in multiview reconstruction. In: CVPR (2007)
22. Moulon, P., Monasse, P., Marlet, R.: Global fusion of relative motions for robust, accurate and scalable structure from motion. In: ICCV, pp. 3248–3255 (2013)
23. Mur-Artal, R., Montiel, J.M.M., Tardos, J.D.: ORB-SLAM: a versatile and accurate monocular slam system. IEEE Trans. Robot. **31**(5), 1147–1163 (2015)
24. Philbin, J., Chum, O., Isard, M., Sivic, J., Zisserman, A.: Object retrieval with large vocabularies and fast spatial matching. In: CVPR (2007)
25. Raguram, R., Chum, O., Pollefeys, M., Matas, J., Frahm, J.M.: USAC: a universal framework for random sample consensus. IEEE Trans. Pattern Anal. Mach. Intell. **35**(8), 2022–2038 (2013)
26. Roberts, R., Sinha, S.N., Szeliski, R., Steedly, D.: Structure from motion for scenes with large duplicate structures. In: CVPR, pp. 3137–3144 (2011)
27. Schönberger, J.L., Radenovič, F., Chum, O., Frahm, J.M.: From single image query to detailed 3d reconstruction. In: CVPR, pp. 5126–5134, June 2015
28. Schönberger, J.L., Frahm, J.M.: Structure-from-motion revisited. In: CVPR (2016)
29. Sinha, S.N., Steedly, D., Szeliski, R.: A multi-stage linear approach to structure from motion. In: Kutulakos, K.N. (ed.) ECCV 2010. LNCS, vol. 6554, pp. 267–281. Springer, Heidelberg (2012). https://doi.org/10.1007/978-3-642-35740-4_21
30. Sivic, J., Zisserman, A.: Video Google: a text retrieval approach to object matching in videos. In: ICCV (2003)
31. Snavely, N., Seitz, S.M., Szeliski, R.: Modeling the world from internet photo collections. Int. J. Comput. Vis. **80**(2), 189–210 (2008)
32. Sweeney, C.: Theia Multiview Geometry Library: Tutorial & Reference. http://theia-sfm.org
33. Sweeney, C., Fragoso, V., Höllerer, T., Turk, M.: Large scale SFM with the distributed camera model. In: 3DV, pp. 230–238. IEEE (2016)
34. Sweeney, C., Sattler, T., Tobias, H., Turk, M., Pollefeys, M.: Optimizing the viewing graph for structure-from-motion. In: ICCV, pp. 801–809 (2015)

35. Wilson, K., Snavely, N.: Robust global translations with 1DSfM. In: Fleet, D., Pajdla, T., Schiele, B., Tuytelaars, T. (eds.) ECCV 2014. LNCS, vol. 8691, pp. 61–75. Springer, Cham (2014). https://doi.org/10.1007/978-3-319-10578-9_5

36. Wu, C.: Towards linear-time incremental structure from motion. In: 3DV, pp. 127–134 (2013)

37. Zach, C., Irschara, A., Bischof, H.: What can missing correspondences tell us about 3D structure and motion? In: CVPR (2008)

38. Zach, C., Klopschitz, M., Pollefeys, M.: Disambiguating visual relations using loop constraints. In: CVPR (2010)

Monocular Depth Estimation Using Whole Strip Masking and Reliability-Based Refinement

Minhyeok Heo[1(✉)], Jaehan Lee[2], Kyung-Rae Kim[2], Han-Ul Kim[2],
and Chang-Su Kim[2]

[1] NAVER LABS, Seongnam, South Korea
heo.minhyeok@naverlabs.com
[2] School of Electrical Engineering, Korea University, Seoul, Korea
{jaehanlee,krkim,hanulkim}@mcl.korea.ac.kr, changsukim@korea.ac.kr

Abstract. We propose a monocular depth estimation algorithm based on whole strip masking (WSM) and reliability-based refinement. First, we develop a convolutional neural network (CNN) tailored for the depth estimation. Specifically, we design a novel filter, called WSM, to exploit the tendency that a scene has similar depths in horizontal or vertical directions. The proposed CNN combines WSM upsampling blocks with a ResNet encoder. Second, we measure the reliability of an estimated depth, by appending additional layers to the main CNN. Using the reliability information, we perform conditional random field (CRF) optimization to refine the estimated depth map. Experimental results demonstrate that the proposed algorithm provides the state-of-the-art depth estimation performance.

Keywords: Monocular depth estimation · Whole strip masking
Reliability · Depth map refinement

1 Introduction

Estimating depth information from images is a fundamental problem in computer vision [1–3]. Humans can infer depths with ease, since we intuitively use various cues and have an innate sense. However, it is very challenging to imitate this ability computationally. Especially, in comparison with stereo matching [4] and video-based approaches, monocular (or single-image) depth estimation is even more difficult due to the lack of reliable visual cues, such as the disparity between matching points.

Early studies for monocular depth estimation attempted to compensate for this lack of information. Some techniques depend on scene assumptions, *e.g.* box models [5] and typical indoor rooms [6], which make the techniques useful for limited situations only. Some use additional data, *e.g.* user annotations [7] and semantic labels [8], which are not always available. Also, hand-crafted features

© Springer Nature Switzerland AG 2018
V. Ferrari et al. (Eds.): ECCV 2018, LNCS 11208, pp. 39–55, 2018.
https://doi.org/10.1007/978-3-030-01225-0_3

based on geometric and semantic cues were designed [9–11]. For example, since a depth map often has similar values in horizontal or vertical directions, an elongated rectangular patch was used in [9]. However, these hand-crafted features have become obsolete and replaced by machine learning approaches recently.

As labeled data increase, many data-based techniques have been proposed. In [12], a depth map was transferred from aligned candidates in an image pool. More recently, many convolutional neural networks (CNNs) have been proposed for monocular depth estimation [13–19]. They learn features to represent depths automatically and implicitly, without requiring the traditional feature engineering. Also, several techniques combine CNNs with conditional random field (CRF) optimization to improve the accuracy of a depth map [15–18].

In this work, we propose a novel CNN-based algorithm, which achieves accurate depth estimation by exploiting the characteristics of depth information to a greater extent. First, we develop a novel upsampling block, referred to as the whole strip masking (WSM), to exploit the tendency that depths are flat horizontally or vertically in scenes. We estimate a depth map by cascading these upsampling blocks together with the deep network ResNet [20]. Second, we use the notion of reliability of an estimated depth. Specifically, we measure the reliability (or confidence) of the estimated depth of each pixel and use the information to define unary and pairwise potentials of a CRF. Through the reliability-based CRF optimization, we refine the estimated depth map and improve its accuracy. We highlight our main contributions as follows:

- We propose a deep CNN with the novel WSM upsampling blocks for monocular depth estimation.
- We measure the reliability of an estimated depth and use the information for the depth refinement.
- The proposed algorithm yields the state-of-the-art depth estimation performance, outperforming conventional algorithms [8, 12–19, 21] significantly.

2   Related Work

Before the widespread adoption of CNNs, hand-crafted features had been used to estimate the depth information from a single image. An early method, proposed by Saxena et al. [9], adopted a Markov random field (MRF) model to predict the depth from multi-scale patches and a column patch of a vertically long shape. Saxena et al. [10] also predicted the depth, by assuming that a scene consists of small planes and inferring the set of plane parameters. Liu et al. [11] estimated the depth based on class-related depth and geometry priors, obtained through semantic segmentation. Assuming that semantically similar images have similar depth distributions, Karsch et al. [12] extracted a depth map by finding similar images from a database and warping them.

Recently, with the remarkable success of deep learning in many applications [22–24], various CNN-based methods for monocular depth estimation have been proposed. Eigen et al. [13] first applied a CNN to monocular depth estimation. They predicted a coarse depth map based on AlexNet [25] and refined it with another network in a fine scale. Eigen and Fergus [14] replaced AlexNet with the deeper VGGNet [26] and used the common network to predict depths, semantic labels, and surface normals jointly. Laina *et al.* [19] improved the depth estimation performance by combining upsampling blocks with ResNet [20], which is about three times deeper than VGGNet. Also, Lee *et al.* [27] introduced the notion of Fourier domain analysis into monocular depth estimation. These methods have gradually improved the estimation performance by adopting deeper networks in general. However, they often yield blurry depth maps.

Sharper depth maps can be obtained by combining CNNs with CRF optimization. Liu *et al.* [15] proposed a superpixel-based algorithm, which divides an image into superpixels and learns unary and pairwise potentials of a CRF during the network training. Li *et al.* [17] adopted hierarchical CRFs. They estimated depths at a superpixel level and then refined them at a pixel level. Also, Wang *et al.* [16] proposed a CNN for joint depth estimation and semantic segmentation, and refined a depth map using a two-layer CRF. These CNN-based methods [13–17,19] provide decent depth maps. In this work, by exploiting the characteristics of depth information to a greater extent, as well as by adopting the merits of the conventional methods, we attempt to further improve the depth estimation performance.

3   Proposed Algorithm

Figure 1 is an overview of the proposed monocular depth estimation algorithm. We first encode an input image into a feature vector based on the ResNet-50 architecture [20]. We then decode the feature vector using four WSM upsampling blocks. Then, we use the decoded result for two purposes: (1) to estimate the depth map $\hat{d}$ and (2) to obtain the reliability map α. Finally, we perform the CRF optimization using α to process $\hat{d}$ into the refined depth map $\tilde{d}$.

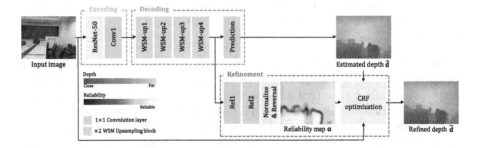

Fig. 1. Overview of the proposed depth estimation algorithm.

3.1   Depth Map Estimation

Most CNNs for generating a high-resolution image (or map) as the output are composed of encoding and decoding parts. The encoding part decreases the spatial resolution of an input image through pooling or convolution layers with strides. For the encoding part, in general, pre-trained networks on a very large dataset, *e.g.* ImageNet [28], are used without modification or fine-tuned with a smaller dataset to speed up the learning and alleviate the need for a large training dataset for each specific task. On the other hand, the decoding part processes input activations to yield a higher-resolution output map using unpooling layers or deconvolution layers. In other words, the encoder contracts a signal, whereas the decoder expands a signal. It is known that the contraction enables a network to have a theoretically large receptive field without demanding unnecessarily many parameters [29]. Also, as a network depth increases, the receptive field gets larger. Therefore, recent deep networks, such as VGGNet and ResNet-50, have theoretical receptive fields larger than input image sizes [29,30].

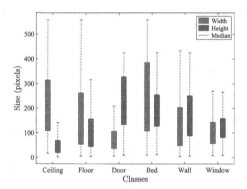

Fig. 2. The width and height distributions of six object classes, which are often observed in indoor scenes. A central red line indicates the median, and the bottom and top edges of a box indicate the 1st and 3rd quartiles.

However, even in the case of a deep CNN, the effective range is smaller than the theoretical receptive field. Luo *et al.* [30] observed that not all pixels in the receptive field affect an output response meaningfully. Thus, the information in a local image region only is used to yield a response. This is undesirable especially in the depth estimation task, which requires global information to estimate the depth of each pixel. Note that depths in a typical image exhibit very strong horizontal or vertical correlations. In Fig. 2, we analyze the width and height distributions of six object classes, which are observed in indoor scenes in the NYU Depth Dataset V2 [31], in which the semantic labels are available. For instance, a ceiling is horizontally wide, while a door is vertically long. Also, the average depth variation within such an object is very small, less than 0.3. Hence, to estimate the depth of a pixel reliably, all information in the entire rows or columns within an image is required. The limited effective receptive fields of conventional CNNs may degrade the depth estimation performance.

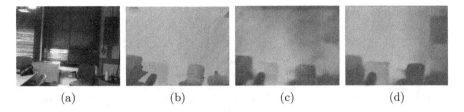

(a)   (b)   (c)   (d)

Fig. 3. The efficacy of WSM layers: (a) an image, (b) its ground-truth depths, (c) estimated depths using convolution layers only, and (d) estimated depths using both convolution and WSM layers.

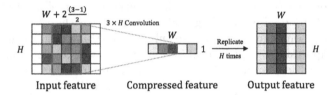

Fig. 4. Illustration of the proposed $3 \times H$ WSM layer.

To overcome this problem, we propose a novel filter, called WSM, for upsampling blocks. Note that a typical convolution layer performs zero-padding to maintain the same output resolution as the input resolution and uses a square kernel of a small size, *e.g.* 1×1, 3×3, or 5×5. Thus, an output value of the typical convolution layer merges only the local information of the input feature. Hence, in Fig. 3(c), although the wall has similar features and depths, the estimation result of a network using convolution layers only does not yield flat depths on the wall. In contrast, to consider horizontally or vertically flat characteristics of depth maps, the proposed WSM adopts long rectangular kernels and replicates the kernel responses in the horizontal or vertical direction. Consequently, as shown in Fig. 3(d), the proposed WSM facilitates more faithful reconstruction of vertically flat depths on the wall.

Suppose an input feature of spatial resolution $W \times H$. Figure 4 shows the $3 \times H$ WSM layer. We first apply zero-padding in the horizontal direction only. Then, we perform the horizontal convolution using the $3 \times H$ mask, which yields a compressed feature map of size $W \times 1$. This compressed feature map summarizes the information in the vertical strips of the input feature map and is forced to have the largest receptive field in the vertical direction. Next, we replicate the compressed feature to yield the output feature map that has the same size as the input. As a result, each response in the output feature map combines all information in the corresponding vertical strip, and all responses in the same column have an identical value. The $W \times 3$ WSM is also performed similarly.

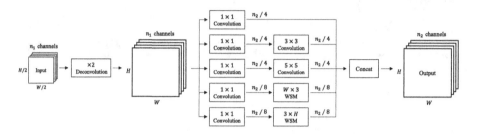

Fig. 5. The structure of the proposed WSM upsampling block.

We use both $3 \times H$ and $W \times 3$ WSM layers in each upsampling block in Fig. 1. Note that the proposed upsampling is also referred to as the WSM upsampling. However, it has some limitations to use only the WSM layers in the upsampling. First, it is important to exploit local information, as well as global information, when estimating depths. Second, a great number of parameters are required for the large $3 \times H$ and $W \times 3$ masks. To alleviate these limitations, we adopt the inception structure in [32]. The inception structure merges the results of various convolutions of different kernel sizes, but applies 1×1 convolution layers first to lower the dimension of the input feature and thus reduce the number of parameters. By incorporating the WSM layers into the inception structure, the proposed WSM upsampling attempts to maximize the network capacity and integrate both global and local information, while requiring a moderate number of parameters. Figure 5 shows the WSM upsampling block. First, we double the spatial resolution of a feature map using a deconvolution layer. Then, we adopt 1×1 convolution layers to lower the feature dimension, before applying the conventional 3×3 and 5×5 convolutional layers and the proposed $W \times 3$ and $3 \times H$ WSM layers. We concatenate all results to yield the output feature map.

The WSM upsampling is employed by the entire network in Fig. 1. We use the ResNet-50 architecture in the encoding step, but remove the last two fully-connected layers and instead add a 1×1 convolution layer to lower the feature dimension since the last convolution layer of ResNet-50 yields a relative high feature dimension. For the decoding step, we cascade four WSM upsampling blocks to increase the output spatial resolution to 160×128. Finally, through a 1×1 convolution layer, we obtain an estimated depth map $\hat{\mathbf{d}}$. To train the network in an end-to-end manner, we adopt the Euclidean loss to minimize the sum of squared differences between the ith estimated depth $\hat{d}_i$ and the corresponding ground truth d_i^{gt}. Table 1 presents detailed network configurations.

Table 1. Configurations of the proposed network. Input and output sizes are given by $W \times H \times C$, where W, H, and C are the width, height, and number of channels, respectively.

	Layer Name	Input	Input Size	Output Size
Encoding	ResNet-50	Image	$304 \times 228 \times 3$	$10 \times 8 \times 2048$
Decoding	Conv1	ResNet-50	$10 \times 8 \times 2048$	$10 \times 8 \times 1024$
	WSM-up1	Conv1	$10 \times 8 \times 1024$	$20 \times 16 \times 1024$
	WSM-up2	WSM-up1	$20 \times 16 \times 1024$	$40 \times 32 \times 512$
	WSM-up3	WSM-up2	$40 \times 32 \times 512$	$80 \times 64 \times 256$
	WSM-up4	WSM-up3	$80 \times 64 \times 256$	$160 \times 128 \times 128$
	Prediction	WSM-up4	$160 \times 128 \times 128$	$160 \times 128 \times 1$
Refinement	Rel1	WSM-up4	$160 \times 128 \times 128$	$160 \times 128 \times 128$
	Rel2	Rel1	$160 \times 128 \times 128$	$160 \times 128 \times 1$

3.2 Depth Map Refinement

As shown in Fig. 6, even though the proposed depth estimation provides a promising result, the estimated depth map $\hat{\mathbf{d}}$ still contains residual errors especially around object boundaries. In a wide variety of estimation problems, attempts have been made not only to make an estimate, but also to measure the reliability or confidence (or inversely uncertainty) of the estimate. For example, in the classical depth-from-motion technique in [33], Matthies *et al.* predicted depth and depth uncertainty at each pixel and incrementally refined the estimates to reduce the uncertainty. In this work, we observe that the reliability of an estimated depth can be quantified, surprisingly, using the same features from the decoder for the depth estimation itself, as shown in Fig. 1.

We augment the network to learn the reliability. In Fig. 1, the reliability map is obtained by adding only two 1×1 convolution layers 'Rel1' and 'Rel2' after the final upsampling layer 'WSM-up4.' To train the two convolutional layers, the absolute prediction error, $|\hat{d}_i - d_i^{\mathrm{gt}}|$, is defined as the ground-truth and the Euclidean loss is employed. Thus, the output of the added convolution layers is not a reliability value but an error estimate (or uncertainty). We hence normalize the error estimate to $[0, 1]$, and subtract the normalized result from 1 to yield the reliability value. Figure 6(d) shows a reliability map $\boldsymbol{\alpha}$. We see that the reliability map yields low values in erroneous areas in the actual error map in Fig. 6(c).

Next, based on the reliability map $\boldsymbol{\alpha}$, we model the conditional probability distribution of the depth field $\mathbf{d}$ for the CRF optimization as $p(\mathbf{d}|\hat{\mathbf{d}}, \boldsymbol{\alpha}) = \frac{1}{Z} \cdot \exp\left(-E(\mathbf{d}, \hat{\mathbf{d}}, \boldsymbol{\alpha})\right)$ where E is an energy function and Z is the normalization term. The energy function is given by

$$E(\mathbf{d}, \hat{\mathbf{d}}, \boldsymbol{\alpha}) = U(\mathbf{d}, \hat{\mathbf{d}}, \boldsymbol{\alpha}) + \lambda \cdot V(\mathbf{d}, \boldsymbol{\alpha}) \tag{1}$$

where U is a unary term to make the refined depth $\mathbf{d}$ similar to the estimated depth $\hat{\mathbf{d}}$ and V is a pairwise term to make each refined depth similar to the weighted sum of adjacent depths. Also, λ controls a tradeoff between the two terms. The unary term is defined as

$$U(\mathbf{d}, \widehat{\mathbf{d}}, \boldsymbol{\alpha}) = \sum_i \alpha_i \left(d_i - \hat{d}_i \right)^2 \tag{2}$$

where d_i, $\hat{d}_i$, and α_i denote the refined depth, estimated depth, and reliability of pixel i, respectively. By employing α_i, we strongly encourage a refined depth to be similar to an estimated depth only if the estimated depth is reliable. In other words, when an estimated depth is unreliable, it can be modified significantly to yield a refined depth during the CRF optimization.

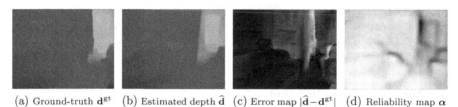

(a) Ground-truth $\mathbf{d}^{gt}$ (b) Estimated depth $\hat{\mathbf{d}}$ (c) Error map $|\hat{\mathbf{d}} - \mathbf{d}^{gt}|$ (d) Reliability map $\boldsymbol{\alpha}$

Fig. 6. An example of the reliability map. In (c) and (d), a bright color indicates a higher value than a dark one.

To model the relation between neighboring pixels, we use the auto-regression model, which are employed in various applications, such as image matting [34], depth recovery [35], and monocular depth estimation [17]. In addition, to take advantage of the different characteristics of image and depth map, we use the color similarity introduced in [36,37]. In this work, we generalize the color-guided auto-regression model in [35], based on the reliability map, to define the pairwise term

$$V(\mathbf{d}, \boldsymbol{\alpha}) = \sum_i \left(d_i - \sum_{j \in \mathcal{N}_i} \omega_{ij} d_j \right)^2 \tag{3}$$

where $\mathcal{N}_i$ is the 11×11 neighborhood of pixel i. Also, ω_{ij} is the similarity between pixel i and its neighbor j, given by

$$\omega_{ij} = \frac{\alpha_j}{T} \cdot \exp\left(-\frac{\sum_{c \in \mathcal{C}} \|\mathbf{B}_i \circ (\mathcal{S}_i^c - \mathcal{S}_j^c)\|_2^2}{2 \cdot 3 \cdot \sigma_1^2} \right) \tag{4}$$

where $\mathcal{S}_i^c$ denotes the 5×5 patch centered at pixel i, extracted from color channel c of the image, and $\mathcal{C}$ is the set of three YUV color channels. Also, $\circ$ represents the element-wise multiplication, σ_1 is a weighting parameter, and T is the normalization factor. The color-guided kernel $\mathbf{B}_i$ is defined on the 5×5 patch centered at pixel i, and its element corresponding to neighbor pixel k is given by

$$B_{i,k} = \exp\left(-\frac{\sum_{c \in \mathcal{C}} (I_i^c - I_k^c)^2}{2 \cdot 3 \cdot \sigma_2^2} \right) \tag{5}$$

where I_i^c is the image value of pixel i in channel c, and σ_2 is a parameter. The exponential term in (4), through the pairwise term V in (3), encourages neighboring pixels with similar colors to have similar depths. Moreover, because of α_j in (4), we constrain the depth of pixel i to be more similar to that of neighbor pixel j, when neighbor pixel j is more reliable. This causes the depths of reliable pixels to propagate to those of unreliable ones, improving the accuracy of the overall depth map.

We can rewrite the energy function in (1) in vector notations.

$$E(\mathbf{d}, \widehat{\mathbf{d}}, \boldsymbol{\alpha}) = (\mathbf{d} - \widehat{\mathbf{d}})^T \mathbf{A}(\mathbf{d} - \widehat{\mathbf{d}}) + \lambda \, (\mathbf{d} - \mathbf{W}\mathbf{d})^T(\mathbf{d} - \mathbf{W}\mathbf{d}) \qquad (6)$$

where $\mathbf{A}$ is the diagonal matrix whose ith diagonal element is α_i, and $\mathbf{W} \triangleq [\omega_{ij}]$ is the weight matrix. Finally, the refined depth $\widetilde{\mathbf{d}}$ can be obtained by solving the maximum *a posteriori* (MAP) inference problem:

$$\widetilde{\mathbf{d}} = \arg\max_{\mathbf{d}} p(\mathbf{d}|\widehat{\mathbf{d}}, \boldsymbol{\alpha}) = \arg\min_{\mathbf{d}} E(\mathbf{d}, \widehat{\mathbf{d}}, \boldsymbol{\alpha}). \qquad (7)$$

Since the energy function is quadratic, the closed-form solution is given by

$$\widetilde{\mathbf{d}} = (\mathbf{A} + \lambda \, (\mathbf{I} - \mathbf{W})^T(\mathbf{I} - \mathbf{W}))^{-1}\mathbf{A}\widehat{\mathbf{d}}. \qquad (8)$$

4 Experiments

4.1 Experimental Setup

Implementation details: We implement the proposed network using the Caffe library [38] on an NVIDIA GPU with 12GB memory. We initialize the backbone network in the encoder with the pre-trained weights, and initialize the other parameters randomly. We train the network in two phases. First, we train the depth estimation network, composed of the encoding and decoding parts. The learning rate is initialized at 10^{-7} and decreased by 10 times when training errors converge. The batch size is set to 4. The momentum and the weight decay are set to typical values of 0.9 and 0.0005. Second, we fix the parameters of the encoding and decoding parts and then train the refinement part. The learning rate starts at 10^{-8}, while the batch size, the momentum, and the weight decay are the same as the first phase. The parameters λ in (1), σ_1 in (4), and σ_2 in (5) is set to 1.5, 6.5, and 0.1. It takes about two days to train the whole network.

Evaluation metrics: For quantitative evaluation, we assess the proposed monocular depth estimation algorithm based on the four evaluation metrics [8,13,14].

- Average absolute relative error (rel): $\frac{1}{N}\sum_i \frac{|\hat{d}_i - d_i^{\text{gt}}|}{d_i^{\text{gt}}}$
- Average $\log_{10}$ error ($\log_{10}$): $\frac{1}{N}\sum_i |\log_{10}(\hat{d}_i) - \log_{10}(d_i^{\text{gt}})|$
- Root mean squared error (rms): $\sqrt{\frac{1}{N}\sum_i (\hat{d}_i - d_i^{\text{gt}})^2}$
- Accuracy with threshold t: percentage of $\hat{d}_i$ such that $\max\{\frac{d_i^{\text{gt}}}{\hat{d}_i}, \frac{\hat{d}_i}{d_i^{\text{gt}}}\} = \delta < t$

Table 2. Comparison of various network models on the NYU dataset. A number in the third column is the number of parameters in both encoder and decoder.

Encoding	Decoding	Parameters	rel	rms
AlexNet	FC	106M	0.215	0.833
	Deconv	6.7M	0.204	0.842
VGGNet-16	FC	60M	0.183	0.776
	Deconv	18.5M	0.194	0.746
ResNet-50	FC	74M	0.160	0.626
	Deconv	53.5M	0.152	0.602
	Deconv-Conv	66.0M	0.149	0.604
	UpProj [19]	63.6M	0.145	0.596
	Inception	62.1M	0.148	0.607
	Equivalent	61.0M	0.150	0.595
	WSM	61.1M	**0.141**	**0.582**

4.2   NYU Depth Dataset V2

We evaluate the proposed algorithm on the large RGB-D dataset, NYU Depth Dataset V2 [31]. It contains 120 K pairs of RGB and depth images, captured with Microsoft Kinect devices, with 249 scenes for training and 215 scenes for testing. Each image or depth has a spatial resolution of 640 × 480. We uniformly sample frames from the entire training scenes and extract approximately 24 K unique pairs. Using the colorization tool [34] provided with the dataset, we fill in missing values of depth maps automatically. Since an image and its depth map are not perfectly synchronized, we eliminate top 2 K erroneous samples, after training the depth estimation network for one epoch. We perform the online data augmentation schemes *Scale, Flip,* and *Translataion,* introduced in [13]. Also, as in [15,21], we center-crop images to 561 × 427 pixels containing valid depths, and then downsample them to 304 × 228 pixels, which are used as the input to the network. For the evaluation, we upsample the estimated depth map to the original size 561 × 427 through the bilinear interpolation and compare the result against the ground-truth depth map.

Comparison of network models: Table 2 compares the proposed algorithm with other network models. First, we test how the depth estimation performance is affected when a different backbone network (AlexNet [25], VGGNet16 [26], or ResNet-50 [20]) is adopted as the encoder. In this test, we use the fully-connected layer 'FC' or the deconvolution block 'Deconv' as the decoder. Specifically, FC is a fully-connected layer of 1280 (= 40 × 32) dimensions directly connected to an output feature map of the encoder. Deconv is the upsampling block, composed of four 3 × 3 deconvolution layers only. As the backbone network gets deeper from AlexNet to ResNet-50, the depth estimation performance is improved.

Next, we compare the performances of various decoders, after fixing ResNet-50 as the encoder. 'Deconv-Conv' is the decoder, composed of four pairs of 3 × 3

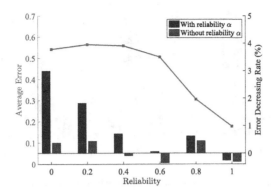

Fig. 7. Verifying reliability values and the reliability-based refinement. The line plot with the left axis shows the average absolute error for each quantized reliability value. The bar plot with the right axis shows the decreasing rate of the average error due to the refinement with or without reliability α.

deconvolution layer and 5×5 convolution layer. 'UpProj' is the Laina *et al.*'s decoder [19]. 'Inception' [32] uses a 7×7 convolution layer instead of the $W \times 3$ and $3 \times H$ WSM layers in Fig. 5. Similarly, 'Equivalent' replaces the two WSM layers with a square convolution layer, but set the square size to be about the same as the sum of $3 \times H$ and $W \times 3$. Consequently, Equivalent and the proposed WSM decoder require similar numbers of parameters. The output resolution is 160×128 except for FC, which yields 40×32 output because of GPU memory constraints. The WSM decoder provides outstanding performances. Especially, note that WSM significantly outperforms Equivalent, which is another method using large kernels. This indicates that the improved performance of WSM is made possible not only by the use of large kernels, but also because horizontally or vertically flat characteristics of depth maps are exploited. Moreover, despite the large kernels, the proposed WSM algorithm requires a moderate number of parameters, and in fact demands less than Deconv-Conv, UpProj, and Inception.

Efficacy of Refinement Step: The line graph in Fig. 7 shows the absolute average error for each quantized reliability value. As the reliability value increases, the average error decreases. This indicates that the proposed algorithm correctly predicts the confidence of an estimated depth using the reliability map.

The bar graph in Fig. 7 plots how the proposed reliability-based refinement decreases the average error. To confirm its impacts comparatively, we also provide the refinement result without the reliability, *i.e.* when α is fixed to 1 in (2) and (4). With the adaptive reliability, we see that the error decreases by up to 2.9%. In particular, estimation errors are significantly decreased by the refinement step, especially for the pixels with low reliability values. On the other hand, without the reliability, there are only little changes in the errors.

Figure 8 shows point cloud rendering results of depth maps with and without the refinement step. We see that the refinement separates the objects from the background more clearly and more accurately.

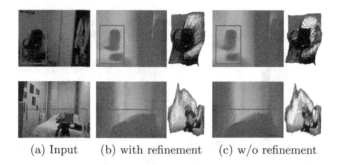

(a) Input   (b) with refinement   (c) w/o refinement

Fig. 8. Point cloud rendering of depth maps with or without the refinement step.

Comparison with the State-of-the-Arts: Table 3 compares the proposed algorithm with eleven conventional algorithms [8, 12–19, 21, 39]. We report the performances of two versions of the proposed algorithm: 'WSM' uses only the depth estimation network and 'WSM-Ref' performs the reliability-based refinement additionally. Note that both WSM and WSM-Ref outperform all conventional algorithms.

Figure 9 compares the depth maps of the proposed algorithm with those of the state-of-the-art monocular depth estimation algorithms [14, 18, 19] qualitatively. The proposed WSM and WSM-Ref generate more faithful depth maps than the conventional algorithms. Through WSM, both WSM and WSM-Ref reconstruct flat depths on the walls more accurately. Moreover, WSM-Ref improves the depth maps through the reliability-based refinement. For instance, WSM-Ref reconstructs the detailed depths of the objects on the desk in the first row and the chairs in the second and third rows more precisely.

4.3   Make3D

We also test the proposed algorithm on the outdoor dataset Make3D [10], which contains 534 pairs of RGB and depth images: 400 pairs for training and 134 for testing. There is a difference of resolutions between RGB images (1704 × 2272) and depth images (305 × 55). Since the dataset is not large enough for training a deep network, training on Make3D needs a careful strategy. We follow the strategy of [15, 19]. Specifically, we resize RGB images to 345 × 460 pixels and downsample them to 173 × 230 pixels. Since Make3D expresses depths up to 80 m only, the depths of far objects, *e.g.* sky, are often inaccurate. Thus, we train the network after masking out pixels with depths over 70m. This criterion, called C1, was first suggested by [21] and has been used in [15, 19, 21]. We perform online data augmentation, as done in the case of the NYU dataset. All the other parameters are the same. For evaluation, we upsample an estimated depth map to 345 × 460 and compare the result against the ground-truth depth map, which is also upsampled to 345 × 460. We only compute the errors in regions of depths less than 70 m (C1 criterion).

Table 4 compares the proposed algorithm with conventional algorithms [12, 15, 17, 19, 21]. Again, the proposed WSM-Ref outperforms all conventional algo-

Table 3. Quantitative comparison on the NYU Depth Dataset V2 [31]. The best performance is boldfaced, and the second best is underlined.

Methods	Error ($\downarrow$)			Accuracy ($\uparrow$)		
	rel	$\log_{10}$	rms	$\delta < 1.25$	$\delta < 1.25^2$	$\delta < 1.25^3$
Karsch et al. [12]	0.374	0.134	1.12	-	-	-
Ladicky et al. [8]	-	-	-	0.542	0.829	0.941
Liu et al. [21]	0.335	0.127	1.06	-	-	-
Li et al. [17]	0.232	0.094	0.821	0.621	0.886	0.968
Liu et al. [15]	0.230	0.095	0.824	0.614	0.883	0.971
Wang et al. [16]	0.220	0.094	0.745	0.605	0.890	0.970
Eigen et al. [13]	0.215	0.095	0.907	0.611	0.887	0.971
Eigen et al. [14]	0.158	0.067	0.641	0.769	0.950	0.988
Chakrabarti et al. [18]	0.149	0.062	0.620	0.806	0.958	0.988
Li et al. [39]	0.143	0.063	0.635	0.788	0.958	<u>0.991</u>
Laina et al. [19]	<u>0.140</u>	<u>0.060</u>	0.597	<u>0.811</u>	0.953	0.988
WSM	0.141	<u>0.060</u>	<u>0.582</u>	<u>0.811</u>	<u>0.962</u>	<u>0.991</u>
WSM-Ref	**0.135**	**0.058**	**0.571**	**0.816**	**0.964**	**0.992**

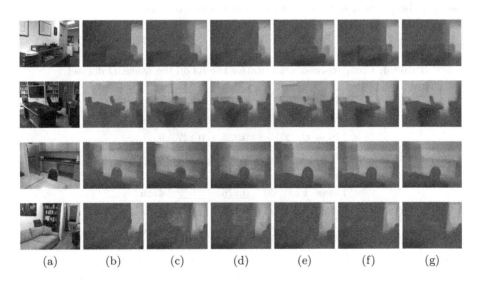

| (a) | (b) | (c) | (d) | (e) | (f) | (g) |

Fig. 9. Qualitative comparison: (a) input image, (b) ground-truth, (c) Eigen et al. [14], (d) Chakrabarti et al. [18], (e) Laina et al. [19], and (f) the proposed WSM, and (g) the proposed WSM-Ref.

rithms. Figure 10 shows qualitative results. The proposed WSM-Ref yields faithful depth maps, and the reliability maps detect erroneous regions effectively. These experimental results indicate that the proposed algorithm is a promising solution to monocular depth estimation for both indoor and outdoor scenes.

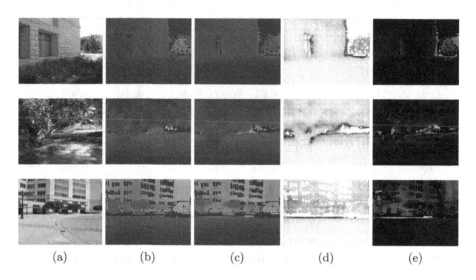

| (a) | (b) | (c) | (d) | (e) |

Fig. 10. Depth estimation of the proposed WSM-Ref on the Make3D dataset: (a) input, (b) ground-truth, (c) estimation result, (d) reliability map, and (e) error map. In (d) and (e), a bright color indicates a higher value than a dark one.

Table 4. Comparison of quantitative results on the Make3D dataset.

Methods	rel	$\log_{10}$	rms
Karsch et al. [12]	0.355	0.127	9.20
Liu et al. [21]	0.335	0.137	9.49
Liu et al. [15]	0.314	0.119	8.60
Li et al. [17]	0.278	0.092	7.19
Laina et al. [19]	<u>0.176</u>	<u>0.072</u>	**4.46**
WSM	0.185	0.073	4.85
WSM-Ref	**0.171**	**0.063**	**4.46**

5   Conclusions

In this work, we proposed a monocular depth estimation algorithm based on the WSM upsampling and the reliability-based refinement. First, we developed the

WSM layers to exploit the horizontally or vertically flat characteristics of depth maps. We constructed the depth estimation network by stacking WSM upsampling blocks upon the ResNet-50 encoder. Second, we measured the reliability of each estimated depth, and exploited the information to refine the depth map through the CRF optimization. Experimental results showed that the proposed algorithm significantly outperforms the conventional algorithms on both indoor and outdoor datasets, while requiring a moderate number of parameters.

Acknowledgement. This work was supported partly by the Cross-Ministry Giga KOREA Project Grant funded by the Korean Government (MSIT) (development of 4D reconstruction and dynamic deformable action model based hyper-realistic service technology) under Grant GK18P0200, partly by the National Research Foundation of Korea Grant funded by the Korean Government (MSIP) under Grant NRF-2015R1A2A1A10055037 and Grant NRF-2018R1A2B3003896, and partly by NAVER LABS.

References

1. Yang, S., Maturana, D., Scherer, S.: Real-time 3D scene layout from a single image using convolutional neural networks. In: ICRA, pp. 2183–2189 (2016)
2. Shao, T., Xu, W., Zhou, K., Wang, J., Li, D., Guo, B.: An interactive approach to semantic modeling of indoor scenes with an RGBD camera. ACM Trans. Graph. **31**(6), 136 (2012)
3. Porzi, L., Buló, S.R., Penate-Sanchez, A., Ricci, E., Moreno-Noguer, F.: Learning depth-aware deep representations for robotic perception. IEEE Robot. Autom. Lett. **2**(2), 468–475 (2017)
4. Kim, K.R., Koh, Y.J., Kim, C.S.: Multiscale feature extractors for stereo matching cost computation. IEEE Access **6**, 27971–27983 (2018)
5. Gupta, A., Efros, A.A., Hebert, M.: Blocks world revisited: image understanding using qualitative geometry and mechanics. In: Proceedings ECCV, pp. 482–496 (2010)
6. Lee, D.C., Gupta, A., Hebert, M., Kanade, T.: Estimating spatial layout of rooms using volumetric reasoning about objects and surfaces. In: Proceedings NIPS, pp. 1288–1296 (2010)
7. Russell, B.C., Torralba, A.: Building a database of 3D scenes from user annotations. In: Proceedings IEEE CVPR, pp. 2711–2718 (2009)
8. Ladicky, L., Shi, J., Pollefeys, M.: Pulling things out of perspective. In: Proceedings IEEE CVPR, pp. 89–96 (2014)
9. Saxena, A., Chung, S.H., Ng, A.Y.: Learning depth from single monocular images. In: Proceedings NIPS, pp. 1161–1168 (2005)
10. Saxena, A., Sun, M., Ng, A.Y.: Make3D: learning 3D scene sctructure from a single still image. IEEE Trans. Pattern Anal. Mach. Intell. **31**(5), 824–840 (2009)
11. Liu, B., Gould, S., Koller, D.: Single image depth estimation from predicted semantic labels. In: Proceedings IEEE CVPR, pp. 1253–1260 (2010)
12. Karsch, K., Liu, C., Kang, S.B.: Depth transfer: depth extraction from video using non-parametric sampling. IEEE Trans. Pattern Anal. Mach. Intell. **36**(11), 2144–2158 (2014)
13. Eigen, D., Puhrsch, C., Fergus, R.: Depth map prediction from a single image using a multi-scale deep network. In: Proceedings NIPS, pp. 2366–2374 (2014)

14. Eigen, D., Fergus, R.: Predicting depth, surface normals and semantic labels with a common multi-scale convolutional architecture. In: Proceedings IEEE ICCV, pp. 2650–2658 (2015)
15. Liu, F., Shen, C., Lin, G.: Deep convolutional neural fields for depth estimation from a single image. In: Proceedings IEEE CVPR, pp. 5162–5170 (2015)
16. Wang, P., Shen, X., Lin, Z., Cohen, S., Price, B., Yuille, A.: Towards unified depth and semantic prediction from a single image. In: Proceedings IEEE CVPR, pp. 2800–2809 (2015)
17. Li, B., Shen, C., Dai, Y., van den Hengel, A., He, M.: Depth and surface normal estimation from monocular images using regression on deep features and hierarchical CRFs. In: Proceedings IEEE CVPR, pp. 1119–1127 (2015)
18. Chakrabarti, A., Shao, J., Shakhnarovich, G.: Depth from a single image by harmonizing overcomplete local network predictions. In: Proceedings NIPS, pp. 2658–2666 (2016)
19. Laina, I., Rupprecht, C., Belagiannis, V.: Deeper depth prediction with fully convolutional residual networks. In: Proceedings IEEE 3DV, pp. 239–248 (2016)
20. He, K., Zhang, X., Ren, S., Sun, J.: Deep residual learning for image recognition. In: Proceedings IEEE CVPR, pp. 770–778 (2016)
21. Liu, M., Salzmann, M., He, X.: Discrete-continuous depth estimation from a single image. In: Proceedings IEEE CVPR, pp. 716–723 (2014)
22. Kim, H.U., Kim, C.S.: CDT: Cooperative detection and tracking for tracing multiple objects in video sequences. In: Proceedings ECCV, pp. 851–867 (2016)
23. Jang, W.D., Kim, C.S.: Online video object segmentation via convolutional trident network. In: Proceedings IEEE CVPR, pp. 5849–5856 (2017)
24. Lee, J.T., Kim, H.U., Lee, C., Kim, C.S.: Semantic line detection and its applications. In: Proceedings IEEE ICCV, pp. 3229–3237 (2017)
25. Krizhevsky, A., Sutskever, I., Hinton, G.E.: ImageNet classification with deep convolutional neural networks. In: Proceedings NIPS, pp. 1097–1105 (2012)
26. Simonyan, K., Zisserman, A.: Very deep convolutional networks for large-scale image recognition. In: ICLR (2012)
27. Lee, J.H., Heo, M., Kim, K.R., Kim, C.S.: Single-image depth estimation based on Fourier domain analysis. In: Proceedings IEEE CVPR, pp. 330–339 (2018)
28. Deng, J., Dong, W., Socher, R., Li, L.J., Li, K., Fei-Fei, L.: ImageNet: a large-scale hierarchical image database. In: Proceedings IEEE CVPR, pp. 248–255 (2009)
29. Long, J., Shelhamer, E., Darrell, T.: Fully convolutional networks for semantic segmentation. In: Proceedings IEEE CVPR, pp. 3431–3440 (2015)
30. Luo, W., Li, Y., Urtasun, R., Zemel, R.: Understanding the effective receptive field in deep convolutional neural networks. In: Proceedings NIPS, pp. 4898–4906 (2016)
31. Silberman, N., Hoiem, D., Kohli, P., Fergus, R.: Indoor segmentation and support inference from RGBD images. In: Fitzgibbon, A., Lazebnik, S., Perona, P., Sato, Y., Schmid, C. (eds.) ECCV 2012. LNCS, vol. 7576, pp. 746–760. Springer, Heidelberg (2012). https://doi.org/10.1007/978-3-642-33715-4_54
32. Szegedy, C., Ioffe, S., Vanhoucke, V., Alemi, A.: Inception-v4, Inception-ResNet and the impact of residual connections on learning. AAA I, 4278–4284 (2016)
33. Matthies, L., Kanade, T., Szeliski, R.: Kalman filter-based algorithms for estimating depth from image sequences. Int. J. Comput. Vis. **3**(3), 209–238 (1989)
34. Levin, A., Lischinski, D., Weiss, Y.: A closed-form solution to natural image matting. IEEE Trans. Pattern Anal. Mach. Intell. **30**(2), 228–242 (2008)
35. Yang, J., Ye, X., Li, K., Hou, C., Wang, Y.: Color-guided depth recovery from RGB-D data using an adaptive autoregressive model. IEEE Trans. Image Process. **23**(8), 3443–3458 (2016)

36. Diebel, J., Thrun, S.: An application of markov random fields to range sensing. In: Advances in Neural Information Processing Systems, pp. 291–298 (2006)
37. Park, J., Kim, H., Tai, Y.W., Brown, M.S., Kweon, I.: High quality depth map upsampling for 3D-TOF cameras. In: 2011 IEEE International Conference on Computer Vision (ICCV), pp. 1623–1630. IEEE (2011)
38. Jia, Y., Shelhamer, E., Donahue, J., Karayev, S., Long, J., Girshick, R.: Caffe: Convolutional architecture for fast feature embedding. In: ACM Multimedia, pp. 675–678 (2014)
39. Li, J., Klein, R., Yao, A.: A two-streamed network for estimating fine-scaled depth maps from single RGB images. In: Proceedings of the 2017 IEEE International Conference on Computer Vision, Venice, Italy, pp. 22–29 (2017)

Local Spectral Graph Convolution
for Point Set Feature Learning

Chu Wang, Babak Samari, and Kaleem Siddiqi[✉]

School of Computer Science and Center for Intelligent Machines, McGill University,
Montreal, Canada
{chuwang,babak,siddiqi}@cim.mcgill.ca

Abstract. Feature learning on point clouds has shown great promise, with the introduction of effective and generalizable deep learning frameworks such as pointnet++. Thus far, however, point features have been abstracted in an independent and isolated manner, ignoring the relative layout of neighboring points as well as their features. In the present article, we propose to overcome this limitation by using spectral graph convolution on a local graph, combined with a novel graph pooling strategy. In our approach, graph convolution is carried out on a nearest neighbor graph constructed from a point's neighborhood, such that features are jointly learned. We replace the standard max pooling step with a recursive clustering and pooling strategy, devised to aggregate information from within clusters of nodes that are close to one another in their spectral coordinates, leading to richer overall feature descriptors. Through extensive experiments on diverse datasets, we show a consistent demonstrable advantage for the tasks of both point set classification and segmentation. Our implementations are available at https://github.com/fate3439/LocalSpecGCN.

Keywords: Point set features · Graph convolution
Spectral filtering · Spectral coordinates · Clustering · Deep learning

1 Introduction

With the present availability of registered depth and appearance images of complex real-world scenes, there is tremendous interest in feature processing algorithms for classic computer vision problems including object detection, classification and segmentation. In their latest incarnation, for example, depth sensors are now found in the Apple iPhone X camera, making a whole new range of computer vision technology available to the common user. For such data it is particularly attractive to work *directly* with the unorganized 3D point clouds and to not require an intermediate representation such as a surface mesh. The processing of 3D point clouds from such sensors remains challenging, since the sensed depth points can vary in spatial density, can be incomplete due to occlusion or perspective effects and can suffer from sensor noise.

V. Ferrari et al. (Eds.): ECCV 2018, LNCS 11208, pp. 56–71, 2018.
https://doi.org/10.1007/978-3-030-01225-0_4

Motivated by the need to handle unstructured 3D point clouds while leveraging the power of deep neural networks, the pointnet++ framework has shown promise for 3D point cloud feature processing for the tasks of recognition and segmentation [1]. In this approach a network structure is designed to work directly with point cloud data, while aggregating information in a hierarchical fashion, in the spirit of traditional CNNs on regular grids. To do so, a centroid sampling is first applied on the input point cloud, followed by a radius search to form point neighborhoods. Then the point neighborhoods are processed by multi-layer perceptrons [2] and the resulting point features are abstracted by a pooling operation. Through hierarchical multi-layer learning on the point cloud data, the pointnet++ framework exhibits impressive performance in both segmentation and classification on challenging benchmarks, while treating the input data as an unorganized point cloud.

In a parallel development, Defferrard *et al.* have sought to extend CNNs, traditionally applied on regular domains, such as sampled image pixels in 2D or voxels in 3D, to irregular domains represented as graphs [3]. Their approach uses Chebyshev polynomials to approximate spectral graph filters. Here an initial graph is processed by convolutional operations to yield features which are then coarsened using sub-sampling and pooling methods. Kipf and Welling [4] simplify the higher order polynomial approximations in Defferrard *et al.* and propose a first order linear approximation of spectral graph filters. The aforementioned spectral approaches operate on the full graph and have the limitation that the graph Laplacian and the graph coarsening hierarchy have to be precomputed, in an offline manner, before network training or testing. This adds significant overhead when the full graph is large.

In this article we propose to leverage the power of spectral graph CNNs in the pointnet++ framework, while adopting a different pooling strategy. This allows us to address two limitations of present deep learning methods from point clouds: (1) the fact that for each point sample the learning of features is carried out in an isolated manner in a local neighborhood and (2) that the aggregation of information in later layers uses a greedy winner-take-all max pooling strategy. Instead, we adopt a different pooling module, as illustrated by the example in Fig. 1. Further, our method requires no precomputation, in contrast to existing spectral graph CNN approaches [3,4]. Our combination of local spectral feature learning with recursive clustering and pooling provides a novel architecture for point set feature abstraction from unorganized point clouds. Our main methodological contributions are the following:

- The use of local spectral graph convolution in point set feature learning to incorporate structural information in the neighborhood of each point.
- An implementation of the local spectral graph convolution layer that requires no offline computation and is trainable in an end-to-end manner. We build the graph dynamically during runtime and compute the Laplacian and pooling hierarchy on the fly.
- The use of a novel and effective graph pooling strategy, which aggregates features at graph nodes by recursively clustering the spectral coordinates.

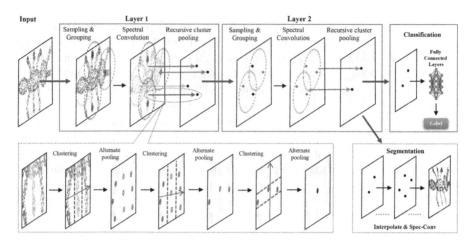

Fig. 1. TOP: Starting from a point cloud, farthest point sampling leads to centroids, from which k-NN's are sampled. Then, for each neighborhood, spectral convolution is carried out followed by recursive cluster pooling. After several layers of sampling, spectral convolution and cluster pooling, we perform segmentation or classification. BOTTOM: The green dashed box details the process of recursive spectral cluster pooling on the Fiedler vector of a sample neighborhood. See text in Sect. 4 for a discussion.

The proposed architecture leads to new state-of-the-art object recognition and segmentation results on diverse datasets, as demonstrated by extensive experiments.

2 Challenges in Point Set Feature Learning

A limitation of feature learning in the pointnet++ framework [1], is that features from the k nearest neighbors (k-NN) of a point are learned in an isolated fashion. Let h represent the output of an arbitrary hidden layer in a deep network, typically a multilayer perceptron. In pointnet++ the individual features for each point in the k-NN are achieved with $h(x_i), i \in 1, 2, ..., k$. Unfortunately, this hidden layer function does not model the joint relationship between points in the k-NN. A convolution kernel that jointly learns features from all points in the k-NN would capture topological information related to the geometric layout of the points, as well as features related to the input point samples themselves, e.g., color, texture, or other attributes. In the following section we shall extend approaches such as the pointnet++ framework to achieve this goal by using local graph convolution, but in the spectral domain.

Another limitation in pointnet++ is that the set activation function for the k-NN is achieved by max pooling across the hidden layer's output for each point, such that

$$f(x_1, x_2, ..., x_k) = \max_{i \in 1, ..., k} h(x_i). \qquad (1)$$

Max pooling does not allow for the preservation of information from disjoint sets of points within the neighborhood, as the legs of the ant in the example in Fig. 1. To address this limitation we introduce a recursive spectral clustering and pooling module that yields an improved set activation function for the k-NN, as discussed in Sect. 4. The combined point set feature abstraction operation in this paper can be summarized by

$$f(x_1, x_2, ..., x_k) = \oplus(h_1, h_2, ..., h_k), \tag{2}$$

where h_i is the convolution output $h(x_1, x_2, ..., x_k)$ evaluated at the i-th point and $\oplus$ represents our set activation function.

Figure 2 provides a comparison between the point-wise MLP in pointnet++ [1] and our spectral graph convolution, to highlight the differences. Whereas pointnet++ abstracts point features in an isolated manner, spectral graph convolution considers all points in a local neighborhood in a joint manner, incorporating both features at neighboring points as well as structural information encoded in the graph topology. This is accomplished via the graph Fourier transform and spectral modulation steps, which blend neighborhood features using the eigenspace of the graph Laplacian (see Fig. 3). In the following section we provide theoretical background and discuss implementation details of our spectral graph convolution kernel.

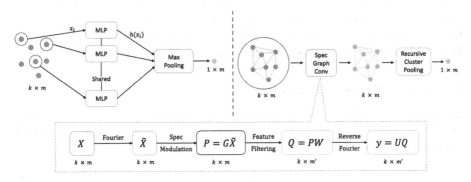

Fig. 2. TOP: A comparison between the point-wise MLP of pointnet++ (left) and our spectral graph convolution (right) for a local neighborhood of a point. The spectral graph convolution output depends on all points in the neighborhood, whereas in point-wise MLP the output depends only on the point itself. BOTTOM: The network operations in a spectral graph convolutional layer along with the input/output dimensions.

3 Graph Convolution

The convolution operation on vertices in the graph is described by

$$h = X * g, \tag{3}$$

where X stands for the input point set features and g for a graph convolution kernel. This is equivalent to an element-wise Hadamard product in the graph spectral domain, as shown in Defferrard *et al.* [3] and Shuman *et al.* [5]:

$$\tilde{h} = \tilde{X} \odot \tilde{g}. \tag{4}$$

Here $\tilde{X}$ stands for the graph Fourier transform of the point set features, $\tilde{g}$ stands for the filter in the graph Fourier domain and $\tilde{h}$ for the filtered output. In order to acquire the filtered output in the original (vertex) domain, an inverse Fourier transform is required. We elaborate on the graph Fourier transform and spectrum filtering steps below.

3.1 Graph Formulation of a Local Neighborhood

Given a set of k points $x_1, x_2, ..., x_k$ in a local neighborhood, we build a representation graph G_k whose vertices V are the points and whose edges $E \subseteq V \times V$ carry weights $a : E \rightarrow \mathbb{R}_+^*$ which represent pair-wise distance between vertices in a feature space. This provides a $k \times k$ nonnegative symmetric graph adjacency matrix A, with entries $A_{ij} = dist(x_i, x_j)$. We then compute the graph spectrum based on this adjacency matrix and perform a graph Fourier transform, spectral filtering and finally an inverse Fourier transform.

3.2 Graph Fourier Transform

To compute a graph Fourier Transform of the point features $X \in \mathbb{R}^{k \times m}$, which are graph signals on vertices of G_k, we first need to compute the normalized graph Laplacian defined as

$$\mathcal{L} = I - D^{-1/2} A D^{-1/2}, \tag{5}$$

where I is the identity matrix and $D \in \mathbb{R}^{k \times k}$ is the diagonal degree matrix with entries $D_{ii} = \sum_j A_{ij}$. It follows that $\mathcal{L}$ is a real symmetric positive semidefinite matrix, and has a complete set of orthonormal eigenvectors which comprise the graph Fourier basis

$$U = [u_0, u_1, ..., u_{k-1}] \in \mathbb{R}^{k \times k}. \tag{6}$$

The eigenvalues can be used to construct a diagonal matrix

$$\Lambda = diag([\lambda_0, \lambda_1, ..., \lambda_{k-1}]) \in \mathbb{R}^{k \times k} \tag{7}$$

which contains the frequencies of the graph. Then it follows that $\mathcal{L} = U \Lambda U^T$. The graph Fourier transform of X is then defined as $\tilde{X} = U^T X$ and its inverse as $X = U \tilde{X}$.

3.3   Spectral Filtering

The convolution operation is defined in the Fourier domain as

$$x * g = U((U^T x) \odot (U^T g)), \tag{8}$$

following Shuman *et al.* [5], where $\odot$ is the element-wise Hadamard product, x is an arbitrary graph signal and g is a spatial filter. If we define $y = x * g$ as the output of the graph convolution, it follows that a graph signal $X \in \mathbb{R}^{k \times m}$ filtered by g can be written as

$$y = \tilde{g}_\theta(\mathcal{L})X = \tilde{g}_\theta(U \Lambda U^T)X = U\tilde{g}_\theta(\Lambda)\tilde{X}, \tag{9}$$

where θ stands for an arbitrary parametrization. In the following section, we describe our implementation of spectral filtering, which is introduced as a module on top of the existing pointnet++ [1] framework, using TensorFlow.

3.4   Implementation of Spectral Filtering

We carry out spectral graph convolution using standard unparametrized Fourier kernels, where the entries of $\tilde{g}_\theta(\Lambda)$ are all learnable. With m the input feature dimension and m' the output dimension, convolution of a graph signal $X \in \mathbb{R}^{k \times m}$ with spectral filters can be achieved by the following three steps:

1. **Spectral modulation** which outputs $P = G\tilde{X}$, with the diagonal matrix G being the unparametrized kernel $\tilde{g}_\theta(\Lambda)$. The k diagonal entries of G are all free parameters in the unparametrized Fourier kernel formulation.
2. **Feature filtering** which expands the input dimension from m to m'. The output of this step is a feature matrix $Q \in \mathbb{R}^{k \times m'}$. The entry $q_{k,i}$ is the i-th output feature of the k-th point and is given by $q_{k,i} = \sum_{j=1}^{m} p_{k,j} w_{j,i}$. Here $p_{k,j}$ is the entry of P corresponding to the j-th input feature of the k-th point defined in the previous step and $w_{j,i}$ is the filter coefficient between the i-th input feature with j-th output feature. This step can be represented by $Q = PW$, where W is the matrix of learnable filter parameters. The filtering operation in steps 1 and 2 can be summarized as

$$Q = (G\tilde{X})W. \tag{10}$$

3. **Reverse Fourier transform** which provides convolution outputs in the spatial graph signal domain via $y = UQ$.

The above formulation resembles that of [3,4], with the difference that we build the k-NN graph during runtime, computing its Laplacian and pooling hierarchy on the fly, so that no offline precomputation is required. We further note that the weights of the feature filter W, as well as the spectral modulation matrix G, are shared by all the different local neighborhoods in a given graph convolution layer. Thus, unlike [3,4], the learned parameters in our work do not depend on the underlying graph structure. Figure 2 (bottom) summarizes the above spectral filtering process.

While the more sophisticated efficient kernels of [3] could be used, our goal was to demonstrate the improvement obtained by graph CNNs in general. The overhead due to eigenvalue decomposition (EVD) in our unparametrized spectral kernel does not significantly affect runtime since the EVD is computed on local k-NN graphs, with k being very small. This computation is easily handled by parallel computing on GPUs, as demonstrated by the experiments which describe training time cost in our model ablation study in Sect. 5.3. Our approach is also robust to potential ambiguity in eigenvector sign in EVD computation, for both the spectral graph convolution and cluster pooling operations, as discussed in the arXiv version of this paper at https://arxiv.org/abs/1803.05827.

4   Pooling on Local k-NN Graph

The set activation function discussed in Sect. 2, whose aim is to summarize information from a k-NN graph, is essentially a form of graph pooling, where a graph of k vertices is abstracted via feature pooling to a single vertex. We propose a novel k-NN graph pooling algorithm using hierarchical clustering and within-cluster pooling. Our method is inspired by the results in [6], where the benefit of recursive cluster pooling across multiple views in 3D object recognition is demonstrated.

The general strategy is to pool information during learning in a manner that does so only *within* a cluster of similar abstract point features, in contrast to the greedy strategy of max pooling, which is commonly applied in regular CNNs as well as in pointnet++. The intuition here is that multiple sets of distinct features may together contribute towards a salient property for the task at hand, and that the detection of these clusters combined with within cluster pooling will improve performance. For example, for the task of classifying a point set sampled from a human head one would want to simultaneously learn and capture nose-like, chin-like and ear-like features and not assume that only one of these would be discriminative for this object category. We discuss each of our steps in turn.

4.1   Spectral Clustering

We propose to group features into clusters according to a local k-NN's geometric information that is embedded using spectral coordinates. The spectral coordinates we use are based on the low frequency eigenvectors of the Graph Laplacian $\mathcal{L}$, which capture coarse shape properties since the Laplacian itself encodes pairwise distances in the k-NN graph. As exploited in [7,8] for computing point-to-point correspondences on meshes or for feature description, the low frequency spectral coordinates provide a discriminative spectral embedding of an object's local geometry (see Fig. 1 bottom and Fig. 3). The eigenvector corresponding to the second smallest eigenvalue, the Fiedler vector [9], is widely used for spectral clustering [10].

λ_1 λ_2 λ_3 λ_1 λ_2 λ_3

Fig. 3. A visualization of spectral coordinates for models of a bird (left) and a human (right), both from the McGill Shape Benchmark. $\lambda_i, i \in \{0, 1, ..., k-1\}$ is the i-th eigenvalue of the graph Laplacian.

4.2 Clustering, Pooling and Recurrence

Following the normalized cuts clustering algorithm [10], we partition the Fiedler vector to perform spectral clustering in a local k-NN. We first sort the entries of the Fiedler vector in ascending order of their numerical value, and then evenly cut it into k_1 sections in the first iteration. The points in the neighborhood whose Fiedler vector entries fall in the same section will be clustered together. This results in k_1 clusters with a cluster size of $c = \frac{k}{k_1}$. After obtaining a partition into k_1 clusters, we perform pooling operations only *within* each cluster. This allows the network to take advantage of separated features from possibly disjoint components in the k-NN graph.

Algorithm 1. Recursive Cluster Pooling

Inputs: pts ← point features ($\mathbb{R}^{k \times m}$), csize ← cluster size, and POOL ← the Pool method.

Output: Pooled point features ($\mathbb{R}^{1 \times m}$).

Methods: ARG_SORT(x) returns the sorted indices of x, REARRANGE(x,y) permutes x along its 1st dimension according to the given indices y, POOL(x) pools x along its 1st dimension.

procedure CLUSTER(pts, csize, POOL)
    G ← ADJ_MATRIX(pts)
    L ← LAPLACIAN(G)
    $[\Lambda, U]$ ← EVD(L)
    fiedler_vector← $U[:, 1]$
    inds← ARG_SORT(fiedler_vector)
    REARRANGE(pts, inds)
    RESHAPE(pts, [:, csize])
    return POOL(pts)

procedure MAIN(pts, csize)
    POOL← MAX_POOL
    while COUNT(pts)>csize **do**
        pts←CLUSTER(pts, csize, POOL)
        if POOL == MAX_POOL **then**
            POOL← AVG_POOL
        else
            POOL← MAX_POOL
    return POOL(pts)

The above steps result in a coarsened k_1-NN graph with aggregated point features. The same process is then repeated on the coarsened graph in a recursive manner, to obtain k_i clusters for each iteration i. We alternate between max pooling and average pooling between different recurrences to further increase the discriminative power of the graph pooling algorithm. The proposed algorithm terminates when the number of vertices remaining is smaller or equal to a pre-scribed cluster size. A regular full stride pooling is then applied on the resultant graph signals. We formalize the above steps in Algorithm 1.

In practice, we found that using $k = 2c^2$ as a relationship between cluster size c and neighborhood k size gave good results, with two recurrences of cluster pooling and a final pooling of size 2. We used max pooling as the first stage in the alternating pooling scheme, and fixed these configurations for all our experiments in Sect. 5. We implemented the recursive cluster pooling module in TensorFlow, integrating it fully with the spectral graph convolution layer to make the entire network end-to-end trainable.

5   Experiments

5.1   Datasets

We evaluate our approach against present state-of-the-art methods on:

- MNIST, which contains images of handwritten digits with 60k training and 10k testing samples. It has been used to benchmark related graph CNN approaches [3,11] as well as pointnet++ [1].
- ModelNet40 [12], which contains CAD models of 40 categories, sampled as point clouds. We use the official split, with 9,843 training and 2,468 testing examples.
- McGill Shape Benchmark [13], which contains 254 articulated object models and 202 non-articulated ones, from 19 categories. We sample the meshes into point clouds and use the first two-thirds of the examples in each category for training and the remaining one-third for testing.
- ShapeNet part segmentation dataset [14], which contains 16,881 shapes from 16 classes, with the points in each model labeled into one of 50 part types. We use the official training/testing split, following [2,14,15], where the challenge is to assign a part label to each point in the test set.
- ScanNet Indoor Scene dataset [16], which contains 1513 scanned and recon-structed indoor scenes, with annotations including semantic voxel labels. We follow the experimental settings for segmentation in [1,16] and use 1201 scenes for training, and 312 scenes for testing.

5.2   Network Architecture and Training

We provide details of our network structures for the case of 1024 input points (1k) and 2048 input points (2k). The network structure for the 2k experiments is designed to be "wider" to better accommodate the increased input point density. Table 1 lists all the variations of the pointnet++ and our spectral point convolution network structures, which we will later to refer to when presenting

Table 1. Network architectures for the 1k experiments (top) and the 2k experiments (bottom). Here, for each layer, C stands for the number of centroids, k stands for the size of the k-NN, and m stands for the output feature dimension.

1k Structure		L1	L2	L3	L4	Kernel	Pooling
3l-pointnet++	C	512	128	1	-		
	k	64	64	128	-	point MLP	max
	m	128	256	1024	-		
4l-pointnet++	C	512	128	32	1		
	k	32	32	8	32	point MLP	max
	m	128	256	512	1024		
2k Structure		L1	L2	L3	L4	Kernel	Pooling
3l-pointnet++	C	1024	256	1	-		
	k	64	64	256	-	point MLP	max
	m	128	256	1024	-		
4l-pointnet++	C	1024	256	64	1		
	k	32	32	8	64	point MLP	max
	m	128	256	512	1024		

experimental results. The 3l-pointnet++ is defined in the "pointnet2_cls_ssg.py" model file on the pointnet++ GitHub page. We replace the kernels from 4l-pointnet++ with spectral graph convolution kernels to acquire the *4l-spec-max* model. Replacing max pooling with recursive cluster pooling in the 4l-spec-max model results in the *4l-spec-cp* model. Details of the network structures and the parameters used in the training process are described in the arXiv version of this paper at https://arxiv.org/abs/1803.05827.

5.3 Ablation Study for Network Models

We first evaluate the effect of the novel components in our framework: (1) local spectral filtering on a k-NN and (2) recursive cluster pooling for local outputs. We apply a 4 layer pointnet++ structure as the baseline method, then add spectral filters to each layer, and then replace max pooling with recursive cluster pooling. We also include results obtained using the 3 layer structure used in [1]. In addition, we consider the scalability of both approaches as well as their training time, under the conditions of varying the number of input points and including additional features such as surface normals. These results are presented in Table 2.

From the model ablation study in Table 2 it is evident that our proposed model, which incorporates spectral graph convolution together with recursive cluster pooling, provides a non-trivial improvement over pointnet++ on both the classification and segmentation tasks. We make the following observations: (1) *3l-pointnet++ performs better than the 4 layer version*. This is likely because in the 4 layer version the neighborhood size is half of that in the 3 layer version. Since features are learned at each point in an isolated fashion in pointnet++, the use of larger neighborhoods gives an advantage. (2) *Spectral graph convolution on local k-NNs performs better than point-wise MLP.* The 4l-spec-max model outperforms 4l-pointnet++. This implies that the topological information encoded by spectral graph convolution improves feature learning. (3) *Recursive cluster pooling further boosts the performance of the spectral graph convolution layer.* This suggests that information aggregation following spectral coordinates increases the discriminative power of the learned point features, benefiting both classification and segmentation. (4) *The runtime of our model is comparable to those of pointnet++.* The eigenvalue decomposition used in spectral convolution and recursive cluster pooling could in theory be costly, but since we use local neighborhoods the impact is not severe. Our best model, 4l-spec-cp, has roughly the same training time as that of 3l-pointnet++, which is the best model from pointnet++. Spectral graph convolution kernels are as fast as the point-wise MLP kernels, which can be seen by comparing the runtime of the 4l-spec-max and 4l-pointnet++ models.

Table 2. Model Ablation Study on ModelNet40 (classification) and ShapeNet (segmentation). Acc stands for classification accuracy, 1k/2k refers to the number of points used and "+N" indicates the addition of surface normal features to xyz spatial coordinates. The "2k + N" column shows results averaged over 5 runs. For the segmentation experiments, mIOU stands for mean intersection over union. Here we only compare the best models from pointnet++ with ours. Training time is with respect to the number of epochs used in each experiment. Adding normals only increases the training time by a negligible amount, therefore only one runtime column is provided for the 1k experiments. The network structures for these experiments are described in Table 1.

ModelNet40	Acc 1k	Acc 1k +N	Time 250ep	Acc 2k +N	Time 250ep
3l-pointnet++	90.7	91.3	11h	91.47 ± 0.11	20h
4l-pointnet++	90.6	91.1	7.5h	91.19 ± 0.11	11h
4l-spec-max	91.2	91.6	8h	91.83 ± 0.08	12h
4l-spec-cp	91.5	91.8	12h	92.03 ± 0.09	20h
ShapeNet Seg	mIOU 1k	mIOU 1k +N	Time 100ep	mIOU 2k +N	Time 100ep
3l-pointnet++	84.2	84.7	7.5h	84.84 ± 0.10	14h
4l-spec-cp	84.6	85.0	8h	85.37 ± 0.09	14h

We now provide comparisons against the present state-of-the-art methods in classification and segmentation, using the datasets described in Sect. 5.1. When comparing against pointnet++, unless stated otherwise, we apply the 3l-pointnet++ model since it gives better results than the 4 layer version in our model ablation study in Table 2.

5.4   Classification Experiments

McGill Shape Benchmark. The classification results for the McGill Shape Benchmark are presented in Table 3, using 1024 xyz points as the inputs in all cases. Spectral graph convolution on point sets provides a consistent boost in both average instance level accuracy and category level accuracy. The use of recursive cluster pooling gives our model another 0.7% boost in overall instance level accuracy over max pooling. Since the k-NNs may contain disjoint sets of points, a recursive aggregation of k-NN features by clustering the spectral coordinates appears to increase discriminative power for articulated objects.

Table 3. McGill Shape Benchmark classification results. We report the instance and category level accuracy on both the entire database and on subsets (see Table 1 for network structures).

Model	Kernel	Pooling	Instance Level Accuracy (%)			Category Level Accuracy (%)		
			Arti	Non-Arti	Combined	Arti	Non-Arti	Combined
3l-pointnet++	point-MLP	max	91.25	95.31	93.06	91.33	95.44	93.27
4l-pointnet++	point-MLP	max	92.50	92.19	92.36	92.83	92.74	92.79
4l-spec-cp	spec-conv	max	92.50	98.44	95.14	92.75	98.41	95.43
	spec-conv	cp	93.75	98.44	95.83	93.30	98.41	95.74

Table 4. MNIST classification results. To obtain the pointnet++ results we reproduced the experiments discussed in [1].

Method	Domain	Kernel	Error Rate(%)
Multi-layer perceptron [17]	full image	spatial MLP	1.60
LeNet5 [18]	local img patch	spatial conv	0.80
Network in Network [19]	local img patch	spatial conv	0.47
ChebNet [3]	full graph	spectral graph conv	0.86
MoNet [11]	local graph	spatial graph conv	0.81
3l-pointnet++ [1]	local points	spatial point-MLP	0.55
4l-spec-cp	local k-NN graph	spectral graph conv	0.42

MNIST Dataset. 2D images can be treated as a grid graph [3,11] or a 2D point cloud [1]. We provide results on the MNIST dataset using our proposed best model, 4l-spec-cp, from the previous model ablation study. We compare our results with the state-of-the-art methods in graph CNNs [3,11], in point sets [1] (our 0.55% error rate using pointnet++ is very close to that reported by the authors) and with regular neural network/CNN approaches applied on the 2D image domain [17–19].

For both pointnet++ and our method, 784 points are provided as inputs to the network and we use the 1k experimental network, where the first layer samples 512 centroids (see Table 1). The results in Table 4 show that approaches which favor local operations on the input domain usually yield better performance, for instance, MLP vs. LeNet, and our method vs. ChebNet. Our approach gives a 20% error rate reduction over pointnet++, demonstrating the advantage of spectral convolution on a local k-NN graph over the isolated learning process in point-wise MLP. In addition, our performance surpasses that of the Network in Network model [19], which is a strong regular image CNN model.

ModelNet40 Dataset. We present ModelNet40 3D shape recognition results in Table 5, where we compare our method with representative competitive approaches. We were able to reproduce the results from pointnet++, to get very similar performance to that reported by the authors in [1]. We report two sets of accuracy results. In the first 1024 xyz point coordinates are used as inputs, with the network structure following the 1k configurations in Table 1. In the second 2048 xyz points along with their surface normals are used as inputs, with the network structure following the 2k configurations in Table 1. Our use of spectral graph convolution and recursive cluster pooling provides a consistent improvement over pointnet++, and leads to state-of-the-art level classification performance on the ModelNet40 Benchmark.

Table 5. ModelNet40 results. "Acc" stands for 1k experiments with only xyz points as input features. "Acc + N" stands for 2k experiments with xyz points along with their surface normals as input features. "graph-cp" stands for recursive cluster pooling.

Method	Domain	Kernel	Pooling	Acc (%)	Acc + N (%)
Subvolume [20]	Voxel Grid	3D conv	3D-max	89.2	-
MVCNN [21]	2D views	2D conv	view-max	90.1	-
PointNet [2]	Full Points	point-MLP	point-max	89.2	-
3l-pointnet++ [1]	Local Points	point-MLP	point-max	90.7	91.5
4l-spec-max	Local k-NN graph	graph conv	graph-max	91.2	91.9
4l-spec-cp	Local k-NN graph	graph conv	graph-cp	91.5	92.1

5.5   Segmentation Experiments

Point segmentation is a labeling task for each point in a 3D point set, and is more challenging than point set classification. We present experimental results on ShapeNet [14] and ScanNet [16] in Table 6. We then provide details on experimental settings for each case.

Table 6. Segmentation Results. We compare our method with the state-of-the-art approaches, as well as with the results from pointnet++, which we have been able to reproduce experimentally. For ShapeNet, mIOU stands for mean intersection over union on points, and for ScanNet, Acc stands for voxel label prediction accuracy.

Method	Domain	Kernel	ShapeNet-mIOU (%)	ScanNet-Acc (%)
Yi *et al.* [14]	-	-	81.4	-
Dai *et al.* [16]	Voxel Grid	3D conv	-	73.0
SynSpecCNN [22]	Full *k*-NN Graph	graph conv	84.7	-
PointNet [2]	Full Points	point-MLP	83.7	73.9
Pointnet++ [1]	Local Points	point-MLP	84.9	84.0
4l-spec-cp	Local *k*-NN Graphs	graph conv	85.4	84.8

Shapenet Part Segmentation Dataset. Following the setting in [14], we evaluate our approach assuming that a category label for each shape is already known and we use the same mIoU (mean intersection over union) measurement on points. 2048 xyz points and their surface normals are used as input features and the network structure follows that of the 2k configurations in Table 1. More specifically, the 3l-pointnet++ model is applied for pointnet++ and the 4l-spec-cp is applied for our method.

ScanNet Dataset. ScanNet is a large-scale semantic segmentation dataset constructed from real-world 3D scans of indoor scenes, and as such is more challenging than the synthesized 3D models in ShapeNet. Following [1,16], we remove RGB information in our experiments in Table 6 and we use the semantic voxel label prediction accuracy for evaluation. The training and testing procedures follow those in pointnet++ [1]. 8192 xyz points are used as input features and the network structure is that of the 2k configurations in Table 1. More specifically, the 4l-pointnet++ model is applied for pointnet++ and the 4l-spec-cp is applied for our method.[1]

The use of spectral graph convolution combined with cluster pooling in our approach once again provides a non-trivial improvement over pointnet++, achieving state-of-the-art level performance on part segmentation on the ShapeNet dataset and indoor scene semantic segmentation on the ScanNet dataset. We provide an illustrative visualization of the part segmentation results on selected models in Fig. 4. In these examples, when compared to pointnet++, our approach gives results that are closer to the ground truth overall and it better captures fine local structures, such as the axles of the skateboard, and the feet of the table. In addition, spectral graph convolution with cluster pooling provides a more faithful representation of changes in local geometry. This allows us to successfully segment connected parts of a 3D object, such as the strap from

---

[1] The 3l-pointnet++ model leads to inferior performance on this large-scale indoor dataset. For both networks, for all experiments reported in this paper, single scale grouping (SSG in [1]) is applied for a fair comparison.

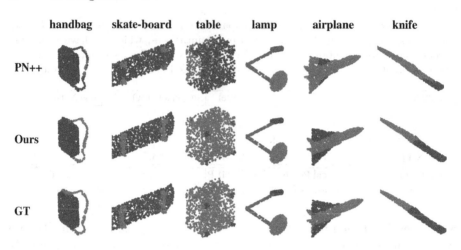

Fig. 4. A visualization of segmentation results on ShapeNet using pointnet++ (top row, 84.9% in Table 6), our 41-spec-cp model (middle row, 85.4% in Table 6), and the ground truth labels (bottom row). Our method appears to better capture fine local structures (see text for a discussion).

the body of the handbag, the wings from the tail fins of the airplane and the handle from the blade of the knife.

6   Conclusion

The use of spectral graph convolution on local point neighborhoods, followed by recursive cluster pooling on the derived representations, holds great promise for feature learning from unorganized point sets. Our method's ability to capture local structural information and geometric cues from such data presents an advance in deep learning approaches to feature abstraction for applications in computer vision. With its strong experimental performance, acceptable runtime, and versatility in handling a variety of datasets and tasks, our approach could have considerable practical value as 3D depth sensors begin to become more and more commonplace. The approach is not limited in application to point sets derived from cameras. It can also be applied in settings where the vertices carry a more abstract interpretation, such as nodes in a graph representing a social network, where local feature attributes could play an important role.

Acknowledgments. We thank Charles Ruizhongtai Qi who not only released the pointnet++ implementation upon which our own work is based, but was also kind enough to provide many helpful hints on how to use it. We are also grateful to the Natural Sciences and Engineering Research Council of Canada for research funding.

References

1. Qi, C.R., Yi, L., Su, H., Guibas, L.J.: Pointnet++: deep hierarchical feature learning on point sets in a metric space. In: NIPS (2017)

2. Qi, C.R., Su, H., Mo, K., Guibas, L.J.: PointNet: deep learning on point sets for 3D classification and segmentation. In: CVPR (2016)
3. Defferrard, M., Bresson, X., Vandergheynst, P.: Convolutional neural networks on graphs with fast localized spectral filtering. In: NIPS (2016)
4. Kipf, T.N., Welling, M.: Semi-supervised classification with graph convolutional networks. In: ICLR (2017)
5. Shuman, D.I., Narang, S.K., Frossard, P., Ortega, A., Vandergheynst, P.: The emerging field of signal processing on graphs: extending high-dimensional data analysis to networks and other irregular domains. IEEE Sig. Process. Mag. 30(3), 83–98 (2013)
6. Wang, C., Pelillo, M., Siddiqi, K.: Dominant set clustering and pooling for multi-view 3D object recognition. In: BMVC (2017)
7. Lombaert, H., Grady, L., Cheriet, F.: FOCUSR: feature oriented correspondence using spectral regularization-a method for precise surface matching. IEEE Trans. Pattern Anal. Mach. Intell. (2013)
8. Bronstein, A.M., Bronstein, M.M., Kimmel, R.: Numerical Geometry of Non-rigid Shapes. Monographs in Computer Science. Springer, New York (2008). https:// doi.org/10.1007/978-0-387-73301-2
9. Chung, F.R.: Spectral Graph Theory. Number 92 in Regional Conference Series in Mathematics. Am. Mathe. Soc. (1997)
10. Shi, J., Malik, J.: Normalized cuts and image segmentation. IEEE Trans. Pattern Anal. Mach. Intell. 22(8), 888–905 (2000)
11. Monti, F., Boscaini, D., Masci, J., Rodolà, E., Svoboda, J., Bronstein, M.M.: Geometric deep learning on graphs and manifolds using mixture model CNNs. In: CVPR (2017)
12. Wu, Z., et al.: 3D shapenets: a deep representation for volumetric shapes. In: CVPR (2015)
13. Siddiqi, K., Zhang, J., Macrini, D., Shokoufandeh, A., Bouix, S., Dickinson, S.: Retrieving articulated 3D models using medial surfaces. Mach. Vis. Appl. 19(4), 261–274 (2008)
14. Yi, L., et al.: A scalable active framework for region annotation in 3D shape collections. ACM Trans. Graph. (TOG) (2016)
15. Yi, L., Su, H., Guo, X., Guibas, L.: SyncSpecCNN: synchronized spectral CNN for 3D shape segmentation. In: CVPR (2017)
16. Dai, A., Chang, A.X., Savva, M., Halber, M., Funkhouser, T., Nießner, M.: ScanNet: richly-annotated 3D reconstructions of indoor scenes. In: CVPR (2017)
17. Simard, P.Y., Steinkraus, D., Platt, J.C., et al.: Best practices for convolutional neural networks applied to visual document analysis. In: ICDAR (2003)
18. LeCun, Y., Bottou, L., Bengio, Y., Haffner, P.: Gradient-based learning applied to document recognition. Proc. IEEE 86(11), 2278–2324 (1998)
19. Lin, M., Chen, Q., Yan, S.: Network in network. In: ICLR (2014)
20. Qi, C.R., Su, H., Niessner, M., Dai, A., Yan, M., Guibas, L.J.: Volumetric and multi-view CNNs for object classification on 3D data. In: CVPR (2016)
21. Su, H., Maji, S., Kalogerakis, E., Learned-Miller, E.: Multi-view convolutional neural networks for 3D shape recognition. In: ICCV (2015)

Piggyback: Adapting a Single Network to Multiple Tasks by Learning to Mask Weights

Arun Mallya[✉], Dillon Davis, and Svetlana Lazebnik

University of Illinois at Urbana-Champaign, Champaign, USA
{amallya2,ddavis14,slazebni}@illinois.edu

Abstract. This work presents a method for adapting a single, fixed deep neural network to multiple tasks without affecting performance on already learned tasks. By building upon ideas from network quantization and pruning, we learn binary masks that "piggyback" on an existing network, or are applied to unmodified weights of that network to provide good performance on a new task. These masks are learned in an end-to-end differentiable fashion, and incur a low overhead of 1 bit per network parameter, per task. Even though the underlying network is fixed, the ability to mask individual weights allows for the learning of a large number of filters. We show performance comparable to dedicated fine-tuned networks for a variety of classification tasks, including those with large domain shifts from the initial task (ImageNet), and a variety of network architectures. Our performance is agnostic to task ordering and we do not suffer from catastrophic forgetting or competition between tasks.

Keywords: Incremental learning · Binary networks

1 Introduction

The most popular method used in prior work for training a deep network for a new task or dataset is fine-tuning an established pre-trained model, such as the VGG-16 [1] trained on ImageNet classification [2]. A major drawback of fine-tuning is the phenomenon of "*catastrophic forgetting*" [3], by which performance on the old task degrades significantly as the new task is learned, necessitating one to store specialized models for each task or dataset. For achieving progress towards continual learning [4,5], we need better methods for augmenting capabilities of an existing network while avoiding catastrophic forgetting and requiring as few additional parameters as possible.

Prior methods for avoiding catastrophic forgetting, such as Learning without Forgetting (LwF) [6] and Elastic Weight Consolidation (EWC) [4], maintain performance on older tasks through proxy losses and regularization terms while modifying network weights. Another recent work, PackNet [7], adopts a different route of iteratively pruning unimportant weights and fine-tuning them for

© Springer Nature Switzerland AG 2018
V. Ferrari et al. (Eds.): ECCV 2018, LNCS 11208, pp. 72–88, 2018.
https://doi.org/10.1007/978-3-030-01225-0_5

learning new tasks. As a result of pruning and weight modifications, a binary parameter usage mask is produced by PackNet. We question whether the weights of a network have to be changed at all to learn a new task, or whether we can get by with just selectively masking, or setting certain weights to 0, while keeping the rest of the weights the same as before. Based on this idea, we propose a novel approach in which we learn to mask weights of an existing *"backbone"* network for obtaining good performance on a new task, as shown in Fig. 1. Binary masks that take values in $\{0, 1\}$ are learned in an end-to-end differentiable fashion while optimizing for the task at hand. These masks are elementwise applied to backbone weights, allowing us to learn a large range of different filters, even with fixed weights. We find that a well-initialized backbone network is crucial for good performance and that the popular ImageNet pre-trained network generalizes to multiple new tasks. After training for a new task, we obtain a per-task binary mask that simply *"piggybacks"* onto the backbone network.

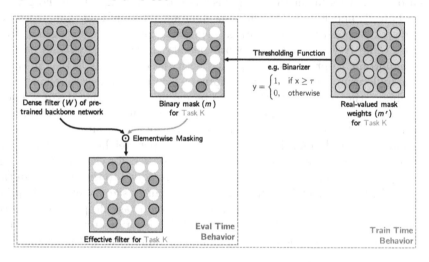

Fig. 1. Overview of our method for learning piggyback masks for fixed backbone networks. During training, we maintain a set of real-valued weights m^r which are passed through a thresholding function to obtain binary-valued masks m. These masks are applied to the weights W of the backbone network in an elementwise fashion, keeping individual weights active, or masked out. The gradients obtained through backpropagation of the task-specific loss are used to update the real-valued mask weights. After training, the real-valued mask weights are discarded and only the thresholded mask is retained, giving one network mask per task.

Our experiments conducted on image classification, and presented in Sect. 4, show that this proposed method obtains performance similar to using a separate network per task, for a variety of datasets considered in prior work [7] such as CUBS birds [8], Stanford cars [9], Oxford flowers [10], as well datasets with a significant departure from the natural image domain of the ImageNet dataset such as WikiArt paintings [11] and human sketches [12]. We demonstrate the applicability of our method to multiple network architectures including

VGG-16 [1], ResNets [13,14], and DenseNets [15]. Section 5 tries to offer some insight into the workings of the proposed method, and analyzes design choices that affect performance. As presented in Sect. 6, we also obtain performance competitive with the best methods [16] on the Visual Decathlon challenge [17] while using the least amount of additional parameters. Finally, we show that our method can be used to train a fully convolutional network for semantic segmentation starting from a classification backbone.

2   Related Work

While multiple prior works [18–20] have explored multi-task training, wherein data of all tasks is available at the time of training, we consider the setting in which new tasks are available sequentially, a more realistic and challenging scenario. Prior work under this setting is based on Learning without Forgetting (LwF) [5,6,21] and Elastic Weight Consolidation (EWC) [4,22]. LwF uses initial network responses on new data as regularization targets during new task training, while EWC imposes a smooth penalty on changing weights deemed to be important to prior tasks. An issue with these methods is that it is not possible to determine the change in performance on prior tasks beforehand since all weights of the network are allowed to be modified to varying degrees. Pack-Net [7] avoids this issue by identifying weights important for prior tasks through network pruning, and keeping the important weights fixed after training for a particular task. Additional information is stored per weight parameter of the network to indicate which tasks it is used by. However, for each of these methods, performance begins to drop as many tasks are added to the network. In the case of LwF, a large domain shift for a new task causes significant drop in prior task performance [6]. For PackNet, performance on a task drops as it is added later to the network due to the lack of available free parameters, and the total number of tasks that can be added is ultimately limited due to the fixed size of the network [7].

Our proposed method does not change weights of the initial backbone network and learns a different mask per task. As a result, it is agnostic to task ordering and the addition of a task does not affect performance on any other task. Further, an unlimited number of tasks can piggyback onto a backbone network by learning a new mask. The parameter usage masks in PackNet were obtained as a by-product of network pruning [23], but we learn appropriate masks based on the task at hand. This idea of masking is related to PathNet [24], which learns selective routing through neurons using evolutionary strategies. We achieve similar behavior through an end-to-end differentiable method, which is less computationally demanding. The learning of separate masks per task decouples the learning of multiple tasks, freeing us from having to choose hyperparameters such as batch mixing ratios [20], pruning ratios [7], and cost weighting [6].

Similar to our proposed method, another set of methods adds new tasks by learning additional task-specific parameters. For a new task, Progressive Neural Networks [25] duplicates the base architecture while adding lateral connections to layers of the existing network. The newly added parameters are optimized for the new task, while keeping old weights fixed. This method incurs a large overhead as the network is replicated for the number of tasks added. The method of Residual Adapters [17] develops on the observation that linearly parameterizing a convolutional filter bank of a network is the same as adding an additional per-task convolutional layer to the network. The most recent Deep Adaptation Networks (DAN) [16] allows for learning new filters that are linear combinations of existing filters. Similar to these methods, we enable the learning of new per-task filters. However, these new filters are constrained to be masked versions of existing filters. Our learned binary masks incur an overhead of 1 bit per network parameter, smaller than all of the prior work. Further, we do not find it necessary to learn task-specific layer biases and batch normalization parameters.

Our method for training binary masks is based on the technique introduced by Courbariaux *et al.* [26,27] for the training of a neural network with binary-valued weights from scratch. The authors maintain a set of real-valued weights that are passed through a binarizer function during the forward pass. Gradients are computed with respect to the binarized weights during the backward pass through the application of the chain rule, and the real-valued weights are updated using the gradients computed for the binarized versions. In [26], the authors argue that even though the gradients computed in this manner are noisy, they effectively serve as a regularizer and quantization errors cancel out over multiple iterations. Subsequent work including [28,29] has extended this idea to ternary-valued weights. Unlike these works, we do not train a quantized network from scratch but instead learn quantized masks that are applied to fixed, real-valued filter weights. Work on sparsifying dense neural networks, specifically [30], has used the idea of masked weight matrices. However, only their weight matrix was trainable and their mask values were a fixed function of the magnitude of the weight matrix and not explicitly trainable. In contrast, we treat the weight matrix of the backbone network as a fixed constant.

3   Approach

The key idea behind our method is to learn to selectively mask the fixed weights of a base network, so as to improve performance on a new task. We achieve this by maintaining a set of real-valued weights that are passed through a deterministic thresholding function to obtain binary masks, that are then applied to existing weights. By updating the real-valued weights through backpropagation, we hope to learn binary masks appropriate for the task at hand. This process is illustrated in Fig. 1. By learning different binary-valued $\{0, 1\}$ masks per task, which are element-wise applied to network parameters, we can re-use the same underlying base network for multiple tasks, with minimal overhead. Even though we do not modify the weights of the network, a large number of different filters can be obtained through masking. For example, a dense weight vector such as $[0.1, 0.9, -0.5, 1]$ can give rise to filters such as $[0.1, 0, 0, 1]$, $[0, 0.9, -0.5, 0]$, and $[0, 0.9, -0.5, 1]$ after binary masking. In practice, we begin with a network such as the VGG-16 or ResNet-50 pre-trained on the ImageNet classification task as our base network, referred to as the *backbone* network, and associate a real-valued mask variable with each weight parameter of all the convolutional and fully-connected layers. By combining techniques used in network binarization [26, 27] and pruning [30], we train these mask variables to learn the task at hand in an end-to-end fashion, as described in detail below. The choice of the initialization of the backbone network is crucial for obtaining good performance, and is further analyzed in Sect. 5.1.

For simplicity, we describe the mask learning procedure using the example of a fully-connected layer, but this idea can easily be extended to a convolutional layer as well. Consider a simple fully-connected layer in a neural network. Let the input and output vectors be denoted by $\mathbf{x} = (x_1, x_2, \cdots, x_m)^T$ of size $m \times 1$, and $\mathbf{y} = (y_1, y_2, \cdots, y_n)^T$ of size $n \times 1$, respectively. Let the weight matrix of the layer be $\mathbf{W} = [w]_{ji}$ of size $n \times m$. The input-output relationship is then given by $\mathbf{y} = \mathbf{W}\mathbf{x}$, or $y_j = \sum_{i=1}^{m} w_{ji} \cdot x_i$. The bias term is ignored for ease of notation. Let δv denote the partial derivative of the error function E with respect to the variable v. The backpropagation equation for the weights $\mathbf{W}$ of this fully-connected layer is given by

$$\delta w_{ji} \triangleq \frac{\partial E}{\partial w_{ji}} = \left(\frac{\partial E}{\partial y_j}\right) \cdot \left(\frac{\partial y_j}{\partial w_{ji}}\right) \tag{1}$$

$$= \delta y_j \cdot x_i \tag{2}$$

$$\therefore \delta \mathbf{W} \triangleq \left[\frac{\partial E}{\partial w}\right]_{ji} = \delta \mathbf{y} \cdot \mathbf{x}^T, \tag{3}$$

where $\delta \mathbf{y} = (\delta y_1, \delta y_2, \cdots, \delta y_n)^T$ is of size $n \times 1$.

Our modified fully-connected layer associates a matrix of real-valued mask weights $\mathbf{m^r} = [m^r]_{ji}$ with every weight matrix $\mathbf{W}$, of the same size as $\mathbf{W}$ ($n \times m$), as indicated by the rightmost filter in Fig. 1. We obtain thresholded mask matrices $\mathbf{m} = [m]_{ji}$ by passing the real-valued mask weight matrices $\mathbf{m^r}$ through a hard binary thresholding function given by

$$m_{ji} = \begin{cases} 1, & \text{if } m^r{}_{ji} \geq \tau \\ 0, & \text{otherwise} \end{cases}, \tag{4}$$

where τ is a selected threshold. The binary-valued matrix $\mathbf{m}$ activates or switches off contents of $\mathbf{W}$ depending on whether a particular value m_{ji} is 0 or 1. The layer's input-output relationship is given by the equation $\mathbf{y} = (\mathbf{W} \odot \mathbf{m})\mathbf{x}$, or $y_j = \sum_{i=1}^{m} w_{ji} \cdot m_{ji} \cdot x_i$, where $\odot$ indicates elementwise multiplication or masking. As mentioned previously, we set the weights $\mathbf{W}$ of our modified layer to those from the same architecture pre-trained on a task such as ImageNet classification. We treat the weights $\mathbf{W}$ as fixed constants throughout, while only training the real-valued mask weights $\mathbf{m^r}$. The backpropagation equation for the thresholded mask weights $\mathbf{m}$ of this fully-connected layer is given by

$$\delta m_{ji} \triangleq \frac{\partial E}{\partial m_{ji}} = \left(\frac{\partial E}{\partial y_j}\right) \cdot \left(\frac{\partial y_j}{\partial m_{ji}}\right) \tag{5}$$

$$= \delta y_j \cdot w_{ji} \cdot x_i \tag{6}$$

$$\therefore \delta \mathbf{m} \triangleq \left[\frac{\partial E}{\partial m}\right]_{ji} = (\delta \mathbf{y} \cdot \mathbf{x}^T) \odot \mathbf{W}. \tag{7}$$

Even though the hard thresholding function is non-differentiable, the gradients of the thresholded mask values $\mathbf{m}$ serve as a noisy estimator of the gradients of the real-valued mask weights $\mathbf{m^r}$, and can even serve as a regularizer, as shown in prior work [26,27]. We thus update the real-valued mask weights $\mathbf{m^r}$ using gradients computed for $\mathbf{m}$, the thresholded mask values. After adding a new final classification layer for the new task, the entire system can be trained in an end-to-end differentiable manner. In our experiments, we did not train per-task biases as prior work [7] showed that this does not have any significant impact on performance. We also did not train per-task batch-normalization parameters for simplicity. Section 5.3 analyzes the benefit of training per-task batchnorm parameters, especially for tasks with large domain shifts.

After training a mask for a given task, we no longer require the real-valued mask weights. They are discarded, and only the thresholded masks associated with the backbone network layers are stored. A typical neural network parameter is represented using a 32-bit float value (including in our PyTorch implementation). A binary mask only requires 1 extra bit per parameter, leading to an approximate per-task overhead of 1/32 or 3.12% of the backbone network size.

Practical Optimization Details. From Eq. 7, we observe that $|\delta\mathbf{m}|, |\delta\mathbf{m^r}| \propto |\mathbf{W}|$. The magnitude of pre-trained weights varies across layers of a network, and as a result, the mask gradients would also have different magnitudes at different layers. This relationship requires us to be careful about the manner in which we initialize and train mask weights $\mathbf{m^r}$. There are two possible approaches:

(1) Initialize $\mathbf{m^r}$ with values proportional to the weight matrix $\mathbf{W}$ of the corresponding layer. In this case, the ratio $|\delta\mathbf{m^r}|/|\mathbf{m^r}|$ will be similar across layers, and a constant learning rate can be used for all layers.
(2) Initialize $\mathbf{m^r}$ with a constant value, such as 0.01, for all layers. This would require a separate learning rate per layer, due to the scaling of the mask gradient by the layer weight magnitude. While using SGD, scaling gradients obtained at each layer by a factor of $1/\mathrm{avg}(|\mathbf{W}|)$, while using a constant learning rate, has the same effect as layer-dependent learning rates. Alternatively, one could use adaptive optimizers such as Adam, which would learn appropriate scaling factors.

The second initialization approach combined with the Adam optimizer produced the best results, with a consistent gain in accuracy by $\sim 2\%$ compared to the alternatives. We initialized the real-valued weights with a value of 1e-2 with a binarizer threshold (τ, in Eq. 4) of 5e-3 in all our experiments. Randomly initializing the real-valued mask weights such that the thresholded binary masks had an equal number of 0s and 1s did not give very good performance. Ensuring that all thresholded mask values were 1 provides the same network initialization as that of the baseline methods.

We also tried learning ternary masks $\{-1, 0, 1\}$ by using a modified version of Eq. 4 with two cut-off thresholds, but did not achieve results that were significantly different from those obtained with binary masks. As a result, we only focus on results obtained with binary masks in the rest of this work.

4   Experiments and Results

We consider a wide variety of datasets, statistics of which are summarized in Table 1, to evaluate our proposed method. Similar to PackNet [7], we evaluate our method on two large-scale datasets, the ImageNet object classification dataset [2] and the Places365 scene classification dataset [31], each of which has over a million images, as well as the CUBS [8], Stanford Cars [9], and Flowers [10] fine-grained classification datasets. Further, we include two more datasets with significant domain shifts from the natural images of ImageNet, the WikiArt Artists classification dataset, created from the WikiArt dataset [11], and the Sketch classifcation dataset [12]. The former includes a wide genre of painting styles, as shown in Fig. 2a, while the latter includes black-and-white sketches drawn by humans, as shown in Fig. 2b. For all these datasets, we use networks with an input image size of 224×224 px.

Table 1. Summary of datasets used.

Dataset	#Train	#Eval	#Classes
ImageNet [2]	1,281,144	50,000	1,000
Places365 [31]	1,803,460	36,500	365
CUBS [8]	5,994	5,794	200
Stanford Cars [9]	8,144	8,041	196
Flowers [10]	2,040	6,149	102
WikiArt [11]	42,129	10,628	195
Sketch [12]	16,000	4,000	250

(a) WikiArt   (b) Sketch

Fig. 2. Datasets unlike ImageNet.

Table 2 reports the errors obtained on fine-grained classification tasks by learning binary-valued piggyback masks for a VGG-16 network pre-trained on ImageNet classification. The first baseline considered is **Classifier Only**, which only trains a linear classifier using fc7 features extracted from the pre-trained VGG-16 network. This is a commonly used method that has low overhead as all layers except for the last classification layer are re-used amongst tasks. The second and more powerful baseline is **Individual Networks**, which finetunes a separate network per task. We also compare our method to the recently introduced **PackNet** [7] method, which adds multiple tasks to a network through iterative pruning and re-training. We train all methods for 30 epochs. We train the piggyback and classifier only, using the Adam optimizer with an initial learning rate of 1e-4, which is decayed by a factor of 10 after 15 epochs. We found SGDm with an initial learning rate of 1e-3 to work better for the individual VGG network baseline. For PackNet, we used a 50% pruned initial network trained with SGDm with an initial learning rate of 1e-3 using the same decay scheme as before. We prune the network by 75% and re-train for 15 epochs with a learning rate of 1e-4 after each new task is added. All errors are averaged over 3 independent runs.

Table 2. Errors obtained by starting from an ImageNet-trained VGG-16 network and then using various methods to learn new fine-grained classification tasks. PackNet performance is sensitive to order of task addition, while the rest, including our proposed method, are agnostic. ↓ and ↑ indicate that tasks were added in the CUBS → Sketch, and Sketch → CUBS order, resp. Values in parentheses are top-5 errors, rest are top-1 errors.

Dataset	Classifier Only	PackNet [7]		Piggyback (ours)	Individual Networks
		↓	↑		
ImageNet	28.42 (9.61)	29.33 (9.99)		28.42 (9.61)	28.42 (9.61)
CUBS	36.49	22.30	29.69	20.99	21.30
Stanford Cars	54.66	15.81	21.66	11.87	12.49
Flowers	20.01	10.33	10.25	7.19	7.35
WikiArt	49.53	32.80	31.48	29.91	29.84
Sketch	58.53	28.62	24.88	22.70	23.54
# Models (Size)	1 (537 MB)	1 (587 MB)		1 (621 MB)	6 (3,222 MB)

As seen in Table 2, training individual networks per task clearly provides a huge benefit over the classifier only baseline for all tasks. PackNet significantly improves over the classifier only baseline, but begins to suffer when more than 3 tasks are added to a single network. As PackNet is sensitive to the ordering of tasks, we try two settings - adding tasks in order from CUBS to Sketch (top to bottom in Table 2), and the reverse. The order of new task addition has a large impact on the performance of PackNet, with errors increasing by 4–7% as the addition of a task is delayed from first to last (fifth). The error on ImageNet is also higher in the case of PackNet, due to initial network pruning. By training binary piggyback masks, we are able to obtain errors slightly lower than the individual network case. We believe that this is due to the regularization effect caused by the constrained filter modification allowed by our method. Due to the learning of independent masks per task, the obtained performance is agnostic to the ordering of new tasks, albeit at a slightly higher storage overhead as compared to PackNet. The number of weights switched off varies per layer and by dataset depending on its similarity to the ImageNet dataset. This effect is further examined in Sect. 5.2.

While the results above were obtained by adding multiple smaller fine-grained classification tasks to a network, the next set of results in Table 3 examines the effect of adding a large-scale dataset, the Places365 scene classification task with 1.8M images, to a network. Here, instead of the Classifier Only baseline, we compare against the **Jointly Trained Network** of [31], in which a single network is simultaneously trained for both tasks. Both PackNet and Piggyback were trained for 20 epochs on Places365. Once again, we are able to achieve close to best-case performance on the Places365 task, obtaining top-1 errors within 0.36% of the individual network, even though the baselines were trained for 60–90 epochs [31]. The performance is comparable to PackNet, and for the case of adding just one task, both incur a similar overhead.

Table 3. Adding a large-scale dataset to an ImageNet-trained VGG-16 network. Values in parentheses are top-5 errors, rest are top-1 errors. * indicates models downloaded from https://github.com/CSAILVision/places365, trained by [31].

Dataset	Jointly Trained Network*	PackNet [7]	Piggyback (ours)	Individual Networks
ImageNet	33.49 (12.25)	29.33 (9.99)	28.42 (9.61)	28.42 (9.61)
Places365	45.98 (15.59)	46.64 (15.92)	46.71 (16.18)	46.35 (16.14)*
# Models (Size)	1 (537 MB)	1 (554 MB)	1 (554 MB)	2 (1,074 MB)

The previous results were obtained using the large VGG-16 network, and it is not immediately obvious whether the piggyback method would work for much deeper networks that have batch normalization layers. Masking out filter weights can change the average magnitude of activations, requiring changes to batchnorm parameters. We present results obtained with a VGG-16 network with batch normalization layers, the ResNet-50, and DenseNet-121 networks in Table 4. We observe that the method can be applied without any changes to these network architectures with batchnorm, residual, and skip connections. In the presented results, we do not learn task-specific batchnorm parameters. We however notice that the deeper a network gets, the larger the gap between the performance of piggyback and individual networks. For the VGG-16 architecture, piggyback can often do as well as or better than individual models, but for the ResNet and DenseNet architectures, the gap is ~2%. In Sect. 5.3 we show that learning task-specific batchnorm parameters in the case of datasets that exhibit a large domain shift, such as WikiArt, for which the performance gap is 4–5% (as seen in Table 4), helps further close the gap.

Table 4. Results on other network architectures. Values in parentheses are top-5 errors, rest are top-1 errors. ↑ and ↓ indicate order of task addition for PackNet.

Dataset	Classifier Only	PackNet [7] ↓	↑	Piggyback (ours)	Individual Networks
VGG-16 BN					
ImageNet	26.63	27.18		26.63	26.63
	(8.49)	(8.69)		(8.49)	(8.49)
CUBS	33.88	20.21	23.82	18.37	19.57
Stanford Cars	51.62	14.05	17.60	9.87	9.41
Flowers	19.38	7.82	7.85	4.84	4.55
WikiArt	48.05	30.21	29.59	27.50	26.68
Sketch	59.96	25.47	23.53	21.41	21.92
# Models (Size)	1 (537 MB)	1 (587 MB)		1 (621 MB)	6 (3,222 MB)
ResNet-50					
ImageNet	23.84	24.29		23.84	23.84
	(7.13)	(7.18)		(7.13)	(7.13)
CUBS	29.97	19.59	28.62	18.41	17.17
Stanford Cars	47.20	13.89	19.99	10.38	8.17
Flowers	14.01	6.96	9.45	5.23	3.44
WikiArt	44.40	30.60	29.69	28.67	24.40
Sketch	49.14	23.83	21.30	20.09	19.22
# Models (Size)	1 (94 MB)	1 (103 MB)		1 (109 MB)	6 (564 MB)
DenseNet-121					
ImageNet	25.56	25.60		25.56	25.56
	(8.02)	(7.89)		(8.02)	(8.02)
CUBS	26.55	19.26	30.36	19.50	18.08
Stanford Cars	43.19	15.35	22.09	10.87	8.64
Flowers	16.56	8.94	8.46	5.31	3.49
WikiArt	45.08	33.66	30.81	29.56	23.59
Sketch	46.88	25.35	21.08	20.30	19.48
# Models (Size)	1 (28 MB)	1 (31 MB)		1 (33 MB)	6 (168 MB)

5   Analysis

5.1   Does Initialization Matter?

Here, we analyze the importance of the initialization of the backbone network. It is well known that training a large network such as the VGG-16 from scratch on a small dataset such as CUBS, or Flowers leads to poor performance, and the most

popular approach is to fine-tune a network pre-trained on the ImageNet classification task. It is not obvious whether initialization is just as important for the
piggyback method. Table 5 presents the errors obtained by training piggyback
masks for tasks using the ResNet-50 as the backbone network, but with different
initializations. We consider 3 different initializations: (1) a network trained on
the ImageNet classification task, the popular initialization for fine-tuning, (2) a
network trained from scratch on the Places365 scene classification task, a dataset
larger than ImageNet (1.8 M v/s 1.3 M images), but with fewer classes (365 v/s
1000), and lastly (3) a randomly initialized network.

We observe in Table 5 that initialization does indeed matter, with the
ImageNet-initialized network outperforming both the Places365 and randomly
initialized network on all tasks. In fact, by training a piggyback mask for the
Places365 dataset on an ImageNet-initialized backbone network, we obtain an
accuracy very similar to a network trained from scratch on the Places365 dataset.
The ImageNet dataset is very diverse, with classes ranging from animals, to
plants, cars and other inanimate objects, whereas the Places365 dataset is solely
devoted to the classification of scenes such as beaches, bedrooms, restaurants,
etc. As a result, the features of the ImageNet-trained network serve as a very
general and flexible initialization A very interesting observation is that even a
randomly initialized network obtains non-trivial accuracies on all datasets. This
indicates the learning a mask is indeed a powerful technique of utilizing fixed
filters and weights for adapting a network to a new task.

Table 5. Errors obtained by piggyback masks for the ResNet-50 backbone network
with different initializations. Errors in parentheses are top-5 errors, the rest are top-1
errors.

Dataset	Pre-training/Initialization		
	ImageNet	Places365	Random
CUBS	18.41	28.50	66.24
Stanford Cars	10.38	13.70	77.79
Flowers	5.23	10.92	71.17
WikiArt	28.67	31.24	64.74
Sketch	20.09	23.17	43.75
ImageNet	23.84	32.56	71.48
	(7.13)	(11.92)	(46.73)
Places365	45.17	45.39	60.41
	(15.12)	(15.05)	(28.94)

5.2   Learned Sparsity and Its Distribution Across Network Layers

Table 6 reports the total sparsity, or the number of mask values set to 0 in
a binary piggyback mask learned for the corresponding choice of dataset and

network architecture. This measures the amount of change that is required to be made to the backbone network, or the deviation from the ImageNet pre-trained initialization, in order to obtain good performance on a given dataset. We note that the amount of sparsity obtained on fine-grained datasets seems to be proportional to the errors obtained by the Classifier Only method on the respective datasets. The easiest Flowers dataset requires the least number of changes, or a sparsity of 4.51%, while the harder WikiArt dataset leads to a 34.14% sparsity for a VGG-16 network mask. Across network architectures, we observe a similar pattern of sparsity based on the difficulty of the tasks. The sparsity obtained is also a function of the magnitude of the real-valued mask initialization and threshold used for the binarization (See Eq. 4), with a higher threshold leading to higher sparsity. The numbers in Table 6 were obtained using our default settings of a binarizer threshold of 5e-3 and a uniform real-valued mask initialization of 1e-2.

Table 6. Percentage of zeroed out weights after training a binary mask for the respective network architectures and datasets.

Dataset	VGG-16	VGG-16 BN	ResNet-50		Dense-Net-121
			ImNet-init.	Places-init.	
CUBS	14.09%	13.24%	12.21%	15.22%	12.01%
Stanford Cars	17.03%	16.70%	15.65%	17.72%	15.80%
Flowers	4.51%	4.52%	4.48%	6.45%	5.28%
WikiArt	34.14%	33.01%	30.47%	30.04%	29.11%
Sketch	27.23%	26.05%	23.04%	24.23%	22.24%
ImageNet	–	–	–	37.59%	–
Places365	43.47%	–	37.99%	–	–

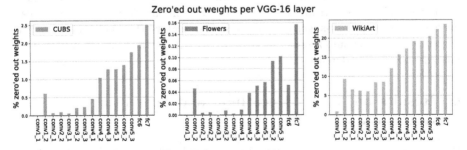

Fig. 3. Percentage of weights masked out per ImageNet pre-trained VGG-16 layer. Datasets similar to ImageNet share a lot of the lower layers, and require fewer changes. The number of masked out weights increases with depth of layer.

We observe that a Places365-initialized network requires more changes as compared to an ImageNet-initialized network (refer to the ResNet-50 column of Table 6). This once again indicates that features learned on ImageNet are more diverse and serve as better initialization than those learned on Places365. Figure 3 shows the sparsity obtained per layer of the ImageNet pre-trained VGG-16 network, for three datasets considered. While the total amount of sparsity obtained per dataset is different, we observe a consistent pattern of sparsity across the layers. In general, the number of changes increases with depth of the network layer. For datasets similar to ImageNet, such as CUBS, and Flowers, we observe that the low-level features (conv1-conv3) are mostly re-used without any major changes. WikiArt, which has a significant domain shift from ImageNet, requires some changes in the low-level features. All tasks seem to require changes to the mid-level (conv4-conv5) and high-level features (fc6-fc7) in order to learn new task-specific features. Similar behavior was also observed for the deeper ResNet and DenseNet networks.

5.3   Handling Large Input Domain Shifts

In Table 4, we observe that WikiArt, which has a large domain shift from the ImageNet dataset on which the backbone network was trained on, has a larger gap in performance (4–5%) between the piggyback and individual network methods, especially for the deeper ResNet and DenseNet networks. Those numbers are duplicated in the Piggyback - Fixed BN and Individual Network columns of Table 7. We suspect that keeping batchnorm parameters fixed while training the piggyback masks might be a reason for the gap in performance, as the domain shift is likely to cause a larger discrepancy between the ideal batchnorm parameter values and those inherited from ImageNet, the effect of which is cascaded through the large number of layers. We performed these experiments again, but while updating batchnorm parameters, and report the results in the Piggyback - Trained BN column of Table 7. The top-1 error on WikiArt reduces from 28.67% to 25.92% for the ResNet-50 network, and from 29.56% to 25.90% for the DenseNet-121 network if the batchnorm parameters are allowed to update. For the Sketch dataset, training separate batchnorm parameters leads to a small decrease in error. Task-specific batchnorm parameters thus help improve performance, while causing a small increase of ∼1 MB in the storage overhead for both networks considered.

6   Results on Visual Decathlon and Semantic Segmentation

We also evaluate our proposed method on the newly introduced Visual Decathlon challenge [17] consisting of 10 classification tasks. While the images of this task are of a lower resolution (72 × 72 px), they contain a wide variety of tasks such as pedestrian, digit, aircraft, and action classification, making it perfect for testing the generalization abilities of our method. Evaluation on this challenge reports per-task accuracies, and assigns a cumulative score with a maximum value of 10,000 (1,000 per task) based on the per-task accuracies. The goal is to learn models for maximizing the total score over the 10 tasks while using the least number of parameters. Complete details about the challenge settings, evaluation, and datasets used can be found at http://www.robots.ox.ac.uk/~vgg/decathlon/.

Table 7. Effect of task-specific batch normalization layers on the top-1 error.

Dataset	Piggyback (ours)		Individual
	Fixed BN	Trained BN	Network
ResNet-50			
WikiArt	28.67	25.92	24.40
Sketch	20.09	19.82	19.22
DenseNet-121			
WikiArt	29.56	25.90	23.59
Sketch	20.30	20.12	19.48

Table 8. Top-1 accuracies obtained on the Visual Decathlon online test set.

Method	#par	ImNet.	Airc.	C100	DPed	DTD	GTSR	Flwr	Oglt	SVHN	UCF	Mean	Score
Scratch [17]	10	59.87	57.1	75.73	91.2	37.77	96.55	56.3	88.74	96.63	43.27	70.32	1625
Feature [17]	1	59.67	23.31	63.11	80.33	45.37	68.16	73.69	58.79	43.54	26.8	54.28	544
Finetune [17]	10	59.87	60.34	82.12	92.82	55.53	97.53	81.41	87.69	96.55	51.2	76.51	2500
Res. Adapt. [17]	2	59.67	56.68	81.2	93.88	50.85	97.05	66.24	89.62	96.13	47.45	73.88	2118
Res. Adapt. (J) [17]	2	59.23	63.73	81.31	93.3	57.02	97.47	83.43	89.82	96.17	50.28	77.17	2643
DAN [16]	2.17	57.74	64.12	80.07	91.3	56.54	98.46	86.05	89.67	96.77	49.38	77.01	2851
Piggyback (Ours)	1.28	57.69	65.29	79.87	96.99	57.45	97.27	79.09	87.63	97.24	47.48	76.60	2838

Table 8 reports the results obtained on the online test set of the challenge. Consistent with prior work [17], we use a Wide Residual Network [14,16] with a depth of 28, widening factor of 4, and a stride of 2 in the first convolutional layer of each block. We use the 64 × 64 px ImageNet-trained network of [16] as our backbone network, and train piggyback masks for the remaining 9 datasets. We train for a total of 60 epochs per dataset, with learning rate decay by a factor of 10 after 45 epochs. Adam with a base learning rate of 1e-4 was used for updating the real-valued piggyback masks. Data augmentation by random cropping, horizontal flipping, and resizing the entire image was chosen based on cross-validation. As observed in Table 8, our method obtains performance competitive with the state-of-the-art, while using the least amount of additional parameters. Assuming that the base network uses 32-bit parameters, it accounts for a parameter cost of $32n$ bits, where n is the number of parameters. A binary mask per dataset requires n bits, leading to a total cost of approximately $(32n + 9n) = 41n$ bits, or a parameter ratio of $(41/32) = 1.28$, as reported.

The results presented in Sect. 4 only required a single fully connected layer to be added on top of the backbone network. Our method can also be extended to cases where more than one layers are added and trained from scratch on top of a backbone network, as shown in Fig. 4. We tested our method on the task of pixelwise segmentation using the basic Fully Convolutional Network architecture [32] which has fully connected layer followed by a deconvolutional layer of stride 32. We trained our networks on the

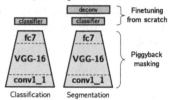

Fig. 4. Mixed training of layers using finetuning from scratch and piggyback masking.

21-class PASCAL 2011 + SBD dataset, using the official splits provided by [33] for 15 epochs. Using the VGG-16 finetuned network, we obtain a mean IOU of 61.08[1]. Using the piggyback method, we obtain a competitive mean IOU of 61.41. Instead of replicating the whole VGG-16 network of $\sim$500 MB, we only need an overhead of 17 MB for masking the backbone network and 7.5 MB for the newly added layers. These results show that piggyback does not face any issues due to mixed training schemes.

7 Conclusions

We have presented a novel method for utilizing the fixed weights of a network for obtaining good performance on a new task, empirically showing that the proposed method works for multiple datasets and network architectures. We hope that the piggyback method will be useful in practical scenarios where new skills need to be learned on a deployed device without having to modify existing weights or download a new large network. The re-usability of the backbone network and learned masks should help simplify and scale the learning of a new task across large numbers of potential users and devices. One drawback of our current method is that there is no scope for added tasks to benefit from each other. Apart from addressing this issue, another interesting area for future work is the extension to tasks such as object detection that require specialized layers, and expanding existing layers with more capacity.

Acknowledgments. This material is based upon work supported in part by the National Science Foundation under Grants No. 1563727 and 1718221, Amazon Research Award, AWS Machine Learning Research Award, and Google Research Award.

---

[1] This is lower than the 63.6 mIOU obtained by [32] owing to differences in the Caffe and PyTorch VGG-16 initializations, as documented at https://goo.gl/quvmm2.

References

1. Simonyan, K., Zisserman, A.: Very deep convolutional networks for large-scale image recognition. CoRR abs/1409.1556 (2014)
2. Russakovsky, O., et al.: ImageNet large scale visual recognition challenge. IJCV (2015)
3. French, R.M.: Catastrophic forgetting in connectionist networks. Trends Cogn. Sci. **3**(4), 128–135 (1999)
4. Kirkpatrick, J., et al.: Overcoming catastrophic forgetting in neural networks. In: PNAS (2017)
5. Rannen, A., Aljundi, R., Blaschko, M.B., Tuytelaars, T.: Encoder based lifelong learning. In: ICCV (2017)
6. Li, Z., Hoiem, D.: Learning without forgetting. In: Leibe, B., Matas, J., Sebe, N., Welling, M. (eds.) ECCV 2016. LNCS, vol. 9908, pp. 614–629. Springer, Cham (2016). https://doi.org/10.1007/978-3-319-46493-0_37
7. Mallya, A., Lazebnik, S.: PackNet: adding multiple tasks to a single network by iterative pruning. arXiv:1711.05769 (2017)
8. Wah, C., Branson, S., Welinder, P., Perona, P., Belongie, S.: The Caltech-UCSD Birds-200-2011 Dataset. Technical report CNS-TR-2011-001, California Institute of Technology (2011)
9. Krause, J., Stark, M., Deng, J., Fei-Fei, L.: 3D object representations for fine-grained categorization. In: CVPRW (2013)
10. Nilsback, M.E., Zisserman, A.: Automated flower classification over a large number of classes. In: ICCVGIP (2008)
11. Saleh, B., Elgammal, A.: Large-scale classification of fine-art paintings: Learning the right metric on the right feature. In: ICDMW (2015)
12. Eitz, M., Hays, J., Alexa, M.: How do humans sketch objects? In: SIGGRAPH (2012)
13. He, K., Zhang, X., Ren, S., Sun, J.: Deep residual learning for image recognition. In: CVPR (2016)
14. Zagoruyko, S., Komodakis, N.: Wide residual networks. In: BMVC (2016)
15. Huang, G., Liu, Z., van der Maaten, L., Weinberger, K.Q.: Densely connected convolutional networks. In: CVPR (2017)
16. Rosenfeld, A., Tsotsos, J.K.: Incremental learning through deep adaptation. arXiv:1705.04228 (2017)
17. Rebuffi, S.A., Bilen, H., Vedaldi, A.: Learning multiple visual domains with residual adapters. In: NIPS (2017)
18. Bilen, H., Vedaldi, A.: Integrated perception with recurrent multi-task neural networks. In: NIPS (2016)
19. Caruana, R.: Multitask learning. Learn. Learn (1998)
20. Kokkinos, I.: Ubernet: training a universal convolutional neural network for low-, mid-, and high-level vision using diverse datasets and limited memory. In: CVPR (2017)
21. Shmelkov, K., Schmid, C., Alahari, K.: Incremental learning of object detectors without catastrophic forgetting. In: ICCV (2017)
22. Lee, S.W., Kim, J.H., Ha, J.W., Zhang, B.T.: Overcoming catastrophic forgetting by incremental moment matching. In: NIPS (2017)
23. Han, S., Pool, J., Tran, J., Dally, W.: Learning both weights and connections for efficient neural network. In: NIPS (2015)

24. Fernando, C., et al.: PathNet: evolution channels gradient descent in super neural networks. arXiv:1701.08734 (2017)
25. Rusu, A.A., et al.: Progressive neural networks. arXiv:1606.04671 (2016)
26. Courbariaux, M., Bengio, Y., David, J.P.: BinaryConnect: training deep neural networks with binary weights during propagations. In: NIPS (2015)
27. Hubara, I., Courbariaux, M., Soudry, D., El-Yaniv, R., Bengio, Y.: Binarized neural networks. In: NIPS (2016)
28. Li, F., Zhang, B., Liu, B.: Ternary weight networks. arXiv:1605.04711 (2016)
29. Zhu, C., Han, S., Mao, H., Dally, W.J.: Trained ternary quantization. In: ICLR (2017)
30. Guo, Y., Yao, A., Chen, Y.: Dynamic network surgery for efficient DNNs. In: NIPS (2016)
31. Zhou, B., Lapedriza, A., Khosla, A., Oliva, A., Torralba, A.: Places: A 10 million image database for scene recognition. TPAMI (2017)
32. Long, J., Shelhamer, E., Darrell, T.: Fully convolutional networks for semantic segmentation. In: CVPR (2015)
33. BerekeleyVision: Segmentation data splits. https://github.com/shelhamer/fcn. berkeleyvision.org/tree/master/data/pascal Accessed 11 Mar 2018

Real-Time MDNet

Ilchae Jung[1], Jeany Son[1], Mooyeol Baek[1], and Bohyung Han[2(✉)]

[1] Department of CSE, POSTECH, Pohang, Korea
{chey0313,jeany,mooyeol}@postech.ac.kr
[2] Department of ECE and ASRI, Seoul National University, Seoul, Korea
bhhan@snu.ac.kr

Abstract. We present a fast and accurate visual tracking algorithm based on the multi-domain convolutional neural network (MDNet). The proposed approach accelerates feature extraction procedure and learns more discriminative models for instance classification; it enhances representation quality of target and background by maintaining a high resolution feature map with a large receptive field per activation. We also introduce a novel loss term to differentiate foreground instances across multiple domains and learn a more discriminative embedding of target objects with similar semantics. The proposed techniques are integrated into the pipeline of a well known CNN-based visual tracking algorithm, MDNet. We accomplish approximately 25 times speed-up with almost identical accuracy compared to MDNet. Our algorithm is evaluated in multiple popular tracking benchmark datasets including OTB2015, UAV123, and TempleColor, and outperforms the state-of-the-art real-time tracking methods consistently even without dataset-specific parameter tuning.

Keywords: Visual tracking · Multi-domain learning · RoIAlign
Instance embedding loss

1 Introduction

Convolutional Neural Networks (CNNs) are very effective in visual tracking [1–10], but, unfortunately, highly accurate tracking algorithms based on CNNs are often too slow for practical systems. There are only a few methods [11–13] that achieve two potentially conflicting goals—accuracy and speed—at the same time.

MDNet [1] is a popular CNN-based tracking algorithm with state-of-the-art accuracy. This algorithm is inspired by an object detection network, R-CNN [14]; it samples candidate regions, which are passed through a CNN pretrained on a large-scale dataset and fine-tuned at the first frame in a test video. Since every candidate is processed independently, MDNet suffers from high computational complexity in terms of time and space. In addition, while its multi-domain learning framework concentrates on saliency of target against background in each domain, it is not optimized to distinguish potential target instances across multiple domains. Consequently, a learned model by MDNet is not effective to discriminatively represent unseen target objects with similar semantics in test sequences.

© Springer Nature Switzerland AG 2018
V. Ferrari et al. (Eds.): ECCV 2018, LNCS 11208, pp. 89–104, 2018.
https://doi.org/10.1007/978-3-030-01225-0_6

A straightforward way to avoid redundant observations and accelerate inference is to perform RoIPooling from a feature map [23], but naïve implementations result in poor localization due to coarse quantization of the feature map. To alleviate such harsh quantization for RoI pooling, [15] proposes RoI alignment (RoIAlign) via bilinear interpolation. However, it may also lose useful localization cues within target if the size of RoI is large. On the other hand, since most CNNs are pretrained for image classification tasks, the networks are competitive to predict semantic image labels but insensitive to tell differences between object instances in low- or mid-level representations. A direct application of such CNNs to visual tracking often yields degradation of accuracy since the embedding generated by pretrained CNNs for image classification task is not effective to differentiate two objects in the same category.

To tackle such critical limitations, we propose a novel real-time visual tracking algorithm based on MDNet by making the following contributions. First, we employ an RoIAlign layer to extract object representations from a preceding fully convolutional feature map. To maintain object representation capacity, the network architecture is updated to construct a high resolution feature map and enlarge the receptive field of each activation. The former is helpful to represent candidate objects more precisely, and the latter is to learn rich semantic information of target. Second, we introduce an instance embedding loss in pretraining stage and aggregate to the existing binary foreground/background classification loss employed in the original MDNet. The new loss function plays an important role to embed observed target instances apart from each other in a latent space. It enables us to learn more discriminative representations of unseen objects even in the case that they have identical class labels or similar semantics.

Our main contributions are summarized as follows:

- We propose a real-time tracking algorithm inspired by MDNet and Fast R-CNN, where an improved RoIAlign technique is employed to extract more accurate representations of targets and candidates from a feature map and improve target localization.
- We learn shared representations using a multi-task loss in a similar way to MDNet, but learn an embedding space to discriminate object instances with similar semantics across multiple domains more effectively.
- The proposed algorithm demonstrates outstanding performance in multiple benchmark datasets without dataset-specific parameter tuning. Our tracker runs real-time with 25 times speed-up compared to MDNet while maintaining almost identical accuracy.

The rest of the paper is organized as follows. We first discuss related work in Sect. 2. Section 3 discusses our main contribution for target representation via the improved RoIAlign and the instance embedding loss. We present overall tracking algorithm in Sect. 4, and provide experimental results in Sect. 5. We conclude this paper in Sect. 6.

2 Related Work

2.1 Visual Tracking Algorithms

CNN-based visual tracking algorithms typically formulate object tracking as discriminative object detection problems. Some methods [1,2,5,6,9,10] draw a set of samples corresponding to candidate regions and compute their likelihoods independently using CNNs. Recent techniques based on discriminative correlation filters boost accuracy significantly by incorporating representations from deep neural networks [3,4,16–18]. Although various tracking algorithms based on CNNs are successful in terms of accuracy, they often suffer from high computational cost mainly due to critical time consuming components within the methods including feature computation of multiple samples, backpropagation for model updates, feature extraction from deep networks, etc. While some CNN-based techniques [13,19,20] for visual tracking run real-time by employing offline representation learning without online model updates, their accuracy is not competitive compared to the state-of-the-art methods.

There are only a few real-time trackers [3,11,12] that present competitive accuracy. Galoogahi *et al.* [11] incorporate background region to learn more discriminative correlation filters using hand-crafted features. Fan *et al.* [12] design a robust tracking algorithm through interactions between a tracker and a verifier. Tracker estimates target states based on the observation using hand-crafted features efficiently while verifier double-checks the estimation using the features from deep neural networks. Danelljan *et al.* [3] propose a discriminative correlation filter for efficient tracking by integrating multi-resolution deep features. Since its implementation with deep representations is computationally expensive, they also introduce a high-speed tracking algorithm with competitive accuracy based on hand-crafted features. Note that most real-time trackers with competitive accuracy rely on hand-crafted features or limited use of deep representations. Contrary to such real-time tracking methods, our algorithm has a simpler inference pipeline within a pure deep neural network framework.

2.2 Representation Learning for Visual Tracking

MDNet [1] pretrains class-agnostic representations appropriate for visual tracking task by fine-tuning a CNN trained originally for image classification. It deals with label conflict issue across videos by employing multi-domain learning, and achieves the state-of-the-art performance in multiple datasets. Since the great success of MDNet [1], there have been several attempts to learn representations for visual tracking [20–22] using deep neural networks. Bertinetto *et al.* [20] learn to maximize correlation scores between the same objects appearing in different frames. Valmadre *et al.* [21] regress response maps between target objects and input images to maximize the score at the ground-truth target location. Similarly, Gundogdu *et al.* [22] train deep features to minimize difference between the response map from a tracker based on correlation filters and the ground-truth map that has a peaky maximum value at target location.

All the efforts discussed above focus on how to make target objects salient against backgrounds. While this strategy is effective to separate target from background, it is still challenging to discrimninate between object instances with similar semantics. Therefore, our algorithm encourages our network to achieve the two objectives jointly by proposing a novel loss function with two terms.

2.3 Feature Extraction in Object Detection

Although R-CNN [14] is successful in object detection, it has significant overhead to extract features from individual regions for inference. Fast R-CNN [23] reduces its computational cost for feature extraction using RoIPooling, which computes fixed-size feature vectors by applying max pooling to the specific regions in a feature map. While the benefit in terms of computational cost is impressive, RoIPooling is not effective to localize targets because it relies on a coarse feature map. To alleviate this limitation, mask R-CNN [15] introduces a new feature extraction technique, RoI alignment (RoIAlign), which approximates features via bilinear interpolation for better object localization. Our work proposes a modified network architecture for an adaptive RoIAlign to extract robust features corresponding to region proposals.

3   Efficient Feature Extraction and Discriminative Feature Learning

This section describes our CNN architecture with an improved RoiAlign layer, which accelerates feature extraction while maintaining quality of representations. We also discuss a novel multi-domain learning approach with discriminative instance embedding of foreground objects.

3.1   Network Architecture

Figure 1 illustrates architecture of our model. The proposed network consists of fully convolutional layers (conv1-3) for constructing a shared feature map, an adaptive RoIAlign layer for extracting feature of each RoI, and three fully connected layers (fc4-6) for binary classification. Given a whole image with a set of proposal bounding boxes as an input, the network computes a shared feature map of the input image through a single forward pass. A CNN feature corresponding to each RoI is extracted from the shared feature map using an adaptive RoIAlign operation. Through this feature computation strategy, we reduce computational complexity significantly while improving quality of features.

The extracted feature representation from each RoI is fed to two fully connected layers for classification between target and background. We create multiple branches of domain specific layers ($fc6^1$-$fc6^D$) for multi-domain learning, and learn a discriminative instance embedding. During online tracking, a set of the domain-specific fully connected layers are replaced by a single binary classification layer with softmax cross-entropy loss, which will be fine-tuned using the examples from an initial frame.

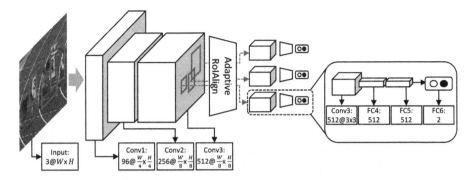

Fig. 1. Network architecture of the proposed tracking algorithm. The network is composed of three convolutional layers for extracting a shared feature map, adaptive RoIAlign layer for extracting a specific feature using regions of interest (RoIs), and three fully connected layers for binary classification. The number of channels and the size of each feature map are shown with the name of each layer.

3.2 Improved RoIAlign for Visual Tracking

Our network has an RoIAlign layer to obtain object representations from a fully convolutional feature map constructed from a whole image. However, features extracted by RoIAlign are inherently coarse compared to the ones from individual proposal bounding boxes. To improve quality of representations of RoIs, we need to construct a feature map with high resolution and rich semantic information. These requirements can be addressed by computing a denser fully convolutional feature map and enlarging the receptive field of each activation. To these end s, we remove a max pooling layer followed by conv2 layer in VGG-M network [24] and perform dilated convolutions [25] in conv3 layer with rate $r = 3$. This strategy results in a twice larger feature map than the output of conv3 layer in the original VGG-M network. It allows to extract high resolution features and improve quality of representation. Figure 2 compares our network for dense feature map computation with the original VGG-M network.

Our adaptive RoIAlign layer computes more reliable features, especially for large objects, using a modified bilinear interpolation. Since ordinary RoIAlign only utilizes nearby grid points on the feature map to compute the interpolated value, it may lose useful information if the interval of the sampled points for RoI is larger than the one of the feature map grid. To handle this issue, we adjust the interval of the grid points from the shared dense feature map adaptively. In specific, the bandwidth of the bilinear interpolation is determined by the size of RoIs; it is proportional to $[\frac{w}{w'}]$, where w and w' denote the width of RoI after the conv3 layer and the width of RoI's output feature in the RoIAlign layer, respectively, and $[\cdot]$ is a rounding operator.

The technique integrating a network to employ a dense feature map and the adaptive RoIAlign is referred to as improved RoIAlign. Our adaptive RoIAlign layer produces a 7×7 feature map, and a max pooling layer is applied after the layer to produce a 3×3 feature map. Although the improved RoIAlign makes

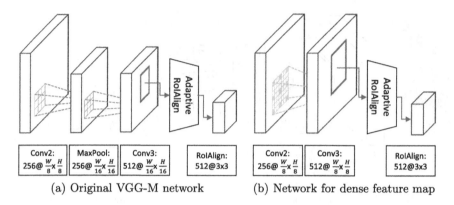

(a) Original VGG-M network   (b) Network for dense feature map

Fig. 2. Network architecture of the part of our fully convolutional network for extracting a shared feature map. Max pooling layer is removed after conv2 layer in original VGG-M network, and dilated convolution with rate $r = 3$ is applied for extracting a dense feature map with a higher spatial resolution.

minor changes, it improves performance of our tracking algorithm significantly in practice. This is partly because, on the contrary to object detection, tracking errors originated from subtle differences in target representations are propagated over time and create large errors to make trackers fail eventually.

3.3   Pretraining for Discriminative Instance Embedding

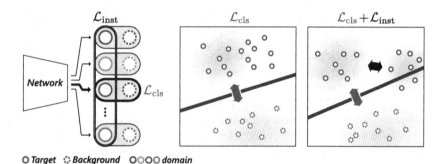

Fig. 3. Multi-task learning for binary classification of the target object and instance embedding across multiple domains. The binary classification loss is designed to distinguish the target and background, while the instance embedding loss separates target instances. Note that a minibatch in each iteration for training is constructed by sampling from a single domain.

The goal of our learning algorithm is to train a discriminative feature embedding applicable to multiple domains. MDNet has the separate shared and domain-specific layers to learn the representations distinguishing between target and background. In addition to this objective, we propose a new loss term, referred to as an instance embedding loss, which enforces target objects in different domains to be embedded far from each other in a shared feature space and enables to learn discriminative representations of the unseen target objects in new test sequences. In other words, MDNet only attempts to discriminate target and background in individual domains, and may not be powerful to discriminate foreground objects in different domains, especially when the foreground objects belong to the same semantic class or have similar appearances. This is partly because the original CNNs are trained for image classification. To handle this issue, our algorithm incorporates an additional constraint, which embeds foreground objects from multiple videos to be apart from each other.

Given an input image $\mathbf{x}^d$ in domain d and a bounding box R, the output score of the network, denoted by $\mathbf{f}^d$, is constructed by concatenating the activations from the last fully connected layers ($\mathtt{fc6}^1\text{-}\mathtt{fc6}^D$) as

$$\mathbf{f}^d = [\phi^1(\mathbf{x}^d; R), \phi^2(\mathbf{x}^d; R), \ldots, \phi^D(\mathbf{x}^d; R)] \in \mathbb{R}^{2 \times D}, \tag{1}$$

where $\phi^d(\cdot; \cdot)$ is a 2D binary classification score from the last fully connected layer $\mathtt{fc6}^d$ in domain d, and D is the number of domains in a training dataset. The output feature is given to a softmax function for binary classification, which determines whether a bounding box R is a target or a background patch in domain d. Additionally, the output feature is passed through another softmax operator for discriminating instances in multiple domains. The two softmax functions are given by

$$[\sigma_{\text{cls}}(\mathbf{f}^d)]_{ij} = \frac{\exp(f_{ij}^d)}{\sum_{k=1}^{2} \exp(f_{kj}^d)} \quad \text{and} \quad [\sigma_{\text{inst}}(\mathbf{f}^d)]_{ij} = \frac{\exp(f_{ij}^d)}{\sum_{k=1}^{D} \exp(f_{ik}^d)}, \tag{2}$$

where $\sigma_{\text{cls}}(\cdot)$ compares scores of target and background in each domain whereas $\sigma_{\text{inst}}(\cdot)$ compares the positive scores of the objects across all domains.

Our network minimizes a multi-task loss $\mathcal{L}$ on the two softmax operators, which is given by

$$\mathcal{L} = \mathcal{L}_{\text{cls}} + \alpha \cdot \mathcal{L}_{\text{inst}}, \tag{3}$$

where $\mathcal{L}_{\text{cls}}$ and $\mathcal{L}_{\text{inst}}$ are loss terms for binary classification and discriminative instance embedding, respectively, and α is a hyper-parameter that controls balance between the two loss terms. Following MDNet, we handle a single domain in each iteration; the network is updated based on a minibatch collected from the $(k \bmod D)^{\text{th}}$ domain only in the kth iteration.

The binary classification loss with domain $\hat{d}(k) = (k \bmod D)$ in the kth iteration is given by

$$\mathcal{L}_{\text{cls}} = -\frac{1}{N} \sum_{i=1}^{N} \sum_{c=1}^{2} [\mathbf{y}_i]_{c\hat{d}(k)} \cdot \log\left(\left[\sigma_{\text{cls}}\left(\mathbf{f}_i^{\hat{d}(k)} \right) \right]_{c\hat{d}(k)} \right), \tag{4}$$

where $\mathbf{y}_i \in \{0,1\}^{2 \times D}$ is a one-hot encoding of a ground-truth label; its element $[\mathbf{y}_i]_{cd}$ is 1 if a bounding box R_i in domain d corresponds to class c, otherwise 0. Also, the loss for discriminative instance embedding is given by

$$\mathcal{L}_{\text{inst}} = -\frac{1}{N} \sum_{i=1}^{N} \sum_{d=1}^{D} [\mathbf{y}_i]_{+d} \cdot \log \left(\left[\sigma_{\text{inst}} \left(\mathbf{f}_i^d \right) \right]_{+d} \right). \tag{5}$$

Note that the instance embedding loss is applied only to positive examples using the positive channel denoted by + in Eq. (5). As a result of the proposed loss, the positive scores of target objects in current domain become larger while their scores in other domains get smaller. It leads to a distinctive feature embedding of target instances and makes it effective to distinguish similar objects potentially appearing in new testing domains.

Figure 3 illustrates impact of the multi-task learning for discriminative feature embedding of target instances across multiple domains.

4   Online Tracking Algorithm

We discuss the detailed procedure of our tracking algorithm including implementation details. The pipeline of our tracking algorithm is almost identical to MDNet [1].

4.1   Main Loop of Tracking

Once pretraining is completed, we replace multiple branches of domain-specific layers ($\mathtt{fc6}^1$-$\mathtt{fc6}^D$) with a single branch for each test sequence. Given the first frame with ground-truth of target location, we fine-tune fully connected layers ($\mathtt{fc4\text{-}6}$) and customize the network to a test sequence. For the rest of frames, we update the fully connected layers in an online manner while convolutional layers are fixed. Given an input frame at time t, a set of samples, denoted by $\{\mathbf{x}_t^i\}_{i=1...N}$, are drawn from a Gaussian distribution centered at the target state of the previous frame, the optimal target state is given by

$$\mathbf{x}_t^* = \arg\max_{\mathbf{x}_t^i} f^+(\mathbf{x}_t^i), \tag{6}$$

where $f^+(\mathbf{x}_t^i)$ indicates the positive score of the ith sample drawn from the current frame at time step t. Note that tracking is performed in a three dimensional state space for translation and scale change.

We also train a bounding box regressor to improve target localization accuracy motivated by the success in [1]. Using a set of extracted features from RoIs from the first frame of a video, $\mathcal{F}_i^{\text{RoI}}$, we train a simple linear regressor in the same way to [14,26]. We apply the learned bounding box regressor from the second frame and adjust the estimated target regions if the estimated target state is sufficiently reliable, $f^+(\mathbf{x}_t^*) > 0.5$.

4.2   Online Model Updates

We perform two complementary update strategies as in MDNet [1]: long-term and short-term updates to maintain robustness and adaptiveness, respectively. Long-term updates are regularly applied using the samples collected for a long period of time, while short-term updates are triggered whenever the score of the estimated target is below a threshold and the result is unreliable.

A minibatch is composed of 128 examples—32 positive and 96 negative samples, for which we employ hard minibatch mining in each iteration of online learning procedure. The hard negative examples are identified by testing 1024 negative examples and selecting the ones with top 96 positive scores.

4.3   Implementation Details

Network Initialization and Input Management. The weights of three convolutional layers are transferred from the corresponding parts in VGG-M network [24] pretrained on ImageNet [27] while fully connected layers are initialized randomly. An input image is resized to make the size of target object fit to 107×107, and cropped to the smallest rectangle enclosing all sample RoIs. The receptive field size of a single unit in the last convolutional layer is equal to 75×75.

Offline Pretraining. For each iteration of offline pretraining, we construct a minibatch with samples collected from a single domain. We first sample 8 frames randomly in the selected domain, and draw 32 positive and 96 negative examples from each frame, which results in 256 positive and 768 negative data altogether in a minibatch. The positive bounding boxes have overlap larger than 0.7 with ground-truths in terms of Intersection over Union (IoU) measure while the negative samples have less than 0.5 IoUs. Instead of backpropagating gradients in each iteration, we accumulate the gradients from backward passes in multiple iterations; the network is updated at every 50 iteration in our experiments. We train our models on ImageNet-Vid [27], which is a large-scale video dataset for object detection. Since this dataset contains a lot of video sequences, almost 4500 videos, we randomly choose 100 videos for an instance embedding loss in each iteration. Hyper-parameter α in Eq. (3) is set to 0.1.

Online Training. Since pretraining stage aims to learn generic representation for visual tracking, we have to fine-tune the pretrained network at the first frame of each testing video. We draw 500 positive and 5000 negative samples based on the same IoU criteria with the pretraining stage. From the second frame, the training data for online updates are collected after tracking is completed in each frame. The tracker gather 50 positive and 200 negative examples that have larger than 0.7 IoU and less than 0.3 IoU with the estimated target location, respectively. Instead of storing the original image patches, our algorithm keep their feature representations to save time and memory by avoiding redundant computation. Long-term updates are executed every 10 frame.

Optimization. Our network is trained by a Stochastic Gradient Descent (SGD) method. For offline representation learning, we train the network for 1000 epochs with learning rate 0.0001 while it is trained for 50 iterations at the first frame of a test video. For online updates, the number of iterations for fine-tuning is 15 and the learning rate is set to 0.0003. The learning rate for fc6 is 10 times bigger than others (fc4-5) to facilitate convergence in practice. The weight decay and momentum are fixed to 0.0005 and 0.9, respectively. Our algorithm is implemented in PyTorch with 3.60 GHz Intel Core I7-6850K and NVIDIA Titan Xp Pascal GPU.

5 Experiments

This section presents our results on multiple benchmark datasets with comparisons to the state-of-the-art tracking algorithms, and analyzes performance of our tracker by ablation studies.

5.1 Evaluation Methodology

We evaluate our tracker, denoted by real-time MDNet or RT-MDNet, on three standard datasets including OTB2015 [28], UAV123 [29] and TempleColor [30]. For comparison, we employ several state-of-the-art trackers including ECO [3], MDNet [1], MDNet+IEL, SRDCF [31], C-COT [4], and top performing real-time trackers, ECO-HC [3], BACF [11], PTAV [12], CFNet [21], SiamFC [20] and DSST [32]. ECO-HC is a real-time variant of ECO based on hand-crafted features, HOG and color names, while MDNet+IEL is a version of MDNet with the instance embedding loss. Both MDNet and MDNet+IEL are pretrained on IMAGENET-VID.

We follow the evaluation protocol presented in a standard benchmark [28], where performance of trackers is evaluated based on two criteria—bounding box overlap ratio and center location error—and is visualized by success and precision plots. The two plots are generated by computing ratios of successfully tracked frames at a set of different thresholds in the two metrics. The Area Under Curve (AUC) scores of individual trackers are used to rank the trackers in the success plot. In the precision plots, the ranks of trackers are determined by the accuracy at 20 pixel threshold. In both plots, real-time trackers are represented with solid lines while the rests are denoted by dashed lines. Note that the parameters of our algorithm are fixed throughout the experiment; we use the same parameters for all three tested datasets while others may have the different parameter setting for each dataset.

5.2 Evaluation on OTB2015

We first analyze our algorithm on OTB2015 dataset [28], which consists of 100 fully annotated videos with various challenging attributes. Figure 4 presents precision and success plots on OTB2015 dataset.

The results clearly show that real-time MDNet outperforms all the tested real-time trackers significantly in terms of both measures. It also has competitive accuracy compared to the top-ranked trackers while it is approximately 130, 25, and 8 times faster than C-COT, MDNet, and ECO, respectively. Our algorithm is slightly less accurate than the competitors when the overlap threshold is larger than 0.8. It implies that the estimated target bounding boxes given by our tracker are not very tight compared to other state-of-the-art methods; possible reasons are inherent drawback of CNN-based trackers and the limitation of our RoIAlign for target localization at high precision area.

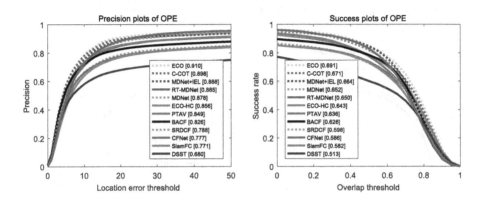

Fig. 4. Quantitative results on OTB2015 [28].

Table 1. Quantitative comparisons of real-time trackers on OTB2015

Trackers	DSST [32]	SiamFC [20]	CFNet [21]	BACF [11]	PTAV [12]	ECO-HC [3]	RT-MDNet
Succ (%)	51.3	58.2	58.6	62.7	63.5	64.3	65.0
Prec (%)	68.0	77.1	77.7	82.7	84.8	85.6	88.5
FPS	24	86	43	35	25	60	46/52

Table 1 presents overall performance of real-time trackers including our algorithm in terms of AUC for success rate, precision rate at 20 pixel threshold, and speed measured by FPS. The proposed method outperforms all other real-time trackers by substantial margins in terms of two accuracy measures. It runs very fast, 46 FPS in average, while speed except the first frame is approximately 52 FPS. Note that our tracker needs extra computational cost at the first frame for fine-tuning the network and learning a bounding box regressor.

We also illustrate the qualitative results of multiple real-time algorithms on a subset of sequences in Fig. 7. Our approach shows consistently better performance in various challenging scenarios including illumination change, scale variation and background clutter. Some failure cases are presented in Fig. 8.

Our algorithm loses target in *Soccer* sequence due to significant occlusion and in *Biker* sequence due to sudden large motion and out-of-plane rotation. Objects with similar appearances make our tracker confused in *Coupon* sequence, and dramatic non-rigid appearance changes in *Jump* cause drift problems.

5.3   Evaluation on TempleColor

Figure 5 illustrates the precision and success plots on TempleColor dataset [30], which is containing 128 color videos while most of sequences are overlapped with OTB2015 dataset [28]. Our method again surpass all real-time trackers[1] and has a substantial improvement over ECO-HC.

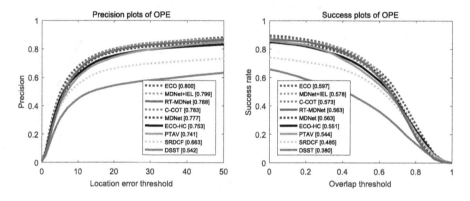

Fig. 5. Quantitative results on TempleColor [30].

5.4   Evaluation on UAV123

We also evaluate real-time MDNet on the aerial video benchmark, UAV123 [29] whose characteristics inherently differ from other datasets such as OTB2015 and TempleColor. It contains 123 aerial videos with more than 110 K frames altogether. Figure 6 illustrates the precision and success plots of the trackers that have publicly available results on this dataset. Surprisingly, in the precision rate, our tracker outperforms all the state-of-the-art methods including non-real-time tracker while it is very competitive in the success rate as well. In particular, our tracker beats ECO, which is a top ranker in OTB2015 and TempleColor, on the both metrics with a approximately 8 times speed-up. It shows that our algorithm has better generalization capability without parameter tuning to a specific dataset.

---

[1] The AUC score of BACF is reported in their paper by 52.0%, which is much lower than the score of our tracker.

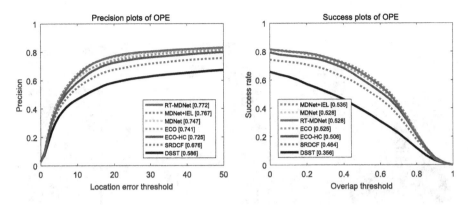

Fig. 6. Quantitative results on UAV123 [29].

Table 2. Impacts of different feature extraction methods on accuracy of RT-MDNet

Pooling operation	align	adaRoI	denseFM	AUC (%)	Prec (%)
RoIPooling [23]				35.4	53.8
RoIAlign [15]	√			56.1	80.4
Adaptive RoIAlign	√	√		59.0	83.8
RoIAlign with denseFM	√		√	60.7	84.3
Improved RoIAlign	√	√	√	61.9	85.3

5.5 Ablation Study

We perform several ablation studies on OTB2015 [28] to investigate the effectiveness of individual components in our tracking algorithm. We first test the impact of the proposed RoIAlign on the quality of our tracking algorithm. For this experiments, we pretrain our network using VOT-OTB dataset, which consist of 58 videos collected from VOT2013 [33], VOT2014 [34] and VOT2015 [35] excluding the videos in OTB2015. Table 2 presents several options to extract target representations, which depend on choice between RoIPooling and RoIAlign, use of adaptive RoIAlign layer (adaRoI) and construction of dense feature map (denseFM). All results consistently support that each component of our improved RoIAlign makes meaningful contribution to tracking performance improvement.

We also investigated two additional versions of our tracking algorithm—one is without bounding box regression (Ours–BBR) and the other is without bounding box regression and instance embedding loss (Ours–BBR–IEL). Table 3 summarizes the results from this internal comparison. According to our experiment, the proposed multi-task loss (binary classification loss and instance embedding loss) and bounding box regression are both helpful to improve localization[2].

---

[2] As illustrated in Figs. 4 and 5, and 6, we verified that applying instance embedding loss to MDNet also improves performances.

RT-MDNet   BACF   PTAV   ECO-HC   DSST   SiamFC   CFNet

Fig. 7. Qualitative results of the proposed method on several challenging sequences (*Matrix, MotorRolling, Skiing, Sylvester*) in OTB2015 dataset.

Fig. 8. Failure cases of RT-MDNet in *Soccer, Biker, Coupon,* and *Jump* sequence. Magenta and blue bounding boxes denote ground-truths and our results, respectively.

Table 3. Internal comparison results pretrained on ImageNet-Vid dataset.

Method	$\mathcal{L}_{cls}$	$\mathcal{L}_{inst}$	BBreg	Succ (%)	Prec (%)
Ours–BBR–IEL	$\checkmark$			61.9	84.2
Ours–BBR	$\checkmark$	$\checkmark$		64.1	87.7
Ours	$\checkmark$	$\checkmark$	$\checkmark$	65.0	88.5

6   Conclusions

We presented a novel real-time visual tracking algorithm based on a CNN by learning discriminative representations of target in a multi-domain learning framework. Our algorithm accelerates feature extraction procedure by an improved RoIAlign technique. We employ a multi-task loss effective to discriminate object instances across domains in the learned embedding space. The proposed algorithm was evaluated on the public visual tracking benchmark datasets and demonstrated outstanding performance compared to the state-of-the-art techniques, especially real-time trackers.

Acknowledgement. This research was supported in part by Research Resettlement Fund for the new faculty of Seoul National University and the IITP grant [2014-0-00059, Development of Predictive Visual Intelligence Technology (DeepView); 2016-0-00563, Research on Adaptive Machine Learning Technology Development for Intelligent Autonomous Digital Companion; 2017-0-01780, The Technology Development for Event Recognition/Relational Reasoning and Learning Knowledge based System for Video Understanding].

References

1. Nam, H., Han, B.: Learning multi-domain convolutional neural networks for visual tracking. In: CVPR (2016)
2. Nam, H., Baek, M., Han, B.: Modeling and propagating CNNs in a tree structure for visual tracking. arXiv preprint arXiv:1608.07242 (2016)
3. Danelljan, M., Bhat, G., Shahbaz Khan, F., Felsberg, M.: ECO: efficient convolution operators for tracking. In: CVPR (2017)
4. Danelljan, M., Robinson, A., Shahbaz Khan, F., Felsberg, M.: Beyond correlation filters: learning continuous convolution operators for visual tracking. In: Leibe, B., Matas, J., Sebe, N., Welling, M. (eds.) ECCV 2016. LNCS, vol. 9909, pp. 472–488. Springer, Cham (2016). https://doi.org/10.1007/978-3-319-46454-1_29
5. Yun, S., Choi, J., Yoo, Y., Yun, K., Young Choi, J.: Action-decision networks for visual tracking with deep reinforcement learning. In: CVPR (2017)
6. Fan, H., Ling, H.: SANet: structure-aware network for visual tracking. In: CVPRW (2017)
7. Wang, L., Ouyang, W., Wang, X., Lu, H.: Visual tracking with fully convolutional networks. In: ICCV (2015)
8. Hong, S., You, T., Kwak, S., Han, B.: Online tracking by learning discriminative saliency map with convolutional neural network. In: ICML (2015)
9. Teng, Z., Xing, J., Wang, Q., Lang, C., Feng, S., Jin, Y.: Robust object tracking based on temporal and spatial deep networks. In: ICCV (2017)
10. Han, B., Sim, J., Adam, H.: BranchOut: regularization for online ensemble tracking with convolutional neural networks. In: CVPR (2017)
11. Galoogahi, H., Fagg, A., Lucey, S.: Learning background-aware correlation filters for visual tracking. In: ICCV (2017)
12. Fan, H., Ling, H.: Parallel tracking and verifying: a framework for real-time and high accuracy visual tracking. In: ICCV (2017)
13. Huang, C., Lucey, S., Ramanan, D.: Learning policies for adaptive tracking with deep feature cascades. In: ICCV (2017)

14. Girshick, R., Donahue, J., Darrell, T., Malik, J.: Rich feature hierarchies for accurate object detection and semantic segmentation. In: CVPR (2014)
15. He, K., Gkioxari, G., Dollár, P., Girshick, R.: Mask R-CNN. In: ICCV (2017)
16. Ma, C., Huang, J.B., Yang, X., Yang, M.H.: Hierarchical convolutional features for visual tracking. In: ICCV (2015)
17. Song, Y., Ma, C., Gong, L., Zhang, J., Lau, R., Yang, M.H.: CREST: convolutional residual learning for visual tracking. In: ICCV (2017)
18. Zhang, T., Xu, C., Yang, M.H.: Multi-task correlation particle filter for robust object tracking. In: CVPR (2017)
19. Held, D., Thrun, S., Savarese, S.: Learning to track at 100 FPS with deep regression networks. In: Leibe, B., Matas, J., Sebe, N., Welling, M. (eds.) ECCV 2016. LNCS, vol. 9905, pp. 749–765. Springer, Cham (2016). https://doi.org/10.1007/978-3-319-46448-0_45
20. Bertinetto, L., Valmadre, J., Henriques, J.F., Vedaldi, A., Torr, P.: Fully-convolutional siamese networks for object tracking. In: ECCVW (2016)
21. Valmadre, J., Bertinetto, L., Henriques, J.F., Vedaldi, A., Torr, P.: End-to-end representation learning for correlation filter based tracking. In: CVPR (2017)
22. Gundogdu, E., Alatan, A.A.: Good features to correlate for visual tracking. TIP (2018)
23. Girshick, R.: Fast R-CNN. In: ICCV (2015)
24. Chatfield, K., Simonyan, K., Vedaldi, A., Zisserman, A.: Return of the devil in the details: delving deep into convolutional nets. In: BMVC (2014)
25. Chen, L.C., Papandreou, G., Kokkinos, I., Murphy, K., Yuille, A.L.: DeepLab: semantic image segmentation with deep convolutional nets, atrous convolution, and fully connected CRFs. TPAMI 40(4), 834–848 (2017)
26. Felzenszwalb, P.F., Girshick, R.B., McAllester, D., Ramanan, D.: Object detection with discriminatively trained part-based models. TPAMI 32(9), 1627–1645 (2010)
27. Russakovsky, O., et al.: ImageNet large scale visual recognition challenge. IJCV 115(3), 211–252 (2015)
28. Wu, Y., Lim, J., Yang, M.: Object tracking benchmark. TPAMI 37(9), 1834–1848 (2015)
29. Mueller, M., Smith, N., Ghanem, B.: A benchmark and simulator for UAV tracking. In: Leibe, B., Matas, J., Sebe, N., Welling, M. (eds.) ECCV 2016. LNCS, vol. 9905, pp. 445–461. Springer, Cham (2016). https://doi.org/10.1007/978-3-319-46448-0_27
30. Liang, P., Blasch, E., Ling, H.: Encoding color information for visual tracking: algorithms and benchmark. TIP 24(12), 5630–5644 (2015)
31. Danelljan, M., Häger, G., Khan, F.S., Felsberg, M.: Learning spatially regularized correlation filters for visual tracking. In: ICCV (2015)
32. Danelljan, M., Häger, G., Khan, F.S., Felsberg, M.: Discriminative scale space tracking. TPAMI 39(8), 1561–1575 (2017)
33. Kristan, M., et al.: The visual object tracking VOT2013 challenge results. In: ICCVW (2013)
34. Kristan, M., et al.: The visual object tracking VOT2014 challenge results. In: Agapito, L., Bronstein, M.M., Rother, C. (eds.) ECCV 2014. LNCS, vol. 8926, pp. 191–217. Springer, Cham (2015). https://doi.org/10.1007/978-3-319-16181-5_14
35. Kristan, M., et al.: The visual object tracking VOT2015 challenge results. In: ICCVW (2015)

Real-Time Hair Rendering Using Sequential Adversarial Networks

Lingyu Wei[1,2], Liwen Hu[1,2], Vladimir Kim[3], Ersin Yumer[4], and Hao Li[1,2]([✉])

[1] Pinscreen Inc., Los Angeles, CA 90025, USA
[2] University of Southern California, Los Angeles, CA 90089, USA
[3] Adobe Research, San Jose, CA 95110, USA
[4] Argo AI, Pittsburgh, PA 15222, USA
`hao@hao-li.com`

Abstract. We present an adversarial network for rendering photoreal-istic hair as an alternative to conventional computer graphics pipelines. Our deep learning approach does not require low-level parameter tun-ing nor ad-hoc asset design. Our method simply takes a strand-based 3D hair model as input and provides intuitive user-control for color and lighting through reference images. To handle the diversity of hairstyles and its appearance complexity, we disentangle hair structure, color, and illumination properties using a sequential GAN architecture and a semi-supervised training approach. We also introduce an intermediate edge activation map to orientation field conversion step to ensure a successful CG-to-photoreal transition, while preserving the hair structures of the original input data. As we only require a feed-forward pass through the network, our rendering performs in real-time. We demonstrate the syn-thesis of photorealistic hair images on a wide range of intricate hairstyles and compare our technique with state-of-the-art hair rendering methods.

Keywords: Hair rendering · GAN

1 Introduction

Computer-generated (CG) characters are widely used in visual effects and games, and are becoming increasingly prevalent in photo manipulation and in virtual reality applications. Hair is an essential visual component of virtual char-acters. However, while significant advancements in hair rendering have been made in the computer graphics community, the production of aesthetically real-istic and desirable hair renderings still relies on a careful design of strand models, shaders, lights, and composites, generally created by experienced look develop-ment artists. Due to the geometric complexity and volumetric structure of hair,

Electronic supplementary material The online version of this chapter (https://doi.org/10.1007/978-3-030-01225-0_7) contains supplementary material, which is available to authorized users.

© Springer Nature Switzerland AG 2018
V. Ferrari et al. (Eds.): ECCV 2018, LNCS 11208, pp. 105–122, 2018.
https://doi.org/10.1007/978-3-030-01225-0_7

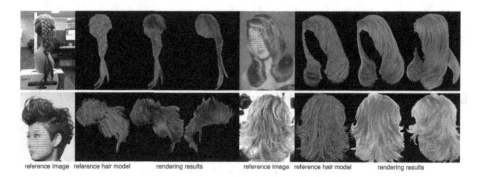

reference image reference hair model   rendering results   reference image reference hair model   rendering results

Fig. 1. We propose a real-time hair rendering method. Given a reference image, we can render a 3D hair model with the referenced color and lighting in real-time. Faces in this paper are obfuscated to avoid copyright infringement

modern hair rendering pipelines often combine the use of efficient hair representation, physically-based shading models, shadow mapping techniques, and scattering approximations, which not only increase the computational cost, but also the difficulty for tweaking parameters. In high-end film production, it is not unusual that a single frame for a photorealistic hair on a rendering farm takes several minutes to generate. While compelling real-time techniques have been introduced recently, including commercial solutions (e.g., NVIDIA HairWorks, Unity Hair Tools), the results often appear synthetic and are difficult to author, even by skilled digital artists. For instance, several weeks are often necessary to produce individualized hair geometries, textures, and shaders for hero hair assets in modern games, such as Uncharted 4 and Call of Duty: Ghosts.

Inspired by recent advances in generative adversarial networks (GANs), we introduce the first deep learning-based technique for rendering photorealistic hair. Our method takes a 3D hair model as input in strand representation and uses an example input photograph to specify the desired hair color and lighting. In addition to our intuitive user controls, we also demonstrate real-time performance, which makes our approach suitable for interactive hair visualization and manipulation, as well as 3D avatar rendering.

Compared to conventional graphics rendering pipelines, which are grounded on complex parametric models, reflectance properties, and light transport simulation, deep learning-based image synthesis techniques have proven to be a promising alternative for the efficient generation of photorealistic images. Successful image generations have been demonstrated on a wide range of data including urban scenes, faces, and rooms, but fine level controls remain difficult to implement. For instance, when conditioned on a semantic input, arbitrary image content and visual artifacts often appear, and variations are also difficult to handle due to limited training samples. This problem is further challenged by the diversity of hairstyles, the geometric intricacy of hair, and the aesthetic complexity of hair in natural environments. For a viable photorealistic hair rendering solution, we need to preserve the intended strand structures of a given 3D hair model, as well as provide controls such as color and lighting.

Furthermore, the link between CG and real-world images poses another challenge, since such training data is difficult to obtain for supervised learning. Photoreal simulated renderings are time-consuming to generate and often difficult to match with real-world images. In addition, capturing photorealistic hair models is hard to scale, despite advances in hair digitization techniques.

In this work, we present an approach, based on a sequential processing of a rendered input hair models using multiple GANs, that converts a semantic strand representation into a photorealistic image (See Fig. 1 and Sect. 5). Color and lighting parameters are specified at intermediate stages. The input 3D hair model is first rendered without any shading information, but strand colors are randomized to reveal the desired hair structures. We then compute an edge activation map, which is an important intermediate representation based on adaptive thresholding, which allows us to connect the strand features between our input CG representation and a photoreal output for effective semi-supervised training. A conditional GAN is then used to translate this edge activation map into a dense orientation map that is consistent with those obtained from real-world hair photographs. We then concatenate two multi-modal image translation networks to disentangle color and lighting control parameters in latent space. These high-level controls are specified using reference hair images as input, which allows us to describe complex hair color variations and natural lighting conditions intuitively. We provide extensive evaluations of our technique and demonstrate its effectiveness on a wide range of hairstyles. We compare our rendered images to ground truth photographs and renderings obtained from state-of-the-art computer graphics solutions. We also conduct a user study to validate the achieved level of realism.

Contributions: We demonstrate that a photorealistic and directable rendering of hair is possible using a sequential GAN architecture and an intermediate conversion from edge activation map to orientation field. Our network decouples color, illumination, and hair structure information using a semi-supervised approach and does not require synthetic images for training. Our approach infers parameters from input examples without tedious explicit low-level modeling specifications. We show that color and lighting parameters can be smoothly interpolated in latent space to enable fine-level and user-friendly control. Compared to conventional hair rendering techniques, our method does not require any low-level parameter tweaking or ad-hoc texture design. Our rendering is computed in a feed forward pass through the network, which is fast enough for real-time applications. Our method is also significantly easier to implement than traditional global illumination techniques. We plan to release the code and data to the public.[1]

---

[1] Available on project page: http://cosimo.cn/#hair_render.

2 Related Work

In this section we provide an overview of state-of-the-art techniques for hair rendering and image manipulation and synthesis.

Fiber-level hair renderings produce highly realistic output, but incurs substantial computational cost [8,31,42–44], but also require some level of expertise for asset preparation and parameter tuning by a digital artist. Various simplified models have been proposed recently, such as dual scattering [54], but its real-time variant have a rather plastic and solid appearance. Real-time rendering techniques generally avoid physically-based models, and instead rely on approximations that only mimics its appearance, by modeling hair as parametric surfaces [24,25], meshes [18,46], textured morphable models [2], or multiple semi-transparent layers [40,45]. Choosing the right parametric model and setting the parameters for the desired appearance requires substantial artist expertise. Converting across different hair models can be casted as a challenging optimization or learning problem [43]. Instead, in this work, we demonstrate that one can directly learn a representation for hair structure, appearance, and illumination using a sequence of GANs, and that this representation can be intuitively manipulated by using example images.

Substantial efforts have been dedicated to estimating hair structures from natural images, such as with multi-view hair capturing methods [15,17,28–30,34,35,47]. Recently, single-view hair reconstruction methods [3–6,16] are becoming increasingly important because of the popularity in manipulating internet portraits and selfies. We view our work as complementary to these hair capturing methods, since they rely on existing rendering techniques and do not estimate the appearance and illumination for the hair. Our method can be used in similar applications, such as hair manipulation in images [5,6], but with simpler control over the rendering parameters.

Neural networks are increasingly used for the manipulation and synthesis of visual data such as faces [19,39], object views [50], and materials [27]. Recently, Nalbach et al. [32] proposed how to render RGB images using CNN, but it requires aligned attributes e.g. normal and reflectance per pixel, which are not well-defined for hair strands with sub-pixel details. Generative models with an adversary [12,36] can successfully learn a data representation without explicit supervision. To enable more control these models have been further modified to consider user input [51] or to condition on a guiding image [20]. While the latter provides a powerful manipulation tool via image-to-image translation, it requires strong supervision in the form of paired images. This limitation has been further addressed by enforcing cycle-consistency across unaligned datasets [52]. Another limitation of the original image translation architecture is that it does not handle multimodal distributions which are common in synthesis tasks. This is addressed by encouraging bijections between the output and latent spaces [53] in a recently introduced architecture known as BicycleGAN. We assess this architecture as part of our sequential GAN for hair rendering.

Our method is also related to unsupervised learning methods that remove part of the input signal, such as color [48], and then try to recover it via an auto-encoder architecture. However, in this work we focus on high quality hair renderings instead of generic image analysis, and unlike SplitBrain [48], we use image processing to connect two unrelated domains (CG hair models and real images).

Variants of these models have been applied to many applications including image compositing [26], font synthesis [1], texture synthesis [41], facial texture synthesis [33], sketch colorization [38], makeup transfer [7], and many more. Hair has a more intricate appearance model due to its thin semi-transparent structures, inter-reflections, scattering effects, and very detailed geometry.

3   Method

We propose a semi-supervised approach to train our hair rendering network using only real hair photographs during training. The key idea of our approach is to gradually reduce the amount of information by processing the image, eventually

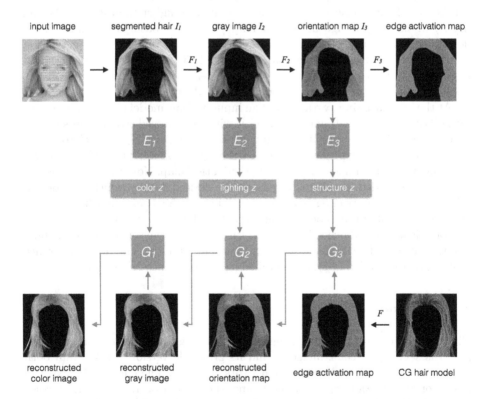

Fig. 2. Overview of our method. Given a natural image, we first use simple image processing to strip it off salient details such as color, lighting, and fiber-level structure, leaving only coarse structure captured in activation map (top row). We encode each simplified image into its own latent space which are further used by generators. The CG hair is rendered in a style mimicking the extracted coarse structure, and generators are applied in inverse order to add the details from real hair encoded in the latent space yielding the realistic reconstruction (bottom row)

bringing it to a simple low dimensional representation, *edge activation map*. This representation can also be trivially derived from a CG hair model, enabling us to connect two domains. The encoder-decoder architecture is applied to each simplified representation, where the encoder captures the information removed by the image processing and the decoder recovers it (see Fig. 2).

Given a 2D image I_1 we define image processing filters $\{F_i\}_{i=1}^3$ that generate intermediate simplified images $I_{i+1} := F_i(I_i)$. Each intermediate image I_i is first encoded by a network $E_i(I_i)$ to a feature vector z_i and then decoded with a generator $G_i(z_i, I_i)$. The decoder is trained to recover the information, that is lost in a particular image processing step. We use a conditional variational autoencoder GAN [53] for each encoder-decoder pair.

Our sequential image processing operates in the following three steps. First, $I_2 := F_1(I_1)$ desaturates a segmented hair region of an input photograph to produce a *grayscale image*. Second, $I_3 := F_2(I_2)$ is the *orientation map* using the maximal response of a rotating DoG filter [28]. Third, $F_3(I_3)$ is an *edge activation map* obtained using adaptive thresholding, and each pixel contains only the values 1 or -1 indicating if it is activated (response higher than its neighboring pixels) or not. This edge activation map provides a basic representation for describing hair structure from a particular viewpoint, and the edge activation map derived from natural images or rendering of CG model with random strand colors can be processed equally well with our generators. Figure 3 demonstrates some examples of our processing pipeline applied to real hair.

At the inference time, we are given an input 3D hair model in strand representation (100 vertices each) and we render it with randomized strand colors from a desired viewpoint. We apply the full image processing stack $F_3 \circ F_2 \circ F_1$ to obtain the edge activation map. We then can use the generators $G_1 \circ G_2 \circ G_3$ to recover the realistic looking image from the edge activation map. Note that these generators rely on encoded features z_i to recover the desired details, which provides an effective tool for controlling rendering attributes such as color and lighting. We demonstrate that our method can effectively transfer these attributes by encoding an example image and by feeding the resulting vector to the generator (where fine-grained hair structure is encoded in z_3, natural illumination and hair appearance properties are encoded in z_2, and detailed hair color is encoded in z_1).

4   Implementation

Given a pair of input/output images for each stage in the rendering pipeline (e.g. the segmented color image I_1 and its grayscale version I_2) we train both the encoder network and generator network together. The encoder E_1 extracts the color information $z_1 := E_1(I_1)$, and the generator reconstructs a color image identical to I_1 using only the gray scaled image I_2 and the parameter z_1, $I_1 \approx G_1(z_1, I_2)$. These pairs of encoder and generator networks enable us to extract information available in higher dimensional image (e.g., color), represent it with a vector z_1, and then use it convert an image in the lower-dimensional domain (e.g., grayscale) back to the higher-dimensional representation.

Fig. 3. Examples of our training data. For each set of images from left to right, we show input image; segmented hair; gray image; orientation map; and edge activation map

We train three sets of networks (E_i, G_i) in a similar manner, using the training images I_i, I_{i+1} derived from the input image I via filters F_i. Since these filters are fixed, we can treat these three sets of networks independently and train them in parallel. For the rest of this section, we focus on training only a single encoder and generator pair, and thus use a simplified notation: $G := G_i, E := E_i, I := I_i, I' := I_{i+1} = F_i(I_i), z := z_i = E_i(I_i)$.

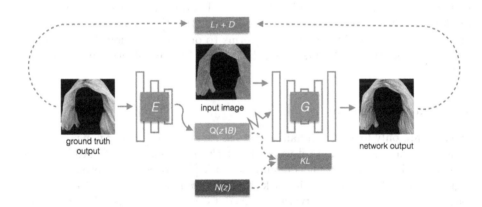

Fig. 4. Our entire network is composed of three encoder and generator pairs (E_i, D_i) with the same cVAE-GAN architecture depicted in this figure

4.1 Architecture

We train the encoder and generator network pair $((E, G))$ using the conditional variational autoencoder GAN (cVAE-GAN) architecture [53] (see Fig. 4).

A ground truth image I is being processed by an encoder E, producing the latent vector z. This z and the filtered input image I' are both inputs to the generator G. Our loss function is composed of three terms:

$$\mathcal{L}_1^{\text{VAE}}(G, E) = \|I - G(E(I), I')\|_1$$

penalizes the reconstruction error between I and the generated image produced by $G(z, I')$.

$$\mathcal{L}_{\text{KL}}(E) = \mathcal{D}_{\text{KL}}(E(I)\|\mathcal{N}(0,1))$$

favors $z = E(I)$ to come from the normal distribution in the latent space, where $\mathcal{D}_{KL}$ is the KL-divergence of two probability distributions. This loss preserves the diversity of z and allows us to efficiently re-sample a random z from the normal distribution. Finally, an adversarial loss is introduced by training a patch-based discriminator [21] D. The discriminator takes either I or $G(z, I')$ and classifies whether the input comes from real data or from the generator. A path-based discriminator will learn to distinguish the local feature from its receptive field, and penalize artifacts produced in the local regions of $G(z, I')$.

We use the add_to_input method from the work of [53] to replicate z. For a tensor I' with size $H \times W \times C$ and z with size $1 \times Z$, we copy value of z, extending it to a $H \times W \times Z$ tensor, and concatenate this with the tensor I' on the channel dimension, resulting a $H \times W \times (Z + C)$ tensor. This tensor is used as G's input. We considered additional constraints, such as providing a randomly drawn latent vector to the generator [10, 11], but we did not achieve visible improvements by adding more terms to our loss function. We provide a comparison between cVAE-GAN and the BicycleGAN architecture in the results section.

4.2   Data Preparation

Since we are only focusing on hair synthesis, we mask non-hair regions to ignore their effect, and set their pixel values to black. To avoid manual mask annotation, we train Pyramid Scene Parsing Network [49] to perform automatic hair segmentation. We annotate hair masks for 3000 random images from CelebA-HQ dataset [23], and train our network on this data. We use the network to compute masks for the entire 30,000 images in CelebA-HQ dataset, and manually remove images with wrong segmentation, yielding about 27,000 segmented hair images.[1] We randomly sampled 5,000 images from this dataset to use as our training data.

We apply same deterministic filters F_i on each image in the training data, to obtain the corresponding gray image, orientation maps, and edge activation maps.

4.3   Training

We apply data augmentation including random rotation, translation, and color perturbation (only for input RGB images) to add more variations to the training set. Scaling is not applied, as the orientation map depends on the scale of the texture details from the gray-scaled image. We choose the U-net [37] architecture for generator G, which has an encoder-decoder architecture with symmetric skip connections allowing generation of pixel-level details as well as preserving the global information. ResNet [13] is used for encoder E, which consists of 6 groups of residual blocks. In all experiments, we use a fixed resolution 512×512 for all images, and the dimension of z is 8 in each transformation, following the choice from the work of Zhu et al. [53]. We train each set of networks from 5000 images for 100 epochs, with a learning rate gradually decreasing from 0.0001 to zero. The training time for each set is around 24 hours. Lastly, we also add random Gaussian noise withdrawn from $\mathcal{N}(0, \sigma 1)$ with gradually decreasing σ to the image, before feeding them to D, to stabilize the GAN training.

5   Results

Geometric hair models used in Figs. 1, 6 and 9 are generated using various hair modeling techniques [15–17]. The traditional computer graphic models used for comparison in Fig. 10 are manually created in Maya with XGen. We use the model from USC Hair Salon [14] in Fig. 7.

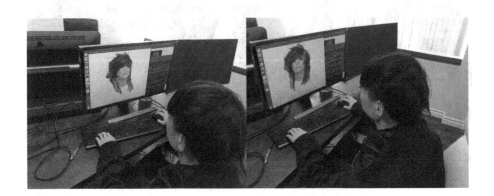

Fig. 5. Our interactive interface

Real-Time Rendering System. To demonstrate the utility of our method, we developed a real-time rendering interface for hair (see Fig. 5 and supplemental video). The user can load a CG hair model, pick the desired viewpoint, and then provide an example image for color and lighting specification. This example-based approach is user friendly as it is often difficult to describe hair colors using a single RGB value as they might have dyed highlights or natural variations in follicle pigmentations. Figures 1 and 6 demonstrate the rendering results with our method. Note that our method successfully handles a diverse set of hairstyles, complex hair textures, and natural lighting conditions. One can further refine the color and lighting by providing additional examples for these attributes and interpolate between them in latent space (Fig. 7). This feature provides an intuitive user control when a desired input example is not available.

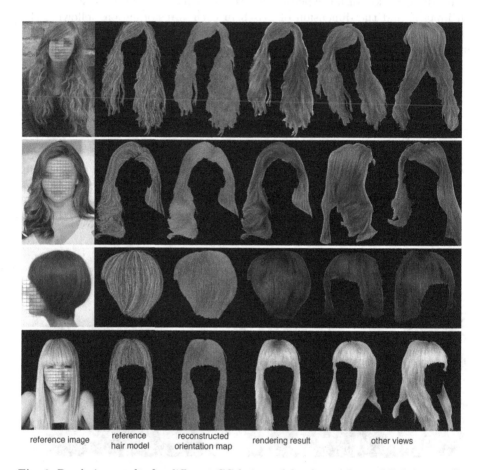

reference image   reference   reconstructed   rendering result   other views
                   hair model   orientation map

Fig. 6. Rendering results for different CG hair models where color and lighting conditions are extracted from a reference image

Comparison. We compare our sequential network to running BicycleGAN to directly render the colored image from the orientation field without using the sequential network pairs (Fig. 8). Even if we double the number of parameters and training time, we still notice that only the lighting, but not color, is accurately captured. We believe that the lighting parameters are much harder to be captured than the color parameters, hence the combined network may always

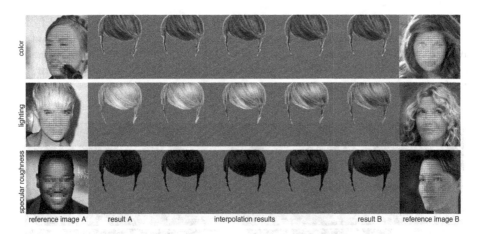

Fig. 7. We demonstrate rendering of the same CG hair model where material attributes and lighting conditions are extracted from different reference images, and demonstrate how the appearance can be further refined by interpolating between these attributes in latent space

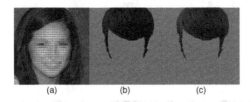

Fig. 8. Comparisons between our method with BicycleGAN (i.e., no sequential network). From left to right, we show (a) reference image; (b) rendering result with BicycleGAN; (c) rendering result with our sequential pipeline

try to minimize the error brought by lighting changes first, without considering the change of color as an equally important factor. To qualitatively evaluate, our system we compare to state-of-the-art rendering techniques. Unfortunately, these rendering methods do not take reference images as input, and thus lack similar level of control. We asked a professional artist to tweak the lighting and shading parameters to match our reference images. We used an enhanced version of Unity's *Hair Tool*, a high-quality real-time hair rendering plugin based on Kajiya-Kay reflection model [22] (Fig. 9). Note that a similar real-time shading technique that approximates multiple scattering components was used in the state-of-the-art real-time avatar digitization work of [18]. Our approach appears less synthetic and contains more strand-scale texture variations. Our artist used the default hair shader in Solid Angle's Arnold renderer, which is a commercial implementation of a hybrid shaded based on the works of [9] and [54], to match the reference image. This is an offline system and it takes about 5 min to render a single frame (Fig. 10) on an 8-core AMD Ryzen 1800x machine with 32

GB RAM. While our renderer may not reach the level of fidelity obtained from high-end offline rendering systems, it offers real time performance, and instantaneously, produces a realistic result. It also matching the lighting and hair color of a reference image, a task that took our experienced artist over an hour to perform.

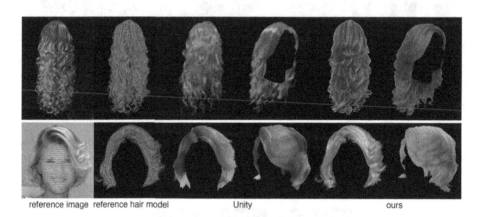

reference image reference hair model   Unity   ours

Fig. 9. Comparisons between our method with real-time rendering technique in Unity

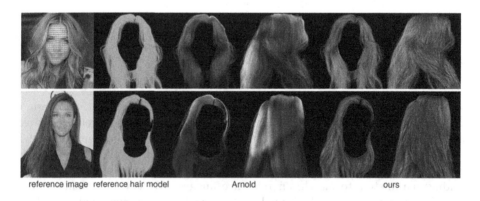

reference image reference hair model   Arnold   ours

Fig. 10. Comparisons between our method with offline rendering Arnold

User Study. We further conduct a user study to evaluate the quality of our renderings in comparison to real hair extracted from images. We presented our synthesized result and an image crop to MTurk workers side by side for 1 s, and asked them to pick an image that contained the real hair. We tested this with edge activation fields coming from either CG model or a reference image (in both

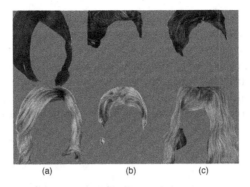

Fig. 11. User study example. From left to right, we show (a) real image, which is used to infer latent space z; (b) rendering result generated with z and the activation map of another real image; (c) rendering result of z and a CG model

cases we used a latent space from another image). If the synthetic images are not distinguishable from real images, the expected fraction of MTurk workers being "fooled" and think they are real is 50%. This is the same evaluation method as Zhu et al. work [53], and we showed 120 sets of randomly generated subjects to over over 100 testers (a subset of 10 subjects is provided to each person). We present qualitative results in Fig. 11 and the rate of selecting the synthetic images in Table 1. Note that in all cases, the users had a hard time distinguishing our results from real hair, and that our system successfully rendered hair produced from a CG model or a real image. We further test how human judgments change if people spend more time (3 s) evaluating our rendering of a CG model. We found that crowd workers become more accurate at identifying generated results, but still mislabel a significant number of examples as being real.

Table 1. MTurk workers were provided two images in a random order and were asked to select one that looked more real to them. Either CG models or images were used to provide activation fields. Note that in all cases MTurk users had a hard time distinguishing our results from real hair, even if we extend the time that images are visible to 3 s

Hair source	AMT fooling rate [%]
Image	49.9%
CG model	48.5%
CG model (3 s)	45.6%

Performance. We measure the performance of our feed forward networks on an real-time hair rendering application. We use a desktop with 2 Titan Xp each with 12 GB of GPU memory. All online processing steps including F_1, F_2, F_3 and all generator are running per frame. The average amount of time used in F_2 is 9 ms for looping over all possible rotating angles, and the computation time for F_1 and F_3 are negligible. The three networks have identical architecture and thus runs in consistent speed, each taking around 15 ms. For a single GPU, our demo runs at around 15 fps with GPU memory consumption 2.7 GB. Running the demo on multiple GPUs allows real-time performance with fps varying between 24 to 27 fps. Please refer to the video included in the supplemental material.

6   Discussion

We presented the first deep learning approach for rendering photorealistic hair, which performs in real-time. We have shown that our sequential GAN architecture and semi-supervised training approach can effectively disentangle strand-level structures, appearance, and illumination properties from the highly complex and diverse range of hairstyles. In particular, our evaluations show that without our sequential architecture, the lighting parameter would dominate over color, and color specification would no longer be effective. Moreover, our trained latent space is smooth, which allows us to interpolate continuously between arbitrary color and lighting samples. Our evaluations also suggests that there are no significant differences between a vanilla conditional GAN and a state-of-the-art network such as bicycleGAN, which uses additional smoothness constraints in the training. Our experiments further indicate that a direct conversion from a CG rendering to a photoreal image using existing adversarial networks would lead to significant artifacts or unwanted hairstyles. Our intermediate conversion step from edge activation to orientation map has proven to be an effective way for semi-supervised training and transitioning from synthetic input to photoreal output while ensuring that the intended hairstyle structure is preserved.

Limitations and Future Work. As shown in the video demo, the hair rendering is not entirely temporally coherent when rotating the view. While the per frame predictions are reasonable and most strand structure are consistent between frames, there are still visible flickering artifacts. We believe that temporal consistency could be trained with augmentations with 3D rotations, or video training data.

We believe that our sequential GAN architecture for parameter separation and our intermediate representation for CG-to-photoreal conversion could be generalized for the rendering of other objects and scenes beyond hair. Our method presents an interesting alternative and complementary solution for many applications, such as hair modeling with interactive visual feedback, photo manipulation, and image-based 3D avatar rendering.

While we do not provide the same level of fine-grained control as conventional graphics pipelines, our efficient approach is significantly simpler and generates more realistic output without any tedious fine tuning. Nevertheless, we would like to explore the ability to specify precise lighting configurations and advanced shading parameters for a seamless integration of our hair rendering into virtual environments and game engines. We believe that additional training with controlled simulations and captured hair data would be necessary.

Like other GAN techniques, our results are also not fully indistinguishable from real ones for a trained eye and an extended period of observation, but we are confident that our proposed approach would benefit from future advancements in GANs.

Acknowledgments. This work was supported in part by the ONR YIP grant N00014-17-S-FO14, the CONIX Research Center, one of six centers in JUMP, a Semiconductor Research Corporation (SRC) program sponsored by DARPA, the Andrew and Erna Viterbi Early Career Chair, the U.S. Army Research Laboratory (ARL) under contract number W911NF-14-D-0005, and Adobe. The content of the information does not necessarily reflect the position or the policy of the Government, and no official endorsement should be inferred. We thank Radomír Měch for insightful discussions.

References

1. Azadi, S., Fisher, M., Kim, V.G., Wang, Z., Shechtman, E., Darrell, T.: Multi-content GAN for few-shot font style transfer. CVPR (2018)
2. Cao, C., Wu, H., Weng, Y., Shao, T., Zhou, K.: Real-time facial animation with image-based dynamic avatars. ACM Trans. Graph. **35**(4), 126:1–126:12 (2016). https://doi.org/10.1145/2897824.2925873
3. Chai, M., Luo, L., Sunkavalli, K., Carr, N., Hadap, S., Zhou, K.: High-quality hair modeling from a single portrait photo. ACM Trans. Graph. (Proceedings SIGGRAPH Asia) **34**(6), November 2015
4. Chai, M., Shao, T., Wu, H., Weng, Y., Zhou, K.: AutoHair: fully automatic hair modeling from a single image. ACM Trans. Graph. (TOG) **35**(4), 116 (2016)
5. Chai, M., Wang, L., Weng, Y., Jin, X., Zhou, K.: Dynamic hair manipulation in images and videos. ACM Trans. Graph. **32**(4), 75:1–75:8 (2013). https://doi.org/10.1145/2461912.2461990
6. Chai, M., Wang, L., Weng, Y., Yu, Y., Guo, B., Zhou, K.: Single-view hair modeling for portrait manipulation. ACM Trans. Graph. (TOG) **31**(4), 116 (2012)
7. Chang, H., Lu, J., Yu, F., Finkelstein, A.: Makeupgan: makeup transfer via cycle-consistent adversarial networks. CVPR (2018)
8. d'Eon, E., Francois, G., Hill, M., Letteri, J., Aubry, J.M.: An energy-conserving hair reflectance model. In: Proceedings of the Twenty-Second Eurographics Conference on Rendering, EGSR 2011, pp. 1181–1187. Eurographics Association, Aire-la-Ville (2011). https://doi.org/10.1111/j.1467-8659.2011.01976.x
9. d'Eon, E., Marschner, S., Hanika, J.: Importance sampling for physically-based hair fiber models. In: SIGGRAPH Asia 2013 Technical Briefs, SA 2013, pp. 25:1–25:4. ACM, New York (2013). https://doi.org/10.1145/2542355.2542386
10. Donahue, J., Krähenbühl, P., Darrell, T.: Adversarial feature learning. CoRR abs/1605.09782 (2016). http://arxiv.org/abs/1605.09782
11. Dumoulin, V., et al.: Adversarially learned inference. CoRR abs/1606.00704 (2016)
12. Goodfellow, I.J., et al.: Generative adversarial nets. In: Proceedings of the 27th International Conference on Neural Information Processing Systems, NIPS 2014, vol. 2, pp. 2672–2680. MIT Press, Cambridge (2014). http://dl.acm.org/citation.cfm?id=2969033.2969125

13. He, K., Zhang, X., Ren, S., Sun, J.: Deep residual learning for image recognition. CoRR abs/1512.03385 (2015). http://arxiv.org/abs/1512.03385
14. Hu, L.: (2015). http://www-scf.usc.edu/~liwenhu/shm/database.html
15. Hu, L., Ma, C., Luo, L., Li, H.: Robust hair capture using simulated examples. ACM Trans. Graph. (Proceedings SIGGRAPH) **33**(4) (2014)
16. Hu, L., Ma, C., Luo, L., Li, H.: Single-view hair modeling using a hairstyle database. ACM Trans. Graph. (Proceedings SIGGRAPH) **34**(4) (2015)
17. Hu, L., Ma, C., Luo, L., Wei, L.Y., Li, H.: Capturing braided hairstyles. ACM Trans. Graph. **33**(6), 225:1–225:9 (2014)
18. Hu, L.: Avatar digitization from a single image for real-time rendering. ACM Trans. Graph. **36**(6), 195:1–195:14 (2017). https://doi.org/10.1145/3130800.31310887
19. Huynh, L., et al.: Photorealistic facial texture inference using deep neural networks. In: Computer Vision and Pattern Recognition (CVPR). IEEE (2018)
20. Isola, P., Zhu, J.Y., Zhou, T., Efros, A.A.: Image-to-image translation with conditional adversarial networks. CVPR (2016)
21. Isola, P., Zhu, J., Zhou, T., Efros, A.A.: Image-to-image translation with conditional adversarial networks. CoRR abs/1611.07004 (2016). http://arxiv.org/abs/1611.07004
22. Kajiya, J.T., Kay, T.L.: Rendering fur with three dimensional textures. SIGGRAPH Comput. Graph. **23**(3), 271–280 (1989). https://doi.org/10.1145/74334.74361
23. Karras, T., Aila, T., Laine, S., Lehtinen, J.: Progressive growing of GANs for improved quality, stability, and variation. In: International Conference on Learning Representations (2018). https://openreview.net/forum?id=Hk99zCeAb
24. Kim, T.Y., Neumann, U.: Interactive multiresolution hair modeling and editing. ACM Trans. Graph. **21**(3), 620–629 (2002). https://doi.org/10.1145/566654.566627
25. Lee, D.W., Ko, H.S.: Natural hairstyle modeling and animation. Graph. Models **63**(2), 67–85 (2001). https://doi.org/10.1006/gmod.2001.0547
26. Lin, C., Lucey, S., Yumer, E., Wang, O., Shechtman, E.: ST-GAN: spatial transformer generative adversarial networks for image compositing. In: IEEE Conference on Computer Vision and Pattern Recognition, CVPR 2018 (2018)
27. Liu, G., Ceylan, D., Yumer, E., Yang, J., Lien, J.M.: Material editing using a physically based rendering network. In: ICCV (2017)
28. Luo, L., Li, H., Paris, S., Weise, T., Pauly, M., Rusinkiewicz, S.: Multi-view hair capture using orientation fields. In: Computer Vision and Pattern Recognition (CVPR), June 2012
29. Luo, L., Li, H., Rusinkiewicz, S.: Structure-aware hair capture. ACM Trans. Graph. (Proceeding SIGGRAPH) **32**(4), July 2013
30. Luo, L., Zhang, C., Zhang, Z., Rusinkiewicz, S.: Wide-baseline hair capture using strand-based refinement. In: Computer Vision and Pattern Recognition (CVPR), June 2013
31. Marschner, S.R., Jensen, H.W., Cammarano, M., Worley, S., Hanrahan, P.: Light scattering from human hair fibers. ACM Trans. Graph. **22**(3), 780–791 (2003). https://doi.org/10.1145/882262.882345
32. Nalbach, O., Arabadzhiyska, E., Mehta, D., Seidel, H.P., Ritschel, T.: Deep shading: convolutional neural networks for screen space shading. Comput. Graph. Forum **36**, 65–78 (2017)
33. Olszewski, K., et al.: Realistic dynamic facial textures from a single image using GANs. In: ICCV (2017)

34. Paris, S., Briceño, H.M., Sillion, F.X.: Capture of hair geometry from multiple images. ACM Trans. Graph. (TOG) **23**, 712–719 (2004)
35. Paris, S., et al.: Hair photobooth: geometric and photometric acquisition of real hairstyles. ACM Trans. Graph. (TOG) 27, **30** (2008)
36. Radford, A., Metz, L., Chintala, S.: Unsupervised representation learning with deep convolutional generative adversarial networks. In: ICLR (2016)
37. Ronneberger, O., Fischer, P., Brox, T.: U-Net: convolutional networks for biomedical image segmentation. CoRR abs/1505.04597 (2015). http://arxiv.org/abs/1505.04597
38. Sangkloy, P., Lu, J., Fang, C., Yu, F., Hays, J.: Scribbler: controlling deep image synthesis with sketch and color. In: Computer Vision and Pattern Recognition, CVPR (2017)
39. Shu, Z., Yumer, E., Hadap, S., Sunkavalli, K., Shechtman, E., Samaras, D.: Neural face editing with intrinsic image disentangling. In: The IEEE Conference on Computer Vision and Pattern Recognition (CVPR), July 2017
40. Sintorn, E., Assarsson, U.: Hair self shadowing and transparency depth ordering using occupancy maps. In: Proceedings of the 2009 Symposium on Interactive 3D Graphics and Games, I3D 2009, pp. 67–74. ACM, New York (2009). https://doi.org/10.1145/1507149.1507160
41. Xian, W., et al.: TextureGAN: controlling deep image synthesis with texture patches. In: CVPR (2018)
42. Yan, L.Q., Jensen, H.W., Ramamoorthi, R.: An efficient and practical near and far field fur reflectance model. ACM Trans. Graph. (Proceedings of SIGGRAPH 2017) **36**(4) (2017)
43. Yan, L.Q., Sun, W., Jensen, H.W., Ramamoorthi, R.: A BSSRDF model for efficient rendering of fur with global illumination. ACM Trans. Graph. (Proceedings of SIGGRAPH Asia 2017) (2017)
44. Yan, L.Q., Tseng, C.W., Jensen, H.W., Ramamoorthi, R.: Physically-accurate fur reflectance: modeling, measurement and rendering. ACM Trans. Graph. (Proceedings of SIGGRAPH Asia 2015) **34**(6) (2015)
45. Yu, X., Yang, J.C., Hensley, J., Harada, T., Yu, J.: A framework for rendering complex scattering effects on hair. In: Proceedings of the ACM SIGGRAPH Symposium on Interactive 3D Graphics and Games, I3D 2012, pp. 111–118. ACM, New York (2012). https://doi.org/10.1145/2159616.2159635
46. Yuksel, C., Schaefer, S., Keyser, J.: Hair meshes. ACM Trans. Graph. (Proceedings of SIGGRAPH Asia 2009) **28**(5), 166:1–166:7 (2009). https://doi.org/10.1145/1661412.1618512
47. Zhang, M., Chai, M., Wu, H., Yang, H., Zhou, K.: A data-driven approach to four-view image-based hair modeling. ACM Trans. Graph. (TOG) **36**(4), 156 (2017)
48. Zhang, R., Isola, P., Efros, A.A.: Split-brain autoencoders: Unsupervised learning by cross-channel prediction. In: CVPR (2017)
49. Zhao, H., Shi, J., Qi, X., Wang, X., Jia, J.: Pyramid scene parsing network. In: 2017 IEEE Conference on Computer Vision and Pattern Recognition (CVPR), pp. 6230–6239, July 2017. https://doi.org/10.1109/CVPR.2017.660
50. Zhou, T., Tulsiani, S., Sun, W., Malik, J., Efros, A.A.: View synthesis by appearance flow. In: Leibe, B., Matas, J., Sebe, N., Welling, M. (eds.) ECCV 2016. LNCS, vol. 9908, pp. 286–301. Springer, Cham (2016). https://doi.org/10.1007/978-3-319-46493-0_18

51. Zhu, J.-Y., Krähenbühl, P., Shechtman, E., Efros, A.A.: Generative visual manipulation on the natural image manifold. In: Leibe, B., Matas, J., Sebe, N., Welling, M. (eds.) ECCV 2016. LNCS, vol. 9909, pp. 597–613. Springer, Cham (2016). https://doi.org/10.1007/978-3-319-46454-1_36

52. Zhu, J.Y., Park, T., Isola, P., Efros, A.A.: Unpaired image-to-image translation using cycle-consistent adversarial networks. In: ICCV (2017)

53. Zhu, J.Y., et al.: Toward multimodal image-to-image translation. In: Advances in Neural Information Processing Systems, vol. 30 (2017)

54. Zinke, A., Yuksel, C., Weber, A., Keyser, J.: Dual scattering approximation for fast multiple scattering in hair. ACM Trans. Graph. (Proceedings of SIGGRAPH 2008) **27**(3), 32:1–32:10 (2008). https://doi.org/10.1145/1360612.1360631

Model-free Consensus Maximization
for Non-Rigid Shapes

Thomas Probst[1(✉)], Ajad Chhatkuli[1], Danda Pani Paudel[1],
and Luc Van Gool[1,2]

[1] Computer Vision Lab, ETH Zürich, Zürich, Switzerland
{probstt,ajad.chhatkuli,paudel,vangool}@vision.ee.ethz.ch
[2] VISICS, ESAT/PSI, KU Leuven, Leuven, Belgium

Abstract. Many computer vision methods use consensus maximization
to relate measurements containing outliers with the correct transformation model. In the context of rigid shapes, this is typically done using
Random Sampling and Consensus (RANSAC) by estimating an analytical model that agrees with the largest number of measurements (inliers).
However, small parameter models may not be always available. In this
paper, we formulate the model-free consensus maximization as an Integer Program in a graph using 'rules' on measurements. We then provide a method to solve it optimally using the Branch and Bound (BnB)
paradigm. We focus its application on non-rigid shapes, where we apply
the method to remove outlier 3D correspondences and achieve performance superior to the state of the art. Our method works with outlier
ratio as high as 80%. We further derive a similar formulation for 3D
template to image matching, achieving similar or better performance
compared to the state of the art.

1 Introduction

Consensus maximization is a powerful tool in computer vision that has
enabled practical applications of highly complex algorithms such as Structure-
from-Motion (SfM) [1–3] to work despite incorrect measurements and noise.
Apart from heuristic strategies such as Random Sampling and Consensus
(RANSAC) [4], globally optimal consensus maximizers [5–11] have been widely
studied for rigid shapes, where there exists a simple analytical transformation
between two sets of measurements. In contrast, such tools have not been explored
in earnest for the model-free scenario, where simple analytical transformation
models cannot explain the measurements. An important field where model-free
approaches are needed is in non-rigid shape registration. Consensus maximization in non-rigid shapes have applications in augmented reality, object animations and shape analysis, among others.

Electronic supplementary material The online version of this chapter (https://
doi.org/10.1007/978-3-030-01225-0_8) contains supplementary material, which is
available to authorized users.

While a large number of works have tackled non-rigid registration problem between images or shapes [12–16], little attention has been given to identifying outliers in matching correspondences. A few methods solve the problem in the images of non-rigid shapes [17,18] and between a template shape and an image [19] through locally optimal approaches. The difficulty of assigning a suitable minimal parameter model to non-rigid transformations makes it highly challenging to devise a consensus maximizer.

In this paper, we propose a common framework of seeking consensus in a model-free correspondence set. Our key idea is that despite lacking a model which can explain each instance in a matching set individually, one can consider the agreement between two or more instances using certain rules to formulate constraints. In non-rigid shapes, a rule widely applied for reconstruction and registration is the isometric deformation prior. Isometry implies that the geodesic distances are preserved despite deformations. Using these theoretical understandings, we provide our contributions in three different aspects. First we show how a model-free consensus maximization problem can be posed as a graph problem and solved as an Integer Program if we have inlier/outlier rules on the matching sets. Such an Integer Program can be solved optimally using a BnB approach. Second, we apply this formulation for removing outliers in non-rigid shape correspondences under the isometry prior. We show that our method can handle as much as 80% outlier correspondences on isometric surfaces. We provide extensive experiments on several isometric and partial shapes, as well as 'loosely' isometric partial inter-subject human shapes, where we obtain results that improve over the state-of-the-art methods. To show the generic nature of the introduced consensus maximizer, we also formulate a 3D template-to-image outlier removal problem using the piecewise rigidity and smoothness prior. We conduct extensive experiments in order to analyze the behavior of the proposed algorithms and to compare with the state-of-the-art methods.

2   Related Work

We briefly highlight the related works that are relevant to non-rigid registration problems. The first problem is that of maximizing consensus between matched 3D surface points in non-rigid 3D shapes using the isometry prior. Isometry is a widely used prior in registration [14,15,20–22] as well as 3D reconstruction [23,24]. Most non-rigid shape registration methods [15,20–22] start with a 3D descriptor such as the SHOT descriptor [25] or heat kernels [26] and establish correspondences between shapes through energy minimization. Others compute the registration by blending conformal maps [14,27]. Any such matching method results in good and bad matches. In the following sections, we study how the outlier matches from various methods can be removed in practical cases, including complete, partial and inter-subject scenarios.

3D template-to-image matching is yet another important problem in non-rigid shapes that can be used to localize cameras [28] or for template-based 3D reconstruction [19,24,29,30]. Eliminating outlier matches in such cases is addressed in [19] by using a local iterative approach. Most other methods which solve image registration [12, 18] do not use a 3D geometric prior explicitly. We address the problem of consensus maximization in this setting with piece-wise rigidity and smoothness prior. A recent method [16] solves the combinatorial matching problem with similar constraints but does not focus on the problem of identifying outlier matches.

3   Background and Theory

Notations. We represent sets and graphs as special Latin characters, e.g., $\mathcal{V}$. We use lowercase Latin letters i, j, k or l to represent indices or sets of indices. For example, $\mathcal{V}_i$ is an element of the set $\mathcal{V}$. We write known or unknown scalars also in lowercase letters, such as z. We use uppercase bold Latin letters to represent matrices (e.g., M) and lowercase bold Latin letters to represent vectors (e.g., v). We use lowercase Greek letter ϵ to represent thresholds. We use uppercase Greek letters to represent mappings or functions (e.g., Φ). We use $\|.\|$ to denote the ℓ_2 – norm and $| \, . \, |$ to denote the ℓ_1 – norm of a vector or the cardinality of a set. Unless stated otherwise, we write primed letters to represent quantities related to the transformed set.

3.1   Outliers

Let $\Phi : \Omega \to \Omega'$ be a transformation function between two spatial domains. Φ is related to the matching sets $\mathcal{P} = \{\mathcal{P}_i : \mathcal{P}_i \in \Omega, \ i = 1, \ldots, p\}$ and $\mathcal{P}' = \{\mathcal{P}'_i : \mathcal{P}'_i \in \Omega', \ i = 1, \ldots, p\}$. In practice, Φ may be a rigid or non-rigid transformation function or such transformations followed by camera projection. Each member $\mathcal{P}_i$ corresponds to the member $\mathcal{P}'_i$ in the second set. This defines a set of matches $\mathcal{C} \subset \mathcal{P} \times \mathcal{P}'$ that may contain outliers. The outlier set $\mathcal{O}$ is defined with a distance function Δ as:

$$\forall i \in \{1 \ldots p\}, \quad \Delta\left(\Phi(\mathcal{P}_i), \mathcal{P}'_i\right) \geq \epsilon \implies i \in \mathcal{O}. \tag{1}$$

A correspondence pair $(\mathcal{P}_i, \mathcal{P}'_i)$, also simply denoted as i, is an outlier if the distance between the mapping of $\mathcal{P}_i$ and its correspondence $\mathcal{P}'_i$, is greater than the threshold ϵ.

3.2   Consensus Maximization

Using the definition of outliers in (1), the problem of consensus maximization is defined as the minimization of the cardinality of the set $\mathcal{O}$ for the unknown Φ:

$$\begin{aligned} \underset{\Phi}{\text{minimize}} \quad & |\mathcal{O}| \\ \text{subject to} \quad & \Delta\left(\Phi(\mathcal{P}_i), \mathcal{P}'_i\right) \geq \epsilon \implies i \in \mathcal{O}. \end{aligned} \tag{2}$$

Problem (2) implies that we wish to find the mapping Φ which results in the least number of disagreements given by the cardinality of $\mathcal{O}$, in the given matching set $\mathcal{C}$. In rigid SfM related problems, Φ can be often expressed using a linear or non-linear function with a small fixed number of parameters. This means that Eq. (1) can be evaluated point-wise[1] and also estimated using a very small size of point correspondence set, known as the minimal set. There is no doubt that such problems can be efficiently solved using RANSAC and other globally optimal methods highlighted in Sect. 1. It should be noted that even if Φ can be parameterized, very recently problem (2) was shown to be NP-hard with W[1]-complexity [31,32], meaning that solving it optimally is very expensive. We call such a problem, when Φ can be parameterized (with a reasonably small number of parameters), as model-based consensus maximization. In the sections below we focus on the model-free case. Note that most formulations on consensus maximization are written as maximization of the inlier set cardinality rather than the minimization of the outlier set cardinality. However, these definitions are equivalent and we choose the latter for convenience.

3.3   Generic Rules-Based Consensus Maximization

In contrast to model-based problems, for many applications such as those related to non-rigid shapes, Φ cannot be represented with a small size of parameters and therefore it cannot be estimated using a minimal point set. As a consequence, Δ cannot be evaluated point-wise. For example, consider the case when Φ represents the mapping between the two instances of a non-rigid surface. Such a map may be represented by Free-Form Deformation (FFD) [18,33] or specialized latent space models such as SMPL [34] for human body, both requiring a large number of points to fit the latent parameters. In such cases problem (2) is impractical to solve in its original form.

Therefore, we offer an alternative consensus maximization formulation which is easier to solve for a special class of problems. A problem belongs to this special class if the sets $\mathcal{P}$ and $\mathcal{P}'$ have a common underlying structure which can be measured using subsets of the match set $\mathcal{C}$, without explicitly computing the transformation function Φ. To obtain a tractable formulation, we define a set of binary variables $\{z\}, z_i \in \{0,1\}$ and $i \in \{1,\ldots,p\}$ such that $z_i = 1 \iff i \in \mathcal{O}$. Let a binary valued function $\Theta : (\mathcal{S}_a, \mathcal{S}_b) \to \{0,1\}$ measure the agreement between two small subsets $\mathcal{S}_a, \mathcal{S}_b \subset \mathcal{C}$. Θ evaluates to 1 if the subsets $\mathcal{S}_a$ and $\mathcal{S}_b$ agree up to some threshold ϵ and 0 otherwise. Then the following is an alternative of the original problem (2):

$$\underset{\{z\}}{\text{minimize}} \quad \sum_i z_i$$

$$\text{subject to} \tag{3}$$

$$\Theta(\mathcal{S}_a, \mathcal{S}_b) = 0 \implies \exists (\mathcal{P}_i, \mathcal{P}'_i) \in \mathcal{S}_a \cup \mathcal{S}_b : z_i = 1,$$

$$\forall (\mathcal{S}_a, \mathcal{S}_b) : \mathcal{S}_a \neq \mathcal{S}_b,$$

---

[1] Although in some cases such as that of the Fundamental Matrix, Φ cannot be determined point-wise, it can be estimated for a minimal set. Thus, a RANSAC problem can be formulated.

The function Θ can be thought of as a rule which uses priors on the sets $\mathcal{P}$ and $\mathcal{P}'$ to measure the agreement on the matched subsets. The subsets $\mathcal{S}_a$ and $\mathcal{S}_b$ sampled from the match set $\mathcal{C}$, are the minimal sets such that Θ can be evaluated. Problem (3) simply means, in case two subsets chosen on the basis of a prior do not agree with each other, *at least one member from the union of those subsets must be an outlier.* This is the key idea of our work. Although solving problem (3) optimally does not guarantee an optimal solution for problem (2), the latter is a close relaxation of the former. Therefore solving problem (3) amounts to solving the model-free consensus maximization. Problem (3) is still a combinatorial problem and is NP-hard. In the next section we give more insights into the problem with a graph structure and provide a globally optimal method for solving it with integer programming.

4   Consensus Maximization with a Graph

We represent the union of all samples $\mathcal{S}_a$ and $\mathcal{S}_b$ as the nodes and the connection between them as the edges of a graph $\mathcal{G} = \{\mathcal{V}, \mathcal{E}\}$. The node set $\mathcal{V}$ consists of all unique sampled subsets $\mathcal{S}_a$ and $\mathcal{S}_b$. An edge $(\mathcal{S}_a, \mathcal{S}_b) \in \mathcal{E}$ connects the nodes $\mathcal{S}_a$ and $\mathcal{S}_b$ and induces the agreement function $\Theta(\mathcal{S}_a, \mathcal{S}_b)$. We use the index $k \in \{1 \dots v\}$ to denote the nodes $\mathcal{V}$ and the index $l \in \{1 \dots e\}$ to denote the edges $\mathcal{E}$. Figure 1 illustrates this representation of the problem.

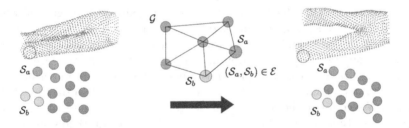

Fig. 1. Graph formulation for consensus maximization. The selected point sets (nodes) are drawn as orange and purple circles in the graph, connected by edges representing the compatibility between the sets. The point clouds are taken from [35].

4.1   Graph Formulation

Given the graph $\mathcal{G}$, we would still like to compute the original binary variable set $\{z\}$. With a slight abuse of notations, we define the binary variable set of a node as $z_k \triangleq \{z_i\} : (\mathcal{P}_i, \mathcal{P}_i') \in \mathcal{V}_k$. Similarly we define the binary variable set of an edge as $z_l \triangleq \{z_i\} : (\mathcal{P}_i, \mathcal{P}_i') \in \mathcal{V}_{k_a} \cup \mathcal{V}_{k_b}$ for $\mathcal{E}_l = (\mathcal{V}_{k_a}, \mathcal{V}_{k_b})$. The constraint on the binary variables can then be compactly expressed as:

$$\Sigma z_l + \Theta(\mathcal{E}_l) \geq 1, \tag{4}$$

where Σz_l represents the sum of all the elements in the set z_l. Problem (3) with constraint (4) is an example of graph optimization where we need to compute the node properties z_k for each node k using the edge measurements $\Theta(\mathcal{E}_l)$.

4.2   Integer Programming

Using the constraint of (4) in a graph, we propose an efficient way to solve the consensus maximization problem, under the framework of Integer Programming, as:

$$
\begin{aligned}
&\underset{\{z\}}{\text{minimize}} \quad \sum z_i \\
&\text{subject to} \quad \sum z_l \geq 1, \quad \forall l \in \{1 \ldots e\}, \quad \text{if } \Theta(\mathcal{E}_l) = 0.
\end{aligned}
\tag{5}
$$

Problem (5) can be optimally solved using any off-the-shelf solver for Integer Programming. This is done using the popular BnB method. Often such problems in consensus maximization are solved using the so-called big M method [36]. Such a method is needed when a binary decision function Θ cannot be defined for a given edge $\mathcal{E}_l$. In that case, the integer inequality in problem (5) is written as $M \sum z_l + \epsilon \geq \Lambda(\mathcal{E}_l)$ using the scalar-valued function Λ and a scalar threshold ϵ. Here, M is a chosen large scalar number that makes the problem feasible when Λ is large. However, in this work we consider only those problems that can be expressed with a binary rule Θ.

Relaxed Alternatives and BnB. Integer programming problems are generally non-convex in nature. They can be simplified by further relaxing the binary or integer constraint with real bounds. In contrast, we opt for the BnB approach keeping the integer constraint in order to obtain a globally optimal solution even in case of high outlier ratio. Such an approach computes the lower and upper bound of the cost iteratively and terminates with a certificate of ϵ sub-optimality if they are equal. We compare the relaxed and the globally optimal methods in Sect. 6. In the next section, we describe two different problems in non-rigid shapes which can be expressed in the form of problem (5).

5   Non-Rigid Shapes

Non-rigid objects have deformations that cannot be parameterized with a small fixed set of parameters. Nevertheless, they do obey some shape priors. We provide our methods for two problems in non-rigid shapes below, based on such deformation priors.

5.1   Shape Matching with Isometry

We consider two different shapes $\mathcal{P}$ and $\mathcal{P}'$ related by an unknown deformation Φ. We want to establish the set of outlier points $\mathcal{O}$ on the matching set $\mathcal{C}$.

Such problems may arise, for example, when registering 3D non-rigid surfaces using image matches [28] or when registering different shapes with a 3D feature point descriptor [25,26]. In order to solve the problem, we consider the isometric deformation prior which assumes that the surface distances are preserved under deformations. The prior allows us to use the following graph attributes:

$$\mathcal{V}_k = (\mathcal{P}_i, \mathcal{P}'_i)$$

$$\Theta(\mathcal{E}_l) = \begin{cases} 1 & \text{if} \quad \|\Psi(\mathcal{P}_{i_1}, \mathcal{P}_{i_2}) - \Psi(\mathcal{P}'_{i_1}, \mathcal{P}'_{i_2})\| \leq \epsilon \\ 0 & \text{otherwise.} \end{cases} \tag{6}$$

where Ψ is the function that measures the geodesic distance between two points on a surface. Each graph node consists of a single matching pair in $\mathcal{C}$. Therefore each graph constraint in (6) obtained for an edge consists of only two binary variables, making the problem highly sparse. Although, we only show the problem formulation using isometry, other deformation priors such as conformality may be used in problem (6).

Practical Considerations. While the method works perfectly for isometric surfaces, objects which are undergoing topological changes such as a tearing piece of paper or loosely isometric surfaces such as a human body pose additional difficulty, as isometry is not always satisfied in such cases. We therefore provide a more practical approach to solve the problem in Algorithm 1. In Algorithm 1, separately applying the method for different clusters also addresses the non-linear time complexity of the integer programming problem. This allows us to use the method in dense point surfaces as the time complexity with the number of clusters is always linear. To estimate the geodesics, we compute a mesh by Delaunay triangulation when a mesh is not provided.

Algorithm 1. $\{z\}$ = shapeRegistration $(\mathcal{P}, \mathcal{P}', \mathcal{C})$

---

1. Cluster initial matches $\mathcal{C}$ into m disjoint clusters using k-means.
2. For each cluster $c \in \{1 \dots m\}$,
   (a) Compute nearest neighbors and establish edges $\mathcal{E}_l$.
   (b) For each edge compute the agreement function $\Theta(\mathcal{E}_l)$.
   (c) Formulate constraints (6) with Θ.
3. Aggregate all the results from each cluster c.

5.2   Template to Image Matching

Template-based reconstruction is a well-studied problem [19,23,24,30] which uses matches between the template shape $\mathcal{P}$ and the deformed shape's image $\mathcal{I}$ to reconstruct the deformed surface. Again, the matches established may consist of outliers, in which case the reconstruction obtained can be of poor quality. Here, we propose the use of piece-wise rigidity and surface smoothness as the priors to define the agreement function Θ. Despite non-rigidity, surface smoothness has been successfully used in the state-of-the-art template-based reconstruction methods [19,30]. We use a similar approach by considering that the relative camera to object pose changes smoothly over the surface. Using these priors we define the graph attributes as follows:

$$\mathcal{V}_{k_1} = \{(\mathcal{P}_i, \mathcal{I}_i)\}, \quad i = \{i_1, i_2, i_3\}, \quad i_1, i_2, i_3 \in \{1\ldots p\}$$
$$\mathcal{V}_{k_2} \in \mathcal{N}(\mathcal{V}_{k_1})$$
$$\Theta(\mathcal{E}_l) = \begin{cases} 1 & \text{if} \quad \Delta\left(\mathsf{R}_{k_1}^\top, \mathsf{R}_{k_2}\right) \leq \epsilon_1 \text{ and } |\mathsf{t}_{k_1} - \mathsf{t}_{k_2}| \leq \epsilon_2 \\ 0 & \text{otherwise} \end{cases} \quad (7)$$

where R_{k_1} and R_{k_2} represent the rotations of the absolute pose estimated using the nodes $\mathcal{V}_{k_1}$ and $\mathcal{V}_{k_2}$ respectively, for the image $\mathcal{I}$. We define $\mathcal{N}(.)$ to be the set valued function giving neighboring nodes in the graph. Similarly t_{k_1} and t_{k_2} represent the camera translations. The rule Θ measures how well the poses agree for the two nodes. To that end, Δ is the function used to measure the distance between two rotations. We use two hyperparameters ϵ_1 and ϵ_2 to threshold the change in rotation and translation respectively. Local rigidity and surface smoothness imply that the poses should also change smoothly. The absolute pose problem can be solved using any of the so-called PnP methods [37–39]. We consider only the minimal problem that uses three non-collinear matched points and is also known as the P3P method [37]. The solutions obtained with P3P have a 4-fold ambiguity. This can be disambiguated either by using an additional matching point pair or by simply choosing the solution that minimizes Δ. The nodes are sampled such that each edge requires only four unique point matches and therefore each inequality constraint will consist of four binary variables.

Practical Considerations. Piecewise rigidity is a stronger prior compared to isometry. For non-rigid shapes, this holds true only for close neighbors. In contrast to the shape matching problem of 5.1, each edge here requires four point matches. For that reason, it requires the matching set to be dense enough so that the points obey rigidity at least locally. Algorithm 2 describes the implementation of the method. A very naive simplification of Algorithm 2 can be made by considering all points that produce a high number of 1's in the agreement function Θ to be inliers. We term such a voting method as local filtering which can find obvious inliers in the template-image matching problem.

Algorithm 2. $\{z\}$ = templateImageRegistration $(\mathcal{P}, \mathcal{I}, \mathcal{C})$

　　1. Cluster initial matches $\mathcal{C}$ into m disjoint clusters using k-means.
　　2. For each cluster $c \in \{1\ldots m\}$,
　　(a) Compute various triangulations of the point clusters and establish edges with two triangles.
　　(b) For each such pair of triangles with shared edge, evaluate $\Theta(\mathcal{E}_l)$.
　　(c) Formulate constraints (7) with Θ.
　　3. Aggregate all the results from m clusters.

5.3   Complexity Analysis

The combinatorial complexity of problem (5) depends on four main aspects: the number of points p, the neighborhood size q, the cluster size r and the cardinality of the minimal set required to represent a vertex set $\mathcal{S}$, say s in the graph (see Fig. 1). The complexity for a single Integer Program as reported in Table 1 can be directly obtained from the combinatorics in graph. Although the template-to-image matching complexity ($s = 3$) is high, the problem demands only local agreement, which allows us to use a small local neighborhood ($q = 15$) for creating the vertices (triangles in this case) with on average 30 edges per point. This is not the case in the shape matching and we use a fully-connected graph ($q = p/r - 1$) on any cluster as the geodesic measurements are valid irrespective of the points' proximity.

Table 1. Complexity Analysis. Solving for n points and minimal set size s with full connectivity (cluster size $r = 1$) and q-connectivity (cluster size r).

Full-connectivity		q-connectivity	
Vertices	Edges	Vertices	Edges
$\binom{p}{s}$	$\binom{\binom{p}{s}}{2}$	$\frac{p}{sr}\binom{q}{s-1}$	$\frac{\frac{p}{sr}\binom{q}{s-1}}{2}$

6   Experimental Results

We present the results and analysis of our proposed methods in this section on several standard datasets. We refer to the integer program based methods as *exact* or the proposed method. We also compare with the simplified method where the binary constraints in problem (5) have been relaxed to real, which we refer to as the *relaxed* method. We compare and use several matching or outlier removal methods. We write the spline-warp based image outlier removal method [18] as *featds*. We write the graph matching method [12] as *maxpoolm*. We test the template-image outlier removal method based on mesh Laplacian [19] as *laplacian*. Apart from these image-based methods we also use shape matching methods. We write the recent deformable shape kernel matching method [15] as KM. We write the deep functional map [22] as DFM and the blended intrinsic maps [14] as BIM. We implement our methods in MATLAB with YALMIP [40] and MOSEK [41] for integer programming. Below we describe in detail the experiments for each of the discussed non-rigid registration problems.

Clustering and Threshold Parameters. For some experiments, we apply clustering to handle the high number of point matches. For template-to-image matching and the Hand dataset, the number of point matches is low ($n < 200$) and therefore the number of clusters is 1. For the human shapes and the newspaper dataset we choose the number of clusters as 5 based on neighborhood (k-means clustering). Note that the result aggregation is straight forward, since the clusters are disjoint. For Fig. 2, to vary the number of points, we randomly sub-sampled the points to a fixed number. Regarding thresholds, we fix $\epsilon = 20\%$ distance error relative to the template for shape matching (Sect. 6.1) unless stated otherwise. In the template-to-image (Sect. 6.2) matching case, we use $\epsilon_1 = 10°$ and $\epsilon_2 = 40\%$ for all datasets.

6.1   Non-rigid Shape Matching

We begin by analyzing the behavior of the proposed methods on synthetic data where the ground truth correspondences are available for the shape matching problem. We also compare the proposed methods with the state-of-the-art methods on several real datasets. All these are outlined below.

Mocap Data. We test with two cloth-capture data [35]. The datasets consist of a cloth falling (toss) and a moving pair of trousers (stepping trousers). The datasets are generated with mocap and consist of registered real 3D points. We synthetically generate outliers by randomly re-assigning matches to evaluate our methods.

Figure 2 (a) compares the *relaxed* and *exact* versions of the proposed method. We observe that, for low outlier ratio, it is possible to remove all the outliers using the *relaxed* method. However, it breaks down as the percentage of outliers increase beyond 50%, while the *exact* solution still correctly detects the inliers even in conditions with 80% outliers. Note that the proposed method does not detect any false positive inliers. Figure 2 (b) shows how the *exact* method behaves with the number of iterations. We observe that the method quickly computes the upper bound cost or the pessimistic inlier set while it takes a while to obtain the certificate of optimality. We find this behavior to be consistent to many other experimental setups. Figure 2 (c) shows the number of open nodes at each iteration, describing how BnB evaluates and prunes branches. To investigate time complexity, we also plot the execution time for the *exact* method in Fig. 2 (d). It can be observed that the execution time increases with increase in the number of points. However, this is not a problem in practice thanks to the clustering framework presented in Algorithm 1.

KINECT Newspaper Dataset. The RGB-D data obtained from depth-camera sensors such as KINECT make an important field of application for the method. We investigated our method on the Newspaper dataset[2] [42]. It consists of a double sheet of newspaper being torn into two parts. Figure 3 shows the inliers and outliers for a part of the template image with our method. Due to the local neighborhood computed using both point sets, the *exact* method can robustly handle the topological changes. On the other hand, the *relaxed* method does not work well from lack of enough constraints[3].

---

[2]   Dataset was provided by the authors.

[3]   The complete set of results are provided in the supplementary document.

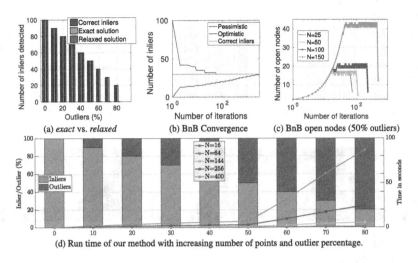

(a) *exact* vs. *relaxed*   (b) **BnB Convergence**   (c) **BnB open nodes (50% outliers)**

(d) Run time of our method with increasing number of points and outlier percentage.

Fig. 2. Analysis of our method. Number of inliers detected, convergence of the proposed method, and time taken for the mocap cloth dataset [35] under various setups. Note that the number of iterations in (b) and (c) are in log-scale.

(a) *exact*

(b) *relaxed*

(c) *laplacian*

Fig. 3. Newspaper dataset. Visualization of inlier and outlier matches from our *exact* and two next best performing methods for an example pair of the Newspaper dataset. Left column shows the inlier detection and the right column shows the outlier detection.

Hand Dataset. The hand dataset [42] consists of two different instances of a hand and their 3D ground truth obtained with SfM. Due to the non-rigid deformation, the detected SIFT correspondences consist of very few matches with a large percentage (more than 70%) of outliers. The shape matching methods [14,15] completely fail on this dataset and we do not show them here. We show the results of the *exact* method in Fig. 4 and the next best performing methods in Fig. 5. These qualitative results clearly show that the compared methods do not perform well in such difficult cases.

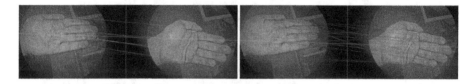

Fig. 4. SfM Hand dataset. Inlier detections (left) and outlier detections (right) of our *exact* method.

Fig. 5. Inlier detections with *laplacian* (left) and *relaxed* (right).

Human Body Shapes. In the next set of experiments, we use our methods on human body scans from the FAUST [43] dataset. To introduce challenging outliers, we consider a partial matching scenario by cutting out one arm and one leg from the mesh, and matching it to the full one. Thanks to the mesh registrations provided by the dataset, we can exactly evaluate inliers and outliers based on geodesic deviations to the ground truth correspondences (deviations greater than 15 cm are considered as outliers). We compare our *relaxed* and *exact* methods against matches estimated by DFM [22], KM [15], and BIM [14]. Although BIM [14] produced visually good correspondences, it suffered from mirror-image ambiguity, that could not be resolved. Therefore we compare to BIM only where proper evaluations were possible.

Since our method is designed for isometric shapes, we conduct the first experiment in the *intra-subject* case (same subject in 9 different poses). We observe that our method can successfully eliminate more than 90% outliers produced by DFM and KM while removing only a few true inliers, as shown in the first column of Table 2.

In inter-subject body shape matching applications however, the isometry assumption holds only to some extent. We use two challenging datasets to test such scenarios. The first one is on *inter-subject* matching on the FAUST data, again in the partial matching setting. Since the body shape varies across subjects, isometry doesn't hold anymore. The results presented in the second column of Table 2 demonstrate that this problem is significantly harder than the isometric matching. We see that the matches resulting from BIM contain outliers that are very hard to detect, and only 15% can be removed without sacrificing many inliers. For DFM and KM, we reliably detect more than 80% and 90% resp., and therefore improve the matching robustness for subsequent tasks.

Our third experiment with human body shapes involves dense correspondence estimation from a depth map to the 3D model. We rendered synthetic depth map mimicking the projection and noise properties of KINECT from an articulated MPII Human Shape model [44] using variations of upright poses and body shapes. To compute the geodesics on this modality, we triangulated the point cloud using 2D Delaunay triangulation. Applying DFM and KM on the raw input does not work well, since SHOT [45] and HKS [46] are not reliable features for depth maps. We therefore take initial matches from a metric regression forest [47] trained on the specific task of dense correspondence estimation. We then compare our methods, KM and ICP on top of these matches in the third column of Table 2. We can conclude that, although provided with initial matches, KM fails to correctly match the two modalities. Our method however shows promising results even though the shapes are non-isometric, and geodesics are computed on the triangulated point cloud. Interestingly, our result is comparable to that of the articulated non-rigid ICP which exploits additional information such as the kinematics and a stronger shape prior. Figure 6 shows a qualitative example from our test set.

In summary, we showed that our method can be used on top of generic matching methods to robustly detect outliers for isometric deformations, and some classes of non-isometric registration such as inter-subject body shapes. Moreover, we can confirm our results on the synthetic data and conclude that even the *relaxed* method provides good results if the proportion of the outliers is below 50%.

6.2   Template to Image Matching

The template 3D to image matching is an important problem in non-rigid geometry. Most reconstruction methods [19, 30] are sensitive to outlying correspondences and proceed by first removing outliers in matches. We use problem (7) to formulate the template to image outlier removal method using the absolute pose. We test our results on three datasets: KINECT Paper [48], T-Shirt [49] and the MPI Sintel [50] all of which contain the groundtruth 3D data and images. We select a random single pair for each dataset and compute the SIFT matches. We count the number of inliers and outlier matches manually for each of the methods' output. We compare our methods with three other state-of-the-art methods *laplacian*, *featds* and *maxpoolm*. Similarly, as discussed in Sect. 5.2 we also report the results of the *relaxed* method. We further report the results of the local-filtering method as another baseline where the inliers are decided based on the local neighborhood voting (Table 3).

Table 2. Non-rigid 3D shape matching. Results on FAUST [43] intra- and inter-subject, as well as matching depth maps to the MPII HumanShape [44] model. We report the number of true positive (inliers) and false positive (remaining outliers) matches.

Method	FAUST					MPII HumanShape	
	Intra-subject			*Inter-subject*		*From rendered depth map*	
	Inliers / Outliers	Time [s]		Inliers / Outliers	Time [s]	Inliers / Outliers	Time [s]
BIM	-	-		3381 / 1602	3	-	-
BIM+Ours (*relaxed*)	-	-		3269 / **1362**	10	-	-
BIM+Ours (*exact*)	-	-		3267 / 1395	32.9	-	-
DFM	4211 / 772	1		3756 / 1227	1	272 / 3728	1
DFM+Ours (*relaxed*)	3918 / **31**	19		3437 / **93**	15	-	-
DFM+Ours (*exact*)	3918 / **31**	24		3437 / **93**	19.4	-	-
KM	4736 / 181	89		4051 / 860	92	572 / 3387	53
KM+Ours (*relaxed*)	4554 / 18	104		3634 / **161**	107	-	-
KM+Ours (*exact*)	4556 / **17**	110		3634 / **161**	115	-	-
RF	-	-		-	-	3220 / 780	<1
RF+KM	-	-		-	-	1162 / 269	3
RF+Ours (*relaxed*)	-	-		-	-	2800 / **137**	14
RF+Ours (*exact*)	-	-		-	-	2800 / **137**	15
RF+ICP	-	-		-	-	3166 / 159	301
	Mostly isometric			Non-isometric			

We test all the methods with favorable parameters. The reported inliers are manually validated. The results show that our method performs in par with *laplacian* designed exactly for the template-based outlier removal. Note that the *exact* method consistently detects more number of inliers than other methods. Our method performs better than *featds* in multi-body situation as *featds* uses a single spline-based warp and computes the residuals to identify outliers. We visualize the results of outlier removal in Fig. 7 for the proposed method and two other best performing methods: *featds* and *laplacian*.

Fig. 6. Qualitative results. Non-isometric shape matching from depth map. Left to right: body mesh model [44], RF [47], RF+KM [15], RF+Ours, RF+ICP, input depth map. Correspondences are color-coded, gray indicates removed matches.

Table 3. 3D template to image matching. Comparison on three different real datasets.

Method	Kinect Paper		T-shirt		Sintel	
	Inliers	Time(s)	Inliers	Time(s)	Inliers	Time(s)
Local-filtering	46 / 142	4.22	95 / 351	6.10	17 / 68	2.03
Relaxed	99 / 142	5.56	291 / 351	7.52	44 / 68	3.51
Exact	114 / 142	7.59	**309** / 351	9.66	**53** / 68	5.01
Laplacian	**126** / 142	**1.15**	301 / 351	7.84	44 / 68	0.53
Featds	76 / 142	3.93	304 / 351	**1.46**	42 / 68	**0.32**
Maxpoolm	3 / 142	159.96	6 / 351	608.55	16 / 68	7.88

Fig. 7. Inliers (left) vs. Outliers (right) for the T-shirt dataset using the *exact* method. The performance of our method is better than that of the two compared methods designed for non-rigid matching. More results are provided in the supplementary material.

7 Conclusions and Future Work

In this paper we brought forward a theory on model-free consensus maximization using integer programming and an optimal method to solve it using Branch and Bound. We formulated two different registration problems using our consensus maximizer: isometric shape outlier removal and template-image outlier removal. We obtained very good results at up to 80% mismatches in non-rigid shape registration and >25% mismatches in template-image registration. We obtained these results by solving a close relaxation of the original problem with guaranteed optimality. We showed with extensive experiments that our methods consistently performs on par or better than the existing methods.

Although the focus of this paper was on non-rigid shapes, many vision problems can be converted to formulation 5 with three or less variables per graph node. A non-exhaustive list includes: *(i)* one variable problems: relative pose on robot navigation [51], *(ii)* two variable problems: robust triangulation [52] and pure translation estimation [53], and *(iii)* three variable problems: image to image affine homography and three-view modulus constraints [54]. For future works, we intend to tackle some of these problems using the formulation we developed in this paper.

Acknowledgements. Research was funded by the EU's Horizon 2020 programme under grant No. 687757– REPLICATE and grant No. 645331– EurEyeCase. Research was also supported by the Swiss Commission for Technology and Innovation (CTI, Grant No. 26253.1 PFES-ES, EXASOLVED).

References

1. Hartley, R.I., Zisserman, A.: Multiple View Geometry in Computer Vision, 2nd edn. Cambridge University Press, New York (2004). ISBN 0521540518
2. Longuet-Higgins, H.: A computer algorithm for reconstructing a scene from two projections. Nature **293**, 133–135 (1981)
3. Nistér, D.: An efficient solution to the five-point relative pose problem. IEEE Trans. Pattern Anal. Mach. Intell. **26**(6), 756–777 (2004)
4. Fischler, M.A., Bolles, R.C.: Random sample consensus: a paradigm for model fitting with applications to image analysis and automated cartography. Commun. ACM **24**(6), 381–395 (1981)
5. Chin, T.J., Kee, Y.H., Eriksson, A., Neumann, F.: Guaranteed outlier removal with mixed integer linear programs. In: CVPR (2016)
6. Speciale, P., Paudel, D.P., Oswald, M.R., Kroeger, T., Gool, L.V., Pollefeys, M.: Consensus maximization with linear matrix inequality constraints. In: CVPR (2017)
7. Bazin, J.C., Li, H., Kweon, I.S., Demonceaux, C., Vasseur, P., Ikeuchi, K.: A branch-and-bound approach to correspondence and grouping problems. IEEE Trans. Pattern Anal. Mach. Intell. **35**(7), 1565–1576 (2013)
8. Hartley, R.I., Kahl, F.: Global optimization through rotation space search. IJCV **82**(1), 64–79 (2009)
9. Bazin, J.-C., Seo, Y., Hartley, R., Pollefeys, M.: Globally optimal inlier set maximization with unknown rotation and focal length. In: Fleet, D., Pajdla, T., Schiele, B., Tuytelaars, T. (eds.) ECCV 2014. LNCS, vol. 8690, pp. 803–817. Springer, Cham (2014). https://doi.org/10.1007/978-3-319-10605-2_52
10. Li, H.: Consensus set maximization with guaranteed global optimality for robust geometry estimation. In: ICCV (2009)
11. Zheng, Y., Sugimoto, S., Okutomi, M.: Deterministically maximizing feasible subsystem for robust model fitting with unit norm constraint. In: CVPR (2011)
12. Cho, M., Sun, J., Duchenne, O., Ponce, J.: Finding matches in a haystack: A max-pooling strategy for graph matching in the presence of outliers. In: CVPR (2013)
13. Collins, T., Mesejo, P., Bartoli, A.: An analysis of errors in graph-based keypoint matching and proposed solutions. In: Fleet, D., Pajdla, T., Schiele, B., Tuytelaars, T. (eds.) ECCV 2014. LNCS, vol. 8695, pp. 138–153. Springer, Cham (2014). https://doi.org/10.1007/978-3-319-10584-0_10
14. Kim, V.G., Lipman, Y., Funkhouser, T.: Blended intrinsic maps. ACM Trans. Graph. (TOG) **30** (2011). 79
15. Lähner, Z., et al.: Efficient deformable shape correspondence via kernel matching. In: 3DV (2017)
16. Bernard, F., Schmidt, F.R., Thunberg, J., Cremers, D.: A combinatorial solution to non-rigid 3D shape-to-image matching. In: CVPR (2017)
17. Pilet, J., Lepetit, V., Fua, P.: Fast non-rigid surface detection, registration and realistic augmentation. Int. J. Comput. Vis. **76**(2), 109–122 (2008)

18. Pizarro, D., Bartoli, A.: Feature-based deformable surface detection with self-occlusion reasoning. Int. J. Comput. Vis. **97**(1), 54–70 (2012)
19. Ngo, T.D., Östlund, J.O., Fua, P.: Template-based monocular 3D shape recovery using laplacian meshes. IEEE Trans. Pattern Anal. Mach. Intell. **38**(1), 172–187 (2016)
20. Aflalo, Y., Dubrovina, A., Kimmel, R.: Spectral generalized multi-dimensional scaling. Int. J. Comput. Vis. **118**(3), 380–392 (2016)
21. Vestner, M., Litman, R., Rodolá, E., Bronstein, A., Cremers, D.: Product manifold filter: non-rigid shape correspondence via kernel density estimation in the product space. In: CVPR (2017)
22. Litany, O., Remez, T., Rodola, E., Bronstein, A.M., Bronstein, M.M.: Deep functional maps: structured prediction for dense shape correspondence. In: ICCV (2017)
23. Salzmann, M., Fua, P.: Linear local models for monocular reconstruction of deformable surfaces. IEEE Trans. Pattern Anal. Mach. Intell. **33**(5), 931–944 (2011)
24. Bartoli, A., Gérard, Y., Chadebecq, F., Collins, T., Pizarro, D.: Shape-from-template. IEEE Trans. Pattern Anal. Mach. Intell. **37**(10), 2099–2118 (2015)
25. Salti, S., Tombari, F., Di Stefano, L.: SHOT: unique signatures of histograms for surface and texture description. Comput. Vis. Image Underst. **125**, 251–264 (2014)
26. Ovsjanikov, M., Mérigot, Q., Mémoli, F., Guibas, L.: One point isometric matching with the heat kernel. Comput. Graph. Forum (2010)
27. Le, H., Chin, T.J., Suter, D.: Conformal surface alignment with optimal mobius search. In: CVPR (2016)
28. Innmann, M., Zollhöfer, M., Nießner, M., Theobalt, C., Stamminger, M.: VolumeDeform: real-time volumetric non-rigid reconstruction. In: Leibe, B., Matas, J., Sebe, N., Welling, M. (eds.) ECCV 2016. LNCS, vol. 9912, pp. 362–379. Springer, Cham (2016). https://doi.org/10.1007/978-3-319-46484-8_22
29. Wandt, B., Ackermann, H., Rosenhahn, B.: 3D reconstruction of human motion from monocular image sequences. IEEE Trans. Pattern Anal. Mach. Intell. **38**(8), 1505–1516 (2016)
30. Chhatkuli, A., Pizarro, D., Bartoli, A., Collins, T.: A stable analytical framework for isometric shape-from-template by surface integration. IEEE Trans. Pattern Anal. Mach. Intell. **39**(5), 833–850 (2017)
31. Chin, T.J., Suter, D.: The Maximum Consensus Problem: Recent Algorithmic Advances, vol. 7. Morgan & Claypool Publishers (2017)
32. Chin, T.J., Cai, Z., Neumann, F.: Robust fitting in computer vision: easy or hard? arXiv preprint arXiv:1802.06464 (2018)
33. Brunet, F., Bartoli, A., Hartley, R.: Monocular template-based 3D surface reconstruction: convex inextensible and nonconvex isometric methods. Comput. Vis. Image Underst. **125**, 138–154 (2014)
34. Loper, M., Mahmood, N., Romero, J., Pons-Moll, G., Black, M.J.: SMPL: a skinned multi-person linear model. ACM Trans. Graphics (Proceedings SIGGRAPH Asia) **34**(6), 248:1–248:16 (2015)
35. White, R., Crane, K., Forsyth, D.: Capturing and animating occluded cloth. In: SIGGRAPH (2007)
36. McCormick, G.P.: Computability of global solutions to factorable nonconvex programs: Part i—convex underestimating problems. Mathe. Program. **10**(1), 147–175 (1976)

37. Kneip, L., Li, H., Seo, Y.: UPnP: an optimal $O(n)$ solution to the absolute pose problem with universal applicability. In: Fleet, D., Pajdla, T., Schiele, B., Tuytelaars, T. (eds.) ECCV 2014. LNCS, vol. 8689, pp. 127–142. Springer, Cham (2014). https://doi.org/10.1007/978-3-319-10590-1_9

38. Lepetit, V., Moreno-Noguer, F., Fua, P.: EP nP: an accurate O(n) solution to the PnP problem. Int. J. Comput. Vision **81**(2), 155–166 (2009)

39. Urban, S., Leitloff, J., Hinz, S.: MLPnP - a real-time maximum likelihood solution to the perspective-n-point problem. In: ISPRS Annals of Photogrammetry, Remote Sensing & Spatial Information Sciences, vol. 3, pp. 131–138 (2016)

40. Löfberg, J.: YALMIP: a toolbox for modeling and optimization in MATLAB. In: Proceedings of the CACSD Conference (2004)

41. ApS, M.: The MOSEK optimization toolbox for MATLAB manual. Version 7.1 (Revision 28) (2015)

42. Chhatkuli, A., Pizarro, D., Collins, T., Bartoli, A.: Inextensible non-rigid shape-from-motion by second-order cone programming. In: CVPR (2016)

43. Bogo, F., Romero, J., Loper, M., Black, M.J.: FAUST: dataset and evaluation for 3D mesh registration. In: Proceedings IEEE Conference on Computer Vision and Pattern Recognition (CVPR), Piscataway, NJ, USA. IEEE (2014)

44. Pishchulin, L., Wuhrer, S., Helten, T., Theobalt, C., Schiele, B.: Building statistical shape spaces for 3D human modeling. Pattern Recogn. (2017)

45. Tombari, F., Salti, S., Di Stefano, L.: Unique signatures of histograms for local surface description. In: Daniilidis, K., Maragos, P., Paragios, N. (eds.) ECCV 2010. LNCS, vol. 6313, pp. 356–369. Springer, Heidelberg (2010). https://doi.org/10.1007/978-3-642-15558-1_26

46. Sun, J., Ovsjanikov, M., Guibas, L.: A concise and provably informative multi-scale signature based on heat diffusion. Comput. Graph. Forum **28**, 1383–1392 (2009)

47. Pons-Moll, G., Taylor, J., Shotton, J., Hertzmann, A., Fitzgibbon, A.: Metric regression forests for correspondence estimation. Int. J. Comput. Vis., 1–13 (2015)

48. Varol, A., Salzmann, M., Fua, P., Urtasun, R.: A constrained latent variable model. In: CVPR (2012)

49. Chhatkuli, A., Pizarro, D., Bartoli, A.: Non-rigid shape-from-motion for isometric surfaces using infinitesimal planarity. In: BMVC (2014)

50. Butler, D.J., Wulff, J., Stanley, G.B., Black, M.J.: A naturalistic open source movie for optical flow evaluation. In: Fitzgibbon, A., Lazebnik, S., Perona, P., Sato, Y., Schmid, C. (eds.) ECCV 2012. LNCS, vol. 7577, pp. 611–625. Springer, Heidelberg (2012). https://doi.org/10.1007/978-3-642-33783-3_44

51. Scaramuzza, D.: 1-point-ransac structure from motion for vehicle-mounted cameras by exploiting non-holonomic constraints. Int. J. Comp. Vision **95**(1), 74–85 (2011)

52. Li, H.: A practical algorithm for L_∞ triangulation with outliers. In: CVPR (2007)

53. Fredriksson, J., Enqvist, O., Kahl, F.: Fast and reliable two-view translation estimation. In: CVPR (2014)

54. Pollefeys, M., Gool, L.V.: Stratified self-calibration with the modulus constraint. IEEE Trans. Pattern Anal. Mach. Intell. **21**(8), 707–724 (1999)

Relaxation-Free Deep Hashing
via Policy Gradient

Xin Yuan, Liangliang Ren, Jiwen Lu$^{(\boxtimes)}$, and Jie Zhou

Department of Automation, Tsinghua University, Beijing, China
{yuanx16,renll16}@mails.tsinghua.edu.cn,
{lujiwen,jzhou}@tsinghua.edu.cn

Abstract. In this paper, we propose a simple yet effective relaxation-free method to learn more effective binary codes via policy gradient for scalable image search. While a variety of deep hashing methods have been proposed in recent years, most of them are confronted by the dilemma to obtain optimal binary codes in a truly end-to-end manner with non-smooth sign activations. Unlike existing methods which usually employ a general relaxation framework to adapt to the gradient-based algorithms, our approach formulates the non-smooth part of the hashing network as sampling with a stochastic policy, so that the retrieval performance degradation caused by the relaxation can be avoided. Specifically, our method directly generates the binary codes and maximizes the expectation of rewards for similarity preservation, where the network can be trained directly via policy gradient. Hence, the differentiation challenge for discrete optimization can be naturally addressed, which leads to effective gradients and binary codes. Extensive experimental results on three benchmark datasets validate the effectiveness of the proposed method.

Keywords: Deep hashing · Relaxation-free · Policy gradient

1 Introduction

With the rapid development of information technology, large-scale and high-dimensional image data have been widespread on the Internet. A variety of efforts have been made to deal with the large scale similarity search, which is shown to be useful for many practical applications (*e.g.* computer vision [3,25,37], machine learning [9,27,39], and data mining [44]). The hashing technique [1,5, 6,16,32,34,35,38] is a popular approach of encoding high-dimensional data as low-dimensional binary codes, which benefits from its computation and storage efficiencies. Learning based hashing [10,11,20,23,29,45] which mines the data properties and the semantic affinities shows better performance than data-independent hashing methods [8].

© Springer Nature Switzerland AG 2018
V. Ferrari et al. (Eds.): ECCV 2018, LNCS 11208, pp. 141–157, 2018.
https://doi.org/10.1007/978-3-030-01225-0_9

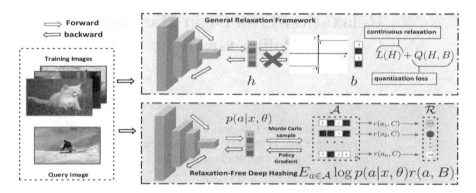

Fig. 1. Illustration of our approach. Unlike most existing learning-based hashing methods (on the top) which solve the differential difficulty by continuous relaxations, our method (on the bottom) modifies the non-smooth part as a stochastic policy, where samples for binary codes are encouraged to earn maximum rewards for similarity preservation. The network is trained via policy gradient directly

Most previous learning-based hashing methods encode data samples with shallow architectures [11,20,29], which map similar samples to close in the learned hamming space by learning a single projection matrix. While encouraging performance can be obtained, most of them suffer from the non-linear feature representation, scalability and non-linearity issues. Recently, deep learning based hashing methods [17,42] have been proposed to learn discriminative feature representations and nonlinear hash mappings, which have shown state-of-the-art performance on various scalable image retrieval datasets. However, the binary constraint of the non-smooth discrete optimization is a challenging problem in these methods, which prevents deep hashing to be learned in a truly end-to-end manner. By continuous relaxation, the non-smooth optimization can be transformed to a continuous one which can be solved by standard gradient methods, leading to the deviation from the optimal binary codes. While many methods have been proposed to control the quantization errors, they still cannot learn exactly binary hash codes in an optimization procedure. Hence this may lead to substantial performance loss due to the sub-optimal of the learned binary codes.

In this paper, we present a relaxation-free deep hashing method via policy gradient (PGDH) for scalable image search. Figure 1 shows the key idea of our proposed method. Specifically, we formulate the non-smooth part of the hashing network as sampling with a stochastic policy, so that the relaxation procedure used in most previous hashing methods can be removed. We directly generate binary codes and maximize the expectation of rewards for similarity preservation, which leads to more effective gradient and binary hash codes and the differentiation issue for discrete optimization can be naturally addressed. Extensive evaluations on three benchmark datasets show that our method significantly improves the state-of-the-arts.

2   Related Work

A variety of learning-based hashing methods have been proposed in recent years, which can be mainly classified into unsupervised hashing and supervised hashing.

Unsupervised hashing methods learn binary codes by exploiting data properties such as distributions and manifold structures. For example, spectral hashing (SH) [40] formulated hashing learning as a graph partitioning problem and approximately solved the problem with the assumption of the uniform data distribution. Anchor graph hashing (AGH) [26] approximated neighborhoods by using a tractable graph based method. Deep hashing (DH) [21] employed a multi-layer neural network to learn hash functions to preserve the nonlinear relationship of samples. Iterative quantization (ITQ) [9] minimized quantization loss by seeking a rotation matrix in an iterative manner. Manifold hashing (MH) [31] learned binary embeddings from cluster centers and mapped data into a low-dimension manifold. Discrete graph hashing (DGH) [24] presented a tractable alternating optimization method for similarity preservation in the discrete code space.

Supervised hashing methods learn binary codes by exploiting the label information of samples, which have shown superior performance than unsupervised approaches. For example, kernelized supervised hashing (KSH) [25] utilized the equivalence between code inner products and Hamming distances, which aims to keep the inner product of hash codes consistent with the pairwise supervision. Fast supervised hashing [19] employed boosted decision trees to iteratively perform alternative optimization on a subset of binary codes. Supervised discrete hashing (SDH) [30] formulated the discrete optimization objective by introducing an auxiliary variable and used a kernel based hashing function to learn binary codes. The supervised extension of deep hashing [21] learned multi-layer functions by considering the label information of samples. Recent advances in deep learning [12,15,33] show that deep convolutional networks learn robust and powerful feature representations for complex data, which has gained great successes in many computer vision applications. Hence, it is natural to leverage deep learning to obtain compact binary codes. For example, CNNH [42] adopted a two-stage strategy in which the first stage learned hash codes and the second stage learned a deep network based hash function to obtain the codes. DNNH [17] improved the two-stage CNNH with a simultaneous feature learning and hash coding pipeline so that representations and hash codes can be optimized in a joint learning procedure. DSH [22] improved DNNH by adding a max-margin loss and a quantization loss which jointly preserved pairwise similarity and controlled the quantization error. HashNet [2] gradually approximated the non-smooth sign activation with a smoothed activation by a continuation method.

3   Approach

3.1   Overview of General Relaxation Framework

Given a training set of N points (images) $\boldsymbol{X} = \{\boldsymbol{x}_i\}_{i=1}^{N}$, each sample is represented by either a D-dimensional feature vector or raw pixels. A set of pairwise labels $\boldsymbol{S} = \{s_{ij}\}$ is provided, where $s_{ij} = 1$ if $\boldsymbol{x}_i$ and $\boldsymbol{x}_j$ are similar while $s_{ij} = -1$

if x_i and x_j are dissimilar. For supervised hashing, $\mathcal{S}$ can be constructed from semantic labels of data points or the relevance feedback from click-through data. We aim to learn a mapping function $f : x \mapsto b \in \{-1, 1\}^K$ from the input space to the Hamming space $\{-1, 1\}^K$, where each data point x is encoded as a compact K-bit binary hash code. The binary codes $B = \{b_i\}_{i=1}^N$ should preserve some notion of similarity in $\mathcal{S}$. Hence, the hashing learning problem can be generally formulated as follows:

$$\min_{f,B} \mathcal{L}(B), \qquad s.t. \qquad B \in \{-1, 1\}^{n \times K} \qquad (1)$$

where $\mathcal{L}$ is the predefined loss function with similarity preservation.

To directly optimize the problem in Eq. (1) with the discrete constrain on B, we need to adopt the sign function $b = \text{sgn}(h)$ as the activation function to convert the continuous representation h to the binary hash code b. However, the sign function is non-differentiable at zero and with zero gradient for all nonzero inputs, which makes standard back-propagation infeasible. As a result, it is inappropriate to directly solve the discrete optimization problem by standard gradient-based methods. Most existing hashing methods relax the intractable optimization problem mainly in two ways: (1) continuous relaxation by introducing a quantization function, and (2) approximating the sign function with sigmoid or tanh relaxation [2,17]. For the first strategy, these methods derive an optimization problem $\mathcal{L}(H)$ from the hashing objective $\mathcal{L}(B)$ by continuous relaxation and control the quantization loss between B and H, which is denoted as $\mathcal{Q}(B, H)$. The objective of these methods can be usually reformulated as:

$$\min_{f,H,B} \mathcal{L}(\cdot) + \mathcal{Q}(B, H), \qquad s.t. \qquad B \in \{-1, 1\}^{n \times K} \qquad (2)$$

where $\mathcal{L}(\cdot)$ indicates $\mathcal{L}(H)$ for continuous optimization [18] or $\mathcal{L}(B)$ for discrete optimization [22]. However, since $\mathcal{Q}(B, H)$ is NP-complete and cannot be minimized to zero, there still exists a gap between B and H. Thus a local minimum is usually obtained by such relaxation optimization problems.

For the second strategy, the non-smooth sign function is approximated by continuation method, which leads to a convergence to the original hash learning objective. However, to obtain feasible gradients, such relaxation inevitably becomes more non-smooth and slows down or suppresses the convergence, which makes it difficult to optimize the learning model.

3.2   Relaxation-Free Deep Hashing via Policy Gradient

In this section, we propose a new architecture for deep learning to hash with policy gradient inspired by the REINFORCE algorithm [41]. The architecture of our proposed framework contains: (1) a convolutional network (CNN) for learning deep representations of images, and (2) a fully-connected policy layer with a sigmoid activation function for transforming each feature representation into a K-dimensional vector, where each dimension represents the probability of taking the binary action. The proposed end-to-end learning framework can be viewed as an *agent* that interacts with an external *environment* (images in our case). The aim of the agent is to get maximum possible similarity preservation with difference minimization, which can be considered as the reward to the agent.

We define a policy as $\boldsymbol{\pi}(\boldsymbol{x}_i, \theta) = \{\pi_{\boldsymbol{x}_i, \theta}^{(k)}\}_{k=1:K}$, which is parametrized by network parameter θ with i-th input $\boldsymbol{x}_i$. The policy generates a sequence of actions $\boldsymbol{a}_i = \{a_{i,k}\}_{k=1:K} \sim P_\theta(\boldsymbol{x}_i)$, where $a_{i,k} = \{0, 1\}$ represents a binary action value. $\pi_{\boldsymbol{x}_i, \theta}^{(k)}$ only outputs the probability of the hash code $+1$, which is different from most existing reinforcement learning methods which predict the probability distribution for each possible action (e.g. softmax probability). Hence, the probability distribution in our method can be formulated as follows:

$$p(a_{i,k}) = \begin{cases} \pi_{\boldsymbol{x}_i, \theta}^{(k)}, & \text{if } a_{i,k} = 1 \\ 1 - \pi_{\boldsymbol{x}_i, \theta}^{(k)}, & \text{if } a_{i,k} = 0 \end{cases} \tag{3}$$

Having generated *action* $\boldsymbol{a}_i$, the agent observes a *reward* $r(\boldsymbol{a}_i)$ that is related to the similarity preservation. The reward is computed by an evaluation metric by comparing the similarity relationship in the Hamming space with ground-truth similarity function $\mathcal{S}$.

We adopt a minibatch-based strategy for learning and sample a minibatch of points from the whole training set in each iteration. For each mini-batch with m training samples, we aim to utilize the global information by maximizing the preserved information between each binary code $\boldsymbol{b}_i = 2 * (\boldsymbol{a}_i - 0.5)$ and the codebook $C = \{\hat{\boldsymbol{b}}_j\}_{j=1}^n$ of all the training points in the Hamming space. For a pair of binary codes $\boldsymbol{b}_i$ and $\hat{\boldsymbol{b}}_j$, we represent the Hamming distance $dist_H(\cdot, \cdot)$ by inner product $\langle \cdot, \cdot \rangle$ as: $dist_H(\boldsymbol{b}_i, \hat{\boldsymbol{b}}_j) = \frac{1}{2}(K - \langle \boldsymbol{b}_i, \hat{\boldsymbol{b}}_j \rangle)$. The weighted reward of learning to effective hash codes can be written as follows:

$$r(\boldsymbol{a}_i) = -\frac{1}{2} \sum_{j=1}^n \hat{s}_{ij}(K - \boldsymbol{b}_i^T \hat{\boldsymbol{b}}_j)$$

$$s.t. \quad \boldsymbol{b}_i, \hat{\boldsymbol{b}}_j \in \{-1, +1\}^K \tag{4}$$

where

$$\hat{s}_{ij} = \begin{cases} \beta, & \text{if } s_{ij} = 1 \\ \beta - 1, & \text{otherwise} \end{cases} \tag{5}$$

is the weighted similarity measurement to compensate the imbalance of positive and negative pairs. The parameter β allows different weights on the positive and negative pairs. Note that the codebook C is updated slower than the learning model θ during the training process, which will be discussed later.

The goal of training is to minimize the negative expected reward of the minibatch:

$$\mathcal{L}(\theta) = -\sum_i \mathbb{E}_{\boldsymbol{a}_i \sim P_\theta(\boldsymbol{x}_i)}[r(\boldsymbol{a}_i)] \tag{6}$$

Note that in our framework the description of the environment consists of images, which is not determined by the previous states or actions. Strictly speaking, this formulation is not a full reinforcement learning framework where a state transition is clearly defined. Here we only focus on the optimization under the guidance of the rewards related to similarity preservation and improving performance of hash learning.

Policy Gradient with REINFORCE: In our proposed hash learning method, the expected reward r is non-differentiable. In order to compute $\nabla L(\theta)$ directly, we use the REINFORCE algorithm, which computes the expected gradient of the non-differentiable reward function as follows:

$$\nabla_\theta \mathcal{L}(\theta) = -\sum_i \mathbb{E}_{a_i \in \mathcal{A}_i}[r(a_i)\nabla_\theta \log(P_\theta(a_i|x_i))] \tag{7}$$

where $\mathcal{A}_i$ is the set of all possible actions for i-th input data in the minibatch. The expected gradient can be approximated using Monte Carlo sample. We represent a T-samples Monte Carlo on a_i as:

$$\mathcal{A}_i = \{a_i^1, a_i^2, ..., a_i^T\} = MC^{P_\theta(a_i|x_i)}(T) \tag{8}$$

For training examples in a minibatch, the expected policy gradient can be computed as:

$$\nabla_\theta \mathcal{L}(\theta) \approx -\frac{1}{T}\sum_i \sum_t [r(a_i^t)\nabla_\theta \log(P_\theta(a_i^t|x_i))] \tag{9}$$

where the log probability in Eq. (9) can be calculated by the binary cross entropy over the Bernoulli distribution in Eq. (3).

REINFORCE with a Baseline: The above gradient estimator is simple but suffers from high variance because of the difficulty of credit assignment. To reduce the variance of the gradient estimation, we again approximate the expected gradient with widely used Baseline method in policy gradient. For each training minibatch:

$$\nabla_\theta \mathcal{L}(\theta) \approx -\frac{1}{T}\sum_i \sum_t [(r(a_i^t) - r')\nabla_\theta \log(P_\theta(a_i^t|x_i))] \tag{10}$$

where the baseline r' should be the value which is independent on the action. Adding such a baseline term will not change the expectation of the gradient [1] but can reduce the variance of the gradient estimation. Here we choose average of all

---

[1] $\sum_i \mathbb{E}_{a_i \in \mathcal{A}_i}[r'\nabla_\theta \log(P_\theta(a_i^t|x_i))] = \sum_i r'\nabla_\theta \sum_{a_i} P_\theta(a_i^t|x_i) = \sum_i r'\nabla_\theta 1 = 0.$

Algorithm 1. PGDH

Input: Training set: $\boldsymbol{X} = \{\boldsymbol{x}_i\}_{i=1}^n$, pairwise labels: $\mathcal{S} = \{s_{ij}\}$ and codebook update interval $R > 1$.
Output: Learning model θ and codebook $\boldsymbol{C}$
1: Initialize p_θ and $\boldsymbol{C}$;
2: **for** $iter = 1, 2, \ldots, M$ **do**
3:     Sample random minibatch from $\boldsymbol{X}$;
4:     Compute the action probability by feeding minibatch to the model;
5:     Compute the rewards for MC samples of the minibatch according to Eq. (4)
6:     Compute policy gradient according to Eq. (10);
7:     Update the model θ according to Eq. (11);
8:     **if** iter $\% R = 0$ **then**
9:         Update codebook $\boldsymbol{C}$;
10:    **end if**
11: **end for**
12: **return** model θ and codebook $\boldsymbol{C}$;

---

rewards in each mini-batch as the baseline. The binary codes that preserve more similarity information with the codebook $\boldsymbol{C}$ than the baseline will get positive rewards, while those that with less similarity information will be penalized by negative rewards. We then update the network's parameters as:

$$\theta \leftarrow \theta - \lambda \nabla_\theta \mathcal{L}(\theta) \tag{11}$$

where λ denotes the learning rate.

During the learning process, the codebook $\boldsymbol{C}$ is updated slower than the model for the training stability and performance improvement. We can formulate the codebook update as:

$$\hat{\boldsymbol{b}}_j = 2 * (\hat{\boldsymbol{a}}_j - 0.5), \hat{\boldsymbol{a}}_i \sim P(\boldsymbol{x}_j | \theta^-) \tag{12}$$

This strategy is motived by [28] which introduces a target network θ^- with slower updating rate than the online network θ to gain more stable performance.

In summary, **Algorithm 1** shows full details of the proposed method.

3.3 Out-of-Sample Extensions

Having completed the learning procedure, we only generate the optimized hash codes for the training points by maximizing the expectation of rewards. How to perform out-of-sample extensions to generate hash codes for the points which are not in the training dataset remains unclear. To address this, we perform the out-of-sample extensions in two ways: Deterministic and Stochastic.

Deterministic Generation: Denote a data point which is not in the training dataset as x_q, we feed it to our proposed architecture and get a vector with K values $\pi_{x_q,\theta}$, each represents the probability of the binary action 1 (sigmoid activation ranges from 0 to 1). We can directly obtain the binary codes in the deterministic way:

$$b_q^k = \begin{cases} +1, & \text{if } \pi_{x_q,\theta}^{(k)} > 0.5 \\ -1, & \text{otherwise} \end{cases} \tag{13}$$

Stochastic Generation: Having obtained the probability vector, we can write the stochastic code generation function as:

$$b_q^k = \begin{cases} +1, & \text{with probability} \quad \pi_{x_q,\theta}^{(k)} \\ -1, & \text{with probability} \quad 1 - \pi_{x_q,\theta}^{(k)} \end{cases} \tag{14}$$

The stochastic way seems more appealing than the deterministic one but in practice the performance differs slightly after the learning model converges. In our experiments, we report the performance directly using deterministic generation and we also conduct investigation on the two ways to generate hash codes.

4   Experiments

4.1   Datasets and Experimental Settings

We conduct extensive empirical evaluation on three public widely used benchmark datasets: CIFAR-10 [14], NUS-WIDE [43] and ImageNet [4]. **CIFAR10** contains 60,000 manually single-labeled color images belonging to 10 classes (6000 images per class). Following the same setting in [36], we construct the query set by randomly sampling 1,000 images with 100 images per category and use the remaining 59,000 images to form the database. Then we uniformly select 500 images per class to form the training set from the database. **NUS-WIDE**[2] is a public Web image dataset of 269,648 images collected from Flickr. This is a multi-label dataset, namely, each image is associated with one or multiple labels from a given 81 concepts. We follow the settings in [42,46] and use the subset of 195,834 images that are associated with the 21 most frequent concepts, where each concept consists of at least 5,000 images. We randomly sample 2,100 images with 100 images per category to form the test set and use the remaining images as the database. We uniformly sample 500 images per category out of the database to form a training set. **ImageNet** is a large dataset for visual recognition which contains over 1.2M images in the training set and 50K images in the validation

---

[2] http://lms.comp.nus.edu.sg/research/NUS-WIDE.htm.

set covering 1,000 categories. Following the same setting in [2], we randomly select 100 categories, use all the images of these categories in the training set as the database and all the images in the validation set as the queries. To train hashing methods, we randomly select 100 images per category from the database as the training points.

Following the same evaluation protocol as previous work [22], the similarity information, which is constructed from image labels, is used for ground truth evaluation and constructing the pairwise similarity matrix for training. For both single and multiple labeled dataset, we define the ground truth semantic neighbors as images sharing at least one label. Note that by constructing the training data in this way, all three datasets exhibit the data imbalance problem because of the imbalance of positive and negative pairs, which can be used to evaluate the effects of our weighted rewards controlled by β.

We evaluate the retrieval performance of generated binary codes with the following metrics: mean average precision (MAP), precision-recall (P-R) curve, precision at top retrieved samples (P@N), and Hamming lookup precision within a Hamming radius $r = 2$ (HLP@2). We choose to evaluate the performance over binary codes with lengths of 16, 32, 48, and 64 bits. Note that for the ImageNet dataset we calculate the MAP@1000 as each category has only 1,300 images, and for NUS-WIDE we adopt MAP@5000.

In our implementation of PGDH, we utilize the AlexNet network structure and implement it in the Pytorch framework. We initialize first seven layers of PGDH by copying the parameters of convolutional layers $conv1 - conv5$ and fully-connected layers $fc6 - fc7$ in the pre-trained model on ImageNet and fine-tuned these layers. We also initialize the final policy layer with the Guassian distribution and train this layer from scratch. In the training phase, we use Adam [13] with the initial learning rate as 0.005 and set the batch size as 128. For parameter tuning, we evenly split the training set into ten parts to cross validate the parameters. We fix the Monte Carlo samples T as 10 in each iteration and codebook update interval R as 5.

4.2   Results and Analysis

Comparison with the State-of-the-Arts: We compare the proposed PGDH with twelve state-of-the-art hashing methods, including unsupervised methods: LSH [8], SH [40], ITQ [9], supervised methods: KSH [25], CCA-ITQ [9], FastH [19], SDH [30], and supervised deep methods: CNNH [42], DNNH [17], DPSH [18], DSH [22], HashNet [2]. We report their results by running the source codes provided by their respective authors to train the models by ourselves, except for DNNH due to the inaccessibility of the source code. For conventional hashing methods, we use $DeCAF_7$ [7] features as input. For deep hashing methods, we directly use raw images as input and resize images to fit the adopted network. Note that we adopt the AlexNet architecture for all deep hashing for fair comparison.

Table 1. The comparison of the retrieval performance among all compared hashing methods in terms of mean average precision (MAP %) on the three image datasets for different number of bits of 16, 32, 48, and 64

Methods	CIFAR-10 (%)				NUS-WIDE (%)				ImageNet (%)			
	16	32	48	64	16	32	48	64	16	32	48	64
LSH [8]	12.9	15.2	16.9	17.8	40.3	49.2	49.3	55.1	10.1	23.5	30.1	34.9
SH [40]	12.2	13.5	12.1	12.6	47.9	49.1	49.8	51.5	20.8	32.7	39.5	42.0
ITQ [9]	21.3	23.4	23.8	25.3	56.7	60.3	62.2	62.6	32.5	46.2	51.3	55.6
CCA-ITQ [9]	31.4	36.1	36.6	37.9	50.9	54.4	56.8	67.6	26.6	43.6	54.8	58.0
KSH [25]	35.6	40.8	53.1	44.1	40.6	40.8	38.7	39.8	16.0	28.8	34.2	39.4
FastH [19]	45.3	46.1	48.7	50.3	51.9	61.0	64.7	65.2	22.8	44.7	51.7	55.6
SDH [30]	40.2	42.0	44.9	45.6	53.4	61.8	63.1	64.5	29.9	45.1	54.9	59.3
CNNH [42]	48.8	51.2	53.4	53.6	61.2	62.3	62.1	63.7	28.8	44.7	52.8	55.6
DNNH [17]	55.5	55.8	58.1	62.3	68.1	71.3	71.8	72.0	29.7	46.3	54.0	56.6
DPSH [18]	64.6	66.1	67.7	68.6	71.5	72.6	73.8	75.3	32.6	54.6	61.7	65.4
DSH [22]	68.9	69.1	70.3	71.6	71.8	72.3	74.2	75.6	34.8	55.0	62.9	66.5
HashNet [2]	70.3	71.1	71.6	73.9	73.3	75.2	76.2	77.6	50.6	62.9	66.3	68.4
PGDH	**73.6**	**74.1**	**74.7**	**76.2**	**76.1**	**78.0**	**78.6**	**79.2**	**51.8**	**65.3**	**70.7**	**71.6**

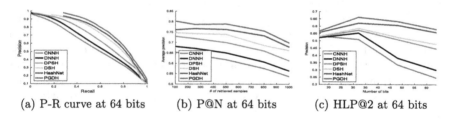

(a) P-R curve at 64 bits   (b) P@N at 64 bits   (c) HLP@2 at 64 bits

Fig. 2. The experimental results of PGDH and comparison methods on the CIFAR-10 dataset under three evaluation metrics

Table 1 shows the overall retrieval performance of different hashing methods in terms of MAP at different code lengths. We can observe that our proposed PGDH outperforms all compared methods. Compared with the best competitor in deep learning based hashing methods, PGDH consistently outperforms by around 3%. The significant performance improvement attributes to the effective binary codes obtained via policy gradient instead of the general relaxation framework. Note that our PGDH also utilizes the weighted rewards function to attack the data imbalance problem which is ignored by many existing methods. Also, we see that the recently proposed HashNet boosts the performance of other deep learning methods (e.g. DSH and DPSH) because HashNet tackles the optimization difficulty by continuation method and the data imbalance problem by weighted maximum likelihood. Compared with the best conventional hashing methods, PGDH also boosts the performance by a large improvement. Note that the deep hashing methods sustainably outperform the conventional hash learning methods on both datasets by a large margin even though the conventional ones utilize the CNN features, which suggests the end-to-end learning scheme is advantageous.

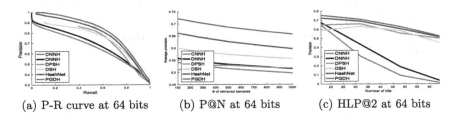

(a) P-R curve at 64 bits   (b) P@N at 64 bits   (c) HLP@2 at 64 bits

Fig. 3. The experimental results of PGDH and comparison methods on the NUSWIDE dataset under three evaluation metrics

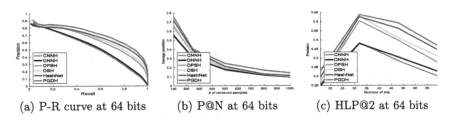

(a) P-R curve at 64 bits   (b) P@N at 64 bits   (c) HLP@2 at 64 bits

Fig. 4. The experimental results of PGDH and comparison methods on the ImageNet dataset under three evaluation metrics

The performance on CIFAR-10, NUS-WIDE and ImageNet datasets in terms of Precision-Recall (PR) curves for 64-bit binary codes are shown in Figs. 2(a), 3(a) and 4(a). Here we only show the results in terms of PR curves on the deep learning based hashing methods to evaluate the effectiveness of the hashing learning. The results show that PGDH outperforms all the compared methods by large margins. PGDH achieves much higher precision at the same recall level than compared methods which suggests that effective hash codes are learnt via policy gradient. This attribute is appreciated in practical precision-first image retrieval system where high probability of finding true neighbors is more important.

The performance on the three datasets in terms of the average precision with respect to different numbers of top retrieved results(P@N) of deep learning methods for 64-bit binary codes are shown in Figs. 2(b), 3(b) and 4(b). Note that the maximum of N is set to 1,000 here for the consistency on all the three datasets. From the result figures, we can see that PGDH consistently provides superior precision than the compared hashing methods for the same amount of retrieved samples. This stands for that more semantic neighbors are retrieved, which is desirable in practical use.

The performance in terms of Hamming lookup precision within Hamming radius 2 (HLP@2) for deep learning based hashing methods at different bit lengths on three datasets are shown in Figs. 2(c), 3(c) and 4(c). This evaluation metric measures the precision of the retrieved results falling into the buckets within the Hamming radius 2. The results validate the compactness of the binary codes learnt by PGDH. We also observe that the best performance is achieved at a moderate length of binary codes. This is because that longer binary code makes the data distribution in Hamming space sparse and fewer samples fall within the set Hamming ball.

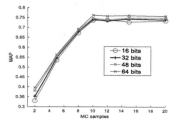

Fig. 5. Effects of the number of Monte Carlo samples in terms of MAP with 16, 32, 48 and 64-bit binary codes on the CIFAR-10 dataset

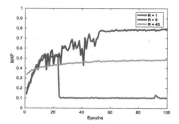

Fig. 6. Effects of the frequency of codebook update by setting R as 1, 5 and 40 in terms of MAP with 64-bit binary codes on CIFAR-10 (Color figure online)

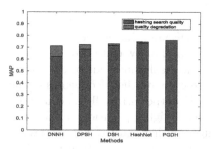

Fig. 7. Loss of search quality in MAP (by red bars) due to conversion from continuous features to 64-bit binary codes on the CIFAR-10 dataset (Color figure online)

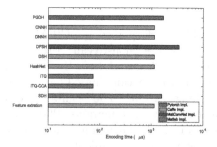

Fig. 8. Time cost to encode one newcoming image of different hashing methods on the CIFAR-10 dataset with 64-bit binary codes

Investigation on Samples: We study the effects of the number of Monte Carlo samples in the optimization procedure by changing the parameter T in PGDH. Note that it costs more time to train a minibatch of data as T increases. We report the performance results of different T values selected from $\{2, 5, 8, 10, 12, 15, 20\}$ in Fig. 5 in terms of MAP on the CIFAR-10 dataset. The results show that when T is small, the search quality degrades because efficient gradients cannot be obtained without enough MC samples. We also observe that the performance exhibits saturation when we keep enlarging T. For a tradeoff of the search quality and the training efficiency, we choose to fix T as 10 during training.

Investigation on Codebook Update: We study the effects of the frequency of codebook update during training by changing the interval parameter R in PGDH. Figure 6 shows MAP performance evolution of the first 60 epochs during training with respect to R on the CIFAR-10 dataset with length of binary codes set as 64 bits. The network is hard to optimize and MAP exhibits a very low value during training (red curve) when we update the codebook C every iteration ($R = 1$). When we update the codebook C once a epoch ($R = 40$), the network can be trained steadily but MAP raises up very slowly (green curve). We also observe that the best performance (blue curve) is achieved at a moderate value of $R = 5$.

Table 2. MAP (%) for different code generation schemes related to different training epochs on the CIFAR-10 dataset with 64-bit binary codes

Training Epochs	1	5	10	40	50	60	70	80	90	100
Deterministic	24.51	47.18	66.56	72.13	74.73	74.78	74.77	75.17	75.50	75.54
Stochastic	10.10	18.18	58.32	73.54	74.18	74.93	75.12	75.18	74.90	75.21

Table 3. MAP (%) for different β on the three datasets with 64-bits binary codes

β	0.1	0.2	0.3	0.4	0.5	0.6	0.7	0.8	0.9
CIFAR-10	10.12	18.38	20.08	49.43	73.65	70.32	**75.23**	75.12	34.12
NUS-WIDE	31.32	43.65	54.13	66.12	77.95	76.12	77.32	**79.18**	78.80
ImageNet	1.14	1.14	33.12	43.64	69.65	68.69	**70.32**	70.11	70.03

Deterministic vs. Stochastic: We investigate the deterministic and stochastic generation during the testing phase. Table 2 shows the MAP performance of the 64-bit codes generated by these two ways at different epochs on the CIFAR-10 dataset. We can observe that the performance differs a lot during the first decades of epochs. This is because that the stochastic way generates binary codes by sampling in an uncertain manner, which will influence results if the model doesn't converge. We also observe that the MAP differs slightly when the learning model converges as the epochs increase. Although the stochastic way seems more appealing in PGDH, it will take more time for code generation during testing because of the sampling operation in practice.

Investigation on Weighted Rewards: We investigate the effect of weighted rewards on dealing with the imbalance problem. The weight is controlled by the parameter β in Eq. (5). The algorithm merely utilizes the positive pairs to learn hash codes when we set β to a large value. Setting β close to 0, the algorithm merely utilizes the negative pairs to learn hash codes. With the definition of semantic similarity and the datasets, the imbalance problem substantially deteriorates the performance of hashing methods. Table 3 shows the variation of performance in terms of MAP with respect to β on three datasets with the length of binary codes set as 64 bits. The retrieval performance ascends when setting $\beta > 0.5$, which shows the effect of introducing weighted rewards in our method.

Comparison of Search Quality Degradation: A crucial superiority of PGDH over the comparison methods lies in that PGDH directly learns effective compact binary codes via policy gradient, while comparison methods relax the discrete objective to adopt to the gradient-based algorithm. Intuitively, searching with binary codes using Hamming distance is evidently inferior to searching with continuous features using Euclidean distance, due to substantial information loss by relaxation. The search quality loss in terms of MAP due to binarization is shown in Fig. 7. Note that since PGDH directly outputs the binary codes, we only show the absolute MAP value for PGDH. From the result figure, we see that DNNH (9 % degradation), DPSH (3.85 % degradation), DSH (1.56 % degradation) and HashNet (0.9 % degradation) suffer from MAP loss while our PGDH can even break the bottleneck of the search quality with continuous features obtained by the compared methods. In other words, PGDH can learn more effective binary codes which are more accurate than all other methods.

Comparison of Encoding Time: The time to generate the binary code for a new-coming sample is an important factor to evaluate retrieval system in practical use. In this part, we compare the encoding time of our PGDH with (1) five deep learning based hashing methods, CNNH, DNNH, DPSH, DSH and HashNet, and (2) three conventional hashing methods, ITQ, ITQ-CCA, SDH, including the unsupervised and supervised hashing with linear and nonlinear hashing functions. For deep hashing methods, which directly take the raw images as input, we report the encoding time on GPUs. For conventional hashing methods, we take into consideration both the time cost for deep feature extraction on GPUs and the time cost for hashing encoding on CPUs. Figure 8 shows the comparison of the encoding time of involved hashing methods in logarithmic scale on the CIFAR-10 dataset with 64-bit binary codes. Our computing platform is equipped with a 4.0 GHz Intel CPU, 32 GB RAM, and NVIDIA GTX 1080Ti. Although HashNet and DSH are faster than our PGDH because of the higher computational efficiency in Caffe implementation, we can easily convert the trained Pytorch model into a Caffe version during the test phase to realize the encoding acceleration while keeping the retrieval performance.

5 Conclusion

In this paper, we have proposed a new relaxation-free framework for deep hashing via policy gradient. We modified the non-smooth part of the hashing network for sampling as a stochastic policy to address the back-propagation difficulty. We directly generated binary codes through the network and maximized the expectation of the rewards related to the similarity preservation. We trained the proposed network via policy gradient, which naturally avoids the differentiation difficulty for discrete optimization, leading to more effective binary codes. We have conducted extensive experiments to validate the superiority of the proposed PGDH through comparison with the state-of-the-art hashing methods.

Acknowledgements. This work was supported in part by the National Key Research and Development Program of China under Grant 2017YFA0700802, in part by the National Natural Science Foundation of China under Grant 61672306, Grant U1713214, Grant 61572271, and in part by the Shenzhen Fundamental Research Fund (Subject Arrangement) under Grant JCYJ20170412170602564.

References

1. Çakir, F., He, K., Bargal, S.A., Sclaroff, S.: MIHash: online hashing with mutual information. In: ICCV, pp. 437–445 (2017). https://doi.org/10.1109/ICCV.2017. 55

2. Cao, Z., Long, M., Wang, J., Yu, P.S.: HashNet: deep learning to hash by continuation. In: ICCV, pp. 5609–5618 (2017). https://doi.org/10.1109/ICCV.2017. 598

3. Dean, T.L., Ruzon, M.A., Segal, M., Shlens, J., Vijayanarasimhan, S., Yagnik, J.: Fast, accurate detection of 100, 000 object classes on a single machine. In: CVPR, pp. 1814–1821 (2013). https://doi.org/10.1109/CVPR.2013.237

4. Deng, J., Dong, W., Socher, R., Li, L., Li, K., Li, F.: ImageNet: a large-scale hierarchical image database. In: CVPR, pp. 248–255 (2009). https://doi.org/10. 1109/CVPRW.2009.5206848

5. Do, T.-T., Doan, A.-D., Cheung, N.-M.: Learning to hash with binary deep neural network. In: Leibe, B., Matas, J., Sebe, N., Welling, M. (eds.) ECCV 2016. LNCS, vol. 9909, pp. 219–234. Springer, Cham (2016). https://doi.org/10.1007/978-3-319-46454-1_14

6. Do, T., Tan, D.L., Pham, T.T., Cheung, N.: Simultaneous feature aggregating and hashing for large-scale image search. In: CVPR, pp. 4217–4226 (2017). http://doi. ieeecomputersociety.org/10.1109/CVPR.2017.449

7. Donahue, J., et al.: DeCAF: a deep convolutional activation feature for generic visual recognition. In: ICML, pp. 647–655 (2014)
8. Gionis, A., Indyk, P., Motwani, R.: Similarity search in high dimensions via hashing. In: VLDB, pp. 518–529 (1999)
9. Gong, Y., Lazebnik, S., Gordo, A., Perronnin, F.: Iterative quantization: a procrustean approach to learning binary codes for large-scale image retrieval. TPAMI **35**(12), 2916–2929 (2013). https://doi.org/10.1109/TPAMI.2012.193
10. Gui, L., Wang, Y., Hebert, M.: Few-shot hash learning for image retrieval. In: ICCVW, pp. 1228–1237 (2017). http://doi.ieeecomputersociety.org/10.1109/ICCVW.2017.148
11. He, K., Wen, F., Sun, J.: K-means hashing: an affinity-preserving quantization method for learning binary compact codes. In: CVPR, pp. 2938–2945 (2013). https://doi.org/10.1109/CVPR.2013.378
12. He, K., Zhang, X., Ren, S., Sun, J.: Deep residual learning for image recognition. In: CVPR (2016). https://doi.org/10.1109/CVPR.2016.90
13. Kingma, D.P., Ba, J.: Adam: a method for stochastic optimization. CoRR abs/1412.6980 (2014). http://arxiv.org/abs/1412.6980
14. Krizhevsky, A., Hinton, G.: Learning multiple layers of features from tiny images. Technical report (2009)
15. Krizhevsky, A., Sutskever, I., Hinton, G.E.: Imagenet classification with deep convolutional neural networks. In: NIPS, pp. 1106–1114 (2012). http://papers.nips.cc/paper/4824-imagenet-classification-with-deep-convolutional-neural-networks
16. Kulis, B., Jain, P., Grauman, K.: Fast similarity search for learned metrics. TPAMI **31**(12), 2143–2157 (2009). https://doi.org/10.1109/TPAMI.2009.151
17. Lai, H., Pan, Y., Liu, Y., Yan, S.: Simultaneous feature learning and hash coding with deep neural networks. In: CVPR, pp. 3270–3278 (2015). https://doi.org/10.1109/CVPR.2015.7298947
18. Li, W., Wang, S., Kang, W.: Feature learning based deep supervised hashing with pairwise labels. In: IJCAI, pp. 1711–1717 (2016). http://www.ijcai.org/Abstract/16/245
19. Lin, G., Shen, C., Shi, Q., van den Hengel, A., Suter, D.: Fast supervised hashing with decision trees for high-dimensional data. In: CVPR, pp. 1971–1978 (2014). https://doi.org/10.1109/CVPR.2014.253
20. Lin, Z., Ding, G., Hu, M., Wang, J.: Semantics-preserving hashing for cross-view retrieval. In: CVPR, pp. 3864–3872 (2015). https://doi.org/10.1109/CVPR.2015.7299011
21. Liong, V.E., Lu, J., Wang, G., Moulin, P., Zhou, J.: Deep hashing for compact binary codes learning. In: CVPR, pp. 2475–2483 (2015). https://doi.org/10.1109/CVPR.2015.7298862
22. Liu, H., Wang, R., Shan, S., Chen, X.: Deep supervised hashing for fast image retrieval. In: CVPR, June 2016
23. Liu, H., Ji, R., Wu, Y., Huang, F., Zhang, B.: Cross-modality binary code learning via fusion similarity hashing. In: CVPR, pp. 6345–6353 (2017). https://doi.org/10.1109/CVPR.2017.672
24. Liu, W., Mu, C., Kumar, S., Chang, S.: Discrete graph hashing. In: NIPS, pp. 3419–3427 (2014)
25. Liu, W., Wang, J., Ji, R., Jiang, Y., Chang, S.: Supervised hashing with kernels. In: CVPR, pp. 2074–2081 (2012). https://doi.org/10.1109/CVPR.2012.6247912
26. Liu, W., Wang, J., Kumar, S., Chang, S.: Hashing with graphs. In: ICML (2011)
27. Liu, W., Wang, J., Mu, Y., Kumar, S., Chang, S.: Compact hyperplane hashing with bilinear functions. In: ICML (2012)

28. Mnih, V., et al.: Human-level control through deep reinforcement learning. Nature **518**(7540), 529–533 (2015). https://doi.org/10.1038/nature14236
29. Norouzi, M., Fleet, D.J.: Minimal loss hashing for compact binary codes. In: ICML, pp. 353–360 (2011)
30. Shen, F., Shen, C., Liu, W., Shen, H.T.: Supervised discrete hashing. In: CVPR, pp. 37–45 (2015). https://doi.org/10.1109/CVPR.2015.7298598
31. Shen, F., Shen, C., Shi, Q., van den Hengel, A., Tang, Z.: Inductive hashing on manifolds. In: CVPR, pp. 1562–1569 (2013). https://doi.org/10.1109/CVPR.2013. 205
32. Shen, Y., Liu, L., Shao, L., Song, J.: Deep binaries: encoding semantic-rich cues for efficient textual-visual cross retrieval. In: ICCV, pp. 4117–4126 (2017). http:// doi.ieeecomputersociety.org/10.1109/ICCV.2017.441
33. Simonyan, K., Zisserman, A.: Very deep convolutional networks for large-scale image recognition. CoRR abs/1409.1556 (2014). http://arxiv.org/abs/1409.1556
34. Song, J.: Binary generative adversarial networks for image retrieval. CoRR abs/1708.04150 (2017). http://arxiv.org/abs/1708.04150
35. Wang, J., Zhang, T., Song, J., Sebe, N., Shen, H.T.: A survey on learning to hash. CoRR abs/1606.00185 (2016). http://arxiv.org/abs/1606.00185
36. Wang, J., Kumar, S., Chang, S.: Semi-supervised hashing for large-scale search. TPAMI **34**(12), 2393–2406 (2012). https://doi.org/10.1109/TPAMI.2012.48
37. Wang, J., Liu, W., Kumar, S., Chang, S.: Learning to hash for indexing big data - a survey. Proc. IEEE **104**(1), 34–57 (2016). https://doi.org/10.1109/JPROC.2015. 2487976
38. Wang, Q., Si, L., Zhang, D.: Learning to hash with partial tags: exploring correlation between tags and hashing bits for large scale image retrieval. In: Fleet, D., Pajdla, T., Schiele, B., Tuytelaars, T. (eds.) ECCV 2014. LNCS, vol. 8691, pp. 378–392. Springer, Cham (2014). https://doi.org/10.1007/978-3-319-10578-9_25
39. Weinberger, K.Q., Dasgupta, A., Langford, J., Smola, A.J., Attenberg, J.: Feature hashing for large scale multitask learning. In: ICML, pp. 1113–1120 (2009). https:// doi.org/10.1145/1553374.1553516
40. Weiss, Y., Torralba, A., Fergus, R.: Spectral hashing. In: NIPS, pp. 1753–1760 (2008)
41. Williams, R.J.: Simple statistical gradient-following algorithms for connectionist reinforcement learning. Mach. Learn. **8**, 229–256 (1992). https://doi.org/10.1007/ BF00992696
42. Xia, R., Pan, Y., Lai, H., Liu, C., Yan, S.: Supervised hashing for image retrieval via image representation learning. In: AAAI (2014). http://www.aaai.org/ocs/index. php/AAAI/AAAI14/paper/view/8137
43. Xiao, J., Hays, J., Ehinger, K.A., Oliva, A., Torralba, A.: SUN database: large-scale scene recognition from abbey to zoo. In: CVPR, pp. 3485–3492 (2010). https:// doi.org/10.1109/CVPR.2010.5539970
44. Zhang, D., Li, W.: Large-scale supervised multimodal hashing with semantic correlation maximization. In: AAAI, pp. 2177–2183 (2014). http://www.aaai.org/ocs/ index.php/AAAI/AAAI14/paper/view/8382
45. Zhang, R., Lin, L., Zhang, R., Zuo, W., Zhang, L.: Bit-scalable deep hashing with regularized similarity learning for image retrieval and person re-identification. IEEE Trans. Image Process. **24**(12), 4766–4779 (2015). https://doi.org/10.1109/ TIP.2015.2467315
46. Zhu, H., Long, M., Wang, J., Cao, Y.: Deep hashing network for efficient similarity retrieval. In: AAAI, pp. 2415–2421 (2016). http://www.aaai.org/ocs/index.php/ AAAI/AAAI16/paper/view/12039

Question Type Guided Attention in Visual Question Answering

Yang Shi[1]([✉]), Tommaso Furlanello[2], Sheng Zha[3],
and Animashree Anandkumar[3,4]

[1] University of California, Irvine, Irvine, USA
shiy4@uci.edu
[2] University of Southern California, Los Angeles, USA
furlanel@usc.edu
[3] Amazon AI, Seattle, USA
{zhasheng,anima}@amazon.com
[4] California Institute of Technology, Pasadena, USA

Abstract. Visual Question Answering (VQA) requires integration of feature maps with drastically different structures. Image descriptors have structures at multiple spatial scales, while lexical inputs inherently follow a temporal sequence and naturally cluster into semantically different question types. A lot of previous works use complex models to extract feature representations but neglect to use high-level information summary such as question types in learning. In this work, we propose Question Type-guided Attention (QTA). It utilizes the information of question type to dynamically balance between bottom-up and top-down visual features, respectively extracted from ResNet and Faster R-CNN networks. We experiment with multiple VQA architectures with extensive input ablation studies over the TDIUC dataset and show that QTA systematically improves the performance by more than 5% across multiple question type categories such as "Activity Recognition", "Utility" and "Counting" on TDIUC dataset compared to the state-of-art. By adding QTA on the state-of-art model MCB, we achieve 3% improvement in overall accuracy. Finally, we propose a multi-task extension to predict question types which generalizes QTA to applications that lack question type, with a minimal performance loss.

Keywords: Visual question answering · Attention · Question type Feature selection · Multi-task

1 Introduction

The relative maturity and flexibility of deep learning allow us to build upon the success of computer vision [17] and natural language [13,20] to face new complex and multimodal tasks. Visual Question Answering (VQA) [4] focus on providing

---

Y. Shi—Work partially done while the author was working at Amazon AI.

V. Ferrari et al. (Eds.): ECCV 2018, LNCS 11208, pp. 158–175, 2018.
https://doi.org/10.1007/978-3-030-01225-0_10

a natural language answer given any image and any free-form natural language question. To achieve this goal, information from multiple modalities must be integrated. Visual and lexical inputs are first processed using specialized encoding modules and then integrated through differentiable operators. Image features are usually extracted by convolution neural networks [7], while recurrent neural networks [13,26] are used to extract question features. Additionally, attention mechanism [30–32] forces the system to *look at* informative regions in both text and vision. Attention weight is calculated from the correlation between language and vision features and then is multiplied to the original feature.

Previous works explore new features to represent vision and language. Pre-trained ResNet [12] and VGG [24] are commonly used in VQA vision feature extraction. The authors in [27] show that post-processing CNN with region-specific image features [3] such as Faster R-CNN [22] can lead to an improvement of VQA performance. Along with generating language feature from either sentence-level or word-level using LSTM [13] or word embedding, Lu *et al.* [19] propose to model the question from word-level, phrase-level, and entire question-level in a hierarchical fashion.

Through extensive experimentation and ablation studies, we notice that the role of "raw" visual features from ResNet and processed region-specific features from Faster R-CNN is complementary and leads to improvement over different subsets of question types. However, we also notice that trivial information in VQA dataset: question/answer type is omitted in training. Generally, each sample in any VQA dataset contains one image file, one natural language question/answer and sometimes answer type. A lot of work use the answer type to analyze accuracy per type in result [4] but neglect to use it during learning. TDIUC [15] is a recently released dataset that contains question type for each sample. Compared to answer type, question type has less variety and is easier to interpret when we only have the question.

The focus of this work is the development of an attention mechanism that exploits high-level semantic information on the question type to guide the visual encoding process. This procedure introduces information leakage between modalities before the classical integration phase that improves the performance on VQA task. Specifically, We introduce a novel VQA architecture **Question Type-guided Attention** (QTA) that dynamically gates the contribution of ResNet and Faster R-CNN features based on the question type. Our results with QTA allow us to integrate the information from multiple visual sources and obtain gains across all question types. A general VQA network with our QTA is shown in Fig. 1.

The contributions of this paper are: (1) We propose question type-guided attention to balance between bottom-up and top-down visual features, which are respectively extracted from ResNet and Faster R-CNN networks. Our results show that QTA systematically improves the performance by more than 5% across multiple question type categories such as "Activity Recognition", "Utility" and "Counting" on TDIUC dataset. By adding QTA to the state-of-art model MCB, we achieve 3% improvement in overall accuracy. (2) We propose a multi-task extension that is trained to predict question types from the lexical inputs during training time that do not require ground truth labels during inference. We get more than 95% accuracy for the question type prediction while keeping the VQA task accuracy almost same as before. (3) Our analysis reveals some problems in the TDIUC VQA dataset. Though the "Absurd" question is intended to help reduce bias, it contains too many similar questions, specifically, questions regarding color. This will mislead the machine to predict wrong question types. Our QTA model gets 17% improvement on simple accuracy compared to the baseline in [15] when we exclude absurd questions in training.

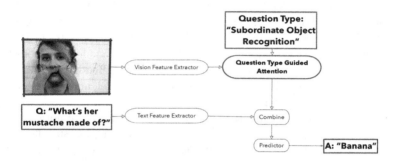

Fig. 1. General VQA network with QTA

2   Related Works

VQA task is first proposed in [4]. It focuses on providing a natural language answer given any image and any free-form natural language question. Collecting data and solving the task are equally challenging as they require the understanding of the joint relation between image and language without any bias.

Datasets. VQA dataset v1 is first released by Antol *et al.* [4]. The dataset consists of two subsets: real images and abstract scenes. However, the inherent structure of our world is biased and it results in a biased dataset. In another word, a specific question tends to have the same answer regardless of the image. For example, when people ask about the color of the sky, the answer is most likely blue or black. It is unusual to see the answer be yellow. This is the bottleneck when we give a yellow color sky and ask the machine to answer it. Goyal *et al.* [10] release VQA dataset v2. This dataset pairs the same question with similar images that lead to different answers to reduce the sample bias. Agrawal *et al.* [2] also noticed that every question type has different prior distributions of answers. Based on that they propose GVQA and new splits of the VQA v1/v2. In the new split, the distribution of answers per question type is different in the test data compared to the training data. Zhang *et al.* [33,34] also propose a method to reduce bias in abstract scenes dataset at question level. By extracting representative word tuples from questions, they can identify and control the balance for each question. Vizwiz [11] is another recently released dataset that uses pictures taken by blind people. Some pictures are of poor quality, and the questions are spoken. These data collection methods help reduce bias in the dataset.

Johnson et al. [14] introduce Compositional Language and Elementary Visual Reasoning (CLEVR) diagnostic dataset that focuses on reasoning. Strub et al. [25] propose a two-player guessing game: guess a target in a given image with a sequence of questions and answers. This requires both visual question reasoning and spatial reasoning.

The Task Driven Image Understanding Challenge dataset (TDIUC) [15] contains a total of over 1.6 million questions in 12 different types. It contains images and annotations from MSCOCO [18] and Visual genome [16]. The key difference between TDIUC and the previous VQA v1/v2 dataset is the categorization of questions: Each question belongs to one of the 12 categories. This allows a task-oriented evaluation such as per question-type accuracies. They also include an "Absurd" question category in which questions are irrelevant to the image contents to help balance the dataset.

Feature Selection. VQA requires solving several tasks at once involving both visual and textual inputs: visual perception, question understanding, and reasoning. Usually, features are extracted respectively with convolutional neural networks [7] from the image, and with recurrent neural networks [13,26] from the text.

Pre-trained ResNet and VGG are commonly used in VQA vision feature extraction. The authors in [27] show that post-processing CNN with region-specific image features [3] can lead to an improvement of VQA performance. Specifically, they use pre-trained Faster R-CNN model to extract image features for VQA task. They won the VQA challenge 2017.

On the language side, pre-trained word embeddings such as Word2Vec [20] are used for text feature extraction. There is a discussion about the sufficiency of language input for VQA task. Agrawal et al. [1] have shown that state-of-art VQA models converge to the same answer even if only given half of the question compared to if given the whole sentence.

Generic Methods. Information of both modalities are used jointly through means of combination, such as concatenation, product or sum. In [4], authors propose a baseline that combines LSTM embedding of the question and CNN embedding of the image via a point-wise multiplication followed by a multi-layer perceptron classifier.

Pooling Methods. Pooling methods are widely used in visual tasks to combine information for various streams into one final feature representation. Common pooling methods such as average pooling and max pooling bring the property of translation invariance and robustness to elastic distortions at the cost of spatial locality. Bilinear pooling can preserve spatial information, which is performed with the outer product between two feature maps. However, this operation entails high output dimension ($O(MN)$ for feature maps of dimension M and N). This exponential growth with respect to the number of feature maps renders it too costly to be applied to huge real image datasets. There have been several proposals for new pooling techniques to address this problem:

– Count sketch [5] is applied as a feature hashing operator to avoid dimension expanding in bilinear pooling. Given a vector $a \in \mathcal{R}^n$, random hash function $f \in \mathcal{R}^n$: $[n] \rightarrow [b]$ and binary variable $s \in \mathcal{R}^n$: $[n] \rightarrow \pm 1$, the **count sketch** [5] operator $cs(a, h, s) \in \mathcal{R}^b$ is:

$$cs(a, f, s)[j] = \sum_{f[i]=j} s[i]a[i], \quad j \in 1, \cdots, b \tag{1}$$

Gao *et al.* [9] use convolution layers from two different neural networks as the local descriptor extractors of the image and combine them using count sketch. "α-pooling" [23] allows the network to learn the pooling strategy: a continuous transition between linear and polynomial pooling. They show that higher α gives larger gain for fine-grained image recognition tasks. However, as α goes up, the computation complexity increases in polynomial order.

– Fukui *et al.* [8] use count sketch as a pooling method in VQA tasks and obtains the best results on VQA dataset v1 in VQA challenge 2016. They compute count sketch approximation of the visual and textual representation at each spatial location. Given text feature $v \in \mathcal{R}^L$ and image features $I \in \mathcal{R}^{C \times H \times W}$, Fukui *et al.* [8] propose **MCB** as:

$$
\begin{aligned}
MCB(I[:, h, w] &\otimes v)[t_1, h, w] \\
&= (cs(I[:, h, w], f, s) \star cs(v, f, s))[t_1, h, w] \\
&= IFFT1(FFT1(cs(I[:, h, w], f, s))[t_1, h, w] \circ FFT1(cs(v, f, s))[t_1]) \\
&h \in \{1, \cdots H\}, w \in \{1, \cdots W\}, t_1 \in \{1, \cdots, b\}
\end{aligned}
\tag{2}
$$

$\otimes$ denotes outer product. $\circ$ denotes element-wise product. $\star$ denotes convolution operator. This procedure preserves spatial information in the image feature.

Attention. Focusing on the objects in the image that are related to the question is the key to understand the correlation between the image and the question. Attention mechanism is used to address this problem. There are soft attention and hard attention [31] based on whether the attention term/loss function is differentiable or not. Yang *et al.* [32] and Xu *et al.* [30] propose word guided spatial attention specifically for VQA task. Attention weight at each spatial location is calculated by the correlation between the embedded question feature and the embedded visual features. The attended pixels are at the maximum correlations. Wang *et al.* [28] explore mechanisms of triplet attention that interact between the image, question and candidate answers based on image-question pairs.

3   Question Type Guided Visual Attention

Question type is very important in predicting the answer regardless whether we have the corresponding image or not. For example, questions starting with "how many" will mostly lead to numerical answers. Agrawal *et al.* [1] have shown that state-of-art VQA models converge to the same answer even if only given half of the question compared to if given the whole sentence. Besides that, inspired by [27], we are curious about combining bottom-up and top-down visual features in VQA task. To get a deep understanding of visual feature preference for different questions, we try to find an attention mechanism between these two. Since question type is representing the question, we propose Question Type-guided Attention (QTA).

Given several independent image features $F_1, F_2, \cdots F_k$, such as features from ResNet, VGG or Faster R-CNN, we concatenate them as one image feature: $F = [F_1, F_2, \cdots F_k] \in \mathcal{R}^M$. Assume there are N different question types, QTA is defined as $F \circ WQ$, where $Q \in \mathcal{R}^N$ is the one-hot encoding of the question type, and $W \in \mathcal{R}^{M \times N}$ is the hidden weight. We can learn the weight by back propagation through the network. In other words, we learn a question type embedding and use it as attention weight.

QTA can be used in both generic and complex pooling models. In Fig. 2, we show a simple concatenation model with question type as input. We describe it in detail in Sect. 4. To fully exploit image features in different channels and preserve spatial information, we also propose MCB with question type-guided image attention in Fig. 4.

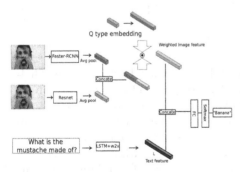

Fig. 2. Concatenation model with QTA structure for VQA task (CATL-QTA^W in Sect. 4)

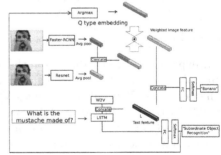

Fig. 3. Concatenation model with QTA structure for multi-task (CATL-QTA-M^W in Sect. 4)

One obvious limitation of QTA is that it requires question type label. In the real world scenario, the question type for each question may not be available. In this case, it is still possible to predict the question type from the text, and use it as input to the QTA network. Thus, we propose a multi-task model that focuses on VQA task along with the prediction of the question type in Fig. 3.

This model operates in the setting where true question type is available only at training time. In Sect. 5, we also show through experiment that it is a relatively easy task to predict the question type from question text, and thus making our method generalizable to those VQA settings that lack question type.

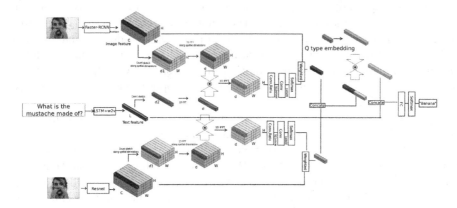

Fig. 4. MCB model with QTA structure (MCB-QTA in Sect. 4)

4   Experiments

In this section, we describe the dataset in Sect. 4.1, evaluation metrics in Sect. 4.2, model features in Sect. 4.3, and model structures are explained in Sect. 4.4.

4.1   Dataset

Our experiments are conducted on the Task Driven Image Understanding Challenge dataset (TDIUC) [15], which contains over 1.6 million questions in 12 different types. This dataset includes VQA v1 and Visual Genome, with a total of 122429 training images and 57565 test images. The annotation sources are MSCOCO (VQA v1), Visual genome annotations, and manual annotations. TDIUC introduces absurd questions that force an algorithm to determine if a question is valid for a given image. There are 1115299 total training questions and 538543 total test questions. The total number of samples is 3 times larger than that in VQA v1 dataset.

4.2   Evaluation Metrics

There are total 12 different question types in TDIUC dataset as we mentioned in Sect. 2. We calculate the simple accuracy for each type separately and also report the arithmetic and harmonic means across all per question-type (MPT) accuracies.

4.3   Feature Representation

Image Feature. We use the output of "pool" of a 152-layer ResNet as an image feature baseline. The output dimension is $2048 \times 14 \times 14$. Faster R-CNN [22] focuses on object detection and classification. Teney *et al.* [27] use it to extract object-oriented features for VQA dataset and show better performance compared to the ones using ResNet feature. We fix the number of detected objects to be 36 and extract the image features based on their pre-trained Faster R-CNN model. As a result, the extracted image feature is a 36×2048 matrix. To fit in MCB model, which requires spatial representation, we reshape it into a $6 \times 6 \times 2048$ tensor.

Text Feature. We use common word embedding library: 300-dim Word2Vec [20] as a pre-trained text feature: we sum over the word embeddings for all words in the sentence. A two-layer LSTM is used as an end-to-end text feature extractor. We also use the encoder of google neural machine translation (NMT) system [29] as a pre-trained text feature and compare it with Word2Vec. The pre-trained NMT model is trained on UN parallel corpus 1.0 in MXnet [6]. Its BLEU score is 34. The output dimension of the encoder is 1024.

4.4   Models

Baseline Models. Baseline models are based on a one-layer MLP: A fully connected network classifier with one hidden layer with ReLu non-linearity, followed by a softmax layer. The input is a concatenation of image and text feature. There are 8192 units in the hidden state.

Table 1. Baseline models

Name	Image feature	Text feature	Model
CAT1	ResNet/Faster R-CNN vector feature	Skipthought/NMT/Word2Vec pre-trained feature	MLP
CAT1L	ResNet/Faster R-CNN vector feature	End-to-end 2-layer LSTM's last hidden state	MLP
CATL	Concatenation of ResNet and Faster R-CNN vector features	End-to-end 2-layer LSTM's last hidden state	MLP
CAT2	Concatenation of ResNet and Faster R-CNN vector features	NMT pre-trined feature	MLP

To compare different image and text feature, we have **CAT1**, **CAT1L** and **CATL**. To check the complementarity of different features between ResNet and Faster R-CNN and show how they perform differently across question types, we set up baseline **CAT2**. In LSTM, the hidden state length is 1024. The word embedding dimension is 300. Detailed definitions are in Table 1.

To further exam and explain our QTA proposal, we use more sophisticate feature integration operators as a strong baseline to compare with. **MCB-A**, as we mentioned in Sect. 2, is proposed in [8]. **RAU** [21] is a framework that combines the embedding, attention and predicts operation together inside a recurrent network. We reference results of these two models from [15].

QTA Models. From the baseline analysis, we realize that ResNet and Faster R-CNN features are complementary to each other. Using question type as guidance for image feature selection is the key to make image feature stronger. Therefore, we propose QTA networks in MLP model (**CATL-QTA**) and MCB model (**MCB-QTA**). The out dimension of the count sketch in the MCB is 8000. The structures are in Figs. 2 and 4. The descriptions are in Table 2.

To check whether the model benefits from the QTA mechanism or from added question type information itself, we design a network that only uses question type embedding without attention. **CAT-QT** and **CATL-QT** are the two proposed network using Word2Vec and LSTM lexical features.

As mentions in Sect. 3, we propose a multi-task network for QTA in case we don't have question type label at inference. **CATL-QTA-M** is a multi-task model based on CATL-QTA. The output of LSTM is connected to a one-layer MLP to predict question type for the input question. The prediction result is then fed into QTA part through argmax. The Multi-task MLP is in Fig. 3.

Table 2. QTA models

Name	Image feature	Text feature	Model
CATL-QTA	QTA weighted pre-trained vector features from ResNet and Faster R-CNN	End-to-end 2-layer LSTM's last hidden state	MLP
MCB-QTA	QTA weighted pre-trained spatial features from ResNet and Faster R-CNN	End-to-end 2-layer LSTM's last hidden state	MCB
CAT-QT	Concatenation of ResNet and Faster R-CNN vector features	Concatenation of Word2Vec pre-trined feature and a 1024-dim question type embedding	MLP
CATL-QT	Concatenation of ResNet hidden state and Faster R-CNN vector features	Concatenation of end-to-end 2-layer LSTM's last and a 1024-dim question type embedding	MLP
CATL-QTA-M	QTA weighted pre-trained spatial features from ResNet and Faster R-CNN	End-to-end 2-layer LSTM's last hidden state	Multi-task MLP

5   Results and Analysis

We first focus in Sects. 5.1 and 5.2 on results concerning the complementarity of different features across question category types. For the visual domain, we explore the use of Faster R-CNN and ResNet features, while for the lexical domain we use NMT, LSTM and pre-trained Word2Vec features. We then analyze the effect of question type both as input and with QTA in VQA tasks in Sect. 5.3. Finally, in the remaining subsections, we extend the basic concatenation QTA model to MCB style pooling; introduce question type as both input and output during training such that the network can produce predicted question types during inference; and study more in depth the effect of the question category "Absurd" on the overall model performance across categories.

5.1   Faster R-CNN and ResNet Features

Table 3 reports our extensive ablation analysis of simple concatenation models using multiple visual and lexical feature sources. From the results in the second and third columns, we see that overall the model with Faster R-CNN features outperform the one using ResNet features when using NMT features. We show in column 4 that the features sources are complementary, and their combination is better across most categories (in bold) with respect to the single source models in columns 2 and 3. In columns 5, 6; 7, 8 and 9, 10 we replicate the same comparison between ResNet and R-CNN features using more sophisticate models to embed the lexical information. We reach more than 10 % accuracy increase, from 69.53 % to 80.16 % using a simple concatenation model with an accurate selection of the feature type.

5.2   Pre-trained and Jointly-Trained Text Feature Extractors

The first four columns in Table 3 show the results of models with text features from NMT. To fully explore the text feature extractor in VQA system, we substitute the NMT pre-trained language feature extractor with a jointly-trained two layer LSTM model. The improved performance of jointly-training text feature extractor can be appreciated by comparing the results of the 1–4 and 5–10 columns in Table 3. For example, comparing second column and fifth column in Table 3, we get 6% improvement using LSTM while keeping image feature and network same.

Table 3. Benchmark results of concatenation models on TDIUC dataset using different image features and pre-trained language feature. 1: Use ResNet feature and Skip-Gram feature 2: Use ResNet feature and NMT feature 3: Use Faster R-CNN feature and NMT feature 4: Use ResNet feature and end-to-end LSTM feature 5: Use Faster R-CNN feature and end-to-end LSTM feature. N denotes that additional NMT embedding is concatenated to LSTM output. W denotes that additional Word2Vec embedding is concatenated to LSTM output (Following tables also use the same notation)

Columns Accuracy(%)	1 $CAT1^1$ [15]	2 $CAT1^2$	3 $CAT1^3$	4 $CAT2$	5 $CAT1L^4$	6 $CAT1L^5$	7 $CAT1L^{4N}$	8 $CAT1L^{5N}$	9 $CAT1L^{4W}$	10 $CAT1L^{5W}$
Scene Recognition	72.19	68.51	68.81	**69.06**	91.62	**92.27**	91.16	**92.33**	91.57	**92.45**
Sport Recognition	85.16	89.67	92.36	**93.15**	90.94	**93.84**	89.62	**93.52**	90.77	**94.05**
Color Attributes	43.69	32.90	34.35	**34.99**	45.62	**49.43**	44.07	**47.78**	47.33	**49.47**
Other Attributes	42.89	38.05	**39.76**	39.67	40.89	**43.49**	39.60	**42.35**	41.92	**45.19**
Activity Recognition	24.16	39.34	45.75	**46.87**	42.95	**49.25**	40.12	**44.11**	42.13	**49.25**
Positional Reasoning	25.15	25.63	27.16	**28.02**	26.22	**29.35**	24.17	**27.50**	25.72	**28.59**
Sub. Object Recognition	80.92	83.94	85.67	**86.78**	82.20	**85.06**	81.85	**84.47**	82.52	**85.05**
Absurd	96.96	94.98	94.77	**95.82**	90.87	87.10	**95.38**	93.28	**93.59**	91.95
Utility and Affordances	24.56	25.93	**27.78**	27.16	15.43	25.93	**25.31**	18.52	16.05	**17.28**
Object Presence	69.43	77.21	77.90	**78.29**	89.40	**91.14**	90.13	**91.95**	91.08	**91.81**
Counting	44.82	48.46	52.18	**52.57**	45.95	**50.27**	44.26	**49.24**	44.93	**51.30**
Sentiment Understanding	53.00	43.45	46.49	**47.28**	46.49	**48.72**	41.85	**42.81**	44.89	**46.01**
Overall (Arithmetic MPT)	55.25	55.67	57.57	58.31	59.05	62.15	58.96	60.66	59.38	**61.80**
Overall (Harmonic MPT)	44.13	45.37	47.99	48.44	44.09	**51.66**	46.84	46.84	44.42	47.70
Overall Accuracy	69.53	71.41	72.44	**73.05**	77.55	78.66	78.35	79.94	78.94	**80.16**

We obtain the best model by concatenating the output of the LSTM and the pre-trained NMT/Word2Vec feature, as shown in Table 3. It gives us 10% improvement for "Utility and Affordances" when we look at the fifth and seventh column. We find the use of Word2Vec is better than NMT feature in last four columns in Table 3. We think the better performance of Word2Vec with respect to the NMT encoder, might be due to the more similar structure of single sentence samples of Word2Vec training set with those from classical VQA dataset with respect to those used for training NMT models.

Table 4. QTA in concatenation models on TDIUC dataset

Accuracy(%)	CATL	CATL-QTA	CATL^W	CATL-QTA^W
Scene Recognition	93.18	93.45	93.31	93.80
Sport Recognition	94.69	95.45	94.96	95.55
Color Attributes	54.66	56.08	57.59	60.16
Other Attributes	48.52	50.30	52.25	54.36
Activity Recognition	53.36	58.43	54.59	60.10
Positional Reasoning	32.73	31.94	33.63	34.71
Sub. Object Recognition	86.56	86.76	86.52	86.98
Absurd	95.03	100.00	98.01	100.00
Utility and Affordances	29.01	23.46	29.01	31.48
Object Presence	93.34	93.48	94.13	94.55
Counting	50.08	49.93	52.97	53.25
Sentiment Understanding	56.23	56.87	62.62	64.38
Overall (Arithmetic MPT)	65.62	66.34	67.46	69.11
Overall (Harmonic MPT)	55.95	54.60	57.83	60.08
Overall Accuracy	82.23	83.62	83.92	85.03

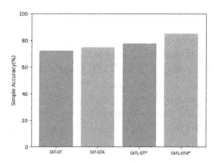

Fig. 5. Evaluation of different ways to utilize information from question type

5.3   QTA in Concatenation Models

We use QTA in concatenation models to study the effect of QTA. The framework is in Fig. 2. We compare the network using a weighted feature with the same network using an unweighted concatenated image feature in Table 4. As we can see, the model using the weighted feature has more power than the one using the unweighted feature. 9 out of 12 categories get improved results. "Color" and "Activity Recognition" get around 2% and 6% accuracy increases.

To ensure that the improvement is not because of the added question type information but the attention mechanism using question type, we show the comparison of QTA with QT in Fig. 5. With same text feature and image feature and approximately same number of parameters in the network, QTA is 3–5% better than QT.

We show the effect of QTA on image feature norms in Fig. 6. By weighing the image features by question type, we find that our model relies more on Faster R-CNN features for "Absurd" question samples while it relies more on ResNet features for "Color" questions.

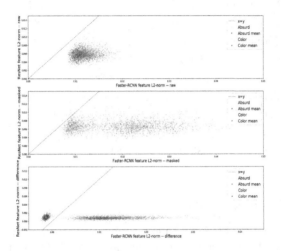

Fig. 6. Effects of weighting by QTA. Top: raw feature norms, Middle: feature norms weighted by QTA, Bottom: differences of norms after weighting vs before weighting. For color questions, the feature norms shift towards ResNet features, while for absurd questions they shift towards Faster-RCNN features.

The best setting we get in concatenation model is using a weighted image feature concatenated with the output of the LSTM and Word2Vec feature (CATL-QTA^W). It gets 5% improvement compared to complicated deep network such as RAU and MCB-A in Table 5.

Table 5. Results of QTA models on TDIUC dataset compared to state-of-art models

Accuracy (%)	CATL-QTA^W	MCB-QTA	MCB-A [15]	RAU [15]
Scene Recognition	93.80	93.56	93.06	**93.96**
Sport Recognition	95.55	**95.70**	92.77	93.47
Color Attributes	60.16	59.82	**68.54**	66.86
Other Attributes	54.36	54.06	**56.72**	56.49
Activity Recognition	60.10	**60.55**	52.35	51.60
Positional Reasoning	34.71	34.00	**35.40**	35.26
Sub. Object Recognition	86.98	**87.00**	85.54	86.11
Absurd	**100.00**	100.00	84.82	96.08
Utility and Affordances	31.48	**37.04**	35.09	31.58
Object Presence	**94.55**	94.34	93.64	94.38
Counting	53.25	**53.99**	51.01	48.43
Sentiment Understanding	64.38	65.65	**66.25**	60.09
Overall (Arithmetic MPT)	69.11	**69.69**	67.90	67.81
Overall (Harmonic MPT)	60.08	**61.56**	60.47	59.00
Overall Accuracy	**85.03**	84.97	81.86	84.26

5.4   QTA in Pooling Models

To show how to combine QTA with more complicated feature integration operator, we propose MCB-QTA structure. Even though MCB-QTA in Table 5 doesn't
win with simple accuracy, it shows great performance in many categories such as
"Object Recognition" and "Counting". Accuracy in "Utility and Affordances"
is improved by 6% compared to our CATL-QTA model. It gets 8% improvement
in "Activity recognition" compared to state-of-art model MCB-A and also gets
the best Arithmetic and Harmonic MPT value.

5.5   Multi-task Analysis

In this part, we will discuss how we use QTA when we have questions without
specific question types. It is quite easy to predict the question type from the
question itself. We use a 2-layer LSTM followed by a classifier and the test
accuracy is 96% after 9 epochs. The problem is whether we can predict the
question type while keeping the same performance for VQA task or not. As
described in Fig. 3, we use the predicted question type as input of the QTA
network in a multi-task setting. We get 84.33% test simple accuracy for VQA
task as shown in Table 9. When we compare it to MCB-A or RAU in Table 5,
though accuracy gets a little affected for most of the categories, we still get 2%
improvement in "Sports Recognition" and "Counting".

We fine-tune our model on VQA v1 using a pre-trained multi-task model that was trained on TDIUC. We use the question type predictor in the multi-task model as the input of QTA. Our model's performance is better than MCB in Table 6 with an approximately same number of parameters in the network.

Table 6. Results of test-dev accuracy on VQA v1. Models are trained on the VQA v1 train split and tested on test-dev

	Accuracy (%)
Element-wise Sum [8]	56.50
Concatenation [8]	57.49
Concatenation + FC [8]	58.40
Element-wise Product [8]	58.57
Element-wise Product + FC [8]	56.44
MCB (2048 × 2048 → 16K) [8]	59.83
CATL-QTA-M + FC	**60.32**

5.6   Findings on TDIUC Dataset

To further analyze the effects of the question type prediction part in this multi-task framework, we list the confusion matrix for the question type prediction results in Table 7. "Color" and "Absurd" question type predictions are most often bi-directionally confused. The reason for this is that among all absurd questions, more than 60% are questions start with "What color". To avoid this bias, we remove all absurd questions and run our multi-task model again. In this setting, our question type prediction did much better than before. Almost all categories get 99% accuracy as shown in Table 8. We also compare our QTA models' performance without absurd questions in Table 9. In CATL-QTA network, removing absurd questions doesn't help much because in test we feed in the true question type labels. But it is useful when we consider the multi-task model. From fourth and fifth columns, we see that without absurd questions, we get improved performance among all categories. This is because we remove the absurd questions that may mislead the network to predict "color" question type in the test.

Table 7. Confusion matrix for test question types prediction in CATL-QTA-M using TDIUC dataset. 1. Other Attributes 2. Sentiment Understanding 3. Sports Recognition 4. Position Reasoning 5. Object Utilities/Affordances 6. Activity Recognition 7. Scene Classification 8. Color 9. Object Recognition 10. Object Presence 11. Counting 12. Absurd

Target	Predicted												Acc(%)
	1	2	3	4	5	6	7	8	9	10	11	12	95.66
1	77.76	0.00	0.89	3.20	0.00	0.08	0.42	1.15	0.12	0.00	0.00	16.38	
2	0.80	60.51	1.77	8.83	0.00	2.25	2.57	0.00	1.44	0.96	0.16	20.71	
3	0.31	0.00	73.08	0.37	0.00	0.17	0.00	0.03	0.02	0.00	0.01	26.01	
4	2.95	0.02	0.01	89.52	0.00	0.01	0.02	0.19	1.88	0.03	0.03	5.35	
5	12.50	0.63	3.12	45.62	0.00	0.00	3.12	0.00	11.25	0.00	0.00	23.75	
6	0.79	0.00	14.56	1.76	0.00	13.18	0.00	0.00	2.21	0.00	0.07	67.43	
7	0.04	0.00	0.04	0.40	0.00	0.01	99.40	0.02	0.00	0.00	0.06	0.03	
8	0.32	0.00	0.18	0.13	0.00	0.00	0.00	86.10	0.00	0.00	0.00	13.28	
9	0.01	0.00	0.00	0.31	0.00	0.00	0.00	0.00	98.96	0.01	0.00	0.71	
10	0.00	0.00	0.00	0.00	0.00	0.00	0.00	0.00	0.00	100.00	0.00	0.00	
11	0.00	0.00	0.00	0.01	0.00	0.00	0.02	0.00	0.02	0.05	99.90	0.00	
12	0.35	0.00	0.18	0.41	0.00	0.03	0.00	3.18	0.40	0.00	0.00	95.46	

Table 8. Confusion matrix for test question types prediction in CATL-QTA-M using TDIUC dataset without absurd questions. Numbers represent same categories as in Table 7

Target	Predicted												Acc(%)
	1	2	3	4	5	6	7	8	9	10	11	12	99.50
1	98.39	0.00	0.07	0.15	0.00	0.13	0.08	0.63	0.55	0.00	0.00	N/A	
2	0.16	84.03	3.67	0.00	0.00	3.35	5.59	0.00	0.48	0.00	2.72	N/A	
3	0.00	0.08	97.31	0.00	0.00	2.37	0.01	0.00	0.10	0.02	0.11	N/A	
4	1.01	0.00	0.00	98.07	0.00	0.01	0.00	0.51	0.41	0.00	0.00	N/A	
5	8.64	3.70	14.81	0.00	0.00	59.26	7.41	1.23	4.94	0.00	0.00	N/A	
6	0.45	0.15	31.42	0.00	0.00	67.39	0.04	0.04	0.45	0.00	0.07	N/A	
7	0.02	0.03	0.00	0.00	0.00	0.03	99.86	0.02	0.00	0.00	0.04	N/A	
8	0.06	0.00	0.00	0.13	0.00	0.04	0.07	99.70	0.00	0.00	0.00	N/A	
9	0.06	0.00	0.13	0.01	0.00	0.02	0.00	0.00	99.76	0.01	0.00	N/A	
10	0.00	0.00	0.00	0.00	0.00	0.00	0.00	0.00	0.00	100.00	0.00	N/A	
11	0.00	0.00	0.01	0.00	0.00	0.00	0.00	0.00	0.00	0.01	99.98	N/A	
12	N/A	N/A	N/A	N/A	N/A	N/A	N/A	N/A	N/A	N/A	N/A	N/A	

Table 9. Results of test accuracy when question type is hidden with/without absurd questions in training. We compare them with similar QTA models. * denotes training and testing without absurd questions

	CATL-QTA^W	CATL^{W*}	CATL-QTA^{W*}	CATL-QTA-M	CATL-QTA-M*	CAT1^{1*} [15]
Scene Recognition	93.80	93.46	93.62	93.74	93.82	72.75
Sport Recognition	95.55	94.97	95.47	94.80	95.31	89.40
Color Attributes	60.16	57.84	58.63	57.62	59.73	50.52
Other Attributes	54.36	53.90	53.44	52.05	56.17	51.47
Activity Recognition	60.10	57.38	59.43	53.13	58.61	48.55
Positional Reasoning	34.71	33.98	34.63	33.90	34.70	27.73
Sub. Object Recognition	86.98	86.62	86.74	86.89	86.80	81.66
Absurd	100.00	N/A	N/A	98.57	N/A	N/A
Utility and Affordances	31.48	27.78	34.57	24.07	35.19	30.99
Object Presence	94.55	93.87	94.22	94.57	94.60	69.50
Counting	53.25	52.33	52.20	53.59	55.30	44.84
Sentiment Understanding	64.38	64.06	65.81	60.06	61.31	59.94
Overall (Arithmetic MPT)	69.11	65.11	66.25	66.92	66.88	57.03
Overall (Harmonic MPT)	60.08	55.89	58.51	55.77	58.82	50.30
Simple Accuracy	85.03	79.79	80.13	84.33	80.95	63.30

6 Conclusion

We propose a question type-guided visual attention (QTA) network. We show empirically that with the question type information, models can balance between bottom-up and top-down visual features and achieve state-of-the-art performance. Our results show that QTA systematically improves the performance by more than 5% across multiple question type categories such as "Activity Recognition", "Utility" and "Counting" on TDIUC dataset. We consider the case when we don't have question type for test and propose a multi-task model to overcome this limitation by adding question type prediction task in the VQA task. We get around 95% accuracy for the question type prediction while keeping the VQA task accuracy almost same as before.

Acknowledgements. We thank Amazon AI for providing computing resources. Yang Shi is supported by Air Force Award FA9550-15-1-0221.

References

1. Agrawal, A., Batra, D., Parikh, D.: Analyzing the behavior of visual question answering models. In: EMNLP (2016)
2. Agrawal, A., Batra, D., Parikh, D., Kembhavi, A.: Don't just assume; look and answer: overcoming priors for visual question answering. In: CVPR (2018)
3. Anderson, P., et al.: Bottom-up and top-down attention for image captioning and VQA. http://arxiv.org/abs/1707.07998
4. Antol, S., et al.: VQA: visual question answering. In: International Conference on Computer Vision (ICCV) (2015)

5. Charikar, M., Chen, K., Farach-Colton, M.: Finding frequent items in data streams. In: Proceedings of ICALP (2002)
6. Chen, T., et al.: MXNet: a flexible and efficient machine learning library for heterogeneous distributed systems. In: Neural Information Processing Systems, Workshop on Machine Learning Systems (2015)
7. Donahue, J., et al.: DECAF: a deep convolutional activation feature for generic visual recognition. http://arxiv.org/abs/1310.1531
8. Fukui, A., Park, D.H., Yang, D., Rohrbach, A., Darrell, T., Rohrbach, M.: Multimodal compact bilinear pooling for visual question answering and visual grounding. In: EMNLP (2016)
9. Gao, Y., Beijbom, O., Zhang, N., Darrell, T.: Compact bilinear pooling. In: Computer Vision and Pattern Recognition (CVPR) (2016)
10. Goyal, Y., Khot, T., Summers-Stay, D., Batra, D., Parikh, D.: Making the V in VQA matter: elevating the role of image understanding in Visual Question Answering. In: Conference on Computer Vision and Pattern Recognition (CVPR) (2017)
11. Gurari, D., et al.: VizWiz grand challenge: answering visual questions from blind people. https://arxiv.org/abs/1802.08218
12. He, K., Zhang, X., Ren, S., Sun, J.: Deep residual learning for image recognition. In: Proceedings of the IEEE Conference on Computer Vision and Pattern Recognition (CVPR)
13. Hochreiter, S., Schmidhuber, J.: Long short-term memory. Neural Comput. **9**(8), 1735–1780 (1997)
14. Johnson, J., et al.: CLEVR: a diagnostic dataset for compositional language and elementary visual reasoning. http://arxiv.org/abs/1612.06890
15. Kafle, K., Kanan, C.: An analysis of visual question answering algorithms. In: ICCV (2017)
16. Krishna, R., et al.: Visual genome: connecting language and vision using crowdsourced dense image annotations. https://arxiv.org/abs/1602.07332
17. Krizhevsky, A., Sutskever, I., Hinton, G.E.: ImageNet classification with deep convolutional neural networks. In: Pereira, F., Burges, C.J.C., Bottou, L., Weinberger, K.Q. (eds.) Advances in Neural Information Processing Systems, vol. 25, pp. 1097–1105. Curran Associates, Inc. (2012)
18. Lin, T.-Y., et al.: Microsoft COCO: common objects in context. In: Fleet, D., Pajdla, T., Schiele, B., Tuytelaars, T. (eds.) ECCV 2014. LNCS, vol. 8693, pp. 740–755. Springer, Cham (2014). https://doi.org/10.1007/978-3-319-10602-1_48
19. Lu, J., Yang, J., Batra, D., Parikh, D.: Hierarchical question-image co-attention for visual question answering. In: NIPS (2016)
20. Mikolov, T., Sutskever, I., Chen, K., Corrado, G., Dean, J.: Distributed representations of words and phrases and their compositionality. In: Advances in neural information processing systems, pp. 3111–3119
21. Noh, H., Han, B.: Training recurrent answering units with joint loss minimization for VQA. https://arxiv.org/abs/1606.03647
22. Ren, S., He, K., Girshick, R.B., Sun, J.: Faster R-CNN: towards real-time object detection with region proposal networks. http://arxiv.org/abs/1506.01497
23. Simon, M., Gao, Y., Darrell, T., Denzler, J., Rodner, E.: Generalized orderless pooling performs implicit salient matching. In: International Conference on Computer Vision (ICCV) (2017)
24. Simonyan, K., Zisserman, A.: Very deep convolutional networks for large-scale image recognition. http://arxiv.org/abs/1409.1556

25. Strub, F., de Vries, H., Mary, J., Piot, B., Courville, A.C., Pietquin, O.: End-to-end optimization of goal-driven and visually grounded dialogue systems. In: International Joint Conference on Artificial Intelligence (IJCAI) (2017)

26. Sutskever, I., Vinyals, O., Le, Q.V.: Sequence to sequence learning with neural networks. In: Proceedings of the 27th International Conference on Neural Information Processing Systems, NIPS 2014, pp. 3104–3112. MIT Press, Cambridge (2014). http://dl.acm.org/citation.cfm?id=2969033.2969173

27. Teney, D., Anderson, P., He, X., van den Hengel, A.: Tips and tricks for visual question answering: learnings from the 2017 challenge. http://arxiv.org/abs/1708.02711

28. Wang, Z., et al.: Structured triplet learning with POS-tag guided attention for visual question answering. In: IEEE Winter Conference on Applications of Computer Vision (2018)

29. Wu, Y., et al.: Google's neural machine translation system: bridging the gap between human and machine translation. http://arxiv.org/abs/1609.08144

30. Xu, H., Saenko, K.: Ask, attend and answer: exploring question-guided spatial attention for visual question answering. In: Leibe, B., Matas, J., Sebe, N., Welling, M. (eds.) ECCV 2016. LNCS, vol. 9911, pp. 451–466. Springer, Cham (2016). https://doi.org/10.1007/978-3-319-46478-7_28

31. Xu, K., et al.: Show, attend and tell: Neural image caption generation with visual attention. In: International Conference on Machine Learning (2015)

32. Yang, Z., He, X., Gao, J., Deng, L., Smola, A.: Stacked attention networks for image question answering. https://arxiv.org/abs/1511.02274

33. Zhang, P.: Towards interpretable vision systems. Ph.D. thesis. Virginia Polytechnic Institute and State University (2017)

34. Zhang, P., Goyal, Y., Summers-Stay, D., Batra, D., Parikh, D.: Yin and Yang: balancing and answering binary visual questions. In: Conference on Computer Vision and Pattern Recognition (CVPR) (2016)

Estimating Depth from RGB and Sparse Sensing

Zhao Chen$^{(\boxtimes)}$ ⬤, Vijay Badrinarayanan⬤, Gilad Drozdov⬤,
and Andrew Rabinovich⬤

Magic Leap, Sunnyvale, CA 94089, USA
{zchen,vbadrinarayanan,gdrozdov,arabinovich}@magicleap.com

Abstract. We present a deep model that can accurately produce dense
depth maps given an RGB image with known depth at a very sparse
set of pixels. The model works *simultaneously* for both indoor/outdoor
scenes and produces state-of-the-art dense depth maps at nearly real-
time speeds on both the NYUv2 and KITTI datasets. We surpass the
state-of-the-art for monocular depth estimation even with depth values
for only 1 out of every ∼10000 image pixels, and we outperform other
sparse-to-dense depth methods at all sparsity levels. With depth values for 1/256 of the image pixels, we achieve a mean error of less than
1% of actual depth on indoor scenes, comparable to the performance of
consumer-grade depth sensor hardware. Our experiments demonstrate
that it would indeed be possible to efficiently transform sparse depth
measurements obtained using e.g. lower-power depth sensors or SLAM
systems into high-quality dense depth maps.

Keywords: Sparse-to-dense depth · Depth estimation · Deep learning

1 Introduction

Efficient, accurate and real-time depth estimation is essential for a wide variety of scene understanding applications in domains such as virtual/mixed reality, autonomous vehicles, and robotics. Currently, a consumer-grade Kinect v2
depth sensor consumes ∼15 W of power, only works indoors at a limited range of
∼4.5 m, and degrades under increased ambient light [8]. For reference, a future
VR/MR head mounted depth camera would need to consume 1/100th the power
and have a range of 1–80 m (indoors and outdoors) at the full FOV and resolution of an RGB camera. Such requirements present an opportunity to jointly
develop energy-efficient depth hardware and depth estimation models. Our work
begins to address depth estimation from this perspective.

Electronic supplementary material The online version of this chapter (https://
doi.org/10.1007/978-3-030-01225-0_11) contains supplementary material, which is
available to authorized users.

V. Ferrari et al. (Eds.): ECCV 2018, LNCS 11208, pp. 176–192, 2018.
https://doi.org/10.1007/978-3-030-01225-0_11

Due to its intrinsic scale ambiguity, monocular depth estimation is a challenging problem, with state-of-the-art models [4,17] still producing >12% mean absolute relative error on the popular large-scale NYUv2 indoor dataset [24]. Such errors are prohibitive for applications such as 3D reconstruction or tracking, and fall very short of depth sensors such as the Kinect that boast relative depth error on the order of ~1% [14,25] indoors.

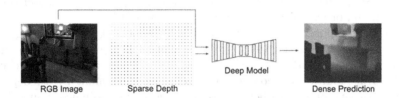

RGB Image   Sparse Depth   Deep Model   Dense Prediction

Fig. 1. From Sparse to Dense Depth. An RGB Image and very sparse depth map are input into a deep neural network. We obtain a high-quality dense depth prediction as our final output.

Acknowledging the limitations of monocular depth estimation, we provide our depth model with a sparse amount of measured depth along with an RGB image (See Fig. 1) in order to estimate the full depth map. Such sparse depth resolves the depth scale ambiguity, and could be obtained from e.g. a sparser illumination pattern in Time-of-Flight sensors [8], confident stereo matches, LiDAR-like sensors, or a custom-designed sparse sensor. We show that the resultant model can provide comparable performance to a modern depth sensor, despite only observing a small fraction of the depth map. We believe our results can thus motivate the design of smaller and more energy-efficient depth sensor hardware. As the objective is now to *densify* a sparse depth map (with additional cues from an RGB image), we call our model Deep Depth Densification, or D^3.

One advantage of our D^3 model is that it accommodates for arbitrary sparse depth input patterns, each of which may correspond to a relevant physical system. A regular grid of sparse depth may come from a lower-power depth sensor, while certain interest point sparse patterns such as ORB [27] or SIFT [21] could be output from modern SLAM systems [23]. In the main body of this work, we will focus on regular grid patterns due to their ease of interpretation and immediate relevance to existing depth sensor hardware, although we detail experiments on ORB sparse patterns in the Supplementary Materials.

Our contributions to the field of depth estimation are as follows:

1. A deep network model for dense scene depth estimation that achieves accuracies comparable to conventional depth sensors.
2. A depth estimation model which works *simultaneously* for indoors and outdoors scenes and is robust to common measurement errors.
3. A flexible, invertible method of parameterizing sparse depth inputs that can accommodate arbitrary sparse input patterns during training and testing.

2   Related Work

Depth estimation has been tackled in computer vision well before the advent of deep learning [28,29]; however, the popularization of encoder-decoder deep net architectures [1,20], which produce full-resolution pixel-wise prediction maps, make deep neural networks particularly well-suited for this task. Such advances have spurred a flurry of research into deep methods for depth estimation, whether through fusing CRFs with deep nets [37], leveraging geometry and stereo consistency [5,16], or exploring novel deep architectures [17].

Depth in computer vision is often used as a component for performing other perception tasks. One of the first approaches to deep depth estimation also simultaneously estimates surface normals and segmentation in a multitask architecture [4]. Other multitask vision networks [3,12,34] also commonly use depth as a complementary output to benefit overall network performance. Using depth as an explicit input is also common in computer vision, with plentiful applications in tracking [30,33], SLAM systems [13,36] and 3d reconstruction/detection [7,19]. There is clearly a pressing demand for high-quality depth maps, but current depth hardware solutions are power-hungry, have severe range limitations [8], and the current traditional depth estimation methods [4,17] fail to achieve the accuracies necessary to supersede such hardware.

Such challenges naturally lead to depth densification, a middle ground that combines the power of deep learning with energy-efficient sparse depth sensors. Depth densification is related to depth superresolution [10,31], but superresolution generally uses a bilinear or bicubic downsampled depth map as input, and thus still implicitly contains information from all pixels in the low-resolution map. This additional information would not be accessible to a true sparse sensor, and tends to make the estimation problem easier (see Supplementary Material). Work in [22,23] follows the more difficult densification paradigm where only a few pixels of measured depth are provided. We will show that our densification network outperforms the methods in both [22,23].

3   Methodology

3.1   Input Parametrization for Sparse Depth Inputs

We desire a parametrization of the sparse depth input that can accommodate arbitrary sparse input patterns. This should allow for varying such patterns not only across different deep models but even within the same model during training and testing. Therefore, rather than directly feeding a highly discontinuous sparse depth map into our deep depth densification (D^3) model (as in Fig. 1), we propose a more flexible parametrization of the sparse depth inputs.

At each training step, the inputs to our parametrization are:

1. $I(x,y)$ and $D(x,y)$: RGB vector-valued image I and ground truth depth D. Both maps have dimensions H × W. Invalid values in D are encoded as zero.

Algorithm 1. Sparse Inputs for the Deep Depth Densification (D^3) Model

---

INPUT image $I(x,y)$, depth $D(x,y)$, and pattern mask $M(x,y)$.

INITIALIZE $S_1(x,y) = 0$, $S_2(x,y) = 0$ for all (x,y).

FOR $\mathbf{r} := (x,y)$ s.t. $D(\mathbf{r}) = 0$ AND $M(\mathbf{r}) = 1$:

$\quad \mathbf{r}_{new} = \text{argmin}_{\mathbf{r}'} ||\mathbf{r} - \mathbf{r}'||_2$ s.t. $D(\mathbf{r}') > 0$;   ($|| \cdot ||_2$ *denotes the L_2 norm.*)

$\quad M(\mathbf{r}) = 0; \quad M(\mathbf{r}_{new}) = 1$;

ENDFOR   (*All depth locations are now valid.*)

FOR $\mathbf{r} := (x,y)$:

$\quad \mathbf{r}_{nearest} = \text{argmin}_{\mathbf{r}'} ||\mathbf{r}' - \mathbf{r}||_2$ s.t. $M(\mathbf{r}') = 1$;

$\quad S_1(x,y) = D(\mathbf{r}_{nearest}); \quad S_2(x,y) = \sqrt{||\mathbf{r}_{nearest} - \mathbf{r}||_2}$;

ENDFOR

OUTPUT **concatenate**(S_1, S_2)

---

2. $M(x,y)$: Binary pattern mask of dimensions H × W, where $M(x,y) = 1$ defines (x,y) locations of our desired depth samples. $M(x,y)$ is preprocessed so that all points where $M(x,y) = 1$ must correspond to valid depth points ($D(x,y) > 0$). (see Algorithm 1).

From I, D, and M, we form *two maps* for the sparse depth input, $S_1(x,y)$ and $S_2(x,y)$. Both maps have dimension H × W (see Fig. 2 for examples).

- $S_1(x,y)$ is a NN (nearest neighbor) fill of the sparse depth $M(x,y) * D(x,y)$.
- $S_2(x,y)$ is the Euclidean Distance Transform of $M(x,y)$, i.e. the L_2 distance between (x, y) and the closest point (x', y') where $M(x',y') = 1$.

The final parametrization of the sparse depth input is the concatenation of $S_1(x,y)$ and $S_2(x,y)$, with total dimension H × W × 2. This process is described in Algorithm 1. The parametrization is fast and involves at most two Euclidean Transforms. The resultant NN map S_1 is nonzero everywhere, allowing us to treat the densification problem as a *residual prediction* with respect to S_1. The distance map S_2 informs the model about the pattern mask $M(x,y)$ and acts as a prior on the residual magnitudes the model should output (i.e. points farther from a pixel with known depth tend to incur higher residuals). Inclusion of S_2 can substantially improve model performance and training stability, especially when multiple sparse patterns are used during training (see Sect. 5.3).

In this work, we primarily focus on regular grid patterns, as they are high-coverage sparse maps that enable straightforward comparisons to prior work (as in [22]) which often assume a grid-like sparse pattern, but our methods fully generalize to other patterns like ORB (see Supplementary Materials).

3.2 Sparse Pattern Selection

For regular grid patterns, we try to ensure minimal spatial bias when choosing the pattern mask $M(x,y)$ by enforcing equal spacing between subsequent pattern points in both the x and y directions. This results in a checkerboard

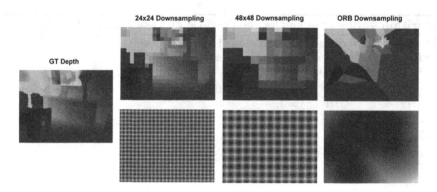

Fig. 2. Various Sparse Patterns. NN fill maps $\mathcal{S}_1$ (top row) and the sampling pattern Euclidean Distance transforms $\mathcal{S}_2$ (bottom row) are shown for both regular and irregular sparse patterns. Dark points in $\mathcal{S}_2$ correspond to the pixels where we have access to depth information.

pattern of square regions in the sparse depth map $\mathcal{S}_1$ (see Fig. 2). Such a strategy is convenient when one deep model must accommodate images of different resolutions, as we can simply extend the square pattern in $M(x, y)$ from one resolution to the next. For ease of interpretation, we will always use sparse patterns close to an integer level of downsampling; for a downsampling factor of $A \times A$, we take $\sim H * W/A^2$ depth values as the sparse input. For example, for 24×24 downsampling on a 480×640 image, this would be 0.18% of the total pixels.

Empirically we observed that it is beneficial to vary the sparse pattern $M(x, y)$ during training. For a desired final pattern of N sparse points, we employ a slow decay learning schedule following $N_{\text{sparse}}(t) = \lfloor 5Ne^{-0.0003t} + N \rfloor$ for training step $0 \leq t \leq 80000$. Such a schedule begins training at six times the desired sparse pattern density and smoothly decays towards the final density as training progresses. Compared to a static sparse pattern, we see a relative decrease of $\sim3\%$ in the training L_2 loss and also in the mean relative error when using this decay schedule. We can also train with randomly varying sampling densities at each training step. This we show in Sect. 5.3 results in a deep model which performs well *simultaneously* at different sampling densities.

4   Experimental Setup

4.1   Architecture

We base our network architecture (see Fig. 3) on the network used in [2] but with DenseNet [9] blocks in place of Inception [32] blocks. We empirically found it critical for our proposed model to carry the sparse depth information throughout the deep network, and the residual nature of DenseNet is well-suited for this requirement. For optimal results, our architecture retains feature maps at multiple resolutions for addition back into the network during the decoding phase.

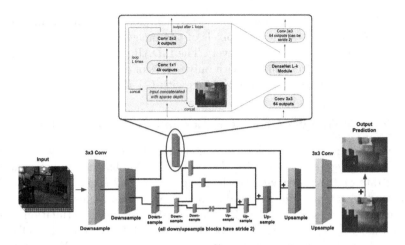

Fig. 3. D³ Network Architecture. Our proposed multi-scale deep network takes an RGB image concatenated with $\mathcal{S}_1$ and $\mathcal{S}_2$ as inputs. The first and last computational blocks are simple 3×3 stride-2 convolutions, but all other blocks are DenseNet modules [9] (see inset). All convolutional layers in the network are batch normalized [11] and ReLU activated. The network outputs a residual that is added to the sparse depth map $\mathcal{S}_1$ to produce the final dense depth prediction.

Each block in Fig. 3 represents a DenseNet Module (see Fig. 3 inset for a precise module schematic) except for the first and last blocks, which are simple 3×3 stride-2 convolutional layers. A copy of the sparse input $[\mathcal{S}_1, \mathcal{S}_2]$ is presented as an additional input to each module, downsampled to the appropriate resolution. Each DenseNet module consists of $2L$ layers and k feature maps per layer; we use $L = 5$ and $k = 12$. At downsample/upsample blocks, the final convolution has stride 2. The (residual) output of the network is added to the sparse input map $\mathcal{S}_1$ to obtain the final depth map estimate.

4.2   Datasets

We experiment extensively with both indoor and outdoor scenes. For indoor scenes, we use the NYUv2 [24] dataset, which provides high-quality 480×640 depth data taken with a Kinect V1 sensor with a range of up to 10m. Missing depth values are filled using a standard approach [18]. We use the official split of 249/215 train/validation scenes, and sample 26331 images from the training scenes. We further augment the training set with horizontal flips. We test on the standard validation set of 654 images to compare against other methods.

For outdoor scenes, we use the KITTI road scenes dataset [35], which has a depth range up to $\sim$85 m. KITTI provides over 80000 images for training, which we further augment with horizontal flips. We test on the full validation set ($\sim$10% the size of the training set). KITTI images have resolution 1392×512, but we take random 480×640 crops during training to enable joint training with

NYUv2 data. The 640 horizontal pixels are sampled randomly while the 480 vertical pixels are the 480 bottom pixels of the image (as KITTI only provides LiDAR GT depth towards ground level). The LiDAR projections used in KITTI result in very sparse depth maps (with only ∼10% of depths labeled per image), and we only evaluate our models on points with GT depth.

4.3   General Training Characteristics and Performance Metrics

In all our experiments we train with a batch size of 8 across 4 Maxwell Titan X GTX GPUs using Tensorflow 1.2.1. We train for 80000 batches and start with a learning rate of 1e−3, decaying the learning rate by 0.2 every 25000 steps. We use Adam [15] as our optimizer, and standard pixel-wise L_2 loss to train.

Standard metrics are used [4,23] to evaluate our depth estimation model against valid GT depth values. Let $\hat{y}$ be the predicted depth and y the GT depth for N pixels in the dataset. We measure: (1) Root Mean Square Error (RMSE): $\sqrt{\frac{1}{N}\sum[\hat{y}-y]^2}$, (2) Mean Absolute Relative Error (MRE): $\frac{100}{N}\sum\left(\frac{|\hat{y}-y|}{y}\right)$, and (3) Delta Thresholds (δ_i): $\frac{|\{\hat{y}|\max(\frac{y}{\hat{y}},\frac{\hat{y}}{y})<1.25^i\}|}{|\{\hat{y}\}|}$. δ_i is the percentage of pixels with relative error under a threshold controlled by the constant i.

5   Results and Analysis

Here we present results and analysis of the D^3 model for both indoor (NYUv2) and outdoor (KITTI) datasets. We further demonstrate that D^3 is robust to input errors and also generalizes to multiple sparse input patterns.

5.1   Indoor Scenes from NYUv2

From Table 1 we see that, at all pattern sparsities, the D^3 network offers superior performance for all metrics[1] compared to the results in [23] and in [22][2]. The accuracy metrics for the D^3 *mixed* network represent the NYUv2 results for a network that has been simultaneously trained on the NYUv2 (indoors) and KITTI (outdoors) datasets (more details in Sect. 5.4). We see that incorporating an outdoors dataset with significantly different semantics only incurs a mild degradation in accuracy. Figure 4 has comparative results for additional sparsities, and once again demonstrates that our trained models are more accurate than other recent approaches.

At 16×16 downsampling our absolute mean relative error falls below 1% (at 0.99%). At this point, the error of our D^3 model becomes comparable to the error in consumer-grade depth sensors [8]. Figure 5(a) presents a more detailed

---

[1] A model trained with 0.18% sparsity performs very well on a larger NYUv2 test set of 37K images: RMSE 0.116 m/ MRE 1.34%/δ_1 99.52%/δ_2 99.93%/δ_3 99.986%.

[2] As results in [22] were computed on a small subset of the NYUv2 val set, metrics were normalized to each work's reported NN fill RMSE to ensure fair comparison.

Table 1. D^3 Performance on NYUv2. Lower RMSE and MRE is better, while higher δ_i is better. NN Fill corresponds to using the sparse map $\mathcal{S}_1$ as our final prediction. If no sparse depth is provided, the D^3 model falls short of [4,17], but even at 0.01% points sampled the D^3 model offers significant improvements over state-of-the-art non-sparse methods. D^3 additionally performs the best compared to other sparse depth methods at all input sparsities.

Model	% Points sampled	Downsampling factor	RMSE (m)	MRE (%)	δ_1 (%)	δ_2 (%)	δ_3 (%)
Eigen et al. [4]	0	N/A	0.641	15.8	76.9	95.0	98.8
Laina et al. [17]	0	N/A	**0.573**	**12.7**	**81.1**	**95.3**	**98.8**
D^3 No Sparse	0	N/A	0.711	22.37	67.32	89.68	96.73
NN Fill	0.011	96 × 96	0.586	11.69	86.8	95.8	98.4
D^3 (Ours)	0.011	96 × 96	**0.318**	**7.20**	**94.2**	**98.9**	**99.8**
Ma et al. [23]	0.029	∼59 × 59	0.351	7.8	92.8	98.4	99.6
NN Fill	0.043	48 × 48	0.383	6.23	94.42	98.20	99.35
D^3 Mixed (Ours)	0.043	48 × 48	0.217	3.77	97.90	99.65	99.93
D^3 (Ours)	0.043	48 × 48	**0.193**	**3.21**	**98.31**	**99.73**	**99.95**
NN Fill	0.174	24 × 24	0.250	3.20	97.5	99.3	99.8
Lu et al. [22]	-	24 × 24	0.171	-	-	-	-
D^3 Mixed (Ours)	0.174	24 × 24	0.131	1.76	99.31	99.90	99.98
D^3 (Ours)	0.174	24 × 24	**0.118**	**1.49**	**99.45**	**99.92**	**99.98**
Ma et al. [23]	0.289	∼19 × 19	0.23	4.4	97.1	99.4	99.8
NN Fill	0.391	16 × 16	0.192	2.10	98.5	99.6	99.88
Lu et al. [22]	-	16 × 16	0.108	-	-	-	-
D^3 (Ours)	0.391	16 × 16	**0.087**	**0.99**	**99.72**	**99.97**	**99.99**

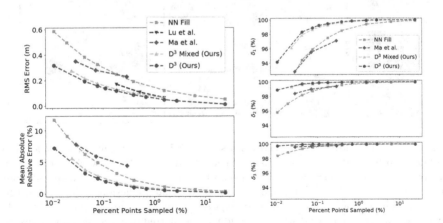

Fig. 4. Performance on the NYUv2 Dataset. RMSE and MRE are plotted on the left (lower is better), while the δ_i are plotted on the right (higher is better). Our D^3 models achieve the best performance at all sparsities, while joint training on outdoor data (D^3 mixed) only incurs a minor performance loss.

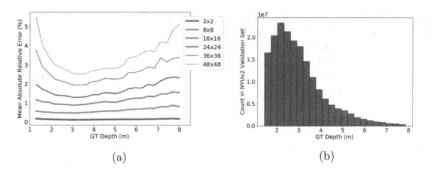

(a)   (b)

Fig. 5. NYUv2 MRE performance at different depths. (a) MRE at different depths for varying levels of sparsity. At 0.39% sparsity the average MRE is less than 1% which is comparable to depth sensors. (b) Histogram of GT depths in the validation dataset; higher relative errors correspond to rarer depth values.

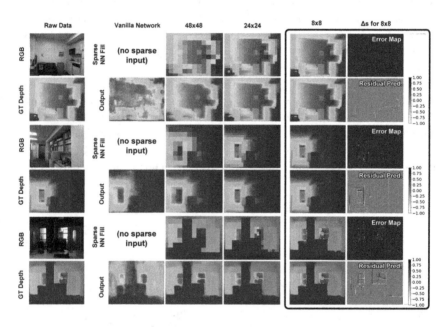

Fig. 6. Visualization of D^3 Predictions on NYUv2. Left column: Sample RGB and GT depths. Middle columns: sparse $\mathcal{S}_1$ map on top and D^3 network prediction on bottom for different sparsities. Vanilla network denotes the case with no sparse input (monocular depth estimation). Final column: D^3 residual predictions (summed with $\mathcal{S}_1$ to obtain the final prediction) and error maps of the final estimate with respect to GT. Errors are larger at farther distances. Residuals are plotted in grayscale and capped at $|\delta| \leq 1$ for better visualization; they exhibit similar sharp features as $\mathcal{S}_1$, showing how a D^3 model cancels out the nonsmoothness of $\mathcal{S}_1$.

plot of relative error at different values of GT depth. Our model performs well at most common indoor depths (around 2–4 m), as can be assessed from the histogram in Fig. 5(b). At farther depths the MRE deteriorates, but these depth values are rarer in the dataset. This suggests that using a more balanced dataset can improve those MRE values as well.

Table 2. Timing for D^3 and other architectures. Models are evaluated assuming 0.18% sparsity and using 1 Maxwell Titan X. The D^3 network achieves the lowest RMSE compared to other well known efficient network architectures. A slim version of D^3 runs at a near real-time 16 fps for VGA resolution.

Model	L	k	RMSE (m)	FPS	Forward Pass (s)	Model	L	k	RMSE (m)	FPS	Forward Pass (s)
D^3	5	12	**0.118**	10	0.11	SegNet [1]	-	-	0.150	5	0.20
D^3	3	8	0.127	13	0.08	ENet [26]	-	-	0.237	25	0.04
D^3	2	6	0.131	16	0.06						

Visualizations of our network predictions on the NYUv2 dataset are shown in Fig. 6. At a highly sparse 48 × 48 downsampling, our D^3 network already shows a dramatic improvement over a vanilla network without any sparse input. We note here that although network outputs are added as residuals to a sparse map with many first order discontinuities, the final predictions appear smooth and relatively free of sharp edge artifacts. Indeed, in the final column of Fig. 6, we can see how the direct residual predictions produced by our networks also contain sharp features which cancels out the non-smoothness in the sparse maps.

5.2   Computational Analysis

In Table 2 we show the forward pass time and accuracy for a variety of models at 0.18% points sampled. Our standard D^3 model with $L = 5$ and $k = 12$ achieves the lowest error and takes 0.11s per VGA frame per forward pass. Slimmer versions of the D^3 network incur mild accuracy degradation but still outperform other well known efficient architectures [1,26]. The baseline speed for our D^3 networks can thus approach real-time speeds for full-resolution 480 × 640 inputs, and we expect these speeds can be further improved by weight quantization and other optimization methods for deep networks [6]. Trivially, operating at half resolution would result in our slimmer D^3 networks operating at a real-time speed of >60fps. This speed is important for many application areas where depth is a critical component for scene understanding.

5.3   Generalizing D^3 to Multiple Patterns and the Effect of $\mathcal{S}_2$

We train a D^3 network with a different input sparsity (sampled uniformly between 0.065% and 0.98% points) for each batch. Figure 7(a) shows how this multi-sparsity D^3 network performs relative to the 0.18% and 0.39% sparsity models. The single-sparsity trained D^3 networks predictably perform the best near the sparsity they were tuned for. However, the multi-sparsity D^3 network only performs slightly worse at those sparsities, and dramatically outperforms the single-sparsity networks away from their training sparsity value. Evidently, a random sampling schedule effectively regularizes our model to work *simultaneously at all sparsities within a wide range*. This robustness may be useful in scenarios where different measurement modes are used in the same device.

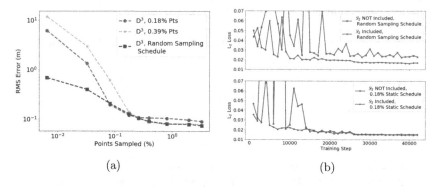

(a)   (b)

Fig. 7. Multi-sparsity D^3 models. (a) The Random Sampling network was trained with a different sparse pattern (between 0.065% and 0.98% points sampled) on every iteration, and performs well at all sparsity levels while being only mildly surpassed by single-density networks at their specialized sparsities. (b) Validation loss curves (for 0.18% points sampled) for a D^3 models trained with and without inclusion of distance map S_2. S_2 is clearly crucial for stability and performance, especially when training with complex pattern schedules.

Inclusion of the distance map S_2 gives our network spatial information of the sparse pattern, which is especially important when the sparse pattern changes during training. Figure 7(b) shows validation L_2 loss curves for D^3 networks trained with and without S_2. S_2 improves relative L_2 validation loss by 34.4% and greatly stabilizies training when the sparse pattern is varied randomly during training. For a slow decay sampling schedule (i.e. what is used for the majority of our D^3 networks), the improvement is 8.8%, and even for a static sampling schedule (bottom of Fig. 7(b)) there is a 2.8% improvement. The inclusion of the distance map is thus clearly essential to train our model well.

5.4   Generalizing D^3 to Outdoor Scenes

We extend our model to the challenging outdoor KITTI dataset [35]. All our KITTI D^3 models are initialized to a pre-trained NYUv2 model. We then train either with only KITTI data (KITTI-exclusive) or with a 50/50 mix of NYUv2 and KITTI data for each batch (mixed model). Since NYUv2 images have a max depth of 10 m, *depth values are scaled by 0.1* for the KITTI-exclusive model. For the mixed model we use a scene-agnostic scaling rule; we scale all images down to have a max depth of $\leq$10 m, and invert this scaling at inference. Our state-of-the-art results are shown in Table 3. Importantly, as for NYUv2, our mixed model only performs slightly worse than the KITTI-exclusive network. More results for additional sparsities are presented in the Supplementary Material.

Table 3. D^3 Model Performance on the KITTI Dataset. Lower values of RMSE and MRE are better, while higher values of δ_i are better. For competing methods we show results at the closest sparsity. The performance of our models, including the mixed models, is superior by a large margin.

Model	% Points sampled	Downsample factor	RMSE (m)	MRE (%)	δ_1 (%)	δ_2 (%)	δ_3 (%)
NN Fill	0.077	36 × 36	4.441	9.306	91.88	97.75	99.04
D^3 Mixed (Ours)	0.077	36 × 36	1.906	3.14	98.62	99.65	99.88
D^3 (Ours)	0.077	36 × 36	**1.600**	**2.50**	**99.12**	**99.76**	**99.91**
Ma et al. [23]	0.096	~32 × 32	3.851	8.3	91.9	97.0	98.6
NN Fill	0.174	24 × 24	3.203	5.81	96.62	99.03	99.57
D^3 Mixed (Ours)	0.174	24 × 24	1.472	2.22	99.30	99.83	99.94
D^3 (Ours)	0.174	24 × 24	**1.387**	**2.09**	**99.40**	**99.85**	**99.95**
Ma et al. [23]	0.240	~20 × 20	3.378	7.3	93.5	97.6	98.9
NN Fill	0.391	16 × 16	2.245	3.73	98.67	99.60	99.81
D^3 Mixed (Ours)	0.391	16 × 16	1.120	1.62	99.67	99.92	99.97
D^3 (Ours)	0.391	16 × 16	**1.008**	**1.42**	**99.76**	**99.94**	**99.98**

Visualizations of the our model outputs are shown in Fig. 8. The highlight here is that the mixed model produces high-quality depth maps for both NYUv2 and KITTI. Interestingly, even the KITTI-exclusive model (bottom row of Fig. 8) produces good qualitative results on the NYUv2 dataset. Perhaps more strikingly, even an NYUv2 pretrained model with no KITTI data training (third-to-last row of Fig. 8) produces reasonable results on KITTI. This suggests that our D^3 models intrinsically possess some level of cross-domain generalizability.

5.5   Robustness Tests

Thus far, we have sampled depth from high-quality Kinect and LiDAR depth maps, but in practice sparse depth inputs may come from less reliable sources. We now demonstrate how our D^3 network performs given the following common errors within the sparse depth input:

1. Spatial misregistration between the RGB camera and depth sensor.
2. Random Gaussian error.
3. Random holes (dropout), e.g. due to shadows, specular reflection, etc.

Fig. 8. Joint Predictions on NYUv2 and KITTI. The RGB, Depth GT, and Sparse Input $\mathcal{S}_1$ are given in the first three rows. Predictions by three models on both indoors and outdoors scenes are given in the final three rows, with the second-to-last row showing the mixed model trained on both datasets simultaneously. All sparse maps have a density of 0.18% ($\sim 24 \times 24$ downsampling).

In Fig. 9 we show examples of each of these potential sources of error, and in Fig. 10 we show how D^3 performs when trained with such errors in the sparse depth input (see Supplementary Material for for tabulated metrics). The D^3 network degrades gracefully under all sources of error, with most models still outperforming the other baselines in Table 1 (none of which were subject to input errors). It is especially encouraging that network performs robustly under constant mis-registration error, a very common issue when multiple imaging sensors are active in the same visual system. The network effectively learns to fix the calibration between the different visual inputs. Predictably, the error is much higher when the mis-registration is randomly varying per image.

Fig. 9. Potential Errors in Sparse Depth. The three sparse depth maps on the right all exhibit significant errors that are common in real sensors.

5.6   Discussion

Through our experiments, we've shown how the D^3 model performs very well at taking a sparse depth measurement in a variety of settings and turning it into a dense depth map. Most notably, our model can simultaneously perform well both on indoor and outdoor scenes. We attribute the overall performance of the model to a number of factors. As can be gathered from Table 2, the design of our multi-scale architecture, in which the sparse inputs are ingested at various scales and outputs are treated as residuals with respect to $\mathcal{S}_1$, is important for optimizing performance. Our proposed sparse input parameterization clearly allows for better and more stable training as seen in Fig. 7. Finally, the design of the training curriculum, in which we use varying sparsities in the depth input during training, also plays an important role. Such a strategy makes the model robust to test time variations in sparsity (see Fig. 7) and reduces overall errors.

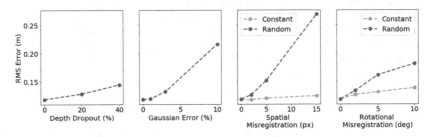

Fig. 10. Accuracy of D^3 Networks under Various Sparse Depth Errors. Under all potential error sources (with the exception of the unlikely random spatial mis-registration error), the D^3 network exhibits graceful error degradation. This error degradation is almost negligible for constant spatial mis-registration.

6   Conclusions

We have demonstrated that a trained deep depth densification (D^3) network can use sparse depth information and a registered RGB image to produce high-quality, dense depth maps. Our flexible parametrization of the sparse depth information leads to models that generalize readily to multiple scene types (working simultaneously on indoor and outdoor images, from depths of 1 m to 80 m) and to diverse sparse input patterns. Even at fairly aggressive sparsities for indoor scenes, we achieve a mean absolute relative error of under 1%, comparable to the performance of consumer-grade depth sensor hardware. We also found that our model is fairly robust to various input errors.

We have thus shown that sparse depth measurements can be sufficient for applications that require an RGBD input, whether indoors or outdoors. A natural next step in our line of inquiry would be to evaluate how densified depth maps perform in 3d-reconstruction algorithms, tracking systems, or perception models for related vision tasks such as surface normal prediction. We hope that our work motivates additional research into uses for sparse depth from both the software and hardware perspectives.

References

1. Badrinarayanan, V., Kendall, A., Cipolla, R.: SegNet: a deep convolutional encoder-decoder architecture for image segmentation. IEEE Trans. Pattern Anal. Mach.Intell. **39**(12), 2481–2495 (2017)
2. Chen, W., Fu, Z., Yang, D., Deng, J.: Single-image depth perception in the wild. In: Advances in Neural Information Processing Systems, pp. 730–738 (2016)
3. Chen, Z., Badrinarayanan, V., Lee, C.Y., Rabinovich, A.: GradNorm: gradient normalization for adaptive loss balancing in deep multitask networks. arXiv preprint arXiv:1711.02257 (2017)
4. Eigen, D., Fergus, R.: Predicting depth, surface normals and semantic labels with a common multi-scale convolutional architecture. In: Proceedings of the IEEE International Conference on Computer Vision, pp. 2650–2658 (2015)
5. Garg, R., B.G., V.K., Carneiro, G., Reid, I.: Unsupervised CNN for single view depth estimation: geometry to the rescue. In: Leibe, B., Matas, J., Sebe, N., Welling, M. (eds.) ECCV 2016. LNCS, vol. 9912, pp. 740–756. Springer, Cham (2016). https://doi.org/10.1007/978-3-319-46484-8_45
6. Han, S., Mao, H., Dally, W.J.: Deep compression: compressing deep neural networks with pruning, trained quantization and Huffman coding. arXiv preprint arXiv:1510.00149 (2015)
7. Hermans, A., Floros, G., Leibe, B.: Dense 3d semantic mapping of indoor scenes from RGB-D images. In: 2014 IEEE International Conference on Robotics and Automation (ICRA), pp. 2631–2638. IEEE (2014)
8. Horaud, R., Hansard, M., Evangelidis, G., Ménier, C.: An overview of depth cameras and range scanners based on time-of-flight technologies. Mach. Vis. Appl. **27**(7), 1005–1020 (2016)
9. Huang, G., Liu, Z., Weinberger, K.Q., van der Maaten, L.: Densely connected convolutional networks. In: Proceedings of the IEEE Conference on Computer Vision and Pattern Recognition, vol. 1, p. 3 (2017)
10. Hui, T.-W., Loy, C.C., Tang, X.: Depth map super-resolution by deep multi-scale guidance. In: Leibe, B., Matas, J., Sebe, N., Welling, M. (eds.) ECCV 2016. LNCS, vol. 9907, pp. 353–369. Springer, Cham (2016). https://doi.org/10.1007/978-3-319-46487-9_22
11. Ioffe, S., Szegedy, C.: Batch normalization: accelerating deep network training by reducing internal covariate shift. In: International Conference on Machine Learning, pp. 448–456 (2015)
12. Kendall, A., Gal, Y., Cipolla, R.: Multi-task learning using uncertainty to weigh losses for scene geometry and semantics. arXiv preprint arXiv:1705.07115 (2017)
13. Kerl, C., Sturm, J., Cremers, D.: Dense visual slam for RGB-D cameras. In: 2013 IEEE/RSJ International Conference on Intelligent Robots and Systems (IROS), pp. 2100–2106. IEEE (2013)
14. Khoshelham, K., Elberink, S.O.: Accuracy and resolution of kinect depth data for indoor mapping applications. Sensors **12**(2), 1437–1454 (2012)
15. Kingma, D.P., Ba, J.: Adam: a method for stochastic optimization. arXiv preprint arXiv:1412.6980 (2014)

16. Kuznietsov, Y., Stückler, J., Leibe, B.: Semi-supervised deep learning for monocular depth map prediction. In: Proceedings of the IEEE Conference on Computer Vision and Pattern Recognition, pp. 6647–6655 (2017)
17. Laina, I., Rupprecht, C., Belagiannis, V., Tombari, F., Navab, N.: Deeper depth prediction with fully convolutional residual networks. In: 2016 Fourth International Conference on 3D Vision (3DV), pp. 239–248. IEEE (2016)
18. Levin, A., Lischinski, D., Weiss, Y.: Colorization using optimization. ACM Trans. Graph. (ToG) **23**, 689–694 (2004)
19. Lin, D., Fidler, S., Urtasun, R.: Holistic scene understanding for 3d object detection with RGBD cameras. In: 2013 IEEE International Conference on Computer Vision (ICCV), pp. 1417–1424. IEEE (2013)
20. Long, J., Shelhamer, E., Darrell, T.: Fully convolutional networks for semantic segmentation. In: Proceedings of the IEEE Conference on Computer Vision and Pattern Recognition, pp. 3431–3440 (2015)
21. Lowe, D.G.: Distinctive image features from scale-invariant keypoints. Int. J. Comput. Vis. **60**(2), 91–110 (2004)
22. Lu, J., Forsyth, D.A., et al.: Sparse depth super resolution. In: CVPR, vol. 6 (2015)
23. Ma, F., Karaman, S.: Sparse-to-dense: depth prediction from sparse depth samples and a single image. arXiv preprint arXiv:1709.07492 (2017)
24. Silberman, N., Hoiem, D., Kohli, P., Fergus, R.: Indoor segmentation and support inference from RGBD images. In: Fitzgibbon, A., Lazebnik, S., Perona, P., Sato, Y., Schmid, C. (eds.) ECCV 2012. LNCS, vol. 7576, pp. 746–760. Springer, Heidelberg (2012). https://doi.org/10.1007/978-3-642-33715-4_54
25. Nguyen, C.V., Izadi, S., Lovell, D.: Modeling kinect sensor noise for improved 3d reconstruction and tracking. In: 2012 Second International Conference on 3D Imaging, Modeling, Processing, Visualization and Transmission (3DIMPVT), pp. 524–530. IEEE (2012)
26. Paszke, A., Chaurasia, A., Kim, S., Culurciello, E.: ENet: a deep neural network architecture for real-time semantic segmentation. arXiv preprint arXiv:1606.02147 (2016)
27. Rublee, E., Rabaud, V., Konolige, K., Bradski, G.: ORB: an efficient alternative to SIFT or SURF. In: 2011 IEEE International Conference on Computer Vision (ICCV), pp. 2564–2571. IEEE (2011)
28. Saxena, A., Chung, S.H., Ng, A.Y.: Learning depth from single monocular images. In: Advances in Neural Information Processing Systems, pp. 1161–1168 (2006)
29. Sinz, F.H., Candela, J.Q., Bakır, G.H., Rasmussen, C.E., Franz, M.O.: Learning depth from stereo. In: Rasmussen, C.E., Bülthoff, H.H., Schölkopf, B., Giese, M.A. (eds.) DAGM 2004. LNCS, vol. 3175, pp. 245–252. Springer, Heidelberg (2004). https://doi.org/10.1007/978-3-540-28649-3_30
30. Song, S., Xiao, J.: Tracking revisited using RGBD camera: unified benchmark and baselines. In: 2013 IEEE International Conference on Computer Vision (ICCV), pp. 233–240. IEEE (2013)
31. Song, X., Dai, Y., Qin, X.: Learning depth super resolution using deep convolutional neural network. In: Lai, S.-H., Lepetit, V., Nishino, K., Sato, Y. (eds.) ACCV 2016. LNCS, vol. 10114, pp. 360–376. Springer, Cham (2017). https://doi.org/10.1007/978-3-319-54190-7
32. Szegedy, C., et al.: Going deeper with convolutions. In: CVPR (2015)
33. Teichman, A., Lussier, J.T., Thrun, S.: Learning to segment and track in RGBD. IEEE Trans. Autom. Sci. Eng. **10**(4), 841–852 (2013)

34. Teichmann, M., Weber, M., Zoellner, M., Cipolla, R., Urtasun, R.: Multi-Net: real-time joint semantic reasoning for autonomous driving. arXiv preprint arXiv:1612.07695 (2016)
35. Uhrig, J., Schneider, N., Schneider, L., Franke, U., Brox, T., Geiger, A.: Sparsity invariant CNNS. In: International Conference on 3D Vision (3DV) (2017)
36. Whelan, T., Kaess, M., Johannsson, H., Fallon, M., Leonard, J.J., McDonald, J.: Real-time large-scale dense RGB-D slam with volumetric fusion. Int. J. Robot. Res. **34**(4–5), 598–626 (2015)
37. Xu, D., Ricci, E., Ouyang, W., Wang, X., Sebe, N.: Multi-scale continuous CRFS as sequential deep networks for monocular depth estimation. In: Proceedings of CVPR (2017)

Specular-to-Diffuse Translation
for Multi-view Reconstruction

Shihao Wu[1], Hui Huang[2]([✉]), Tiziano Portenier[1], Matan Sela[3],
Daniel Cohen-Or[2,4], Ron Kimmel[3], and Matthias Zwicker[5]

[1] University of Bern, Bern, Switzerland
[2] Shenzhen University, Shenzhen, China
hhzhiyan@gmail.com
[3] Technion - Israel Institute of Technology, Haifa, Israel
[4] Tel-Aviv University, Tel Aviv, Israel
[5] University of Maryland, College Park, USA

Abstract. Most multi-view 3D reconstruction algorithms, especially when shape-from-shading cues are used, assume that object appearance is predominantly diffuse. To alleviate this restriction, we introduce S2Dnet, a generative adversarial network for transferring multiple views of objects with specular reflection into diffuse ones, so that multi-view reconstruction methods can be applied more effectively. Our network extends unsupervised image-to-image translation to multi-view "specular to diffuse" translation. To preserve object appearance across multiple views, we introduce a Multi-View Coherence loss (MVC) that evaluates the similarity and faithfulness of local patches after the view-transformation. In addition, we carefully design and generate a large synthetic training data set using physically-based rendering. During testing, our network takes only the raw glossy images as input, without extra information such as segmentation masks or lighting estimation. Results demonstrate that multi-view reconstruction can be significantly improved using the images filtered by our network.

Keywords: Generative adversarial network
Multi-view reconstruction · Multi-view coherence · Specular-to-diffuse
Image translation

1 Introduction

Three-dimensional reconstruction from multi-view images is a long standing problem in computer vision. State-of-the-art shape-from-shading techniques achieve impressive results [1,2]. These techniques, however, make rather strong

Electronic supplementary material The online version of this chapter (https://doi.org/10.1007/978-3-030-01225-0_12) contains supplementary material, which is available to authorized users.

© Springer Nature Switzerland AG 2018
V. Ferrari et al. (Eds.): ECCV 2018, LNCS 11208, pp. 193–211, 2018.
https://doi.org/10.1007/978-3-030-01225-0_12

assumptions about the data, mainly that target objects are predominantly diffuse with almost no specular reflectance. Multi-view reconstruction of glossy surfaces is a challenging problem, which has been addressed by adding specialized hardware (e.g., coded pattern projection [3] and two-layer LCD [4]), imposing surface constraints [5,6], or making use of additional information like silhouettes and environment maps [7], or the Blinn-Phong model [8].

In this paper, we present a generative adversarial neural network (GAN) that translates multi-view images of objects with specular reflection to diffuse ones. The network aims to generate a specular-free surface, which then can be reconstructed by a standard multi-view reconstruction technique as shown in Fig. 1. We name our translation network, S2Dnet, for Specular-to-Diffuse. Our approach is inspired by recent GAN-based image translation methods, like pix2pix [9] or cycleGAN [10], that can transform an image from one domain to another. Such techniques, however, are not designed for multi-view image translation. Directly applying these translation techniques to individual views is prone to reconstruction artifacts due to the lack of coherence among the transformed images. Hence, instead of using single views, our network considers a triplet of nearby views as input. These triplets allow learning the mutual information of neighboring views. More specifically, we introduce a global-local discriminator and a perceptual correspondence loss that evaluate the multi-view coherency of local corresponding image patches. Experiments show that our method outperforms baseline image translation methods.

Fig. 1. Specular-to-diffuse translation of multi-view images. We show eleven views of a glossy object (top), and the specular-free images generated by our network (bottom).

Another obstacle of applying image translation techniques to specularity removal is the lack of good training data. It is rather impractical to take enough paired or even unpaired photos to successfully train a deep network. Inspired by the recent works of simulating training data by physically-based rendering [11–14] and domain adaptation [15–18], we present a fine-tuned process for generating training data, then adapting it to real world data. Instead of using Shapenet [19], we develop a new training dataset that includes models with richer geometric details, which allows us to apply our method to complex real-world data. Both quantitative and qualitative evaluations demonstrate that the performance of multi-view reconstruction can be significantly improved using the images filtered by our network. We show also the performance of adapting our network on real world training and testing data with some promising results.

2 Related Work

Specular Object Reconstruction. Image based 3D reconstruction has been widely used for AR/VR applications, and the reconstruction speed and quality have been improved dramatically in recent years. However, most photometric stereo methods are based on the assumption that the object surface is diffuse, that is, the appearance of the object is view independent. Such assumptions, however, are not valid for glossy or specular objects in uncontrolled environments. It is well known that modeling the specularity is difficult as the specular effects are largely caused by the complicated global illumination that is usually unknown. For example, Godard et al. [7] first reconstruct a rough model by silhouette and then refine it using the specified environment map. Their method can reconstruct high quality specular surfaces from HDR images with extra information, such as silhouette and environment map.

In contrast, our method requires only the multi-view images as input. Researchers have proposed sophisticated equipment, such as a setup with two-layer LCDs to encode the directions of the emitted light field [4], taking advantages of the IR images recorded by RGB-D scanners [20,21] or casting coded patterns onto mirror-like objects [3]. While such techniques can effectively handle challenging non-diffuse effects, they require additional hardware and user expertise. Another way to tackle this problem is by introducing additional assumptions, such as surface constraints [5,6], the Blinn-Phong model [8], and shape-from-specularity [22]. These methods can also benefit from our network that outputs diffuse images, where strong specularities are removed from uncontrolled illumination. Please refer to [23] for a survey on specular object reconstruction.

GAN-based Image-to-Image Translation. We are inspired by the latest success of learning based image-to-image translation methods, such as ConditionalGAN [9], cycleGAN [10], [24] dualGAN, and discoGAN [17]. The remarkable capacity of Generative Adversarial Networks (GANs) [25] in modeling data distributions allows these methods to transform images from one domain to another with relatively small amounts of training data, while preserving the intrinsic structure of original images faithfully. With improved multi-scale training techniques, such as Progressive GAN [26] and pix2pixHD [27], image-to-image translation can be performed at mega pixel resolutions and achieve results of stunning visual quality.

Recently, modified image-to-image translation architectures have been successfully applied to ill-posed or underconstrained vision tasks, including face frontal view synthesis [28], facial geometry reconstruction [29–32], raindrop removal [33], or shadow removal [34]. These applications motivate us to develop a glossiness removal method based on GANs to facilitate multi-view 3D reconstruction of non-diffuse objects.

Learning-based Multi-view 3D Reconstruction. Learning surface reconstruction from multi-view images end-to-end has been an active research direction recently [35–38]. Wu et al. [39] and Gwak et al. [40] use GANs to learn the latent space of shapes and apply it to single image 3D reconstruction. 3D-R2N2 [36] designs a recurrent network for unified single and multi-view reconstruction. Image2Mesh [41] learns parameters of free-form-deformation of a base model. Nonetheless, in general, the reconstruction quality of these methods cannot really surpass that of traditional approaches that exploit multiple-view geometry and heavily engineered photometric stereo pipelines. To take the local image feature coherence into account, we focus on removing the specular effect on the image level and resort to the power of multi-view reconstruction as a post-processing and also a production step.

On the other hand, there are works, closer to ours, that focus on applying deep learning on subparts of the stereo reconstruction pipeline, such as depth and pose estimation [42], feature point detection and description [43,44], semantic segmentation [45], and bundle adjustment [46,47]. These methods still impose the Lambertian assumption for objects or scenes, where our method can serve as a preprocessing step to deal with glossiness.

Learning-based Intrinsic Image Decomposition. Our method is also loosely related to some recent works on learning intrinsic image decomposition. These methods include training a CNN to reconstruct rendering parameters, e.g., material [48,49], reflectance maps [50], illumination [51], or some combination of those components [13,48,52]. These methods are often trained on synthetic data and are usually applied to the re-rendering of single images. Our method shares certain similarity with these methods. However, our goal is not to recover intrinsic images with albedos. Disregarding albedo, we aim for output images with a consistent appearance across the entire training set that reflects the structure of the object.

3 Multi-view Specular-to-Diffuse GAN

In this section, we introduce S2Dnet, a conditional GAN that translates multi-view images of highly specular scenes into corresponding diffuse images. The input to our model is a multi-view sequence of a glossy scene without any additional input such as segmentation masks, camera parameters, or light probes.

This enables our model to process real-world data, where such additional information is not readily available. The output of our model directly serves as input to state-of-the-art photometric stereo pipelines, resulting in improved 3D reconstruction without additional effort. Figure 2 shows a visualization of the proposed model. We discuss the training data, one of our major contributions, in Sect. 3.1. In Sect. 3.2 we introduce the concept of inter-view coherence that enables our model to process multiple views of a scene in a consistent manner, which is important in the context of multi-view reconstruction. Then, we outline in Sect. 3.3 the overall end-to-end training procedure. Implementation details are discussed in Sect. 3.4. Upon publication we will release both our data (synthetic and real) and the proposed model to foster further work.

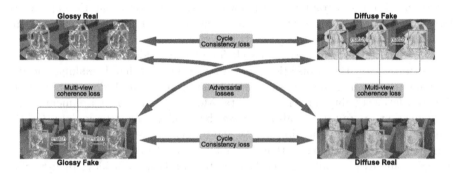

Fig. 2. Overview of S2Dnet. Two generators and two discriminators are trained simultaneously to learn cross-domain translations between the glossy and the diffuse domain. In each training iteration, the model randomly picks and forwards a real glossy and diffuse image sequence, computes the loss functions and updates the model parameters.

Fig. 3. Gallery of our synthetically rendered specular-to-diffuse training data.

3.1   Training Data

To train our model to translate multi-view glossy images to diffuse correspondents, we need appropriate data for both domains, i.e., glossy source domain images as inputs, and diffuse images as the target domain. Yi et al.[24] propose a MATERIAL dataset consisting of unlabeled data grouped in different material classes, such as plastic, fabric, metal, and leather, and they train GANs to perform material transfer. However, the MATERIAL dataset does not contain multi-view images and thus is not suited for our application. Moreover, the dataset is rather small and we expect our deep model to require a larger amount of training data. Hence, we propose a novel synthetic dataset consisting of multi-view images, which is both sufficiently large to train deep networks and complex to generalize to real-world objects. For this purpose, we collect and align 91 watertight and noise-free geometric models featuring rich geometric details from SketchFab (Fig. 3). We exclude three models for testing and use the remaining 88 models for training. To obtain a dataset that generalizes well to real-world images, we use PBRT, a physically based renderer [53] to render these geometric models in various environments with a wide variety of glossy materials applied to form our source domain. Next, we render the target domain images by applying a Lambertian material to our geometric models.

Our experiments show that the choice of the rendering parameters has a strong impact on the translation performance. On one hand, making the two domains more similar by choosing similar materials for both domains improves the translation quality on synthetic data. Moreover, simple environments, such as a constant ground plane, also increase the quality on synthetic data. On the other hand, such simplifications cause the model to overfit and prevent generalization to real-world data. Hence, a main goal of our dataset is to provide enough complexity to allow generalization to real data. To achieve realistic illumination, we randomly sample one of 20 different HDR indoor environment maps and randomly rotate it for each scene. In addition, we orient a directional light source pointing from the camera approximately towards the center of the scene and position two additional light sources above the scene. The intensities, positions, and directions of these additional light sources are randomly jittered. This setup guarantees a rather even, but still random illumination. To render the source domain images, we applied the various metal materials defined in PBRT, including copper, silver, and gold. Material roughness and index of refraction are randomly sampled to cover a large variety of glossy materials. We randomly sample camera positions on the upper hemisphere around the scene pointing towards the center of the scene. To obtain multi-view data, we always sample 5 close-by, consecutive camera positions in clock-wise order while keeping the scene parameters fixed to mimic the common procedure of taking photos for stereo reconstruction. Since we collect 5 images of the same scene and the input to our network consists of 3 views, we obtain 3 training samples per scene. All rendered images are of 512×512 resolution, which is the limit for our GPU memory. However, it is likely that higher resolutions would further improve the reconstruction quality. Finally, we render the exact same images again with a white, Lambertian material, i.e., the mapping from the source to the target domain is bijective. The proposed procedure results in a training dataset of more than 647k images, i.e., more than 320k images per domain. For testing, we rendered 2k sequences of images, each consisting of 50 images. All qualitative results on synthetic data shown in this paper belong to this test set.

3.2   Inter-view Coherence

Multi-view reconstruction algorithms leverage corresponding features in different views to accurately estimate the 3D geometry. Therefore, we cannot expect good reconstruction quality if the glossy images in a multi-view sequence are translated independently using standard image translation methods, e.g., [9,10]. This will introduce inconsistencies along the different views, and thus cause artifacts in the subsequent reconstruction. We therefore propose a novel model that enforces inter-view coherence by processing multiple views simultaneously. Our approach consists of a global and local consistency constraint: the global constraint is implemented using an appropriate network architecture, and the local consistency is enforced using a novel loss function.

Global Inter-view Coherence. A straightforward idea to incorporate multiple views is to stack them pixel-by-pixel before feeding them to the network. We found that this does not lead to strong enough constraints, since the network can still learn independent filter weights for the different views. This results in blurry translations, especially if corresponding pixels in different views are not aligned, which is typically the case. Instead, we concatenate the different views along the spatial axis before feeding them to the network. This solution, although simple, enforces the network to use the same filter weights for all views, and thus effectively avoids inconsistencies on a global scale.

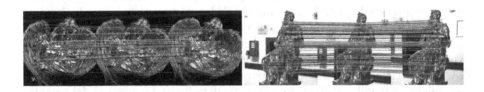

Fig. 4. Two examples of the SIFT correspondences pre-computed for our training

Local Inter-view Coherence. Incorporating loss functions based on local image patches has been successfully applied to generative adversarial models, such as image completion [54] or texture synthesis [55]. However, comparing image patches at random locations is not meaningful in a multi-view setup for stereo reconstruction. Instead, we encourage the network to maintain feature point correspondences in the input sequence, i.e., inter-view correspondences should be invariant to the translation. Since the subsequent reconstruction pipeline relies on such correspondences, maintaining them during translation should improve reconstruction quality. To achieve this, we first extract SIFT feature correspondences for all training images. For each training sequence consisting of three views, we compute corresponding feature points between the

different views in the source domain; see Fig. 4 for two examples. During training, we encourage the network output at the SIFT feature locations to be similar
along the views using a perceptual loss in VGG feature space [27,56–58]. The
key idea is to measure both high- and low-level similarity of two images by considering their feature activations in a deep CNN like VGG. We adopt this idea
to keep local image patches around corresponding SIFT features perceptually
similar in the translated output. The perceptual loss in VGG feature space is
defined as:

$$\mathcal{L}_{VGG}(x, \hat{x}) = \sum_{i=1}^{N} \frac{1}{M_i} \|F^{(i)}(x) - F^{(i)}(\hat{x})\|_1, \tag{1}$$

where $F^{(i)}$ denotes the i-th layer in the VGG network consisting of M_i elements.
Now consider a glossy input sequence consisting of three images X_1, X_2, X_3, and
the corresponding diffuse sequence $\tilde{X}_1, \tilde{X}_2, \tilde{X}_3$ produced by our model. A SIFT
correspondence for this sequence consists of three image coordinates p_1, p_2, p_3,
one in each glossy image, and all three pixels at the corresponding coordinates
represent the same feature. We then extract local image patches $\tilde{x}_i$ centered at
p_i from $\tilde{X}_i$, and define the perceptual correspondence loss as:

$$\mathcal{L}_{corr}(\tilde{X}_1, \tilde{X}_2, \tilde{X}_3) = \mathcal{L}_{VGG}(\tilde{x}_1, \tilde{x}_2) + \mathcal{L}_{VGG}(\tilde{x}_2, \tilde{x}_3) + \mathcal{L}_{VGG}(\tilde{x}_1, \tilde{x}_3). \tag{2}$$

3.3   Training Procedure

Given two sets of data samples from two domains, a source domain A and a target
domain B, the goal of image translation is to find a mapping T that transforms data
points $X_i \in A$ to B such that $T(X_i) = \tilde{X}_i \in B$, while the intrinsic structure of X_i
should be preserved under T. Training GANs has been proven to produce aston-
ishing results on this task, both in supervised settings where the data of the two
domains are paired [9], and in unsupervised cases using unpaired data [10]. In our
experiments, we observed that both approaches (ConditionalGAN [9] and cycle-
GAN [10]) perform similarly well on our dataset. However, while paired training
data might be readily available for synthetic data, paired real-world data is difficult to obtain. Therefore we come up with a design for unsupervised learning that
can easily be fine-tuned on unpaired real-world data.

Cycle-consistency Loss. Similar to CycleGAN [10], we learn the mapping
between domain A and B with two translators $G_B : A \rightarrow B$ and $G_A : B \rightarrow A$
that are trained simultaneously. The key idea is to train with cycle-consistency
loss, i.e., to enforce that $G_A(G_B(X)) \approx X$ and $G_B(G_A(Y)) \approx Y$, where $X \in A$
and $Y \in B$. This cycle-consistency loss guarantees that data points preserve their
intrinsic structure under the learned mapping. Formally, the cycle-consistency
loss is defined as:

$$\mathcal{L}_{cyc}(X, Y) = \|G_A(G_B(X)) - X\|_1 + \|G_B(G_A(Y)) - Y\|_1. \tag{3}$$

Adversarial Loss. To enforce the translation networks to produce data that is indistinguishable from genuine images, we also include an adversarial loss to train our model. For both translators, in GAN context often called generators, we train two additional discriminator networks D_A and D_B that are trained to distinguish translated from genuine images. To train our model, we use the following adversarial term:

$$\mathcal{L}_{adv} = \mathcal{L}_{GAN}(G_A, D_A) + \mathcal{L}_{GAN}(G_B, D_B), \tag{4}$$

where $\mathcal{L}_{GAN}(G, D)$ is the LSGAN formulation [59].

Overall, we train our model using the following loss function:

$$\mathcal{L} = \lambda_{adv}\mathcal{L}_{adv} + \lambda_{cyc}\mathcal{L}_{cyc} + \lambda_{corr}\mathcal{L}_{corr}, \tag{5}$$

where λ_{adv}, λ_{cyc}, and λ_{corr} are user-defined hyperparameters.

3.4   Implementation Details

Our model is based on cycleGAN and implemented in Pytorch. We experimented with different architectures for the translation networks, including U-Net [60], ResNet [61], and RNN-blocks [62]. Given enough training time, we found that all networks produce similar results. Due to its memory efficiency and fast convergence, we chose U-Net for our final model. As shown in Fig. 5, we use the multi-scale discriminator introduced in [27] that downsamples by a rate of 2, which generally works better for high resolution images. Our discriminator also considers the local correspondence patches as additional input, which helps to produce coherent translations. Followed by the training guidances proposed in [26], we use pixel-wise normalization in the generators and add a 1-strided convolutional layer after each deconvolutional layer. For computing the correspondence loss, we use a patch size of 256×256 and sample a single SIFT correspondence per training iteration randomly. The discriminator follows the architecture as: C64-C128-C256-C512-C1. The generator's encoder architecture is: C64-C128-C256-C512-C512-C512-C512-C512. We use $\lambda_{adv} = 1, \lambda_{cyc} = 10, \lambda_{corr} = 5$ in all our experiments and train using the ADAM optimizer with a learning rate of 0.0002.

4   Evaluation

In this section, we present qualitative and quantitative evaluations of our proposed S2Dnet. For this purpose, we evaluate the performance of our model on both the translation task and the subsequent 3D reconstruction, and we compare to several baseline systems. In Sect. 4.1 we report results on our synthetic test set and we also perform an evaluation on real-world data in Sect. 4.2.

To evaluate the benefit of our proposed inter-view coherence, we perform a comparison to a single-view translation baseline by training a cycleGAN network [10] on glossy to diffuse translation. Since our synthetic dataset features a bijective mapping between glossy and diffuse images, we also train a pix2pix

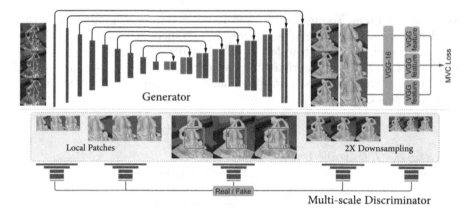

Fig. 5. Illustration of the generator and discriminator network. The generator uses the U-net architecture and both input and output are a multi-view sequence consisting of three views. A random SIFT correspondence is sampled during training to compute the correspondence loss. The multi-scale joint discriminator examines three scales of the image sequence and two scales of corresponding local patches. The width and height of each rectangular block indicate the channel size and the spatial dimension of the output feature map, respectively.

network [9] for a supervised baseline on synthetic data. In addition, we compare reconstruction quality to performing stereo reconstruction directly on the glossy multi-view sequence to demonstrate the benefit of translating the input as a preprocessing step. For 3D reconstruction, we apply a state-of-the-art multi-view surface reconstruction method [1] on input sequences consisting of 10 to 15 views. For our method, we translate each input view sequentially but we feed the two neighboring views as additional inputs to our multi-view network. For the two baseline translation methods, we translate each view independently. The 3D reconstruction pipeline then uses the entire translated multi-view sequence as input.

4.1 Synthetic Data

For a quantitative evaluation of the image translation performance, we compute MSE with respect to the ground truth diffuse renderings on our synthetic test set. Table 1 shows a comparison of our S2Dnet to pix2pix and cycleGAN. Unsurprisingly, the supervised pix2pix network performs best, closely followed by our S2Dnet, which outperforms the unsupervised baseline by a significant margin. In Fig. 6 we show qualitative translation results. Note that the output of pix2pix is generally blurry. Since MSE penalizes outliers and prefers a smooth solution, pix2pix still achieves a low MSE error. While the output of cycleGAN is sharper, the translated sequence lacks inter-view consistency, whereas our S2Dnet produces both highly detailed and coherent translations.

Table 1. Quantitative evaluation of the image error on our synthetic testing data.

	Glossy	pix2pix	cycleGAN	S2Dnet
Image MSE	118.39	56.20	69.15	57.78

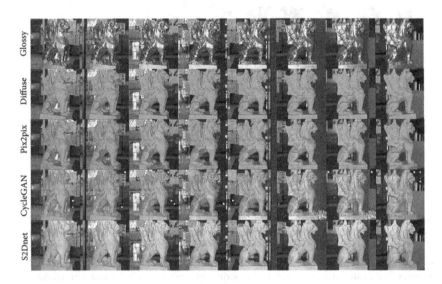

Fig. 6. Qualitative translation results on a synthetic input sequence consisting of 8 views. From top down: the glossy input sequence, the ground truth diffuse rendering, and the translation results for the baselines pix2pix and cycleGAN, and our S2Dnet. The output of pix2pix is generally blurry. The cycleGAN output, although sharp, lacks inter-view consistency. Our S2Dnet produces both crisp and coherent translations.

Table 2. Quantitative evaluation of surface reconstruction performance on 10 different scenes. The error metric is the percentage of bounding box diagonal. Our S2Dnet performs best, and the translation baseline still performs significantly better than directly reconstructing from the glossy images. The numbering of the models follows the visualization in Fig. 7, using the same left to right order.

Model	1	2	3	4	5	6	7	8	9	10	AVG
Glossy	0.67	0.88	1.35	0.76	1.15	1.13	1.15	0.78	0.54	0.66	0.90
cycleGAN	1.18	0.72	0.89	0.59	1.35	0.72	0.99	0.62	0.51	0.42	0.80
S2Dnet	0.52	0.67	0.72	0.43	0.87	0.54	0.92	0.65	0.55	0.56	0.64

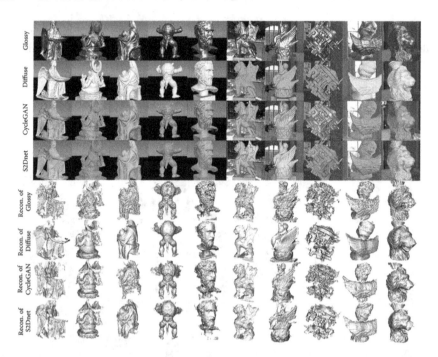

Fig. 7. Qualitative surface reconstruction results on 10 different scenes. From top to bottom: glossy input, ground truth diffuse renderings, cycleGAN translation outputs, our S2Dnet translation outputs, reconstructions from glossy images, reconstructions from ground truth diffuse images, reconstructions from cycleGAN output, and reconstructions from our S2Dnet output. All sequences are excluded from our training set, and the objects in column 3 and 4 have not even been seen during training.

Next, we evaluate the quality of the surface reconstruction by feeding the translated sequences to the reconstruction pipeline. We found that the blurry output of pix2pix is not suitable for stereo reconstruction, since already the first step, estimating camera parameters based on feature correspondences, fails on this data. We therefore exclude pix2pix from the surface reconstruction evaluation but include the trivial baseline of directly reconstructing from the glossy input sequence to demonstrate the benefit of the translation step. In order to compute the geometric error of the surface reconstruction output, we register the reconstructed geometry to the ground truth mesh using a variant of ICP [63]. Next, we compute the Euclidean distance of each reconstructed surface point to its nearest neighbor in the ground truth mesh and report the per-model mean value. Table 2 shows the surface reconstruction error for our S2Dnet in comparison to the three baselines. The numbers show that our S2Dnet performs best, and that preprocessing the glossy input sequences clearly helps to obtain a more accurate reconstruction, even when using the cycleGAN baseline. In Fig. 7 we show qualitative surface reconstruction results for 10 different scenes in various environments.

4.2   Real-World Data

Since we do not have real-world ground truth data, we compile a real-world test set and perform a qualitative comparison on it. For all methods, we compare generalization performance when training on our synthetic dataset. Moreover, we evaluate how the different models perform when fine-tuning on real-world data, or training on real-world data from scratch. For this purpose, we compile a dataset by shooting photos of real-world objects. We choose 5 diffuse real-world objects and take 5k pictures in total from different camera positions and under varying lighting conditions. Next, we use a glossy spray paint to cover our objects with a glossy coat and shoot another 5k pictures to represent the glossy domain. The resulting dataset consists of unpaired samples of glossy and diffuse objects under real-world conditions, see Fig. 10(a) and (b).

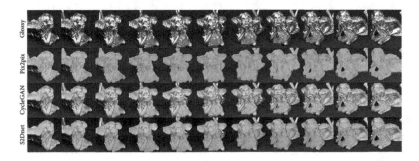

Fig. 8. Qualitative translation results on a real-world input sequence consisting of 11 views. The first row shows the glossy input sequence and the remaining rows show the translation results of pix2pix, cycleGAN, and our S2Dnet. All networks are trained on synthetic data only. Similar to the synthetic case, cycleGAN outperforms pix2pix, but it produces high-frequency artifacts that are not consistent along the views. Our S2Dnet is able to remove most of the specular effects and preserves all the geometric details in a consistent manner.

In Fig. 8 we show qualitative translation results on real-world data. All networks are trained on synthetic data only here, and they all manage to generalize to some extent to real-world data, thanks to our high-quality synthetic dataset. Similar to the synthetic results in Fig. 6, pix2pix produces blurry results, while cycleGAN introduces inconsistent high-frequency artifacts. S2Dnet is able the remove most of the specular effects and preserves geometric details in a consistent manner. In Fig. 9 we show qualitative surface reconstruction results for 7 different scenes. Artifacts occur mainly close to the object silhouettes in complex background environments. This could be mitigated by training with segmentation masks.

Finally, we evaluate performance when either fine-tuning or training from scratch on real-world data. We retrain or fine-tune S2Dnet and cycleGAN on our real-world dataset, but cannot retrain pix2pix for this purpose, since it relies on

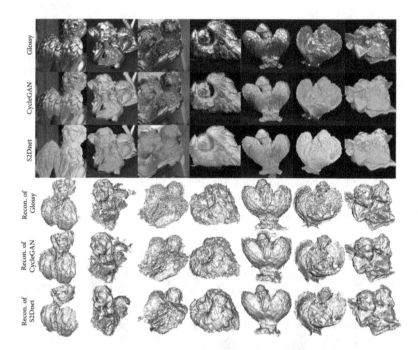

Fig. 9. Qualitative surface reconstruction results on 7 different real-world scenes. Top to bottom: glossy input, cycleGAN translation outputs, our S2Dnet translation outputs, reconstructions from glossy images, reconstructions from cycleGAN output, and reconstructions from our S2Dnet output. All networks are trained on synthetic data only.

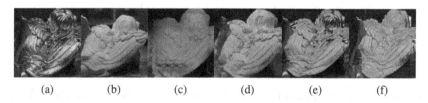

Fig. 10. (a), (b) A sample of our real-world dataset. (c) translation result of cycleGAN when training from scratch on our real-world dataset. (d) S2Dnet output, trained from scratch on our real-world dataset. (e) S2Dnet output, trained on synthetic data only. (f) S2Dnet output, trained on synthetic data, fine-tuned on real-world data.

a supervision signal that is not present in our unpaired real-world dataset. Our experiments show that training or fine-tuning using such a small dataset leads to heavy overfitting. The translation performance for real-world objects that were not seen during training decreases significantly compared to the models trained on synthetic data only. In Fig. 10(c) and (d) we show image translation results of cycleGAN and S2Dnet when training from scratch on our real-world dataset. Since the scene in Fig. 10 is part of the training set (although the input image itself is excluded from the training set), our S2Dnet produces decent translation results, which is not the case for scenes not seen during training. Fine-tuning our S2Dnet produces similar results (Fig. 10(f)).

5   Limitations and Future Work

Although the proposed framework enables reconstructing glossy and specular objects more accurately compared to state-of-the-art 3D reconstruction algorithms, a few limitations do exist. First, since the network architecture contains an encoder and a decoder with skip connections, the glossy-to-Lambertian image translation is limited to images of a fixed resolution. This resolutions might be too low for certain types of applications. Next, due to the variability of the background in real images, the translation network might treat a portion of the background as part of the reconstructed object. Similarly, the network occasionally misclassifies the foreground as part of the background, especially in very light domains on specular objects. Finally, as the simulated training data was rendered by assuming a fixed albedo, the network cannot consistently translate glossy materials with spatially varying albedo into a Lambertian surface. We predict that given a larger and more diverse training set in terms of shapes, backgrounds, albedos and materials, the accuracy of the proposed method in recovering real object would be largely enhanced. Our current training dataset includes the most common types of specular material. The proposed translation network has potential to be extended to other more challenging materials, such as transparent objects, given proper training data.

Acknowledgement. We thank the anonymous reviewers for their constructive comments. This work was supported in parts by Swiss National Science Foundation (169151), NSFC (61522213, 61761146002, 61861130365), 973 Program (2015CB352501), Guangdong Science and Technology Program (2015A030312015), ISF-NSFC Joint Research Program (2472/17) and Shenzhen Innovation Program (KQJSCX20170727101233642).

References

1. Langguth, F., Sunkavalli, K., Hadap, S., Goesele, M.: Shading-aware multi-view stereo. In: Leibe, B., Matas, J., Sebe, N., Welling, M. (eds.) ECCV 2016. LNCS, vol. 9907, pp. 469–485. Springer, Cham (2016). https://doi.org/10.1007/978-3-319-46487-9_29
2. Maier, R., Kim, K., Cremers, D., Kautz, J., Niessner, M.: Intrinsic3D: high-quality 3D reconstruction by joint appearance and geometry optimization with spatially-varying lighting. In: 2017 IEEE International Conference on Computer Vision (ICCV), pp. 3133–3141 (2017)
3. Tarini, M., Lensch, H.P.A., Goesele, M., Seidel, H.P.: 3D acquisition of mirroring objects using striped patterns. Graph. Models **67**(4), 233–259 (2005)

4. Tin, S.K., Ye, J., Nezamabadi, M., Chen, C.: 3D reconstruction of mirror-type objects using efficient ray coding. In: 2016 IEEE International Conference on Computational Photography (ICCP), pp. 1–11, May 2016

5. Ikeuchi, K.: Determining surface orientations of specular surfaces by using the photometric stereo method. IEEE Trans. Pattern Anal. Mach. Intell. **6**, 661–669 (1981)

6. Savarese, S., Perona, P.: Local analysis for 3D reconstruction of specular surfaces. In: Proceedings of the 2001 IEEE Computer Society Conference on Computer Vision and Pattern Recognition, CVPR 2001, vol. 2, pp. II-738–II-745 (2001)

7. Godard, C., Hedman, P., Li, W., Brostow, G.J.: Multi-view reconstruction of highly specular surfaces in uncontrolled environments. In: 3DV (2015)

8. Khanian, M., Boroujerdi, A.S., Breuß, M.: Photometric stereo for strong specular highlights. Comput. Vis. Media **4**(1), 83–102 (2018)

9. Isola, P., Zhu, J.Y., Zhou, T., Efros, A.A.: Image-to-image translation with conditional adversarial networks. In: The IEEE Conference on Computer Vision and Pattern Recognition (CVPR), July 2017

10. Zhu, J.Y., Park, T., Isola, P., Efros, A.A.: Unpaired image-to-image translation using cycle-consistent adversarial networks. In: The IEEE International Conference on Computer Vision (ICCV), October 2017

11. Zhang, Y., et al.: Physically-based rendering for indoor scene understanding using convolutional neural networks. In: The IEEE Conference on Computer Vision and Pattern Recognition (CVPR), July 2017

12. Movshovitz-Attias, Y., Kanade, T., Sheikh, Y.: How useful is photo-realistic rendering for visual learning? In: Hua, G., Jégou, H. (eds.) ECCV 2016. LNCS, vol. 9915, pp. 202–217. Springer, Cham (2016). https://doi.org/10.1007/978-3-319-49409-8_18

13. Shi, J., Dong, Y., Su, H., Yu, S.X.: Learning non-Lambertian object intrinsics across shapeNet categories. In: The IEEE Conference on Computer Vision and Pattern Recognition (CVPR), July 2017

14. Meka, A., Maximov, M., Zollhoefer, M., Chatterjee, A., Richardt, C., Theobalt, C.: Live intrinsic material estimation. arXiv preprint arXiv:1801.01075 (2018)

15. Hoffman, J., et al.: CYCADA: cycle-consistent adversarial domain adaptation. arXiv preprint arXiv:1711.03213 (2017)

16. Benaim, S., Wolf, L.: One-sided unsupervised domain mapping. In: Guyon, I., et al. (eds.) Advances in Neural Information Processing Systems, vol. 30, pp. 752–762. Curran Associates, Inc. (2017)

17. Kim, T., Cha, M., Kim, H., Lee, J.K., Kim, J.: Learning to discover cross-domain relations with generative adversarial networks. In: Precup, D., Teh, Y.W. (eds.) Proceedings of the 34th International Conference on Machine Learning. Volume 70 of Proceedings of Machine Learning Research, PMLR. International Convention Centre, Sydney, Australia, 06–11 August 2017, pp. 1857–1865 (2017)

18. Kang, G., Zheng, L., Yan, Y., Yang, Y.: Deep adversarial attention alignment for unsupervised domain adaptation: the benefit of target expectation maximization. arXiv preprint arXiv:1801.10068 (2018)

19. Chang, A.X., et al.: ShapeNet: an information-rich 3D model repository. Technical report arXiv:1512.03012 [cs.GR]. Stanford University - Princeton University - Toyota Technological Institute at Chicago (2015)

20. Or-El, R., Hershkovitz, R., Wetzler, A., Rosman, G., Bruckstein, A.M., Kimmel, R.: Real-time depth refinement for specular objects. In: Proceedings of IEEE Conference on Computer Vision & Pattern Recognition, pp. 4378–4386 (2016)

21. Or-El, R., Rosman, G., Wetzler, A., Kimmel, R., Bruckstein, A.M.: RGBD-fusion: real-time high precision depth recovery. In: Proceedings of IEEE Conference on Computer Vision & Pattern Recognition, pp. 5407–5416 (2015)
22. Chen, T., Goesele, M., Seidel, H.P.: Mesostructure from specularity. In: 2006 IEEE Computer Society Conference on Computer Vision and Pattern Recognition (CVPR 2006), vol. 2, pp. 1825–1832 (2006)
23. Ihrke, I., Kutulakos, K.N., Lensch, H.P.A., Magnor, M., Heidrich, W.: Transparent and specular object reconstruction. In: Computer Graphics Forum. Blackwell Publishing Ltd., Oxford (2010)
24. Yi, Z., Zhang, H., Tan, P., Gong, M.: DualGAN: unsupervised dual learning for image-to-image translation. In: The IEEE International Conference on Computer Vision (ICCV), October 2017
25. Goodfellow, I., et al.: Generative adversarial nets. In: Ghahramani, Z., Welling, M., Cortes, C., Lawrence, N.D., Weinberger, K.Q. (eds.) Advances in Neural Information Processing Systems, vol. 27, pp. 2672–2680. Curran Associates, Inc. (2014)
26. Karras, T., Aila, T., Laine, S., Lehtinen, J.: Progressive growing of GANs for improved quality, stability, and variation. In: International Conference on Learning Representations (2018)
27. Wang, T.C., Liu, M.Y., Zhu, J.Y., Tao, A., Kautz, J., Catanzaro, B.: High-resolution image synthesis and semantic manipulation with conditional gans. arXiv preprint arXiv:1711.11585 (2017)
28. Huang, R., Zhang, S., Li, T., He, R.: Beyond face rotation: global and local perception GAN for photorealistic and identity preserving frontal view synthesis. In: The IEEE International Conference on Computer Vision (ICCV), October 2017
29. Richardson, E., Sela, M., Kimmel, R.: 3D face reconstruction by learning from synthetic data. In: 2016 Fourth International Conference on 3D Vision (3DV), pp. 460–469. IEEE (2016)
30. Sela, M., Richardson, E., Kimmel, R.: Unrestricted facial geometry reconstruction using image-to-image translation. In: The IEEE International Conference on Computer Vision (ICCV), October 2017
31. Richardson, E., Sela, M., Or-El, R., Kimmel, R.: Learning detailed face reconstruction from a single image. In: Proceedings of IEEE Conference on Computer Vision & Pattern Recognition, pp. 5553–5562. IEEE (2017)
32. Sengupta, S., Kanazawa, A., Castillo, C.D., Jacobs, D.: SFSNet: learning shape, reflectance and illuminance of faces in the wild. arXiv preprint arXiv:1712.01261 (2017)
33. Qian, R., Tan, R.T., Yang, W., Su, J., Liu, J.: Attentive generative adversarial network for raindrop removal from a single image. arXiv preprint arXiv:1711.10098 (2017)
34. Wang, J., Li, X., Hui, L., Yang, J.: Stacked conditional generative adversarial networks for jointly learning shadow detection and shadow removal. arXiv preprint arXiv:1712.02478 (2017)
35. Tatarchenko, M., Dosovitskiy, A., Brox, T.: Multi-view 3D models from single images with a convolutional network. In: European Conference on Computer Vision (ECCV) (2016)
36. Choy, C.B., Xu, D., Gwak, J.Y., Chen, K., Savarese, S.: 3D-R2N2: a unified approach for single and multi-view 3D object reconstruction. In: Leibe, B., Matas, J., Sebe, N., Welling, M. (eds.) ECCV 2016. LNCS, vol. 9912, pp. 628–644. Springer, Cham (2016). https://doi.org/10.1007/978-3-319-46484-8_38

37. Lin, C.H., Kong, C., Lucey, S.: Learning efficient point cloud generation for dense 3D object reconstruction. In: AAAI Conference on Artificial Intelligence (AAAI) (2018)
38. Tulsiani, S., Zhou, T., Efros, A.A., Malik, J.: Multi-view supervision for single-view reconstruction via differentiable ray consistency. In: The IEEE Conference on Computer Vision and Pattern Recognition (CVPR), July 2017
39. Wu, J., Zhang, C., Xue, T., Freeman, B., Tenenbaum, J.: Learning a probabilistic latent space of object shapes via 3D generative-adversarial modeling. In: Advances in Neural Information Processing Systems (NIPS), pp. 82–90 (2016)
40. Gwak, J., Choy, C.B., Chandraker, M., Garg, A., Savarese, S.: Weakly supervised 3D reconstruction with adversarial constraint. In: 2017 Fifth International Conference on 3D Vision 3D Vision (3DV) (2017)
41. Pontes, J.K., Kong, C., Sridharan, S., Lucey, S., Eriksson, A., Fookes, C.: Image2Mesh: a learning framework for single image 3D reconstruction. arXiv preprint arXiv:1711.10669 (2017)
42. Zhou, T., Brown, M., Snavely, N., Lowe, D.G.: Unsupervised learning of depth and ego-motion from video. In: The IEEE Conference on Computer Vision and Pattern Recognition (CVPR), July 2017
43. Yi, K.M., Trulls, E., Lepetit, V., Fua, P.: LIFT: learned invariant feature transform. In: Leibe, B., Matas, J., Sebe, N., Welling, M. (eds.) ECCV 2016. LNCS, vol. 9910, pp. 467–483. Springer, Cham (2016). https://doi.org/10.1007/978-3-319-46466-4_28
44. DeTone, D., Malisiewicz, T., Rabinovich, A.: SuperPoint: self-supervised interest point detection and description. arXiv preprint arXiv:1712.07629 (2017)
45. Ma, L., Stueckler, J., Kerl, C., Cremers, D.: Multi-view deep learning for consistent semantic mapping with RGB-D cameras. In: IROS, Vancouver, Canada, September 2017
46. Zhu, R., Wang, C., Lin, C.H., Wang, Z., Lucey, S.: Object-centric photometric bundle adjustment with deep shape prior. arXiv preprint arXiv:1711.01470 (2017)
47. Zhu, R., Wang, C., Lin, C.H., Wang, Z., Lucey, S.: Semantic photometric bundle adjustment on natural sequences. arXiv preprint arXiv:1712.00110 (2017)
48. Liu, G., Ceylan, D., Yumer, E., Yang, J., Lien, J.M.: Material editing using a physically based rendering network. In: The IEEE International Conference on Computer Vision (ICCV), October 2017
49. Yu, Y., Smith, W.A.: PVNN: a neural network library for photometric vision. In: Proceedings of the IEEE Conference on Computer Vision and Pattern Recognition, pp. 526–535 (2017)
50. Rematas, K., Ritschel, T., Fritz, M., Gavves, E., Tuytelaars, T.: Deep reflectance maps. In: The IEEE Conference on Computer Vision and Pattern Recognition (CVPR), June 2016
51. Georgoulis, S., Rematas, K., Ritschel, T., Fritz, M., Van Gool, L., Tuytelaars, T.: Delight-Net: decomposing reflectance maps into specular materials and natural illumination. arXiv preprint arXiv:1603.08240 (2016)
52. Georgoulis, S., Rematas, K., Ritschel, T., Fritz, M., Tuytelaars, T., Van Gool, L.: What is around the camera? In: Proceedings of IEEE Conference on Computer Vision & Pattern Recognition, pp. 5170–5178 (2017)
53. Pharr, M., Humphreys, G.: Physically Based Rendering, Second Edition: From Theory to Implementation. Morgan Kaufmann Publishers, San Francisco (2010)
54. Iizuka, S., Simo-Serra, E., Ishikawa, H.: Globally and locally consistent image completion. ACM Trans. Graph. (TOG) 36(4), 107 (2017)

55. Xian, W., Sangkloy, P., Lu, J., Fang, C., Yu, F., Hays, J.: TextureGAN: controlling deep image synthesis with texture patches. arXiv preprint arXiv:1706.02823 (2017)
56. Gatys, L.A., Ecker, A.S., Bethge, M.: Image style transfer using convolutional neural networks. In: 2016 IEEE Conference on Computer Vision and Pattern Recognition (CVPR), pp. 2414–2423. IEEE (2016)
57. Wang, C., Xu, C., Wang, C., Tao, D.: Perceptual adversarial networks for image-to-image transformation. arXiv preprint arXiv:1706.09138 (2017)
58. Vansteenkiste, E., Kern, P.: Taming adversarial domain transfer with structural constraints for image enhancement. arXiv preprint arXiv:1712.00598 (2017)
59. Mao, X., Li, Q., Xie, H., Lau, R.Y., Wang, Z., Smolley, S.P.: Least squares generative adversarial networks. In: ICCV, pp. 2813–2821. IEEE (2017)
60. Ronneberger, O., Fischer, P., Brox, T.: U-Net: convolutional networks for biomedical image segmentation. In: Navab, N., Hornegger, J., Wells, W.M., Frangi, A.F. (eds.) MICCAI 2015. LNCS, vol. 9351, pp. 234–241. Springer, Cham (2015). https://doi.org/10.1007/978-3-319-24574-4_28
61. He, K., Zhang, X., Ren, S., Sun, J.: Deep residual learning for image recognition. In: Proceedings of IEEE Conference on Computer Vision & Pattern Recognition, June 2016
62. Chaitanya, C.R.A., et al.: Interactive reconstruction of Monte Carlo image sequences using a recurrent denoising autoencoder. ACM Trans. Graph. **36**(4), 98:1–98:12 (2017)
63. Rusinkiewicz, S., Levoy, M.: Efficient variants of the ICP algorithm. In: Proceedings of Third International Conference on 3-D Digital Imaging and Modeling, pp. 145–152. IEEE (2001)

Stacked Cross Attention
for Image-Text Matching

Kuang-Huei Lee[1]([✉]), Xi Chen[1], Gang Hua[1], Houdong Hu[1], and Xiaodong He[2]

[1] Microsoft AI and Research, Redmond, USA
{kualee,chnxi,ganghua,houhu}@microsoft.com
[2] JD AI Research, Beijing, China
xiaodong.he@jd.com

Abstract. In this paper, we study the problem of image-text matching. Inferring the latent semantic alignment between objects or other salient stuff (*e.g.* snow, sky, lawn) and the corresponding words in sentences allows to capture fine-grained interplay between vision and language, and makes image-text matching more interpretable. Prior work either simply aggregates the similarity of all possible pairs of regions and words without attending differentially to more and less important words or regions, or uses a multi-step attentional process to capture limited number of semantic alignments which is less interpretable. In this paper, we present *Stacked Cross Attention* to discover the full latent alignments using both image regions and words in a sentence as context and infer image-text similarity. Our approach achieves the state-of-the-art results on the MS-COCO and Flickr30K datasets. On Flickr30K, our approach outperforms the current best methods by 22.1% relatively in text retrieval from image query, and 18.2% relatively in image retrieval with text query (based on Recall@1). On MS-COCO, our approach improves sentence retrieval by 17.8% relatively and image retrieval by 16.6% relatively (based on Recall@1 using the 5K test set). Code has been made available at: (https://github.com/kuanghuei/SCAN).

Keywords: Attention · Multi-modal · Visual-semantic embedding

1 Introduction

In this paper we study the problem of image-text matching, central to image-sentence cross-modal retrieval (*i.e.* image search for given sentences with visual descriptions and the retrieval of sentences from image queries).

When people describe what they see, it can be observed that the descriptions make frequent reference to objects and other salient stuff in the images, as well as

---

X. He—Work performed while working at Microsoft Research.

Electronic supplementary material The online version of this chapter (https://doi.org/10.1007/978-3-030-01225-0_13) contains supplementary material, which is available to authorized users.

V. Ferrari et al. (Eds.): ECCV 2018, LNCS 11208, pp. 212–228, 2018.
https://doi.org/10.1007/978-3-030-01225-0_13

their attributes and actions (as shown in Fig. 1). In a sense, sentence descriptions are weak annotations, where words in a sentence correspond to some particular, but unknown regions in the image. Inferring the latent correspondence between image regions and words is a key to more interpretable image-text matching by capturing the fine-grained interplay between vision and language.

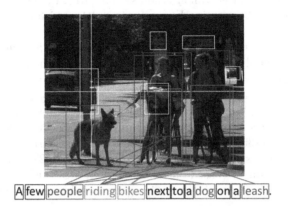

A few people riding bikes next to a dog on a leash.

Fig. 1. Sentence descriptions make frequent reference to some particular but unknown salient regions in images, as well as their attributes and actions. Reasoning the underlying correspondence is a key to interpretable image-text matching.

Similar observations motivated prior work on image-text matching [19,20,32]. These models often detect image regions at object/stuff level and simply aggregate the similarity of all possible pairs of image regions and words in sentence to infer the global image-text similarity; *e.g.* Karpathy and Fei-Fei [19] proposed taking the maximum of the region-word similarity scores with respect to each word and averaging the results corresponding to all words. It shows the effectiveness of inferring the latent region-word correspondences, but such aggregation does not consider the fact that the importance of words can depend on the visual context.

We strive to take a step towards attending differentially to important image regions and words with each other as context for inferring the image-text similarity. We introduce a novel *Stacked Cross Attention* that enables attention with context from both image and sentence in two stages. In the proposed *Image-Text* formulation, given an image and a sentence, it first attends to words in the sentence with respect to each image region, and compares each image region to the attended information from the sentence to decide the importance of the image regions (*e.g.* mentioned in the sentence or not). Likewise, in the proposed *Text-Image* formulation, it first attends to image regions with respect to each word and then decides to pay more or less attention to each word.

Compared to models that perform fixed-step attentional reasoning and thus only focus on limited semantic alignments (one at a time) [16,31], Stacked Cross

Attention discovers all possible alignments simultaneously. Since the number of semantic alignments varies with different images and sentences, the correspondence inferred by our method is more comprehensive and thus making image-text matching more interpretable.

To identify the salient regions in image, we follow Anderson *et al.* [1] to analogize the detection of salient regions at object/stuff level to the spontaneous bottom-up attention in the human vision system [4, 6, 21], and practically implement bottom-up attention using Faster R-CNN [34], which represents a natural expression of a bottom-up attention mechanism.

To summarize, our primary contribution is the novel Stacked Cross Attention mechanism for discovering the full latent visual-semantic alignments. To evaluate the performance of our approach in comparison to other architectures and perform comprehensive ablation studies, we look at the MS-COCO [29] and Flickr30K [43] datasets. Our model, Stacked Cross Attention Network (SCAN) that uses the proposed attention mechanism, achieves the state-of-the-art results. On Flickr30K, our approach outperforms the current best methods by 22.1% relatively in text retrivel from image query, and 18.2% relatively in image retrieval with text query (based on Recall@1). On MS-COCO, it improves sentence retrieval by 17.8% relatively and image retrieval by 16.6% relatively (based on Recall@1 using the 5K test set).

2   Related Work

A rich line of studies have explored mapping whole images and full sentences to a common semantic vector space for image-text matching [2, 8–11, 13, 22, 23, 27, 33, 38, 39, 44]. Kiros *et al.* [22] made the first attempt to learn cross-view representations with a hinge-based triplet ranking loss using deep Convolutional Neural Networks (CNN) to encode images and Recurrent Neural Networks (RNN) to encode sentences. Faghri *et al.* [10] leveraged hard negatives in the triplet loss function and yielded significant improvement. Peng *et al.* [33] and Gu *et al.* [13] suggested incorporating generative objectives into the cross-view feature embedding learning. As opposed to our proposed method, the above works do not consider the latent vision-language correspondence at the level of image regions and words. Specifically, we discuss two lines of research addressing this problem using attention mechanism as follows.

Image-Text Matching with Bottom-Up Attention. Bottom-up attention is a terminology that Anderson *et al.* [1] proposed in their work on image captioning and Visual Question-Answering (VQA), referring to purely visual feed-forward attention mechanisms in analogy to the spontaneous bottom-up attention in human vision system [4, 6, 21] (*e.g.* human attention tends to be attracted to salient instances like objects instead of background). Similar observation had motivated this study and several other works [17, 19, 20, 32]. Karpathy and Fei-Fei [19] proposed detecting and encoding image regions at object level with R-CNN [12], and then inferring the image-text similarity by aggregating the similarity scores of all possible region-word pairs. Niu *et al.* [32] presented a model that maps noun phrases within sentences and objects in images into a shared embedding space on top of full sentences and whole images embeddings. Huang *et al.* [17] combined image-text matching and sentence generation for model learning with an improved image representation including objects, properties, actions, etc. In contrast to our model, these studies do not use the conventional attention mechanism (*e.g.* [40]) to learn to focus on image regions for given semantic context.

Conventional Attention-Based Methods. The attention mechanism focuses on certain aspects of data with respect to a task-specific context (*e.g.* looking for something). In computer vision, visual attention aims to focus on specific images or subregions [1,26,40,41]. Similarly, attention methods for natural language processing adaptively select and aggregate informative snippets to infer results [3,25,28,35,42]. Recently, attention-based models have been proposed for the image-text matching problem. Huang *et al.* [16] developed a context-modulated attention scheme to selectively attend to a pair of instances appearing in both the image and sentence. Similarly, Nam *et al.* [31] proposed Dual Attentional Network to capture fine-grained interplay between vision and language through multiple steps. However, these models adopt multi-step reasoning with a predefined number of steps to look at one semantic matching (*e.g.* an object in the image and a phrase in the sentence) at a time, despite the number of semantic matchings change for different images and sentence descriptions. In contrast, our proposed model discovers all latent alignments, thus is more interpretable.

3   Learning Alignments with Stacked Cross Attention

In this section, we describe the Stacked Cross Attention Network (SCAN). Our objective is to map words and image regions into a common embedding space to infer the similarity between a whole image and a full sentence. We begin with bottom-up attention to detect and encode image regions into features. Also, we map words in sentence along with the sentence context to features. We then apply Stacked Cross Attention to infer the image-sentence similarity by aligning image region and word features. We first introduce Stacked Cross Attention in Sect. 3.1 and the objective of learning alignments in Sect. 3.2. Then we detail image and sentence representations in Sects. 3.3 and 3.4, respectively.

3.1   Stacked Cross Attention

Stacked Cross Attention expects two inputs: a set of image features $V = \{v_1, ..., v_k\}, v_i \in \mathbb{R}^D$, such that each image feature encodes a region in an image; a set of word features $E = \{e_1, ..., e_n\}, e_i \in \mathbb{R}^D$, in which each word feature encodes a word in a sentence. The output is a similarity score, which measures the similarity of an image-sentence pair. In a nutshell, Stacked Cross Attention attends differentially to image regions and words using both as context to each other while inferring the similarity. We define two complimentary formulations of Stacked Cross Attention below: *Image-Text* and *Text-Image*.

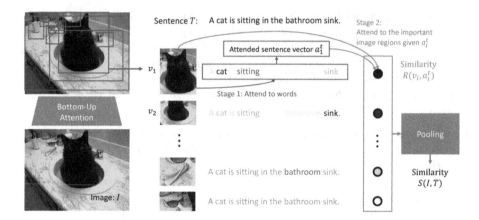

Fig. 2. Image-Text Stacked Cross Attention: At stage 1, we first attend to words in the sentence with respect to each image region feature v_i to generate an attended sentence vector a_i^t for i-th image region. At stage 2, we compare a_i^t and v_i to determine the importance of each image region, and then compute the similarity score.

Image-Text Stacked Cross Attention. This formulation is illustrated in Fig. 2, entailing two stages of attention. First, it attends to words in the sentence with respect to each image region. In the second stage, it compares each image region to the corresponding attended sentence vector in order to determine the importance of the image regions with respect to the sentence. Specifically, given an image I with k detected regions and a sentence T with n words, we first compute the cosine similarity matrix for all possible pairs, *i.e.*

$$s_{ij} = \frac{v_i^T e_j}{||v_i||||e_j||}, i \in [1, k], j \in [1, n].\tag{1}$$

Here, s_{ij} represents the similarity between the i-th region and the j-th word. We empirically find it beneficial to threshold the similarities at zero [20] and normalize the similarity matrix as $\bar{s}_{ij} = [s_{ij}]_+ / \sqrt{\sum_{i=1}^{k} [s_{ij}]_+^2}$, where $[x]_+ \equiv max(x, 0)$.

To attend on words with respect to each image region, we define a weighted combination of word representations (*i.e.* the attended sentence vector a_i^t, with respect to the i-th image region)

$$a_i^t = \sum_{j=1}^{n} \alpha_{ij} e_j,\tag{2}$$

where

$$\alpha_{ij} = \frac{exp(\lambda_1 \bar{s}_{ij})}{\sum_{j=1}^{n} exp(\lambda_1 \bar{s}_{ij})},\tag{3}$$

and λ_1 is the inversed temperature of the softmax function [5] (Eq. (3)). This definition of attention weights is a variant of dot product attention [30].

To determine the importance of each image region given the sentence context, we define relevance between the i-th region and the sentence as cosine similarity between the attended sentence vector a_i^t and each image region feature v_i, *i.e.*

$$R(v_i, a_i^t) = \frac{v_i^T a_i^t}{||v_i||||a_i^t||}. \tag{4}$$

Inspired by the minimum classification error formulation in speech recognition [15,18], the similarity between image I and sentence T is calculated by LogSum-Exp pooling (LSE), *i.e.*

$$S_{LSE}(I, T) = log(\sum_{i=1}^{k} exp(\lambda_2 R(v_i, a_i^t)))^{(1/\lambda_2)}, \tag{5}$$

where λ_2 is a factor that determines how much to magnify the importance of the most relevant pairs of image region feature v_i and attended sentence vector a_i^t. As $\lambda_2 \to \infty$, $S(I, T)$ approximates to $max_{i=1}^{k} R(v_i, a_i^t)$. Alternatively, we can summarize $R(v_i, a_i^t)$ with average pooling (AVG), *i.e.*

$$S_{AVG}(I, T) = \frac{\sum_{i=1}^{k} R(v_i, a_i^t)}{k}. \tag{6}$$

Essentially, if region i is not mentioned in the sentence, its feature v_i would not be similar to the corresponding attended sentence vector a_i^t since it would not be able to collect good information while computing a_i^t. Thus, comparing a_i^t and v_i determines how important region i is with respect to the sentence.

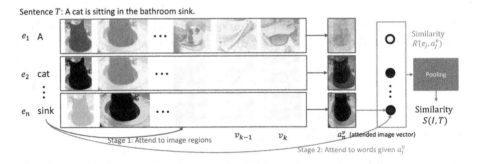

Fig. 3. Text-Image Stacked Cross Attention: At stage 1, we first attend to image regions with respect to each word feature e_i to generate an attended image vector a_j^v for j-th word in the sentence (The images above the symbol a_n^v represent the attended image vectors). At stage 2, we compare a_j^v and e_j to determine the importance of each image region, and then compute the similarity score.

Text-Image Stacked Cross Attention. Likewise, we can first attend to image regions with respect to each word, and compare each word to the corresponding attended image vector to determine the importance of each word.

We call this formulation *Text-Image*, which is depicted in Fig. 3. Specifically, we normalize cosine similarity $s_{i,j}$ between the i-th region and the j-th word as $\bar{s}'_{i,j} = [s_{i,j}]_+ / \sqrt{\sum_{j=1}^{n}[s_{i,j}]_+^2}$.

To attend on image regions with respect to each word, we define a weighted combination of image region features (*i.e.* the attended image vector a_j^v with respect to j-th word): $a_j^v = \sum_{i=1}^{k} \alpha'_{ij} v_i$, where $\alpha'_{ij} = exp(\lambda_1 \bar{s}'_{i,j}) / \sum_{i=1}^{k} exp(\lambda_1 \bar{s}'_{i,j})$. Using the cosine similarity between the attended image vector a_j^v and the word feature e_j, we measure the relevance between the j-th word and the image as $R'(e_j, a_j^v) = (e_j^T a_j^v)/(\|e_j\|\|a_j^v\|)$. The final similarity score between image I and sentence T is summarized by LogSumExp pooling (LSE), *i.e.*

$$S'_{LSE}(I,T) = log(\sum_{j=1}^{n} exp(\lambda_2 R'(e_j, a_j^v)))^{(1/\lambda_2)}, \tag{7}$$

or alternatively by average pooling (AVG)

$$S'_{AVG}(I,T) = \frac{\sum_{j=1}^{n} R'(e_j, a_j^v)}{n}. \tag{8}$$

In prior work, Karpathy and Fei-Fei [19] defined region-word similarity as a dot product between v_i and e_j, *i.e.* $s_{ij} = v_i^T e_j$ and image-text similarity by aggregating all possible pairs without attention as

$$S'_{SM}(I,T) = \sum_{j=1}^{n} \max_i (s_{ij}). \tag{9}$$

We revisit this formulation in our ablation studies in Sect. 4.4, dubbed *Sum-Max Text-Image*, and also the symmetric form, dubbed *Sum-Max Image-Text*

$$S_{SM}(I,T) = \sum_{i=1}^{k} \max_j (s_{ij}). \tag{10}$$

3.2   Alignment Objective

Triplet loss is a common ranking objective for image-text matching. Previous approaches [19,22,37] have employed a hinge-based triplet ranking loss with margin α, *i.e.*

$$l(I,T) = \sum_{\hat{T}} [\alpha - S(I,T) + S(I,\hat{T})]_+ + \sum_{\hat{I}} [\alpha - S(I,T) + S(\hat{I},T)]_+, \tag{11}$$

where $[x]_+ \equiv max(x,0)$ and S is a similarity score function (*e.g.* S_{LSE}). The first sum is taken over all negative sentences $\hat{T}$ given an image I; the second sum considers all negative images $\hat{I}$ given a sentence T. If I and T are closer to one another in the joint embedding space than to any negatives pairs, by the margin α, the hinge loss is zero. In practice, for computational efficiency, rather than summing over all the negative samples, it usually considers only the hard negatives in a mini-batch of stochastic gradient descent.

In this study, we focus on the hardest negatives in a mini-batch following Fagphri *et al.* [10]. For a positive pair (I, T), the hardest negatives are given by $\hat{I}_h = argmax_{m \neq I} S(m, T)$ and $\hat{T}_h = argmax_{d \neq T} S(I, d)$. We therefore define our triplet loss as

$$l_{hard}(I, T) = [\alpha - S(I, T) + S(I, \hat{T}_h)]_+ + [\alpha - S(I, T) + S(\hat{I}_h, T)]_+. \quad (12)$$

3.3 Representing Images with Bottom-Up Attention

Given an image I, we aim to represent it with a set of image features $V = \{v_1, ..., v_k\}, v_i \in \mathbb{R}^D$, such that each image feature encodes a region in an image. The definition of an image region is generic. However, in this study, we focus on regions at the level of object and other entities. Following Anderson *et al.* [1]. We refer to detection of salient regions as bottom-up attention and practically implement it with a Faster R-CNN [34] model.

Faster R-CNN is a two-stage object detection framework. In the first stage of Region Proposal Network (RPN), a grid of anchors tiled in space, scale and aspect ratio are used to generate bounding boxes, or Region Of Interests (ROIs), with high objectness scores. In the second stage the representations of the ROIs are pooled from the intermediate convolution feature map for region-wise classification and bounding box regression. A multi-task loss considering both classification and localization are minimized in both the RPN and final stages.

We adopt the Faster R-CNN model in conjunction with ResNet-101 [14] pre-trained by Anderson *et al.* [1] on Visual Genomes [24]. In order to learn feature representations with rich semantic meaning, instead of predicting the object classes, the model predicts attribute classes and instance classes, in which instance classes contain objects and other salient stuff that is difficult to localize (*e.g.* stuff like 'sky', 'grass', 'building' and attributes like 'furry').

For each selected region i, f_i is defined as the mean-pooled convolutional feature from this region, such that the dimension of the image feature vector is 2048. We add a fully-connect layer to transform f_i to a h-dimensional vector

$$v_i = W_v f_i + b_v. \quad (13)$$

Therefore, the complete representation of an image is a set of embedding vectors $v = \{v_1, ..., v_k\}, v_i \in \mathbb{R}^D$, where each v_i encodes an salient region and k is the number of regions.

3.4 Representing Sentences

To connect the domains of vision and language, we would like to map language to the same h-dimensional semantic vector space as image regions. Given a sentence T, the simplest approach is mapping every word in it individually. However, this approach does not consider any semantic context in the sentence. Therefore, we employ an RNN to embed the words along with their context.

For the i-th word in the sentence, we represent it with an one-hot vector showing the index of the word in the vocabulary, and embed the word into a 300-dimensional vector through an embedding matrix W_e. $x_i = W_e w_i, i \in [1, n]$. We then use a bi-directional GRU [3,36] to map the vector to the final word feature along with the sentence context by summarizing information from both directions in the sentence. The bi-directional GRU contains a forward GRU which reads the sentence T from w_1 to w_n

$$\overrightarrow{h_i} = \overrightarrow{GRU}(x_i), i \in [1, n] \tag{14}$$

and a backward GRU which reads from w_n to w_1

$$\overleftarrow{h_i} = \overleftarrow{GRU}(x_i), i \in [1, n]. \tag{15}$$

The final word feature e_i is defined by averaging the forward hidden state $\overrightarrow{h_i}$ and backward hidden state $\overleftarrow{h_i}$, which summarizes information of the sentence centered around w_i

$$e_i = \frac{(\overrightarrow{h_i} + \overleftarrow{h_i})}{2}, i \in [1, n]. \tag{16}$$

4   Experiments

We carry out extensive experiments to evaluate Stacked Cross Attention Network (SCAN), and compare various formulations of SCAN to other state-of-the-art approaches. We also conduct ablation studies to incrementally verify our approach and thoroughly investigate the behavior of SCAN. As is common in information retrieval, we measure performance of sentence retrieval (image query) and image retrieval (sentence query) by recall at K (R@K) defined as the fraction of queries for which the correct item is retrieved in the closest K points to the query. The hyperparameters of SCAN, such as λ_1 and λ_2, are selected on the validation set. Details of training and the bottom-up attention implementation are presented in the supplementary material.

4.1   Datasets

We evaluate our approach on the MS-COCO and Flickr30K datasets. Flickr30K contains 31,000 images collected from Flickr website with five captions each. Following the split in [10,19], we use 1,000 images for validation and 1,000 images for testing and the rest for training. MS-COCO contains 123,287 images, and each image is annotated with five text descriptions. In [19], the dataset is split into 82,783 training images, 5,000 validation images and 5,000 test images. We follow [10] to add 30,504 images that were originally in the validation set of MS-COCO but have been left out in this split into the training set. Each image comes with 5 captions. The results are reported by either averaging over 5 folds of 1K test images or testing on the full 5K test images. Note that some early works such as [19] only use a training set containing 82,783 images.

4.2 Results on Flickr30K

Table 1 presents the quantitative results on Flickr30K where all formulations of our proposed method outperform recent approaches in all measures. We denote the Text-Image formulation by t-i, Image-Text formulation by i-t, LogSumExp pooling by LSE, and average pooling by AVG. The best R@1 of sentence retrieval given an image query is 67.9, achieved by SCAN i-t AVG, where we see a 22.1% relative improvement comparing to DPC [44]. Furthermore, we combine t-i and i-t models by averaging their predicted similarity scores. The best result of model ensembles is achieved by combining t-i AVG and i-t LSE, selected on the validation set. The combined model gives 48.6 at R@1 for image retrieval, which is a 18.2% relative improvement from the current state-of-the-art, SCO [17]. Our assumption is that different formulations of Stacked Cross Attention (t-i and i-t; AVG/LSE pooling) approach different aspects of data, such that the model ensemble further improves the results.

Table 1. Comparison of the cross-modal retrieval results in terms of Recall@K (R@K) on Flickr30K. t-i denotes Text-Image. i-t denotes Image-Text. AVG and LSE denotes average and LogSumExp pooling respectively.

Method	Sentence retrieval			Image retrieval		
	R@1	R@5	R@10	R@1	R@5	R@10
DVSA (R-CNN, AlexNet) [19]	22.2	48.2	61.4	15.2	37.7	50.5
HM-LSTM (R-CNN, AlexNet) [32]	38.1	-	76.5	27.7	-	68.8
SM-LSTM (VGG) [16]	42.5	71.9	81.5	30.2	60.4	72.3
2WayNet (VGG) [9]	49.8	67.5	-	36.0	55.6	-
DAN (ResNet) [31]	55.0	81.8	89.0	39.4	69.2	79.1
VSE++ (ResNet) [10]	52.9	-	87.2	39.6	-	79.5
DPC (ResNet) [44]	55.6	81.9	89.5	39.1	69.2	80.9
SCO (ResNet) [17]	55.5	82.0	89.3	41.1	70.5	80.1
Ours (Faster R-CNN, ResNet):						
SCAN t-i LSE ($\lambda_1 = 9, \lambda_2 = 6$)	61.1	85.4	91.5	43.3	71.9	80.9
SCAN t-i AVG ($\lambda_1 = 9$)	61.8	87.5	93.7	45.8	74.4	83.0
SCAN i-t LSE ($\lambda_1 = 4, \lambda_2 = 5$)	67.7	88.9	94.0	44.0	74.2	82.6
SCAN i-t AVG ($\lambda_1 = 4$)	**67.9**	89.0	94.4	43.9	74.2	82.8
SCAN t-i AVG + i-t LSE	67.4	**90.3**	**95.8**	**48.6**	**77.7**	**85.2**

4.3 Results on MS-COCO

Table 2 lists the experimental results on MS-COCO and a comparison with prior work. On the 1K test set, the single SCAN t-i AVG achieves comparable results to the current state-of-the-art, SCO. Our best result on 1K test set is achieved by combining t-i LSE and i-t AVG which improves 4.0% on image query and 8.0% relatively comparing to SCO. On the 5K test set, we choose to list the best single model and ensemble selected on the validation set due to space limitation. Both models outperform SCO on all metrics, and SCAN t-i AVG + i-t LSE improves 17.8% on sentence retrieval (R@1) and 16.6% on image retrieval (R@1) relatively.

Table 2. Comparison of the cross-modal retrieval restuls in terms of Recall@K(R@K) on MS-COCO. t-i denotes Text-Image. i-t denotes Image-Text. AVG and LSE denotes average and LogSumExp pooling respectively.

Method	Sentence retrieval			Image retrieval		
	R@1	R@5	R@10	R@1	R@5	R@10
1K test images						
DVSA (R-CNN, AlexNet) [19]	38.4	69.9	80.5	27.4	60.2	74.8
HM-LSTM (R-CNN, AlexNet) [32]	43.9	-	87.8	36.1	-	86.7
Order-embeddings (VGG) [38]	46.7	-	88.9	37.9	-	85.9
SM-LSTM (VGG) [16]	53.2	83.1	91.5	40.7	75.8	87.4
2WayNet (VGG) [9]	55.8	75.2	-	39.7	63.3	-
VSE++ (ResNet) [10]	64.6	-	95.7	52.0	-	92.0
DPC (ResNet) [44]	65.6	89.8	95.5	47.1	79.9	90.0
GXN (ResNet) [13]	68.5	-	97.9	56.6	-	94.5
SCO (ResNet) [17]	69.9	92.9	97.5	56.7	87.5	**94.8**
Ours (Faster R-CNN, ResNet):						
SCAN t-i LSE ($\lambda_1 = 9, \lambda_2 = 6$)	67.5	92.9	97.6	53.0	85.4	92.9
SCAN t-i AVG ($\lambda_1 = 9$)	70.9	94.5	97.8	56.4	87.0	93.9
SCAN i-t LSE ($\lambda_1 = 4, \lambda_2 = 20$)	68.4	93.9	98.0	54.8	86.1	93.3
SCAN i-t AVG ($\lambda_1 = 4$)	69.2	93.2	97.5	54.4	86.0	93.6
SCAN t-i LSE + i-t AVG	**72.7**	**94.8**	**98.4**	**58.8**	**88.4**	**94.8**
5K test images						
Order-embeddings (VGG) [38]	23.3	-	84.7	31.7	-	74.6
VSE++ (ResNet) [10]	41.3	-	81.2	30.3	-	72.4
DPC (ResNet) [44]	41.2	70.5	81.1	25.3	53.4	66.4
GXN (ResNet) [13]	42.0	-	84.7	31.7	-	74.6
SCO (ResNet) [17]	42.8	72.3	83.0	33.1	62.9	75.5
Ours (Faster R-CNN, ResNet):						
SCAN i-t LSE	46.4	77.4	87.2	34.4	63.7	75.7
SCAN t-i AVG + i-t LSE	**50.4**	**82.2**	**90.0**	**38.6**	**69.3**	**80.4**

4.4 Ablation Studies

To begin with, we would like to incrementally validate our approach by revisiting a basic formulation of inferring the latent alignments between image regions and words without attention; *i.e.* the Sum-Max Text-Image proposed in [19] and its compliment, Sum-Max Image-Text (See Eqs. (9) (10)). Our Sum-Max models adopt the same learning objectives with hard negatives sampling, bottom-up attention-based image representation, and sentence representation as SCAN. The only difference is that it simply aggregates the similarity scores of all possible pairs of image regions and words. The results and a comparison are presented in Table 3. VSE++ [10] matches whole images and full sentences on a single embedding vector. It uses pre-defined ResNet-152 trained on ImageNet [7] to extract one feature per image for training (single crop) and also leveraged hard negatives sampling, same as SCAN. Essentially, it represents the case without considering the latent correspondence but keeping other configurations similar to our Sum-Max models. The comparison between Sum-Max and VSE++ shows the effectiveness of inferring the latent alignments. With a better bottom-up attention model (compared to R-CNN in [19]), Sum-Max t-i even outperforms the current state-of-the-art. By comparing SCAN and Sum-Max models, we show that Stacked Cross Attention can further improve the performance significantly.

Table 3. Effect of inferring the latent vision-language alignment at the level of regions and words. Results are reported in terms of Recall@K(R@K). Refer to Eqs. (9) (10) for the definition of Sum-Max. t-i denotes Text-Image. i-t denotes Image-Text.

Method	Sentence retrieval			Image retrieval		
	R@1	R@5	R@10	R@1	R@5	R@10
VSE++ (fixed ResNet, 1 crop) [10]	31.9	-	68.0	23.1	-	60.7
Sum-Max t-i	59.6	85.2	92.9	44.1	70.0	79.0
Sum-Max i-t	56.7	83.5	89.7	36.8	65.6	74.9
SCO [17] (current state-of-the-art)	55.5	82.0	89.3	41.1	70.5	80.1
SCAN t-i AVG ($\lambda_1 = 9$)	61.8	87.5	93.7	45.8	74.4	83.0
SCAN i-t AVG ($\lambda_1 = 10$)	67.9	89.0	94.4	43.9	74.2	82.8

We further investigate in several different configurations with SCAN i-t AVG as our baseline model, and present the results in Table 4. Each experiment is performed with one alternation. It is observed that the gain we obtain from hard negatives in the triplet loss is very significant for our model, improving the model by 48.2% in terms of sentence retrieval R@1. Not normalizing the image embedding (See Eq. (1)) changes the importance of image sample [10], but SCAN is not significantly affected by this factor. Using summation (SUM) or maximum (MAX) instead of average or LogSumExp as the final pooling function yields weaker results. Finally, we find that using bi-directional GRU improves sentence retrieval R@1 by 4.3 and image retrieval R@1 by 0.7.

Table 4. Effect of different SCAN configurations on Flickr30K. Results are reported in terms of Recall@K(R@K). i-t denotes Image-Text. SUM and MAX denote summation and max pooling instead of AVG/LSE at the pooling step, respectively.

Method	Sentence retrieval			Image retrieval		
	R@1	R@5	R@10	R@1	R@5	R@10
Baseline: SCAN i-t AVG	67.9	89.0	94.4	43.9	74.2	82.8
No hard negatives	45.8	77.8	86.2	33.9	63.7	73.4
Not normalize image embedding	67.8	89.3	94.6	43.3	73.7	82.7
SCAN i-t SUM	63.9	89.0	93.9	45.0	73.1	82.0
SCAN i-t MAX	59.7	83.9	90.8	43.3	72.0	80.9
One-directional GRU	63.6	87.7	93.7	43.2	73.1	82.3

5   Visualization and Analysis

5.1   Visualizing Attention

By visualizing the attention component learned by the model, we are able to showcase the interpretablity of our model. In Fig. 4, we qualitatively present the attention changes predicted by our Text-Image model. For the selected image, we visualize the attention weights with respect to each word in the sentence description "A young boy is holding a tennis racket." in different sub-figures.

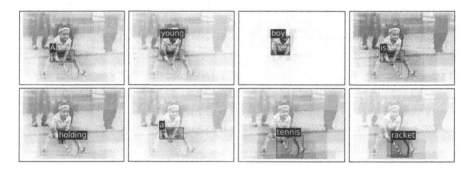

Fig. 4. Visualization of the attended image regions with respect to each word in the sentence description, outlining the region with the maximum attention weight in red. The regional brightness represents the attention strength, which considers the importance of both region and word estimated by our model. Our model generates interpretable focus shift and stresses on words like "boy" and "tennis racket", as well as the attributes (young) and actions (holding). (Best viewed in color) (Color figure online)

The regional brightness represents the attention weights which considers both importance of the region and the word corresponding to the sub-figure. We can observe that "boy", "holding", "tennis" and "racket" receive strong and focused attention on the relatively precise locations, while attention weights corresponding to "a" and "is" are weaker and less focused. This shows that our attention component learns interpretable alignments between image regions and words, and is able to generate reasonable focus shift and attention strength to weight regions and words by their importance while inferring image-text similarity.

5.2   Image and Sentence Retrieval

Figure 5 shows the qualitative results of sentence retrieval given image queries on Flickr30K. For each image query, we show the top-5 retrieved sentences ranked by the similarity scores predicted by our model. Figure 6 illustrates the qualitative results of image retrieval given sentence queries on Flickr30K. Each sentence corresponds to a ground-truth image. For each sentence query we show the top-3 retrieved images, ranking from left to right. We outline the true matches in green and false matches in red.

(a)

1:Older women and younger girl are opening presents up .
2:Two ladies and a little girl in her pajamas opening gifts
3:A family opening up their Christmas presents .
4:A mother and two children opening gifts on a Christmas morning .
5:A little girl opening a Christmas present .

(b)

1:Two men dressed in green are preparing food in a restaurant .
2:A man , wearing a green shirt , is cooking food in a restaurant .
3:A check with a green shirt uses a blowtorch on some food .
4:An Asian man in a green uniform shirt with a white speckled headband is using a torch to cook food in a restaurant .
5:An Asian man wearing gloves is working at a food stall .

(c)

1:A female runner dressed in blue athletic wear is running in a competition , while spectators line the street .
2:A lady dressed in blue running a marathon .
3:A young woman is running a marathon in a light blue tank top and spandex shorts .
4:A lady standing at a crosswalk .
5:A woman who is running , with blue shorts .

Fig. 5. Qualitative results of sentence retrieval given image queries on Flickr30K dataset. For each image query we show the top-5 ranked sentences. We observe that our Stacked Cross Attention model retrieves the correct results in the top ranked sentences even for image queries of complex and cluttered scenes. The model outputs some reasonable mismatches, *e.g.* (b.5). On the other hand, there are incorrect results such as (c.4), which is possibly due to a poor detection of action in static images. (Best viewed in color when zoomed in.) (Color figure online)

Fig. 6. Qualitative results of image retrieval given sentence queries on Flickr30K. For each sentence query, we show the top-3 ranked images, ranking from left to right. We outline the true matches in green boxes and false matches in red boxes. In the examples we show, our model retrieves the ground truth image in the top-3 list. Note that other results are also reasonable outputs. (Best viewed in color.) (Color figure online)

6   Conclusions

We propose Stacked Cross Attention that gives the state-of-the-art performance on the Flickr30K and MS-COCO datasets in all measures. We carry out comprehensive ablation studies to verify that Stacked Cross Attention is essential to the performance of image-text matching, and revisit prior work to confirm the importance of inferring the latent correspondence between image regions and words. Furthermore, we show how the learned Stacked Cross Attention can be leveraged to give more interpretablity to such vision-language models.

Acknowledgement. The authors would like to thank Po-Sen Huang and Yokesh Kumar for helping the manuscript. We also thank Li Huang, Arun Sacheti, and Bing Multimedia team for supporting this work. Gang Hua is partly supported by National Natural Science Foundation of China under Grant 61629301.

References

1. Anderson, P., et al.: Bottom-up and top-down attention for image captioning and VQA. In: CVPR (2018)
2. Ba, J.L., Kiros, J.R., Hinton, G.E.: Layer normalization. arXiv preprint arXiv:1607.06450 (2016)
3. Bahdanau, D., Cho, K., Bengio, Y.: Neural machine translation by jointly learning to align and translate. In: ICLR (2015)
4. Buschman, T.J., Miller, E.K.: Top-down versus bottom-up control of attention in the prefrontal and posterior parietal cortices. Science **315**(5820), 1860–1862 (2007)
5. Chorowski, J.K., Bahdanau, D., Serdyuk, D., Cho, K., Bengio, Y.: Attention-based models for speech recognition. In: NIPS (2015)
6. Corbetta, M., Shulman, G.L.: Control of goal-directed and stimulus-driven attention in the brain. Nat. Rev. Neurosci. **3**(3), 201 (2002)

7. Deng, J., Dong, W., Socher, R., Li, L.J., Li, K., Fei-Fei, L.: ImageNet: a large-scale hierarchical image database. In: CVPR (2009)
8. Devlin, J., et al.: Language models for image captioning: the quirks and what works. In: ACL (2015)
9. Eisenschtat, A., Wolf, L.: Linking image and text with 2-way nets. In: CVPR (2017)
10. Faghri, F., Fleet, D.J., Kiros, J.R., Fidler, S.: VSE++: improved visual-semantic embeddings. arXiv preprint arXiv:1707.05612 (2017)
11. Fang, H., et al.: From captions to visual concepts and back. In: CVPR (2015)
12. Girshick, R., Donahue, J., Darrell, T., Malik, J.: Rich feature hierarchies for accurate object detection and semantic segmentation. In: CVPR (2014)
13. Gu, J., Cai, J., Joty, S., Niu, L., Wang, G.: Look, imagine and match: improving textual-visual cross-modal retrieval with generative models. In: CVPR (2018)
14. He, K., Zhang, X., Ren, S., Sun, J.: Deep residual learning for image recognition. In: CVPR (2016)
15. He, X., Deng, L., Chou, W.: Discriminative learning in sequential pattern recognition. IEEE Sig. Process. Mag. **25**(5), 1436 (2008)
16. Huang, Y., Wang, W., Wang, L.: Instance-aware image and sentence matching with selective multimodal LSTM. In: CVPR (2017)
17. Huang, Y., Wu, Q., Wang, L.: Learning semantic concepts and order for image and sentence matching. In: CVPR (2018)
18. Juang, B.H., Hou, W., Lee, C.H.: Minimum classification error rate methods for speech recognition. IEEE Trans. Speech Audio process. **5**(3), 257–265 (1997)
19. Karpathy, A., Fei-Fei, L.: Deep visual-semantic alignments for generating image descriptions. In: CVPR (2015)
20. Karpathy, A., Joulin, A., Fei-Fei, L.: Deep fragment embeddings for bidirectional image sentence mapping. In: NIPS (2014)
21. Katsuki, F., Constantinidis, C.: Bottom-up and top-down attention: different processes and overlapping neural systems. Neuroscientist **20**(5), 509–521 (2014)
22. Kiros, R., Salakhutdinov, R., Zemel, R.S.: Unifying visual-semantic embeddings with multimodal neural language models. arXiv preprint arXiv:1411.2539 (2014)
23. Klein, B., Lev, G., Sadeh, G., Wolf, L.: Associating neural word embeddings with deep image representations using fisher vectors. In: CVPR (2015)
24. Krishna, R., et al.: Visual Genome: connecting language and vision using crowd-sourced dense image annotations. Int. J. Comput. Vis. **123**(1), 32–73 (2017)
25. Kumar, A., et al.: Ask me anything: dynamic memory networks for natural language processing. In: ICML (2016)
26. Lee, K.H., He, X., Zhang, L., Yang, L.: CleanNet: transfer learning for scalable image classifier training with label noise. In: CVPR (2018)
27. Lev, G., Sadeh, G., Klein, B., Wolf, L.: RNN Fisher vectors for action recognition and image annotation. In: Leibe, B., Matas, J., Sebe, N., Welling, M. (eds.) ECCV 2016. LNCS, vol. 9910, pp. 833–850. Springer, Cham (2016). https://doi.org/10.1007/978-3-319-46466-4_50
28. Li, J., Luong, M.T., Jurafsky, D.: A hierarchical neural autoencoder for paragraphs and documents. In: ACL (2015)
29. Lin, T.-Y., et al.: Microsoft COCO: common objects in context. In: Fleet, D., Pajdla, T., Schiele, B., Tuytelaars, T. (eds.) ECCV 2014. LNCS, vol. 8693, pp. 740–755. Springer, Cham (2014). https://doi.org/10.1007/978-3-319-10602-1_48
30. Luong, M.T., Pham, H., Manning, C.D.: Effective approaches to attention-based neural machine translation. In: EMNLP (2015)
31. Nam, H., Ha, J.W., Kim, J.: Dual attention networks for multimodal reasoning and matching. In: CVPR (2017)

32. Niu, Z., Zhou, M., Wang, L., Gao, X., Hua, G.: Hierarchical multimodal LSTM for dense visual-semantic embedding. In: ICCV (2017)
33. Peng, Y., Qi, J., Yuan, Y.: CM-GANs: cross-modal generative adversarial networks for common representation learning. arXiv preprint arXiv:1710.05106 (2017)
34. Ren, S., He, K., Girshick, R., Sun, J.: Faster R-CNN: towards real-time object detection with region proposal networks. In: NIPS (2015)
35. Rush, A.M., Chopra, S., Weston, J.: A neural attention model for abstractive sentence summarization. In: EMNLP (2015)
36. Schuster, M., Paliwal, K.K.: Bidirectional recurrent neural networks. IEEE Trans. Sig. Process. **45**(11), 2673–2681 (1997)
37. Socher, R., Karpathy, A., Le, Q.V., Manning, C.D., Ng, A.Y.: Grounded compositional semantics for finding and describing images with sentences. In: ACL (2014)
38. Vendrov, I., Kiros, R., Fidler, S., Urtasun, R.: Order-embeddings of images and language. In: ICLR (2016)
39. Wang, L., Li, Y., Lazebnik, S.: Learning deep structure-preserving image-text embeddings. In: CVPR (2016)
40. Xu, K., et al.: Show, attend and tell: neural image caption generation with visual attention. In: ICML (2015)
41. Xu, T., et al.: AttnGAN: fine-grained text to image generation with attentional generative adversarial networks. In: CVPR (2018)
42. Yang, Z., Yang, D., Dyer, C., He, X., Smola, A., Hovy, E.: Hierarchical attention networks for document classification. In: NAACL-HLT (2016)
43. Young, P., Lai, A., Hodosh, M., Hockenmaier, J.: From image descriptions to visual denotations: new similarity metrics for semantic inference over event descriptions. In: ACL (2014)
44. Zheng, Z., Zheng, L., Garrett, M., Yang, Y., Shen, Y.D.: Dual-path convolutional image-text embedding. arXiv preprint arXiv:1711.05535 (2017)

Deep Texture and Structure Aware Filtering Network for Image Smoothing

Kaiyue Lu[1,2]($\boxtimes$), Shaodi You[1,2], and Nick Barnes[1,2]

[1] Research School of Engineering, Australian National University,
Canberra, Australia
[2] Data61, CSIRO, Canberra, Australia
{Kaiyue.Lu,Shaodi.You,Nick.Barnes}@data61.csiro.au

Abstract. Image smoothing is a fundamental task in computer vision, that attempts to retain salient structures and remove insignificant textures. In this paper, we aim to address the fundamental shortcomings of existing image smoothing methods, which cannot properly distinguish textures and structures with similar low-level appearance. While deep learning approaches have started to explore structure preservation through image smoothing, existing work does not yet properly address textures. To this end, we generate a large dataset by blending natural textures with clean structure-only images, and use this to build a texture prediction network (TPN) that predicts the location and magnitude of textures. We then combine the TPN with a semantic structure prediction network (SPN) so that the final texture and structure aware filtering network (TSAFN) is able to identify the textures to remove ("texture-awareness") and the structures to preserve ("structure-awareness"). The proposed model is easy to understand and implement, and shows good performance on real images in the wild as well as our generated dataset.

Keywords: Image smoothing · Texture prediction · Deep learning

1 Introduction

Image smoothing, a fundamental technology in image processing and computer vision, aims to clean images by retaining salient structures (to the ***structure-only image***) and removing insignificant textures (to the ***texture-only image***), with various applications including denoising [15], detail enhancement [14], image abstraction [38] and segmentation [36].

There are mainly two types of methods for image smoothing: (1) kernel-based methods, that calculate the average of the neighborhood for texture pixels while trying to retain the original value for structural pixels, such as the guided filter (GF) [18], rolling guidance filter (RGF) [46], segment graph filter (SGF) [45] and so on; and (2) separation-based methods, which decompose the image into a structure layer and a texture layer, such as relative total variation (RTV) [42],

© Springer Nature Switzerland AG 2018
V. Ferrari et al. (Eds.): ECCV 2018, LNCS 11208, pp. 229–245, 2018.
https://doi.org/10.1007/978-3-030-01225-0_14

fast L0 [27], and static and dynamic guidance filter (SDF) [16,17]. Traditional approaches rely on hand-crafted features and/or prior knowledge to distinguish textures from structures. These features are largely based on low-level appearance, and generally assume that structures always have larger gradients, and textures are just smaller oscillations in color intensities.

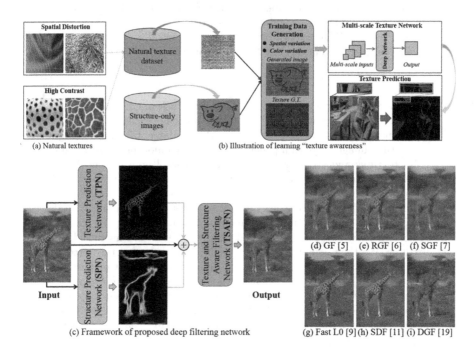

Fig. 1. (a) Texture in natural images is often hard to identify due to spatial distortion and high contrast. (b) Illustration of learning "texture awareness". We generate training data by adding spatial and color variations to natural texture patterns and blending them with structure-only images, and then use the result to train a multi-scale texture network with texture ground-truth. We test the network on both generated data and natural images. (c) Our proposed deep filtering network is composed of a texture prediction network (TPN) for predicting textures (white stripes with high-contrast); a structure prediction network (SPN) for extracting structures (the giraffe's boundary, which has relatively low contrast to the background); and a texture and structure aware filtering network (TSAFN) for image smoothing. (d)–(i) Existing methods cannot distinguish low-contrast structures from high-contrast textures effectively. (Color figure online)

In fact, it is quite difficult to identify textures. The main reasons are twofold: (1) textures are essentially repeated patterns regularly or irregularly distributed within object structures, and they may show significant spatial distortions in an image (as shown in Fig. 1(a)), making it hard to fully define them mathematically; (2) in some images there are strong textures with large gradients and color contrast to the background, which are easy to confuse with structures (such as the white stripes on the giraffe's body in Fig. 1(c)). We see from Fig. 1 that GF, RGF, SGF, fast L0, and SDF perform poorly on the giraffe image. The textures are either not removed, or suppressed with the structure severely blurred. This is because the hand-crafted nature of these filters makes them less robust when applied to various types of textures, and also leads to poor discrimination of textures and structures. Some other methods [6,11,12,21,23,31,41] take advantage of deep neural networks, and aim for better performance by extracting richer information. However, existing networks use the output of various hand-crafted filters as ground-truth during training. These deep learning approaches are thus limited by the shortcomings of hand-crafted filters, and cannot learn how to effectively distinguish textures from structures.

A recently-proposed double-guided filter (DGF) [25] addresses this issue by introducing the idea of "texture guidance", which infers the location of texture, and combines it with "structure guidance" to achieve both goals of texture removal and structure preservation. However, DGF uses a hand-crafted separation-based algorithm called Structure Gradient and Texture Decorrelating (SGTD) [22] to construct the texture confidence map that still cannot essentially overcome the natural deficiency. We argue that this is not true "texture awareness", because in many cases, some structures are inevitably blurred when the filter tries to remove strong textures after several iterations. As can be seen in Fig. 1(i), although the stripe textures are largely smoothed out, the structure of the giraffe is unexpectedly blurred, especially around the head and the tail (red boxes).

In this paper, we hold the idea that "texture awareness" should reflect both the *texture region* (where the texture is) and *texture magnitude* (texture with high contrast to the background is harder to remove). Thus, we take advantage of deep learning and propose a texture prediction network (TPN) that aims to learn textures from natural images. However, since there are no available datasets containing natural images with labeled texture regions, we make use of texture-only datasets [8,10]. The process of learning "texture awareness" is shown in Fig. 1(b). Specifically, we generate the training data by adding spatial and color variations to natural texture patterns and blending them with the structure-only image. Then we construct a multi-scale network (containing different levels of contextual information) to train these images with texture ground-truth (G.T. in short). The proposed TPN is able to predict textures through a full consideration of both low-level appearance, *e.g.*, gradient, and other statistics, *e.g.*, repetition, tiling, spatial varying distortion. The network achieves good performance on our generated testing data, and can also generalize well to natural images, effectively locating texture regions and measuring texture magnitude by assigning different confidence, as shown in Fig. 1(b). More details can be found in Sect. 3.

For the full problem, we are inspired by the idea of "double guidance" introduced in [25] and propose a deep neural network based filter that learns to predict textures to remove ("texture-awareness" by our TPN) and structures to preserve ("structure-awareness" by HED semantic edge detection [39]). This is an end-to-end image smoothing architecture which we refer to as "Texture and Structure Aware Filtering Network" (TSAFN), as shown in Fig. 1(c). The network is trained with our own generated dataset. Different from the work in [25], we generate texture and structure guidance with deep learning approaches, and replace the hand-crafted kernel filter with a deep learning model to achieve a more consistent and effective combination of these two types of guidance. Experimental results show that our proposed filter outperforms DGF [25] in terms of both effectiveness and efficiency, achieves state-of-the-art performance on our dataset, and generalizes well to natural images.

The main contributions of this paper are: (1) We propose a deep neural network to robustly predict textures in natural images. (2) We present a large dataset that enables training texture prediction and image smoothing. (3) We propose an end-to-end deep neural network for image smoothing that achieves both "texture-awareness" and "structure-awareness", and outperforms existing methods on challenging natural images.

2   Related Work

Texture Extraction from Structures. The basic assumption of this type of work is that an image can be decomposed into structure and texture layers (the structure layer is a smoothed version of the input and contains salient structures, while the texture layer contains insignificant details or textures). The pioneering work, Total Variation [30], aims to minimize the quadratic difference between the input and output images to maintain structure consistency with the gradient loss as an additional penalty. Later works retain the quadratic form and propose other regularizer terms or features (*gradient loss is still necessary to keep the structures as sharp as possible*), such as weighted least squares (WLS) [13], ℓ_0 norm smoothing [27,40], ℓ_1 norm smoothing [3], local extrema [32], structure gradient and texture decorrelating (SGTD) [22]. Other works also focuses on accelerating the optimization [4] or improving existing algorithms [24]. There are two general issues that have not been handled effectively in existing work. Firstly, as they are largely dependent on gradient information, these methods *lack discrimination of textures and structures*, especially when they have similar low-level appearance, particularly in terms of scale or magnitude. Secondly, all the objective functions are *manually defined*, and may not be adaptive and robust to the huge variety of possible textures, especially in natural images.

Image Smoothing with Guidance. The guidance image can provide structure information to help repair and sharpen structures in the target image. Since adding guidance into separation-based methods may make it harder to optimize, this idea is more widely used in kernel-based methods. Static guidance refers to the use of a fixed guidance image, such as the bilateral filter [35], joint bilateral filter [28], and guided filter [18]. To make the guidance more structure-aware, existing filters also employ techniques such as leverage tree distance [2], super-pixels [45], region covariances [20], co-occurrence matrix [19], propagation distance [29], multipoint estimation [34], fully connected regions [9] and edge maps [7,43,44]. In contrast, dynamic guidance methods update the guidance image to suppress more details [16,17,46] by iteratively refining the target image. Overall, the aforementioned guidance methods only address structure information, or assume that structures and textures can be sufficiently distinguished with a single guidance. However, in most cases, structures and textures interfere with each other severely. Lu et al. [25] address this issue by introducing the concept of "texture guidance", which infers texture regions by normalizing the texture layer separated by SGTD [22] to construct the texture confidence map. They then naively combine it with structure guidance to form a double-guided kernel filter. However, this method is still largely dependent on hand-crafted features (in particular it relies on the hand-crafted SGTD to infer textures, which is not robust in essence). Structures may be blurred when the filter tries to smooth out strong textures after several iterations.

Deep Image Smoothing. Deep learning has been widely used in low-level vision tasks, such as super resolution [33], deblurring [26] and dehazing [5]. Compared with non-learning approaches, deep learning is able to extract richer information from images. In image smoothing, current deep filtering models all focus on approximating and accelerating existing non-learning filters. [41] is a pioneering paper, where the learning is performed on the gradient domain and the output is reconstructed from the refined gradients produced by the deep network. Liu et al. [23] take advantage of both convolutional networks (for perceiving salient structures) and recurrent networks (for producing smoothing output in a data-driven manner). Li et al. [21] fuse the features from the original input and guidance image together and then produce the guided smoothing result (this work is mainly for upsampling). Fan et al. [12] first construct a network called E-CNN to predict the edge/structure confidence map based on gradients, and then use it to guide the filtering network called I-CNN. Similar work can be found in [11] by the same authors. Most recent works mainly focus on extracting richer information from input images ([31] introduces a convolutional neural pyramid to extract features of different scales, and [6] utilizes context aggregation networks to include more contextual information) and yielding more satisfying results. One common issue is all of these approaches have to take the output of existing filters as ground-truth. Hence, they are unable to overcome their deficiency in discriminating textures.

3   Texture Prediction

In this section, we give insights into textures in natural images, which inspire the design of the texture prediction network (TPN) and the dataset for training.

3.1   What Is Texture?

Appearance of Texture. It is well known that many different types of textures occur in nature and it is difficult to fully define them mathematically. Generally speaking, textures are repeated patterns regularly or irregularly distributed within object structures. For example, in Fig. 1(c), the white stripes on the giraffe's surface are recognized as textures. In Fig. 2, textures are widely spread in the image on clothes, books, and the table cloth. For cognition and vision tasks, an intuitive observation is that the removal of these textures will not affect the spatial structure of objects. Thus, they can be removed by image smoothing as a preprocessing step for other visual tasks.

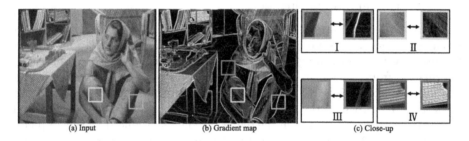

(a) Input   (b) Gradient map   (c) Close-up

Fig. 2. Close observation of structures and textures. In contrast with the assumptions used in existing methods, large gradients do not necessarily indicate structures (IV), and small gradients may also belong to structures (III). The challenge to distinguish them motivates us to propose two independent texture and structure guidance.

Textures do not Necessarily have Small Gradients. Existing methods generally assume that textures are minor oscillations and have small gradients. Thus, they can easily hand-craft the filter or loss function. However, in many cases, textures may also have large gradients, *e.g.*, the white stripes on the giraffe's body in Fig. 1(b), and the stripes occurring on the books in close-up IV of Fig. 2(c). Therefore, defining textures purely based on local contrast is insufficient.

Mathematically Modeling Texture Repetition is Non-trivial. By definition, textures are patterns with spatial repetitions. However, modeling and describing the repetition is non-trivial due to the existence of various distortions (see Fig. 1(a)).

Learn to Predict Textures. To tackle these issues, we take advantage of deep neural networks. Provided sufficient training examples are available, the network is able to learn to predict textures without explicit modeling.

3.2   Dataset Generation

We aim to provide a dataset so that a deep network can learn to predict textures. Ideally, we would like to learn directly from natural images. However, manually annotating pixel-wise labels plus alpha-matting would be costly. Moreover, it would require a full range of textures, each with a full range of distortions in a broad array of natural scenes. Therefore, we propose a strategy to generate the training and testing data. Later, we will demonstrate that the proposed network is able to predict textures in the wild effectively.

We observe that cartoon images have only structural edges filled with pure color, and can be safely considered "structure-only images". Specifically, we select 174 cartoon images from the Internet and 233 different types of natural texture-only images from public datasets [8,10]. The data generation process is illustrated in Fig. 3(a). Note that texture images in these datasets show textures only and all have simple backgrounds, so that separating them from the colored background is simple and efficient even using Relative Total Variation (RTV) [42]. The texture layer separated by RTV is normalized to $[0, 1]$.

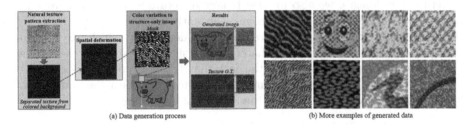

(a) Data generation process   (b) More examples of generated data

Fig. 3. Illustration of dataset generation. We blend-in natural texture patterns to structure-only images, adding spatial and color variation to increase texture diversity. We mainly focus on image patches motivated by the fact that textures are always clustered in certain regions.

Texture itself can be irregular, and textures in the wild may be distorted because of geometric projection. This arises because textures can appear on planar surfaces that are not orthogonal to the viewing direction, as well as being projected onto object with complex 3D surfaces. Therefore, we apply both spatial and color variation to the regular textures during dataset generation. As shown in Fig. 3(a), we blend-in the texture to the structure-only image. In detail, we rescale all the texture images to 100×100 and extract texture patterns with RTV. We model spatial variation, capturing projected texture at patch level by performing geometric transforms including rotation, scaling, shearing, and linear and non-linear distortion. We randomly select the geometric transform and parameters for the operation. Based on the deformed result, we generate a binary mask $\mathbf{M}$.

As for color variation, given the structure-only image $\mathbf{S}$, the value of pixel i in the jth channel of the generated image $\mathbf{I}_i^{(j)}$ is determined by both $\mathbf{S}$ and the mask $\mathbf{M}$. If $\mathbf{M}_i = 1$, $\mathbf{I}_i^{(j)} = rand[\kappa \cdot (1 - \mathbf{S}_i^{(j)}), 1 - \mathbf{S}_i^{(j)}]$, where κ is used to control the range of random generation and empirically set as 0.75. Otherwise, $\mathbf{I}_i^{(j)} = \mathbf{S}_i^{(j)}$. We repeat this by sliding the mask over the whole image without overlapping. The ground-truth texture confidence is calculated by averaging the values of the three channels of the texture layer:

$$\mathbf{T}_i^* = \delta(\frac{1}{3}\sum_{j=1}^{3}\left|\mathbf{I}_i^{(j)} - \mathbf{S}_i^{(j)}\right|),\tag{1}$$

where $\delta(x) = 1/(1 + exp(-x))$ is the sigmoid function to scale the value to $[0, 1]$. We use this color variation to generate significant contrast between the textures and the background. Using this method, it is unlikely that two images have the same textures even when the textures come from the same original pattern. Figure 3(b) shows eight generated image patches.

Finally, we generate 30,000 images in total (a handful of low-quality images have been manually removed). For ground-truth, besides the purely-clean structure-only images, we also provide binary structure maps and texture confidence maps of all the generated images. Currently we distribute textures over the entire image and the textures are not object-dependent, which may be typical appearance in natural images. Later we will show the use of patch learning can bridge the gap, motivated by the fact that textures are always clustered in certain regions. Moreover, we aim to let the network learn the statistics of appearance of local textures rather than the global structure.

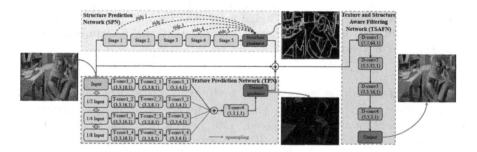

Fig. 4. Our proposed network architecture. The outputs of the texture prediction network (TPN) and structure prediction network (SPN) are concatenated with the original input, and then fed to the texture and structure aware filtering network (TSAFN) to produce the final smoothing result. (k,k,c,s) for a convolutional layer means the kernel is $k \times k$ in size with c feature maps, and the stride is s.

3.3   Texture Prediction Network

Network Design. We propose the texture prediction network (TPN), which is trained on our generated dataset. Considering that textures have various colors, scales, and shapes, we employ a multi-scale learning strategy. Specifically, we apply 1/2, 1/4, and 1/8 down-sampling to the input respectively. For each image, we use 3 convolutional layers for feature extraction, with the same size 3×3 kernel and different number of feature maps. Then, all the feature maps are resized to the original input size and concatenated to form a 16-channel feature map. They are further convolved with a 3×3 layer to yield the final 1-channel result. Note that each convolutional layer is followed by ReLU except for the output layer, which is followed by a sigmoid activation function to scale the values to $[0, 1]$. The architecture of TPN is shown in Fig. 4. Consequently, given the input image **I**, the predicted texture guidance **T̃** is obtained by:

$$\tilde{\mathbf{T}} = g\left(\mathbf{I}, \frac{1}{2}\mathbf{I}, \frac{1}{4}\mathbf{I}, \frac{1}{8}\mathbf{I}\right). \tag{2}$$

Network Training. The network is trained by minimizing the mean squared error (MSE) between the predicted texture guidance map and the ground-truth:

$$\ell_T(\theta) = \frac{1}{N} \sum_i \left\| \tilde{\mathbf{T}}_i - \mathbf{T}_i^* \right\|_2^2, \tag{3}$$

where N is the number of pixels in the image, $*$ denotes the ground-truth, and θ represents parameters. More training details can be found in the experiment section.

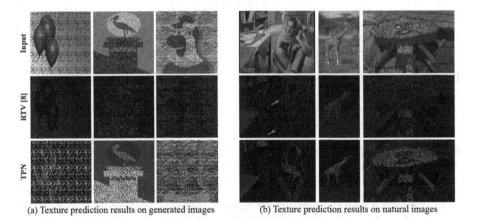

(a) Texture prediction results on generated images   (b) Texture prediction results on natural images

Fig. 5. Texture prediction results. First row: input (including both generated and natural images). Second row: texture extraction results by RTV [42] (we compare it because we use it to extract textures from texture-only images). Third row: texture prediction results by our proposed TPN. The network is able to find textures in both generated and natural images effectively, and indicate the magnitude of textures by assigning pixel-level confidence.

Texture Prediction Results. We present the texture prediction results on our generated images in Fig. 5(a) and natural images in Fig. 5(b). The network is able to find textures in both the generated and natural images effectively, and indicate the magnitude of textures by assigning pixel-level confidence (the third row). For comparison, we also list the texture extraction results from these examples by RTV [42] in the second row. RTV performs worse on the more complex scenes, because just like other hand-crafted filters, RTV also assumes structures have large gradients and hence has poor discrimination of strong textures.

3.4   Texture and Structure Aware Filtering Network

Network Design. Once the structure and texture guidance are generated, the texture and structure aware filtering network (TSAFN) concatenates them with the input to form a 5-channel tensor. TSAFN consists of 4 layers. We set a relatively large kernel (7×7) in the first layer to take more original information into account. The kernel size decreases in the following two layers (5×5, 3×3 respectively). In the last layer, the kernel size is increased to 5×5 again. The first three layers are followed by ReLU, while the last layer has no activation function (transforming the tensor into the 3-channel output). Empirically, we remove all the pooling layers, the same as [6,12,21,41]. We set the filtering network without any guidance as the baseline. The whole process can be denoted as:

$$\tilde{\mathbf{I}} = h(\mathbf{I}, \tilde{\mathbf{E}}, \tilde{\mathbf{T}}). \tag{4}$$

Network Training. The network is trained by minimizing:

$$\ell_D(\theta) = \frac{1}{N} \sum_i (\left\| \tilde{\mathbf{I}}_i - \mathbf{I}_i^* \right\|_2^2). \tag{5}$$

More details can be found in the experiment section.

4   Experiments and Analysis

In this section, we demonstrate the effectiveness of our proposed deep image smoothing network through.

Environment Setup. We construct the networks in Tensorflow [1], and train and test all the data on a single NVIDIA Titan X graphics card.

Dataset. Because there is no publicly-available texture removal dataset, we perform training using our generated images. More specifically, we select 19,505 images (65%) from the dataset for training, 2,998 (10%) for validation, and 7,497 (25%) for testing (all test images are resized to 512×512). There is no overlapping of structure-only and texture images between training, validation and testing samples.

Training. We first train the three networks separately. 300,000 patches with the size 64 × 64 are randomly and sparsely collected from training images. We use gradient descent with a learning rate of 0.0001, and momentum of 0.9. Finally, we perform fine-tuning by jointly training the whole network with a smaller learning rate of 0.00001, and the same momentum 0.9. The fine-tuning loss is

$$\ell(\theta) = \gamma \cdot \ell_D(\theta) + \lambda \cdot (\ell_T(\theta) + \ell_E(\theta)), \tag{6}$$

where we empirically set $\gamma = 0.6$, and $\lambda = 0.2$.

4.1 Existing Methods to Compare

Non-learning Methods. We compare our filter with 2 classical filters: Total Variation (TV) [30], bilateral filter (BLF) [35], and 9 recently-proposed filters: L0 [40], Relative Total Variation (RTV) [42], guided filter (GF) [18], Structure Gradient and Texture Decorrelation (SGTD) [22], rolling guidance filter (RGF) [46], fast L0 [27], segment graph filter (SGF) [45], static and dynamic filter (SDF) [17], double-guided filter (DGF) [25]. Note that, BLF, GF, RGF, SGF, DGF are kernel-based, while TV, L0, RTV, SGTD, fast L0, SDF are separation-based. We use the default parameters defined in the open-source code for each method.

Deep Learning Methods. We select 5 state-of-the-art deep filtering models: deep edge-aware filter (DEAF) [41], deep joint filter (DJF) [21], deep recursive filter (DRF) [23], deep fast filter (DFF) [6], and cascaded edge and image learning network (CEILNet) [12]. **We retrain all the models with our dataset.**

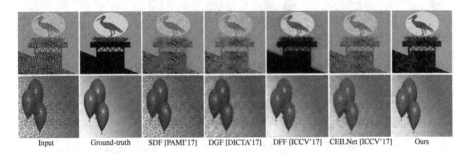

Input   Ground-truth   SDF [PAMI'17]   DGF [DICTA'17]   DFF [ICCV'17]   CEILNet [ICCV'17]   Ours

Fig. 6. Smoothing results on generated images. Our filter can smooth out various types of textures while preserving structures more effectively than other approaches.

4.2 Results

Quantitative Results on Generated Images. We first compare the average MSE, PSNR, SSIM [37], and processing time (in seconds) of 11 non-learning filters on our testing data in Table 1. Our method achieves the smallest MSE (closest to ground-truth), largest PSNR and SSIM (removing textures and preserving main structures most effectively), and lowest running time, indicating its superiority in both effectiveness and efficiency. Note that although the double-guided filter (DGF) [25] achieves better quantitative results than other hand-crafted approaches, it runs quite slowly (more than *50 times* slower than ours). We also compare the quantitative results on different deep models trained and tested on our dataset in Table 2. Our model achieves the best MSE, PSNR and SSIM, with comparable efficiency to the other methods. We additionally select 4 state-of-the-art methods (SDF [17], DGF [25], DFF [6], and CEILNet [12]) for visual comparison in Fig. 6. Our method gives favorable qualitative results.

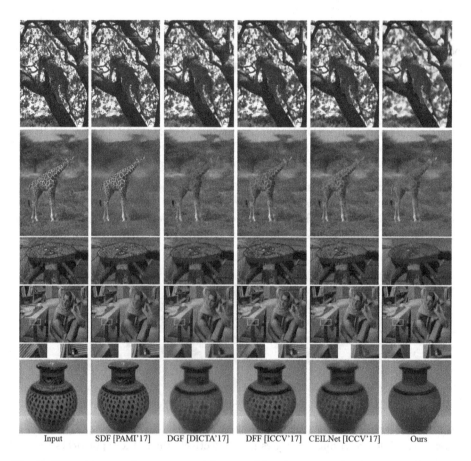

| Input | SDF [PAMI'17] | DGF [DICTA'17] | DFF [ICCV'17] | CEILNet [ICCV'17] | Ours |

Fig. 7. Smoothing results on natural images. The first example shows the ability of weak structure preservation and enhancement in textured scenes. The next four examples present various texture types with different shapes, contrast, and distortion. Our filter performs consistently better than state-of-the-art methods in all the examples.

Qualitative Comparison on Real Images in the Wild. We visually compare smoothing results of 5 challenging natural images with SDF [17], DGF [25], DFF [6], and CEILNet [12] in Fig. 7. In the first example, the leopard is covered with black texture, and it has relatively low contrast to the background (weak structure). Only our filter smooths out most of the textures while effectively preserving and enhancing the structure. The next four examples present various texture types with different shapes, contrast, and distortion, and our filter performs consistently well. We analyze the last challenging vase example in more detail. The vase is covered with strong dotted textures, densely wrapped on the surface. SDF fails to remove these textures since they are regarded as structures with large gradients. DGF smooths out the black dots more effectively but the entire image looks blurry. This is because just as [25] points out, a larger kernel size and more iterations are required to remove more textures, resulting in the blurred structure as a penalty. Also, the naive combination of structure and texture kernels makes the filter not robust to various types of textures. The two deep filters do not demonstrate much improvement over the hand-crafted approaches because "texture-awareness" is not specially emphasized in their network design. Only our filter removes textures without blurring the main structure.

Table 1. Quantitative evaluation of different non-learning filters tested on our dataset

	MSE	PSNR	SSIM	Time		MSE	PSNR	SSIM	Time
TV [30]	0.2791	11.33	0.6817	2.44	RGF [46]	0.2094	15.73	0.7173	0.87
BLF [35]	0.3131	10.89	0.6109	4.31	Fast L0 [27]	0.2068	15.50	0.7359	1.36
L0 [40]	0.2271	14.62	0.7133	0.94	SGF [45]	0.2446	13.92	0.7002	2.26
RTV [42]	0.2388	14.07	0.7239	1.23	SDF [17]	0.1665	16.82	0.7633	3.71
GF [18]	0.2557	12.22	0.6948	0.83	DGF [25]	0.1247	17.89	0.7552	8.66
SGTD [22]	0.1951	16.14	0.7538	1.59	Ours	**0.0051**	**25.07**	**0.9152**	**0.16**

Table 2. Quantitative evaluation of deep models trained and tested on our dataset

	MSE	PSNR	SSIM	Time		MSE	PSNR	SSIM	Time
DEAF [41]	0.0297	20.62	0.8071	0.35	DFF [6]	0.0172	22.21	0.8675	**0.07**
DJF [21]	0.0352	19.01	0.7884	0.28	CEILNet [12]	0.0156	22.65	0.8712	0.13
DRF [23]	0.0285	21.14	0.8263	0.12	Ours	**0.0051**	**25.07**	**0.9152**	0.16

Ablation Study of Each Guidance. To investigate the effect of guidance, we train the filtering network with no guidance, only structure guidance, only texture guidance, and double guidance respectively. We list the average MSE, PSNR, and SSIM of the testing results compared with ground-truth in Table 3, demonstrating that the results with double guidance have smaller MSE, larger

| Input | No guidance | Structure guidance only | Texture guidance only | Double guidance (trained separately) | Double guidance (fine-tuned) |

Fig. 8. Image smoothing results with no guidance, single guidance, double guidance (trained separately, and fine-tuned). With only structure guidance, the main structures are retained as well as the textures. With only texture guidance, all the textures are smoothed out but the structures are severely blurred. The result with double guidance performs well in both structure preservation and texture removal. Fine-tuning the whole network can further improve the performance.

PSNR, and larger SSIM. Also, the fine-tuning process improves the filtering network. Further, we show two natural images in Fig. 8. Compared with the baseline without guidance, the result only with structure guidance retains more structure, as well as the texture (this is mainly because HED may also be negatively affected by strong textures, resulting in a larger MSE loss when training the network). In contrast, the structures are severely blurred with only texture guidance, even though most textures are removed. Combining both structure and texture guidance produces a better result due to the good discrimination of structures and textures. Fine-tuning further improves the result (in the red rectangle of the first example, the structures are sharper; in the second example, the textures within the red region are further suppressed) because it takes all the three networks as a whole and this synergistic strategy allows different features to support and complement each other for better performance. All the observations are consistent with the quantitative evaluation in Table 3.

Table 3. Ablation study of image smoothing effects with no guidance, only structure guidance, only texture guidance, and double guidance (trained separately and fine-tuned)

	MSE	PSNR	SSIM
No guidance (Baseline)	0.0316	20.32	0.7934
Only structure guidance	0.0215	21.71	0.8671
Only texture guidance	0.0118	23.23	0.8201
Double guidance (trained separately)	0.0059	24.78	0.9078
Double guidance (fine-tuned)	**0.0051**	**25.07**	**0.9152**

5   Conclusion

In this paper, we propose an end-to-end texture and structure aware filtering network that is able to smooth images with both "texture-awareness" and "structure-awareness". The "texture-awareness" benefits from the newly-proposed texture prediction network. To facilitate training, we blend-in natural textures onto structure-only cartoon images with spatial and color variations. The"structure-awareness" is realized by semantic edge detection. Experiments show that the texture network can predict textures effectively. And our filtering network outperforms other filters on both generated images and natural images. The network structure is intuitive and easy to implement. In future work, we will introduce object-based texture cues - moving to a more object-based approach for texture prediction and image smoothing.

Acknowledgements. This work has been partially funded by NHMRC (National Health and Medical Research Council) under Grant No. 1082358.

References

1. Abadi, M., et al.: Tensorflow: large-scale machine learning on heterogeneous distributed systems. arXiv preprint arXiv:1603.04467 (2016)
2. Bao, L., Song, Y., Yang, Q., Yuan, H., Wang, G.: Tree filtering: efficient structure-preserving smoothing with a minimum spanning tree. IEEE Trans. Image Process. **23**(2), 555–569 (2014)
3. Bi, S., Han, X., Yu, Y.: An l 1 image transform for edge-preserving smoothing and scene-level intrinsic decomposition. ACM Trans. Graph. (TOG) **34**(4), 78 (2015)
4. Buades, A., Le, T.M., Morel, J.M., Vese, L.A.: Fast cartoon + texture image filters. IEEE Trans. Image Process. **19**(8), 1978–1986 (2010)
5. Cai, B., Xu, X., Jia, K., Qing, C., Tao, D.: Dehazenet: an end-to-end system for single image haze removal. IEEE Trans. Image Process. **25**(11), 5187–5198 (2016)
6. Chen, Q., Xu, J., Koltun, V.: Fast image processing with fully-convolutional networks. In: The IEEE International Conference on Computer Vision (ICCV), October 2017
7. Cho, H., Lee, H., Kang, H., Lee, S.: Bilateral texture filtering. ACM Trans. Graph. (TOG) **33**(4), 128 (2014)
8. Cimpoi, M., Maji, S., Kokkinos, I., Mohamed, S., Vedaldi, A.: Describing textures in the wild. In: Proceedings of the IEEE Conference on Computer Vision and Pattern Recognition (CVPR) (2014)
9. Dai, L., Yuan, M., Zhang, F., Zhang, X.: Fully connected guided image filtering. In: Proceedings of the IEEE International Conference on Computer Vision, pp. 352–360 (2015)
10. Dana, K.J., Van Ginneken, B., Nayar, S.K., Koenderink, J.J.: Reflectance and texture of real-world surfaces. ACM Trans. Graph. (TOG) **18**(1), 1–34 (1999)
11. Fan, Q., Wipf, D.P., Hua, G., Chen, B.: Revisiting deep image smoothing and intrinsic image decomposition. CoRR abs/1701.02965 (2017). http://arxiv.org/abs/1701.02965
12. Fan, Q., Yang, J., Hua, G., Chen, B., Wipf, D.: A generic deep architecture for single image reflection removal and image smoothing. In: The IEEE International Conference on Computer Vision (ICCV), October 2017

13. Farbman, Z., Fattal, R., Lischinski, D., Szeliski, R.: Edge-preserving decompositions for multi-scale tone and detail manipulation. ACM Trans. Graph. (TOG) **27**, 67 (2008)
14. Fattal, R., Agrawala, M., Rusinkiewicz, S.: Multiscale shape and detail enhancement from multi-light image collections. ACM Trans. Graph. **26**(3), 51 (2007)
15. Gu, S., Zhang, L., Zuo, W., Feng, X.: Weighted nuclear norm minimization with application to image denoising. In: Proceedings of the IEEE Conference on Computer Vision and Pattern Recognition, pp. 2862–2869 (2014)
16. Ham, B., Cho, M., Ponce, J.: Robust image filtering using joint static and dynamic guidance. In: Proceedings of the IEEE Conference on Computer Vision and Pattern Recognition, pp. 4823–4831 (2015)
17. Ham, B., Cho, M., Ponce, J.: Robust guided image filtering using nonconvex potentials. IEEE Trans. Pattern Anal. Mach. Intell. (2017)
18. He, K., Sun, J., Tang, X.: Guided image filtering. IEEE Trans. Pattern Anal. Mach. Intell. **35**(6), 1397–1409 (2013)
19. Jevnisek, R.J., Avidan, S.: Co-occurrence filter. In: The IEEE Conference on Computer Vision and Pattern Recognition (CVPR), July 2017
20. Karacan, L., Erdem, E., Erdem, A.: Structure-preserving image smoothing via region covariances. ACM Trans. Graph. (TOG) **32**(6), 176 (2013)
21. Li, Y., Huang, J.-B., Ahuja, N., Yang, M.-H.: Deep joint image filtering. In: Leibe, B., Matas, J., Sebe, N., Welling, M. (eds.) ECCV 2016. LNCS, vol. 9908, pp. 154–169. Springer, Cham (2016). https://doi.org/10.1007/978-3-319-46493-0_10
22. Liu, Q., Liu, J., Dong, P., Liang, D.: SGTD: structure gradient and texture decorrelating regularization for image decomposition. In: Proceedings of the IEEE International Conference on Computer Vision, pp. 1081–1088 (2013)
23. Liu, S., Pan, J., Yang, M.-H.: Learning recursive filters for low-level vision via a hybrid neural network. In: Leibe, B., Matas, J., Sebe, N., Welling, M. (eds.) ECCV 2016. LNCS, vol. 9908, pp. 560–576. Springer, Cham (2016). https://doi.org/10.1007/978-3-319-46493-0_34
24. Liu, W., Chen, X., Shen, C., Liu, Z., Yang, J.: Semi-global weighted least squares in image filtering. In: The IEEE International Conference on Computer Vision (ICCV), October 2017
25. Lu, K., You, S., Barnes, N.: Double-guided filtering: Image smoothing with structure and texture guidance. In: The IEEE International Conference on Digital Image Computing: Techniques and Applications (DICTA), December 2017
26. Nah, S., Hyun Kim, T., Mu Lee, K.: Deep multi-scale convolutional neural network for dynamic scene deblurring. In: The IEEE Conference on Computer Vision and Pattern Recognition (CVPR), July 2017
27. Nguyen, R.M., Brown, M.S.: Fast and effective L0 gradient minimization by region fusion. In: Proceedings of the IEEE International Conference on Computer Vision, pp. 208–216 (2015)
28. Petschnigg, G., Szeliski, R., Agrawala, M., Cohen, M., Hoppe, H., Toyama, K.: Digital photography with flash and no-flash image pairs. ACM Trans. Graph. (TOG) **23**(3), 664–672 (2004)
29. Rick Chang, J.H., Frank Wang, Y.C.: Propagated image filtering. In: Proceedings of the IEEE Conference on Computer Vision and Pattern Recognition, pp. 10–18 (2015)
30. Rudin, L.I., Osher, S., Fatemi, E.: Nonlinear total variation based noise removal algorithms. Physica D **60**(1–4), 259–268 (1992)
31. Shen, X., Chen, Y., Tao, X., Jia, J.: Convolutional neural pyramid for image processing. CoRR abs/1704.02071 (2017). http://arxiv.org/abs/1704.02071

32. Subr, K., Soler, C., Durand, F.: Edge-preserving multiscale image decomposition based on local extrema. ACM Trans. Graph. (TOG) **28**(5), 147 (2009)
33. Tai, Y., Yang, J., Liu, X.: Image super-resolution via deep recursive residual network. In: The IEEE Conference on Computer Vision and Pattern Recognition (CVPR), July 2017
34. Tan, X., Sun, C., Pham, T.D.: Multipoint filtering with local polynomial approximation and range guidance. In: Proceedings of the IEEE Conference on Computer Vision and Pattern Recognition, pp. 2941–2948 (2014)
35. Tomasi, C., Manduchi, R.: Bilateral filtering for gray and color images. In: Sixth International Conference on Computer Vision, pp. 839–846. IEEE (1998)
36. Wang, Y., He, C.: Image segmentation algorithm by piecewise smooth approximation. EURASIP J. Image Video Process. **2012**(1), 16 (2012)
37. Wang, Z., Bovik, A.C., Sheikh, H.R., Simoncelli, E.P.: Image quality assessment: from error visibility to structural similarity. IEEE Trans. Image Process. **13**(4), 600–612 (2004)
38. Winnemöller, H., Olsen, S.C., Gooch, B.: Real-time video abstraction. ACM Trans. Graph. (TOG) **25**, 1221–1226 (2006)
39. Xie, S., Tu, Z.: Holistically-nested edge detection. In: Proceedings of the IEEE International Conference on Computer Vision, pp. 1395–1403 (2015)
40. Xu, L., Lu, C., Xu, Y., Jia, J.: Image smoothing via l 0 gradient minimization. ACM Trans. Graph. (TOG)**30**, 174 (2011)
41. Xu, L., Ren, J., Yan, Q., Liao, R., Jia, J.: Deep edge-aware filters. In: Proceedings of the 32nd International Conference on Machine Learning (ICML-2015), pp. 1669–1678 (2015)
42. Xu, L., Yan, Q., Xia, Y., Jia, J.: Structure extraction from texture via relative total variation. ACM Trans. Graph. (TOG) **31**(6), 139 (2012)
43. Yang, Q.: Semantic filtering. In: Proceedings of the IEEE Conference on Computer Vision and Pattern Recognition, pp. 4517–4526 (2016)
44. Zang, Y., Huang, H., Zhang, L.: Guided adaptive image smoothing via directional anisotropic structure measurement. IEEE Trans. Vis. Comput. Graph. **21**(9), 1015–1027 (2015)
45. Zhang, F., Dai, L., Xiang, S., Zhang, X.: Segment graph based image filtering: Fast structure-preserving smoothing. In: Proceedings of the IEEE International Conference on Computer Vision, pp. 361–369 (2015)
46. Zhang, Q., Shen, X., Xu, L., Jia, J.: Rolling guidance filter. In: Fleet, D., Pajdla, T., Schiele, B., Tuytelaars, T. (eds.) ECCV 2014. LNCS, vol. 8691, pp. 815–830. Springer, Cham (2014). https://doi.org/10.1007/978-3-319-10578-9_53

VSO: Visual Semantic Odometry

Konstantinos-Nektarios Lianos[1], Johannes L. Schönberger[2], Marc Pollefeys[2,3], and Torsten Sattler[2(✉)]

[1] Geomagical Labs, Inc., Mountain View, USA
nelianos@geomagical.com
[2] Department of Computer Science, ETH Zürich, Zürich, Switzerland
{jsch,marc.pollefeys,sattlert}@inf.ethz.ch
[3] Microsoft, Wallisellen, Switzerland

Abstract. Robust data association is a core problem of visual odometry, where image-to-image correspondences provide constraints for camera pose and map estimation. Current state-of-the-art direct and indirect methods use short-term tracking to obtain continuous frame-to-frame constraints, while long-term constraints are established using loop closures. In this paper, we propose a novel visual semantic odometry (VSO) framework to enable medium-term continuous tracking of points using semantics. Our proposed framework can be easily integrated into existing direct and indirect visual odometry pipelines. Experiments on challenging real-world datasets demonstrate a significant improvement over state-of-the-art baselines in the context of autonomous driving simply by integrating our semantic constraints.

Keywords: Visual odometry · SLAM · Semantic segmentation

1 Introduction

Visual Odometry (VO) algorithms track the movement of one or multiple cameras using visual measurements. Their ability to determine the current position based on a camera feed forms a key component of any type of embodied artificial intelligence, *e.g.*, self-driving cars or other autonomous robots, and of any type of intelligent augmentation system, *e.g.*, Augmented or Mixed Reality devices.

At its core, VO is a data association problem, as it establishes pixel-level associations between images. These correspondences are simultaneously used to build a 3D map of the scene and to track the pose of the current camera frame relative to the map. Naturally, such a local tracking and mapping approach introduces small errors in each frame. Accumulating these errors over time leads to drift in the pose and map estimates. In order to reduce this drift, constraints

---

This work was done while Konstantinos-Nektarios Lianos was at ETH Zürich.

Electronic supplementary material The online version of this chapter (https://doi.org/10.1007/978-3-030-01225-0_15) contains supplementary material, which is available to authorized users.

ⓒ Springer Nature Switzerland AG 2018
V. Ferrari et al. (Eds.): ECCV 2018, LNCS 11208, pp. 246–263, 2018.
https://doi.org/10.1007/978-3-030-01225-0_15

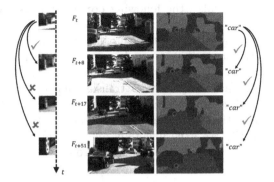

Fig. 1. Patch trackability under severe scale variation. Each row shows an image at time $t + \tau$. The point in red is tracked. Its patch appearance changes drastically but its semantic identity remains the same. While appearance-based tracking fails, image semantics can be used to establish medium-term constraints. (Color figure online)

between corresponding image observations are used to jointly optimize poses and map, *e.g.*, using an extended Kalman Filter [33] or bundle adjustment [26,46].

In general, there are two orthogonal approaches to reduce drift in VO. The first uses short-term correspondences between images to enable temporal drift correction by transitively establishing constraints between subsequent camera frames. This is especially useful in automotive scenarios where a car drives along a straight path for a significant amount of time. The second approach establishes long-term constraints between temporally far-away frames using loop closure detection. The latter is only effective if the camera intersects its previous trajectory multiple times or in the case of localization against a pre-built map [30].

In this paper, we propose an approach to improve upon the first drift correction strategy using semantics for *medium-term continuous tracking* of points. The main limitation of the existing state of the art in this scenario is a lack of invariant representations: Both feature-based approaches, *e.g.*, ORB-SLAM [34,35], and direct methods based on minimizing a photometric error, *e.g.*, LSD-SLAM [13] or DSO [12], are not able to continuously track a point over long distances as both representations are not fully invariant to viewpoint and illumination changes. An example for such a scenario is shown in Fig. 1, where the missing invariance of patch representations to scale changes prevents us from establishing medium-term correspondences while a car drives down a road.

The main idea of this paper is to use semantics as an invariant scene representation. The underlying intuition is that changes in viewpoint, scale, illumination, *etc.* only affect the low-level appearance of objects but not their semantic meaning. As illustrated in Fig. 1, scene semantics thus enable us to establish longer-term constraints, enabling us to significantly reduce drift in VO systems. Based on this idea, this paper derives a novel visual *semantic* odometry (VSO) approach that integrates semantic constraints into pose and map optimization.

In detail, this paper makes the following **contributions**: (**1**) We derive a novel cost function for minimizing *semantic* reprojection errors and show that it can be minimized using an expectation maximization (EM) scheme. Our approach is flexible in the sense that it can be combined with any semantic segmentation algorithm. (**2**) We demonstrate that including our semantic cost term into VO algorithms significantly reduces translational drift in the context of autonomous driving. Our approach can be readily integrated into existing VO approaches, independently of whether they rely on direct or indirect methods for data association. (**3**) We experimentally analyze the behavior of our approach, explain under which conditions it offers improvements, and discuss current restrictions.

2   Related Work

The large body of existing visual odometry systems can be categorized based on the employed optimization approach [46] (filtering or non-linear optimization), the sampling of observations (sparse or dense), and the data association approach (direct or indirect). In this paper, we aim at improving data association by introducing a semantic error term. As shown in Sect. 4, this allows us to reduce drift for both direct and indirect methods. As such, our proposed approach is orthogonal to the existing VO methods we review below. Most related to our work are methods that use semantics for VO or for image-to-model alignment.

Direct methods minimize the photometric error of corresponding pixels in consecutive camera frames [2,12–14,36,48,53]. The optimization objective is to align the camera poses such that the reprojected scene optimally explains the observed image intensities. The underlying energy functional is based on image gradients and thus typically requires a good initialization of the camera pose and scene structure to converge. In contrast, our proposed system aims to increase the convergence radius of the energy by incorporating longer-term constraints derived from semantic segmentation. In addition, photometric error metrics are generally not robust to even small viewpoint or illumination changes [37]. As a consequence, most direct methods track points only over a short time window. Our semantic constraints complement the accurate, short-term photometric constraints by increasing the trackability of points to larger time windows.

Indirect methods minimize the reprojection error between 3D map points and their observed projections in the image [10,20,21,34,35]. Indirect visual odometry methods typically use a sparse sampling of observations in the image by detecting and matching local features. As a result, (sparse) indirect methods are typically more robust to viewpoint and illumination changes [37]. Due to their local nature, feature detectors and descriptors are not fully invariant against such changes [31,32]. Thus, indirect methods are still subject to the same principal limitation of direct methods and fail to track points over longer time frames. In contrast, we incorporate semantic information that is derived globally from the entire image. Section 4 shows that incorporating such global information into a state-of-the-art indirect visual odometry system [35] significantly reduces drift due to adding medium-term constraints between images.

Semantic mapping approaches focus on constructing semantic 3D maps from images and their known poses [6,18,24,44,47,52]. The maps are built by jointly reasoning about semantics and geometry using fixed camera positions. As a by-product, our approach also generates a semantically annotated 3D map. However, we focus on jointly optimizing semantics, geometry, and camera poses.

Semantic visual odometry methods use higher-level features, such as lines [22], planes [4,19,28], or objects [3–5,7,16,43] to improve the robustness of VO or to obtain richer map representations [39,42]. Conversely, VO can be used to improve object detection [11,15,25,38]. Most similar to our approach are object-based SLAM [3,5,7,15,40,43] and Structure-from-Motion [4,16] approaches. They use object detections as higher-level semantic features to improve camera pose tracking [4,7,15,16] and/or to detect and handle loop closures [3,5,15,43]. While some approaches rely on a database of specific objects that are detected online [7,15,43], others use generic object detectors [3,5,16]. The former require that all objects are known and mapped beforehand. The latter need to solve a data association problem to resolve the ambiguities arising from detecting the same object class multiple times in an image. Bowman *et al.* were the first to jointly optimize over continuous camera poses, 3D point landmarks, and object landmarks (represented by bounding volumes [5,16]) as well as over discrete data associations [5]. They use a probabilistic association model to avoid the need for hard decisions. In contrast, our approach does not need a discrete data association by considering continuous distances to object boundaries rather than individual object detections. By focusing on the boundaries of semantic objects, we are able to handle a larger corpus of semantic object classes. Specifically, we are able to use both convex objects as well as semantic classes that cannot be described by bounding boxes, such as street, sky, and building. Compared to [5], who focus on handling loop closures, our approach aims at reducing drift through medium-term continuous data associations.

Semantic image-to-model alignment methods use semantics to align images with 3D models [8,45,50,51]. Cohen *et al.* stitch visually disconnected models by measuring the quality of an alignment using 3D point projections into a semantically segmented image. Taneja *et al.* estimate an initial alignment between a panorama and a 3D model based on semantic segmentation [50]. They then alternate between improving the segmentation and the alignment. Most closely related to our approach is concurrent work by Toft *et al.* [51], who project semantically labeled 3D points into semantically segmented images. Similar to us, they construct error maps for each class via distance fields. Given an initial guess for the camera pose, the errors associated with the 3D points are then used to refine the pose. They apply their approach to visual localization and thus assume a pre-built and pre-labeled 3D model. In contrast, our approach is designed for VO and optimizes camera poses via a semantic error term while simultaneously constructing a labeled 3D point cloud. Toft *et al.* incrementally include more classes in the optimization and fix parts of the pose at some point. In contrast, our approach directly considers all classes.

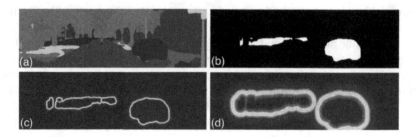

Fig. 2. Illustration of the semantic likelihood derivation. The example regards the
car class (blue) in the input segmentation in (a) and its binary image $\mathbb{I}_{S=car}$ in (b).
Semantic likelihoods $p(S|X, T, z = car)$ are shown for $\sigma = 10$ in (c) and for $\sigma = 40$ in
(d), where red corresponds to value 1 and blue to value 0. (Color figure online)

3   Visual Semantic Odometry

The goal of this paper is to reduce drift in visual odometry by establishing
continuous medium-term correspondences. Since both direct and indirect VO
approaches are often not able to track a point over a long period of time continuously, we use scene semantics to establish such correspondences.

The idea behind this approach is illustrated in Fig. 1: Consider a 3D point
(marked by the red circle) situated on the wheel of a parking car. As we move
closer, the appearance of the patch surrounding the point changes so drastically
that we are soon unable to associate it with the point's first observation. As
a result, we cannot establish sufficient constraints between frame F_t and later
frames to effectively prevent drift in the estimated trajectory. While the image-
level appearance of the point changes, its semantic identity, *i.e.*, being part of a
car, remains the same. Associating the point with a semantic label and enforcing consistency, *i.e.*, that the point labeled as *car* projects into an image region
labeled as *car*, thus enables the creation of medium-term constraints. The scenario shown in Fig. 1 is prevalent in the case of forward motion in the automotive
domain, where points are often visible for a long time. As our experiments show,
the illustrated problem affects both direct and indirect methods.

In the following, we formalize our semantic constraints: Sect. 3.1 proposes
our visual semantic odometry framework. Sects. 3.2 and 3.3 derive our semantic
cost function and its optimization. Finally, Sect. 3.4 describes how the semantic
cost function can be integrated into existing VO pipelines.

3.1   Visual Semantic Odometry Framework

In general, we can integrate our proposed system into any standard window-
based visual odometry system, which we denote as the *base* system in the following. Given a set of input images $\mathcal{I} = \{I\}_{k=1}^{K}$, visual odometry tackles the problem
of jointly optimizing the set of camera poses $\mathcal{T} = \{T\}_{k=1}^{K}$, with $T_k \in SE(3)$, and
map points $\{P\}_{i=1}^{N}$ using a given set of corresponding observations $z_{i,k}$. Each

map point is typically represented by its location $X_i \in \mathbb{R}^3$. An observation is either defined as a keypoint location in an image (in the case of indirect methods) or an image intensity (in the case of direct methods). To make real-time optimization feasible, point cross-correlations are typically ignored and the odometry objective functional is thus formulated as

$$E_{base} = \sum_k \sum_i e_{base}(k, i) \ . \tag{1}$$

Here, the function $e_{base}(k, i)$ is the cost of the i-th point induced in the k-th camera. This function is either defined as a photometric (direct methods) or geometric error (indirect methods).

We now describe our proposed semantic cost function that can be readily combined with E_{base}. For each input image I_k, we require a dense pixel-wise semantic segmentation $S_k : \mathbb{R}^2 \rightarrow \mathcal{C}$, where each pixel is labeled as one of $|\mathcal{C}|$ classes from the set $\mathcal{C}$. In addition to its location X_i, each map point is thus also associated with a categorical variable $Z_i \in \mathcal{C}$. $p(Z_i = c|X_i)$ is the probability of a point P_i at position X_i to be of class c. We denote the label probability vector for each point P_i as $w_i \in \mathbb{R}^C$, where $w_i^{(c)} = p(Z_i = c|X_i)$ is the probability that point P_i belongs to class c. This probability vector is estimated online from semantic segmentations. Intuitively, the objective of our proposed semantic energy encourages point projections to be both semantically and photometrically/geometrically consistent.

To incorporate our semantic constraints into the odometry optimization functional, we define the *semantic cost function*

$$E_{sem} = \sum_k \sum_i e_{sem}(k, i) \ , \tag{2}$$

where each term associates the camera pose T_k and point P_i, represented by its label Z_i and location X_i, with the semantic image observation S_k. We optimize the base and semantic costs in the joint functional

$$\{\hat{X}\}, \{\hat{T}\} = \arg \min \ E_{base} + \lambda E_{sem} \ , \tag{3}$$

where λ weights the different terms, as explained in detail in the following section.

3.2 Semantic Cost Function

We follow a probabilistic approach and first define the observation likelihood model $p(S_k|T_k, X_i, Z_i = c)$, associating the semantic observations S_k with the camera pose T_k and point P_i. The intuition behind our observation model is that a semantic point observation $p(S_k|T_k, X_i, Z_i = c)$ should be likely if the pixel corresponding to X_i's projection $\pi(T_k, X_i)$ into S_k is labeled with c. The likelihood should decrease with the distance of $\pi(T_k, X_i)$ to the nearest region labeled as c. To implement this concept, we make use of the distance transform

$DT_B(p) : \mathbb{R}^2 \rightarrow \mathbb{R}$, where $p \in \mathbb{R}^2$ is the pixel location and B the binary image on which the distance transform is defined (c.f. Fig. 2). More precisely, we compute a binary image $\mathbb{I}_{S_k=c}$ for each semantic class c such that pixels with label c in S_k have a value of 1 and all other pixels have value 0 (c.f. Fig. 2(b)). We then define a distance transform $DT_k^{(c)}(p) = DT_{\mathbb{I}_{S_k=c}}(p)$ based on this binary image (c.f. Fig. 2(c)). Using $DT_k^{(c)}(p)$, we define the observation likelihood as

$$p(S_k|T_k, X_i, Z_i = c) \propto e^{-\frac{1}{2\sigma^2} DT_k^{(c)}(\pi(T_k, X_i))^2} \quad , \tag{4}$$

where π again is the projection operator from world to image space and σ models the uncertainty in the semantic image classification. For brevity, we omit the normalization factor that ensures that the sum over the probability space is 1. For a detailed derivation of Eq. 4, including its underlying assumptions, we refer to the supplementary material[1]. Figure 2 illustrates the semantic likelihood for an example image. For a point with label c, the likelihood decreases proportionally to the distance from the image area labeled as c. Intuitively, maximizing the likelihood thus corresponds to adjusting the camera pose and point position such that the point projection moves towards the correctly labeled image area.

Using the observation likelihood (Eq. 4), we define a semantic cost term as

$$\begin{aligned} e_{sem}(k, i) &= \sum_{c \in C} w_i^{(c)} \log(p(S_k|T_k, X_i, Z_i = c)) \\ &= -\sum_{c \in C} w_i^{(c)} \cdot \frac{1}{\sigma^2} DT_k^{(c)}(\pi(T_k, X_i))^2 \quad , \end{aligned} \tag{5}$$

where $w_i^{(c)}$ again is the probability that P_i is of class $c \in C$. Intuitively, the semantic cost $e_{sem}(k, i)$ for a given the semantic image S_k and point P_i is a weighted average of 2D distances. Each distance $DT_k^{(c)}(\pi(T_k, X_i))$ of the point projection $\pi(T_k, X_i)$ to the nearest area of class c is weighted by the probability w_i that P_i is of class c. For example, if P_i has label car with high certainty, then its cost is the distance of the point projection to the closest area labelled as car in S_k. If P_i has labels $sidewalk$ and $road$ with equal probability, its cost is lowest on the boundary between the two classes.

The label probability vector w_i for point P_i is computed by jointly considering all of its observations. Concretely, if P_i is observed by a set of cameras $\mathcal{T}_i$, then

$$w_i^{(c)} = \frac{1}{\alpha} \prod_{k \in \mathcal{T}_i} p(S_k|T_k, X_i, Z_i = c) \quad . \tag{6}$$

The constant α ensures that $\sum_c w_i^{(c)} = 1$. This rule allows for incremental refinement of the label vector w_i by accumulating semantic observations. If the observations have the same mode, i.e., they have their maximum value for the same

---

[1] The supplementary material for this work is available online at http://cvg.ethz.ch/research/visual-semantic-odometry/.

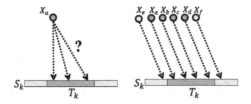

Fig. 3. *Left:* The optimization of a camera pose and a single point using semantics has infinitely many solutions. *Right:* Using multiple fixed points to optimize the camera pose constrains the solution and semantic optimization becomes feasible.

class, then the element-wise multiplication and normalization will cause the vector w_i to converge to a single mode corresponding to the true label.

The uncertainty parameter σ in Eq. 5 plays an important role as it defines the level of trust in the segmentation and thus in the label assignment for point P_i. For an example, consider a point projecting outside the *car* class in Fig. 2. We consider only two existing classes, *car* and *no_car*. The point is of class Z_i = *car*, with $w_i^{(car)}$ = 1. Then the weight of the residual in Eq. 5 is inversely proportional to the value of σ. What is more, if σ is high, then from Eq. 4, the class likelihood for a point will be almost uniform, canceling out the semantic residual for a point for competing classes (*i.e.*, close to the boundary of objects).

3.3   Optimization

Equations 5 and 6 result in a coupled structure for the optimization as both depend on the 3D point positions, the associated categorical variables, and the camera poses. For tractability, we use expectation maximization (EM) to minimize the functional E_{joint} in an alternating fashion: The E-step computes the weight vector w_i for each point P_i based on Eq. 6 while keeping the point positions and camera poses fixed. The M-step in turn optimizes the point positions and camera poses while fixing the weights. Since E_{sem} has a sparse structure, the M-step is implemented efficiently by using the Levenberg-Marquardt algorithm [27,29] inside a sparse non-linear solver, *e.g.*, Ceres [1] or G^{2}o [23].

The presented optimization framework can be formally derived by modeling the point labels Z_i as latent variables and performing maximum likelihood inference using EM. Due to space constraints, we skip this derivation and directly explain the resulting optimization strategy. We refer the interested reader to the supplementary material for the derivation.

Using our proposed semantic formulation, we benefit from invariance but lack structural information. Optimizing the map points and camera poses with only the semantic term thus makes the problem under-constrained, as the likelihood (Eq. 4) is uniform inside object boundaries. This is illustrated in Fig. 3(left), where any projection of the 3D point into the blue image area will result in the same cost. To avoid this problem, the optimization of E_{sem} is performed as follows: (1) The semantic optimization is performed jointly with the base visual odometry functional. (2) Multiple points and semantic constraints are used to optimize a single camera pose. (3) As mentioned above, our semantic cost is under-constrained by itself. Points providing only semantic constraints and no base constraints, *i.e.*, points that are no longer optimized by the base system, are thus fixed and we optimize only their corresponding camera poses to reduce drift. This approach not only keeps the number of optimizable variables bounded, but introduces structural correlation between points as well, thus constraining the pose solution (see Fig. 3). (4) By frequent semantic optimization, we reduce the probability of associating a point to a wrong object instance. Since the optimization is based on the gradient of the distance transform, we ensure that a point stays close to a correctly labelled area and is thus pulled towards it.

3.4   Obtaining Semantic Constraints and System Integration

The semantic objective of Eq. 5 assumes the creation of constraints between a camera k with semantic image S_k and a point P_i. To establish these correspondences, we follow a standard approach: The base VO system creates a set of visible points $V(k)$ for each frame k. For each point in $V(k)$, an optimizable camera-point constraint is created. To update this list, direct VO methods compare the intensity of a candidate point P_i with the intensity of the image I_k at the projected location, while indirect methods use feature matching. Analogously, we also maintain a semantic visibility list $V_{sem}(k)$ for each frame k. A candidate point P_i is inserted into $V_{sem}(k)$ if the projection of the point i into the image k is sufficiently close to an area with the semantic class of the point. Here, allowing a certain amount of semantic reprojection error when establishing semantic constraints is necessary to be able to handle drift.

VO approaches typically maintain an *active window* (AW) of a few (key-)frames that are used to optimize the trajectory based on photometric/geometric constraints. Similarly, we define an *active semantic window* (ASW) of (key-)frames. Once a frame leaves the AW, we consider adding it to the ASW. We thereby try to limit the number of frames in the ASW while trying to cover as large a part of the trajectory as possible. The poses of frames in the ASW are not optimized anymore as they usually lack photometric/geometric constraints with the current frame. A more detailed description on how to obtain semantic correspondences from existing VO pipelines and on integrating our approach into existing systems can be found in the supplementary material.

4   Experimental Evaluation

In this section, we experimentally demonstrate that integrating our semantic medium-term constraints into state-of-the-art VO approaches significantly reduces translational drift. The focus of our experiments is an autonomous driving scenario with long periods without turns as this is the case where our semantic constraints can be most useful. We use the KITTI [17] and PlayingForBenchmarks (P4B) [41] datasets. A laptop with a quad-core 2.50 GHz CPU, 8 GB RAM, and a NVIDIA 1080 GPU was used for our experimental evaluation.

4.1 Experimental Setup

For semantic segmentation, we use the raw output of an off-the-shelf semantic classifier [54] pre-trained offline on the Cityscapes dataset [9]. While this semantic classifier achieves state-of-the-art performance on Cityscapes, it often introduces severe errors on the KITTI dataset (see Fig. 5). To account for the classification errors, the uncertainty is modeled by the parameters λ (weighting the relative importance of the semantic cost term) and σ (modeling the uncertainty of the classifier) in Eqs. 3 and 4, which we choose empirically per sequence. σ is measured in pixels and depends on the quality of the segmentation and the image resolution. λ depends on the type of base cost (reprojection/photometric) and the classifier performance. For the P4B experiments, we show results using the ground truth semantic labels, thus establishing an upper bound on the potential of our method. To outline the versatility of our proposed framework, we implemented it on top of two VO pipelines, as detailed in the following.

We chose **ORB-SLAM2** [34] as a state-of-the-art representative of indirect VO methods. As shown in [53], stereo ORB-SLAM2 is state-of-the-art in terms of translation accuracy. We run the system with the default real-time settings and de-activate loop closing and global bundle adjustment, as we focus on showing the benefits of our semantic constraints in a pure VO setting. Notice that our constraints are complimentary to loop closure constraints as the latter only reduce drift in the case a place is re-visited. We experiment both with stereo and monocular ORB-SLAM2, denoting the latter as "mono-ORB-SLAM2".

We chose **PhotoBundle** [2] as a direct VO method. In contrast to LSD-SLAM [13] and DSO [12], which use custom-made optimizers, PhotoBundle uses Ceres [1] as its backend, allowing for an easy integration of our semantic constraints. For comparability with [2], we also use 3× downsampled KITTI images. Equivalent to the original PhotoBundle approach, we use stereo depth maps to initialize 3D points, but do not enforce stereo constraints during the optimization. Depth maps are solely computed using static and not temporal stereo, resulting in failures in scenarios where horizontal lines are dominant. As such, the PhotoBundle base framework fails on one of the KITTI sequences and performs slightly worse than ORB-SLAM2. However, we are primarily interested in demonstrating the relative improvement by integrating our method. In contrast to ORB-SLAM2, PhotoBundle executes the tracking and mapping threads serially and is missing the SIMD parallelization of other direct approaches, e.g., [13]. Thus, it does not operate in real-time.

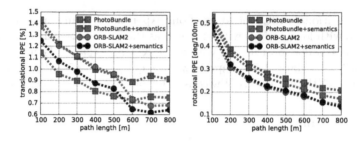

Fig. 4. Translation (left) and rotation (right) RPE as a function of the trajectory length, averaged over the sequences of the KITTI dataset. We report results for stereo ORB-SLAM2 and PhotoBundle with and without our semantic constraints. As can be seen, semantic constraints reduce the translational drift for both methods. The average was computed without sequences 01, 04, 06, 10.

Table 1. KITTI RPE results for translation t_{rel} (%) and rotation r_{rel} (deg./100 m), averaged over 100 m to 800 m intervals (lower is better). We also report the relative improvements $t_{rel}^{(\%)}$ and $r_{rel}^{(\%)}$ (in %, higher is better) obtained with semantic constraints. The mean RPEs exclude sequences 01, 04 and 10

Seq.	ORB-SLAM2		+semantics				PhotoBundle		+semantics			
	t_{rel}	r_{rel}	t_{rel}	r_{rel}	$t_{rel}^{(\%)}$	$r_{rel}^{(\%)}$	t_{rel}	r_{rel}	t_{rel}	r_{rel}	$t_{rel}^{(\%)}$	$r_{rel}^{(\%)}$
00	1.00	**0.42**	**0.97**	**0.42**	2.51	-0.13	1.17	0.46	1.03	0.45	11.94	1.94
01	**1.79**	**0.31**	1.95	**0.31**	-8.76	0.62	-	-	-	-	-	-
02	1.05	**0.32**	**1.02**	0.34	2.10	-6.49	1.47	0.39	1.36	0.40	7.15	-1.54
03	1.93	**0.24**	**1.86**	0.27	3.52	-12.84	3.67	0.35	3.25	0.35	11.37	0.75
04	1.19	0.13	1.30	**0.10**	-9.52	17.31	0.81	0.28	**0.80**	0.27	1.60	3.36
05	0.87	**0.30**	0.82	**0.30**	6.64	1.92	0.94	0.41	**0.81**	0.41	13.48	-0.16
06	1.10	0.29	**0.98**	**0.26**	10.55	8.96	1.87	0.33	1.03	0.30	44.79	11.17
07	0.81	**0.38**	0.75	0.41	6.96	-7.03	0.70	0.42	**0.65**	0.40	7.38	5.05
08	1.33	**0.35**	1.26	**0.35**	5.11	-1.08	1.25	0.43	**1.18**	0.44	5.75	-0.84
09	1.10	0.29	1.07	**0.28**	3.09	4.22	1.04	0.35	**0.93**	0.34	10.97	3.02
10	1.25	**0.37**	1.28	0.38	-2.24	-1.88	**1.15**	**0.37**	1.17	**0.37**	-2.00	-0.62
mean	1.15	**0.33**	1.09	**0.33**	5.06	-1.56	1.51	0.39	1.28	0.39	14.10	2.42

Evaluation Metrics. Following standard practice [49], we measure the RMSE of the Relative Pose Error (RPE) and the Absolute Trajectory Error (ATE) for each method. RPE measures the average deviation of the estimated from the ground truth trajectory over intervals of fixed length. ATE measures the absolute difference between points on the two trajectories. For the monocular experiments, we follow the literature [14,34] and calculate the ATE after performing 7-DoF alignment. For the stereo experiments, we measure the *Relative RPE* in % in order to quantify the relative reduction in drift obtained using semantic constraints. For the translational error, the *Relative RPE* $t_{rel}^{(\%)}$ is defined as $t_{rel}^{(\%)} = 100 \cdot (t_{rel}^{base} - t_{rel}^{joint})/t_{rel}^{base}$, where t_{rel}^{base} and t_{rel}^{joint} are the translation RPE values obtained without and with our constraints, respectively. The relative rotational RPE $r_{rel}^{(\%)}$ is defined accordingly.

Fig. 5. Consecutive frames from KITTI sequence 10 with inconsistent semantic segmentations. Increasing the uncertainty σ in the semantic segmentation places less weight on our semantic constraints and allows us to handle such scenes. In general, small values for σ are preferable if shape details are consistent.

4.2 Results

We quantitatively measure the impact of integrating our semantic constraints on drift accumulated during VO using relative and absolute error metrics.

KITTI Dataset. Figure 4 shows the RPE of ORB-SLAM2 and PhotoBundle as a function of the trajectory length for the KITTI dataset. The plots were obtained by averaging over sub-trajectories of different lengths over different KITTI sequences. Using semantic constraints significantly reduces the translational drift for both direct and indirect VO methods.

We observe that our semantic constraints have limited impact on the rotational RPE. This is not surprising as we observe little rotational drift when the car travels along a straight path. Rotational drift mainly occurs during turns, *i.e.*, in situations in which semantics cannot provide medium-term constraints as the 3D points quickly leave the field-of-view of the cameras.

Table 1 shows the RPEs for the individual sequences of the KITTI benchmark. For most of the scenes, we observe a consistent improvement of up to 45% for the translational errors compared to the baselines. This improvement is consistent for both ORB-SLAM2 and PhotoBundle. For the few scenes that perform worse in terms of translational error, the negative impact is comparatively small, with the exception of sequences 01 and 04, as discussed in detail further below.

Table 2 shows the ATE metric for PhotoBundle, ORB-SLAM2, and mono-ORB-SLAM2. Especially for the latter, major improvement can be observed. Monocular VO is particularly challenging in the automotive domain, due to the forward motion which lacks significant parallax. Scale drift is usually a major source of error, as map points leave the field of view and scale information is discarded. Semantics help to preserve camera-point associations and thus the scale for longer intervals. The absolute improvement is further visualized in Fig. 6 for sequences 00 and 09.

P4B Dataset. This dataset consists of monocular synthetic images in an urban environment with ground-truth semantic segmentations. Due to high speed and sudden rotations, this benchmark is particularly challenging. In this evaluation,

Table 2. ATE, in meters, on KITTI without/with semantics. The mean reductions in ATE are 0.55 m, 0.51 m, and 9.06 m for ORB-SLAM2, PhotoBundle, and mono-ORB-SLAM2, respectively. We skip sequence 01 as PhotoBundle fails to handle it

	00	02	03	04	05
ORB-SLAM2	3.99 / 3.11	9.71 / 7.90	3.20 / 3.15	1.21 / 1.36	2.36 / 2.20
PhotoBundle	4.67 / 4.45	14.10 / 13.41	6.32 / 5.40	0.62 / 0.80	3.52 / 3.35
mono-ORB-SLAM2	56 / 45	25 / 23	2.0 / 2.1	1.4 / 1.9	27 / 19

	06	07	08	09	10
ORB-SLAM2	2.64 / 2.14	1.11 / 1.06	4.04 / 3.74	4.22 / 3.34	1.99 / 2.10
PhotoBundle	4.81 / 2.72	0.94 / 0.84	6.38 / 6.26	6.78 / 5.80	1.45 / 1.45
mono-ORB-SLAM2	47.1 / 40.5	13.6 / 12.5	50 / 42	43 / 43	6.8 / 7.7

Table 3. ATE error, in meters, on the Playing For Benchmarks (P4B) dataset for mono-ORB-SLAM2 without/with semantics. Each sequence is run 5 times. The ATE is calculated after 7-DoF alignment with the ground truth trajectory. Only the day sequences of P4B dataset for which at least 80% of the sequence can be tracked are considered. The results are obtained using the ground truth semantic labels

001	002	003	005	065	067
1.48 / 1.12	13 / 12	22 / 17	1.07 / 0.97	4 / 3.5	51 / 38

006	044	045	051	069
14 / 8.5	6.0 / 3.0	68 / 57	25 / 16	57 / 51

we select a subset of sequences to showcase the improvement obtained by incorporating semantics into mono-ORB-SLAM2. For all experiments, we ignore the *unlabeled* and *void* class and exclude any moving objects with labels 20-31. Figure 6 shows trajectories of representative sequences, where monocular tracking using the base framework was feasible, while Table 3 shows numeric ATE results.

Failure Cases. While our method leads to a large overall improvement in relative and absolute error metrics, we observed a few interesting failure cases in the KITTI sequences that we analyze in the following. In sequence 01, the classification in the highway segment is erroneous. Thus, outliers located in the background are introduced, which remain in the field of view for a long time. The resulting incorrect medium-term constraints lead to an increase in translational drift for ORB-SLAM2. Furthermore, PhotoBundle fails for sequence 01 due to perceptual aliasing caused by horizontal lines in the highway segment. In sequence 04, another car drives in front of the camera over the whole trajectory. Semantic constraints are successfully created on this moving object that remain in the field of view for a long period of time. As our approach implicitly assumes that the scene remains static, moving objects naturally lead to wrong semantic associations and thus an increase in drift. Excluding the "car" class from the semantic optimization for ORB-SLAM2+semantics solves this problem and reduces the translational and rotational RPE to 1.23% and 0.13 deg./100 m,

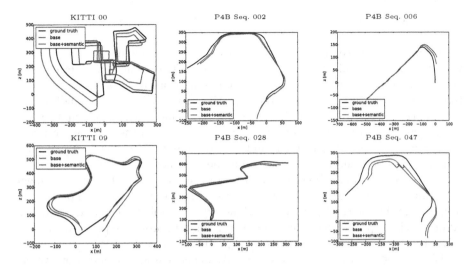

Fig. 6. Trajectory plots for mono-ORB-SLAM2 on sequences from KITTI and PlayingForBenchmarks (P4B). All sequences are 7-DoF aligned with the ground truth.

respectively. As shown qualitatively in the supplementary material, this slightly larger drift compared to pure ORB-SLAM2 is caused by inconsistent semantic segmentations. We observed that stationary cars typically provide excellent semantic constraints as they are typically well-segmented and visible for a long time. Rather than excluding entire semantic classes, instance-level segmentation should be used in practice to distinguish between moving and stationary objects. In sequence 10, the semantic classifier performs particularly bad (see Fig. 5), resulting in an increase of the RPEs. In such cases, the reason for the decrease in performance is an over-estimation of the classification accuracy by setting a low uncertainty σ in Eq. 4. Choosing a larger value for σ down-weights the influence of the semantic cost, resulting in the same performance as the baselines.

Runtime Results. The runtime of our system directly depends on the number of semantic constraints in the optimization. In general, the number of semantic constraints is scene and motion dependent, as shown in the supplementary material. For ORB-SLAM2, we use an average of 35 semantic constraints for KITTI, leading to a negligible computational overhead over the baseline. As a result, we achieve real-time performance when integrating semantic constraints into ORB-SLAM2. In contrast to the sparse measurements in ORB-SLAM2, PhotoBundle uses dense intensity-based measurements, resulting in 944 semantic constraints on average. In this setting, the joint optimization is on average (over all frames and sequences) 1.5× slower than base PhotoBundle. Executing the semantic optimization every 4th frame reduces the overhead to 1.125× at negligible loss in accuracy, allowing for real-time execution using PhotoBundle.

5 Conclusion

In this paper, we have proposed a novel visual semantic odometry (VSO) framework that can be readily integrated into existing VO systems. Our method harnesses the invariance of semantic object representations to incorporate medium-term constraints into the odometry objective. By appropriately handling the lack of structure of the semantic identity, we are able to effectively and significantly reduce translational drift. We have demonstrated consistent performance improvements for both direct and indirect systems in a challenging real-world scenario. The bottleneck of our method is the accuracy of the semantic segmentation, especially along object boundaries. In the future, we plan to experiment with multi-camera systems, for which we expect an even bigger improvement using semantics, since objects are continuously trackable for longer duration. In addition, class-specific uncertainty modeling could improve the performance and solve some of the current failure cases, *e.g.*, due to dynamic objects. Finally, we envision a system where geometry not only benefits from semantics but where both modalities are tightly coupled, thereby facilitating end-to-end learning of a geometric and semantic understanding of the world in real-time.

Acknowledgements. This project received funding from the European Union's Horizon 2020 research and innovation program under grant No. 688007 (TrimBot2020).

References

1. Agarwal, S., Mierle, K., et al.: Ceres solver. http://ceres-solver.org
2. Alismail, H., Browning, B., Lucey, S.: Photometric bundle adjustment for vision-based SLAM. In: Lai, S.-H., Lepetit, V., Nishino, K., Sato, Y. (eds.) ACCV 2016. LNCS, vol. 10114, pp. 324–341. Springer, Cham (2017). https://doi.org/10.1007/978-3-319-54190-7_20
3. Atanasov, N., Zhu, M., Daniilidis, K., Pappas, G.J.: Semantic Localization Via the Matrix Permanent. In: Robotics: Science and Systems (RSS) (2014)
4. Bao, S.Y., Savarese, S.: Semantic structure from motion. In: IEEE Conference on Computer Vision and Pattern Recognition (CVPR) (2011)
5. Bowman, S.L., Atanasov, N., Daniilidis, K., Pappas, G.J.: Probabilistic data association for semantic SLAM. In: IEEE International Conference on Robotics and Automation (ICRA) (2017)
6. Cherabier, I., Schönberger, J.L., Oswald, M., Pollefeys, M., Geiger, A.: Learning priors for semantic 3D reconstruction. In: Ferrari, V., Hebert, M., Sminchisescu, C., Weiss, Y. (eds.) ECCV 2018, Part XII. LNCS, vol. 11216, pp. 325–341. Springer, Cham (2018)
7. Civera, J., Gálvez-López, D., Riazuelo, L., Tardós, J.D., Montiel, J.: Towards semantic SLAM using a monocular camera. In: IEEE/RSJ International Conference on Intelligent Robots and Systems (IROS) (2011)
8. Cohen, A., Sattler, T., Pollefeys, M.: Merging the unmatchable: stitching visually disconnected SfM models. In: IEEE International Conference on Computer Vision (ICCV) (2015)

9. Cordts, M., et al.: The Cityscapes Dataset for Semantic Urban Scene Understanding. In: IEEE Conference on Computer Vision and Pattern Recognition (CVPR) (2016)
10. Davison, A.J., Reid, I.D., Molton, N.D., Stasse, O.: MonoSLAM: real-time single camera SLAM. IEEE Trans. Pattern Anal. Mach. Intell. (PAMI) **29**(6), 1052–1067 (2007)
11. Dong, J., Fei, X., Soatto, S.: Visual inertial semantic scene representation for 3D object detection. In: IEEE Conference on Computer Vision and Pattern Recognition (CVPR) (2017)
12. Engel, J., Koltun, V., Cremers, D.: Direct sparse odometry. IEEE Trans. Pattern Anal. Mach. Intell. (PAMI) **40**(3), 611–625 (2018)
13. Engel, J., Schöps, T., Cremers, D.: LSD-SLAM: large-scale direct monocular SLAM. In: Fleet, D., Pajdla, T., Schiele, B., Tuytelaars, T. (eds.) ECCV 2014. LNCS, vol. 8690, pp. 834–849. Springer, Cham (2014). https://doi.org/10.1007/978-3-319-10605-2_54
14. Forster, C., Zhang, Z., Gassner, M., Werlberger, M., Scaramuzza, D.: SVO: Semidirect Visual Odometry for monocular and multicamera systems. IEEE Trans. Robot. (T-RO) **33**(2), 249–265 (2017)
15. Gálvez-López, D., Salas, M., Tardós, J.D., Montiel, J.: Real-time monocular object slam. Robot. Auton. Syst. **75**, 435–449 (2016)
16. Gay, P., Rubino, C., Bansal, V., Del Bue, A.: Probabilistic structure from motion with objects (PSfMO). In: IEEE International Conference on Computer Vision (ICCV) (2017)
17. Geiger, A., Lenz, P., Urtasun, R.: Are we ready for autonomous driving? The KITTI vision benchmark suite. In: Conference on Computer Vision and Pattern Recognition (CVPR) (2012)
18. Häne, C., Zach, C., Cohen, A., Pollefeys, M.: Dense semantic 3D reconstruction. IEEE Trans. Pattern Anal. Mach. Intell. (PAMI) **39**(9), 1730–1743 (2017)
19. Henry, P., Krainin, M., Herbst, E., Ren, X., Fox, D.: RGB-D mapping: using kinect-style depth cameras for dense 3D modeling of indoor environments. Int. J. Robot. Res. (IJRR) **31**(5), 647–663 (2012)
20. Jin, H., Favaro, P., Soatto, S.: Real-time 3D motion and structure of point features: a front-end system for vision-based control and interaction. In: IEEE Conference on Computer Vision and Pattern Recognition (CVPR) (2000)
21. Klein, G., Murray, D.: Parallel tracking and mapping for small AR workspaces. In: IEEE and ACM International Symposium on Mixed and Augmented Reality (ISMAR) (2007)
22. Kottas, D.G., Roumeliotis, S.I.: Efficient and consistent vision-aided inertial navigation using line observations. In: IEEE International Conference on Robotics and Automation (ICRA) (2013)
23. Kümmerle, R., Grisetti, G., Strasdat, H., Konolige, K., Burgard, W.: G²o: a general framework for graph optimization. In: IEEE International Conference on Robotics and Automation (ICRA) (2011)
24. Kundu, A., Li, Y., Dellaert, F., Li, F., Rehg, J.M.: Joint semantic segmentation and 3D reconstruction from monocular video. In: Fleet, D., Pajdla, T., Schiele, B., Tuytelaars, T. (eds.) ECCV 2014. LNCS, vol. 8694, pp. 703–718. Springer, Cham (2014). https://doi.org/10.1007/978-3-319-10599-4_45
25. Leibe, B., Cornelis, N., Cornelis, K., Van Gool, L.: Dynamic 3d scene analysis from a moving vehicle. In: IEEE Conference on Computer Vision and Pattern Recognition (CVPR) (2007)

26. Leutenegger, S., Lynen, S., Bosse, M., Siegwart, R., Furgale, P.: Keyframe-based visual-inertial odometry using nonlinear optimization. Int. J. Robot. Res. (IJRR) **34**(3), 314–334 (2015)
27. Levenberg, K.: A method for the solution of certain non-linear problems in least squares. Q. Appl. Math. **2**(2), 164–168 (1944)
28. Ma, L., Kerl, C., Stückler, J., Cremers, D.: CPA-SLAM: consistent plane-model alignment for direct RGB-D SLAM. In: IEEE International Conference on Robotics and Automation (ICRA) (2016)
29. Marquardt, D.W.: An algorithm for least-squares estimation of nonlinear parameters. J. Soc. Ind. Appl. Math. **11**(2), 431–441 (1963)
30. Middelberg, S., Sattler, T., Untzelmann, O., Kobbelt, L.: Scalable 6-DOF localization on mobile devices. In: Fleet, D., Pajdla, T., Schiele, B., Tuytelaars, T. (eds.) ECCV 2014. LNCS, vol. 8690, pp. 268–283. Springer, Cham (2014). https://doi.org/10.1007/978-3-319-10605-2_18
31. Mikolajczyk, K., Schmid, C.: A performance evaluation of local descriptors. IEEE Trans. Pattern Anal. Mach. Intell. (PAMI) **27**(10), 1615–1630 (2005)
32. Mikolajczyk, K., et al.: A comparison of affine region detectors. Int. J. Comput. Vis. (IJCV) **65**(1), 43–72 (2005)
33. Mourikis, A.I., Trawny, N., Roumeliotis, S.I., Johnson, A.E., Ansar, A., Matthies, L.: Vision-aided inertial navigation for spacecraft entry, descent, and landing. IEEE Trans. Robot. (T-RO) **25**(2), 264–280 (2009)
34. Mur-Artal, R., Montiel, J.M.M., Tardos, J.D.: ORB-SLAM: a versatile and accurate monocular SLAM system. IEEE Trans. Robot. (T-RO) **31**(5), 1147–1163 (2015)
35. Mur-Artal, R., Tardós, J.D.: ORB-SLAM2: an open-source SLAM system for monocular, stereo and RGB-D cameras. IEEE Trans. Robot. (T-RO) **33**(5), 1255–1262 (2017)
36. Newcombe, R.A., Lovegrove, S.J., Davison, A.J.: DTAM: Dense tracking and mapping in real-time. In: IEEE International Conference on Computer Vision (ICCV), pp. 2320–2327 (2011)
37. Park, S., Schöps, T., Pollefeys, M.: Illumination change robustness in direct visual SLAM. In: IEEE International Conference on Robotics and Automation (ICRA) (2017)
38. Pillai, S., Leonard, J.: Monocular SLAM Supported Object Recognition. In: Robotics: Science and Systems (RSS) (2015)
39. Pronobis, A.: Semantic Mapping with Mobile Robots. Ph.D. thesis, KTH Royal Institute of Technology, Stockholm, Sweden (2011)
40. Reid, I.: Towards semantic visual SLAM. In: International Conference on Control Automation Robotics & Vision (ICARCV) (2014)
41. Richter, S.R., Hayder, Z., Koltun, V.: Playing for Benchmarks. In: IEEE International Conference on Computer Vision (ICCV) (2017)
42. Rusu, R.B., Marton, Z.C., Blodow, N., Dolha, M., Beetz, M.: Towards 3D point cloud based object maps for household environments. Robot. Auton. Syst. **56**(11), 927–941 (2008)
43. Salas-Moreno, R.F., Newcombe, R.A., Strasdat, H., Kelly, P.H., Davison, A.J.: Slam++: Simultaneous localisation and mapping at the level of objects. In: IEEE Conference on Computer Vision and Pattern Recognition (CVPR) (2013)
44. Savinov, N., Häne, C., Ladický, L., Pollefeys, M.: Semantic 3D reconstruction with continuous regularization and ray potentials using a visibility consistency constraint. In: IEEE Conference on Computer Vision and Pattern Recognition (CVPR) (2016)

45. Schönberger, J.L., Pollefeys, M., Geiger, A., Sattler, T.: Semantic Visual Localization. In: Conference on Computer Vision and Pattern Recognition (CVPR) (2018)
46. Strasdat, H., Montiel, J.M.M., Davison, A.J.: Visual slam: why filter? Image Vision Comput. **30**(2), 65–77 (2012)
47. Stückler, J., Waldvogel, B., Schulz, H., Behnke, S.: Dense real-time mapping of object-class semantics from RGB-D video. J. Real-Time Image Process. **10**(4), 599–609 (2015)
48. Stühmer, J., Gumhold, S., Cremers, D.: Real-time dense geometry from a handheld camera. In: Joint Pattern Recognition Symposium (2010)
49. Sturm, J., Engelhard, N., Endres, F., Burgard, W., Cremers, D.: A benchmark for the evaluation of RGB-D SLAM systems. In: IEEE/RSJ International Conference on Intelligent Robot Systems (IROS) (2012)
50. Taneja, A., Ballan, L., Pollefeys, M.: Registration of spherical panoramic images with cadastral 3D models. In: International Conference on 3D Imaging, Modeling, Processing, Visualization Transmission (3DIMPVT) (2012)
51. Toft, C., Olsson, C., Kahl, F.: Long-term 3D localization and pose from semantic labellings. In: IEEE International Conference on Computer Vision (ICCV) Workshops (2017)
52. Vineet, V., et al.: Incremental dense semantic stereo fusion for large-scale semantic scene reconstruction. In: IEEE International Conference on Robotics and Automation (ICRA) (2015)
53. Wang, R., Schwörer, M., Cremers, D.: Stereo DSO: large-scale direct sparse visual odometry with stereo cameras. In: IEEE International Conference on Computer Vision (ICCV) (2017)
54. Yu, F., Koltun, V.: Multi-scale context aggregation by dilated convolutions. In: International Conference on Learning Representations (ICLR) (2016)

MPLP++: Fast, Parallel Dual Block-Coordinate Ascent for Dense Graphical Models

Siddharth Tourani[1]([✉]), Alexander Shekhovtsov[2], Carsten Rother[1], and Bogdan Savchynskyy[1]

[1] Visual Learning Lab, IWR, University of Heidelberg, Heidelberg, Germany
{siddharth.tourani,Carsten.Rother,bogdan.savchynskyy}@iwr.uni-heidelberg.de
[2] Centre for Machine Perception, Czech Technical University,
Prague, Czech Republic
shekhovtsov@gmail.com

Abstract. Dense, discrete Graphical Models with pairwise potentials are a powerful class of models which are employed in state-of-the-art computer vision and bio-imaging applications. This work introduces a new MAP-solver, based on the popular Dual Block-Coordinate Ascent principle. Surprisingly, by making a small change to a low-performing solver, the Max Product Linear Programming (MPLP) algorithm [7], we derive the new solver MPLP++ that significantly outperforms all existing solvers by a large margin, including the state-of-the-art solver Tree-Reweighted Sequential (TRW-S) message-passing algorithm [17]. Additionally, our solver is highly parallel, in contrast to TRW-S, which gives a further boost in performance with the proposed GPU and multi-thread CPU implementations. We verify the superiority of our algorithm on dense problems from publicly available benchmarks as well as a new benchmark for 6D Object Pose estimation. We also provide an ablation study with respect to graph density.

Keywords: Graphical models · Block-Coordinate-Ascent · Message passing algorithms

1 Introduction

Undirected discrete graphical models with dense neighbourhood structure are known to be much more expressive than their sparse counterparts. A striking example is the fully-connected Conditional Random Field (CRF) model with Gaussian pairwise potentials [23], significantly improving the image segmentation field, once an efficient solver for the model was proposed. More recently,

---

Electronic supplementary material The online version of this chapter (https://doi.org/10.1007/978-3-030-01225-0_16) contains supplementary material, which is available to authorized users.

V. Ferrari et al. (Eds.): ECCV 2018, LNCS 11208, pp. 264–281, 2018.
https://doi.org/10.1007/978-3-030-01225-0_16

various applications in computer vision and bio-imaging have successfully used fully-connected or densely-connected, pairwise models with non-Gaussian potentials. Non-Gaussian potentials naturally arise from application-specific modelling or the necessity of robust potentials. A prominent application of the non-Gaussian fully-connected CRF case achieved state-of-the-art performance in 6D object pose estimation [29], with an efficient *application-specific* solver. Other examples of densely connected models were proposed in the area of stereo-reconstruction [19], body pose estimation [2,16,30], bio-informatics [12] etc.

An efficient solver is a key condition to make such expressive models efficient in practice. This work introduces such a solver, which outperforms all existing methods for a class of dense and semi-dense problems with non-Gaussian potentials. This includes Tree-Reweighted Sequential (TRW-S) message passing, which is typically used for general pairwise models. We would like to emphasize that efficient solvers for this class are highly desirable, even in the age of deep learning. The main reason is that such expressive graphical models can encode information which is often hard to learn from data, since very large training datasets are needed to learn the application specific prior knowledge. In the above mentioned 6D object pose estimation task, the pairwise potentials encode length-consistency between the observed data and the known 3D model and the unary potentials are learned from data. Other forms of combining graphical models with CNNs such as Deep-Structured-Models [3] can also benefit from the proposed solver.

Linear Programming (LP) relaxation is a powerful technique that can solve exactly all known tractable maximum a posteriori (MAP) inference problems for undirected graphical models (those known to be polynomially solvable) [20]. Although there are multiple algorithms addressing MAP inference, which we discuss in Sect. 2, the linear programs obtained by relaxing the MAP-inference problem are not any simpler than general linear programs [31]. This implies that algorithms solving it exactly are bounded by the computational complexity of the general LP and do not scale well to problems of large size. Since LP relaxations need not be tight, solving it optimally is often impractical. On the other hand, block coordinate ascent (BCA) algorithms for the LP dual problem form an approach delivering fast and practically useful approximate solutions. TRW-S [17] is probably the most well-known and efficient solver of this class, as shown in [14]. Since due to the graph density the model size grows quadratically with the number of variables, a scalable solver must inevitably be highly parallelizable to be of practical use. Our work improves another well-known BCA algorithm of this type, MPLP [7] (Max Product Linear Programming algorithm) and proposes a parallel implementation as explained next.

Contribution. We present a new state-of-the-art parallel BCA algorithm of the same structure as MPLP, *i.e.* an elementary step of our algorithm updates all dual variables related to a single graph edge. We explore the space of such edge-wise updates and propose that a different update rule inspired by [43] can be employed, which significantly improves the practical performance of MPLP. Our method with the new update is termed MPLP++. The difference in the updates stems from the fact that the optimization in the selected block of variables is non-unique and the way the update utilizes the degrees of freedom to which the block objective is not sensitive significantly affects subsequent updates and thus the whole performance.

We propose the following theoretical analysis. We show that MPLP++ converges towards arc-consistency, similarly to the convergence result of [36] for min-sum diffusion. We further show that given any starting point, an iteration of the MPLP++ algorithm, which processes all edges of the graph in a specified order always results in a better objective than the same iteration of MPLP. For multiple iterations this is not theoretically guaranteed, but empirically observed in all our test cases. All proofs relating to the main paper are given in the supplement.

Another important aspect that we address is parallelization. TRW-S is known as a "sequential" algorithm. However, it admits parallelization especially for bipartite graphs [17], which is exploited in specialized implementations [5,9] for 4-connected grid graphs. The parallelization there gives a speed-up factor of $O(n)$, where n is the number of nodes in the graph. A parallel implementation for dense graphs has not been proposed. We observe that in MPLP a group of non-incident edges can be updated in parallel. We pre-compute a schedule maximizing the number of edges that can be processed in parallel using an exact or a greedy maximum matching. The obtainable theoretical speed-up is at least $n/2$ for *any* graph, including dense ones. We consider two parallel implementations, suitable for CPU and GPU architectures respectively. A further speed-up is possible by utilizing parallel algorithms for lower envelopes in message passing (see Sect. 4 and [4]).

The new MPLP++ method consistently outperforms all its competitors, including TRW-S [17], in the case of densely (not necessarily fully) connected graphs, even in the sequential setting: In our experiments it is 2 to 10 times faster than TRW-S and 5 to 150 times faster than MPLP depending on the dataset and the required solution precision. The empirical comparison is conducted on several datasets. As there are only few publicly available ones, we have created a new dataset related to the 6D pose estimation problem [29].

2   Related Work

The general MAP inference problem for discrete graphical models (formally defined in Sect. 3) is NP-hard and is also hard to approximate [24]. A natural linear programming relaxation is obtained by formulating it as a 0-1 integer linear program (ILP) and relaxing the integrality constraints [38] (see also the recent review [47]). A hierarchy of relaxations is known [49], from which the so-called Base LP relaxation, also considered in our work, is the simplest one. It was shown [20,46] that this relaxation is tight for all tractable subclasses of the problem. For many other classes of problems it provides approximation guarantees, reviewed in [24].

Apart from general LP solvers, a number of specialized algorithms exist that take advantage of the problem structure and guarantee convergence to an optimal solution of the LP relaxation. This includes proximal [26,27,33,40], dual subgradient [21,37,44], bundle [15], mirror-descent [25] smoothing-based [28,34,35] and (quasi-) Newton [13] methods.

However, as it was shown in [32], the linear programs arising from the relaxation of the MAP inference problem have the same computational complexity as general LPs. At the same time, if the problem is hard, solving the relaxation to optimality may be of low practical utility. A comparative study [14] notes that TRW-S [17] is the most efficient solver for the relaxation in practice. It belongs to the class of BCA methods for the LP dual that includes also MPLP [7], min-sum diffusion [22,36] and DualMM [43] algorithms. BCA methods are not guaranteed to solve the LP dual to optimality. They may get stuck in a suboptimal point and be unable to compute primal LP solutions unless integer solutions are found (which is not always the case). However, they scale extremely well, take advantage of fast dynamic programming techniques, solve exactly all submodular problems [39] and provide good approximate solutions in general vision benchmarks.

3 Preliminaries

Notation. $\mathcal{G} = (\mathcal{V}, \mathcal{E})$ denotes an undirected graph, with vertex set $\mathcal{V}$ (we assume $\mathcal{V} = \{1, \ldots, n\}$) and edge set $\mathcal{E}$. The notation $uv \in \mathcal{E}$ will mean that $\{u, v\} \in \mathcal{E}$ and $u < v$ with respect to the order of $\mathcal{V}$. Each node $u \in \mathcal{V}$ is associated with a label from a finite *set of labels* $\mathcal{Y}$ (for brevity w.l.o.g. we will assume that it is the same set for all nodes). The label space for a pair of nodes $uv \in \mathcal{E}$ is $\mathcal{Y}^2$ and for all nodes it is $\mathcal{Y}^{\mathcal{V}}$.

For each node and edge the *unary* $\theta_u : \mathcal{Y} \to \mathbb{R}$, $u \in \mathcal{V}$ and *pairwise* cost functions $\theta_{uv} : \mathcal{Y}^2 \to \mathbb{R}$, $uv \in \mathcal{E}$, assign a cost to a label or label pair, respectively. Let $\mathcal{I} = (\mathcal{V} \times \mathcal{Y}) \cup (\mathcal{E} \times \mathcal{Y}^2)$ be the index set enumerating all labels and label pairs in neighbouring graph nodes. Let the *cost vector* $\theta \in \mathbb{R}^{\mathcal{I}}$ contain all values of the functions θ_u and θ_{uv} as its coordinates.

The *MAP-inference* problem for the graphical model defined by the triple $(\mathcal{G}, \mathcal{Y}^{\mathcal{V}}, \theta)$ consists in finding the labelling with the smallest total cost, *i.e.*:

$$y^* = \arg\min_{y \in \mathcal{Y}^{\mathcal{V}}} \left[E(y|\theta) := \sum_{v \in \mathcal{V}} \theta_v(y_v) + \sum_{uv \in \mathcal{E}} \theta_{uv}(y_{uv}) \right]. \tag{1}$$

This problem is also known as *energy minimization* for graphical models and is closely related to weighted and valued constraint satisfaction problems. The total cost E is also often called *energy*.

The problem (1) is in general NP-hard and is also hard to approximate [24]. A number of approaches to tackle it in different practical scenarios are reviewed in [10,14]. One of the widely applicable techniques is based on (approximately) solving its linear programming (LP) relaxation as discussed in Sect. 2.

Dual Problem. Most existing solvers for the LP relaxation tackle its dual form, which we introduce now. It is based on the fact that the representation of the energy function $E(y|\theta)$ using unary θ_u and pairwise θ_{uv} costs is not unique. There exist other costs $\hat{\theta} \in \mathbb{R}^{\mathcal{I}}$ such that $E(y|\hat{\theta}) = E(y|\theta)$ for all labelings $y \in \mathcal{Y}^{\mathcal{V}}$.

It is known (see e.g. [47]) and straightforward to check that such *equivalent* costs can be obtained with an arbitrary vector $\phi := (\phi_{v \to u}(s) \in \mathbb{R} \mid u \in \mathcal{V}, v \in \mathrm{Nb}(u), s \in \mathcal{Y})$, where $\mathrm{Nb}(u)$ is the set of neighbours of u in $\mathcal{G}$, as follows:

$$\hat{\theta}_u(s) \equiv \theta_u^\phi(s) := \theta_u(s) + \sum\nolimits_{v \in \mathrm{Nb}(u)} \phi_{v \to u}(s) \qquad (2)$$

$$\hat{\theta}_{uv}(s, t) \equiv \theta_{uv}^\phi(s, t) := \theta_{uv}(s, t) - \phi_{v \to u}(s) - \phi_{u \to v}(t).$$

The cost vector θ^ϕ is called *reparametrized* and the vector ϕ is known as *reparametrization*. Costs related by (2) are also called *equivalent*. Other established terms for reparametrization are *equivalence preserving* [6] or *equivalent transformations* [38].

By swapping min and $\sum$ operations in (1) one obtains a lower bound on the energy $D(\theta^\phi) \leq E(y|\theta)$ for all y, which reads

$$D(\theta^\phi) := \sum_{u \in \mathcal{V}} \min_{s \in \mathcal{Y}} \theta_u^\phi(s) + \sum_{uv \in \mathcal{E}} \min_{(s,t) \in \mathcal{Y}^2} \theta_{uv}^\phi(s, t). \qquad (3)$$

Although the energy $E(y|\theta)$ remains the same for all equivalent cost vectors (i.e. $E(y|\theta) = E(y|\theta^\phi)$), the lower bound $D(\theta^\phi)$ depends on the reparametrization, which is $D(\theta) \neq D(\theta^\phi)$. Therefore, a natural maximization problem arises as maximization of the lower bound over all equivalent costs: $\max_\phi D(\theta^\phi)$. It is known (see [47]) that this maximization problem can be seen as a dual formulation of the LP relaxation of (1). We will write $D(\phi)$ to denote $D(\theta^\phi)$, since the cost vector θ is clear from the context. The function $D(\phi)$ is concave, piecewise linear and therefore, non-smooth. In many applications the dimensionality of ϕ often exceeds 10^5 to 10^6 and the respective dual problem $\max_\phi D(\phi)$ is large scale.

4   Dual Block-Coordinate Ascent

As we discussed in Sect. 2, BCA methods, although not guaranteed to solve the dual to the optimality, provide good solutions for many practical instances and scale very well to large problems. The fastest such methods are represented by methods working with chain subproblems [17,43] or their generalizations [18].

The TRW-S algorithm can be seen as updating a block of dual variables $(\phi_{v \to u}, v \in \mathrm{Nb}(u))$ "attached" to a node u during each elementary step. The same block of variables is also used in the *min-sum diffusion* algorithm [36], as well as in *convex message passing* [8], and [18] gives a generalization of such methods.

However, the update coefficients in TRW-S are related to the density of the graph and its advantage diminishes when the graph becomes dense. We show that for dense graphs updating a block of dual variables $\phi_{u\leftrightarrow v} = (\phi_{v\rightarrow u}, \phi_{u\rightarrow v})$ associated to an edge $uv \in \mathcal{E}$ can be more efficient. Such updates were previously used in the MPLP algorithm [7]. We show that our MPLP++ updates differ in detail but bring a significant improvement in performance.

Block Optimality Condition. For further analysis of BCA algorithms we will require a sufficient condition of optimality w.r.t. the selected block of dual variables. The restriction of the dual to the block of variables $\phi_{u\leftrightarrow v}$ is given by the function:

$$D_{uv}(\phi_{u\leftrightarrow v}) := \min_{(s,t)\in\mathcal{Y}^2} \theta_{uv}^{\phi}(s,t) + \min_{s\in\mathcal{Y}} \theta_u^{\phi}(s) + \min_{t\in\mathcal{Y}} \theta_v^{\phi}(t), \tag{4}$$

Maximizing D_{uv} is equivalent to performing a BCA w.r.t. $\phi_{u\leftrightarrow v}$ for $D(\phi)$. The necessary and sufficient condition of a maximum of D_{uv} are given by the following.

Proposition 1. *Reparametrization* $\phi_{u\leftrightarrow v}$ *maximizes* $D_{uv}(\cdot)$ *iff there exist* $(s,t) \in \mathcal{Y}^2$ *such that s minimizes $\theta_u^{\phi}(\cdot)$, t minimizes $\theta_v^{\phi}(\cdot)$ and (s,t) minimizes* $\theta_{uv}^{\phi}(\cdot,\cdot)$.

This condition is trivial to check, it is a special case of arc consistency [47] or weak tree-agreement [17] when considering a simple graph with one edge. It is also clear that $\phi_{u\leftrightarrow v}$ satisfying this condition is not unique. For BCA algorithms it means that there are degrees of freedom in the block which do not directly affect the objective. By moving on a plateau, they can nevertheless affect subsequent BCA updates. Therefore, the performance of the algorithm will be very much dependent on the particular BCA update rule satisfying Proposition 1.

Block Coordinate Ascent Updates. Given the form of the restricted dual (4) on the edge uv, all BCA-updates can be described as follows. Assume θ is the current reparametrized cost vector, *i.e.* $\theta = \bar{\theta}^{\bar{\phi}}$ for some initial $\bar{\theta}$ and the current reparametrization $\bar{\phi}$.

Definition 1. *A BCA update takes as the input an edge $uv \in \mathcal{E}$ and costs* $\theta_{uv}(s,t)$, $\theta_u(s)$ and $\theta_v(t)$ and outputs a reparametrization $\phi_{u\leftrightarrow v}$ satisfying Proposition 1. W.l.o.g., we assume that it will also satisfy $\min_{(s,t)} \theta_{uv}^{\phi}(s,t) = 0$.[1]

According to (2) a BCA-update results in the following reparametrized potentials:

$$\theta_u^{\phi} = \theta_u + \phi_{v\rightarrow u}, \quad \theta_v^{\phi} = \theta_v + \phi_{u\rightarrow v}, \quad ,\theta_{uv}^{\phi}(s,t) = \theta_{uv} - \phi_{v\rightarrow u} - \phi_{u\rightarrow v}. \tag{5}$$

Note that since all reparametrizations constitute a vector space, after a BCA-update ϕ we can update the current total reparametrization as $\bar{\phi} := \bar{\phi} + \phi$.

---

[1] This fixes the ambiguity w.r.t. a constant that can be otherwise added to the edge potential and subtracted from one of the unary potentials. This constant does not affect the performance of algorithms.

We will consider BCA-updates of the following form: first construct the aggregated cost $g_{uv}(s,t) = \theta_{uv}(s,t) + \theta_u(s) + \theta_v(t)$. This corresponds to applying a reparametrization $\mathring{\phi}_{u \leftrightarrow v} = (-\theta_u, -\theta_v)$, which gives $\theta_{uv}^{\mathring{\phi}} = g_{uv}$, $\theta_u^{\mathring{\phi}} = \theta_v^{\mathring{\phi}} = 0$. After that, a BCA update forms a new reparametrization $\phi_{u \leftrightarrow v}$ such that $\theta^{\mathring{\phi}+\phi}$ satisfies Proposition 1.

Such BCA-updates can be represented in the following form, which will be simpler for defining and analysing the algorithms.

Definition 2. *Consider a BCA-update using a composite reparametrization $\mathring{\phi}_{u \leftrightarrow v} + \phi_{u \leftrightarrow v}$. It can then be fully described by the reparametrization mapping $\gamma : g_{uv} \to (\theta_u^\gamma, \theta_v^\gamma)$, where $g_{uv} \in \mathbb{R}^{\mathcal{Y}_{uv}}$, $\theta_u^\gamma = \phi_{v \to u}$ and $\theta_v^\gamma = \phi_{u \to v}$.*

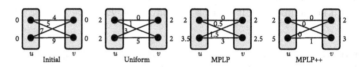

Fig. 1. Illustration of the considered BCA-updates. The gray boxes in the figure represent graph nodes. The black dots in them are the labels. The edges connecting the black dots make up the pairwise costs. The numbers adjacent to the edges and labels are the pairwise and unary costs, respectively.

By construction, θ_u^γ matches the reparametrized unary term $\theta_u^{\mathring{\phi}+\phi}$, θ_v^γ is alike and the reparametrized pairwise term is given by $\theta_{uv}^\gamma = g_{uv} - \phi_{v \to u} - \phi_{u \to v} = g_{uv} - \theta_u^\gamma - \theta_v^\gamma$. In what follows, BCA-update will mean specifically the reparametrization mapping γ. We define now several BCA-updates that will be studied further.

- The **uniform** BCA-update is given by the following reparametrization mapping $\mathcal{U}$:

$$\theta_u^{\mathcal{U}}(s) = \theta_v^{\mathcal{U}}(t) := \tfrac{1}{2} \min_{(s',t') \in \mathcal{Y}^2} g_{uv}(s',t'), \quad \forall s', t' \in \mathcal{Y}. \qquad (\mathcal{U})$$

This is indeed just an example, to illustrate the problem of non-uniqueness of the minimizer. It is easy to see that this update satisfies Proposition 1 since both $\theta_u^{\mathcal{U}}(\cdot)$ and $\theta_v^{\mathcal{U}}(\cdot)$ are constant and therefore any pairwise minimizer of $\theta_{uv}^{\mathcal{U}}$ is consistent with them.

- The **MPLP** BCA-update is given by the following reparametrization mapping $\mathcal{M}$:

$$\begin{aligned}\theta_u^{\mathcal{M}}(s) &:= \tfrac{1}{2} \min_{t \in \mathcal{Y}} g_{uv}(s,t), \quad \forall s \in \mathcal{Y}, \\ \theta_v^{\mathcal{M}}(t) &:= \tfrac{1}{2} \min_{s \in \mathcal{Y}} g_{uv}(s,t), \quad \forall t \in \mathcal{Y}.\end{aligned} \qquad (\mathcal{M})$$

The MPLP algorithm [7] can now be described as performing iterations by applying BCA-update $\mathcal{M}$ to all edges of the graph in a sequence.

- The new MPLP++ BCA-update, that we propose, is based on the *handshake* operation [43]. It is given by the following procedure defining the reparametrization mapping $\mathcal{H}$:

$$\theta_u^{\mathcal{H}}(s) := \theta_u^{\mathcal{M}}(s), \quad \theta_v^{\mathcal{H}}(s) := \theta_v^{\mathcal{M}}(s), \ \forall s \in \mathcal{Y},$$
$$\theta_v^{\mathcal{H}}(t) := \theta_v^{\mathcal{H}}(t) + \min_{s \in \mathcal{Y}} [g_{uv}(s,t) - \theta_v^{\mathcal{H}}(t) - \theta_u^{\mathcal{H}}(s)], \ \forall t \in \mathcal{Y}, \qquad (\mathcal{H})$$
$$\theta_u^{\mathcal{H}}(s) := \theta_u^{\mathcal{H}}(s) + \min_{t \in \mathcal{Y}} [g_{uv}(s,t) - \theta_v^{\mathcal{H}}(t) - \theta_u^{\mathcal{H}}(s)], \ \forall s \in \mathcal{Y}.$$

In other words, the MPLP++ update first performs the MPLP update and then pushes as much cost from the pairwise factor to the unary ones as needed to fulfill $\min_t \theta_{uv}^{\mathcal{M}}(s,t) = \min_s \theta_{uv}^{\mathcal{M}}(s,t) = 0$ for all labels s and t in the nodes u and v respectively. It is also easy to see that the assignment $\theta_v^{\mathcal{H}}(s) := \theta_v^{\mathcal{M}}(s)$ together with the second line in $(\mathcal{H})$ can be equivalently substituted by $\theta_v^{\mathcal{H}}(t) := \min_{s \in \mathcal{Y}} [g_{uv}(s,t) - \theta_u^{\mathcal{H}}(s)], \ \forall t \in \mathcal{Y}$. This allows to perform the MPLP++ update with 3 minimizations over $\mathcal{Y}^2$ instead of 4. Figure 1 shows the result of applying the three BCA-updates on a simple two-node graph.

It is straightforward to show that $\mathcal{M}$ and $\mathcal{H}$ also satisfy Definition 1 (see supplement) and therefore are liable BCA-updates. In spite of that, the behavior of all three updates is notably different, as it is shown by the example in Fig. 2. Therefore, proving only that some algorithm is a BCA, does not imply its efficiency.

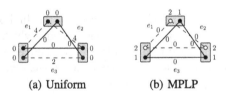

(a) Uniform   (b) MPLP

Fig. 2. Choosing the right BCA-update is important. Notation has the same meaning as in Fig. 1. Solid lines correspond to the locally optimal pairwise costs connected to the locally optimal labels. Omitted lines in pairwise interactions denote infinite pairwise costs. e_i denotes edge indexes, edge processing order is according to the subscript i. **(a)** Uniform update gets stuck and is unable to optimize the dual further. **(b)** MPLP and MPLP++ attain the dual optimum in one iteration.

Message Passing. Importantly for performance, updates $\mathcal{U}$, $\mathcal{M}$ and $\mathcal{H}$ can be computed using a subroutine computing $\min_t [\theta_{uv}(s,t) + a(t)]$ for all s, where θ is a fixed initial pairwise potential and a is an arbitrary input unary function. This operation occurring in dynamic programming and all of the discussed BCA algorithms, is known as *message passing*. In many cases of practical interest it can be implemented in time $O(|\mathcal{Y}|)$ (e.g. for Potts, absolute difference and quadratic costs) rather than $O(|\mathcal{Y}|^2)$ in the general case, using efficient sequential algorithms, *e.g.*, [1].

Primal Rounding. BCA-algorithms iterating BCA-updates give only a lower bound to the MAP-inference problem (1). To obtain a primal solution, we use a sequential rounding procedure similar to the one proposed in [17]. Assuming we have already computed a primal integer solution x_u^* for all $u < v$, we want to compute x_v^*. To do so, we use the following equation for the assignment

$$x_v^* \in \arg\min\nolimits_{x_u \in \mathcal{Y}} \left[\theta_v(x_v) + \sum\nolimits_{u<v|uv\in\mathcal{E}} \theta_{uv}(x_u^*, x_v) \right], \tag{6}$$

where θ is the reparametrized potential produced by the algorithm.

5   Theoretical Analysis

As we prove below, MPLP++ in the limit guarantees to fulfill a necessary optimality condition related to *arc-consistency* [47] and *weak tree-agreement* [17].

Arc-Consistency. Let $[\![\cdot]\!]$ be the Iverson bracket, *i.e.* $[\![A]\!] = 1$ if A holds. Otherwise $[\![A]\!] = 0$. Let $\bar{\theta}_u(s) := [\![\theta_u(s) = \min_{s'} \theta_u(s')]\!]$ and $\bar{\theta}_{uv}(s,t) := [\![\theta_{uv}(s,t) = \min_{s',t'} \theta_{uv}(s',t')]\!]$ be binary vectors with values 1 assigned to the locally minimal labels and label pairs. Let also logical *and* and *or* operations be denoted as $\wedge$ and $\vee$. To the binary vectors they apply coordinate-wise.

Definition 3. *A vector* $\bar{\theta} \in \{0,1\}^{\mathcal{I}}$ *is called* arc-consistent, *if* $\bigvee_{t\in\mathcal{Y}} \bar{\theta}_{uv}(s,t) = \bar{\theta}_u(s)$ *for all* $\{u,v\} \in \mathcal{E}$ *and* $s \in \mathcal{Y}$.

However, arc-consistency itself is not necessary for dual optimality. The necessary condition is existence of node-edge agreement, which is a special case of weak tree agreement [17] when individual nodes and edges are considered as the trees in a problem decomposition. This condition is also known as a non-empty *kernel* [47]/*arc-consistent closure* [6] of the cost vector θ.

Definition 4. *We will say that the costs* $\theta \in \mathbb{R}^{\mathcal{I}}$ *fulfill* node-edge agreement, *if there is an arc-consistent vector* $\xi \in \{0,1\}^{\mathcal{I}}$ *such that* $\xi \wedge \bar{\theta} = \xi$.

Convergence of MPLP++. It is clear that all BCA algorithms are monotonous and converge in the dual objective value as soon as the dual is bounded (*i.e.*, the primal is feasible). However, this is a weaker convergence than the desired *node-edge agreement*. To this end we were able to show something in between the two: the convergence of MPLP++ in a measure quantifying violation of the node-edge agreement, a result analogous to [36].

Theorem 1. *The* MPLP++ *algorithm converges to node-edge agreement.*

When comparing different algorithms, the ultimate goal is to prove faster convergence of one compared to the other. We cannot show that the new MPLP++ algorithm has a better theoretical convergence rate. First, such rates are generally unknown for BCA algorithms for non-smooth functions. Second, the considered algorithms are all of the same family and it is likely that their asymptotic rates are the same. Instead, we study the *dominance*, a condition that allows to rule out BCA updates which are always inferior to others. Towards this end we show that given the same starting dual point, one iteration of MPLP++ always results in a better objective value than that of MPLP and uniform BCA. While this argument does not extend theoretically to multiple iterations of each method, we show that it is still true in practice for all used datasets and a significant speed-up (up to two orders) is observed. The experimental comparison in Sect. 7 gives results in wall-clock time as well as in a machine-independent count of the message passing updates performed.

5.1 Analysis of BCA-updates

Definition 5. *A BCA-iteration α is defined by the BCA-update γ applied to all edges $\mathcal{E}$ in some chosen order. Let also $D(\alpha)$ represent the dual objective value with the reparametrization defined by the iteration α on the input costs θ.*

We will analyze BCA-iterations of different BCA-updates w.r.t. the same sequence of edges. The goal is to show that an iteration of the new update dominates the baselines in the dual objective. This property is formally captured by the following definition.

Definition 6. *We will say that a BCA-iteration α dominates a BCA-iteration β, if for any input costs it holds $D(\alpha) \geq D(\beta)$.*

In order to show it, we introduce now and prove later the dominance relations of individual BCA-updates. They are defined not on the dual objective but on all unary components.

Definition 7. *Let γ and δ be two BCA-updates. We will say that update γ dominates δ (denoted as $\gamma \geq \delta$) if for any $g_{uv} \in \mathbb{R}^{\mathcal{Y}^2}$ it holds that $\gamma[g_{uv}] \geq \delta[g_{uv}]$, where the inequality is understood as component-wise inequalities $\theta_u^\gamma[g_{uv}] \geq \theta_u^\delta[g_{uv}]$ and $\theta_v^\gamma[g_{uv}] \geq \theta_v^\delta[g_{uv}]$.*

We can show the following dominance results. Recall that $\mathcal{U}$, $\mathcal{H}$ and $\mathcal{M}$ are the uniform, MPLP and MPLP++ BCA-updates, respectively.

Proposition 2. *The following BCA-dominances hold: $\mathcal{H} \geq \mathcal{M} \geq \mathcal{U}$.*

It is easy to see that the dominance Definition 7 is transitive and so also $\mathcal{H} \geq \mathcal{U}$. We will prove that such coordinate-wise dominance of BCA-updates implies also the dominance in the dual objective whenever the following monotonicity property holds:

Definition 8. *A BCA-update γ is called* monotonous *if $(\theta_u \geq \theta_u', \theta_v \geq \theta_v')$ implies $\gamma[\theta_u + \theta_{uv} + \theta_v] \geq \gamma[\theta_u' + \theta_{uv} + \theta_v']$ for all θ, θ'.*

Proposition 3. *Updates $\mathcal{U}$ and $\mathcal{M}$ are monotonous. The update $\mathcal{H}$ is not monotonous.*

With these results we can formulate our main claim about domination in the objective value for the whole iteration.

Theorem 2. *Let BCA-update γ dominate BCA-update μ and let μ be monotonous. Then a BCA-iteration with γ dominates a BCA-iteration with μ.*

From Proposition 2, Propostion 3 and Theorem 2 it follows now that BCA-iteration of MPLP++ dominates that of MPLP, which in its turn dominates uniform.

6 Parallelization

To optimize $D(\theta^{\phi})$, we have to perform local operations on a graph, that per reparametrization influence only one edge $uv \in \mathcal{E}$ and it's incident vertices u and v. The remaining graph $\mathcal{G}' = (\mathcal{V} - \{u,v\}, \mathcal{E} - \{I_u \cup I_v\})$, (where I_u and I_v are the index sets for vertices u and v) remains unchanged. This gives rise to opportunities for parallelization. However, special care has to be taken to prevent a *race condition* which occurs when two or more threads access shared data and they try to change it at the same time.

Consider the case of Fig. 3, choosing edges 1 and 2 or 1 and 6 to process in parallel. These edges have vertex A in common, which would lead to a race condition. Processing edges 1 and 3 in parallel would lead to more parallelization as there are no conflicting nodes.

Finding such edges without intersecting vertices is a well-studied problem in combinatorial optimization [41]. A *matching* $\mathcal{M} \subset \mathcal{E}$ in graph $\mathcal{G}$ is a set of edges such that no two edges in $\mathcal{M}$ share a common vertex. A matching is *maximum* if it includes the largest number of edges, $|\mathcal{M}|$. Every edge in a matching can be processed in parallel without race conditions ensuing. There exist efficient greedy algorithms to find a maximum matching which we use. This gives rise to Algorithm 1 for covering all edges of the graph while ensuring good parallelization. To cover the entire graph, we call a matching algorithm repeatedly, until all edges are exhausted.

Initially, in line 1 the edge queue $\mathcal{Q}_{\mathcal{E}}$ is empty. In line 3, a maximum matching $\mathcal{E}_{\mathcal{M}}$ is found. This is added to $\mathcal{Q}_{\mathcal{E}}$ in line 4. This continues until all edges have been exhausted, *i.e.* the edges remaining $\mathcal{E}_{\mathcal{R}}$ is empty. The queue thus has a structure $\mathcal{Q}_{\mathcal{E}} = (\mathcal{E}_{\mathcal{M}}^1, \mathcal{E}_{\mathcal{M}}^2, ..., \mathcal{E}_{\mathcal{M}}^n)$, ordered left to right. $\mathcal{E}_{\mathcal{M}}^i$ being the ith matching computed. The threads running in parallel can keep popping edges from $\mathcal{Q}_{\mathcal{E}}$ and processing them without much need for mutex locking.

We have different implementation algorithms for GPUs and multi-core CPUs.

CPU Implementation: Modern CPUs consist of multiple cores with each core having one hardware thread. Hyper-threading allows for an additional lower-performing thread per core.

Processing an edge is a short-lived task and launching a separate thread for each edge would have excessive overhead. To process lightweight tasks we use the *thread-pool* design pattern. A thread-pool keeps multiple threads waiting for tasks to be executed concurrently by a supervising program. The threads are launched only once and continuously process tasks from a task-queue. As

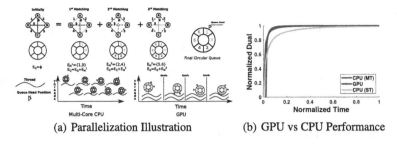

(a) Parallelization Illustration   (b) GPU vs CPU Performance

Fig. 3. This figure shows parallelization details and a performance comparison for CPU and GPU. (a) shows the details of how the edge schedule is computed for maximizing throughput. The first row shows how edge selection is carried out by finding matchings and adding the edges in these matchings to the queue. The second row shows how the threads are launched for the CPU and GPU. For the CPU, threads are launched dynamically at different time instances, and no synchronization is carried out across all threads. This is due to a local memory locking mechanism (mutex) for the CPU. For the GPU, many threads are launched simultaneously and synchronized simultaneously via a memory barrier. This barrier is shown as the vertical line with **Synch.** (b) shows the running time comparison between single-threaded, multi-threaded and GPU versions of the MPLP++ algorithm. The GPU takes some time to load memory from the host (CPU) to device (GPU)..

Algorithm 1 Compute Edge Schedule

Require: $\mathcal{G} = (\mathcal{V}, \mathcal{E})$
1: **Initial:** $\mathcal{Q}_\mathcal{E} := \emptyset$ (Empty edge queue),
    $\mathcal{E}_\mathcal{R} := \mathcal{E}$ (Initial pool of edges)
2: **while** $\mathcal{E}_\mathcal{R}! = \emptyset$ **do**
3:     $\mathcal{E}_\mathcal{M} := \text{Maximum\_Matching}(\mathcal{V}, \mathcal{E}_\mathcal{R})$
4:     $\mathcal{Q}_\mathcal{E}.push(\mathcal{E}_\mathcal{M})$ (Push maximum-matching $\mathcal{E}_\mathcal{M}$ to the queue)
5:     $\mathcal{E}_\mathcal{R} := \mathcal{E}_\mathcal{R} - \mathcal{E}_\mathcal{M}$ (Remove matched edges from $\mathcal{E}_\mathcal{R}$)
6: **end while**

---

they are launched only once, the latency in execution due to overhead in thread creation and destruction is avoided.

In the case of our algorithm the task queue is $\mathcal{Q}_\mathcal{E}$. The thread picks up the index of the edge to process and performs the MPLP++ operation ($\mathcal{H}$). During the MPLP++ operation the node and edge structures are locked by mutexes. One iteration of the algorithm is complete when all edges have been processed. Since multiple iterations may be required to reach convergence, our task queue is circular, letting the threads restart the reparameterization process from the first element of $\mathcal{Q}_\mathcal{E}$. The ordering of $\mathcal{Q}_\mathcal{E}$ prevents heavy lock contention of mutexes.

GPU Implementation: Unlike CPUs, GPUs do not use mutexes for synchronization. The threads in each GPU processor are synchronized via a hardware barrier synchronization. A barrier for a group of threads stops the threads at this point and prevents them from proceeding until all other threads/processes reach this barrier.

This is where the ordering of $\mathcal{Q}_{\mathcal{E}}$ comes in handy. Recall the structure of $\mathcal{Q}_{\mathcal{E}} = (\mathcal{E}_{\mathcal{M}}^1, \mathcal{E}_{\mathcal{M}}^2, ..., \mathcal{E}_{\mathcal{M}}^n)$. Barrier synchronization can be used between the matchings $\mathcal{E}_{\mathcal{M}}^i$ and $\mathcal{E}_{\mathcal{M}}^{i+1}$, allowing for the completion of the MPLP++ BCA update operations for $\mathcal{E}_{\mathcal{M}}^i$, before beginning the processing of $\mathcal{E}_{\mathcal{M}}^{i+1}$. This minimizes the time threads spend waiting while the other threads complete, as they have no overlapping areas to write to in the memory.

7   Experimental Evaluation

In our experiments, we use a 4-core Intel i7-4790K CPU @ 4.00GHz, with hyper-threading, giving 8 logical cores. For GPU experiments, we used the NVIDIA Tesla K80 GPU with 4992 cores.

Compared Algorithms. We compare different algorithms in two regimes: the wall-clock time and the machine-independent regime, where we count the number of operations performed. For the latter one we use the notion of the *oracle call*, which is an operation like $\min_{t \in \mathcal{Y}} g_{uv}(s, t)$, $\forall s \in \mathcal{Y}$ involving a single evaluation of all costs of a pairwise factor. When speaking about *oracle complexity* we mean the number of oracle calls per single iteration of the algorithm. As different algorithms have different oracle complexities we define a *normalized iteration* as exactly $|\mathcal{E}|$ messages for an even comparison across algorithms. We compare the following BCA schemes:

- The Tree-Reweighted Sequential (TRWS) message passing algorithm [17] has consistently been the best performing method on several benchmarks like [14]. Its oracle complexity is $2|\mathcal{E}|$. We use the multicore implementation introduced in [42] for comparison, which is denoted as TRWS(MT) when run on multiple cores.
- The Max-Product Linear Programming (MPLP) algorithm [7] with BCA-updates ($\mathcal{M}$). It's oracle complexity is thus $2|\mathcal{E}|$. For MPLP we have our own multi-threaded implementation that is faster than the original one by a factor of 4.
- The Min-Sum Diffusion Algorithm (MSD) [36], is one of the earliest (in the 70s) proposed BCA algorithms for graphical models. The oracle complexity of the method is $4|\mathcal{E}|$.
- The MPLP++ algorithm with BCA-updates ($\mathcal{H}$) has the oracle complexity of $3|\mathcal{E}|$. The algorithm is parallelized as described in Sect. 6 for both CPU and GPU. The corresponding legends are MPLP++(MT) and MPLP++(GPU).

Dense Datasets. To show the strength of our method we consider the following datasets with underlying densely connected graphs:

- The worms dataset [11] consists of 30 problem instances coming from the field of bioimaging. The problems' graphs are dense but not fully connected with about $0.1|\mathcal{V}|^2$ of edges, up to 600 nodes and up to 1500 labels.
- The protein-folding dataset [48] taken from the OpenGM benchmark [14] has 21 problem instances with 33 to 1972 variables. The models are fully connected and have 81 to 503 labels per node.

- **pose** is the dataset inspired by the recent work [29] showing state-of-the-art performance on the 6D object pose estimation problem. In [29] this problem is formulated as MAP-inference in a fully connected graphical model. The set of nodes of the underlying graph coincides with the set of pixels of the input image (up to some downscale factor), which requires specialized heuristics to solve the problem. Contrary to the original work, we assume that the position of the object is given by its mask (we used ground-truth data from the validation set, but assume the mask could be provided by some segmentation method) and treat only the pixels inside the mask as the nodes of the corresponding graphical model. The unary and pairwise costs are constructed in the same way as in [29] but with different hyper-parameters. This dataset has 32 problem instances with 600 to 4800 variables each and 13 labels per node. The models are all fully connected.

Sparse Datasets. Although our method is not the best performing one on sparse graphical models, we include the comparison on the following four-connected grid-graph based benchmark datasets for fairness:

- **color-seg** from [14] has Potts pairwise costs. The nodes contain up to 12 labels.
- **stereo** from the Middlebury MRF benchmark [45] consists of 3 models with truncated linear pairwise costs and 16, 20 and 60 labels respectively.

Algorithm Convergence. Figure 4 shows convergence of the considered algorithms in a sequential setting for the **protein** and **stereo** datasets as representatives of the dense and sparse problems. For other datasets the behavior is similar, therefore we moved the corresponding plots to the supplement. The proposed **MPLP++** method outperforms all its competitors on *all* dense problem instances and is inferior to TRWS only on sparse ones. This holds for both comparisons: the implementation-independent *normalized iteration* and the implementation-dependent *running time* ones. Figure 5 shows relative time speed-ups of the considered methods as a function of the attained dual precision. The speed of MPLP, as typically the slowest one, is taken to be 1, *i.e.*, for other algorithms the speed-up compared to MPLP is plotted. This includes also the CPU-parallel versions of MPLP++, TRWS and the GPU-parallel MPLP++. Figure 5 also shows that for dense models MPLP++ is 2 to 10 times faster than TRWS in the sequential setting and 7 to 40 times in the parallel setting. The speed-up w.r.t. MPLP is 5 to 150 times depending on the dataset and the required precision.

Performance Degradation with Graph Sparsification. In this test we gradually and randomly removed edges from the graphs of the **pose** dataset and measured performance of all algorithms. Figure 6 shows that down to atleast 10% of all possible edges MPLP++ leads the board. Only when the number of edges drops to 5% and less, TRWS starts to outperform MPLP++. Note, the density of edges in grid graphs considered above does not exceed the 0.007% level.

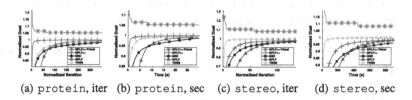

(a) protein, iter   (b) protein, sec   (c) stereo, iter   (d) stereo, sec

Fig. 4. Improvement in dual as a function of time and iterations for the protein-folding and stereo dataset. The algorithms we compare have different message-passing schemes and end up doing different amounts of work per iteration. Hence, for a fair comparison across algorithms we define a normalized iteration as exactly $|\mathcal{E}|$ messages. This is also equal to number of messages passed in a normal iteration divided by its oracle complexity. (a) and (b) are for the dense protein-folding dataset, where both per unit time and per iteration, MPLP++ outperforms TRWS and all other algorithms. In the sparse stereo dataset (c,d) TRWS beats all other algorithms. Results are averaged over the entire dataset. The dual is normalized to 1 for equal weighing of every instance in the dataset.

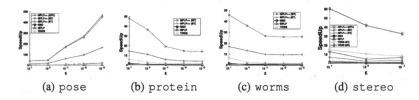

(a) pose   (b) protein   (c) worms   (d) stereo

Fig. 5. Relative speed w.r.t the MPLP algorithm in converging to within ε of the best attained dual optima $D^*(\theta^\phi)$, i.e. $D^*(\theta^\phi) - \varepsilon$. The plot shows the speedups of all the algorithms relative to MPLP for ε's 0.001, 0.01, 0.1, 1 and 10 of $D^*(\theta^\phi)$. Figure (a) shows MPLP++ is 50× faster than MPLP in converging to within 10% of $D^*(\theta^\phi)$. Figure (b) and (c) likewise show an order of magnitude speedup. Figure (d) shows that for the stereo dataset consisting of sparse graphs TRWS dominates MPLP++. Convergence only till 0.1% of $D^*(\theta^\phi)$ is shown for stereo as only TRWS converges to the required precision.

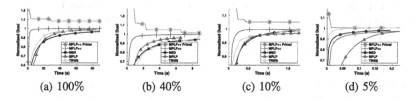

(a) 100%   (b) 40%   (c) 10%   (d) 5%

Fig. 6. Degradation with Sparsity (Dual vs Time): (a)–(d) show graphs with decreasing average connectivity given as percentage of possible edges in the figure subcaption. In (a)–(c) MPLP++ outperforms TRWS. MPLP++ is resilient to graph sparsification even when 90% of the edges have been removed. Only when more than 95% of the edges have been removed as in (d) TRWS outperforms MPLP++.

8   Conclusions and Outlook

Block-coordinate ascent methods remain a perspective research direction for creating efficient parallelizable dual solvers for MAP-inference in graphical models. We have presented one such solver beating the state-of-the-art on dense graphical models with arbitrary potentials. The method is directly generalizable to higher order models, which we plan to investigate in the future.

Acknowledgements. A. Shekhovtsov was supported by Czech Science Foundation grant 18-25383S.

References

1. Aggarwal, A., Klawe, M.M., Moran, S., Shor, P., Wilber, R.: Geometric applications of a matrix-searching algorithm. Algorithmica **2**(1), 195–208 (1987). https://doi.org/10.1007/BF01840359
2. Bergtholdt, M., Kappes, J., Schmidt, S., Schnörr, C.: A study of parts-based object class detection using complete graphs. Int. J. Comput. Vis. **87**(1–2), 93 (2010)
3. Chen, L.C., Schwing, A., Yuille, A., Urtasun, R.: Learning deep structured models. In: International Conference on Machine Learning, pp. 1785–1794 (2015)
4. Chen, W., Wada, K.: On computing the upper envelope of segments in parallel. In: Proceedings. 1998 International Conference on Parallel Processing (Cat. No. 98EX205), pp. 253–260, August 1998. https://doi.org/10.1109/ICPP.1998.708493
5. Choi, J., Rutenbar, R.A.: Hardware implementation of MRF map inference on an FPGA platform. In: 2012 22nd International Conference on Field Programmable Logic and Applications (FPL), pp. 209–216. IEEE (2012)
6. Cooper, M., Schiex, T.: Arc consistency for soft constraints. Artif. Intell. **154**(1–2), 199–227 (2004)
7. Globerson, A., Jaakkola, T.S.: Fixing max-product: convergent message passing algorithms for MAP LP-relaxations. In: Advances in Neural Information Processing Systems, vol. 20 (2008)
8. Hazan, T., Shashua, A.: Norm-Product Belief Propagation: Primal-Dual Message-Passing for approximate inference (2008)
9. Hurkat, S., Choi, J., Nurvitadhi, E., Martínez, J.F., Rutenbar, R.A.: Fast hierarchical implementation of sequential tree-reweighted belief propagation for probabilistic inference. In: 2015 25th International Conference on Field Programmable Logic and Applications (FPL), pp. 1–8. IEEE (2015)
10. Hurley, B., et al.: Multi-language evaluation of exact solvers in graphical model discrete optimization. Constraints **21**(3), 413–434 (2016)
11. Kainmueller, D., Jug, F., Rother, C., Meyers, G.: Graph matching problems for annotating c. elegans (2017). https://doi.org/10.15479/AT:ISTA:57. Accessed 10 Sept 2017
12. Kainmueller, D., Jug, F., Rother, C., Myers, G.: Active graph matching for automatic joint segmentation and annotation of *C. elegans*. In: Golland, P., Hata, N., Barillot, C., Hornegger, J., Howe, R. (eds.) MICCAI 2014. LNCS, vol. 8673, pp. 81–88. Springer, Cham (2014). https://doi.org/10.1007/978-3-319-10404-1_11
13. Kannan, H., Komodakis, N., Paragios, N.: Newton-type methods for inference in higher-order markov random fields. In: IEEE International Conference on Computer Vision and Pattern Recognition (2017)

14. Kappes, J.H., et al.: A comparative study of modern inference techniques for structured discrete energy minimization problems. Int. J. Comput. Vis., 1–30 (2015). https://doi.org/10.1007/s11263-015-0809-x
15. Kappes, J.H., Savchynskyy, B., Schnörr, C.: A bundle approach to efficient MAP-inference by lagrangian relaxation. In: 2012 IEEE Conference on Computer Vision and Pattern Recognition (CVPR), pp. 1688–1695. IEEE (2012)
16. Kirillov, A., Schlesinger, D., Zheng, S., Savchynskyy, B., Torr, P.H.S., Rother, C.: Joint training of generic CNN-CRF models with stochastic optimization. In: Lai, S.-H., Lepetit, V., Nishino, K., Sato, Y. (eds.) ACCV 2016. LNCS, vol. 10112, pp. 221–236. Springer, Cham (2017). https://doi.org/10.1007/978-3-319-54184-6_14
17. Kolmogorov, V.: Convergent tree-reweighted message passing for energy minimization. IEEE Trans. Pattern Anal. Mach. Intell. **28**(10), 1568–1583 (2006)
18. Kolmogorov, V.: A new look at reweighted message passing. IEEE Trans. Pattern Anal. Mach. Intell. **37**(5), 919–930 (2015)
19. Kolmogorov, V., Rother, C.: Comparison of energy minimization algorithms for highly connected graphs. In: Leonardis, A., Bischof, H., Pinz, A. (eds.) ECCV 2006. LNCS, vol. 3952, pp. 1–15. Springer, Heidelberg (2006). https://doi.org/10.1007/11744047_1
20. Kolmogorov, V., Thapper, J., Zivny, S.: The power of linear programming for general-valued CSPs. SIAM J. Comput. **44**(1), 1–36 (2015)
21. Komodakis, N., Paragios, N., Tziritas, G.: MRF optimization via dual decomposition: message-passing revisited. In: IEEE 11th International Conference on Computer Vision, ICCV 2007, pp. 1–8. IEEE (2007)
22. Kovalevsky, V., Koval, V.: A diffusion algorithm for decreasing energy of max-sum labeling problem. Glushkov Institute of Cybernetics, Kiev, USSR (1975). unpublished
23. Krähenbühl, P., Koltun, V.: Efficient inference in fully connected CRFs with gaussian edge potentials. In: Advances in Neural Information Processing Systems, pp. 109–117 (2011)
24. Li, M., Shekhovtsov, A., Huber, D.: Complexity of discrete energy minimization problems. In: Leibe, B., Matas, J., Sebe, N., Welling, M. (eds.) ECCV 2016. LNCS, vol. 9906, pp. 834–852. Springer, Cham (2016). https://doi.org/10.1007/978-3-319-46475-6_51
25. Luong, D.V.N., Parpas, P., Rueckert, D., Rustem, B.: Solving MRF minimization by mirror descent. In: Bebis, G., et al. (eds.) ISVC 2012. LNCS, vol. 7431, pp. 587–598. Springer, Heidelberg (2012). https://doi.org/10.1007/978-3-642-33179-4_56
26. Martins, A.F.T., Figueiredo, M.A.T., Aguiar, P.M.Q., Smith, N.A., Xing, E.P.: An augmented lagrangian approach to constrained MAP inference. In: ICML (2011)
27. Meshi, O., Globerson, A.: An alternating direction method for dual MAP LP relaxation. In: Gunopulos, D., Hofmann, T., Malerba, D., Vazirgiannis, M. (eds.) ECML PKDD 2011. LNCS (LNAI), vol. 6912, pp. 470–483. Springer, Heidelberg (2011). https://doi.org/10.1007/978-3-642-23783-6_30
28. Meshi, O., Globerson, A., Jaakkola, T.S.: Convergence rate analysis of MAP coordinate minimization algorithms. In: Advances in Neural Information Processing Systems, pp. 3014–3022 (2012)
29. Michel, F., et al.: Global hypothesis generation for 6D object pose estimation. arXiv preprint (2017)
30. Nowozin, S., Rother, C., Bagon, S., Sharp, T., Yao, B., Kohli, P.: Decision Tree Fields. In: 2011 IEEE International Conference on Computer Vision (ICCV), pp. 1668–1675. IEEE (2011)

31. Průša, D., Werner, T.: LP relaxation of the potts labeling problem is as hard as any linear program. IEEE Trans. Pattern Anal. Mach. Intell. **39**(7), 1469–1475 (2017)

32. Prusa, D., Werner, T.: Universality of the local marginal polytope. PAMI **37**(4), April 2015

33. Ravikumar, P., Agarwal, A., Wainwright, M.: Message-passing for graph-structured linear programs: proximal methods and rounding schemes. JMLR **11**, 1043–1080 (2010)

34. Savchynskyy, B., Kappes, J., Schmidt, S., Schnörr, C.: A study of Nesterov's scheme for Lagrangian decomposition and MAP labeling. In: 2011 IEEE Conference on Computer Vision and Pattern Recognition (CVPR), pp. 1817–1823. IEEE (2011)

35. Savchynskyy, B., Schmidt, S., Kappes, J., Schnörr, C.: Efficient MRF energy minimization via adaptive diminishing smoothing. arXiv preprint arXiv:1210.4906 (2012)

36. Schlesinger, M., Antoniuk, K.: Diffusion algorithms and structural recognition optimization problems. Cybern. Syst. Anal. **47**(2), 175–192 (2011)

37. Schlesinger, M., Giginyak, V.: Solution to structural recognition (max,+)-problems by their equivalent transformations. in 2 Parts. Control Syst, Comput. (1–2) (2007)

38. Schlesinger, M.I.: Syntactic analysis of two-dimensional visual signals in noisy conditions. Kibernetika **4**(113–130), 1 (1976)

39. Schlesinger, M.I., Flach, B.: Some solvable subclasses of structural recognition problems. In: Czech Pattern Recognition Workshop. 2000, pp. 55–62 (2000)

40. Schmidt, S., Savchynskyy, B., Kappes, J., Schnörr, C.: Evaluation of a first-order primal-dual algorithm for MRF energy minimization. In: EMMCVPR 2011 (2011)

41. Schrijver, A.: Combinatorial Optimization: Polyhedra and Efficiency, vol. 24. Springer, Heidelberg (2003)

42. Shekhovtsov, A., Swoboda, P., Savchynskyy, B.: Maximum persistency via iterative relaxed inference with graphical models. PAMI (2017)

43. Shekhovtsov, A., Reinbacher, C., Graber, G., Pock, T.: Solving dense image matching in real-time using discrete-continuous optimization. In: CVWW, p. 13 (2016)

44. Storvik, G., Dahl, G.: Lagrangian-based methods for finding MAP solutions for MRF models. IEEE Trans. Image Process. **9**(3), 469–479 (2000)

45. Szeliski, R., et al.: A comparative study of energy minimization methods for markov random fields with smoothness-based priors. IEEE Trans. Pattern Anal. Mach. Intell. **30**(6), 1068–1080 (2008)

46. Thapper, J., Živný, S.: The power of linear programming for valued CSPs. In: Symposium on Foundations of Computer Science (FOCS), pp. 669–678 (2012)

47. Werner, T.: A linear programming approach to max-sum problem: A review. IEEE Trans. Pattern Anal. Mach. Intell. **29**(7) (2007)

48. Yanover, C., Schueler-Furman, O., Weiss, Y.: Minimizing and learning energy functions for side-chain prediction. J. Comput. Biol. **15**(7), 899–911 (2008)

49. Živný, S., Werner, T., Průša, D.a.: The Power of LP Relaxation for MAP Inference, pp. 19–42. The MIT Press, Cambridge (2014)

Single Image Highlight Removal with a Sparse and Low-Rank Reflection Model

Jie Guo[1], Zuojian Zhou[2], and Limin Wang[1]($\boxtimes$)

[1] State Key Lab for Novel Software Technology, Nanjing University, Nanjing, China
guojie@nju.edu.cn, 07wanglimin@gmail.com
[2] School of Information Technology, Nanjing University of Chinese Medicine,
Nanjing, China
lygzzj@163.com

Abstract. We propose a sparse and low-rank reflection model for specular highlight detection and removal using a single input image. This model is motivated by the observation that the specular highlight of a natural image usually has large intensity but is rather sparsely distributed while the remaining diffuse reflection can be well approximated by a linear combination of several distinct colors with a sparse and low-rank weighting matrix. We further impose the non-negativity constraint on the weighting matrix as well as the highlight component to ensure that the model is purely additive. With this reflection model, we reformulate the task of highlight removal as a constrained nuclear norm and l_1-norm minimization problem which can be solved effectively by the augmented Lagrange multiplier method. Experimental results show that our method performs well on both synthetic images and many real-world examples and is competitive with previous methods, especially in some challenging scenarios featuring natural illumination, hue-saturation ambiguity and strong noises.

Keywords: Highlight removal · Low-rank · Sparse · Diffuse reflection

1 Introduction

A vast majority of objects in real-world scenes exhibit both diffuse and specular reflections. The existence of specular reflection is recognized as a hindrance for a variety of computer vision tasks including image segmentation, pattern recognition, and object detection, since it creates undesired discontinuities and reduces image contrast. Therefore, separating specular highlights from diffuse reflection is of crucial importance and forms the core of many high-level vision tasks. Although highlights can be well suppressed by some special facilities such as polarizing filters [1–4] or multi-spectral light stages [5], it is more appealing

Electronic supplementary material The online version of this chapter (https://doi.org/10.1007/978-3-030-01225-0_17) contains supplementary material, which is available to authorized users.

to remove them using just a single color image without any hardware assistance. However, highlight removal from a single image constitutes an ill-posed problem with more unknowns than equations to solve.

Our goal in this paper is to separate reflection components of a single input image based on the dichromatic reflection model [6]. We notice that highlight regions in many real-world scenes are contiguous pieces with relatively small size while colors of diffuse reflection can be well approximated by a small number of distinct colors. The former observation implies that highlight regions in an image tend to be sparse. The latter observation, which resembles the observation in non-local image dehazing [7], reveals that diffuse colors form tight clusters in RGB space with a low-rank and sparse weighting matrix. This inspires us to separate diffuse and specular reflections with sparse and low-rank matrix decomposition [8–10].

Based on the insights gained from these observations, we propose a sparse and low-rank reflection (SLRR) model. This model assumes that specular highlights have the same spectral distribution with the incident illumination (*i.e.*, the neutral interface reflection assumption [11]) and are rather sparse in the spatial domain of a given image. We also assume that each diffuse color can be represented by a linear combination of several "basis colors" from a "color dictionary" and the weighting matrix formed by the coefficients is low-rank and sparse. The low-rankness indicates some global structures in the weighting matrix [12,13] while the sparsity stems from the fact that the diffuse colors are clustered as blocks in the image. In this context, the highlight removal process is formulated as a constrained nuclear norm and l_1-norm minimization problem, which can be efficiently solved by the augmented Lagrange multiplier (ALM) method with alternating direction minimizing (ADM) strategy [14]. To ensure that our model is purely additive and avoids counteracting each other by subtraction, we further explicitly impose the non-negativity constraint on it. This will bring in some inequality constraints that are difficult for optimization. We address this issue by introducing slack variables and converting inequalities into equalities. These equalities are added into the augmented Lagrange function.

To demonstrate the effectiveness and robustness of our method, we conduct an extensive evaluation using various synthetic and real-world images from several public image datasets. Experimental results show that our method achieves better performance on many tasks than state-of-the-art. Particularly, it can effectively handle some challenging scenarios including natural illumination and hue-saturation ambiguity.

2 Related Work

Highlight removal has been paid much attention in recent years [15]. Existing work on highlight removal is generally grouped into two high-level categories based on the number of images used.

In the first category are approaches that remove highlight with multiple images. As highlight regions are direction-dependent, it is natural to use image sequences from different points of view [16,17] or from multiple light positions [5,18,19] to restore the diffuse reflection. The polarization based methods

[1–4] require a set of images captured with different polarization orientations for accurate highlight removal, considering that specular and diffuse reflections hold different degrees of polarization. Other auxiliary data, such as that generated by a multi-spectral light stage [16,17] or a flash system [20,21], also benefits this task. Despite their effectiveness, these methods are less appealing to everyday users because such image datasets are not often available in practice.

The second line of work focuses on removing highlight from a single image. As this problem is inherently ill-posed, prior knowledge or assumptions on the characteristics of natural images should be exploited to make the problem tractable. Early work relies on color space analysis [22–24] which is only limited to dealing with uniform surface colors and probably involves image segmentation.

In order to handle textured surfaces, Tan and Ikeuchi [25] pioneered the idea of specular-free image which has been widely studied ever since. A specular-free image is a pseudo-diffuse image that has the same geometrical profile as the true diffuse component of the input image. It can be generated by setting the diffuse maximum chromaticity of each pixel to an arbitrary value [25, 26] or by subtracting the minimum value of the RGB channels for each pixel [27–30]. Kim *et al.* [31] obtained an approximated specular-free image via applying the dark channel prior. Suo et al. [32] defined l_2 chromaticity and used it to generate the specular-free image. Yang *et al.* [26] proposed a fast bilateral filter adopting the specular-free image as the range weighting function. Several methods [28,30,33] use the specular-free image for pixel clustering and then recover the diffuse colors in each cluster. The main drawback of the specular-free image is it suffers from hue-saturation ambiguity which exists in many natural images. Liu *et al.* [33] suggested using an additional compensation step to raise the achromatic component of the diffuse chromaticity.

Some single image based methods do not explicitly rely on a specular-free image. For instance, Mallick *et al.* [34] proposed a PDE algorithm, which iteratively erodes the specular component in the SUV color space. But this method performs poorly on large specular regions. Ren *et al.* [35] introduced the color-lines constraint into the dichromatic reflection model and proposed a fast highlight removal method. Li *et al.* [36] made use of specialized domain knowledge to guide the removal of specular highlights in facial images. Inpainting techniques which synthetically fill in the missing regions using the neighboring patterns have also been applied to recover diffuse colors [37,38]. Our method bears some similarity to that of Akashi and Okatani [39] which formulates the separation of reflections as a sparse non-negative matrix factorization (NMF) problem. However, current algorithms for NMF are sensitive to initial values and only guarantee finding a local minimum rather than a global minimum. Therefore this method requires running several times to get the most reasonable result. Furthermore, since NMF is highly sensitive to outliers in general cases, this method may fail in the presence of strong specularity or noises. Oppositely, our method relies on sparse and low-rank decomposition which is much more robust to outliers.

3   Sparse and Low-Rank Reflection Model

To exploit sparse and low-rank structures in an image, we derive a new reflection model following the formulation of the dichromatic reflection model [6]. This model states that the observed image intensity $\mathbf{I}$ of a pixel p is the sum of a diffuse component $\mathbf{I}_d$ and a specular component $\mathbf{I}_s$:

$$\mathbf{I}(p) = \mathbf{I}_d(p) + \mathbf{I}_s(p) = m_d(p)\mathbf{\Lambda}(p) + m_s(p)\mathbf{\Gamma}(p) \tag{1}$$

where $\mathbf{\Lambda}(p)$ and $\mathbf{\Gamma}(p)$ respectively denote the chromaticities of the diffuse and specular components. $m_d(p)$ and $m_s(p)$ represent their corresponding coefficients which are achromatic and only depend on imaging geometry.

The specular chromaticity could be assumed to be uniform for a given image and equals to the chromaticity of the incident illumination [11]. Like many other specular removal methods, we estimate the illumination chromaticity $\mathbf{\Gamma}$ of a real-world image via the color constancy algorithm in [40], and then normalize the original image by $\mathbf{I}(p)/(3\mathbf{\Gamma})$ in a preprocessing step. After that, we have a pure white illumination color, i.e., $\mathbf{\Gamma}_r = \mathbf{\Gamma}_g = \mathbf{\Gamma}_b = 1/3$. Often, we observe that highlight regions are small in size and are distributed rather sparsely. This implies that $m_s(p)$ is non-zero only for a low density of pixels.

On the contrary, the diffuse component $\mathbf{I}_d$ usually has a high density of valid data. However, since the diffuse reflectance of natural objects is commonly piecewise constant, the number of distinct colors of $\mathbf{I}_d$ is orders of magnitude smaller than the number of pixels [7]. Therefore, given a proper color dictionary $\mathbf{\Phi}_d = [\phi_1, \phi_2, \cdots, \phi_K]$, $\mathbf{I}_d$ can be faithfully reconstructed by $\mathbf{I}_d(p) = \sum_{k=1}^{K} \phi_k w_k(p)$ in which $w_k(p) \geq 0$ is the weighting coefficient of the pixel p w.r.t. the basis color ϕ_k. The non-negativity constraint makes every pixel value stay in the convex hull of the dictionary, avoiding counteracting each other by subtraction. Ideally, w_k is non-zero for only one basis color, implying that w_k is sparse. Meanwhile, as the color dictionary $\mathbf{\Phi}_d$ is often over-complete, the best choice of w_k should be drawn from a low-rank subspace.

We finally come up with the following sparse and low-rank reflection model:

$$\mathbf{X} = \mathbf{\Phi}_d\mathbf{W}_d + \mathbf{\Gamma}\mathbf{M}_s \tag{2}$$

where $\mathbf{X}$ is a $3 \times N$ matrix with each column representing a pixel color. N is the total number of pixels in an image. $\mathbf{W}_d$ is a $K \times N$ matrix formed by the weighting coefficients of all pixels. As the specular chromaticity $\mathbf{\Gamma}$ is assumed to be a constant column vector for a given image, we represent the specular component using a rank-one expression in which $\mathbf{M}_s$ is a row vector of size $1 \times N$ encoding the position and intensity of specular highlights.

The above analysis reveals that $\mathbf{M}_s$ tends to be sparse while $\mathbf{W}_d$ is both sparse and low-rank. Furthermore, since pixel values are non-negative, we also impose the non-negativity constraint on $\mathbf{M}_s$ and $\mathbf{W}_d$. In this way, the reflection separation problem of an input image can be formulated as the following optimization problem with both equality and inequality constraints:

$$\min_{\mathbf{W}_d, \mathbf{M}_s} \text{rank}(\mathbf{W}_d) + \lambda\|\mathbf{M}_s\|_0 + \tau\|\mathbf{W}_d\|_0$$
$$\text{s.t. } \mathbf{X} = \boldsymbol{\Phi}_d\mathbf{W}_d + \boldsymbol{\Gamma}\mathbf{M}_s, \mathbf{W}_d \geq 0, \mathbf{M}_s \geq 0 \tag{3}$$

in which λ and τ are parameters used to balance the effect of different components. $\|\cdot\|_0$ denotes the l_0 norm of a matrix, which counts the number of non-zero entries in the matrix.

4   Model Optimization

Unfortunately, Eq. 3 is highly non-convex and no efficient solution is available. To make the optimization tractable, we relax Eq. 3 via replacing rank($\cdot$) with $\|\cdot\|_*$ and $\|\cdot\|_0$ with $\|\cdot\|_1$ as in the sparse and low-rank matrix decomposition. Here $\|\cdot\|_*$ is the nuclear norm of a matrix defined by the sum of its singular values and $\|\cdot\|_1$ is the l_1 norm. We also introduce two auxiliary variables $\mathbf{J}$ and $\mathbf{H}$ to make the objective function separable:

$$\min_{\mathbf{J}, \mathbf{M}_s, \mathbf{H}, \mathbf{W}_d} \|\mathbf{J}\|_* + \lambda\|\mathbf{M}_s\|_1 + \tau\|\mathbf{H}\|_1$$
$$\text{s.t. } \mathbf{X} = \boldsymbol{\Phi}_d\mathbf{W}_d + \boldsymbol{\Gamma}\mathbf{M}_s, \mathbf{J} = \mathbf{W}_d, \mathbf{H} = \mathbf{W}_d, \mathbf{W}_d \geq 0, \mathbf{M}_s \geq 0. \tag{4}$$

This optimization problem involves two non-negativity constraints. To cope with these inequalities, a straightforward strategy, as suggested by Zhuang et al. [41], is to clamp the negative entries in $\mathbf{W}_d$ and $\mathbf{M}_s$ to zero directly during each iteration. Unfortunately, we find that such a simple strategy shows poor convergence as shown in Fig. 8. Instead, we introduce two non-negative slack variables $\mathbf{S}_1$ and $\mathbf{S}_2$ to convert the non-negativity constraints into two equality constraints: $\mathbf{W}_d - \mathbf{S}_1 = 0$ and $\mathbf{M}_s - \mathbf{S}_2 = 0$.

Various algorithms have been developed to solve the optimization problem, among which the ALM method [8,14] is most widely used. This method replaces the original constrained optimization problem by a sequence of unconstrained subproblems which can be efficiently solved by soft-thresholding or singular value thresholding (SVT) [42].

The augmented Lagrange function of the above optimization problem with two slack variables is

$$\mathcal{L}(\mathbf{J}, \mathbf{M}_s, \mathbf{H}, \mathbf{W}_d, \mathbf{Y}_i, \mathbf{S}_1, \mathbf{S}_2, \mu) =$$
$$\|\mathbf{J}\|_* + \lambda\|\mathbf{M}_s\|_1 + \tau\|\mathbf{H}\|_1 + \sum_{i=1}^{5} < \mathbf{Y}_i, \mathbf{E}_i > + \frac{\mu}{2}(\|\mathbf{E}_i\|_F^2) \tag{5}$$

where $\mathbf{Y}_i$ are Lagrange multipliers and $\mu > 0$ is a penalty parameter. $\mathbf{E}_i$ are five equality constraints, namely, $\mathbf{E}_1 = \mathbf{X} - \boldsymbol{\Phi}_d\mathbf{W}_d - \boldsymbol{\Gamma}\mathbf{M}_s$, $\mathbf{E}_2 = \mathbf{J} - \mathbf{W}_d$, $\mathbf{E}_3 = \mathbf{H} - \mathbf{W}_d$, $\mathbf{E}_4 = \mathbf{W}_d - \mathbf{S}_1$, and $\mathbf{E}_5 = \mathbf{M}_s - \mathbf{S}_2$. $< \cdot, \cdot >$ denotes the standard inner product between two matrices while $\|\cdot\|_F$ represents the Frobenius norm of a matrix. The ALM method with ADM strategy decomposes the minimization of $\mathcal{L}$ into several subproblems in which the variables are updated alternately with other variables fixed.

4.1 Update J

With some algebra, the optimization problem over $\mathbf{J}$, keeping other variables fixed, is rearranged as

$$\mathbf{J}^* = \arg\min_{\mathbf{J}} \frac{1}{\mu}\|\mathbf{J}\|_* + \frac{1}{2}\left\|\mathbf{J} - \left(\mathbf{W}_d - \frac{\mathbf{Y}_2}{\mu}\right)\right\|_F^2. \tag{6}$$

For conventional nuclear norm, the solution to this subproblem is given analytically by

$$\mathbf{J}^* = \mathcal{D}_{1/\mu}\left(\mathbf{W}_d - \mathbf{Y}_2/\mu\right). \tag{7}$$

Here $\mathcal{D}_{1/\mu}$ is an SVT operator [42] defined as $\mathcal{D}_{1/\mu}(\mathbf{A}) = \mathbf{U}[\mathrm{sgn}(\boldsymbol{\Sigma})\max(|\boldsymbol{\Sigma}| - \mu^{-1}, 0)]\mathbf{V}^\top$, in which $\mathbf{U}\boldsymbol{\Sigma}\mathbf{V}^\top$ is a singular value decomposition of $\mathbf{A}$. For weighted nuclear norm, we can also obtain a similar analytical solution if the weights are in a non-ascending order [43]. In this paper, we prefer the weighted version for better performance, and the weight $\mathbf{w}$ is set as

$$w_i = \sqrt{N}/(|\boldsymbol{\Sigma}_{i,i}| + \delta) \tag{8}$$

where a small constant δ is used to avoid dividing by zero. With the weight $\mathbf{w}$, we have $\mathcal{D}_{1/\mu}(\mathbf{A}) = \mathbf{U}[\mathrm{sgn}(\boldsymbol{\Sigma})\max(|\boldsymbol{\Sigma}| - \mu^{-1}\mathrm{diag}(\mathbf{w}), 0)]\mathbf{V}^\top$.

4.2 Update $\mathbf{M}_s$

$\mathbf{M}_s$ in our context is a N-dimensional row vector. Suppose $\boldsymbol{\Gamma}$ is known in advance, we can formulate the update of $\mathbf{M}_s$ as

$$\mathbf{M}_s^* = \arg\min_{\mathbf{M}_s} \frac{\lambda}{\mu g}\|\mathbf{M}_s\|_1 + \frac{1}{2}\left\|\mathbf{M}_s - \frac{1}{g}\left(\boldsymbol{\Gamma}^\top\left(\mathbf{X} - \boldsymbol{\Phi}_d\mathbf{W}_d + \frac{\mathbf{Y}_1}{\mu}\right) - \frac{\mathbf{Y}_5}{\mu} + \mathbf{S}_2\right)\right\|_2^2 \tag{9}$$

in which $g = \boldsymbol{\Gamma}^\top\boldsymbol{\Gamma}$. By employing the soft-thresholding operator $\mathcal{S}_\tau(x) = \mathrm{sgn}(x)\max(|x| - \tau, 0)$, this subproblem also has an analytical solution:

$$\mathbf{M}_s^* = \mathcal{S}_{\frac{\lambda}{\mu g}}\left(\left(\boldsymbol{\Gamma}^\top\left(\mathbf{X} - \boldsymbol{\Phi}_d\mathbf{W}_d + \mathbf{Y}_1/\mu\right) - \mathbf{Y}_5/\mu + \mathbf{S}_2\right)/g\right). \tag{10}$$

4.3 Update H

Similarly, we can rearrange the subproblem optimizing $\mathbf{H}$ as

$$\mathbf{H}^* = \arg\min_{\mathbf{H}} \frac{\tau}{\mu}\|\mathbf{H}\|_1 + \frac{1}{2}\left\|\mathbf{H} - \left(\mathbf{W}_d - \frac{\mathbf{Y}_3}{\mu}\right)\right\|_F^2 \tag{11}$$

and solve it efficiently with the soft-thresholding operator:

$$\mathbf{H}^* = \mathcal{S}_{\tau/\mu}(\mathbf{W}_d - \mathbf{Y}_3/\mu). \tag{12}$$

Note that this operator is performed element-wise for a matrix.

4.4 Update $\mathbf{W}_d$

With other variables fixed, the subproblem w.r.t. $\mathbf{W}_d$ is quadratic. Therefore, this is a standard least squares regression problem with a closed-form solution:

$$\mathbf{W}_d^* = (\boldsymbol{\Phi}_d^\top\boldsymbol{\Phi}_d+3\mathbf{I})^{-1}(\boldsymbol{\Phi}_d^\top\mathbf{X}-\boldsymbol{\Phi}_d^\top\boldsymbol{\Gamma}\mathbf{M}_s+\mathbf{J}+\mathbf{H}+\mathbf{S}_1+(\boldsymbol{\Phi}_d^\top\mathbf{Y}_1+\mathbf{Y}_2+\mathbf{Y}_3-\mathbf{Y}_4)/\mu).\tag{13}$$

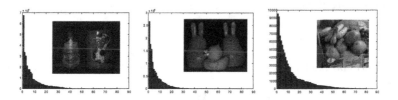

Fig. 1. Sorted color histograms of three typical natural images.

4.5 Update Slack Variables

The subproblems w.r.t. two slack variables ($\mathbf{S}_1$ and $\mathbf{S}_2$) are also standard least squares regression problems. Their solutions are given by

$$\mathbf{S}_1^* = \max(\mathbf{W}_d + \mathbf{Y}_4/\mu, 0) \quad \text{and} \quad \mathbf{S}_2^* = \max(\mathbf{M}_s + \mathbf{Y}_5/\mu, 0)\tag{14}$$

respectively. The max function is added to ensure that both $\mathbf{S}_1$ and $\mathbf{S}_2$ are non-negative.

4.6 Construct Color Dictionary

In sparse and low-rank representations, constructing a proper dictionary is important. A simple option would take the entire input date as the dictionary [12]. However, such a large dictionary is computationally expensive and consumes too much storage space. Inspired by the non-local prior [7] of natural images, we adopt the following histogram binning method to construct a color dictionary $\boldsymbol{\Phi}_d$.

This method requires constructing a 2-dimensional binning of longitude θ and latitude ϕ on a unit sphere. We use the same strategy as in [7] to uniformly tessellate a unit sphere. For an input image, we view each pixel $\mathbf{I}(p)$ as a 3-dimensional vector and transform it into spherical coordinates: $\mathbf{I}(p) = [r(p), \theta(p), \phi(p)]$. Then, each pixel is assigned into a proper bin based on $\theta(p)$ and $\phi(p)$. After that, we sort all the bins in a descending order according to their densities (see Fig. 1) and select the top K bins. The bin centers are regarded as atoms of the dictionary $\boldsymbol{\Phi}_d \in \mathbb{R}^{3\times K}$. Figure 1 shows sorted color histograms of three typical natural images used in this paper. Obviously, there are only a limited number of distinct colors in an image.

4.7   Highlight Removal Algorithm

The complete steps of our highlight removal method are outlined in Algorithm 1. The input of this algorithm is a single image that is reshaped into a $3 \times N$ matrix in which each column stores a pixel value. The output includes a color dictionary $\mathbf{\Phi}_d$, a weighting matrix $\mathbf{W}_d$, and a specular coefficient matrix $\mathbf{M}_s$. With these outputs, we can easily obtain the diffuse component and the specular component according to Eq. 2. Note that an adaptive updating strategy for the penalty parameter μ is used as shown in line 10, which makes the convergence faster.

Algorithm 1. Highlight Removal with the SLRR Model

Input: Image data $\mathbf{X} \in \mathbb{R}^{3 \times N}$.

1: **Initialize:** $\mathbf{W}_d = \mathbf{J} = \mathbf{H} = 0$, $\mathbf{M}_s = 0$, $\mathbf{S}_1 = 0$, $\mathbf{S}_2 = 0$, $\mathbf{Y}_i = 0$, $\mu = 0.1$,
     $\mu_{max} = 10^{10}$, $\rho = 1.1$, $\epsilon = 10^{-6}$, $K = 50$;
2: Construct a color dictionary $\mathbf{\Phi}_d$;
3: **while** not converged **do**
4:      Update $\mathbf{J}$ according to Eq. 7;
5:      Update $\mathbf{M}_s$ according to Eq. 10;
6:      Update $\mathbf{H}$ according to Eq. 12;
7:      Update $\mathbf{W}_d$ according to Eq. 13;
8:      Update slack variables $\mathbf{S}_1$ and $\mathbf{S}_2$ according to Eq. 14;
9:      Update Lagrange multipliers: $\mathbf{Y}_i \leftarrow \mathbf{Y}_i + \mu \mathbf{E}_i$, $i = 1$ to 5;
10:     Update μ: $\mu \leftarrow \min(\mu_{max}, \rho\mu)$;
11:     Check convergence: $\max_i(\|\mathbf{E}_i\|_F / \|\mathbf{X}\|_F) < \epsilon$;

Output: $\mathbf{\Phi}_d \in \mathbb{R}^{3 \times K}$, $\mathbf{W}_d \in \mathbb{R}^{K \times N}$, and $\mathbf{M}_s \in \mathbb{R}^{1 \times N}$.

---

5   Experimental Results and Discussions

To verify the effectiveness and robustness of the proposed method, we evaluate it on both synthetic images and many real and practical scenarios. We also present comparisons to some recent methods proposed by Tan and Ikeuchi [25], Shen et al. [28], Yang et al. [26], Shen and Zheng [30], Akashi and Okatani [39], and Ren et al. [35]. Unless otherwise stated, λ is set as $0.1/\sqrt{N}$ while τ is set as $1/\sqrt{N}$. This is a good starting point for many cases.

5.1   Study on Illumination Chromaticity

Recall that we use the color constancy algorithm proposed in [40] to estimate the illumination chromaticity $\mathbf{\Gamma}$. Figure 2 and Table 1 show that our method is robust to a certain amount of estimation error of $\mathbf{\Gamma}$. To demonstrate this, we provide two scenes rendered with four different lighting configurations. The accurate values of the illumination chromaticity are listed in the second column of Table 1 while the estimated values for the two scenes are listed in the third and sixth columns, respectively. As expected, using accurate values of $\mathbf{\Gamma}$ in our method (the third row of Fig. 2) leads to high-quality results that closely match the ground truth results (the second row of Fig. 2). Although the estimation error of Γ has negative influence on our method (the fourth row of Fig. 2), we still achieve satisfactory results with a small decline in PSNR (see Table 1).

5.2 Comparisons on Synthetic and Laboratory Images

Figure 3 conducts experiments on two synthetic images. The first scene includes a single rendered sphere. Diffuse reflectances of the upper and lower hemisphere are set as $[0.8, 0.5, 0.5]$ and $[0.8, 0.2, 0.2]$, respectively, such that they share the same hue but different saturation. As shown in Fig. 3, when the diffuse reflectance is close to the incident illumination color, the separation will be error-prone for many methods, especially those based on a specular-free image. These methods will mistakenly regard the entire region of the upper hemisphere as contaminated by specular reflection, making this region very dim after separation. Although the NMF method [39] tries to preserve the saturation of such regions, the separation is not sufficient in this experiment. In contrast, our method based on the SLRR model regards strong highlights as sparse outliers and encodes remaining diffuse colors using a color dictionary in which both colors: $[0.8, 0.5, 0.5]$ and $[0.8, 0.2, 0.2]$ after normalization are present. Consequently, we successfully remove highlights with less color distortions. Compared to other methods, our method achieves the best separation result that is very close to the ground truth (G.T.). Further discussions on the ball scene are given in the supplemental material. Another challenge

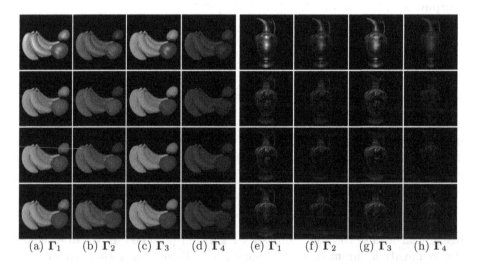

(a) Γ_1 (b) Γ_2 (c) Γ_3 (d) Γ_4 (e) Γ_1 (f) Γ_2 (g) Γ_3 (h) Γ_4

Fig. 2. Influence of the illumination chromaticity on highlight removal. The first row shows two rendered scenes under four different illumination chromaticities and the second row gives the corresponding diffuse component of each input image. The third and fourth rows present our method's results using the accurate and estimated illumination chromaticities, respectively.

Table 1. Illumination chromaticities of four different lighting configurations in Fig. 2 and the corresponding PSNR values. Here PSNR1 and PSNR2 are calculated for our method with the accurate and estimated values of Γ, respectively.

	Accurate	Fig. 2 left			Fig. 2 right		
		Estimated	PSNR1	PSNR2	Estimated	PSNR1	PSNR2
Γ_1	$[1/3, 1/3, 1/3]$	$[0.36, 0.29, 0.35]$	33.1	31.9	$[0.34, 0.35, 0.31]$	34.9	34.0
Γ_2	$[0.6, 0.2, 0.2]$	$[0.64, 0.19, 0.17]$	37.1	33.0	$[0.63, 0.20, 0.17]$	37.4	35.1
Γ_3	$[0.2, 0.6, 0.2]$	$[0.21, 0.63, 0.16]$	37.3	35.6	$[0.20, 0.63, 0.17]$	37.6	33.8
Γ_4	$[0.2, 0.2, 0.6]$	$[0.22, 0.23, 0.55]$	37.0	33.0	$[0.22, 0.22, 0.56]$	37.4	35.1

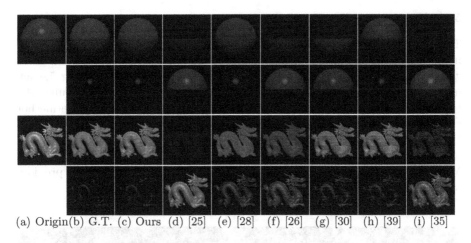

(a) Origin (b) G.T. (c) Ours (d) [25] (e) [28] (f) [26] (g) [30] (h) [39] (i) [35]

Fig. 3. Highlight removal results of two synthetic images. From (c) to (i), we compare our method to those of Tan and Ikeuchi [25], Shen *et al.* [28], Yang *et al.* [26], Shen and Zheng [30], Akashi and Okatani [39], and Ren *et al.* [35].

scene shown in the third and fourth rows of Fig. 3 also contains hue-saturation ambiguity. Again, our method outperforms previous work and retains most of the texture details.

Figure 4 presents the results of different highlight removal methods on four laboratory captured images with well-controlled lighting configurations. These images accompanied with ground truth results are captured by Shen and Zheng [30] and have already been normalized w.r.t. the illumination color. Therefore, the accurate value of the illumination chromaticity is $\Gamma = [1/3, 1/3, 1/3]$. Figure 4 compares our method to three competing methods that perform well on this dataset. For a fair comparison, the accurate illumination chromaticity is used in each method. We also provide the results generated by our method using the estimated illumination chromaticity. Visual comparisons reveal that the separated diffuse components of our method using either accurate or estimated illumination chromaticity match the ground truth results quite well. The differences are subtle although errors exist in illumination estimation.

To further validate the accuracy of our method, we provide quantitative analysis for Figs. 3 and 4 in Table 2. The error metrics used for evaluation are PSNR and SSIM w.r.t. the ground truth. As seen, our method using accurate illumination chromaticity achieves the highest scores for the two synthetic images, and also achieves two highest scores both in PSNR and SSIM for the laboratory images. Similarly, the errors of illumination estimation do not affect our results apparently. The results demonstrate the superiority of the proposed method, and are consistent with the visual impression in Figs. 3 and 4.

5.3   Robustness Exploration

To demonstrate that our method is robust to strong noises, we conduct an experiment in Fig. 5. We generate a noisy image by adding zero-mean Gaussian noises with variance 0.1 to each channel of a real-world image. As shown in Fig. 5, some methods, in particular those based on material clustering [28,30], are vulnerable to noises and produce separation results with degraded accuracy. The method of Akashi and Okatani [39] also fails in the presence of strong noises because the NMF is highly sensitive to outliers. In comparison, our method can generate high quality results even in this tough case. For this image, we set $\tau = 5/\sqrt{N}$. More results testing the sensitivity of our method to image noises are provided in the supplemental material.

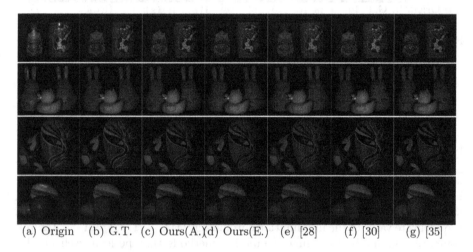

(a) Origin   (b) G.T.   (c) Ours(A.)(d) Ours(E.)   (e) [28]   (f) [30]   (g) [35]

Fig. 4. Highlight removal results of four laboratory images with ground truth (G.T.). We compare our method using either accurate (A.) or estimated (E.) illumination chromaticity to three competing methods. See Table 2 for quantitative comparisons.

Table 2. Quantitative evaluation in terms of PSNR and SSIM for the images in Fig. 3 (Ball and Dragon) and Fig. 4 (Cups, Animals, Masks and Fruit). The highest scores are in red and the second highest scores are in blue.

Scenes	PSNR								SSIM							
	Ours(A.)	Ours(E.)	[25]	[28]	[26]	[30]	[39]	[35]	Ours(A.)	Ours(E.)	[25]	[28]	[26]	[30]	[39]	[35]
Ball	39.6	38.9	18.8	28.4	19.1	20.0	27.1	17.3	0.998	0.997	0.780	0.974	0.813	0.856	0.885	0.644
Dragon	31.8	30.5	11.4	21.1	17.3	25.4	27.6	13.5	0.972	0.964	0.638	0.933	0.883	0.945	0.952	0.738
Cups	39.1	38.6	29.3	37.5	34.1	38.9	35.7	38.0	0.963	0.959	0.767	0.962	0.941	0.966	0.937	0.957
Animals	35.7	34.4	26.1	34.2	33.0	37.4	26.8	30.6	0.975	0.938	0.929	0.974	0.970	0.971	0.802	0.896
Masks	34.4	31.5	23.9	32.1	28.4	33.9	32.3	30.0	0.955	0.911	0.789	0.943	0.899	0.941	0.657	0.913
Fruit	36.4	36.5	29.2	38.0	32.4	39.2	30.8	37.5	0.930	0.921	0.912	0.961	0.939	0.960	0.765	0.952

Our method is also robust to the response function of the camera. In Fig. 6, we simulate the error of camera calibration by transforming each pixel value I to $I^{1/\gamma}$. γ is set to 1.5 (the first row) and 2.2 (the second row), respectively. As seen, our method still works well even if there are some errors in the calibration of the cameras response function. It clearly outperforms some previous methods (*e.g.*, [25,26] and [30]).

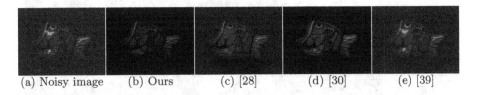

(a) Noisy image   (b) Ours   (c) [28]   (d) [30]   (e) [39]

Fig. 5. Influence of strong noises. Zero-mean Gaussian noises with variance 0.1 are added to each channel of a real-world image. Some methods (*e.g.*, [28], [30], and [39]) are vulnerable to strong noises while our method is much more robust.

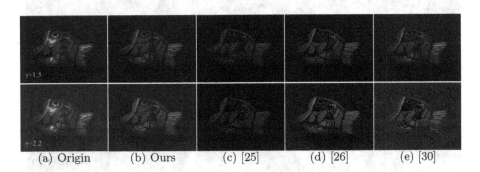

(a) Origin   (b) Ours   (c) [25]   (d) [26]   (e) [30]

Fig. 6. Influence of the response function of the camera. Each pixel value I of the original images is transformed to $I^{1/\gamma}$.

5.4   Test on Images in the Wild

Qualitative results on images in the wild are provided in Fig. 7 where we compare our method with those of Yang *et al.* [26], Shen and Zheng [30], Akashi and Okatani [39], and Ren *et al.* [35]. We do not provide quantitative comparisons since ground truth results are unavailable for these images. Overall, our method performs well on a diversity of natural images which may contain various materials, heavy textures, occlusion, overexposure and natural illumination. Note that many methods produce obvious visual artifacts in those regions having a close-to-white diffuse reflectance (*e.g.* the labels of cardboard boxes in the fourth scene and the color palette in the fifth scene) such that the diffuse chromaticity is almost identical to the illumination chromaticity. As shown, our method can still handle this challenging situation without introducing annoying artifacts. In comparison, our method well suppresses the specular highlights and preserves the saturation and image details as much as possible. Results for additional real-world images are provided in the supplemental material.

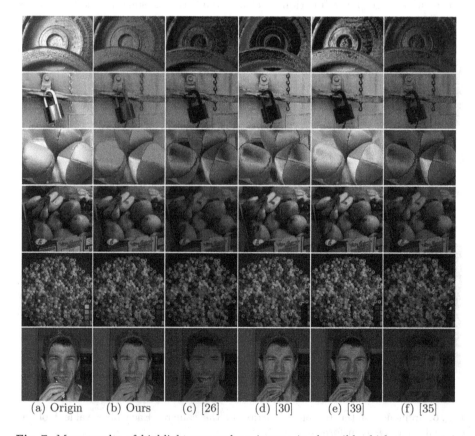

(a) Origin   (b) Ours   (c) [26]   (d) [30]   (e) [39]   (f) [35]

Fig. 7. More results of highlight removal on images in the wild which may contain natural illumination, heavy textures, hue-saturation ambiguity and overexposed pixels.

5.5   Study on Convergence

In this work, we use slack variables to explicitly convert non-negativity constraints into equality constraints. This leads to a fast convergence rate as evidence in Fig. 8. Here we show two examples. Compared to Zhuang *et al.* [41]'s strategy which simply clamps the negative entries to zero, our method converges faster in both cases. Empirically, $200 \sim 300$ iterations are sufficient for most images. Increasing the iteration number has little effect on the final results once the algorithm converges.

We also test the influence of the color dictionary size K on the convergence rate in Fig. 9. Here, we provide the results of four real world images that have ground truths. We see that a very small K leads to low accuracy for diffuse color reconstruction. Both PSNR and SSIM obtain an obvious improvement as varying K from 1 to 10. After this, the scores of PSNR and SSIM almost saturate when K increases from 10 to 80. In practice, although high PSNR and SSIM scores could be obtained when K is relatively small (e.g., $K = 10$), the visual quality of reconstructed image is not satisfying. For a much larger K (e.g., from 60 to 80) it hardly affects the numerical results (PSNR, SSIM) as well as visual quality, but will significantly increase the computational cost. Taking these factors into account, we generally set K as 50 without any specific tuning.

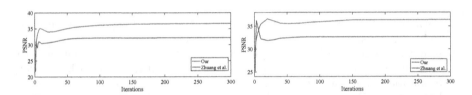

Fig. 8. Convergence rate comparisons with Zhuang *et al.* [41]'s strategy on two images: Animals (left) and Fruit (right).

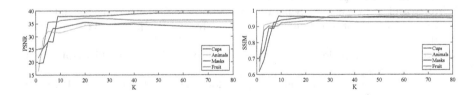

Fig. 9. Influence of K on the convergence rate. The line plots show the PSNR (left) and SSIM (right) w.r.t. K after 300 iterations.

6   Conclusion

We have presented a new method for automatically separating an original image into a diffuse component and a specular component with no user intervention. This method is built upon a sparse and low-rank reflection (SLRR) model in which we assume that highlight regions in an image are sparse while diffuse colors can be well represented by a limited number of distinct colors. We then cast the task of highlight removal into a constrained nuclear norm and l_1-norm minimization problem which can be solved effectively by the ALM method. Different from some previous work, our method do not require a specular-free image which is vulnerable to hue-saturation ambiguity. With the SLRR model and proper parameter settings, we tend to avoid this problem and preserve scene details as much as possible. Experimental results using various synthetic and real-world images validate the accuracy and robustness of our method.

Acknowledgement. We would like to thank the anonymous reviewers for their valuable feedback. This work was partially supported by the National Key Research and Development Program of China (No. 2018YFB1004901) and NSFC (No. 61502223).

References

1. Nayar, S.K., Fang, X.S., Boult, T.: Separation of reflection components using color and polarization. Int. J. Comput. Vision **21**(3), 163–186 (1997)
2. Kim, D.W., Lin, S., Hong, K.S., Shum, H.Y.: Variational specular separation using color and polarization. In: Proceedings of the IAPR Conference on Machine Vision Applications, pp. 176–179 (2002)
3. Umeyama, S., Godin, G.: Separation of diffuse and specular components of surface reflection by use of polarization and statistical analysis of images. IEEE Trans. Pattern Anal. Mach. Intell. **26**(5), 639–647 (2004)
4. Wang, F., Ainouz, S., Petitjean, C., Bensrhair, A.: Specularity removal: a global energy minimization approach based on polarization imaging. Comput. Vis. Image Underst. **158**(Suppl. C), 31–39 (2017)
5. Kobayashi, N., Okabe, T.: Separating reflection components in images under multispectral and multidirectional light sources. In: ICPR, pp. 3210–3215, December 2016
6. Shafer, S.A.: Using color to separate reflection components. Color Res. Appl. **10**(4), 210–218 (1985)
7. Berman, D., Treibitz, T., Avidan, S.: Non-local image dehazing. In: CVPR (2016)
8. Candès, E.J., Li, X., Ma, Y., Wright, J.: Robust principal component analysis? J. ACM **58**(3), 11:1–11:37 (2011)
9. Chandrasekaran, V., Sanghavi, S., Parrilo, P.A., Willsky, A.S.: Rank-sparsity incoherence for matrix decomposition. SIAM J. Optim. **21**(2), 572–596 (2011)
10. Zhou, X., Yang, C., Zhao, H., Yu, W.: Low-rank modeling and its applications in image analysis. ACM Comput. Surv. **47**(2) (2015)
11. Lee, H.C., Breneman, E.J., Schulte, C.P.: Modeling light reflection for computer color vision. IEEE Trans. Pattern Anal. Mach. Intell. **12**(4), 402–409 (1990)

12. Liu, G., Lin, Z., Yu, Y.: Robust subspace segmentation by low-rank representation. In: ICML, pp. 663–670 (2010)
13. Zhang, Y., Jiang, Z., Davis, L.S.: Learning structured low-rank representations for image classification. In: CVPR, June 2013
14. Lin, Z., Chen, M., Ma, Y.: The augmented lagrange multiplier method for exact recovery of corrupted low-rank matrices. Technical report, UIUC (2009)
15. Artusi, A., Banterle, F., Chetverikov, D.: A survey of specularity removal methods. Comput. Graph. Forum (2011)
16. Lin, S., Li, Y., Kang, S.B., Tong, X., Shum, H.-Y.: Diffuse-specular separation and depth recovery from image sequences. In: Heyden, A., Sparr, G., Nielsen, M., Johansen, P. (eds.) ECCV 2002. LNCS, vol. 2352, pp. 210–224. Springer, Heidelberg (2002). https://doi.org/10.1007/3-540-47977-5_14
17. Weiss, Y.: Deriving intrinsic images from image sequences. In: ICCV, pp. 68–75 (2001)
18. Lin, S., Shum, H.Y.: Separation of diffuse and specular reflection in color images. In: CVPR, pp. 341–346 (2001)
19. Sato, Y., Ikeuchi, K.: Temporal-color space analysis of reflection. J. Opt. Soc. Am. A 11(11), 2990–3002 (1994)
20. Feris, R., Raskar, R., Tan, K.H., Turk, M.: Specular reflection reduction with multi-flash imaging. SIBGRAP I, 316–321 (2004)
21. Agrawal, A., Raskar, R., Nayar, S.K., Li, Y.: Removing photography artifacts using gradient projection and flash-exposure sampling. ACM Trans. Graph. 24(3), 828–835 (2005)
22. Klinker, G.J., Shafer, S.A., Kanade, T.: The measurement of highlights in color images. Int. J. Comput. Vision 2(1), 7–32 (1988)
23. Schlüns, K., Teschner, M.: Analysis of 2D color spaces for highlight elimination in 3D shape reconstruction. In: ACCV, 801–805 (1995)
24. Bajcsy, R., Lee, S.W., Leonardis, A.: Detection of diffuse and specular interface reflections and inter-reflections by color image segmentation. Int. J. Comput. Vision 17(3), 241–272 (1996)
25. Tan, R.T., Ikeuchi, K.: Separating reflection components of textured surfaces using a single image. IEEE Trans. Pattern Anal. Mach. Intell. 27(2), 178–193 (2005)
26. Yang, Q., Wang, S., Ahuja, N.: Real-time specular highlight removal using bilateral filtering. In: Daniilidis, K., Maragos, P., Paragios, N. (eds.) ECCV 2010. LNCS, vol. 6314, pp. 87–100. Springer, Heidelberg (2010). https://doi.org/10.1007/978-3-642-15561-1_7
27. j. Yoon, K., Choi, Y., Kweon, I.S.: Fast separation of reflection components using a specularity-invariant image representation. In: ICIP, pp. 973–976 (2006)
28. Shen, H.L., Zhang, H.G., Shao, S.J., Xin, J.H.: Chromaticity-based separation of reflection components in a single image. Pattern Recogn. 41(8), 2461–2469 (2008)
29. Shen, H.L., Cai, Q.Y.: Simple and efficient method for specularity removal in an image. Appl. Opt. 48(14), 2711–2719 (2009)
30. Shen, H.L., Zheng, Z.H.: Real-time highlight removal using intensity ratio. Appl. Opt. 52(19), 4483–4493 (2013)
31. Kim, H., Jin, H., Hadap, S., Kweon, I.: Specular reflection separation using dark channel prior. In: CVPR, pp. 1460–1467, June 2013
32. Suo, J., An, D., Ji, X., Wang, H., Dai, Q.: Fast and high quality highlight removal from a single image. IEEE Trans. Image Process. 25(11), 5441–5454 (2016)
33. Liu, Y., Yuan, Z., Zheng, N., Wu, Y.: Saturation-preserving specular reflection separation. In: CVPR, pp. 3725–3733 (2015)

34. Mallick, S.P., Zickler, T., Belhumeur, P.N., Kriegman, D.J.: Specularity removal in images and videos: a pde approach. In: Leonardis, A., Bischof, H., Pinz, A. (eds.) ECCV 2006. LNCS, vol. 3951, pp. 550–563. Springer, Heidelberg (2006). https://doi.org/10.1007/11744023_43
35. Ren, W., Tian, J., Tang, Y.: Specular reflection separation with color-lines constraint. IEEE Trans. Image Process. **26**(5), 2327–2337 (2017)
36. Li, C., Lin, S., Zhou, K., Ikeuchi, K.: Specular highlight removal in facial images. In: CVPR, July 2017
37. Tan, P., Lin, S., Quan, L., Shum, H.Y.: Highlight removal by illumination-constrained inpainting. In: ICCV, pp. 164–169, October 2003
38. Tan, P., Quan, L., Lin, S.: Separation of highlight reflections on textured surfaces. In: CVPR, pp. 1855–1860 (2006)
39. Akashi, Y., Okatani, T.: Separation of reflection components by sparse non-negative matrix factorization. Comput. Vis. Image Underst. **146**(C), 77–85 (2016)
40. Tan, T.T., Nishino, K., Ikeuchi, K.: Illumination chromaticity estimation using inverse-intensity chromaticity space. In: Proceedings of the 2003 IEEE Computer Society Conference on Computer Vision and Pattern Recognition, vol. 1, pp. I-673–I-680 (2003)
41. Zhuang, L., Gao, H., Lin, Z., Ma, Y., Zhang, X., Yu, N.: Non-negative low rank and sparse graph for semi-supervised learning. In: CVPR, pp. 2328–2335 (2012)
42. Cai, J.F., Candès, E.J., Shen, Z.: A singular value thresholding algorithm for matrix completion. SIAM J. Optim. **20**(4), 1956–1982 (2010)
43. Gu, S., Xie, Q., Meng, D., Zuo, W., Feng, X., Zhang, L.: Weighted nuclear norm minimization and its applications to low level vision. Int. J. Comput. Vision **121**(2), 183–208 (2017)

Spatio-temporal Channel Correlation Networks for Action Classification

Ali Diba[1,4], Mohsen Fayyaz[2]($\boxtimes$), Vivek Sharma[3], M. Mahdi Arzani[4],
Rahman Yousefzadeh[4], Juergen Gall[2], and Luc Van Gool[1,4]

[1] ESAT-PSI, KU Leuven, Leuven, Belgium
{ali.diba,luc.vangool}@kuleuven.be
[2] University of Bonn, Bonn, Germany
{fayyaz,gall}@iai.uni-bonn.de
[3] CV:HCI, KIT, Karlsruhe, Germany
vivek.sharma@kit.edu
[4] Sensifai, Bruxelles, Belgium
{diba,arzani,ryzadeh,vangool}@sensifai.com

Abstract. The work in this paper is driven by the question if spatio-temporal correlations are enough for 3D convolutional neural networks (CNN)? Most of the traditional 3D networks use local spatio-temporal features. We introduce a new block that models correlations between channels of a 3D CNN with respect to temporal and spatial features. This new block can be added as a residual unit to different parts of 3D CNNs. We name our novel block 'Spatio-Temporal Channel Correlation' (STC). By embedding this block to the current state-of-the-art architectures such as ResNext and ResNet, we improve the performance by 2–3% on the Kinetics dataset. Our experiments show that adding STC blocks to current state-of-the-art architectures outperforms the state-of-the-art methods on the HMDB51, UCF101 and Kinetics datasets. The other issue in training 3D CNNs is about training them from scratch with a huge labeled dataset to get a reasonable performance. So the knowledge learned in 2D CNNs is completely ignored. Another contribution in this work is a simple and effective technique to transfer knowledge from a pre-trained 2D CNN to a randomly initialized 3D CNN for a stable weight initialization. This allows us to significantly reduce the number of training samples for 3D CNNs. Thus, by fine-tuning this network, we beat the performance of generic and recent methods in 3D CNNs, which were trained on large video datasets, e.g. Sports-1M, and fine-tuned on the target datasets, e.g. HMDB51/UCF101.

1 Introduction

Compelling advantages of exploiting temporal rather than merely spatial cues for video classification have been shown lately [1–3]. In recent works, researchers

---

Ali Diba and Mohsen Fayyaz contributed equally to this work. Mohsen Fayyaz contributed to this work while he was at Sensifai.

© Springer Nature Switzerland AG 2018
V. Ferrari et al. (Eds.): ECCV 2018, LNCS 11208, pp. 299–315, 2018.
https://doi.org/10.1007/978-3-030-01225-0_18

have focused on improving modeling of spatio-temporal correlations. Like 2D CNNs, 3D CNNs try to learn local correlation along input channels. Therefore, 3D CNNs neglect the hidden information in between channels correlations in both directions: space and time, which limits the performance of these architectures. Another major problem in using 3D CNNs is training the video architectures calls for extra large labeled datasets. All of these issues negatively influence their computational cost and performance. To avoid these limitations, we propose (i) a new network architecture block that efficiently captures both spatial-channels and temporal-channels correlation information throughout network layers; and (ii) an effective supervision transfer that bridges the knowledge transfer between different architectures, such that training the networks from scratch is no longer needed.

Motivated by the above observations, we introduce the spatio-temporal channel correlation (STC) block. The aim of this block is considering the information of inter channels correlations over the spatial and temporal features simultaneously. For any set of transformation in the network (e.g. convolutional layers) a STC block can be used for performing spatio-temporal channel correlation feature learning. The STC block has two branches: a spatial correlation branch (SCB) and a temporal correlation branch (TCB). The SCB considers spatial channel-wise information while TCB considers the temporal channel-wise information. The input features $I \in \mathbb{R}^{H \times W \times T \times C}$ are fed to SCB and TCB. In SCB a spatial global pooling operation is done to generate a representation of the global receptive field which plays two vital roles in the network: (i) considering global correlations in I by aggregating the global features over the input, (ii) providing a channel-wise descriptor for analyzing the between channels correlations. This channel-wise feature vector is then fed to two bottleneck fully connected layers which learn the dependencies between channels. The same procedure happens in TCB, however, for the first step a temporal global pooling is used instead of the spatial global pooling. Output features of these two branches are then combined and returned as the output of the STC block. These output features can be combined with the output features of the corresponding layer(s). By employing such features along-side traditional features available inside a 3D CNN, we enrich the representation capability of 3D CNNs. Therefore, the STC block equipped 3D CNNs are capable of learning channel wise dependencies which enables them to learn better representations of videos. We have added the STC block to the current state-of-the-art 3D CNN architectures such as 3D-ResNext and 3D-ResNet [4]. The STC block is inserted after each residual block of these networks.

As mentioned before, training 3D CNNs from scratch needs a large labeled dataset. It has been shown that training 3D Convolution Networks [2] from scratch takes two months [5] for them to learn a good feature representation from a large scale dataset like Sports-1M, which is then finetuned on target datasets to improve performance. Another major contribution of our work therefore is to achieve supervision transfer across architectures, thus avoiding the need to train 3D CNNs from scratch. Specifically, we show that a 2D CNN pre-trained on ImageNet can act as 'a teacher' for supervision transfer to a randomly initialized

3D CNN for a stable weight initialization. In this way we avoid the excessive computational workload and training time. Through this transfer learning, we outperform the performance of generic 3D CNNs (C3D [2]) which was trained on Sports-1M and finetuned on the target datasets HMDB51 and UCF101.

2   Related Work

Video Classification with and without CNNs: Video classification and understanding has been studied for decades. Several techniques have been proposed to come up with efficient spatio-temporal feature representations that capture the appearance and motion propagation across frames in videos, such as HOG3D [6], SIFT3D [7], HOF [8], ESURF [9], MBH [10], iDTs [11], and more. These were all hand-engineered. Among these, iDTs yielded the best performance, at the expense of being computationally expensive and lacking scalability to capture semantic concepts. It is noteworthy that recently several other techniques [12] have been proposed that also try to model the temporal structure in an efficient way.

Using deep learning, the community went beyond hand-engineered representations and learned the spatio-temporal representations in an end-to-end manner. These methods operate on 2D (frame-level) or 3D (video-level) information. In the 2D setting, CNN-based features of individual frames are modeled via LSTMs/RNNs to capture long-term temporal dependencies [3,13], or via feature aggregation and encoding using Bilinear models [1], VLAD [14], Fisher encoding [15] etc. Recently, several temporal architectures have been proposed for video classification, where the input to the network consists of either RGB video clips or stacked optical-flow frames. The filters and pooling kernels for these architectures are 3D (x, y, time). The most intuitive are 3D convolutions ($s \times s \times d$) [3] where the kernel temporal depth d corresponds to the number of frames used as input, and s is the kernel spatial size. Simonyan et al. [16] proposed a two-stream network, cohorts of RGB and flow CNNs. In their flow stream CNNs, the 3D convolution has d set to 10. Tran et al. [2] explored 3D CNNs with filter kernel of size $3 \times 3 \times 3$ and in [5] extended the ResNet architecture with 3D convolutions. Feichtenhofer et al. [17] propose 3D pooling. Sun et al. [18] decomposed the 3D convolutions into 2D spatial and 1D temporal convolutions. Carreira et al. [19] proposed converting a pre-trained 2D Inception-V1 [20] architecture to 3D by inflating all the filters and pooling kernels with an additional temporal dimension d. The Non-local Neural Networks [21] proposes a new building block for CNNs which captures long range dependencies. Feichtenhofer et al. [22] introduce residual connections for learning the dependencies between motion and appearance stream of a two stream CNN. Varol et al. [23] have studied the long-term temporal convolutions for learning better representations of long-term activities in video. The spatio-temporal feature gating method introduced in [24] addresses a similar issue by introducing the feature gating module. Miech et al. [25] introduce the context gating method which applies gating to the features of the output layer. Most of these architectures neglect the channel wise information throughout the whole architecture. To the best of our knowledge, our STC block is the first 3D block that integrates channel wise information over 3D networks' layers.

Transfer Learning: Finetuning or specializing the learned feature representations of a pre-trained network trained on another dataset to a target dataset is commonly referred to as transfer learning. Recently, several works have shown that transferring knowledge within or across modalities (e.g. RGB→RGB [26] vs. RGB→Depth [27], RGB→Optical-Flow [27,28], RGB→Sound [29], Near-Infrared→RGB [30]) is effective, and leads to significant improvements in performance. They typically amount to jointly learning representations in a shared feature space. Mansimov et al. [31] have studied various methods of weight initialization which are the principle idea for inflation approaches. Our work differs substantially. Our goal is to transfer supervision across architectures (i.e. 2D→3D CNNs), not necessarily limited to transferring information between RGB models only, as our solution can be easily adopted across modalities too (Fig. 1).

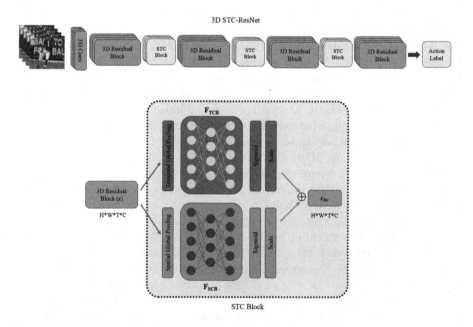

Fig. 1. STC-ResNet. Our STC block is applied to the 3D ResNet. The 3D network uses video clips as input. The 3D feature-maps from the clips are densely propagated throughout the network. The STC operates on the different levels of feature maps in the network to extract spatial and temporal channel relations as new source of information. The output of the network is a video-level prediction.

3 Proposed Method

Our approach with the newly proposed neural block, STC, is to capture different and new information in deep CNNs from videos. The spatio-temporal channel correlation block is meant to extract relations between different channels in the different layers of 3D CNNs. The STC block considers these relations in space and time dimensions. In addition, as another major contribution of our work, we show knowledge transfer between cross architectures (i.e. 2D→3D CNNs), thus avoiding the need to train 3D CNNs from scratch. Details about the transfer learning is given in Sect. 3.2.

3.1 Spatio-Temporal Channel Correlation (STC) Block

STC is a computational block which can be added to any 3D CNN architecture. Therefore, we have added our STC block to the ResNet and ResNext 3D CNNs introduced by [4]. After each convolutional block in ResNet and ResNext, the STC blocks are inserted to enrich the feature representation. As it was mentioned previously, this new block is exploiting both spatial and temporal information by considering the filters correlation in both spatial and temporal dimension. As input to the STC block, we consider feature maps coming from previous convolution layers.

The STC block has a dual path structure which represents different levels of concept and information. Each of these paths have different modules; channel or filter information embedding and capturing dependencies. Our approach is inspired by the Squeeze-and-Excitation [32] method which uses global average pooling (spatial and temporal) following with two bottleneck fully connected layers and sigmoid activation. In contrast to [32], the STC block has two branches or in other words a dual path; one considering pure channel-wise information and the other takes temporal channel-wise information. Since we are solving video classification, it makes sense to extract more meaningful representations in both spatial and temporal approaches. The STC is capturing channel dependencies information based on this theory. In the following we describe both branches and their integration into the known 3D architectures like 3D-ResNet [4].

Notation. The output feature-maps of the 3D convolutions and pooling kernels at the lth layer extracted for an input video is a tensor $X \in \mathbb{R}^{H \times W \times T \times C}$ where H, W, T and C are the height, width, temporal depth and number of channels of the feature maps, respectively. The 3D convolution and pooling kernels are of size $(s \times s \times d)$, where d is the temporal depth and s is the spatial size of the kernels.

Temporal Correlation Branch (TCB): In this path the feature map will be squeezed by both spatial and temporal dimensions to extract channel descriptors. If we consider X as the input to STC, the output of the first stage, which is a global spatio-temporal pooling is:

$$z_{tcb} = \frac{1}{W \times H \times T} \sum_i^W \sum_j^H \sum_t^T x_{ijt} \, . \tag{1}$$

To obtain the filters non-linear relations, we apply two fully connected layers. The feature dimension is reduced in the first FC layer to C/r (r is reduction ratio) and is increased again to C by the second FC layer. Since we used global spatial-temporal pooling over all dimensions of receptive fields, in the next operation, channel-wise information will be extracted. Right after the sigmoid function, the output of the temporal branch (x_{tcb}) will be calculated by rescaling X using the s_{tcb} vector. So s_{tcb}, output of the bottleneck layers, and x_{tcb}, the branch output, are calculated in this way:

$$s_{tcb} = F_{tcb}(z_{tcb}, W) = W_2(W_1 z_{tcb}) \tag{2}$$

$$x_{tcb} = s_{tcb} \cdot X . \tag{3}$$

W is the parameter set for the bottleneck layers, including $W_1 \in \mathbb{R}^{\frac{C}{r} \times C}$, $W_2 \in \mathbb{R}^{C \times \frac{C}{r}}$ which are FC layers parameters respectively. F_{tcb} is the symbol of fully-connected functions to calculate the s_{tcb}.

Table 1. 3D ResNet vs. STC-ResNet and STC-ResNext. All the proposed architectures incorporate 3D filters and pooling kernels. Each convolution layer shown in the table corresponds the composite sequence BN-ReLU-Conv operations.

Layers	Output Size	3D-ResNet101	3D STC-ResNet101	3D STC-ResNext101
3D Convolution	$56 \times 56 \times 8$	\multicolumn{3}{c}{$7 \times 7 \times 7$ conv, stride 2}		
3D Pooling	$56 \times 56 \times 8$	\multicolumn{3}{c}{$3 \times 3 \times 3$ max pool, stride 1}		
Res_1	$28 \times 28 \times 8$	$\begin{bmatrix} conv, 1 \times 1 \times 1, 64 \\ conv, 3 \times 3 \times 3, 64 \\ conv, 1 \times 1 \times 1, 256 \end{bmatrix} \times 3$	$\begin{matrix} conv, 1 \times 1 \times 1, 64 \\ conv, 3 \times 3 \times 3, 64 \\ conv, 1 \times 1 \times 1, 256 \\ fc, [16, 256] \end{matrix} \times 3$	$\begin{matrix} conv, 1 \times 1 \times 1, 128 \\ conv, 3 \times 3 \times 3, 128 \quad C = 32 \\ conv, 1 \times 1 \times 1, 256 \\ fc, [16, 256] \end{matrix} \times 3$
Res_2	$14 \times 14 \times 4$	$\begin{bmatrix} conv, 1 \times 1 \times 1, 128 \\ conv, 3 \times 3 \times 3, 128 \\ conv, 1 \times 1 \times 1, 512 \end{bmatrix} \times 4$	$\begin{matrix} conv, 1 \times 1 \times 1, 128 \\ conv, 3 \times 3 \times 3, 128 \\ conv, 1 \times 1 \times 1, 512 \\ fc, [32, 512] \end{matrix} \times 4$	$\begin{matrix} conv, 1 \times 1 \times 1, 256 \\ conv, 3 \times 3 \times 3, 256 \quad C = 32 \\ conv, 1 \times 1 \times 1, 512 \\ fc, [32, 512] \end{matrix} \times 4$
Res_3	$7 \times 7 \times 2$	$\begin{bmatrix} conv, 1 \times 1 \times 1, 256 \\ conv, 3 \times 3 \times 3, 256 \\ conv, 1 \times 1 \times 1, 1024 \end{bmatrix} \times 23$	$\begin{matrix} conv, 1 \times 1 \times 1, 256 \\ conv, 3 \times 3 \times 3, 256 \\ conv, 1 \times 1 \times 1, 1024 \\ fc, [64, 1024] \end{matrix} \times 23$	$\begin{matrix} conv, 1 \times 1 \times 1, 512 \\ conv, 3 \times 3 \times 3, 512 \quad C = 32 \\ conv, 1 \times 1 \times 1, 1024 \\ fc, [64, 1024] \end{matrix} \times 23$
Res_4	$4 \times 4 \times 1$	$\begin{bmatrix} conv, 1 \times 1 \times 1, 512 \\ conv, 3 \times 3 \times 3, 512 \\ conv, 1 \times 1 \times 1, 2048 \end{bmatrix} \times 3$	$\begin{matrix} conv, 1 \times 1 \times 1, 512 \\ conv, 3 \times 3 \times 3, 512 \\ conv, 1 \times 1 \times 1, 2048 \\ fc, [128, 2048] \end{matrix} \times 3$	$\begin{matrix} conv, 1 \times 1 \times 1, 512 \\ conv, 3 \times 3 \times 3, 512 \quad C = 32 \\ conv, 1 \times 1 \times 1, 2048 \\ fc, [128, 2048] \end{matrix} \times 3$
Classification	$1 \times 1 \times 1$	\multicolumn{3}{c}{$4 \times 4 \times 1$ avg pool}		
Layer		\multicolumn{3}{c}{400D softmax}		

Spatial Correlation Branch (SCB): The main difference in this branch compared to the temporal branch is in the aggregation method. The spatial branch shrinks the channel-wise information with respect to the temporal dimension and does global spatial pooling on the input feature map. Therefore this branch is considering the temporal-channel information extraction to enrich the representation in each layer. The calculation of the first operation of the branch comes as following:

$$z_{scb} = \frac{1}{W \times H} \sum_{i}^{W} \sum_{j}^{H} x_{ijT} \tag{4}$$

After the pooling layer, we obtain z_{scb} which is a vector with size of $T \times C$. Afterward, there are the fully connected layers to extract the temporal based channel relations. In this branch the first FC layer size is $(T \times C)/r$ and the second FC size is C. Here is the computation description:

$$s_{scb} = F_{scb}(z_{scb}, W) = W_2(W_1 z_{scb}) \tag{5}$$

$$x_{scb} = s_{scb} \cdot X \tag{6}$$

with $W_1 \in \mathbb{R}^{\frac{(T \times C)}{r} \times (T \times C)}$ and $W_2 \in \mathbb{R}^{C \times \frac{T \times C}{r}}$. By considering both of the branches, the final output of the block (x_{stc}) is computed by averaging over x_{tcb} and x_{scb}.

$$x_{stc} = avg(x_{tcb}, x_{scb}) \tag{7}$$

In the case of 3D ResNet or ResNext, this output will be added to the residual layer to have the final output of the Convolution (Conv) blocks (Table 1).

3.2   Knowledge Transfer

In this section, we describe our method for transferring knowledge between architectures, i.e. pre-trained 2D CNNs to 3D CNNs. Therefore we bypass the need to train the 3D CNNs from scratch with supervision or training with large datasets.

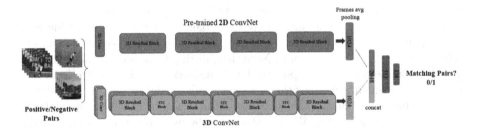

Fig. 2. Architecture for knowledge transfer from a pre-trained 2D CNN to a 3D CNN. The 2D network operates on RGB frames, and the 3D network operates on video clips for the same time stamp. The 2D CNN acts as a teacher for knowledge transfer to the 3D CNN, by teaching the 3D CNN to learn mid-level feature representation by solving an image-video correspondence task. The model parameters of the 2D CNN are frozen, while the task is to effectively learn the model parameters of the 3D CNN only.

Lets $\mathcal{I}$ be a pre-trained 2D CNN which has learned a rich representation from labeled images dataset, while $\mathcal{V}$ being a 3D CNN which is randomly initialized using [33] and we want to transfer the knowledge of the representation from $\mathcal{I}$ to $\mathcal{V}$ for a stable weight initialization. This allows us to avoid training $\mathcal{V}$ from scratch, which has million more parameters, and would require heavy computational workload and training time of months [5]. In the current setup, $\mathcal{I}$ acts as a teacher for knowledge transfer to the $\mathcal{V}$ architecture.

Intuitively, our method uses correspondence between frames and video clips available by the virtue of them appearing together at the same time. Given a pair of X frames and video clip for the same time stamp, the visual information in both frames and video are the same. We leverage this for learning mid-level feature representations by an image-video correspondence task between the 2D and 3D CNN architecture, as depicted in Fig. 2. We use 2D ResNet [34] pretrained on ImageNet [35] as $\mathcal{I}$, and the STC-ResNet network as $\mathcal{V}$. The 2D ResNet CNN has 4 convolution blocks and one fully connected layer at the end, while our 3D architecture has 4 3D-convolution blocks with an STC block and we add a fully-connected layer after the last block. We concatenate the last fc layers of both architectures, and connect them with the 2048-dimensional fc layer which is in turn connected to two fully connected layers with 512 and 128 sizes (fc1, fc2) and to the final binary classifier layer. We use a binary matching classifier: given X frames and a video clip, decide whether the pairs belong to each other or not. For a given pair, X frames are fed sequentially into the network $\mathcal{I}$ and we average the last 2D fc features over the X frames, resulting in a 1024-D feature representation. In parallel the video clip is fed to the network $\mathcal{V}$, and we extract the 3D fc features (1024-D), and concatenate them, which is then passed to the fully connected layers for classification. For training, we use a binary classification loss.

During the training, the model parameters of $\mathcal{I}$ are frozen, while the task is to effectively learn the model parameters of $\mathcal{V}$ without any additional supervision than correspondences between frames and video. The pairs belonging to the same time stamp from the same video are positive pairs, while the pairs coming from two different videos by randomly sampling X frames and video clips from two different videos is a negative pair. Note that, during back-propagation, only the model parameters for $\mathcal{V}$ are updated, i.e., transferring the knowledge from $\mathcal{I}$ to $\mathcal{V}$. In our experiments we show that a stable weight initialization of $\mathcal{V}$ is achieved, and when fine-tuned on the target dataset, it adapts quickly, thus avoiding training the model from scratch. We also show that by using our proposed knowledge transfer method, 3D CNNs can be trained directly on small datasets like UCF101 and achieve a better performance than training from scratch.

Since our transfer learning is unsupervised and there is no need of video label, we have applied on a collection of unlabeled videos. Further, our experiments in Sect. 4 demonstrate that our proposed transfer learning of STC-ResNext outperforms the generic 3D CNNs by a significant margin which was trained on a large video dataset, Sports-1M [36], and finetuned on the target datasets, HMDB51 or UCF101.

4   Experiments

In this section, we first introduce the datasets and implementation details of our proposed approach. Afterwards, we provide an extensive study on the architecture of the proposed STC-ResNet and STC-ResNext, which are 3D CNNs. Following, we evaluate and compare our proposed methods with the baselines and other state-of-the-art methods. Finally, we compare our transfer learning: $2D \rightarrow 3D$ CNN performance with generic state-of-the-art 3D CNN methods.

4.1   Datasets

We evaluate our proposed method on three challenging video datasets with human actions, namely HMDB51 [37], UCF101 [38], and Kinetics [19]. Table 2 shows the details of the datasets. For all of these datasets, we use the standard training/testing splits and protocols provided by the datasets. For HMDB51 and UCF101, we report the average accuracy over the three splits and for Kinetics, we report the performance on the validation and test set.

Kinetics: Kinetics is a new challenging human action recognition dataset introduced by [19], which contains 400 action classes. There are two versions of this dataset: untrimmed and trimmed. The untrimmed videos contain the whole video in which the activity is included in a short period of it. However, the trimmed videos contain the activity part only. We evaluate our models on the trimmed version. We use all training videos for training our models from scratch.

UCF101: For evaluating our STC-Nets architectures, we first trained them on the Kinetics dataset, and then fine-tuned them on UCF101. Furthermore, we also evaluate our models by training them from scratch on UCF101 using randomly initialized weights to be able to investigate the effect of pre-training on a huge dataset, such as Kinetics.

HMDB51: Same as UCF101 evaluation we fine-tune the models on HMDB51, which were pre-trained from scratch on Kinetics. Also, we similarly evaluate our models by training them from scratch on HMDB51 using randomly initialized weights.

Table 2. Details of the datasets used for evaluation. The 'Clips' shows the total number of short video clips extracted from the 'Videos' available in the dataset.

Data-set	# Clips	# Videos	# Classes
HMDB51 [37]	6,766	3,312	51
UCF101 [38]	13,320	2,500	101
Kinetics [19]	306,245	306,245	400

4.2   Implementation Details

We use the PyTorch framework for the implementation and all the networks are trained on 8 Tesla P100 NVIDIA GPUs. Here, we describe the implementation details of our two schemes, 3D CNN architectures and knowledge transfer from 2D to 3D CNNs for stable weight initialization.

STC-Nets.

Training: We train our STC-Nets (STC-ResNet/ResNext) from scratch on Kinetics. Our STC-Net operates on a stack of 16/32/64 RGB frames. We resize the video to 122px when smaller, and then randomly apply 5 crops (and their horizontal flips) of size 112×112. For the network weight initialization, we adopt the same technique proposed in [33]. For the network training, we use SGD, Nesterov momentum of 0.9, weight decay of 10^{-4} and batch size of 128. The initial learning rate is set to 0.1, and reduced by a factor of 10 manually when the validation loss is saturated. The maximum number of epochs for the whole Kinetics dataset is set to 200. Batch normalization also has been applied. The reduction parameter in STC blocks, r, is set to 4.

Testing: For video prediction, we decompose each video into non-overlapping clips of 16/32/64 frames. The STC-Net is applied over the video clips by taking a 112×112 center-crop, and finally we average the predictions over all clips to make a video-level prediction.

Knowledge Transfer: $2D \rightarrow 3D$ **_CNNs._** We employ 2D ResNet architecture, pre-trained on ImageNet [35], while the 3D CNN is our STC-ResNet network. To the 2D CNN, 16 RGB frames are fed as input. The input RGB images are randomly cropped to the size 112×112, and then mean-subtracted for the network training. To supervise transfer to the STC-ResNet, we replace the previous classification layer of the 2D CNN with a 2-way softmax layer to distinguish between positive and negative pairs. We use stochastic gradient descent (SGD) with mini-batch size of 32 with a fixed weight decay of 10^{-4} and Nesterov momentum of 0.9. For network training, we start with learning rate set to 0.1 and decrease it by a factor of 10 every 30 epochs. The maximum number of epochs is set to 150. For training data, we use approx. 500 K unlabeled videos from YouTube8m dataset [39].

4.3 Ablation Study on Architecture Design

To evaluate our STC block on 3D CNNs model, we conducted an architecture study and evaluated different configurations. For this work, we mainly focused on 3D versions for ResNet and ResNext with different input size and depth. Our choice is based on the recently presented good performance of these networks in video classification [4].

Model Depth: We first analyze the impact of the architecture depth with 3D-ResNet and 3D-ResNext and we have done a series of evaluations on the network size. For the architecture study, the model weights were initialized using [33].

We employ three different sizes of 3D STC-ResNet; 18, 50, 101 with STC blocks. Evaluations results of these 3D STC-ResNet models are reported in the Table 3. As it can be observed, by adding small overhead of STC blocks, STC-Nets can achieve reasonable performance even in a smaller version of ResNet, since our STC-ResNet50 is comparable in accuracy with a regular ResNet101.

Table 3. Evaluation results of 3D STC-ResNet model with network sizes of 18, 50, and 101 on UCF101 split 1. All models were trained from scratch.

Model Depth	Accuracy %
3D-ResNet 101	46.7
STC-ResNet 18	42.8
STC-ResNet 50	46.2
STC-ResNet 101	**47.9**

Temporal Input Size: The number of input frames plays a key role in activity recognition. Therefore, we have reported the performance of our 3D STC-ResNet and 3D STC-ResNext with different number of input frames in Table 4. Our evaluation shows that longer clips as input will yield better performance, which confirms the observations made in [4, 19].

Table 4. Evaluation results of STC-ResNet and 3D STC-ResNext models with temporal depths of 16, 32, and 64 frames for all three splits of UCF101 and HMDB51.

Model	UCF101	HMDB51
STC-ResNet 101 (16 frames)	90.1	62.6
STC-ResNet 101 (32 frames)	93.2	68.9
STC-ResNet 101 (64 frames)	93.7	70.5
STC-ResNext 101 (16 frames)	92.3	65.4
STC-ResNext 101 (32 frames)	95.8	72.6
STC-ResNext 101 (64 frames)	96.5	74.9

TCB vs SCB: We also have studied the impact of the TCB and SCB branches in our STC-Nets. Since each of them considers a different concept in the branch, we evaluated the performance for three settings: SCB only, TCB only, and SCB-TCB combination (STC). In Table 5, the importance of the channel correlation branches is shown. As it is shown, incorporating both branches to capture different types of correlations is performing better than SCB or TCB alone.

Table 5. Performance comparison using different channel correlation blocks (TCB vs SCB) for UCF101 split 1.

Channel correlation branch	Accuracy %
SCB	46.1
TCB	47.2
TCB + SCB	**47.9**

Frame Sampling Rate: Finding the right configuration of input-frames which are fed to the CNNs for capturing the appearance and temporal information plays a very critical role in temporal CNNs. For this reason, we investigated the impact of the frame sampling rate for the input stream. The STC-ResNet101 has been used for the ablation study on frame sampling rate for training and testing. We evaluate the model by varying the temporal stride of the input frames in the following set {1, 2, 4, 16}. Table 6 presents the accuracy of STC-ResNet101 trained on inputs with different sampling rates. The best results are obtained with sampling rate of 2, which we also used for other 3D CNNs in the rest of the experiments.

Table 6. Evaluation results of different frame sampling rates for the STC-ResNet101 model. Trained and tested on UCF101 split 1.

Input Stride	1	2	4	16
Accuracy %	44.6%	**47.9%**	46.8%	40.3%

4.4   Knowledge Transfer

To apply our proposed supervision transfer, we have tested 2D ResNet as basic pre-trained model on ImageNet, while 3D-ResNet and our STC-ResNet are randomly initialized using [33] and used as target 3D CNNs. We show that a stable weight initialization via transfer learning is possible for 3D CNN architectures, which can be used as a good starting model for training on small datasets like UCF101 or HMDB51. Since the transfer learning pipeline for 3D CNNs have been tested with two different deep architectures (3D-ResNet and STC-Nets), we clearly show the generalization capacity of our method in deep architectures, which can be easily adopted for other deep networks and tasks which use the similar architectures.

Table 7. Transfer learning results for 3D CNNs by 2D CNNs over all three splits of UCF101 and HMDB51. All models have the same depth of 101.

3D CNNs	UCF101	HMDB51
3D-ResNet-Baseline	88.9	61.7
3D-ResNet-Inflation	90.4	62.6
3D-ResNet-**Transfered**	91.3	64.2
STC-ResNet-Baseline	90.1	62.6
STC-ResNet-**Transfered**	92.6	66.1

Table 7 shows the results. The baseline is trained from scratch using random initialization. As it is shown, our transfer method performs better than the baseline for the standard 3D-ResNet as well as for our proposed STC-ResNet. Using inflation also improves the baseline, but it is outperformed by our approach. Note that inflation can only be used if the structure of the 2D and 3D network are the same, while our approach allows to transfer the knowledge from any 2D CNN to a 3D CNN, e.g., from 2D-ResNet to the 3D STC-ResNet as in Table 7, which is not possible by inflation.

Table 8. Comparison results of our models with other state-of-the-art methods on Kinetics dataset. * denotes the pre-trained version of C3D on the Sports-1M.

Method	Top1-Val	Top5-Val
DenseNet3D	59.5	-
Inception3D	58.9	-
C3D* [4]	55.6	-
3D ResNet101 [4]	62.8	83.9
3D ResNext101 [4]	65.1	85.7
RGB-I3D [19]	68.4	88
STC-ResNet101 (16 frames)	64.1	85.2
STC-ResNext101 (16 frames)	66.2	86.5
STC-ResNext101 (32 frames)	**68.7**	**88.5**

4.5 Comparison with the State-of-the-art

Finally, after exploring and studying on STC-Net architectures and the configuration of input-data and architecture, we compare our STC-ResNet and STC-ResNext with the state-of-the-art methods by pre-training on Kinetics and fine-tuning on all three splits of the UCF101 and HMDB51 datasets. For UCF101 and HMDB51, we report the average accuracy over all three splits. The results for supervision transfer technique experiments were reported in the previous part of experiments.

Table 8 shows the result on Kinetics dataset for STC-Nets compared with state-of-the-art methods. The STC-ResNext101 with 32 frames input depth achieves higher accuracies than RGB-I3D which has the input size of 64 frames.

Table 9 shows the results on the UCF101 and HMDB51 datasets for comparison of STC-Nets with other RGB based action recognition methods. Our STC-ResNext101 (64 frames) model outperforms the 3D-ResNet [5], Inception3D, RGB-I3D [19] and C3D [2] on both UCF101 and HMDB51 and achieves 96.5% and 74.9% accuracy respectively. We also trained Inception3D, a similar architecture to the I3D [19], without using ImageNet on Kinetics and fine-tuned it on UCF101 and HMDB51 to be able to have a fair comparison. As shown in Table 9, STC-ResNext performs better than 3D-ResNext by almost 2% on UCF101. Moreover, we note that the state-of-the-art CNNs [19,42] use expensive optical-flow maps in addition to RGB input-frames, as in I3D which obtains a performance of 98% on UCF101 and 80% on HMDB51. Because of such a high computation needs, we are not able to run the similar experiments, but as it can be concluded from Table 9, our best RGB model has superior performance than the other RGB based models.

Table 9. Accuracy (%) performance comparison of STC-Nets (STC-ResNet/ResNext) with state-of-the-art methods over all three splits of UCF101 and HMDB51.

Method	UCF101	HMDB51
DT+MVSM [40]	83.5	55.9
iDT+FV [11]	85.9	57.2
C3D [2]	82.3	56.8
Conv Fusion [17]	82.6	56.8
Two Stream [16]	88.6	–
TDD+FV [41]	90.3	63.2
RGB+Flow-TSN [42]	94.0	68.5
P3D [43]	88.6	–
RGB-I3D [19]	95.6	74.8
RGB+Flow-I3D [19]	**98.0**	**80.7**
Inception3D	87.2	56.9
3D ResNet 101 (16 frames)	88.9	61.7
3D ResNet 101-Transfered Knowledge	91.3	64.2
3D ResNext 101 (16 frames)	90.7	63.8
STC-ResNext 101 (16 frames)	92.3	65.4
STC-ResNext 101 (64 frames)	96.5	74.9

Note that in our work we have not used dense optical-flow maps, and still achieving comparable performance to the state-of-the-art methods [42]. This shows the effectiveness of our STC-Nets to exploit temporal information and spatio-temporal channel correlation in deep CNNs for video clips. This calls for efficient methods like ours instead of computing the expensive optical-flow information (beforehand) which is very computationally demanding, and therefore difficult to obtain for large scale datasets.

5   Conclusion

In this work, we introduced a new 'Spatio-Temporal Channel Correlation' (STC) block that models correlations between the channels of a 3D CNN. We clearly show the benefit of exploiting spatio-temporal channel correlations features using the STC block. We equipped 3D-ResNet and 3D-ResNext with our STC block and improved the accuracies by 2–3% on the Kinetics dataset. Our STC blocks are added as a residual unit to other parts of networks and learned in an end-to-end manner. The STC feature-maps model the feature interaction in a more expressive and efficient way without an undesired loss of information throughout the network. Our STC-Nets are evaluated on three challenging action recognition datasets, namely HMDB51, UCF101, and Kinetics. The STC-Net architectures achieve state-of-the-art performance on HMDB51, UCF101 and comparable results on Kinetics in comparison to other temporal deep neural network models. We expect that the proposed STC blocks will also improve other 3D CNNs. Further, we show the benefit of transfer learning between cross architectures, specifically supervision transfer from 2D to 3D CNNs. This provides a valuable and stable weight initialization for 3D CNNs instead of training them from scratch which is also very expensive. Our transfer learning approach is not limited to transfer supervision between RGB models only, as our approach for transfer learning can be easily adopted for transfer across modalities.

Acknowledgements. This work was supported by DBOF PhD scholarship, KU Leuven:CAMETRON project, and KIT:DFG-PLUMCOT project. The authors would like to thank Sensifai engineering team. Mohsen Fayyaz and Juergen Gall have been financially supported by the DFG project GA 1927/4-1 (Research Unit FOR 2535) and the ERC Starting Grant ARCA (677650).

References

1. Diba, A., Sharma, V., Van Gool, L.: Deep temporal linear encoding networks. In: CVPR (2017)
2. Tran, D., Bourdev, L., Fergus, R., Torresani, L., Paluri, M.: Learning spatiotemporal features with 3D convolutional networks. In: ICCV (2015)
3. Yue-Hei Ng, J., Hausknecht, M., Vijayanarasimhan, S., Vinyals, O., Monga, R., Toderici, G.: Beyond short snippets: Deep networks for video classification. In: CVPR (2015)
4. Hara, K., Kataoka, H., Satoh, Y.: Can spatiotemporal 3D CNNS retrace the history of 2D CNNS and imagenet? In: CVPR (2018)
5. Tran, D., Ray, J., Shou, Z., Chang, S.F., Paluri, M.: Convnet architecture search for spatiotemporal feature learning. arXiv:1708.05038 (2017)
6. Klaser, A., Marszałek, M., Schmid, C.: A spatio-temporal descriptor based on 3D-gradients. In: BMVC (2008)
7. Scovanner, P., Ali, S., Shah, M.: A 3-dimensional sift descriptor and its application to action recognition. In: ACM'MM (2007)
8. Laptev, I., Marszalek, M., Schmid, C., Rozenfeld, B.: Learning realistic human actions from movies. In: CVPR (2008)

9. Willems, G., Tuytelaars, T., Van Gool, L.: An efficient dense and scale-invariant spatio-temporal interest point detector. In: Forsyth, D., Torr, P., Zisserman, A. (eds.) ECCV 2008. LNCS, vol. 5303, pp. 650–663. Springer, Heidelberg (2008). https://doi.org/10.1007/978-3-540-88688-4_48

10. Dalal, N., Triggs, B., Schmid, C.: Human detection using oriented histograms of flow and appearance. In: Leonardis, A., Bischof, H., Pinz, A. (eds.) ECCV 2006. LNCS, vol. 3952, pp. 428–441. Springer, Heidelberg (2006). https://doi.org/10.1007/11744047_33

11. Wang, H., Schmid, C.: Action recognition with improved trajectories. In: ICCV (2013)

12. Fernando, B., Gavves, E., Oramas, J.M., Ghodrati, A., Tuytelaars, T.: Modeling video evolution for action recognition. In: CVPR (2015)

13. Donahue, J., et al.: Long-term recurrent convolutional networks for visual recognition and description. In: CVPR (2015)

14. Girdhar, R., Ramanan, D., Gupta, A., Sivic, J., Russell, B.: Actionvlad: Learning spatio-temporal aggregation for action classification. In: CVPR (2017)

15. Tang, P., Wang, X., Shi, B., Bai, X., Liu, W., Tu, Z.: Deep fishernet for object classification. arXiv:1608.00182 (2016)

16. Simonyan, K., Zisserman, A.: Two-stream convolutional networks for action recognition in videos. In: NIPS (2014)

17. Feichtenhofer, C., Pinz, A., Zisserman, A.: Convolutional two-stream network fusion for video action recognition. In: CVPR (2016)

18. Sun, L., Jia, K., Yeung, D.Y., Shi, B.E.: Human action recognition using factorized spatio-temporal convolutional networks. In: ICCV (2015)

19. Carreira, J., Zisserman, A.: Quo vadis, action recognition? a new model and the kinetics dataset. In: CVPR (2017)

20. Ioffe, S., Szegedy, C.: Batch normalization: Accelerating deep network training by reducing internal covariate shift. In: ICML (2015)

21. Wang, X., Girshick, R., Gupta, A., He, K.: Non-local neural networks. In: CVPR (2018)

22. Feichtenhofer, C., Pinz, A., Wildes, R.: Spatiotemporal residual networks for video action recognition. In: Advances in Neural Information Processing Systems, pp. 3468–3476 (2016)

23. Varol, G., Laptev, I., Schmid, C.: Long-term temporal convolutions for action recognition. IEEE Trans. Pattern Anal. Mach. Intell. (2017)

24. Xie, S., Sun, C., Huang, J., Tu, Z., Murphy, K.: Rethinking spatiotemporal feature learning for video understanding. arXiv preprint arXiv:1712.04851 (2017)

25. Miech, A., Laptev, I., Sivic, J.: Learnable pooling with context gating for video classification. arXiv preprint arXiv:1706.06905 (2017)

26. Hinton, G., Vinyals, O., Dean, J.: Distilling the knowledge in a neural network. arXiv:1503.02531 (2015)

27. Gupta, S., Hoffman, J., Malik, J.: Cross modal distillation for supervision transfer. In: CVPR (2016)

28. Diba, A., Pazandeh, A.M., Van Gool, L.: Efficient two-stream motion and appearance 3D CNNS for video classification. In: ECCV Workshops (2016)

29. Arandjelović, R., Zisserman, A.: Look, listen and learn. In: ICCV (2017)

30. Limmer, M., Lensch, H.P.: Infrared colorization using deep convolutional neural networks. In: ICMLA (2016)

31. Mansimov, E., Srivastava, N., Salakhutdinov, R.: Initialization strategies of spatio-temporal convolutional neural networks. arXiv preprint arXiv:1503.07274 (2015)

32. Hu, J., Shen, L., Sun, G.: Squeeze-and-excitation networks. arXiv preprint arXiv:1709.01507 (2017)
33. He, K., Zhang, X., Ren, S., Sun, J.: Delving deep into rectifiers: Surpassing human-level performance on imagenet classification. In: ICCV (2015)
34. He, K., Zhang, X., Ren, S., Sun, J.: Deep residual learning for image recognition. In: CVPR (2016)
35. Deng, J., Dong, W., Socher, R., Li, L.J., Li, K., Fei-Fei, L.: Imagenet: a large-scale hierarchical image database. In: CVPR (2009)
36. Karpathy, A., Toderici, G., Shetty, S., Leung, T., Sukthankar, R., Fei-Fei, L.: Large-scale video classification with convolutional neural networks. In: CVPR (2014)
37. Kuehne, H., Jhuang, H., Stiefelhagen, R., Serre, T.: HMDB51: a large video database for human motion recognition. In: Nagel, W., Kröner, D., Resch, M. (eds.) High Performance Computing in Science and Engineering'12. Springer, Heidelberg (2013). https://doi.org/10.1007/978-3-642-33374-3_41
38. Soomro, K., Zamir, A.R., Shah, M.: Ucf101: A dataset of 101 human actions classes from videos in the wild. arXiv:1212.0402 (2012)
39. Abu-El-Haija, S., et al.: Youtube-8m: A large-scale video classification benchmark. arXiv:1609.08675 (2016)
40. Cai, Z., Wang, L., Peng, X., Qiao, Y.: Multi-view super vector for action recognition. In: CVPR (2014)
41. Wang, L., Qiao, Y., Tang, X.: Action recognition with trajectory-pooled deep-convolutional descriptors. In: CVPR (2015)
42. Wang, L., et al.: Temporal segment networks: towards good practices for deep action recognition. In: Leibe, B., Matas, J., Sebe, N., Welling, M. (eds.) ECCV 2016. LNCS, vol. 9912, pp. 20–36. Springer, Cham (2016). https://doi.org/10.1007/978-3-319-46484-8_2
43. Qiu, Z., Yao, T., Mei, T.: Learning spatio-temporal representation with pseudo-3D residual networks. In: 2017 IEEE International Conference on Computer Vision (ICCV) (2017)

A Zero-Shot Framework for Sketch Based Image Retrieval

Sasi Kiran Yelamarthi$^{(\boxtimes)}$, Shiva Krishna Reddy, Ashish Mishra,
and Anurag Mittal

Indian Institute of Technology Madras, Chennai, India
sasikiran1996@gmail.com, shivakrishnam912@gmail.com,
{mishra,amittal}@cse.iitm.ac.in

Abstract. Sketch-based image retrieval (SBIR) is the task of retrieving images from a natural image database that correspond to a given hand-drawn sketch. Ideally, an SBIR model should learn to associate components in the sketch (say, feet, tail, etc.) with the corresponding components in the image having similar shape characteristics. However, current evaluation methods simply focus only on coarse-grained evaluation where the focus is on retrieving images which belong to the same class as the sketch but not necessarily having the same shape characteristics as in the sketch. As a result, existing methods simply learn to associate sketches with classes seen during training and hence fail to generalize to unseen classes. In this paper, we propose a new benchmark for zero-shot SBIR where the model is evaluated on novel classes that are not seen during training. We show through extensive experiments that existing models for SBIR that are trained in a discriminative setting learn only class specific mappings and fail to generalize to the proposed zero-shot setting. To circumvent this, we propose a generative approach for the SBIR task by proposing deep conditional generative models that take the sketch as an input and fill the missing information stochastically. Experiments on this new benchmark created from the "Sketchy" dataset, which is a large-scale database of sketch-photo pairs demonstrate that the performance of these generative models is significantly better than several state-of-the-art approaches in the proposed zero-shot framework of the coarse-grained SBIR task.

Keywords: Image retrieval · Zero-shot learning

1 Introduction

The rise in the number of internet users coupled with increased storage capacity, better internet connectivity and higher bandwidths has resulted in an exponential growth in multimedia content on the Web. In particular, image content

---

S. K. Yelamarthi and S. K. Reddy—Equal Contribution.

Electronic supplementary material The online version of this chapter (https:// doi.org/10.1007/978-3-030-01225-0_19) contains supplementary material, which is available to authorized users.

© Springer Nature Switzerland AG 2018
V. Ferrari et al. (Eds.): ECCV 2018, LNCS 11208, pp. 316–333, 2018.
https://doi.org/10.1007/978-3-030-01225-0_19

has become ubiquitous and plays an important role in engaging users on social media as well as customers on various e-commerce sites. With this growth in image content, the information needs and search patterns of users have also evolved. Specifically, it is now common for users to search for images (instead of documents) either by providing a textual description of the image or by providing another image which is similar to the desired image. The former is known as text based image retrieval and the latter as content based image retrieval [17].

The motivation for content based image retrieval can be easily understood by taking an example from online fashion. Here, it is often hard to provide a *textual description* of the desired product but easier to provide a *visual description* in the form of a matching image. The visual description/query need not necessarily be an image but can also be a sketch of the desired product, if no image is available. The user can simply draw the sketch on-the-fly on touch based devices. This convenience in expressing a visual query has led to the emergence of Sketch-based image retrieval (SBIR) as an active area of research [3–5,9,13,14,16,23, 29,30,34,35,43,47,50]. The primary challenge here is the domain gap between images and sketches wherein sketches contain only an outline of the object and hence have less information compared to images. The second challenge is the large intra-class variance present in sketches due to the fact that humans tend to draw sketches with varied levels of abstraction. Ideally, for better generalization, a model for SBIR must learn to discover the alignments between the components of the sketch and the corresponding image. For example, in Fig. 1, we would want the model to associate the head of the cow in the sketch to that in the image. However, current evaluation methodology [7,25,36] focuses only on class-based retrieval rather than shape or attribute-based retrieval. Specifically, during evaluation, the model is given credit if it simply fetches an image which belongs to the same class as the sketch. The object in the image need not have the same outline, etc. as in the sketch. For example, for the query (sketch) shown in Fig. 1, there is no guarantee that the model fetches the image of the cow with the same number of feet visible or the tail visible, even if it has high evaluation score.

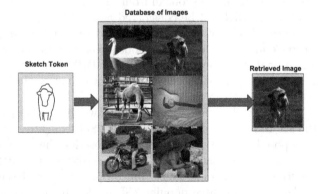

Fig. 1. Illustration of sketch based image retrieval

Thus, a model could possibly achieve good performance by simply learning a class specific mapping from sketches to class labels and retrieve all the images from the same class as that of the query sketch. This is especially so, when the unseen sketches seen at test time belong to the same set of classes as seen during training. Furthermore, existing methods evaluate their models on a set of randomly selected sketches that are withheld during training. However, the images corresponding to the withheld sketches could still occur in the training set, and that would make the task easier.

One way to discourage such class specific learning is to employ a fine-grained evaluation [29,47]. For a given sketch, the retrieved results are evaluated by comparing the estimated ranking of images in the database with a human anno-tated rank list. However, creating such annotations for large datasets such as "Sketchy" [36] requires extensive human labor. Also, such evaluation metrics are subject to human biases. In this work, we propose coarse-grained evaluation in the zero-shot setting as a surrogate to fine-grained evaluation to circumvent both these drawbacks. The idea is to test the retrieval on sketches of unseen classes to discourage class-specific learning during training. The evaluation is automatic, *i.e.*, it requires no human labor for each retrieval, apart from having no biases. The model has to learn to associate the latent alignments in the sketch and the image in order to perform well. This is also important from a practical standpoint wherein, in some domains, all possible classes many not be available at training time. For example, new product classes emerge every day in the fashion industry. Thus, the *Zero-Shot Sketch Based Image Retrieval (ZS-SBIR)* task introduced in this paper provides a more realistic setup for the sketch-based retrieval task.

Towards this end, we propose a new benchmark for the ZS-SBIR task by cre-ating a careful split of the Sketchy database. We first evaluate several existing SBIR models on this task and observe that the performance of these models drops significantly in the zero-shot setting thereby pointing to class-specific learning occurring in these models. We hypothesize that one reason for this could be that the existing methods are essentially formulated in the discriminative setup, which encourages class specific learning. To circumvent the problems in these existing models, we approach the problem from the point of view of a generative model. Specifically, ZS-SBIR can be considered as the task of generating addi-tional information that is absent in the sketch in order to retrieve similar images. We propose Deep Conditional Generative Models based on Adversarial Autoen-coders and Variational Autoencoders for the ZS-SBIR task. Our experiments show that the proposed generative approach performs better than all existing state-of-the-art SBIR models in the zero-shot setting.

The paper is organized as follows: In Sect. 2, we give a brief overview of the state-of-the-art techniques in SBIR and ZSL. Subsequently, in Sect. 3, we introduce the proposed zero-shot framework and describe the proposed dataset split. Section 4 shows the evaluation of existing state-of-the-art SBIR models in this proposed setting. Section 5 introduces our proposed generative modeling of ZS-SBIR and adaptations of three popular ZSL models to this setting. Finally, in Sect. 6, we present an empirical evaluation of these models on the proposed zero shot splits on the Sketchy dataset.

2   Related Work

Since we propose a zero-shot framework for the SBIR task, we briefly review the literature from both sketch-based image retrieval as well as zero-shot learning in this section.

Conventional pipeline in SBIR involves projecting images and sketches into a common feature space. These features or binary codes extracted from them are used for the retrieval task. Hand-crafted feature based models include the gradient field HOG descriptor proposed by Hu and Collomose [13], the histogram of edge orientations (HELO) proposed by Saavendra [34], the learned key shapes (LKS) proposed by Saavendra et al. [35] which are used in Bag of Visual Words (BoVW) framework as feature extractors for SBIR. Yu et al. [48] were the first to use Convolutional Neural Networks (CNN) for the sketch classification task. Qi et al. [7] introduced the use of siamese architecture for coarse-grained SBIR. Sangkloy et al. [36] used triplet ranking loss for training the features for coarse-grained SBIR. Yu et al. [47] used triplet network for instance level SBIR evaluating the performance on shoe and chair dataset. They use a pseudo fine-grained evaluation where they only look at the position of the correct image for a sketch in the retrieved images. Liu et al. [25] propose a semi-heterogeneous deep architecture for extracting binary codes from sketches and images that can be trained in an end-to-end fashion for coarse-grained SBIR task.

We now review the zero-shot literature. Zero-shot learning in Image Classification [21,22,27] refers to learning to recognize images of novel classes although no examples from these classes are present in the training set. Due to the difficulty in collecting examples of every class in order to train supervised models, zero-shot learning has received significant interest from the research community recently [1,10,20,22,33,39,42,44,45]. We refer the reader to [46] for a comprehensive survey on the subject. Recently, zero shot learning has been gaining increasing attention for a number of other computer vision tasks such as image tagging [24,49], visual question answering [28,31,41] etc. To the best of our knowledge, the zero-shot framework has not been previously explored in the SBIR task.

3   Zero Shot Setting for SBIR

We now provide a formal definition of the zero shot setting in SBIR. Let $S = \{(x_i^{sketch}, x_i^{img}, y_i) | y_i \in \mathcal{Y}\}$ be the triplets of sketch, image and class label where $\mathcal{Y}$ is the set of all class labels in S. We partition the class labels in the data into $\mathcal{Y}_{train}$ and $\mathcal{Y}_{test}$ data respectively. Correspondingly, let $S_{tr} = \{(x_i^{sketch}, x_i^{img}) | y_i \in Y_{train}\}$ and $S_{te} = \{(x_i^{sketch}, x_i^{img}) | y_i \in Y_{test}\}$ be the partition of S into train and test sets. This way, we partition the paired data into train and test set such that none of the sketches from the test classes occur in the train set. Since the model has no access to class labels, the model needs to learn latent alignments between the sketches and the corresponding images to perform well on the test data.

Let D be the database of all images and g_I be the mapping from images to class labels. We split D into $D_{tr} = \{x_i^{img} \in D | g_I(x_i^{img}) \in Y_{train}\}$ and $D_{te} = \{x_i^{img} \in D | g_I(x_i^{img}) \in Y_{test}\}$. This is similar to other zero-shot literature [22] in image classification. The retrieval model in this framework can only be trained on S_{tr}. The database D_{tr} may be used for validating the retrieval results in order to tune the hyper-parameters. Given an x^{sketch} taken from sketches of S_{te}, the objective of zero shot setting in SBIR is to retrieve images from D_{te} that belong to same class as that of the query sketch. This evaluation setting ensures that the model can not just learn the mapping from sketches to class labels and retrieve all the images using the label information. The model now has to learn the salient common features between sketches and images and use this to retrieve images for the query that are from the unseen classes.

3.1 Benchmark

Since we are introducing the task of zero-shot sketch based retrieval, there is no existing benchmark for evaluating this setting. Hence, we first propose a new benchmark for evaluation by making a careful split of the "Sketchy" dataset [36]. Sketchy is a dataset consisting of 75,471 hand-drawn sketches and 12,500 images belonging to 125 classes collected by Sangkloy *et al.* [36]. Each image has approximately 6 hand-drawn sketches. The original Sketchy dataset uses the same 12,500 images as the database. Liu *et al.* [25] augment the database with 60,502 images from Imagenet to create a retrieval database with a total of 73,002 images. We use the augmented dataset provided by Liu *et al.* [25] in this work.

Next, we partition the 125 classes into 104 train classes and 21 test classes. This peculiar split is not arbitrary. We make sure that the 21 test classes are not present in the 1000 classes of Imagenet [8]. This is done to ensure that researchers

Table 1. Statistics of the proposed dataset split of Sketchy database for ZS-SBIR task

Dataset statistics	#
Train classes	104
Test classes	21
Train images	10400
Train sketches	62787
Avg. sketches per image	6.03848
Test sketches	12694
DB images for training	62549
DB images for testing	10453

can still pre-train their models on the 1000 classes of Imagenet without violating the zero-shot assumption. Such a split was motivated by the recently proposed benchmark for standard datasets used in the zero shot image classification task by Xian *et al.* [46]. The details of the proposed dataset split are summarized in Table 1.

4   Limitations of Existing SBIR Methods

Next we evaluate whether the existing approaches to the sketch-based image retrieval task generalize well to the proposed zero-shot setting. To this end, we evaluate three state-of-the-art SBIR methods described below on the above proposed benchmark.

4.1   A Siamese Network

The Siamese network proposed by Hadsell *et al.* [12] maps both the sketches and images into a common space where the semantic distance is preserved. Let $(S, I, Y = 1)$ and $(S, I, Y = 0)$ be the pairs of images and sketches that belong to same and different class respectively and $D_\theta(S, I)$ be the l2 distance between the image and sketch features where θ are the parameters of the mapping function. The loss function $L(\theta)$ for training is given by:

$$L(\theta) = (Y)\frac{1}{2}(D_\theta)^2 + (1 - Y)\frac{1}{2}\{max(0, m - D_\theta)\}^2 \tag{1}$$

where m is the margin. Chopra *et al.* [7] and Qi *et al.* [30] use a modified version of the above loss function for training the Siamese network for the tasks of face verification and SBIR respectively, which is given below:

$$L(\theta) = (Y)\alpha D_\theta^2 + (1 - Y)\beta e^{\gamma D_\theta} \tag{2}$$

where $\alpha = \dfrac{2}{Q}$, $\beta = 2Q$, $\gamma = -\dfrac{2.77}{Q}$ and constant Q is set to the upper bound on D_θ estimated from the data. We explore both these formulations in the proposed zero-shot setting. We call the former setting as Siamese-1 and the latter as Siamese-2.

4.2   A Triplet Network

Triplet loss [36,37] is defined in a max-margin framework, where, the objective is to minimize the distance between sketch and positive image that belong to the same class and simultaneously maximize the distance between the sketch and negative image which belong to different classes. The triplet training loss for a given triplet $t(s, p^+, p^-)$ is given by:

$$L_\theta(t) = max(0, m + D_\theta(s, p^+) - D_\theta(s, p^-)) \tag{3}$$

where m is the margin and D_θ is the distance measure used.

Table 2. Precision and mAP are estimated by retrieving 200 images. - indicates that the authors do not present results on that metric. 1: Using 128 bit hash codes

Method	Precision@200		mAP@200	
	Traditional	Zero-Shot	Traditional	Zero-Shot
Baseline	-	0.106	-	0.054
Siamese-1	-	0.243	-	0.134
Siamese-2	0.690	0.251	0.518	0.149
Coarse-grained triplet	0.761	0.169	0.573	0.083
Fine-grained triplet	-	0.155	-	0.081
DSH[1]	0.866	0.153	0.783	0.059

To sample the negative images during training, we follow two strategies (i) we consider only images from different class and (ii) we consider all the images that do not directly correspond to the sketch, resulting in coarse-grained and fine-grained training of triplet network respectively. We explore both these training methods in the proposed zero-shot setting for SBIR.

4.3   Deep Sketch Hashing(DSH)

Liu *et al.* [25] propose an end-to-end framework for learning binary codes of sketches and images which is the current state-of-the-art in SBIR. The objective function consists of the following three terms: (i) cross-view pairwise loss which tries to bring binary codes of images and sketches of the same class to be close (ii) semantic factorization loss which tries to preserve the semantic relationship between classes in the binary codes and (iii) the quantization loss.

4.4   Experiments

We now present the results of the above described models on our proposed partitions of the "Sketchy" dataset [36] in order to evaluate them in the zero-shot setting.

While evaluating each model, for a given test sketch, we retrieve the top $K = 200$ images from the database that are closest to the sketch in the learned feature space. We use inverse of the cosine similarity as the distance metric. We present the experimental details for the evaluated methods below.

Baseline: We take a VGG-16 network [38] trained on image classification task on ImageNet-1K [8] as the baseline. The score for a given sketch-image pair is given by the cosine similarity between their VGG features.

Training: We re-implement the above described models to evaluate them for the ZS-SBIR task. For sanity check, we first reproduce the results on the traditional SBIR task reported in [25] successfully. We follow the training methodology described in [7,25,36] closely.

We observe that the validation performance saturates after 20 epochs in case of Siamese network and after 80 epochs for the Triplet network. We also employ data augmentation for training the Triplet network because the available training data is insufficient for proper training. We explore the hyper-parameters via grid search.

In the case of DSH, we use the CNNs proposed by Liu *et al.* [25] for feature extraction. We train the network for 500 epochs, validating on the train database after every 10 epochs. We explored the hyper-parameters and found that $\lambda = 0.01$ and $\gamma = 10^{-5}$ give the best results similar to the original SBIR training.

The performance of these models on the ZS-SBIR task are shown in Table 2. For comparative purposes, we also present the performance in the traditional SBIR setting [25] where the models are trained on the sketch-image pairs of all the classes. We observe that the performance of these models dips significantly, indicating the non-generalizability of existing approaches to SBIR. This performance drop of more than 50% in the zero-shot setting may be due to the fact that these models trained in a discriminative setting may learn to associate the sketches and images to class labels.

Among the compared methods we notice that the Siamese network preforms the best among the existing SBIR methods in the zero-shot setting. We also observe that the Triplet loss gives poorer performance compared to the Siamese network. This can be attributed to the presence of only about $60,000$ images during training, which is not sufficient for properly training a triplet network as observed by Schroff *et al.* [37]. We also observe that the coarse-grained training of triplet performs better compared to fine-grained triplet. This may be because the fine-grained training considers all the images other than those that correspond directly to the sketch as negative samples making the training harder.

Our next observation is that DSH, which is the state-of-the-art model in SBIR does not perform well compared to either Siamese or Triplet networks in ZS-SBIR task. This may be due to the fact that the semantic factorization loss in DSH takes only the training class embeddings into account and does not reduce the semantic gap for the test classes.

Thus, one can claim that there exists a problem of class-based learning inherent in the existing models, which leads to inferior performance in the ZS-SBIR task.

5 Generative Models for ZS-SBIR

Having noticed that the existing approaches do not generalize well to the ZS-SBIR task, we now propose the use of generative models for the ZS-SBIR task. The motivation for such an approach is that while a sketch gives a basic outline of the image, additional details could possibly be generated from the latent prior vector via a generative model. This is inline with the recent work on similar image translation tasks [6,15,32] in computer vision.

Let G_θ model the probability distribution of the image features (x_{img}) conditioned on the sketch features (x_{sketch}) and parameterized by θ, i.e.

$\mathbb{P}(x_{img}|x_{sketch}; \theta)$. G_θ is trained using paired data of sketch-image pairs from the training classes. Since we do not provide the model with class label information, it is hoped that the model learns to associate the characteristics of the sketch such as the general outline, local shape, etc. with that of the image. We would like to emphasize here that G_θ is trained to generate image features but not the images themselves using the sketch. We consider two popular generative models: Variational Autoencoders [19,40] and Adversarial Autoencoders [26] as described below:

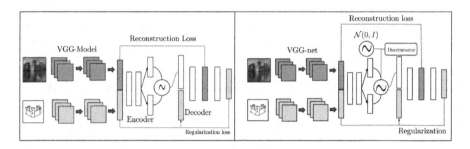

Fig. 2. The architectures of CVAE and CAAE are illustrated in the left and right diagrams respectively

5.1   Variational Autoencoders

The Variational Autoencoders (VAE) [19] map a prior distribution on a hidden latent variable $p(z)$ to the data distribution $p(x)$. The intractable posterior $p(z|x)$ is approximated by the variational distribution $q(z|x)$ which is assumed to be Gaussian in this work. The parameters of the variational distribution are estimated from x via the encoder which is a neural network parameterized by ϕ. The conditional distribution $p(x|z)$ is modeled by the decoder network parameterized by θ. Following the notation in [19], the variational lower bound for $p(x)$ can be written as:

$$
\begin{aligned}
p(x) \geq \mathcal{L}(\phi, \theta; x) \\
= -D_{KL}\left(q_\phi(z|x)||p_\theta(z)\right) + \mathbb{E}_{q_\phi(z|x)}\left[\log p_\theta(x|z)\right]
\end{aligned}
\tag{4}
$$

Similarly, it is possible to model the conditional probability $p(x|y)$ as proposed by [40]. In this work, we model the probability distribution over images conditioned on the sketch i.e. $P(x_{img}|x_{sketch})$. The bound now becomes:

$$
\mathcal{L}(\phi, \theta; x_{img}, x_{sketch}) =
$$

$$
\begin{aligned}
- D_{KL}\left(q_\phi\left(z|x_{img}, x_{sketch}\right)||p_\theta\left(z|x_{sketch}\right)\right) + \\
\mathbb{E}\left[\log p_\theta\left(x_{img}|z, x_{sketch}\right)\right]
\end{aligned}
\tag{5}
$$

Furthermore, to encourage the model to preserve the latent alignments of the sketch, we add the reconstruction regularization to the objective. In other words, we force the reconstructibility of the sketch features from the generated image features via a one-layer neural network f_{NN} with parameters ψ. All the parameters $\theta, \psi \& \phi$ are trained end-to-end. The regularization loss can be expressed as

$$\mathcal{L}_{recons} = \lambda. ||f_{NN}(\widehat{x}_{img}) - x_{sketch}||_2^2 \tag{6}$$

Here, λ is a hyper-parameter which is to be tuned. The architecture of the conditional variational autoencoder used is shown in Fig. 2. We call this CVAE from here on.

5.2   Adversarial Autoencoders

Adversarial Autoencoders [26] are similar to the variational autoencoder, where the KL-Divergence term is replaced with an adversarial training procedure. Let E, D be the encoder and decoder of the autoencoder respectively. E maps input x_{img} to the parameters of the hidden latent vector distribution $P(z|x_{img})$, whereas, D maps the sampled z to x_{img} (both are conditioned on the sketch vector x_{sketch}). We have an additional network $\mathcal{D}$: the discriminator. The networks E & D try to minimize the following loss:

$$\mathbb{E}_z \left[\log p_\theta \left(x_{img}|z, x_{sketch}\right)\right] + \mathbb{E}_{x_{img}} \left[\log \left(1 - \mathcal{D}(E(x_{img}))\right)\right] \tag{7}$$

The discriminator $\mathcal{D}$ tries to maximize the following similar to the original GAN formulation [11]:

$$\mathbb{E}_z \left[\log \left[\mathcal{D}(z)\right]\right] + \mathbb{E}_{x_{img}} \left[\log \left[1 - \mathcal{D}\left(E(x_{img})\right)\right]\right] \tag{8}$$

We add the reconstructibility regularization described in the above section to the loss of the encoder. The architecture of the adversarial autoencoder used is shown in Fig. 2. We call this CAAE from here on.

5.3   Retrieval Methodology

G_θ is trained on the sketch-image feature pairs from the seen classes. During test time, the decoder part of the network is used to generate a number of image feature vectors x_{gen}^I conditioned on the test sketch by sampling latent vectors from the prior distribution $p(z) = \mathcal{N}(0, I)$. For a test sketch x_S corresponding to a test class, we generate the set $\mathcal{I}_{x_S}$ consisting of N (a hyper-parameter) such samples of x_{gen}^I. We then cluster these generated samples $\mathcal{I}_{x_S}$ using K-Means clustering and obtain K cluster centers $C_1, C_2, \ldots, C_k$ for each test sketch. We retrieve 200 images x_{db}^I from the image database based on the following distance metric:

$$\mathcal{D}(x_I^{db}, \mathcal{I}_{x_S}) = min_{k=1}^K cosine \left(\theta(x_I^{db}), C_k\right) \tag{9}$$

where θ is the VGG-16 [38] function. We empirically observe that $K = 5$ gives the best results for retrieval. Other distance metrics typically used in clustering were considered but this gave the best results.

5.4   Experiments

We conduct an evaluation of the generative models on the proposed zero-shot setting and compare the results with those of existing methods in SBIR. We use the same metrics i.e. Precision and mAP, for evaluation. We use the VGG-16 [38] model pre-trained on the Imagenet-1K dataset to obtain 4096 dimensional features for images. To extract the sketch features, we tune the network for sketch classification task using only the training sketches. We observed that this training gives only a marginal improvement in the performance and is hence optional.

Baselines. Along with the state-of-the-art models for the SBIR task, we consider three popular algorithms [46] from the zero-shot image classification literature that do not explicitly use class label information and can be easily adopted to the zero-shot SBIR task. Let $(X_I, X_S) \in (\mathbb{R}^{N \times d_I}, \mathbb{R}^{N \times d_S})$ represent the image and sketch feature pairs from the training data respectively. We learn a mapping f from sketch features to image features, i.e. $f : \mathbb{R}_I^d \to \mathbb{R}_S^d$ where d_I, d_S are the dimensions of the image and sketch vectors respectively. We describe these models below:

Direct Regression: The ZS-SBIR task is formulated as a simple regression problem, where each feature of the image feature vector is learnt from the sketch features. This is similar to the Direct Attribute prediction [22] which is a widely used baseline for zero-shot image classification.

Embarrassingly Simple Zero-Shot Learning: ESZSL was introduced by Romera-Paredes & Torr [33] as a method of learning bilinear compatibility matrix between images and attribute vectors in the context of zero-shot classification. In this work, we adapt the model to the ZS-SBIR task by mapping the sketch features to the image features using parallel training data from the train classes. The objective is to estimate $W \in \mathbb{R}^{d_S \times d_I}$ that minimizes the following loss:

$$||X_S W - X_I||_F^2 + \gamma \left|\left|X_I W^T\right|\right|_F^2 + \lambda \left|\left|X_S W\right|\right|_F^2 + \beta \left|\left|W\right|\right|_F^2 \tag{10}$$

where γ, λ, β are hyper-parameters.

Semantic Autoencoder: The Semantic Autoencoder (SAE) [20] proposes an autoencoder framework to encourage the re-constructibility of the sketch vector from the generated image vector. The loss term is given by:

$$||X_I - X_S W||_F^2 + \lambda \left|\left|X_I W^T - X_S\right|\right|_F^2 \tag{11}$$

We would like to note here that SAE, though simple, is currently the state-of-the-art among published models for zero-shot image classification task to the best of our knowledge.

Training. We use Adam optimizer [18] with learning rate $\alpha = 2 \times 10^{-4}$, $\beta_1 = 0.5$, $\beta_2 = 0.999$ and a batch size of 64 and 128 for training the CVAE and CAAE respectively. We observe that the validation performance saturates at 25 epochs for the CVAE model and at 6000 iterations for the CAAE model. While training CAAE, we train the discriminator for 32 iterations for each training iteration of the encoder and decoder. We found that $N = 200$ i.e. generating 200 image features for a given input sketch gives optimal performance and saturates afterwards. The reconstructibility parameter λ is set via cross-validation.

SAE has a single hyper-parameter and is solved using the Bartels-Stewart algorithm [2]. ESZSL has three hyper parameters γ, λ & β. We set $\beta = \gamma\lambda$ following the authors to get a closed form solution. We tune these hyper-parameters via a grid search from 10^{-6} to 10^7.

6   Results

The results of the evaluated methods for ZS-SBIR are summarized in Table 3. As observed in Sect. 4.4, existing SBIR models perform poorly in the ZS-SBIR task. Both the proposed generative models out-perform the existing models indicating better latent alignment learning in the generative approach.

Qualitative Analysis: We show some of the retrieved images for sketch inputs of the unseen classes using the CVAE model in ZS-SBIR in Fig. 3. We observe that the retrieved images closely match the outline of the sketch. We also observe that our model makes visually reasonable mistakes in the case of false positives wherein the retrieved images do have a significant similarity with the sketch even though they belong to a different class. For instance, in the last example the false positive that belongs to the class rhinoceros has a similar outline as

Table 3. The Precision and MAP evaluated on the retrieved 200 images in ZS-SBIR on the proposed split

Type	Evaluation methods	Precision@200	mAP@200
SBIR methods	Baseline	0.106	0.054
	Siamese-1	0.243	0.134
	Siamese-2	0.251	0.149
	Coarse-grained triplet	0.169	0.083
	Fine-grained triplet	0.155	0.081
	DSH	0.153	0.059
ZSL methods	Direct regression	0.066	0.022
	ESZSL	0.187	0.117
	SAE	0.238	0.136
Ours	CAAE	**0.260**	**0.156**
	CVAE	**0.333**	**0.225**

Fig. 3. Top 6 images retrieved for some input sketches using CVAE in the proposed zero-shot setting. Note that these sketch classes have never been encountered by the model during training. The red border indicates that the retrieved image does not belong to sketch's class. However, we would like to emphasize that the retrieved false positives do match the outline of the sketch

that of the sketch. These may be considered not as an error but rather as a positive retrieval, but can only be evaluated qualitatively by an arduous manual task and may be attributed to data bias.

Human Evaluation: We aim to see how well the proposed zero-shot evaluation can substitute the fine-grained human evaluation. We randomly select 50 test sketches spanning all the unseen classes and then retrieve top 10 images per sketch from the database using the trained CVAE model. We compute the precision@10 for each of these sketches to get 50 such precision values (henceforth referred to as zero-shot scores).

Next, we present these sketch-image pairs to ten human evaluators. They were asked to evaluate each pair based on the outline, texture and overall shape associations, giving each pair a subjective score between 0 (no associations whatsoever) to 5 (perfect associations). We compute the average rating for the 10 retrieved images of each sketch and scale it down on a scale of 0–1. We compute the Pearson Correlation Coefficient (PCC) between the two scores across sketches, which was observed to be **0.65** indicating strong positive correlation between the two evaluation scores. The average human score across 50 sketches was observed to be **0.547**, whereas the average zero-shot score was **0.454**.

We repeat the above experiment using one of the baseline models, Coarse-grained Triplet Network. We observe a PCC of **0.69**. The average human score was **0.37** and the average zero-shot score was **0.238**. Across the two models studied, we observe that the scores are both high or both low, thus further strengthening the claim that methods working well on ZS-SBIR work well on fine-grained evaluation.

Feature Visualization: To understand the kinds of features generated by the model, we visualize the generated image features of the test sketches in Fig. 4 via the t-sne method. We make two observations, (i) the generated features are largely close to the true test image features (ii) multiple modalities of the distribution are captured by our model.

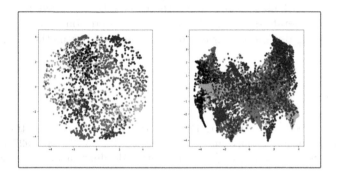

Fig. 4. T-SNE visualization of generated image features. Test data features are presented on the left and the predicted image features are on the right. Each color represents a particular class

Performance Comparisons: Comparison among the current state-of-the-art models in the zero-shot setting of SBIR was already done in Sect. 4.4.

Direct regression from sketch to image feature space gives a precision value of 0.066. This serves as a baseline to evaluate other explicitly imposed regularizations in ESZSL and SAE. Our first observation is that the simple zero-shot learning models adapted to the ZS-SBIR task perform better than two state-of-the-art sketch based image retrieval models i.e. Triplet network and DSH. SAE, which is the current state-of-the-art for zero-shot image classification, achieves the best performance among all the prior methods considered. SAE maps the sketches to images and hence generates a single image for a given sketch. This is similar to our proposed models except that our models generate a number of samples for a single sketch by filling the missing details from the latent distribution. Furthermore our model is non-linear whereas SAE is a simple linear projection. We believe that these generalizations over the SAE in our model leads to superior performance.

Among the two models proposed, we observe that the CVAE models performs significantly better than the CAAE model. This may be attributed to the issue of instability while training adversarial models. We observe that the training error of the CVAE models is much more smoother compared to the CAAE model. We observe that using the reconstruction loss leads to a 3% improvement on the precision.

7   Conclusion

We identified major drawbacks in current evaluation schemes in sketch-based image retrieval (SBIR) task. To this end, we pose the problem of sketch-based retrieval in a zero-shot evaluation framework (ZS-SBIR). By making a careful split in the "Sketchy" dataset, we provide a benchmark for this task. We then evaluate current state-of-the-art SBIR models in this framework and show that the performance of these models drop significantly, thus exposing the class-specific learning which is inherent to these models. We then pose the SBIR problem as a generative task and propose two conditional generative models which achieve significant improvement over the existing methods in ZS-SBIR setting.

References

1. Akata, Z., Reed, S.E., Walter, D., Lee, H., Schiele, B.: Evaluation of output embeddings for fine-grained image classification. In: CVPR, pp. 2927–2936. IEEE Computer Society (2015). http://dblp.uni-trier.de/db/conf/cvpr/cvpr2015.html#AkataRWLS15
2. Bartels, R.H., Stewart, G.W.: Solution of the matrix equation $AX + XB = C$. Comm. ACM **15**, 820–826 (1972)
3. Cao, X., Zhang, H., Liu, S., Guo, X., Lin, L.: SYM-FISH: a symmetry-aware flip invariant sketch histogram shape descriptor. In: ICCV, pp. 313–320. IEEE Computer Society (2013). http://dblp.uni-trier.de/db/conf/iccv/iccv2013.html#CaoZLGL13
4. Cao, Y., Wang, C., Zhang, L., Zhang, L.: Edgel index for large-scale sketch-based image search. In: CVPR, pp. 761–768. IEEE Computer Society (2011). http://dblp.uni-trier.de/db/conf/cvpr/cvpr2011.html#CaoWZZ11
5. Cao, Y., Wang, H., Wang, C., Li, Z., Zhang, L., Zhang, L.: MindFinder: interactive sketch-based image search on millions of images. In: Bimbo, A.D., Chang, S.F., Smeulders, A.W.M. (eds.) ACM Multimedia, pp. 1605–1608. ACM (2010). http://dblp.uni-trier.de/db/conf/mm/mm2010.html#CaoWWLZZ10
6. Chidambaram, M., Qi, Y.: Style transfer generative adversarial networks: Learning to play chess differently. CoRR abs/1702.06762 (2017). http://dblp.uni-trier.de/db/journals/corr/corr1702.html#ChidambaramQ17
7. Chopra, S., Hadsell, R., LeCun, Y.: Learning a similarity metric discriminatively, with application to face verification. In: 2005 IEEE Computer Society Conference on Computer Vision and Pattern Recognition, CVPR 2005, vol. 1, pp. 539–546. IEEE (2005)
8. Deng, J., Dong, W., Socher, R., Li, L.J., Li, K., Fei-Fei, L.: ImageNet: a large-scale hierarchical image database. In: CVPR 2009 (2009)

9. Eitz, M., Hildebrand, K., Boubekeur, T., Alexa, M.: Sketch-based image retrieval: benchmark and bag-of-features descriptors. IEEE Trans. Vis. Comput. Graph. **17**(11), 1624–1636 (2011). http://dblp.uni-trier.de/db/journals/tvcg/tvcg17.html#EitzHBA11

10. Frome, A., et al.: Devise: a deep visual-semantic embedding model. In: Burges, C.J.C., Bottou, L., Ghahramani, Z., Weinberger, K.Q. (eds.) NIPS, pp. 2121–2129 (2013). http://dblp.uni-trier.de/db/conf/nips/nips2013.html#FromeCSBDRM13

11. Goodfellow, I.J., et al.: Generative adversarial nets. In: Ghahramani, Z., Welling, M., Cortes, C., Lawrence, N.D., Weinberger, K.Q. (eds.) NIPS, pp. 2672–2680 (2014). http://dblp.uni-trier.de/db/conf/nips/nips2014.html#GoodfellowPMXWOCB14

12. Hadsell, R., Chopra, S., LeCun, Y.: Dimensionality reduction by learning an invariant mapping. In: CVPR (2), pp. 1735–1742. IEEE Computer Society (2006). http://dblp.uni-trier.de/db/conf/cvpr/cvpr2006-2.html#HadsellCL06

13. Hu, R., Collomosse, J.P.: A performance evaluation of gradient field hog descriptor for sketch based image retrieval. Comput. Vis. Image Underst. **117**(7), 790–806 (2013). http://dblp.uni-trier.de/db/journals/cviu/cviu117.html#HuC13

14. Hu, R., Wang, T., Collomosse, J.P.: A bag-of-regions approach to sketch-based image retrieval. In: Macq, B., Schelkens, P. (eds.) ICIP, pp. 3661–3664. IEEE (2011). http://dblp.uni-trier.de/db/conf/icip/icip2011.html#HuWC11

15. Isola, P., Zhu, J.Y., Zhou, T., Efros, A.A.: Image-to-image translation with conditional adversarial networks. arxiv (2016)

16. James, S., Fonseca, M.J., Collomosse, J.P.: ReEnact: sketch based choreographic design from archival dance footage. In: Kankanhalli, M.S., Rueger, S., Manmatha, R., Jose, J.M., van Rijsbergen, K. (eds.) ICMR, p. 313. ACM (2014). http://dblp.uni-trier.de/db/conf/mir/icmr2014.html#JamesFC14

17. John Eakins, M.G.: Content-based image retrieval

18. Kingma, D.P., Ba, J.: Adam: a method for stochastic optimization. CoRR abs/1412.6980 (2014). http://dblp.uni-trier.de/db/journals/corr/corr1412.html#KingmaB14

19. Kingma, D.P., Welling, M.: Auto-encoding variational bayes. arXiv preprint arXiv:1312.6114 (2013)

20. Kodirov, E., Xiang, T., Gong, S.: Semantic autoencoder for zero-shot learning. CoRR abs/1704.08345 (2017). http://dblp.uni-trier.de/db/journals/corr/corr1704.html#KodirovXG17

21. Kumar Verma, V., Arora, G., Mishra, A., Rai, P.: Generalized zero-shot learning via synthesized examples. In: The IEEE Conference on Computer Vision and Pattern Recognition (CVPR), June 2018

22. Lampert, C.H., Nickisch, H., Harmeling, S.: Attribute-based classification for zero-shot visual object categorization. IEEE Trans. Pattern Anal. Mach. Intell. **36**(3), 453–465 (2014). http://dblp.uni-trier.de/db/journals/pami/pami36.html#LampertNH14

23. Li, K., Pang, K., Song, Y.Z., Hospedales, T.M., Zhang, H., Hu, Y.: Fine-grained sketch-based image retrieval: the role of part-aware attributes. In: WACV, pp. 1–9. IEEE Computer Society (2016). http://dblp.uni-trier.de/db/conf/wacv/wacv2016.html#LiPSHZH16

24. Li, X., Liao, S., Lan, W., Du, X., Yang, G.: Zero-shot image tagging by hierarchical semantic embedding. In: Baeza-Yates, R.A., Lalmas, M., Moffat, A., Ribeiro-Neto, B.A. (eds.) SIGIR, pp. 879–882. ACM (2015). http://dblp.uni-trier.de/db/conf/sigir/sigir2015.html#LiLLDY15

25. Liu, L., Shen, F., Shen, Y., Liu, X., Shao, L.: Deep sketch hashing: fast free-hand sketch-based image retrieval. CoRR abs/1703.05605 (2017). http://dblp.uni-trier. de/db/journals/corr/corr1703.html#LiuSSLS17
26. Makhzani, A., Shlens, J., Jaitly, N., Goodfellow, I.: Adversarial autoencoders. In: International Conference on Learning Representations (2016). http://arxiv.org/ abs/1511.05644
27. Mishra, A., Reddy, M., Mittal, A., Murthy, H.A.: A generative model for zero shot learning using conditional variational autoencoders. arXiv preprint arXiv:1709.00663 (2017)
28. Mishra, A., Verma, V.K., Reddy, M., Rai, P., Mittal, A., et al.: A generative approach to zero-shot and few-shot action recognition. arXiv preprint arXiv:1801.09086 (2018)
29. Parui, S., Mittal, A.: Similarity-invariant sketch-based image retrieval in large databases. In: Fleet, D., Pajdla, T., Schiele, B., Tuytelaars, T. (eds.) ECCV 2014. LNCS, vol. 8694, pp. 398–414. Springer, Cham (2014). https://doi.org/ 10.1007/978-3-319-10599-4_26. http://dblp.uni-trier.de/db/conf/eccv/eccv2014-6.html#ParuiM14
30. Qi, Y., Song, Y.Z., Zhang, H., Liu, J.: Sketch-based image retrieval via siamese convolutional neural network. In: ICIP, pp. 2460–2464. IEEE (2016). http://dblp. uni-trier.de/db/conf/icip/icip2016.html#QiSZL16
31. Ramakrishnan, S.K., Pal, A., Sharma, G., Mittal, A.: An empirical evaluation of visual question answering for novel objects. CoRR abs/1704.02516 (2017). http:// dblp.uni-trier.de/db/journals/corr/corr1704.html#RamakrishnanPSM17
32. Reed, S., Akata, Z., Yan, X., Logeswaran, L., Schiele, B., Lee, H.: Generative adversarial text-to-image synthesis. In: Proceedings of the 33rd International Conference on Machine Learning (2016)
33. Romera-Paredes, B., Torr, P.H.S.: An embarrassingly simple approach to zero-shot learning. In: Bach, F.R., Blei, D.M. (eds.) ICML, JMLR Workshop and Conference Proceedings, vol. 37, pp. 2152–2161. JMLR.org (2015). http://dblp.uni-trier.de/ db/conf/icml/icml2015.html#Romera-ParedesT15
34. Saavedra, J.M.: Sketch based image retrieval using a soft computation of the histogram of edge local orientations (S-HELO). In: ICIP, pp. 2998–3002. IEEE (2014). http://dblp.uni-trier.de/db/conf/icip/icip2014.html#Saavedra14
35. Saavedra, J.M., Barrios, J.M.: Sketch based image retrieval using learned keyshapes (LKS). In: Xie, X., Jones, M.W., Tam, G.K.L. (eds.) BMVC, pp. 164.1–164.11. BMVA Press (2015). http://dblp.uni-trier.de/db/conf/bmvc/bmvc2015. html#SaavedraB15
36. Sangkloy, P., Burnell, N., Ham, C., Hays, J.: The sketchy database: learning to retrieve badly drawn bunnies. ACM Trans. Graph. 35(4), 119 (2016). http://dblp.uni-trier.de/db/journals/tog/tog35.html#SangkloyBHH16
37. Schroff, F., Kalenichenko, D., Philbin, J.: FaceNet: a unified embedding for face recognition and clustering. In: CVPR, pp. 815–823. IEEE Computer Society (2015). http://dblp.uni-trier.de/db/conf/cvpr/cvpr2015.html#SchroffKP15
38. Simonyan, K., Zisserman, A.: Very deep convolutional networks for large-scale image recognition. CoRR abs/1409.1556 (2014)
39. Socher, R., Ganjoo, M., Manning, C.D., Ng, A.Y.: Zero-shot learning through cross-modal transfer. In: Burges, C.J.C., Bottou, L., Ghahramani, Z., Weinberger, K.Q. (eds.) NIPS, pp. 935–943 (2013). http://dblp.uni-trier.de/db/conf/nips/nips2013. html#SocherGMN13

40. Sohn, K., Lee, H., Yan, X.: Learning structured output representation using deep conditional generative models. In: Cortes, C., Lawrence, N.D., Lee, D.D., Sugiyama, M., Garnett, R. (eds.) NIPS, pp. 3483–3491 (2015). http://dblp.uni-trier.de/db/conf/nips/nips2015.html#SohnLY15

41. Teney, D., van den Hengel, A.: Zero-shot visual question answering. CoRR abs/1611.05546 (2016). http://dblp.uni-trier.de/db/journals/corr/corr1611.html#TeneyH16a

42. Verma, V.K., Rai, P.: A simple exponential family framework for zero-shot learning. In: Ceci, M., Hollmén, J., Todorovski, L., Vens, C., Džeroski, S. (eds.) ECML PKDD 2017. LNCS (LNAI), vol. 10535, pp. 792–808. Springer, Cham (2017). https://doi.org/10.1007/978-3-319-71246-8_48

43. Wang, F., Kang, L., Li, Y.: Sketch-based 3D shape retrieval using convolutional neural networks. CoRR abs/1504.03504 (2015). http://dblp.uni-trier.de/db/journals/corr/corr1504.html#WangKL15

44. Wang, W., et al.: Zero-shot learning via class-conditioned deep generative models. arXiv preprint arXiv:1711.05820 (2017)

45. Xian, Y., Akata, Z., Sharma, G., Nguyen, Q., Hein, M., Schiele, B.: Latent embeddings for zero-shot classification. CoRR abs/1603.08895 (2016). http://dblp.uni-trier.de/db/journals/corr/corr1603.html#XianA0N0S16

46. Xian, Y., Schiele, B., Akata, Z.: Zero-shot learning - the good, the bad and the ugly. In: IEEE Computer Vision and Pattern Recognition (CVPR) (2017)

47. Yu, Q., Liu, F., Song, Y.Z., Xiang, T., Hospedales, T.M., Loy, C.C.: Sketch me that shoe. In: CVPR, pp. 799–807. IEEE Computer Society (2016). http://dblp.uni-trier.de/db/conf/cvpr/cvpr2016.html#YuLSXHL16

48. Yu, Q., Yang, Y., Liu, F., Song, Y.Z., Xiang, T., Hospedales, T.M.: Sketch-a-Net: a deep neural network that beats humans. Int. J. Comput. Vis. **122**(3), 411–425 (2017). http://dblp.uni-trier.de/db/journals/ijcv/ijcv122.html#YuYLSXH17

49. Zhang, Y., Gong, B., Shah, M.: Fast zero-shot image tagging. CoRR abs/1605.09759 (2016). http://dblp.uni-trier.de/db/journals/corr/corr1605.html#ZhangGS16

50. Zhou, R., Chen, L., Zhang, L.: Sketch-based image retrieval on a large scale database. In: Babaguchi, N., et al. (eds.) ACM Multimedia, pp. 973–976. ACM (2012). http://dblp.uni-trier.de/db/conf/mm/mm2012.html#ZhouCZ12

Lambda Twist: An Accurate Fast Robust Perspective Three Point (P3P) Solver

Mikael Persson$^{(\boxtimes)}$ (iD) and Klas Nordberg

Computer Vision Laboratory, Linköping University, Linköping, Sweden
{mikael.persson,klas.nordberg}@liu.se

Abstract. We present Lambda Twist; a novel P3P solver which is accurate, fast and robust. Current state-of-the-art P3P solvers find all roots to a quartic and discard geometrically invalid and duplicate solutions in a post-processing step. Instead of solving a quartic, the proposed P3P solver exploits the underlying elliptic equations which can be solved by a fast and numerically accurate diagonalization. This diagonalization requires a single real root of a cubic which is then used to find the, up to four, P3P solutions. Unlike the direct quartic solvers our method never computes geometrically invalid or duplicate solutions.

Extensive evaluation on synthetic data shows that the new solver has better numerical accuracy and is faster compared to the state-of-the-art P3P implementations. Implementation and benchmark are available on github.

Keywords: P3P · PnP · Visual odometry · Camera geometry

1 Introduction

Pose estimation from projective observations of known model points, also known as the Perspective n-point Problem (PnP), is extensively used in geometric computer vision systems. In particular, finding the camera pose (orientation and position) from observations of n 3D points in relation to a world coordinate system is often the first step in visual odometry and augmented reality systems [7,12]. It is also an important part in structure from motion and reconstruction of unordered images [1]. The minimal PnP case with a finite number of solutions requires three ($n = 3$) observations in a nondegenerate configuration and is known as the P3P problem (Fig. 1).

We are concerned with the latency and accuracy critical scenarios of odometry on low power hardware and AR/VR. Since both latency and localization errors independently not only break immersion, but also cause nausea, accurate solutions and minimal latency are crucial. As an example application, vision based localization for AR/VR places a few markers/beacons on a target, which are then found using a high speed camera. Ideally we would then solve the pose directly on chip without sending the full image stream elsewhere, mandating minimal cost. Further, because the markers are placed on a small area and

© Springer Nature Switzerland AG 2018
V. Ferrari et al. (Eds.): ECCV 2018, LNCS 11208, pp. 334–349, 2018.
https://doi.org/10.1007/978-3-030-01225-0_20

the camera is of relatively low resolution, the markers are close to each other, meaning numerical issues due to near degenerate cases are common and the algorithm must be robust. The experiments will show that we have made substantial progress on both speed and accuracy compared to state-of-the-art.

Surveying the literature we find that P3P solvers are either direct or triangulating. Triangulating methods first triangulate the points in the camera coordinate system using a pose invariant, leaving only distances as unknowns and then solve for the pose. In this case the rotation is solved for as either a quaternion or $\mathbf{R} \in SO(3)$ depending on end user preference. This allows the geometric feasibility constraints, i.e. each point must lie in front of the camera, to limit the solutions prior to computing the pose. In contrast, direct methods parametrize the pose in the input coefficients using a projective invariant. Therefore, they have to apply the feasibility constraint after the solutions are found, as a post processing step.

To our knowledge, all direct methods, including state-of-the-art [6,8], are based on finding the four roots of a quartic. This requires complex arithmetics and root polishing to achieve high numerical accuracy. In contrast, triangulating methods can find all P3P solutions by diagonalizing a three by three matrix. Further, the methods by Kneip and Ke output $\mathbf{R} \in SO(3)$, which if unit quaternion representation is desired requires careful conversion. Thus, triangulating methods have a potential advantage in terms of numerical complexity and accuracy. This motivates us to revisit the P3P problem. To this end we derive a novel triangulating P3P solution designed to provide high numerical accuracy and computational performance. Unlike earlier approaches based on similar pose invariants, we use a novel solution path. This allows us to discard infeasible and duplicate solutions at an earlier stage, thereby saving computation. We explicitly exploit that only a single real root of the diagonalizing cubic is required. We find this root using Newton's method with an initializing heuristic. This improves the numerical accuracy and again saves computation.

We believe that the main strength of our algorithm is the relative numerical stability of solving for one root of a cubic compared to the multiple iterative solvers used in the solution of a quartic. Note that while discarding invalid and duplicate solutions in advance saves us time, there is another more subtle problem which our solution avoids. Note that the numeric accuracy of quartic solver roots decrease severely with increasing root multiplicity. Because such roots correspond to duplicate or near duplicate solutions and because such duplicates are common see Sect. 4.4, this reduces the numerical accuracy of the quartic based solvers beyond what might otherwise be expected. Further this predicts the behavior seen in the experiments where a incorrect solution found by Ke's solver will be refined to a duplicate root with further iterations. Since we compute the single root we need iteratively, the multiplicity of the cubic does not significantly affect the numerical accuracy of our solver. Further, since the different roots of the cubic do not correspond to different or duplicate solutions, higher multiplicities are rare. Finally, the initialization used makes it very likely that the root we converge to is the one with the best numerical properties.

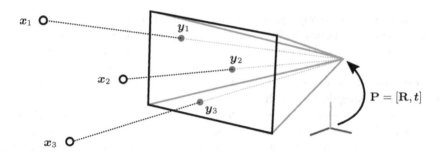

Fig. 1. The P3P setup, where each pair $\{\boldsymbol{x}_1, \boldsymbol{y}_1\}$, $\{\boldsymbol{x}_2, \boldsymbol{y}_2\}$ and $\{\boldsymbol{x}_3, \boldsymbol{y}_3\}$ are used in the calculation of the camera pose $\mathbf{P} = [\mathbf{R}, \boldsymbol{t}]$.

Although grounded in geometry, the proposed method is derived using methods from linear algebra. The method is parameterized simply in the signed distance to the three 3D points. Although difficult to compare, we believe that the proposed approach is comparatively simple to understand.

Through extensive experiments we show that our solver achieves superior computational and significantly better numerical performance over prior state of the art.

1.1   Related Work

Several methods for solving P3P can be found in the literature. The first solution for P3P was published 1841 by Grunert [4], which demonstrated that P3P has up to 4 feasible solutions. Since then, a large number of solvers have been published, which improve the original formulation in various ways. An overview of several of the relevant P3P algorithms until 1991 is presented in the paper by Haralick et al. [5]. More recent methods can be found in the work by Gao et al. [2], Kneip et al. [8], and by Ke et al. [6].

A common theme in a majority of P3P solvers is that each valid solution is associated with a root of a quartic. What differs between the solvers is how this quartic is formulated from the known data, and how the solution are associated with the roots. To find all valid solutions to P3P these methods thus need to find all real roots to a quartic.

A few of the proposed methods, e.g. the one by Finsterwalder, accounted for by Haralick et al. [5], and the one by Grafarend et al. [3], have observed that pairs of P3P solutions can be associated with the roots of a cubic. This observation has not been given much attention in the literature on P3P. In particular, it has not been discussed in the more recent P3P methods.

In this paper we present a novel P3P solver that, while it shares the projective invariant beginnings with Grafarend et al. [9], follows a different solution path which enables an efficient implementation.

2   Problem Formulation

Given a calibrated pinhole camera, three 3D points $x_i = (x_i, y_i, z_i)$, and corresponding homogeneous image coordinates $y_i \sim (u_i, v_i, 1)$ such that $|y_i| = 1$, then:

$$\lambda_i y_i = \mathbf{R} x_i + t, \ i \in \{1, 2, 3\}, \tag{1}$$

where the rotation $\mathbf{R} \in SO(3)$ together with the translation $t \in \mathbb{R}^3$ define the pose of the camera. In short a P3P solver is a function $[\mathbf{R}_k, t_k] = $ P3P$(x_{1:3}, y_{1:3})$. Depending on the configuration of the points, P3P has up to four solutions.

2.1   Requirements

It is well known that a necessary condition to assure a finite set of solutions, is that neither the 3D points nor the 2D points are collinear [5]. In addition there are two specific requirements any solution should meet. First, they should be real. Second, since the parameters λ_k is the signed distance from the camera center for each 3D point, λ_1, λ_2, and λ_3 are required to be positive and real. This is a geometric feasibility condition on the solutions, which implies that all three 3D points are "in front of" the camera.

3   Lambda Twist Derivation

In this section we derive the proposed algorithm for solving P3P. The starting point is (1), and the first step is to eliminate t and $\mathbf{R}$, leaving only the signed distance parameters λ_i as unknowns. More precisely, they have to solve a system of three inhomogeneous quadratic equations. As we will see, the solutions to the three inhomogeneous equations can be determined by first reducing the problem to a pair of homogeneous quadratic equations. Solving these homogeneous quadratic equations is isomorphic to finding the intersection of two ellipses in the plane. We diagonalize the elliptic equations by finding a rank 2 linear combination of the constraints. Finding this rank 2 combination requires a single root of a cubic polynomial. In general, this root gives us up to four sets of positive $(\lambda_1, \lambda_2, \lambda_3)$, corresponding to a vector $\mathit{\Lambda} \in \mathbb{R}^3$, an element of the "lambda-space". Finally, for each geometrically feasible set of $\mathit{\Lambda}_k$ parameters, we determine a corresponding camera pose $(\mathbf{R}_k, t_k)$.

3.1   Pose Invariant Constraints

In principle, the homogeneous image coordinates y_i in (1) can be multiplied by an arbitrary non-zero scalar. By doing so, the parameters λ_i have to scale inversely. If the scaling is positive, each λ_i then represents a scaled depth, but the sign rules described in Sect. 2.1 still apply. In the following, we scale each y_i such that $\|y_i\| = 1$.

We begin the elimination with the translation t, by taking the pairwise differences of the three equations in (1), then taking into account that $\mathbf{R} \in SO(3)$ and $\|\boldsymbol{y}_i\| = 1$:

$$\lambda_i \boldsymbol{y}_i - \lambda_j \boldsymbol{y}_j = \mathbf{R}(\boldsymbol{x}_i - \boldsymbol{x}_j), \implies \tag{2}$$

$$|\lambda_i \boldsymbol{y}_i - \lambda_j \boldsymbol{y}_j|^2 = |\boldsymbol{x}_i - \boldsymbol{x}_j|^2 \overset{def}{=} a_{ij}, \implies$$

$$\lambda_i^2 + \lambda_j^2 - 2b_{ij}\lambda_i\lambda_j = a_{ij}, \tag{3}$$

$$b_{ij} \overset{def}{=} \boldsymbol{y}_i^T \boldsymbol{y}_j.$$

This leaves us with only λ_i as free variables to be determined from the three non-trivial ij i.e. $\{12, 13, 23\}$. This is what we will do next.

3.2   Three Inhomogeneous Quadratic Polynomials

The constraints on the scaled depth parameters λ_i in (3) can be formulated in a more compact way as

$$\boldsymbol{\Lambda}^\top \mathbf{M}_{12} \boldsymbol{\Lambda} = a_{12}, \qquad \boldsymbol{\Lambda}^\top \mathbf{M}_{13} \boldsymbol{\Lambda} = a_{13}, \qquad \boldsymbol{\Lambda}^\top \mathbf{M}_{23} \boldsymbol{\Lambda} = a_{23}, \tag{4}$$

where

$$\mathbf{M}_{12} = \begin{pmatrix} 1 & -b_{12} & 0 \\ -b_{12} & 1 & 0 \\ 0 & 0 & 0 \end{pmatrix}, \quad \mathbf{M}_{13} = \begin{pmatrix} 1 & 0 & -b_{13} \\ 0 & 0 & 0 \\ -b_{13} & 0 & 1 \end{pmatrix}, \quad \mathbf{M}_{23} = \begin{pmatrix} 0 & 0 & 0 \\ 0 & 1 & -b_{23} \\ 0 & -b_{23} & 1 \end{pmatrix}.$$

There is a geometric interpretation of the variables: $b_{ij} = \boldsymbol{y}_i^T \boldsymbol{y}_j$ is the cosine of the angle between the projection rays of image point i and j, and a_{ij} is the squared distance between 3D points $\boldsymbol{x}_i$ and $\boldsymbol{x}_j$. Since we require that the 3D points are not collinear, it follows that $a_{ij} > 0, \forall ij$.

Some observations can be made from (4). First, we see that if $\boldsymbol{\Lambda}$ solves these three equations, then so does $-\boldsymbol{\Lambda}$. However as mentioned in Sect. 2.1 only solutions where all $\lambda_i > 0$ are of interest. A second observation is that the set of $\boldsymbol{\Lambda}$ which solves an equation in (4) forms an elliptic cylinder centered on each of the three axes in the lambda-space. Each solution $\boldsymbol{\Lambda}$ is a point where all three cylinders intersect each other. In general there are 8 such points, taking the sign flip of $\boldsymbol{\Lambda}$ into account, though some of these intersection points may be complex. As mentioned in Sect. 2.1, we want to remove complex $\boldsymbol{\Lambda}$ and also any $\boldsymbol{\Lambda}$ which does not lie in the "positive octant" of the lambda-space, where $\lambda_1, \lambda_2, \lambda_3 > 0$.

3.3   Two Homogeneous Quadratic Polynomials

A linear combination of Eq. (4) provide a set of homogeneous polynomials which are compactly formulated as

$$\mathbf{D}_1 = \mathbf{M}_{12} a_{23} - \mathbf{M}_{23} a_{12} = \begin{pmatrix} \boldsymbol{d}_{11} \boldsymbol{d}_{12} \boldsymbol{d}_{13} \end{pmatrix}, \tag{5}$$

$$\mathbf{D}_2 = \mathbf{M}_{13} a_{23} - \mathbf{M}_{23} a_{13} = \begin{pmatrix} \boldsymbol{d}_{21} \boldsymbol{d}_{22} \boldsymbol{d}_{23} \end{pmatrix}, \tag{6}$$

$$\boldsymbol{\Lambda}^\top \mathbf{D}_i \boldsymbol{\Lambda} = 0, \forall i \in \{1, 2\}, \tag{7}$$

where $\boldsymbol{d}_{ij}$ is column j of the matrix $\mathbf{D}_i$.

Since (7) are homogeneous polynomials, any requirement on the norm of Λ is lost. By substituting the solution into one of the equations in (4) the proper scale is found. The equations in (7) specify two ellipses in (λ_1, λ_2) if $\lambda_3 = 1$. Thus the solution represents the intersections of the ellipses.

3.4   The Cubic Polynomial

We now turn to the problem of finding Λ that solves (7). For now we assume that $\mathbf{D}_1$ and $\mathbf{D}_2$ are indefinite as the rare cases when this is not true is either trivial or degenerate. In Eq. (7), each quadratic form has a solutions set in the form of an elliptic double cone in the lambda-space. These two cones intersect along, at most, four lines. This is true for any quadratic form specified as a linear combination of $\mathbf{D}_1$ and $\mathbf{D}_2$ as well. A special case of such a double cone is a pair of planes, where each plane intersects with two of the lines. Such a degenerate case occurs precisely when the linear combination has rank 2. A plane which includes Λ is then an extra linear constraint in addition to the previous quadratic relations. This observation is key for the proposed solver, and we will next consider how to determine these planes, and how they can be used to find all valid Λ.

We form $\mathbf{D}_0 = \mathbf{D}_1 + \gamma \mathbf{D}_2$ that has a corresponding solution space which is simple to determine. We find this $\mathbf{D}_0$ by solving

$$0 = \det(\mathbf{D}_0) = \det(\mathbf{D}_1 + \gamma \mathbf{D}_2). \tag{8}$$

This corresponds to a cubic polynomial in γ:

$$c_3 \gamma^3 + c_2 \gamma^2 + c_1 \gamma + c_0. \tag{9}$$

The four coefficients are given by

$$c = \begin{pmatrix} c_3 \\ c_2 \\ c_1 \\ c_0 \end{pmatrix} = \begin{pmatrix} \det(\mathbf{D}_2) \\ d_{21}^T(d_{12} \times d_{13}) + d_{22}^T(d_{13} \times d_{11}) + d_{23}^T(d_{11} \times d_{12}) \\ d_{11}^T(d_{22} \times d_{23}) + d_{12}^T(d_{23} \times d_{21}) + d_{13}^T(d_{21} \times d_{22}) \\ \det(\mathbf{D}_1) \end{pmatrix}. \tag{10}$$

In the special case that either of $\mathbf{D}_1$ or $\mathbf{D}_2$ are semi-definite, or indefinite with one eigenvalue equal to zero, we get $c_0 = 0$ or $c_3 = 0$. In this case, is not necessary to form and solve this cubic, we simply set $\mathbf{D}_0 = \mathbf{D}_1$ or $\mathbf{D}_0 = \mathbf{D}_2$. In the general case, we may still want to avoid being close to a case where $c_3 \approx 0$, as the cubic then becomes numerically unstable. In this case the real root of the inverse polynomial, i.e. $\mu = \gamma^{-1}$, is found instead. In practice these are near non-existent cases and the polynomial is well conditioned.

In general, we can assume that neither c_3 nor c_0 vanish, and the cubic polynomial is well-defined and has one, two, or three distinct roots. Diagonalizing $\mathbf{D}_0$ requires only one real root γ_0 which can be found with any of several standard methods. With γ_0 at hand, we set $\mathbf{D}_0 = \mathbf{D}_1 + \gamma_0 \mathbf{D}_2$.

We recall that $\mathbf{D}_0$ specifies two planes, each intersecting with two distinct lines that includes Λ solving (7). In the case of four such lines, there are *three* ways to specify the two planes. Therefore we should expect the problem of finding the degenerate cone, specified by $\mathbf{D}_0$, to have three solutions. As we have seen, finding this $\mathbf{D}_0$ can be formulated as finding a root of a cubic. Although additional roots provide more constraints on Λ, we will in the next step see that one case of $\mathbf{D}_0$ is sufficient for finding all solutions to P3P.

3.5   Diagonalization of $\mathbf{D}_0$

An eigenvalue decomposition of $\mathbf{D}_0$ results in

$$\mathbf{D}_0 = \mathbf{E}\mathbf{S}\mathbf{E}^\top, \text{ where } \mathbf{E} = \begin{pmatrix} e_0 & e_1 & e_2 \\ e_3 & e_4 & e_5 \\ e_6 & e_7 & e_8 \end{pmatrix} = (e_1, e_2, e_3,). \tag{11}$$

The matrix $\mathbf{E}$ holds an orthogonal basis of $\mathbb{R}^3$ in its columns e_i, and $\mathbf{S}$ holds the corresponding eigenvalues in its diagonal. Since $\det(\mathbf{D}_0) = 0$, at least one of the eigenvalues are zero, and we can assume $\mathbf{S}$ to have the following form:

$$\mathbf{S} = \mathbf{E}^T\mathbf{D}_0\mathbf{E} = \begin{pmatrix} \sigma_1 & 0 & 0 \\ 0 & -\sigma_2 & 0 \\ 0 & 0 & 0 \end{pmatrix}, \tag{12}$$

and $\sigma_1 > 0, \sigma_2 \geq 0$. The fact that there is at least one non-zero eigenvalue, and that if there is more than one they have opposite sign, is a general observation. This property holds when a rigid transform relates the observations.

We exploit that we know one eigenvalue of $\mathbf{D}_0$ is zero for a efficient eigenvalue decomposition in Algorithm 2. This algorithm also reorders the eigenvectors to ensure that $|\sigma_1| \leq |\sigma_2|$. This improves numerical performance in later steps.

3.6   Solving for Λ

We use the eigenvalue decomposition of $\mathbf{D}_0$ to solve $\Lambda^T\mathbf{D}_0\Lambda = 0$ by first solving the simpler equation $p^T\mathbf{S}p = 0$ using the substitution $p = \mathbf{E}^T\Lambda$ where $p = (p_1, p_2, p_3)^T$. With $p_1 = sp_2$ we find that $s = \pm\sqrt{\frac{-\sigma_2}{\sigma_1}}$ for any p_3.

Each solution of s gives us a linear relation between $\lambda_1, \lambda_2, \lambda_3$ using $p = \mathbf{E}^T\Lambda$:

$$e_1\Lambda = p_1 = sp_2,$$
$$e_2\Lambda = p_2, \implies$$
$$se_2\Lambda = sp_2, \implies$$
$$e_1\Lambda - se_2\Lambda = 0, \implies$$
$$\lambda_1 = \underbrace{\frac{e_3 - se_4}{se_1 - e_0}}_{w_0}\lambda_2 + \underbrace{\frac{e_6 - se_7}{se_1 - e_0}}_{w_1}\lambda_3 = w_0\lambda_2 + w_1\lambda_3. \tag{13}$$

The two solutions for s gives two possible expressions for λ_1 in Eq. (13).

Next let: $\lambda_3 = \tau\lambda_2$. This implies $\tau > 0$ since we only seek the solutions where $\lambda_i > 0$ which satisfy the geometric feasibility constraint. Inserting $\lambda_3 = \tau\lambda_2$ and Eq. (13) in e.g. $\Lambda\mathbf{D}_1\Lambda = 0$ gives

$$\lambda_2^2 \begin{pmatrix} w_0 + \tau w_1 \\ 1 \\ \tau \end{pmatrix}^{\top} \mathbf{D}_1 \begin{pmatrix} w_0 + \tau w_1 \\ 1 \\ \tau \end{pmatrix} = 0. \tag{14}$$

This leads to a quadratic equation in $\tau : a\tau^2 + b\tau + c = 0$ with coefficients:

$$\begin{aligned} a &= ((a_{13} - a_{12})w_1^2 + 2a_{12}b_{13}w_1 - a_{12}), \\ b &= (2a_{12}b_{13}w_0 - 2a_{13}b_{12}w_1 - 2w_0w_1(a_{12} - a_{13})), \\ c &= ((a_{13} + a_{13} - a_{12})w_0^2 - 2a_{13}b_{12}w_0). \end{aligned} \tag{15}$$

In summary, for each of the two possible values of s, we get two solutions for τ. This gives up to four solutions. Complex and negative τ are discarded at this point since they will never lead to real and geometrically feasible poses. We denote the surviving solutions as τ_k.

Next we determine λ_{2k} for each τ_k using $\lambda_{3k} = \tau_k\lambda_{2k}$ and Eq. (4). Specifically we use $\Lambda^T\mathbf{M}_{23}\Lambda^T = a_{12}$ because it does not depend on λ_1. The result is

$$\lambda_{2k}^2 \begin{pmatrix} 1 \\ \tau_k \end{pmatrix}^T \begin{pmatrix} 1 & -b_{23} \\ -b_{23} & 1 \end{pmatrix} \begin{pmatrix} 1 \\ \tau_k \end{pmatrix} = a_{23}, \quad \lambda_{2k} > 0, \tag{16}$$

which is solved by $\lambda_{2k} = \sqrt{\frac{a_{23}}{\tau_k(b_{23}+\tau_k)+1}}$. This gives us a λ_{2k} for each τ_k. Note that $a_{23} > 0$ and $(\tau_k(b_{23} + \tau_k) + 1) > 0$ since $|b_{23}| \leq 1$.

Finally we compute $\lambda_{3k} = \tau_k\lambda_{2k}$ and λ_{1k} from Eq. (13). To summarize, for each τ_k we get a Λ_k. So far we have only guaranteed that λ_2 and λ_3 are positive. If $\lambda_{1k} < 0$ then Λ_k is discarded. This ensures that the remaining Λ_k are geometrically feasible.

3.7 Recovering R and t

At this point we have a set of up to four geometrically feasible solutions Λ_k. For each Λ_k, it remains to determine the corresponding camera pose $(\mathbf{R}_k, \mathbf{t}_k)$. The rotation $\mathbf{R}_k$ can be recovered from $ij \in \{12, 13, 23\}$ in (2), but since the differences of the 3D points that appear in the right hand sides of these equations are linearly dependent, these three equations are of rank two. To increase the rank, we can take the cross product of the entries in the left hand side of the first two equations. This must equal the cross product of the corresponding entries in the right hand side:

$$\mathbf{z}_1 \times \mathbf{z}_2 = \mathbf{R}\Big((\mathbf{x}_1 - \mathbf{x}_2) \times (\mathbf{x}_2 - \mathbf{x}_3)\Big), \tag{17}$$

where $\mathbf{z}_1 = \lambda_1\mathbf{y}_1 - \lambda_2\mathbf{y}_2$ and $\mathbf{z}_2 = \lambda_2\mathbf{y}_2 - \lambda_3\mathbf{y}_3$.

The first two equations in (2) together with (17) gives:

$$\mathbf{Y} = \mathbf{RX}, \tag{18}$$

$$\mathbf{Y} = \left(\boldsymbol{z}_1, \boldsymbol{z}_2, \boldsymbol{z}_1 \times \boldsymbol{z}_2 \right), \tag{19}$$

$$\mathbf{X} = \left(\boldsymbol{x}_1 - \boldsymbol{x}_2, \boldsymbol{x}_2 - \boldsymbol{x}_3, (\boldsymbol{x}_1 - \boldsymbol{x}_2) \times (\boldsymbol{x}_2 - \boldsymbol{x}_3) \right), \tag{20}$$

$$\mathbf{R} = \mathbf{YX}^{-1}. \tag{21}$$

This solution only provides $\mathbf{R} \in SO(3)$ if the correspondences are exact. This is guaranteed by Eq. (1).

Finally, the translation part of the pose can be solved from any of the three equations in (1):

$$\boldsymbol{t} = \lambda_i \boldsymbol{y}_i - \mathbf{R}\boldsymbol{x}_i. \tag{22}$$

In the end, this produces one pose $(\mathbf{R}_k, \boldsymbol{t}_k)$ that solves (1) for each feasible vector $\boldsymbol{\Lambda}_k$ that is generated by the previous step.

If desired, the corresponding unit quaternions $\boldsymbol{q}_k$ can be extracted given the two 3D correspondences in (17), see Appendix A.2. We use the rotation matrix representation to make the algorithm more closely comparable to the alternatives.

Algorithm 1. Lambda Twist P3P

1: **function** MIX$(\boldsymbol{n}, \boldsymbol{m}) = \left(\boldsymbol{n}, \boldsymbol{m}, \boldsymbol{n} \times \boldsymbol{m} \right)$

2: **function** P3P$(\boldsymbol{y}_{1:3}, \boldsymbol{x}_{1:3})$
3:     Normalize $\boldsymbol{y}_i = \boldsymbol{y}_i / |\boldsymbol{y}_i|$
4:     Compute a_{ij} and b_{ij} according to (3)
5:     Construct $\mathbf{D}_1$ and $\mathbf{D}_2$ from (5) and (6)
6:     Compute a real root γ to (8)–(10) of the cubic equation
7:     $\mathbf{D}_0 = \mathbf{D}_1 + \gamma \mathbf{D}_2$
8:     $[\mathbf{E}, \sigma_1, \sigma_2] = $ EIG3X3KNOWN0 $(\mathbf{D}_0)$. See Algorithm 2
9:     $s = \pm\sqrt{\frac{-\sigma_2}{\sigma_1}}$
10:     Compute the $\tau_k > 0, \tau_k \in \mathbb{R}$ for each s using Eq. (14) with coefficients in Eq. (15)
11:     Compute $\boldsymbol{\Lambda}_k$ according to Eq. (16), $\lambda_{3k} = \tau_k \lambda_{2k}$ and Eq. (13), $\lambda_{1k} > 0$
12:     $\mathbf{X}_{\text{inv}} = (\text{mix}(\boldsymbol{x}_1 - \boldsymbol{x}_2, \boldsymbol{x}_1 - \boldsymbol{x}_3))^{-1}$
13:     **for each** valid $\boldsymbol{\Lambda}_k$ **do**
14:         Gauss-Newton-Refine$(\boldsymbol{\Lambda}_k)$, see Sect. 3.8
15:         $\mathbf{Y}_k = $ MIX$(\lambda_{1k}\boldsymbol{y}_1 - \lambda_{2k}\boldsymbol{y}_2, \lambda_{1k}\boldsymbol{y}_1 - \lambda_{3k}\boldsymbol{y}_3)$
16:         $\mathbf{R}_k = \mathbf{Y}_k \mathbf{X}_{\text{inv}}$
17:         $\boldsymbol{t}_k = \lambda_{1k}\boldsymbol{y}_1 - \mathbf{R}_k\boldsymbol{x}_1$
18:     Return all $\mathbf{R}_k, \boldsymbol{t}_k$

3.8   Implementation Details

We find the diagonalizing γ as a root of the cubic in Eq. (9) by using Newton-Raphson's method initialized using a simple heuristic.

Algorithm 2. eig3x3known0

1: **function** GETEIGVECTOR(m, r)
2:     $c = (r^2 + m_1 m_5 - r(m_1 + m_5) - m_2^2)$
3:     $a_1 = (r m_3 + m_2 m_6 - m_3 m_5)/c$
4:     $a_2 = (r m_6 + m_2 m_3 - m_1 m_6)/c$
5:     $v = (a_1 \ a_2 \ 1)$
6:     Return $v/|v|$

7: **function** EIG3X3KNOWN0(M)
8:     $b_3 = M(:,2) \times M(:,3);$
9:     $b_3 = b_3/|b_3|$
10:     $m = M(:)$
11:     $p_1 = m_1 - m_5 - m_9$
12:     $p_0 = -m_2^2 - m_3^2 - m_6^2 + m_1 m_5 + m_9 + m_5 m_9$
13:     $[\sigma_1, \sigma_2]$ as the roots of $\sigma^2 + p_1 \sigma + p_0 = 0$
14:     $b_1 = $ GETEIGVECTOR(m, σ_1)
15:     $b_2 = $ GETEIGVECTOR(m, σ_2)
16:     **if** $|\sigma_1| > |\sigma_2|$ **then**
17:         Return $([b_1, b_2, b_3], \sigma_1, \sigma_2)$
18:     **else**
19:         Return $([b_2, b_1, b_3], \sigma_2, \sigma_1)$

Once the Λ_k have been computed they are also refined in accordance with standard praxis [13]. Specifically, we refine the solution using a few verified steps of Gauss-Newton optimization on the sum of squares of Eq. (4). A similar refinement is used in the P3P solver by Ke et al. Note that for both algorithms the accuracy rarely improves after 2 iterations.

This concludes the Lambda Twist P3P algorithm, summarized in Algorithms 1 and 2.

4   Experiments

We have performed three experiments: one to evaluate the numerical accuracy of the proposed method, and two to evaluate the execution time. In order to demonstrate the performance of the proposed method, the experiments were performed on random synthetic data. The proposed method is implemented in C++ and is compared to the state-of-the-art P3P solver by Ke et al. [6], and the P3P solver Kneip et al. [8]. The publicly available C++ implementations of the two state-of-the-art methods have been used. The method by Ke et al. [6] is available as part of OpenCV [10] and the method by Kneip et al. [8] is available at [11]. These solvers both show that they provide superior computational and numerical performance compared to earlier work. The algorithms are compiled with gcc using the same optimization settings as part of the same program. The numerical and time benchmarks are available along with the code on the main authors github page. The comparison is performed using a Intel Core i7-6700 3.40 GHz CPU and the code compiled using gcc 4.4 on ubuntu 14.04 with the compile options: $-O3$ and -march $=$ native.

The implementations by Ke and by Kneip always output four solutions, not all of which are correct. The user must determine which of these are valid. Thus we extend these implementations with a minimal post-processing step. This removes solutions which do not satisfy the geometric feasibility constraint, i.e. $\lambda_i > 0$. We also remove solutions which contains NaN or do not approximately contain rotation matrices, i.e. $|\det(\mathbf{R}) - 1| < 10^{-6}$ and $|\mathbf{R}^T\mathbf{R} - \mathbf{I}|_{L1} < 10^{-6}$. This step takes a total of 40ns per sample. This cost is included in the timings since this step must always be performed before the result can be used. Table 1 shows that there is approximately 1.7 unique valid solutions on average per sample. Note that the solutions output by our algorithm intrinsically fulfill these criterion by construction.

We time the system in two ways. First we time the computation of each sample resulting in a time distribution graph. Second we take the total runtime over the same samples providing an average time without the overhead of per sample timing. The timing is performed using high resolution stable timers.

4.1 Synthetic Data

We generate random rigid transforms and random reasonably distributed observations. There are two goals with the sampling. First, the samples should uniformly cover both the image, and the set of rotations. Second, we want substantial depth and translation direction variation within reasonable limits. This resembles data found in the reconstruction of unordered images, a challenging application. Specifically we generate a P3P observation as follows: The rotation $\mathbf{R}$ is represented by a unit quaternion $\mathbf{q} \in \mathbb{R}^4$. Each sample of $\mathbf{q}$ is drawn from a isotropic Gaussian distribution in $\mathbb{R}^4$, before being normalized to unit norm and then converted to a matrix. This assures that the rotations have a uniform distribution in $SO(3)$ [9]. The translation components $\mathbf{t}$ are sampled from a normal distribution with $\sigma = 1$. Combined, $[\mathbf{R}_{gen}, \mathbf{t}_{gen}]$ is the generating pose of the sample. Observations are generated by a uniform sampling of the normalized image coordinates (u_i, v_i) in the range $[-1,1]$, and the corresponding 3D point is computed as $\mathbf{x}_i = \mathbf{R}^T(\mathbf{y}_i z - \mathbf{t})$ for a uniform random positive depth $z \in [0.1, 10]$.

Note that P3P is algebraically complete in the sense that it has the same number of constraints as there are free parameters, i.e. it is a minimal solver. Therefore there is no coherent interpretation of adding noise to the observations. We do not remove near degenerate data but instead rely on their presence to strain the algorithms. Strictly degenerate cases, i.e. exactly collinear samples, are removed. It is worth pointing out that this dataset strains the algorithms far more than the "near degenerate" samples experiment of Ke et al., which fails to find the problem cases we find.

The resulting data set consists of 10^7 samples, and the same set is used in all experiments. The experiments are performed sequentially but caching cannot occur due to the size of the dataset. Note, one sample is 104 Byte and the full dataset is therefore 1 GB.

4.2 Experiment 1: Numerical Accuracy

The numerical accuracy is evaluated by letting the three methods determine their solutions for each sample. Each valid solution $[\mathbf{R}_k, \mathbf{t}_k]$ is then compared to the generating pose $[\mathbf{R}_{gen}, \mathbf{t}_{gen}]$ of the sample. For each algorithm, the total pose error $\|\mathbf{t}_{gen} - \mathbf{t}_k\|_{L1} + \|\mathbf{R}_{gen} - \mathbf{R}_k\|_{L1}$ of the solution with the error are compared. We are primarily interested in the error in $\mathbf{R}$ but add the translation error to avoid hiding errors in the computation of $\mathbf{t}$. The matrix differences are used to avoid the angle conversion from contaminating the comparison. Similarly the L1 norm is used to reduce numerical error in the norm computation and provide a fair comparison for the smaller errors. Larger errors above 10^{-6} simply indicate failure. The numerical ranking of the algorithms does not change if the L2 norm, or the delta angle, is used. The latter case favors our solution since the $\mathbf{R}$ to quaternion conversion can be avoided in using the method in Appendix A.2.

Figure 2a shows the numerical errors of the three methods. The graph shows that lower errors are more likely with our method than either of the other methods. The number of successes, shown in Table 1, is the number of samples with an error $\leq 10^{-6}$. The table support that failures are significantly less likely with our method. It also shows that the rate of outright failure is far less likely with our algorithm than either of the other two. In particular its interesting to note that Kneip's algorithm has fewer extreme failures than the method by Ke et al. It also turns out the algorithm by Kneip et al. occasionally returns NaN rather than any correct solution. NaNs are replaced by a error of 1 and partially explain the increase at the end of Fig. 2a for Kneip's algorithm. Finally we note that for every single sample our error is lower than the errors of both Ke and Kneip. In short, the numerical performance of our solver is substantially better than the other two methods.

Table 1. Output statistics over 10^7 samples.

Method	Mean[ns]	Successes	Failures	Unique
Lambda twist	278	9999968	32	16934510
Ke et al. 2 iters	342	9995790	4210	16924141
Ke et al. 10 iters	435	9996105	3895	16925025
Kneip et al.	1042	9994973	5027	16909306

Table 2. Timing statistics over 10^7 samples iterated 1000 times.

Method	Median[ns]	Min[ns]	Max[ns]
Lambda twist	277	271	289
Ke et al. 2 iters	341	335	353

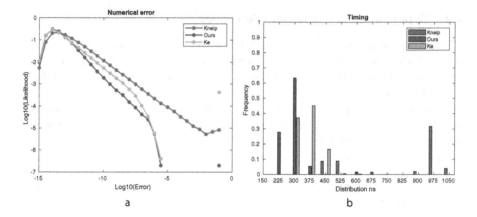

Fig. 2. a Solver numerical precision likelihoods. b Time comparison over 10^7 samples.

4.3   Experiment 2: Execution Time Comparison

We provide each algorithm with identical sequences of synthetic data. Since timing a function interferes with performance, we have sampled both a total time and each sample separately. Figures 2a–b and Table 1 show that the new method is faster than the method by Ke et al., and that both methods are substantially faster than the method by Kneip et al. Note that excluding the post processing step does not change the ranking. In order to show that the timings are stable the primary comparison has been repeated 1000 times on the same data while keeping the computer otherwise idle. The result is shown in Table 2.

4.4   Solutions and Successes

First and foremost, Table 1 shows that we have less than one hundredth the number of failures for this data. Further Table 1 shows that we find more unique solutions, i.e. where $|\mathbf{R}_i - \mathbf{R}_j|_{L1} > 10^{-6}$ and $\mathbf{R}_i, \mathbf{R}_j \in SO(3)$, than either of the other methods. This is largely, but not entirely, due to the samples for which the other algorithms do not find any accurate solution. It is worth mentioning that we do not find duplicate solutions, unlike Ke et al. Their algorithm finds about 0.3% duplicates and 36% incorrect solutions in the standard configuration with two root refinement iterations. Interestingly, if the number of root refinement iterations are increased, Ke's methods only finds slightly more solutions. Instead it refines solutions, which otherwise would not satisfy the solution criteria, into duplicates which do. This results in a duplicate ratio of 36%. Arguably, duplicates should be removed in most applications, but this step was not added to the post-processing as they are technically correct.

We make two additional observations: First, any sample which results in a failure for our method, results in a failure for both other methods, i.e. we are never worse. Second: Every failure for our algorithm and the algorithm of

Ke et al. are near known degenerate cases. This is not the case for the algorithm by Kneip et al. where a rare cancellation of terms causing a division by zero can occur in a nondegenerate case.

When Ke's algorithm fails, the most common reason is that the method does not ensure that the output matrix is in SO(3) due to numerical noise after the quartic root. The benchmark by Ke et al. unfortunately hides this error as it normalizes/converts the resulting rotation matrix to a unit quaternion as part of the evaluation. This step is costly and not included in their timing measurements. The degradation of performance seen here compared to their work is because our metric does not hide this issue. While we understand the appeal of a geometrically interpretable error, we conclude that for the estimation of numerical accuracy, the measure which minimizes error estimation error is preferable.

5 Conclusions

We have presented a novel P3P method with substantially better numerical performance that is faster than previous state-of-the-art. We believe that both the speed and the accuracy are a result of avoiding the quartic and instead going for a cubic. We have shown the performance of the method using extensive synthetic tests. The test stresses the algorithms sufficiently to find failures. Further, the method lets the user select if a unit quaternion or $\mathbf{R} \in SO(3)$ rotation is desired as output without conversion. The method and the benchmark will be available at: https://github.com/midjji/lambdatwist-p3p.

Acknowledgments. This work was funded in part by Daimler Ag, Singulareye AB and Linköping University as well as by CENTAURO: European Union's Horizon 2020 Programme under Grant Agreement 644839.

A Appendix

A.1 Degeneracy of (7)

The two equations in (7) become degenerate when $\mathbf{D}_1$ is a scalar multiplied with $\mathbf{D}_2$, in which case the set of solutions is infinite. Taking into account that $a_{ij} > 0$, a straight-forward inspection of the two matrices in (5)–(6) shows that the degenerate case implies $\mathbf{D}_1 = \mathbf{D}_2$. This happens if and only if

$$b_{12} = b_{13} = b_{23} = 0, \quad \text{and} \quad a_{23} = 0. \tag{23}$$

This means that degeneracy requires $a_{23} = 0$, which in turn implies that the 3D points are collinear.

A.2   Quaternion from two 3D Correspondences

The rotation can be found as a unit quaternion q given the two 3D correspondences a_i, b_i:

$$a_i = \mathbf{R}b_i \iff \begin{pmatrix} 0 \\ a_i \end{pmatrix} = q * \begin{pmatrix} 0 \\ b_i \end{pmatrix} * q^c = \mathbf{Q}\mathbf{B}_i q^c \iff$$

$$\mathbf{Q}^T a_i = \mathbf{B}_i q^c \iff \mathbf{A}_i q^c = \mathbf{B}_i q^c \implies$$

$$(\mathbf{A}_i - \mathbf{B}_i)q^c \overset{def}{=} \mathbf{Z}_i q = 0 \implies$$

$$(\mathbf{Z}_1 \; \mathbf{Z}_2) \begin{pmatrix} \mathbf{Z}_1 \\ \mathbf{Z}_2 \end{pmatrix} q \overset{def}{=} \mathbf{K}q = 0$$

q is then extracted from $\mathbf{K}$ using a specialized solver which exploits that $\mathbf{K}$ has exactly one zero singular value.

References

1. Agarwal, S., Snavely, N., Simon, I., Sietz, S.M., Szeliski, R.: Building Rome in a day. In: Twelfth IEEE International Conference on Computer Vision (ICCV 2009). IEEE, Kyoto, September 2009. https://www.microsoft.com/en-us/research/publication/building-rome-in-a-day/
2. Gao, X.S., Hou, X.R., Tang, J., Cheng, H.F.: Complete solution classification for the perspective-three-point problem. IEEE Trans. Patt. Anal. Mach. Intell. **25**(8), 930–943 (2003)
3. Grafarend, E.W., Lohse, P., Schaffarin, B.: Dreidimensionaler Rückwärtsschnitt, Teil I: Die Projectiven Gleichungen. Technical report, Geodätisches Institut, Universität Stuttgart (1989)
4. Grunert, J.A.: Das Pothenotische Problem in erweiterter Gestalt nebst über seine Anwendungen in der Geodäsie. In: Grunerts Archiv für Mathematik und Physik (1841)
5. Haralick, R.M., Lee, C., Ottenberg, K.: Analysis and solutions of the three point perspective pose estimation problem. In: IEEE Computer Society Conference on Computer Vision and Pattern Recognition, pp. 592–598 (1999)
6. Ke, T., Roumeliotis, S.: An efficient algebraic solution to the perspective-three-point problem. In: 2017 IEEE Conference on Computer Vision and Pattern Recognition (CVPR). IEEE (2017)
7. Klein, G., Murray, D.: Parallel tracking and mapping for small AR workspaces. In: Proceedings of Sixth IEEE and ACM International Symposium on Mixed and Augmented Reality (ISMAR 2007), Nara, Japan, November 2007
8. Kneip, L., Scarmuzza, D., Siegwart, R.: A novel parametrization of the perspective-three-point problem for a direct computation of absolute camera position and orientation. In: IEEE Computer Society Conference on Computer Vision and Pattern Recognition, pp. 4546–4553 (2011)
9. Muller, M.E.: A note on a method for generating points uniformly on N-dimensional spheres. Commun. ACM **2**(4), 19–20 (1959)

10. Web page: https://opencv.org/
11. Web page: http://www.laurentkneip.com/software/
12. Persson, M., Piccini, T., Mester, R., Felsberg, M.: Robust stereo visual odometry from monocular techniques. In: IEEE Intelligent Vehicles Symposium (2015)
13. Press, W.H., Teukolsky, S.A., Vetterling, W.T., Flannery, B.P.: Numerical Recipes in C++: The Art of Scientific Computing. Cambridge University Press, Cambridge (2002)

Linear RGB-D SLAM
for Planar Environments

Pyojin Kim[1], Brian Coltin[2], and H. Jin Kim[1(✉)]

[1] ASRI, Seoul National University, Seoul, South Korea
{rlavywls,hjinkim}@snu.ac.kr
[2] SGT, Inc., NASA Ames Research Center, Mountain View, USA
brian.j.coltin@nasa.gov

Abstract. We propose a new formulation for including orthogonal planar features as a global model into a linear SLAM approach based on sequential Bayesian filtering. Previous planar SLAM algorithms estimate the camera poses and multiple landmark planes in a pose graph optimization. However, since it is formulated as a high dimensional nonlinear optimization problem, there is no guarantee the algorithm will converge to the global optimum. To overcome these limitations, we present a new SLAM method that jointly estimates camera position and planar landmarks in the map within a linear Kalman filter framework. It is rotations that make the SLAM problem highly nonlinear. Therefore, we solve for the rotational motion of the camera using structural regularities in the Manhattan world (MW), resulting in a linear SLAM formulation. We test our algorithm on standard RGB-D benchmarks as well as additional large indoors environments, demonstrating comparable performance to other state-of-the-art SLAM methods *without* the use of expensive nonlinear optimization.

Keywords: Linear SLAM · Manhattan world · Bayesian filtering

1 Introduction

Visual simultaneous localization and mapping (vSLAM) is the problem of estimating the six degrees of freedom (DoF) rotational and translational camera motion while simultaneously building a map of a surrounding unknown environment from a sequence of images. They are fundamental building blocks for various applications from autonomous robots to virtual and augmented reality (VR/AR).

Many typical visual RGB-D SLAM approaches such as DVO-SLAM [17] and ORB-SLAM2 [23], which are based on the pose graph optimization [19], have shown promising results in the environments with rich texture. However, they fare poorly in textureless scenes, which are commonly encountered in indoor environments with large planar structures [13]. They also rely on pose graph optimization methods, which are computationally expensive, and sometimes fail.

Electronic supplementary material The online version of this chapter (https:// doi.org/10.1007/978-3-030-01225-0_21) contains supplementary material, which is available to authorized users.

© Springer Nature Switzerland AG 2018
V. Ferrari et al. (Eds.): ECCV 2018, LNCS 11208, pp. 350–366, 2018.
https://doi.org/10.1007/978-3-030-01225-0_21

For working well in low-texture environments, recent visual SLAM methods [13,20,33] utilize additional geometric information like planar features. They combine plane measurements and scene layout with graph-based SLAM approaches [10,16] to improve robustness and accuracy. Although these SLAM approaches show better accuracy for low-texture environments, there are some limitations: they are still dependent on the pose graph optimization, which is the non-convex and nonlinear optimization problem [4]. Since their SLAM is formulated as a high dimensional nonlinear optimization problem for jointly refining 6-DoF camera poses and multiple landmarks, there is no guarantee that the algorithm can converge to the global optimum [34]. Also, if the nonlinearity of pose graph optimization is too high due to the rotational components of the camera and the landmarks, they will fail to find the true solution.

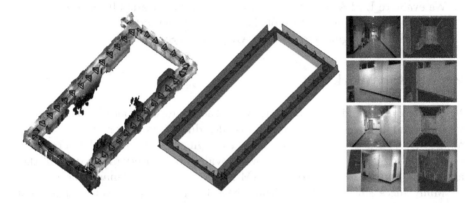

Fig. 1. Linear RGB-D SLAM: L-SLAM generates a consistent global planar map using a linear Kalman filter framework instead of expensive pose graph optimization. Left: Accumulated 3D point cloud is rendered by back-projecting the RGB-D images from the estimated camera trajectory with L-SLAM. Right: The detected orthogonal planar features are overlaid on top of the RGB images. Note that we omit the ceiling planar features for visibility.

To address these issues, we propose *Linear RGB-D SLAM* (L-SLAM), a novel method that jointly estimates camera position and planar landmarks in the map within a linear Bayesian filter as shown in Fig. 1. To separate the need for rotational motion estimation, which is a main source of nonlinearity in SLAM formulation, from the SLAM problem, we first track drift-free 3-DoF rotation and initial 3-DoF translational movement separately using Manhattan world (MW) assumption [5] from VO algorithm [18]. Given the absolute camera orientation, L-SLAM identifies the horizontal and vertical planes in structured environments, and measures the distance to these orthogonal planes from the current camera pose at every frame. With the distance measurements from the orthogonal planes, we simultaneously update the 3-DoF camera translation and the 1-D distance of the associated global planes in the map within a linear Kalman filter (KF) framework. We present a simple, linear KF SLAM formulation by fully compensating for the 3-DoF rotational camera motion obtained from [18], resulting in very low computational complexity while working well in textureless regions.

Extensive evaluations show that L-SLAM produces comparable estimation results compared to other state-of-the-art SLAM methods without expensive SLAM techniques (loop detection, pose graph optimization). Furthermore, we apply L-SLAM to augmented reality (AR) without any external infrastructure. We highlight our main contributions below:

– We develop an orthogonal plane detection method in structured environments when the absolute camera orientation is given.
– We propose a new, linear KF SLAM formulation for localizing the camera translation and mapping the global infinite planes.
– We evaluate L-SLAM on the RGB-D benchmark datasets from room-size to building-size with other state-of-the-art SLAM methods.
– We implement augmented reality (AR) using L-SLAM.

2   Related Work

Visual SLAM methods have been actively studied in the robotics and computer vision communities for the past two decades due to its importance in various applications such as autonomous UAV to augmented reality (AR). From the vast literature in the visual SLAM, we provide a brief overview of state-of-the-art typical approaches and some SLAM methods utilizing planar structures.

Many successful SLAM algorithms have been developed using either point features (indirect) or high gradient pixels (direct). Representatives of them are direct LSD-SLAM [7], DSO [30], and feature-based ORB-SLAM2 [23]. But their performance can be severely degraded in challenging low-texture environments.

Some research in early years of SLAM exploits planes within an extended Kalman filter (EKF) based SLAM approaches [6]. In [8,9], tracked points lying on the same plane are reformulated as a planar feature to reduce the state size in EKF-SLAM. [24] includes planar features in the EKF state vector with a priori structural information. [22] proposes a unified parameterization for points and planes within an EKF monocular SLAM. [31] uses planar features extracted from 2D laser scanner in an EKF-based SLAM. However, these EKF-SLAM methods utilizing planar features have some problems. They cannot avoid local linearization error [2] because the estimation of camera rotation and translation together results in non-linearity of the measurement model. Also, since both distance and orientation are used to represent the planar features, the state vector and covariance matrix size (computational complexity) grows rapidly over time, which limits applications to a small room-scale environment.

Several recent planar SLAM studies apply graph-based SLAM [10,16,19], which is a nonlinear and non-convex optimization problem [4]. To avoid singularities in pose graph optimization, [15] presents a minimal plane representation of infinite planes. With the help of the GPU, [21] tracks keyframe camera pose and global plane model by performing direct image alignment and global graph optimization. [33] performs graph-based SLAM with the plane measurements coming from scene layout understanding using convolutional neural networks (CNN). In [13], a keyframe-based factor graph optimization is performed to achieve real-time operation on a CPU only. Although these approaches demonstrate superior estimation results in structured environments, they require expensive and difficult pose graph optimization since they estimate the camera rotation and translation together [4].

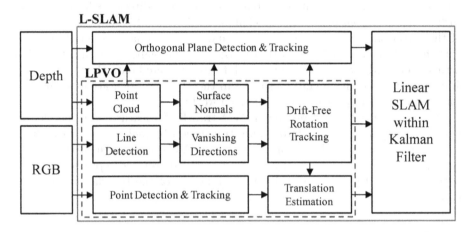

Fig. 2. Overview of the complete L-SLAM algorithm.

The most relevant planar SLAM approach to the proposed L-SLAM is [20], which first estimates the 3-DoF camera rotation by recognizing the piecewise planar models, and utilizes graph SLAM optimization to recover the 2-DoF camera translation. However, unlike the proposed L-SLAM which estimates full 6-DoF camera motion, there is an assumption that the translational motion of the camera is always planar.

3   Proposed Method

Our proposed L-SLAM method builds on the previous *Line and Plane based Visual Odometry* (LPVO) algorithm [18]. However, while LPVO cannot avoid drift over time due to the nature of VO, we extend it to the SLAM formulation in which the planar features are directly modeled as landmarks in order to further constrain the camera motion and significantly reduce drift in translation.

We start by giving a brief description of the previous LPVO algorithm in Sect. 3.1. As a first contribution, we present a method of detecting orthogonal planes in structured environments in Sect. 3.2, which plays an important role in our SLAM method. Next, we introduce L-SLAM, a novel SLAM approach using orthogonal planar features within a linear Kalman filter (KF) framework in Sect. 3.3. Figure 2 shows an overview of the L-SLAM.

3.1   Line and Plane Based Visual Odometry

We summarize the LPVO algorithm briefly (for full details, refer to [18]). LPVO has two main steps: (1) structural regularities (Manhattan frame) are tracked to obtain the drift-free rotation with a SO(3)-manifold constrained mean shift algorithm; and (2) it estimates translation by minimizing a de-rotated reprojection error from tracked points.

The core of the drift-free rotation estimation in LPVO is to track the Manhattan frame (MF) jointly from both lines and planes by exploiting environmental regularities. Given the density distribution of vanishing directions from lines and surface normals from planes on the Gaussian sphere $\mathbb{S}^2$, LPVO infers the mean of the directional vector distribution around each dominant Manhattan frame axis through a mean shift algorithm in the tangent plane $\mathbb{R}^2$ with a Gaussian kernel. The modes found by the mean shift are projected onto the SO(3) manifold to maintain orthogonality, resulting in the absolute orientation estimate of the camera with respect to the Manhattan world.

For the translation estimation, LPVO transforms feature correspondences between consecutive frames into a pure translation by making use of the drift-free rotation estimation in the previous step. LPVO estimates the 3-DoF translational motion of the camera by minimizing the de-rotated reprojection error from the tracked points, which is only a function of the translational camera motion.

3.2   Orthogonal Plane Detection

Once the Manhattan world orientation of the scene with respect to the camera pose has been established from LPVO, we can easily identify the dominant orthogonal planes in current structured environments. Given the surface normals for each pixel used when we track the Manhattan frame in LPVO, we find the relevant normal vectors inside a conic section of each Manhattan frame axis. We perform the plane RANSAC [32] with the pixels corresponding to the surface normals near each axis of the tracked Manhattan frame. We model the plane [29] as:

$$n_x u + n_y v + n_z = w \qquad (u = \frac{X}{Z}, v = \frac{Y}{Z}, w = \frac{1}{Z}) \tag{1}$$

where X, Y, Z denote the 3D coordinates, u, v, w correspond to the normalized image coordinates and the measured disparity at that coordinate. n_x, n_y, n_z are the model parameters representing the distance and orientation of the plane. The error function of the plane RANSAC is the distance between the 3D point and the plane. We fit the plane to the given inlier 3D points from the plane RANSAC in the least-squares sense.

If the angle difference between the normal vector of the plane and one of the three Manhattan frame axes is less than 5 degrees, we refit this plane again to a set of disparity values (w) subject to the constraint that it must be parallel to the corresponding Manhattan frame axis. We compute the optimal scale factor in the least-squares sense that minimizes:

$$s^* = \arg\min_s \|s\left(r_x u + r_y v + r_z\right) - w\| \tag{2}$$

where s is the scale factor representing the reciprocal of the distance (offset) from the plane to the origin, and r_x, r_y, r_z denote the unit vector of the corresponding Manhattan frame axis. In this way, we can find the orthogonal planar features in the scene whose normals are aligned with the tracked Manhattan frame as shown in Fig. 3.

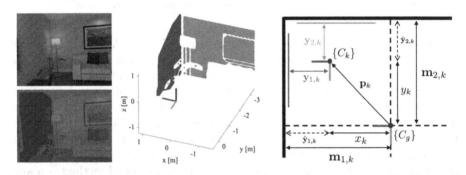

Fig. 3. Results of orthogonal plane detection are overlaid on top of the RGB images (left). Color-coded orthogonal planar features are drawn in a 3-D space (middle), and top view (right). The detailed descriptions of each variable, definition of the state vector, and the measurement model are given in Sect. 3.3. (Color figure online)

3.3   Linear RGB-D SLAM

KF State Vector Definition. The state vector in the KF consists of the current 3-DoF translational motion of the camera and a 1-D representation of the orthogonal planar features in the map. We denote the state vector by $\mathbf{X}$ with its associated covariance $\mathbf{P}$:

$$\mathbf{X} = \begin{bmatrix} \mathbf{p}^\top & \mathbf{m}_1 \cdots \mathbf{m}_n \end{bmatrix}^\top \in \mathbb{R}^{3+n} \qquad \mathbf{P} = \begin{bmatrix} \mathbf{P}_{\mathbf{pp}} & \mathbf{P}_{\mathbf{pm}} \\ \mathbf{P}_{\mathbf{mp}} & \mathbf{P}_{\mathbf{mm}} \end{bmatrix} \in \mathbb{R}^{(3+n)\times(3+n)} \tag{3}$$

where $\mathbf{p} = \begin{bmatrix} x & y & z \end{bmatrix}^\top \in \mathbb{R}^3$ denotes the 3-DoF camera translation in the global Manhattan map frame where the rotation of the camera is completely compensated. Unlike the previous planar SLAM approaches, we do not include the camera orientation in the state vector, which is the main factor that increases the nonlinearity in the SLAM problem [4] because we already obtain accurate and drift-free camera rotation from LPVO in Sect. 3.1.

The map $\mathbf{m}_i = [o_i] \in \mathbb{R}^1$ denotes the 1-D distance (offset) of the orthogonal planar feature from the origin in the global Manhattan map frame, and n is the number of orthogonal planes in the global map. Although each orthogonal planar feature in Sect. 3.2 consists of the 1-D distance and the alignment for the Manhattan frame, we only track and update the distance since the alignment of the orthogonal planes does not change over time. A newly detected orthogonal planar feature $\mathbf{m}_{new}$ is additionally augmented after the last map component of the state vector. Note that there are no variables related to the camera or plane orientation in the state vector $\mathbf{X}$, resulting in a linear KF formulation.

Table 1. Advantages of L-SLAM over existing EKF-SLAM methods

	L-SLAM (Ours)	[9]	[8]	[24]	[22]
State size	$3 + n$	$7 + 7n$	$7 + 9n$	$15 + 3n$	$12 + 10n$
Linearity	Linear	Nonlinear	Nonlinear	Nonlinear	Nonlinear

One of the problems of using the Kalman filter (KF) in SLAM is the quadratic update complexity in the number of features that can limit the ability to use multiple measurements [26]. Since we model only large and dominant planar structures such as a wall or floor with a single variable per plane, the size of the state vector $\mathbf{X}$ is very small compared to other EKF-SLAM approaches as shown in Table 1. While other EKF-SLAM methods [8,9,22,24] in Table 1 represent the plane using a 3 to 10-D vector, the proposed method models the planar feature with only one parameter (offset), resulting in very low complexity. If the number of the planar features (n) is 10, the state size of the proposed method is about ten times smaller than that of Martinez's EKF-SLAM method [22], meaning the EKF update is expected to be ~100 times faster.

Process Model. We predict the next state based on the 3-DoF translational movement estimated from LPVO between the consecutive frames. We propagate the 3-DoF camera translation, and assume the map does not change. Our process model can be written as follows:

$$\mathbf{X}_k = \mathbf{F}\mathbf{X}_{k-1} + \left[\triangle \mathbf{p}_{k,k-1}^\top \ \mathbf{0}_{1\times n} \right]^\top \tag{4}$$

where $\mathbf{F}$ denotes the identity matrix, and $\triangle \mathbf{p}_{k,k-1}$ is the estimated 3-DoF translational movement between the k and $k - 1$ image frame from LPVO.

Measurement Model. We update the state vector in the KF by observing the distance between the currently detected orthogonal planar features and the current camera pose. A measurement model $\mathbf{y}$ for the $\mathbf{m}_i$ is defined by:

$$\mathbf{y} = \begin{bmatrix} \mathbf{m}_1 - x \\ \mathbf{m}_2 - y \\ \mathbf{m}_3 - z \\ \vdots \end{bmatrix} = \mathbf{HX} \in \mathbb{R}^m \qquad \mathbf{H} = \begin{bmatrix} -1 & 0 & 0 & 1 & 0 & 0 & \cdots \\ 0 & -1 & 0 & 0 & 1 & 0 & \cdots \\ 0 & 0 & -1 & 0 & 0 & 1 & \cdots \\ \vdots & \vdots & \vdots & \vdots & \vdots & \vdots & \ddots \end{bmatrix} \in \mathbb{R}^{(m)\times(3+n)} \tag{5}$$

where **H** is the observation model which maps the state space into the observed space, and m is the number of matched orthogonal planar features. For the sake of presentation, we assume that each orthogonal planar feature corresponds to the x or y or z axis of the Manhattan frame in the Eq. (5). A value of the measurement model **y** is the observed distance from the orthogonal planar features computed with the current state vector. We perform the KF update (SLAM) for all associated orthogonal planes with the global planes in the map. Since all formulas and calculations are *perfectly* linear from the Eqs. (3) to (5), there is no local linearization error, and we can easily calculate the optimal Kalman gain [25]. In this manner, we can consistently track the 3-DoF camera translation and 1-D planar map position efficiently and reliably.

Our KF SLAM algorithm relies on the drift-free rotation estimates from LPVO [18] in Sect. 3.1, which shows accurate and stable rotation tracking performance (about 0.2 degrees error in average) in structured environments. This small orientation error is treated as the measurement noise by the Kalman filter, which removes the need to explicitly take into account the correlations [3]. The measurement noise includes not only the error in orientation but also the distance measurement noise of the RGB-D camera. Currently, the measurement error is manually tuned to 2 cm.

Planar Map Management. At the beginning of L-SLAM, we initialize a state vector and its covariance with the orthogonal planar features detected at the first frame. When constructing a global planar map, we only utilize the orthogonal planes that have a sufficiently large area in order to accurately recognize the dominant structural characteristics such as walls, floor, and ceiling in the current structured environments. We perform plane matching using the distance (offset) and alignment from the currently detected orthogonal planar features and the global plane map in the state vector. If the metric distance between the two planes is less than a certain length (in our experiments, 10 cm), and they have the same alignment, the detected planar feature is associated with an existing global planar map to update the state vector. The global planar map can be extended incrementally as new orthogonal planes are detected.

4   Evaluation

We evaluate the proposed L-SLAM on various RGB-D datasets from room-size (∼10 m) to building-size (∼100 m) for planar environments:

- *ICL-NUIM* [11] is a room-size RGB-D dataset providing RGB and depth images rendered in a synthetic living room and office with ground-truth camera trajectories. It is challenging to accurately estimate the camera pose due to the low-texture and artificial noise in the depth images.
- *TUM RGB-D* [28] is the de facto standard RGB-D dataset for VO/vSLAM evaluation consisting of ground-truth camera poses and RGB-D images captured in room-scale environments with various objects.

– *Author-collected RGB-D dataset* contains RGB and depth images at 30 Hz in
large building-scale planar environments with an Asus Xtion RGB-D camera.
We start and end at the same position to evaluate loop closing and consistency
since ground-truth trajectories and maps are not available.

We compare our L-SLAM to other state-of-the-art RGB-D SLAM and
planar SLAM approaches, namely ORB-SLAM2 [23], DVO-SLAM [17], CPA-
SLAM [21], KDP-SLAM [13], and DPP-SLAM [20]. Unlike the proposed L-
SLAM, which is based on a linear formulation, they all perform a high dimensional nonlinear pose graph optimization. We also show an improvement compared to LPVO [18], which our new SLAM approach builds on. Note that we test
each SLAM method with the original source code provided by the authors while
we include the result of CPA-SLAM and KDP-SLAM taken directly from [13].

We implement the proposed L-SLAM in unoptimized MATLAB code for fast
prototyping. Our L-SLAM operates at above 20 Hz throughout the sequence on a
desktop computer with an Intel Core i5 (3.20 GHz) and 8 GB memory, suggesting
a potential of the proposed method when implemented in C/C++.

4.1   ICL-NUIM Dataset

We report the root mean square error (RMSE) of the absolute trajectory error
(ATE) [28] for the resulting camera trajectories of all living room and office
sequences with noise in Table 2. The smallest error for each sequence is highlighted. The results of the CPA-SLAM and KDP-SLAM for the office are not
available. Although CPA-SLAM, which requires GPU for expensive computation, shows the best quantitative results in most living room sequences, L-SLAM
presents comparable estimation results. We plot the estimated camera trajectories using L-SLAM in Fig. 4, showing that L-SLAM is comparable to other
state-of-the-art SLAM approaches without a nonlinear pose graph optimization.

Table 2. Evaluation results of ATE RMSE (unit: m) on ICL-NUIM Benchmark

Sequence	lr-kt0n	lr-kt1n	lr-kt2n	lr-kt3n	of-kt0n	of-kt1n	of-kt2n	of-kt3n
ORB-SLAM2	0.010	0.185	**0.028**	0.014	0.049	0.079	**0.025**	0.065
DVO-SLAM	0.108	0.059	0.375	0.433	0.244	0.178	0.099	0.079
CPA-SLAM	**0.007**	**0.006**	0.089	**0.009**	–	–	–	–
KDP-SLAM	0.009	0.019	0.029	0.153	–	–	–	–
LPVO	0.015	0.039	0.034	0.102	0.061	0.052	0.039	0.030
L-SLAM (Ours)	0.012	0.027	0.053	0.143	**0.020**	**0.015**	0.026	**0.011**

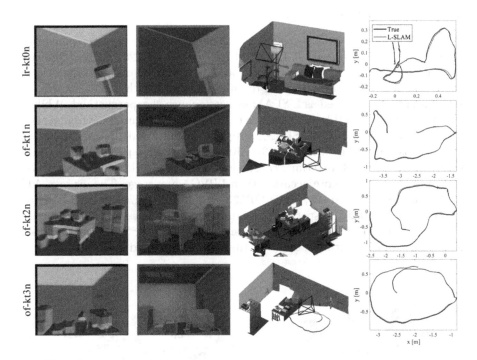

Fig. 4. Selected motion estimation results of the proposed algorithm in the ICL-NUIM dataset. The first column shows the per-pixel surface normal map with respect to the currently tracked Manhattan world. The second and third columns show the orthogonal planar features for mapping and localizing the camera position in the proposed SLAM algorithm. Vertical surfaces are red or green and horizontal surfaces are blue depending on their orientation. The magenta and black lines in the fourth column represent the estimated and the ground-truth trajectories, respectively. (Color figure online)

In the office sequences, L-SLAM achieves more accurate or similar performance to other SLAM methods since the office environments consist of sufficient orthogonal planar features. Reconstruction results of the 'office room' sequences are shown in Fig. 5. Although ORB-SLAM2 performs the best thanks to sufficient texture in 'of-kt2n', L-SLAM also performs nearly as well. The average ATE RMSE of L-SLAM is 0.038, while ORB-SLAM2, DVO-SLAM, CPA-SLAM, KDP-SLAM, and LPVO are 0.057, 0.197, 0.028, 0.053, and 0.046, respectively. Among the CPU-only RGB-D and planar SLAM methods (except for CPA-SLAM, which requires a GPU), L-SLAM presents the lowest average trajectory error. The resulting camera trajectories with L-SLAM are plotted in Fig. 4, showing that L-SLAM, with an efficient and linear KF, is comparable to other recent SLAM approaches especially for highly-planar environments.

4.2   TUM RGB-D Dataset

We choose several RGB-D sequences in the environments where the planar features are sufficiently present in the TUM RGB-D dataset [28]. Table 3 compares estimation results of the SLAM approaches. ORB-SLAM2 outperforms the proposed and other SLAM methods in texture-rich scenes such as 'fr3/str_tex_far', which is entirely expected as L-SLAM utilizes a much cheaper method. While L-SLAM shows comparable performance even in poorly-featured environments of Fig. 6, the accuracy of ORB-SLAM2 drops drastically, and the trajectory estimation fails (marked as × in Table 3). Although inaccurate planar distance measurements in L-SLAM sometimes cause slight performance degradation of LPVO, L-SLAM is generally more accurate than LPVO on average. The average ATE RMSE of L-SLAM is 0.168, while ORB-SLAM2, DVO-SLAM, and LPVO are 0.230, 0.340, and 0.205, respectively. Figure 7 presents the estimated trajectories using L-SLAM from 'fr3/large_cabinet', showing that other SLAM methods perform poorly in low-texture scenes, but the proposed method does not.

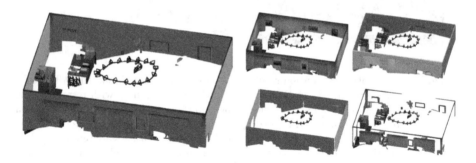

Fig. 5. Left: Synthetic scene 3D reconstruction of an office room from the ICL-NUIM dataset, displaying both planar and non-planar regions with the estimated (magenta) and the ground-truth (black) trajectories. Right, in clockwise order: Color output, surface normal map, non-planar regions only with gray scale, and orthogonal planar regions only with RGB scale. The ceilings are not shown for visibility. (Color figure online)

Table 3. Evaluation results of ATE RMSE (unit: m) on TUM RGB-D Benchmark

Sequence	fr3/str_notex_far	fr3/str_notex_near	fr3/str_tex_far	fr3/str_tex_near	fr3/cabinet	fr3/large_cabinet
ORB-SLAM2	0.276	0.652	**0.024**	**0.019**	×	0.179
DVO-SLAM	0.213	0.076	0.048	0.031	0.690	0.979
LPVO	**0.075**	0.080	0.174	0.115	0.520	0.279
L-SLAM (Ours)	0.141	**0.066**	0.212	0.156	**0.291**	**0.140**

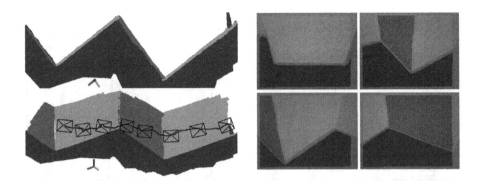

Fig. 6. Top and side views of the global 3D planar map generated by the proposed L-SLAM algorithm from 'fr3/str_notex_near' (left). The orthogonal planar features are overlaid on top of the original images of the respective scenes in clockwise order (right).

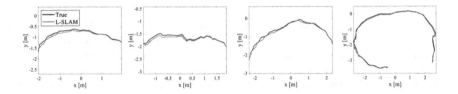

Fig. 7. The resulting camera trajectories with L-SLAM (magenta) and the ground-truth (black) for the TUM RGB-D dataset: fr3/str_notex_far, fr3/str_notex_near, fr3/str_tex_far, and fr3/large_cabinet. (Color figure online)

4.3   Author-Collected RGB-D Dataset

We provide the qualitative 3D reconstruction results generated by L-SLAM with other SLAM methods' trajectories of square corridor sequence, with trajectory lengths of 90 m as shown in Fig. 8. L-SLAM maintains the orthogonal planar structure and significantly reduces the drift error in the final position compared to DVO-SLAM and LPVO. ORB-SLAM2 performs a wrong loop closing in pose graph optimization, resulting in the entire estimated camera trajectory breaking. Although DPP-SLAM [20] shows the second best trajectory estimation results, it only works well in such a 2-D environment with little change in camera height; otherwise, it fails in all sequences from ICL-NUIM and TUM RGB-D dataset. With L-SLAM, the starting and ending points nearly match without loop closure detection; for the others, they do not. Our final drift error is under 0.1%. Figure 9 shows a roughly 120 m long corridor trajectory which consists of the forward camera motion and on-the-spot rotations. We demonstrate that L-SLAM can accurately track the camera pose and the global infinite planes in the map by preserving the planar geometric structure of indoor environments in a much more efficient and cheaper way within a linear KF framework.

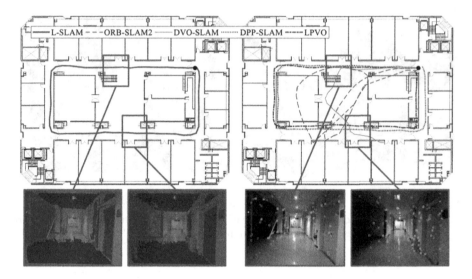

Fig. 8. Estimated trajectories with the proposed (left) and other SLAM methods (right) on the author-collected RGB-D dataset in a square corridor sequence. We start and end at the same position marked in the black circle to check loop closing and the consistency in the resulting trajectories. In the bottom, two images from different locations which look the same and break ORB-SLAM2's loop closing step are shown. Our L-SLAM recognizes the orientation of the current structured environments correctly without expensive SLAM techniques (loop closure, pose graph optimization).

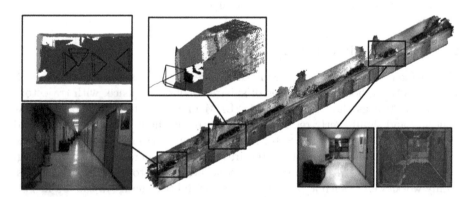

Fig. 9. Accumulated 3D point cloud with the estimated trajectory (magenta) on the author-collected RGB-D dataset in a long corridor sequence. The 3D geometry of the long corridor with the doors is consistently aligned over time while the challenging on-the-spot rotations (top-left) occur. The ceilings in blue are not shown in the 3D point cloud for visibility. (Color figure online)

4.4   Augmented Reality with Linear RGB-D SLAM

We further apply the proposed L-SLAM to augmented reality (AR) to effectively demonstrate its usefulness in a practical application. Currently, most commercial VR/AR products such as Oculus Rift and HTC Vive must use external devices to track the 3-DoF translational movements of the head. However, the AR implemented using the proposed L-SLAM algorithm enables full 6-DoF head tracking only with the onboard RGB-D sensor similar to HoloLens, which is one of the most advanced AR headsets. What the proposed method requires is only the highly-planar environments, and such geometric characteristics can be found easily in most structured indoor environments.

To perceptually assess better, we carefully select a 3D object fixed to the wall or floor in the tested environments. We obtain the international space station (ISS), Elk's head, and Hiroshima sofa 3D models from the 3D Warehouse website [1], and render the 3D objects as an image with the Open Scene Graph [12]. Figure 10 shows a consistent view of the 3D models no matter where we look thanks to the accurate 6-DoF camera motion tracking with respect to the current structured environments from the proposed SLAM method, suggesting a potential in VR/AR applications.

Please refer to the video clips submitted with this paper showing more details about the experiments.[1]

Fig. 10. Augmented reality (AR) implementation results on the ICL-NUIM dataset (left), and the author-collected RGB-D dataset (right) with the ISS, Elk's head, and Hiroshima sofa 3D models. Note that any arbitrary 3D models can be used.

---

[1] Video available at https://youtu.be/GO0Q0ZiBiSE.

5   Conclusion

We present a new, linear KF SLAM formulation that jointly estimates the camera position and the global infinite planes in the map by compensating the rotational motion of the camera from structural regularities in the Manhattan world. By measuring the distance from the orthogonal planar features, we update the 3-DoF camera translation and the position of associated global planes in the map. The extensive evaluation demonstrates the superior performance of the proposed SLAM algorithm in a variety of planar environments, especially in keeping its efficiency *without* the use of expensive nonlinear SLAM techniques. Future work will further consider more general and relaxed planar environments including multiple groups of Manhattan frames such as a mixture of Manhattan frames (MMF) [27] and Atlanta world (AW) [14].

Acknowledgements. This work was supported by the Samsung Smart Campus Research Center (0115-20170013) and Samsung Research, Samsung Electronics Co.,Ltd. Special thanks to Phi-Hung Le for his assistance with the DPP-SLAM code.

References

1. https://3dwarehouse.sketchup.com/?hl=en
2. Bailey, T., Nieto, J., Guivant, J., Stevens, M., Nebot, E.: Consistency of the EKF-SLAM algorithm. In: 2006 IEEE/RSJ International Conference on Intelligent Robots and Systems (IROS) (2006)
3. Camposeco, F., Pollefeys, M.: Using vanishing points to improve visual-inertial odometry. In: 2015 IEEE International Conference on Robotics and Automation (ICRA) (2015)
4. Carlone, L., Tron, R., Daniilidis, K., Dellaert, F.: Initialization techniques for 3D SLAM: a survey on rotation estimation and its use in pose graph optimization. In: 2015 IEEE International Conference on Robotics and Automation (ICRA) (2015)
5. Coughlan, J.M., Yuille, A.L.: Manhattan world: compass direction from a single image by Bayesian inference. In: IEEE International Conference on Computer Vision (ICCV) (1999)
6. Davison, A.J., Reid, I.D., Molton, N.D., Stasse, O.: MonoSLAM: real-time single camera SLAM. IEEE Trans. Patt. Anal. Mach. Intell. **29**, 1052–1067 (2007)
7. Engel, J., Schöps, T., Cremers, D.: LSD-SLAM: large-scale direct monocular SLAM. In: Fleet, D., Pajdla, T., Schiele, B., Tuytelaars, T. (eds.) ECCV 2014. LNCS, vol. 8690, pp. 834–849. Springer, Cham (2014). https://doi.org/10.1007/978-3-319-10605-2_54
8. Gee, A.P., Chekhlov, D., Calway, A., Mayol-Cuevas, W.: Discovering higher level structure in visual SLAM. IEEE Trans. Robot. **24**, 980–990 (2008)
9. Gee, A.P., Chekhlov, D., Mayol-Cuevas, W.W., Calway, A.: Discovering planes and collapsing the state space in visual SLAM. In: British Machine Vision Conference (2007)
10. Grisetti, G., Kummerle, R., Stachniss, C., Burgard, W.: A tutorial on graph-based SLAM. IEEE Intell. Transp. Syst. Mag. **2**, 31–43 (2010)
11. Handa, A., Whelan, T., McDonald, J., Davison, A.J.: A benchmark for RGB-D visual odometry, 3D reconstruction and SLAM. In: 2014 IEEE International Conference on Robotics and Automation (ICRA) (2014)

12. Hassner, T., Assif, L., Wolf, L.: When standard RANSAC is not enough: cross-media visual matching with hypothesis relevancy. Mach. Vis. Appl. **25**, 971–983 (2014)
13. Hsiao, M., Westman, E., Zhang, G., Kaess, M.: Keyframe-based dense planar SLAM. In: 2017 IEEE International Conference on Robotics and Automation (ICRA) (2017)
14. Joo, K., Oh, T.H., Kweon, I.S., Bazin, J.C.: Globally optimal inlier set maximization for Atlanta frame estimation. In: Proceedings of the IEEE Conference on Computer Vision and Pattern Recognition (2018)
15. Kaess, M.: Simultaneous localization and mapping with infinite planes. In: 2015 IEEE International Conference on Robotics and Automation (ICRA) (2015)
16. Kaess, M., Ranganathan, A., Dellaert, F.: iSAM: incremental smoothing and mapping. IEEE Trans. Robot. **24**, 1365–1378 (2008)
17. Kerl, C., Sturm, J., Cremers, D.: Dense visual SLAM for RGB-D cameras. In: 2013 IEEE/RSJ International Conference on Intelligent Robots and Systems (IROS) (2013)
18. Kim, P., Coltin, B., Kim, H.J.: Low-drift visual odometry in structured environments by decoupling rotational and translational motion. In: 2018 IEEE International Conference on Robotics and Automation (ICRA) (2018)
19. Kümmerle, R., Grisetti, G., Strasdat, H., Konolige, K., Burgard, W.: g2o: a general framework for graph optimization. In: 2011 IEEE International Conference on Robotics and Automation (ICRA) (2011)
20. Le, P.H., Košecka, J.: Dense piecewise planar RGB-D SLAM for indoor environments. In: 2017 IEEE/RSJ International Conference on Intelligent Robots and Systems (IROS) (2017)
21. Ma, L., Kerl, C., Stückler, J., Cremers, D.: CPA-SLAM: consistent plane-model alignment for direct RGB-D SLAM. In: 2016 IEEE International Conference on Robotics and Automation (ICRA) (2016)
22. Martínez-Carranza, J., Calway, A.: Unifying planar and point mapping in monocular SLAM. In: British Machine Vision Conference (2010)
23. Mur-Artal, R., Tardós, J.D.: ORB-SLAM2: an open-source SLAM system for monocular, stereo, and RGB-D cameras. IEEE Trans. Robot. **33**, 1255–1262 (2017)
24. Servant, F., Marchand, E., Houlier, P., Marchal, I.: Visual planes-based simultaneous localization and model refinement for augmented reality. In: 2008 19th International Conference on Pattern Recognition, ICPR 2008. IEEE (2008)
25. Simon, D.: Optimal State Estimation: Kalman, H Infinity, and Nonlinear Approaches. Wiley, New York (2006)
26. Strasdat, H., Montiel, J., Davison, A.J.: Real-time monocular SLAM: why filter? In: 2010 IEEE International Conference on Robotics and Automation (ICRA) (2010)
27. Straub, J., Rosman, G., Freifeld, O., Leonard, J.J., Fisher, J.W.: A mixture of Manhattan frames: beyond the Manhattan world. In: Proceedings of the IEEE Conference on Computer Vision and Pattern Recognition (2014)
28. Sturm, J., Engelhard, N., Endres, F., Burgard, W., Cremers, D.: A benchmark for the evaluation of RGB-D SLAM systems. In: 2012 IEEE/RSJ International Conference on Intelligent Robots and Systems (IROS) (2012)
29. Taylor, C.J., Cowley, A.: Parsing indoor scenes using RGB-D imagery. In: Robotics: Science and Systems (2013)
30. Wang, R., Schwörer, M., Cremers, D.: Stereo DSO: large-scale direct sparse visual odometry with stereo cameras. In: IEEE International Conference on Computer Vision (ICCV) (2017)

31. Weingarten, J., Siegwart, R.: 3D SLAM using planar segments. In: 2006 IEEE/RSJ International Conference on Intelligent Robots and Systems (IROS) (2006)
32. Yang, M.Y., Förstner, W.: Plane detection in point cloud data. In: Proceedings of the 2nd International Conference on Machine Control Guidance, Bonn (2010)
33. Yang, S., Song, Y., Kaess, M., Scherer, S.: Pop-up SLAM: semantic monocular plane SLAM for low-texture environments. In: 2016 IEEE/RSJ International Conference on Intelligent Robots and Systems (IROS) (2016)
34. Zhao, L., Huang, S., Dissanayake, G.: Linear SLAM: a linear solution to the feature-based and pose graph SLAM based on submap joining. In: 2013 IEEE/RSJ International Conference on Intelligent Robots and Systems (IROS) (2013)

Attentive Semantic Alignment with Offset-Aware Correlation Kernels

Paul Hongsuck Seo[1], Jongmin Lee[1], Deunsol Jung[1], Bohyung Han[2], and Minsu Cho[1(✉)]

[1] Pohang University of Science and Technology (POSTECH), Pohang, Korea
{hsseo,ljm1121,hesedjds,mscho}@postech.ac.kr
[2] Department of ECE and ASRI, Seoul National University, Seoul, Korea
bhhan@snu.ac.kr

Abstract. Semantic correspondence is the problem of establishing correspondences across images depicting different instances of the same object or scene class. One of recent approaches to this problem is to estimate parameters of a global transformation model that densely aligns one image to the other. Since an entire correlation map between all feature pairs across images is typically used to predict such a global transformation, noisy features from different backgrounds, clutter, and occlusion distract the predictor from correct estimation of the alignment. This is a challenging issue, in particular, in the problem of semantic correspondence where a large degree of image variations is often involved. In this paper, we introduce an attentive semantic alignment method that focuses on reliable correlations, filtering out distractors. For effective attention, we also propose an offset-aware correlation kernel that learns to capture translation-invariant local transformations in computing correlation values over spatial locations. Experiments demonstrate the effectiveness of the attentive model and offset-aware kernel, and the proposed model combining both techniques achieves the state-of-the-art performance.

Keywords: Semantic correspondence · Attention process
Offset-aware correlation kernels · Attentive semantic alignment
Local transformation

1 Introduction

Semantic correspondence is the problem of establishing correspondences across images depicting different instances of the same object or scene class. Compared to conventional correspondence tasks handling pictures of the same scene, such as stereo matching [1,2] and motion estimation [3–5], the problem of semantic correspondence involves substantially larger changes in appearance and spatial

Electronic supplementary material The online version of this chapter (https://doi.org/10.1007/978-3-030-01225-0_22) contains supplementary material, which is available to authorized users.

© Springer Nature Switzerland AG 2018
V. Ferrari et al. (Eds.): ECCV 2018, LNCS 11208, pp. 367–383, 2018.
https://doi.org/10.1007/978-3-030-01225-0_22

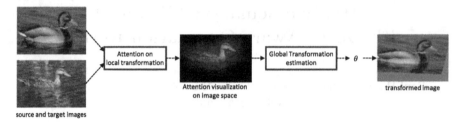

Fig. 1. The proposed attentive semantic alignment. Our model estimates dense correspondences of objects by predicting a set of global transformation parameters via an attention process. The attention process spatially focuses on the reliable local transformation features, filtering out irrelevant backgrounds and clutter.

layout, thus remaining very challenging. For this reason, traditional approaches based on hand-crafted features such as SIFT [6,7] and HOG [8–10] do not produce satisfactory results on this problem due to lack of high-level semantics in local feature representations.

While previous approaches to the problem focus on introducing an effective spatial regularizer in matching [7,9,11], recent convolutional neural networks have advanced this area by learning high-level semantic features [12–24]. One of the main approaches [13] is to estimate parameters of a global transformation model that densely aligns one image to the other. In contrast to other approaches, it casts the whole correspondence problem for all individual features into a simple regression problem with a global transformation model, thus predicting dense correspondences through the efficient pipeline. On the other hand, however, the global alignment approach may be easily distracted; An entire correlation map between all feature pairs across images is used to predict such a global transformation, and thus noisy features from different backgrounds, clutter, and occlusion, may distract the predictor from correct estimation of the alignment. This is a challenging issue, in particular, in the problem of semantic correspondence where a large degree of image variations is often involved.

In this paper, we introduce an attentive semantic alignment method that focuses on reliable correlations, filtering out distractors as shown in Fig. 1. For effective attention, we also propose an offset-aware correlation kernel that learns to capture translation-invariant local transformations in computing correlation values over spatial locations. The resultant feature map of offset-aware correlation (OAC) kernels is computed from two input features, where each activation of the feature map represents how smoothly a source feature is transformed spatially to the target feature map. This use of OAC kernels greatly improves a subsequent attention process. Experiments demonstrate the effectiveness of the attentive model and offset-aware kernel, and the proposed model combining both techniques achieves the state-of-the-art performance.

Our contribution in this work is threefold:

- The proposed algorithm incorporates an attention process to estimate a global transformation from a set of inconsistent and noisy local transformations for semantic image alignment.
- We introduce offset-aware correlation kernels to guide the network in capturing local transformations at each spatial location effectively, and employ the kernels to compute feature correlations between two images for better representation of semantic alignment.
- The proposed network with the attention module and offset-aware correlation kernels achieves the state-of-the-art performances on semantic correspondence benchmarks.

The rest of the paper is organized as follows. We overview the related work in Sect. 2. Section 3 describes our proposed network with the attention process and the offset-based correlation kernels. Finally, we show the experimental results of our method and conclude the paper in Sects. 4 and 5.

2 Related Work

Most approaches to semantic correspondence are based on dense matching of local image features. Early methods extract local features of patches using handcrafted feature descriptors [25] such as SIFT [7, 11, 26, 27] and HOG [9, 10, 28, 29]. In spite of some success, the lack of high-level semantics in the feature representation makes the approaches suffer from non-rigid deformation and large appearance changes of objects. While such challenges have been mainly investigated in the area of graph-based image matching [28, 30–32], recent methods [15–24] rely on deep neural networks to extract high-level features of patches for robust matching. More recently, Han et al. [14] propose a deep neural network that learns both a feature extractor and a matching model for semantic correspondence. In spite of these developments, all these approaches detect correspondences by matching patches or region proposals based on their local features. In contrast, Rocco et al. [13] propose a global transformation estimation method that is the most relevant work to ours. Their model in [13] predicts the transformation parameters from a correlation map obtained by computing correlations of every pair of features in source and target feature maps. Although this model is similar to ours in that it estimates the global transformation based on correlations of feature pairs, our model is distinguished by the attention process suppressing irrelevant features and the use of the OAC kernels constructing local transformation features.

There are some related studies on other tasks using feature correlations such as optical flow estimation [3] and stereo matching [33, 34]. Dosovitskiy et al. [3] use correlations between features of two video frames to estimate optical flow, while Zbontar et al. [33] and Luo et al. [34] extract feature correlations from patches of images for stereo matching. Although all these methods utilize the correlations, they extract correlations from features in a limited set of candidate regions. Moreover, unlike ours, they do not explore the attentive process and the offset-based correlation kernels.

Lately, attention models have been widely explored for various tasks with multi-modal inputs such as image captioning [35,36], visual question answering [37,38], attribute prediction [39] and machine translation [40,41]. In these studies, models attend to the relevant regions referred and guided by another modality such as language, while the proposed model attends based on a self-guidance. Noh *et al.* [42] use an attention process for image retrieval to extract deep local features, where the attention is obtained from the features themselves as in our work.

3   Deep Attentive Semantic Alignment Network

We propose a deep neural network architecture for semantic alignment incorporating an attention process with a novel offset-aware correlation kernel. Our network takes as inputs two images and estimates a set of global transformation parameters using three main components: feature extractor, local transformation encoder, and attentive global transformation estimator as presented in Fig. 2. We describe each of these components in details.

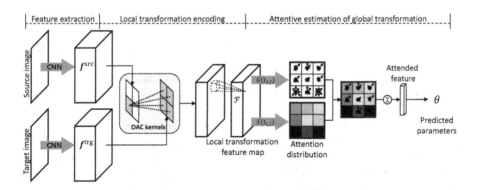

Fig. 2. Overall architecture of the proposed network. It consists of three main components: feature extractor, local transformation encoder, and attentive global transformation estimator. For details, see text.

3.1   Feature Extractor

Given source and target images, we first extract their image feature maps $f^{\mathrm{src}}, f^{\mathrm{trg}} \in \mathbb{R}^{D \times H \times W}$ using a fully convolutional image feature extractor, where H and W are height and width of input images, respectively. We use a VGG-16 [43] model pretrained on ImageNet [44] and extract features from its pool4 layer. We share the weights of the feature extractor for both source and target images. Input images are resized into 240×240 and fed to the feature extractor resulting in 15×15 feature maps with 512 channels. After extracting the features, we normalize them using L_2 norm.

3.2   Local Transformation Encoder

Given source and target feature maps from the feature extractor, the model encodes local transformations of the source features with respect to the target feature map. The encoding is given by introducing a novel offset-aware correlation (OAC) kernel, which facilitates to overcome limitations of conventional correlation layers [13]. We briefly describe details of the correlation layer including its limitations and discuss the proposed OAC kernel.

Correlation Layer. The correlation layer computes correlations of all pairs of features from the source and the target images [13]. Specifically, the correlation layer takes two feature maps as its inputs and constructs a correlation map $c \in \mathbb{R}^{HW \times H \times W}$, which is given by

$$c_{i,j} = f_{i,j}^{\mathrm{src}\top} \hat{f}^{\mathrm{trg}}, \tag{1}$$

where $c_{i,j} \in c$ is a HW dimensional correlation vector at a spatial location (i,j), $f_{i,j}^{\mathrm{src}} \in f^{\mathrm{src}}$ is a feature vector at a location (i,j) of the source image, and $\hat{f}^{\mathrm{trg}} \in \mathbb{R}^{D \times HW}$ is a spatially flattened feature map of f^{trg} of the target image. In other words, each correlation vector $c_{i,j}$ consists of correlations between a single source feature $f_{i,j}^{\mathrm{src}}$ and all target features of f^{trg}. Although each element of a correlation vector maintains the correspondence likelihood of a source feature onto a certain location in the target feature map, the order of elements in the correlation vector is based on the absolute coordinates of individual target features regardless of the source feature location. This means that decoding the local displacement of the source feature requires not only the vector itself but also the spatial location of the source feature. For example, consider a correlation vector $c_{i,j} = [1,0,0,0]^\top$ between 2×2 feature maps, each element of which is the correlation of $f_{i,j}^{\mathrm{src}}$ with $f_{0,0}^{\mathrm{trg}}$, $f_{0,1}^{\mathrm{trg}}$, $f_{1,0}^{\mathrm{trg}}$ and $f_{1,1}^{\mathrm{trg}}$. The displacement represented by the vector varies with the coordinate of the source feature (i,j). When $(i,j) = (0,0)$, it indicates that the source feature $f_{0,0}^{\mathrm{src}}$ remains at the same location $(0,0)$ in the target feature map. When $(i,j) = (0,1)$, it implies that $f_{0,1}^{\mathrm{src}}$ is moved to the left of its original location in the target feature map.

Given a correlation map, decoding the local displacement of a source feature requires incorporating the offset information from the source feature to individual target features. And, this local process is crucial for subsequent spatial attention process in the next section. Therefore, we first introduce an offset-aware correlation kernel that utilizes the offset of features during the kernel application.

Offset-Aware Correlation Kernels. Similarly to the correlation layer, our OAC kernels also take two input feature maps and utilize correlations of all feature pairs between these feature maps. The kernels naturally capture the displacement of a source feature in the target feature map by aligning kernel weights based on the offset between the source and target features for each

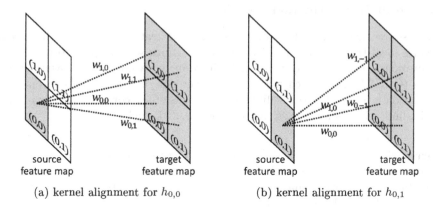

(a) kernel alignment for $h_{0,0}$ (b) kernel alignment for $h_{0,1}$

Fig. 3. Offset-aware correlation kernel at different source locations: (a) at $(0,0)$ and (b) at $(0,1)$. Each dotted line connects source and target features to compute correlation, and $w_{i,j}$ represents a kernel weight for the dotted line. Note that kernel weights are associated with different correlation pairs when source locations vary.

correlation as illustrated in Fig. 3. Formally speaking, an OAC kernel captures feature displacement of a source feature $f_{i,j}^{\text{src}}$ by

$$h_{i,j}^{(n)} = \sum_{k=1}^{H}\sum_{l=1}^{W} w_{i-k,j-l}^{(n)} c_{i,j;k,l} \tag{2}$$

$$= \sum_{k=1}^{H}\sum_{l=1}^{W} w_{i-k,j-l}^{(n)} f_{i,j}^{\text{src}\top} f_{k,l}^{\text{trg}}, \tag{3}$$

where $h_{i,j}^{(n)}$ is the kernel output with the kernel index n, $c_{i,j;k,l}$ is the correlation between a source feature $f_{i,j}^{\text{src}}$ and a target feature $f_{k,l}^{\text{trg}}$, and $\Phi^{(n)} = \{w_{s,t}^{(n)}\}$ is a set of the kernel weights. Note that the kernel weights are indexed by offset between the source and target features, and shared for correlations of any feature pair with the same offset. For example, in Fig. 3a, $w_{0,0}$ is associated with the target feature at $(0,0)$ because the source location is $(0,0)$. The same weight $w_{0,0}$ is associated with the target feature at $(0,1)$ when the source location is $(0,1)$ as in Fig. 3b because the offset between these features is $(0,0)$. Also note that each kernel output $h_{i,j}^{(n)}$ at a location (i,j) captures the displacement of its corresponding source feature $f_{i,j}^{\text{src}}$ at the same location.

While a proposed kernel captures a single aspect of feature displacement, a set of the proposed kernels produce a dense feature representation of feature displacement for each source feature. We use 128 OAC kernels resulting in a feature displacement map $\boldsymbol{h} \in \mathbb{R}^{128 \times 15 \times 15}$ encoding the displacement of each source feature. We set ReLU as the activation functions of the kernel outputs, and compute normalized correlations in OAC kernels since normalization further improves the scores as observed in [13].

In practice, the proposed OAC kernels are implemented by two sub-procedures. We first compute the normalized correlation map reordered based on the offsets between the locations of the source and target features. In this reordered correlation map, every correlation with the same relative displacement is arranged in the same channel. This reordering results in $(2H - 1)(2W - 1)$ possible offsets and thus the size of the output tensor becomes $(2H - 1)(2W - 1) \times H \times W$ where many of the values are zeros due to non-existing pairs for some offsets. Then, we use a 1×1 convolutional layer to compute the dense feature representation from the raw displacement information captured in the reordered correlation map. Note that this process significantly reduces the number of channels by compactly encoding various aspects of the local displacements into dense representations.

Encoding Local Transformation Features. Since the feature displacement map conveys the movement of each source feature independently, each feature alone is not sufficient to predict the global transformation parameters. To allow the network predicts the global transformation from local features in the attention process, we construct a local transformation feature map by combining spatially adjacent feature displacement information captured by h. That is, the proposed network feeds the feature displacement map h to a 7×7 convolution layer with 128 output channels applied without padding. This convolution layer results in a local transformation feature map $\mathcal{F} \in \mathbb{R}^{128 \times 9 \times 9}$. Note that each feature $t_{i,j} \in \mathcal{F}$ captures transformations occurred in a local region. We utilize this local transformation feature map to predict the global transformation through an attention process.

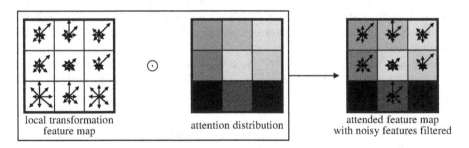

local transformation
feature map

attention distribution

attended feature map
with noisy features filtered

Fig. 4. Illustration of attention process. Noisy features in local transformation feature map are filtered by assigning lower probabilities to these locations. Arrows in boxes of local transformation feature map demonstrate features encoding local transformations, and grayscale colors in attention distribution represent magnitudes of probabilities where brighter colors mean higher probabilities.

3.3   Attentive Global Transformation Estimator

After local transformation encoding, a set of global transformation parameters is estimated with an attention process. Given a local transformation feature map $\mathcal{F} \in \mathbb{R}^{\hat{D} \times \hat{H} \times \hat{W}}$ extracted by OAC kernels with a convolution layer, the network focuses on reliable local transformation features by filtering out distracting regions as depicted in Fig. 4 to predict the parameters from the aggregation of those features. Although a feature map $\mathcal{F}$ gives sufficient information to predict the global transformation from source to target, local transformation features extracted from a real image pair is noisy due to image variations such as background clutter and intra-class variations. Therefore, we propose a model that suppresses unreliable features by the attention process and extracts an attended feature vector that summarizes local transformations from all reliable locations to estimate an accurate global transformation. In other words, the model computes an attended transformation feature τ^{att} by

$$\tau^{\text{att}} = \sum_{i=1}^{\hat{H}} \sum_{j=1}^{\hat{W}} \alpha_{i,j} G(t_{i,j}), \tag{4}$$

where $G : \mathbb{R}^{\hat{D}} \to \mathbb{R}^{D'}$ is a projection function of $t_{i,j}$ into a D' dimensional vector space and $\alpha = \{\alpha_{i,j}\}$ is an attention probability distribution over feature map. The model computes the attention probabilities by

$$\alpha_{i,j} = \frac{\exp\left(S(t_{i,j})\right)}{\sum_{k=1}^{\hat{H}} \sum_{l=1}^{\hat{W}} \exp\left(S(t_{k,l})\right)}, \tag{5}$$

where $S : \mathbb{R}^{\hat{D}} \to \mathbb{R}$ is an attention score function producing a single scalar given a local transformation feature. Note that the model learns to suppress noisy features by assigning low attention scores and reducing their contribution to the attended feature.

Once the attended feature τ^{att} over all local transformations is obtained, we compute the global transformation $\theta \in \mathbb{R}^Q$ by a simple matrix-vector multiplication as

$$\theta = W\tau^{\text{att}}, \tag{6}$$

where $W \in \mathbb{R}^{Q \times D'}$ is a weight matrix for linear projection of the attended feature τ^{att}.

In summary, we first compute local transformation between two images and perform a nonlinear embedding using a projection function $G(\cdot)$. The embedded vector is weighted by spatial attention to compute an attended feature τ^{att} as shown in Eq. (4). The global transformation vector is obtained by linear projection of the attended feature, which is parametrized by a matrix as presented in Eq. (6).

We use multi-layer perceptrons (MLPs) for G and S in Eqs. (4) and (5). G is a two-layer MLP with 128 hidden and output ReLU activations. Since the feature representations produced by G is directly used for the final estimation as a linear mapping in Eq. (6), we additionally concatenate 5-dimensional index embedding to the feature $t_{i,j} \in \mathcal{F}$ to better estimate the global transformation from local transformation features. While S is another two-layer MLP with 64 hidden ReLU activations, its output is a scalar without non-linearity; this is due to the application of softmax normalization outside S. Note that we do not use the index embedding to avoid strong biases of attentions on certain regions. Since G and S are applied to all feature vectors across the spatial dimensions, we implement them by multiple 1×1 convolutions with batch normalizations.

Network Training. We build two of the proposed networks with different parametric global transformations: affine and thin-plate spline (TPS) transformations. To train the network, we adapt the average transformed grid distance loss proposed in [13], which indirectly measures the distance from the predicted transformation parameters θ to the ground-truth transformation parameters θ_{GT}. Given θ and θ_{GT}, the transformed grid distance $\mathrm{TGD}(\theta, \theta_{\mathrm{GT}})$ is obtained by

$$\mathrm{TGD}(\theta, \theta_{\mathrm{GT}}) = \frac{1}{|\mathcal{G}|} \sum_{g \in \mathcal{G}} d\left(\mathcal{T}_\theta\left(g\right), \mathcal{T}_{\theta_{\mathrm{GT}}}\left(g\right)\right)^2 \tag{7}$$

where $\mathcal{G}$ is a set of points in a regular grid, $\mathcal{T}_\theta$ is the transformation parameterized by θ and $d(\cdot)$ is a distance measure. We minimize the average TGD of training examples to train the network. Since every operation within the proposed network is differentiable, the network is trainable end-to-end using a gradient-based optimization algorithm. We use ADAM [45] with initial learning rate of 2×10^{-4} and batch size of 32 for 50 epochs. During training, the pretrained feature extractor is fixed and only the other parts of the network are finetuned.

4   Experiments

We evaluate the proposed method on public benchmarks for semantic correspondence estimation. The experiments demonstrate that the proposed attentive method and OAC kernels are effective in semantic alignment, substantially improving the baseline models. The codes are publicly released at http://cvlab.postech.ac.kr/research/A2Net/.

4.1   Experimental Settings

Training with Self-supervision. While the loss function requires the full supervision of θ_{GT}, it is very expensive or even impractical to collect exact ground-truth transformation parameters for non-rigid objects involving intraclass variations. Therefore, it is hard to scale up to numerous instances and classes, restricting generalization. For example, the largest annotation dataset at this time, PF-PASCAL, only contains total 1,351 image pairs from 20 classes, and furthermore their dense annotations are extrapolated from sparse keypoints, thus being not fully exact. To work around this problem, we adopt the self-supervised learning for semantic alignment, which is free from the burden of any manual annotation, is an appealing alternative introduced in [13]. In this framework, given a public image dataset $\mathcal{D}$ without any annotations, we synthetically generate a training example $(I_{\text{src}}, I_{\text{trg}})$ by randomly sampling an image I_{src} from $\mathcal{D}$ and computing a transformed image I_{trg} by applying a random transformation θ_{GT}. We also use mirror padding and center cropping following [13] to avoid border artifacts. The synthetic image pairs generated by this process are annotated with the ground-truth transformation parameters θ_{GT} allowing us to train the network with full supervision. Note that, however, this training scheme can be considered unsupervised since no annotated real dataset is used during training.

For the synthetic dataset generation, we use PASCAL VOC 2011 [46], and build two variations of training datasets with either affine or TPS transformation each for its corresponding network. A set of PASCAL VOC images is kept separate to generate another set of synthetic examples for validation and the best performing models on the validation set is evaluated.

Evaluation. Two public benchmarks called PF-WILLOW and PF-PASCAL [9] are used for the evaluation. PF-WILLOW consists of about 900 image pairs generated from 100 images of 5 object classes. PF-PASCAL contains 1351 image pairs of 20 object classes. Each image pair in both datasets contains different instances of the same object class such as ducks and motorbikes, e.g., left two images in Fig. 1. The objects in these datasets have large intra-class variations and many background clutters making the task more challenging. The image pairs of both PF-WILLOW and PF-PASCAL are annotated with sparse key points that establishe correspondences between two images. Following the standard evaluation metric, the probability of correct keypoint (PCK) [47] of these benchmarks, our goal is to correctly transform the key points in the source image to their corresponding ones in the target image. A transformed source key point is considered correct if its distance to its corresponding target key point is less than $\alpha \cdot \max(h, w)$, where $\alpha = 0.1$, and h and w are height and width of the object bounding box. Formally, PCK of a proposed model $\mathcal{M}$ is measured by

$$\text{PCK}(\mathcal{M}) = \frac{\sum_{i=1}^{N} \sum_{(p_s, p_t) \in \mathcal{P}_i} \mathbb{1}\left[d\left(\mathcal{T}_{\theta_i}(p_s), p_t\right) < \alpha \cdot \max(h, w)\right]}{\sum_{i=1}^{N} |\mathcal{P}_i|}, \quad (8)$$

where N is the total number of image pairs, $\mathcal{P}_i$ is a set of source and target key point pairs (p_s, p_t) for i^{th} example, θ_i is predicted transformation, and $\mathbb{1}$ is the indicator function which returns 1 if the expression inside brackets is true and 0 otherwise.

We evaluate three different versions of the proposed model as in [13]. The first two versions are the models with different transformations: affine and TPS transformations. The other version sequentially merges these two models. That is, the input image pair are first fed to the network with affine transformation, and the image pair transformed by its out is then fed to the network with TPS transformation.

4.2 Results

Comparisons to Other Models. Table 1 shows the comparative results on both PF-WILLOW and PF-PASCAL benchmarks. It includes (i) previous methods using hand-crafted features: DeepFlow [5], GMK [31], SIFTFlow [7], DSP [11], and ProposalFlow [9], (ii) self-supervised alignment methods: GeoCNN [13] and the proposed attentive alignment network (A2Net), (iii) supervised methods: UCN [12], FCSS [17], and SCNet [14]. Note that the supervised methods are trained with either a weakly or strongly annotated data and that many of their PCKs are measured under a different criterion that are not directly comparable to the other scores. By contrast, our method is only trained using synthetic data with

Table 1. Experimental results on PF-WILLOW and PF-PASCAL. PCK is measured with $\alpha = 0.1$. Scores for other models are brought from [9,13,14] while scores marked with an asterisk (*) are drawn from the reproduced models by released official codes. The PCK scores marked with a star ($\star$) are measured with height and width of the image size instead of the bounding box size. Note that the PCK measure with the bounding box size is more conservative than the one with the image size resulting in lower scores.

	Models	PCK ($\alpha = 0.1$)	
		PF-WILLOW	PF-PASCAL
Hand-crafted	DeepFlow [5]	0.20	0.21
	GMK [31]	0.27	0.27
	SIFTFlow [7]	0.38	0.33
	DSP [11]	0.29	0.30
	ProposalFlow (NAM) [9]	0.53	–
	ProposalFlow (PHM) [9]	0.55	–
	ProposalFlow (LOM) [9]	0.56	0.45
Self Sup.	GeoCNN (affine) [13]	0.49	0.50*
	GeoCNN (affine+TPS) [13]	0.56	0.60*
	A2Net (affine)	0.52	0.57
	A2Net (affine+TPS)	0.63	0.63
	A2Net (affine+TPS; ResNet101)	**0.68**	**0.68**
Supervised	UCN [12]	0.42$\star$	0.56$\star$
	FCSS [17]	0.58	–
	SCNet-A [14]	0.73$\star$	0.66$\star$
	SCNet-AG [14]	0.72$\star$	0.70$\star$
	SCNet-AG+ [14]	0.70$\star$	0.72$\star$

self-supervision. As shown in Table 1, the proposed method substantially outperforms all the other methods that are directly comparable. Using VGG-16 feature extractor, the proposed method improves 12.5% and 5% of PCK over the non-attentive alignment method [13] on PF-WILLOW and PF-PASCAL, respectively. This reveals the effect of the proposed attention model for semantic alignment. The quality of the model is further improved when incorporated with a more advanced feature extractor such as ResNet101. It is notable that the proposed model outperforms some of supervised methods, UCN [12] and FCSS [17], while it is trained without any real datasets.

Ablation Study. As our proposed model combines two distinct techniques we perform ablation studies to demonstrate their effects. We mainly compare the proposed model to GeoCNN as it directly predicts the global transformation parameters using the correlation layer. To see the effect of the proposed OAC kernels, we build a model, referred to as GeoCNN+OACK, by replacing the correlation layer of GeoCNN with the OAC kernels. As shown in Table 2, the use of the OAC kernels already improves the performances of GeoCNN for all three versions. Moreover, the OAC kernels reduce the number of parameters in the network since it uses dense representations of local transformations allowing channel compression. Applying attention process on top of correlation layer (GeoCNN+Attention) drops the performance. This is because the correlation map does not encode local transformations in a translation invariant representations. On the other hand, the attention process with the OAC kernels, which is the proposed model, further improves the performances as the distracting regions can be suppressed during the transformation estimation thanks to the

Table 2. PCKs of ablations on PF-WILLOW trained with PASCAL VOC 2011. Scores of GeoCNN are obtained from the code released by the authors. The numbers of network parameters exclude the feature extractors since all models share the same feature extractor.

Models	# of params	Affine	TPS	Affine+TPS
GeoCNN [13]	1.63M (x1.7)	0.430	0.539	0.560
GeoCNN+Attention	1.41M (x1.5)	0.423	0.478	0.476
GeoCNN+OACK	1.12M (x1.2)	0.491	0.555	0.609
Attention+OACK (A2Net)	**0.95M (x1.0)**	**0.521**	**0.563**	**0.626**

Table 3. PCKs of affine models on PF-WILLOW with different training datasets: PASCAL VOC 2011 and Tokyo Time Machine. Scores for GeoCNN are brought from [13].

Models	PASCAL VOC 2011	Tokyo time machine
GeoCNN [13]	0.45	0.49
A2Net	**0.52**	**0.51**

local transformation feature map obtained by the OAC kernels. It is also notable that applying the attention process reduces the number of model parameters because the model does not need extra layers that combine all local information to produce the global estimation; instead, the models simply aggregate local features with attention distribution. This additional parameter reduction results in 70% fewer parameters than GeoCNN while the models maintain superior performance improvements.

Sensitivity to Training Datasets. While both our model and GeoCNN are generally applicable to any image datasets, we experiment the sensitivity of the models to changing training datasets. We train both models with the affine transformation on another image dataset, called Tokyo Time Machine [48], using the same synthetic generation process, and show how much the performances change depending on the datasets. Table 3 shows that the proposed model is less dependent on the choice of the training dataset compared to GeoCNN.

Qualitative Results with Attention Visualizations. Figure 5 presents some qualitative examples of our model on PF-PASCAL. In our experimental setting, the models learn to predict inverse transformation. Therefore, we transform

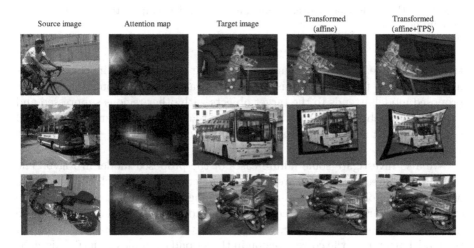

Fig. 5. Qualitative results of the attentive semantic alignment. Each row shows an example of PF-PASCAL benchmark. Given the source and target images shown in first and third columns, we visualize the attention maps of the affine model (second column), the transformed image by the affine model (fourth column) and the final transformed image by the affine+TPS model (last column). Since the models learn inverse transformation, the target image is transformed toward the source image while the attention distribution is drawn over the source image. The model attends to the objects to match and estimates dense correspondences despite intra-class variations and background clutters.

Fig. 6. Some failure cases of the proposed model with the affine transformation. Each row shows an example of PF-PASCAL. Each example contains (1) source image, (2) source image masked by attention distribution, (3) target image and (4) target image transformed by the predicted affine parameters. Even though the model attends to the matching objects, the model fails to find the correct correspondences due to multiple objects of the same class causing ambiguity or hard examples that are difficult to visually percept.

the target image toward the source image using the estimated inverse transformation whereas the attention distribution is drawn over the source image. The proposed model attends to the target objects with other regions suppressed and predicts the global transformation based on reliable local features. The model estimates the transformation despite large intra-class variations such as an adult vs. a kid.

We also investigate some failure cases of the proposed model in Fig. 6. The model is confused when there are multiple objects of the same class in an image or have a large obstacles occluding the matching objects. Also, objects in some examples are hard to visually recognize and lead mismatches. For instance, the model fails to correctly match a wooden chair to a transparent chair although the model attends to the correct region in the second example of Fig. 6. It is challenging even for human to recognize the transparent chair and its corresponding key points.

5   Conclusion

We propose a novel approach for semantic alignment. Our model facilitates an attention process to estimate global transformation from reliable local transformation features by suppressing distracting features. We also propose offset-aware correlation kernels that reorder correlations of feature pairs and produce a dense feature representation of local transformations. The experimental results show the attentive model with the proposed kernels achieves the state-of-the-art performances with large margins over previous methods on the PF-WILLOW and PF-PASCAL benchmarks.

Acknowledgement. This research was supported by Next-Generation Information Computing Development Program (NRF-2017M3C4A7069369) and Basic Science Research Program (NRF-2017R1E1A1A01077999) through the National Research Foundation of Korea (NRF) funded by the Ministry of Science, ICT, and Institute for Information & communications Technology Promotion (IITP) funded by the Korea government (MIST) (No. 2017-0-01778, Development of Explainable Human-level Deep Machine Learning Inference Framework).

References

1. Hosni, A., Rhemann, C., Bleyer, M., Rother, C., Gelautz, M.: Fast cost-volume filtering for visual correspondence and beyond. IEEE Trans. Patt. Anal. Mach. Intell. **35**(2), 504–511 (2013)
2. Okutomi, M., Kanade, T.: A multiple-baseline stereo. IEEE Trans. Patt. Anal. Mach. Intell. **15**(4), 353–363 (1993)
3. Dosovitskiy, A., et al.: FlowNet: learning optical flow with convolutional networks. In: ICCV (2015)
4. Weinzaepfel, P., Revaud, J., Harchaoui, Z., Schmid, C.: DeepFlow: large displacement optical flow with deep matching. In: ICCV (2013)
5. Revaud, J., Weinzaepfel, P., Harchaoui, Z., Schmid, C.: DeepMatching: hierarchical deformable dense matching. Int. J. Comput. Vis. **120**(3), 300–323 (2016)
6. Lowe, D.G.: Distinctive image features from scale-invariant keypoints. Int. J. Comput. Vis. **60**(2), 91–110 (2004)
7. Liu, C., Yuen, J., Torralba, A.: SIFT flow: dense correspondence across scenes and its applications. In: Hassner, T., Liu, C. (eds.) Dense Image Correspondences for Computer Vision, pp. 15–49. Springer, Cham (2016). https://doi.org/10.1007/978-3-319-23048-1_2
8. Dalal, N., Triggs, B.: Histograms of oriented gradients for human detection. In: CVPR (2005)
9. Ham, B., Cho, M., Schmid, C., Ponce, J.: Proposal flow. In: CVPR (2016)
10. Taniai, T., Sinha, S.N., Sato, Y.: Joint recovery of dense correspondence and cosegmentation in two images. In: CVPR (2016)
11. Kim, J., Liu, C., Sha, F., Grauman, K.: Deformable spatial pyramid matching for fast dense correspondences. In: CVPR (2013)
12. Choy, C.B., Gwak, J., Savarese, S., Chandraker, M.: Universal correspondence network. In: Advances in Neural Information Processing Systems, pp. 2414–2422 (2016)
13. Rocco, I., Arandjelovic, R., Sivic, J.: Convolutional neural network architecture for geometric matching. In: CVPR (2017)
14. Han, K., et al.: SCNet: learning semantic correspondence. In: ICCV (2017)
15. Ufer, N., Ommer, B.: Deep semantic feature matching. In: CVPR (2017)
16. Kim, S., Min, D., Lin, S., Sohn, K.: DCTM: discrete-continuous transformation matching for semantic flow. In: ICCV (2017)

17. Kim, S., Min, D., Ham, B., Jeon, S., Lin, S., Sohn, K.: FCSS: fully convolutional self-similarity for dense semantic correspondence. In: CVPR (2017)
18. Novotny, D., Larlus, D., Vedaldi, A.: AnchorNet: a weakly supervised network to learn geometry-sensitive features for semantic matching. In: CVPR (2017)
19. Zagoruyko, S., Komodakis, N.: Learning to compare image patches via convolutional neural networks. In: CVPR (2015)
20. Zbontar, J., LeCun, Y.: Computing the stereo matching cost with a convolutional neural network. In: CVPR (2015)
21. Han, X., Leung, T., Jia, Y., Sukthankar, R., Berg, A.C.: MatchNet: unifying feature and metric learning for patch-based matching. In: CVPR (2015)
22. Long, J.L., Zhang, N., Darrell, T.: Do convnets learn correspondence? In: NIPS (2014)
23. Zhou, T., Krahenbuhl, P., Aubry, M., Huang, Q., Efros, A.A.: Learning dense correspondence via 3D-guided cycle consistency. In: CVPR (2016)
24. Kanazawa, A., Jacobs, D.W., Chandraker, M.: WarpNet: weakly supervised matching for single-view reconstruction. In: CVPR (2016)
25. Yang, H., Lin, W.Y., Lu, J.: Daisy filter flow: a generalized discrete approach to dense correspondences. In: CVPR (2014)
26. Hur, J., Lim, H., Park, C., Chul Ahn, S.: Generalized deformable spatial pyramid: Geometry-preserving dense correspondence estimation. In: CVPR (2015)
27. Bristow, H., Valmadre, J., Lucey, S.: Dense semantic correspondence where every pixel is a classifier. In: ICCV (2015)
28. Berg, A.C., Berg, T.L., Malik, J.: Shape matching and object recognition using low distortion correspondences. In: CVPR (2005)
29. Yang, F., Li, X., Cheng, H., Li, J., Chen, L.: Object-aware dense semantic correspondence. In: CVPR (2017)
30. Cho, M., Lee, J., Lee, K.M.: Reweighted random walks for graph matching. In: Daniilidis, K., Maragos, P., Paragios, N. (eds.) ECCV 2010. LNCS, vol. 6315, pp. 492–505. Springer, Heidelberg (2010). https://doi.org/10.1007/978-3-642-15555-0_36
31. Duchenne, O., Joulin, A., Ponce, J.: A graph-matching kernel for object categorization. In: ICCV (2011)
32. Cho, M., Alahari, K., Ponce, J.: Learning graphs to match. In: ICCV (2013)
33. Zbontar, J., LeCun, Y.: Stereo matching by training a convolutional neural network to compare image patches. J. Mach. Learn. Res. 17(1–32), 2 (2016)
34. Luo, W., Schwing, A.G., Urtasun, R.: Efficient deep learning for stereo matching. In: Proceedings of the IEEE Conference on Computer Vision and Pattern Recognition, pp. 5695–5703 (2016)
35. Xu, K., et al.: Show, attend and tell: neural image caption generation with visual attention. In: ICML (2015)
36. Mun, J., Cho, M., Han, B.: Text-guided attention model for image captioning. In: AAAI (2017)
37. Xu, H., Saenko, K.: Ask, attend and answer: exploring question-guided spatial attention for visual question answering. In: Leibe, B., Matas, J., Sebe, N., Welling, M. (eds.) ECCV 2016. LNCS, vol. 9911, pp. 451–466. Springer, Cham (2016). https://doi.org/10.1007/978-3-319-46478-7_28
38. Yang, Z., He, X., Gao, J., Deng, L., Smola, A.: Stacked attention networks for image question answering. In: CVPR (2016)
39. Seo, P.H., Lin, Z., Cohen, S., Shen, X., Han, B.: Progressive attention networks for visual attribute prediction. arXiv preprint arXiv:1606.02393 (2016)

40. Bahdanau, D., Cho, K., Bengio, Y.: Neural machine translation by jointly learning to align and translate. In: ICLR (2015)
41. Luong, T., Pham, H., Manning, C.D.: Effective approaches to attention-based neural machine translation. In: EMNLP (2015)
42. Noh, H., Araujo, A., Sim, J., Weyand, T., Han, B.: Large-scale image retrieval with attentive deep local features. In: ICCV (2017)
43. Simonyan, K., Zisserman, A.: Very deep convolutional networks for large-scale image recognition. In: ICLR (2015)
44. Deng, J., Dong, W., Socher, R., Li, L.J., Li, K., Fei-Fei, L.: ImageNet: a large-scale hierarchical image database. In: CVPR (2009)
45. Kingma, D.P., Ba, J.: Adam: a method for stochastic optimization. arXiv preprint arXiv:1412.6980 (2014)
46. Everingham, M., Van Gool, L., Williams, C.K.I., Winn, J., Zisserman, A.: The PASCAL Visual Object Classes Challenge 2011 (VOC2011) Results. http://www.pascal-network.org/challenges/VOC/voc2011/workshop/index.html
47. Yang, Y., Ramanan, D.: Articulated human detection with flexible mixtures of parts. IEEE Trans. Patt. Anal. Mach. Intell. 35(12), 2878–2890 (2013)
48. Arandjelovic, R., Gronat, P., Torii, A., Pajdla, T., Sivic, J.: NetVLAD: CNN architecture for weakly supervised place recognition. In: CVPR (2016)

Mancs: A Multi-task Attentional Network with Curriculum Sampling for Person Re-Identification

Cheng Wang[1], Qian Zhang[2], Chang Huang[2], Wenyu Liu[1],
and Xinggang Wang[1(✉)]

[1] School of EIC, Huazhong University of Science and Technology, Wuhan, China
{wangcheng,liuwy,xgwang}@hust.edu.cn
[2] Horizon Robotics Inc., Beijing, China
{qian01.zhang,chang.huang}@hobot.cc

Abstract. We propose a novel deep network called Mancs that solves the person re-identification problem from the following aspects: fully utilizing the attention mechanism for the person misalignment problem and properly sampling for the ranking loss to obtain more stable person representation. Technically, we contribute a novel fully attentional block which is deeply supervised and can be plugged into any CNN, and a novel curriculum sampling method which is effective for training ranking losses. The learning tasks are integrated into a unified framework and jointly optimized. Experiments have been carried out on Market1501, CUHK03 and DukeMTMC. All the results show that Mancs can significantly outperform the previous state-of-the-arts. In addition, the effectiveness of the newly proposed ideas has been confirmed by extensive ablation studies.

Keywords: Person re-ID · Attention · Curriculum sampling
Multi-task learning

1 Introduction

Person re-identification (re-ID), aims at spotting a person of interest in a camera network, is a well-established research problem in computer vision [39]. Due to its great impact in the application of video surveillance [16], and the public available large-scale re-ID datasets and the encouraging re-ID results of deep learning systems, person re-ID has become increasingly popular in computer vision.

However, the person re-ID problem is quite challenging in the situations of large viewpoint variation, large misalignment, and occlusion, etc. Thus, lots of works have been proposed to learn an effective person representation based on the training images with person identities are given. The learning problem is naturally formulated as a distance metric learning problem [6,40]. It aims to find a

---

C. Wang—The work was done when Cheng Wang was an intern in Horizon Robotics.

© Springer Nature Switzerland AG 2018
V. Ferrari et al. (Eds.): ECCV 2018, LNCS 11208, pp. 384–400, 2018.
https://doi.org/10.1007/978-3-030-01225-0_23

new distance metric to transform the original person feature (such as HOG [9] and SIFT [24]) into a new space in which the examples have the same identity are closer and otherwise have large distances. In deep learning person re-ID systems, the idea of distance metric learning is usually formulated as a ranking loss and has been proven to be effective. A typical ranking loss is triplet loss, such as [27]. Given an anchor example with a positive example that has the same identity as the anchor and a negative example that has a different identity, triplet loss enforces the anchor-positive distance is smaller than the anchor-negative distance. Besides the triplet loss, there are other types of metric learning losses have been proposed, such as the histogram loss [30] and the quadruplet loss [6]. Due to the unbalanced number of positive and negative sample pairs, when training with the metric learning losses, the strategy of example sampling is an essential issue. Recent studies show that mining hard negative is beneficial to learn a robust deep person representation [11,27]. In addition, another loss function, the classification loss function which directly classifies the person images into its own identity class, is still very useful [19]. The deep re-ID networks can provide great global deep person representation. However, aligning and matching discriminative local features for person re-ID is still very necessary due to the inaccurate person detection, person pose variation etc. To achieve this goal, there are different ways, such as in-explicitly feature aligning and matching using spatial attention [37] and explicitly feature aligning using LSTM [4] or aligning by finding the shortest path [35].

By reviewing the current person re-ID research works, we can find that, due to challenges in the problem, there exists at least the following issues need to be handled: (1) the choices of loss functions; (2) the misalignment problems; (3) finding discriminative local features; and (4) how to sample training examples during the optimization of the ranking loss functions. In current person re-ID research works, few of them have addressed all these issues in the same framework. Therefore, in this paper, we propose Mancs, a unified person re-ID deep network, to deal with the mentioned issues at the same time.

Mancs has the following building blocks. It has a backbone network, such as ResNet-50, to extract deep feature hierarchies for the input person image. The backbone network is supervised with a ranking loss and a classification loss. The ranking loss is a triplet loss; we propose a novel curriculum sampling strategy to train with the triplet loss; the curriculum sampling method is motivated by curriculum learning [5] that helps to train the network by sampling examples from easy to hard. The classification loss is a focal loss which has been proven to be helpful for dense object detection [21]. To deal with the misalignment problem and localize discriminative local features, we propose a new fully attentional block (FAB) which creates both channel-wise and spatial-wise attention information to mine the useful features for re-ID. To better learn the FABs in our network, we further propose to use the deep supervision idea [14] by adding a classification loss function for each FAB; thus, the classification loss function is termed as attention loss. In the end, the triplet loss, the focal loss, and the attention loss are combined for training our person re-ID network in a multi-task manner.

In the experiments, we have studied the Mancs on three large-scale person re-ID datasets, which are Market-1501 [38], CUHK03 [17], and DukeMTMC-reID [42]. The results clearly demonstrate the contribution of newly proposed triplet loss with curriculum sampling, the deeply supervised fully attentional block, the focal loss, and the unified multi-task learning framework. Besides, Mancs obtains significant better accuracies than the previous state-of-the-arts on all the datasets.

2   Related Work

Attentional Network. Recently, lots of works have adopted attentional deep learning approaches to tackle the misalignment problem in person re-ID. Usually, they use an additional subnet to obtain a region of interest and extract features from those attention areas. MSCAN [15] uses a spatial transformation network (STN) [13] to get several attention regions and then extracts local feature from the regions. HA-CNN [19] combines both soft attention methods and hard attention methods. Apart from acquiring hard attention region, they also rely on channel-wise attention and spatial-wise attention, which are complementary to previous hard attention. CAN [23] combines attention methods with LSTM to obtain discriminative attention feature of the whole image. The proposed Mancs adopts a 1×1 convolution to acquire an attention mask with the same shape of the feature map.

Metric Learning. It is widely used for learning image embeddings, such as [3,4,6,27,35,40]. In face recognition, [27] uses triplet loss to push the negative pair further and pull the positive pair closer. Except triplet loss, contrastive loss [40] and quadruplet loss [6] are also used in person re-ID task. For triplet loss, online hard examples mining (OHEM) is important, namely selecting the furthest positive examples and closet negative examples for training. In the proposed Mancs framework, we sample training examples in a curriculum way.

Multi-task Learning. Since metric learning and representation learning can both be applied to person re-identification task, [4,10] combine softmax loss with triplet loss to train model for a robust performance. [1] adopts two losses but divides them into two stages. The proposed Mancs combines focal loss with triplet loss and can be trained in an end-to-end way.

3   Method

In this section, we present the proposed Mancs person re-ID framework by first describing the training framework and its building blocks, then describing the multi-task learning strategy and finally describing the inference network.

3.1 Training Architecture

The network architecture for training is shown in Fig. 1. Basically, it has three major components. The backbone network, the attention module, and the loss functions, which are described as follows.

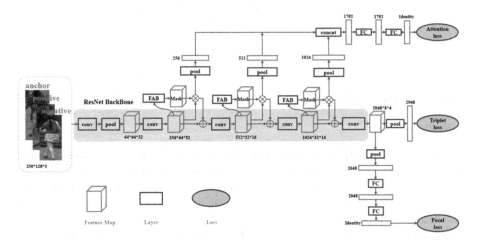

Fig. 1. The Mancs training architecture: its backbone network is ResNet-50; the pooling layers are all spatially average pooling; the FAB block is an attention module which is described in Fig. 2; and it has three loss functions: attention loss, triplet loss and focal loss

The backbone network is served as a multi-scale feature extractor. Without loss of generality, here we apply the popular ResNet-50. As shown in Fig. 1, we take the conv-2, conv-3 and conv-4 feature maps to generate attention masks which are added back into the mainstream. The last conv-5 feature map is used for generating the final person identity feature.

3.2 Fully Attentional Block

Attention is very useful in person re-ID, which has been proved in the previous studies [15,15,19]. In our understanding, attention can localize the most discriminative local regions for person re-ID. To fully illustrate the usage of attention, we propose a fully attentional block (FAB). FAB is motivated by the recent Squeeze-and-Excitation Network (SENet) [12] method, which illustrates that different channels of a feature map play different roles in specifying objects. In consideration of that, the SE block (Fig. 2(a)) in SENet utilizes the preference of channels and gives a weighting coefficient to each channel of the feature map. However, the initial SE block only re-calibrates feature response on channel-wise while ignores the spatial-wise response on the account of using global pooling which leads to losing the spatial structure information. To remedy this problem,

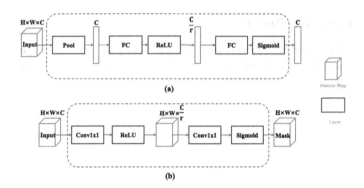

Fig. 2. (a) is a SE Block and the reduction factor r is set to 16; (b) is our Fully Attentional Block where $r = 16$

the proposed FAB discards the pooling layer and employs 1×1 convolutional layers instead of fully-connected layers to regain spatial information. Therefore we can get an attention mask with the same size of input feature map and this attention model is called fully attentional block. FAB is illustrated in Fig. 2(b) and formulated as follows.

Given a convolutional feature map F_i, its attention map is computed as:

$$M = \text{Sigmoid}\left(\text{Conv}(\text{ReLU}(\text{Conv}(F_i)))\right), \tag{1}$$

where the two Conv operators are 1×1 convolution. The inner Conv is used for squeeze and the outer Conv is used for excitation. After obtaining the attention map M the output feature map of F_i is calculated as:

$$F_o = F_i * M + F_i, \tag{2}$$

where the operator $*$ and $+$ are performed in an element-wise manner. This means that the attention induced feature map is added into the original feature map to emphasize discriminative features. It is worth to note that the proposed FAB is pluggable and can be applied to any existing CNN, since FAB does not change the size of the convolutional feature map.

3.3 ReID Task #1: Triplet Loss with Curriculum Sampling

A ranking loss is essential for a person re-ID deep network since it has better generalization ability than the contractive/classification loss especially when the training dataset is not large enough. Thus, we firstly introduce a ranking branch with triplet loss to our model. To clearly describe the proposed triplet loss method, we denote the feature of image I_i for the triplet loss as $f_{\text{rank}}(I_i)$, where $f_{\text{rank}}(\cdot)$ means the feature extraction network for ranking features. As shown in Fig. 1, $f_{\text{rank}}(\cdot)$ shares the backbone network with other branches and has a pooling layer and a FC layer owned by itself. When applying a triplet loss, its sampling algorithm matters (Fig. 3).

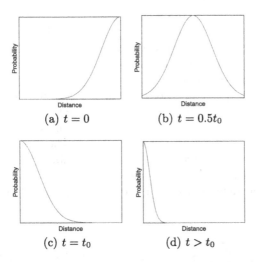

Fig. 3. Different selecting probabilities on negative examples under a given t. X-axis represents the distance between negative examples and anchor, while Y-axis represents the probability of a negative example being selected

Most person re-ID works [4,11,35] adopt the triplet loss proposed by [27]. The main idea of [27] is to do online hard triplets sampling through the so-called PK sampling method, which randomly samples P identities and then randomly K images for each identity to form a mini-batch with the size of $P \times K$. In a mini-batch $\mathcal{I} = \{I_i\}_{i=1}^{PK}$, for each image, it is considered as an anchor image denoted as I_i^a, and the hardest positive image and the hardest negative of the anchor are found in $\mathcal{I}$ which are denoted as I_i^p and I_i^n respectively. Thus, $T_i = \{I_i^a, I_i^p, I_i^n\}$ is a triplet and PK triplets can be obtained. The above sampling procedure is also called online hard examples mining (OHEM). It is widely used in many visual application problems. However, it is easy to collapse according to [25]. Inspired by curriculum learning [5], we propose a new sampling way named curriculum sampling. The idea is to train a person re-ID network in a progress from easy triplets to hard triplets.

More specifically, we discard the method of sampling hardest instances in the beginning of training and start from easy instances. Given an anchor instance I_i^a, firstly, we randomly select one of its positive instances as I_i^p; secondly, we sort negative instances according to their distances to the anchor from small to large, which means that the negatives are sorted from hard to easy; thirdly, we give each negative instance a probability of being selected. These probabilities obey a Gaussian distribution $\mathcal{N}(\mu, \sigma)$, where μ and σ are defined as below:

$$\mu = [N_n - \frac{N_n}{t_0}t]_+, \tag{3}$$

$$\sigma = a \times b^{[\frac{t-t0}{t_1-t_0}]_+}, \tag{4}$$

where $[\cdot]_+ = max(\cdot, 0)$, N_n is the numbers of negative instances. a is initial std value and b is the decay exponent when $t > t_0$. t_0 and t_1 are hyper-parameters that control the speed of learning process from easy to hard. The above procedure selects an anchor, a positive instance and a negative instance to form a triplet. Next, the aim is still the same; we randomly select another different positive instance as the second procedure does. Then, we select another negative example based on the previous probability distribution (since the anchor is still the same). Now, we have selected our second triplet. When all positive instances of this anchor are selected, we move to the next anchor. The process described above totally gives us $PK(K-1)$ triplets. PK is the number of anchors. $K-1$ is the number of positive instances of each anchor.

Based on the curriculum sampling method, the final loss for ranking branch can be defined as:

$$L_{\text{rank}} = \frac{1}{P(K-1)K} \sum_{i=1}^{P(K-1)K} [m + D(f_{\text{rank}}(I_i^a), f_{\text{rank}}(I_i^p)) - D(f_{\text{rank}}(I_i^a), f_{\text{rank}}(I_i^n))]_+,$$

(5)

where $D(\cdot, \cdot)$ is the Euclidean distance between two feature vectors. The probability of I_i^n being chose is defined as below:

$$Pr(I_i^{n*} = I_i^n \mid I_i^a) \propto \mathcal{N}(\mu, \sigma)$$

(6)

3.4   ReID Task #2: Person Classification with Focal Loss

Recent studies show that combining both ranking loss and classification loss is helpful for person re-ID [4]. In Mancs, we also have a classification branch. Since hard examples mining is essential in the ranking loss, we think it can also be applied in the classification task. Now that hard examples are more important than easy examples in learning, we decide to increase the ratio that negative examples take up in the total loss. Apparently, the newly proposed focal loss [21] for dense object detection is an appropriate option, since it is able to let hard examples have a higher weight than easy examples.

We denote the feature extractor of the classification branch as $f_{\text{cls}}(\cdot)$. Given an image I_i and its ground-truth identity c_i, the probability of I_i belonging to the c_i-th class is denoted as follows:

$$p_i = \text{Sigmoid}_{c_i}\left(\text{FC}\left(f_{\text{cls}}(I_i)\right)\right),$$

(7)

where the subscript c_i of Sigmoid means taking the output value in its c_i-th dimension. Then, the focal loss for classification can be defined as follows:

$$L_{cls} = -\frac{1}{PK} \sum_{i=1}^{PK} (1 - p_i)^\gamma \log(p_i).$$

(8)

3.5 ReID Task #3: Deep Supervision for Better Attention

As shown in Fig. 1, we can acquire different scales of attention responses based on different level of intermediate features. Besides, in order to acquire accurate attention maps, we use person identity information to deeply supervised them. The idea is inspired by the deeply-supervised nets work [14]. The deep supervision is helpful in alleviating the problem of gradient vanishing.

To implement this goal, the multi-scale attention maps are spatially and averagely pooling into a one-dimensional feature vector; then, the feature vectors are concatenated into an attention feature vector. We denote the attention feature extractor as $f_{att}(\cdot)$. Similar to the setting in the Sect. 3.4, the probability of I_i belonging to the c-th class is given as:

$$q_i^c = \text{Sigmoid}_c\left(\text{FC}\left(f_{att}(I_i)\right)\right). \tag{9}$$

Then, we define the loss function of the attention branch as:

$$L_{att} = -\frac{1}{PKC}\sum_{i=1}^{PK}\sum_{c=1}^{C} y_i^c \log(q_i^c) + (1 - y_i^c)\log(1 - q_i^c) \tag{10}$$

where $y_i^c = 1$ if I_i belongs to the c-class and otherwise $y_i^c = 0$.

3.6 Multi-task Learning

As shown in Fig. 1, the three tasks share the same backbone network. In training, the corresponding three loss functions are optimized jointly. The final loss is given by:

$$\mathcal{L} = \lambda_{rank}L_{rank} + \lambda_{cls}L_{cls} + \lambda_{att}L_{att}, \tag{11}$$

where λ_{rank}, λ_{cls}, and λ_{att} weight factors for the loss functions.

3.7 Inference

In testing the inference network is quite simple which is shown in Fig. 4. We choose the deep feature for ranking loss, i.e., f_{rank}, as the final re-ID feature for each instance. This is mainly because the proposed triplet loss with curriculum sampling can produce deep feature with better generalization ability. The choice of using ranking features has been confirmed in many other research works, such as [4,32].

4 Experiments

4.1 Datasets

We mainly focus on three large-scale reID datasets, which are Market1501, CUHK03 and DukeMTMC-reID. The details of the three datasets are given as follows.

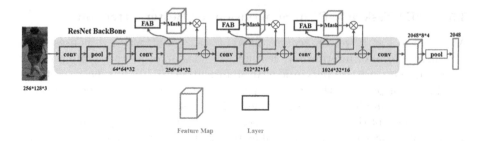

Fig. 4. The architecture of the inference network in Mancs.

Market-1501 [38]: It contains 32,668 images of 1,501 identities captured by six camera views. The whole dataset is divided into a training set containing 12,936 images of 751 identities and a testing set containing 19,732 images of 750 identities. For each identity in testing set, we select one image from each camera as a query image, forming 3,368 queries following the standard setting in [38].

CUHK03 [17]: It contains 14,097 images of 1,467 identities. It provides person bounding boxes detected both from the deformable part model detector and from manual labeling. We conduct experiments both on the labeled dataset and detected dataset. The dataset offers a 20-splits dividing, resulting in a training set with 1,367 identities and a testing set with 100 identities. The average performance of 20 splits is adopted as the final result of this dataset. Similar with [44], we also evaluate a division way with the training set of 767 identities and the testing set of 700 identities.

DukeMTMC-reID [42]: Similar to Market-1501, DukeMTMC-reID contains 36,411 images of 1,812 identities taken by 8 cameras, where only 1,404 identities appeared in more than 2 cameras. The other 408 identities are regarded as distractors. The training set contains 16,522 images of 702 identities while the testing set contains 2,228 query images of 702 identities and 17,661 gallery images.

4.2 Evaluation Protocol

We follow the official training and evaluation protocols in Market-1501, CUHK03 and DukeMTMC-reID. We use the cumulative matching characteristics (CMC) and mean Average Precision (mAP) metrics. We conduct experiments on Market-1501 under both single query and multi-query mode. While on CUHK03 and DukeMTMC-reID, we conduct experiments only in single query mode. Especially in CUHK03, there are 2 different ways of dividing the training set and testing set. One is dividing to 1,367/100 split, the other is dividing to 767/700 split. The former needs to run 20 rounds and get an averaged result which we use rank1, rank5 and rank10 matching rate to evaluate. The later is similar to

Market-1501 and DukeMTMC-reID and only need to run once which is evaluated by rank1 matching rate and mAP. We perform experiments for both splits.

4.3 Implementation Details

We implement Mancs based on Pytorch [26]. We take the ResNet-50 model pretrained on ImageNet as the backbone. As described above, we insert a fully-connected layer with channel numbers of 2048 before the last classification layer.

Data Augmentation. We first resize training images to 256×128. Then we randomly crop each image with scale in the interval $[0.64, 1.0]$ and aspect ratio in $[2, 3]$. Third, we resize these cropped images back to the size of 256×128 and randomly horizontally flip them with the probability of 0.5. Finally, we add a random erasing data augmentation method as described in [45]. Before sent to the network, each image is subtracted the mean value and divided by the standard deviation according to standard normalization procedure when using the pretrained model on ImageNet.

Training Configurations. As described in Sect. 3.3, we adopt *PK Sampling* strategy to form every mini-batch. The values of both P and K is set distinguished among different datasets. For Market1501, P and K is set to 16 and 16, respectively. For CUHK03, P is set to 32 and K is set to 8. DukeMTMC-ReID shares the same configurations with Market1501. Each epochs includes $[N_c/P]$ mini-batches. We train our models for 160 epochs. t_0, t_1, a and b described in Eqs. (3) and (4) are set to $30, 60, 15$ and 0.001, respectively. $\lambda_{rank}, \lambda_{cls}$ and λ_{att} are set to $1, 1$ and 0.2, respectively. The margin m in Eq. (5) is set to 0.5. γ in Eq. (11) is set to 2. We adopt Adam optimizer with an initial learning rate of 3×10^{-4} in our experiments to minimize the three losses. In addition, we add gradient clipping to prevent model collision. The activation function of the last convolutional layer is changed from ReLU to PReLU, which can enrich the expressiveness of the final feature. All the experiments run on a server with 4 TITAN XP GPUs.

4.4 Comparisons with the State-of-art Methods

Evaluation On Market-1501. We evaluated our proposed Mancs against 13 existing methods on Market-1501. As showed in Table 1, our model outperforms HA-CNN which also uses an attention subnetwork by 6.6% on mAP and 1.9% on rank1 matching rate under single query mode, respectively. Compared with Deep-Person which also adopts multi-task learning, our Mancs outperforms it by 2.7% in mAP and 0.8% in rank1 matching rate under the single query model, respectively. Under multiple query mode, Mancs outperforms Deep-Person by 2.4% on mAP and 0.9% on rank1 matching rate, respectively. With the combination of re-ranking approach, the performance can be further improved. Under the single query mode, mAP and rank1 can be boosted to 92.3% and 94.9%, respectively. While under multiple query mode, it can reach 94.5% and 95.8% (Tables 2 and 3).

Table 1. Comparisons on Market-1501 with state-of-art methods. SQ: single query, MQ: multiple queries. Mancs obtains the best results.

Methods	SQ		MQ	
	rank1	mAP	rank1	mAP
CAN [23]	60.3	35.9	72.1	47.9
DNS [34]	61.0	35.6	71.5	46.0
Gated S-CNN [31]	65.9	39.6	76.0	48.4
CRAFT [8]	68.7	42.3	77.0	50.3
Spindle [36]	76.9	-	-	-
MSCAN [15]	80.3	57.5	86.8	66.7
SVDNet [29]	82.3	62.1	-	-
PDC [28]	84.1	63.4	-	-
TriNet [11]	84.9	69.1	90.5	76.4
JLML [18]	85.1	65.5	89.7	74.5
HA-CNN [19]	91.2	75.7	93.8	82.8
Deep-Person [4]	92.3	79.6	94.5	85.1
AlignedReID [35]	92.6	82.3	-	-
Mancs(Ours)	**93.1**	**82.3**	**95.4**	**87.5**

Table 2. Comparisons on the CUHK03 dataset in terms of mAP and rank1 matching rate, using both manually labeled person bounding boxes and automatic detections by DPM, under the setting of 767/700 split. Mancs gets the best results.

Settings	767/700 split			
	Labeled		Detected	
Methods	rank1	mAP	rank1	mAP
BoW+XQDA [33]	7.9	7.3	6.4	6.4
LOMO+XQDA [20]	14.8	13.6	12.8	11.5
IDE(C) [44]	15.6	14.9	15.1	14.2
IDE(C)+XQDA [44]	21.9	20.0	21.1	19.0
IDE(R) [44]	22.2	21.0	21.3	19.7
IDE(R)+XQDA [44]	32.0	29.6	31.1	28.2
DPFL [7]	43.0	40.5	40.7	37.0
SVDNet-ResNet50 [29]	-	-	41.5	37.6
HA-CNN [19]	44.4	41.0	41.7	38.6
TriNet+Random Erasing [11,45]	58.1	53.8	55.5	50.7
Mancs(Ours)	**69.0**	**63.9**	**65.5**	**60.5**

Table 3. Comparisons on CUHK03 in terms of rank1, rank5, rank10 matching rate, using both manually labeled person bounding boxes and automatic detections by DPM, under the setting of 1367/100 split. Mancs obtains the best results.

Settings	1367/100 split					
Models	Labeled			Detected		
	r1	r5	r10	r1	r5	r10
DNS [34]	62.5	90.0	94.8	54.7	84.7	94.8
Gated-SCNN [31]	-	-	-	68.1	88.1	94.6
MSCAN [15]	74.2	94.3	97.5	68.0	91.0	95.4
Quadruplet [6]	75.5	95.2	99.2	-	-	-
SSM [2]	76.6	94.6	98.0	72.7	92.4	96.1
SVDNet [29]	-	-	-	81.8	95.2	97.2
CRAFT [8]	-	-	-	84.3	97.1	98.3
JLML [18]	83.2	98.0	99.4	80.6	96.9	98.7
DPFL [7]	86.7	-	-	82.0	-	-
PDC [28]	88.7	98.6	99.2	78.3	94.8	97.2
Deep-Person [4]	91.5	99.0	99.5	89.4	98.2	99.1
AlignedReID [35]	91.9	98.7	99.4	-	-	-
Mancs(Ours)	**93.8**	**99.3**	**99.8**	**92.4**	**98.8**	**99.4**

Evaluation On CUHK03. As mentioned in Sect. 4.1, there are two ways of dividing the CUHK03 dataset into training and testing set. Typically, the 767/700 split setting is harder than the 1367/100 setting. Because the former split has less training images and more testing images than the later. We evaluate Mancs in both settings. Without the help of re-ranking, in the detected split, Mancs can reach to 92.4% under the 1367/100 split and 65.5% under the 767/700 split on rank1 target, respectively. Especially under the 767/700 split, Mancs is 23.8% higher than HA-CNN and 10.0% higher than TriNet with Random Erasing.

Evaluation On DukeMTMC-reID. Similar to Market-1501, the comparisons with related methods is depicted in Table 4. Compared with the state-of-art method Deep-Person [4], Mancs achieves an improvement of 7.0% on mAP and 4.0% on rank1 performance.

From the above experiment results, we can observe that Mancs obtains excellent person re-ID performance. However, to future discovery the limitations, we visualize some randomly selected failure cases of Mancs in Fig. 5, in which the results of 4 probes in DukeMTMC-reID are listed. From the results in the second and the third row, we can observe that Mancs may be affected by some unusual situations, such as multi-person in one image and a car occupies the image, which is very unusual in the training set. So, when applying Mancs in real applications, it is better to have an accurate person detector. From the results in the first and

Fig. 5. Some failure cases (missed in the rank1 matching) on DukeMTMC-reID. Left are probes, right are the ranking results. Persons surrounded by green box have the same identities as their probes. (Color figure online)

the fourth row, we can observe that there are still some very similar distractors may affect Mancs, which will be deeply investigated in future research. However, these failure cases can be remedied by a re-ranking post process.

4.5   Ablation Study

We further perform several extra experiments to verify the effectiveness of each individual component of our proposed model. Market-1501 and CUHK03 are used in experiments of ablation study. Specifically, we perform all experiments under single query mode. In addition, we use the 767/700 split of CUHK03 with

Table 4. Comparisons with state-of-art results on DukeMTMC-reID.

Methods	rank1	mAP
BoW+XQDA [33]	25.1	12.2
LOMO+XQDA [20]	30.8	17.0
LSRO [43]	67.7	47.1
AttIDNet [22]	70.7	51.9
PAN [41]	71.6	51.5
SVDNet [29]	76.7	56.8
DPFL [7]	79.2	60.6
HA-CNN [19]	80.5	63.8
Deep-Person [4]	80.9	64.8
Mancs(Ours)	**84.9**	**71.8**

Table 5. Ablation studies of the modules of Mancs, based on both Market-1501 and CUHK03 datasets. Specifically, the results below are under single query mode and the detected part and the 767/700 split are used in CUHK03. f_{cls}: global branch, RE: random erasing, f_{rank}: ranking branch, FL: using Focal Loss instead of cross-entropy loss, f_{att}: fully attentional block, OHEM: online hard example mining, CS: curriculum sampling.

Components			baseline			
f_{cls}	√	√	√	√	√	√
RE		√	√	√	√	√
f_{rank}			√	√	√	√
OHEM			√	√	√	
FL				√	√	√
f_{att}					√	√
CS						√

rank1/mAP							
	Market-1501	69.5/46.1	71.6/47.6	92.4/80.4	92.7/81.0	92.9/81.7	**93.1/82.3**
	CUHK03	33.9/30.8	42.2/38.9	63.8/58.4	63.9/59.2	64.4/60.1	**65.5/60.5**

bounding boxes extracted by DPM. Table 5 shows the results and effectiveness of each component.

Effectiveness of Curriculum Sampling. We further evaluate the effect of CS by comparing with the popular OHEM sampling way. As can be seen in the Table 5, with Market-1501, CS outperforms OHEM by 0.6% on mAP and 0.2% in rank1 matching rate. The improvement can even reach 0.4% and 1.1% in CUHK03, respectively. This shows that the proposed curriculum sampling can help model learn a better representation.

Effectiveness of Full Attentional Block. We verify the effectiveness of attention branch in Table 5. mAP/rank1 are improved 0.7%/0.2% and 0.9%/0.5% on Market-1501 and CUHK03, respectively. FAB provides a fine-grained attention to emphasize the irregular discriminative part of the pedestrian object in an end-to-end way. It is also pluggable and can be added to any existing models.

Effectiveness of Focal Loss. As Table 5 depicts, on Market-1501, focal loss exceeds cross-entropy loss by 0.6%/0.3% in mAP/rank1, respectively. And in CUHK03, the benefit reaches 0.8%/0.1% in mAP/rank1, respectively. Similar to OHEM in triplet loss, focal loss can also mine more information from examples that are hard to classify, which is essential in improving the generalization of the model.

Effectiveness of Random Erasing. Random erasing is not only a way of data augmentation but also helps alleviate occlusion problem by artificially adding occlusion patch to initial image. It makes our model more robust to occlusion situation. Figure 5 also shows that, when combined with a simple classification branch, random erasing can still obtain an obvious improvement.

5   Conclusions

In this paper, we introduce a novel deep network called Mancs to learn stable features for person re-ID. The experiment results on three popular datasets show that Mancs is superior to the previous state-of-art methods. In addition, the effectiveness of the proposed fully attentional block with deep supervision and curriculum sampling have been confirmed in the ablation studies. In the future, we would like jointly investigate the sampling problem for ranking loss and data augmentation methods to obtain more generalizable person re-ID features.

Acknowledgements. This work was partly supported by HUST-Horizon Computer Vision Research Center and NSFC (No. 61733007, 61503145 and 61572207). Xinggang Wang was sponsored by the Program for HUST Academic Frontier Youth Team.

References

1. Almazan, J., Gajic, B., Murray, N., Larlus, D.: Re-ID done right: towards good practices for person re-identification. ArXiv e-prints, January 2018
2. Bai, S., Bai, X., Tian, Q.: Scalable person re-identification on supervised smoothed manifold. In: CVPR, vol. 6, p. 7 (2017)
3. Bai, S., Bai, X., Tian, Q., Latecki, L.J.: Regularized diffusion process on bidirectional context for object retrieval. TPAMI **37**, 803–815 (2018)
4. Bai, X., Yang, M., Huang, T., Dou, Z., Yu, R., Xu, Y.: Deep-Person: Learning Discriminative Deep Features for Person Re-Identification. ArXiv e-prints, November 2017
5. Bengio, Y., Louradour, J., Collobert, R., Weston, J.: Curriculum learning. In: Proceedings of the 26th Annual International Conference on Machine Learning, pp. 41–48. ACM (2009)
6. Chen, W., Chen, X., Zhang, J., Huang, K.: Beyond triplet loss: a deep quadruplet network for person re-identification. In: Proceedings of CVPR, vol. 2 (2017)
7. Chen, Y., Zhu, X., Gong, S.: Person re-identification by deep learning multi-scale representations. In: Proceedings of the IEEE Conference on Computer Vision and Pattern Recognition, pp. 2590–2600 (2017)
8. Chen, Y.C., Zhu, X., Zheng, W.S., Lai, J.H.: Person re-identification by camera correlation aware feature augmentation. IEEE Trans. Patt. Anal. Mach. Intell. **40**(2), 392–408 (2018)
9. Dalal, N., Triggs, B.: Histograms of oriented gradients for human detection. In: 2005 IEEE Computer Society Conference on Computer Vision and Pattern Recognition, CVPR 2005, vol. 1, pp. 886–893. IEEE (2005)
10. Geng, M., Wang, Y., Xiang, T., Tian, Y.: Deep Transfer Learning for Person Re-identification. ArXiv e-prints, November 2016
11. Hermans, A., Beyer, L., Leibe, B.: In defense of the triplet loss for person re-identification. arXiv preprint arXiv:1703.07737 (2017)
12. Hu, J., Shen, L., Sun, G.: Squeeze-and-excitation networks. In: IEEE Conference on Computer Vision and Pattern Recognition (2018)
13. Jaderberg, M., Simonyan, K., Zisserman, A., et al.: Spatial transformer networks. In: Advances in Neural Information Processing Systems, pp. 2017–2025 (2015)
14. Lee, C.Y., Xie, S., Gallagher, P., Zhang, Z., Tu, Z.: Deeply-supervised nets. In: Artificial Intelligence and Statistics, pp. 562–570 (2015)

15. Li, D., Chen, X., Zhang, Z., Huang, K.: Learning deep context-aware features over body and latent parts for person re-identification. In: Proceedings of the IEEE Conference on Computer Vision and Pattern Recognition, pp. 384–393 (2017)

16. Li, J., Zhang, S., Wang, J., Gao, W., Tian, Q.: LVreID: Person Re-Identification with Long Sequence Videos. ArXiv e-prints, December 2017

17. Li, W., Zhao, R., Xiao, T., Wang, X.: DeepReID: deep filter pairing neural network for person re-identification. In: Proceedings of the IEEE Conference on Computer Vision and Pattern Recognition, pp. 152–159 (2014)

18. Li, W., Zhu, X., Gong, S.: Person re-identification by deep joint learning of multi-loss classification. In: Proceedings of the Twenty-Sixth International Joint Conference on Artificial Intelligence, IJCAI 2017, pp. 2194–2200 (2017)

19. Li, W., Zhu, X., Gong, S.: Harmonious attention network for person re-identification. In: CVPR, vol. 1, p. 2 (2018)

20. Liao, S., Hu, Y., Zhu, X., Li, S.Z.: Person re-identification by local maximal occurrence representation and metric learning. In: Proceedings of the IEEE Conference on Computer Vision and Pattern Recognition, pp. 2197–2206 (2015)

21. Lin, T., Goyal, P., Girshick, R.B., He, K., Dollár, P.: Focal loss for dense object detection. In: IEEE International Conference on Computer Vision, ICCV, pp. 2999–3007 (2017)

22. Lin, Y., Zheng, L., Zheng, Z., Wu, Y., Yang, Y.: Improving person re-identification by attribute and identity learning. arXiv preprint arXiv:1703.07220 (2017)

23. Liu, H., Feng, J., Qi, M., Jiang, J., Yan, S.: End-to-end comparative attention networks for person re-identification. IEEE Trans. Image Process. **26**(7), 3492–3506 (2017)

24. Lowe, D.G.: Object recognition from local scale-invariant features. In: 1999 The Proceedings of the Seventh IEEE International Conference on Computer Vision, vol. 2, pp. 1150–1157. IEEE (1999)

25. Manmatha, R., Wu, C., Smola, A.J., Krähenbühl, P.: Sampling matters in deep embedding learning. In: IEEE International Conference on Computer Vision, ICCV, pp. 2859–2867 (2017)

26. Paszke, A., et al.: Automatic differentiation in pytorch (2017)

27. Schroff, F., Kalenichenko, D., Philbin, J.: FaceNet: a unified embedding for face recognition and clustering. In: Proceedings of the IEEE Conference on Computer Vision and Pattern Recognition, pp. 815–823 (2015)

28. Su, C., Li, J., Zhang, S., Xing, J., Gao, W., Tian, Q.: Pose-driven deep convolutional model for person re-identification. In: 2017 IEEE International Conference on Computer Vision (ICCV), pp. 3980–3989. IEEE (2017)

29. Sun, Y., Zheng, L., Deng, W., Wang, S.: Svdnet for pedestrian retrieval. In: IEEE International Conference on Computer Vision, ICCV 2017, Venice, Italy, 22–29 October 2017, pp. 3820–3828 (2017)

30. Ustinova, E., Lempitsky, V.S.: Learning deep embeddings with histogram loss. In: Advances in Neural Information Processing Systems 29: Annual Conference on Neural Information Processing Systems, pp. 4170–4178 (2016)

31. Varior, R.R., Haloi, M., Wang, G.: Gated siamese convolutional neural network architecture for human re-identification. In: Leibe, B., Matas, J., Sebe, N., Welling, M. (eds.) ECCV 2016. LNCS, vol. 9912, pp. 791–808. Springer, Cham (2016). https://doi.org/10.1007/978-3-319-46484-8_48

32. Vo, N., Hays, J.: Generalization in Metric Learning: Should the Embedding Layer be the Embedding Layer? ArXiv e-prints, March 2018

33. Wang, H., Gong, S., Xiang, T.: Highly efficient regression for scalable person re-identification. In: Proceedings of the British Machine Vision Conference 2016, BMVC (2016)

34. Zhang, L., Xiang, T., Gong, S.: Learning a discriminative null space for person re-identification. In: Proceedings of the IEEE Conference on Computer Vision and Pattern Recognition, pp. 1239–1248 (2016)

35. Zhang, X., et al.: AlignedReID: Surpassing human-level performance in person re-identification. arXiv preprint arXiv:1711.08184 (2017)

36. Zhao, H., et al.: Spindle net: person re-identification with human body region guided feature decomposition and fusion. In: Proceedings of the IEEE Conference on Computer Vision and Pattern Recognition, pp. 1077–1085 (2017)

37. Zhao, L., Li, X., Zhuang, Y., Wang, J.: Deeply-learned part-aligned representations for person re-identification. In: IEEE International Conference on Computer Vision, ICCV, pp. 3239–3248 (2017)

38. Zheng, L., Shen, L., Tian, L., Wang, S., Wang, J., Tian, Q.: Scalable person re-identification: a benchmark. In: Proceedings of the IEEE International Conference on Computer Vision, pp. 1116–1124 (2015)

39. Zheng, L., Yang, Y., Hauptmann, A.G.: Person re-identification: Past, present and future. arXiv preprint arXiv:1610.02984 (2016)

40. Zheng, Z., Zheng, L., Yang, Y.: A discriminatively learned CNN embedding for person reidentification, vol. 14, p. 13. ACM (2017)

41. Zheng, Z., Zheng, L., Yang, Y.: Pedestrian alignment network for large-scale person re-identification. arXiv preprint arXiv:1707.00408 (2017)

42. Zheng, Z., Zheng, L., Yang, Y.: Unlabeled samples generated by GAN improve the person re-identification baseline in vitro. In: Proceedings of the IEEE International Conference on Computer Vision (2017)

43. Zheng, Z., Zheng, L., Yang, Y.: Unlabeled samples generated by GAN improve the person re-identification baseline in vitro. In: IEEE International Conference on Computer Vision, ICCV 2017, pp. 3774–3782 (2017)

44. Zhong, Z., Zheng, L., Cao, D., Li, S.: Re-ranking person re-identification with k-reciprocal encoding. In: 2017 IEEE Conference on Computer Vision and Pattern Recognition (CVPR), pp. 3652–3661. IEEE (2017)

45. Zhong, Z., Zheng, L., Kang, G., Li, S., Yang, Y.: Random erasing data augmentation. arXiv preprint arXiv:1708.04896 (2017)

Deep Discriminative Model
for Video Classification

Mohammad Tavakolian$^{(\boxtimes)}$ and Abdenour Hadid

Center for Machine Vision and Signal Analysis (CMVS),
University of Oulu, Oulu, Finland
{mohammad.tavakolian,abdenour.hadid}@oulu.fi

Abstract. This paper presents a new deep learning approach for video-based scene classification. We design a Heterogeneous Deep Discriminative Model (HDDM) whose parameters are initialized by performing an unsupervised pre-training in a layer-wise fashion using Gaussian Restricted Boltzmann Machines (GRBM). In order to avoid the redundancy of adjacent frames, we extract spatiotemporal variation patterns within frames and represent them sparsely using Sparse Cubic Symmetrical Pattern (SCSP). Then, a pre-initialized HDDM is separately trained using the videos of each class to learn class-specific models. According to the minimum reconstruction error from the learnt class-specific models, a weighted voting strategy is employed for the classification. The performance of the proposed method is extensively evaluated on two action recognition datasets; UCF101 and Hollywood II, and three dynamic texture and dynamic scene datasets; DynTex, YUPENN, and Maryland. The experimental results and comparisons against state-of-the-art methods demonstrate that the proposed method consistently achieves superior performance on all datasets.

1 Introduction

Through the recent surge in digital content, video data has become an indisputable part of today's life. This has stimulated the evolution of advanced approaches for a wide range of video understanding applications. In this context, the understanding and classification of video content have gained a substantial research interest among the computer vision community. However, the automatic classification of scene in videos is subject to a number of challenges, including a range of natural variations in short videos such as illumination variations, viewpoint changes, and camera motions. Moreover, scene classification differs from the conventional object detection or classification, because a scene is composed of several entities which are often organized in a random layout. Therefore, devising an accurate, efficient and robust representation of videos is essential to deal with these challenges.

To achieve an effective representation of a scene in videos, we can model videos' spatiotemporal motion patterns using the concept of dynamic textures. Videos comprise dynamic textures which inherently exhibit spatial and temporal

© Springer Nature Switzerland AG 2018
V. Ferrari et al. (Eds.): ECCV 2018, LNCS 11208, pp. 401–418, 2018.
https://doi.org/10.1007/978-3-030-01225-0_24

regularities of a scene or an object. Dynamic textures widely exist in real-world video data, e.g. regular rigid motion like windmill, chaotic motion such as smoke and water turbulences, and sophisticated motion caused by camera panning and zooming. The modeling of dynamic textures in videos is challenging but very important for computer vision applications such as video classification, dynamic texture synthesis, and motion segmentation.

Despite all challenges, great efforts have been devoted to find a robust and powerful solution for video-based scene classification tasks. Furthermore, it has been commonly substantiated that an effective representation of the video content is a crucial step towards resolving the problem of dynamic texture classification. In previous years, a substantial number of approaches for video representation have been proposed, e.g. Linear Dynamic System (LDS) based methods [1], Local Binary Pattern (LBP) based methods [2], and Wavelet-based methods [3]. Unfortunately, the current methods are sensitive to a wide range of variations such as viewpoint changes, object deformations, and illumination variations. Coupled with these drawbacks, other methods frequently model the video information within consecutive frames on a geometric surface represented by a subspace [4], a combination of subspaces [5], a point on the Grassmann manifold [6], or Lie Group of Riemannian manifold [7]. These require prior assumptions regarding specific category of the geometric surface on which samples of the video are assumed to lie.

On the other hand, deep learning has recently achieved significant success in a number of areas [8–10], including video scene classification [11–14]. Unlike the conventional methods, which fail to model discontinuous rigid motions, deep learning based approaches have a great modeling capacity and can learn discriminative representations in videos. However, the current techniques have mostly been devised to deal with fixed-length video sequences. They fail to deal with long sequences due to their limited temporal coverage. This paper presents a novel deep learning approach, which does not assume any biased knowledge about the concept of data and it automatically explores the structure of the complex non-linear surface on which the samples of the video are present. According to the block diagram in Fig. 1, our proposed method defines a Heterogeneous Deep Discriminative Model (HDDM) whose weights are initialized by an unsupervised layer-wise pre-training stage using Gaussian Restricted Boltzmann Machines (GRBM) [15]. The initialized HDDM is then separately trained for each class using all videos of that class in order to learn a Deep Discriminative Model (DDM) for every class. The training is done so that the DDM learns to specifically represent videos of that class. Therefore, a class specific model is made to learn the structure and the geometry of the complex non-linear surface on which video sequences of that class exist. Also, we represent the raw video data using Sparse Cubic Symmetrical Pattern (SCSP) to capture long-range spatiotemporal patterns and reduce the redundancy between adjacent frames. For the classification of a given query video, we first represent the video based on the learnt class-specific DDMs. The representation errors from the respective DDMs are then computed and a weighted voting strategy is used to assign a class label to the query video.

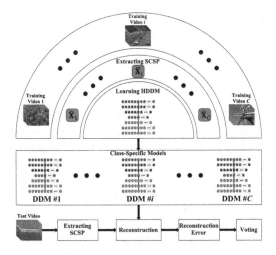

Fig. 1. The block diagram of the proposed DDM framework for video classification.

The main contributions of our proposed Deep Discriminative Model (DDM) are the followings. First, a novel deep learning based framework is introduced for video classification (Sect. 3). Moreover, we develop a Sparse Cubic Symmetrical Pattern (SCSP) to avoid the redundancy in video sequences and reduce the computational cost, and a weighted voting strategies is utilized for classification (Sect. 4). Finally, extensive experiments are conducted along with comparisons against state-of-the-art methods for video classification. The experimental results demonstrate that the proposed method achieves superior performance compared to the state-of-the-art methods (Sect. 5).

2   Related Work

Several approaches have been proposed for video classification [3,16,17]. A popular approach is Linear Dynamic System (LDS) [1,16], which is known as a probabilistic generative model defined over space and time. LDS approximates hidden states using Principal Component Analysis (PCA), and describes their trajectory as time evolves. LDS has obvious drawbacks due to its sensitivity to external variations. In order to overcome this limitation, Closed-Loop LDS (CLDS) [18] was proposed. However, CLDS tends to fail to capture some discontinuous rigid motions due to its simplistic linearity. Local Binary Pattern (LBP) based methods [2] have been widely used in texture analysis. Zhao *et al.* [19] extended LBP to the space and the time domains and proposed two LBP variants: (1) Volume Local Binary Pattern (VLBP) [19] which combines both the spatial and the temporal variations of the video; (2) Local Binary Pattern on Three Orthogonal Planes (LBP-TOP) [19], which computes LBP in three individual $x - y$, $x - t$, and $y - t$ planes to describe the video. Likewise, other versions of LBP-TOP, such as Local Ternary Pattern on Three Orthogonal Planes (LTP-TOP) [20] and Local Phase Quantization on Three Orthogonal Planes (LPQ-TOP) [20], have been proposed. Although they are all effective in capturing the spatiotemporal information, they rarely achieve a satisfactory performance in the presence of camera motions.

Recently, there is a huge growing research interest in deep learning methods in various areas of computer vision, beating the state-of-the-art techniques [9, 11–14]. Deep learning methods set up numerous recognition records in image classification [21], object detection [22], face recognition and verification [23], and image set classification [10]. Deep models, such as Deep Belief Networks and stacked autoencoders, have much more expressive power than traditional shallow models and can be effectively trained with layer-wise pre-training and fine-tuning [24]. Stacked autoencoders have been successfully used for feature extraction [25]. Also, they can be used to model complex relationships between variables due to the composition of several levels of non-linearity [25]. Xie *et al.* [26] modeled relationships between noisy and clean images using stacked denoising autoencoders. Although, deep autoencoders are rarely used to model time series data, there are researches on using variants of Restricted Boltzmann Machine (RBM) [27] for specific time series data such as human motion [28]. On the other hand, some convolutional architectures have been used to learn spatiotemporal features from video data [29]. Kaparthy *et al.* [11] used a deep structure of Convolutional Neural Networks (CNN) and tested it on a large scale video dataset. By learning long range motion features via training a hierarchy of multiple convolutional layers, they showed that their framework is just marginally better than single frame-based methods. Simonyan *et al.* [12] designed Two-Stream CNN which includes the spatial and the temporal networks. They took advantage of ImageNet dataset for pre-training and calculated the optical flow to explicitly capture the motion information. Tran *et al.* [13] investigated 3D CNNs [30] on realistic (captured in the wild) and large-scale video datasets. They tried to learn both the spatial and temporal features with 3D convolution operations. Sun *et al.* [14] proposed a factorized spatiotemporal CNN and exploited different ways to decompose 3D convolutional kernels.

The long-range temporal structure plays an important role in understanding the dynamics of events in videos. However, mainstream CNN frameworks usually focus on appearances and short-term motions. Thus, they lack the capacity to incorporate the long-range temporal structure. Recently, few other attempts (mostly relying on dense temporal sampling with a pre-defined sampling interval) have been proposed to deal with this problem [31, 32]. This approach would incur excessive computational cost and is not applicable to real-world long video sequences. It also poses the risk of missing important information for videos that are longer than the maximal sequence length. Our proposed method deals with this problem by extracting Sparse Cubic Symmetrical Patterns (SCSP) from video sequences to feed its autoencoder structure (Sect. 4.1). In terms of spatiotemporal structure modeling, a key observation is that consecutive frames are highly redundant. Therefore, dense temporal sampling, which results in highly similar sampled frames, is unnecessary. Instead, a sparse spatiotemporal representation will be more favorable in this case. Also, autoencoders reduce the dimension and keep as much important information as possible, and remove noise. Furthermore, combining them with RBMs helps the model to learn more complicated video structures based on their non-linearity.

3   The Proposed Deep Discriminative Model

We first define a Heterogeneous Deep Discriminative Model (HDDM) which will be used to learn the underlying structure of the data in Sect. 4.2. The architecture of the HDDM is shown in Fig. 2. Generally, an appropriate parameter initialization is inevitable for deep neural networks to have a satisfactory performance. Therefore, we initialize the parameters of HDDM by performing pre-training in a greedy layer-wise framework using Gaussian Restricted Boltzmann Machines. The initialized HDDM is separately fine-tuned for each of the C classes of the training videos. Therefore, we end up with a total of C fine-tuned Deep Discriminative Models (DDMs). Then, the fined-tuned models are used for video classification.

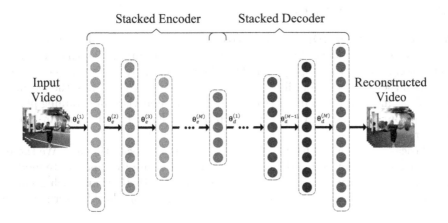

Fig. 2. The configuration of the proposed Heterogeneous Deep Discriminative Model.

3.1   The Heterogeneous Deep Discriminative Model

As can be seen in Fig. 2, the proposed HDDM is based on an autoencoder which comprises multiple encoder and decoder layers. In the proposed autoencoder structure, both the encoder and the decoder have M hidden layers each such that the M-th layer of the encoder is considered as the first layer of the decoder. The encoder section represents the input data in a lower dimension. The encoder consists of a combination of non-linear functions $s\,(\cdot)$ used to map the input data $\mathbf{x}$ to a representation $\mathbf{h}$ given by

$$\mathbf{h} = s\left(\mathbf{x}\middle|\boldsymbol{\theta}_e^{(1)}, \boldsymbol{\theta}_e^{(2)}, \ldots, \boldsymbol{\theta}_e^{(M)}\right) \tag{1}$$

where $\boldsymbol{\theta}_e^{(i)} = \left\{\mathbf{W}_e^{(i)}, \mathbf{b}_e^{(i)}\right\}$ denotes the parameters of the i-the encoder layer. So, $\mathbf{W}_e^{(i)} \in \mathbb{R}^{n_i \times n_{i-1}}$ is the encoder weight matrix for layer i having n_i nodes, $\mathbf{b}_e^{(i)} \in \mathbb{R}^{n_i}$ is the bias vector and $s(\cdot)$ is a non-linear sigmoid activation function. The encoder parameters are learnt by combining the encoder with the decoder and jointly train the encoder-decoder structure to represent the input data by optimizing a cost function. Hence, the decoder can be defined as series of non-linear functions, which calculate an approximation of the input $\mathbf{x}$ from the encoder output $\mathbf{h}$. The approximated output $\tilde{\mathbf{x}}$ of the decoder is obtained by

$$\tilde{\mathbf{x}} = s\left(\mathbf{h}\middle|\boldsymbol{\theta}_d^{(1)}, \boldsymbol{\theta}_d^{(2)}, \ldots, \boldsymbol{\theta}_d^{(M)}\right) \tag{2}$$

where $\boldsymbol{\theta}_d^{(j)} = \left\{\mathbf{W}_d^{(j)}, \mathbf{b}_d^{(j)}\right\}$ are the parameters of the j-the decoder layer. Consequently, we represent the complete encoder-decoder structure by its parameters $\boldsymbol{\theta}_{HDDM} = \{\boldsymbol{\theta}_{\mathbf{W}}, \boldsymbol{\theta}_{\mathbf{b}}\}$, where $\boldsymbol{\theta}_{\mathbf{W}} = \left\{\mathbf{W}_e^{(i)}, \mathbf{W}_d^{(i)}\right\}_{i=1}^{M}$ and $\boldsymbol{\theta}_{\mathbf{b}} = \left\{\mathbf{b}_e^{(i)}, \mathbf{b}_d^{(i)}\right\}_{i=1}^{M}$.

3.2   Parameter Initialization

We train the defined HDDM with videos of each class individually, which results in class-specific models. The training is performed through stochastic gradient descent with back propagation [33]. The training may not yield to desirable results if the HDDM is initialized with inappropriate weights. Thus, the parameters of the model are first initialized through an unsupervised pre-training phase. For this purpose, a greedy layer-wise approach is adopted and Gaussian RBMs [15] are used.

Basically, a standard RBM [27] is used for binary stochastic data. We therefore use an extension of RBM to process real valued data by appropriate modifications in its energy function. Gaussian RBM (GRBM) [15] is one such popular extension whose energy function is defined by changing the bias term of the visible layer.

$$E_{GRBM}(v, h) = \sum_i \frac{(v_i - b_i)^2}{2\sigma_i^2} - \sum_j c_j h_j - \sum_{ij} w_{ij} \frac{v_i}{\sigma_i} h_j \tag{3}$$

where $\mathbf{W}$ is the weight matrix, and $\mathbf{b}$ and $\mathbf{c}$ are the biases of the visible and the hidden layer, respectively. We use a numerical technique called Contrastive Divergence (CD) [34] to learn the model parameter $\{\mathbf{W}, \mathbf{b}, \mathbf{c}\}$ of the GRBM in the training phase. v_i and h_j denote the visible layer and the hidden layer's nodes, respectively. Also, σ_i is the standard deviation of the real valued Gaussian distributed inputs to the visible node v_i. It is possible to learn σ_i for each visible unit but it becomes arduous when using CD for GRBM parameter learning. We therefore use another approach and set σ_i to a constant value.

Since there are no intra-layer node connections, result derivation becomes easily manageable for the RBM to the contrary of most directed graphical models. The probability distributions for GRBM are given by

$$\rho\left(h_j \mid \mathbf{v}\right) = s\left(\sum_i w_{ij} v_i + c_j\right) \tag{4}$$

$$\rho\left(v_i \mid \mathbf{h}\right) = \frac{1}{\sigma_i \sqrt{2\pi}} \exp\left(\frac{-(v_i - u_i)^2}{2\sigma_i^2}\right) \tag{5}$$

where

$$u_i = b_i + \sigma_i^2 \sum_i w_{ij} h_j \tag{6}$$

Since our data are real-valued, we use GRBMs to initialize the parameters of the proposed HDDM. In this case, we consider two stacked layers at a time to obtain the GRBM parameters during the learning process. First, the input layer nodes and the first hidden layer nodes are considered as the visible units v and the hidden unit h of the first GRBM, respectively, and their respective parameters are obtained. The activations of the first GRBM's hidden units are then used as an input to train the second GRBM. We repeat this process for all four encoder hidden layers. The weights learnt for the encoder layers are then tied to the corresponding decoder layers.

4   Video Classification Procedure

In this section, we describe how to classify query videos using the representation error. Assume that there are C training videos $\{\mathbf{X}_c\}_{c=1}^C$ with the corresponding class labels $y_c \in \{1, 2, \cdots, C\}$. A video sequence is denoted by $\mathbf{X}_c = \{\mathbf{x}^{(t)}\}_{t=1}^T$, where $\mathbf{x}^{(t)}$ contains raw pixel values of the frame at time t. The problem is to assign class y_q to the query video $\mathbf{X}_q$.

4.1   Sparse Cubic Symmetrical Patterns

We represent dynamic textures by video blocks, video volumes spanning over both the spatial and temporal domains, to jointly model the spatial and temporal information. Since there are strong correlations between adjacent regions of scenes (which cause redundancy), we devise an approach to extract a sparse representation of the spatiotemporal encoded features. As a result, the less important information is discarded which makes the deep discriminative model representation more efficacious. For this purpose, we design a volumetric based descriptor to capture the spatiotemporal variations in the scene. Given a video, we first decompose it into a batch of small cubic spatiotemporal volumes. We only consider the video cubes of small size ($w \times h \times d$ pixels), which consists of relatively simple content that can be generated with few components.

Figure 3 illustrates the feature extraction process. We divide each series of frames $\mathbf{X} = \{\mathbf{x}^{(t)}\}_{t=1}^T$ into $w \times h \times d$ distinct non-overlapping uniformly spaced

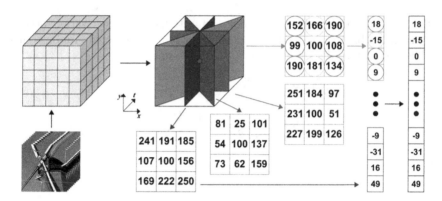

Fig. 3. An example of extracting symmetric signed magnitude variation pattern in a volumetric block of the video sequence.

cubic blocks and extract symmetric spatiotemporal variation pattern for every block which results in a feature vector of the corresponding block. Consequently, each video sequence $\mathbf{X}$ is encoded in terms of the symmetric signed magnitude variation patterns, denoted as $\mathbf{x}_E \in \mathbb{R}^d$, obtained by concatenating the feature vectors of all cubic blocks spanning over the entire video sequence. We do not consider the last one or two frames of video sequence if they do not fit in the cubic block structure. This does not affect the algorithm's performance due to the correlation between consecutive frames.

Given any pixel $x_o^{(t)}$, we represent the neighboring pixels by $x_1^{(t)}, \cdots, x_P^{(t)}$. The symmetric spatiotemporal variations for j-th plane is calculated as

$$F_j\left(x_o^{(t)}\right) = \biguplus_{p=1}^{\frac{P}{2}} \left(x_p^{(t)} - x_{p+\frac{P}{2}}^{(t)}\right) \tag{7}$$

where $x_p^{(t)}$ and $x_{p+\frac{P}{2}}^{(t)}$ are two symmetric neighbors of pixel $x_o^{(t)}$. Also, $\biguplus$ denotes the concatenation operator.

The aforementioned feature vectors are organized into the columns of a matrix $\mathbf{D} \in \mathbb{R}^{d \times N}$, where d is the dimension of the feature vectors and N is the total number of videos. In variable-length videos, we temporally partition the video sequences into non-overlapping segments with a fixed length k and extract features from the cubic blocks within each segment, separately. Then, we place the extracted features of each section into a column of the matrix $\mathbf{D}$. Here, we call matrix $\mathbf{D}$ the dictionary and aim to find a sparse representation $\hat{\mathbf{x}}$ of the encoded video $\mathbf{x}_E$, $\mathbf{x}_E = \mathbf{D}\hat{\mathbf{x}}$ by basis matching pursuit [35] such that

$$\min_{\hat{\mathbf{x}}} \frac{1}{2} \|\mathbf{x}_E - \mathbf{D}\hat{\mathbf{x}}\|_2^2 + \lambda\|\hat{\mathbf{x}}\|_1 \tag{8}$$

where λ is a slack variable and $\|\cdot\|_1$ is the sparsity including ℓ_1 norm. The slack variable balances the trade-off between fitting data perfectly and employing a sparse solution. For further improvements, we represent each color channel, individually. Also, we reshape the sparsely represented vector $\hat{\mathbf{x}}$ into a 3D structure of $\hat{\mathbf{X}} = \{\hat{\mathbf{x}}^{(l)}\}_{l=1}^{L}$, where L is the length of the structure. We feed the proposed deep model with Sparse Cubic Symmetrical Patterns (SCSP) instead of raw videos.

For notational simplicity, we will consider the sparsely represented $\hat{\mathbf{X}} = \{\hat{\mathbf{x}}^{(l)}\}_{l=1}^{L}$ as a sequence of frames with length L and denote it by $\mathbf{X} = \{\mathbf{x}^{(l)}\}_{l=1}^{L}$ hereafter.

4.2 Learning DDMs of the Training Classes

In order to initialize the parameters of the HDDM using GRBMs, we randomly shuffle a small subset, containing video sequences from all classes (of the training video sequences). We use this subset for layer-wise GRBM training of all encoder layers. The parameters of the decoder layers are then configured with their corresponding tied parameters of the encoder layers. This process assures us that rarely does the proposed network gets stuck in a local minimum.

We define a cost function based on the representation error over all frames of the video for learning class-specific parameters. In order to avoid over-fitting and enhance the generalization of the learnt model to unseen test data, the regularization terms are added to the cost function of the HDDM. A weight decay penalty term J_{wd} and a sparsity constraint J_{sp} are added.

$$J_{reg}\left(\theta_{HDDM}\left|x^{(l)} \in X_c\right.\right) = \sum \left\|x^{(l)} - \tilde{x}^{(l)}\right\|^2 + \lambda_{wd}J_{wd} + \lambda_{sp}J_{sp} \qquad (9)$$

where λ_{wd} and λ_{sp} are regularization parameters. J_{wd} guarantees small values of weights for all hidden units and ensures that dropping out will not happen for hidden layers' units. It is defined as the summation of the Frobenius norm of all weight matrices:

$$J_{wd} = \sum_{i=1}^{M} \left\|\mathbf{W}_e^{(i)}\right\|_F^2 + \sum_{i=1}^{M} \left\|\mathbf{W}_d^{(i)}\right\|_F^2 \qquad (10)$$

Moreover, J_{sp} enforces that the mean activation $\bar{\rho}_j^{(i)}$ (over all training samples) of the j-th unit of the i-th hidden layer is as close as possible to the sparsity target ρ which is a very small constant. J_{sp} is further defined based on the KL divergence as

$$J_{sp} = \sum_{i=1}^{2M-1} \sum_{j} \rho \log \frac{\rho}{\bar{\rho}_j^{(i)}} + (1 - \rho) \log \frac{1 - \rho}{1 - \bar{\rho}_j^{(i)}} \qquad (11)$$

Therefore, a class specific model θ_c is obtained by optimizing the regularized cost function J_{reg} over all frames of the class $\mathbf{X}_c$.

$$\theta_c = \arg \min_{\theta_{HDDM}} J_{reg}\left(\theta_{HDDM}\left|x^{(l)} \in \mathbf{X}_C\right.\right) \qquad (12)$$

We note that our proposed model is easily scalable. Enrolling new classes would not require re-training on the complete database. Instead, the class-specific models for the added classes can be learnt independently of the existing classes.

4.3   Classification

Given a query video sequence $\mathbf{X}_q = \left\{\mathbf{x}^{(t)}\right\}_{t=1}^{T_q}$, we first extract SCSPs and then separately reconstruct them using all class-specific DDMs $\boldsymbol{\theta}_c$, $c = 1, \cdots, C$, using Eqs. (1) and (2). Suppose $\tilde{\mathbf{x}}_c^{(l)}$ is the l-th frame of the reconstructed query video sequence $\tilde{\mathbf{X}}_{q_c}$ based on the c-th class model $\boldsymbol{\theta}_c$. We obtain the reconstruction errors, i.e. $\left\|x^{(l)} - \tilde{x}_c^{(l)}\right\|_2$, from all class specific models; then, a weighted voting strategy is employed to determine the class label of the given query video sequence $\mathbf{X}_q$. Each query video sequence's frame $\mathbf{x}^{(l)}$ casts a vote to all classes. Using the reconstruction error of each class's model, we assign a weight to the casted vote to each class. The weight $\mu_c\left(x^{(l)}\right)$ of the vote casted by a frame $\mathbf{x}^{(l)}$ to class c is defined as

$$\mu_c\left(\mathbf{x}^{(l)}\right) = \exp\left(-\left\|\mathbf{x}^{(l)} - \tilde{\mathbf{x}}_c^{(l)}\right\|_2\right) \tag{13}$$

The candidate class which achieves the highest accumulated weight from all frames of $\mathbf{X}_q$ is declared as the class y_q of the query video sequence:

$$y_q = \arg\max_c \sum_{\mathbf{X}_q} \mu_c\left(\mathbf{x}^{(l)}\right) \tag{14}$$

5   Experimental Analysis

We extensively evaluate the performance of the proposed method on five benchmarking datasets including UCF101 [36] and Hollywood II [37] datasets for action recognition, DynTex dataset [17] for dynamic texture recognition, and YUPENN [38] and Maryland [39] datasets for dynamic scene classification task.

5.1   Parameter Setting

We performed a grid search to obtain the optimal parameters and conducted experiments on a validation set. To be specific, the initial weights for layer-wise GRBM training are drawn from a uniform random distribution in the range of $[-0.005, 0.005]$. Contrastive Divergence (CD) was used to train GRBMs on 200 randomly selected videos from the training data. Mini-batches of 32 videos were used and the training was done for 50 epochs. A fixed learning rate of 10^{-3} was used. To train the pre-initialized HDDM to learn class-specific models, we used an annealed learning rate that is started with 2×10^{-3} and multiplied by a factor of 0.6 per epoch. We chose ℓ_2 weight decay (λ_{wd}) to be 0.01, a sparsity target (ρ) of 0.001, and non-sparsity penalty term (λ_{sp}) of 0.5. The training was performed by considering a mini-batch of 10 videos for 20 epochs.

Table 1. Comparison of the proposed method's accuracy (%) on the UCF101 database [36] with different block sizes for SCSP.

Block size	$1 \times 1 \times 3$	$1 \times 1 \times 5$	$3 \times 3 \times 3$	$3 \times 3 \times 5$	$5 \times 5 \times 3$	$5 \times 5 \times 5$	$7 \times 7 \times 5$
Accuracy	87.3	91.2	94.3	92.5	89.4	84.3	79.5

The size of volumetric blocks in SCSP also affects the performance of the algorithm. Therefore, we conducted an empirical study on different sizes of video blocks in Table 1. It is observed from Table 1 that the best result is achieved with the block size of $3 \times 3 \times 3$. With very small blocks (e.g. $1 \times 1 \times 3$), few spatiotemporal regions are captured and the model will have problems on dealing with the scene variations. Moreover, the blocks of large sizes (e.g. $7 \times 7 \times 5$) carry too much information that does not improve the model's performance.

In order to determine the number of layers and the number of units in each layer, we employed a multi-resolution search strategy. The ideas is to test some values from a large parameter range, choose a few best configurations, and then test again with smaller steps around these values. We tested the model with the escalating number of layers [40] and stopped where the performance reaches the highest rate on the validation set. The hidden layers sizes varies in the range of [250, 1000].

5.2 Human Action Recognition

We conducted experiments on two benchmark action recognition datasets, i.e. UCF101 [36] and Hollywood II [37] datasets, and compared the performance of the proposed method against state-of-the-art approaches.

The UCF101 dataset [36] is composed of realistic web videos which are typically captured with large variations in camera motion, object appearance/scale, viewpoint, cluttered background, and illumination variations. It has 101 categories of human actions ranging from daily life to sports. The UCF101 contains 13,320 videos with an average length of 180 frames. It has three splits setting to separate the dataset into training and testing videos. We report the average classification accuracy over these three splits.

We compare the average accuracy performance of our proposed DDM with both the traditional and deep learning-based benchmark methods for human action recognition in Table 2. Our model obtains an average accuracy of 91.5%. However, the accuracy of DDM on the UCF101 is less than that of KVMF [41] by 1.6%. We argue that the performance of DDM degrades since it only captures short range spatiotemporal information in the video sequence. The videos in UCF101 exhibit significant temporal variations. Moreover, the severe camera movements increase the complexity of video's dynamics and make data reconstruction challenging. These issues bring up difficulties for the algorithm to focus on the action happening at each time instance.

To tackle this problem, we feed the extracted SCSP features to our DDM. The proposed SCSP extracts detailed spatiotemporal information by capturing the

Table 2. Comparison of the average classification accuracy of DDM against state-of-the-art methods on the UCF101 dataset [36].

Method	Average accuracy (%)
iDT+HSV [42]	87.9
MoFAP [43]	88.3
Two-Stream CNN [12]	88.0
C3D (3 nets) [13]	85.2
C3D (3 nets)+iDT [13]	90.4
F_{ST}CN (SCI Fusion) [14]	88.1
TDD+FV [44]	90.3
KVMF [41]	93.1
DDM	**91.5**
DDM+SCSP	**94.3**

spatiotemporal variations of the video sequence within small volumetric blocks. By representing this information sparsely, it not only covers the whole length of the video sequence, but also decreases the redundancy of data. In this way, SCSP increases the discriminability of samples in the feature space in which the similar samples are mapped close to each other and dissimilar ones are mapped far apart. Therefore, the DDM can readily learn the underlying structure of each class. As can be seen from Table 2, the performance of our DDM improves by using SCSP features.

The Hollywood II dataset [37] has been constructed from 69 different Hollywood movies and includes 12 activity classes. It contains a total of 1,707 videos with 823 training videos and 884 testing videos. The length of videos varies from hundreds to several thousand frames. According to the test protocol, the performance is measured by the mean average precession over all classes [37].

To compare our approach with the benchmark, we obtain the average precession performance for each class and take the mean average precession (mAP) as indicated in Table 3. The best result is obtained using DDM with a 0.4 mAP improvement in the overall accuracy. The superior performance of the proposed method in action recognition task demonstrates the effectiveness of our long-term spatiotemporal modeling of videos approach.

5.3 Dynamic Texture and Dynamic Scene Recognition

We evaluated the capability of our proposed method in the case of dynamic texture and dynamic scene classification using DynTex [17] dataset, and YUPENN [38] and Maryland [39] datasets, respectively. In order to follow the standard comparison protocol, we use Leave-One-Out (LOO) cross validation. Note that the results are drawn from the related papers.

Table 3. Comparison of the mean average precession (mAP) of DDM with the state-of-the-art methods on the Hollywood II dataset [37].

Method	mAP (%)
DL-SFA [45]	48.1
iDT [46]	64.3
Actons [47]	64.3
MIFS [48]	68.0
NL-RFDRP+CNN [49]	70.1
HRP [14]	76.7
DDM	**75.3**
DDM+SCSP	**77.1**

The DynTex dataset [17] is a standard database for dynamic texture analysis containing high-quality dynamic texture videos such as windmill, waterfall, and sea waves. It includes over 650 videos recorded in PAL format in various conditions. Each video has 250 frames length with a 25 frames per second frame rate. Table 4 compares the rank-1 recognition rates of DDM with the benchmark approaches. It can be clearly seen that our proposed approach yields in the best results compared to all other methods.

The YUPENN dataset [38] is a stabilized dynamic scene dataset. This dataset was created with an emphasis on scene-specific temporal information. YUPENN contains 14 dynamic scene categories with 30 videos per category. There are significant variations in this dataset's video sequences such as frame rate, scene appearance, scaling, illumination, and camera viewpoint. We report the experimental results on this dataset in Table 5. It can be observed from Table 5 that DDM outperforms the existing state-of-the-art methods in the case of dynamic scene classification. The results confirm that the proposed DDM is effective for dynamic scene data classification in a stabilized setting.

Table 4. Comparison of the rank-1 recognition rates on the DynTex dataset [17].

Method	Recognition rate (%)
VLBP [19]	95.71
LBP-TOP [19]	97.14
DFS [50]	97.63
BoS Tree [51]	98.86
MBSIF-TOP [52]	98.61
st-TCoF [9]	98.20
DDM	**98.05**
DDM+SCSP	**99.27**

Table 5. Comparison of the classification results (%) on the YUPENN [38] and Maryland [39] dynamic scene datasets.

Method	YUPENN	Maryland
CSO [53]	85.95	67.69
SFA [54]	85.48	60.00
SOE [3]	80.71	43.10
BoSE [3]	96.19	77.69
LBP-TOP [19]	84.29	39.23
C3D [13]	98.10	N/A
st-TCoF [9]	99.05	88.46
DDM	**97.52**	**86.33**
DDM+SCSP	**99.18**	**90.27**

The Maryland dataset [39] is a dynamic scene database which consist of 13 natural scene categories containing 10 videos each with 617 frames on average. The dataset has videos showing a wide range of variations in natural dynamic scenes, e.g. avalanches, traffic, and forest fire. One notable difference between the Maryland dataset and the YUPENN dataset is that the former includes camera motions, while the latter does not.

We present the comparison between our proposed method and the state-of-the-art methods in Table 5. Since most of the videos in the Maryland dataset show significant temporal variations, the experimental results suggest that, for highly dynamic data, DDM is able to outperform its strongest rival st-TCoF by a margin of 1.81%. The promising performance of st-TCoF in the dynamic scene classification (Table 5) is due to incorporating the spatial and the temporal information of the video sequence. However, the results on Maryland dataset suggests that st-TCoF is sensitive to the significant camera motions. On the other hand, our DDM is strongly robust when the structure of the images drastically changes their position with time. Therefore, the DDM can effectively learn the complex underlying structure of the dynamic scene in the presence of severe camera movements.

5.4 Discriminability Analysis

In order to illustrate the discriminability power of the SCSP, Fig. 4 shows the distribution of the sampled data from different classes of UCF101 database before and after applying SCSP in a 3D space. Thanks to the existing redundancy, the samples are correlated before applying SCSP, which makes the data reconstruction a non-trivial task. However, the samples become scattered in the feature space after applying SCSP, i.e. the similar samples are closer to each other and dissimilar samples are far apart. This strategy makes the process of learning class-specific models easier for DDM by learning the underlying structure of each class from the feature space instead of raw video data.

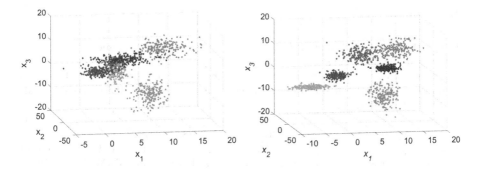

Fig. 4. An example of the distribution of the learnt classes from UCF101 dataset [36] before (**Left**) and after (**Right**) applying the proposed SCSP. The SCSP reduces the correlation between similar classes by condensing and scattering their samples in the feature space.

By enlarging the inter-class similarity of data, the proposed DDM reconstructs the videos of each class more effectively by learning the class-specif models. According to the distances between samples in the new feature space, the DDM can easily learn the pattern and the structure of each class, since the correlation and the redundancy are lessened by applying SCSP.

6   Conclusion

We proposed a novel deep learning approach for video-based scene classification. Specifically, a multi-layer deep autoencoder structure was presented which is first pre-trained for appropriate parameter initialization and then fine-tuned for learning class-specific Deep Discriminative Models (DDMs). Capturing the underlying non-linear complex geometric surfaces, the DDMs can effectively model the spatiotemporal variations within video sequences. In order to discard the redundant information in video sequences and avoid the strong correlations between adjacent frames, we captured the spatiotemporal variations in the video sequences and represented them sparsely using Sparse Cubic Symmetrical Pattern (SCSP). The learnt DDMs are used for a minimum reconstruction error-based classification technique during the testing phase. The proposed method has been extensively evaluated on a number of benchmark video datasets for action recognition, dynamic texture and dynamic scene classification tasks. Comparisons against state-of-the-art approaches showed that our proposed method achieves very interesting performance.

Acknowledgement. The financial support of the Academy of Finland and Infotech Oulu is acknowledged.

References

1. Ravichandran, A., Chaudhry, R., Vidal, R.: Categorizing dynamic textures using a bag of dynamical systems. IEEE Trans. PAMI **35**(2), 342–353 (2013)
2. Ojala, T., Pietikäinen, M., Mäenpää, T.: Multiresolution gray-scale and rotation invariant texture classification with local binary patterns. IEEE Trans. PAMI **24**(7), 971–987 (2002)
3. Feichtenhofer, C., Pinz, A., Wildes, R.P.: Bags of spacetime energies for dynamic scene recognition. In: IEEE CVPR, pp. 2681–2688 (2014)
4. Kim, T.K., Kittler, J., Cipolla, R.: Discriminative learning and recognition of image set classes using canonical correlations. IEEE Trans. PAMI **29**(6), 1005–1018 (2007)
5. Wang, R., Shan, S., Chen, X., Dai, Q., Gao, W.: Manifold-manifold distance and its application to face recognition with image sets. IEEE Trans. Image Process. **21**(10), 4466–4479 (2012)
6. Harandi, M., Sanderson, C., Shirazi, S., Lovell, B.C.: Graph embedding discriminant analysis on grassmannian manifolds for improved image set matching. In: IEEE CVPR, pp. 2705–2712 (2011)
7. Wang, R., Guo, H., Davis, L.S., Dai, Q.: Covariance discriminative learning: a natural and efficient approach to image set classification. In: IEEE CVPR, pp. 2496–2503 (2012)
8. Bengio, Y., Courville, A., Vincent, P.: Representation learning: a review and new perspectives. IEEE Trans. PAMI **35**(8), 1798–1828 (2013)
9. Qi, X., Li, C.G., Zhao, G., Hong, X., Pietikäinen, M.: Dynamic texture and scene classification by transferring deep image features. Neurocomputing **171**, 1230–1241 (2016)
10. Hayat, M., Bennamoun, M., An, S.: Deep reconstruction models for image set classification. IEEE Trans. PAMI **37**(7), 713–727 (2015)
11. Karpathy, A., Toderici, G., Shetty, S., Leung, T., Sukthankar, R., Fei-Fei, L.: Large-scale video classification with convolutional neural networks. In: IEEE CVPR, pp. 1725–1732 (2014)
12. Simonyan, K., Zisserman, A.: Two-stream convolutional networks for action recognition in videos. In: NIPS, pp. 568–576 (2014)
13. Tran, D., Bourdev, L., Fergus, R., Torresani, L., Paluri, M.: Learning spatiotemporal features with 3D convolutional networks. In: IEEE ICCV, pp. 4489–4497 (2015)
14. Sun, L., Jia, K., Yeung, D.Y., Shi, B.E.: Human action recognition using factorized spatio-temporal convolutional networks. In: IEEE ICCV, pp. 4597–4605 (2015)
15. Welling, M., Rosen-Zvi, M., Hinton, G.: Exponential family harmoniums with an application to information retrieval. In: NIPS, pp. 1481–1488 (2004)
16. Chaudhry, R., Hager, G., Vidal, R.: Dynamic template tracking and recognition. IJCV **105**(1), 19–48 (2013)
17. Péteri, R., Fazekas, S., Huiskes, M.J.: DynTex: a comprehensive database of dynamic textures. Patt. Recogn. Lett. **31**(12), 1627–1632 (2010)
18. Yuan, L., Wen, F., Liu, C., Shum, H.-Y.: Synthesizing dynamic texture with closed-loop linear dynamic system. In: Pajdla, T., Matas, J. (eds.) ECCV 2004. LNCS, vol. 3022, pp. 603–616. Springer, Heidelberg (2004). https://doi.org/10.1007/978-3-540-24671-8_48
19. Zhao, G., Pietikäinen, M.: Dynamic texture recognition using local binary patterns with an application to facial expressions. IEEE Trans. PAMI **29**(6), 915–928 (2007)

20. Rahtu, E., Heikkilä, J., Ojansivu, V., Ahonen, T.: Local phase quantization for blur-insensitive image analysis. Image Vis. Comput. **30**(8), 501–512 (2012)
21. Azizpour, H., Razavian, A.S., Sullivan, J., Maki, A., Carlsson, S.: From generic to specific deep representations for visual recognition. In: IEEE CVPR, pp. 36–45 (2015)
22. Sermanet, P., Eigen, D., Zhang, X., Mathieu, M., Fergus, R., LeCun, Y.: OverFeat: integrated recognition, localization and detection using convolutional networks. CoRR abs/1312.6229 (2013)
23. Sun, Y., Wang, X., Tang, X.: Deep learning face representation from predicting 10,000 classes. In: IEEE CVPR, pp. 1891–1898 (2014)
24. Bengio, Y.: Learning deep architectures for AI. Found. Trends Mach. Learn. **2**(1), 1–127 (2013)
25. Vincent, P., Larochelle, H., Lajoie, I., Bengio, Y., Manzagol, P.A.: Stacked denoising autoencoders: learning useful representations in a deep network with a local denoising criterion. J. Mach. Learn. Res. **11**, 3371–3408 (2010)
26. Xie, J., Xu, L., Chen, E.: Image denoising and inpainting with deep neural networks. In: Advances in Neural Information Processing Systems, pp. 350–358 (2012)
27. Smolensky, P.: Parallel Distributed Processing: Explorations in the Microstructure of Cognition, vol. 1. MIT Press, Cambridge (1986). 194–281
28. Taylor, G.W., Hinton, G.E., Roweis, S.: Modeling human motion using binary latent variables. In: Advances in Neural Information Processing Systems, pp. 1345–1352 (2007)
29. Taylor, G.W., Fergus, R., LeCun, Y., Bregler, C.: Convolutional learning of spatiotemporal features. In: Daniilidis, K., Maragos, P., Paragios, N. (eds.) ECCV 2010. LNCS, vol. 6316, pp. 140–153. Springer, Heidelberg (2010). https://doi.org/10.1007/978-3-642-15567-3_11
30. Ji, S., Xu, W., Yang, M., Yu, K.: 3D convolutional neural networks for human action recognition. IEEE Trans. PAMI **35**(1), 221–231 (2013)
31. Ng, J.Y.H., Hausknecht, M., Vijayanarasimhan, S., Vinyals, O., Monga, R., Toderici, G.: Beyond short snippets: deep networks for video classification. In: IEEE CVPR, pp. 4694–4702 (2015)
32. Varol, G., Laptev, I., Schmid, C.: Long-term temporal convolutions for action recognition. CoRR abs/1604.04494 (2016)
33. Hinton, G.E., Osindero, S., Teh, Y.W.: A fast learning algorithm for deep belief nets. Neural Comput. **18**(7), 1527–1554 (2006)
34. Hinton, G.E., Osindero, S., Welling, M., Teh, Y.W.: Unsupervised discovery of nonlinear structure using contrastive backpropagation. Cogn. Sci. **30**(4), 725–731 (2006)
35. Chen, S.S., Donoho, D.L., Saunders, M.A.: Atomic decomposition by basis pursuit. SIAM Rev. **43**(1), 129–159 (2001)
36. Soomro, K., Zamir, A.R., Shah, M.: UCF101: A dataset of 101 human actions classes from videos in the wild. CoRR abs/1212.0402 (2012)
37. Marszalek, M., Laptev, I., Schmid, C.: Actions in context. In: IEEE CVPR, pp. 2929–2936 (2009)
38. Derpanis, K.G., Lecce, M., Daniilidis, K., Wildes, R.P.: Dynamic scene understanding: the role of orientation features in space and time in scene classification. In: IEEE CVPR, pp. 1306–1313 (2012)
39. Shroff, N., Turaga, P., Chellappa, R.: Moving vistas: exploiting motion for describing scenes. In: IEEE CVPR, pp. 1911–1918 (2010)

40. Larochelle, H., Erhan, D., Courville, A., Bergstra, J., Bengio, Y.: An empirical evaluation of deep architectures on problems with many factors of variation. In: ICML, pp. 473–480 (2007)
41. Zhu, W., Hu, J., Sun, G., Cao, X., Qiao, Y.: A key volume mining deep framework for action recognition. In: IEEE CVPR, 1991–1999 (2016)
42. Peng, X., Wang, L., Wang, X., Qiao, Y.: Bag of visual words and fusion methods for action recognition: comprehensive study and good practice. Comput. Vis. Image Underst. 150, 109–125 (2016)
43. Wang, L., Qiao, Y., Tang, X.: MoFAP: a multi-level representation for action recognition. IJCV 119(3), 254–271 (2016)
44. Wang, L., Qiao, Y., Tang, X.: Action recognition with trajectory-pooled deep-convolutional descriptors. In: IEEE CVPR, pp. 4305–4314 (2015)
45. Sun, L., Jia, K., Chan, T.H., Fang, Y., Wang, G., Yan, S.: DL-SFA: deeply-learned slow feature analysis for action recognition. In: IEEE CVPR, pp. 2625–2632 (2014)
46. Wang, H., Schmid, C.: Action recognition with improved trajectories. In: IEEE ICCV, pp. 3551–3558 (2013)
47. Zhu, J., Wang, B., Yang, X., Zhang, W., Tu, Z.: Action recognition with actons. In: IEEE ICCV, pp. 3559–3566 (2013)
48. Zhenzhong, L., Ming, L., Xuanchong, L., Hauptmann, A.G., Raj, B.: Beyond Gaussian pyramid: multi-skip feature stacking for action recognition. In: IEEE CVPR, pp. 204–212 (2015)
49. Fernando, B., Gavves, E., Oramas, J., Ghodrati, A., Tuytelaars, T.: Rank pooling for action recognition. IEEE Trans. PAMI 39(4), 773–787 (2017)
50. Yong, X., Yuhui, Q., Haibin, L., Hui, J.: Dynamic texture classification using dynamic fractal analysis. In: IEEE ICCV, pp. 1219–1226 (2011)
51. Coviello, E., Mumtaz, A., Chan, A.B., Lanckriet, G.R.G.: Growing a bag of systems tree for fast and accurate classification. In: IEEE CVPR, pp. 1979–1986 (2012)
52. Arashloo, S.R., Kittler, J.: Dynamic texture recognition using multiscale binarized statistical image features. IEEE Trans. Multimedia 16(8), 2099–2109 (2014)
53. Feichtenhofer, C., Pinz, A., Wildes, R.P.: Spacetime forests with complementary features for dynamic scene recognition. In: BMVC, pp. 1–12 (2013)
54. Thériault, C., Thome, N., Cord, M.: Dynamic scene classification: learning motion descriptors with slow features analysis. In: IEEE CVPR, pp. 603–2610 (2013)

Task-Aware Image Downscaling

Heewon Kim, Myungsub Choi, Bee Lim, and Kyoung Mu Lee[✉]

Department of ECE, ASRI, Seoul National University, Seoul, Korea
{ghimhw,cms6539,biya999,kyoungmu}@snu.ac.kr
https://cv.snu.ac.kr

Abstract. Image downscaling is one of the most classical problems in computer vision that aims to preserve the visual appearance of the original image when it is resized to a smaller scale. Upscaling a small image back to its original size is a difficult and ill-posed problem due to information loss that arises in the downscaling process. In this paper, we present a novel technique called *task-aware image downscaling* to support an upscaling task. We propose an auto-encoder-based framework that enables joint learning of the downscaling network and the upscaling network to maximize the restoration performance. Our framework is efficient, and it can be generalized to handle an arbitrary image resizing operation. Experimental results show that our task-aware downscaled images greatly improve the performance of the existing state-of-the-art super-resolution methods. In addition, realistic images can be recovered by recursively applying our scaling model up to an extreme scaling factor of x128. We also validate our model's generalization capability by applying it to the task of image colorization.

Keywords: Image downscaling · Image super-resolution
Deep learning

1 Introduction

Scaling or resizing is one of the most frequently used operations when handling digital images. When sharing images via the Internet, we rarely use the original high-resolution (HR) images because of the low resolution of display screens; most images are downscaled to save the data transfer cost while maintaining adequate image qualities. However, the loss of information from the downscaling process makes the inverse problem of super-resolution (SR) highly ill-posed, and zooming in to a part of the downscaled image usually shows a blurry restoration.

Previous works normally consider downscaling and super-resolution (upscaling) as separate problems. Studies on image downscaling [16, 23, 24, 34] only focus on obtaining visually pleasing low-resolution (LR) images. Likewise, recent studies on SR [5, 7, 13, 18, 20, 22, 31, 36, 37] tend to fix the downscaling kernel

Electronic supplementary material The online version of this chapter (https://doi.org/10.1007/978-3-030-01225-0_25) contains supplementary material, which is available to authorized users.

V. Ferrari et al. (Eds.): ECCV 2018, LNCS 11208, pp. 419–434, 2018.
https://doi.org/10.1007/978-3-030-01225-0_25

SRGAN [8]	EDSR+ [9]	TAU(Ours)	GT

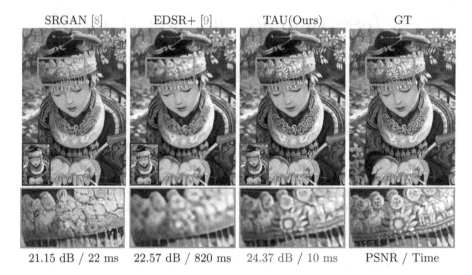

21.15 dB / 22 ms	22.57 dB / 820 ms	24.37 dB / 10 ms	PSNR / Time

Fig. 1. Our task-aware downscaled (TAD) image (red box) generates more realistic and accurate HR image compared with the state-of-the-art methods that use bicubic-downscaled LR images (blue box). TAD image shows good LR image quality and, when upscaled with our jointly trained upscaling method TAU, outperforms EDSR+ by a large margin with considerably faster runtime. The scaling factor (We use the term *scaling factor* (denoted as *sc*) as "upscaling" factor unless otherwise mentioned. Then, downscaling an image from $H \times W$ to $\frac{H}{2} \times \frac{W}{2}$ is noted to have a scaling factor of $sc = \frac{1}{2}$. When indicated in a joint model, the images are downscaled to $\frac{1}{sc}$ and upscaled again to $\frac{sc}{sc} = 1$.) is ×4. (Color figure online)

(to *e.g.* bicubic downscaling) and optimize the restoration performance of the HR images with the given training LR-HR image pairs. However, the predetermined downscaling kernel may not be optimal for the SR task. Figure 1 shows an example of the importance of choosing an appropriate downscaling method, where the downscaled LR images in blue and red look similar, but the restored HR image from the red LR image shows much more accurate result where the shapes and details are consistent with the original ground truth image.

In this paper, we address the problem of task-aware image downscaling and show the importance of learning the optimal image downscaling method for the target tasks. For the SR task, the goal is to find the optimal LR image that maximizes the restoration performance of the HR image. To achieve this goal, we use a deep convolutional auto-encoder model where the encoder is the downscaling network and the decoder is the upscaling network. The auto-encoder is trained end-to-end, and the output of the encoder (output of the downscaling network) will be our final task-aware downscaled (TAD) image. We also guarantee that the latent representation of the auto-encoder resembles the downscaled version of its original input image by introducing the *guidance image*.

In SR, the guidance image is an LR image made by a predefined downscaling algorithm (*e.g.* bicubic, Lanczos), and it can be used to control the trade-off between HR image reconstruction performance and LR image quality. Our whole framework has only 20 convolution layers and can be run in real-time.

Our framework can also be generalized to other resizing tasks aside from SR. Note that the rescaling can be done not only in the spatial dimension but also in the channel dimension of an image. So we can apply our proposed framework to the grayscale-color conversion problem. In this setting, the downscaling task becomes RGB to grayscale conversion, and the upscaling task becomes image colorization. Our final grayscale image achieves visually much more pleasing results when re-colorized.

Overall, our contributions are as follows:

- To the best of our knowledge, our proposed method is the first deep learning-based image downscaling method that is jointly learned to boost the accuracy of an upscaling task. Applying our TAD images to train an SR model improves the reconstruction performance of the previous state-of-the-art (SotA) by a large margin.
- Our downscaling and upscaling networks operate efficiently and cover multiple scaling factors. In particular, our method achieves the best SR performance in extreme scaling factors up to ×128.
- Our framework can be generalized to various computer vision tasks with scale changes in any dimension.

2 Related Work

In this section, we review studies on super-resolution and image downscaling.

2.1 Image Super-Resolution (SR)

Single image super-resolution (SR) is a standard inverse problem in computer vision with a long history. Most previous works discuss which methodology is used to obtain HR images from LR images, but we categorize SR methods according to the inherent assumptions they used with regard to the process of acquiring LR images in the first place. First, approaches without any such assumptions at all exist. These approaches include early methods that use interpolation [2,12,19,38], which estimates filter kernels from local pixels/patch to the HR image pixel values with respect to the scaling factor. Interpolation-based methods are typically fast but yield blurry results. Many methods used priors from natural image statistics for more realistic textures [14,28,29]. One exceptional case of Ulyanov *et al.* [32] showed that a different structural image prior is inherent in deep CNN architecture.

Second, a line of work attempts to estimate the LR image acquisition process via self-similarities. These studies assume the fractal structures inherent in images, which means that considerable internal path redundancies exist within a single image. Glasner *et al.* [7] proposed a novel SR framework that exploits recurrent patches within and across image scales. Michaeli and Irani [22] improved this approach by jointly estimating the unknown downscaling blur kernel with the HR image, and Huang *et al.* [10] extended this approach to incorporate transformed self-exemplars for added expressive power. Shocher *et al.* [27] recently proposed a "zero-shot" SR (ZSSR) using deep learning, which trains an image-specific CNN with HR-LR pairs of patches extracted from the test image itself. ZSSR shares our motivation of handling the problem of fixed downscaling process in generating HR-LR pairs when training deep models. However, the main objective is different in that our model focuses on restoring HR images *from previously downscaled images*.

The third and last category includes the majority of SR methods, wherein the process of obtaining LR images is predetermined (in most cases, MATLAB bicubic). Fixing the downscaling method is inevitable when creating a large HR-LR paired image dataset, especially when training a model needs a vast amount of data. Many advanced works that use neighbor embedding [3,4,6, 25,31,37], sparse coding [31,35–37], and deep learning [5,13,17,18,20,30] fall into this category, where many HR-LR paired patches are needed to learn the mapping function between them. With regard to more recent deep learning based methods, Dong *et al.* [5] proposed SRCNN as the first attempt to solve the SR problem with CNN. Accordingly, CNN-based SR architectures expanded, and they have greatly boosted the performance. Kim *et al.* (VDSR) [13] suggested the concept of residual learning to ease the difficulty in optimization, which was later improved by Ledig *et al.* (SRResNet) [18] with intermediate residual connections [8]. Following this line of work, Lim *et al.* [20] proposed an enhanced model called EDSR, which achieved SotA performance in the recent NTIRE challenge [30]. Ledig *et al.* proposed another distinctive method called SRGAN, which introduces adversarial loss with perceptual loss [11] and raised the problem of the current metric that we use for evaluating SR methods: peak signal-to-noise ratio (PSNR). Although these methods generate visually more realistic images than previous works regardless of their PSNR value, the generated textures can differ considerably from the original HR image (as shown in Fig. 1).

2.2   Image Downscaling

Image downscaling aims to preserve the appearance of HR images in LR images. Conventional methods use smoothing filters and resampling for anti-aliasing [23]. Although these classical methods are still dominant in practical usage, more recent approaches have also attempted to improve the sharpness of LR images. Kopf *et al.* [16] proposed a content-adaptive method, wherein filter kernel coefficients are adapted with respect to image content. Öztireli and Gross [24] proposed an optimization framework to minimize SSIM [33] between the nearest-neighbor upsampled LR image and the HR image. Weber *et al.* [34] uses convolutional filters to preserve important visual details, and Hou *et al.* [9] recently proposed perceptual loss based method using deep learning.

However, a high similarity value does not imply good results when an image is restored to high resolution. Zhang *et al.* [39] proposed interpolation-dependent image downsampling (IDID) where given an interpolation method, the downsampled image that minimizes the sum of squared errors between the original input HR image and the obtained LR image interpolated to the input scale is obtained. Our method is most similar to IDID, but we mitigate its limitations in that the upscaling process considers only simple interpolation methods and take full advantage of the recent advancements in deep learning-based SR.

3   Task-Aware Downscaling (TAD)

3.1   Formulation

We aim to study a *task-aware downscaled* (TAD) image that can be efficiently reconstructed to its original HR input. Let I^{TAD} denote our TAD image and I^{HR} as the original HR image. Our ultimate goal is to study the optimal downscaling function $g : I^{HR} \mapsto I^{TAD}$ with respect to the upscaling function f, which denotes our task of interest. The process of obtaining input I^{HR} is shown in the following equation:

$$I^{HR} = f(I^{TAD}) = f(g(I^{HR})).$$

The downscaling and upscaling functions g and f are both image-to-image mappings, and the input to g and the output of f are the same HR image I^{HR}. Thus, f and g are naturally modeled with a deep convolutional auto-encoder, each becoming the decoder and encoder part of the network.

Let θ_f and θ_g be the parameters of the convolutional decoder and encoder f and g, respectively. With the training dataset of N images $I_n^{HR}, n = 1, ..., N$ and L^{task} as the loss function that can differ task by task, our learning objective becomes:

$$\theta_f^*, \theta_g^* = \operatorname*{argmin}_{\theta_f, \theta_g} \frac{1}{N} \sum_{n=1}^{N} L^{task}\left(f_{\theta_f}\left(g_{\theta_g}\left(I_n^{HR}\right)\right), I_n^{HR}\right). \tag{1}$$

The desired I^{TAD} for downscaling and the reconstructed image I^{TAU} (taskaware upscaled image) can be calculated accordingly:

$$I^{TAD} = g_{\theta_g^*}\left(I^{HR}\right), \tag{2}$$

$$I^{TAU} = f_{\theta_f^*}\left(I^{TAD}\right). \tag{3}$$

3.2   Network Architecture and Training

In this section, we describe the network architecture and the training details. In this work, we mainly focus on the SR task and present SR-specific operations and configurations. The overall architecture is outlined in Fig. 2.

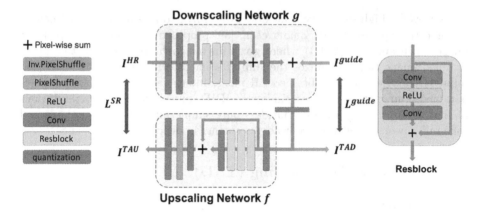

Fig. 2. Our convolutional auto-encoder architecture with three parts: downscaling network (g_{θ_g}, encoder), compression module, and upscaling network (f_{θ_f}, decoder). *Two* outputs, I^{TAD} and I^{TAU}, are obtained from Eqs. 2 and 3, and used to calculate the two loss terms in Eq. 4.

Guidance Image for Better Downscaling. In our framework, TAD images are obtained as the latent representation of the deep convolutional auto-encoder. However, without proper constraints, the latent representation may be arbitrary and does not look like the original HR image. Therefore, we propose a *guidance* image I^{guide}, which is basically a bicubic-downsampled LR image obtained from I^{HR}, to ensure visual similarity of our learned TAD image I^{TAD} with I^{HR}. The guidance image is used as a ground truth image to calculate the L1 loss with the predicted I^{TAD}. Incorporating I^{guide} and the new loss term, L^{guide}, changes the loss function in the original objective of Eq. 1 to:

$$L^{task}\left(f(g(I_n^{HR})), I_n^{guide}, I_n^{HR}\right) = L^{SR}\left(f(I_n^{TAD}), I_n^{HR}\right) + \lambda L^{guide}\left(I_n^{TAD}, I_n^{guide}\right),$$
(4)

where L^{SR} is the standard L1 loss function for the SR task. θ_f and θ_g are omitted for the simplicity of notation. The hyperparameter λ is introduced to control the weights for the loss imposed by the guidance image w.r.t. the original SR loss. We can set the amount of trade-off between the reconstructed HR image quality and the LR TAD image quality by changing the value of λ. The effect of λ can be seen in Fig. 4, and this will be analyzed more extensively in the experiment section.

Simple Residual Blocks as Base Networks. Our final deep convolutional auto-encoder model is composed of three parts: a downscaling network (encoder), a compression module, and an upscaling network (decoder). We jointly optimize all parts in an end-to-end manner, for the scaling factor of ×2.

The encoder (g_{θ_g}) consists of a downscaling layer, three residual blocks, and a residual connection. The downscaling layer is a reverse version of sub-pixel convolution (also called pixel shuffle layer) [26], so that the feature channels are properly aligned and the number of channels is reduced by a factor of ×4.

We used two convolution layers with one ReLU activation for each residual block without batch normalization and bottleneck, which is the same as that used in EDSR [20]. Note that in our downscaling network g, the final output I^{TAD} is obtained by the addition of the output of the last conv. layer and the I^{guide} in a pixel-wise manner.

The decoder has almost the same simple architecture as the encoder, except the downscaling layer changes to the upscaling layer. The sub-pixel convolution layer [26] is used to upscale the output feature map by a factor of ×2. Note that each scaling layer is located at the beginning (downscaling layer) and the end (upscaling layer) of the network to reduce the overall computational complexity of our model.

All our networks' convolution layers have a fixed channel size of 64, except for upscaling/downscaling layers, where we set the output activation map to have 64 channels. That is, for sub-pixel convolution with a scaling factor of ×2, we first apply a 3 × 3 convolution layer to increase the number of channels to 256, and then align the pixels to reduce it again to 64.

Compression Module. Most deep networks have floating-point values for both feature activations and weights. Our TAD image output from the downscaling network is also represented with the default floating-point values. However, when displayed on a screen, most of the images are represented in true color (8 bits for each R, G, and B color channels). Considering that the objective of this work is to save a TAD image that is suitable for future application to SR, saving the obtained TAD image in RGB format is helpful for wider usage. We propose a compression module to achieve this goal.

A compression module is a structure for converting an image into a bitstream and storing it. We use a simple differentiable quantization layer that converts the floating-point values into 8-bit unsigned int (uint8) for this module. However, in the early iterations when the training is unstable, adding a quantization layer can result in training failure. Therefore, we omit it the layer until almost at the end of the training stage and insert our compression module again to fine-tune the network for a few hundred more iterations. The fine-tuned output TAD image then becomes a true-color RGB image that can be stored by lossless image compression methods, such as PNG. Although we used a single quantization layer for the compression module and saved the images in PNG format, this process can be generalized to the use of more complex image compression models as long as it is differentiable; thus, we call this part the *compression* module.

Multi-scale SR with Extreme Scaling Factors. To deal with multiple scaling factors, we simply placed the original HR image in our downscaling model recursively, with minor changes in our architecture. Therefore, our model can (down)scale the HR image to the scaling factors of negative powers of 2. We even test our model with an extreme scaling factor of $\frac{1}{128}$ and show that our method can recover a reasonable ×128 HR image from a tiny LR image. To the best of our knowledge, this work is the first to present the SR results for scaling factors of such an extreme level (over 16). Qualitative result and discussion can be seen in Fig. 5.

Our architectural changes for multi-scale SR are as follows:

1. We omit the compression module during the recursive execution of the down-scaling network, and replace the compression module of the final downscaling network to a simple rounding operation because a more beneficial alternative is to preserve the full information in floating-point values until the end where the final TAD image has to be saved.
2. The output of the downscaling network is modified to predict the guidance image itself directly by removing the pixelwise addition of the guidance image.
3. During the recursive process, the network is fine-tuned for a few hundred iterations once every scaling factor of ×4.

Upscaling the TAD image again requires the same recursive process, this time with the upscaling network. Although the exact downscaling and upscaling for our model, including recursive executions, are only for the scaling factors of powers of 2, combining our model with small-scale changes handled by a simple bicubic interpolation can still work. As shown in the experiments, this problem can be solved by applying a scale-invariant model, such as VDSR [13], to the obtained TAD image.

3.3   Extending to General Tensor Resizing Operations

Note that the goal of the SR task is to reconstruct the HR image I^{HR} from the corresponding LR image I^{LR}. Assuming I^{LR} (input low resolution image) with spatial size $H \times W$ and channels C, the upscaling function becomes $f : \mathbb{R}^{H \times W \times C} \mapsto \mathbb{R}^{sH \times sW \times C}$ where s denotes the scaling factor.

In this section, we formulate a generalized resizing operation, so that the proposed model can handle arbitrary resizing of an image tensor. Specifically, we consider the general *upscaling* task of $f : \mathbb{R}^{H \times W \times C} \mapsto \mathbb{R}^{sH \times rW \times tC}$, where s, r, and t are the scaling factors for the image height, width, and channels, respectively. $I^{HR} \in \mathbb{R}^{sH \times rW \times tC}$ is denoted again as a *high-resolution*[1]image tensor, and θ_f and θ_g are denoted as the parameters of our *new* models f_{θ_f} and g_{θ_g}, respectively. Training these models jointly with the same objective function of Eq. 1 completes our generalized formulation.

Note that if we constrain the scaling factor to $s = t = 1$, then the task becomes the image color space conversion. For example, if we consider the colorization task, the *downscaling* network g_{θ_g} performs a RGB to grayscale conversion where the spatial resolution is fixed and only the feature channel dimension is downsized. The *upscaling* network, f_{θ_f}, performs a colorization task. We use the similar model of a deep convolutional auto-encoder to obtain the TAD image I^{TAD}, which becomes a grayscale image that is optimal for the reconstruction of original RGB color image. For the colorization task, one major change in the

---

[1]   We keep using the term *high-resolution* for the input tensor of its original scale, to have a consistent notation with the formulation in Sect. 3.1, although tensors in general don't use the word "resolution" to indicate its dimensions. Likewise, HR and LR image tensors represent the high-dimensional and the low-dimensional tensors.

network architecture is the removal of the downscaling layer in the encoder (g_{θ_g}) and the upscaling layer in the decoder (f_{θ_f}), because no spatial dimensionality change occurs in the color space conversions and the sub-convolution layers are not needed. Thus, the resulting network each has nine convolution layers. Other changes in the model configurations follow naturally: the guidance image I^{guide} becomes a grayscale image obtained using the conventional RGB to grayscale conversion method, and the task-aware *upscaled* image I^{TAU} becomes the colorized output image. For the compression module, a simple rounding scheme is used instead of a differentiable quantization layer.

4 Experiment

In this section, we report the results of our TAD model for SR (Sect. 4.1), analyze the results of our model thoroughly (Sect. 4.2), and apply our generalized model shown in Sect. 3.3 to the colorization task (Sect. 4.3).

4.1 TAD for Super-Resolution

Datasets and Evaluation Metrics. We evaluate the performance on five widely used benchmark datasets: Set5 [3], Set14 [37], B100 [21], Urban100 [10], and the validation set of DIV2K [1]. All benchmark datasets are evaluated with scaling factors of ×2 and ×4 between LR and HR images. For the validation set of DIV2K that consists of 2 K resolution images, we also perform experiments with extreme scaling factors of ×8-×128. All the models we present in this section are trained on the 800 images from DIV2K training set [1]. No image overlap exists between our training set of images and the data we use for evaluation.

For the evaluation metric, we use PSNR to compare similarities between (1) the bicubic downscaled LR image and our predicted I^{TAD} (Eq. 2); and (2) the ground truth HR image and our predicted I^{TAU} (Eq. 3). To ensure a fair comparison with previous works, the input LR images of the reproduced SotA networks [13,20] are downscaled by MATLAB's default `imresize` operation, which is implemented to perform bicubic downsampling with antialiasing. We apply the networks for both single channel (Y from YCbCr) and RGB color channel images. To obtain a single-channel image, an RGB color image is first converted to YCbCr color space, and the chroma channels (Cb, Cr) are discarded.

Comparison With the SotA. We compare our downscaling method **TAD** and upscaling method (**TAU**) with recent SotA models for single (VDSR [13]) and color (EDSR [20]) channel images. Since the single channel performance of EDSR+ and the color channel performance of VDSR are not provided in the reference papers, we reproduced them for the comparison. For *VDSR and *EDSR+ under TAD as the downscaling method, we re-train the reproduced networks using TAD-HR image pairs, instead of conventional LR-HR pairs for bicubic-downsampled LR images. Quantitative evaluations are summarized in Table 1.

Table 1. Quantitative PSNR (dB) results on benchmark datasets: Set5, Set14, B100, Urban100, and DIV2K. The red color indicates the best performance, and the blue color indicates the second best.   (*: reproduced performance)

Downscaling		Single Channel Results / Color Channel Results					
		Bicubic			TAD(Ours)		
Upscaling		TAU(baseline)	VDSR [13]	EDSR+ [20]	TAU	*VDSR	*EDSR+
Set5	×2	35.84/36.04	37.53/35.08	37.95/36.09	37.69/38.46	37.68/38.76	37.98/39.44
	×4	31.20/29.52	31.35/29.39	32.17/30.71	31.59/31.81	31.60/31.96	32.36/32.49
Set14	×2	32.89/30.99	33.03/30.93	33.65/31.97	33.90/35.52	33.88/35.92	34.07/36.58
	×4	27.92/26.28	28.01/26.26	28.50/27.14	28.36/28.63	28.38/28.76	28.82/29.24
B100	×2	31.74/30.40	31.90/30.42	32.22/31.40	32.62/36.68	32.65/36.87	32.83/37.59
	×4	27.20/25.88	27.29/25.87	27.54/26.45	27.57/28.51	27.57/28.53	27.86/28.97
Urban100	×2	30.64/29.13	30.76/29.19	32.51/31.47	31.96/35.03	32.16/35.50	32.86/35.55
	×4	25.08/23.66	25.18/23.68	26.25/25.34	25.56/26.63	25.66/26.98	26.50/27.76
DIV2K	×2	35.17/33.91	35.29/33.79	35.91/35.12	36.13/39.01	36.18/39.42	36.52/40.21
	×4	29.73/28.40	29.63/28.31	30.29/29.38	30.25/31.16	30.25/31.34	30.73/31.88

The results show that our jointly trained TAD-TAU for the color image SR outperforms all previous methods in all datasets. Moreover, EDSR+ trained with TAD-HR images (*down- and up-scaling* **not** *jointly trained as an auto-encoder*) boosts reconstruction performance considerably, gaining over 5 dB additional PSNR in some benchmarks. The same situation holds for the single channel settings. The TAU network architecture is much more efficient (comprising 10 convolution layers) than the compared networks, VDSR (20 convolution layers) and EDSR+ (68 convolution layers).

The qualitative results in Fig. 3 show that only TAU for the color image perfectly reconstructs the word, "presentations". TAU for the single-channel image also provides clearer characters than the previous SotA methods.

Training Details. We trained all models with a GeForce GTX 1080 Ti GPU using 800 images from the DIV2K training data [1]. For both training and testing, we first crop the input HR images from the upper and left sides so that the height and width of the image are divisible by the scaling factors. Then, we obtain the guidance images (single channel or color channel LR images with regard to the experiment setting) by using MATLAB `imresize` command. We randomly crop 16 patches of 96 × 96 HR sub images, with each patch coming from a different HR image, to construct the training mini-batch. Our downscaling and upscaling networks are fully convolutional and can handle images of arbitrary size. We normalized the range of the input pixel values to [−0.5, 0.5] and output pixel values to [0,1], and the L1 loss is calculated to be in the range of [0, 1]. To optimize our network, we use the ADAM [15] optimizer with $\beta_1 = 0.9$. The network parameters are updated with a learning rate of 10^{-4} for 3×10^5 iterations.

Fig. 3. Qualitative SR results of "ppt3"(Set14). The top and bottom rows show the results for single (Y) and color (RGB) channel images, respectively. In both gray and color images, TAD produces more decent LR images compared with Bicubic and guarantees much better HR reconstructions when upscaled with TAU. This figure is best viewed in color, and by zooming into the electronic copy. The scaling factor is ×2.

4.2   Analysis

In this section, we perform two experiments to improve understanding of our TAD model and discuss the results.

Investigating LR-HR Image Quality Trade-off. The objective for training our model is given in Sect. 3.1, Eq. 4. The hyperparameter λ controls the weight between two loss terms: L^{SR} for HR image reconstruction and L^{guide} for LR image guidance. If $\lambda = 0$, then our framework becomes a simple deep convolutional auto-encoder model for the task of SR, without any constraint in producing a high quality downscaled image. Conversely, if $\lambda = \infty$, L^{SR} is ignored, then and our framework becomes a downscaling CNN with ground truth downscaling method as bicubic downsampling. In this study, we explore the effect of the influence of guidance image I^{guide}, and find that changing the weight λ allows us to control the quality of generated HR (I^{TAU}) and LR (I^{TAD}) images. This effect is visualized in Fig. 4.

We train our TAD model for the scaling factor of ×2, first with $\lambda = 0$ and gradually increase its value up to 10^2. For each λ, we measure the average PSNR for 10 validation images of DIV2K [1] and plot the values, as shown in the top-left corner of Fig. 4. We chose $\lambda = 10^{-1}$ where the PSNR for HR images (39.81 dB) and LR images (40.69 dB) are similar, as the default value for our model and use it throughout all the SR experiments. The compression module is not used for this experiment. The exact PSNR accuracy for different values of λ will be reported in the supplementary materials due to the space limit.

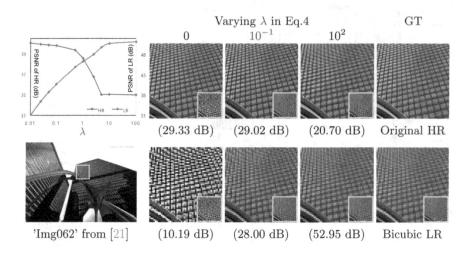

Fig. 4. TAD-TAU reconstruction performance trade-off. Smaller values of λ give a high upscaling performance with noisy TAD image. We choose λ from the intersection of the curves, where both TAD/TAU images give satisfactory results. PSNR for LR image is measured with bicubic-downsampled image, and for HR images with the original GT.

Multi-scale Extreme SR. The results of recursive multi-scale SR operation with extreme scaling factors described in Sect. 3.2 are shown in Fig. 5. In this experiment, the last conv. of our downscaling network predicts TAD images directly. As the guidance image for each scaling factors is not needed to produce TAD/TAU images, it improves practical applicability of our model. Quantitative analysis and more of qualitative results will be provided in the supplementary materials due to the page limit.

Runtime Analysis. Our model efficiently achieves near real-time performance while still maintaining SotA SR accuracy. Each of our scaling networks consists of 10 convolution layers and one sub-convolution (pixel shuffle) layer, and a full HD image (1920×1080) can be upscaled in 0.14 s with a single GeForce GTX 1080 GPU Ti. Our model clearly has a major advantage over the recent EDSR+ (70.88 s), which is a heavy model with 68 convolution layers.

4.3 Extension: TAD for Colorization

We follow the exact formulation described in Sect. 3.3 and perform the color space conversion experiments accordingly. All experiments use the DIV2K training image dataset [1] for training, and B100 and Urban100 datasets for evaluation. We use a single Y channel image from YCbCr color space as I^{guide}, and we choose our hyper-parameter $\lambda = 5$ to place a strong constraint on our TAD image.

Bicubic ↓	Bicubic ↑	TAU ↑	TAD ↓

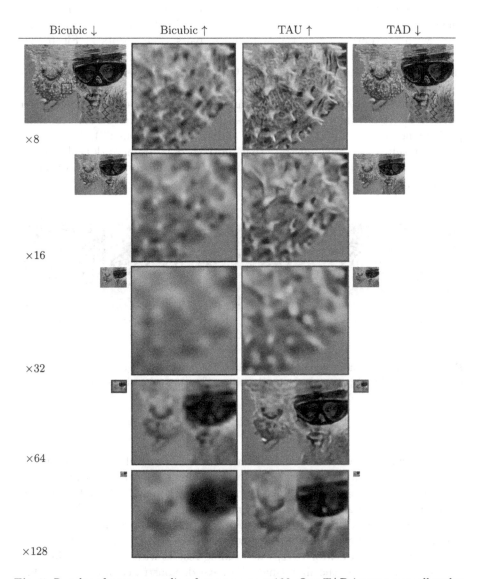

Fig. 5. Results of extreme scaling factors up to ×128. Our TAD images over all scales have decent visual quality with respect to Bicubic↓, and our TAU images are much cleaner and sharper than those of Bicubic ↑. All resized results are produced by **a single joint network of TAU and TAD** (Fig. 2), with a scaling factor of ×2. Considering that the ×64 and ×128 downscaled images have only 31×24 and 15×12 pixels respectively, we visualize the full image for these extreme scaling factors. The generated I^{TAU} is downscaled again - with Bicubic↓ - for visualization. Note the detailed recovery of the spines of the pufferfish in ×8 and surprisingly realistic global structures reconstructed in ×64.

To demonstrate the effectiveness of our proposed framework, we train another image colorization network that has the same architecture as our upscaling network with conventional grayscale-HR image pairs. The results in Fig. 6 show that the colorization network trained in a standard way clearly cannot resolve the color ambiguities, whereas our TAD Gray image contains the necessary information for restoring original pleasing colors as demonstrated in the reconstructed TAD color. Quantitatively, while the baseline model achieves an average PSNR of 24.21 dB (B100) and 23.29 dB (Urban100), our model outputs much higher performance values of 36.14 dB (B100) and 33.68 dB (Urban100).

The results clearly demonstrate that the TAD-TAU framework is also practically very useful for both the color to gray conversion and gray to color conversion (colorization) tasks.

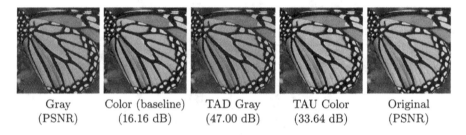

| Gray | Color (baseline) | TAD Gray | TAU Color | Original |
| (PSNR) | (16.16 dB) | (47.00 dB) | (33.64 dB) | (PSNR) |

Fig. 6. Qualitative image colorization results. The leftmost image is used as I^{guide} for our model and input grayscale for the baseline. The channel scale factor ×3.

5   Conclusion

In this work, we present a novel *task-aware* image downscaling method using a deep convolutional auto-encoder. By jointly training the downscaling and upscaling processes, our task-aware downscaling framework greatly alleviates the difficulties in solving highly ill-posed resizing problems such as image SR. We have shown that our upscaling method outperforms previous works in SR by a large margin, and our downscaled image also aids the existing methods to achieve much higher accuracy. Moreover, valid scaling results with extreme scaling factors are provided for the first time. We have demonstrated how our method can be generalized and verified our framework's capability in image color space conversion. Apart from the tasks examined in this study, we believe that our approach provides a useful framework for handling images of various sizes. Promising future work may include deep learning based image compression.

Acknowledgment. This work was partly supported by the National Research Foundation of Korea (NRF) grant funded by the Korea Government(MSIT) (No. NRF-2017R1A2B2011862)

References

1. Agustsson, E., Timofte, R.: Ntire 2017 challenge on single image super-resolution: dataset and study. In: CVPRW (2017)
2. Allebach, J., Wong, P.W.: Edge-directed interpolation. In: ICIP (1996)
3. Bevilacqua, M., Roumy, A., Guillemot, C., Alberi-Morel, M.L.: Low-complexity single-image super-resolution based on nonnegative neighbor embedding. In: BMVC (2012)
4. Chang, H., Yeung, D.Y., Xiong, Y.: Super-resolution through neighbor embedding. In: CVPR (2004)
5. Dong, C., Loy, C.C., He, K., Tang, X.: Learning a deep convolutional network for image super-resolution. In: Fleet, D., Pajdla, T., Schiele, B., Tuytelaars, T. (eds.) ECCV 2014. LNCS, vol. 8692, pp. 184–199. Springer, Cham (2014). https://doi.org/10.1007/978-3-319-10593-2_13
6. Gao, X., Zhang, K., Tao, D., Li, X.: Image super-resolution with sparse neighbor embedding. IEEE Trans. Image Process. **21**(7), 3194–3205 (2012)
7. Glasner, D., Bagon, S., Irani, M.: Super-resolution from a single image. In: ICCV (2009)
8. He, K., Zhang, X., Ren, S., Sun, J.: Deep residual learning for image recognition. In: CVPR (2016)
9. Hou, X., Duan, J., Qiu, G.: Deep feature consistent deep image transformations: Downscaling, decolorization and HDR tone mapping. arXiv:1707.09482 (2017)
10. Huang, J., Singh, A., Ahuja, N.: Single image super-resolution from transformed self-exemplars. In: CVPR (2015)
11. Johnson, J., Alahi, A., Fei-Fei, L.: Perceptual losses for real-time style transfer and super-resolution. In: ECCV (2016)
12. Keys, R.G.: Cubic convolution interpolation for digital image processing. In: IEEE Transactions on Acoustics, Speech, and Signal Processing, pp. 1153–1160 (1981)
13. Kim, J., Lee, J., Lee, K.M.: Accurate image super-resolution using very deep convolutional networks. In: CVPR (2016)
14. Kim, K.I., Kwon, Y.: Single-image super-resolution using sparse regression and natural image prior. TPAMI **32**(6), 1127–1133 (2010)
15. Kingma, D.P., Ba, J.: Adam: a method for stochastic optimization. In: ICLR (2015)
16. Kopf, J., Shamir, A., Peers, P.: Content-adaptive image downscaling. ACM Trans. Graph. **32**(6), 173 (2013)
17. Lai, W.S., Huang, J.B., Ahuja, N., Yang, M.H.: Deep laplacian pyramid networks for fast and accurate super-resolution. In: CVPR (2017)
18. Ledig, C., et al.: Photo-realistic single image super-resolution using a generative adversarial network. In: CVPR (2017)
19. Li, X., Orchard, M.T.: New edge-directed interpolation. IEEE Trans. Image Process. **10**(10), 1521–1527 (2001)
20. Lim, B., Son, S., Kim, H., Nah, S., Lee, K.M.: Enhanced deep residual networks for single image super-resolution. In: CVPRW (2017)
21. Martin, D.R., Fowlkes, C.C., Tal, D., Malik, J.: A database of human segmented natural images and its application to evaluating segmentation algorithms and measuring ecological statistics. In: ICCV (2001)
22. Michaeli, T., Irani, M.: Nonparametric blind super-resolution. In: ICCV (2013)
23. Mitchell, D.P., Netravali, A.N.: Reconstruction filters in computer-graphics. In: SIGGRAPH, pp. 221–228 (1988)

24. Öztireli, A.C., Gross, M.: Perceptually based downscaling of images. ACM Trans. Graph. **34**(4), 77:1–77:10 (2015)
25. Roweis, S.T., Saul, L.K.: Nonlinear dimensionality reduction by locally linear embedding. Science **290**(5500), 2323–2326 (2000)
26. Shi, W., et al.: Real-time single image and video super-resolution using an efficient sub-pixel convolutional neural network. In: CVPR (2016)
27. Shocher, A., Cohen, N., Irani, M.: "Zero-Shot" super-resolution using deep internal learning. In: CVPR (2018)
28. Sun, J., Xu, Z., Shum, H.Y.: Image super-resolution using gradient profile prior. In: CVPR (2008)
29. Tai, Y.W., Liu, S., Brown, M.S., Lin, S.: Super resolution using edge prior and single image detail synthesis. In: CVPR (2010)
30. Timofte, R., et al.: Ntire 2017 challenge on single image super-resolution: methods and results. In: CVPRW (2017)
31. Timofte, R., Smet, V.D., Gool, L.J.V.: A+: adjusted anchored neighborhood regression for fast super-resolution. In: ACCV (2014)
32. Ulyanov, D., Vedaldi, A., Lempitsky, V.: Deep image prior. In: CVPR (2018)
33. Wang, Z., Bovik, A.C., Sheikh, H.R., Simoncelli, E.P.: Image quality assessment: from error measurement to structural similarity. IEEE Trans. Image Process. **13**, 600–612 (2004)
34. Weber, N., Waechter, M., Amend, S.C., Guthe, S., Goesele, M.: Rapid, detail-preserving image downscaling. ACM Trans. Graph. **35**(6), 205:1–205:6 (2016)
35. Yang, J., Wang, Z., Lin, Z., Cohen, S., Huang, T.: Coupled dictionary training for image super-resolution. IEEE Trans. Image Process. **21**(8), 3467–3478 (2012)
36. Yang, J., Wright, J., Huang, T.S., Ma, Y.: Image super-resolution via sparse representation. IEEE Trans. Image Process. **19**(11), 2861–2873 (2010)
37. Zeyde, R., Elad, M., Protter, M.: On single image scale-up using sparse-representations. In: Proceedings of the International Conference on Curves and Surfaces (2010)
38. Zhang, L., Wu, X.: An edge-guided image interpolation algorithm via directional filtering and data fusion. IEEE Trans. Image Process. **15**(8), 2226–2238 (2006)
39. Zhang, Y., Zhao, D., Zhang, J., Xiong, R., Gao, W.: Interpolation-dependent image downsampling. IEEE Trans. Image Process. **20**(11), 3291–3296 (2011)

Self-calibration of Cameras with Euclidean Image Plane in Case of Two Views and Known Relative Rotation Angle

Evgeniy Martyushev[⊠] [ID]

South Ural State University, 454080 Chelyabinsk, Russia
mev@susu.ac.ru

Abstract. The internal calibration of a pinhole camera is given by five parameters that are combined into an upper-triangular 3×3 calibration matrix. If the skew parameter is zero and the aspect ratio is equal to one, then the camera is said to have Euclidean image plane. In this paper, we propose a non-iterative self-calibration algorithm for a camera with Euclidean image plane in case the remaining three internal parameters — the focal length and the principal point coordinates — are fixed but unknown. The algorithm requires a set of $N \geq 7$ point correspondences in two views and also the measured relative rotation angle between the views. We show that the problem generically has six solutions (including complex ones).

The algorithm has been implemented and tested both on synthetic data and on publicly available real dataset. The experiments demonstrate that the method is correct, numerically stable and robust.

Keywords: Multiview geometry · Self-calibration · Essential matrix
Euclidean image plane · Relative rotation angle · Gröbner basis

1 Introduction

The problem of camera calibration is an essential part of numerous computer vision applications including 3d reconstruction, visual odometry, medical imaging, etc. At present, a number of calibration algorithms and techniques have been developed. Some of them require to observe a planar pattern viewed at several different positions [5,9,25]. Other methods use 3d calibration objects consisting of two or three pairwise orthogonal planes, which geometry is known with good accuracy [24]. Also, there are calibration algorithms assuming that a scene involves the pairs of mutually orthogonal directions [3,14]. In contrast with the just mentioned methods, *self-calibration* does not require any special

The work was supported by Act 211 Government of the Russian Federation, contract No. 02.A03.21.0011.

calibration objects or scene restrictions [6,16,18,23], so only image feature correspondences in several uncalibrated views are required. This provides the self-calibration approach with a great flexibility and makes it indispensable in some real-time applications.

In two views, camera calibration is given by ten parameters — five internal and five external, whereas the fundamental matrix describing the epipolar geometry in two views has only seven degrees of freedom [6]. This means that self-calibration in two views is only possible under at least three further assumptions on the calibration parameters. For example, we can assume that the skew parameter is zero and so is the translation vector, i.e. the motion is a pure rotation. Then, the three orientation angles and the remaining four internals can be self-calibrated from at least seven point matches [7]. Another possibility is that all the internal parameters except common focal length are known. Then, there exist a minimal self-calibration solution operating with six matched points [2,11,13,20].

The five internal calibration parameters have different interpretation. The skew parameter and the aspect ratio describe the pixel's shape. In most situations, e.g. under zooming, these internals do not change. Moreover, for modern cameras the pixel's shape is very close to a square and hence the skew and aspect ratio can be assumed as given and equal to 0 and 1 respectively. Following [10], we say that a camera in this case has *Euclidean image plane*. On the other hand, the focal length and the principal point coordinates describe the relative placement of the camera center and the image plane. The focal length is the distance between the camera center and the image plane, whereas the principal point is an orthographic projection of the center onto the plane. All these internals should be considered as unknown, since even for modern cameras the principal point can be relatively far from the geometric image center. Besides, it is well known that the focal length and the principal point always vary together by zooming [22].

The aim of this paper is to propose an efficient solution to the self-calibration problem of a camera with Euclidean image plane. As it was mentioned above, in two views at most seven calibration parameters can be self-calibrated. Since a camera with Euclidean image plane has eight parameters, we conclude that one additional assumption should be made. In this paper we reduce the number of external parameters assuming that the *relative rotation angle* between the views is known. The problem thus becomes minimally constrained from seven point correspondences in two views. In practice, the relative rotation angle can be reliably found from e.g. the readings of an inertial measurement unit (IMU) sensor. The possibility of using such additional data in structure-from-motion has been demonstrated in [12].

In general, the joint usage of a camera and an IMU requires *external calibration* between the devices, i.e. we have to know the transformation matrix between their coordinate frames. However, if only relative rotation angle is used, then the external calibration is unnecessary, provided that both devices are fixed on some rigid platform. Thus, the rotation angle of the IMU can be directly used as the rotation angle of the camera [12]. This fact makes the presented self-calibration method more convenient and flexible for practical use.

To summarize, we propose a new non-iterative solution to the self-calibration problem in case of at least seven matched points in two views, provided the following assumptions:

- the camera intrinsic parameters are the same for both views;
- the camera has Euclidean image plane;
- the relative rotation angle between the views is known.

Our self-calibration method is based on the ten quartic equations. Nine of them are well-known and follow from the famous cubic constraint on the essential matrix. The novel last one (see Eq. (13)) arises from the condition that the relative angle is known.

Finally, throughout the paper it is assumed that the cameras and scene points are in *sufficiently general position*. There are critical camera motions for which self-calibration is impossible, unless some further assumptions on the internal parameters or the motion are made [21]. Also there exist degenerate configurations of scene points. However, in this paper we restrict ourselves to the generic case of camera motions and points configurations.

The rest of the paper is organized as follows. In Sect. 2, we recall some definitions and results from multiview geometry and deduce our self-calibration constraints. In Sect. 3, we describe in detail the algorithm. In Sects. 4 and 5, the algorithm is validated in a series of experiments on synthetic and real data. In Sect. 6, we discuss the results and make conclusions.

2 Preliminaries

2.1 Notation

We preferably use $\alpha, \beta, \ldots$ for scalars, $a, b, \ldots$ for column 3-vectors or polynomials, and $A, B, \ldots$ both for matrices and column 4-vectors. For a matrix A the entries are $(A)_{ij}$, the transpose is A^{T}, the determinant is $\det A$, and the trace is $\operatorname{tr} A$. For two 3-vectors a and b the cross product is $a \times b$. For a vector a the notation $[a]_\times$ stands for the skew-symmetric matrix such that $[a]_\times b = a \times b$ for any vector b. We use I for the identity matrix.

2.2 Fundamental and Essential Matrices

Let there be given two cameras $P = \begin{bmatrix} I & 0 \end{bmatrix}$ and $P' = \begin{bmatrix} A & a \end{bmatrix}$, where A is a 3×3 matrix and a is a 3-vector. Let Q be a 4-vector representing homogeneous coordinates of a point in 3-space, q and q' be its images, that is

$$q \sim PQ, \quad q' \sim P'Q, \tag{1}$$

where $\sim$ means an equality up to non-zero scale. The *coplanarity constraint* for a pair (q, q') says

$$q'^{\mathrm{T}} F q = 0, \tag{2}$$

where matrix $F = [a]_\times A$ is called the *fundamental matrix*.

It follows from the definition of matrix F that $\det F = 0$. This condition is also sufficient. Thus we have

Theorem 1 ([8]). *A non-zero 3×3 matrix F is a fundamental matrix if and only if*

$$\det F = 0. \tag{3}$$

The *essential matrix* E is the fundamental matrix for *calibrated cameras* $\hat{P} = [I\ 0]$ and $\hat{P}' = [R\ t]$, where $R \in SO(3)$ is called the *rotation matrix* and t is called the *translation vector*. Hence, $E = [t]_\times R$. Matrices F and E are related by

$$E \sim K'^{\mathrm{T}} F K, \tag{4}$$

where K and K' are the upper-triangular *calibration matrices* of the first and second camera respectively.

The fundamental matrix has seven degrees of freedom, whereas the essential matrix has only five degrees of freedom. It is translated into extra constraints on the essential matrix. The following theorem gives one possible form of such constraints.

Theorem 2 ([15]). *A 3×3 matrix E of rank two is an essential matrix if and only if*

$$\frac{1}{2}\operatorname{tr}(EE^{\mathrm{T}})E - EE^{\mathrm{T}}E = 0_{3\times3}. \tag{5}$$

2.3 Self-calibration Constraints

Let θ be the angle of rotation between two calibrated camera frames. In case θ is known, the trace of rotation matrix $\tau = 2\cos\theta + 1$ is known too. This leads to an additional quadratic constraint on the essential matrix.

Proposition 1. *Let $E = [t]_\times R$ be a real non-zero essential matrix and $\operatorname{tr} R = \tau$. Then E satisfies the equation*

$$\frac{1}{2}(\tau^2 - 1)\operatorname{tr}(EE^{\mathrm{T}}) + (\tau + 1)\operatorname{tr}(E^2) - \tau\operatorname{tr}^2 E = 0. \tag{6}$$

Proof. Let $U \in SO(3)$ be such that $Ut = [0\ 0\ 1]^{\mathrm{T}}$. Then,

$$\hat{E} = UEU^{\mathrm{T}} = U[t]_\times U^{\mathrm{T}} U R U^{\mathrm{T}} = [Ut]_\times \hat{R} = \begin{bmatrix} 0 & 1 & 0 \\ -1 & 0 & 0 \\ 0 & 0 & 0 \end{bmatrix} \hat{R}, \tag{7}$$

where $\hat{R} = URU^{\mathrm{T}}$. It is clear that if E satisfies Eq. (6), then so does $\hat{E}$ and vice versa. Let us represent $\hat{R}$ in terms of a unit quaternion $s + u\mathbf{i} + v\mathbf{j} + w\mathbf{k}$, i.e.

$$\hat{R} = \begin{bmatrix} 1 - 2v^2 - 2w^2 & 2uv - 2ws & 2uw + 2vs \\ 2uv + 2ws & 1 - 2u^2 - 2w^2 & 2vw - 2us \\ 2uw - 2vs & 2vw + 2us & 1 - 2u^2 - 2v^2 \end{bmatrix}, \tag{8}$$

where $s^2 + u^2 + v^2 + w^2 = 1$. Then,

$$\hat{E} = \begin{bmatrix} 2uv + 2ws & 1 - 2u^2 - 2w^2 & 2vw - 2us \\ -1 + 2v^2 + 2w^2 & -2uv + 2ws & -2uw - 2vs \\ 0 & 0 & 0 \end{bmatrix}. \tag{9}$$

Substituting this into (6), after some computation, we get

$$\text{l.h.s. of (6)} = (\tau + 1 - 4s^2)(\tau + 1 - 4w^2). \tag{10}$$

This completes the proof, since $\tau = \text{tr}\, R = \text{tr}\, \hat{R} = 4s^2 - 1$.

It is well known [8,15] that for a given essential matrix E there is a "twisted pair" of rotations R_a and R_b so that $E \sim [\pm t]_\times R_a \sim [\pm t]_\times R_b$. By Proposition 1, $\tau_a = \text{tr}\, R_a$ and $\tau_b = \text{tr}\, R_b$ must be roots of Eq. (6). Since the equation is quadratic in τ there are no other roots. Thus we have

Proposition 2. *Let E be a real non-zero essential matrix satisfying Eq. (6) for a certain $\tau \in [-1, 3]$. Then, either $\tau = \text{tr}\, R_a$ or $\tau = \text{tr}\, R_b$, where (R_a, R_b) is the twisted pair of rotations for E.*

Now suppose that we are given two cameras with unknown but identical calibration matrices K and $K' = K$. Then we have

$$E \sim K^T F K, \tag{11}$$

where F is the fundamental matrix. Substituting this into Eqs. (5)–(6), we get the following ten equations:

$$\frac{1}{2}\, \text{tr}(F\omega^* F^T \omega^*) F - F\omega^* F^T \omega^* F = 0_{3\times 3}, \tag{12}$$

$$\frac{1}{2}(\tau^2 - 1)\, \text{tr}(F\omega^* F^T \omega^*) + (\tau + 1)\, \text{tr}(\omega^* F \omega^* F) - \tau\, \text{tr}^2(\omega^* F) = 0, \tag{13}$$

where $\omega^* = KK^T$. Constraints (12)–(13) involve the internal parameters of a camera and hence can be used for its self-calibration. We notice that not all of these constraints are necessarily linearly independent.

Proposition 3. *If the fundamental matrix F is known, then Eq. (12) gives at most three linearly independent constraints on the entries of ω^*.*

Proof. Recall that matrix F is generically of rank two. Let the right and left null vectors of F be e and e' respectively. Denote by G the l.h.s. of Eq. (12). Then it is clear that

$$Ge = G^T e' = 0_{3\times 1}. \tag{14}$$

It follows that, given F, at least six of $(G)_{ij}$ are linearly dependent. Proposition 3 is proved.

3 Description of the Algorithm

The initial data for our algorithm is $N \geq 7$ point correspondences $q_i \leftrightarrow q_i'$, $i = 1, \ldots, N$, and also the trace τ of the rotation matrix R.

3.1 Data Pre-normalization

To significantly improve the numerical stability of our algorithm, points q_i and q_i' are first normalized as follows, adapted from [8]. We construct a 3×3 matrix S of the form

$$S = \begin{bmatrix} \gamma & 0 & \alpha \\ 0 & \gamma & \beta \\ 0 & 0 & 1 \end{bmatrix} \tag{15}$$

so that the $2N$ new points, represented by the columns of matrix

$$S \begin{bmatrix} q_1 \cdots q_N \; q_1' \cdots q_N' \end{bmatrix}, \tag{16}$$

satisfy the following conditions:

- their centroid is at the coordinate origin;
- their average distance from the origin is $\sqrt{2}$.

From now on we assume that q_i and q_i' are normalized.

3.2 Polynomial Equations

The fundamental matrix F is estimated from $N \geq 7$ point correspondences in two views. The algorithm is well known, see [8] for details. In the minimal case $N = 7$ there are either one or three real solutions. Otherwise, the solution is generically unique.

Let both cameras be identically calibrated and have Euclidean image planes, i.e.

$$K = K' = \begin{bmatrix} f & 0 & a \\ 0 & f & b \\ 0 & 0 & 1 \end{bmatrix}, \tag{17}$$

where f is the focal length and (a, b) is the principal point. It follows that

$$\omega^* = KK^{\mathrm{T}} = \begin{bmatrix} a^2 + p & ab & a \\ ab & b^2 + p & b \\ a & b & 1 \end{bmatrix}, \tag{18}$$

where we introduce a new variable $p = f^2$.

Substituting F and ω^* into constraints (12) and (13), we get ten quartic equations in variables a, b and p. Let G be the l.h.s. of (12). By Proposition 3, up to three of $(G)_{ij}$ are linearly independent. Let $f_1 = (G)_{11}$, $f_2 = (G)_{22}$,

$f_3 = (G)_{33}$ and $f_4 = $ l.h.s. of (13). The objective is to find all feasible solutions of the following system of polynomial equations

$$f_1 = f_2 = f_3 = f_4 = 0. \tag{19}$$

Let us define the ideal $J = \langle f_1, f_2, f_3, f_4 \rangle \subset \mathbb{C}[a, b, p]$. Unfortunately, ideal J is not zero-dimensional. There is a one-parametric family of solutions of system (19) corresponding to the unfeasible case $p = 0$. We state without proof the decomposition

$$\sqrt{J} = J' \cap \langle p, \operatorname{tr}(F\omega^*) \rangle, \tag{20}$$

where $\sqrt{J}$ is the radical of J and $J' = J/\langle p \rangle$ is the quotient ideal, which is already zero-dimensional. By (20), the affine variety of J is the union of a finite set of points in $\mathbb{C}^3$ and a conic in the plane $p = 0$.

3.3   Gröbner Basis

In this subsection, the Gröbner basis of ideal J' will be constructed. We start from rewriting equations (19) in form

$$B_0 y_0 = 0, \tag{21}$$

where B_0 is a 4×22 coefficient matrix, and

$$y_0 = \begin{bmatrix} a^3b & a^2b^2 & ab^3 & a^2b & a^4 & b^4 & a^3 & ab^2 & b^3 & a^2p & abp & b^2p \\ & & & a^2 & ab & b^2 & ap & bp & p^2 & a & b & p & 1 \end{bmatrix}^{\mathrm{T}} \tag{22}$$

is a monomial vector. Let us consider the following sequence of transformations:

$$(B_i, y_i) \rightarrow (\tilde{B}_i, y_i) \rightarrow (B_{i+1}, y_{i+1}), \qquad i = 0, \ldots, 4. \tag{23}$$

Here each $\tilde{B}_i$ is the *reduced row echelon form* of B_i. The monomials in y_i are ordered so that the left of matrix $\tilde{B}_i$ is an identity matrix for each i.

We exploit below some properties of the intermediate polynomials in sequence (23), e.g. they can be factorized or have degree lower than one expects from the corresponding monomial vector. All of these properties have been verified in Maple by using randomly generated instances of the problem over the field of rationals.

Let us denote by $(A)_i$ the ith row of matrix A. Now we describe in detail each transformation $(\tilde{B}_i, y_i) \rightarrow (B_{i+1}, y_{i+1})$ of sequence (23).

– The last row of $\tilde{B}_0$ corresponds to a 3rd degree polynomial. Matrix B_1 of size 7×32 is obtained from $\tilde{B}_0$ by appending 3 new rows and 10 new columns. The rows are: $a(\tilde{B}_0)_4$, $b(\tilde{B}_0)_4$ and $p(\tilde{B}_0)_4$. Monomial vector

$$y_1 = \begin{bmatrix} a^3b & a^2b^2 & ab^3 & a^2b & \underline{a^3p} & \underline{a^2bp} & \underline{ab^2p} & a^4 \\ & b^4 & a^3 & ab^2 & b^3 & a^2p & \underline{b^2p^2} & \underline{ap^2} & abp & b^2p & \underline{b^3p} & a^2 \\ & \underline{abp^2} & \underline{a^2p^2} & ab & b^2 & \underline{bp^2} & \underline{p^3} & ap & bp & p^2 & a & b & p & 1 \end{bmatrix}^{\mathrm{T}}, \tag{24}$$

where we underlined the new monomials (columns) of matrix B_1.

- The polynomials corresponding to the last three rows of $\tilde{B}_1$ are divisible by p. Matrix B_2 of size 13×32 is obtained as follows. We append 6 new rows to $\tilde{B}_1$, which are $(\tilde{B}_1)_i/p$, $a(\tilde{B}_1)_i/p$ and $b(\tilde{B}_1)_i/p$ for $i = 6, 7$. Monomial vector $y_2 = y_1$.
- Matrix B_3 of size 19×32 is obtained from $\tilde{B}_2$ by appending 6 new rows: $a(\tilde{B}_2)_i$, $b(\tilde{B}_2)_i$ and $p(\tilde{B}_2)_i$ for $i = 12, 13$. Monomial vector $y_3 = y_1$.
- The last row of $\tilde{B}_3$ corresponds to a 2nd degree polynomial. Thus we proceed with the polynomials of degree up to 3. We eliminate from $\tilde{B}_3$ rows and columns corresponding to all 4th degree polynomials and monomials respectively. Matrix B_4 of size 11×20 is obtained from $\tilde{B}_3$ as follows. We hold the rows of $\tilde{B}_3$ with numbers 4, 10, 11, 12, 13, 16, 17, 19, and append 3 new rows: $a(\tilde{B}_3)_{19}$, $b(\tilde{B}_3)_{19}$ and $p(\tilde{B}_3)_{19}$. Monomial vector

$$y_4 = \begin{bmatrix} a^2b & a^3 & ab^2 & b^3 & a^2p & ap^2 & abp & b^2p \\ a^2 & ab & b^2 & bp^2 & p^3 & ap & bp & p^2 & a & b & p & 1 \end{bmatrix}^{\mathrm{T}}. \quad (25)$$

- Finally, matrix B_5 of size 14×20 is obtained from $\tilde{B}_4$ by appending 3 new rows: $a(\tilde{B}_4)_{11}$, $b(\tilde{B}_4)_{11}$ and $p(\tilde{B}_4)_{11}$. Monomial vector $y_5 = y_4$.

The last six rows of matrix $\tilde{B}_5$ constitute the (reduced) Gröbner basis of ideal J' w.r.t. the graded reverse lexicographic order with $a > b > p$.

3.4   Internal and External Parameters

Given the Gröbner basis of J', the 6×6 action matrix M_p for multiplication by p in the quotient ring $\mathbb{C}[a, b, p]/J'$ can be easily constructed as follows. We denote by C the 6×6 right lower submatrix of $\tilde{B}_5$. Then the first three rows of M_p are the last three rows of $(-C)$. The rest of M_p consists of almost all zeros except

$$(M_p)_{41} = (M_p)_{52} = (M_p)_{65} = 1. \quad (26)$$

The six solutions are then found from the eigenvectors of matrix M_p, see [4] for details. Complex solutions and the ones with $p < 0$ are excluded.

Having found the calibration matrix K, we compute the essential matrix E from formula (11) and then the externals R and t using the standard procedure, see e.g. [17]. Note that, due to Proposition 2 and the *cheirality constraint* [8,17], the trace of the estimated matrix R must equal τ.

Finally, the denormalized entities (see Subsect. 3.1 and the definition of matrix S) are found as follows:

- fundamental matrix is $S^{\mathrm{T}}FS$;
- calibration matrix is $S^{-1}K$;
- essential matrix is unchanged, as $K^{\mathrm{T}}S^{-\mathrm{T}}S^{\mathrm{T}}FSS^{-1}K = K^{\mathrm{T}}FK \sim E$;
- externals R and t are also unchanged.

4 Experiments on Synthetic Data

In this section we test the algorithm on synthetic image data. The default data setup is given in the following table:

Distance to the scene	1
Scene depth	0.5
Baseline length	0.1
Image dimensions	1280 × 720

4.1 Numerical Accuracy

First we verify the numerical accuracy of our method. The numerical error is defined as the minimal relative error in the calibration matrix, that is

$$\min_{i}\left(\frac{\|K_i - K_{\mathrm{gt}}\|}{\|K_{\mathrm{gt}}\|}\right). \tag{27}$$

Here $\|\cdot\|$ stands for the Frobenius norm, i counts all real solutions, and

$$K_{\mathrm{gt}} = \begin{bmatrix} 1000 & 0 & 640 \\ 0 & 1000 & 360 \\ 0 & 0 & 1 \end{bmatrix} \tag{28}$$

is the ground truth calibration matrix. The numerical error distribution is reported in Fig. 1.

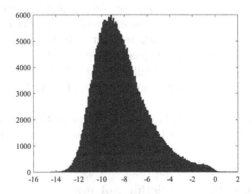

Fig. 1. $\log_{10}$ of numerical error for noise free data. The median error is 2.5×10^{-9}

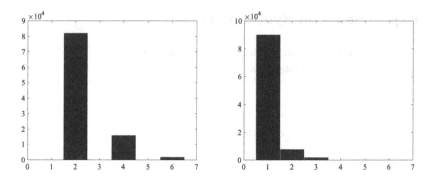

Fig. 2. The number of real (left) and feasible (right) solutions for the internal calibration. Noise free data

4.2 Number of Solutions

In general, the algorithm outputs six solutions for the calibration matrix, counting both real and complex ones. The number of real solutions is usually two or four. The number of real solutions with positive p (we call such solutions feasible) is equal to one in most cases. The corresponding distributions are demonstrated in Fig. 2.

4.3 Behaviour Under Noise

To evaluate the robustness of our solver, we add two types of noise to the initial data. First, the image noise which is modelled as zero-mean, Gaussian distributed with a standard deviation varying from 0 to 1 pixel in a 1280×720 image. Second, the angle noise resulting from inaccurately found relative rotation angle θ. In practice, θ is computed by integrating the angular velocity measurements obtained from a 3d gyroscope. Therefore, a realistic model for the angle noise is quite complicated and depends on a number of factors such as the value of θ, the measurement rates, the inertial sensor noise model, etc. In a very simplified manner, the angle noise can be modelled as θs [12], where s has the Gaussian distribution with zero mean and standard deviation σ. In our experiments σ ranges from 0 to 0.09.

Figure 3 demonstrates the behaviour of the algorithm under increasing the image and angle noise. Here and below each point on the diagram is a median of 10^4 trials.

4.4 Comparison with the Existing Solvers

We compare our algorithm for the minimal number of points ($N = 7$) with the 6-point solver from [20] and the 5-point solver from [19].

Figure 4 depicts the relative focal length error $|f - 1000|/1000$ at varying levels of image noise. Here and below $\alpha = 0.1$ means a 10%-miscalibration in

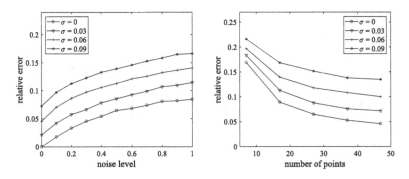

Fig. 3. The relative error in the calibration matrix at varying level of noise (left) and at varying number of points (right). The number of image points on the left figure is $N = 20$. The standard deviation for the image noise on the right figure is 1 pixel

the parameters a and b, i.e. the data was generated using the ground truth calibration matrix K_{gt}, whereas the solutions were found assuming that

$$K = \begin{bmatrix} 1000 & 0 & (1+\alpha)640 \\ 0 & 1000 & (1+\alpha)360 \\ 0 & 0 & 1 \end{bmatrix}. \tag{29}$$

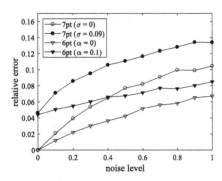

Fig. 4. The relative focal length error against noise standard deviation in pixels

In Fig. 5, the rotational and translational errors of the algorithms are reported. As it can be seen, for realistic levels of image noise, the 5-point algorithm expectedly outperforms as our solution as the 6-point solver. However, it is worth emphasizing that our solution is more suitable for the internal self-calibration of a camera rather than for its pose estimation. Once the self-calibration is done, it is more efficient to switch to the 5- or even 4-point solvers from [12,17].

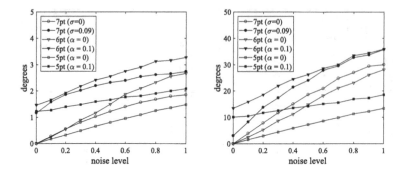

Fig. 5. The rotational (left) and translational (right) errors in degrees against noise standard deviation in pixels

We also compared the speed of the algorithms. The average running times over 10^5 trials are 2.0 ms (our 7pt), 1.6 ms (6pt) and 0.4 ms (5pt) on a system with 2.3 GHz processor. The most expensive step of our algorithm is the computation of the five reduced row echelon forms in sequence (23).

5 Experiments on Real Data

In this section we validate the algorithm by using the publicly available EuRoC dataset [1]. This dataset contains sequences of the data recorded from an IMU and two cameras on board a micro-aerial vehicle and also a ground truth. Specifically, we used the "Machine Hall 01" dataset (easy conditions) and only the images taken by camera "0". The image size is 752×480 (WVGA) and the ground truth calibration matrix is

$$K_{\mathrm{gt}} = \begin{bmatrix} 458.654 & 0 & 367.215 \\ 0 & 457.296 & 248.375 \\ 0 & 0 & 1 \end{bmatrix}. \tag{30}$$

Fig. 6. The pair of undistorted images with the time stamps "1403636646263555584" and "1403636646613555456" from the EuRoC dataset and the matched points

The sequence of 68 image pairs was derived from the dataset and the algorithm was applied to every image pair, see example in Fig. 6. Here it is necessary to make a few remarks.

- Since the algorithm assumes the pinhole camera model, every image was first undistorted using the ground truth parameters.
- As it was mentioned in Subsect. 4.2, the feasible solution is almost always unique. However in rare cases multiple solutions are possible. To reduce the probability of getting such solutions we additionally assumed that the principal point is sufficiently close to the geometric image center. More precisely, the solutions with

$$(a, b) \notin \{|x - 376| < 50, |y - 240| < 50\} \tag{31}$$

were marked as unfeasible and hence discarded. This condition almost guarantees that the algorithm outputs at most one solution.
- Given the readings of a triple-axis gyroscope the relative rotation angle can be computed as follows. The gyroscope reading at time ξ_i is an angular rate 3-vector w_i. Let $\Delta\xi_i = \xi_i - \xi_{i-1}$, where $i = 1, \ldots, n$. Then the relative rotation matrix R_n between the 0th and nth frames is approximately found from the recursion

$$R_i = \exp([w_i]_\times \Delta\xi_i) R_{i-1}, \tag{32}$$

where $R_0 = I$ and the matrix exponential is computed by the Rodrigues formula

$$\exp([v]_\times) = I + \frac{\sin\|v\|}{\|v\|} [v]_\times + \frac{1 - \cos\|v\|}{\|v\|^2} [v]_\times^2. \tag{33}$$

The relative rotation angle is then derived from $\operatorname{tr} R_n$.
- The image pairs with the relative rotation angle less than 5 degrees were discarded, since the motion in this case is close to a pure translation and self-calibration becomes unstable.

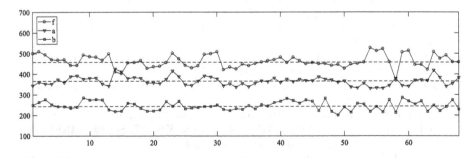

Fig. 7. The estimated focal length and principal point coordinates for the 68 image pairs. The dashed horizontal lines represent the average values

The estimated internal parameters for each image pair are shown in Fig. 7. The calibration matrix averaged over the entire sequence is given by

$$K = \begin{bmatrix} 457.574 & 0 & 366.040 \\ 0 & 457.574 & 243.616 \\ 0 & 0 & 1 \end{bmatrix} . \tag{34}$$

Hence the relative error in the calibration matrix is about 0.6 %.

6 Conclusions

We have presented a new practical solution to the problem of self-calibration of a camera with Euclidean image plane. The solution operates with at least seven point correspondences in two views and also with the known value of the relative rotation angle.

Our method is based on a novel quadratic constraint on the essential matrix, see Eq. (6). We expect that there could be other applications of that constraint. In particular, it can be used to obtain an alternative solution of the problem from paper [12]. The investigation of that possibility is left for further work.

We have validated the solution in a series of experiments on synthetic and real data. Under the assumption of generic camera motion and points configuration, it is shown that the algorithm is numerically stable and demonstrates a good performance in the presence of noise. It is also shown that the algorithm is fast enough and in most cases it produces a unique feasible solution for camera calibration.

References

1. Burri, M., et al.: The EuRoC micro aerial vehicle datasets. Int. J. Robot. Res. **35**(10), 1157–1163 (2016)
2. Byröd, M., Josephson, K., Åström, K.: Improving numerical accuracy of Gröbner basis polynomial equation solver. In: IEEE 11th International Conference on Computer Vision ICCV 2007, pp. 1–8. IEEE (2007)
3. Caprile, B., Torre, V.: Using vanishing points for camera calibration. Int. J. Comput. Vis. **4**(2), 127–139 (1990)
4. Cox, D., Little, J., O'Shea, D.: Ideals, Varieties, and Algorithms, vol. 3. Springer, New York (2007). https://doi.org/10.1007/978-1-4757-2181-2
5. Faugeras, O.: Three-Dimensional Computer Vision: A Geometric Viewpoint. MIT Press, London (1993)
6. Hartley, R.I.: Estimation of relative camera positions for uncalibrated cameras. In: Sandini, G. (ed.) ECCV 1992. LNCS, vol. 588, pp. 579–587. Springer, Heidelberg (1992). https://doi.org/10.1007/3-540-55426-2_62
7. Hartley, R.I.: Self-calibration from multiple views with a rotating camera. In: Eklundh, J.-O. (ed.) ECCV 1994. LNCS, vol. 800, pp. 471–478. Springer, Heidelberg (1994). https://doi.org/10.1007/3-540-57956-7_52
8. Hartley, R., Zisserman, A.: Multiple View Geometry in Computer Vision. Cambridge University Press, Cambridge (2003)

9. Heikkilä, J.: Geometric camera calibration using circular control points. IEEE Trans. Pattern Anal. Mach. Intell. **22**(10), 1066–1077 (2000)
10. Heyden, A., Åström, K.: Euclidean reconstruction from image sequences with varying and unknown focal length and principal point. In: Conference on Computer Vision and Pattern Recognition, pp. 438–443. IEEE (1997)
11. Kukelova, Z., Bujnak, M., Pajdla, T.: Polynomial eigenvalue solutions to the 5-pt and 6-pt relative pose problems. In: British Machine Vision Conference, vol. 2 (2008)
12. Li, B., Heng, L., Lee, G., Pollefeys, M.: A 4-point algorithm for relative pose estimation of a calibrated camera with a known relative rotation angle. In: IEEE/RSJ International Conference on Intelligent Robots and Systems, pp. 1595–1601. IEEE (2013)
13. Li, H.: A simple solution to the six-point two-view focal-length problem. In: Leonardis, A., Bischof, H., Pinz, A. (eds.) ECCV 2006. LNCS, vol. 3954, pp. 200–213. Springer, Heidelberg (2006). https://doi.org/10.1007/11744085_16
14. Liebowitz, D., Zisserman, A.: Combining scene and auto-calibration constraints. In: The Proceedings of the Seventh IEEE International Conference on Computer Vision, vol. 1, pp. 293–300. IEEE (1999)
15. Maybank, S.: Theory of Reconstruction from Image Motion. Springer, Heidelberg (1993). https://doi.org/10.1007/978-3-642-77557-4
16. Maybank, S., Faugeras, O.: A theory of self calibration of a moving camera. Int. J. Comput. Vis. **8**(2), 123–151 (1992)
17. Nistér, D.: An efficient solution to the five-point relative pose problem. IEEE Trans. Pattern Anal. Mach. Intell. **26**(6), 756–770 (2004)
18. Quan, L., Triggs, B.: A unification of autocalibration methods. In: Asian Conference on Computer Vision, pp. 917–922 (2000)
19. Stewénius, H., Engels, C., Nistér, D.: Recent developments on direct relative orientation. ISPRS J. Photogramm. Remote Sens. **60**(4), 284–294 (2006)
20. Stewénius, H., Nistér, D., Kahl, F., Schaffalitzky, F.: A minimal solution for relative pose with unknown focal length. Image and Vis. Comput. **26**(7), 871–877 (2008)
21. Sturm, P.: Critical motion sequences for monocular self-calibration and uncalibrated Euclidean reconstruction. In: Conference on Computer Vision and Pattern Recognition, pp. 1100–1105. IEEE (1997)
22. Sturm, P.: Self-calibration of a moving zoom-lens camera by pre-calibration. Image and Vis. Comput. **15**(8), 583–589 (1997)
23. Triggs, B.: Autocalibration and the absolute quadric. In: Conference on Computer Vision and Pattern Recognition, pp. 609–614. IEEE (1997)
24. Tsai, R.: A versatile camera calibration technique for high-accuracy 3D machine vision metrology using off-the-shelf TV cameras and lenses. IEEE J. Robot. Autom. **3**(4), 323–344 (1987)
25. Zhang, Z.: A flexible new technique for camera calibration. IEEE Trans. Pattern Anal. Mach. Intell. **22**(11), 1330–1334 (2000)

Learning to Detect and Track Visible and Occluded Body Joints in a Virtual World

Matteo Fabbri$^{(\boxtimes)}$, Fabio Lanzi, Simone Calderara, Andrea Palazzi,
Roberto Vezzani, and Rita Cucchiara

Department of Engineering "Enzo Ferrari", University of Modena and Reggio Emilia,
Modena, Italy
{matteo.fabbri, fabio.lanzi, simone.calderara, andrea.palazzi,
roberto.vezzani, rita.cucchiara}@unimore.it

Abstract. Multi-People Tracking in an open-world setting requires a
special effort in precise detection. Moreover, temporal continuity in the
detection phase gains more importance when scene cluttering introduces
the challenging problems of occluded targets. For the purpose, we propose a deep network architecture that jointly extracts people body parts
and associates them across short temporal spans. Our model explicitly
deals with occluded body parts, by hallucinating plausible solutions of
not visible joints. We propose a new end-to-end architecture composed
by four branches (*visible heatmaps, occluded heatmaps, part affinity fields*
and *temporal affinity fields*) fed by a *time linker* feature extractor. To
overcome the lack of surveillance data with tracking, body part and
occlusion annotations we created the vastest Computer Graphics dataset
for people tracking in urban scenarios by exploiting a photorealistic
videogame. It is up to now the vastest dataset (about 500.000 frames,
almost 10 million body poses) of human body parts for people tracking in urban scenarios. Our architecture trained on virtual data exhibits
good generalization capabilities also on public real tracking benchmarks,
when image resolution and sharpness are high enough, producing reliable
tracklets useful for further batch data association or re-id modules.

Keywords: Pose estimation · Tracking · Surveillance · Occlusions

1 Introduction

Multi-People Tracking (MPT) is one of the most established fields in computer
vision. It has been recently fostered by the availability of comprehensive public
benchmarks and data [2,25]. Often, MPT approaches have been casted in the

---

M. Fabbri, F. Lanzi and S. Calderara—Equally contributed.

Electronic supplementary material The online version of this chapter (https://
doi.org/10.1007/978-3-030-01225-0_27) contains supplementary material, which is
available to authorized users.

© Springer Nature Switzerland AG 2018
V. Ferrari et al. (Eds.): ECCV 2018, LNCS 11208, pp. 450–466, 2018.
https://doi.org/10.1007/978-3-030-01225-0_27

tracking by detection paradigm where a pedestrian detector extracts candidate objects and a further association mechanism arranges them in a temporally consistent trajectory [10,14,35]. Nevertheless, in the last years several researchers [11,35] raised the question on whether these two phases would be disentangled or considered two sides of the same problem. The strong influence between detection accuracy and tracking performance [35] suggests considering detection and tracking as two parts of a unique problem that should be addressed end-to-end at least for short-term setups. In this work, we advocate for an integrated approach between detection and short-term tracking that can serve as a proxy for more complex association method either belonging to the tracking or re-id family of techniques. To this aim, we propose:

- an end-to-end deep network, called *THOPA-net (Temporal Heatmaps and Occlusions based body Part Association)* that jointly locates people body parts and associates them across short temporal spans. This is achievable with modern deep learning architectures that exhibit terrific performance in body part location [6] but, mostly, neglect the temporal contribution. For the purpose, we propose a bottom-up human pose estimation network with a temporal coherency module that jointly enhances the detection accuracy and allows for short-term tracking;
- an explicit method for dealing with occluded body parts that exploits the capability of deep networks of hallucinating feasible solutions;

Results are very encouraging in their precision also in crowded scenes. Our experiments tell us that the problem is less dependent on the details or the realism of the shape than one could imagine; instead, it is more affected by the image quality and resolution that are extremely high in Computer Graphics (CG) generated datasets. Nevertheless, experiments on real MPT dataset [2,25] demonstrate that the model can transfer positively towards real scenarios.

2   Related Works

Human pose estimation in images has made important progress over the last few years [5,7,15,27,36]. However, those techniques assume only one person per image and are not suitable for videos of multiple people that occlude each other. The natural extension of single-person pose estimation, i.e., multi-person pose estimation, has therefore gained much importance recently being able of handling situations with a varying number of people [6,17,18,23,26,28,30]. Among them, [28] uses graph decomposition and node labeling with local search while [26] introduces associative embeddings to simultaneously generate and group body joints detections. An end-to-end architecture for jointly learning body parts and their association is proposed by [6] while [28], instead, exploits a two-stage approach, consisting of a person detection stage followed by a keypoint estimation for each person. Moreover, [17,18,30] jointly estimate multiple poses in the image, while also handling truncations and occlusions. However, those methods still rely on a separate people detector and do not perform well in cluttered situations.

Table 1. Overview of the publicly available datasets for Pose Estimation and MPT in videos. For each dataset we reported the numbers of clips, annotated frames and people per frame, as well as the availability of 3D data, occlusion labels, tracking information, pose estimation annotations and data type

Dataset	#Clips	#Frames	#PpF	3D	Occl.	Tracking	Pose Est.	Type
Penn Action [40]	2,326	159,633	1				✓	sports
JHMDB [22]	5,100	31,838	1				✓	diverse
YouTube Pose [8]	50	5,000	1				✓	diverse
Video Pose 2.0 [33]	44	1,286	1				✓	diverse
Posetrack [2]	514	23,000	1–13			✓	✓	diverse
MOT-16 [25]	14	11,235	6–51		✓	✓		urban
JTA	512	460,800	0–60	✓	✓	✓	✓	urban

Single person pose estimation in videos has been addressed by several researchers, [13,21,29,39]. Nevertheless, all those methods improve the pose estimation accuracy by exploiting temporal smoothing constraints or optical flow data, but neglect the case of multiple overlapping people.

In recent years, online tracking has been successfully extended to scenarios with multiple targets [4,9,31,32,37,38]. In contrast to single target tracking approaches, which rely on sophisticated appearance models to track a single entity in subsequent frames, multiple target tracking does not rely solely on appearance models. [38] exploits a high-performance detector with a deep learning appearance feature while [31] presents an online method that encodes long-term temporal dependencies across multiple cues. [9], on the other hand, introduces spatial-temporal attention mechanism to handle the drift caused by occlusion and interaction among targets. [4] solves the online multi-object tracking problem by associating tracklets and detections in different ways according to their confidence values and [32] exploits both high and low confidence target detections in a probability hypothesis density particle filter framework.

In this work, we address the problem of multi-person pose estimation in videos jointly with the goal of multiple people tracking. Early works that approach the problem [3,20] do not tackle pose estimation and tracking simultaneously, but rather target on multi-person tracking alone. More recent methods [16,19], which rely on graph partitioning approaches closely related to [17,18,30], simultaneously estimate the pose of multiple people and track them over time but do not cope with urban scenarios that are dominated by targets occlusions, scene clutterness and scale variations. In contrast to [16,19] we do not tackle the problem as a graph partitioning approach. Instead, we aim at simplifying the tracking problem by providing accurate detections robust to occlusions by reasoning directly at video level.

The most widely used publicly available datasets for human pose estimation in videos are presented in Table 1. [8,22,40] provide annotations for the single-person subtask of person pose estimation. Only Posetrack [2] has a multi-person perspective with tracking annotations but not provide them in the surveillance context. The reference benchmark for evaluation of multi-person tracking is [25] which provides challenging sequences of crowded urban scenes with severe occlusions and scale variations. However, it pursuits no pose estimation task and only provides bounding boxes as annotations. Our virtual world dataset instead, aim at taking the best of both worlds by merging precise pose and tracking annotations in realistic urban scenarios. This is indeed feasible when the ground truth can be automatically computed exploiting highly photorealistic CG environments.

3   JTA Dataset

We collected a massive dataset JTA (Joint Track Auto) for pedestrian pose estimation and tracking in urban scenarios by exploiting the highly photorealistic video game *Grand Theft Auto V* developed by *Rockstar North*. The collected videos feature a vast number of different body poses, in several urban scenarios at varying illumination conditions and viewpoints, Fig. 1. Moreover, every clip comes with a precise annotation of visible and occluded body parts, people tracking with 2D and 3D coordinates in the game virtual world. In terms of completeness, our JTA dataset overcomes all the limitation of existing dataset in terms of number of entities and available annotations, Table 1. In order to virtually re-create real-world scenarios we manually directed the scenes by developing a game modification that interacts synchronously with the video game's engine. The developed module allowed us to generate and record natural pedestrian flows recreating people behaviors specific to the most crowded areas. Moreover, exploiting the game's APIs, the software can handle people actions: in clips, people occasionally perform natural actions like sitting, running, chatting, talking on the phone, drinking or smoking. Each video contains a number of people ranging between 0 and 60 with an average of more than 21 people, totaling almost 10M annotated body poses over 460,800 densely annotated frames. The distance from the camera ranges between 0.1 and 100 m, resulting in pedestrian heights between 20 and 1100 pixels (see supplementary material for further details). We collected a set of 512 Full HD videos, 30 s long, recorded at 30 fps. We halve the sequences into 256 videos for training and 256 for testing purposes. Through the game modification, we access the game renderer for automatically annotating the same 14 body parts in [1] and [2] in order to foster cross-dataset experiments. In each video, we assigned a unique identifier to every pedestrian that appears in the scene. The identifier remains the same throughout the entire video even if the pedestrian moves out the field-of-view. This feature could foster person re-identification research despite not being the target of this work. Our dataset also provides *occlusion* and *self-occlusion* flags. Each joint is marked as occluded if it is not directly visible from the camera point of view and it is occluded by objects or other pedestrians. Instead, a joint is marked as self-occluded if it is occluded by the same person to whom the joint belongs. As for joints annotation, occlusion annotation is captured by accessing the game renderer. JTA

Dataset also provides accurate 3D information: for each annotated joint, as well as having the 2D coordinates of the location in the image, we also provide the 3D coordinates of the location in the simulator's space. Differently from Pose-track [2], which uses the annotated head bounding boxes as an estimation of the absolute scale of the person, we provide the precise scale of each pedestrian through the 3D annotation. The dataset, along with the game modification, are freely accessible[1].

Fig. 1. Examples from the JTA dataset exhibiting its variety in viewpoints, number of people and scenarios. Ground truth joints are superimposed to the original images. See supplementary material for further examples

4   THOPA-net

Our approach exploits both intra-frame and inter-frame information in order to jointly solve the problem of multi-person pose estimation and tracking in videos. For individual frames, we extended the architecture in [6] by integrating a branch for handling occluded joints in the detection process. Subsequently, we propose a temporal linking network to integrate temporal consistency in the process and jointly achieve detection and short-term tracking. The Single Image model, Fig. 2, takes an RGB frame of size $w \times h$ as input and produces, as output, the pose prediction for every person in the image. Conversely, the complete architecture, Fig. 3, takes a clip of N frames as input and outputs the pose prediction for the last frame of the clip and the temporal links with the previous frame.

4.1   Single Image Pose Prediction

Our single image model, Fig. 2, consists of an initial feature extractor based on the first 10 layers of VGG-19 [34] pretrained on COCO 2016 keypoints dataset [24]. The computed feature maps are subsequently processed by a three-branch multi-stage CNN where each branch focuses on a different aspect of body pose estimation: the first branch predicts the heatmaps of the visible parts, the second branch predicts the heatmaps of the occluded parts and the third branch predicts the part affinity fields (PAFs), which are vector fields used to link parts together. Note that, oppositely to [6], we employed a different branch for the occlusion

---

[1] http://imagelab.ing.unimore.it/jta.

detection task. It is straightforward that visible and occluded body parts detection are two related but distinct tasks. The features used by the network in order to detect the location of a body part are different from those needed to estimate the location of an occluded one. Nevertheless, the two problems are entangled together since visible parts allow to estimate the missing ones. In fact, the network exploits contextual cues in order to perform the desired prediction, and the presence of a joint is indeed strongly influenced by the person's silhouette (e.g. a foot detection mechanism relies heavily on the presence of a leg, thus a visible foot detection may trigger even though the foot is not completely visible). Each branch is, in turn, an iterative predictor that refines the predictions at each subsequent stage applying intermediate supervision in order to address the vanishing gradient problem. Apart from the first stage, which takes as input only the features provided by VGG-19, the consecutive stages integrate the same features with the predictions from the branches at the previous stage. Consequently, information flow across the different branches and in particular both visible and occluded joints detection are entangled in the process.

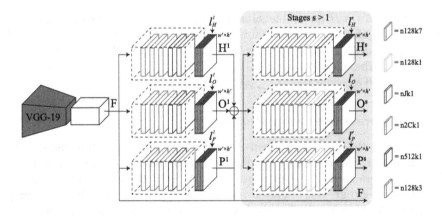

Fig. 2. Architecture of the three-branch multi-stage CNN with corresponding kernel size (k) and number of feature maps (n) indicated for each convolutional layer

We apply, for each branch, a different loss function at the end of each stage. The loss is a SSE loss between estimated predictions and ground truth, masked by a mask M in order to not penalize occluded joints in the visible branch. Specifically, for the generic output of each branch X^s of stage $s \in \{1, \ldots, S\}$ and the ground truth X^* we have the loss function:

$$l_X^s = \sum_i \sum_{x=1}^{w'} \sum_{y=1}^{h'} M(x,y) \odot (X_i^s(x,y) - X_i^*(x,y))^2, \tag{1}$$

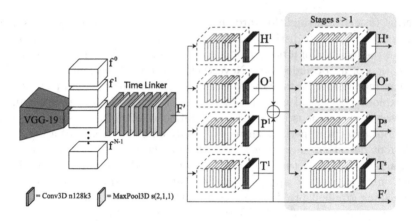

Fig. 3. Architecture of our method that encompass pose estimation and tracking in an end-to-end fashion. The MaxPool3D perform pooling operations only in the temporal dimension with stride s

where X is in turn H for visible joints heatmaps, O for occluded ones and P for affinity fields; the outer summation spans the J number of joints for H and O and the C number of limbs for P. H^s, O^s and P^s sizes (w', h') are eight times smaller than the input due to VGG19 max pooling operations. Eventually, the overall objective becomes $L = \sum_{s=1}^{S}(l_H^s + l_O^s + l_P^s)$.

4.2 Temporal Consistency Branch

In order to jointly solve the problem of multi-person pose estimation and tracking we enhance the Single Image model by adding our novel temporal network, Fig. 3. The temporal model takes as input N RGB frames of size $w \times h$ and produces, as output, the temporal affinity fields (TAFs), as well as heatmaps and part affinity fields. TAFs, like PAFs, are vector fields that link body parts but, oppositely to PAFs, are focused on temporal links instead of spatial ones. In detail, PAFs connect different types of body parts intra-frame while TAFs, instead, connect the same types of body parts inter-frame, e.g., they connect heads belonging to the same person in two subsequent frames. The TAF field is, in fact, a proxy of the motion of the body parts and provide the expected location of the same body part in the previous frame and can be used both for boosting the body parts detection and for associating body parts detections in time. At a given time t_0, our architecture takes frames $I^t \in \mathbb{R}^{w \times h \times 3}$ with $t \in \{t_0, t_{-\tau}, t_{-2\tau}, \dots, t_{-N\tau+1}\}$ and pushes them through the VGG19 feature extractor, described in Sect. 4.1, to obtain N feature tensors $f^t \in \mathbb{R}^{w' \times h' \times r}$ where r is the number of channels of the feature tensor. Those tensors are then concatenated over the temporal dimension obtaining $F \in \mathbb{R}^{w' \times h' \times r \times N}$. F is consecutively fed to a cascade of 3D convolution blocks that, in turn, capture the temporal patterns of the body part features and distill them by temporal max pooling until we achieve a feature tensor $F' \in \mathbb{R}^{w' \times h' \times r}$, Fig. 3. As in Sect. 4.1, the feature maps are passed through a multi-branch multi-stage CNN. Moreover, we add to the Single Image architecture a fourth branch for handling the TAFs prediction. As a consequence, after the first stage, temporal information flow to all the branches of the network and acts as a prior for body part estimation (visible and occluded) and PAFs computation. The complete network objective function then becomes $L = \sum_{s=1}^{S}(l_H^s + l_O^s + l_P^s + l_T^s)$ where

$$l_T^s = \sum_{j=1}^{J} \sum_{x=1}^{w'} \sum_{y=1}^{h'} M(x,y) \odot (T_j^s(x,y) - T_j^*(x,y))^2 \tag{2}$$

is the loss function computed between the ground truth T_j^* and the prediction T_j^s at each stage s. The set $T = (T_1, T_2, \ldots, T_j)$ has J vector fields, one for each part, with $T_j \in \mathbb{R}^{w \times h}, j \in \{1, \ldots, J\}$.

4.3   Training Procedure

During training, we generate both the ground truth heatmaps H^* and O^* from the annotated keypoint coordinates by placing at the keypoint location a 2D Gaussian with its variance conditioned by the true metric distance, d, of the keypoint from the camera. Oppositely to [6], by smoothing the Gaussian using distances, it is possible to achieve heatmaps of different sizes proportional to the scale of the person itself. This process is of particular importance to force scale awareness in the network and avoiding the need of multi scale branches. For example, given a visible heatmap H_j, let $q_{j,k} \in \mathbb{R}^2$ be the ground truth location of the body part j of the person k. For each body part j the ground truth H_j^* at location $p \in \mathbb{R}^2$ results:

$$H_j^*(p) = \max_k \exp\left(-\frac{\|p - q_{j,k}\|_2^2}{\sigma^2}\right), \qquad \sigma = \exp\left(1 - \frac{d}{\alpha}\right) \tag{3}$$

where σ regulates the spread of the peak in function of the distance d of each joint from the camera. In our experiments we choose α equals to 20.

Instead, each location p of ground truth part affinity fields $P_{c,k}^*$ is equal to the unit vector (with the same direction of the limb) if the point p belongs to the limb. The points belonging to the limb are those within a distance threshold of the line segment that connect the pair of body parts. For each frame, the ground truth part affinity fields are the two channels image containing the average of the PAFs of all people. As previously stated, by extending the concept of PAFs to the temporal dimension, we propose the novel TAFs representation which encodes short-term tubes of body parts across multiple frames (as shown in Fig. 4(b)). The temporal affinity field is a 2D vector field, for each body part, that points to the location of the same body part in the previous frame. Consider a body part j of a person k at frame t and let $q_{j,k}^{t-1}$ and $q_{j,k}^t$ be their ground truth positions at frame $t-1$ and t respectively. If a point p lies on the path crossed by the body part j between $t-1$ and t, the value at $T_{j,k}^*(p)$ is a unit vector pointing from j at time t to j at time $t-1$; for all other points the vector is zero. We computed ground truth TAFs using the same strategy exploited for PAFs.

4.4   Spatio-Temporal Multi-Person Joints Association

In order to connect body parts into skeletons we take into account two different contributions both at frame level (PAF) and at temporal level (TAF). First, the joints heatmaps are non-maxima suppressed to obtain a set of discrete locations, D_j, for multiple people, where $D_j = \{d_j^m : \text{for } j \in \{1, \ldots, J\}, m \in \{1, \ldots, N_j\}\}$ and N_j is the number of candidates of part j, and J the number of joint types.

(a)   (b)

Fig. 4. (a) Visualization of TAFs for different parts: for clarity, we show a single joint TAF for each person where color encodes direction. (b) Pose prediction performed on JTA dataset which distinguish between visible and occluded joints

We associate joints by defining a variable $z_{j_1 j_2}^{mn} \in \{0, 1\}$ to indicate whether two joints candidates $d_{j_1}^m$ and $d_{j_2}^n$ are connected. Consequently, the objective is to find the optimal assignment for the set of possible connections, $Z = \{z_{j_1 j_2}^{mn} : \text{for } j_1, j_2 \in \{1, \ldots, J\}, m \in \{1, \ldots, N_{j_1}\}, n \in \{1, \ldots, N_{j_2}\}\}$. To this aim we score every candidate limb (i.e. a pair of joints) spatially and temporally by computing the line integral along PAFs, E and TAFs, G:

$$E(d_{j_1}, d_{j_2}) = \int_{u=0}^{u=1} PAF(p(u)) \cdot \frac{d_{j_2} - d_{j_1}}{\left\| d_{j_2} - d_{j_1} \right\|_2} du \tag{4}$$

$$G(d_j, \hat{d}_j) = \int_{u=0}^{u=1} TAF(t(u)) \cdot \frac{\hat{d}_j - d_j}{\left\| \hat{d}_j - d_j \right\|_2} du \tag{5}$$

where $p(u)$ linearly interpolates the locations along the line connecting two joints d_{j_2} and d_{j_1} and $t(u)$ acts analogously for two joints $\hat{d}_j$ at frame $t-1$ and d_j at frame t.

We then maximize the overall association score E_c for limb type c and every subset of allowed connection Z_c (i.e. anatomically plausible connections):

$$\max_{Z_c} E_c = \max_{Z_c} \sum_{m \in D_{j_1}} \sum_{n \in D_{j_2}} (E(d_{j_1}^m, d_{j_2}^n) + \alpha E(\hat{d}_{j_1}^m, \hat{d}_{j_2}^n)) \cdot z_{j_1 j_2}^{mn}, \tag{6}$$

subject to $\sum_{n \in D_{j_2}} z_{j_1 j_2}^{mn} \leq 1, \forall m \in D_{j_1}$ and $\sum_{n \in D_{j_2}} z_{j_1 j_2}^{mn} \leq 1, \forall m \in D_{j_1}$ where

$$\hat{d}_{j_1}^m = \arg\max_{\hat{d}_{j_1}^b} G(d_{j_1}^m, \hat{d}_{j_1}^b), \qquad \hat{d}_{j_2}^n = \arg\max_{\hat{d}_{j_2}^q} G(d_{j_2}^n, \hat{d}_{j_2}^q) \tag{7}$$

are the joints at frame $t-1$ that maximize the temporal consistency along the TAF where b and q span the indexes of the people detected at the previous frame.

In principle, Eq. (6) mixes both the contribution coming from the PAF in the current frame and the contribution coming from the PAF obtained by warping, in the previous frame, the candidate joints along the best TAF lines.

In order to speed up the computation, we maximize iteratively Eq. (6) by considering only the subsets of joints inside a radius at twice the size of the skeletons in the previous frame at the same location. The complete skeletons are then built, by maximizing, for the limbs type set C, $E = \sum_{c=1}^{C} \max_{Z_c} E_c$.

Fig. 5. Qualitative results of THOPA-net on JTA (top row), MOT-16 (middle row) and PoseTrack (bottom row)

5   Experiments

We conducted experiments in two different contexts, either on our virtual world dataset JTA and on real data. In the virtual world scenario, we evaluated the capability of the proposed architecture of both reliably extracting people joints and successfully associating them along the temporal dimension. Real data experiments instead, aimed at empirically demonstrating that our virtual world dataset can function as a good proxy for training deep models and to which extent it is necessary to fine-tune the network on real data. In fact, we purposely conducted the experiments either without retraining the network and testing it out-of-the-box or by fine-tuning the network on real data. Moreover, all the tracking experiments do not explicitly model the target appearance, but visual appearance is only taken into account when extracting TAFs, thus exploited only for very short-term target association (namely tracklet construction).

5.1   Experiments on JTA

We tested our proposal on our virtual world scenario in order to evaluate both the joints extraction accuracy and the tracking capabilities. We started from the pre-trained VGG19 weights as the feature extractor and we trained our model end-to-end allowing features fine-tuning. For the temporal branch we randomly split every sequence into 1 s long clips. Subsequently, we uniformly subsampled every clip obtaining 8 frames that are inputted to the temporal branch. The train was performed by using ADAM optimizer with a learning rate of 10^{-4} and batch size equal to 16. We purposely kept the batch size relatively small because every frame carries a high number of different joints at different scales and locations leading to a reliable average gradient for the task.

Table 2. Detection results on JTA Dataset

	Joints	Detection		
	Mean Average Prec.	Precision	Recall	F1 Score
Single Image no occ	50.9	81.5	64.1	71.6
Single Image + occ	56.3	87.9	71.8	78.4
Complete	**59.3**	**92.1**	**77.4**	**83.9**
[6]	50.1	86.3	55.8	69.5

Detection Experiment. We first performed a detection experiment in order to quantify the contribution of the individual branch of our architecture. The detection experiment evaluated the location of people joints and the overall bounding box accuracy in terms of detection metrics. Analogously to [19], we used the PCKh (head-normalized probability of correct keypoint) metric, which considers a body joint to be correctly localized if the predicted location of the joint is within a certain threshold from the true location. Table 2 reports the results in term of mean average precision of joints location and bounding box detection metrics such as precision, recall and F1-score with an intersection over union threshold of 50%. We additionally ablated different branch of our architecture in order to empirically measure the contribution of every individual branch (i.e. the occlusion branch and the temporal branch). By observing the Table we can confirm that the network benefits from the presence of the occlusion estimation branch both in terms of joints location accuracy and detection performances. This is due to two different positive effects given by occluded joints. The first is the chance of estimate/guess the position of a person even if visually strong occluded, the second is about maximizing the presence of body joints that greatly simplifies their clustering into skeletons and consequently the detection metrics results improved, Fig. 4(b). Moreover, the temporal branch strengthens this process by adding short-term temporal consistency to the joints location. In fact, results indicate this boosts the performance leading to a more accurate joints detection in presence of people that overlaps in the scene. The improvement is due to the TAFs contribution that helps to disambiguate the association among body joints on the basis of the target direction, Fig. 4(a). Additionally we compared with [6] that was retrained on JTA and tested at 2 different scales (since the method does not deal with multiple scales), against which we score positively. The architecture in [6] is the same as our *Single Image no occ* model in Table 2, with the only difference that the latter has been trained with distance rescaled versions of heatmaps and PAFs, according to Sect. 4.3, and it deals with multiple scales without any input rescaling operation.

Tracking Experiment. We additionally tested the extent of disentanglement between temporal short-term detection and people tracking by performing a complete tracking experiments on the JTA test set. The experiments have been carried out by processing 1 s clips with a stride of 1 frame and associating targets using a local nearest neighbour approach maximizing the TAFs scores. As previously introduced, the purpose of the experiment was to empirically validate the claim that mixing short-term tracking and detection can still provide acceptable overall tracking performance even when adopting a simple association frame-by-frame method. Secondly, this is indeed more evident when the association algorithm exploits more than a single control point (e.g. usually the bounding box lower midpoint), which is the case of tracking sets of joints. For the purpose, we compared against a hungarian based baseline (acting on the lower midpoint of the bounding box), [35], inputed with either our detections and DPM [12] ones. Table 3 reports results in terms of Clear MOT tracking metrics [25]. Results indicate that the network trained on the virtual world scores positively in terms of tracked entities but suffers of a high number of IDs and FRAGS. This behavior is motivated by the absence of a strong appearance model capable of re-associating the targets after long occlusions. Additionally, the motion model is purposely simple suggesting that a batch tracklet association procedure can lead to longer tracks and reduce switches and fragmentations.

Table 3. Tracking results on JTA dataset

	MOTA	IDF1	MT	ML	FP	FN	IDs	FRAG
[35] + our det	57.4	57.3	45.3	21.7	40096	103831	15236	15569
[35] + DPM det	31.5	27.6	25.3	41.7	80096	170662	10575	19069
THOPA-net	**59.3**	**63.2**	**48.1**	**19.4**	**40096**	**103662**	**10214**	**15211**

5.2 Tracking People in Real Data

We tested our solution on real data with the purpose of evaluating the generalization capabilities of our model and its effectiveness in real surveillance scenarios. We choose to adopt two datasets: the commonly used MOT-16 Challenge Benchmark [25] and the new PoseTrack Dataset [2].

MOT-16. The MOT-16 Challenge Benchmark consists of 7 sequences in urban areas with varying resolution from 1980 × 1024 to 640 × 480 for a total number of approx 5000 frames and 3.5 min length. The benchmark exhibits strong challenges in terms of viewpoint changes, from top-mounted surveillance cameras to street level ones, Fig. 5. All results are expressed in terms of Clear MOT metrics according to the benchmark protocol [25] and as for the virtual world tracking experiment the tracks were associated by maximizing the TAF scores between detections. The network was end-to-end fine-tuned, with the exception of the occlusion branch. Fine-tuning was performed by considering the ground truth detections and inserting a default skeleton when our Single Image model scored a false negative obtaining an automatically annotated dataset.

Table 4. Results on MOT-16 benchmark ranked by MOTA score

	MOTA	IDF1	MT	ML	FP	FN	IDs	FRAG
[38]	**66.1**	**65.1**	**34.0**	20.8	5061	**55914**	805	3093
[37]	61.4	62.2	32.8	**18.2**	12852	56668	781	2008
THOPA-net	56.0	29.2	25.2	27.9	9182	67059	4064	5557
[31]	47.2	46.3	14.0	41.6	**2681**	92856	774	1675
[9]	46.0	50.0	14.6	43.6	6895	91117	**473**	**1422**
[4]	43.9	45.1	10.7	44.4	6450	95175	676	1795
[32]	38.8	42.4	7.9	49.1	8114	102452	965	1657

Table 4 reports the results of our fine-tuned network compared with the best published state of the art competitors up to now. We include in the Table only online trackers, that are referred on the benchmark website as causal methods. The motivation is that our method performs tracking at low level, using TAFs, for framewise temporal association thus it configures as an online tracker. Additionally, it is always possible to consider our tracklets as an intermediate output and perform a subsequent global association by possibly assessing additional high level information such as strong appearance cues and re-id techniques. Our method performs positively in terms of MOTA placing at the top positions. We observe a high IDS value and FRAG given by the fact that our output is an intermediate step between detections and long-term tracking. Nevertheless, we remark that we purposely choose a trivial association method that does not force any strong continuity in terms of target trajectories, instead, we argue that given temporal consistency to the target detections the association among them results satisfying for short-term tracking applications. This is possible also thanks to the fact that we use several control points for association (i.e. the joints) that are in fact reliable cues when objects are close each other and the scene is cluttered. Contrary to [38] and [37] our model do not employ strong appearance cues for re-identification. This suggests that the performance can be further improved by plugging a re-id module that connects tracks when targets are lost. Moreover, contrary to [31] we do not employ complex recurrent architecture to encode long-term dynamics. Nevertheless, the performances are comparable suggesting that when a tracker disposes of a plausible target candidate, even if occluded, the association simplify to keep subsequent frames temporally consistent that is indeed what our TAF branch do. Figure 5 shows qualitative results of our proposal.

PoseTrack. The PoseTrack Dataset is a large-scale benchmark for multi-person pose estimation and tracking in videos. It contains 550 videos including around 23,000 annotated frames, split into 292, 50, 208 videos for training, validation and testing, respectively. The annotations include 15 body keypoints location, a unique person id and a head bounding box for each person instance. We tested our solution on a subset of PoseTrack Dataset with surveillance like features (e.g. people standing, walking, etc.). We remark that PoseTack exhibits different features w.r.t. surveillance context in which the targets number is higher and the camera FoV is mostly a far FoV. In Fig. 6 we show MOTA and mAP results of THOPA-net on PoseTrack sequences (solely using synthetic data for training). We used training and validation sequences in order to obtain per-sequence results. The results are satisfying (see Fig. 5) even if the network is trained solely on CG data suggesting it could be a viable solution for fostering research in the joint tracking field, especially for urban scenarios where real joint tracking datasets are missing.

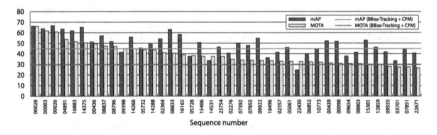

Fig. 6. Results on PoseTrack dataset compared with a BBox-Tracking + CPM (trained on MPII) baseline (used also in [19]; red/green lines are the average of performances on the selected sequences to avoid plot clutter) (Color figure online)

6   Conclusion

In this paper, we presented a massive CG dataset for human pose estimation and tracking which simulates realistic urban scenarios. The precise annotation of occluded joints provided by our dataset allowed us to extend a state-of-the-art network by handling occluded parts. We further integrate temporal coherency and propose a novel network capable of jointly locate people body parts and associate them across short temporal spans. Results suggest that the network, even if trained solely on synthetic data, adapts to real world scenarios when the image resolution and sharpness are high enough. We believe that the proposed dataset and architecture jointly constitute a starting point for considering tracking in surveillance as a unique process composed by detection and temporal association and can provide reliable tracklets as the input for batch optimization and re-id techniques.

Acknowledgments. The work is supported by the Italian MIUR, Ministry of Education, Universities and Research, under the project COSMOS PRIN 2015 programme 201548C5NT. We also gratefully acknowledge the support of Panasonic Silicon Valley Lab and Facebook AI Research with the donation of the GPUs used for this research. We finally thank Marco Gianelli and Emanuele Frascaroli for developing part of the mod used to acquire JTA dataset.

References

1. Andriluka, M., Pishchulin, L., Gehler, P., Schiele, B.: 2D human pose estimation: new benchmark and state of the art analysis. In: CVPR (2014)
2. Andriluka, M., et al.: Posetrack: a benchmark for human pose estimation and tracking. In: Proceedings of the IEEE Conference on Computer Vision and Pattern Recognition, pp. 5167–5176 (2018)
3. Andriluka, M., Roth, S., Schiele, B.: People-tracking-by-detection and people-detection-by-tracking. In: IEEE Conference on Computer Vision and Pattern Recognition CVPR 2008, pp. 1–8. IEEE (2008)
4. Bae, S.H., Yoon, K.J.: Confidence-based data association and discriminative deep appearance learning for robust online multi-object tracking. IEEE Trans. Pattern Anal. Mach. Intell. **40**(3), 595–610 (2018). https://doi.org/10.1109/TPAMI.2017. 2691769
5. Bulat, A., Tzimiropoulos, G.: Human pose estimation via convolutional part heatmap regression. In: Leibe, B., Matas, J., Sebe, N., Welling, M. (eds.) ECCV 2016. LNCS, vol. 9911, pp. 717–732. Springer, Cham (2016). https://doi.org/10. 1007/978-3-319-46478-7_44
6. Cao, Z., Simon, T., Wei, S.E., Sheikh, Y.: Realtime multi-person 2D pose estimation using part affinity fields. In: CVPR, vol. 1, p. 7 (2017)
7. Carreira, J., Agrawal, P., Fragkiadaki, K., Malik, J.: Human pose estimation with iterative error feedback. In: Proceedings of the IEEE Conference on Computer Vision and Pattern Recognition, pp. 4733–4742 (2016)
8. Charles, J., Pfister, T., Magee, D., Hogg, D., Zisserman, A.: Personalizing human video pose estimation. In: 2016 IEEE Conference on Computer Vision and Pattern Recognition (CVPR), pp. 3063–3072. IEEE (2016)
9. Chu, Q., Ouyang, W., Li, H., Wang, X., Liu, B., Yu, N.: Online multi-object tracking using CNN-based single object tracker with spatial-temporal attention mechanism. In: 2017 IEEE International Conference on Computer Vision (ICCV), pp. 4846–4855, October 2017. https://doi.org/10.1109/ICCV.2017.518
10. Dehghan, A., Tian, Y., Torr, P.H.S., Shah, M.: Target identity-aware network flow for online multiple target tracking. In: 2015 IEEE Conference on Computer Vision and Pattern Recognition (CVPR), pp. 1146–1154, June 2015. https://doi.org/10. 1109/CVPR.2015.7298718

11. Feichtenhofer, C., Pinz, A., Zisserman, A.: Detect to track and track to detect. In: IEEE International Conference on Computer Vision, ICCV 2017, Venice, Italy, pp. 3057–3065, 22–29 October 2017. https://doi.org/10.1109/ICCV.2017.330

12. Felzenszwalb, P.F., Girshick, R.B., McAllester, D., Ramanan, D.: Object detection with discriminatively trained part-based models. IEEE Trans. Pattern Anal. Mach. Intell. **32**(9), 1627–1645 (2010). https://doi.org/10.1109/TPAMI.2009.167

13. Gkioxari, G., Toshev, A., Jaitly, N.: Chained predictions using convolutional neural networks. In: Leibe, B., Matas, J., Sebe, N., Welling, M. (eds.) ECCV 2016. LNCS, vol. 9908, pp. 728–743. Springer, Cham (2016). https://doi.org/10.1007/978-3-319-46493-0_44

14. Hamid Rezatofighi, S., Milan, A., Zhang, Z., Shi, Q., Dick, A., Reid, I.: Joint probabilistic data association revisited. In: The IEEE International Conference on Computer Vision (ICCV), December 2015

15. Hu, P., Ramanan, D.: Bottom-up and top-down reasoning with hierarchical rectified gaussians. In: Proceedings of the IEEE Conference on Computer Vision and Pattern Recognition, pp. 5600–5609 (2016)

16. Insafutdinov, E., et al.: Arttrack: articulated multi-person tracking in the wild. In: IEEE Conference on Computer Vision and Pattern Recognition (CVPR), vol. 4327 (2017)

17. Insafutdinov, E., Pishchulin, L., Andres, B., Andriluka, M., Schiele, B.: DeeperCut: a deeper, stronger, and faster multi-person pose estimation model. In: Leibe, B., Matas, J., Sebe, N., Welling, M. (eds.) ECCV 2016. LNCS, vol. 9910, pp. 34–50. Springer, Cham (2016). https://doi.org/10.1007/978-3-319-46466-4_3

18. Iqbal, U., Gall, J.: Multi-person pose estimation with local joint-to-person associations. In: Hua, G., Jégou, H. (eds.) ECCV 2016. LNCS, vol. 9914, pp. 627–642. Springer, Cham (2016). https://doi.org/10.1007/978-3-319-48881-3_44

19. Iqbal, U., Milan, A., Gall, J.: Posetrack: joint multi-person pose estimation and tracking. In: Proceedings of the IEEE Conference on Computer Vision and Pattern Recognition, vol. 1 (2017)

20. Izadinia, H., Saleemi, I., Li, W., Shah, M.: $(MP)^2T$: multiple people multiple parts tracker. In: Fitzgibbon, A., Lazebnik, S., Perona, P., Sato, Y., Schmid, C. (eds.) ECCV 2012. LNCS, vol. 7577, pp. 100–114. Springer, Heidelberg (2012). https://doi.org/10.1007/978-3-642-33783-3_8

21. Jain, A., Tompson, J., LeCun, Y., Bregler, C.: MoDeep: a deep learning framework using motion features for human pose estimation. In: Cremers, D., Reid, I., Saito, H., Yang, M.-H. (eds.) ACCV 2014. LNCS, vol. 9004, pp. 302–315. Springer, Cham (2015). https://doi.org/10.1007/978-3-319-16808-1_21

22. Jhuang, H., Gall, J., Zuffi, S., Schmid, C., Black, M.J.: Towards understanding action recognition. In: 2013 IEEE International Conference on Computer Vision (ICCV), pp. 3192–3199. IEEE (2013)

23. Levinkov, E., et al.: Joint graph decomposition & node labeling: problem, algorithms, applications. In: IEEE Conference on Computer Vision and Pattern Recognition (CVPR) (2017)

24. Lin, T.-Y., et al.: Microsoft COCO: common objects in context. In: Fleet, D., Pajdla, T., Schiele, B., Tuytelaars, T. (eds.) ECCV 2014. LNCS, vol. 8693, pp. 740–755. Springer, Cham (2014). https://doi.org/10.1007/978-3-319-10602-1_48

25. Milan, A., Leal-Taixé, L., Reid, I., Roth, S., Schindler, K.: MOT16: a benchmark for multi-object tracking. arXiv: 1603.00831 (2016)

26. Newell, A., Huang, Z., Deng, J.: Associative embedding: end-to-end learning for joint detection and grouping. In: Advances in Neural Information Processing Systems, pp. 2274–2284 (2017)

27. Newell, A., Yang, K., Deng, J.: Stacked hourglass networks for human pose estimation. In: Leibe, B., Matas, J., Sebe, N., Welling, M. (eds.) ECCV 2016. LNCS, vol. 9912, pp. 483–499. Springer, Cham (2016). https://doi.org/10.1007/978-3-319-46484-8_29

28. Papandreou, G., et al.: Towards accurate multiperson pose estimation in the wild. arXiv preprint arXiv:1701.01779, vol. 8 (2017)

29. Pfister, T., Charles, J., Zisserman, A.: Flowing convnets for human pose estimation in videos. In: Proceedings of the IEEE International Conference on Computer Vision, pp. 1913–1921 (2015)

30. Pishchulin, L., et al.: Deepcut: joint subset partition and labeling for multi person pose estimation. In: Proceedings of the IEEE Conference on Computer Vision and Pattern Recognition, pp. 4929–4937 (2016)

31. Sadeghian, A., Alahi, A., Savarese, S.: Tracking the untrackable: learning to track multiple cues with long-term dependencies. In: 2017 IEEE International Conference on Computer Vision (ICCV), pp. 300–311, October 2017. https://doi.org/10.1109/ICCV.2017.41

32. Sanchez-Matilla, R., Poiesi, F., Cavallaro, A.: Online multi-target tracking with strong and weak detections. In: Hua, G., Jégou, H. (eds.) ECCV 2016. LNCS, vol. 9914, pp. 84–99. Springer, Cham (2016). https://doi.org/10.1007/978-3-319-48881-3_7

33. Sapp, B., Weiss, D., Taskar, B.: Parsing human motion with stretchable models. In: 2011 IEEE Conference on Computer Vision and Pattern Recognition (CVPR), pp. 1281–1288. IEEE (2011)

34. Simonyan, K., Zisserman, A.: Very deep convolutional networks for large-scale image recognition. arXiv preprint arXiv:1409.1556 (2014)

35. Solera, F., Calderara, S., Cucchiara, R.: Towards the evaluation of reproducible robustness in tracking-by-detection. In: 2015 12th IEEE International Conference on Advanced Video and Signal Based Surveillance (AVSS), pp. 1–6, August 2015. https://doi.org/10.1109/AVSS.2015.7301755

36. Wei, S.E., Ramakrishna, V., Kanade, T., Sheikh, Y.: Convolutional pose machines. In: Proceedings of the IEEE Conference on Computer Vision and Pattern Recognition, pp. 4724–4732 (2016)

37. Wojke, N., Bewley, A., Paulus, D.: Simple online and realtime tracking with a deep association metric. In: 2017 IEEE International Conference on Image Processing (ICIP), pp. 3645–3649 (2017)

38. Yu, F., Li, W., Li, Q., Liu, Y., Shi, X., Yan, J.: POI: multiple object tracking with high performance detection and appearance feature. In: Hua, G., Jégou, H. (eds.) ECCV 2016. LNCS, vol. 9914, pp. 36–42. Springer, Cham (2016). https://doi.org/10.1007/978-3-319-48881-3_3

39. Zhang, D., Shah, M.: Human pose estimation in videos. In: Proceedings of the IEEE International Conference on Computer Vision, pp. 2012–2020 (2015)

40. Zhang, W., Zhu, M., Derpanis, K.G.: From actemes to action: a strongly-supervised representation for detailed action understanding. In: Proceedings of the IEEE International Conference on Computer Vision, pp. 2248–2255 (2013)

DeepJDOT: Deep Joint Distribution Optimal Transport for Unsupervised Domain Adaptation

Bharath Bhushan Damodaran[1]([✉]), Benjamin Kellenberger[2], Rémi Flamary[3], Devis Tuia[2], and Nicolas Courty[1]

[1] Université de Bretagne Sud, IRISA, UMR 6074, CNRS, Lorient, France
bharath-bhushan.damodaran@irisa.fr
[2] Wageningen University, Wageningen, The Netherlands
benjamin.kellenberger@wur.nl
[3] Université Côte d'Azur, OCA, UMR 7293, CNRS, Laboratoire Lagrange,
Nice, France

Abstract. In computer vision, one is often confronted with problems of domain shifts, which occur when one applies a classifier trained on a source dataset to target data sharing similar characteristics (e.g. same classes), but also different latent data structures (e.g. different acquisition conditions). In such a situation, the model will perform poorly on the new data, since the classifier is specialized to recognize visual cues specific to the source domain. In this work we explore a solution, named DeepJDOT, to tackle this problem: through a measure of discrepancy on joint deep representations/labels based on optimal transport, we not only learn new data representations aligned between the source and target domain, but also simultaneously preserve the discriminative information used by the classifier. We applied DeepJDOT to a series of visual recognition tasks, where it compares favorably against state-of-the-art deep domain adaptation methods.

Keywords: Deep domain adaptation · Optimal transport

1 Introduction

The ability to generalize across datasets is one of the holy grails of computer vision. Designing models that can perform well on datasets sharing similar characteristics such as classes, but also presenting different underlying data structures (for instance different backgrounds, colorspaces, or acquired with different devices) is key in applications where labels are scarce or expensive to obtain. However, traditional learning machines struggle in performing well out of the datasets (or *domains*) they have been trained with. This is because models generally assume that both training (or *source*) and test (or *target*) data are issued

B.B. Damodaran and B. Kellenberger—Equally contributed.

from the same generating process. In vision problems, factors such as objects position, illumination, number of channels or seasonality break this assumption and call for adaptation strategies able to compensate for such shifts, or *domain adaptation* strategies [1].

In a first rough subdivision, domain adaptation strategies can be separated into *unsupervised* and *semi-supervised* domain adaptation: the former assumes that no labels are available in the target domain, while the latter assumes the presence of a few labeled instances in the target domain that can be used as reference points for the adaptation. In this paper, we propose a contribution for the former, more challenging case. Let $\mathbf{x}^s \in \mathbb{X}^S$ be the source domain examples with the associated labels $y^s \in \mathbb{Y}^S$. Similarly, let $\mathbf{x}^t \in \mathbb{X}^T$ be the target domain images, but with unknown labels. The goal of the unsupervised domain adaptation is to learn the classifier f in the target domain by leveraging the information from the source domain. To this end, we have access to a source domain dataset $\{\mathbf{x}_i^s, y_i^s\}_{i=1,\dots,n^s}$ and a target domain dataset $\{\mathbf{x}_i^t\}_{i=1,\dots,n^t}$ with only observations and no labels.

Early unsupervised domain adaptation research tackled the problem as the one of finding a common representation between the domains, or a latent space, where a single classifier can be used independently from the datapoint's origin [2,3]. In [4], the authors propose to use discrete optimal transport to match the shifted marginal distributions of the two domains under constraints of class regularity in the source. In [5] a similar logic is used, but the joint distributions are aligned directly using a coupling accounting for the marginals and the class-conditional distributions shift *jointly*. However, the method has two drawbacks, for which we propose solutions in this paper: (1) first, the JDOT method in [5] scales poorly, as it must solve a $n_1 \times n_2$ coupling, where n_1 and n_2 are the samples to be aligned; (2) secondly, the optimal transport coupling γ is computed between the input spaces (and using a ℓ_2 distance), which is a poor representation to be aligned, since we are interested in matching more semantic representations supposed to ease the work of the classifier using them to take decisions.

We solve the two problems above by a strategy based on deep learning. On the one hand, using deep learning algorithms for domain adaptation has found an increasing interest and has shown impressive results in recent computer vision literature [6–9]. On the other hand (and more importantly), a Convolutional Neural Network (CNN) offers the characteristics needed to solve our two problems: (1) by gradually adapting the optimal transport coupling along the CNN training, we obtain a scalable solution, an approximated and stochastic version of JDOT; (2) by learning the coupling in a deep layer of the CNN, we align the representation the classifier is using to take its decision, which is a more semantic representation of the classes. In summary, we learn jointly the embedding between the two domains and the classifier in a single CNN framework. We use a domain adaptation-tailored loss function based on optimal transport and therefore call our proposition *Deep Joint Distribution Optimal Transportation (DeepJDOT)*.

We test DeepJDOT on a series of visual domain adaptation tasks and compare favorably against several recent state of the art competitors.

2   Related Works

Unsupervised Domain Adaptation. Unsupervised domain adaptation studies the situation where the source domain carries labeled instances, while the target domain is unlabeled, yet accessible during training [10]. Earlier approaches consider projections aligning data spaces to each other [2,11,12], thus trying to exploit shift-invariant information to match the domains in their original (input) space. Later works extended such logic to deep learning, typically by weight sharing [6]/reconstruction [13], by adding Maximum Mean Discrepancy (MMD) and association-based losses between source and target layers [14–16]. Other major developments focus on the inclusion of adversarial loss functions pushing the CNN to be unable to discriminate whether a sample comes from the source or the target domain [7,8,17]. Finally, the most recent works extend this adversarial logic to the use of GANs [18,19], for example using two GAN modules with shared weights [9], forcing image to image architectures to have similar activation distributions [20] or simply fooling a GAN's discriminator discerning between domains [21]. These adversarial image generation based methods [18–20] use a class-conditioning or cycle consistency term to learn the discriminative embedding, such that semantically similar images in both domains are projected closeby in the embedding space. Our proposed DeepJDOT uses the concept of a shared embedding for both domains [17] and is built on a similar logic as the MMD-based methods, yet adding a clear discriminative component to the alignment: the proposed DeepJDOT associates representation and discriminative learning, since the optimal transport coupling ensures that distributions are matched, while *(i)* the JDOT class loss performs source label propagation to the target samples and *(ii)* the fact of learning the coupling in deep layers of the CNN ensures discrimination power.

Optimal Transport in Domain Adaptation. Optimal transport [22–24] has been used in domain adaptation to learn the transformation between domains [4,25, 26], with associated theoretical guarantees [27]. In those works, the coupling γ is used to transport (i.e. transform) the source data samples through an estimated mapping called barycentric mapping. Then, a new classifier is trained on the transported source data representation. But those different methods can only address problems of small to medium sizes because they rely on the exact solution of the OT problem on all samples. Very recently, Shen *et al.* [28] used the Wasserstein distance as a loss in a deep learning setting to promote similarities between embedded representations using the dual formulation of the problem exposed in [29]. However, none of those approaches considers an adaptation w.r.t. the discriminative content of the representation, as we propose in this paper.

3 Optimal Transport for Domain Adaptation

Our proposal is based on optimal transport. After recalling the associated basic notions and its relation with domain adaptation, we detail the JDOT method [5], which is the starting point of our proposition.

3.1 Optimal Transport

Optimal transport [24] (OT) is a theory that allows to compare probability distributions in a geometrically sound manner. It permits to work on empirical distributions and to exploit the geometry of the data embedding space. Formally, OT searches a probabilistic coupling $\gamma \in \Pi(\mu_1, \mu_2)$ between two distributions μ_1 and μ_2 which yields a minimal displacement cost

$$OT_c(\mu_1, \mu_2) = \inf_{\gamma \in \Pi(\mu_1, \mu_2)} \int_{\mathcal{R}^2} c(\mathbf{x}_1, \mathbf{x}_2) d\gamma(\mathbf{x}_1, \mathbf{x}_2) \tag{1}$$

w.r.t. a given cost function $c(\mathbf{x}_1, \mathbf{x}_2)$ measuring the dissimilarity between samples $\mathbf{x}_1$ and $\mathbf{x}_2$. Here, $\Pi(\mu_1, \mu_2)$ describes the space of joint probability distributions with marginals μ_1 and μ_2. In a discrete setting (both distributions are empirical) this becomes:

$$OT_c(\mu_1, \mu_2) = \min_{\gamma \in \Pi(\mu_1, \mu_2)} < \gamma, \mathbf{C} >_F, \tag{2}$$

where $\langle \cdot, \cdot \rangle_F$ is the Frobenius dot product, $\mathbf{C} \geq 0$ is a cost matrix $\in \mathbb{R}^{n_1 \times n_2}$ representing the pairwise costs $c(\mathbf{x}_i, \mathbf{x}_j)$, and γ is a matrix of size $n_1 \times n_2$ with prescribed marginals. The minimum of this optimization problem can be used as a distance between distributions, and, whenever the cost c is a norm, it is referred to as the Wasserstein distance. Solving Eq. (2) is a simple linear programming problem with equality constraints, but scales super-quadratically with the size of the sample. Efficient computational schemes were proposed with entropic regularization [30] and/or stochastic versions using the dual formulation of the problem [29,31,32], allowing to tackle small to middle sized problems.

3.2 Joint Distribution Optimal Transport

Courty et al. [5] proposed the joint distribution optimal transport (JDOT) method to prevent the two-steps adaptation (i.e. first adapt the representation and then learn the classifier on the adapted features) by directly learning a classifier embedded in the cost function c. The underlying idea is to align the joint features/labels distribution instead of only considering the features distribution. Consequently, μ_s and μ_t are measures of the product space $\mathcal{X} \times \mathcal{Y}$. The generalized cost associated to this space is expressed as a weighted combination of costs in the feature and label spaces, reading

$$d\left(\mathbf{x}_i^s, \mathbf{y}_i^s; \mathbf{x}_j^t, \mathbf{y}_j^t\right) = \alpha c(\mathbf{x}_i^s, \mathbf{x}_j^t) + \lambda_t L(\mathbf{y}_i^s, \mathbf{y}_j^t) \tag{3}$$

for the i-th source and j-th target element, and where $c(\cdot, \cdot)$ is chosen as a ℓ_2^2 distance and $L(\cdot, \cdot)$ is a classification loss (e.g. hinge or cross-entropy). Parameters α and λ_t are two scalar values weighing the contributions of distance terms. Since target labels $\mathbf{y}_j^t$ are unknown, they are replaced by a surrogate version $f(\mathbf{x}_j^t)$, which depends on a classifier $f : \mathcal{X} \to \mathcal{Y}$. Accounting for the classification loss leads to the following minimization problem:

$$\min_{f, \gamma \in \Pi(\mu_s, \mu_t)} \; < \gamma, \mathbf{D}_f >_F, \tag{4}$$

where $\mathbf{D}_f$ depends on f and gathers all the pairwise costs $d(\cdot, \cdot)$. As a by-product of this optimization problem, samples that share a common representation and a common label (through classification) are matched, yielding better discrimination. Interestingly, it is proven in [5] that minimizing this quantity is equivalent to minimizing a learning bound on the domain adaptation problem. However, JDOT has two major drawbacks: (i) on large datasets, solving for γ becomes intractable because γ scales quadratically in size to the number of samples; (ii) the cost $c(\mathbf{x}_i^s, \mathbf{x}_j^t)$ is taken in the input space as the squared Euclidean norm on images and can be uninformative of the dissimilarity between two samples. Our proposed DeepJDOT solves those two issues by introducing a stochastic version computing only small couplings along the iterations of a CNN, and by the fact that the optimal transport is learned between the semantic representations in the deeper layers of the CNN, rather than in the image space.

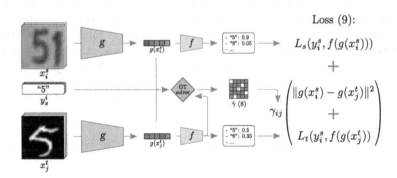

Fig. 1. Overview of the proposed DeepJDOT method. While the structure of the feature extractor g and the classifier f are shared by both domains, they are represented twice to distinguish between the two domains. Both the latent representations and labels are used to compute per batch a coupling matrix γ that is used in the global loss function.

4   Proposed Method

4.1   Deep Joint Distribution Optimal Transport(DeepJDOT)

The DeepJDOT model, illustrated in Fig. 1, is composed of two parts: an embedding function $g : \mathbf{x} \to \mathbf{z}$, where the input is mapped into the latent space Z, and the classifier $f : \mathbf{z} \rightarrow \mathbf{y}$, which maps the latent space to the label space on the target domain. The latent space can be any feature layer provided by a model, as in our case the penultimate fully connected layer of a CNN. DeepJ-DOT optimizes jointly this feature space and the classifier to provide a method that performs well on the target domain. The solution to this problem can be achieved by minimizing the following objective function:

$$\min_{\gamma \in \Pi(\mu_s, \mu_t), f, g} \sum_i \sum_j \gamma_{ij} d\left(g(\mathbf{x}_i^s), \mathbf{y}_i^s; g(\mathbf{x}_j^t), f(g(\mathbf{x}_j^t))\right), \tag{5}$$

where $d\left(g(\mathbf{x}_i^s), \mathbf{y}_i^s; g(\mathbf{x}_j^t), f(g(\mathbf{x}_j^t))\right) = \alpha \|g(x_i^s) - g(x_j^t)\|^2 + \lambda_t L\left(y_i^s, f(g(x_j^t))\right)$, and α and λ_t are the parameters controlling the tradeoff between the two terms, as in Eq. (3). Similarly to JDOT, the first term in the loss compares the compatibility of the embeddings for the source and target domain, while the second term considers the classifier f learned in the target domain and its regularity with respect to the labels available in the source. Despite similarities with the formulation of JDOT [5], our proposition comes with the notable difference that, in DeepJDOT, the Wasserstein distance is minimized between the joint (embedded space/label) distributions within the CNN, rather than between the original input spaces. As the deeper layers of a CNN encode both spatial and semantic information, we believe them to be more apt to describe the image content for both domains, rather than the original features that are affected by a number of factors such as illumination, pose or relative position of objects.

One can note that the formulation reported in Eq. (5) only depends on the classifier learned in the target domain. By doing so, one puts the emphasis on learning a good classifier for the target domain, and disregards the performance of the classifier when considering source samples. In recent literature, such a degradation in the source domain has been named as '*catastrophic forgetting*' [33, 34]. To avoid such forgetting, one can easily re-incorporate the loss on the source domain in (5), leading to the final DeepJDOT objective:

$$\min_{\gamma, f, g} \frac{1}{n^s} \sum_i L_s\left(y_i^s, f(g(x_i^s))\right) + \sum_{i,j} \gamma_{ij} \left(\alpha \|g(x_i^s) - g(x_j^t)\|^2 + \lambda_t L_t\left(y_i^s, f(g(x_j^t))\right)\right). \tag{6}$$

This last formulation is the optimization problem solved by DeepJDOT. However, for large sample sizes the constraint of computing a full γ yields a computationally infeasible problem, both in terms of memory and time complexity. In the next section, we propose an approximation method based on stochastic optimization.

4.2   Solving the Optimization Problem with Stochastic Gradients

In this section, we describe the approximate optimization procedure for solving DeepJDOT. Eq. (6) involves two groups of variables to be optimized: the OT matrix γ and the models f and g. This suggest the use of an alternative minimization approach (as proposed in the original JDOT). Indeed, when $\hat{g}$ and $\hat{f}$

are fixed, solving Eq. (6) boils down to a standard OT problem with associated cost matrix $C_{ij} = \alpha\|\hat{g}(x_i^s) - \hat{g}(x_j^t)\|^2 + \lambda_t L_t\left(y_i^s, \hat{f}(\hat{g}(x_j^t))\right)$. When fixing $\hat{\gamma}$, optimizing g and f is a classical deep learning problem. However, computing the optimal coupling with the classical OT solvers is not scalable to large-scale datasets. Despite some recent development for large scale OT with general ground loss [31,32], the model does not scale sufficiently to meet requirements of recent computer vision tasks.

Therefore, in this work we propose to solve the problem with a stochastic approximation using minibatches from both the source and target domains [35]. This approach has two major advantages: it is scalable to large datasets and can be easily integrated in modern deep learning frameworks. More specifically, the objective function (6) is approximated by sampling a mini-batch of size m, leading to the following optimization problem:

$$\min_{f,g} \mathbb{E}\left[\frac{1}{m}\sum_{i=1}^{m} L_s\left(y_i^s, f(g(x_i^s))\right) + \min_{\gamma \in \Delta}\sum_{i,j}^{m} \gamma_{ij}\left(\alpha\|g(x_i^s) - g(x_j^t)\|^2 + \lambda_t L_t\left(y_i^s, f(g(x_j^t))\right)\right)\right] \quad (7)$$

where $\mathbb{E}$ is the expected value with respect to the randomly sampled minibatches drawn from both source and target domains. The classification loss functions for the source (L_s) and target (L_t) domains can be any general class of loss functions that are twice differentiable. We opted for a traditional cross-entropy loss in both cases. Note that, as discussed in [35], the expected value over the minibtaches does not converge to the true OT coupling between every pair of samples, which might then lead to the appearance of connections between samples that would not have been connected in the full coupling. However, this can also be seen as a regularization that will promote sharing of the mass between neighboring samples. Finally note that we did not use the regularized version of OT as in [35], since it introduces an additional regularization parameter that should be cross-validated, which can make the model calibration even more complex. Still, the extension of DeepJDOT to regularized OT is straightforward and could be beneficial for high-dimensional embeddings g.

Consequently, we propose to obtain the stochastic update for Eq. (7) as follows (and summarized in Algorithm 4):

1. With fixed CNN parameters $(\hat{g}, \hat{f})$ and for every randomly drawn minibatch (of m samples), obtain the coupling

$$\min_{\gamma \in \Pi(\mu_s, \mu_t)} \sum_{i,j=1}^{m} \gamma_{ij}\left(\alpha\|\hat{g}(x_i^s) - \hat{g}(x_j^t)\|^2 + \lambda_t L_t\left(y_i^s, \hat{f}(g(x_j^t))\right)\right) \quad (8)$$

using the network simplex flow algorithm.

Algorithm 1. DeepJDOT stochastic optimization

Require: $\mathbf{x}^s$: source domain samples, $\mathbf{x}^t$: target domain samples, $\mathbf{y}^s$: source domain labels

1: **for** each batch of source $(\mathbf{x_b}^s, \mathbf{y_b}^s)$ and target samples $(\mathbf{x_b}^t)$ **do**
2:      fix $\hat{g}$ and $\hat{f}$, solve for γ as in equation (8)
3:      fix $\hat{\gamma}$, and update for g and f according to equation (9)
4: **end for**

---

2. With fixed coupling $\hat{\gamma}$ obtained at the previous step, update the embedding function (g) and classifier (f) with stochastic gradient update for the following loss on the minibatch:

$$\frac{1}{m}\sum_{i=1}^{m} L_s\left(y_i^s, f(g(x_i^s))\right) + \sum_{i,j=1}^{m} \hat{\gamma}_{ij}\left(\alpha\|g(x_i^s) - g(x_j^t)\|^2 + \lambda_t L_t\left(y_i^s, f(g(x_j^t))\right)\right).$$

$$(9)$$

The domain alignment term aligns only the source and target samples with similar activation/labels and the sparse matrix $\hat{\gamma}$ will automatically perform label propagation between source and target samples. The classifier f is simultaneously learnt in both source and target domain.

5   Experiments and Results

We evaluate DeepJDOT on three adaptation tasks: digits classification (Sect. 5.1), the OfficeHome dataset (Sect. 5.2), and the Visual Domain Adaptation challenge (visDA; Sect. 5.3). For each dataset, we first present the data, then detail the implementation and finally present and discuss the results.

5.1   Digit Classification

Datasets. We consider four data sources (domains) from the digits classification field: MNIST [36], USPS [37], MNIST-M, and the Street View House Numbers (SVHN) [38] dataset. Each dataset involves a 10-class classification problem (retrieving numbers 0-9):

- *USPS.* The USPS datasets contains 7'291 training and 2'007 test grayscale images of handwritten images, each one of size 16×16 pixels.
- *MNIST.* The MNIST dataset contains 60'000 training and 10'000 testing grayscale images of size 28×28.
- *MNIST M.* We generated the MNIST-M images by following the protocol in [8]. MNIST-M is a variation on MNIST, where the (black) background is replaced by random patches extracted from the Berkeley Segmentation Data Set (BSDS500) [39]. The number of training and testing samples are the same as the MNIST dataset discussed above.

- *SVHN.* The SVHN dataset contains house numbers extracted from Google Street View images. We used the *Format2* version of SVHN, where the images are cropped into 32 × 32 pixels. Multiple digits can appear in a single image, the objective is to detect the digit in the center of the image. This dataset contains 73'212 training images, and 26'032 testing images of size 32× 32×3. The respective examples of the each dataset is shown in Fig. 2.

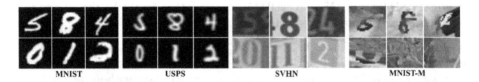

Fig. 2. Examples from the MNIST, USPS, SVHN and MNIST-M datasets.

The three following experiments were run (the arrow direction corresponds to the sense of the domain adaptation):

- *USPS↔MNIST.* The USPS images are zero-padded to reach the same size as MNIST dataset. The adaptation is considered in both directions: USPS → MNIST, and MNIST → USPS.
- *SVHN→MNIST.* The single-channel MNIST images are replicated three times to form a gray 3 channels image, and resized to match the resolution of the SVHN images. Here, the adaptation is considered in only one direction: SVHN→MNIST. Adapting SVHN images to MNIST is challenging due to the variations in the SVHN images [8]
- *MNIST→MNIST-M.* MNIST is considered as the source domain and MNIST-M as the target domain. The color MNIST-M images can be easily identified by a human, however it is challenging for the CNN trained on MNIST, which is only grayscale. Again, the gray scale MNIST images are replicated three times to match the color resolution of the MNIST-M images.

Model. For all digits adaptation experiments, our embedding function g is trained from scratch with six 3 × 3 convolutional layers containing 32, 32, 64, 64, 128 and 128 filters, and one fully-connected layer of 128 hidden units followed by a sigmoid nonlinearity respectively. Classifier f then consists of a fully-connected layer, followed by a softmax to provide the class scores. The Adam optimizer ($lr = 2e-4$) is used to update our model using mini-batch sizes of $m_S = m_T = 500$ for the two domains (50 samples per class in the source mini-batch). The hyper-parameters of DeepJDOT, $\alpha = 0.001$ and $\lambda_t = 0.0001$, are fixed experimentally.

We compare DeepJDOT with the following methods:

- non-adversarial discrepancy methods: DeepCORAL [6], MMD [14], DRCN [40], DSN [41], AssocDA [16], Self-ensemble [42][1],
- adversarial discrepancy methods: DANN [8], ADDA [21],
- adversarial image generation methods: CoGAN [9], UNIT [18], GenToAdapt [19] and I2I Adapt [20].

To ensure fair comparison, we re-implemented the most relevant competitors (CORAL, MMD, DANN, and ADDA). For the other methods, the results are directly reported from the respective articles.

Results. The performance of DeepJDOT on the four digits adaptation tasks is reported in Table 1. The first row (`source only`) shows the accuracies on target test data achieved with classifiers trained on source data without adaptation, and the row (`target only`) reports accuracies on the target test data achieved with classifiers trained on the target training data. This method is considered as an upper bound for our proposed method and can be seen as our gold standard. `StochJDOT` (stochastic adaptation of JDOT) refers to the accuracy of our proposed method, when the discrepancy between source and target domain is computed with an ℓ_2 distance in the original image space. Lastly, `DeepJDOT-source` indicates the source data accuracy, after adapting to the target domain, and can be considered a measure of catastrophic forgetting.

The experimental results show that DeepJDOT achieves accuracies comparable or higher to the current state-of-the-art methods. When the methods in the first block of Table 1 are considered, `DeepJDOT` outperforms the competitors by large margins, with the exception of `DANN` that have similar performance on the MNIST→USPS task. In the more challenging adaptation settings (SVHN→MNIST and MNIST→MNIST-M), the state-of-the-art methods[2] were not able to adapt well to the target domain. Next, when the methods in the second block of Table 1 is considered, our method showed impressive performance, despite `DeepJDOT` not using any complex procedure for generating target images to perform the adaptation.

t-**SNE Embeddings.** We visualize the quality of the embeddings for the source and target domain learnt by `DeepJDOT`, `StochJDOT` and `DANN` using *t*-SNE embedding on the MNIST→MNIST-M adaptation task (Fig. 3). As expected, in the source model the samples from the source domain are well clustered and target samples are more scattered. The *t*-SNE embeddings with the `DANN` were not able to align the distributions well, and this observation also holds for `StochJDOT`. It is noted that `StochJDOT` does not align the distributions, but learns the classifier in target domain directly. The poor embeddings of the target samples with

---

[1] we report a comparison against [42] by using minimal data augmentation (corresponding to MT+CT* in Table 1 of [42]). We do not compare against their full model, as they use a much heavier data augmentation and different networks.

[2] For `ADDA`[21] in the SVHN→MNIST adaptation task the accuracy is reported from the paper, as we were not able to further improve the source only accuracy.

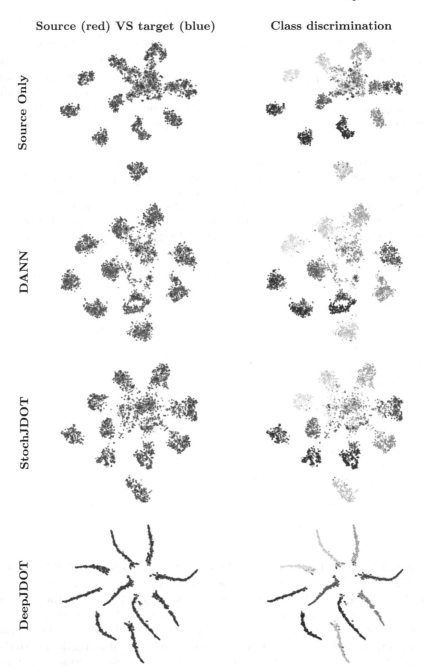

Fig. 3. t-SNE embeddings of 2'000 test samples for MNIST (source) and MNIST-M (target) for Source only classifier, DANN, StochJDOT and DeepJDOT. The left column shows domain comparisons, where colors represent the domain. The right column shows the ability of the methods to discriminate classes (samples are colored w.r.t. their classes).

StochJDOT shows the necessity of computing the ground metric (cost function) of optimal transport in the deep CNN layers. Finally, DeepJDOT perfectly aligns the source domain samples and target domain samples to each other, which explains the good numerical performances reported above. The "tentacle"-shaped and near-perfect separation of the classes in the embedding illustrate the fact that DeepJDOT finds an embedding that both aligns the source/target distribution, but also maximizes the margin between the classes.

Table 1. Classification accuracy on the target test datasets for the digit classification tasks. *Source only* and *target only* refer to training on the respective datasets without domain adaptation and evaluating on the target test dataset. The accuracies reported in the first block are our own implementations, while the second block reports performances from the respective articles. **Bold** and *italic* indicates the best and second best results. The last line reports the performance of DeepJDOT on the source domain.

Method	Adaptation:source→target			
	MNIST → USPS	USPS → MNIST	SVHN → MNIST	MNIST → MNIST-M
Source only	94.8	59.6	60.7	60.8
DeepCORAL [6]	89.33	91.5	59.6	66.5
MMD [14]	88.5	73.5	64.8	72.5
DANN [8]	*95.7*	90.0	70.8	75.4
ADDA [21]	92.4	93.8	76.0[b]	78.8
AssocDA [16]	-	-	*95.7*	*89.5*
Self-ensemble[a] [42]	88.14	92.35	93.33	-
DRCN [40]	91.8	73.6	81.9	-
DSN [41]	91.3	-	82.7	83.2
CoGAN [9]	91.2	89.1	-	-
UNIT [18]	**95.9**	*93.5*	90.5	-
GenToAdapt [19]	95.3	90.8	92.4	-
I2I Adapt [20]	92.1	87.3	80.3	-
StochJDOT	93.6	90.5	67.6	66.7
DeepJDOT (ours)	*95.7*	**96.4**	**96.7**	**92.4**
target only	95.8	98.7	98.7	96.8
DeepJDOT-source	98.5	94.9	75.7	97.8

[a] See footnote 1
[b] See footnote 2.

Ablation Study. Table 2 reports the results obtained in the USPS→MNIST and MNIST→ MNIST-M cases for models using only parts of our proposed loss (Eq. (6)). When only the JDOT loss is considered ($\alpha d + L_t$ case), the accuracy drops in both adaptation cases. This behavior might be due to overfitting of the target classifier to the noisy pseudo- (propagated) labels. However, the performance is comparable to non-adversarial discrepancy-based methods reported in Table 1. On the contrary, when only the feature space distribution is included in Eq. (6), i.e. the $L_s + \alpha d$ experiment, the accuracy is close to our full model in USPS→MNIST direction, but drops in the MNIST→ MNIST-M one. Overall the accuracies are improved compared to the original JDOT model, which highlights the importance of including the information from the source domain. Moreover, this also highlights the importance of simultaneously updating the classifier both in the source and target domain. Summarizing, this ablation study showed that the individual components bring complimentary information to achieve the best classification results.

Table 2. Ablation study of DeepJDOT.

Method	USPS → MNIST	MNIST → MNIST-M
$L_s + (\alpha d + L_t)$	96.4	92.4
$\alpha d + L_t$	86.41	73.6
$L_s + \alpha d$	95.53	82.3

5.2   Office-Home

Dataset. The Office-Home dataset [43] contains around 15'500 images in 65 categories from four different domains: artistic paintings, clipart, product and real-world images.

Model. In this case, we use a pre-trained VGG-16 model [44] with the last layer replaced, but perform no data augmentation. We use 3'250 samples per domain to compute the optimal couplings. We compared our model with following state-of-the-art methods: CORAL [45], JDA [46], DAN [47], DANN [8], and DAH [43].

Results. Table 3 lists the performance of DeepJDOT compared to a series of other adaptation methods. As can be seen, DeepJDOT outperforms all other models by a margin on all tasks, except for the adaptation from domain "product" to "clipart".

5.3   VisDA-2017

Dataset. The Visual Domain Adaptation classification challenge of 2017 (VisDA-2017; [48]) requires training a model on renderings of 3D models for each of the 12 classes and adapting to natural images sampled from MS-COCO [49] (validation set) and YouTube BoundingBoxes [50] (test set), respectively. The test set performances reported here were evaluated on the official server.

Model. Due to VisDA's strong adaptation complexity, we employ ResNet-50 [51] as a base model, replacing the last layer with two MLPs that map to 512 hidden an then to the 12 classes, respectively. We train a model on the source domain and then freeze it to calculate source feature vectors, adapting an intially identical copy to the target set. We use 4'096 samples per domain to calculate the couplings. Data augmentation follows the scheme of [42].

Results. DeepJDOT's performance on VisDA-2017 is reported in Table 4 along with the baselines (DeepCORAL, DAN) from the evaluation server[3] . Our entry

---

[3] https://competitions.codalab.org/competitions/17052#results.

Table 3. Performance of DeepJDOT on the Office-Home dataset. "Ar" = artistic paintings, "Cl" = clipart, "Pr" = product, "Rw" = real-world images. Performance figures of competitive methods are reported from [43].

Method	Ar→Cl	Ar→Pr	Ar→Rw	Cl→Ar	Cl→Pr	Cl→Rw	Pr→Ar	Pr→Cl	Pr→Rw	Rw→Ar	Rw→Cl	Rw→Pr	Mean
CORAL[45]	27.10	36.16	44.32	26.08	40.03	40.33	27.77	30.54	50.61	38.48	36.36	57.11	37.91
JDA [46]	25.34	35.98	42.94	24.52	40.19	40.90	25.96	32.72	49.25	35.10	35.35	55.35	36.97
DAN [47]	30.66	42.17	54.13	32.83	47.59	49.58	29.07	34.05	56.70	43.58	38.25	62.73	43.46
DANN [8]	33.33	42.96	54.42	32.26	49.13	49.76	30.44	38.14	56.76	44.71	42.66	64.65	44.94
DAH [43]	31.64	40.75	51.73	34.69	51.93	52.79	29.91	**39.63**	60.71	44.99	45.13	62.54	45.54
DeepJDOT	**39.73**	**50.41**	**62.49**	**39.52**	**54.35**	**53.15**	**36.72**	39.24	**63.55**	**52.29**	**45.43**	**70.45**	**50.67**

in the evaluation server is mentioned as `oatmil`. We can see that our method achieved better accuracy than the distribution matching methods (DeepCORAL [6], DAN [47]) with all the classes, expect `knife`. We observe a negative transfer for the class `car` for DeepJDOT, however this phenomena is also valid with the most of the current methods (see the evaluation server results). For a fair comparison with the rest of the methods in the evaluation server, we also showed (values in bracket of Table 4) the accuracy difference between the source model and target model. Our method is ranked sixth when the mean accuracy is considered, and third when the difference between the source model and target model is considered at the time of publication. It is noted that the performance of our method depends on the capacity of the source model: if a larger CNN is used, the performance of our method could be improved further.

Table 4. Performance of DeepJDOT on the VisDA 2017 classification challenge. The scores in the bracket indicate the accuracy difference between the source (unadapted) model and target (adapted) model. The respective values of CORAL and DAN are reported from the evaluation server (See footnote 3).

Method	plane	bcycl	bus	car	horse	knife	mcycl	person	plant	sktbd	train	truck	Mean
Source only	36.0	4.0	19.9	**94.7**	14.8	0.42	38.7	3.8	37.4	8.1	71.9	6.7	28.0
DeepCORAL [6]	62.5	21.7	66.3	64.6	31.1	36.7	54.2	24.9	73.8	29.9	43.4	34.2	45.3 (19.0)
DAN [47]	55.3	18.4	59.8	68.6	55.3	**41.4**	63.4	30.4	78.8	23.0	62.9	40.2	49.8 (19.5)
DeepJDOT	**85.4**	**50.4**	**77.3**	87.3	**69.1**	14.1	**91.5**	**53.3**	**91.9**	**31.2**	**88.5**	**61.8**	**66.9 (38.9)**

6   Conclusions

In this paper, we proposed the DeepJDOT model for unsupervised deep domain adaptation based on optimal transport. The proposed method aims at learning a common latent space for the source and target distributions, that conveys discriminant information for both domains. This is achieved by minimizing the discrepancy of joint deep feature/labels domain distributions by means of optimal transport. We propose an efficient stochastic algorithm that solves this problem, and despite being simple and easily integrable into modern deep learning frameworks, our method outperformed the state-of-the-art on cross domain digits and office-home adaptation, and provided satisfactory results on the VisDA-2017 adaptation.

Future works will consider the evaluation of this method in multi-domains scenario, as well as more complicated cost functions taking into account similarities of the representations across the embedding layers and/or similarities of labels across different classifiers.

Acknowledgement. This work benefited from the support of Region Bretagne grant and OATMIL ANR-17-CE23-0012 project of the French National Research Agency (ANR). The constructive comments and suggestions of anonymous reviewers are gratefully acknowledged.

References

1. Patel, V.M., Gopalan, R., Li, R., Chellappa, R.: Visual domain adaptation: a survey of recent advances. IEEE SPM **32**(3), 53–69 (2015)
2. Saenko, K., Kulis, B., Fritz, M., Darrell, T.: Adapting visual category models to new domains. In: Daniilidis, K., Maragos, P., Paragios, N. (eds.) ECCV 2010. LNCS, vol. 6314, pp. 213–226. Springer, Heidelberg (2010). https://doi.org/10.1007/978-3-642-15561-1_16
3. Gopalan, R., Li, R., Chellappa, R.: Domain adaptation for object recognition: an unsupervised approach. In: ICCV, pp. 999–1006 (2011)
4. Courty, N., Flamary, R., Tuia, D., Rakotomamonjy, A.: Optimal transport for domain adaptation. IEEE TPAMI **39**(9), 1853–1865 (2017)
5. Courty, N., Flamary, R., Habrard, A., Rakotomamonjy, A.: Joint distribution optimal transportation for domain adaptation. In: NIPS (2017)
6. Sun, B., Saenko, K.: Deep CORAL: correlation alignment for deep domain adaptation. In: Hua, G., Jégou, H. (eds.) ECCV 2016. LNCS, vol. 9915, pp. 443–450. Springer, Cham (2016). https://doi.org/10.1007/978-3-319-49409-8_35
7. Luo, Z., Zou, Y., Hoffman, J., Fei-Fei, L.: Label efficient learning of transferable representations across domains and tasks. In: NIPS (2017)
8. Ganin, Y., et al.: Domain-adversarial training of neural networks. J. Mach. Learn. Res. **17**(1), 2030–2096 (2016)
9. Liu, M.Y., Tuzel, O.: Coupled generative adversarial networks. In: Lee, D.D., Sugiyama, M., Luxburg, U.V., Guyon, I., Garnett, R. (eds.) NIPS, pp. 469–477 (2016)
10. Ben-David, S., Blitzer, J., Crammer, K., Pereira, F.: Analysis of representations for domain adaptation. In: NIPS, pp. 137–144 (2007)
11. Jhuo, I.H., Liu, D., Lee, D.T., Chang, S.F.: Robust visual domain adaptation with low-rank reconstruction. In: CVPR, pp. 2168–2175 (2012)
12. Hoffman, J., Rodner, E., Donahue, J., Saenko, K., Darrell, T.: Efficient learning of domain-invariant image representations. In: ICLR (2013)
13. Aljundi, R., Tuytelaars, T.: Lightweight unsupervised domain adaptation by convolutional filter reconstruction. In: Hua, G., Jégou, H. (eds.) ECCV 2016. LNCS, vol. 9915, pp. 508–515. Springer, Cham (2016). https://doi.org/10.1007/978-3-319-49409-8_43
14. Long, M., Cao, Y., Wang, J., Jordan, M.I.: Learning transferable features with deep adaptation networks. In: ICML, pp. 97–105 (2015)
15. Long, M., Wang, J., Jordan, M.I.: Unsupervised domain adaptation with residual transfer networks. In: NIPS (2016)

16. Haeusser, P., Frerix, T., Mordvintsev, A., Cremers, D.: Associative domain adaptation. In: ICCV (2017)
17. Tzeng, E., Hoffman, J., Darrell, T., Saenko, K.: Simultaneous deep transfer across domains and tasks. In: ICCV (2015)
18. Liu, M.Y., Breuel, T., Kautz, J.: Unsupervised image-to-image translation networks. In: Guyon, I., et al. (eds.) NIPS, pp. 700–708 (2017)
19. Sankaranarayanan, S., Balaji, Y., Castillo, C.D., Chellappa, R.: Generate to adapt: Aligning domains using generative adversarial networks. CoRR abs/1704.01705 (2017)
20. Murez, Z., Kolouri, S., Kriegman, D., Ramamoorthi, R., Kim, K.: Image to Image Translation for Domain Adaptation. ArXiv e-prints, December 2017
21. Tzeng, E., Hoffman, J., Darrell, T., Saenko, K.: Adversarial discriminative domain adaptation. In: CVPR (2017)
22. Monge, G.: Mémoire sur la théorie des déblais et des remblais. De l'Imprimerie Royale (1781)
23. Kantorovich, L.: On the translocation of masses. C.R. (Doklady) Acad. Sci. URSS (N.S.) **37**, 199–201 (1942)
24. Villani, C.: Optimal Transport: Old and New, Grundlehren der mathematischen Wissenschaften. Springer, Heidelberg (2009). https://doi.org/10.1007/978-3-540-71050-9
25. Courty, N., Flamary, R., Tuia, D.: Domain adaptation with regularized optimal transport. In: ECML (2014)
26. Perrot, M., Courty, N., Flamary, R., Habrard, A.: Mapping estimation for discrete optimal transport. In: NIPS, pp. 4197–4205 (2016)
27. Redko, I., Habrard, A., Sebban, M.: Theoretical analysis of domain adaptation with optimal transport. In: ECML/PKDD, pp. 737–753 (2017)
28. Shen., J., Qu, Y., Zhang, W., Yu, Y.: Wasserstein distance guided representation learning for domain adaptation. In: AAAI (2018)
29. Arjovsky, M., Chintala, S., Bottou, L.: Wasserstein generative adversarial networks. In: ICML, pp. 214–223 (2017)
30. Cuturi, M.: Sinkhorn distances: lightspeed computation of optimal transportation. In: NIPS, pp. 2292–2300 (2013)
31. Genevay, A., Cuturi, M., Peyré, G., Bach, F.: Stochastic optimization for large-scale optimal transport. In: NIPS, pp. 3432–3440 (2016)
32. Seguy, V., Damodaran, B.B., Flamary, R., Courty, N., Rolet, A., Blondel, M.: Large-scale optimal transport and mapping estimation. In: ICLR (2018)
33. Shmelkov, K., Schmid, C., Alahari, K.: Incremental learning of object detectors without catastrophic forgetting. In: ICCV, Venice, Italy (2017)
34. Li, Z., Hoiem, D.: Learning without forgetting. IEEE TPAMI (in press)
35. Genevay, A., Peyré, G., Cuturi, M.: Sinkhorn-autodiff: tractable wasserstein learning of generative models. arXiv preprint arXiv:1706.00292 (2017)
36. Lecun, Y., Bottou, L., Bengio, Y., Haffner, P.: Gradient-based learning applied to document recognition. Proc. IEEE **86**(11), 2278–2324 (1998)
37. Hull, J.J.: A database for handwritten text recognition research. IEEE TPAMI **16**(5), 550–554 (1994)
38. Netzer, Y., Wang, T., Coates, A., Bissacco, A., Wu, B., Ng, A.Y.: Reading digits in natural images with unsupervised feature learning. In: NIPS worksophs (2011)
39. Arbelaez, P., Maire, M., Fowlkes, C., Malik, J.: Contour detection and hierarchical image segmentation. IEEE TPAMI **33**(5), 898–916 (2011)

40. Ghifary, M., Kleijn, W.B., Zhang, M., Balduzzi, D., Li, W.: Deep reconstruction-classification networks for unsupervised domain adaptation. In: Leibe, B., Matas, J., Sebe, N., Welling, M. (eds.) ECCV 2016. LNCS, vol. 9908, pp. 597–613. Springer, Cham (2016). https://doi.org/10.1007/978-3-319-46493-0_36
41. Bousmalis, K., Trigeorgis, G., Silberman, N., Krishnan, D., Erhan, D.: Domain separation networks. In: NIPS (2016) 343–351
42. French, G., Mackiewicz, M., Fisher, M.: Self-ensembling for visual domain adaptation. In: International Conference on Learning Representations (2018)
43. Venkateswara, H., Eusebio, J., Chakraborty, S., Panchanathan, S.: Deep hashing network for unsupervised domain adaptation. In: IEEE Conference on Computer Vision and Pattern Recognition (CVPR) (2017)
44. Simonyan, K., Zisserman, A.: Very deep convolutional networks for large-scale image recognition. arXiv preprint arXiv:1409.1556 (2014)
45. Sun, B., Feng, J., Saenko, K.: Return of frustratingly easy domain adaptation. In: Proceedings of the Thirtieth AAAI Conference on Artificial Intelligence. AAAI 2016, AAAI Press, pp. 2058–2065 (2016)
46. Long, M., Wang, J., Ding, G., Sun, J., Yu, P.S.: Transfer feature learning with joint distribution adaptation. In: 2013 IEEE International Conference on Computer Vision, pp. 2200–2207, December 2013
47. Long, M., Cao, Y., Wang, J., Jordan, M.: Learning transferable features with deep adaptation networks. In: Bach, F., Blei, D., (eds.) Proceedings of the 32nd International Conference on Machine Learning, Volume 37 of Proceedings of Machine Learning Research., Lille, France, PMLR, pp. 97–105, 07–09 July 2015
48. Peng, X., Usman, B., Kaushik, N., Hoffman, J., Wang, D., Saenko, K.: Visda: the visual domain adaptation challenge (2017)
49. Lin, T.-Y., et al.: Microsoft COCO: common objects in context. In: Fleet, D., Pajdla, T., Schiele, B., Tuytelaars, T. (eds.) ECCV 2014. LNCS, vol. 8693, pp. 740–755. Springer, Cham (2014). https://doi.org/10.1007/978-3-319-10602-1_48
50. Real, E., Shlens, J., Mazzocchi, S., Pan, X., Vanhoucke, V.: Youtube-boundingboxes: a large high-precision human-annotated data set for object detection in video. In: 2017 IEEE Conference on Computer Vision and Pattern Recognition (CVPR), pp. 7464–7473. IEEE (2017)
51. He, K., Zhang, X., Ren, S., Sun, J.: Deep residual learning for image recognition. In: Proceedings of the IEEE Conference on Computer Vision and Pattern Recognition, pp. 770–778 (2016)

Two at Once: Enhancing Learning and Generalization Capacities via IBN-Net

Xingang Pan$^{1(\boxtimes)}$, Ping Luo^1, Jianping Shi^2, and Xiaoou Tang^1

^{1} CUHK-SenseTime Joint Lab, The Chinese University of Hong Kong,
Shatin, Hong Kong
{px117, pluo, xtang}@ie.cuhk.edu.hk
^{2} SenseTime Group Limited, Beijing, China
shijianping@sensetime.com

Abstract. Convolutional neural networks (CNNs) have achieved great successes in many computer vision problems. Unlike existing works that designed CNN architectures to improve performance on a single task of a single domain and not generalizable, we present IBN-Net, a novel convolutional architecture, which remarkably enhances a CNN's modeling ability on one domain (*e.g.* Cityscapes) as well as its generalization capacity on another domain (*e.g.* GTA5) without finetuning. IBN-Net carefully integrates Instance Normalization (IN) and Batch Normalization (BN) as building blocks, and can be wrapped into many advanced deep networks to improve their performances. This work has three key *contributions*. (1) By delving into IN and BN, we disclose that IN learns features that are invariant to appearance changes, such as colors, styles, and virtuality/reality, while BN is essential for preserving content related information. (2) IBN-Net can be applied to many advanced deep architectures, such as DenseNet, ResNet, ResNeXt, and SENet, and consistently improve their performance without increasing computational cost. (3) When applying the trained networks to new domains, *e.g.* from GTA5 to Cityscapes, IBN-Net achieves comparable improvements as domain adaptation methods, even without using data from the target domain. With IBN-Net, we won the 1st place on the WAD 2018 Challenge Drivable Area track, with an mIoU of 86.18%.

Keywords: Instance normalization · Invariance · Generalization
CNNs

1 Introduction

Deep convolutional neural networks (CNNs) have improved performance of many tasks in computer vision, such as image recognition [17], object detection [21],

Electronic supplementary material The online version of this chapter (https://doi.org/10.1007/978-3-030-01225-0_29) contains supplementary material, which is available to authorized users.

V. Ferrari et al. (Eds.): ECCV 2018, LNCS 11208, pp. 484–500, 2018.
https://doi.org/10.1007/978-3-030-01225-0_29

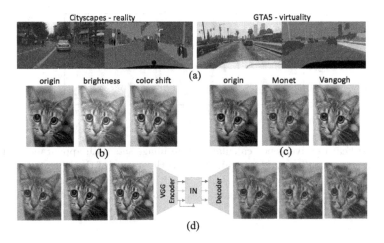

Fig. 1. (a) visualizes two example images (left) and their segmentation maps (right) selected from Cityscapes [2] and GTA5 [22] respectively. These samples have similar categories and scene configurations when comparing their segmentation maps, but their images are from different domains, *i.e.* reality and virtuality. (b) shows simple appearance variations, while those of complex appearance variations are provided in (c). (d) proves that Instance Normalization (IN) is able to filter out complex appearance variance. The style transfer network used here is AdaIN [14]. (Best viewed in color)

and semantic segmentation [1]. However, existing works mainly design network architectures to solve the above problems on a single domain, for example, improving scene parsing on the real images of Cityscape dataset [2,20]. When these networks are applied to the other domain of this scene parsing task, such as the virtual images of GTA5 dataset [22], their performance would drop notably. This is due to the appearance gap between the images of these two datasets, as shown in Fig. 1(a).

A natural solution to solve the appearance gap is by using transfer learning. For instance, by finetuning a CNN pretrained on Cityscapes using the data from GTA5, we are able to adapt the features learned from Cityscapes to GTA5, where accuracy can be increased. But even so, the appearance gap is not eliminated, because when applying the finetuned CNN back to Cityscapes, the accuracy would be significantly degraded. How to address large diversity of appearances by designing deep architectures? It is a key challenge in computer vision.

The answer is to induce appearance invariance into CNNs. This solution is obvious but non-trivial. For example, there are many ways to produce the property of spatial invariance in deep networks, such as max pooling [17], deformable convolution [3], which are invariant to spatial variations like poses, viewpoints, and scales, but are not invariant to variations of image appearances. As shown in Fig. 1(b), when the appearance variance of two datasets are simple and known beforehand, such as lightings and infrared, they can be reduced by explicitly

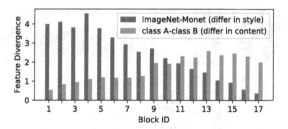

Fig. 2. (a) Feature divergence calculated from image sets with appearance difference (blue) and content difference (orange). We show the results of the 17 features after the residual blocks of ResNet50. The detailed definition of feature divergence is given in Sect. 4.3. The orange bars are enlarged 10 times for better visualization. (Color figure online)

augmenting data. However, as shown in Fig. 1(c), when appearance variance are complex and unknown, such as arbitrary image styles and virtuality, the CNNs have to learn to reduce them by introducing new component into their deep architectures.

To this end, we present IBN-Net, a novel convolutional architecture, which learns to *capture* and *eliminate* appearance variance, while *maintains* discrimination of the learned features. IBN-Net carefully integrates Instance Normalization (IN) and Batch Normalization (BN) as building blocks, enhancing both its learning and generalization capacity. It has two appealing benefits that previous deep architectures do not have.

First, different from previous CNN structures that isolate IN and BN, IBN-Net unifies them by delving into their learned features. For example, many recent advanced deep architectures employed BN as a key component to improve their learning capacity in high-level vision tasks such as image recognition [8,12,13,30], while IN was often combined with CNNs to remove variance of images on low-level vision tasks such as image style transfer [5,14,29]. But the different characteristics of their learned features and the impact of their combination have not been disclosed in existing works. In contrast, IBN-Net shows that combining them in an appropriate manner improves both learning and generalization capacities.

Second, our IBN-Net keeps IN and BN features in shallow layer and BN features in higher layer, inheriting from the statistical merit of feature divergence under different depth of a network. As shown in Fig. 2, the x-axis denotes the depth of a network and the y-axis shows feature divergence calculated via symmetric KL divergence. When analyzing the depth-vs-divergence in ImageNet original with its Monet version (blue bars), the divergence decreases as layer depth increases, manifesting the appearance difference mainly lies in shallow layers. On the contrary, compared with two disjoint ImageNet splits (orange bar), the object level difference attributes to majorly higher layer divergence and partially low layer ones. Based on these observations, we introduce IN layers to CNNs following two rules. Firstly, to reduce feature variance caused by appearance in shallow layers while not interfering the content discrimination in deep layers, we only add IN layers to the shallow half of the CNNs. Secondly, to also preserve image content information in shallow layers, we replace the original BN layers to IN for a half of features and BN for the other half. These give rise to our IBN-Net.

Our **contributions** can be summarized as follows:

(1) A novel deep structure, IBN-Net, is proposed to *improve both* learning and generalization capacities of deep networks. For example, IBN-Net50 achieves 22.54%/6.32% and 51.57%/27.15% top1/top5 errors on the original validation set of ImageNet [4] and a new validation set after style transformation respectively, outperforming ResNet50 by 1.73%/0.76% and 2.17%/2.94%, when they have similar numbers of parameters and computational cost.

(2) By delving into IN and BN, we disclose the key characteristics of their learned features, where IN provides visual and appearance *invariance*, while BN accelerates training and preserves *discriminative* features. This finding is important to understand them, and helpful to design the architecture of IBN-Net, where IN is preferred in shallow layers to remove appearance variations, whereas its strength in deep layers should be reduced in order to maintain discrimination. The component of IBN-Net can be used to re-develop many recent deep architectures, improving both their learning and generalization capacities, but keeping their computational cost unchanged. For example, by using IBN-Net, DenseNet169 [13], ResNet101 [8], ResNeXt101 [30], and SE-ResNet101 [12], outperform their original versions by 0.79%, 1.09%, 0.43%, and 0.43% on ImageNet respectively. These re-developed networks can be utilized as *strong backbones* in many tasks in future researches.

(3) IBN-Net significantly improves performance across domains. By taking scene understanding as an example under a cross-evaluation setting, *i.e.* training a CNN on Cityscapes and evaluating it on GTA5 without finetuning and vice versa, ResNet50 integrated with IBN-Net improves its counterpart by 8.5% and 7.5% respectively. It also notably reduces sample size when finetuning GTA5 pretrained model on Cityscapes. For instance, it achieves a segmentation accuracy of 65.5% when finetuning using just 30% training data from Cityscapes, compared to 63.8% of ResNet50 alone, which is finetuned using all training data.

2   Related Works

The previous work related to IBN-Net are described in three aspects, including invariance of CNNs, network architectures, and methods of domain adaptation and generalization.

Invariance in CNNs. Several modules [3,15,17,24,29] have been proposed to improve a CNN's modeling capacity, or reduce overfitting to enhance its generalization capacity on a single domain. These methods typically achieved the above purposes by introducing specific kinds of invariance into the architectures of CNNs. For example, max pooling [17] and deformable convolution [3] introduce spatial invariance to CNNs, thus increasing their robustness to spatial variations such as affine, distortion, and viewpoint transformations. And dropout [24] and batch normalization (BN) [15] can be treated as regularizers to reduce the effects of sample noise in training. When image appearances are presented, simple appearance variations such as color or brightness shift could simply be eliminated by normalizing each RGB channel of an image with its mean and standard deviation. For more complex appearance transforms such as style transformations, recent studies have found that such information could be encoded in the mean and variance of the hidden feature maps [5,14]. Therefore, the instance normalization (IN) [29] layer shows potential to eliminate such appearance differences.

CNN Architectures. Since CNNs have shown compelling modeling capacity over traditional methods, their architectures have gone through a number of developments. Among them one of the most widely used is the residual network (ResNet) [8], which uses short cut to alleviate training difficulties of very deep networks. Since then a number of variants of ResNet were proposed. Compared to ResNet, ResNeXt [30] improves modeling capacity by increasing 'cardinality' of ResNet. It is implemented by using group convolutions. In practice, increasing cardinality increases runtime in modern deep learning frameworks. Moreover, squeeze-and-excitation network (SENet) [12] introduces channel wise attention into ResNet. It achieves better performance on ImageNet compared to ResNet, but it also increases number of network parameters and computations. The recently proposed densely connected networks (DenseNet) [13] uses concatenation to replace short-cut connections. It was proved to be more efficient than ResNet.

However, there are two limitations in the above CNN architectures. Firstly, the limited basic modules prevent them from gaining more appealing properties. For example, all these architectures are simply composed of convolutions, BNs, ReLUs, and poolings. The only difference among them is how these modules are organized. However, the composition of these layers are naturally vulnerable by appearance variations. Secondly, the design goal of these models is to achieve strong modeling capacity on a single task of a single domain, while their capacities to generalize to new domains are still limited.

In the field of image style transfer, some methods employ IN to help remove image contrast [5,14,29]. Basically, this helps the models transfer images to different styles. However, the invariance property of image appearance has not been successfully introduced to aforementioned CNNs, especially in high-level tasks such as image classification or semantic segmentation. This is because IN drops useful content information presented in the hidden features, impeding modeling capacity as proved in [29].

Improve Performances Across Domains. Alleviating the drop of performances caused by appearance gap between different domains is an important problem. One natural approach is to use transfer learning such as finetuning the model on the target domain. However, this requires human annotations of the target domain, and the performances of the finetuned models would then drop when they are applied on the source domain. There are a number of domain adaptation approaches which use the statistics of the target domain to facilitate adaptation. Most of these works address the problem by reducing feature divergences between two domains through carefully designed loss functions, like maximum mean discrepancy (MMD) [18,28], correlation alignment (CORAL) [25], and adversarial loss [11,27]. Besides, [10,23] use generative adversarial networks (GAN) to transfer images between two domains to help adaptation, but required independent models for the two domains. There are two main limitations in transfer learning and domain adaptation. First, in real applications it is difficult to obtain the statistics of the target domain. It is also difficult to collect data that covers all possible scenarios in the target domain. Second, most state-of-the-art methods employ different model weights for the source and target domains in order to improve performance. But the ideal case is that one model could adapt to all domains.

Another paradigm towards this problem is domain generalization, which aims to acquire knowledge from a number of related source domains and apply it to a new target domain whose statistics is unknown during training. Existing methods typically design algorithms to learn domain agnostic representations or design models that capture common aspects from the domains, such as [6,16,19]. However, for real applications it is often hard to acquire data from a number of related source domains, and the performance highly depends on the series of source domains.

In this work, we increase the modeling capacity and generalization ability across domains by designing a new CNN architecture, IBN-Net. The benefit is that we do not require either target domain data or related source domains, unlike existing domain adaptation and generalization methods. The improvement of generalization across domains is achieved by designing architectures with built-in appearance invariance. Our method is extremely useful for the situations that the target domain data are unobtainable, where traditional domain adaptation cannot be applied. For more detailed comparison of our method with related works, please refer to our supplementary material.

3   Method

3.1   Background

Batch Normalization [15] enables larger learning rate and faster convergence by reducing the internal covariate shift during training CNNs. It uses the mean and variance of a mini-batch to normalize each feature channels during training, while in inference phase, BN uses the global statistics to normalize features. Experiments have shown that BN significantly accelerates training, and could improve the final performance meanwhile. It has become a standard component in most prevalent CNN architectures like Inception [26], ResNet [8], DenseNet [13], etc.

Unlike batch normalization, **instance normalization** [29] uses the statistics of an individual sample instead of mini-batch to normalize features. Another important difference between IN and BN is that IN applies the same normalize procedure for both training and inference. Instance normalization has been mainly used in the style transfer field [5,14,29]. The reason for IN's success in style transfer and similar tasks is that, these tasks trying to change image appearance while preserving content, and IN allows to filter out instance-specific contrast information from the content. Despite these successes, IN has not shown benefits for high-level vision tasks like image classification and semantic segmentation. Ulyanov *et al.* [29] have given primary attempt adopting IN for image classification, but got worse results than CNNs with BN.

In a word, batch normalization preserves discrimination between individual samples, but also makes CNNs vulnerable to appearance transforms. And instance normalization eliminates individual contrast, but diminishes useful information at the same time. Both methods have their limitations. In order to introduce appearance invariance to CNNs without hurting feature discrimination, here we carefully unify them in a single deep hierarchy.

3.2 Instance-Batch Normalization Networks

Our architecture design is based on an important observation: as shown in Fig. 2(a)(b), for BN based CNNs, the feature divergence caused by appearance variance mainly lies in shallow half of the CNN, while the feature discrimination for content is high in deep layers, but also exists in shallow layers. Therefore we introduce INs following two rules. Firstly, in order not to diminish the content discrimination in deep features, we do not add INs in the last part of CNNs. Secondly, in order to also preserve content information in shallow layers, we keep part of the batch normalized features.

To provide instance for discussion, we describe our method based on the classic residual networks (ResNet). ResNet mainly consists of four groups of residual blocks, with each block having the structure as shown in Fig. 3(a). Following our first rule, we only add IN to the first three groups (conv2_x-conv4_x) and leave the fourth group (conv5_x) as before. For a residual block, we apply BN for half channels and IN for the others after the first convolution layer in the residual path, as Fig. 3(b) shows. There are three reasons to do so. Firstly, as [9] pointed out, a clean identity path is essential for optimizing ResNet, so we add IN to the residual path instead of identity path. Secondly, in the residual learning function $\mathbf{y} = \mathcal{F}(\mathbf{x}, \{W_i\}) + \mathbf{x}$, the residual function $\mathcal{F}(\mathbf{x}, \{W_i\})$ is learned to align with $\mathbf{x}$ in the identity path. Therefore IN is applied to the first normalization layer instead of the last to avoid misalignment. Thirdly, the half BN half IN scheme comes from our second design rule as discussed before. This gives rise to our instance-batch normalization network (IBN-Net).

This design is a pursuit of model capacity. On one hand, INs enable the model to learn appearance invariant features so that it could better utilize the images with high appearance diversity within one dataset. On the other hand, INs are added in a moderate way so that content related information could be

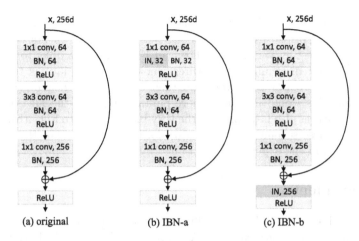

Fig. 3. Instance-batch normalization (IBN) block.

well preserved. We denote this model as IBN-Net-a. To take full use of IN's potential for generalization, in this work we also study another version, which is IBN-Net-b. Since appearance information could be either preserved in residual path or identity path, we add IN right after the addition operation, as shown in Fig. 3(c). To not deteriorate optimization for ResNet, we only add three IN layers after the first convolution layer (conv1) and the first two convolution groups (conv2_x, conv3_x).

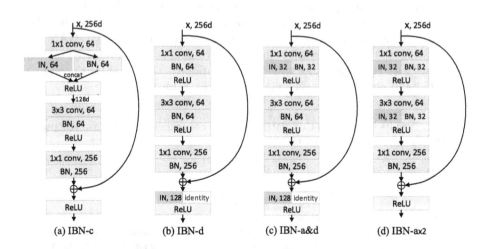

Fig. 4. Variants of IBN block.

Variants of IBN-Net. The two types of IBN-Net described above are not the only ways to utilize IN and BN in CNNs. In the experiments we will also study some interesting variants, as shown in Fig. 4. For example, to keep both generalizable and discriminative features, another natural idea is to feed the feature to both IN and BN layers and then concatenate their outputs, as in Fig. 4(a), but this would introduce more parameters. And the idea of keeping two kind of features also be applied to the IBN-b, giving rise to Fig. 4(b). We may also combine these schemes as Fig. 4(c)(d) do. Discussions about these variants would be given in the experiments section.

4   Experiments

We evaluate IBN-Net on both classification and semantic segmentation tasks on the ImageNet and Cityscapes-GTA5 dataset respectively. In both tasks, we study our models' modeling capacity within one dataset and their generalization under appearance transforms.

4.1   ImageNet Classification

We evaluate our method on the ImageNet [4] 2012 classification dataset with 1000 object classes. It has 1.28 million images for training and 50k images for validation. Data augmentation includes random scale, random aspect ratio, random crop, and random flip. We use the same training policy as in [7], and apply 224×224 center crop during testing.

Generalization to Appearance Transforms. We first evaluate the models' generalization to many kinds of appearance transforms including shift in color, brightness, contrast, and style transform, which is realized using CycleGAN [32]. The models are trained merely on ImageNet training set and evaluated on validation set with the appearance transforms mentioned. The result for the original ResNet50 and our IBN-Net versions are given in Table 1.

Table 1. Results on ImageNet validation set with appearance transforms. The performance drops are given in brackets.

Appearance transform	ResNet50 [8]	IBN-Net50-a	IBN-Net50-b
	top1/top5 err	top1/top5 err	top1/top5 err
Origin	24.27/7.08	**22.54/6.32**	23.64/6.86
RGB+50	28.22/9.64 (3.94/2.56)	25.54/8.03 (3.00/1.71)	**23.82/6.96 (0.18/0.10)**
R+50	27.53/8.78 (3.26/1.70)	25.20/7.56 (2.66/1.24)	**25.10/7.43 (1.46/0.57)**
std ×1.5	40.01/19.08 (15.74/12.00)	35.97/16.22 (13.43/9.90)	**23.64/6.86 (0.00/0.00)**
Monet	54.51/29.32 (30.24/22.24)	51.57/27.15 (29.03/20.83)	**50.45/25.22 (26.81/18.36)**

From the results we can see that IBN-Net-a achieves both better generalization and stronger capacity. When applied to images with new appearance domains, it shows less performance drop than the original ResNet. Meanwhile, its top1/top5 error on the original images is significantly improved by 1.73%/0.76%, showing that the model capacity is also improved. For IBN-Net-b, generalization is significantly enhanced, as the performance drops on new image domains are largely reduced. This shows that IN does help CNNs to generalize. Meanwhile, its performance on the original images also increases a little, showing that although IN removed discrepancy of feature mean and variance, content information could be well preserved in the spatial dimension.

Table 2. Results of IBN-Net over other CNNs on ImageNet validation set. The performance gains are shown in the brackets. More detailed descriptions of these IBN-Nets are provided in the supplementary material.

Model	Original	Re-implementation	IBN-Net-a
	top1/top5 err	top1/top5 err	top1/top5 err
DenseNet121 [13]	25.0/-	24.96/7.85	24.47/7.25 (0.49/0.60)
DenseNet169 [13]	23.6/-	24.02/7.06	23.25/6.51 (0.79/0.55)
ResNet50 [8]	24.7/7.8	24.27/7.08	22.54/6.32 (1.73/0.76)
ResNet101 [8]	23.6/7.1	22.48/6.23	21.39/5.59 (1.09/0.64)
ResNeXt101 [30]	21.2/5.6	21.31/5.74	20.88/5.42 (0.43/0.32)
SE-ResNet101 [12]	22.38/6.07	21.68/5.88	21.25/5.51 (0.43/0.37)

Table 3. Results of IBN-Net variants on ImageNet validation set and Monet style set.

Model	Origin	Monet
	top1/top5 err	top1/top5 err
ResNet50	24.26/7.08	54.51/29.32 (30.24/22.24)
IBN-Net50-a	**22.54/6.32**	51.57/27.15 (29.03/20.83)
IBN-Net50-b	23.64/6.86	**50.45/25.22 (26.81/18.36)**
IBN-Net50-c	22.78/**6.32**	51.83/27.09 (29.05/20.77)
IBN-Net50-d	22.86/6.48	50.80/26.16 (27.94/19.68)
IBN-Net50-a& d	22.89/6.48	51.27/26.64 (28.38/20.16)
IBN-Net50-a×2	22.81/6.46	51.95/26.98 (29.14/20.52)

Model Capacity. To demonstrate the stronger model capacity of IBN-Net over traditional CNNs, we compare its performance with a number of recently prevalent CNN architectures on the ImageNet validation set. As Table 2 shows, IBN-Net achieves consistent improvement over these CNNs, indicating stronger model

Table 4. Comparison of IBN-Net50-a with IN layers added to different amount of residual groups.

Residual groups	none	1	1-2	1-3	1-4
top1 err		24.27	23.58	22.94	**22.54**	22.96
top5 err		7.08	6.72	6.40	**6.32**	6.49

Table 5. Effects of the ratio of IN channels in the IBN layers. 'full' denotes ResNet50 with all BN layers replaced by IN.

IN ratio	0	0.25	0.5	0.75	1	full
top1 err	24.27	**22.49**	22.54	23.11	23.44	28.56
top5 err	7.08	6.39	**6.32**	6.57	6.94	9.83

capacity. Specifically, IBN-ResNet101 gives comparable or higher accuracy than ResNeXt101 and SE-ResNet101, which either requires more time consumption or introduces additional parameters. Note that our method brings no additional parameters while only add marginal calculations during inference phase. Our results show that, dropping out some mean and variance statistics in features helps the model to learn from images with high appearance diversity.

IBN-Net Variants. We further study some other variants of IBN-Net. Table 3 shows results for IBN-Net variants described in the method section. All our IBN-Net variants show better performance than the original ResNet50 and less performance drop under appearance transform. Specifically, IBN-Net-c achieves similar performance as IBN-Net-a, providing an alternative feature combining approach. The modeling and generalization capacity of IBN-Net-d lies in between IBN-Net a and b, which demonstrates that preserving some BN features help improve performance, but loses generalization meanwhile. The combination of IBN-Net a and d makes little difference with d, showing that the effects of INs on the main path of ResNet would dominate, eliminating the effects of those on the residual path. Finally, adding additional IBN layers to IBN-Net-a brings no good, a moderate amount of IN features would suffice.

On the Amount of IN and BN. Here we study IBN-Nets with different amount of IN layers added. Table 4 gives performance of IBN-Net50-a with IN layers added to different amount of residual groups. It can be seen that the performance is improved with more IN layers added to shallow layers, but decreased when IN layers are added to the last residual group. This indicates that IN in shallow layers help to improve modelling capacity, while in deep layers BN should be kept to preserve important content information. Furthermore, we study the effects of IN-BN ratio on the performance, as shown in Table 5. Again, the best performance is achieved at a moderate ratio 0.25–0.5, demonstrating the trade-off relationship between IN and BN.

4.2 Cross Domain Experiments

If models trained with synthetic data could be applied to the real world, it would save much effort for data collection and labelling. In this section we study our model's capacity to generalize across real and synthetic domains on Cityscapes and GTA5 datasets.

Cityscapes [2] is a traffic scene dataset collect from a number of European cities. It contains high resolution 2048×1024 images with pixel level annotations of 34 categories. The dataset is divided into 2975 for training, 500 for validation, and 1525 for testing.

GTA5 [22] is a similar street view dataset generated semi-automatically from the realistic computer game Grand Theft Auto V (GTA5). It has 12403 training images, 6382 validation images, and 6181 testing images of resolution 1914×1052 and the labels have the same categories as in Cityscapes.

Implementation. During training, we use random scale, aspect ratio and mirror for data augmentation. We apply random crop on full resolution images for Cityscapes and 1024×563 resized images for GTA5, because this leads to better performance for both datasets. We use the "poly" learning rate policy with base learning rate set to 0.01 and power set to 0.9. We train the models for 80 epochs. Batch size, momentum and weight decay are set to 16, 0.9, and 0.0001 respectively. When training on GTA5, we use a quarter of the train data so that the data scale matches that of Cityscapes.

As in [1], we use ResNet50 with atrous convolution strategy as our baseline, and our IBN-Net follows the same modification. We train the models on each dataset and evaluate on both, the results are given in Table 6.

Table 6. Results on Cityscapes-GTA dataset. Mean IoU for both within domain evaluation and cross domain evaluation is reported.

Train	Test	Model	mIoU(%)	Pixel Acc.(%)
Cityscapes	Cityscapes	ResNet50	64.5	93.4
		IBN-Net50-a	**69.1**	**94.4**
		IBN-Net50-b	67.0	94.3
	GTA5	ResNet50	29.4	71.9
		IBN-Net50-a	32.5	71.4
		IBN-Net50-b	**37.9**	**78.8**
GTA5	GTA5	ResNet50	61.0	91.5
		IBN-Net50-a	**64.8**	**92.5**
		IBN-Net50-b	64.2	92.4
	Cityscapes	ResNet50	22.2	53.5
		IBN-Net50-a	26.0	60.9
		IBN-Net50-b	**29.6**	**66.8**

Table 7. Comparison with domain adaptation methods. Note that our method does not use target data to help adaptation.

Method	mIoU	mIoU gain	Target data
Source only [11]	21.2	5.9	w/
FCN wild [11]	27.1		
Source only [31]	22.3	6.6	w/
Curr. DA [31]	28.9		
Source only [23]	29.6	**7.5**	w/
GAN DA [23]	37.1		
Ours - Source only	22.17	**7.5**	**w/o**
Ours - IBN - Source only	29.64		

Table 8. Finetune with different data percent.

Data for finetune (%)	10	20	30	100
ResNet50		52.7	54.2	58.7	63.84
IBN-Net50-a		56.5	60.5	65.5	68.78

Results. Our results are consistent with those on the ImageNet dataset. IBN-Net shows both stronger modeling capacity within one dataset and better generalization across datasets of different domains. Specifically, IBN-Net-a shows stronger model capacity, outperforming ResNet50 by 4.6% and 3.8% on the two datasets. And IBN-Net-b's generalization is better, as the cross evaluation performance is increased by 8.5% from Cityscapes to GTA5 and 7.5% for the opposite direction.

Comparison with Domain Adaptation Methods. It should be mentioned that our method is under the different setting with the domain adaptation works. Domain adaptation is target domain oriented and requires target domain data during training, while our method does not. Despite so, we show that the performance gain of our method is comparable with those of domain adaptation methods, as Table 7 shows. Our approach takes an important step towards more generalizable models since we introduce built-in appearance invariance to the model instead of forcing it to fit into a specific data domain.

Finetune on Cityscapes. Another commonly used approach to apply a model on new data domain is to finetune it with a small amount of target domain annotations. Here we show that with our more generalizable model, the data required for finetuning could be significantly reduced. We finetune the models pretrained on the GTA5 dataset with different amount of Cityscapes data and labels. The initial learning rate and the number of epochs is set to 0.003 and 80 respectively. As Table 8 shows, with only 30% of Cityscapes training data, IBN-Net50-a outperforms resnet50 finetuned on all the data.

4.3   Feature Divergence Analysis

In order to understand how IBN-Net achieves better generalization, we analyse the feature divergence caused by domain bias in this section. Our metric for feature divergence is as follows. For the output feature of a certain layer in a CNN, we denote the mean value of a channel as F, which basically describes how much this channel is activated. We assume a Gaussian distribution of F, with mean μ and variance σ^2. Then the symmetric KL divergence of this channel between domain A and B would be:

$$D(F_A\|F_B) = KL(F_A\|F_B) + KL(F_B\|F_A) \tag{1}$$

$$KL(F_A\|F_B) = log\frac{\sigma_A}{\sigma_B} + \frac{\sigma_A^2 + (\mu_A - \mu_B)^2}{2\mu_B^2} - \frac{1}{2} \tag{2}$$

Denote $D(F_{iA}\|F_{iB})$ as the symmetric KL divergence of the ith channel, then the average feature divergence of the layer would be:

$$D(L_A\|L_B) = \frac{1}{C}\sum_{i=1}^{C} D(F_{iA}\|F_{iB}) \tag{3}$$

where C is the number of channels in this layer. This metric provides a measurement of the distance between feature distribution for domain A and that for domain B.

To capture the effects of instance normalization on appearance information and content information, here we consider three groups of domains. The first two groups are "Cityscapes-GTA5" and "photo-Monet", which differs in complex appearance. To build two domains with different contents, we split the ImageNet-1k validation set into two parts, with the first part containing images with 500 object categories and the second part containing those with the other 500 categories. Then we calculate the feature divergence of the 17 ReLU layers on the main path of ResNet50 and IBN-Net50. The results are shown in Fig. 5.

It can be seen from Fig. 5(a)(b) that in our IBN-Net, the feature divergence caused by appearance difference is significantly reduced. For IBN-Net-a the divergence decreases moderately while for IBN-Net-b it encounters sudden drop after IN layer at position 2,4,8. And this effect lasts till deep layers where IN is not added, which implies that the variance encoding appearance is reduced in deep features, so that their interference with classification is reduced. On the other hand, the feature divergence caused by content difference does not drop in IBN-Net, as Fig. 5(c) shows, showing that the content information in features are well preserved in BN layers.

Discussions. These results give us an intuition of how IBN-Net gains stronger generalization. By introducing IN layers to CNNs in a clever and moderate way, they could work in a manner that helps to filter out the appearance variance within features. In this way the models' robustness to appearance transforms is improved, as shown in our experiments.

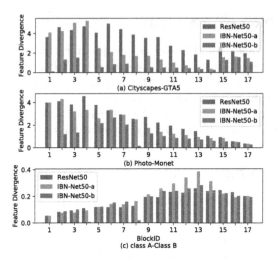

Fig. 5. Feature divergence caused by (a) real-virtual appearance gap, (b) style gap, (c) object class difference.

Note that generalization and modelling capacity are not uncorrelated properties. On one hand, intuitively appearance invariance could also help the model to better adapt to the training data of high appearance diversity and extract their common aspects. On the other hand, even within one dataset, appearance gap exists between the training and testing set, in which case stronger generalization would also improve performance. These could be the reasons for the stronger modelling capacity of IBN-Net.

5   Conclusions

In this work we propose IBN-Net, which carefully unifies instance normalization and batch normalization layers in a single deep network to increase both modeling and generalization capacity. We show that IBN-Net achieves consistent improvement over a number of classic CNNs including VGG, ResNet, ResNeXt, and SENet on ImageNet dataset. Moreover, the built-in appearance invariance introduced by IN helps our model to generalize across image domains even without the use of target domain data. Our work concludes the role of IN and BN layers in CNNs: IN introduces appearance invariance and improves generalization while BN preserves content information in discriminative features.

Acknowledgement. This work is partially supported by SenseTime Group Limited, the Hong Kong Innovation and Technology Support Programme, and the National Natural Science Foundation of China (61503366).

References

1. Chen, L., Papandreou, G., Kokkinos, I., Murphy, K., Yuille, A.: Deeplab: Semantic image segmentation with deep convolutional nets, atrous convolution, and fully connected CRFS. In: TPAMI (2017)
2. Cordts, M., et al.: The cityscapes dataset for semantic urban scene understanding. In: CVPR (2016)
3. Dai, J., et al.: Deformable convolutional networks. In: ICCV (2017)
4. Deng, J., Dong, W., Socher, R., Li, L.J., Li, K., Fei-Fei, L.: Imagenet: a large-scale hierarchical image database. In: CVPR (2009)
5. Dumoulin, V., Shlens, J., Kudlur, M.: A learned representation for artistic style. In: ICLR (2017)
6. Ghifary, M., Bastiaan Kleijn, W., Zhang, M., Balduzzi, D.: Domain generalization for object recognition with multi-task autoencoders. In: ICCV (2015)
7. Gross, S., Wilber, M.: Training and investigating residual nets (2016). https://github.com/facebook/fb.resnet.torch
8. He, K., Zhang, X., Ren, S., Sun, J.: Deep residual learning for image recognition. In: CVPR (2016)
9. He, K., Zhang, X., Ren, S., Sun, J.: Identity mappings in deep residual networks. In: Leibe, B., Matas, J., Sebe, N., Welling, M. (eds.) ECCV 2016. LNCS, vol. 9908, pp. 630–645. Springer, Cham (2016). https://doi.org/10.1007/978-3-319-46493-0_38
10. Hoffman, J., et al.: Cycada: cycle-consistent adversarial domain adaptation. arXiv preprint arXiv:1711.03213 (2017)
11. Hoffman, J., Wang, D., Yu, F., Darrell, T.: Fcns in the wild: pixel-level adversarial and constraint-based adaptation. arXiv preprint arXiv:1612.02649 (2016)
12. Hu, J., Shen, L., Sun, G.: Squeeze-and-excitation networks. arXiv preprint arXiv:1709.01507 (2017)
13. Huang, G., Liu, Z., Weinberger, K.Q., van der Maaten, L.: Densely connected convolutional networks. In: CVPR (2017)
14. Huang, X., Belongie, S.: Arbitrary style transfer in real-time with adaptive instance normalization. In: ICCV (2017)
15. Ioffe, S., Szegedy, C.: Batch normalization: accelerating deep network training by reducing internal covariate shift. In: ICML (2015)
16. Khosla, A., Zhou, T., Malisiewicz, T., Efros, A.A., Torralba, A.: Undoing the damage of dataset bias. In: ECCV (2012)
17. Krizhevsky, A., Sutskever, I., Hinton, G.E.: Imagenet classification with deep convolutional neural networks. In: NIPS (2012)
18. Long, M., Cao, Y., Wang, J., Jordan, M.: Learning transferable features with deep adaptation networks. In: ICML (2015)
19. Muandet, K., Balduzzi, D., Schölkopf, B.: Domain generalization via invariant feature representation. In: ICML (2013)
20. Pan, X., Shi, J., Luo, P., Wang, X., Tang, X.: Spatial as deep: spatial CNN for traffic scene understanding. In: AAAI (2018)
21. Ren, S., He, K., Girshick, R., Sun, J.: Faster R-CNN: towards real-time object detection with region proposal networks. In: NIPS (2015)
22. Richter, S.R., Vineet, V., Roth, S., Koltun, V.: Playing for data: ground truth from computer games. In: Leibe, B., Matas, J., Sebe, N., Welling, M. (eds.) ECCV 2016. LNCS, vol. 9906, pp. 102–118. Springer, Cham (2016). https://doi.org/10.1007/978-3-319-46475-6_7

23. Sankaranarayanan, S., Balaji, Y., Jain, A., Lim, S.N., Chellappa, R.: Unsupervised domain adaptation for semantic segmentation with GANS. arXiv preprint arXiv:1711.06969 (2017)
24. Srivastava, N., Hinton, G., Krizhevsky, A., Sutskever, I., Salakhutdinov, R.: Dropout: a simple way to prevent neural networks from overfitting. J. Mach. Learn. Res. (2014)
25. Sun, B., Saenko, K.: Deep CORAL: correlation alignment for deep domain adaptation. In: Hua, G., Jégou, H. (eds.) ECCV 2016. LNCS, vol. 9915, pp. 443–450. Springer, Cham (2016). https://doi.org/10.1007/978-3-319-49409-8_35
26. Szegedy, C., et al.: Going deeper with convolutions. In: CVPR (2015)
27. Tzeng, E., Hoffman, J., Saenko, K., Darrell, T.: Adversarial discriminative domain adaptation. In: CVPR (2017)
28. Tzeng, E., Hoffman, J., Zhang, N., Saenko, K., Darrell, T.: Deep domain confusion: maximizing for domain invariance. arXiv preprint arXiv:1412.3474 (2014)
29. Ulyanov, D., Vedaldi, A., Lempitsky, V.: Improved texture networks: maximizing quality and diversity in feed-forward stylization and texture synthesis. In: CVPR (2017)
30. Xie, S., Girshick, R., Dollár, P., Tu, Z., He, K.: Aggregated residual transformations for deep neural networks. In: CVPR (2017)
31. Zhang, Y., David, P., Gong, B.: Curriculum domain adaptation for semantic segmentation of urban scenes. In: ICCV (2017)
32. Zhu, J.Y., Park, T., Isola, P., Efros, A.A.: Unpaired image-to-image translation using cycle-consistent adversarial networks. In: ICCV (2017)

Beyond Part Models: Person Retrieval with Refined Part Pooling (and A Strong Convolutional Baseline)

Yifan Sun[1], Liang Zheng[2], Yi Yang[3], Qi Tian[4], and Shengjin Wang[1(✉)]

[1] Department of Electronic Engineering, Tsinghua University, Beijing, China
sunyf15@mails.tsinghua.edu.cn, wgsgj@tsinghua.edu.cn
[2] Research School of Computer Science, Australian National University,
Canberra, Australia
[3] Centre for Artificial Intelligence, University of Technology Sydney,
Ultimo, Australia
[4] Huawei Noah's Ark Lab, University of Texas at San Antonio, San Antonio, USA

Abstract. Employing part-level features offers fine-grained information for pedestrian image description. A prerequisite of part discovery is that each part should be well located. Instead of using external resources like pose estimator, we consider content consistency within each part for precise part location. Specifically, we target at learning discriminative part-informed features for person retrieval and make two contributions. (i) A network named Part-based Convolutional Baseline (PCB). Given an image input, it outputs a convolutional descriptor consisting of several part-level features. With a uniform partition strategy, PCB achieves competitive results with the state-of-the-art methods, proving itself as a strong convolutional baseline for person retrieval. (ii) A refined part pooling (RPP) method. Uniform partition inevitably incurs outliers in each part, which are in fact more similar to other parts. RPP re-assigns these outliers to the parts they are closest to, resulting in refined parts with enhanced within-part consistency. Experiment confirms that RPP allows PCB to gain another round of performance boost. For instance, on the Market-1501 dataset, we achieve (77.4+4.2)% mAP and (92.3+1.5)% rank-1 accuracy, surpassing the state of the art by a large margin. Code is available at: https://github.com/syfafterzy/PCB_RPP

Keywords: Person retrieval · Part-level feature · Part refinement

1 Introduction

Person retrieval, also known as person re-identification (re-ID), aims at retrieving images of a specified pedestrian in a large database, given a query person-of-interest. Presently, deep learning methods dominate this community, with convincing superiority against hand-crafted competitors [44]. Deeply-learned representations provide high discriminative ability, especially when aggregated from deeply-learned part features. The latest state of the art on re-ID benchmarks are achieved with part-informed deep features [31,39,41].

© Springer Nature Switzerland AG 2018
V. Ferrari et al. (Eds.): ECCV 2018, LNCS 11208, pp. 501–518, 2018.
https://doi.org/10.1007/978-3-030-01225-0_30

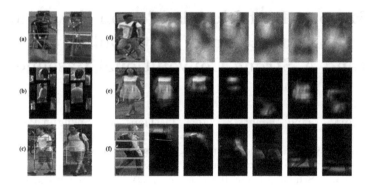

Fig. 1. Partition strategies of several deep part models in person retrieval. (a) to (e): Partitioned parts by GLAD [35], PDC [31], DPL [39], Hydra-plus [25] and PAR [41], respectively. (f): Our method employs a uniform partition and then refines each stripe. Both PAR [41] and our method conduct "soft" partition, but our method differs significantly from [41], as detailed in Sect. 2.

An essential prerequisite of learning discriminative part features is that parts should be accurately located. Recent state-of-the-art methods vary on their partition strategies and can be divided into two groups accordingly. The first group [31,35,42] leverage external cues, *e.g.,* assistance from human pose estimation [2,16,26,29,36]. They rely on external human pose estimation datasets and sophisticated pose estimator. The underlying datasets bias between pose estimation and person retrieval remains an obstacle against ideal semantic partition on person images. The other group [25,39,41] abandon cues from semantic parts. They require no part labeling and yet achieve competitive accuracy with the first group. Some partition strategies are compared in Fig. 1. Against this background of progress on learning part-level deep features, we rethink the problem of what makes well-aligned parts. Semantic partitions may offer stable cues to good alignment but are prone to noisy pose detections. This paper, from another perspective, lays emphasis on the consistency within each part, which we speculate is vital to the spatial alignment. Then we arrive at our motivation that given coarsely partitioned parts, we aim to refine them to reinforce within-part consistency. Specifically, we make the following two contributions:

First, we propose a network named Part-based Convolutional Baseline (PCB) which conducts uniform partition on the conv-layer for learning part-level features. It does not explicitly partition the images. PCB takes a whole image as the input and outputs a convolutional feature. Being a classification net, the architecture of PCB is concise, with slight modifications on the backbone network. The training procedure is standard and requires no bells and whistles. We show that the convolutional descriptor has much higher discriminative ability than the commonly used fully-connected (FC) descriptor. On the Market-1501 dataset, for instance, the performance increases from 85.3% rank-1 accuracy and 68.5% mAP to 92.3% (+7.0%) rank-1 accuracy and 77.4% (+8.9%) mAP, surpassing many state-of-the-art methods by a large margin.

Second, we propose an adaptive pooling method named Refined Part Pooling (RPP) to improve the uniform partition. We consider the motivation that within each part the contents should be consistent. We observe that under uniform partition, there exist outliers in each part. These outliers are, in fact, closer to contents in some other part, implying within-part inconsistency. Therefore, we refine the uniform partition by relocating those outliers to the part they are closest to, so that the within-part consistency is reinforced. An example of the refined parts is illustrated in Fig. 1(f). RPP does not require part labels for training and improves the retrieval accuracy over the high baseline achieved by PCB. For example on Market-1501, RPP further increases the performance to 93.8% (+1.5%) rank-1 accuracy and 81.6% (+4.2%) mAP.

2   Related Works

Hand-crafted Part Features for Person Retrieval. Before deep learning methods dominated the re-ID research community, hand-crafted algorithms had developed approaches to learn part or local features. Gray and Tao [13] partition pedestrians into horizontal stripes to extract color and texture features. Similar partitions have then been adopted by many works [9,23,28,45]. Some other works employ more sophisticated strategy. Gheissari et al. [12] divide the pedestrian into several triangles for part feature extraction. Cheng et al. [4] employ pictorial structure to parse the pedestrian into semantic parts. Das et al. [6] apply HSV histograms on the head, torso and legs to capture spatial information.

Deeply-Learned Part Features. The state of the art on most person retrieval datasets is presently maintained by deep learning methods [44]. When learning part features for re-ID, the advantages of deep learning over hand-crafted algorithms are two-fold. First, deep features generically obtain stronger discriminative ability. Second, deep learning offers better tools for parsing pedestrians, which further benefits the part features. In particular, human pose estimation and landmark detection have achieved impressive progress [2,16,26,29,36]. Several recent works in re-ID employ these tools for pedestrian partition and report encouraging improvement [31,35,42]. However, the underlying gap between datasets for pose estimation and person retrieval remains a problem when directly utilizing these pose estimation methods in an off-the-shelf manner. Others abandon the semantic cues for partition. Yao et al. [39] cluster the coordinates of max activations on feature maps to locate several regions of interest. Both Liu et al. [25] and Zhao et al. [41] embed the attention mechanism [38] in the network, allowing the model to decide where to focus by itself.

Deeply-learned Part with Attention Mechanism. A major contribution of this paper is the refined part pooling. We compare it with a recent work, PAR [39] by Zhao et al. in details. Both works employ a part-classifier to conduct "soft" partition on pedestrian images, as shown in Fig. 1. Two works share the merit of requiring no part labeling for learning discriminative parts. However, the motivation, training methods, mechanism, and final performance of the two methods are quite different, to be detailed below.

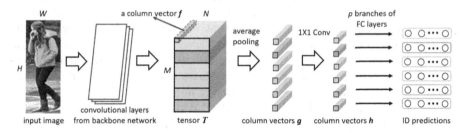

Fig. 2. Structure of PCB. The input image goes forward through the stacked convolutional layers from the backbone network to form a 3D tensor T. PCB replaces the original global pooling layer with a conventional pooling layer, to spatially down-sample T into p pieces of column vectors g. A following 1×1 kernel-sized convolutional layer reduces the dimension of g. Finally, each dimension-reduced column vector h is input into a classifier, respectively. Each classifier is implemented with a fully-connected (FC) layer and a sequential Softmax layer. Either p pieces of g or h are concatenated to form the final descriptor of the input image.

Motivation: PAR aims at directly learning aligned parts while RPP aims to refine the pre-partitioned parts. *Working mechanism:* using attention method, PAR trains the part classifier in an unsupervised manner, while the training of RPP can be viewed as a weakly-supervised process. *Training process:* RPP firstly trains an identity classification model with uniform partition and then utilizes the learned knowledge to induce the training of part classifier. *Performance:* the slightly more complicated training procedure rewards RPP with better interpretation and significantly higher performance. For instance on Market-1501, mAP achieved by PAR, PCB cooperating attention mechanism and the proposed RPP are 63.4%, 74.6% and 81.6%, respectively. In addition, RPP has the potential to cooperate with various partition strategies.

3   Proposed Method

Section 3.1 first proposes a part-based convolutional baseline (PCB). PCB employs the simple strategy of uniform partition on convolutional features. Section 3.2 describes the phenomenon of within-part inconsistency, which reveals the problem of uniform partition. Section 3.3 proposes the refined part pooling (RPP) method. RPP reduces the partition errors by conducting pixel-level refinement on the convolutional feature. RPP is also featured for learning without part label information, which is detailed in Sect. 3.4.

3.1   PCB: A Part-Based Convolutional Baseline

Backbone Network. PCB can take any network without hidden fully-connected layers designed for image classification as the backbone, *e.g.*, Google Inception [33] and ResNet [14]. This paper mainly employs ResNet50 with consideration of its competitive performance as well as its relatively concise architecture.

From Backbone to PCB. We reshape the backbone network to PCB with slight modifications, as illustrated in Fig. 2. The structure before the original global average pooling (GAP) layer is maintained exactly the same as the backbone model. The difference is that the GAP layer and what follows are removed. When an image undergoes all the layers inherited from the backbone network, it becomes a 3D tensor T of activations. In this paper, we define the vector of activations viewed along the channel axis as a **column vector**. Then, with a conventional average pooling, PCB partitions T into p horizontal stripes and averages all the column vectors in a same stripe into a single part-level column vector g_i ($i = 1, 2, \cdots, p$, the subscripts will be omitted unless necessary). Afterwards, PCB employs a convolutional layer to reduce the dimension of g. According to our preliminary experiment, the dimension-reduced column vectors h are set to 256-dim. Finally, each h is input into a classifier, which is implemented with a fully-connected (FC) layer and a following Softmax function, to predict the identity (ID) of the input.

During training, PCB is optimized by minimizing the sum of Cross-Entropy losses over p pieces of ID predictions. During testing, either p pieces of g or h are concatenated to form the final descriptor $\mathcal{G}$ or $\mathcal{H}$, *i.e.*, $\mathcal{G} = [g_1, g_2, \cdots, g_p]$ or $\mathcal{H} = [h_1, h_2, \cdots, h_p]$. As observed in our experiment, employing G achieves slightly higher accuracy, but at a larger computation cost, which is consistent with the observation in [32].

Important Parameters. PCB benefits from fine-grained spatial integration. Several key parameters, *i.e.*, the input image size (*i.e.*, $[H, W]$), the spatial size of the tensor T (*i.e.*, $[M, N]$), and the number of pooled column vectors (*i.e.*, p) are important to the performance of PCB. Note that $[M, N]$ is determined by the spatial down-sampling rate of the backbone model, given the fixed-size input. Some deep object detection methods, *e.g.*, SSD [24] and R-FCN [5], show that decreasing the down-sampling rate of the backbone network efficiently enriches the granularity of feature. PCB follows their success by removing the last spatial down-sampling operation in the backbone network to increase the size of T. This manipulation considerably increases retrieval accuracy with very light computation cost added. The details can be accessed in Sect. 4.4.

Through our experiment, the optimized parameter settings for PCB are:

- The input images are resized to 384×128, with a height to width ratio of 3:1.
- The spatial size of T is set to 24×8.
- T is equally partitioned into 6 horizontal stripes.

3.2   Within-Part Inconsistency

Uniform partition for PCB is simple, effective, and yet to be improved. It inevitably introduces partition errors to each part and consequentially compromises the discriminative ability of the learned feature. We analyze the partition errors from a new perspective: the within-part inconsistency.

With focus on the tensor T to be spatially partitioned, our intuition of within-part inconsistency is: column vector f in a same part of T should be similar to each other and be dissimilar to column vectors in other parts; otherwise the phenomenon of within-part inconsistency occurs, implying that the parts are partitioned inappropriately.

After training PCB to convergence, we compare the similarities between each f and g_i ($i = 1, 2, \cdots, p$), i.e., the average-pooled column vector of each part, by measuring cosine distance. By doing this, we find the closest part to each f, as exampled in Fig. 3. Each column vector is denoted by a small rectangle and painted in the color of its closest part. We observe that there exist many outliers, while designated to a specified horizontal stripe (part) during training, which are more similar to another part. The existence of these outliers suggests that they are inherently more consistent with column vectors in another part.

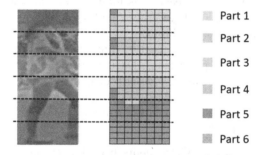

Fig. 3. Visualization of within-part inconsistency. T. Left: T is equally partitioned to $p = 6$ horizontal stripes (parts) during training. Right: Every column vector in T is denoted with a small rectangle and painted in the color of its closest part.

3.3   Refined Part Pooling

We propose the refined part pooling (RPP) to correct within-part inconsistency. Our goal is to assign all the column vectors according to their similarities to each part, so that the outliers will be relocated. More concretely, we quantitatively measure the similarity value $S(f \leftrightarrow P_i)$ between column vector f and each part Pi. Then the column vector f is sampled into part P_i according to the similarity value $S(f \leftrightarrow P_i)$, which is formulated by,

$$P_i = \{S(f \leftrightarrow P_i)f, \forall f \in F\}, \tag{1}$$

where F is the complete set of column vectors in tensor T, $\{\bullet\}$ denotes the sampling operation to form an aggregate.

It is non-trivial to directly measure the similarity value between a given f and each part. Assume that we have performed a sampling operation defined in Eq. 1 to update each part, then the "already-measured" similarities don't stand anymore. We have to perform the "similarity measuring" $\rightarrow$ "sampling" procedure iteratively until convergence, which evolves a non-trivial clustering embedded in deep learning.

So instead of measuring the similarity between each f and each P_i, RPP employs a part classifier to predict the value of $S(f \leftrightarrow P_i)$ (which can also be interpreted as the probability of f belonging to P_i) as follows:

$$S(f \leftrightarrow P_i) = softmax(W_i^T f) = \frac{\exp(W_i^T f)}{\sum\limits_{j=1}^{p} \exp(W_j^T f)}, \qquad (2)$$

where p is the number of pre-defined parts (i.e., $p = 6$ in PCB), and W is the trainable weight matrix of the part classifier.

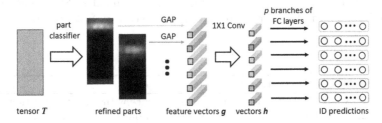

Fig. 4. PCB in combination with refined part pooling. The 3D tensor T is denoted simply by a rectangle instead of a cube as we focus on the spatial partition. Layers before T are omitted as they remain unchanged compared with Fig. 2. A part classifier predicts the probability of each column vector belonging to p parts. Then each part is sampled from all the column vectors with the corresponding probability as the sampling weight. GAP denotes global average pooling.

The proposed refined part pooling conducts a "soft" and adaptive partition to refine the original "hard" and uniform partition, and the outliers originated from the uniform partition will be relocated. In combination with refined part pooling described above, PCB is further reshaped into Fig. 4. Refined part pooling, i.e., the part classifier along with the following sampling operation, replaces the original average pooling. The structure of all the other layers remains exactly the same as in Fig. 2.

W has to be learned without part label information. To this end, we design an induced training procedure, as detailed in the following Sect. 3.4.

3.4 Induced Training for Part Classifier

The key idea of the proposed induced training is that: without part label information, we can use the already-learned knowledge in the pre-trained PCB to induce the training of the newly-appended part classifier. The algorithm is as follows.

- First, a standard PCB model is trained to convergence with T equally partitioned.
- Second, we remove the original average pooling layer after T and append a p-category part classifier on T. New parts are sampled from T according to the prediction of the part classifier, as detailed in Sect. 3.3.
- Third, we set all the already learned layers in PCB fixed, leaving only the part classifier trainable. Then we retrain the model on training set. In this condition, the model still expects the tensor T to be equally partitioned, otherwise it will predict incorrect about the identities of training images. So Step 3 penalizes the part classifier until it conducts partition close to the original uniform partition, whereas the part classifier is prone to categorize inherently similar column vectors into a same part. A state of balance will be reached as a result of Step 3.
- Finally, all the layers are allowed to be updated. The whole net, *i.e.*, PCB along with the part classifier are fine-tuned for overall optimization.

In the above training procedure, PCB model trained in Step1 induces the training of the part classifier. Step3 and 4 converges very fast, requiring 10 more epochs in total.

Algorithm 1. Induced training for part classifier

Step 1. A standard PCB is trained to convergence with uniform partition.
Step 2. A p-category part classifier is appended on the tensor T.
Step 3. All the pre-trained layers of PCB are fixed. Only the part classifier is trainable. The model is trained until convergence again.
Step 4. The whole net is fine-tuned to convergence for overall optimization.

---

4 Experiments

4.1 Datasets and Settings

Datasets. We three datasets for evaluation, *i.e.*, **Market-1501** [43], **DukeMTMC-reID** [30,47], and **CUHK03** [19]. The Market-1501 dataset contains 1,501 identities observed under 6 camera viewpoints, 19,732 gallery images and 12,936 training images detected by DPM [10]. The DukeMTMC-reID dataset contains 1,404 identities, 16,522 training images, 2,228 queries, and 17,661 gallery images. With so many images captured by 8 cameras, DukeMTMC-reID manifests itself as one of the most challenging re-ID datasets up to now. The CUHK03 dataset contains 13,164 images of 1,467 identities. Each identity is observed by 2 cameras. CUHK03 offers both hand-labeled and DPM-detected bounding boxes, and we use the latter in this paper. CUHK03 originally adopts 20 random train/test splits, which is time-consuming for deep learning. So we adopt the new training/testing protocol proposed in [48]. For Market-1501 and DukeMTMC-reID, we use the evaluation packages provided by [43] and [47], respectively. All the experiment evaluates the single-query setting. Moreover, for simplicity we do not use re-ranking algorithms which considerably improve mAP [48]. Our results are compared with reported results without re-ranking.

4.2   Implementation Details

Implementation of IDE for Comparison. We note that the IDE model specified in [44] is a commonly used baseline in deep re-ID systems [11,32,37,42, 44,46,47,49]. In contrast to the proposed PCB, the IDE model learns a global descriptor. For comparison, we implement the IDE model on the same backbone network, *i.e.*, ResNet50, and with several optimizations over the original one in [44], as follows. (1) After the "pool5" layer in ResNet50, we append a fully-connected layer followed by Batch Normalization and ReLU. The output dimension of the appended FC layer is set to 256-dim. (2) We apply dropout on "pool5" layer. Although there are no trainable parameters in "pool5" layer, there is evidence that applying Dropout on it, which outputs a high dimensional feature vector of 2048d, effectively avoids over-fitting and gains considerable improvement [46,47]. We empirically set the dropout ratio to 0.5. On Market-1501, our implemented IDE achieves 85.3% rank-1 accuracy and 68.5% mAP, which is a bit higher than the implementation in [49].

Implementation of Two Potential Alternative Structures of PCB for Comparison. Given a same backbone network, there exist several potential alternative structures to learn part-level features. We enumerate two structures for comparison with PCB.

- Variant 1. Instead of making an ID prediction based on each h_i ($i = 1, 2, \cdots, p$), it averages all h_i into a single vector $\overline{h}$, which is then fully connected to an ID prediction vector. During testing, it also concatenates g or h to form the final descriptor. Variant 1 is featured by learning a convolutional descriptor under a single loss.
- Variant 2. It adopts exactly the same structure as PCB in Fig. 2. However, all the branches of FC classifiers in Variant 2 share a same set of parameters.

Training. The training images are augmented with horizontal flip and normalization. We set batch size to 64 and train the model for 60 epochs with base learning rate initialized at 0.1 and decayed to 0.01 after 40 epochs. The backbone model is pre-trained on ImageNet [7]. The learning rate for all the pre-trained layers are set to 0.1× of the base learning rate. When employing refined part pooling for boosting, we append another 10 epochs with learning rate set to 0.01. With two NVIDIA TITAN XP GPUs and Pytorch as the platform, training an IDE model and a standard PCB on Market-1501 (12,936 training images) consumes about 40 and 50 min, respectively. The increased training time of PCB is mainly caused by the cancellation of the last spatial down-sample operation in the Conv5 layer, which enlarges the tensor T by 4×.

4.3   Performance Evaluation

We evaluate our method on three datasets, with results shown in Table 1. Both uniform partition (PCB) and refined part pooling (PCB+RPP) are tested.

Table 1. Comparison of the proposed method with IDE and 2 variants. pool5: output of Pool5 layer in ResNet50. FC: output of the appended FC layer for dimension reduction. $\mathcal{G}$ ($\mathcal{H}$): feature representation assembled with column vectors g (h). Both g and h are illustrated in Fig. 2

Models	Feature	dim	Market-1501		DukeMTMC-reID		CUHK03	
			R-1	mAP	R-1	mAP	R-1	mAP
IDE	pool5	2048	85.3	68.5	73.2	52.8	43.8	38.9
IDE	FC	256	83.8	67.7	72.4	51.6	43.3	38.3
Variant 1	$\mathcal{G}$	12288	86.7	69.4	73.9	53.2	43.6	38.8
Variant 1	$\mathcal{H}$	1536	85.6	68.3	72.8	52.5	44.1	39.1
Variant 2	$\mathcal{G}$	12288	91.2	75.0	80.2	62.8	52.6	45.8
Variant 2	$\mathcal{H}$	1536	91.0	75.3	80.0	62.6	54.0	47.2
PCB	$\mathcal{G}$	12288	92.3	77.4	81.7	66.1	59.7	53.2
PCB	$\mathcal{H}$	1536	92.4	77.3	81.9	65.3	61.3	54.2
PCB+RPP	$\mathcal{G}$	12288	**93.8**	**81.6**	**83.3**	**69.2**	62.8	56.7
PCB+RPP	$\mathcal{H}$	1536	93.1	81.0	82.9	68.5	**63.7**	**57.5**

PCB is a Strong Baseline. Comparing PCB and IDE, the prior commonly used baseline in many works [11,32,37,42,44,46,47,49], we clearly observe the significant advantage of PCB: mAP on three datasets increases from 68.5%, 52.8% and 38.9% to 77.4% (+8.9%), 66.1% (+13.3%) and 54.2% (+15.3%), respectively. This indicates that integrating part information increases the discriminative ability of the feature. The structure of PCB is as concise as that of IDE, and training PCB requires nothing more than training a canonical classification network. We hope it will serve as a baseline for person retrieval task.

Refined Part Pooling (RPP) Improves PCB Especially in mAP. From Table 1, while PCB already has a high accuracy, RPP brings further improvement to it. On the three datasets, the improvement in rank-1 accuracy is +1.5%, +1.6%, and +3.1%, respectively; the improvement in mAP is +4.2%, +3.1%, and +3.5%, respectively. The improvement is larger in mAP than in rank-1 accuracy. In fact, rank-1 accuracy characterizes the ability to retrieve the easiest match in the camera network, while mAP indicates the ability to find all the matches. So the results indicate that RPP is especially beneficial in finding more challenging matches.

The Benefit of Using p Losses. To validate the usage of p branches of losses in Fig. 2, we compare our method with Variant 1 which learns the convolutional descriptor under a single classification loss. Table 1 suggests that Variant 1 yields much lower accuracy than PCB, implying that employing a respective loss for each part is vital for learning discriminative part features.

The Benefit of NOT Sharing Parameters Among Identity Classifiers. In Fig. 2, PCB inputs each column vector h to a FC layer before the Softmax loss. We compare our proposal (not sharing FC layer parameters) with Variant 2 (sharing FC layer parameters). From Table 1, PCB is higher than Variant 2 by 2.4%, 3.3%, and 7.4% on the three datasets, respectively. This suggests that sharing parameters among the final FC layers is inferior.

Table 2. Comparison of the proposed method with the art on Market-1501. The compared methods are categorized into 3 groups. Group 1: hand-crafted methods. Group 2: deep learning methods employing global feature. Group 3: deep learning methods employing part features. * denotes those requiring auxiliary part labels. Our method is denoted by "PCB" and "PCB+RPP"

Methods	R-1	R-5	R-10	mAP
BoW+kissme [43]	44.4	63.9	72.2	20.8
WARCA [17]	45.2	68.1	76.0	-
KLFDA [18]	46.5	71.1	79.9	-
SOMAnet [1]	73.9	-	-	47.9
SVDNet [32]	82.3	92.3	95.2	62.1
Triplet Loss [15]	84.9	94.2	-	69.1
DML [40]	87.7	-	-	68.8
Cam-GAN [50]	88.1	-	-	68.7
MultiRegion [34]	66.4	85.0	90.2	41.2
PAR [41]	81.0	92.0	94.7	63.4
MultiLoss [20]	83.9	-	-	64.4
PDC* [31]	84.4	92.7	94.9	63.4
MultiScale [3]	88.9	-	-	73.1
GLAD* [35]	89.9	-	-	73.9
HA-CNN [21]	91.2	-	-	75.7
PCB	92.3	97.2	98.2	77.4
PCB+RPP	**93.8**	**97.5**	**98.5**	**81.6**

Comparison with State of the Art. We compare PCB and PCB+RPP with state of the art. Comparisons on Market-1501 are detailed in Table 2. The compared methods are categorized into three groups, *i.e.*, hand-crafted methods, deep learning methods with global feature and deep learning methods with part features. Relying on uniform partition only, PCB surpasses all the prior methods, including [31,35] which require auxiliary part labeling to deliberately align parts. The performance lead is further enlarged by the proposed refined part pooling.

Comparisons on DukeMTMC-reID and CUHK03 (new training/testing protocol) are summarized in Table 3. In the compared methods, PCB exceeds [3] by +5.5% and 17.2% in mAP on the two datasets, respectively. PCB+RPP (refined part pooling) further surpasses it by a large margin of +8.6% mAP on DukeMTMC-reID and +20.5% mAP on CUHK03. PCB+RPP yields higher accuracy than "TriNet+Era" and "SVDNet+Era" [49] which are enhanced by extra data augmentation.

Table 3. Comparison with prior art on DukeMTMC-reID and CUHK03. Rank-1 accuracy (%) and mAP (%) are shown

Methods	DukeMTMC-reID		CUHK03	
	rank-1	mAP	rank-1	mAP
BoW+kissme [43]	25.1	12.2	6.4	6.4
LOMO+XQDA [23]	30.8	17.0	12.8	11.5
GAN [47]	67.7	47.1	-	-
SVDNet [32]	76.7	56.8	41.5	37.3
MultiScale [3]	79.2	60.6	40.7	37.0
SVDNet+Era [49]	79.3	62.4	48.7	43.5
Cam-GAN [50]	75.3	53.5	-	-
HA-CNN [21]	80.5	63.8	41.7	38.6
PCB (UP)	81.8	66.1	61.3	54.2
PCB (RPP)	**83.3**	**69.2**	**63.7**	**57.5**

In this paper, **we report mAP = 81.6%, 69.2%, 57.5% and Rank-1 = 93.8%, 83.3% and 63.7% for Market-1501, Duke and CUHK03**, respectively, setting new state of the art on the three datasets. All the results are achieved under the single-query mode without re-ranking. Re-ranking methods will further boost the performance especially mAP. For example, when "PCB+RPP" is combined with the method in [48], mAP and Rank-1 accuracy on Market-1501 increases to **91.9%** and **95.1%**, respectively.

4.4 Parameters Analysis

We analyze some important parameters of PCB (and with RPP) introduced in Sect. 3.1 on Market-1501. Once optimized, the same parameters are used for all the three datasets.

The Size of Images and Tensor T. We vary the image size from 192×64 to 576×192, using 96×32 as interval. Two down-sampling rates are tested, *i.e.*, the original rate, and a halved rate (larger T). We train all these models on PCB and report their performance in Fig. 5. Two phenomena are observed.

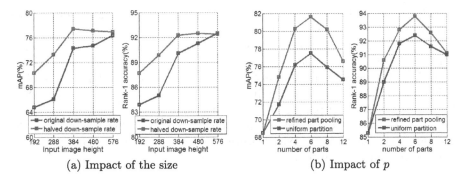

(a) Impact of the size   (b) Impact of p

Fig. 5. Parameter analysis. (a): The impact of image size. We use the original and halved down-sampling rates. (b): The impact of number of parts p. We compare PCB with and without the refined part pooling.

First, a larger image size benefits the learned part feature. Both mAP and rank-1 accuracy increase with the image size until reaching a stable performance.

Second, a smaller down-sampling rate, *i.e.*, a larger spatial size of tensor T enhances the performance, especially when using relatively small images as input. In Fig. 5(a), PCB using 384×128 input and halved down-sampling rate achieves almost the same performance as PCB using 576×192 input and the original down-sampling rate. We recommend the manipulation of halving the down-sampling rate with consideration of the computing efficiency.

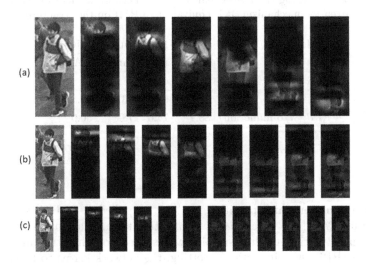

Fig. 6. Visualization of the refined parts under different p values. When $p = 8$ or 12, some parts repeat with others or become empty.

The Number of Parts p. Intuitively, p determines the granularity of the part feature. When $p=1$, the learned feature is a global one. As p increases, retrieval accuracy improves at first. However, accuracy does not always increase with p, as illustrated in Fig. 5(b). When $p = 8$ or 12, the performance drops dramatically, regardless of using refined part pooling. A visualization of the refined parts offers insights into this phenomenon, as illustrated in Fig. 6. When p increases to 8 or 12, some of the refined parts are very similar to others and some may collapse to an empty part. As a result, an over-increased p actually compromises the discriminative ability of the part features. In real-world applications, we would recommend to use $p = 6$ parts.

4.5   Induction and Attention Mechanism

In this work, when training the part classifier in Algorithm 1, a PCB pre-trained with uniform partition is required. The knowledge learned under uniform partition induces the subsequent training of the part classifier. *Without PCB pre-training, the network learns to partition T under no induction and becomes similar to methods driven by attention mechanism.* We conduct an ablation experiment on Market-1501 and DukeMTMC-reID to compare the two approaches. Results are presented in Table 4, from which three observations can be drawn.

Table 4. Ablation study of induction on Market-1501. PAR learns to focus on several parts to discriminate person with attention mechanisms. RPP (w/o induction) means no induction for learning the refined parts and the network learns to focus on several parts with attention mechanism. It is equivalent to PAR on the structure of PCB

Methods	Market-1501		DukeMTMC-reID	
	rank-1	mAP	rank-1	mAP
PAR [41]	81.0	63.4	-	-
IDE	85.3	68.5	73.2	52.8
RPP (w/o induction)	88.7	74.6	78.8	60.9
PCB	92.3	77.4	81.7	66.1
PCB+RPP	93.8	81.6	83.3	69.2

First, no matter which partition strategy is applied in PCB, it significantly outperforms PAR [41], which learns to partition through attention mechanism. Second, the attention mechanism also works based on the structure of PCB. Under the "RPP (w/o induction)" setting, the network learns to focus on several parts through attention mechanism, and achieves substantial improvement over IDE, which learns a global descriptor. Third, the induction procedure (PCB training) is critical. When the part classifier is trained without induction, the retrieval performance drops dramatically, compared with the performance achieved by"PCB+RPP". It implies that the refined parts learned through induction is superior to the parts learned through attention mechanism. Partitioned results with induction and attention mechanism are visualized in Fig. 1.

Moreover, for learning the part classifier without labeling information, we compare RPP with another potential method derived from Mid-level Element Mining [8, 22, 27]. Specifically, we follow [8] by assigning each stripe on tensor T with a pseudo part label to train the part classifier. Then we slide the trained part classifier on T to predict the similarity between every column vector on T and each part. The predicted similarity values are used for refining the uniformly-partitioned stripes of PCB, as the same in RPP. The above described approach achieves 93.0% (82.1%) rank-1 accuracy and 79.0% (66.9%) mAP on Market-1501 (DukeMTMC-reID). It also improves PCB, but is inferior to RPP. We guess the superiority of RPP originates from: given no part labels, the part classifier of RPP and the ID classifier are jointly optimized to recognize training identities, and thus gains better pedestrian discriminative ability.

5 Conclusion

This paper makes two contributions to solving the pedestrian retrieval problem. First, we propose a Part-based Convolutional Baseline (PCB) for learning part-informed features. PCB employs a simple uniform partition strategy and assembles part-informed features into a convolutional descriptor. PCB advances the state of the art to a new level, proving itself as a strong baseline for learning part-informed features. Despite the fact that PCB with uniform partition is simple and effective, it is yet to be improved. We propose the refined part pooling to reinforce the within-part consistency in each part. After refinement, similar column vectors are concluded into a same part, making each part more internally consistent. Refined part pooling requires no part labeling information and improves PCB considerably.

References

1. Barbosa, I.B., Cristani, M., Caputo, B., Rognhaugen, A., Theoharis, T.: Looking beyond appearances: Synthetic training data for deep cnns in re-identification. arXiv preprint arXiv:1701.03153 (2017)
2. Cao, Z., Simon, T., Wei, S.E., Sheikh, Y.: Realtime multi-person 2D pose estimation using part affinity fields. In: CVPR (2017)
3. Chen, Y., Zhu, X., Gong, S.: Person re-identification by deep learning multi-scale representations. In: International Conference on Computer Vision, Workshop on Cross-Domain Human Identification (CHI) (2017)
4. Cheng, D.S., Cristani, M., Stoppa, M., Bazzani, L., Murino, V.: Custom pictorial structures for re-identification. In: BMVC (2011)
5. Dai, J., Li, Y., He, K., Sun, J.: R-FCN: object detection via region-based fully convolutional networks. In: NIPS (2016)

6. Das, A., Chakraborty, A., Roy-Chowdhury, A.K.: Consistent re-identification in a camera network. In: Fleet, D., Pajdla, T., Schiele, B., Tuytelaars, T. (eds.) ECCV 2014. LNCS, vol. 8690, pp. 330–345. Springer, Cham (2014). https://doi.org/10.1007/978-3-319-10605-2_22

7. Deng, J., Dong, W., Socher, R., Li, L.J., Li, K., Li, F.F.: Imagenet: a large-scale hierarchical image database. In: CVPR (2009)

8. Diba, A., Pazandeh, A.M., Pirsiavash, H., Gool, L.V.: Deepcamp: deep convolutional action & attribute mid-level patterns. In: CVPR (2016)

9. Engel, C., Baumgartner, P., Holzmann, M., Nutzel, J.F.: Person re-identification by support vector ranking. In: BMVC (2010)

10. Felzenszwalb, P., McAllester, D., Ramanan, D.: A discriminatively trained, multiscale, deformable part model. In: CVPR (2008)

11. Geng, M., Wang, Y., Xiang, T., Tian, Y.: Deep transfer learning for person reidentification. arXiv preprint arXiv:1611.05244 (2016)

12. Gheissari, N., Sebastian, T.B., Hartley, R.: Person reidentification using spatiotemporal appearance. In: CVPR (2006)

13. Gray, D., Tao, H.: Viewpoint invariant pedestrian recognition with an ensemble of localized features. In: Forsyth, D., Torr, P., Zisserman, A. (eds.) ECCV 2008. LNCS, vol. 5302, pp. 262–275. Springer, Heidelberg (2008). https://doi.org/10.1007/978-3-540-88682-2_21

14. He, K., Zhang, X., Ren, S., Sun, J.: Deep residual learning for image recognition. In: CVPR (2016)

15. Hermans, A., Beyer, L., Leibe, B.: In defense of the triplet loss for person reidentification. arXiv preprint arXiv: 1703.07737 (2017)

16. Insafutdinov, E., Pishchulin, L., Andres, B., Andriluka, M., Schiele, B.: DeeperCut: a deeper, stronger, and faster multi-person pose estimation model. In: Leibe, B., Matas, J., Sebe, N., Welling, M. (eds.) ECCV 2016. LNCS, vol. 9910, pp. 34–50. Springer, Cham (2016). https://doi.org/10.1007/978-3-319-46466-4_3

17. Jose, C., Fleuret, F.: Scalable metric learning via weighted approximate rank component analysis. In: Leibe, B., Matas, J., Sebe, N., Welling, M. (eds.) ECCV 2016. LNCS, vol. 9909, pp. 875–890. Springer, Cham (2016). https://doi.org/10.1007/978-3-319-46454-1_53

18. Karanam, S., Gou, M., Wu, Z., Rates-Borras, A., Camps, O., Radke, R.J.: A comprehensive evaluation and benchmark for person re-identification: features, metrics, and datasets. arXiv preprint arXiv: 1605.09653 (2016)

19. Li, W., Zhao, R., Xiao, T., Wang, X.: Deepreid: deep filter pairing neural network for person re-identification. In: CVPR (2014)

20. Li, W., Zhu, X., Gong, S.: Person re-identification by deep joint learning of multiloss classification. In: IJCAI (2017)

21. Li, W., Zhu, X., Gong, S.: Harmonious attention network for person reidentification. arXiv preprint arXiv:1802.08122 (2018)

22. Li, Y., Liu, L., Shen, C., van den Hengel, A.: Mining mid-level visual patterns with deep CNN activations. Int. J. Comput. Vision (2017)

23. Liao, S., Hu, Y., Zhu, X., Li, S.Z.: Person re-identification by local maximal occurrence representation and metric learning. In: CVPR (2015)

24. Liu, W., et al.: SSD: single shot multibox detector. In: Leibe, B., Matas, J., Sebe, N., Welling, M. (eds.) ECCV 2016. LNCS, vol. 9905, pp. 21–37. Springer, Cham (2016). https://doi.org/10.1007/978-3-319-46448-0_2

25. Liu, X., et al.: Hydraplus-net: attentive deep features for pedestrian analysis. In: ICCV (2017)

26. Long, J., Shelhamer, E., Darrell, T.: Fully convolutional networks for semantic segmentation. In: CVPR (2015)
27. M., J.O., Tuytelaars, T.: Modeling visual compatibility through hierarchical mid-level elements. In: ECCV (2016)
28. Ma, A.J., Yuen, P.C., Li, J.: Domain transfer support vector ranking for person re-identification without target camera label information. In: ICCV (2013)
29. Newell, A., Yang, K., Deng, J.: Stacked hourglass networks for human pose estimation. In: Leibe, B., Matas, J., Sebe, N., Welling, M. (eds.) ECCV 2016. LNCS, vol. 9912, pp. 483–499. Springer, Cham (2016). https://doi.org/10.1007/978-3-319-46484-8_29
30. Ristani, E., Solera, F., Zou, R., Cucchiara, R., Tomasi, C.: Performance measures and a data set for multi-target, multi-camera tracking. In: Hua, G., Jégou, H. (eds.) ECCV 2016. LNCS, vol. 9914, pp. 17–35. Springer, Cham (2016). https://doi.org/10.1007/978-3-319-48881-3_2
31. Su, C., Li, J., Zhang, S., Xing, J., Gao, W., Tian, Q.: Pose-driven deep convolutional model for person re-identification. In: ICCV (2017)
32. Sun, Y., Zheng, L., Deng, W., Wang, S.: SVDNet for pedestrian retrieval. In: ICCV (2017)
33. Szegedy, C., Ioffe, S., Vanhoucke, V., Alemi, A.: Inception-v4, inception-resnet and the impact of residual connections on learning. In: AAAI (2017)
34. Ustinova, E., Ganin, Y., Lempitsky, V.: Multiregion bilinear convolutional neural networks for person re-identification. arXiv preprint arXiv: 1512.05300 (2015)
35. Wei, L., Zhang, S., Yao, H., Gao, W., Tian, Q.: GLAD: Global-local-alignment descriptor for pedestrian retrieval. ACM Multimed. (2017)
36. Wei, S.E., Ramakrishna, V., Kanade, T., Sheikh, Y.: Convolutional pose machines. In: CVPR (2016)
37. Xiao, T., Li, H., Ouyang, W., Wang, X.: Learning deep feature representations with domain guided dropout for person re-identification. In: CVPR (2016)
38. Xu, K., et al.: Show, attend and tell: Neural image caption generation with visual attention. In: ICML (2015)
39. Yao, H., Zhang, S., Zhang, Y., Li, J., Tian, Q.: Deep representation learning with part loss for person re-identification. arXiv preprint arXiv:1707.00798 (2017)
40. Zhang, Y., Xiang, T., Hospedales, T.M., Lu, H.: Deep mutual learning. arXiv preprint arXiv: 1705.00384 (2017)
41. Zhao, L., Li, X., Wang, J., Zhuang, Y.: Deeply-learned part-aligned representations for person re-identification. In: ICCV (2017)
42. Zheng, L., Huang, Y., Lu, H., Yang, Y.: Pose invariant embedding for deep person re-identification. arXiv preprint arXiv:1701.07732 (2017)
43. Zheng, L., Shen, L., Tian, L., Wang, S., Wang, J., Tian, Q.: Scalable person re-identification: a benchmark. In: ICCV (2015)
44. Zheng, L., Yang, Y., Hauptmann, A.G.: Person re-identification: past, present and future. arXiv preprint arXiv:1610.02984 (2016)
45. Zheng, W., Gong, S., Xiang, T.: Reidentification by relative distance comparison. TPAMI (2013)
46. Zheng, Z., Zheng, L., Yang, Y.: Pedestrian alignment network for large-scale person re-identification. arXiv preprint arXiv: 1707.00408 (2017)
47. Zheng, Z., Zheng, L., Yang, Y.: Unlabeled samples generated by gan improve the person re-identification baseline in vitro. In: ICCV (2017)
48. Zhong, Z., Zheng, L., Cao, D., Li, S.: Re-ranking person re-identification with k-reciprocal encoding. In: CVPR (2017)

49. Zhong, Z., Zheng, L., Kang, G., Li, S., Yang, Y.: Random erasing data augmentation. arXiv preprint arXiv: 1708.04896 (2017)
50. Zhong, Z., Zheng, L., Zheng, Z., Li, S., Yang, Y.: Camera style adaptation for person re-identification. arXiv preprint arXiv:1711.10295 (2017)

RefocusGAN: Scene Refocusing Using a Single Image

Parikshit Sakurikar[1(✉)], Ishit Mehta[1], Vineeth N. Balasubramanian[2], and P. J. Narayanan[1]

[1] Center for Visual Information Technology, Kohli Center on Intelligent Systems, International Institute of Information Technology, Hyderabad, India
parikshit.sakurikar@research.iiit.ac.in
[2] Department of Computer Science and Engineering, Indian Institute of Technology, Hyderabad, India

Abstract. Post-capture control of the focus position of an image is a useful photographic tool. Changing the focus of a single image involves the complex task of simultaneously estimating the radiance and the defocus radius of all scene points. We introduce RefocusGAN, a deblur-then-reblur approach to single image refocusing. We train conditional adversarial networks for deblurring and refocusing using wide-aperture images created from light-fields. By appropriately conditioning our networks with a focus measure, an in-focus image and a refocus control parameter δ, we are able to achieve generic free-form refocusing over a single image.

Keywords: Epsilon focus photography · Single image refocusing

1 Introduction

An image captured by a wide-aperture camera has a finite depth-of-field centered around a specific focus position. The location of the focus plane and the size of the depth-of-field depend on the camera settings at the time of capture. Points from different parts of the scene contribute to one or more pixels in the image and the size and shape of their contribution depends on their relative position to the focus plane. Post-capture control of the focus position is a very useful tool for amateur and professional photographers alike. Changing the focus position of a scene using a single image is however an ill-constrained problem as the in-focus intensity and the true point-spread-function for each scene point must be jointly estimated before re-blurring a pixel to the target focus position.

Multiple focused images of a scene, in the form of a focal stack, contain the information required to estimate in-focus intensity and the focus variation for each scene point. Focal stacks have been used in the past for tasks such as estimating a sharp in-focus image of the scene [1,20], computing the depth-map of the scene [19,33], and free-form scene refocusing [11,39]. In this paper, we introduce RefocusGAN, a comprehensive image refocusing framework which takes

© Springer Nature Switzerland AG 2018
V. Ferrari et al. (Eds.): ECCV 2018, LNCS 11208, pp. 519–535, 2018.
https://doi.org/10.1007/978-3-030-01225-0_31

only a single input image and enables post-capture control over its focus position. This is a departure from current methods in computational photography that provide post-capture control over depth-of-field using full focal stacks.

Our work is motivated by the impressive performance of deep neural networks for tasks such as image deblurring, image-to-image translation and depth-map computation from a single image. We propose a two-stage approach to single image refocusing. The first stage of our approach computes the radiance of the scene points by deblurring the input image. The second stage uses the wide-aperture image together with the computed radiance to produce a refocused image based on a refocus control parameter δ. We train conditional adversarial networks for both stages using a combination of adversarial and content loss [15]. Our networks are additionally conditioned by a focus measure response during deblurring and the computed radiance image during refocusing. We train our networks using wide-aperture images created from a large light-field dataset of scenes consisting of flowers and plants [29]. The main contribution of this paper is our novel two-stage algorithm for high-quality scene refocusing over a single input image. To the best of our knowledge, this is the first attempt at comprehensive focus manipulation of a single image using deep neural networks (Fig. 1).

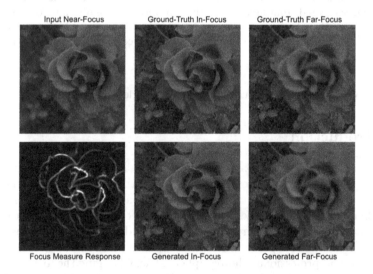

Fig. 1. Refocusing a single-image: We use an input wide-aperture image along with its focus measure response to create a deblurred, in-focus radiance image. The radiance image is then used together with the input image to create a refocused image. The second and third columns show the quality of our deblurring and refocusing stages.

2   Related Work

Controlling the focus position of the scene is possible if multiple focused images of the scene are available, usually in the form of a focal stack. Jacobs et al. [11] propose a geometric approach to refocusing and create refocused images by appropriately blending pixels from different focal slices, while correctly handling halo artifacts. Hach et al. [8] model real point-spread-functions between several pairs of focus positions, using a high quality RGBD camera and dense kernel calibration. They are thereby able to generate production-quality refocusing with accurate bokeh effects. Suwajanakorn et al. [33] compute the depth-map of the scene from a focal stack and then demonstrate scene refocusing using the computed depth values for each pixel. Several methods have been proposed in the past to compute in-focus images and depth maps from focal stacks [4,19,20,26,33]. Most of these methods enable post-capture control of focus but use all the images in the focal stack. Zhang and Cham [38] change the focus position of a single image by estimating the amount of focus at each pixel and use a blind deconvolution framework for refocusing. Methods based on Bae and Durand [3] also estimate the per-pixel focus map but for the task of defocus magnification. These methods are usually limited by the quality of the focus estimation algorithm as the task becomes much more challenging with increasing amounts of blur.

Deep neural networks have been used in the past for refocusing light-field images. Wang et al. [35] upsample the temporal resolution of a light-field video using another aligned 30 fps 2D video. The light-field at intermediate frames is interpolated using both the adjacent light-field frames as well as the 2D video frames using deep convolutional neural networks. Any frame can then be refocused freely as the light-field image at each temporal position is available. Full light-fields can themselves be generated using deep convolutional neural networks using only the four corner images as shown in [13]. A full 4D RGBD light-field can also be generated from a single image using deep neural networks trained over specific scene types as shown in [29]. Srinivasan et al. [28] implicitly estimate the depth-map of a scene by training a neural network to generate a wide-aperture image from an in-focus radiance image. These methods suggest that it is possible to generate light-fields using temporal and spatial interpolation. However, these methods have not been applied for focus interpolation.

Deep neural networks have been used for deblurring an input image to generate an in-focus image. Schuler et al. [27] describe a layered deep neural network architecture to estimate the blur kernel for blind image deblurring. Nimisha et al. [25] propose an end-to-end solution to blind deblurring using an autoencoder and adversarial training. Xu et al. [37] propose a convolutional neural network for deblurring based on separable kernels. Nah et al. [21] propose a multi-scale convolutional neural network with multi-scale loss for generating high-quality deblurring of dynamic scenes. Orest et al. [15] show state-of-the-art deblurring for dynamic scenes using a conditional adversarial network and use perceptual loss as an additional cue to train the deblurring network.

In this paper, we introduce RefocusGAN, a new approach to change the focus position of a single image using deep neural networks. Our approach first

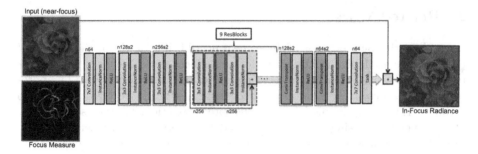

Fig. 2. The architecture of the deblurring cGAN. It receives a wide-aperture image and its focus measure channel as input and computes an in-focus radiance image.

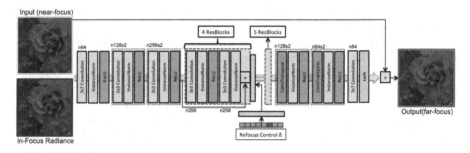

Fig. 3. The architecture of the refocusing cGAN. It uses the generated in-focus image together with the original wide-aperture image and a refocus control parameter δ to compute a refocused image.

deblurs an input wide-aperture image to an in-focus image and then uses this in-focus image in conjunction with the wide-aperture image to simulate geometric refocusing.

3   Single Image Scene Refocusing

A standard approach to scene refocusing uses several wide-aperture images from a focal stack to generate a new image with the target depth-of-field. Refocusing is typically modeled as a composition of pixels from several focal slices to create a new pixel intensity. This reduces the task of refocusing to selecting a set of weights for each pixel across focal slices as is described in [11]. Other methods that use all the slices of a focal stack first estimate the depth map of the scene and a corresponding radiance image, and then convolve the radiance image with geometrically accurate blur kernels, such as in [8]. In the case of single images, it is difficult to simultaneously estimate the true radiance as well as the defocus radius at each pixel. Moreover, the complexity of the size and shape of the defocus kernel at each pixel depends on the scene geometry as well as the quality of the lens. A deep learning approach to refocus a wide-aperture image using a single end-to-end network does not perform very well and this is discussed in more detail in Sect. 5.

Refocusing a wide-aperture image can be modeled as a cascaded operation involving two steps in the image space. The first step is a deblurring operation that computes the true scene radiance $\hat{G}^r$ from a given wide-aperture image G^i, where i denotes the focus position during capture. This involves deblurring each pixel in a spatially varying manner in order to produce locally sharp pixels. The second step applies a new spatially varying blur to all the sharp pixels to generate the image corresponding to the new focus position $G^{i+\delta}$, where δ denotes the change in focus position. The required scene-depth information for geometric refocusing can be assumed to be implicit within this two-stage approach. Srinivasan et al. [28] have shown how the forward process of blurring can actually be used to compute an accurate depth-map of the scene. Our two-stage approach to refocusing a wide-aperture image is briefly described below.

In the first stage, an in-focus radiance image is computed from a given wide-aperture image G^i and an additional focus measure m evaluated over G^i. The focus measure provides a useful cue that improves the quality of deblurring:

$$\hat{G}^r = \mathcal{G}^1_{\theta_G}\left(G^i : m(G^i)\right) \tag{1}$$

In the second stage, the generated in-focus image is used together with the input wide-aperture image to generate the target image corresponding to a shifted focus position $i + \delta$.

$$G^{i+\delta} = \mathcal{G}^2_{\theta_G}\left(G^i : \hat{G}^r, \delta\right) \tag{2}$$

We train end-to-end conditional adversarial networks for both these stages. While the deblurring network $\mathcal{G}^1_\theta$ is motivated by existing blind image-deblurring works in the literature, we provide motivation for our second network $\mathcal{G}^2_\theta$ by producing a far-focused slice from a near-focused slice using a simple optimization method.

Adversarial Learning: Generative adversarial networks (GANs) [6] define the task of learning as a competition between two networks, a generator and a discriminator. The task of the generator is to create an image based on an arbitrary input, typically provided as a noise vector, and the task of the discriminator is to distinguish between a real image and this generated image. The generator is trained to created images that are perceptually similar to real images, such that the discriminator is unable to distinguish between real and generated samples. The objective function of adversarial learning can be defined as:

$$\min_{\mathcal{G}} \max_{\mathcal{D}} \mathcal{L}_{GAN}, \tag{3}$$

where $\mathcal{L}_{GAN}$ is the classic GAN loss function:

$$\mathcal{L}_{GAN} = E_{y \sim p_r(y)}\left[\log \mathcal{D}(y)\right] + E_{z \sim p_z(z)}\left[\log(1 - \mathcal{D}(\mathcal{G}(z)))\right], \tag{4}$$

where $\mathcal{D}$ represents the discriminator, $\mathcal{G}$ is the generator, y is a real sample, z is a noise vector input to the generator, p_r represents the real distribution over target samples and p_z is typically a normal distribution.

Conditional adversarial networks (cGANs), provide additional conditioning to the generator to create images in accordance with the conditioning parameters. Isola et al. [10] provide a comprehensive analysis of GANs for the task of image-to-image translation, and propose a robust cGAN architecture called pix2pix, where the generator learns a mapping from an image x and a noise vector z to an output image y as: $\mathcal{G} : x, z \rightarrow y$. The observed image is provided as conditioning to both the generator and the discriminator. We use cGANs for the tasks of de-blurring and refocusing and provide additional conditioning parameters to both our networks as defined in the following sections.

3.1   Deblurring a Wide-Aperture Image

We use a conditional adversarial network to deblur a wide aperture image G^i and estimate its corresponding scene radiance $\hat{G}^r$ as described in Eq. 1. Our work draws inspiration from several deep learning methods for blind image-deblurring such as [15,21,27,37]. Our network is similar to the state-of-the-art deblurring network proposed by Orest et al. [15]. Our generator network is built on the style transfer network of Johnson et al. [12] and consists of two strided convolution blocks with a stride of $\frac{1}{2}$, nine residual blocks and two transposed convolution blocks. Each residual block is based on the ResBlock architecture [9] and consists of a convolution layer with dropout regularization [30], instance-normalization [34] and ReLU activation [22]. The network learns a residual image since a global skip connection (ResOut) is added in order to accelerate learning and improve generalization [15]. The residual image is added to the input image to create the deblurred radiance image. The discriminator is a Wasserstein-GAN [2] with gradient penalty [7] as defined in [15]. The architecture of the critic discriminator network is identical to that of PatchGAN [10,16]. All convolution layers except for the last layer are followed by instance normalization and Leaky ReLU [36] with an $\alpha = 0.2$.

The cGAN described in [15] is trained to sharpen an image blurred by a motion-blur kernel of the form $I_B = K * I_S + \eta$, where I_B is the blurred image, I_S is the sharp image, K is the motion blur kernel and η represents additive noise. In our case, the radiance image G^r has been blurred by a spatially varying defocus kernel and therefore the task of deblurring is more complex. We thereby append the input image G^i with an additional channel that encodes a focus measure response computed over the input image. We compute $m(G^i)$ as the response of the Sum-of-modified-Laplacian (SML) [23] filter applied over the input image. We also provide the input image along with this additional channel as conditioning to the discriminator. The adversarial loss for our deblurring network can be defined as:

$$\mathcal{L}_{cGAN} = \sum_{n=1}^{N} -\mathcal{D}_{\theta_D}^1(\mathcal{G}_{\theta_G}^1(x^i), x^i), \tag{5}$$

where $x^i = G^i : m(G^i)$ is the input wide-aperture image G^i concatenated with the focus measure channel $m(G^i)$.

In addition to the adversarial loss, we also use perceptual loss [12] as suggested in [15]. Perceptual loss is L2-loss between the CNN feature maps of the generated deblurred image and the target image:

$$\mathcal{L}_X = \frac{1}{W_{ij}H_{ij}} \sum_x \sum_y (\phi_{ij}(I^S)_{xy} - \phi_{ij}(\mathcal{G}_{\theta_G}(I^B))_{xy})^2, \tag{6}$$

where ϕ_{ij} is the feature map in VGG19 trained on ImageNet [5] after the jth convolution and the ith max-pooling layer and W and H denote the size of the feature maps. In this case, I^S and I^B represent the ground truth in-focus image and the input wide-aperture image respectively. The loss function for the generator is a weighted combination of adversarial and perceptual loss $\mathcal{L} = \mathcal{L}_{cGAN} + \lambda\mathcal{L}_X$.

The structure of our deblurring cGAN is shown in Fig. 2. A few wide-aperture images along with the computed in-focus radiance image are shown in Fig. 7.

3.2 Refocusing a Wide-Aperture Image

The in-focus image computed from the above network not only represents the true scene radiance at each pixel, but can also serve as proxy depth information in conjunction with the input wide-aperture image. We motivate our second refocusing network $\mathcal{G}^2_{\theta_G}$ using a simple method that can refocus a near-focus image to a far-focus image and vice versa, using the computed radiance image.

As shown in the example in Fig. 4, a near-focused image G^1 can be converted to a far focused image G^n using the radiance image $\hat{G}^r$ resulting from the deblurring network. Here 1 and n are used to denote the near and far ends of the focus spread of a focal stack. To refocus these images, the first step would be to compute the per-pixel blur radius between the input image G^1 and the radiance image $\hat{G}^r$. This can be achieved using a blur-and-compare framework wherein the in-focus pixels of the radiance image are uniformly blurred by different radii and the best defocus radius σ is estimated for each pixel using pixel-difference between a blurred patch and the corresponding patch in G^1. Inverting these defocus radii as $\sigma' = \sigma_{max} - \sigma$ followed by re-blurring the radiance image is the natural way to create the refocused image. This method can also be used to convert a far-focused image to a near focused image as shown in the second row of Fig. 4. Free-form refocusing between arbitrary focus positions is not trivial though since there is no front-to-back ordering information in the estimated defocus radii.

For free-form scene refocusing, we use a conditional adversarial network similar to our deblurring network. We use the same cGAN architecture of the previous section, with different conditioning and an additional refocus control parameter δ. The refocus control parameter is used to guide the network to produce a target image corresponding to a desired focus position. The input to the network is the original wide-aperture image G^i concatenated with the scene radiance image $\hat{G}^r = \mathcal{G}^1_{\theta_G}(G^i : m(G^i))$ computed by the deblurring network. The refocus parameter δ encodes the shift between the input and output images and is

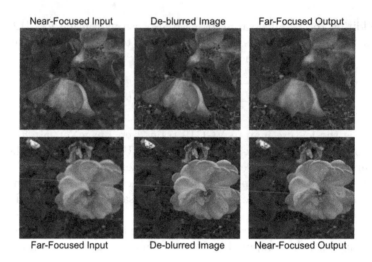

Near-Focused Input   De-blurred Image   Far-Focused Output

Far-Focused Input   De-blurred Image   Near-Focused Output

Fig. 4. Refocusing using a simple image-processing operation over the input wide-aperture image G^1 and the deblurred in-focus image $\hat{G}^r$. The first row shows the input near-focused image, the deblurred in-focus image from the network and the computed far-focused image. The second row shows equivalent far-to-near refocusing.

provided to the network as a one-hot vector. The refocus vector corresponding to δ is concatenated as an additional channel to the innermost layer of the network, using a fully connected layer to convert the one-hot vector into a 64×64 channel.

The structure of the refocusing cGAN is shown in Fig. 3. We use the same structure for the discriminator and the generator as that of the deblurring cGAN. The loss function for the generator is a summation of adversarial loss and perceptual loss. The discriminator network is conditioned using the input image and the in-focus radiance image. The cGAN loss for this network can be defined as:

$$\mathcal{L}_{cGAN} = \sum_{n=1}^{N} -\mathcal{D}^2_{\theta_D}(\mathcal{G}^2_{\theta_G}(x^i), x^i), \tag{7}$$

where $x^i = G^i : \hat{G}^r$ is the input wide-aperture image G^i concatenated with the scene radiance image $\hat{G}^r = \mathcal{G}^1_{\theta_G}(G^i : m(G^i))$. Refocused images generated from the input wide-aperture image, the in-focus image and different refocus parameters are shown in Figs. 8 and 9.

4   Training Details

For training both networks, we compute multiple wide-aperture images from a large light-field dataset of scenes consisting of flowers and plants [29]. The method used to generate training images from light-fields is explained in the following section.

4.1   Focal Stacks from Light-Fields

A focal stack is a sequence of differently focused images of the scene with a fixed focus step between consequent images of the stack. A focal stack can be understood as an ordered collection of differently blurred versions of the scene radiance. A focal slice G^i is a wide-aperture image corresponding to a focus position i and can be defined as:

$$G^i = \int \int h^i(x, y, d_{x,y}) * \hat{G}^r(x, y) \, dx \, dy, \tag{8}$$

where h^i is the spatially varying blur kernel dependent on the spatial location of the pixel and the depth $d_{x,y}$ of its corresponding scene point and $\hat{G}^r$ is the true radiance of the scene point which is usually represented by the in-focus intensity of the pixel.

An ideal focal stack, as defined by Zhou et al. [39], consists of each pixel in focus in one and only one slice. Focal stacks can be captured by manually or programmatically varying the focus position between consequent shots. Programmed control of the focus position is possible nowadays on DSLR cameras as well as high-end mobile devices. Canon DSLR cameras can be programmed using the MagicLantern API [18] and both iOS and Android mobile devices can be controlled using the Swift Camera SDK and Camera2 API respectively. Capturing a focal stack as multiple shots suffers from the limitation that the scene must be static across the duration of capture, which is difficult to enforce for most natural scenes. Handheld capture of focal stacks is also difficult due to the multiple shots involved. Moreover, being able to easily capture focal stacks is a somewhat recent development and there is a dearth of large quantities of focal stack image sequences.

A focal stack can also be created from a light-field image of the scene. The Lytro light-field camera based on Ng et al. [24] captures a 4D light-field of a scene in a single shot, and can thereby be used for dynamic scenes. The different angular views captured by a light-field camera can be merged together to create wide-aperture views corresponding to different focus positions. A large number of light-fields of structurally similar scenes have been captured by Srinivasan et al. [29]. Several other light-field datasets also exist such as the Stanford light-field archive [31] and the light-field saliency dataset [17]. Large quantities of similar focal stacks can be created from such light-field datasets.

Srinivasan et al. [29] captured a large light-field dataset of 3343 light-fields of scenes consisting of flowers and plants using the Lytro Illum Camera. Each image in the dataset consists of the angular views encoded into a single light-field image. A 14 × 14 grid of angular views can be extrapolated from the light-field, each having a spatial resolution of 376 × 541. Typically, only the central 8 × 8 views are useful as the samples towards the corners of the light-field suffer from clipping as they lie outside the camera's aperture. This dataset is described in detail in [29]. A few sample images from this dataset are shown in Fig. 5. For our experiments, we use a central 7 × 7 grid of views to create focal stacks, so as to have a unique geometric center to represent the in-focus image. We generate a focal stack at a high focus resolution for each of these light-field images using the synthetic photography equation defined in [24]:

$$G^i(s,t) = \int \int L\left(u, v, u + \frac{s - u}{\alpha_i}, v + \frac{t - v}{\alpha_i}\right) du\, dv. \qquad (9)$$

Here G^i represents the synthesized focal slice, $L(u, v, s, t)$ is the 4D light-field represented using the standard two-plane parameterization and α_i represents the location of the focus plane. This parameterization is equivalent to the summation of shifted versions of the angular views captured by the lenslets as shown in [24]. We vary the shift-sum parameter linearly between $-s_{max}$ to $+s_{max}$ to generate 30 focal slices between the near and far end of focus.

Fig. 5. A few examples of the light-field images in the Flowers dataset of [29].

To reduce the size of focal stacks to an optimal number of slices, we apply the composite focus measure [26] and study the focus variation of pixels across the stack. We use this measure as it has been shown to be more robust than any single focus measure for the task of depth-from-focus [26]. For each pixel, we record the normalized response of the composite measure at each slice. We build a histogram of the number of pixels that peaked at each of the 30 slices across the 3343 light-field dataset. We find that in close to 90% of the images, all the pixels peak between slices 6 and 15 of the generated focal stack. The depth variation of the captured scenes is mostly covered by these ten focal slices. We thereby subsample each focal stack to consist of ten slices, varying from slice 6 to slice 15 of our original parameterization. Our training experiments use these 10-sliced focal stacks computed from the light-field dataset.

For training, the 3343 focal stacks are partitioned into 2500 training samples and 843 test samples. Each focal slice is cropped to a spatial resolution of 256×256 pixels. The s_{max} parameter while computing focal slices is set to 1.5 pixels. For the deblurring network, we use all the ten focal slices from the 2500 focal stacks for training. For the refocusing network, we experiment with three different configurations. In the first configuration a single refocus parameter of $\delta = +8$ is used. In the second configuration, the refocus parameter has four distinct values: $\delta = \{-9, -5, +5, +9\}$. In the third configuration, the refocus parameter can take any one of 19 possible values from -9 to $+9$. The deblurring network is trained for 30 epochs ($\sim$50 hours) and all configurations of the refocusing network are trained for 60 epochs ($\sim$45 hours). All training experiments were performed on an Nvidia GTX 1080Ti. The learning rate is set to 0.0001

Table 1. Quantitative evaluation of our deblurring network. PSNR and SSIM is reported for the test-split of the light-field dataset. We compare the performance of the deblurring network with and without the additional Sum-of-Modified-Laplacian (SML) focus measure channel. There is a marginal but useful improvement in the quality of deblurring on using the focus measure channel. As an indication of overall performance, we generate an in-focus image using the composite focus measure [26] applied on all slices of the focal stack and report its quality. Note that our method uses only a single image.

Deblurring experiment	PSNR	SSIM
Ours (without additional Focus Measure)	34.88	0.937
Ours (with additional Focus Measure)	35.02	0.938
Composite Focus Measure (uses entire stack)	38.697	0.965

initially for all network configurations. The learning rate is linearly decreased to zero after half the total number of epochs are completed. All networks are trained for a batch size of 1 and the Adam solver [14] is used for gradient descent. The λ parameter for scaling content loss is set to 100 as suggested in [15].

5   Experiments and Results

We provide a quantitative evaluation of the performance of our two-stage refocusing approach in Tables 1 and 2. We compare the peak signal-to-noise ratio (PSNR) and the structural similarity (SSIM) of the refocused images with the ground truth images from the focal stacks. Since this is the first work that comprehensively manipulates the focus position from a single image, there is no direct comparison of the generated refocused images with existing geometric techniques over focal stacks. However, we generate in-focus images using the composite focus measure [26] applied across the full focal stack and report the quantitative reconstruction quality in Table 1. We show the quantitative performance of our networks individually and report the PSNR and SSIM of the computed in-focus radiance image in comparison with the ground-truth central light-field image.

Our two-stage approach to refocusing is motivated by our initial experiments wherein we observed that an end-to-end refocusing network does not work well. Our experiments spanned several network architectures such as the purely convolutional architecture of the disparity estimation network of [13], the separable kernel convolutional architecture of [37], the encoder-decoder style deep network with skip-connections of [32] and the conditional adversarial network of [15]. These networks exhibit poor refocusing performance in both cases of fixed pairs of input-output focal slices as well as for the more complex task of free-form refocusing. Since the networks are only given input wide-aperture images while training, there may be several pixel intensities which do not occur sharply in either the input or output images, and the task of jointly estimating all true intensities and re-blurring them is difficult to achieve within a reasonable compute power/time budget for training. In Table 2, we compare our two-stage approach to refocusing with an equivalent single-stage, end-to-end network. This essentially compares the performance of our refocusing network with and without the additional radiance image computed by the deblurring network. It can be seen that the two-stage method clearly outperforms a single-stage approach to refocusing.

Table 2. Quantitative evaluation of our refocusing network. The PSNR and SSIM values are reported on the test-split of the light-field dataset. The first two rows show the performance of our refocusing network without an additional in-focus image. This corresponds to an end-to-end, single stage approach to refocusing. The next three rows show the performance on using different refocus control parameters in our two-stage experiments. The final row shows the test performance of our refocusing network which was trained using ground truth in-focus images G^r but tested using the radiance images computed by the deblurring network $\hat{G}^r$. Note that the two-stage approaches significantly outperform their single-stage counterparts. The high PSNR and SSIM values quantitatively suggest that our network enables high-quality refocusing.

Experiment	Type	Refocus control steps	PSNR	SSIM
Without G^r	Single-stage	+8	38.73	0.97
Without G^r	Single-stage	$\{-9, -5, +5, +9\}$	38.4	0.956
With G^r	Two-stage	+8	44.225	0.992
With G^r	Two-stage	$\{-9, -5, +5, +9\}$	43.4	0.988
With G^r	Two-stage	$\{-9, -8, .., 0, .., +8, +9\}$	40.42	0.975
With AIF($\hat{G}^r$)	Two-step	$-9, -5, +5, +9$	38.63	0.958

The deblurring network uses an additional focus measure channel to compute the radiance image $\hat{G}^r$. The benefit of using the focus measure is indicated in Table 1. For the refocusing network, we perform experiments on three different configurations. The configurations differ from each other in the number of refocus control parameters and are shown in Table 2. The first configuration is a proof-of-concept network and is trained on a single refocus parameter. This clearly exhibits the best performance as the training samples have a high degree of structural similarity. The network with four control parameters performs better than the network with 19 parameters, which can be seen in Table 2. This can be attributed to two separate issues. The focal stacks created from the light-field dataset consist of ten slices that roughly span the depth range of the scene from near-to-far. However, in the absence of scene content at all depths, certain focal slices may be structurally very similar to adjacent slices. Training these slices with different control parameters can confuse the network. Secondly, in the case of the 19 parameter configuration, the total number of training samples increases to 250000 as there are 100 samples from each focal stack. We use a subset of size 30000 from these training images sampled uniformly at random.

In the case of refocusing with 4 control parameters, the focus shift between input and output images is clearly defined and the network thereby captures the relationship better. All the training samples from the dataset can be used directly to train this network as there are only 12 training samples per focal stack in the four parameter configuration.

We show qualitative deblurring and refocusing results for several test samples in Figs. 7, 8 and 9. In Fig. 6, we show the performance of our refocusing framework on generic images from different light-fields that were not images of flowers or plants, and also show the performance on an image captured using a wide-aperture camera. The performance suggests that our networks are

Fig. 6. The performance of our two-stage refocusing framework on generic images. The first row has the input wide-aperture image and the second row shows the refocused image. The first four columns show the performance on structurally different light-field focal slices from another light-field dataset while the last column shows the performance on an image captured by a wide-aperture camera.

Fig. 7. In-focus radiance images created using the deblurring network. The top row shows the input wide-aperture images and the bottom row shows the deblurred output from our deblurring network.

Fig. 8. Near-to-Far Refocusing generated with $\delta = +9$ using our refocusing network. The top row shows the input wide-aperture images and the bottom row shows the output refocused images.

Fig. 9. Far-to-Near Refocusing generated with $\delta = -9$ using our refocusing network. The top row shows the input wide-aperture images and the bottom row shows the output refocused images.

implicitly learning both tasks quite well and can be used for high-quality refocusing of standalone images.

6   Conclusion

We present a two-stage approach for comprehensive scene refocusing over a single-image. Our RefocusGAN framework uses adversarial training and perceptual loss to train separate deblurring and refocusing networks. We provide a focus measure channel as an additional conditioning for deblurring a wide-aperture image. We use the deblurred in-focus image as an additional conditioning for refocusing. Our quantitative and qualitative results suggest high-quality performance on refocusing. Our networks exhibit useful generalization and can further benefit from fine-tuning and training over multiple datasets together. In the future, we plan to work on creating a refocusing network based on a free-form refocus parameter that is independent of the number and spread of focal slices.

References

1. Agarwala, A., et al.: Interactive digital photomontage. ACM Trans. Graph. **23**, 294–302 (2004)
2. Arjovsky, M., Chintala, S., Bottou, L.: Wasserstein generative adversarial networks. In: Proceedings of the 34th International Conference on Machine Learning. vol. 70, pp. 214–223 (2017)
3. Bae, S., Durand, F.: Defocus magnification. Computer Graphics Forum. **26**, 571–579 (2007)
4. Bailey, S.W., Echevarria, J.I., Bodenheimer, B., Gutierrez, D.: Fast depth from defocus from focal stacks. Visual Comput. **31**(12), 1697–1708 (2015)
5. Deng, J., Dong, W., Socher, R., Li, L.J., Li, K., Fei-Fei, L.: Imagenet: A large-scale hierarchical image database. In: 2009 IEEE Conference on Computer Vision and Pattern Recognition (CVPR), pp. 248–255 (2009)
6. Goodfellow, I., et al.: Generative adversarial nets. In: Advances in neural information processing systems (NIPS), pp. 2672–2680 (2014)
7. Gulrajani, I., Ahmed, F., Arjovsky, M., Dumoulin, V., Courville, A.C.: Improved training of wasserstein gans. In: Advances in Neural Information Processing Systems (NIPS), pp. 5767–5777 (2017)
8. Hach, T., Steurer, J., Amruth, A., Pappenheim, A.: Cinematic bokeh rendering for real scenes. In: Proceedings of the 12th European Conference on Visual Media Production, CVMP 2015, pp. pp. 1:1–1:10 (2015)
9. He, K., Zhang, X., Ren, S., Sun, J.: Deep residual learning for image recognition. In: 2016 IEEE Conference on Computer Vision and Pattern Recognition (CVPR), pp. 770–778 (2016)
10. Isola, P., Zhu, J.Y., Zhou, T., Efros, A.A.: Image-to-image translation with conditional adversarial networks. In: 2017 IEEE Conference on Computer Vision and Pattern Recognition (CVPR), pp. 5967–5976 (2017)
11. Jacobs, D.E., Baek, J., Levoy, M.: Focal stack compositing for depth of field control. Stanford Computer Graphics Laboratory Technical Report 1 (2012)
12. Johnson, J., Alahi, A., Fei-Fei, L.: Perceptual losses for real-time style transfer and super-resolution. In: Leibe, B., Matas, J., Sebe, N., Welling, M. (eds.) ECCV 2016. LNCS, vol. 9906, pp. 694–711. Springer, Cham (2016). https://doi.org/10.1007/978-3-319-46475-6_43
13. Kalantari, N.K., Wang, T.C., Ramamoorthi, R.: Learning-based view synthesis for light field cameras. ACM Trans. Graph. **35**(6), 193:1–193:10 (2016)
14. Kingma, D.P., Ba, J.: Adam: A method for stochastic optimization. CoRR abs/1412.6980 (2014)
15. Kupyn, O., Budzan, V., Mykhailych, M., Mishkin, D., Matas, J.: Deblurgan: Blind motion deblurring using conditional adversarial networks. In: 2018 IEEE Conference on Computer Vision and Pattern Recognition (CVPR), pp. 8183–8192 (2018)

16. Li, C., Wand, M.: Precomputed real-time texture synthesis with markovian generative adversarial networks. In: Leibe, B., Matas, J., Sebe, N., Welling, M. (eds.) ECCV 2016. LNCS, vol. 9907, pp. 702–716. Springer, Cham (2016). https://doi.org/10.1007/978-3-319-46487-9_43

17. Li, N., Ye, J., Ji, Y., Ling, H., Yu, J.: Saliency detection on light field. In: IEEE Conference on Computer Vision and Pattern Recognition, June 2014

18. Magic lantern. http://magiclantern.fm/

19. Möller, M., Benning, M., Schönlieb, C.B., Cremers, D.: Variational depth from focus reconstruction. IEEE Trans. Image Process. 24, 5369–5378 (2015)

20. Nagahara, H., Kuthirummal, S., Zhou, C., Nayar, S.K.: Flexible depth of field photography. In: Forsyth, D., Torr, P., Zisserman, A. (eds.) ECCV 2008. LNCS, vol. 5305, pp. 60–73. Springer, Heidelberg (2008). https://doi.org/10.1007/978-3-540-88693-8_5

21. Nah, S., Kim, T.H., Lee, K.M.: Deep multi-scale convolutional neural network for dynamic scene deblurring. In: 2017 IEEE Conference on Computer Vision and Pattern Recognition (CVPR), pp. 257–265 (2017)

22. Nair, V., Hinton, G.E.: Rectified linear units improve restricted boltzmann machines. In: Proceedings of the 27th International Conference on Machine Learning, ICML, pp. 807–814 (2010)

23. Nayar, S.K., Nakagawa, Y.: Shape from focus. Trans. Pattern Anal. Mach. Intell. (PAMI) 16(8), 824–831 (1994)

24. Ng, R., Levoy, M., Brédif, M., Duval, G., Horowitz, M., Hanrahan, P.: Light field photography with a hand-held plenoptic camera. Comput. Sci. Tech. Rep. CSTR 2(11), 1–11 (2005)

25. Nimisha, T.M., Singh, A.K., Rajagopalan, A.N.: Blur-invariant deep learning for blind-deblurring. In: IEEE International Conference on Computer Vision (ICCV), pp. 4762–4770 (2017)

26. Sakurikar, P., Narayanan, P.J.: Composite focus measure for high quality depth maps. In: IEEE International Conference on Computer Vision (ICCV), pp. 1623–1631 (2017)

27. Schuler, C.J., Hirsch, M., Harmeling, S., Schölkopf, B.: Learning to deblur. Trans. Pattern Anal. Mach. Intell. (PAMI) 38(7), 1439–1451 (2016)

28. Srinivasan, P.P., Garg, R., Wadhwa, N., Ng, R., Barron, J.T.: Aperture supervision for monocular depth estimation. In: 2018 IEEE Conference on Computer Vision and Pattern Recognition (CVPR) (2018)

29. Srinivasan, P.P., Wang, T., Sreelal, A., Ramamoorthi, R., Ng, R.: Learning to synthesize a 4d RGBD light field from a single image. In: IEEE International Conference on Computer Vision, (ICCV), pp. 2262–2270 (2017)

30. Srivastava, N., Hinton, G., Krizhevsky, A., Sutskever, I., Salakhutdinov, R.: Dropout: a simple way to prevent neural networks from overfitting. J. Mach. Learn. Res. 15(1), 1929–1958 (2014)

31. Stanford light-field archive, http://lightfield.stanford.edu/

32. Su, S., Delbracio, M., Wang, J., Sapiro, G., Heidrich, W., Wang, O.: Deep video deblurring for hand-held cameras. In: 2017 IEEE Conference on Computer Vision and Pattern Recognition (CVPR), pp. 237–246 (2017)

33. Suwajanakorn, S., Hernandez, C., Seitz, S.M.: Depth from focus with your mobile phone. In: IEEE Conference on Computer Vision and Pattern Recognition (2015)

34. Ulyanov, D., Vedaldi, A., Lempitsky, V.S.: Instance normalization: The missing ingredient for fast stylization. CoRR abs/1607.08022 (2016)

35. Wang, T.C., Zhu, J.Y., Kalantari, N.K., Efros, A.A., Ramamoorthi, R.: Light field video capture using a learning-based hybrid imaging system. ACM Trans. Graph. (Proc. SIGGRAPH 2017) **36**(4) (2017)
36. Xu, B., Wang, N., Chen, T., Li, M.: Empirical evaluation of rectified activations in convolutional network. CoRR abs/1505.00853 (2015)
37. Xu, L., Ren, J.S.J., Liu, C., Jia, J.: Deep convolutional neural network for image deconvolution. In: Proceedings of the 27th International Conference on Neural Information Processing Systems, NIPS 2014 , vol. 1, pp. 1790–1798 (2014)
38. Zhang, W., Cham, W.K.: Single-image refocusing and defocusing. IEEE Trans. Image Process. **21**(2), 873–882 (2012)
39. Zhou, C., Miau, D., Nayar, S.K.: Focal sweep camera for space-time refocusing. Technical Report, Department of Computer Science, Columbia University CUCS-021-12 (2012)

Zero-Shot Keyword Spotting for Visual Speech Recognition In-the-wild

Themos Stafylakis[✉][ID] and Georgios Tzimiropoulos[ID]

Computer Vision Laboratory, University of Nottingham, Nottingham, UK
themos.stafylakis@nottingham.ac.uk, yorgos.tzimiropoulos@nottingham.ac.uk

Abstract. Visual keyword spotting (KWS) is the problem of estimating whether a text query occurs in a given recording using only video information. This paper focuses on visual KWS for words unseen during training, a real-world, practical setting which so far has received no attention by the community. To this end, we devise an end-to-end architecture comprising (a) a state-of-the-art visual feature extractor based on spatiotemporal Residual Networks, (b) a grapheme-to-phoneme model based on sequence-to-sequence neural networks, and (c) a stack of recurrent neural networks which learn how to correlate visual features with the keyword representation. Different to prior works on KWS, which try to learn word representations merely from sequences of graphemes (i.e. letters), we propose the use of a grapheme-to-phoneme encoder-decoder model which learns how to map words to their pronunciation. We demonstrate that our system obtains very promising visual-only KWS results on the challenging LRS2 database, for keywords unseen during training. We also show that our system outperforms a baseline which addresses KWS via automatic speech recognition (ASR), while it drastically improves over other recently proposed ASR-free KWS methods.

Keywords: Visual keyword spotting · Visual speech recognition · Zero-shot learning

1 Introduction

This paper addresses the problem of visual-only Automatic Speech Recognition (ASR) i.e. the problem of recognizing speech from video information only, in particular, from analyzing the spatiotemporal visual patterns induced by the mouth and lips movement. Visual ASR is a challenging research problem, with decent results being reported only recently thanks to the advent of Deep Learning and the collection of large and challenging datasets [1–3].

In particular, we focus on the problem of Keyword Spotting (KWS) i.e. the problem of finding occurrences of a text query among a set of recordings. In this work we consider only words, however the same architecture can be used for short phrases. Although the problem can be approached with standard ASR methods, recent works aim to address it with more direct and "ASR-free"

© Springer Nature Switzerland AG 2018
V. Ferrari et al. (Eds.): ECCV 2018, LNCS 11208, pp. 536–552, 2018.
https://doi.org/10.1007/978-3-030-01225-0_32

methods [4]. Moreover, such KWS approaches are in line with a recently emerged research direction in ASR (typically termed Acoustics-to-Word) where words are replacing phonemes, triphones or letters as basic recognition units [5,6].

Motivation. One of the main problems regarding the use of words as basic recognition units is the existence of Out-Of-Vocabulary (OOV) words, i.e. words for which the exact phonetic transcription is unknown, as well as words with very few or zero occurrences in the training set. This problem is far more exacerbated in the visual domain where collecting, annotating and distributing large datasets for fully supervised visual speech recognition is a very tedious process. To the best of our knowledge, this paper is the first attempt towards visual KWS under the zero-shot setting.

Relation to Zero-shot Learning. Our approach shares certain similarities with zero-shot learning methods, e.g. for recognizing objects in images without training examples of the particular objects [7]. Different to [7], where representations of the objects encode semantic relationships, we wish to learn word representations that encode merely their phonetic content. To this end, we propose to use a grapheme-to-phoneme (G2P) encoder-decoder model which learns how to map words (i.e. sequences of graphemes or simply letters) to their pronunciation (i.e. to sequences of phonemes)[1]. By training the G2P model using a training set of such pairs (i.e. words and their pronunciation), we obtain a fixed-length representation (embedding) for any word, including words not appearing in the phonetic dictionary or in the visual speech training set.

The proposed system receives as input a video and a keyword and estimates whether the keyword is contained in the video. We use the LRS2 database to train a Recurrent Neural Network (Bidirectional Long Short-Term Memory, BiLSTM) that learns non-linear correlations between visual features and their corresponding keyword representation [8]. The backend of the network is modeling the probability that the video contains the keyword and provides an estimate of its position in the video sequence. The proposed system is trained end-to-end, without information about the keyword boundaries, and once trained it can spot any keyword, even those not included in the LRS2 training set.

In summary, our **contributions** are:

- We are the first to study Query-by-Text visual KWS for words unseen during training.
- We devise an end-to-end architecture comprising (a) a state-of-the-art visual feature extractor based on spatiotemporal Residual Networks, (b) a G2P model based on sequence-to-sequence neural networks, and (c) a stack of recurrent neural networks that learn how to correlate visual features with the keyword representation.
- We demonstrate that our system obtains very promising visual-only KWS results on the challenging LRS2 database.

---

[1] For example, the phonetic transcription of the word "finish" is "F IH1 N IH0 SH", where the numerical values after the vowel "IH" indicate different levels of stretching.

2   Related Work

Visual ASR. During the past few years, the interest in visual and audiovisual ASR has been revived. Research in the field is largely influenced by recent advances in audio-only ASR, as well as by the state-of-the-art in computer vision, mostly for extracting visual features. In [9], CNN features are combined with Gated Recurrent Units (GRUs) in an end-to-end visual ASR architecture, capable of performing sentence-level visual ASR on a relatively easy dataset (GRID [10]). Similarly to several recent end-to-end audio-based ASR approaches, CTC is deployed in order to circumvent the lack of temporal alignment between frames and annotation files [11,12]. In [1,13], the "Listen, attend and spell" ([14]) audio-only ASR architecture is adapted to the audiovisual domain, and tested on recently released in-the-wild audiovisual datasets. The architecture is an attentive encoder-decoder model with the decoder operating directly on letters (i.e. graphemes) rather than on phonemes or visemes (i.e. the visual analogues of phonemes [15]). It deploys a VGG for extracting visual features and the audio and visual modalities are fused in the decoder. The model yields state-of-the-art results in audiovisual ASR. Other recent advances in visual and audiovisual ASR involve residual-LSTMs, adversarial domain-adaptation methods, use of self-attention layers (i.e. Transformer [16]), combinations of CTC and attention, gating neural networks, as well as novel fusion approaches [17–24].

Words as Recognition Units. The general tendency in deep learning towards end-to-end architectures, together with the challenge of simplifying the fairly complex traditional ASR paradigm, has resulted into a new research direction of using words directly as recognition units. In [25], an acoustic deep architecture is introduced, which models words by projecting them onto a continuous embedding space. In this embedding space, words that sound alike are nearby in the Euclidean sense, differentiating it from others word embedding spaces where distances correspond to syntactic and semantic relations [26,27]. In [5,6], two CTC-based ASR architectures are introduced, where CTC maps directly acoustics features to words. The experiments show that CTC word models can outperform state-of-the-art baselines that make use of context-dependent triphones as recognition units, phonetic dictionaries and language models.

In the problem of audio-based KWS, end-to-end word-based approaches have also emerged. In [28], the authors introduce a KWS system based on sequence training, composed of a CNN for acoustic modeling and an aggregation stage, which aggregates the frame-level scores into a sequence-level score for words. However, the system is limited to words seen during training, since it merely associates each word with a label (i.e. one-hot vector) without considering them as sequences of characters. Other recent works aim to spot specific keywords used to activate voice assistant systems [29–31]. The application of BiLSTMs on KWS was first proposed in [32]. The architecture is capable of spotting at least a limited set of keywords, having a softmax output layer with as many output units as keywords, and a CTC loss for training. More recently, the authors in [4] propose an audio-only KWS system capable of generalizing to unseen words, using a CNN/RNN to autoencode sequences of graphemes (corresponding to words or short phrases) into fixed-length representation vectors. The extracted representations, together with audio-feature representations extracted with an acoustic autoencoder are passed to a feed-forward neural network which is trained to predict whether the keyword occurs in the utterance or not. Although this audio-only approach shares certain conceptual similarities with ours, the implementations are different in several ways. Our approach deploys a Grapheme-to-Phoneme model to learn keyword representations, it does not make use of autoencoders for extracting representations of visual sequences, and more importantly it learns how to correlate visual information with keywords from low-level visual features rather than from video-level representations.

The authors in [33] recently proposed a visual KWS approach using words as recognition units. They deploy the ResNet feature extractor with us (proposed by our team in [34,35] and trained on LRW [2]) and they demonstrate the capacity of their network in spotting occurrences of the $N_w = 500$ words in LRW [36]. The bottleneck of their method is the word representation (each word corresponds to a label, without considering words as sequences of graphemes). Such an unstructured word representation may perform well on closed-set word identification/detection tasks, but prevents the method from generalizing to words unseen during training.

Zero-shot Learning. Analogies can be drawn between KWS with unseen words and zero-shot learning for detecting new classes, such as objects or animals. KWS with unseen words is essentially a zero-shot learning problem, where attributes (letters) are shared between classes (words) so that the knowledge learned from seen classes is transferred to unseen ones [37]. Moreover, similarly to a typical zero-shot learning training set-up where bounding boxes of the objects of interest are not given, a KWS training algorithm knows only whether or not a particular word is uttered in a given training video, without having information about the exact time interval. For these reasons, zero-shot learning methods which e.g. learn mappings from an image feature space to a semantic space ([38,39]) are pertinent to our method. Finally, recent methods in action recognition using a representation vector to encode e.g. 3D human-skeleton sequences also exhibit certain similarities with our method [40].

3   Proposed Method

3.1   System Overview

Our system is composed of four different modules. The first module is a visual feature extractor, which receives as input the image frame sequence (assuming a face detector has already been applied, as in LRS2) and outputs features. A spatiotemporal Residual Network is used for this purpose, which has shown remarkable performance in word-level visual ASR [34,35].

The second module of the architecture receives as input a user-defined keyword (or more generally a text query) and outputs a fixed-length representation of the keyword in $\mathbb{R}^{d_e}$. This mapping is learned by a grapheme-to-phoneme (G2P [41]) model, which is a sequence-to-sequence neural network with two RNNs playing the roles of encoder and decoder (similarly to [42]). The two RNNs interact with each other via the last hidden state of the encoder, which is used by the decoder in order to initialize its own hidden state. We claim that this representation is a good choice for extracting word representations, since (a) it contains information about its pronunciation without requiring the phonetic transcription during evaluation, and (b) it generalizes to words unseen during training, provided that the G2P is trained with a sufficiently large vocabulary.

The third module is where the visual features with the keyword representation are combined and non-linear correlations between them are learned. It is implemented by a stack of bidirectional LSTMs, which receives as input the sequence of feature vectors and concatenates each such vector with the word representation vector.

Finally, the forth module is the backend classifier and localizer, whose aims are (a) to estimate whether or not the query occurs in the video, and (b) to provide us with an estimate of its position in the video. Note that we do not train the network with information about the time intervals keywords occur. The only supervision used during training is a binary label indicating whether or not the keyword occurs in the video, together with the grapheme and phoneme sequences of the keyword.

The basic building blocks of the model are depicted in Fig. 1.

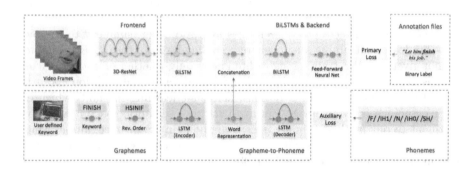

Fig. 1. The block-diagram of the proposed KWS system.

3.2 Modeling Visual Patterns Using Spatiotemporal ResNet

The front-end of the network is an 18-layer Residual Network (ResNet), which has shown very good performance on LRW [34,43] as well as on LRS2 [20]. It has been verified that CNN features encoding spatiotemporal information in their first layers yield much better performance in lipreading, even when combined with deep LSTMs or GRUs in the backend [9,13,34]. For this reason, we replace the first 2D convolutional, batch-normalization and max-pooling layers of the ResNet with their 3D counterparts. The temporal size of the kernel is set equal to $T_r = 5$, and therefore each ResNet feature is extracted over a window of 0.2 s (assuming 25 fps). The temporal stride is equal to 1, since any reduction of time resolution is undesired at this stage. Finally, the average pooling layer of the ResNet output (found e.g. in ImageNet versions of ResNet [43]) is replaced with a fully connected layer. Overall, the spatiotemporal ResNet implements a function $\mathbf{x}_t = f_r([\mathbf{I}_{t-2}, \mathbf{I}_{t-1}, \mathbf{I}_t, \mathbf{I}_{t+1}, \mathbf{I}_{t+2}], \mathbf{W}_r)$, where $\mathbf{W}_r$ denotes the parameters of the ResNet and $\mathbf{I}_t$ the (grayscale and cropped) frames at time t.

We use a pretrained model on LRW which we fine-tune on the pretrain set of LRS2 using closed-set word identification. The pretrain set of LRS2 is useful for this purpose, not merely due to the large number of utterances it contains, but also sue to its more detailed annotation files, which contain information about the (estimated) time each word begins and ends. Word boundaries permits us to excerpt fixed-duration video segments containing specific words and essentially mimic the LRW set-up. To this end, we select the 2000 most frequently appearing words containing at least 4 phonemes and we extract frame sequences of 1.5 s duration, having the target word in the center. The backend is a 2-layer LSTM (jointly pretrained on LRW) which we remove once the training is completed.

Preprocessing. The frames in LRS2 are already cropped according the bounding box extracted by face detector and tracker [1,2]. We crop the frames further with a fixed set of coefficients $C_{crop} = [15, 46, 145, 125]$, we resize them to 122×122, and we finally feed the ResNet with frames of size 112×112, after applying random cropping in training (for data augmentation), and fixed central cropping in testing, as in [34].

3.3 Grapheme-to-phoneme Models for Encoding Keywords

Grapheme-to-phoneme (G2P) models are extensively used in speech technologies in order to learn a mapping $\mathbf{G} \mapsto \mathbf{P}$ from sequences of graphemes $\mathbf{G} \in \mathbb{G}$ to sequences of phonemes $\mathbf{P} \in \mathbb{P}$. Such models are typically trained in a supervised fashion, using a phonetic dictionary, such as the CMU dictionary (for English). The number of different phonemes in the CMU dictionary is equal to $N_{phn} = 69$, with each vowel contributing more than one phoneme, due to the variable level of stretching. The effectiveness of a G2P model is measured by its generalizability, i.e. by its capacity in estimating the correct pronunciation(s) of words unseen during training.

Sequence-to-sequence neural networks have recently shown their strength in addressing this problem [41]. In a sequence-to-sequence G2P model, both sequences are typically modeled by an RNN, such as an LSTM or a GRU. The first RNN is a function $\mathbf{r} = f_e(\mathbf{G}, \mathbf{W}_e)$ parametrized by $\mathbf{W}_e$, which encodes the grapheme sequence in a fixed-size representation $\mathbf{r}|\mathbf{G}$, where $\mathbf{r} \in \mathbb{R}^{d_r}$, while the second RNN estimates the phoneme sequence $\hat{\mathbf{P}} = f_d(\mathbf{r}, \mathbf{W}_d)$. The representation vector is typically defined as the output of the last step, i.e. once the RNN has seen the whole grapheme sequence.

Our implementation of G2P involves two unidirectional LSTMs with hidden size equal to $d_l = 64$. Similarly to sequence-to-sequence models for machine translation (e.g. [42]), the encoder receives as input the (reversed) sequence of graphemes and the decoder received $\mathbf{c}_{e,T}$ and the output $\mathbf{h}_{e,T}$ from the encoder (corresponding to the last time step $t = T$) to initialize its own state, denoted by $\mathbf{c}_{d,0}$ and $\mathbf{h}_{d,0}$. To extract the word representation $\mathbf{r}$, we first concatenate the two vectors, we then project them to $\mathbb{R}^{d_r}$ to obtain $\mathbf{r}$ and finally we re-project them back to $\mathbb{R}^{2d_l}$, i.e. $\left[\mathbf{c}_{e,T}^t, \mathbf{h}_{e,T}^t\right]^t \mapsto \mathbf{r} \mapsto \left[\mathbf{c}_{d,0}^t, \mathbf{h}_{d,0}^t\right]^t$, where $\mathbf{x}^t$ denotes the transpose of $\mathbf{x}$. For the projections we use two linear layers with square matrices (since $d_r = 2d_l$), while biases are omitted for having a more compact notation.

The G2P model is trained by minimizing the cross-entropy (CE) between the true $\mathbf{P}^*$ and posterior probability over sequences $P(\mathbf{P}_t|\mathbf{G})$, averaged across time steps, i.e.

$$L_w\left(\mathbf{P}^*, \mathbf{G}\right) = \frac{1}{T} \sum_{t=1}^{T} \mathrm{CE}\left(\mathbf{P}_t^*, P(\mathbf{P}_t|\mathbf{G})\right). \tag{1}$$

Since the G2P model is trained with back-propagation, its loss function can be added as auxiliary loss to the primary KWS loss function and the overall architecture can be trained jointly. Joint training is highly desired, as it enforces the encoder to learn representations that are optimal not merely for decoding, but for our primary task, too.

During evaluation, the mapping $\mathbf{G} \mapsto \mathbf{z}$ learned by the encoder is all that is required, and therefore the decoder $f_{dec}(\cdot, \mathbf{W}_{dec})$ and the true pronunciation $\mathbf{P}^*$ are not required for KWS.

3.4   Stack of BiLSTMs, Binary Classifier and Loss Function

The backend of the model receives the sequence of visual features $\mathbf{X} = \{\mathbf{x}_t\}_{t=1}^{T}$ of a video and the word representation vector $\mathbf{r}$ and estimates whether the keyword is uttered by the speaker.

Capturing correlations with BiLSTMs. LSTMs have exceptional capacity in modeling long-term correlations between input vectors, as well as correlations between different entries of the input vectors, due to the expressive power of their gating mechanism which controls the memory cell and the output [44]. We use two bidirectional LSTM (BiLSTM), with the first BiLSTM merely applying a transformation of the feature sequence $\mathbf{X} \mapsto \mathbf{Y}$, i.e.

$$\left[\left(\vec{\mathbf{h}}_t, \vec{\mathbf{c}}_t\right), \left(\overleftarrow{\mathbf{h}}_t, \overleftarrow{\mathbf{c}}_t\right)\right] = \left[\vec{f}_{l_0}\left(\mathbf{x}_t, \vec{\mathbf{h}}_{t-1}, \vec{\mathbf{c}}_{t-1}\right), \overleftarrow{f}_{l_0}\left(\mathbf{x}_t, \overleftarrow{\mathbf{h}}_{t+1}, \overleftarrow{\mathbf{c}}_{t+1}\right)\right] \tag{2}$$

and

$$\mathbf{y}_t = \mathbf{W}_{l_0}^t \left[\vec{\mathbf{h}}_t^t, \overleftarrow{\mathbf{h}}_t^t\right]^t \tag{3}$$

where $\mathbf{W}_{l_0}$ is a linear layer of size $(2d_v, d_v)$, $\vec{f}_{l_0}$ and $\overleftarrow{f}_{l_0}$ are functions corresponding to the forward and backward LSTM models (the dependence on their parameters is kept implicit), while $d_v = 256$. The input vectors $\mathbf{X}$ are batch-normalized, and dropouts with $p = 0.2$ are applied by repeating the same dropout mask for all feature vectors of the same sequence [45]. The outputs vectors of the first BiLSTM are concatenated with the word representation vector to obtain $\mathbf{y}_t^+ = [\mathbf{y}_t^t, \mathbf{r}^t]^t$. After applying batch-normalization to $\mathbf{y}_t^+$, we pass them as input to the second BiLSTM, with equations defined as above, resulting in a sequence of output vectors denoted by $\mathbf{Z} = \{\mathbf{z}_t\}_{t=1}^T$, where $\mathbf{z}_t \in \mathbb{R}^{d_v}$.

Note the equivalence between the proposed frame-level concatenation and keyword-based model adaptation. We may consider $\mathbf{r}$ as a means to adapt the biases of the linear layers in the three gates and the input to the cell, in such a way so that the activations of its neurons fire only over subsequences in $\mathbf{Z}$ that correspond to the keyword encoded in $\mathbf{r}$.

Feed-Forward Classifier for Network Initialization. For the first few epochs, we use a simple feed-forward classifier, which we subsequently replace with a BiLSTM backend discussed below. The outputs of the BiLSTM stack are projected to a linear layer $(d_v, d_v/2)$ and are passed to a non-linearity (Leaky Rectified Linear Units, denoted by LReLU) to filter-out those entries with negative values, followed by a summation operator to aggregate over the temporal dimension, i.e. $\mathbf{v} = \sum_{t=1}^T \text{LReLU}(\mathbf{W}^t\mathbf{z}_t)$. After applying dropouts to $\mathbf{v}$ we project them to a linear layer $(d_v/2, d_v/4)$ and we apply again a LReLU layer. Finally, we apply a linear layer to drop the size from $d_v/4$ to 1 and a Sigmoid layer, with which we model the posterior probabilities that the video contains the keyword or not, i.e. $P\left(l|\{\mathbf{I}\}_{t=1}^T, \mathbf{G}\right)$, where $l \in \{0, 1\}$ the binary indicator variable and l^* its true value.

BiLSTM Classifier and Keyword Localization. Once the network with the Feed-Forward Classifier is trained, we replace it with an BiLSTM classifier. The latter does not aggregate over the temporal dimension, because it aims to jointly (a) estimate the posterior probability that the video contains the keyword, and (b) locate the time step that the keyword occurs. Recall that the network is trained without information about the actual time intervals the keyword occurs. Nevertheless, an approximate position of the keyword can still be estimated, even from the output of the BiLSTM stack. As Fig. 2 shows, the average activation of the input of the BiLSTM classifier (after applying the linear layer and ReLU) exhibits a peak, typically within the keyword boundaries. The BiLSTM Classifier aims to model this property, by applying $\max(\cdot)$ and $\operatorname{argmax}(\cdot)$ in order to estimate the posterior that the keyword occurs and localize the keyword, respectively. More analytically, the BiLSTM Classifier receives the output features of the BiLSTM stack and it passes them to a linear layer $\mathbf{W}$ of size (d_v, d_s) where $d_l = 16$, and to a LReLU, i.e. $\mathbf{s}_t = \text{LReLU}(\mathbf{W}^t\mathbf{z}_t)$. The BiLSTM is then applied on the sequence, followed by a linear layer (which drops the dimension from $2d_s$ to 1, i.e. a vector $\mathbf{w}$ and a bias b), the $\max(\cdot)$ and finally the sigmoid $\sigma(\cdot)$ from which we estimate the posterior. More formally, $\mathbf{H} = \text{BiLSTM}(\mathbf{S})$, $y_t = \mathbf{w}^t\mathbf{h}_t + b$ and $p = \sigma(\max(\mathbf{y}))$, $\hat{t} = \operatorname{argmax}(\mathbf{y})$ where $\mathbf{S} = \{\mathbf{s}_t\}_{t=1}^T$, $\mathbf{H} = \{\mathbf{h}_t\}_{t=1}^T$, $\mathbf{y} = \{y_t\}_{t=1}^T$, $p = P\left(l = 1|\{\mathbf{I}_t\}_{t=1}^T, \mathbf{G}\right)$ (i.e. the posterior that the keyword defined by $\mathbf{G}$ occurs in the frame sequence $\{\mathbf{I}_t\}_{t=1}^T$), and $\hat{t}$ is the time step where the maximum occurs, and should be somewhere within the actual keyword boundaries. Note that we did not succeed in training the network with the BiLSTM Classifier from scratch, probably due to the max(·) operator.

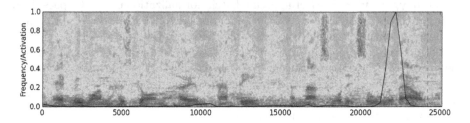

Fig. 2. Localization of the keyword **about** in the phrase "Everyone has gone home happy and that's what it's all **about**". The keyword boundaries are depicted with two vertical lines over the log-spectrogram.

Loss for Joint Training. The primary loss is defined as:

$$L_v\left(l^*, \left[\{\mathbf{I}_t\}_{t=1}^T, \mathbf{G}\right]\right) = \mathrm{CE}\left(l^*, P\left(l|\{\mathbf{I}_t\}_{t=1}^T, \mathbf{G}\right)\right), \tag{4}$$

while the whole model is trained jointly by minimizing a weighted summation of the primary and auxiliary losses, i.e.

$$L\left(\left[l^*, \mathbf{P}^*\right], \left[\{\mathbf{I}_t\}_{t=1}^T, \mathbf{G}\right]\right) = L_v\left(l^*, \left[\{\mathbf{I}_t\}_{t=1}^T, \mathbf{G}\right]\right) + \alpha_w L_w\left(\mathbf{P}^*, \mathbf{G}\right), \tag{5}$$

where α_w a scalar for balancing the two losses. It is worth noting that the representation vectors $\mathbf{r}$ and the encoder's parameters receive gradients from both loss functions, via the decoder of the G2P model and the LSTM backend. Contrarily, the decoder and the binary classifier receive gradients only from $L_w(\cdot, \cdot)$ and $L_v(\cdot, \cdot)$, respectively.

4   Training the Model

In this section we describe our recipe for training the model. We explain how we partition the data, how we create minibatches, and we give details about the optimization parameters.

4.1   LRS2 and CMU Dictionary Partitions

We use the official partition of the LRS2 into pretrain, train, validation and test set. The KWS network is trained on pretrain and train sets. The pretrain set is also used to fine-tune the ResNet, as we discuss in Sect. 3.2. The G2P model is trained from scratch and jointly with the whole KWS network. LRS2 contains about 145 K videos of spoken sentences from BBC TV (96K in pretrain, 46K in train, 1082 in validation, and 1243 in test set). The number of frames per video in the test set varies between 15 and 145.

In terms of keywords, we randomly partition the CMU phonetic dictionary into train, validation and test words (corresponding to 0.75, 0.05 and 0.20, respectively), while words with less that $n_p = 4$ phonemes are removed. Finally, we add to the test set of the dictionary those words we initially assigned to the training and validation sets that do not occur in the LRS2 pretrain or train sets, since they are not used in any way during training.

4.2   Minibatches, Training Sets and Backend

Minibatches for training the KWS model should contain both positive and negative examples, i.e. pairs of videos and keywords where each pair is considered as positive when the video contains the corresponding keyword and negative otherwise. Epochs and minibatches are defined based on the videos, i.e. each epoch contains all videos of the train and pretrain set of LRS2, partitioned into minibatches. The list of keywords in each minibatch is created by all words occurring in the minibatch belonging to the training set of CMU dictionary and having at least n_p number of phonemes. At each minibatch, each video is paired with (a) all its keywords (positive pairs) and (b) an equal number of other randomly chosen keywords from the list (negative pairs). This way we ensure that each video has equal number of positive and negative examples. At each epoch we shuffle the videos in order to create new negative pairs. By feeding the algorithm with the same set of videos and keywords under different binary labels in each minibatch, we enforce it to capture the correlations between videos and words, instead of attempting to correlate the binary label with certain keywords or with irrelevant aspects of specific videos.

For the first 20 epochs we use (a) only the train set of LRS2 (because it contains shorter utterances and much fewer labeling errors compared to the pretrain), (b) $n_p = 4$ and $\alpha_w = 1.0$ (i.e. minimum number of phonemes and weight of auxiliary loss, respectively), and (c) the simple feed-forward backend. After the 20th epoch (a) we add the pretrain set, (b) we set $n_p = 6$ and $\alpha_w = 0.1$, and (c) we replace the backend with the BiLSTM-based (all network parameters but those of the backend are kept frozen during the 21st epoch).

4.3   Optimization

The loss function in Eq. (5) is optimized with backpropagation using the Adam optimizer [46]. The number of epochs is 100, the initial learning rate is 2×10^{-3} and we drop it by a factor of 2 every 20 epochs. The best model is chosen based on the performance on the validation set. The implementation is based on PyTorch and the code together with pretrained models and ResNet features will be released soon. The number of videos in each minibatch is 40, however, as explained in Sect. 4.2, we create multiple training examples per video (equal to twice the number of training keywords it contains). Finally, the ResNet is optimized with the configuration suggested in [34].

5   Experiments

We present here the experimental set-up, the metrics we use and the results we obtain using the proposed KWS model. Moreover, we report baseline results using (a) a visual ASR model with a hybrid CTC/attention architecture, and (b) an implementation of the ASR-free KWS method recently proposed in [4].

5.1   Evaluation Metrics and Keyword Selection

KWS is essentially a detection problem, and in such problems the optimal threshold is application-dependent, typically determined by the desired balance between the false alarm rate (FAR) and the missed detection rate (MDR). Our primary error metric is the Equal Error Rate (EER), defined as the FAR (or MDR) when the threshold is set so that the two rates are equal. We also report MDR for certain low values of FAR (and vice versa) as well as FAR vs. MDR curves.

Apart from EER, FAR and MDR we evaluate the performance based on ranking measures. More specifically, for each text query (i.e. keyword) we report the percentage of times the score of a video containing the query is within the Top-N scores, where $N \in \{1, 2, 4, 8\}$. Since a query q may occur in more than one videos, a positive pair with score $s_{q,v'}$ is considered as Top-N if the number of negative pairs associated with the given query q with score higher than $s_{q,v'}$ is less than N, i.e. if $|\{q, v | l_{q,v} = 0, s_{q,v} > s_{q,v'}\}| < N$.

The evaluation is performed by creating a list of single-word queries, containing all words appearing in the test utterances and having at least 6 phonemes. Keywords appearing in the training and development sets are removed from the list. The final number of queries in the list is $N_q = 635$. Each query is scored against all $N_{test} = 1243$ test videos, so the number of all pairs is $N_q N_{test} = 789305$. The number of positive pairs is $N_p = |\{q, v | l_{q,v} = 1\}| = 873$, and $N_p > N_q$ because some keywords appear in more than one videos.

5.2   Baseline and Proposed Networks

CTC/Attention Hybrid ASR Model. We present here our baseline obtained with a ASR-based model. We use the same ResNet features but a deeper (4-layer) and wider (320-unit) BiLSTM. The implementation is based on the open-source ESPnet Python toolkit presented in [47] using the hybrid CTC/attention character-level network introduced in [48]. The system is trained on the pretrain and train sets of LRS2, while for training the language model we also use the Librispeech corpus [49]. The network attains WER = 71.4% on the LRS2 test set. In decoding, we use the single step decoder beam search (proposed in [48]) with $|H| = 40$ number of decoding hypotheses $h \in H$. Similarly to [50], instead of searching for the keyword only on the best decoding hypothesis we approximate the posterior probability that a keyword q occurs in the video v with feature sequence $\mathbf{X}$ as follows:

$$P(l = 1|\mathbf{q}, \mathbf{X}) = \sum_{h \in H} \mathbf{1}_{[q \in h]} P(h|\mathbf{X}), \tag{6}$$

$$P(h|\mathbf{X}) \approx \frac{\exp(s_h/c)}{\sum_{h' \in H} \exp(s_{h'}/c)}, \tag{7}$$

where $\mathbf{1}_{[q \in h]}$ is the indicator function that the decoding hypothesis h contains q, s_h is the score (log-likelihood) of hypothesis h (combining CTC and attention [48]) and $c = 5.0$ is a fudge factor optimized in the validation set.

Baseline with Video Embeddings. We implement an ASR-free method that is very close to [4] proposed for audio-based KWS. Different to [4] we use our LSTM-based encoder-decoder instead of the proposed CNN-based. A video embedding is extracted from the whole utterance, is concatenated with the word representation and fed to a feed-forward binary classifier as in [4]. This network is useful in order to emphasize the effectiveness of our frame-level concatenation.

Proposed Network and Alternative Encoder-Decoder Losses. To assess the effectiveness of the proposed G2P training method, we examine 3 alternative strategies: (a) The encoder receives gradients merely from the decoder, which is equivalent to training a G2P network separately, using only the words appearing in the training set. (b) The network has no decoder, auxiliary loss or phoneme-based supervision, i.e. the encoder is trained by minimizing the primary loss only. (c) A Grapheme-to-Grapheme (G2G) network is used instead of a G2P. The advantage of this approach over G2P is that it does not require a pronunciation dictionary, i.e. it requires less supervision. The advantage over the second approach is the use of the auxiliary loss (over graphemes instead of phonemes), which acts as a regularizer.

5.3   Experimental Results on LRS2

Our first set of results based on the detection metrics are given in Table 1. We observe that all variants of the proposed network attain much better performance compared to video embeddings. Clearly, video-level representations cannot retain the fine-grained information required to spot individual words. Our best network is the proposed Joint-G2P network (i.e. KWS network jointly trained with G2P), while the degradation of the network when graphemes are used as targets in the auxiliary loss (Joint-G2G) underlines the benefits from using phonetic supervision. Nevertheless, the degradation is relatively small, showing that the proposed architecture is capable of learning basic pronunciation rules even without phonetic supervision. Finally, the variant without a decoder during training is inferior to all other variants (including Joint-G2G), showing the regularization capacity of the decoder. The FAR-MDR tradeoff curves are depicted in Fig. 3(a), obtained by shifting the decision threshold which we apply to the output of the network. The curves show that the proposed architecture with G2P and joint training is superior to all others examined and in all operating points. Finally, we omit results obtained with the ASR-based model as the scoring rule described in Eqs. (6) and (7) is inadequate for measuring EER. The model yields very low FAR ($\approx$ 0.2%) at the cost of very high MDR ($\approx$ 63%) of all reasonable operating points.

Table 1. Equal-Error, False Alarm and Missed Detection Rates

Network	EER	MDR$_{FAR=5\%}$	MDR$_{FAR=1\%}$	FAR$_{MDR=5\%}$	FAR$_{MDR=1\%}$
Video Embed.	32.09%	77.32%	92.67%	66.76%	83.57%
Prop. w/o Dec.	8.46%	14.09%	40.32%	14.25%	36.43%
Prop. G2P-only	7.22%	10.88%	29.21%	10.85%	30.99%
Prop. Joint-G2G	7.26%	10.08%	27.38%	10.51%	40.26%
Prop. Joint-G2P	**6.46%**	**8.93%**	**26.00%**	**8.48%**	**20.11%**

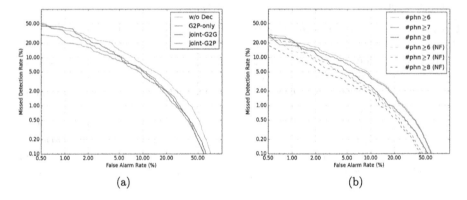

(a)   (b)

Fig. 3. FAR-MDR tradeoff. (a) Comparison between configurations of the proposed network. (b) The effect of the minimum number of phonemes per keyword and the camera view in the performance attained by Joint-G2P. As expected, longer keywords and near frontal (NF) view yield better results.

Length of Keywords and Camera View. We are also interested in examining the extent to which the length of the keyword affects the performance. To this end, we increase the minimum number of phonemes from $n_p = 6$ to 7 and 8. Moreover, we evaluate the network only on those videos labeled as Near-Frontal (NF) view, by removing those labeled as Multi-View (the labeling is given in the annotation files of LRS2). The results are plotted in Fig. 3(b). As expected, the longer the keywords, the lower the error rates. Moreover, the performance is better when only NF views are considered.

Ranking Measures and Localization Accuracy. We measure here the percentage of times videos containing the query are in the top-N scores. The results are given in Table 2. As we observe, our best system scores Top-1 equal to 34.14% meaning that in about 1 out of 3 queries, the video containing the query is ranked first amongst the $N_{test} = 1243$ videos. Moreover, in 2 out of 3 queries the video containing the query is amongst the Top-8. The other training strategies perform well, too, especially the one where the encoder is trained merely with the auxiliary loss (G2P-only). The ranking measures attained by the Video-Embedding method are very bad so we omit them. The ASR-based system attains relatively high Top-1 score, however the rest of the scores are rather poor. We should emphasize though that other ASR-based KWS methods exist for approximating the posterior of a keyword occurrence, e.g. using explicit keyword lattices [51], instead of using the set of decoding hypotheses H created by the beam search in Eqs. (6) and (7).

Finally, we report the localization accuracy for all versions of the proposed network, defined as the percentage of times the estimated location $\hat{t}$ lies within the keyword boundaries (± 2 frames). The reference word boundaries are estimated by applying forced alignment between the audio and the actual text. We observe that although the algorithm is trained without any information about the location of the keywords, it can still provide a very precise estimate of the location of the keyword in the vast majority of cases.

Table 2. Ranking results showing the rate by which the video sequence containing the keyword is amongst the top-N scores. Localization accuracy is also provided

Network	Top-1	Top-2	Top-4	Top-8	Local. Acc.
ASR-based	24.51%	31.39%	33.51%	37.57%	-
Prop. w/o Dec	23.71%	33.68%	43.99%	55.90%	96.20%
Prop. G2P-only	**34.14%**	46.28%	**57.16%**	65.75%	97.39%
Prop. Joint-G2G	31.16%	43.07%	54.98%	65.75%	**97.86%**
Prop. Joint-G2P	**34.14%**	**46.96%**	57.04%	**67.70%**	96.67%

6 Conclusions

We proposed an architecture for visual-only KWS with text queries. Rather than using subword units (e.g. phonemes, visemes) as main recognition units, we followed the direction of modeling words directly. Contrary to other word-based approaches, which treat words merely as classes defined by a label (e.g. [35]), we inject into the model a word representation extracted by a grapheme-to-phoneme model. This zero-shot learning approach enables the model to learn nonlinear correlations between visual frames and word representations and to transfer its knowledge to words unseen during training. The experiments showed that the proposed method is capable of attaining very promising results on the most challenging publicly available dataset (LRS2), outperforming the two baselines by a large margin. Finally, we demonstrated its capacity in localizing the keyword in the frame sequence, even though we do not use any information about the location of the keyword during training.

Acknowledgements. This project has received funding from the European Union's Horizon 2020 research and innovation programme under the Marie Sklodowska-Curie grant agreement No. 706668 (Talking Heads). We are grateful to Dr. Stavros Petridis and Mr. Pingchuan Ma (i-bug, Imperial College London) for their contribution to the ASR-based experiments.

References

1. Chung, J.S., Senior, A., Vinyals, O., Zisserman, A.: Lip reading sentences in the wild. In: Computer Vision and Pattern Recognition (CVPR) (2017)
2. Chung, J.S., Zisserman, A.: Lip reading in the wild. In: Lai, S.-H., Lepetit, V., Nishino, K., Sato, Y. (eds.) ACCV 2016. LNCS, vol. 10112, pp. 87–103. Springer, Cham (2017). https://doi.org/10.1007/978-3-319-54184-6_6
3. Anina, I., Zhou, Z., Zhao, G., Pietikäinen, M.: OuluVS2: a multi-view audiovisual database for non-rigid mouth motion analysis. In: 2015 11th IEEE International Conference and Workshops on Automatic Face and Gesture Recognition (FG), vol. 1, pp. 1–5. IEEE (2015)
4. Audhkhasi, K., Rosenberg, A., Sethy, A., Ramabhadran, B., Kingsbury, B.: End-to-end ASR-free keyword search from speech. IEEE J. Selected Top. Signal Process. **11**(8), 1351–1359 (2017)
5. Audhkhasi, K., Ramabhadran, B., Saon, G., Picheny, M., Nahamoo, D.: Direct acoustics-to-word models for english conversational speech recognition. In: Interspeech (2017)
6. Soltau, H., Liao, H., Sak, H.: Neural speech recognizer: acoustic-to-word LSTM model for large vocabulary speech recognition. In: Interspeech (2017)
7. Socher, R., Ganjoo, M., Manning, C.D., Ng, A.: Zero-shot learning through cross-modal transfer. In: Advances in Neural Information Processing Systems (NIPS) (2013)
8. Chung, J.S., Zisserman, A.: Lipreading Sentences in the wild (link to LRS2). http://www.robots.ox.ac.uk/~vgg/data/lip_reading_sentences/
9. Assael, Y.M., Shillingford, B., Whiteson, S., de Freitas, N.: Lipnet: Sentence-level lipreading. arXiv preprint arXiv:1611.01599 (2016)
10. Cooke, M., Barker, J., Cunningham, S., Shao, X.: An audio-visual corpus for speech perception and automatic speech recognition. J. Acoust. Soc. America **120**(5), 2421–2424 (2006)
11. Graves, A., Jaitly, N.: Towards end-to-end speech recognition with recurrent neural networks. In: International Conference on Machine Learning, pp. 1764–1772 (2014)
12. Zweig, G., Yu, C., Droppo, J., Stolcke, A.: Advances in all-neural speech recognition. In: IEEE International Conference on Acoustics, Speech and Signal Processing (ICASSP), pp. 4805–4809. IEEE (2017)
13. Chung, J.S., Zisserman, A.: Lip reading in profile. In: British Machine Vision Conference (BMVC) (2017)
14. Chan, W., Jaitly, N., Le, Q., Vinyals, O.: Listen, attend and spell: A neural network for large vocabulary conversational speech recognition. In: IEEE International Conference on Acoustics, Speech and Signal Processing (ICASSP), pp. 4960–4964 (2016)

15. Bear, H.L., Harvey, R.: Decoding visemes: improving machine lip-reading. In: IEEE International Conference on Acoustics, Speech and Signal Processing (ICASSP), pp. 2009–2013. IEEE (2016)
16. Vaswani, A., et al.: Attention is all you need. In: Advances in Neural Information Processing Systems (NIPS), pp. 5998–6008 (2017)
17. Koumparoulis, A., Potamianos, G., Mroueh, Y., Rennie, S.J.: Exploring ROI size in deep learning based lipreading. In: AVSP (2017)
18. Petridis, S., Stafylakis, T., Ma, P., Cai, F., Tzimiropoulos, G., Pantic, M.: End-to-end audiovisual speech recognition. In: International Conference on Acoustics, Speech and Signal Processing (ICASSP) (2018)
19. Wand, M., Schmidhuber, J.: Improving speaker-independent lipreading with domain-adversarial training. In: Interspeech (2017)
20. Afouras, T., Chung, J.S., Zisserman, A.: Deep lip reading: a comparison of models and an online application. arXiv preprint arXiv:1806.06053 (2018)
21. Xu, K., Li, D., Cassimatis, N., Wang, X.: LCANet: end-to-end lipreading with cascaded attention-CTC. In: 13th IEEE International Conference on Automatic Face & Gesture Recognition (FG), pp. 548–555. IEEE (2018)
22. Sterpu, G., Saam, C., Harte, N.: Can DNNs learn to lipread full sentences? arXiv preprint arXiv:1805.11685 (2018)
23. Tao, F., Busso, C.: Gating neural network for large vocabulary audiovisual speech recognition. IEEE/ACM Trans. Audio Speech Lang. Process. (TASLP) **26**(7), 1286–1298 (2018)
24. Mroueh, Y., Marcheret, E., Goel, V.: Deep multimodal learning for audio-visual speech recognition. In: IEEE International Conference on Acoustics, Speech and Signal Processing (ICASSP), pp. 2130–2134. IEEE (2015)
25. Bengio, S., Heigold, G.: Word embeddings for speech recognition. In: Interspeech (2014)
26. Pennington, J., Socher, R., Manning, C.: Glove: Global vectors for word representation. In: Proceedings of the 2014 Conference on Empirical Methods in Natural Language Processing (EMNLP), pp. 1532–1543 (2014)
27. Mikolov, T., Sutskever, I., Chen, K., Corrado, G.S., Dean, J.: Distributed representations of words and phrases and their compositionality. In: Advances in Neural Information Processing Systems (NIPS), pp. 3111–3119 (2013)
28. Palaz, D., Synnaeve, G., Collobert, R.: Jointly learning to locate and classify words using convolutional networks. In: Interspeech, pp. 2741–2745 (2016)
29. Sun, M., et al.: Compressed time delay neural network for small-footprint keyword spotting. In: Interspeech, pp. 3607–3611 (2017)
30. Sun, M., Nagaraja, V., Hoffmeister, B., Vitaladevuni, S.: Model shrinking for embedded keyword spotting. In: IEEE 14th International Conference on Machine Learning and Applications (ICMLA), pp. 369–374. IEEE (2015)
31. Chen, G., Parada, C., Heigold, G.: Small-footprint keyword spotting using deep neural networks. In: IEEE International Conference on Acoustics, Speech and Signal Processing (ICASSP), pp. 4087–4091 (2014)
32. Fernández, S., Graves, A., Schmidhuber, J.: An application of recurrent neural networks to discriminative keyword spotting. In: de Sá, J.M., Alexandre, L.A., Duch, W., Mandic, D. (eds.) ICANN 2007. LNCS, vol. 4669, pp. 220–229. Springer, Heidelberg (2007). https://doi.org/10.1007/978-3-540-74695-9_23
33. Jha, A., Namboodiri, V.P., Jawahar, C.: Word spotting in silent lip videos. In: 2018 IEEE Winter Conference on Applications of Computer Vision (WACV), pp. 150–159. IEEE (2018)

34. Stafylakis, T., Tzimiropoulos, G.: Combining Residual Networks with LSTMs for Lipreading. In: Interspeech (2017)
35. Stafylakis, T., Tzimiropoulos, G.: Deep word embeddings for visual speech recognition. In: International Conference on Acoustics, Speech and Signal Processing (ICASSP) (2018)
36. Chung, J.S., Zisserman, A.: Lipreading in the wild (link to LRW), http://www.robots.ox.ac.uk/~vgg/data/lip_reading/
37. Xian, Y., Lampert, C.H., Schiele, B., Akata, Z.: Zero-shot learning-a comprehensive evaluation of the good, the bad and the ugly. arXiv preprint arXiv:1707.00600 (2017)
38. Frome, A., et al.: Devise: A deep visual-semantic embedding model. In: Advances in Neural Information Processing Systems (NIPS), pp. 2121–2129 (2013)
39. Akata, Z., Perronnin, F., Harchaoui, Z., Schmid, C.: Label-embedding for image classification. IEEE Trans. Pattern Anal. Mach. Intell. **38**(7), 1425–1438 (2016)
40. Mahasseni, B., Todorovic, S.: Regularizing long short term memory with 3D human-skeleton sequences for action recognition. In: The IEEE Conference on Computer Vision and Pattern Recognition (CVPR), June 2016
41. Yao, K., Zweig, G.: Sequence-to-sequence neural net models for grapheme-to-phoneme conversion. arXiv preprint arXiv:1506.00196 (2015)
42. Sutskever, I., Vinyals, O., Le, Q.V.: Sequence to sequence learning with neural networks. In: Advances in Neural Information Processing Systems, pp. 3104–3112 (2014)
43. He, K., Zhang, X., Ren, S., Sun, J.: Identity mappings in deep residual networks. In: Leibe, B., Matas, J., Sebe, N., Welling, M. (eds.) ECCV 2016. LNCS, vol. 9908, pp. 630–645. Springer, Cham (2016). https://doi.org/10.1007/978-3-319-46493-0_38
44. Hochreiter, S., Schmidhuber, J.: Long short-term memory. Neural Comput. **9**(8), 1735–1780 (1997)
45. Gal, Y., Ghahramani, Z.: A theoretically grounded application of dropout in recurrent neural networks. In: Advances in Neural Information Processing Systems (NIPS), pp. 1019–1027 (2016)
46. Kingma, D.P., Ba, J.: Adam: a method for stochastic optimization. In: ICLR (2014)
47. Watanabe, S., et al.: ESPnet: end-to-end speech processing toolkit. arXiv preprint arXiv:1804.00015 (2018)
48. Watanabe, S., Hori, T., Kim, S., Hershey, J.R., Hayashi, T.: Hybrid CTC/attention architecture for end-to-end speech recognition. IEEE J. Selected Top. Signal Process. **11**(8), 1240–1253 (2017)
49. Panayotov, V., Chen, G., Povey, D., Khudanpur, S.: Librispeech: an ASR corpus based on public domain audio books. In: IEEE International Conference on Acoustics, Speech and Signal Processing (ICASSP), pp. 5206–5210. IEEE (2015)
50. Miller, D.R., et al.: Rapid and accurate spoken term detection. In: Eighth Annual Conference of the International Speech Communication Association (2007)
51. Zhuang, Y., Chang, X., Qian, Y., Yu, K.: Unrestricted vocabulary keyword spotting using LSTM-CTC. In: Interspeech, pp. 938–942 (2016)

Real-to-Virtual Domain Unification for End-to-End Autonomous Driving

Luona Yang[1], Xiaodan Liang[1,2(✉)], Tairui Wang[2], and Eric Xing[1,2]

[1] Carnegie Mellon University, Pittsburgh, PA, USA
{luonay1,xiaodan1,epxing}@cs.cmu.edu
[2] Petuum Inc., Pittsburgh, PA, USA
tairui.wang@petuum.com

Abstract. In the spectrum of vision-based autonomous driving, vanilla end-to-end models are not interpretable and suboptimal in performance, while mediated perception models require additional intermediate representations such as segmentation masks or detection bounding boxes, whose annotation can be prohibitively expensive as we move to a larger scale. More critically, all prior works fail to deal with the notorious domain shift if we were to merge data collected from different sources, which greatly hinders the model generalization ability. In this work, we address the above limitations by taking advantage of virtual data collected from driving simulators, and present DU-drive, an unsupervised real-to-virtual domain unification framework for end-to-end autonomous driving. It first transforms real driving data to its less complex counterpart in the virtual domain, and then predicts vehicle control commands from the generated virtual image. Our framework has three unique advantages: (1) it maps driving data collected from a variety of source distributions into a unified domain, effectively eliminating domain shift; (2) the learned virtual representation is simpler than the input real image and closer in form to the "minimum sufficient statistic" for the prediction task, which relieves the burden of the compression phase while optimizing the information bottleneck tradeoff and leads to superior prediction performance; (3) it takes advantage of annotated virtual data which is unlimited and free to obtain. Extensive experiments on two public driving datasets and two driving simulators demonstrate the performance superiority and interpretive capability of DU-drive.

Keywords: Domain unification · End-to-end autonomous driving

1 Introduction

The development of a vision-based autonomous driving system has been a longstanding research problem [1–4]. End-to-end models, among many methods, have attracted much research interest [5–7] as they optimize all intermediate procedures simultaneously and eliminate the tedious process of feature engineering. [5] trains a convolutional neural network (CNN) to map raw image pixels from a

© Springer Nature Switzerland AG 2018
V. Ferrari et al. (Eds.): ECCV 2018, LNCS 11208, pp. 553–570, 2018.
https://doi.org/10.1007/978-3-030-01225-0_33

frontal camera to steering commands, which successfully maneuvered the test car in constrained environments. Many attempts have since been made to improve the performance of vanilla end-to-end models by taking advantage of intermediate representations (Fig. 1). For example, [6] uses semantic segmentation as a side task to improve model performance, while [8] first trains a detector to detect nearby vehicles before making driving decisions. However, the collection of driving data and the annotation of intermediate representation can be prohibitively expensive as we move to a larger scale.

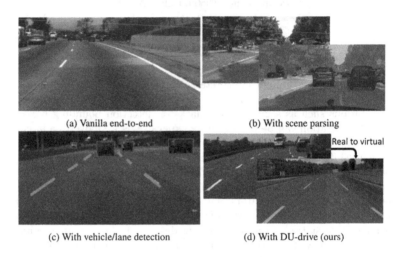

(a) Vanilla end-to-end   (b) With scene parsing

(c) With vehicle/lane detection   (d) With DU-drive (ours)

Fig. 1. Various methods have been proposed for vision-based driving models. While vanilla end-to-end models (a) are not interpretable and suboptimal in performance, scene parsing (b) or object detection (c) requires expensively annotated data. Our method (d) unifies real images from different datasets into their simpler counterparts in the virtual domain that contains less superfluous details, which boosts the performance of vehicle command prediction task.

Moreover, raw images of driving scenes are loaded with nuisance details that are not relevant to the prediction task due to the complexity of the real world. For example, a typical human driver will not change his or her behavior according to the shadow of trees on the road, or the view beyond the road boundaries. Such nuisance information could distract the neural network from what is truly important and negatively impact prediction performance. [9] visualizes the activation of the neural network and shows that the model not only learns driving-critical information such as lane markings, but also unexpected features such as atypical vehicle classes. [7] presents results of the driving model's attention map refined by causal filtering, which seems to include rather random attention blobs.

As pointed out by [10] in the information bottleneck principle, the learning objective for a deep neural network could be formulated as finding the optimal representation that maximally compresses the information in the input while preserving as much information as possible about the output, or in other words, finding an approximate minimal sufficient statistic of the input with respect to the output. Further work [11] shows that the Stochastic Gradient Descent (SGD) optimization of the neural network has two distinct phases, the fitting phase during which the mutual information of the intermediate layers with the output increases and empirical error drops, and the compression phase during which the mutual information of the intermediate layers with the input decreases and the representation becomes closer in form to the minimum sufficient statistic of the output. They also show that most of the training effort is spent on the compression phase, which is the key to good generalization. It is therefore beneficial for the optimization of the network to have a representation that contains less irrelevant complexity, as it could relieve the burden of the compression phase by giving a better "initialization" of the optimal representation.

More critically, all existing work focuses on a single source of data and does not explicitly deal with generalization to an unseen dataset. As noted by [12], datasets could have strong built-in biases, and a well-functioning model trained on one dataset will very likely not work so well on another dataset that is collected differently. This phenomenon is known as domain shift, which characterizes the distance in the distribution of inputs and outputs from different domains. While the existing model could be tuned to gradually fit the new domain with the injection of more and more supervised data from the new environment, this could be extremely data inefficient and prohibitively expensive for tasks with diverse application scenarios like autonomous driving.

We propose to tackle the above challenges by taking advantage of virtual data collected from simulators. Our DU-drive system maps real driving images collected under variant conditions into a unified virtual domain, and then predict vehicle command from the generated fake virtual image. Since all real datasets are mapped to the same domain, we could easily extend our model to unseen datasets while taking full advantage of the knowledge learned from existing ones. Moreover, virtual images are "cleaner" as they are less complex and contain less noise, and are thus closer to the "minimal sufficient statistic" of vehicle command prediction task, which is the target representation that the neural network should learn under the information bottleneck framework. Last but not least, our model could take full use of unlimited virtual data and the simulation environment, and a model learned in the virtual environment could be directly applied to a new dataset after unifying it to the virtual domain. Experimental results on two public driving datasets and two driving simulators under supervised and semi-supervised setting, together with analysis on the efficiency of the learned virtual representation compared to raw image input under the information bottleneck framework clearly demonstrate the performance superiority of our method.

2   Related Work

2.1   Vision-Based Autonomous Driving

Vision-based solutions are believed to be a promising direction for solving autonomous driving due to their low sensor cost and recent developments in computer vision. Since the first successful demonstration in the 1980s [1,3,4], various methods have been investigated in the spectrum of vision-based driving models, from end-to-end methods to full pipeline methods [13]. The ALVINN system [2], first introduced in 1989, is the pioneering work in end-to-end learning for autonomous driving. It shows that an end-to-end model can indeed learn to steer on simple road conditions. The network architecture has since evolved from the small fully-connected network of ALVINN into convolutional networks used by DAVE system [14] and then deep models used by DAVE-2 system [5]. Intermediate representations such as semantic segmentation masks and attention maps are shown to be helpful to improving the performance [6,7].

Pipeline methods separate the parsing of the scene and the control of the vehicle. [8] first trains a vehicle detector to determine the location of adjacent cars and outputs vehicle commands according to a simple control logic. [15] shows that convolutional neural networks can be used to do real-time lane and vehicle detection. While such methods are more interpretable and controllable, the annotation of intermediate representations can be very expensive.

Our method takes advantage of an intermediate representation obtained from unsupervised training and therefore improves the performance of vanilla end-to-end driving models without introducing any annotation cost.

2.2   Domain Adaption for Visual Data

Ideally, a model trained for a specific task should be able to generalize to new datasets collected for the same task, yet research has shown that model performance could seriously degrade when the input distribution changes due to the inherent bias introduced in the data collection process [12]. This phenomenon is known as domain shift or dataset bias. In the world of autonomous driving, it is even more critical to have a model that can generalize well to unseen scenarios.

Domain adaption methods attempt to battle domain shift by bridging the gap between the distribution of source data and target data [16,17]. Recently, generative adversarial network (GAN) based domain adaption, also known as adversarial adaption, has achieved remarkable results in the field of visual domain adaption. [18] introduces a framework that subsumes several approaches as special cases [19–21]. It frames adversarial adaption as training an encoder (generator) that transforms data in the target domain to the source domain at a certain feature level trying to fool the adversarial discriminator, which in turn tries to distinguish the generated data from those sampled from the source domain. The line of work on style transfer [22–24] could also be potentially applied to domain adaption at the pixel level.

One subarea especially to our interest is the adaption of virtual data to real data. As the collection of real-world data can be excessively expensive in certain cases, virtual data rendered with computer graphics technologies can come to remedy if we could adapt knowledge learned in the virtual domain to the real domain. [25] proposed a GAN-based model that transforms data from virtual domain to the real domain in the pixel space in an unsupervised manner by utilizing a content-similarity loss to retain annotation. [26] uses adversarial training to improve the realism of synthetic images with the help a self-regularization term, a local adversarial loss and a buffer of training images for the discriminator. [27] randomizes the texture of objects in the robot simulator and trains a visuomotor policy without using any real-world data. [28] trains a driving policy with reinforcement learning in a simulator by transforming virtual images to real images, retaining the scene structure with an adversarial loss on the segmentation mask.

While existing work aims at transforming virtual images to realistic looking images, we argue that doing it the other way around could be more advantageous for learning a driving policy. The transformation from real to virtual is an easier task as it is more manageable to go from complex to simple, and all real datasets could be unified into their simpler counterparts in the virtual domain.

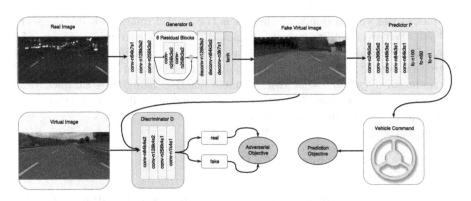

Fig. 2. Model architecture for DU-Drive. The generator network G transforms input real image to fake virtual image, from which vehicle command is predicted by the predictor network P. The discriminator network D tries to distinguish the fake virtual images from true virtual images. Both the adversarial objective and the prediction objective drive the generator G to generate the virtual representation that yields the best prediction performance. For simplicity, instance normalization and activation layers after each convolutional/fully connected layer are omitted. (Abbr: n: number of filters, k: kernel size, s: stride size)

3   Unsupervised Domain Unification

3.1   Network Design and Learning Objective

Learning Objective for DU-Drive. Given a dataset of driving images labeled with vehicle command in the real domain and a similar dataset in the virtual domain, our goal is to transform a real image into the virtual domain and then run prediction algorithm on the transformed fake virtual image. The overall architecture is shown in Fig. 2. Our model is closely related to conditional GAN [29], where the generator and discriminator both take a conditional factor as input, yet different in two subtle aspects. One is that in our model, the discriminator does not depend on the conditional factor. The other is that our generator does not take any noise vector as input. Unlike the mapping from a plain virtual image to a rich real image, where there could be multiple feasible solutions, the mapping from a real image to its less complex virtual counterpart should be more constrained and close to unique. Therefore, we could remove the noise term in conventional GANs and use a deterministic generative network as our generator.

More formally, let $\mathbf{X}^r = \{\mathbf{x}_i^r, \mathbf{y}_i^r\}_{i=1}^{N_r}$ be a labeled dataset with N^r samples in the real domain, and let $\mathbf{X}^v = \{\mathbf{x}_i^v, \mathbf{y}_i^v\}_{i=1}^{N^v}$ be a labeled dataset with N^v samples in the virtual domain, where $\mathbf{x}$ is the frontal image of a driving scene and $\mathbf{y}$ is the corresponding vehicle command. Our DU-drive model consists of a deterministic conditional generator $G(\mathbf{x}^r; \theta_G) \rightarrow \mathbf{x}^f$, parametrized by θ_G, that maps an image $\mathbf{x}^r \in \mathbf{X}^r$ in the real domain to a fake virtual image $\mathbf{x}^f$, a virtual discriminator $D(\mathbf{x}^v; \theta_D)$ that discriminates whether a image is sampled from true virtual images or from fake virtual images, and a predictor $P(\mathbf{x}^v; \theta_P) \rightarrow y^v$, that maps a virtual image to a vehicle control command.

The learning objective of DU-drive is:

$$\min_{\theta_G, \theta_P} \max_{\theta_D} \mathcal{L}_d(D, G) + \lambda L_t(P, G), \tag{1}$$

where $\mathcal{L}_d(D, G)$ is the domain loss, which the generator tries to minimize and the discriminator tries to maximize in the minimax game of GAN. $\mathcal{L}_d(D, G)$ is defined as:

$$\mathcal{L}_d(D, G) = \mathbb{E}_{\mathbf{x}^v} [\log D(\mathbf{x}^v; \theta_D)] + \tag{2}$$
$$\mathbb{E}_{\mathbf{x}^r} [\log(1 - D(G(\mathbf{x}^r; \theta_G); \theta_D))], \tag{3}$$

$\mathcal{L}_t(P, G)$ is the task specific objective for predictor and generator, which in this work is the mean square loss between the predicted control command and the ground truth control command, defined as:

$$\mathcal{L}_t(P, G) = \mathbb{E}_{\mathbf{x}^r} [\|P(G(\mathbf{x}^r; \theta_G), \theta_P) - \mathbf{y}^r\|_2^2] \tag{4}$$

λ is a hyperparameter that controls the weight of task-specific loss and the domain loss.

Network Design. For the GAN part of the model, we mostly adopt the network architecture in [24], which has achieved impressive results in style transfer task. The generator network consists of two convolutional layers with 3×3 kernel and stride size 2, followed by 6 residual blocks. Two deconvolutional layers with stride 1/2 then transform the feature to the same size as the input image. We use instance normalization for all the layers. For the discriminator network, we use a fully convolutional network with convolutional layers of filter size 64, 128, 256 and 1 respectively. Each convolutional layer is followed by instance normalization and Leaky ReLU nonlinearity. We do not use PatchGAN as employed in [23] because driving command prediction needs global structure information.

For the predictor network, we adopt the network architecture used in DAVE-2 system [5], also known as *PilotNet*, as it has achieved decent results in end-to-end driving [5,9,24]. The network contains 5 convolutional layers and 4 fully connected layers. The first three convolutional layers have kernel size 5×5 and stride size 3, while the last two layers have kernel size 3×3 and stride size 1. No padding is used. The last convolutional layer is flattened and immediately followed by four fully connected layers with output size 100, 50, 10 and 1 respectively. All layers use ReLU activation.

3.2   Learning

Our goal is to learn a conditional generator that maps a real image into the virtual domain. However, a naive implementation of conditional GAN is insufficient for two reasons. First, the adversarial loss only provides supervision at the level of image distribution and does not guarantee the retention of the label after transformation. Second, conventional GANs are vulnerable to mode collapse, a common pitfall during the optimization of the GAN objective where the distribution of transformed images degenerates. Previous work on adapting virtual image to real image alleviates those problems by introducing a task-specific loss to add additional constraints to the image generated. For example, [25] uses a content similarity loss to enforce that the foreground of the generated image matches with that of the input image. [26] employs a self-regularization term that minimizes the image difference between the synthetic and refined images.

Unfortunately, we cannot take advantage of similar techniques as the "foreground", or the information critical to retaining the label is not obvious for autonomous driving. Instead, we introduce a joint training scheme, where the conditional generator and the predictor are trained simultaneously, so that the supervision from the prediction task gradually drives the generator to convert the input images from the real domain to its corresponding representation in the virtual domain that retains necessary semantics and yields the best prediction performance. More formally, our objective in Eq. 1 can be decomposed into three parts with respect to the three networks G, P and D:

$$\min_{\theta_G} \mathcal{L}_d(D, G) + \lambda L_t(P, G), \tag{5}$$

$$\min_{\theta_P} L_t(P, G), \tag{6}$$

$$\max_{\theta_D} \mathcal{L}_d(D, G) \tag{7}$$

We omit the weight term λ in Eq. 6, as it is easy to see that only θ_G is influenced by both the domain loss and the prediction loss, and we can train θ_D, θ_G and θ_P with respect to the three objectives above independently. We denote α_P as the learning rate for updating θ_P, and α_{GAN} as the learning rate for updating θ_D and θ_G.

During training, we update θ_D, θ_G and θ_P sequentially by alternately optimizing the above three objectives, so that the generation quality and prediction performance improves hand in hand.

3.3   Domain Unification

Consider the case when we have multiple real datasets $\{\mathbf{x}^{r_1}, \mathbf{y}^{r_1}\}, ..., \{\mathbf{x}^{r_n}, \mathbf{y}^{r_n}\}$. Due to different data distribution depicted by road appearance, lighting conditions or driving scenes, each dataset belongs to a unique domain which we denote as $D_{r_1}, ..., D_{r_n}$ respectively. Prior works on end-to-end driving tend to deal with only one domain rather than a more general reasoning system. DU-drive, however, unifies data from different real domains into a single virtual domain and eliminates the notorious domain shift problem.

For each real domain D_{r_i}, we use our DU-drive model to train a generator that transforms images $\mathbf{x}^{r_i}$ into their counterparts $\mathbf{x}^{f_i}$ in a unified virtual domain D_v (Fig. 3). A global predictor P_v could then be trained to do vehicle command prediction from the transformed virtual images. We fix the generator for each real domain and train the global predictor with labeled data from multiple real domains simultaneously. Same as our training setup for a single domain, we also use *PilotNet* pretrained on virtual data as our initialization for the global predictor.

3.4   Connection with Information Bottleneck Principle

Given a raw image input, what could be a good intermediate representation that could help boost the performance of the prediction task? We try to answer this questions under the information bottleneck framework.

Formally, let X be the raw image input and Y be the vehicle control command that is to be predicted. The information bottleneck objective of learning for a neural network is to find the optimal representation of X w.r.t. Y, which is the minimal sufficient statistic $T(x)$, the simplest sufficient statistic that captures all information about Y in X. However, closed form representation for the minimum

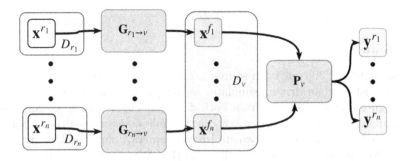

Fig. 3. Domain unification by DU-drive. For each real domain, a generator is trained independently to transform real images to fake virtual images in a unified virtual domain. A single virtual image to vehicle command predictor is trained to do prediction across multiple real domains.

sufficient statistic does not exist in general, and according to [11] this objective could be written as a tradeoff between compression of X and prediction of Y formulated in the following form:

$$\mathcal{L}[p(t|x)] = I(X;T) - \beta I(T;Y) \tag{8}$$

where $I(X;T)$ denotes the mutual information between the learned representation and input, and $I(T;Y)$ denotes the mutual information between the learned representation and output. This objective is optimized successively for each layer. At the beginning of training, the objective at input layer where $T = X$ could be written as

$$\begin{aligned} L_{\{T=X\}} &= I(X;X) - \beta I(X;Y) & (9)\\ &= H(X) - \beta(H(Y) - H(Y|X)) & (10)\\ &= H(X) - \beta H(Y) & (11) \end{aligned}$$

where Eq. 11 follows from the fact that X is a sufficient statistic for Y. Now, consider the case when we have an intermediate representation $G(X)$ of X. We assume that $G(X)$ is also a sufficient statistic of Y, which is reasonable for any meaningful intermediate representation. Then the objective when $T = G(X)$ is

$$\begin{aligned} L_{\{T=G(X)\}} &= I(X;G(X)) - \beta I(G(X);Y) & (12)\\ &= (H(G(X)) - H(G(X)|X)) - \beta(H(Y) - H(Y|X)) & (13)\\ &= H(G(X)) - \beta H(Y) & (14) \end{aligned}$$

Subtract Eq. 12 from Eq. 9 yields:

$$L_{\{T=X\}} - L_{\{T=G(X)\}} = H(X) - H(G(X)) \tag{15}$$

This essentially tells us that an intermediate representation with lower entropy could give a better initialization to the information bottleneck objective, which motivates us to transform real images into their simpler virtual counterparts.

4 Experiments

4.1 Data

We use TORCS [30], an open-source car racing simulator, and Carla [31], a recent realistic urban driving simulator as our platform for virtual data collection. Figure 4 shows samples from both datasets. For TORCS, we construct a virtual dataset by setting up a robot car that follows a simple driving policy as defined in [8] and marking down its frontal camera images and steering commands. We also included twelve traffic cars that follow a simple control logic as defined in [8], with random noise added to the control commands to encourage varied behaviors. We captured our data on six game tracks with different shapes. To account for the imbalance of right turns and left turns in the virtual data, which could introduce bias in the domain transformation process, we augment our data by flipping the image and negate the steering command. For Carla, we use the training dataset provided by [32].

We use two large-scale real-world datasets released by Comma.ai [33] and Udacity [34] respectively (Table 1). Both datasets are composed of several episodes of driving videos. For Comma.ai dataset, we follow the data reader provided by [33] and filter out data points where the steering wheel angle is greater than 200. For Udacity dataset, we use the official release of training/testing data for challenge II at [34]. Large variance could be observed in lighting/road conditions and roadside views.

4.2 Preprocessing

We first crop the input image to 160×320 by removing the extra upper part, which is usually background sky that does not change driving behavior. We then resize the image to 80×160 and normalize the pixel values to $[-1, 1]$.

Instead of predicting the steering angle command directly, we predict the inverse of the radius as it is more stable and invariant to the geometry of the data capturing car [5, 7]. The relationship between the inverse turning radius u_t and steering angle θ_t is characterized by the Ackermann steering geometry:

$$\theta_t = u_t d_w K_s (1 + K_{slip} v_t^2) \tag{16}$$

where θ_t is the steering command in radius, $u_t(1/m)$ is the inverse of the turning radius, $v_t(m/s)$ is the vehicle speed at time t. $d_w(m)$ stands for the wheelbase, which is the distance between the front and the rear wheel. K_{slip} is the slippery coefficient. K_s is the steering ratio between the turn of the steer and the turn of the wheels. We get d_w and K_s from car specifics released by the respective car manufacturer of the data capturing vehicle, and use the K_{slip} provided by Comma.ai [33], which is estimated from real data. After predicting u_t, we transform it back to θ_t according to Eq. 16 and measure the mean absolute error of steering angle prediction.

Fig. 4. Sample data used by our work. From top to down: Carla(virtual), TORCS(virtual), Comma.ai(Real), Udacity(real)

Table 1. Dataset details.

Dataset	Train/test frames	Lighting	Size
Commai.ai	345887/32018	Day/Night	160×320
Udacity	33808/5279	Day	240×320
Carla	657600/74600	Day/Dawn	88×200
TORCS	30183/3354	Day	240×320

4.3 Training Details

All the models are implemented in Tensorflow [35] and trained on an NVIDIA Titan-X GPU. We train all networks with Adam optimizer [36] and set $\beta_1 = 0.5$. We follow the techniques used in [22] to stabilize the training. First, we use LSGAN [37], where the conventional GAN objective is replaced by a least-square loss. Thus the loss function becomes

$$\mathcal{L}_d(D, G) = \mathbb{E}_{\mathbf{x}^v}[D(\mathbf{x}^v; \theta_D)^2] + \tag{17}$$

$$\mathbb{E}_{\mathbf{x}^r}[(1 - D(G(\mathbf{x}^r; \theta_G); \theta_D))^2], \tag{18}$$

Second, we train the discriminator using a buffer of generated images to alleviate model oscillation [26]. We use a buffer size of 50.

In order to take advantage of the labeled data collected from simulators, we initialize the predictor network with a model that is pretrained on virtual images. During pretraining, we set batch size to 2000 and learning rate to 0.01.

At each step, we sequentially update θ_G, θ_P and θ_D with respect to the objective functions in 5, 6 and 7. We use a batch size of 60. We set $\alpha_P = 0.0002$, $\alpha_{GAN} = 0.00002$, and $\lambda = 0.5$ to 1. We train the model for a total of 7 epochs.

After obtaining a real-to-virtual generator for each real domain, we could fix the generator and train a global predictor with all real datasets. We initialize the global predictor with *PilotNet* pretrained on virtual data, and use a learning rate of 0.001 and a batch size of 2000 for training.

4.4   Metrics and Baselines

We evaluate the effectiveness of our model in terms of the quality of generated images in the virtual domain and the mean absolute error of steering angle prediction. We compare the performance of DU-drive with the following baselines. To ensure fairness, we use the same architecture for the predictor network as described in Sect. 3.1.

- **Vanilla end-to-end model *(PilotNet)*** proposed by [5] maps a real driving image directly to the steering command.
- **Finetune from virtual data** We first train a predictor with virtual data only, then finetune it with the real dataset.
- **Conditional GAN** A naive implementation of conditional GAN (cGAN) [29] uses a generator G to transform an image x from the real domain to an image $G(x)$ in the virtual domain. A discriminative network D is set up to discriminate $G(x)$ from y sampled from the virtual domain while G tries to fool the discriminator. No additional supervision is provided other than the adversarial objective. We also train a *PilotNet* to predict steering angle from the fake virtual image generated by cGAN.
- ***PilotNet* joint training** We also directly train a *PilotNet* with two labeled real datasets simultaneously.

4.5   Quantitative Results and Comparisons

We compare the performance of steering command prediction for a single real domain of our DU-drive(single) model with the plain end-to-end model (*PilotNet*), finetuning from virtual data and conditional GAN without joint training (Table 2). Both DU-drive(single) and finetuning from virtual data performs better than the plain end-to-end model, which verifies the effectiveness of leveraging annotated virtual data. DU-drive(single) outperforms finetuning by 12%/20% using TORCS virtual data and 11%/41% using Carla virtual data for Comma.ai/Udacity dataset respectively, despite using the same training data and prediction network. This verifies the superiority of transforming complex real images into their simpler counterparts in the virtual domain for driving command prediction task. Conditional GAN without joint training does not perform well as adversarial objective itself is not enough to ensure the preservation of label. DU-drive runs at 89.2 fps when tested on a Titan-X GPU.

4.6   Information Bottleneck Analysis of Virtual Representation

As shown in Table 2, transforming real images to the virtual domain using our DU-drive model gives superior performance even with the same training data and predictor network. We attribute this to the fact that virtual images are more homogeneous and contains less complexity that is not related to the prediction task. As shown in Fig. 7, superfluous details including views beyond the road and changeable lighting conditions are unified into a clean, homogenious background, while cues critical for steering angle prediction like lane markings are

Table 2. Mean absolute error (MAE) and standard deviation (SD) for steering angle prediction task. DU-drive clearly outperforms all baseline methods.

Simulator		TORCS		Carla	
Dataset	Model	MAE	SD	MAE	SD
Udacity	*PilotNet* [5]	6.018	7.613	6.018	7.613
	Finetune TORCS	5.808	7.721	6.053	8.041
	cGAN [29]	5.921	6.896	4.925	7.100
	PilotNet joint training	15.040	27.636	15.040	27.636
	DU-Drive(single)	4.558	**5.356**	**3.571**	4.958
	DU-Drive(unified)	**4.521**	5.558	3.808	**4.650**
Comma.ai	*PilotNet* [5]	1.208	1.472	1.208	1.472
	Finetune TORCS	1.203	1.500	1.196	1.473
	cGAN [29]	1.215	1.405	1.206	1.404
	PilotNet joint training	5.988	11.670	5.988	11.670
	DU-Drive(single)	**1.061**	1.319	**1.068**	**1.337**
	DU-Drive(unified)	1.079	**1.270**	1.174	1.460

preserved. In the language of information bottleneck theory, this corresponds to a representation that is closer to the optimal minimum sufficient statistic than the raw image with respect to the prediction task.

Following the deduction in 3.4, we now show that $H(X) > H(X_v)$, which infers $L_{\{T=X\}} > L_{\{T=X_v\}}$. While it is unclear how to measure the entropy of an arbitrary set of images, under the mild assumption of normal distribution, the entropy equals to the natural logarithm of the determinant of the covariance matrix up to a constant. We therefore treat each image as a vector and measure the total variance of 50 randomly sampled pairs of real and generated virtual data. As shown in Table 3 and Fig. 5, virtual representation tends to have lower entropy, giving a better initialization to the information bottleneck objective. The performance gain is positively correlated with the decrease in input entropy.

Table 3. Variance of randomly sampled 50 pairs of real and generated virtual images. The generated virtual images have lower variance, which infers lower entropy for input distribution and thus less burden during the compression phase when optimizing the information bottleneck tradeoff.

Variance	Carla		TORCS	
	Udacity	Commaai	Udacity	Commaai
Real	82745	23902	107666	29656
Virtual	31650	23483	62389	22453

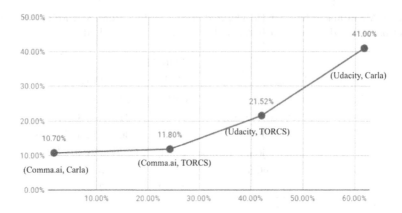

Fig. 5. The percentage decrease in prediction MAE (y-axis) is positively correlated with the percentage decrease in input entropy (x-axis).

Fig. 6. Mode Collapse happens for naively implemented conditional GAN.

4.7   Effectiveness of Domain Unification

A critical advantage of our model is that data collected from different sources could be unified to the same virtual domain. As shown in Fig. 7, images from Comma.ai dataset and those from Udacity dataset are transformed into a unified virtual domain, whose superiority is directly reflected in the performance of steering angle prediction task. As shown in Table 2, directly training a network with data from two real domains together will lead to results much worse than training each one separately due to domain shift. However, with DU-drive(unified), a single network could process data from multiple real domains with comparable results with DU-drive(single). Moreover, DU-drive separates the transformation and prediction process, and a generator could be independently trained for a new real dataset.

To further study the generalization ability of DU-drive, we conducted semi-supervised experiments where labels are limited for an unseen dataset. We first train a DU-drive model with the Comma.ai data, then use 20%/50% of the labeled Udacity data respectively to train the generator with our co-training scheme and report the prediction performance on the test set. We also experimented on joint training with Comma.ai dataset under our domain unification framework. As shown in Table 4, Domain unification outperforms baselines by a large margin, especially when labeled data is scarce. This shows the superiority of domain unification at transferring knowledge across domains and alleviating domain shift.

Table 4. MAE for semi-supervised learning.

% of data used	Carla			TORCS		
	PilotNet	Ours(single)	Ours(unified)	PilotNet	Ours(single)	Ours(unified)
20%	7.86	7.12	**6.02**	7.86	6.85	**6.34**
50%	7.11	6.41	**5.15**	7.11	5.73	**5.42**
100%	6.02	**3.57**	3.81	6.02	4.56	**4.52**

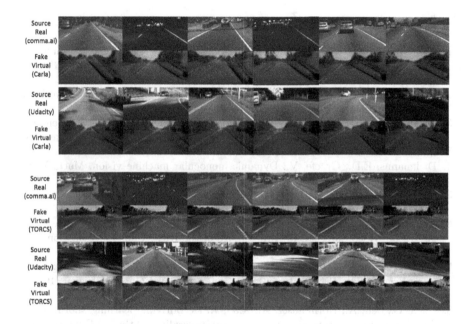

Fig. 7. Image generation results of DU-Drive. Information not critical to driving behavior, e.g. day/night lighting condition and the view beyond road boundary, is unified. Driving critical cues like lane markings are well preserved.

4.8 Prevention of Mode Collapse

Mode collapse is a common pitfall for generative adversarial networks. Due to the lack of additional supervision, a naive implementation of conditional GAN easily suffers from unstable training and mode collapse (Fig. 6). With our novel joint training of steering angle prediction and real-to-virtual transformation, mode collapse for driving critical information like lane markings is effectively prevented.

5 Conclusion

We propose a real to virtual domain unification framework for autonomous driving, or DU-drive, that employs a conditional generative adversarial network to transform real driving images to their simpler counterparts in the virtual domain, from which vehicle control commands are predicted. In the case where there are multiple real datasets, a real-to-virtual generator could be independently trained for each real domain and a global predictor could be trained with data from multiple sources simultaneously. Qualitative and quantitative experiment results show that our model can effectively unify real images from different sources to more efficient representations in the virtual domain, eliminate domain shift and boost the performance of control command prediction task.

References

1. Thorpe, C., Hebert, M.H., Kanade, T., Shafer, S.A.: Vision and navigation for the carnegie-mellon navlab. IEEE Trans. Pattern Anal. Mach. Intell. **10**(3), 360–373 (1988)
2. Pomerleau, D.A.: Alvinn: an autonomous land vehicle in a neural network. In: Advances in Neural Information Processing Systems, pp. 305–313 (1989)
3. Dickmanns, E.D., Mysliwetz, B., Christians, T.: An integrated spatio-temporal approach to automatic visual guidance of autonomous vehicles. IEEE Trans. Syst. Man Cybern. **20**(6), 1273–1284 (1990)
4. Dickmanns, E.D., Graefe, V.: Dynamic monocular machine vision. Mach. Vision Appl. **1**(4), 223–240 (1988)
5. Bojarski, M., et al.: End to end learning for self-driving cars. arXiv preprint arXiv:1604.07316 (2016)
6. Xu, H., Gao, Y., Yu, F., Darrell, T.: End-to-end learning of driving models from large-scale video datasets. In: Proceedings of the IEEE Conference on Computer Vision and Pattern Recognition, pp. 2174–2182 (2017)
7. Kim, J., Canny, J.: Interpretable learning for self-driving cars by visualizing causal attention. In: The IEEE International Conference on Computer Vision (ICCV), October 2017
8. Chen, C., Seff, A., Kornhauser, A., Xiao, J.: Deepdriving: learning affordance for direct perception in autonomous driving. In: Proceedings of the IEEE International Conference on Computer Vision, pp. 2722–2730 (2015)
9. Bojarski, M., et al.: Explaining how a deep neural network trained with end-to-end learning steers a car. arXiv preprint arXiv:1704.07911 (2017)
10. Tishby, N., Zaslavsky, N.: Deep learning and the information bottleneck principle. In: 2015 IEEE Information Theory Workshop (ITW), pp. 1–5. IEEE (2015)
11. Shwartz-Ziv, R., Tishby, N.: Opening the black box of deep neural networks via information. arXiv preprint arXiv:1703.00810 (2017)
12. Torralba, A., Efros, A.A.: Unbiased look at dataset bias. In: 2011 IEEE Conference on Computer Vision and Pattern Recognition (CVPR), pp. 1521–1528. IEEE (2011)
13. Janai, J., Güney, F., Behl, A., Geiger, A.: Computer vision for autonomous vehicles: problems, datasets and state-of-the-art. arXiv preprint arXiv:1704.05519 (2017)
14. Autonomous off-road vehicle control using end-to-end learning. http://net-scale.com/doc/net-scale-dave-report.pdf. Accessed 20 Oct 2017

15. Huval, B., et al.: An empirical evaluation of deep learning on highway driving. arXiv preprint arXiv:1504.01716 (2015)
16. Bickel, S., Brückner, M., Scheffer, T.: Discriminative learning for differing training and test distributions. In: Proceedings of the 24th International Conference on Machine Learning, pp. 81–88. ACM (2007)
17. Patel, V.M., Gopalan, R., Li, R., Chellappa, R.: Visual domain adaptation: a survey of recent advances. IEEE Sig. Process. Mag. **32**(3), 53–69 (2015)
18. Tzeng, E., Hoffman, J., Saenko, K., Darrell, T.: Adversarial discriminative domain adaptation. In: 2017 IEEE Conference on Computer Vision and Pattern Recognition (CVPR), pp. 7167–7176. IEEE (2017)
19. Ganin, Y., Lempitsky, V.: Unsupervised domain adaptation by backpropagation. In: International Conference on Machine Learning, pp. 1180–1189 (2015)
20. Tzeng, E., Hoffman, J., Darrell, T., Saenko, K.: Simultaneous deep transfer across domains and tasks. In: Proceedings of the IEEE International Conference on Computer Vision, pp. 4068–4076 (2015)
21. Liu, M.Y., Tuzel, O.: Coupled generative adversarial networks. In: Advances in Neural Information Processing Systems, pp. 469–477 (2016)
22. Zhu, J.Y., Park, T., Isola, P., Efros, A.A.: Unpaired image-to-image translation using cycle-consistent adversarial networks. In: The IEEE International Conference on Computer Vision (ICCV), October 2017
23. Isola, P., Zhu, J.Y., Zhou, T., Efros, A.A.: Image-to-image translation with conditional adversarial networks. In: The IEEE Conference on Computer Vision and Pattern Recognition (CVPR), July 2017
24. Johnson, J., Alahi, A., Fei-Fei, L.: Perceptual losses for real-time style transfer and super-resolution. In: Leibe, B., Matas, J., Sebe, N., Welling, M. (eds.) ECCV 2016. LNCS, vol. 9906, pp. 694–711. Springer, Cham (2016). https://doi.org/10.1007/978-3-319-46475-6_43
25. Bousmalis, K., Silberman, N., Dohan, D., Erhan, D., Krishnan, D.: Unsupervised pixel-level domain adaptation with generative adversarial networks. In: Proceedings of the IEEE Conference on Computer Vision and Pattern Recognition, pp. 3722–3731 (2017)
26. Shrivastava, A., Pfister, T., Tuzel, O., Susskind, J., Wang, W., Webb, R.: Learning from simulated and unsupervised images through adversarial training. In: The IEEE Conference on Computer Vision and Pattern Recognition (CVPR), July 2017
27. Tobin, J., Fong, R., Ray, A., Schneider, J., Zaremba, W., Abbeel, P.: Domain randomization for transferring deep neural networks from simulation to the real world. arXiv preprint arXiv:1703.06907 (2017)
28. You, Y., Pan, X., Wang, Z., Lu, C.: Virtual to real reinforcement learning for autonomous driving. arXiv preprint arXiv:1704.03952 (2017)
29. Mirza, M., Osindero, S.: Conditional generative adversarial nets. arXiv preprint arXiv:1411.1784 (2014)
30. Wymann, B., Espié, E., Guionneau, C., Dimitrakakis, C., Coulom, R., Sumner, A.: Torcs, the open racing car simulator (2000). Software. http://torcs.sourceforge.net
31. Dosovitskiy, A., Ros, G., Codevilla, F., Lopez, A., Koltun, V.: CARLA: An open urban driving simulator. In: Proceedings of the 1st Annual Conference on Robot Learning, pp. 1–16 (2017)
32. Codevilla, F., Müller, M., López, A., Koltun, V., Dosovitskiy, A.: End-to-end driving via conditional imitation learning. In: International Conference on Robotics and Automation (ICRA) (2018)

33. Santana, E., Hotz, G.: Learning a driving simulator. arXiv preprint arXiv:1608.01230 (2016)
34. Udacity self-driving-car challenge dataset. https://github.com/udacity/self-driving-car/tree/master/datasets. Accessed 20 Oct 2017
35. Abadi, M., et al.: Tensorflow: large-scale machine learning on heterogeneous distributed systems. arXiv preprint arXiv:1603.04467 (2016)
36. Kingma, D., Ba, J.: Adam: a method for stochastic optimization. In: International Conference on Learning Representations (2015)
37. Mao, X., Li, Q., Xie, H., Lau, R.Y., Wang, Z.: Least squares generative adversarial networks. In: Proceedings of the IEEE International Conference on Computer Vision (2017)

The Mutex Watershed: Efficient, Parameter-Free Image Partitioning

Steffen Wolf[1], Constantin Pape[1,2(✉)], Alberto Bailoni[1], Nasim Rahaman[1], Anna Kreshuk[1,2], Ullrich Köthe[1], and Fred A. Hamprecht[1]

[1] HCI/IWR, University of Heidelberg, Heidelberg, Germany
{steffen.wolf,alberto.bailoni,nasim.rahaman,ullrich.kothe,
fred.hamprecht,constantin.pape,anna.kreshuk}@iwr.uni-heidelberg.de
[2] EMBL Heidelberg, Heidelberg, Germany

Abstract. Image partitioning, or segmentation without semantics, is the task of decomposing an image into distinct segments; or equivalently, the task of detecting closed contours in an image. Most prior work either requires seeds, one per segment; or a threshold; or formulates the task as an NP-hard signed graph partitioning problem. Here, we propose an algorithm with empirically linearithmic complexity. Unlike seeded watershed, the algorithm can accommodate not only attractive but also repulsive cues, allowing it to find a previously *unspecified* number of segments without the need for explicit seeds or a tunable threshold. The algorithm itself, which we dub "Mutex Watershed", is closely related to a minimal spanning tree computation. It is deterministic and easy to implement. When presented with short-range attractive and long-range repulsive cues from a deep neural network, the Mutex Watershed gives results that currently define the state-of-the-art in the competitive ISBI 2012 EM segmentation benchmark. These results are also better than those obtained from other recently proposed clustering strategies operating on the very same network outputs.

1 Introduction

Most image partitioning algorithms are defined over a graph encoding purely attractive interactions. No matter whether a segmentation or clustering is then found agglomeratively (as in single linkage clustering/watershed) or divisively (as in spectral clustering or iterated normalized cuts), the user either needs to specify the desired number of segments or a termination criterion. An even stronger form of supervision is in terms of seeds, where one pixel of each segment needs to be designated as such either by a user or automatically. Unfortunately, clustering with automated seed selection remains a fragile and error-fraught process,

---

S. Wolf and C. Pape—Contributed equally.

Electronic supplementary material The online version of this chapter (https://doi.org/10.1007/978-3-030-01225-0_34) contains supplementary material, which is available to authorized users.

because every missed or hallucinated seed causes an under- or oversegmentation error. Although the learning of good edge detectors boosts the quality of classical seed selection strategies (such as finding local minima of the boundary map, or thresholding boundary maps), non-local effects of seed placement along with strong variability in region sizes and shapes make it hard for any learned predictor to place *exactly one* seed in every true region.

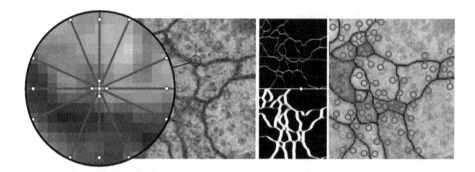

Fig. 1. Left: Overlay of raw data from the ISBI 2012 EM segmentation challenge and the edges for which attractive (green) or repulsive (red) interactions are estimated for each pixel using a CNN. Middle: vertical/horizontal repulsive interactions at intermediate/long range are shown in the top/bottom half. Right: Active mutual exclusion (mutex) constraints that the proposed algorithm invokes during the segmentation process. (Color figure online)

In contrast to the above class of algorithms, multicut/correlation clustering partitions vertices with both attractive and repulsive interactions encoded into the edges of a graph. Multicut has the great advantage that a "natural" partitioning of a graph can be found, without needing to specify a desired number of clusters, or a termination criterion, or one seed per region. Its great drawback is that its optimization is NP-hard.

The main insight of this paper is that when both attractive and repulsive interactions between pixels are available, then a generalization of the watershed algorithm can be devised that segments an image *without* the need for seeds or stopping criteria or thresholds. It examines all graph edges, attractive and repulsive, sorted by their weight and adds these to an active set iff they are not in conflict with previous, higher-priority, decisions. The attractive subset of the resulting active set is a forest, with one tree representing each segment. However, the active set can have loops involving more than one repulsive edge. See Fig. 1 for a visual abstract.

In summary, our principal contribution, the Mutex Watershed, is a "best of both worlds" algorithm that combines the multicut's desirable lack of hyperparameters with the small computational footprint of Kruskal-type watershed algorithm.

The algorithm is presented in Sect. 3. In Sect. 4 we evaluate the algorithm against very strong baselines. We choose a challenging dataset for neuron segmentation from electron microscopy (EM) image stacks as benchmark. For this task, watershed segmentation is a key component: EM staining only highlights membrane boundaries, discouraging the use of region cues for segmentation. By incorporating long-range repulsions into the watershed procedure, we can obtain an accurate segmentation from this step already, avoiding costly post-processing for agglomeration. In addition, we present preliminary results on the BSDS500, demonstrating the applicability of the proposed method to natural images. We describe our future plans, including extensions to semantic segmentation, in Sect. 5. Our implementation is available at https://github.com/hci-unihd/mutex-watershed.git.

2 Related Work

In the original watershed algorithm [1], seeds were automatically placed at all local minima of the boundary map. Unfortunately, this leads to severe oversegmentation. Defining better seeds has been a recurring theme of watershed research ever since. The simplest solution is offered by the seeded watershed algorithm [2]: It relies on an oracle (an external algorithm or a human) to provide seeds and assigns each pixel to its nearest seed in terms of minimax path distance. In the absence of an oracle, automatic seed selection is challenging because *exactly one* seed must be placed in every region. Simple methods, e.g. defining seeds by connected regions of low boundary probability, do not work: The segmentation quality is usually insufficient because multiple seeds are in the same region and/or seeds leak through the boundary.

This problem is typically addressed by biasing seed selection towards oversegmentation (with seeding at all minima being the extreme case). The watershed algorithm then produces superpixels that are merged into final regions by more or less elaborate postprocessing. This works better than using watersheds alone because it exploits the larger context afforded by superpixel adjacency graphs. Many criteria have been proposed to identify the regions to be preserved during merging, e.g. region dynamics [3], the waterfall transform [4], extinction values [5], region saliency [6], and (α, ω)-connected components [7]. A merging process controlled by criteria like these can be iterated to produce a hierarchy of segmentations where important regions survive to the next level. Variants of such hierarchical watersheds are reviewed and evaluated in [8].

These results highlight the close connection of watersheds to hierarchical clustering and minimum spanning trees/forests [9,10], which inspired novel merging strategies and termination criteria. For example, [11] simply terminated hierarchical merging by fixing the number of surviving regions beforehand. [12] incorparate predefined sets of generalized merge constraints into the clustering algorithm. Graph-based segmentation according to [13] defines a measure of quality for the current regions and stops when the merge costs would exceed this measure. Ultrametric contour maps [14] combine the gPb (global probability of boundary) edge detector with an oriented watershed transform. Superpixels are agglomerated until the ultrametric distance between the resulting regions exceeds a learned threshold. An optimization perspective is taken in [15], which introduces h-increasing energy functions and builds the hierarchy incrementally such that merge decisions greedily minimize the energy. The authors prove that the optimal cut corresponds to a different unique segmentation for every value of a free regularization parameter.

An important line of research is based on the observation that superior partitionings are obtained when the graph has both attractive and repulsive edges. Solutions that optimally balance attraction and repulsion do not require external stopping criteria such as predefined number of regions or seeds. This generalization leads to the NP-hard problem of correlation clustering or (synonymous) multicut (MC) partitioning [16]. Fortunately, modern integer linear programming solvers in combination with incremental constraint generation can solve problem instances of considerable size [17], and good approximations exist for even larger problems [18,19].

Another beneficial extension is the introduction of additional long-range edges. Thanks to their larger field of view, the strength of these edges can often be estimated with greater certainty than is achievable for the local edges used in standard watersheds. This has been used in [20] to represent object size constraints by repulsive long-range edges, which is still an MC-type problem. When long-range edges are also allowed to be attractive, the problem turns into the more complicated lifted multicut (LMC) [21]. Realistic problem sizes can only be solved approximately [22,23], but watershed superpixels followed by LMC postprocessing achieve state-of-the-art results on important benchmarks [24]. Long-range edges are also used in [25], as side losses for the boundary detection CNN; but they are not used explicitly in any downstream inference.

In general, striking progress in watershed-based segmentation has been achieved by learning boundary maps with convolutional neural networks (CNNs). This is nicely illustrated by the evolution of neurosegmentation for connectomics, an important field we also address in the experimental section. CNNs were introduced to this application in [26] and became, in much refined form [27], the winning entry of the ISBI 2012 Neuro-Segmentaion Challenge [28]. Boundary maps and superpixels were further improved by progress in CNN architectures and data augmentation methods, using U-Nets [29], FusionNets [30] or inception modules [24]. Subsequent postprocessing with the GALA algorithm [31,32], conditional random fields [33] or the lifted multicut [24] pushed the envelope of final segmentation quality. MaskExtend [34] applied CNNs to both boundary map prediction and superpixel merging, while flood-filling networks [35] eliminated superpixels all together by training a recurrent neural network to perform region growing one region at a time.

Most networks mentioned so far learn boundary maps on pixels, but learning works equally well for edge-based watersheds, as was demonstrated in [36,37] using CNN-generated edge weights according to [38,39]. Tailoring the learning objective to the needs of the watershed algorithm by penalizing critical edges along minimax paths [39] or end-to-end training of edge weights and region growing [40] improved results yet again.

Outside of connectomics, [41] obtained superior boundary maps from CNNs by learning not just boundary strength, but also its gradient direction. Holistically-nested edge detection [42,43] couples the CNN loss at multiple resolutions using deep supervision and is successfully used as a basis for watershed segmentation of medical images in [44].

The present paper combines all these concepts (hierarchical clustering, attractive and repulsive interactions, long-range edges, and CNN-based learning) into a novel efficient segmentation framework. It can be interpreted as a generalization of [12], because we also allow for soft constraints (which can be overridden by strong attractive edges), and constraints are generated on the fly by a neural network rather than predefined. Our method is also related to greedy additive edge contraction (GAEC) according to [22], but we handle attractive and repulsive interactions separately and define edge strength between clusters by a maximum instead of an additive rule.

3   The Mutex Watershed Algorithm

3.1   Definitions and Notation

We consider the problem of clustering a graph $G(V, E^+ \cup E^-, W^+ \cup W^-)$ with both attractive and repulsive edge attributes. The scalar attribute $w_e^+ \in \mathbb{R}_0^+$ associated with edge $e \in E^+$ is a merge affinity: the higher this number, the higher the inclination of the two incident vertices to be assigned to the same cluster. Similarly, $w_e^- \in \mathbb{R}_0^+$ for $e \in E^-$ is a split tendency: the higher this number, the greater the tendency of the incident vertices to be in different clusters.

In our application, each vertex corresponds to one pixel in the image to be segmented. Two vertices may have no edge connecting them; or an attractive edge $e \in E^+$; or a repulsive edge $e \in E^-$; or two edges at the same time, one attractive and one repulsive. Edges can be either *local/short-range* (when connecting two pixels that are immediately adjacent in the image) or *long-range*.

The Mutex Watershed algorithm, defined in Subsect. 3.3, maintains disjunct active sets $A^+ \subseteq E^+$, $A^- \subseteq E^-$, $A^+ \cap A^- = \emptyset$, that encode merges and mutual exclusion constraints, respectively. Clusters are defined via the "connected" predicate:

$$\forall i, j \in V: \qquad \Pi_{i \to j} = \{\text{path } \pi \text{ from } i \text{ to } j \text{ with } \pi \subseteq E^+\}$$
$$\text{connected}(i, j) \Leftrightarrow \exists \text{ path } \pi \in \Pi_{i \to j} \text{ with } \pi \subseteq A^+ \subseteq E^+$$
$$\text{cluster}(i) = \{i\} \cup \{j : \text{connected}(i, j)\}$$

Conversely, the active subset $A^- \subseteq E^-$ of repulsive edges defines mutual exclusion relations by using the following predicate:

$$\text{mutex}(i, j) \Leftrightarrow \exists e = (k, l) \in A^- \text{ with}$$
$$k \in \text{cluster}(i) \text{ and } l \in \text{cluster}(j) \text{ and}$$
$$\text{cluster}(i) \neq \text{cluster}(j)$$

Admissible active edge sets A^+ and A^- must be chosen such that the resulting clustering is consistent, i.e. nodes engaged in a mutual exclusion constraint cannot be in the same cluster: mutex(i,j) ⇒ not connected(i,j). The "connected" and "mutex" predicates can be efficiently evaluated using a union find data structure.

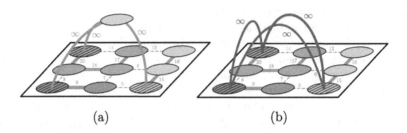

(a)   (b)

Fig. 2. Two equivalent representations of the seeded watershed clustering obtained using (a) a maximum spanning tree computation or (b) Algorithm 1. Both graphs share the weighted attractive (green) edges and seeds (hatched nodes). The infinitely attractive connections to the auxiliary node (gray) in (a) are replaced by infinitely repulsive (red) edges between each pair of seeds in (b). The two final clusterings are defined by the active sets (bold edges) and are identical. Node colors indicate the clustering result, but are arbitrary. (Color figure online)

3.2 Seeded Watershed from a Mutex Perspective

One interpretation of the proposed method is in terms of a generalization of the edge-based watershed algorithm [9,45,46] or image foresting transform [47]. This algorithm can only ingest a graph with purely attractive interations, $G(V, E^+, W^+)$. Without further constraints, the algorithm would yield only the trivial result of a single cluster comprising all vertices. To obtain more interesting output, an oracle needs to provide seeds, namely precisely one node per cluster. These seed vertices are all connected to an auxiliary node (see Fig. 2(a)) by auxiliary edges with infinite merge affinity. A maximum spanning tree (MST) on this augmented graph can be found in linearithmic time; and the maximum spanning tree (or in the case of degeneracy: at least one of the maximum spanning trees) will include the auxiliary edges. When the auxiliary edges are deleted from the MST, a forest results, with each tree representing one cluster [9,45,47].

We now reformulate this well-known algorithm in a way that will later emerge as a special case of the proposed Mutex Watershed: we eliminate the auxiliary node and edges, and replace them by a set of infinitely repulsive edges, one for each pair of seeds (Fig. 2(b)). Algorithm 1 is a variation of Kruskal's MST algorithm operating on the seed mutex graph just defined, and gives results identical to seeded watershed on the original graph.

Input: weighted graph $G(V, E^+, W^+)$ and seeds $S \subseteq V$, such that
$E^- = \{(s_i, s_j) | i, j \in 1, \ldots, |S|; i \neq j\}$ is the set of infinitely repulsive edges
between all pairs of seeds;
Output: clusters defined by activated edges A^+;
Initialization: $A^+ = \emptyset$; $A^- = E^-$;
for $(i, j) = e \in E^+$ in descending order of w^+ **do**
    if not connected(i, j) **and not** mutex(i, j) **then**
        $A^+ \leftarrow A^+ \cup e$;
                ▷ merge i and j and inherit the mutex
                  constraints of the parent clusters
    end
end

Algorithm 1. Mutex version of seeded watershed algorithm.

This algorithm differs from Kruskal's only by the check for mutual exclusion in the if-statement. Obviously, the modified algorithm has the same effect as the original algorithm, because the final set A^+ is exactly the maximum spanning forest obtained after removing the auxiliary edges from the original solution.

In the sequel, we generalize this construction by admitting less-than-infinitely repulsive edges. Importantly, these can be dense and are hence much easier to estimate automatically than seeds with their strict requirement of only-one-per-cluster.

3.3   Mutex Watersheds

We now introduce the core contribution: an algorithm that is empirically no more expensive than a MST computation; but that can ingest both attractive and repulsive cues and partition a graph into a number of clusters that does not need to be specified beforehand. There is no requirement of one seed per cluster, and not even of a hyperparameter that would implicitly determine the number of resulting clusters.

The Mutex Watershed, Algorithm 2, proceeds as follows: given a graph with sets of attractive and repulsive edges E^+ and E^-, with edge weights W^+ and W^- respectively, do the following: sort all edges $E^+ \cup E^-$, attractive or repulsive, by their weight in descending order into a priority queue. Iteratively pop all edges from the queue and add them to the active set one by one, provided that a set of conditions are satisfied. More specifically, if the next edge popped from the priority queue is attractive and its incident vertices are not yet in the same tree, then connect the respective trees provided this is not ruled out by a mutual exclusion constraint. If on the other hand the edge popped is repulsive, and if its incident vertices are not yet in the same tree, then add a mutual exclusion constraint between the two trees.

The crucial difference to Algorithm 1 is that mutex constraints are no longer pre-defined, but created dynamically whenever a repulsive edge is found. However, new exclusion constraints can never override earlier, high-priority merge

---

Input: weighted graph $G(V, E^+ \cup E^-, W^+ \cup W^-)$;
Output: clusters defined by activated edges A^+;
Initialization: $A^+ = \emptyset$; $A^- = \emptyset$;
for $(i,j) = e \in E^+ \cup E^-$ in descending order of $W^+ \cup W^-$ **do**

> **if** $e \in E^+$ **then**
>
>> **if not** connected(i,j) **and not** mutex(i,j) **then**
>>
>>> merge(i, j): $A^+ \leftarrow A^+ \cup e$;
>>>
>>>> ▷ merge i and j and inherit the mutex constraints of the parent clusters
>>
>> **end**
>
> **else**
>
>> **if not** connected(i,j) **then**
>>
>>> addmutex(i, j): $A^- \leftarrow A^- \cup e$;
>>>
>>>> ▷ add mutex constraint between i and j
>>
>> **end**
>
> **end**

end

Algorithm 2. Mutex Watershed

decisions. In this case, the repulsive edge in question is simply ignored. Similarly, an attractive edge must never override earlier and thus higher-priority must-not-link decisions.

3.4   Time Complexity Analysis

Before analyzing the time complexity of Algorithm 2 we first review the complexity of Kruskal's algorithm. Using a union-find data structure the time complexity of merge(i, j) and connected(i, j) is $\mathcal{O}(\alpha(V))$, where α is the slowly growing inverse Ackerman function, and the total runtime complexity is dominated by the initial sorting of the edges $\mathcal{O}(E \log E)$ [48].

To check for mutex constraints efficiently, we maintain a set of all active mutex edges

$$M[C_i] = \{(u,\ v) \in A^- | u \in C_i \vee v \in C_i\}$$

for every C_i = cluster(i) using hash tables, where insertion of new mutex edges (i.e. addmutex) and search have an average complexity of $\mathcal{O}(1)$. Note that every cluster can be efficiently identified by its union-find root node. For mutex(i, j) we check if $M[C_i] \cap M[C_j] = \emptyset$ by searching for all elements of the smaller hash table in the larger hash table. Therefore mutex(i, j) has an average complexity of $\mathcal{O}(\min(|M[C_i]|, |M[C_j]|))$. Similarly, during merge(i, j), mutex constraints are inherited by merging two hash tables, which also has an average complexity $\mathcal{O}(\min(|M[C_i]|, |M[C_j]|))$.

In conclusion, the average runtime contribution of attractive edges $\mathcal{O}(|E^+| \cdot \alpha(V) + |E^+| \cdot M)$ (checking mutex constrains and possibly merging) and repulsive edges $\mathcal{O}(|E^-| \cdot \alpha(V) + |E^-|)$ (insertion of one mutex edge) result in a total average runtime complexity of Algorithm 2:

$$\mathcal{O}(E \log E + E \cdot \alpha(V) + EM). \tag{1}$$

where M is the expected value of $\min(|M[C_i]|, |M[C_j]|)$. Using $\alpha(V) \in \mathcal{O}(\log V) \in \mathcal{O}(\log E)$ this simplifies to

$$\mathcal{O}(E \log E + EM). \tag{2}$$

In the worst case $\mathcal{O}(M) = \mathcal{O}(E)$, the Mutex Watershed Algorithm has a runtime complexity of $\mathcal{O}(E^2)$. Empirically, we find that $\mathcal{O}(EM) \approx \mathcal{O}(E \log E)$ by measuring the runtime of Mutex Watershed for different sub-volumes of the ISBI challenge (see Fig. 3), leading to a

Empirical Mutex Watershed Complexity: $\mathcal{O}(E \log E)$ \hfill (3)

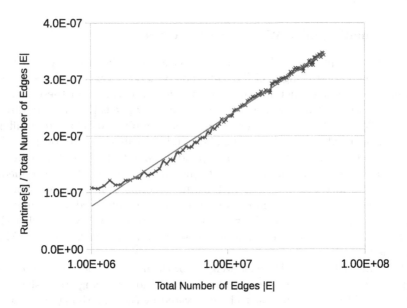

Fig. 3. Runtime T of Mutex Watershed (without sorting of edges) measured on sub-volumes of the ISBI challenge of different sizes (thereby varying the total number of edges E). We plot $\frac{T}{|E|}$ over $|E|$ in a logarithmic plot, which makes $T \sim |E|log(|E|)$ appear as straight line. A logarithmic function (green line) is fitted to the measured $\frac{T}{|E|}$ (blue crosses) with ($R^2 = 0.9896$). The good fit suggests that empirically $T \approx \mathcal{O}(E \log E)$. (Color figure online)

4   Experiments

We evaluate the Mutex Watershed on the challenging task of neuron segmentation in electron microscopy (EM) image volumes. This application is of key interest in connectomics, a field of neuro-science that strives to reconstruct neural wiring diagrams spanning complete central nervous systems. The task requires segmentation of neurons from electron microscopy images of neural tissue – a challenging endeavor, since segmentation has to be based only on boundary information (cell membranes) and some of the boundaries are not very pronounced. Besides, cells contain membrane-bound organelles, which have to be suppressed in the segmentation. Some of the neuron protrusions are very thin, but all of those have to be preserved in the segmentation to arrive at the correct connectivity graph. While a lot of progress has been made recently, only manual tracing yields sufficient accuracy for correct circuit reconstruction [49].

We validated the Mutex Watershed algorithm on the most popular neural segmentation challenge: ISBI2012 [28]. We estimate the edge weights using a CNN as described in Sect. 4.1 and compare with other entries in the leaderboard as well as with other common post-processing methods for the same network predictions Sect. 4.2.

4.1   Estimating Edge Weights with a CNN

The common approach to EM segmentation is to predict which pixels belong to a cell membrane using a CNN. Different post-processing methods are used on top to obtain a segmentation, see Sect. 2 for an overview of these methods. The CNN can be either trained to predict boundary pixels [24,27] or undirected affinities [25,50] which express how likely it is for a pixel to belong to a different cell than its neighbors in the 6-neighborhood. In this case, the output of the network contains three channels, corresponding to left, down and next imaging plane neighbors in 3d. The affinities do not have to be limited to immediate neighbors - in fact, [25] have shown that introduction of long-range affinities is beneficial for the final segmentation even if they are only used as auxiliary loss during training. Building on the work of [25], we train a CNN to predict short and long-range affinities and then use those directly as weights for the Mutex Watershed algorithm.

We estimate the affinities/edge weights for the neighborhood structure shown in Fig. 4. To that end, we define local attractive and long-range repulsive edges. The choice of this structure has to be motivated by the underlying data - we use a different pattern for in-plane and between-plane edges due to the anisotropy of the validation datasets. In more detail, we picked a sparse ring of in-plane repulsive edges and additional longer-range in-plane edges which were necessary to split regions reliably (see Fig. 4a). We also added connections to the indirect neighbors in the lower adjacent slice to ensure correct 3D connectivity (see Fig. 4b).

In total, C^+ attractive and C^- repulsive edges are defined for each pixel, resulting in $C^+ + C^-$ output channels in the network. We partition the set of attractive/repulsive edges into subsets H^+ and H^- that contain all edges at a specific offset, attractive edges: $E^+ = \bigcup_c^{C^+} H_c^+$ and repulsive edges analogously. Each element of the subsets H_c^+ and H_c^- corresponds to a specific channel predicted by the network. We further assume that weights take values in $[0,1]$ and adopt the same conventions for attraciveness/repulsion as in Sect. 3. For more details on network architecture and training see Supplementary 1.

In our experiments, we pick a subset of repulsive edges, by using strides of 2 in the XY-plane in order to avoid artifacts caused by occasional very thick membranes. Note that the stride is not applied to local (attractive) edges, but only to long-range (repulsive) edges.

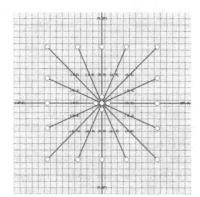

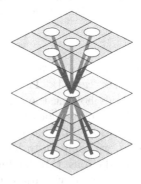

(a) XY-plane neighborhood with local attractive edges, a sparse repulsive edges with approximate radius 9 and further long-range connections with distance 27

(b) Due to the high anisotropy of the data we limit the Z-plane edges to a distance of 1. The direct neighbors are attractive; the indirect neighbors are repulsive.

Fig. 4. Local neighborhood structure of attractive (green) and repulsive (red) edges in the Mutex Watershed graph. Due to point symmetry to the origin, we only predict half of the directions with the neural network. (Color figure online)

4.2 ISBI Challenge

The ISBI 2012 EM Segmentation Challenge [28] is the neuron segmentation challenge with the largest number of competing entries. The challenge data contains two volumes of dimensions $1.5 \times 2 \times 2$ microns with a resolution of $50 \times 4 \times 4$ nm per pixel. The groundtruth is provided as binary membrane labels, which can easily be converted to a 2D, but not 3D segmentation. To train a 3D model, we follow the procedure described in [24].

The test volume has private groundtruth; results can be submitted to the leaderboard. They are evaluated based on the Adapted Rand Score (Rand-Score) and the Variation of Information Score (VI-Score) [28], separately for each 2D slice.

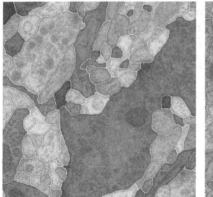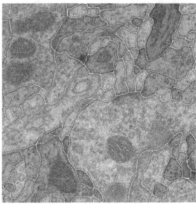

Fig. 5. Mutex Watershed applied on the ISBI Challenge test data. For further images and a detailed comparison to the baseline segmentation methods view Supplementary Sect. 2.

Our method holds the top entry in the challenge's leader board[1] at the time of submission, see Table 1a. This is especially remarkable, because it is simpler than the methods holding the other top entries. Similar to us, they rely on a CNN to predict boundary locations, but postprocess its output with the complex pipeline described in [24], that involves a NP-hard partitioning step.

In addition, we compare to baseline post-processing methods starting from our network predictions: thresholding (THRESH), two watershed variants (WS, WSDT), and one multicut variant (MC-LOCAL) only take into account short-range predictions. Lifed multicut (LMC) and another multicut variant (MC-FULL) also use long-range predictions. For these baseline methods we have only produced 2D segmentations for the individual slices, either because the 3D results were inferior (THRESH, WS, WSDT) or infeasible to obtain (MC, LMC). In contrast, the Mutex Watershed benefited from 3D segmentation. See Table 1b for the evaluation results and see Supplementary 2 for further details on the baseline methods and a qualitative comparison.

The three methods that use short- and long-range connectivty perform significantly better than the other methods. Somewhat surprisingly, MWS performs better than MC-FULL and LMC, which are based on a NP-hard partition problem. This might be explained by the lack of 3D information in the two latter two approaches (solving the 3D model was infeasible).

4.3 Study on Natural Image Segmentation

We conducted preliminary experiments on the Berkeley segmentation dataset BSD500 [53] to study the Mutex Watersheds applicability to natural images. Training a state-of-the-art edge detection network on this small dataset requires

---

[1] http://brainiac2.mit.edu/isbi_challenge/leaders-board-new.

a set of dataset specific optimization tricks such as training with external data, multi resolution architectures and auxiliary losses [43]. In this preliminary study we train a 2D version of the network used for the ISBI experiments to predict the 2D connectivity pattern depicted in Fig. 4a. To alleviate the small size of the training set, we present this network with predictions from [42] as additional input channel.

Table 1. Results on the ISBI 2012 EM Segmentation Challenge.

Method	Rand-Score	VI-Score	Method	Rand-Score	VI-Score	Time [s]
UNet + MWS	**0.98792**	**0.99183**	MWS	**0.98792**	**0.99183**	43.32
M2FCN + LMC [51]	0.98788	0.99072	MC-FULL	0.98029	0.99044	9415.8
SCN + LMC [52]	0.98680	0.99144	LMC	0.97990	0.99007	966.0
FusionNet + LMC [30]	0.98365	0.99130	THRESH	0.91435	0.96961	0.2
ICv1 + LMC [24]	0.98262	0.98945	WSDT	0.88336	0.96312	4.4
			MC-LOCAL	0.70990	0.86874	1410.7
			WS	0.63958	0.89237	4.9

(a) Top five entries at time of submission. Our Mutex Watershed (MWS) is state-of-the-art without relying on complex lifted multicut postprocessing used by all other top entries.

(b) Comparison to other segmentation strategies, all of which are based on our CNN.

In order to isolate the influence of the quality of the underlying affinities, we run ablation experiments where we interpolate (via weighted average) between (a) affinities as predicted by our neural network, (b) those obtained from the ground-truth and (c) uniform noise. We obtain Mutex Watershed segmentations from the interpolated affinities for the BSD testset, size-filter them (as the only post-processing step) and evaluate with the Rand Index. The "phase transition diagram" resulting from these experiments is shown in Fig. 6a; Table 6b shows Rand Index and Variation of Information obtained for several points on this diagram.

Observe that the vertices corresponding to (a) and (c) can be interpreted as structured and unstructured noise on the ground-truth affinities (respectively). Hence, the results of our experiments show that the Mutex Watershed is fairly robust against both types of noise; when mixing the GT with noise, the quality of the segmentations is unaffected up to 60 % noise. When mixing GT with NN predictions, it is unaffected to an even higher degree.

In addition, we compare to the result of [22], who use an approach similar to ours and solve a Lifted Multicut based on long range potentials extracted from a pre-computed probability map. In Supplementary 3, we show the segmentations resulting at different stages of interpolation between GT, NN predictions and noise.

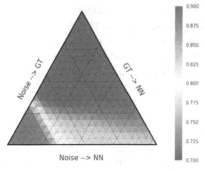

NN	GT	Noise	RI	VI
100%	0%	0%	0.826	1.722
0%	100%	0%	0.901	0.927
0%	38%	62%	0.897	0.976
0%	33%	66%	0.820	1.912
80%	20%	0%	0.878	1.247
43%	0%	57%	0.813	2.127
43%	14%	43%	0.838	1.636
Keuper et al. [22]			0.82	1.75

(a) BSD500 segmentation quality of MWS algorithm, given affinities from ground truth (top corner), from a neural network (right corner) or pure noise (left corner); plus hundreds of experiments on weighted combinations of the above. MWS segmentation quality (evaluated with Rand index) degrades only once a large amount of noise is added to the affinities.

(b) BSD500 scores at various interpolations between the neural network predictions (NN), ground-truth (GT) and noise. See Supplementary Section 3 for example images of the interpolated affinities. We include [22] as a reference point, because they also use long range potentials in their segmentation method.

Fig. 6. (a) BSD500 segmentation quality of MWS algorithm, given affinities from ground truth (top corner), from a neural network (right corner) or pure noise (left corner); plus hundreds of experiments on weighted combinations of the above. MWS segmentation quality (evaluated with Rand index) degrades only once a large amount of noise is added to the affinities. (b) BSD500 scores at various interpolations between the neural network predictions (NN), ground-truth (GT) and noise. See Supplementary Sect. 3 for example images of the interpolated affinities. We include [22] as a reference point, because they also use long range potentials in their segmentation method.

5   Conclusion

We have presented a fast algorithm for the clustering of graphs with both attractive and repulsive edges. The ability to consider both obviates the need for the kind of stopping criterion or even seeds that all popular algorithms except for correlation clustering need. The proposed method has low computational complexity in imitation of its close relative, Kruskal's algorithm.

Finally, we have found that the proposed algorithm, when presented with informative edge costs from a good neural network, outperforms all known methods on a competitive bioimage partitioning benchmark, including methods that operate on the very same network predictions.

In future work we want to generalize our algorithm to semantic instance segmentation commonly found in natural image segmentation challenges [54–56].

Acknowledgements. The authors acknowledge partial support by DFG HA 4364/8-1 and DFG SFB 1129.

References

1. Vincent, L., Soille, P.: Watersheds in digital spaces: an efficient algorithm based on immersion simulations. IEEE Trans. Pattern Anal. Mach. Intell. **6**, 583–598 (1991)
2. Beucher, S., Meyer, F.: The morphological approach to segmentation: the watershed transformation. Opt. Eng. **34**, 433–433 (1992)
3. Grimaud, M.: New measure of contrast: the dynamics. In: Gader, P.D., Dougherty, E.R., Serra, J.C. (eds.), Proceedings of the Image Algebra and Morphological Processing, vol. 1769. SPIE Conference Series, pp. 292–305 (1992)
4. Beucher, S.: Watershed, hierarchical segmentation and waterfall algorithm. In: Serra, J., Soille, P. (eds.) ISMM 1994, vol. 94, pp. 69–76. Springer, Dordrecht (1994). https://doi.org/10.1007/978-94-011-1040-2_10
5. Vachier, C., Meyer, F.: Extinction value: a new measurement of persistence. In: Worksh. Nonlinear Signal and Image Processing, vol. 1, pp. 254–257 (1995)
6. Najman, L., Schmitt, M.: Geodesic saliency of watershed contours and hierarchical segmentation. IEEE Trans. Pattern Anal. Mach. Intell. **18**(12), 1163–1173 (1996)
7. Soille, P.: Constrained connectivity for hierarchical image decomposition and simplification. IEEE Trans. Patt. Anal. Mach. Intell. **30**(7), 1132–1145 (2008)
8. Perret, B., Cousty, J., Guimaraes, S.J., Maia, D.S.: Evaluation of hierarchical watersheds (2017). HAL preprint 01430865
9. Meyer, F.: Morphological multiscale and interactive segmentation. In: WS on Nonlinear Signal and Image Processing, pp. 369–377 (1999)
10. Najman, L.: On the equivalence between hierarchical segmentations and ultrametric watersheds. J. Math. Imaging Vis. **40**(3), 231–247 (2011)
11. Salembier, P., Garrido, L.: Binary partition tree as an efficient representation for image processing, segmentation, and information retrieval. IEEE Trans. Image Proc. **9**, 561–576 (2000)
12. Malmberg, F., Strand, R., Nyström, I.: Generalized hard constraints for graph segmentation. In: Heyden, A., Kahl, F. (eds.) SCIA 2011. LNCS, vol. 6688, pp. 36–47. Springer, Heidelberg (2011). https://doi.org/10.1007/978-3-642-21227-7_4
13. Felzenszwalb, P.F., Huttenlocher, D.P.: Efficient graph-based image segmentation. Int. J. Comput. Vis. **59**(2), 167–181 (2004)
14. Arbelaez, P., Maire, M., Fowlkes, C., Malik, J.: Contour detection and hierarchical image segmentation. IEEE Trans. Patt. Anal. Mach. Intell. **33**(5), 898–916 (2011)
15. Kiran, B.R., Serra, J.: Global-local optimizations by hierarchical cuts and climbing energies. Pattern Recogn. **47**(1), 12–24 (2014)
16. Andres, B., Kappes, J.H., Beier, T., Köthe, U., Hamprecht, F.A.: Probabilistic image segmentation with closedness constraints. In: Proceedings of the ICCV 2011, pp. 2611–26181 (2011)
17. Andres, B., et al.: Globally optimal closed-surface segmentation for connectomics. In: Fitzgibbon, A., Lazebnik, S., Perona, P., Sato, Y., Schmid, C. (eds.) ECCV 2012. LNCS, vol. 7574, pp. 778–791. Springer, Heidelberg (2012). https://doi.org/10.1007/978-3-642-33712-3_56
18. Yarkony, J., Ihler, A., Fowlkes, C.C.: Fast planar correlation clustering for image segmentation. In: Fitzgibbon, A., Lazebnik, S., Perona, P., Sato, Y., Schmid, C. (eds.) ECCV 2012. LNCS, vol. 7577, pp. 568–581. Springer, Heidelberg (2012). https://doi.org/10.1007/978-3-642-33783-3_41
19. Pape, C., Beier, T., Li, P., Jain, V., Bock, D.D., Kreshuk, A.: Solving large multicut problems for connectomics via domain decomposition. In: Proceedings of the IEEE Conference on Computer Vision and Pattern Recognition, pp. 1–10 (2017)

20. Zhang, C., Yarkony, J., Hamprecht, F.A.: Cell detection and segmentation using correlation clustering. In: Golland, P., Hata, N., Barillot, C., Hornegger, J., Howe, R. (eds.) MICCAI 2014. LNCS, vol. 8673, pp. 9–16. Springer, Cham (2014). https://doi.org/10.1007/978-3-319-10404-1_2
21. Horňáková, A., Lange, J.H., Andres, B.: Analysis and optimization of graph decompositions by lifted multicuts. In: International Conference on Machine Learning, pp. 1539–1548 (2017)
22. Keuper, M., Levinkov, E., Bonneel, N., Lavoué, G., Brox, T., Andres, B.: Efficient decomposition of image and mesh graphs by lifted multicuts. In: Proceedings of the ICCV 2015, pp. 1751–1759 (2015)
23. Beier, T., Andres, B., Köthe, U., Hamprecht, F.A.: An efficient fusion move algorithm for the minimum cost lifted multicut problem. In: Leibe, B., Matas, J., Sebe, N., Welling, M. (eds.) ECCV 2016. LNCS, vol. 9906, pp. 715–730. Springer, Cham (2016). https://doi.org/10.1007/978-3-319-46475-6_44
24. Beier, T., Pape, C., Rahaman, N., Prange, T.E.A.: Multicut brings automated neurite segmentation closer to human performance. Nat. Methods 14(2), 101–102 (2017)
25. Lee, K., Zung, J., Li, P., Jain, V., Seung, H.S.: Superhuman accuracy on the snemi3d connectomics challenge. arXiv preprint arXiv:1706.00120 (2017)
26. Jain, V., et al.: Supervised learning of image restoration with convolutional networks. In: Proceedings of the ICCV 2007, pp. 1–8 (2007)
27. Ciresan, D.C., Giusti, A., Gambardella, L.M., Schmidhuber, J.: Deep neural networks segment neuronal membranes in electron microscopy images. In: Proceedings of the NIPS 2012 (2012)
28. Arganda-Carreras, I., Turaga, S., Berger, D.: Crowdsourcing the creation of image segmentation algorithms for connectomics. Front. Neuroanat. 9, 142 (2015)
29. Ronneberger, O., Fischer, P., Brox, T.: U-Net: convolutional networks for biomedical image segmentation. In: Navab, N., Hornegger, J., Wells, W.M., Frangi, A.F. (eds.) MICCAI 2015. LNCS, vol. 9351, pp. 234–241. Springer, Cham (2015). https://doi.org/10.1007/978-3-319-24574-4_28
30. Quan, T.M., Hilderbrand, D.G., Jeong, W.K.: FusionNet: a deep fully residual convolutional neural network for image segmentation in connectomics. arXiv:1612.05360 (2016)
31. Nunez-Iglesias, J., Kennedy, R., Parag, T., Shi, J., Chklovskii, D.: Machine learning of hierarchical clustering to segment 2D and 3D images. PLoS One 8, e71715 (2013)
32. Knowles-Barley, S., et al.: RhoanaNet pipeline: dense automatic neural annotation. arXiv:1611.06973 (2016)
33. Uzunbaş, M.G., Chen, C., Metaxsas, D.: Optree: a learning-based adaptive watershed algorithm for neuron segmentation. In: Golland, P., Hata, N., Barillot, C., Hornegger, J., Howe, R. (eds.) MICCAI 2014. LNCS, vol. 8673, pp. 97–105. Springer, Cham (2014). https://doi.org/10.1007/978-3-319-10404-1_13
34. Meirovitch, Y., et al.: A multi-pass approach to large-scale connectomics. arXiv preprint:1612.02120 (2016)
35. Januszewski, M., Maitin-Shepard, J., Li, P., Kornfeld, J., Denk, W., Jain, V.: Flood-filling networks. arXiv:1611.00421 (2016)
36. Zlateski, A., Seung, H.S.: Image segmentation by size-dependent single linkage clustering of a watershed basin graph. arXiv:1505.00249 (2015)
37. Parag, T., et al.: Anisotropic EM segmentation by 3D affinity learning and agglomeration. arXiv preprint 1707.08935 (2017)
38. Turaga, S.C., et al.: Convolutional networks can learn to generate affinity graphs for image segmentation. Neural Comput. 22(2), 511–538 (2010)

39. Turaga, S.C., Briggman, K.L., Helmstaedter, M., Denk, W., Seung, H.S.: Maximin affinity learning of image segmentation. arXiv:0911.5372 (2009)
40. Wolf, S., Schott, L., Köthe, U., Hamprecht, F.: Learned watershed: End-to-end learning of seeded segmentation. Proceedings of the ICCV 2017 (2017)
41. Bai, M., Urtasun, R.: Deep watershed transform for instance segmentation. arXiv:1611.08303 (2016)
42. Xie, S., Tu, Z.: Holistically-nested edge detection. In: Proceedings of the ICCV 2015, pp. 1395–1403 (2015)
43. Kokkinos, I.: Pushing the boundaries of boundary detection using deep learning. arXiv:1511.07386 (2015)
44. Cai, J., Lu, L., Xie, Y., Xing, F., Yang, L.: Pancreas segmentation in MRI using graph-based decision fusion on convolutional neural networks. In: Descoteaux, M., Maier-Hein, L., Franz, A., Jannin, P., Collins, D.L., Duchesne, S. (eds.) MICCAI 2017. LNCS, vol. 10435, pp. 674–682. Springer, Cham (2017). https://doi.org/10. 1007/978-3-319-66179-7_77
45. Meyer, F.: Topographic distance and watershed lines. Signal Process. **38**(1), 113–125 (1994)
46. Meyer, F.: Minimum spanning forests for morphological segmentation. In: Serra, J., Soille, P. (eds.) Mathematical Morphology and Its Applications to Image Processing, pp. 77–84. Springer, Dordrecht (1994). https://doi.org/10.1007/978-94-011-1040-2_11
47. Falcão, A.X., Stolfi, J., de Alencar Lotufo, R.: The image foresting transform: theory, algorithms, and applications. IEEE Trans. Patt. Anal. Mach. Intell. **26**(1), 19–29 (2004)
48. Cormen, T.H.: Introduction to Algorithms. MIT press, Cambridge (2009)
49. Schlegel, P., Costa, M., Jefferis, G.S.: Learning from connectomics on the fly. Curr. Opin. Insect Sci. (2017)
50. Funke, J., et al.: Large scale image segmentation with structured loss based deep learning for connectome reconstruction. IEEE Trans. Pattern Anal. Mach. Intell. (2018)
51. Shen, W., Wang, B., Jiang, Y., Wang, Y., Yuille, A.: Multi-stage multi-recursive-input fully convolutional networks for neuronal boundary detection. arXiv preprint arXiv:1703.08493 (2017)
52. Weiler, M., Hamprecht, F.A., Storath, M.: Learning steerable filters for rotation equivariant CNNs. arXiv preprint arXiv:1711.07289 (2017)
53. Martin, D., Fowlkes, C., Tal, D., Malik, J.: A database of human segmented natural images and its application to evaluating segmentation algorithms and measuring ecological statistics. In: Proceedings of the 8th International Conference on Computer Vision, vol. 2, pp. 416–423, July 2001
54. Cordts, M., et al.: The cityscapes dataset for semantic urban scene understanding. In: Proceedings of the IEEE Conference on Computer Vision and Pattern Recognition (CVPR) (2016)
55. Lin, T.-Y., et al.: Microsoft COCO: common objects in context. In: Fleet, D., Pajdla, T., Schiele, B., Tuytelaars, T. (eds.) ECCV 2014. LNCS, vol. 8693, pp. 740–755. Springer, Cham (2014). https://doi.org/10.1007/978-3-319-10602-1_48
56. Mottaghi, R., et al.: The role of context for object detection and semantic segmentation in the wild. In: IEEE Conference on Computer Vision and Pattern Recognition (CVPR) (2014)

W-TALC: Weakly-Supervised Temporal Activity Localization and Classification

Sujoy Paul[✉], Sourya Roy, and Amit K. Roy-Chowdhury

University of California, Riverside, CA 92521, USA
{supaul,sroy,amitrc}@ece.ucr.edu

Abstract. Most activity localization methods in the literature suffer from the burden of frame-wise annotation requirement. Learning from weak labels may be a potential solution towards reducing such manual labeling effort. Recent years have witnessed a substantial influx of tagged videos on the Internet, which can serve as a rich source of weakly-supervised training data. Specifically, the correlations between videos with similar tags can be utilized to temporally localize the activities. Towards this goal, we present W-TALC, a Weakly-supervised Temporal Activity Localization and Classification framework using only video-level labels. The proposed network can be divided into two sub-networks, namely the Two-Stream based feature extractor network and a weakly-supervised module, which we learn by optimizing two complimentary loss functions. Qualitative and quantitative results on two challenging datasets - Thumos14 and ActivityNet1.2, demonstrate that the proposed method is able to detect activities at a fine granularity and achieve better performance than current state-of-the-art methods.

Keywords: Weakly-supervised · Activity localization
Co-activity similarity loss

1 Introduction

Temporal activity localization and classification in continuous videos is a challenging and interesting problem in computer vision [1]. Its recent success [62,68] has evolved around a *fully* supervised setting, which considers the availability of frame-wise activity labels. However, acquiring such precise frame-wise information requires enormous manual labor. This may not scale efficiently with a growing set of cameras and activity categories. On the other hand, it is much easier for a person to provide a few labels which encapsulate the content of a video. Moreover, videos available on the Internet are often accompanied by tags which provide semantic discrimination. Such video-level labels are generally termed as *weak* labels, which may be utilized to learn models with the ability to classify and localize activities in continuous videos. In this paper, we propose a novel framework for Temporal Activity Localization and Classification (TALC) from such weak labels. Figure 1 presents the train-test protocol W-TALC.

© Springer Nature Switzerland AG 2018
V. Ferrari et al. (Eds.): ECCV 2018, LNCS 11208, pp. 588–607, 2018.
https://doi.org/10.1007/978-3-030-01225-0_35

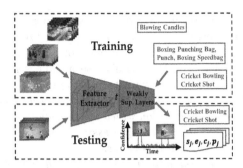

Fig. 1. This figure presents the train-test protocol of W-TALC. The training set consists of videos and the corresponding video-level activity tags. Whereas, while testing, the network not only estimates the labels of the activities in the video, but also temporally locates their occurrence representing the start (s_j) and end time (e_j), category (c_j) and confidence of recognition (p_j) of the jth activity located by the model.

In computer vision, researchers have utilized weak labels to learn models for several tasks including semantic segmentation [18,28,63], visual tracking [69], reconstruction [25,52], video summarization [37], learning robotic manipulations [46], video captioning [41], object boundaries [29], place recognition [2], and so on. The weak TALC problem is analogous to weak object detection in images, where object category labels are provided at the image-level. There have been several works in this domain mostly utilizing the techniques of Multiple Instance Learning (MIL) [70] due to their close relation in terms of the structure of information available for training. The positive and negative bags required for MIL are generated by state-of-the-art region proposal techniques [24,33]. On the other hand, end-to-end learning with categorical loss functions are presented in [13,15,16,47] and recently, the authors in [71] incorporated the proposal generation network in an end-to-end manner.

Temporal localization using weak labels is a much more challenging task compared to weak object detection. The key reason is the additional variation in content as well as the length along the temporal axis in videos. Activity localization from weakly labeled data remains relatively unexplored. Some works [48,50,63] focus on weakly-supervised spatial segmentation of the actor region in short videos. Another set of works [6,20,31,40] considers video-level labels of the activities and their temporal ordering during training. However, such information about the activity order may not be available for a majority of web-videos. A recent work [60] utilizes state-of-the-art object detectors for spatial annotations but considers full temporal supervision. In [57], a soft selection module is introduced for untrimmed video classification along with activity localization and a sparsity constraint is included in [35].

In W-TALC, as we have labels only for the entire video, we need to process them at once. Processing long videos at fine temporal granularity may have considerable memory and computation requirements. On the other hand, coarse temporal processing may result in reduced detection granularity. Thus, there is a trade-off between performance and computation. Over the past few years, networks trained on ImageNet [12] and recently on Kinetics [27], has been used widely in several applications. Based on these advances in literature and the aforementioned trade-off, we may want to ask the question that: *is it possible to utilize these networks just as feature extractors and develop a framework for weakly-supervised activity localization which learns only the task-specific parameters, thus scaling up to long videos and processing them at fine temporal granularity?* To address this question, in this paper, *we present a framework (W-TALC) for weakly-supervised temporal activity localization and video classification, which utilizes pair-wise video similarity constraints via an attention-based mechanism along with multiple instance learning to learn only the task-specific parameters.*

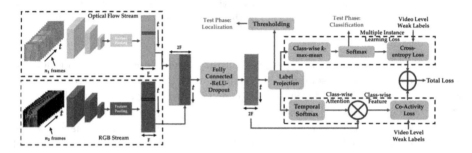

Fig. 2. This figure presents the proposed framework for weakly-supervised activity localization and classification. The number of frames n_1 and n_2 are dependent on the feature extractor used. After concatenating the feature vectors from the RGB and Optical Flow streams, a FullyConnected-ReLU-Dropout operation is applied to get features of dimension 2048 for each time instant. These are then passed through the label projection module to obtain activations over the categories. Using these activations, we compute two loss functions namely Multiple Instance Learning Loss and Co-Activity Similarity Loss, which are optimized jointly to learn the network weights.

Framework Overview. A pictorial representation of W-TALC is presented in Fig. 2. The proposed method utilizes off-the-shelf Two-Stream networks ([9,57]) as a feature extractor. The number of frame inputs depend on the network used and will be discussed in Sect. 3.1. After passing the frames through the networks, we obtain a matrix of feature vectors with one dimension representing the temporal axis. Thereafter, we apply a FullyConnected-ReLU-Dropout layer followed by label space projection layer, both of which is learned for the weakly-supervised task.

The activations over the label space are then used to compute two complimentary loss functions using video-level labels. The first one is Multiple Instance Learning Loss, where the class-wise k-max-mean strategy is employed to pool the class-wise activations and obtain a probability mass function over the categories.

Its cross-entropy with the ground-truth label is the Multiple Instance Learning Loss (MILL). The second one is the Co-Activity Similarity Loss (CASL), which is based on the motivation that a pair of videos having at least one activity category (say biking) in common should have similar features in the temporal regions which correspond to that activity. Also, the features from one video corresponding to biking should be different from features of the other video (of the pair) not corresponding to biking. However, as the temporal labels are not known in weakly-supervised data, we use the attention obtained from the label space activations as weak temporal labels, to compute the CASL. Thereafter, we jointly minimize the two loss functions to learn the network parameters.

Main contributions. The main contributions of the proposed method are as follows.

1. We propose a novel approach for weakly-supervised temporal activity localization and video classification, without fine-tuning the feature extractor, but learning only the task-specific parameters. Our method does not consider any ordering of the labels in the video during training and can detect multiple activities in the same temporal duration.
2. We introduce the Co-Activity Similarity Loss and jointly optimize it with the Multiple Instance Learning Loss to learn the network weights specific to the weakly-supervised task. We empirically show that the two loss functions are complimentary in nature.
3. We perform extensive experimentations on two challenging datasets and show that the proposed method performs better than the current state-of-the-art methods.

2   Related Works

The problem of learning from weakly-supervised data has been addressed in several computer vision tasks including object detection [4,11,16,33,42,47], segmentation [3,28,38,54,59], video captioning [41] and summarization [37]. Here, we discuss in detail the other works which are more closely related to our work.

Weakly-supervised Spatial Action Localization. Some researchers have looked into the problem of spatial localization of actors in mostly short and trimmed videos using weak supervision. In [10] a framework is developed for localization of players in sports videos, using detections from state-of-the-art fully supervised player detector, as inputs to their network. Person detectors are also used in [48,61] to generate person tubes, which is used to learn different Multiple Instance Learning based classifiers. Conditional Random Field (CRF) is used in [63] to perform actor-action segmentation from video-level labels but on short videos.

Scripts as Weak Supervision. Some works in the literature use scripts or subtitles generally available with videos as weak labels for activity localization. In [14,32] words related to human actions are extracted from subtitles to provide coarse temporal localizations of actions for training. In [5], actor-action pairs extracted from movie scripts serve as weak labels for spatial actor-action localization by using discriminative clustering. Our algorithm on the other hand only considers that the label of the video is available as a whole, agnostic to the source from where the labels are acquired, i.e., movie scripts, subtitles, humans or other oracles.

Temporal Localization with Ordering. Few works in the literature have considered the availability of temporal order of activities, apart from the video-level labels during training. The activity orderings in the training videos are used as constraints in discriminative clustering to learn activity detection models in [6]. A similar approach was taken in [7]. In [20], the authors propose a dynamic programming based approach to evaluate and search for possible alignments between video frames and the corresponding labels. The authors in [40] use a Recurrent Neural Network (RNN) to iteratively train and realign the activity regions until convergence. A similar iterative process is presented by the same authors in [31], but without employing an RNN. Unlike these works in literature, our work does not consider any information about the orderings of the activity.

The works in [35,57] are closely related to the problem setting presented in this paper. However, as the framework in [57] is based on the temporal segments network [58], a fixed number of segments, irrespective of the length of the video, are considered during training, which may lead to a reduction in localization granularity. Moreover, they only employ the MILL, which may not be enough to localize activities at fine temporal granularity. A sparsity-based loss function is optimized in [35], along with a loss function similar to that obtained using the soft selection method in [57]. In this paper, we introduce a novel loss function named Co-Activity Similarity Loss (CASL) which imposes pair-wise constraints for better localization performance. We also propose a mechanism for dealing with long videos and yet detecting activities at high temporal granularity. In spite of not finetuning the feature extractor, we can still achieve better performance than state-of-the-art methods on weak TALC. Moreover, experimental results show that CASL is complimentary in nature with MILL.

3   Methodology

In this section, we present our framework (W-TALC) for weakly-supervised activity localization and classification. First, we present the mechanism we use to extract features from the two standard networks, followed by the layers of the network we learn. Thereafter, we present two loss functions MILL and CASL, which we jointly optimize to learn the weights of the network. It may be noted that we compute both the loss functions using only the video-level labels of training videos. Before going into the details of our framework, let us define the notations and problem statement formally.

Problem Statement. Consider that we have a training set of n videos $\mathcal{X} = \{x_i\}_{i=1}^n$ with variable temporal durations denoted by $L = \{l_i\}_{i=1}^n$ (after feature extraction) and activity label set $A = \{a_i\}_{i=1}^n$, where $a_i = \{a_i^j\}_{j=1}^{m_i}$ are the

$m_i(\geq 1)$ labels for the ith video. We also define the set of activity categories as $\mathcal{S} = \bigcup_{i=1}^{n} a_i = \{\alpha_i\}_{i=1}^{n_c}$. During test time, given a video x, we need to predict a set $x_{det} = \{(s_j, e_j, c_j, p_j)\}_{j=1}^{n(x)}$, where $n(x)$ is the number of detections for x. s_j, e_j are the start time and end time of the jth detection, c_j represents its predicted activity category with confidence p_j. With these notations, our proposed framework is presented next.

3.1 Feature Extraction

In this paper, we focus particularly on two architectures - UntrimmedNets [57] and I3D [9] for feature extraction, mainly due to their two stream nature, which incorporates rich temporal temporal information in one of the streams, necessary for activity recognition. Please note that the rest of our framework is agnostic to the features used.

UntrimmedNet Features. In this case, we pass one frame through the RGB stream and 5 frames through the Optical Flow stream as in [57]. We extract the features from just before the classification layer at 2.5 fps. We use the network which is pre-trained on ImageNet [12], and finetuned using weak labels and MILL for task-specific dataset as in [57]. Thus, this feature extractor has no knowledge about activities using strong labels.

I3D Features. As in [35], we also experiment with features extracted from the Kinetics pre-trained I3D network [9]. The input to the two streams are non-overlapping 16 frame chunks. The output is passed through a 3D average pooling layer of kernel size $2 \times 7 \times 7$ to obtain features of dimension 1024 each from the two streams.

At the end of the feature extraction procedure, each video x_i is represented by two matrices X_i^r and X_i^o, denoting the RGB and optical flow features respectively, both of which are of dimension $1024 \times l_i$. Note that l_i is not only dependent on the video index i, but also on the feature extraction procedure used. These matrices become the input to our weakly-supervised learning module.

Memory Constraints. As mentioned previously, natural videos may have large variations in length, from a few seconds to more than an hour. In the weakly-supervised setting, we have information about the labels for the video as a whole, thus requiring it to process the entire video at once. This may be problematic for very long videos due to GPU memory constraints. A possible solution to this problem may be to divide the videos into chunks along the temporal axis [58] and apply a temporal pooling technique to reduce the length of each chunk to a single representation vector. The number of chunks depends on the available GPU memory. However, this will introduce unwanted background activity feature in the representation vectors as the start and end period of the activities in the video will not overlap with the pre-defined chunks for most of the videos. To cope with this problem, we introduce a simple video sampling technique.

Long Video Sampling. As granularity of localizations is important for activity localization, we take an approach alternative to the one mentioned above.

We process the entire video if its length is less than the pre-defined length T necessary to meet the GPU bandwidth. However, if the length of the video is greater than T, we randomly extract from it a clip of length T with contiguous frames and assign all the labels of the entire video to the extracted video clip. It may be noted that although this may introduce some errors in the labels, this way of sampling does have advantages, as will be discussed in more detail in Sect. 4.

Computational Budget and Finetuning. The error introduced by the video sampling strategy will increase with a decrease in the pre-defined length T, which meet the GPU bandwidth constraints. If we want to jointly finetune the feature extractor along with training our weakly-supervised module, T may be very small in order to maintain a reasonable batch size for Stochastic Gradient Descent (SGD) [8]. Although the value of T may be increased by using multiple GPUs simultaneously, it may not be a scalable approach. Moreover, the time to train both the modules may be high. Considering these problems, we do not finetune the feature extractors, but only learn the task-specific parameters, described next, from scratch. The advantages for doing this are twofold - the weakly-supervised module is light-weight in terms of the number of parameters, thus requiring less time to train, and it increases T considerably, thus reducing labeling error while sampling long videos. We next present our weakly-supervised module.

3.2 Weakly Supervised Layer

In this section, we present the proposed weakly-supervised learning scheme, which uses only weak labels to learn models for simultaneous activity localization and classification.

Fully Connected Layer. We introduce a fully connected layer followed by ReLU [34] and Dropout [49] on the extracted features. The operation can be formalized for a video with index i as follows.

$$\boldsymbol{X}_i = \mathcal{D}\left(\max\left(0, \boldsymbol{W}_{fc} \begin{bmatrix} \boldsymbol{X}_i^r \\ \boldsymbol{X}_i^o \end{bmatrix} \oplus \boldsymbol{b}_{fc}\right), k_p\right) \tag{1}$$

where $\mathcal{D}$ represents Dropout with k_p representing its keep probability, $\oplus$ is the addition with broadcasting operator, $\boldsymbol{W}_{fc} \in \mathbb{R}^{2048 \times 2048}$ and $\boldsymbol{b} \in \mathbb{R}^{2048 \times 1}$ are the parameters to be learned from the training data and $\boldsymbol{X}_i \in \mathbb{R}^{2048 \times l_i}$ is the output feature matrix for the entire video.

Label Space Projection We use the feature representation $\boldsymbol{X}_i$ to classify and localize the activities in the videos. We project the representations $\boldsymbol{X}_i$ to the label space ($\in \mathbb{R}^{n_c}$, n_c is the number of categories), using a fully connected layer, with weight sharing along the temporal axis. The class-wise activations we obtain after this projection can be represented as follows.

$$\boldsymbol{A}_i = \boldsymbol{W}_a \boldsymbol{X}_i \oplus \boldsymbol{b}_a \tag{2}$$

where $\boldsymbol{W}_a \in \mathbb{R}^{n_c \times 2048}$, $\boldsymbol{b}_a \in \mathbb{R}^{n_c}$ are to be learned and $\boldsymbol{\mathcal{A}}_i \in \mathbb{R}^{n_c \times l_i}$. These class-wise activations represent the possibility of activities at each of the temporal instants. These activations are used to compute the loss functions as presented next.

3.3 k-max Multiple Instance Learning

As discussed in Sect. 1, the weakly-supervised activity localization and classification problem as addressed in this paper can be directly mapped to the problem of Multiple Instance Learning (MIL) [70]. In MIL, individual samples are grouped in two bags, namely positive and negative bags. A positive bag contains at least one positive instance and a negative bag contains no positive instance. Using these bags as training data, we need to learn a model, which will be able to distinguish each instance to be positive or negative, besides classifying a bag. In our case, we consider the entire video as a bag of instances, where each instance is represented by a feature vector at a certain time instant. In order to compute the loss for each bag, i.e., video in our case, we need to represent each video using a single confidence score per category. For a given video, we compute the activation score corresponding to a particular category as the average of k-max activation over the temporal dimension for that category. As in our case, the number of elements in a bag varies widely, we set k proportional to the number of elements in a bag. Specifically,

$$k_i = \max\left(1, \left\lfloor \frac{l_i}{s} \right\rfloor\right) \tag{3}$$

where s is a design parameter. Thus, our class-wise confidence scores for the jth category of the ith video can be represented as,

$$s_i^j = \frac{1}{k_i} \max_{\substack{\mathcal{M} \subset \mathcal{A}_i[j,:] \\ |\mathcal{M}|=k_i}} \sum_{l=1}^{k_i} \mathcal{M}_l \tag{4}$$

where $\mathcal{M}_l$ indicates the lth element in the set $\mathcal{M}$. Thereafter, a softmax non-linearity is applied to obtain the probability mass function over the all the categories as follows, $p_i^j = \frac{\exp(s_i^j)}{\sum_{j=1}^{n_c} \exp(s_i^j)}$. We need to compare this pmf with the ground truth distribution of labels for each video in order to compute the MILL. As each video can have multiple activities occurring in it, we represent the label vector for a video with ones at the positions if that activity occurs in the video, else zero. We then normalize this ground truth vector in order to convert it to a legitimate pmf. The MILL is then the cross-entropy between the predicted pmf $\boldsymbol{p}_i$ and ground-truth, which can then be represented as follows,

$$\mathcal{L}_{MILL} = \frac{1}{n} \sum_{i=1}^{n} \sum_{j=1}^{n_c} -y_i^j \log(p_i^j) \tag{5}$$

where $\boldsymbol{y}_i = [y_i^1, \ldots, y_i^{n_c}]^T$ is the normalized ground truth vector. This loss function is semantically similar to that used in [57]. We next present the novel Co-Activity Similarity Loss, which enforces constraints to learn better weights for activity localization.

3.4   Co-Activity Similarity

As discussed previously, the W-TALC problem motivates us to identify the correlations between videos of similar categories. Before discussing in more detail, let us define category-specific sets for the jth category as, $\mathcal{S}_j = \{\boldsymbol{x}_i \mid \exists\, a_i^k \in \boldsymbol{a}_i, \text{s.t. } a_i^k = \alpha_j\}$, i.e., the set $\mathcal{S}_j$ contains all the videos of the training set, which has activity α_j as one of its labels. Ideally, we may want the following properties in the learned feature representations $\boldsymbol{X}_i$ in Eq. 1.

-   A video pair belonging to the set $\mathcal{S}_j$ (for any $j \in \{1, \ldots, n_c\}$) should have similar feature representations in the portions of the video where the activity α_j occurs.
-   For the same video pair, feature representation of the portion where α_j occurs in one video should be different from that of the other video where α_j does not occur.

These properties are not directly enforced in MILL. Thus, we introduce Co-Activity Similarity Loss to embed the desired properties in the learned feature representations. As we do not have frame-wise labels, we use the class-wise activations obtained in Eq. 2 to identify the required activity portions. The loss function is designed in a way which helps to learn simultaneously the feature representation as well as the label space projection. We first normalize the per-video class-wise activations scores along the temporal axis using softmax non-linearity as follows:

$$\hat{\boldsymbol{A}}_i[j, t] = \frac{\exp(\boldsymbol{A}_i[j, t])}{\sum_{t'=1}^{l_i} \exp(\boldsymbol{A}_i[j, t'])} \tag{6}$$

where t indicates the time instants and $j \in \{1, \ldots, n_c\}$. We refer to these as *attention*, as they attend to the portions of the video where an activity of a certain category occurs. A high value of attention for a particular category indicates its high occurrence-probability of that category. In order to formulate the loss function, let us first define the class-wise feature vectors of regions with high and low attention as follows:

$$^H\boldsymbol{f}_i^j = \boldsymbol{X}_i \hat{\boldsymbol{A}}_i[j, :]^T$$
$$^L\boldsymbol{f}_i^j = \frac{1}{l_i - 1} \boldsymbol{X}_i \left(1 - \hat{\boldsymbol{A}}_i[j, :]^T\right) \tag{7}$$

where $^H\boldsymbol{f}_i^j, {}^L\boldsymbol{f}_i^j \in \mathbb{R}^{2048}$ represents the high and low attention region aggregated feature representations respectively of video i for category j. It may be noted that in Eq. 7 the low attention feature is not defined if a video contains a certain activity and the number of feature vectors, i.e., $l_i = 1$. This is also conceptually valid and in such cases, we cannot compute the CASL. We use cosine similarity in order to obtain a measure of the degree of similarity between two feature vectors and it may be expressed as follows:

$$d[\boldsymbol{f}_i, \boldsymbol{f}_j] = 1 - \frac{\langle \boldsymbol{f}_i, \boldsymbol{f}_j \rangle}{\langle \boldsymbol{f}_i, \boldsymbol{f}_i \rangle^{\frac{1}{2}} \langle \boldsymbol{f}_j, \boldsymbol{f}_j \rangle^{\frac{1}{2}}} \tag{8}$$

In order to enforce the two properties discussed above, we use the ranking hinge loss. Given a pair of videos $\boldsymbol{x}_m, \boldsymbol{x}_n \in \mathcal{S}_j$, the loss function may be represented as follows:

$$\mathcal{L}_j^{mn} = \frac{1}{2} \Big\{ \max \Big(0, d[^H \boldsymbol{f}_m^j, ^H \boldsymbol{f}_n^j] - d[^H \boldsymbol{f}_m^j, ^L \boldsymbol{f}_n^j] + \delta \Big)$$
$$+ \max \Big(0, d[^H \boldsymbol{f}_m^j, ^H \boldsymbol{f}_n^j] - d[^L \boldsymbol{f}_m^j, ^H \boldsymbol{f}_n^j] + \delta \Big) \Big\} \tag{9}$$

where δ is the margin parameter and we set it to 0.5 in our experiments. The two terms in the loss function are equivalent in meaning, and they represent that the high attention region features in both the videos should be more similar than the high attention region feature in one video and the low attention region feature in the other video. The total loss for the entire training set may be represented as follows:

$$\mathcal{L}_{CASL} = \frac{1}{n_c} \sum_{j=1}^{n_c} \frac{1}{\binom{|S_j|}{2}} \sum_{\boldsymbol{x}_m, \boldsymbol{x}_n \in \mathcal{S}_j} \mathcal{L}_j^{mn} \tag{10}$$

Optimization. The total loss function we need to optimize in order to learn the weights of the weakly supervised layer can be represented as follows:

$$\mathcal{L} = \lambda \mathcal{L}_{MILL} + (1 - \lambda)\mathcal{L}_{CASL} + \alpha ||\boldsymbol{W}||_F^2 \tag{11}$$

where the weights to be learned in our network are lumped to $\boldsymbol{W}$. We use $\lambda = 0.5$ and $\alpha = 5 \times 10^{-4}$ in our experiments. We optimize the above loss function using Adam [30] with a batch size of 10. We create each batch in a way such that it has a minimum of three pairs of videos such that each pair has at least one category in common. We use a constant learning rate of 10^{-4} in all our experiments.

Classification and Localization. After learning the weights of the network, we use them to classify an untrimmed video as well as localize the activities in it during test time. Given a video, we obtain the class-wise confidence scores as in Eq. 4 followed by softmax to obtain a pmf over the possible categories. Then, we can threshold the pmf to classify the video to contain one or more activity categories. However, as defined by the dataset [21] and used in literature [57], we use mAP for comparison, which does not require the thresholding operation, but directly uses the pmf.

For localization, we employ a two-stage thresholding scheme. First, we discard the categories which have confidence score (Eq. 4) below a certain threshold (0.0 used in our experiments). Thereafter, for each of the remaining categories, we apply a threshold on the corresponding activation in $\boldsymbol{A}$ (Eq. 2) along the temporal axis to obtain the localizations. It may be noted that as l_i is generally less than the frame rate of the videos, we upsample the activations to meet the frame rate.

4 Experiments

In this section, we experimentally evaluate the proposed framework for activity localization and classification from weakly labeled videos. We first discuss the datasets we use, followed by the implementation details, quantitative and some qualitative results.

Datasets. We perform experimental analysis on two datasets namely ActivityNet v1.2 [19] and Thumos14 [21]. These two datasets contain untrimmed videos with frame-wise labels of activities occurring in the video. However, as our algorithm is weakly-supervised, we use only the activity tags associated with the videos.

ActivityNet1.2. This dataset has 4819 videos for training, 2383 videos for validation and 2480 videos for testing whose labels are withheld. The number of classes involved is 100, with an average of 1.5 temporal activity segments per video. As in literature [35,57], we use the training videos to train our network, and the validation set to test.

Thumos14. The Thumos14 dataset has 1010 validation videos and 1574 test videos divided into 101 categories. Among these videos, 200 validation videos and 213 test videos have temporal annotations belonging to 20 categories. Although this is a smaller dataset than ActivityNet1.2, the temporal labels are very precise and with an average of 15.5 activity temporal segments per video. This dataset has several videos where multiple activities occur, thus making it even more challenging. The length of the videos also varies widely from a few seconds to more than an hour. The lesser number of videos make it challenging to efficiently learn the weakly-supervised network. Following literature [35,57], we use the validation videos for training and the test videos for testing.

Implementation Details. We use the corresponding repositories to extract the features for UntrimmedNets[1] and I3D[2]. We do not finetune the feature extractors. The weights of the weakly supervised layers are initialized by Xavier method [17]. We use TVL1 optical flow [3]. We train our network on a single Tesla K80 GPU using Tensorflow. We set $s = 8$ in Eq. 3 for both the datasets.

Activity Localization. We first perform a quantitative analysis of our framework for the task of activity localization. We use mAP with different Intersection over Union (IoU) thresholds as a performance metric, as in [21]. We compare our results with several state-of-the-art methods on both strong and weak supervision in Tables 1 and 2 for Thumos14 and ActivityNet1.2 respectively. It may

---

[1] www.github.com/wanglimin/UntrimmedNet.

[2] www.github.com/deepmind/kinetics-i3d.

[3] www.github.com/yjxiong/temporal-segment-networks.

Table 1. Detection performance comparisons over the Thumos14 dataset. UNTF and I3DF are abbreviations for UntrimmedNet features and I3D features respectively. The symbol $\downarrow$ represents that following [35], those models are trained using only the 20 classes having temporal annotations, but without using their temporal annotations.

Supervision	IoU →	0.1	0.2	0.3	0.4	0.5	0.7
Strong	Saliency-Pool [26]	04.6	03.4	02.1	01.4	00.9	00.1
	FV-DTF [36]	36.6	33.6	27.0	20.8	14.4	-
	SLM-mgram [39]	39.7	35.7	30.0	23.2	15.2	-
	S-CNN [44]	47.7	43.5	36.3	28.7	19.0	05.3
	Glimpse [64]	48.9	44.0	27.0	20.8	14.4	-
	PSDF [65]	51.4	42.6	33.6	26.1	18.8	-
	SMS [66]	51.0	45.2	36.5	27.8	17.8	-
	CDC [43]	-	-	40.1	29.4	23.3	**07.9**
	R-C3D [62]	54.5	51.5	44.8	35.6	28.9	-
	SSN [68]	**60.3**	**56.2**	**50.6**	**40.8**	**29.1**	-
Weak	HAS [47]	36.4	27.8	19.5	12.7	06.8	-
	UntrimmedNets [57]	44.4	37.7	28.2	21.1	13.7	-
	STPN (UNTF) [35] $\downarrow$	45.3	38.8	31.1	23.5	16.2	05.1
	STPN (I3DF) [35] $\downarrow$	52.0	44.7	35.5	25.8	16.9	04.3
Weak (Ours)	MILL+CASL+UNTF$\downarrow$	**49.0**	**42.8**	**32.0**	**26.0**	**18.8**	**06.2**
	MILL+I3DF	46.5	39.9	31.2	24.0	16.9	04.4
	MILL+CASL+I3DF	53.7	48.5	39.2	29.9	22.0	07.3
	MILL+CASL+I3DF$\downarrow$	**55.2**	**49.6**	**40.1**	**31.1**	**22.8**	**07.6**

Table 2. Detection performance comparisons over the ActivityNet1.2 dataset. The last column (Avg.) indicates the average mAP for IoU thresholds 0.5:0.05:0.95.

Supervision	IoU →	0.1	0.2	0.3	0.4	0.5	0.7	Avg.
Strong	SSN-SW [68]	-	-	-	-	-	-	24.8
	SSN-TAG [68]	-	-	-	-	-	-	**25.9**
Weak	W-TALC (Ours)	**53.9**	**49.8**	**45.5**	**41.6**	**37.0**	**14.6**	**18.0**

be noted that to the best of our knowledge, we are first to present quantitative results on weakly-supervised temporal activity localization on ActivityNet1.2. We show results for different combinations of features and loss function used. It may be noted that our framework performs much better than the other weakly supervised methods with similar feature usage. It is important to note that although the Kinetics pre-trained I3D features (I3DF) have some knowledge about activities, using only MILL as in [57] along with I3DF performs much worse than combining it with CASL, which is introduced in this paper. Moreover, our framework performs much better than other state-of-the-art methods

Table 3. Classification performance comparisons over Thumos14 dataset. † indicates that the algorithm use both videos from Thumos14 and trimmed videos from UCF101 for training. Without † indicates that the algorithm uses only videos from Thumos14 for training.

Methods	mAP	Supervision
EMV + RGB [67]	61.5	Strong †
iDT+FV [55]	63.1	Strong †
iDT+CNN [56]	62.0	Strong †
Objects + Motion [23]	71.6	Strong †
Feat. Agg. [22]	71.0	Strong †
Extreme LM [53]	63.2	Strong †
Temp. Seg. Net. (TSN) [58]	78.5	Strong †
Two Stream [45]	66.1	Strong †
Temp. Seg. Net. (TSN) [58]	67.7	Strong
UntrimmedNets [57]	74.2	Weak
UntrimmedNets [57]	82.2	Weak †
W-TALC (Ours w. I3D)	**85.6**	Weak

Table 4. Classification performance comparisons over the ActivityNet1.2 dataset. † indicate that the algorithm use the training and validation set of ActivityNet1.2 for training and tested on the server. Without † means that the algorithm is trained on the training set and tested on the validation set.

Algorithms	mAP	Supervision
C3D [51]	74.1	Strong †
iDT+FV [55]	66.5	Strong †
Depth2Action [23]	78.1	Strong †
Temp. Seg. Net. (TSN) [58]	88.8	Strong †
Two Stream [45]	71.9	Strong †
Temp. Seg. Net. (TSN) [58]	86.3	Strong
UntrimmedNets [57]	87.7	Weak
UntrimmedNets [57]	91.3	Weak †
W-TALC (Ours w. I3D)	**93.2**	Weak

even when using UNTF, which is not trained using any strong labels of activities. A detailed analysis of the two loss functions MILL and CASL will be presented subsequently.

Activity Classification. We now present the performance of our framework for activity classification. We use mean average precision (mAP) to compute the classification performance from the predicted videos-level scores in Eq. 4 after applying softmax. We compare with both fully supervised and weakly-supervised methods and the results are presented in Tables 3 and 4 for Thumos14 and ActivityNet1.2 respectively. The proposed method performs significantly better than the other state-of-the-art approaches. Please note that the methods indicated with † utilize a larger training set compared to ours as mentioned in the tables.

Relative Weights on Loss Functions. In our framework, we jointly optimize two loss functions - MILL and CASL defined in Eq. 11 to learn the weights of the weakly-supervised module. It is interesting to investigate the relative contributions of the loss functions to the detection performance. In order to do that, we performed experiments, using the I3D features, with different values of λ (higher value indicate larger weight on MILL) and present the detection results on the Thumos14 dataset in Fig. 3a.

As may be observed from the plot, the proposed method performs best with $\lambda = 0.5$, i.e., when both the loss functions have equal weights. Moreover, using only MILL, i.e., $\lambda = 1.0$, results in a decrease of 7–8% in mAP compared to when both CASL and MILL are given equal weights in the loss function. This shows that the CASL introduced in this work has a major effect towards the better performance of our framework compared to using I3D features along with the loss function in [57], i.e., MILL.

Sensitivity to Maximum Length of Sequence. Natural videos may often be very long. As mentioned previously, in the weakly-supervised setting, we have only video-level labels, so we need to process the entire video at once in order to compute the loss functions. In Sect. 3.1, we discuss a simple sampling strategy, which we use to maintain the length of the videos in a batch to be less than a pre-defined length T to meet GPU memory constraints. This method has the following advantages and disadvantage.

- *Advantages*: First, we can learn from long length videos using this scheme. Secondly, this strategy will act as a data augmentation technique as we randomly crop, along the temporal axis to make it a fixed length sequence, if the length of the video $\geq T$. Also a lower value of T reduces computation time.
- *Disadvantage*: In this sampling scheme, errors will be introduced in the labels of the training batch, which may increase with the number of training videos with length $> T$. The above factors induce a trade-off between performance

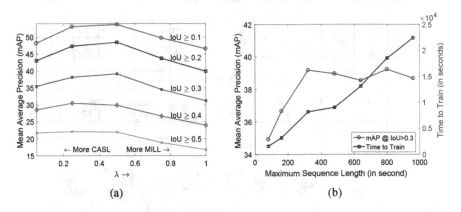

(a)   (b)

Fig. 3. (a) presents the variations in detection performance on Thumos14 by changing weights on MILL and CASL. Higher λ represents more weight on the MILL and vice versa. (b) presents the variations in detection performance (@IoU ≥ 0.3) and training time on Thumos14 dataset by changing the maximum possible length of video sequence during training (T) as discussed in the text.

and computation time. This can be seen in Fig. 3b, wherein the initial portion of the plot, with an increase of T, the detection performance improves, but the computational time increases. However, the detection performance eventually reaches a plateau suggesting $T = 320s$ to be a reasonable choice for this dataset.

Qualitative Results. We present a few interesting example localizations with ground truths in Fig. 4. The figure has four examples from Thumos14 and ActivityNet1.2 datasets. To test how the proposed framework performs on videos outside the datasets used in this paper, we tested the learned networks on randomly collected videos from YouTube. We present two such example detections in Fig. 4, using the model trained on Thumos14.

The first example in Fig. 4 is quite challenging as the localization should precisely be the portions of the video, where Golf Swing occurs, which has very

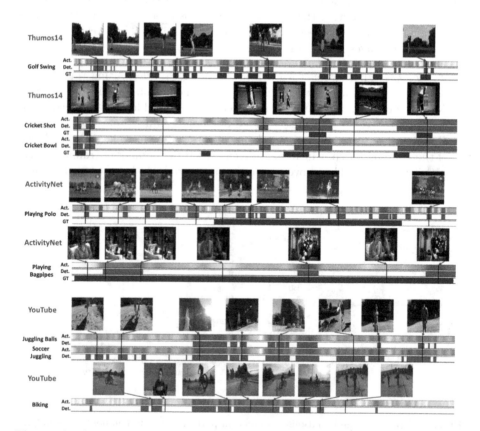

Fig. 4. This figure presents some detection results for qualitative analysis. 'Act.' represents the temporal activations obtained from the final layer of our network, 'Det.' represents the detections obtained after thresholding the activations, and 'GT' represent the ground truth.

similar features in the RGB domain to portions of the video where the player prepares for the swing. In spite of this, our model is able to localize the relevant portions of Golf Swing, potentially based on the flow features. In the second example from Thumos14, the detections of Cricket Shot and Cricket Bowl appear to be correlated in time. This is because Cricket Shot and Bowl are two activities which generally co-occur in videos. To have fine-grained localizations for such activities, videos which have only one of these activities are required. However, in the Thumos14 dataset, very few training examples contain only one of these two activities.

In the third example, which is from ActivityNet1.2, although 'Playing Polo' occurs in the first portion of the video, it is absent in the ground truth. However, our model is able to localize those activity segments as well. The same discussion is also applicable to the fourth example, where 'Bagpiping' occurs in the frames in a sparse manner, and our model's response is aligned with its occurrence, but the ground truth annotations are for almost the entire video. These two examples are motivations behind weakly-supervised localization, because obtaining precise unanimous ground truths from multiple labelers is difficult, costly and sometimes even infeasible.

The fifth example is on a randomly selected video from YouTube. It has a person, who is juggling balls in an outdoor environment. But, most of the examples in Thumos14 of the same category are indoors, with the person taking up a significant portion of the frames spatially. Despite such differences in data, our model is able to localize some portions of the activity. However, the model also predicts some portions of the video to be 'Soccer Juggling', which may be because its training samples in Thumos14 contains a combination of feet, hand, and head, and a subset of such movements are present in 'Juggling Balls'. Moreover, it is interesting to note that the first two frames show some maneuver of a ball with feet and it is detected as 'Soccer Juggling' as well.

5   Conclusions and Future Work

In this paper, we present an approach to learn temporal activity localization and video classification models using only weak supervision with video-level labels. We present the novel Co-Activity Similarity loss, which is empirically shown to be complimentary with the Multiple Instance Learning Loss. We also show a simple mechanism to deal with long length videos, yet processing them at high granularity. Experiments on two challenging datasets demonstrate that the proposed method achieves state-of-the-art results in the weak TALC problem. Future work will concentrate on extending the idea of Co-Activity Similarity Loss to other problems in computer vision.

Acknowledgments. This work was partially supported by ONR contract N00014-15-C5113 through a sub-contract from Mayachitra Inc and NSF grant IIS-1724341. We thank Victor Hill of UCR CS for setting up the computing infrastructure.

References

1. Aggarwal, J.K., Ryoo, M.S.: Human activity analysis: a review. ACM Comput. Surv. (CSUR) **43**(3), 16 (2011)
2. Arandjelovic, R., Gronat, P., Torii, A., Pajdla, T., Sivic, J.: Netvlad: CNN architecture for weakly supervised place recognition. In: CVPR, pp. 5297–5307 (2016)
3. Bearman, A., Russakovsky, O., Ferrari, V., Fei-Fei, L.: What's the Point: semantic segmentation with point supervision. In: Leibe, B., Matas, J., Sebe, N., Welling, M. (eds.) ECCV 2016. LNCS, vol. 9911, pp. 549–565. Springer, Cham (2016). https://doi.org/10.1007/978-3-319-46478-7_34
4. Bilen, H., Vedaldi, A.: Weakly supervised deep detection networks. In: CVPR, pp. 2846–2854 (2016)
5. Bojanowski, P., Bach, F., Laptev, I., Ponce, J., Schmid, C., Sivic, J.: Finding actors and actions in movies. In: ICCV, pp. 2280–2287. IEEE (2013)
6. Bojanowski, P., et al.: Weakly supervised action labeling in videos under ordering constraints. In: Fleet, D., Pajdla, T., Schiele, B., Tuytelaars, T. (eds.) ECCV 2014. LNCS, vol. 8693, pp. 628–643. Springer, Cham (2014). https://doi.org/10.1007/978-3-319-10602-1_41
7. Bojanowski, P., et al.: Weakly-supervised alignment of video with text. In: ICCV, pp. 4462–4470. IEEE (2015)
8. Bottou, L.: Large-scale machine learning with stochastic gradient descent. In: Lechevallier, Y., Saporta, G. (eds.) COMPSTAT, pp. 177–186. Springer, Heidelberg (2010). https://doi.org/10.1007/978-3-7908-2604-3_16
9. Carreira, J., Zisserman, A.: Quo vadis, action recognition? a new model and the kinetics dataset. In: CVPR, pp. 4724–4733. IEEE (2017)
10. Chen, L., Zhai, M., Mori, G.: Attending to distinctive moments: weakly-supervised attention models for action localization in video. In: CVPR, pp. 328–336 (2017)
11. Cinbis, R.G., Verbeek, J., Schmid, C.: Weakly supervised object localization with multi-fold multiple instance learning. PAMI **39**(1), 189–203 (2017)
12. Deng, J., Dong, W., Socher, R., Li, L.J., Li, K., Fei-Fei, L.: Imagenet: a large-scale hierarchical image database. In: CVPR, pp. 248–255. IEEE (2009)
13. Diba, A., Sharma, V., Pazandeh, A., Pirsiavash, H., Van Gool, L.: Weakly supervised cascaded convolutional networks. In: CVPR (2016)
14. Duchenne, O., Laptev, I., Sivic, J., Bach, F., Ponce, J.: Automatic annotation of human actions in video. In: ICCV, pp. 1491–1498. IEEE (2009)
15. Durand, T., Mordan, T., Thome, N., Cord, M.: Wildcat: weakly supervised learning of deep convnets for image classification, pointwise localization and segmentation. In: CVPR (2017)
16. Durand, T., Thome, N., Cord, M.: Weldon: weakly supervised learning of deep convolutional neural networks. In: CVPR, pp. 4743–4752 (2016)
17. Glorot, X., Bengio, Y.: Understanding the difficulty of training deep feedforward neural networks. In: AISTATS, pp. 249–256 (2010)
18. Hartmann, G., et al.: Weakly supervised learning of object segmentations from web-scale video. In: Fusiello, A., Murino, V., Cucchiara, R. (eds.) ECCV 2012. LNCS, vol. 7583, pp. 198–208. Springer, Heidelberg (2012). https://doi.org/10.1007/978-3-642-33863-2_20
19. Heilbron, F.C., Escorcia, V., Ghanem, B., Niebles, J.C.: Activitynet: a large-scale video benchmark for human activity understanding. In: CVPR, pp. 961–970. IEEE (2015)

20. Huang, D.-A., Fei-Fei, L., Niebles, J.C.: Connectionist temporal modeling for weakly supervised action labeling. In: Leibe, B., Matas, J., Sebe, N., Welling, M. (eds.) ECCV 2016. LNCS, vol. 9908, pp. 137–153. Springer, Cham (2016). https://doi.org/10.1007/978-3-319-46493-0_9

21. Idrees, H., Zamir, A.R., Jiang, Y.G., Gorban, A., Laptev, I., Sukthankar, R., Shah, M.: The thumos challenge on action recognition for videos "in the wild". CVIU **155**, 1–23 (2017)

22. Jain, M., van Gemert, J., Snoek, C.G., et al.: University of Amsterdam at Thumos challenge 2014. In: ECCVW 2014 (2014)

23. Jain, M., van Gemert, J.C., Snoek, C.G.: What do 15,000 object categories tell us about classifying and localizing actions? In: CVPR, pp. 46–55 (2015)

24. Jie, Z., Wei, Y., Jin, X., Feng, J., Liu, W.: Deep self-taught learning for weakly supervised object localization. In: CVPR (2017)

25. Kanazawa, A., Jacobs, D.W., Chandraker, M.: Warpnet: weakly supervised matching for single-view reconstruction. In: CVPR, pp. 3253–3261 (2016)

26. Karaman, S., Seidenari, L., Del Bimbo, A.: Fast saliency based pooling of fisher encoded dense trajectories. In: ECCVW, vol. 1, p. 5 (2014)

27. Kay, W., et al.: The kinetics human action video dataset. arXiv preprint arXiv:1705.06950 (2017)

28. Khoreva, A., Benenson, R., Hosang, J., Hein, M., Schiele, B.: Simple does it: weakly supervised instance and semantic segmentation. In: CVPR (2017)

29. Khoreva, A., Benenson, R., Omran, M., Hein, M., Schiele, B.: Weakly supervised object boundaries. In: CVPR, pp. 183–192 (2016)

30. Kingma, D.P., Ba, J.: Adam: a method for stochastic optimization (2014)

31. Kuehne, H., Richard, A., Gall, J.: Weakly supervised learning of actions from transcripts. CVIU **163**, 78–89 (2017)

32. Laptev, I., Marszalek, M., Schmid, C., Rozenfeld, B.: Learning realistic human actions from movies. In: CVPR, pp. 1–8. IEEE (2008)

33. Li, D., Huang, J.B., Li, Y., Wang, S., Yang, M.H.: Weakly supervised object localization with progressive domain adaptation. In: CVPR, pp. 3512–3520 (2016)

34. Nair, V., Hinton, G.E.: Rectified linear units improve restricted Boltzmann machines. In: ICML, pp. 807–814 (2010)

35. Nguyen, P., Liu, T., Prasad, G., Han, B.: Weakly supervised action localization by sparse temporal pooling network. In: CVPR (2018)

36. Oneata, D., Verbeek, J., Schmid, C.: The LEAR submission at Thumos 2014 (2014)

37. Panda, R., Das, A., Wu, Z., Ernst, J., Roy-Chowdhury, A.K.: Weakly supervised summarization of web videos. In: ICCV, pp. 3657–3666 (2017)

38. Pathak, D., Krahenbuhl, P., Darrell, T.: Constrained convolutional neural networks for weakly supervised segmentation. In: ICCV, pp. 1796–1804 (2015)

39. Richard, A., Gall, J.: Temporal action detection using a statistical language model. In: CVPR, pp. 3131–3140 (2016)

40. Richard, A., Kuehne, H., Gall, J.: Weakly supervised action learning with RNN based fine-to-coarse modeling. In: CVPR (2017)

41. Shen, Z., et al.: Weakly supervised dense video captioning. In: CVPR, vol. 2, p. 10 (2017)

42. Shi, Z., Siva, P., Xiang, T.: Transfer learning by ranking for weakly supervised object annotation. BMVC (2012)

43. Shou, Z., Chan, J., Zareian, A., Miyazawa, K., Chang, S.F.: CDC: convolutional-de-convolutional networks for precise temporal action localization in untrimmed videos. In: CVPR, pp. 1417–1426. IEEE (2017)

44. Shou, Z., Wang, D., Chang, S.F.: Temporal action localization in untrimmed videos via multi-stage CNNs. In: CVPR, pp. 1049–1058 (2016)
45. Simonyan, K., Zisserman, A.: Two-stream convolutional networks for action recognition in videos. In: NIPS, pp. 568–576 (2014)
46. Singh, A., Yang, L., Levine, S.: GPLAC: generalizing vision-based robotic skills using weakly labeled images. In: ICCV (2017)
47. Singh, K.K., Lee, Y.J.: Hide-and-seek: forcing a network to be meticulous for weakly-supervised object and action localization. In: ICCV (2017)
48. Siva, P., Xiang, T.: Weakly supervised action detection. In: BMVC, vol. 2, p. 6 (2011)
49. Srivastava, N., Hinton, G., Krizhevsky, A., Sutskever, I., Salakhutdinov, R.: Dropout: a simple way to prevent neural networks from overfitting. JMLR **15**(1), 1929–1958 (2014)
50. Sultani, W., Shah, M.: What if we do not have multiple videos of the same action?-video action localization using web images. In: CVPR, pp. 1077–1085 (2016)
51. Tran, D., Bourdev, L., Fergus, R., Torresani, L., Paluri, M.: Learning spatiotemporal features with 3D convolutional networks. In: ICCV, pp. 4489–4497 (2015)
52. Tulyakov, S., Ivanov, A., Fleuret, F.: Weakly supervised learning of deep metrics for stereo reconstruction. In: CVPR, pp. 1339–1348 (2017)
53. Varol, G., Salah, A.A.: Efficient large-scale action recognition in videos using extreme learning machines. Expert. Syst. Appl. **42**(21), 8274–8282 (2015)
54. Vezhnevets, A., Buhmann, J.M.: Towards weakly supervised semantic segmentation by means of multiple instance and multitask learning. In: CVPR, pp. 3249–3256. IEEE (2010)
55. Wang, H., Schmid, C.: Action recognition with improved trajectories. In: ICCV, pp. 3551–3558 (2013)
56. Wang, L., Qiao, Y., Tang, X.: Action recognition and detection by combining motion and appearance features. THUMOS14 Action Recognition. Challenge **1**(2), 2 (2014)
57. Wang, L., Xiong, Y., Lin, D., Van Gool, L.: Untrimmednets for weakly supervised action recognition and detection. In: CVPR (2017)
58. Wang, L., et al.: Temporal segment networks: towards good practices for deep action recognition. In: Leibe, B., Matas, J., Sebe, N., Welling, M. (eds.) ECCV 2016. LNCS, vol. 9912, pp. 20–36. Springer, Cham (2016). https://doi.org/10.1007/978-3-319-46484-8_2
59. Wei, Y., Liang, X., Chen, Y., Shen, X., Cheng, M.M., Feng, J., Zhao, Y., Yan, S.: STC: a simple to complex framework for weakly-supervised semantic segmentation. PAMI **39**(11), 2314–2320 (2017)
60. Weinzaepfel, P., Martin, X., Schmid, C.: Human action localization with sparse spatial supervision. arXiv preprint arXiv:1605.05197 (2016)
61. Weinzaepfel, P., Martin, X., Schmid, C.: Towards weaklysupervised action localization. 3(7) arXiv preprint arXiv:1605.05197 (2016)
62. Xu, H., Das, A., Saenko, K.: R-C3D: region convolutional 3D network for temporal activity detection. In: ICCV, vol. 6, p. 8 (2017)
63. Yan, Y., Xu, C., Cai, D., Corso, J.: Weakly supervised actor-action segmentation via robust multi-task ranking. In: CVPR, vol. 48, p. 61 (2017)
64. Yeung, S., Russakovsky, O., Mori, G., Fei-Fei, L.: End-to-end learning of action detection from frame glimpses in videos. In: CVPR, pp. 2678–2687 (2016)
65. Yuan, J., Ni, B., Yang, X., Kassim, A.A.: Temporal action localization with pyramid of score distribution features. In: CVPR, pp. 3093–3102 (2016)

66. Yuan, Z., Stroud, J.C., Lu, T., Deng, J.: Temporal action localization by structured maximal sums. In: CVPR (2017)
67. Zhang, B., Wang, L., Wang, Z., Qiao, Y., Wang, H.: Real-time action recognition with enhanced motion vector CNNs. In: CVPR, pp. 2718–2726 (2016)
68. Zhao, Y., Xiong, Y., Wang, L., Wu, Z., Tang, X., Lin, D.: Temporal action detection with structured segment networks. In: ICCV, vol. 8 (2017)
69. Zhong, B., Yao, H., Chen, S., Ji, R., Chin, T.J., Wang, H.: Visual tracking via weakly supervised learning from multiple imperfect oracles. Pattern Recogn. **47**(3), 1395–1410 (2014)
70. Zhou, Z.H.: Multi-instance learning: A survey. Department of Computer Science & Technology, Nanjing University, Technical Report (2004)
71. Zhu, Y., Zhou, Y., Ye, Q., Qiu, Q., Jiao, J.: Soft proposal networks for weakly supervised object localization. arXiv preprint arXiv:1709.01829 (2017)

Value-Aware Quantization for Training and Inference of Neural Networks

Eunhyeok Park[1]([✉]), Sungjoo Yoo[1], and Peter Vajda[2]

[1] Department of Computer Science and Engineering, Seoul National University,
Seoul, South Korea
eunhyeok.park@gmail.com, sungjoo.yoo@gmail.com
[2] Mobile Vision Team, AI Camera Facebook, Bratislava, Slovakia
vajdap@fb.com

Abstract. We propose a novel value-aware quantization which applies aggressively reduced precision to the majority of data while separately handling a small amount of large values in high precision, which reduces total quantization errors under very low precision. We present new techniques to apply the proposed quantization to training and inference. The experiments show that our method with 3-bit activations (with 2% of large ones) can give the same training accuracy as full-precision one while offering significant (41.6% and 53.7%) reductions in the memory cost of activations in ResNet-152 and Inception-v3 compared with the state-of-the-art method. Our experiments also show that deep networks such as Inception-v3, ResNet-101 and DenseNet-121 can be quantized for inference with 4-bit weights and activations (with 1% 16-bit data) within 1% top-1 accuracy drop.

Keywords: Reduced precision · Quantization · Training Inference · Activation · Weight · Accuracy · Memory cost · Runtime

1 Introduction

As neural networks are being widely applied to the server and edge computing, both training and inference need to become more and more efficient regarding runtime, energy consumption and memory cost. On both servers and edge devices, it is critical to reducing computation cost in order to enable fast training, e.g., on-line training of neural networks for click prediction [6,7], and fast inference, e.g., click prediction at less than 10 ms latency constraints [13] and real-time video processing at 30 frames per second [12]. Reducing computation cost is also beneficial to reducing energy consumption in those systems since the energy consumption of GPU is mostly proportional to runtime [8].

E. Park and S. Yoo—Most of this work was done during the authors' visit to Facebook.

© Springer Nature Switzerland AG 2018
V. Ferrari et al. (Eds.): ECCV 2018, LNCS 11208, pp. 608–624, 2018.
https://doi.org/10.1007/978-3-030-01225-0_36

Especially, training is constrained by the memory capacity of GPU. The large batch of a deep and wide model requires large memory during training. For instance, training of a neural network for vision tasks on high-end smartphones or self-driving cars having 4 K images requires 24 MB only for the input to the first layer of the network. During training, we need to store the activations of all the intermediate layers, and the required memory size (batch size × total activation size of the network) can easily exceed the GPU memory capacity. Likewise, the limited GPU capacity also restricts the large-scale training on GPU clusters [15] and the federated learning on embedded devices.

Reduced precision has potential to resolve the problems of runtime, energy consumption, and memory cost by reducing the data size thereby enabling more parallel and energy-efficient computation, e.g., four int8 operations instead of a single fp32 operation, at a smaller memory footprint. The state-of-the-art techniques of quantization are 16-bit training [4] and 8-bit inference [18]. Considering the trend of ever-increasing demand for training and inference on both servers and edge devices, further optimizations in quantization, e.g., 4 bits, will be more and more required [23].

In this paper, we propose a novel quantization method based on the fact that the distributions of weights and activations have the majority of data concentrated in narrow regions while having a small number of large values scattered in large regions. By exploiting the fact, we apply reduced precision only to the narrow regions thereby reducing quantization errors for the majority of data while separately handling large values in high precision. For very deep networks such as ResNet-152 and DenseNet-201, our proposed quantization method enables training with 3-bit activations (2% large values). Our method also offers low-precision inference with 4 to 5-bit weights and activations (1% large values) even for optimized networks such as SqueezeNet-1.1 and MobileNet-v2 as well as deeper networks.

2 Related Work

Recently, there have been presented several methods of memory-efficient training. In [2], Chen et al. propose a checkpointing method of storing intermediate activations of some layers to reduce memory cost of storing activations and re-calculating the other activations during back-propagation. In [5], Gomez et al. present a reversible network which, during back-propagation, re-computes input activations utilizing output activations thereby minimizing the storage of intermediate activations. The existing methods of checkpointing and reversible network are effective in reducing memory cost. However, they have an common critical limitation, the additional computation to re-compute activations during back-propagation. Considering that computation cost determines runtime and energy consumption of training on GPUs, the additional computation cost needs to be minimized. As will be explained in the experiments, our proposed quantization method gives much smaller cost in both memory and computation than the state-of-the-art ones. More importantly, it has a potential of offering less computation cost than the conventional training method.[1]

The state-of-the-art quantization methods of training and inference for deep networks, e.g., ResNet-152 are 16-bit training [4] and 8-bit inference [18]. In [4], Ginsburg et al. propose 16-bit training based on loss scaling (for small activations or local gradients) and fp32 accumulation. In [18], Migacz proposes utilizing Kullback-Leibler (KL) divergence in determining the linear range to apply 8-bit quantization with clipping. There are studies towards more aggressive quantization for training, e.g., [3,30]. In [3], De Sa et al. propose bit centering to exploit the fact that gradients tend to get smaller as training continues. However, these aggressive methods are limited to small networks and do not preserve full-precision accuracy for very deep models such as ResNet-152.

We classify quantization methods for inference into two types, linear and non-linear ones. The linear methods utilize uniform spacing between quantization levels, thereby being more hardware friendly, while the non-linear ones have non-uniform spacing mostly based on clustering. As the purest form of linear quantization, in [27], Rastegari et al. show that a weight binarization of AlexNet does not lose accuracy. In [9], Hubara et al. propose a multi-bit linear quantization method to offer a trade-off between computation cost and accuracy. In [30], Zhou et al. propose a multi-bit quantization which truncates activations to reduce quantization errors for the majority of data.

In [21], Miyashita et al. propose logarithm-based quantization and show that AlexNet can be quantized with 4-bit weights and 5-bit activations at 1.7% additional loss of top-5 accuracy. In [32], Zhu et al. show that deep models can be quantized with separately scaled ternary weights while utilizing full-precision activations. In [22], Park et al. propose a clustering method based on weighted entropy and show 5-bit weight and 6-bit activation can be applied to deep models such as ResNet-101 at less than 1% additional loss of top-5 accuracy. In [31], Zhou et al. propose a clustering method called balanced quantization which tries to balance the frequency of each cluster thereby improving the utility of quantization levels. Recently, several studies report that increasing the number of channels [20] and adopting teacher-student models [19,25] help to reduce the accuracy loss due to quantization. These methods can be utilized together with our proposed quantization method.

Compared with the existing quantization methods, our proposed method, which is a linear method, enables smaller bitwidth, effectively 4 bits for inference in very deep networks such as ResNet-101 and DenseNet-121 for which there is no report of accurate 4-bit quantization in the existing works.

---

[1] Since the writing of this paper, Jain et al. proposed Gist system aiming to reduce activation memory footprint during training [11]. Compared to their work, we give the detailed explanation about the quantized back-propagation, and our method gives smaller memory footprint due to the benefit of value-aware quantization.

3 Motivation

Figure 1(a) and (b) illustrate the distributions (y-axis in log scale) of activations and weights in the second convolutional layer of GoogLeNet. As the figures show, both distributions are wide due to a small number of large values. Given a bitwidth for low precision, e.g., 3 bits, the wider the distribution is, the larger quantization errors we obtain. Figure 1 (c) exemplifies the conventional 3-bit linear quantization applied to the distribution of activations in Fig. 1 (a). As the figure shows, the spacing between quantization levels (vertical bars) is large due to the wide distribution, which incurs large quantization errors.

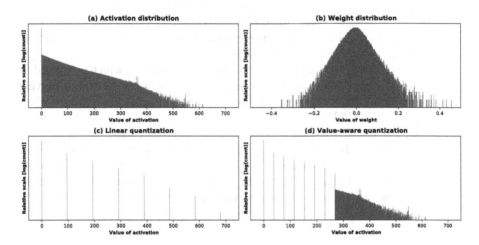

Fig. 1. Activation and weight distributions of second convolutional layer in GoogLeNet.

When comparing Fig. 1 (a) and (c), it is clear that the majority of quantization levels is not fully utilized. Especially, the levels assigned to large values have much fewer data than those assigned to small values, which motivates our idea. Figure 1 (d) illustrates our idea. We propose applying low precision only to small values, i.e., the majority of data, not all. As the figure shows, the spacing between quantization levels gets much smaller than that in the conventional linear quantization in Fig. 1 (c). Such a small spacing can significantly reduce the quantization error for the majority of data. Large values have the more significant impact on the quality of network output. Thus, we propose handling the remaining large values in high precision, e.g., in 32 or 16 bits. The computation and memory overhead of handling high-precision data is small because their frequency, which is called the ratio of large activations, in short, *activation ratio* (AR), is small, e.g., 1–3% of total activation data.[2]

---

[2] We use two ratios of large values, one for large weights and the other for large activations. We use AR to denote the ratio of large activations.

4   Proposed Method

Our basic approach is first to perform value profiling to identify large values during training and inference. Then, we apply reduced precision to the majority of data, i.e., small ones while keeping high precision for the large values. We call this method value-aware quantization (V-Quant).

We apply V-Quant to training to reduce the memory cost of activations. We also apply it to inference to reduce the bitwidth of weights and activations of the trained neural network. To do that, we address new problems as follows.

- (Sects. 4.1 and 4.2) To prevent the quality degradation of training results due to quantization, we propose a novel scheme called *quantized activation back-propagation*, in short, quantized back-propagation. We apply our quantization only to the activations used in the backward pass of training and perform forward pass with full-precision activations.
- (Sects. 4.4 and 4.7) Identifying large values requires sorting which is expensive. To avoid the overhead of global communication between GPUs for sorting during training, we propose performing sorting and identifying large values locally on each GPU.
- (Sects. 4.5 and 4.6) We present new methods for further reduction in memory cost of training. To reduce the overhead of mask information required for ReLU function during back-propagation, we propose ReLU and value-aware quantization. For further reduction in memory cost, we also propose exploiting the fact that, as training continues, the less amount of large activations is required.

4.1   Quantized Back-Propagation

Figure 2 shows how to integrate the proposed method with the existing training pipeline. As the figure shows, we add a new component of value-aware quantization to the existing training flow. In the figure, thick arrows represent the flow of full-precision activations (in black) and gradients (in red).

First, we perform the forward pass with full-precision activations and weights, which gives the same loss as that of the existing full-precision forward pass (step 1 in the figure). During the forward pass, after obtaining the output activations of each layer, e.g., layer l, the next layer (layer $l+1$) of network takes as input the full-precision activations. Then, we apply our quantization method, RV-Quant to them (those of layer l) in order to reduce their size (step 2). As the result of the forward pass, we obtain the loss and the quantized activations.

During the backward pass, when the activations of a layer are required for weight update, we convert the quantized, mostly low-precision, activations, which are stored in the forward pass, into full-precision ones (step 3). Note that this step only converts the data type from low to high precision, e.g., from 3 to 32 bits. Then, we perform the weight update with back-propagated error (thick red arrow) and the activations (step 4).

Note that there is no modification in the computation of the existing forward and backward passes. Especially, as will be explained in the next subsection, when ReLU is used as activation function, the backward error propagation (step 5 in the figure) keeps full-precision accuracy. The added component of value-aware quantization performs conversions between full-precision and reduced-precision activations and compresses a small number of remaining large high-precision activations, which are sparse, utilizing a conventional sparse data representation, e.g., compressed sparse row (CSR).

The conversion from full to reduced precision (step 2) reduces memory cost while that from reduced to full precision (step 3) changes data type back to full precision one thereby increasing memory cost back to that of full precision. Note that the full-precision activations, obtained from the quantized ones, are discarded after weight update for their associated layer. Thus, we need memory resource for the stored quantized activations of the entire network and the full-precision input/output activations of only one layer, which we call working activations, for the forward/backward computation.

As will be explained later in this section, for further reduction in memory cost, the ReLU function consults the value-aware quantization component for the mask information which is required to determine to which neuron to back-propagate the error (step 6).

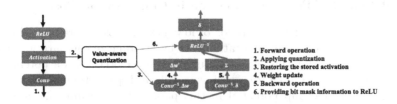

Fig. 2. Value-aware quantization in training pipeline.

4.2   Back-Propagation of Full-Precision Loss

Our proposed method can suffer from quantization error in weight update since we utilize quantized activations. We try to reduce the quantization error by applying reduced precision only to narrow regions, determined by AR, having the majority of data while separately handling the large values in high precision.

Moreover, in state-of-the-art networks where ReLU is utilized as activation function, the back-propagated error is not affected by our quantization of activations as is explained below. Equation (1) shows how we calculate weight update during back-propagation for a multilayer perceptron (MLP).

$$\Delta w_{ji} = \eta \delta_j y_i \tag{1}$$

where Δw_{ji} represents the update of weight from neuron i (of layer l) to neuron j (of layer $l+1$), η learning rate, δ_j the local gradient of neuron j (back-propagated error to this neuron), and y_i the activation of neuron i. Equation (1) shows that the quantization error of activation y_i can affect the weight update. In order to reduce the quantization error in Eq. (1), we apply V-Quant to activations y_i.

The local gradient δ_j is calculated as follows.

$$\delta_j = \varphi'(v_j) \cdot (\Sigma_k \delta_k w_{kj}) \tag{2}$$

where $\varphi'()$ represents the derivative of activation function, v_j the input to neuron j and w_{kj} the weight between neuron j (of layer $l+1$) to neuron k (of layer $l+2$). Eq. (2) shows that the local gradient is a function of the input to neuron, v_j which is the weighted sum of activations. However, if ReLU is used as the activation function, then $\varphi'()$ becomes 1 yielding $\delta_j = \varphi'(v_j) \cdot (\Sigma_k \delta_k w_{kj}) = \Sigma_k \delta_k w_{kj}$, which means *the local gradient becomes independent of activations*. Thus, aggressive quantizations of intermediate activations, e.g., 3-bit activations can hurt only the weight update in Eq. (1), not the local gradient in Eq. (2). This is the main reason why our proposed method can offer full-precision training accuracy even under aggressive quantization of intermediate activations as will be shown in the experiments.

4.3   Potential of Further Reduction in Computation Cost

Compared with the existing methods of low memory cost in training [2,5], our proposed method reduces computation cost by avoiding re-computation during back-propagation. More importantly, our proposed method has a potential for further reduction in computation cost especially in Eq. (1), though we have not yet realized the speedup potential in this paper. It is because the activation y_i is mostly in low precision in our method. Thus, utilizing the capability of 8-bit multiplication on GPUs, our method can transform a single 16-bit x 16-bit multiplication in Eq. (1) into an 8-bit x 16-bit multiplication. In state-of-the-art GPUs, we can perform two 8-bit x 16-bit multiplications at the same computation cost, i.e., execution cycle, of one 16-bit x 16-bit multiplication, which means our proposed method can double the performance of Eq. (1) on the existing GPUs.

Assuming that the forward pass takes M multiplications, the backward pass takes $2M$ multiplications while each of Eqs. (1) and (2) taking M multiplications, respectively. Thus, the 2x improvement in computation cost of Eq. (1) can reduce by up to 1/6 total computation cost of training. In order to realize the potential, further study is needed to prove that our proposed method enables 8-bit low-precision activations (with a small number of 16-bit high-precision activations) without losing the accuracy of 16-bit training [4].

Although our method can currently reduce computation cost utilizing only 8-bit multiplications on GPUs, its reduced-precision computation, e.g., 3-bit multiplications, offers opportunities of further reduction in computation cost for training in future hardware platforms supporting aggressively low precision, e.g., [28].

4.4   Local Sorting in Data Parallel Training

V-Quant requires sorting activations. Assuming that we adopt data parallelism in multi-GPU training, the sorting can incur significant overhead in training runtime since it requires exchanging the activations of each layer between GPUs. What is worse, in reality, such a communication is not easily supported in some training environments, e.g., PyTorch, and it restrict the scalability in any training environments including TensorFlow, Caffe2 and others as well as PyTorch. In order to address the problem of activation exchange, we propose performing sorting locally on each GPU, which eliminates inter-GPU communication for activation exchange. Then, each GPU performs V-Quant locally by applying the same AR, i.e., the same ratio of large activations. Compared with the global solution that collects all the activations and applies the AR to the global distribution of activations, the proposed local solution can lose accuracy in selecting large values. However, our experiments show that the proposed method of local sorting works well, which means that the selection of large values does not need to be accurate.

4.5   ReLU and Value-Aware Quantization (RV-Quant)

The error is back-propagated through the neurons the output activations of which are non-zero. The zero activations result from quantization (called *quantization-induced zero*) as well as ReLU activation function. In order to realize the same back-propagation as the full-precision training, it is required to back-propagate errors in the case of quantization-induced zero. To identify the neurons having quantization-induced zero, we would need a bit mask, i.e., 1-bit memory cost for a neuron. In case that the activations are quantized at a minimal number of bits, e.g., 3 bits, the overhead of the mask bit is significant, e.g., one additional bit for 3-bit activation on each neuron. To reduce the overhead of the mask bit, we exploit the fact that the mask bit is needed only for the case of zero activation. We allocate two states to represent two different types of zero values, i.e., original zero and quantization-induced zero. Thus, given K bits for low precision, we allocate two of 2^K quantization levels to the zero values while representing the positive activation values with $2^K - 2$ levels. We call this quantization ReLU and value-aware quantization (RV-Quant). As will be shown in the experiments, RV-Quant removes the overhead of mask bit while keeping training accuracy.

4.6   Activation Annealing

According to our investigation, the required amount of large activations varies across training phases. To be specific, the early stage of training tends to require more large activations while the later stage tends to need less large activations. We propose exploiting the fact and adjusting AR in a gradual manner from large to small AR across training phases, which we call *activation annealing*. As will be shown in the experiments, activation annealing can maintain training quality while reducing the average memory cost across the entire training phases.

4.7 Quantized Inference

In order to obtain quantized neural networks for inference, we perform V-Quant as a post-processing of training, i.e., we apply V-Quant to the weights and activations of trained networks. To recover from the accuracy loss due to quantization, we perform fine-tuning as follows. We perform forward pass while utilizing the quantized network, i.e., applying V-Quant to weights and activations. During back-propagation, we update full-precision weights. As will be shown in the experiments, the fine-tuning incurs a minimal overhead in training time, i.e., only a few additional epochs of training. Note that we apply local sorting in Sect. 4.4 to avoid communication overhead when multiple GPUs are utilized in fine-tuning.

During fine-tuning, we evaluate candidate ratios for large weights and activations and, among those candidates, select the best configuration which minimizes the bitwidth while meeting accuracy requirements. Note that, as will be explained in the experiments, the total number of candidate combinations is small.

In order to identify large activations meeting the AR, we need to sort activations, which can be expensive in inference. In order to avoid the sorting overhead, we need low-cost sorting solutions, e.g., sampling activations to obtain an approximate distribution of activations. Detailed implementations of quantized models including the low-cost sorting are beyond the scope of this paper and left for further study.

5 Experiments

We evaluate our proposed method on ImageNet classification networks, AlexNet, VGG-16, SqueezeNet-1.1, MobileNet-v2, Inception-v3, ResNet-18/50/101/152 and DenseNet-121/201. We test the trained/quantized networks with ILSVRC2012 validation set (50k images) utilizing a single center crop of 256×256 resized image. We also use an LSTM for word-level language modeling [10, 26, 29]. We implemented our method on PyTorch framework [24] and use the training data at Torchvision [16].

The initial learning rate is set to 0.1 (ResNet-18/50/152 and DenseNet-201), or 0.01 (AlexNet and VGG-16). The learning rate is decreased by 10x at every multiple of 30 epochs and the training stops at 90 epochs. In SqueezeNet-1.1, MobileNet-v2, and Inception-v3, we use the same parameters in the papers except that we use a mini-batch of 256 and SGD instead of RMSprop. In addition, we replace ReLU6 in MobileNet-v2 with ReLU to apply V-Quant.

We apply V-Quant and RV-Quant to training to minimize memory cost. During training, in order to compress the sparse large activations on GPU, we use the existing work in [1]. To obtain quantized networks for inference, we perform fine-tuning with V-Quant for a small number of additional epochs, e.g., 1–3 epochs after total 90 epochs of original training. All networks are initialized in the same condition.

We compare classification accuracy between full-precision models and those under RV-Quant (training) and V-Quant (training/inference). For each network, we use the same randomly initialized condition and perform training for different RV-Quant and V-Quant configurations.

5.1   Training Results

Table 1 shows top-1/top-5 accuracy of ResNet-50 obtained, under V-Quant, varying the bitwidth of low-precision activation and the ratio of large activation, AR. The table shows that the configuration of 3-bit activations with the AR of 2% (in bold) gives training results equivalent to the full-precision (32-bit) training in terms of top-1 accuracy, which corresponds to 6.1X ($=1/((3+1)/32 + 0.04)$) reduction in the memory cost of stored activation at the same quality of training.[3] The table also shows that a very aggressive quantization of 2-bit activation and 1% AR loses only 0.27%/0.24% in top-1/top-5 accuracy, which is comparable to the case of 5-bit quantization without large values (5-bit with AR 0% in the table).

Note that the total memory cost of activations includes that of stored activations of the entire network and that of full-precision working activations (input to the associated layer) required for weight update. Thus, the above-mentioned reduction of 6.1X is only for the memory cost of stored activations. We will give the comparison of the total memory cost of activations later in this section. In addition, we do not compare the accuracy of the state-of-the-art method [2] since it provides the same accuracy as full-precision training. However, we provide the memory consumption of this method later in this section, including that of the conventional linear quantization method (8-bit with AR 0%).

Table 1. Top-1/top-5 accuracy [%] of ResNet-50 with various bitwidth & AR configurations. The full-precision network gives the accuracy of 75.92/92.90%.

AR [%]	0	1	2	3	4	5
1-bit	5.30 / 15.23	74.51 / 92.05	75.17 / 92.50	75.21 / 92.48	75.70 / 92.66	75.57 / 92.66
2-bit	65.75 / 86.72	75.65 / 92.66	75.64 / 92.70	75.66 / 92.51	75.34 / 92.66	75.58 / 92.62
3-bit	75.49 / 92.61	75.71 / 92.59	**75.92 / 92.86**	75.93 / 92.96	75.89 / 92.94	75.73 / 92.63
4-bit	75.70 / 92.75	75.78 / 92.67	75.88 / 92.93	75.79 / 92.71	75.85 / 92.69	75.92 / 92.86

5-bit with AR 0 %	75.60 / 92.61	6-bit with AR 0 %	75.92 / 92.83
7-bit with AR 0 %	75.89 / 92.79	8-bit with AR 0 %	75.67 / 92.85

Table 2 shows top-1/top-5 accuracy of ResNet-50 under RV-Quant. As the table shows, RV-Quant gives similar results to V-Quant, e.g., top-1 accuracy of 3-bit 2% RV-Quant gives an equivalent result to full precision. Compared with V-Quant, RV-Quant reduces the memory cost by 1 bit per neuron. Thus, the

---

[3] Note that V-Quant still requires 1-bit mask information for each neuron. In addition, the sparse data representation of large values, e.g., CSR doubles the size of the original sparse data yielding the memory cost of 4% with the AR of 2%.

Table 2. Top-1/top-5 accuracy [%] of ResNet-50 under RV-Quant. The full-precision network gives the accuracy of 75.92/92.90%.

AR [%]	0	1	2	3	4	5
2-bit	35.52 / 60.86	75.34 / 92.56	75.41 / 92.49	75.67 / 92.59	75.50 / 92.46	75.27 / 92.65
3-bit	75.16 / 92.55	75.88 / 92.80	75.93 / 92.70	75.66 / 92.74	75.91 / 92.75	75.49 / 92.58

configuration of 3-bit 2% RV-Quant gives 7.5X (=1/(3/32 + 0.04)) reduction in the memory cost of stored activations. In addition, we can further reduce the memory cost of stored activations by applying traditional compression techniques to the reduced-precision activations. In the case of 3-bit 2% RV-Quant for ResNet-50, by applying Lempel-Ziv compression, we can further reduce the memory cost of the 3-bit data by 24.4%, which corresponds to 9.0x reduction in the memory cost of the whole stored activations.

Table 3 compares the accuracy of neural networks under full-precision training and two RV-Quant configurations. As the table shows, 3-bit 2% RV-Quant gives almost the same training accuracy as full-precision training for all the networks.

Table 3. Training results. Full means the results of conventional full-precision training, while 3-bit 2% and 8-bit 0% correspond to RV-Quant. The full-precision network gives the accuracy of 75.92/92.90%.

	AlexNet	ResNet-18	SqueezeNet-1.1	MobileNet-v2	VGG-16	Inception-v3	ResNet-152	DenseNet-201
Full	56.35 / 79.02	69.91 / 89.38	58.67 / 81.05	70.10 / 89.74	71.86 / 90.48	74.19 / 91.92	77.95 / 94.02	77.42 / 93.59
3-bit 2%	56.14 / 78.99	69.92 / 89.23	58.53 / 80.94	70.12 / 89.76	71.74 / 90.46	74.14 / 91.92	77.76 / 93.89	77.28 / 93.44
8-bit 0%	56.24 / 78.95	70.01 / 89.28	58.75 / 81.29	70.29 / 89.64	71.77 / 90.66	74.22 / 92.08	78.35 / 93.95	77.32 / 93.51

Table 4 compares the total memory cost of activations (both stored quantized and full-precision working activations) in training with 256 mini-batch sizes. We compare two existing methods and three RV-Quant configurations. 'Full' represents the memory cost of conventional training with full-precision activation. As a baseline, we use the checkpointing method of Chen et al. [2] since it is superior to others including [5], especially for deep neural networks. We calculate the memory cost of the checkpointing method to account for the minimum amount of intermediate activations to re-compute correct activations while having the memory cost of $O(\sqrt{N})$ where N is the number of layers [2].

The table shows that, compared with the checkpointing method, RV-Quant gives significant reductions in the total memory cost of activations. For instance, in the case of ResNet-152 which is favorable to the checkpointing method due to the simple structure as well as a large number of layers, ours reduces the memory cost by 41.6% (from 5.29 GB to 3.09 GB). In networks having more complex sub-networks, e.g., Inception modules, ours gives more reductions. In the case of Inception-v3, ours gives a reduction of 53.7% (3.87 GB to 1.79 GB).

Note that in the case of AlexNet, the reduction is not significant. It is because the input data occupy the majority of stored activations and we store them in full precision. However, the impact of input data storage diminishes in deep networks.

We also measured the training runtime of ResNet-50 with mini-batch of 64 on NVIDIA Tesla M40 GPU. Compared to the runtime of existing full-precision training, our method requires a small additional runtime, 8.8% while the checkpointing method has much larger runtime overhead, 32.4%. Note that as mentioned in Sect. 4.3, our method has a potential for further reduction in training time on hardware platforms supporting reduced-precision computation.

Table 4. Comparison of memory cost (in GB).

	AlexNet	ResNet-18	SqueezeNet-1.1	MobileNet-v2	ResNet-50	VGG-16	Inception-v3	ResNet-152	DenseNet-201
Full	0.35	1.86	1.58	7.34	9.27	9.30	9.75	20.99	24.53
Chen et al. [2]	x	0.98 (52.1 %)	1.05 (66.9 %)	4.21 (52.1 %)	3.70 (39.9 %)	x	3.87 (39.8 %)	5.29 (25.2 %)	6.62 (27.0 %)
(2,0)	0.23 (66.4 %)	0.42 (22.6 %)	0.59 (37.5 %)	0.74 (10.0 %)	1.22 (13.2 %)	3.65 (39.2 %)	1.16 (11.9 %)	1.64 (7.78 %)	2.09 (8.51 %)
(3,0)	0.23 (67.8 %)	0.46 (24.3 %)	0.61 (38.8 %)	0.84 (11.4 %)	1.34 (14.5 %)	3.75 (40.3 %)	1.43 (14.8 %)	2.27 (10.8 %)	2.85 (11.6 %)
(3,2)	0.24 (69.5 %)	0.50 (26.5 %)	0.64 (40.4 %)	1.13 (15.4 %)	1.52 (16.4 %)	3.88 (41.7 %)	1.79 (18.4 %)	3.09 (14.7 %)	3.83 (15.6 %)

Table 5 shows the impact of RV-Quant configurations on training accuracy of ResNet-50. We change the configurations when the learning rate changes (with the initial value of 0.1) at 0.01 and 0.001. For instance, (F)-(3,2)-(2,0) represents the case that, as the initial configuration, we use full-precision activation (F) during back-propagation. After 30 epochs, the configuration is changed to 3-bit 2% RV-Quant. Then, after 60 epochs, it is changed to 2-bit 0% RV-Quant.

Table 5. Sensitivity analysis of RV-Quant configurations (bitwidth and AR [%]) across training phases. The full-precision network gives the accuracy of 75.92/92.90%.

Configuration	Accuracy	Configuration	Accuracy	Configuration	Accuracy	Configuration	Accuracy
(3,2)-(2,1)-(2,0)	75.01 / 92.42	(2,0)-(2,1)-(3,2)	47.35 / 72.31	(3,2)-(3,1)-(3,0)	75.72 / 92.69	(3,0)-(3,1)-(3,2)	75.60 / 92.77
(F)-(3,2)-(2,0)	75.45 / 92.63	(2,0)-(3,2)-(F)	50.36 / 75.02	(3,2)-(3,1)-(2,0)	75.34 / 92.55	(2,0)-(3,1)-(3,2)	48.67 / 73.54
(F)-(2,1)-(2,0)	75.38 / 92.44	(2,0)-(2,1)-(F)	52.72 / 76.76				

In Table 5, the key observation is that it is important to have high precision at the beginning of training. Compared with the case that training starts with full-precision activations and ends with aggressively reduced precision, (F)-(3,2)-(2,0), the opposite case, (2,0)-(3,2)-(F) gives significantly lower accuracy, 75.45% vs. 50.36%. Another important observation is that activation annealing works.

For instance, (3,2)-(3,1)-(3,0) gives almost the same result to (3,2)-(3,2)-(3,2) in Table 2 and, a more aggressive case, (3,2)-(3,1)-(2,0) gives only by 0.58% smaller top-1 accuracy. Thus, as training advances, we need the smaller amount of large values, which means we can have smaller memory cost of activations. This can be exploited for memory management in servers. We expect it can also be utilized in memory-efficient server-mobile co-training in federated learning [14] where the later stage of training requiring smaller memory cost can be performed on memory-limited mobile devices while meeting the requirements of user-specific adaptation using private data.

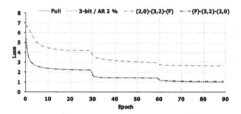

Fig. 3. Training loss of ResNet-50 with various RV-Quant configurations.

Figure 3 shows the training loss of different RV-Quant configurations during training. First, the figure shows that too aggressive quantization at the beginning of training, i.e., (2,0)-(3,2)-(F), does not catch up with the loss of full-precision training (Full in the figure). The figure also shows that the configuration of 3-bit 2% RV-Quant gives almost the same loss as the full-precision training.

5.2   Inference Results

Figure 4 shows the accuracy of quantized models across different configurations of bitwidth and AR. We apply the same bitwidth of low precision to both weights and activations and 16 bits to large values of weights and activations. In addition, we quantize all the layers including the first (quantized weights) and last convolutional layers. As the figure shows, V-Quant with fine-tuning, at 4 bits and an AR of 1%, gives accuracy comparable to full precision in all the networks within 1% of top-1 accuracy. If V-Quant is applied without fine-tuning, the larger AR needs to be used to compensate for accuracy drop due to quantization. However, the figure shows that fine-tuning successfully closes the accuracy gap between V-Quant and full-precision networks.

Figure 5 illustrates the effect of large values on the classification ability. The figure shows the principal component analysis (PCA) results of the last convolutional layer of AlexNet for four classes. Figure 5 (a) shows the PCA result of full-precision network. As Fig. 5 (b) shows, when the conventional 4-bit linear quantization, or 4-bit 0% V-Quant is applied to weights/activations, it is difficult to classify four groups of data successfully. This is because the quantization errors are accumulated across layers thereby deteriorating the quality

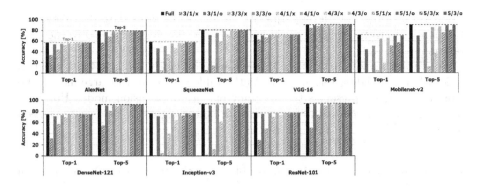

Fig. 4. V-Quant results. The dashed lines and black solid bar represent full-precision accuracy. Legend: bitwidth/AR [%]/fine-tuning or not.

of activations. However, as Fig. 5 (c) shows, only a very small amount (0.1%) of large values can improve the situation. As more large values are utilized, the classification ability continues to improve (3% in Fig. 5 (d)). The figure demonstrates that our idea of reducing quantization errors for the majority of data by separately handling large values is effective in keeping good representations.

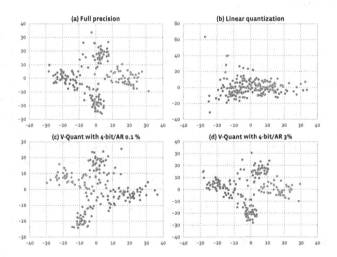

Fig. 5. PCA analysis of the input activations on the last fully-connected layer of AlexNet.

5.3 LSTM Language Model

We apply V-Quant to an LSTM for word-level language modeling [10,26,29]. Table 6 shows the results of the models. Each of the large and small models has two layers. The large model has 1,500 hidden units and the small one 200 units. We measure word-level perplexity on Penn Tree Bank data [17]. We apply V-Quant only to the weights of the models since clipping is applied to the activation.[4]

As Table 6 shows, we evaluate three cases of bitwidth, 2, 3 and 4 bits and two ratios of large weights, 1%, and 3%. As the table shows, for the large model, the 4-bit 1% V-Quant preserves the accuracy of the full-precision model. However, the small model requires the larger ratio of large weights (3%) in order to keep the accuracy.

Table 6. Impact of quantization on word-level perplexity of an LSTM for language modeling.

	Large-1%		Large-3%		Small-1%		Small-3%	
	Valid	Test	Valid	Test	Valid	Test	Valid	Test
float	75.34	72.31	75.34	72.31	103.64	99.24	103.64	99.24
2-bit	79.92	77.31	77.87	74.99	140.70	135.11	122.25	117.76
3-bit	76.19	73.22	75.79	72.72	107.60	102.82	105.99	101.44
4-bit	75.46	72.48	75.44	72.44	104.22	99.83	103.95	99.57

6 Conclusions

We presented a novel value-aware quantization to reduce memory cost in training and computation/memory cost in inference. To realize aggressively low precision, we proposed separately handling a small number of large values and applying reduced precision to the majority of small values, which contributes to reducing quantization errors. In order to apply our idea to training, we proposed quantized back-propagation which utilizes quantized activations only during back-propagation. For inference, we proposed applying fine-tuning to quantized networks to recover from accuracy loss due to quantization. Our experiments show that our proposed method outperforms the state-of-the-art method of low-cost memory in training in deep networks, e.g., 41.6% and 53.7% smaller memory cost in ResNet-152 and Inception-v3, respectively. It also enables 4-bit inference (with 1% large values) for deep networks such as ResNet-101 and DenseNet-121, and 5-bit inference for efficient networks such as SqueezeNet-1.1 and MobileNet-v2 within 1% of additional top-1 accuracy loss.

Acknowledgment. This work was supported in part by National Research Foundation of Korea (NRF-2016M3A7B4909604).

---

[4] The distribution of activations obtained by clipping tends to have the large population near the maximum/minimum values. Considering that clipped activation functions like ReLU6 are useful, it will be interesting to further investigate clipping-aware quantization.

References

1. Bakunas-Milanowski, D.: Efficient algorithms for stream compaction on GPUs. Int. J. Netw. Comput. (IJNC) **7**, 208–226 (2017)
2. Chen, T., et al.: Training deep nets with sublinear memory cost. arXiv:1604.06174 (2016)
3. De Sa, C., et al.: High-accuracy low-precision training. arXiv:1803.03383 (2018)
4. Ginsburg, B., et al.: NVIDIA mixed precision training on volta GPUs. In: GPU Technology Conference (2017)
5. Gomez, A.N., et al.: The reversible residual network: backpropagation without storing activations. In: Advances in Neural Information Processing Systems (NIPS) (2017)
6. Hazelwood, K., et al.: Applied machine learning at facebook: a datacenter infrastructure perspective. In: International Symposium on High-Performance Computer Architecture (HPCA) (2018)
7. He, X., et al.: Practical lessons from predicting clicks on ads at facebook. In: International Workshop on Data Mining for Online Advertising (ADKDD) (2014)
8. Hong, S., Kim, H.: An integrated GPU power and performance model. In: International Symposium on Computer Architecture (ISCA) (2010)
9. Hubara, I., et al.: Quantized neural networks: training neural networks with low precision weights and activations. arXiv:1609.07061 (2016)
10. Inan, H., Khosravi, K., Socher, R.: Tying word vectors and word classifiers: a loss framework for language modeling. arXiv:1611.01462 (2016)
11. Jain, A., et al.: Gist: efficient data encoding for deep neural network training. In: International Symposium on Computer Architecture (ISCA) (2018)
12. Jia, Y., Peter, V.: Delivering real-time AI in the palm of your hand. https://code.facebook.com/posts/196146247499076/delivering-real-time-ai-in-the-palm-of-your-hand/. Accessed 25 July 2018
13. Jouppi, N.P., et al.: In-datacenter performance analysis of a tensor processing unit. In: International Symposium on Computer Architecture (ISCA) (2017)
14. Konečný, J., et al.: Federated learning: Strategies for improving communication efficiency. arXiv:1610.05492 (2016)
15. Mahajan, D., et al.: Exploring the limits of weakly supervised pretraining. arXiv:1805.00932 (2018)
16. Marcel, S., Rodriguez, Y.: Torchvision the machine-vision package of torch. In: ACM Multimedia (2010)
17. Marcus, M.P., Marcinkiewicz, M.A., Santorini, B.: Building a large annotated corpus of English: the Penn Treebank. Comput. Linguist. **19**(2), 313–330 (1993)
18. Migacz, S.: NVIDIA 8-bit inference width TensorRT. In: GPU Technology Conference (2017)
19. Mishra, A., Marr, D.: Apprentice: using knowledge distillation techniques to improve low-precision network accuracy. arXiv:1711.05852 (2017)
20. Mishra, A., et al.: WRPN: Wide reduced-precision networks. arXiv:1709.01134 (2017)
21. Miyashita, D., Lee, E.H., Murmann, B.: Convolutional neural networks using logarithmic data representation. arXiv:1603.01025 (2016)
22. Park, E., Ahn, J., Yoo, S.: Weighted-entropy-based quantization for deep neural networks. In: Computer Vision and Pattern Recognition (CVPR) (2017)
23. Park, E., Kim, D., Yoo, S.: Energy-efficient neural network accelerator based on outlier-aware low-precision computation. In: International Symposium on Computer Architecture (ISCA) (2018)

24. Paszke, A., et al.: Pytorch (2017)
25. Polino, A., Pascanu, R., Alistarh, D.: Model compression via distillation and quantization. In: International Conference on Learning Representation (ICLR) (2018)
26. Press, O., Wolf, L.: Using the output embedding to improve language models. In: European Chapter of the Association for Computational Linguistics (EACL) (2017)
27. Rastegari, M., Ordonez, V., Redmon, J., Farhadi, A.: XNOR-Net: ImageNet classification using binary convolutional neural networks. In: Leibe, B., Matas, J., Sebe, N., Welling, M. (eds.) ECCV 2016. LNCS, vol. 9908, pp. 525–542. Springer, Cham (2016). https://doi.org/10.1007/978-3-319-46493-0_32
28. Umuroglu, Y., et al.: Finn: A framework for fast, scalable binarized neural network inference. Architecture of Field-Programmable Gate Arrays (FPGA) (2017)
29. Zaremba, W., Sutskever, I., Vinyals, O.: Recurrent neural network regularization. arXiv:1409.2329 (2014)
30. Zhou, S., et al.: Dorefa-net: Training low bitwidth convolutional neural networks with low bitwidth gradients. arXiv:1606.06160 (2016)
31. Zhou, S.: Balanced quantization: an effective and efficient approach to quantized neural networks. J. Comput. Sci. Technol. **32**(4), 667–682 (2017)
32. Zhu, C., et al.: Trained ternary quantization. arXiv:1612.01064 (2016)

Fully-Convolutional Point Networks for Large-Scale Point Clouds

Dario Rethage[1][✉], Johanna Wald[1][✉], Jürgen Sturm[2][✉], Nassir Navab[1][✉], and Federico Tombari[1][✉]

[1] Technical University of Munich, Munich, Germany
{dario.rethage,johanna.wald}@tum.de, navab@cs.tum.de, tombari@in.tum.de
[2] Google, Munich, Germany
jsturm@google.com

Abstract. This work proposes a general-purpose, fully-convolutional network architecture for efficiently processing large-scale 3D data. One striking characteristic of our approach is its ability to process unorganized 3D representations such as point clouds as input, then transforming them internally to ordered structures to be processed via 3D convolutions. In contrast to conventional approaches that maintain either unorganized or organized representations, from input to output, our approach has the advantage of operating on memory efficient input data representations while at the same time exploiting the natural structure of convolutional operations to avoid the redundant computing and storing of spatial information in the network. The network eliminates the need to pre- or post process the raw sensor data. This, together with the fully-convolutional nature of the network, makes it an end-to-end method able to process point clouds of huge spaces or even entire rooms with up to $200k$ points at once. Another advantage is that our network can produce either an ordered output or map predictions directly onto the input cloud, thus making it suitable as a general-purpose point cloud descriptor applicable to many 3D tasks. We demonstrate our network's ability to effectively learn both low-level features as well as complex compositional relationships by evaluating it on benchmark datasets for semantic voxel segmentation, semantic part segmentation and 3D scene captioning.

Keywords: Point clouds · 3D deep learning · Scene understanding Fully-convolutional · Semantic segmentation · 3D captioning

1 Introduction

Processing 3D data as obtained from 3D scanners or depth cameras is fundamental to a wealth of applications in the field of 3D computer vision, scene understanding, augmented/mixed reality, robotics and autonomous driving.

Electronic supplementary material The online version of this chapter (https://doi.org/10.1007/978-3-030-01225-0_37) contains supplementary material, which is available to authorized users.

© Springer Nature Switzerland AG 2018
V. Ferrari et al. (Eds.): ECCV 2018, LNCS 11208, pp. 625–640, 2018.
https://doi.org/10.1007/978-3-030-01225-0_37

The extraction of reliable semantic information from a 3D scene is useful, for example, to appropriately add virtual content to the 3D space around us or describe it to a visually-impaired person. Analogously, in robotics, processing of 3D data acquired from a depth camera allows the robot to perform sophisticated tasks, beyond path-planning and collision avoidance, that require intelligent interaction in real world environments (Fig. 1).

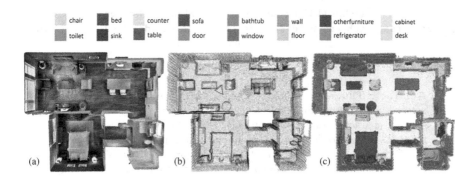

Fig. 1. Example result of our FCPN on semantic voxel labeling and captioning on an Tango 3D reconstruction/point cloud: (a) 3D reconstruction (not used), (b) Input point cloud (c) Output semantic voxel prediction. A possible caption for the camera pose in (b) is *"There is a place to sit in front of you"*

A recent research trend has focused on designing effective learning architectures for processing common 3D data representations such as point clouds, meshes and voxel maps, to be employed in tasks such as voxel-based semantic scene segmentation [1], part-based segmentation of 3D objects [2] and 3D correspondence matching [3]. A primary objective of these models is robustness against typical issues present when working with real world data such as, noise, holes, occlusion and partial scans, as well as viewpoint changes and 3D transformations (rotation and translation). Another challenge more related to semantic inference relates to dealing with the large number of classes that characterize real world scenarios and their typically large intra-class variance.

In pursuit of a versatile 3D architecture, applicable in small- and large-scale tasks, it is not only necessary to extract meaningful features from 3D data at several scales, but also desirable to operate on a large spatial region at once. For this, fully-convolutional networks (FCN) [4] have recently grown to prominence due to their drastic reduction in parameters and flexibility to variable input sizes. However, learning these hierarchical statistical distributions starting at the lowest level requires a huge amount of data. To achieve this, some methods train on synthetic data, but suffer from the domain gap when applied to the real-world [5]. A big step toward closing this gap is ScanNet, a large-scale dataset of indoor scans [1]. Methods that achieve state-of-the-art performance on these challenging tasks quickly reach the memory limits of current GPUs due to the additional dimension present in 3D data [6,7]. While the aforementioned FCN architecture reduces the number of parameters, it requires the input to be in an ordered (dense) form. To bypass the need to convert the raw, unordered data into an ordered representation, PointNet [2] proposes an architecture that directly operates on sets of unordered points. Since PointNet only learns a global descriptor of the point cloud, Qi et. al later introduced a hierarchical point-based network with PointNet++ [8]. While achieving impressive results in several tasks, PointNet++ cannot take advantage of the memory and performance benefits that 3D convolutions offer due to its fully point-based nature. This requires PointNet++ to redundantly compute and store the context of every point even when they spatially overlap.

We present a general-purpose, fully-convolutional network architecture for processing 3D data: Fully-Convolutional Point Network (FCPN). Our network is hybrid, i.e. designed to take as input unorganized 3D representations such as point clouds while processing them internally in an organized fashion through 3D convolutions. This is different from other approaches, which require both input and internal data representation to be either unorganized point sets [2,8,9] or organized data [1,5]. The advantage of our hybrid approach is to take the benefits of both representations. Unlike [1,5], our network operates on memory efficient input representations that scale well with the scene/object size and transforms it to organized internal representations that can be processed via convolutions. A benefit of our method is that it can scale to large volumes while processing point clouds in a single pass. It can also be trained on small regions, e.g. 2.4×2.4×2.4 m and later applied to larger point clouds during inference. A visualization of the output at three different scales of our network trained on semantic voxel labeling is given in Fig. 2. While the proposed method is primarily intended for large-scale, real-world scene understanding applications, demonstrated by the semantic voxel labeling and 3D scene captioning tasks, the method is also evaluated on semantic part segmentation to demonstrate its versatility as a generic feature descriptor capable of operating on a range of spatial scales.

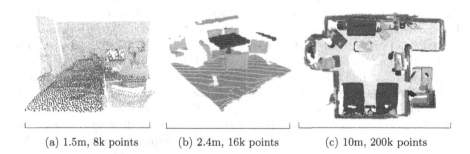

(a) 1.5m, 8k points   (b) 2.4m, 16k points   (c) 10m, 200k points

Fig. 2. Visualization of the semantic segmentation on (a) a depth image, (b) a 2.4 m × 2.4 m × 2.4 m partial reconstruction (c) an entire reconstruction of a hotel suite. Please note that each of these outputs are predicted in a single shot from the same network trained with 2.4 m × 2.4 m × 2.4 m volumes

Our main contributions are (1) a network based on a hybrid unorganized input/organized internal representation; and, (2) the first fully-convolutional network operating on raw point sets. We demonstrate its scalability by running it on full ScanNet scenes regions of up to $80 \, m^2$ in a single pass. In addition, we show the versatility of our learned feature descriptor by evaluating it on both large-scale semantic voxel labeling as well as on 3D part segmentation. In addition, as a third contribution, we explore the suitability of our approach to a novel task which we dub *3D captioning*, that addresses the extraction of meaningful text descriptions out of partial 3D reconstructions of indoor spaces. We demonstrate how our approach is well suited to deal with this task leveraging its ability to embed contextual information, producing a spatially ordered output descriptor from the unordered input, necessary for captioning. For this task, we also publish a novel dataset with human-annotated captions.

2   Related Work

Deep learning has already had a substantial impact on 3D computer vision. Those 3D deep learning approaches can be categorized as either (a) volumetric or voxel-based models that operate on an ordered input (see Sect. 2.1) or (b) point-based models that work entirely with unordered data (see Sect. 2.2). Some approaches do not deal directly with 3D data, but instead operate in 2D or 2.5D (RGB-D), for example, multi-view CNNs [10–12]. Typically, RGB(-D) based methods put more emphasis on color information and less on geometry. This makes it less robust under varying lighting conditions. Instead, our proposed approach is fully geometric and we therefore do not further review RGB-D based methods here.

2.1   Voxel-Based Networks

Most volumetric or voxel-based 3D deep learning methods have proven their value by achieving state of the art accuracy [1,5,13–15] on a variety of tasks. These methods employ convolutional architectures to efficiently process data. This however requires the input data to be organized – stored in a dense grid of predefined order. Each uniformly-sized voxel in this grid is then labeled with a semantic class. Ordered representations of 3D data have the advantage of featuring constant time ($O(1)$) lookup of neighbors. Such a representation usually explicitly models empty space making it memory-intensive. This is particularly inefficient since 3D data is often very sparse. Further, voxelization imposes an explicit resolution on the data. To transform sparse 3D data to a dense representation requires preprocessing: either using a simple occupancy grid or by encoding it, for example, in a truncated signed-distance field (TSDF) as done in KinectFusion [5,16]. This means the model does not see the data itself, but a down-sampled encoding of it.

VoxNet was a pioneering effort using 3D convolutional networks for object recognition [13]. Similarly, Wu et. al learn deep volumetric representations of shapes for shape recognition and completion [17]. Another popular example that applied to medical imaging is 3D U-Net [14]. It processes at a relatively high input resolution of $132 \times 132 \times 116$, but only outputs the center of the volume. With current memory availability, voxelization of larger spaces generally requires labeling at a lower sampling density implying a loss of resolution. Alternatively, a higher density can be achieved if a smaller context is used to inform the prediction of each voxel. For example, ScanNet [1] performs semantic voxel labeling of each approximately 5 cm voxel column in a scene using the occupancy characteristics of the voxel's neighborhood. SSCNet achieves a larger spatial extent of $2.26\,m^3$ for jointly semantically labeling and completing depth images by use of dilated convolutions. However, also in this scenario, the size as well as resolution of the output is reduced [5].

To address this limitation, OctNet propose to use OctTrees, known to efficiently partition 3D space in octants, in a deep learning context by introducing convolutions directly on the OctTree data structure [7]. Klokov and Lempitsky demonstrate another solution using kd-trees [6]. However, these methods still impose a minimum spatial discretization. Our network is flexible and efficient enough to mitigate this memory limitation without discretizing the input in any way.

2.2 Point-Based Networks

A pioneering work that operates on unordered points directly is PointNet [2]. Qi et al. showed the advantages of working with point sets directly, learning more accurate distributions in continuous space, thereby bypassing the need to impose a sampling resolution on the input. PointNet achieves state-of-the-art performance on classification, part segmentation and scene segmentation tasks while operating at a single-scale. They further claim robustness to variable point density and outliers. However, since PointNet does not capture local features the authors later introduced PointNet++ [8] a multi-scale point-based network that uses PointNet as a local feature learner for semantic segmentation, among other tasks. In the semantic segmentation task, point contexts are first abstracted and later propagated through 3NN interpolation in the latent space. For the larger-scale scene segmentation task, it is relevant that PointNet++ redundantly processes and stores the context of points throughout the network. This prevents PointNet++ from being able to process a large space in a single pass. Instead in the semantic scene segmentation task, it processes a sliding region of $1.5 \times 1.5 \times 3\,m$ represented by 8192 points.

Our work is – as the first of its kind – hybrid and therefore positioned between these volumetric and point-based methods. As such, allowing powerful multi-scale feature encoding by using 3D convolutions while still processing point sets directly.

3   Fully-Convolutional Point Network

Our network operates on unorganized input and employs PointNet [2] as a low-level feature descriptor. Contrary to PointNet++ [8], a uniform sampling strategy is applied. This step captures the precise local geometry in each local region and transforms the unordered input internally to an ordered representation for further processing. This transformation is followed by 3D convolutions to then learn compositional relationships at multiple scales. Our network abstracts the space at three scales S_1, S_2 and S_3. Skip connections with $1 \times 1 \times 1$ and $3 \times 3 \times 3$ convolutions at each scale inexpensively double the total number of feature scales the network captures. At the highest abstraction scale, the features are additionally average pooled together weighted by their distance to each voxel. Once features are produced at each scale of abstraction, feature volumes of the same size are concatenated and progressively upsampled by 3D deconvolutions to achieve the desired output sampling density. Figure 3 gives an overview of the proposed architecture. Depending on the scenario, additional convolutions, latent nearest-neighbor interpolation or fully-connected layers can be applied to produce an ordered, end-to-end point mapping or single-value output, respectively. In the following sections, the different components of our network are described in more detail.

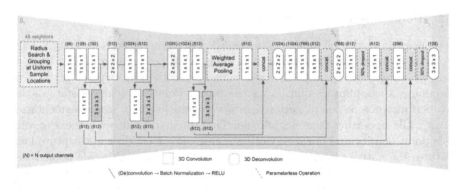

Fig. 3. Fully-convolutional point network architecture

3.1   Architecture

The Fully-Convolutional Point Network consists of four main modules: a series of abstraction layers, feature learners at different scales, a weighted-average pooling layer, and a merging stage where responses are hierarchically merged back together.

Abstraction Layers. Three abstraction layers are used to achieve a hierarchical partitioning, both spatially and conceptually. The first level captures basic geometric features like edges and corners, the second level responds to complex structure and the highest level to structure in context of other structures.

The first level employs a simplified PointNet [8], proven to efficiently capture the geometry in a local region. It consists of a radius search & grouping, $1 \times 1 \times 1$ convolutions followed by a max-pooling layer. Applying PointNet in a uniformly spaced 3D grid produces a 3D feature volume representing the lowest level physical features. This feature volume feeds into the next abstraction layer. Higher level abstraction layers are implemented as 3D convolutions with a kernel size and stride of 2. They are designed to abstract the space in a non-overlapping fashion with 8 features (octants) of the preceding abstraction layer being represented by a single cell in the subsequent layer, just like an OctTree. This non-overlapping spatial-partitioning significantly reduces the memory required to store the space at each abstraction level.

Feature Learners. With three levels of abstraction, we now employ $1 \times 1 \times 1$ and $3 \times 3 \times 3$ convolutions to extract meaningful features at more scales (see Fig. 4). For each abstraction level, skip connections propagate features at the level's inherent spatial scale as well as $3\times$ it to be merged later in the network. This allows the network to better recognize structures at a wider range of scales and to overcome the strictly non-overlapping partitioning of the abstraction layers.

Fig. 4. Visualization of the different spatial scales used to encode indoor spaces within our model on an example apartment scan. For simplification we only show their 2D top-down view. Further, please note that 15 cm features (green) are spherical while the others are cubic (Color figure online)

Weighted Average Pooling. The weighted average pooling layer cost-effectively incorporates long-range contextual information. For every cell in the highest abstraction level, the responses of all other cells in the space are averaged together weighted by their euclidean distance to a 1 m sphere around the cell. Thus, cells positioned closest to the surface of this sphere are weighted most heavily. This puts emphasis on long-range contextual information, instead of information about directly adjacent cells which is already captured by the respective $3 \times 3 \times 3$ skip connection. This improves the discriminative capability of the network by allowing neighboring semantics to influence predictions. For example, distinguishing chairs and toilets by considering the presence of a desk or rather a sink nearby. The parameterless nature of this layer is not only extremely cost-effective, but provides a more informative signal. The average spatial pooling effectively removes the exact configuration of the structures in the vicinity, while retaining their semantic identities. This is a desirable characteristic because the identity of nearby objects or structures help discriminate boundary cases more so than the configuration they are in. In the example of the chair/toilet, it is informative to know the presence of a sink nearby much more than the fact that the sink is to the right of the toilet. We also avoid an inherent challenge: larger-scale spatial contexts ($>1\,\mathrm{m}$) encourage a model to learn entire configurations of spaces, which does not lead to strong generalizability. Finally, the average weighted pooling layer exhibits the flexibility required to scale the network up to larger spaces during inference.

Merging. In the merging stage, skip connections corresponding to each abstraction level are first concatenated and then upsampled to $2\times$ their spatial resolution by 3D deconvolutions. This allows the features at each abstraction level to be progressively merged into each other. $1 \times 1 \times 1$ convolutions add expressive power to the model between deconvolutions.

3.2   Output Representations

Several variants of the network are suitable for different scenarios: For producing organized output, the network is fitted with an additional deconvolution layer to produce the desired output point density. Latent nearest-neighbor interpolation is used in applications where semantics are mapped, for end-to-end processing, to each point in the input cloud. Fully-connected layers are appropriate when summarizing the entire input such as in the case of scene captioning.

3.3   Uniform vs. Furthest Point Sampling

Furthest point sampling is very effective for describing the characteristics of structure (occupied space) because it makes no prior assumptions as to the spatial distribution of the data. However, for describing entire spaces (occupied + unoccupied), a uniform sampling is the only way to ensure we consider every part of it.

3.4   Full-Volume Prediction

Fully-Convolutional Point Network labels the full spatial volume it is given as input. It achieves this by upsampling feature maps to the original sampling density as well as symmetrically padding feature volumes before performing

$3 \times 3 \times 3$ convolutions. This is validated by the fact that regions directly outside of the input volume are most likely to exhibit the same occupancy characteristics as the closest cell within it, since occupancy characteristics present at the edges of the volume are likely to extend beyond it.

3.5 Scalability

The network is flexible in that it can be trained on smaller training samples, then be scaled up during inference to process spaces multiple times larger than it was trained on in a single shot. The network successfully predicts a $80 \, \text{m}^2$ space consisting of $200 \, \text{k}$ points at once. An even larger spatial extent can be processed at sparser point density. This further extends the versatility of the network for other use cases such as autonomous driving.

4   3D Captioning

We introduce a new scene understanding task we call 3D Captioning: generating meaningful textual descriptions of spaces. We envision this as being useful for assistive technology, in particular for the visually impaired when navigating and interacting in unfamiliar environments. To test the model's proficiency on this task, we create a dataset of human-annotated captions based on ScanNet [1], we select the top 25 sentences best describing the diversity of spaces found in ScanNet. They are designed to answer 3 types of questions: *"What is the functional value of the space I'm in?"*, *"How can I move?"*, and *"How can I interact with the space?"*. Every 100th frame of a scene is annotated with 0 or more applicable captions. The dataset was then validated to remove outliers. To accomplish this, a Scene Caption Annotation Tool was built and used to annotate roughly half of ScanNet. We release this dataset together with the source code. The statistics of the captioning dataset are given in the supplementary material.

5   Evaluation

We evaluate our method on (a) small-scale 3D part segmentation as well as (b) large-scale semantic segmentation tasks (see Sect. 5.1). We evaluate semantic segmentation on ScanNet, a 3D dataset containing 1513 RGB-D scans of indoor environments with corresponding surface reconstructions and semantic segmentations [1]. This allows us to compare our results against ScanNet's voxel-based prediction [1] and PointNet++'s point cloud-based semantic segmentation [8]. We achieve comparable performance, while – due to our fully-convolutional architecture – being able to process considerably larger spaces at once. Our second evaluation (b) in Sect. 5.2 on a benchmark dataset for model-based part segmentation shows our networks capability to generalize to other tasks and smaller scales. To further show the usefulness of a spatially ordered descriptor in higher-level scene understanding tasks, we train our network to predict captions for unseen scenes (see Sect. 4) – results for the 3D captioning task are presented here 5.3.

5.1 Semantic Voxel Labeling

In the semantic voxel labeling task, the network is trained to predict the semantics of the occupied space in the input from a set of 20 semantic classes. We present a variant of the network for Semantic Voxel Labeling along with the experimental setup.

Data Preparation. Training samples are generated following the same procedure in ScanNet. We extract volumes exhibiting at least 2% occupancy and 70% valid annotations from 1201 scenes according to the published ScanNet train/set split. Training samples are $2.4\,m^3$ and feature a uniform point spacing of $5\,cm^3$. This produces a training set of $75\,k$ volumes. During training, samples are resampled to a fixed cardinality of $16\,k$ points. Augmentation is performed on the fly: random rotation augmentation along the up-down axis, jitter augmentation in the range $\pm 2\,cm$ and point dropout between 0–80%. Only X, Y, Z coordinates of points are present in the inputs. Ground-truths consist of 20 object classes and 1 class to represent unoccupied space. Each scene in the 312 scene test set is processed by predicting $2.4\,m^3$ cutouts of the scene. Each semantic class is weighted by the inverse log of its per-point frequency in the dataset.

Network. The three spatial scales S1, S2, S3 of the Semantic Voxel Labeling network are 15 cm, 30 cm, 60 cm, respectively. As a result, the network extracts features at 15 cm, 30 cm, 45 cm, 60 cm, 90 cm and 180 cm scales and pools features together at the 60 cm spatial scale. Three $1 \times 1 \times 1$ layers follow each abstraction, feature learning and upsampling layer. An additional deconvolution layer achieves a final output density of $5\,cm^3$. Dropout (50%) is applied before this layer. We also employ a final $3 \times 3 \times 3$ convolution in the last layer to enforce spatial continuity in adjacent predictions, avoiding single point misclassification. The network is trained with an ADAM optimizer starting at a learning rate of 0.01, decaying by half every epoch, for 5 epochs.

Results. Table 1 gives quantitative results of our semantic segmentation on a voxel-basis for 20 classes. Our method achieves a weighted accuracy of 82.6% and an unweighted accuracy of 54.2%; in comparison ScanNet only labels 73% (weighted) or 50.8% (unweighted) of the voxels correctly. The best performing of three PointNet++ variants (MSG+DP) reports 84.5% (weighted) or 60.2% (unweighted). Our method outperforms ScanNet by a large margin particularly in the classes: desk, toilets, chairs and bookshelves. Please note, that our method has the advantage of being able to process all scenes, from small bathrooms up to whole apartments, in a single shot in comparison to PointNet++ who combine the predictions of a sliding volume with a majority voting. Some qualitative results with corresponding ground truth annotations are shown in Fig. 5.

(a)   (b)   (c)

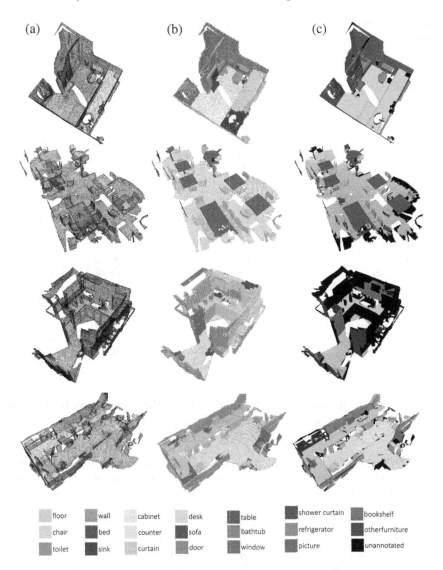

floor	wall	cabinet	desk	table	shower curtain	bookshelf
chair	bed	counter	sofa	bathtub	refrigerator	otherfurniture
toilet	sink	curtain	door	window	picture	unannotated

Fig. 5. Qualitative results of the semantic voxel labeling on an example scene of Scan-Nets test sequences. (a) Input Point Cloud, (b) Semantic Voxel Prediction by our FCPN and (c) Ground Truth Semantic Annotation

5.2 Part Segmentation

We also evaluate our method on a smaller-scale point cloud processing task, model-based semantic part segmentation. To evaluate this, Yi et al. [19] provide a benchmark part segmentation dataset based on ShapeNet. It consists of 50 part

Table 1. Semantic voxel label prediction accuracy on ScanNet test scenes. Please note, ScanComplete only trains on 6 of the 20 classes present in the ScanNet test set

Class	% of Test Scenes	ScanNet[1]	ScanComplete[18]	PointNet++[8]	FCPN (Ours)
Floor	35.7%	90.3%	90.2%	**97.8%**	96.3%
Wall	38.8%	70.1%	88.8%	**89.5%**	87.7%
Chair	3.8%	69.3%	60.3%	**86.0%**	81.6%
Sofa	2.5%	75.7%	72.5%	68.3%	**76.0%**
Table	3.3%	**68.4%**	n/a	59.6%	67.6%
Door	2.2%	**48.9%**	n/a	27.5%	16.6%
Cabinet	2.4%	49.8%	n/a	39.8%	**52.1%**
Bed	2.0%	62.4%	52.8%	**80.7%**	65.9%
Desk	1.7%	36.8%	n/a	**66.7%**	58.5%
Toilet	0.2%	69.9%	n/a	84.8%	**86.7%**
Sink	0.2%	39.4%	n/a	**62.8%**	53.5%
Window	0.4%	20.1%	**36.1%**	23.7%	12.5%
Picture	0.2%	**3.4%**	n/a	0.0%	1.8%
Bookshelf	1.6%	64.6%	n/a	**84.3%**	81.0%
Curtain	0.7%	7.0%	n/a	**48.7%**	6.1%
Shower Curtain	0.04%	46.8%	n/a	**85.0%**	48.0%
Counter	0.6%	32.1%	n/a	**37.6%**	31.6%
Refrigerator	0.3%	**66.4%**	n/a	54.7%	50.5%
Bathtub	0.2%	74.3%	n/a	**86.1%**	79.1%
Other Furniture	2.9%	19.5%	n/a	**30.7%**	30.2%
Weighted Average		73.0%	n/a	**84.5%**	82.6%
Unweighted Average		50.8%	n/a	**60.2%**	54.2%

categories across 16 types of objects. For example, the car category features part classes: hood, roof, wheel and body. (see Table 2).

Table 2. Results of our FCPN on ShapeNet's part segmentation dataset compared to other state-of-the-art methods. Please note, that we outperform all other methods in 12 out of 16 classes

	mean	aero	bag	cap	car	chair	ear phone	guitar	knife	lamp	lap- top	motor	mug	pistol	rocket	skate board	table
Yi [20]	81.4	81.0	78.4	77.7	75.7	87.6	61.9	92.0	85.4	82.5	95.7	70.6	91.9	85.9	53.1	69.8	75.3
SSCNN [21]	84.7	81.6	81.7	81.9	75.2	90.2	**74.9**	93.0	86.1	**84.7**	95.6	66.7	92.7	81.6	60.6	82.9	82.1
PN [2]	83.7	83.4	78.7	82.5	74.9	89.6	73.0	91.5	85.9	80.8	95.3	65.2	93.0	81.2	57.9	72.8	80.6
PN++ [8]	**85.1**	82.4	79.0	**87.7**	77.3	**90.8**	71.8	91.0	85.9	83.7	95.3	71.6	94.1	81.3	58.7	76.4	**82.6**
Ours	84.0	**84.0**	**82.8**	86.4	**88.3**	83.3	73.6	**93.4**	**87.4**	77.4	**97.7**	81.4	95.8	87.7	68.4	83.6	73.4

Data Preparation. For this task, we train directly on the provided data without any preprocessing. During training, the input cloud is first rescaled to maximally fit in the unit sphere (2 m diameter), then augmented with point dropout and jitter as in the previous task as well as randomly shifted (±5 cm) and scaled (±10%) on the fly.

Network. The input spatial extent of the network is 2.8 m to give every point in the cloud full valid context. The three spatial scales S1, S2, S3 are 10 cm, 20 cm, 40 cm, respectively. Three $1 \times 1 \times 1$ layers also follow each abstraction, feature learning and upsampling layer. After upsampling features back to the original sampling resolution, three-nearest-neighbor interpolation is performed in the latent space. Then, like the methods we compare against, the one-hot encoded object class is concatenated to each point's feature vector and followed by three final $1 \times 1 \times 1$ layers with 50% dropout between them.

Results. The method outperforms the state-of-the-art on this benchmark dataset in 12 out of 16 object categories. Visual examples are given in Fig. 6.

Fig. 6. Qualitative results of the part segmentation test set

5.3 Captioning

To demonstrate the usefulness of a spatially ordered output, we evaluate a baseline method for the *3D captioning* task based on the FCPN network. To train the captioning model, we take the semantic voxel labeling network and replace the final upsampling layer and subsequent convolutional layers with three fully-connected layers. We freeze the weights of the semantic voxel labeling network and train only the fully-connected layers on this task. Once again, captions are weighted by the inverse log of their frequency in the training set. We consider the top-3 most confident captions produced by the network. Examples are shown in Fig. 7. Differently from standard image-based captioning, the provided results hint at how the 3D captioning output together with the proposed network can usefully summarize the relevant scene geometry with respect to a specific viewpoint to aid navigation and interaction tasks. Additional results are provided in the supplementary material.

5.4 Memory and Runtime

To complement our evaluation, we estimate the memory footprint and inference speed of our method as a function of the input cloud size (both spatially and in terms of point count), by processing clouds of increasing point counts and surface area on a Titan Xp GPU. The results in Table 3 validate our claim that the proposed method can efficiently process large-scale point clouds, with clouds 5× as large with 10× the amount of points requiring only 40% more memory.

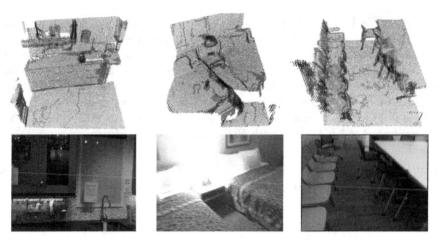

1. You're in a food preparation area.   1. You're in a sleeping area.   1. The space directly ahead of you is clear.
2. You're facing a wall.   2. The space directly ahead of you is clear.   2. You're in a seating area.
3. The space directly ahead of you is clear.   3. You're facing a lounging area.   3. You're in a reading space.

Fig. 7. Example top-3 sentences on 3 frames of the captioning test set. The point cloud in the first row is the input of our captioning model. The RGB image is just illustrated for visualization purposes and not used within our method

Table 3. Memory consumption evaluation

Point count	Surface area	Forward pass	Memory
150 k	80 m^2	9.1 s	9033 MB
36 k	36 m^2	2.9 s	8515 MB
15 k	16 m^2	0.57 s	6481 MB

6   Conclusions

In this paper we presented the first fully-convolutional neural network that operates on unordered point sets. We showed that, being fully convolutional, we are able to process by far larger spaces than the current state of the art in a single shot. We further show that it can be used as a general-purpose feature descriptor by evaluating it on challenging benchmarks at different scales, namely semantic scene and part-based object segmentation. This shows its proficiency in different tasks and application areas. Further, since it learns a spatially ordered descriptor, it opens the door to higher level scene understanding tasks such as captioning. As for future work, we are interested in exploring a wider range of semantic classes and using our network to train a more expressive language model.

References

1. Dai, A., Chang, A.X., Savva, M., Halber, M., Funkhouser, T., Nießner, M.: Scan-Net: richly-annotated 3d reconstructions of indoor scenes (2017)
2. Qi, C.R., Su, H., Mo, K., Guibas, L.J.: PointNet: deep learning on point sets for 3d classification and segmentation. In: Proceedings of the Computer Vision and Pattern Recognition (CVPR). IEEE (2017)
3. Zeng, A., Song, S., Nießner, M., Fisher, M., Xiao, J., Funkhouser, T.: 3DMatch: learning local geometric descriptors from RGB-D reconstructions. In: CVPR (2017)
4. Shelhamer, E., Long, J., Darrell, T.: Fully convolutional networks for semantic segmentation. In: PAMI (2016)
5. Song, S., Yu, F., Zeng, A., Chang, A.X., Savva, M., Funkhouser, T.: Semantic scene completion from a single depth image. In: Proceedings of 30th IEEE Conference on Computer Vision and Pattern Recognition (2017)
6. Klokov, R., Lempitsky, V.: Escape from cells: deep kd-networks for the recognition of 3d point cloud models. In: 2017 IEEE International Conference on Computer Vision (ICCV) (2017)
7. Riegler, G., Ulusoy, O., Geiger, A.: OctNet: learning deep 3d representations at high resolutions. In: IEEE Conference on Computer Vision and Pattern Recognition (CVPR) (2017)
8. Qi, C.R., Yi, L., Su, H., Guibas, L.J.: Pointnet++: deep hierarchical feature learning on point sets in a metric space. arXiv preprint arXiv:1706.02413 (2017)
9. Manessi, F., Rozza, A., Manzo, M.: Dynamic graph convolutional networks (2018). https://arxiv.org/abs/1704.06199
10. Su, H., Maji, S., Kalogerakis, E., Learned-Miller, E.G.: Multi-view convolutional neural networks for 3d shape recognition. In: Proceedings of the ICCV (2015)
11. Qi, C.R., Su, H., Nießner, M., Dai, A., Yan, M., Guibas, L.: Volumetric and multi-view CNNs for object classification on 3d data. In: Proceedings of the Computer Vision and Pattern Recognition (CVPR). IEEE (2016)
12. He, K., Gkioxari, G., Dollár, P., Girshick, R.B.: Mask R-CNN. In: ICCV. IEEE Computer Society (2017)
13. Maturana, D., Scherer, S.: VoxNet: a 3d convolutional neural network for real-time object recognition. In: IEEE/RSJ International Conference on Intelligent Robots and Systems (2015)
14. Çiçek, Ö., Abdulkadir, A., Lienkamp, S.S., Brox, T., Ronneberger, O.: 3D U-Net: learning dense volumetric segmentation from sparse annotation. In: Ourselin, S., Joskowicz, L., Sabuncu, M.R., Unal, G., Wells, W. (eds.) MICCAI 2016. LNCS, vol. 9901, pp. 424–432. Springer, Cham (2016). https://doi.org/10.1007/978-3-319-46723-8_49
15. Milletari, F., Navab, N., Ahmadi, S.: V-Net: fully convolutional neural networks for volumetric medical image segmentation. CoRR (2016)
16. Izadi, S., et al.: KinectFusion: real-time 3d reconstruction and interaction using a moving depth camera. In: Proceedings of the 24th Annual ACM Symposium on User Interface Software and Technology (2011)
17. Wu, Z., et al.: 3d ShapeNets: a deep representation for volumetric shapes. In: CVPR. IEEE Computer Society (2015)
18. Dai, A., Ritchie, D., Bokeloh, M., Reed, S., Sturm, J., Nießner, M.: ScanComplete: large-scale scene completion and semantic segmentation for 3d scans. In: Proceedings of the Computer Vision and Pattern Recognition (CVPR). IEEE (2018)

19. Yi, L., et al.: A scalable active framework for region annotation in 3d shape collections. In: SIGGRAPH Asia (2016)
20. Li, Y., Pirk, S., Su, H., Qi, C.R., Guibas, L.J.: FPNN: field probing neural networks for 3d data. In: NIPS (2016)
21. Yi, L., Su, H., Guo, X., Guibas, L.: SyncSpecCNN: synchronized spectral CNN for 3d shape segmentation. In: CVPR (2016)

Multiple-Gaze Geometry: Inferring Novel 3D Locations from Gazes Observed in Monocular Video

Ernesto Brau[1]($^{(\boxtimes)}$)(iD), Jinyan Guan[1](iD), Tanya Jeffries[2], and Kobus Barnard[2](iD)

[1] CiBO Technologies, Cambridge, MA 02141, USA
{ebrau,jguan}@cibotechnologies.com
[2] University of Arizona, Tucson, AZ 85711, USA
tanyasjeffries@email.arizona.edu,kobus@cs.arizona.edu

Abstract. We develop using person gaze direction for scene understanding. In particular, we use intersecting gazes to learn 3D locations that people tend to look at, which is analogous to having multiple camera views. The 3D locations that we discover need not be visible to the camera. Conversely, knowing 3D locations of scene elements that draw visual attention, such as other people in the scene, can help infer gaze direction. We provide a Bayesian generative model for the temporal scene that captures the joint probability of camera parameters, locations of people, their gaze, what they are looking at, and locations of visual attention. Both the number of people in the scene and the number of extra objects that draw attention are unknown and need to be inferred. To execute this joint inference we use a probabilistic data association approach that enables principled comparison of model hypotheses. We use MCMC for inference over the discrete correspondence variables, and approximate the marginalization over continuous parameters using the Metropolis-Laplace approximation, using Hamiltonian (Hybrid) Monte Carlo for maximization. As existing data sets do not provide the 3D locations of what people are looking at, we contribute a small data set that does. On this data set, we infer what people are looking at with 59% precision compared with 13% for a baseline approach, and where those objects are within about 0.58 m.

Keywords: 3D temporal scene understanding · 3D gaze estimation
Monocular video · Discovering objects · MCMC · Model selection

1 Introduction

Observing people interacting with their environment can provide clues about its 3D structure. Facets of this that have been studied within computer vision include inferring functional objects as "dark matter" [64], ground plane paths [30], and modeling human-object interactions for understanding events and participants from RGB-D video [61]. 3D representations enable answering questions that are awkward or not accessible with 2D representations. For example,

© Springer Nature Switzerland AG 2018
V. Ferrari et al. (Eds.): ECCV 2018, LNCS 11208, pp. 641–659, 2018.
https://doi.org/10.1007/978-3-030-01225-0_38

one might want to ask if there are paths that can be taken that are not visible to security cameras. In this paper, we present a system that infers 3D locations that people look at, including ones not visible to the camera, from monocular, uncalibrated video. For example, we can infer the 3D location of an interesting poster that draws people's gazes by observing the people passing by (Fig. 1).

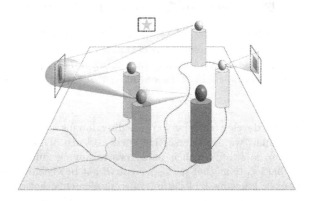

Fig. 1. Temporal 3D scene understanding through joint inference of people's locations, their head posse, and locations of what they're looking at. The gaze cones of the red person for the current (red) and previous times (faded red) intersect to help localize a target in 3D on the left wall. The hypothesis that they are looking at the same object from two different views makes this analogous to stereo vision. The blue person adds a third view. Furthermore, the hypothesis that the green person is looking at the red person enriches our understanding of the scene, and can help improve both the estimate of the green person's head pose as well as the location of the red person. (Color figure online)

To this end, we develop a fully 3D Bayesian modeling approach that represents where people are, their head poses (thus approximate gaze directions), and what 3D location they are looking at, which might be one of the other persons that we are tracking, or an interesting location that attract people's visual attentions in a scene. Our model further embodies the camera parameters of an assumed stationary monocular video camera, so that we can infer it rather than rely on having calibrated cameras.

Our joint inference approach is motivated by the following observations: **(1)** the 3D locations of what people might be looking at can help estimate gaze direction and therefore head pose; **(2)** other people in the scene are possible targets of visual attention, and if we are tracking them in 3D, joint inference of their location and gazes from others should be beneficial; and **(3)** scenes often contain likely locations of visual attention (e.g., a visually interesting poster), and multiple spatio-temporal gaze cones can help pinpoint them in 3D analogously with multiple views (Fig. 1). We also make use of the following observations from Brau et al. [13] regarding tracking of people walking on a ground plane: **(1)** 3D representation simplifies handling occlusions (which become evidence instead of confounds); **(2)** 3D representation allows for a meaningful prior on velocity (and here, head turning angular velocity); and **(3)** one can infer camera parameters jointly with the scene, as people walking tend to maintain fixed height, and thus are like calibration probes that transport themselves to different depths.

We specify the joint probability of the latent model and the association of person detections across frames (Sect. 3). The data association implies a hypothesis for the number of people in the scene at each point in time. To compare models of differing dimensions in a principled way, we approximately marginalize out all the continuous model parameters. These include the locations of each person, their gaze angles, and the locations of the static points drawing visual attention that we are trying to discover from gazing behavior. We compute these approximate marginals using MCMC sampling to maximize the distribution, and then apply the Laplace approximation. We combine this with multiple MCMC sampling strategies to explore the space of models (Sect. 4).

Because our goals are new, we contribute a modest data set with the 3D locations of what participants are looking at, which is not available in other data sets with people walking about (see Sect. 5 for further discussion). In the contributed data set, participants recorded what they were looking at while they were walking around, and we established the ground truth 3D locations for all targets (people and other objects) using ground truth 2D detections (Sect. 6).

Our Contributions include: **(1)** operationalizing the observation that multiple gaze angles estimated from head pose can be used to learn 3D locations that people look at; **(2)** extending the approach proposed by Brau et al. [13] to include head pose, a walking direction prior, and a more efficient sampling approach; **(3)** joint inference of head pose and 3D location of what people are looking at while walking; **(4)** inferring who is looking at whom or what (both anonymously defined); and **(5)** a new data set for what people are looking at while they walk around, and where those objects or people are in 3D.

2   Related Work

Multiple Target Tracking (MOT). Despite significant progress, multiple-target tracking remains a challenge due to issues such as noisy and complex evidence, occlusion, abrupt motion, and an unknown number of targets. This work is in the tracking-by-detection paradigm [3,4,9,13,17,31,37,44,46,54,66,69]. Typically, these approaches first acquire the image locations of people a video sequence, and then find the tracks of each underlying target by solving the data association problem and inferring the target locations. Both 2D and 3D models have been used to represent the underlying targets. Effectively working in 2D requires explicit modeling of occluded targets (e.g., [37,69]). Conversely, 3D models can treat occlusions and smooth motion naturally [13,28].

Head Pose Estimation. There is a rich history in methods to estimate head pose from single images (e.g., [11,12,21,22,25,26,33,34,38,39]). In video, information flow between frames has been exploited by a number of researchers (e.g.,

[6,57,65,70]). More similar to us is model-based tracking methods that fit a 3D model to the tracked features across a video (e.g., [32,45,56,62,63]). Head and body pose have also been estimated jointly via correlations between outputs of body pose and head pose classifiers [14,15]. In contrast, we model this coupling through a joint distribution on 3D body and head poses.

Head pose is a strong cue for visual focus of attention (VFoA) recognition which has potential applications such as measuring the attractiveness of advertisements or shop displays in public spaces as well as analyzing the social dynamics of meetings. Much research in VFoA focuses on dynamic meeting scenarios, where people usually sit around meeting tables while being video recorded by multiple cameras [5,7,8,19,42,43,51–53,58,59]. Most of these methods exploit context-related information from speech and motion activity and the potential VFoA is a predefined discrete set with known locations. In addition, the number of people in the scene is fixed and they are considered to be seated in typically known locations, which makes sense given the application.

VFoA estimation has also been considered in surveillance settings in the context of understanding behavior [10,27,48,49], where, so far, visual attention has been limited to image coordinates, and one person at a time. However, Benfold and Reid [10] use a camera calibrated to the ground plane to estimate a visual attention map representing the amount of attention received by each square meter of the ground in a town center scene. Similar to us, they identify interesting regions in the scene based on the inferred visual attention map. However, while the map can be projected into the video to visualize it, 3D location is not inferred.

Another application of estimating VFoA is human-robot interaction scenarios, which involves both person-to-person and robot-to-person interactions [36, 47,67]. Approaches in this domain often assume known head poses (orientations and locations) of the targets (persons, robots, and objects). For example, Massé et al. proposed a switching Kalman filter formulation to jointly estimate the gaze and the VFoA of several persons from observed head poses and object locations [36]. In addition, they also assume the number of persons and objects are known and remain constant over time. In contrast, we propose simultaneously inferring the number of the targets and their locations in the scene while estimating their VFoAs using image evidence.

3   Statistical Model

Figure 2 shows our generative statistical model for temporal scene understanding using probabilistic graphical modeling notation. The scene consists of **multiple people** moving on the ground plane throughout the video. At each frame, each person may have their visual attention on another person or on one of several static objects that are located in 3D space. We model the **visual focus of attention** and the **static objects** explicitly. At each frame, each person may also generate a detection box, and the **data association** groups these detection boxes by person (or noise). Finally, we model the **camera**, which projects the scene onto the image plane, generating the observed data.

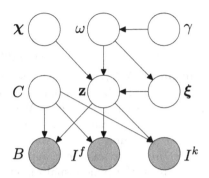

Fig. 2. Generative graphical model for temporal scene understanding. We use bold font for aggregate variables (e.g., **z** represents state vectors for each person for each frame). The data association, ω, specifies the number of people and which detections (body, face) are associated with them. ω depends on hyper-parameters collectively denoted by γ (Sect. 3.1). χ is the set of static 3D points that people look at. The *visual focus of attention* (VFoA), ξ, of each person is, for each frame, either one of these 3D points or another person. The temporal scene **z** consists of the 3D state (location, size, head pose) of each person at each frame (Sect. 3.2). **z** projects onto 2D to create *model frames* via the camera C, generating person detections, B, optical flow, I^f, and face landmarks, I^k (Sect. 3.4).

We place prior distributions on each of the model variables mentioned above. Similarly, for each type of data we use, we have a likelihood function that captures its dependence on the model. We combine these functions to get the posterior distribution, which we maximize (see Sect. 4).

3.1 Association

Following previous work [13], we define an *association* $\omega = \{\tau_r \subset B\}_{r=0}^m$ to be a partition of B, the set of all detections (body, face) for the entire video. Here, each τ_r, $r = 1, \ldots, m$, called a *track*, is the set of detections which are associated to person r, and τ_0 is the set of spurious detections, generated by a noise process [41]. The prior distribution $p(\omega)$ has hyper parameters λ_A, κ, θ, and λ_N representing the expected detections per person per frame, new tracks per frame, track length, and noise detections per frame [13].

3.2 Scene and VFoA

Our 3D scene model consists of a set of moving persons, represented using 3D cylinders and ellipsoids, which we call the temporal scene, and a set of static objects, represented by 3D points. These objects are assumed to command attention from the people in the scene, which we model explicitly for each person at each frame, and call visual focus of attention (VFoA).

Static Objects. The scene contains a set of $\widehat{m}$ static objects, denoted by $\chi = (\chi_1, \ldots, \chi_{\widehat{m}})$, $\chi_r \in \mathbb{R}^3$. Since we do not have any prior information regarding their locations, we set a uniform distribution on their positions over the visible 3D space. We model *interesting locations* as independent from each other by using a joint prior of $p(\chi) = p(\widehat{m}) \prod_{r=1}^{\widehat{m}} p(\chi_r)$, where $p(\widehat{m})$ is Poisson.

Visual Focus of Attention (VFoA). The scene also contains m people, one for each association track $\tau_r \in \omega$. Each person has a VFoA at each frame that encodes who or what they are observing, if anything. We use $\xi_{rj} \in \{0, \ldots, m+\widehat{m}\}$ to denote the VFoA of person r at frame j, e.g., $\xi_{rj} = r'$ indicates person r is looking at person or object r' at frame j, where values of $1 \leq \xi_{rj} \leq m$ indicate focus on a person, $m < \xi_{rj} \leq m+\widehat{m}$ on an object, and $\xi_{rj} = 0$ indicates no focus. A priori, people tend to focus on the same visual target in consecutive frames, and we set a simple Markov prior on $\boldsymbol{\xi}_r = (\xi_{r1}, \ldots, \xi_{ml_m})$, where $\xi_{rj} = \xi_{rj-1}$ with high probability. The prior for the entire VFoA set is $p(\boldsymbol{\xi} \mid \omega) = \prod_{r=1}^{m} p(\boldsymbol{\xi}_r)$.

Temporal Scene. Each person r has temporal 3D state $\mathbf{w}_r = (\mathbf{w}_{r1}, \ldots, \mathbf{w}_{rl_r})$, where each single-frame state consists of the person's ground-plane position $\mathbf{x}_{rj} \in \mathbb{R}^2$, body yaw q_{rj}, head pitch p_{rj}, and head yaw y_{rj}, so that $\mathbf{w}_{rj} = (\mathbf{x}_{rj}, q_{rj}, p_{rj}, y_{rj})$, $j = 1, \ldots, l_r$. Importantly, the head yaw y_{rj} is measured relative to the body yaw q_{rj}, i.e., $y_{rj} = 0$ when person r at frame j is looking straight ahead. Additionally, each person has three size dimensions: width, height, and thickness, denoted by d_r^{w}, d_r^{h}, and d_r^{g}. We will denote the full 3D configuration of track τ_r by $\mathbf{z}_r = (\mathbf{w}_r, d_r^{\mathrm{w}}, d_r^{\mathrm{h}}, d_r^{\mathrm{g}})$. Conceptually, at any given frame j, this can be thought of as a $d_r^{\mathrm{w}} \times d_r^{\mathrm{h}} \times d_r^{\mathrm{g}}$ cylinder whose "front" side is oriented at angle q_{rj}, with an ellipsoid on top that has a pitch of p_{rj} and a yaw of y_{rj} (Fig. 3).

We call $\mathbf{x}_r = (\mathbf{x}_{r1}, \ldots, \mathbf{x}_{rl_r})$ the trajectory of person r, and place a Gaussian process (GP) prior on it to promote smoothness. We use analogous definitions for the body angle trajectory $\mathbf{q}_r$, the head pitch trajectory $\mathbf{p}_r$, and the head yaw trajectory $\mathbf{y}_r$ (e.g., for body angle, $\mathbf{q}_r = (q_{r1}, \ldots, q_{rl_r})$). We use similar smooth GP priors for these trajectories. Importantly, the priors on the head angle trajectories $\mathbf{p}_r$ and $\mathbf{y}_r$ depend on which objects they observe, encoded by $\boldsymbol{\xi}_r$, and their locations, which are contained in χ and $\mathbf{x}_{-r}$ (all trajectories except $\mathbf{x}_r$); e.g., for head pitch, $p(\mathbf{p}_r \mid \boldsymbol{\xi}_r, \chi, \mathbf{x}_{-r})$. We express this dependence by setting the mean of the GP prior to an angle pointing in the direction of the observed object, if any, at each frame.

The prior over a person's full physical state, $p(\mathbf{z}_r \mid \boldsymbol{\xi}_r, \chi, \mathbf{x}_{-r}, \omega)$, expands to $p(d_r^{\mathrm{w}}, d_r^{\mathrm{h}}, d_r^{\mathrm{g}})p(\mathbf{x}_r \mid \omega)p(\mathbf{q}_r \mid \omega)p(\mathbf{p}_r \mid \boldsymbol{\xi}_r, \chi, \mathbf{x}_{-r}, \omega)p(\mathbf{y}_r \mid \boldsymbol{\xi}_r, \chi, \mathbf{x}_{-r}, \omega)$, by conditional independence of the state variables given the context variables. We condition on ω as it encodes track length probability. Our overall state prior includes an energy function that makes trajectory intersection unlikely, which is better for inference than a simple constraint (details omitted). Excluding the energy function, the overall prior is: $p(\mathbf{z} \mid \boldsymbol{\xi}, \chi, \omega) = \prod_{r=1}^{m} p(\mathbf{z}_r \mid \boldsymbol{\xi}_r, \chi, \mathbf{x}_{-r}, \omega)$, where m is the number of people in the scene.

3.3   Camera

We use a standard perspective camera model [23] with the simplifying assumptions used by Del Pero et al. [18]. Specifically, the world coordinate origin is

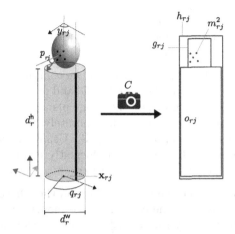

Fig. 3. 3D model for a person (left) and its projection into the image plane (right). Person r at time (frame) j consists of a cylinder at position $\mathbf{x}_{rj}$, of width d_r^w, height d_r^h, and thickness d_r^g (not illustrated) with body angle q_{rj} (the black stripe on the cylinder represents its "front") relative the z-axis of the world. Further, person r's head, represented by the ellipsoid, has yaw y_{rj} relative to the front of the cylinder and pitch p_{rj} indicated by the red arc. Its projection under camera C yields three boxes: model box h_{rj}, model body box o_{rj}, and model face box g_{rj}.

on the ground plane (we use the xz-plane), and the camera center is $(0, \eta, 0)$, with pitch ψ, and focal length f. This simplified camera has unit aspect ratio, and roll, yaw, axis skew, and principal point offset are all zero. We denote the camera parameters as $C = (\eta, \psi, f)$ and give them vague normal priors whose parameters we set manually.

3.4 Data and Likelihood

We use three sources of evidence: person detectors, face landmarks associated with person detections, and optical flow. A person detector [20] provides bounding boxes $B_t = \{b_{t1}, \ldots, b_{tN_t}\}$, $t = 1, \ldots, T$, where N_t is the number of detections at frame t. We define $B = \cup_{t=1}^T B_t$ to be the set of all such boxes. We parameterize each box b_{tj} by $(b_{tj}^x, b_{tj}^{top}, b_{tj}^{bot})$, representing the x-coordinate of the center, and the y-coordinates of the top and bottom, respectively.

A face landmark detector [71] provides five 2D points for each face, $\mathbf{k}_{ti} = (k_{ti}^1, \ldots, k_{ti}^5)$, representing centers of the eyes, the corners of the mouth, and the tip of the nose, of the ith detection at frame t. We use $I_t^k = \{\mathbf{k}_{t1}, \ldots, \mathbf{k}_{tN}\}$ to represent all face landmarks detected at frame t, and define $I^k = \{I_1^k, \ldots, I_T^k\}$. A dense optical flow estimator [35] provides velocity vectors $I_t^f = \{v_{t1}, \ldots, v_{tN_I}\}$ for each frame $t = 1, \ldots, T - 1$, where N_I is the number of pixels in the frame. We also define $I = (I^f, I^k)$.

To compute the data likelihood from evidence in 2D frames, we first convert the 3D model to 2D at each time point, by projecting the 3D scene $\mathbf{z}$ on to the image (via the camera C) as follows.

Model Boxes. For each person r at frame j, we compute a set of points on the surface of their body cylinder and head ellipsoid and project them into the image. We then find a tight bounding box on the image plane, h_{rj}, called the *model box*. Similarly, using the cylinder and ellipsoid separately, we compute a *model body box*, o_{rj}, and a *model face box*, g_{rj} (see Fig. 3). Using this formulation, we can reason about occlusion in 3D, as we can efficiently compute the non-occluded regions of boxes [13], denoted by $\hat{o}_{rj}$ (body) and $\hat{o}_{rj}$ (face).

Face Features. We project five face locations on the ellipsoid representing the centers of the eyes, the nose, the corners of the mouth (see Fig. 3). We denote the projected face features by $\mathbf{m}_{rj} = (m_{rj}^1, \ldots, m_{rj}^5)$, using a special value when a feature is not visible to the camera.

Image Plane Motion Directions. We define two 2D direction vectors, called *model body vector* and *model face vector*, which represent the 3D motion of the body cylinder (respectively, face ellipsoid) projected onto the image. To compute the model face vector for person r at its jth frame, we pick a visible point on the head ellipsoid and project that point onto the image at frames j and $j+1$. Then, the model face vector c_{rj} is given by the difference between the two projected points. We perform the analogous computation using the body cylinder to get the model body vector u_{rj}.

Likelihood. We define a likelihood function for each of the data sources discussed above, $p(B \mid \omega, \mathbf{z}, C)$, $p(I^f \mid \mathbf{z}, C)$, and $p(I^k \mid \mathbf{z}, C)$. Since B, I^f, and I^k are conditionally independent given $\mathbf{z}$ and C (see Fig. 2), the total likelihood function is given by a product of these three functions.

Detection Box Likelihood. We assume each assigned detection box has i.i.d Laplace-distributed errors with respect to their assigned model box in the x-coordinate of its center and the y-coordinates of its top and bottom. Our likelihood includes video specific noise rate for box detections, and detector specific miss rate, both of which are critical for inferring the number of tracks [13].

Face Landmark Likelihood. We associate landmark $\mathbf{k}_{ti}$ to person r at frame t if its centroid is near the center of model face box g_{rt}. Then, we assume a Gaussian noise model around each of the model face features $\mathbf{m}_{rj}$. Specifically, for every $\mathbf{k} \in I^k$, $k^i \sim \mathcal{N}(m_{rj}^i, \Sigma_{I^k}^i)$. for $i = 1, \ldots, 5$, where m_{rj}^i is the model face feature assigned to k^i. Assuming independence of all landmarks, we get a landmark likelihood of

$$p(I^k \mid \mathbf{z}, C) = \prod_{\mathbf{k} \in I^k} p(\mathbf{k} \mid \mathbf{m}(\mathbf{k})), \tag{1}$$

where $\mathbf{m}(\mathbf{k})$ is the predicted face feature for landmark $\mathbf{k}$. Because we link faces to boxes, noisy detections are not relevant. However, the probability of missing a face detection, conditioned on the model (and box) is strongly dependent on whether the face is frontal, or sufficiently in profile that only one eye is visible. Hence we calibrate miss rate for these two cases using held out data.

Optical Flow Likelihood. We place a Laplace distribution on the difference between the **non-occluded** model body vectors and the average optical flow in the corresponding model body box, and similarly for model face vectors [13].

4   Inference

We wish to find the MAP estimate of ω as a good solution to the data association problem. In addition, we need to infer the camera parameters C, and the association prior parameters $\gamma = (\kappa, \theta, \lambda_N)$, which we want to be video specific. We add to this block of parameters, which do not vary in dimension, the discrete VFoA variables $\boldsymbol{\xi}$. Hence, we seek $(\omega, \gamma, C, \boldsymbol{\xi})$ that maximizes the posterior

$$p(\omega, \gamma, C, \boldsymbol{\xi} \mid B, I) \propto p(\omega \mid \gamma)p(\gamma)p(C)p(\boldsymbol{\xi} \mid \omega)p(B, I \mid \omega, C, \boldsymbol{\xi}), \qquad (2)$$

where the marginal data likelihood $p(B, I \mid \omega, C, \boldsymbol{\xi})$ is given by

$$\int p(B \mid \omega, \mathbf{z}, C)p(I \mid \mathbf{z}, C)p(\mathbf{z} \mid \boldsymbol{\xi}, \boldsymbol{\chi}, \omega)p(\boldsymbol{\chi}) \, \mathrm{d}\boldsymbol{\chi} \, \mathrm{d}\mathbf{z}. \qquad (3)$$

4.1   Block Sampling over γ, ω, C and $\boldsymbol{\xi}$

Since expression (2) has no closed form, we approximate its maximum using MCMC block sampling, which successively draws samples from the conditional distributions $p(\gamma \mid \omega)$, $p(\omega \mid \gamma, \boldsymbol{\xi}, C, B, I)$, $p(C \mid \omega, \boldsymbol{\xi}, B, I)$, and $p(\boldsymbol{\xi} \mid \omega, C, B, I)$. During sampling, we are required to evaluate the posterior (2), which contains the integral in expression (3). Since this integral cannot be performed analytically, nor can it be computed numerically due to the high dimensionality of $(\mathbf{z}, \boldsymbol{\chi})$, we estimate its value using the Laplace-Metropolis approximation [24]. This approximation requires obtaining the best 3D scene $(\mathbf{z}^*, \boldsymbol{\chi}^*)$ with respect to the posterior distribution $p(\mathbf{z}, \boldsymbol{\chi} \mid B, I, \omega, C, \boldsymbol{\xi})$, which we estimate using MCMC (see Sect. 4.2), keeping track of the best scene across samples.

We use Gibbs to directly draw samples of the association parameters γ from the conditional posterior $p(\gamma \mid \omega)$, an extension of the MCMCDA algorithm [40] to sample values for ω from $p(\omega \mid \gamma, \boldsymbol{\xi}, C, B, I)$ [13], and random-walk Metropolis-Hastings (MH) to draw samples of the camera parameters η, ψ, and f from the distribution $p(C \mid \omega, \boldsymbol{\xi}, B, I)$.

We also use MH to sample $\boldsymbol{\xi}$ from $p(\boldsymbol{\xi} \mid \omega, C, B, I)$ using the following proposal mechanism. For each person r in the scene, at each frame j, we find the set of objects or persons in the current scene estimate $(\mathbf{z}^*, \boldsymbol{\chi}^*)$ that intersect (up to a threshold) with person r's gaze vector. Then, we build a distribution over these objects, which is biased towards the closer ones, as well as the VFoA in the previous frame. We draw a sample from this distribution and assign it to $\boldsymbol{\xi}_{rj}$. We then accept or reject the sample using the standard MH acceptance probability.

4.2 Estimating $(\mathbf{Z}^*, \mathcal{X}^*)$

To approximate the MAP estimate of $(\mathbf{z}^*, \mathcal{X}^*)$, we alternate sample over $\mathbf{z}$ and $\mathcal{X}$ under the distribution

$$p(\mathbf{z}, \chi \mid B, I, \omega, C, \xi) \propto p(\chi)p(\mathbf{z} \mid \xi, \chi, \omega)p(B, I \mid \mathbf{z}, \chi, \omega, C). \qquad (4)$$

To sample over χ, we use random-walk MH to perturb the position of each interesting point χ_r. We also perform a birth move to introduce new points in the scene. First, we construct a set of candidate points by intersecting all gaze rays across all frames using the current estimate of the temporal 3D state of the persons in the scene $\mathbf{z}$ (see Fig. 4). Then, we choose a point from the candidates uniformly at random and add it to χ. We also use a death move, where we remove an element from χ is uniformly at random.

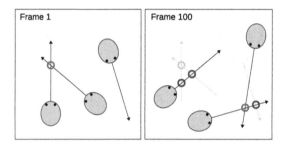

Fig. 4. Proposing static objects. On the left we show a bird's eye view of three people with their corresponding gaze vectors at frame 1. The intersection of two of them creates a candidate static object (red circle). On the right, we show frame 100 of the same video, which also contains three subjects generating four additional candidates. The three lighter lines are gazes recorded in at previous times. The red circles is a candidate generated solely by gazes in the current frame. The three blue circles are candidates generated by intersecting gaze at the current frame with gazes from the previous frames. Finally, the light red circle is the candidate from frame 1. (Color figure online)

To explore the space of $\mathbf{z}$, we use an efficient Gaussian process posterior sampling mechanism based on inducing points [55]. The basic idea is to construct a proposal distribution by drawing samples from the conditional GP prior and a set of inducing point locations that provide a low-dimensional representation of the function. We iterate over persons $r = 1, \ldots, m$ and over the different trajectories of each $\mathbf{x}_r$, $\mathbf{q}_r$, $\mathbf{p}_r$, and $\mathbf{y}_r$, drawing a sample at each iteration. More specifically, for a given trajectory, say $\mathbf{q}_r = (q_{r1}, \ldots, q_{rl_r})$, we arbitrarily choose a subset of $(1, \ldots, l_r)$ as *inducing points*, denoted by $(j_1, \ldots, j_{l'_r})$. Then, for each inducing point j_c, we draw a sample from the conditional GP prior $q'_{rj_c} \sim p(q_{rj} \mid \mathbf{q}_{rj-c})$, and a sample from the predictive distribution $\mathbf{q}'_r \sim p(\mathbf{q}_r \mid \mathbf{q}_{rj-c}, q'_{rj_c})$, where $\mathbf{q}_{rj-c}$ represents $\mathbf{q}_r$ at the set of inducing points excluding j_c. The sample is accepted or rejected using the MH acceptance probability ratio using only the likelihood function $p(B, I \mid \mathbf{z}, \chi, \omega, C)$.

5   Evaluation Dataset and Measures

Several datasets exist for evaluating VFoA recognition in meeting scenarios [5, 7, 8, 29, 58, 59]. Since most of the participants in available meeting datasets are seated throughout the videos, these datasets are not well-suited for evaluating our system, which relies on the ability to detect standing people, and is targeted for scenarios with a diversity of gaze directions in both pitch and yaw. Similarly, datasets such as the Vernissage Corpus dataset [29], which simulates an art gallery scenario, contain many frames where only the upper bodies of the participants are visible. Data sets with walking persons on the other hand uniformly do not encode 3D locations of what people are looking at. While data sets like the challenging SALSA [1], cocktail party [68] and coffee break [16], have head pose annotations, this does not suffice for our goals. Thus we created a new dataset with multiple participants moving freely about while looking at different static targets and each other.

5.1   A New Dataset for 3D Gaze

We captured and annotated six indoor and two outdoor video sequences. Each setting contained several static object locations, several of which were not visible to the camera. Video participants were asked to walk around and look at each other or the stationary objects, indicating when they started and stopped focusing on each target with an audio recording device. All 8 of our videos were between 40 and 90 seconds long with 3 to 4 people and 5 to 8 objects total (including objects that were not visible). Indoor videos had an image resolution of 1920 × 1080. Outdoor video resolution was 1440 × 1080 (Fig. 5).

Fig. 5. From left to right, sample frames from two outdoor videos and two indoor videos. The outdoor videos were taken on top of a garage rooftop and within a library courtyard. The indoor videos were shot in a classroom and within a hallway. Each video participant walks inside the scene and records (via an audio recorder) what they are looking at – either another person or a stationary object. All objects in the indoor videos are visible to the camera and can be seen in the frames. Some of the objects in the outdoor videos are not visible to the camera.

Annotation and Ground Truth. We annotated bounding boxes around each target at each frame using the VATIC annotation tool [60]. We then estimated the ground truth for the 3D positions of each target and the camera parameters in each video by minimizing the reprojection error with respect to 3D locations and heights using the tops and the bottoms of the ground truth boxes. We also used the VFoA audio annotations described above to estimate the ground truth head orientations (pitch and yaw) of each person at every frame where the person was looking at a target. To determine the locations of points not visible to the camera, we measured their locations, and locations that were visible in a shared coordinate system. We then mapped the locations of invisible points to the camera coordinate system.

5.2   Evaluation Measures

Trajectory and Head Pose Evaluation. To evaluate the 3D trajectories of the inferred targets, we first find the best match between the inferred tracks and the ground truth tracks using the Hungarian method with pairwise Euclidean distances. We then use two conventional metrics for tracking: MOTA (for accuracy of the data associations) and MOTP (for precision of the estimated 3D tracks) [50]. Per convention, we set the MOTP threshold to 1 m. To evaluate head pose estimation, we compute the the equivalent of MOTP for both yaw and pitch between the inferred head poses and their corresponding ground truth head poses (measured in degrees) at frames in which they are available.

To Evaluate VFoA Estimation, we compare the inferred VFoA of a tracked person to the ground truth VFoA at each frame where it exists. Let N_c be the number of frames where the VFoA is correctly estimated, N_m be the number of frames where we fail to infer a VFoA (misses), and N_e be the number of frames where we infer an incorrect VFoA. We then compute the following three scores for the VFoA estimation: accuracy $= N_c/N$, mistakes $= N_e/N$, missed $= N_m/N$, where N is the total number of frames that the ground truth for that person records that they were looking at one of the scene VFoA targets. Note that this excludes evaluating the VFoA when the tracked person is transitioning from looking at one target to another. For each video, we compute the average scores over all the tracked persons.

Evaluating Inferring Interesting Locations. Finally, we evaluate how well we can infer the interesting locations in a scene by first finding the best matching between the inferred interesting locations and the preset ground truth locations using the Hungarian method with 1 meter threshold. We then compute the recall and precision for the inferred interesting locations and their average distance to the ground truth locations.

6   Experiments and Results

We ran two sets of experiments to evaluate the performance of our method. We do not compare to others on our main tasks since we are not aware of any relevant published results. We first ran our algorithm and ablated variants on our dataset to assess the impact of different aspects of our approach. We then compare our person tracking performance against our previously published results [13] for people tracking alone to check the effect of the extensions for gaze tracking and object discovery on basic tracking on the well known TUD dataset [2].

Experiments on Our Dataset. We experiment with enabling and disabling inference over three different parts of the model: the 3D head pose $(\mathbf{p}, \mathbf{y})$, the VFoA $\boldsymbol{\xi}$, and the static objects $\boldsymbol{\chi}$, and replace each with a baseline algorithm. We denote the entire model MGG (for "multiple gaze geometry").

When we disable inference over $(\mathbf{p}, \mathbf{y})$, we simply set the head pose same as the walking direction at each frame (MGG-NO-HEAD). When disabling inference over $\boldsymbol{\xi}$, we set the VFoA of each person at each frame to the object or person first intersects their gaze ray (MGG-NO-VO). Finally, when turning off inference over $\boldsymbol{\chi}$, we estimate the static objects by computing a histogram of the intersections of all the 3D gaze directions of all the people across all the frames, then taking the locations of the top 5 bins with the highest votes (MGG-BASELINE).

Table 1. Performance of different modes of our algorithm on our dataset. Numbers are averaged over eight videos. The first row shows our method with all parts enabled, while the next three rows each shows the algorithm with different aspects disabled, e.g., MGG-NO-HEAD is the stereo gaze algorithm without inferring head pose (see Sect. 6 for details). Each column shows a different evaluation measure. We evaluate using the MOTA (with 1.0 m threshold) and MOTP for distance and angles. For VFoA we use the measures defined in Sect. 5.2.

Algorithm	MOTA	MOTP			VFoA		
		pos	yaw	pitch	accuracy	mistakes	missed
MGG	0.95	0.07	28.1	16.8	0.48	0.35	0.17
MGG-NO-HEAD	0.93	0.08	67.3	19.3	0.14	0.45	0.41
MGG-NO-VO	0.95	0.07	29.9	19.2	0.31	0.39	0.30
MGG-BASELINE	0.92	0.10	70.1	20.8	0.13	0.46	0.41

Table 1 provides the tracking and head pose estimation results on our dataset. While MOTA and MOTP on position are comparable across all algorithms, the estimated yaw of the head is poor without head pose data. This is not surprising, as the participants in our videos often do not look straight ahead, partly due to the construction of the experiment. By jointly modeling position and pose, we maintain good performance on tracking, while obtaining reasonable accuracy of head yaw, surpassing MGG-NO-HEAD by a significant amount ($\sim 40°$). The gain for pitch was more modest, but the absolute error in pitch was less to begin with, which was biased by our instructions and our environment. However, this is ecologically valid, as typical viewing angles are not that far from level.

Table 1 also provides the results for the estimated VFoA. On average, we can correctly identify the VFoA target 48% of the time, much better than the baseline (13%), and better than the ablated MGG-NO-VO version (31%). The later result suggests, perhaps not surprisingly, that learning the 3D locations

Table 2. Object discovery performance. Numbers are averaged over eight videos. The algorithms are the same as in Table 1, and the measures are defined in Sect. 5.2. We tabulate performance separately for objects not visible in any frame. The performance here may be favorably biased towards invisible objects because they tended to be behind the camera, and looking at them meant a more frontal image of the viewer, which entails better pose estimation.

Algorithm	All static objects			Objects in video			Objects not in video		
	recall	prec	dist	recall	prec	dist	recall	prec	dist
MGG	0.48	0.59	0.58	0.45	0.54	0.59	0.57	0.67	0.51
MGG-NO-HEAD	0.10	0.23	0.35	0.10	0.25	0.35	0.10	0.22	0.34
MGG-NO-VO	0.14	0.15	0.17	0.15	0.18	0.18	0.14	0.14	0.17
MGG-BASELINE	0.13	0.12	0.40	0.14	0.11	0.40	0.13	0.12	0.39

that people might be looking at provides additional information beyond gaze angles determined from image data alone.

Results for object discovery are shown in Table 2. Here we define success by correctly estimating the location within one meter. We correctly identified 48% of the instances that are available to be identified across the eight videos (recall). In addition, among the ones our method proposes as interesting locations, 59% are correct (precision). The average distance error is a little more than half a meter, which is driven by the choice of the one-meter threshold. Figure 6 shows some example frames of the resulting inferred 3D scene when running the full algorithm (MGG) compared with the baseline (MGG-BASELINE).

Experiments on TUD Benchmark Videos. We compared tracking performance to a similar system for tracking only [13], to evaluate whether incorporating gaze tracking and object inference reduce the tracking performance. We found that we in fact do better on the TUD data, suggesting that the joint inference is helpful (Table 3).

Table 3. Tracking results on the TUD dataset. We compare to [13], which shows that joint inference over additional scene attributes yielded a tracking performance boost as well.

Video	Brau et al. [13]		Proposed	
	MOTA	MOTP	MOTA	MOTP
TUD-Campus	0.84	0.19	0.91	0.11
TUD-Crossing	0.80	0.22	0.80	0.10
TUD-Stadtmitte	0.70	0.27	0.76	0.06
Mean	0.78	0.23	0.82	0.08

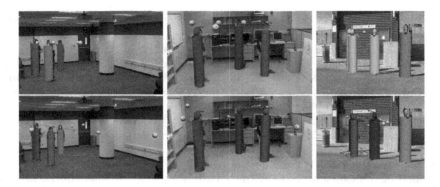

Fig. 6. Visualization of the inferred 3D targets in three scene settings. The top row shows a visualization of the results of the baseline algorithm (MGG-BASELINE), in which the yaw of the gaze direction is set based on the walking directions, and the static objects are estimated from the gaze intersections. The bottom row shows the results of the proposed method on the same frames of the same videos. The arrow on the head indicates the gaze direction and the arrow on the body cylinder indicates the body direction. A tracked person's VFoA is indicated by a line segment from their head connecting to one of the discovered 3D points (yellow spheres) or one of the other tracked people. In the last column, the objects are outside the visible image area. (Color figure online)

7   Conclusion

We demonstrated the feasibility of discovering interesting visual locations, specified in 3D, from multiple person gazes observed in monocular video. In particular, on a data set developed for the task, we found that we can infer what people are looking at 59% of the time, and where it is within about .58 m. We also found that joint inference over the various scene attributes generally improved the accuracy of the individual estimates. In brief, gaze is both part of scene semantics, and can help determine other aspects of scene semantics.

References

1. Alameda-Pineda, X., et al.: Salsa: a novel dataset for multimodal group behavior analysis. IEEE Trans. Pattern Anal. Mach. Intell. **38**(8), 1707–1720 (2016)
2. Andriluka, M., Roth, S., Schiele, B.: People-tracking-by-detection and people-detection-by-tracking. In: IEEE Conference on Computer Vision and Pattern Recognition, CVPR 2008, pp. 1–8. IEEE (2008)
3. Andriyenko, A., Schindler, K.: Globally optimal multi-target tracking on a hexagonal lattice. In: Daniilidis, K., Maragos, P., Paragios, N. (eds.) ECCV 2010. LNCS, vol. 6311, pp. 466–479. Springer, Heidelberg (2010). https://doi.org/10.1007/978-3-642-15549-9_34
4. Andriyenko, A., Schindler, K., Roth, S.: Discrete-continuous optimization for multi-target tracking. In: CVPR, pp. 1926–1933 (2012)

5. Ba, S.O., Hung, H., Odobez, J.M.: Visual activity context for focus of attention estimation in dynamic meetings. In: IEEE International Conference on Multimedia and Expo, ICME 2009, pp. 1424–1427. IEEE (2009)
6. Ba, S.O., Odobez, J.-M.: Probabilistic head pose tracking evaluation in single and multiple camera setups. In: Stiefelhagen, R., Bowers, R., Fiscus, J. (eds.) CLEAR/RT -2007. LNCS, vol. 4625, pp. 276–286. Springer, Heidelberg (2008). https://doi.org/10.1007/978-3-540-68585-2_26
7. Ba, S.O., Odobez, J.M.: Recognizing visual focus of attention from head pose in natural meetings. IEEE Trans. Syst. Man Cybern. Part B Cybern. **39**(1), 16–33 (2009)
8. Ba, S.O., Odobez, J.M.: Multiperson visual focus of attention from head pose and meeting contextual cues. IEEE Trans. Pattern Anal. Mach. Intell. **33**(1), 101–116 (2011)
9. Benfold, B., Reid, I.: Stable multi-target tracking in real-time surveillance video. In: CVPR, pp. 3457–3464 (2011)
10. Benfold, B., Reid, I.: Guiding visual surveillance by tracking human attention. In: BMVC, pp. 1–11 (2009)
11. Beymer, D.J.: Face recognition under varying pose. In: Proceedings of the IEEE Computer Society Conference on Computer Vision and Pattern Recognition, CVPR 1994, pp. 756–761. IEEE (1994)
12. Blanz, V., Vetter, T.: Face recognition based on fitting a 3D morphable model. IEEE Trans. Pattern Anal. Mach. Intell. **25**(9), 1063–1074 (2003)
13. Brau, E., Guan, J., Simek, K., Del Pero, L., Dawson, C.R., Barnard, K.: Bayesian 3D tracking from monocular video. In: 2013 IEEE International Conference on Computer Vision (ICCV), pp. 3368–3375. IEEE (2013)
14. Chen, C., Heili, A., Odobez, J.M.: A joint estimation of head and body orientation cues in surveillance video. In: 2011 IEEE International Conference on Computer Vision Workshops (ICCV Workshops), pp. 860–867. IEEE (2011)
15. Chen, C., Odobez, J.M.: We are not contortionists: coupled adaptive learning for head and body orientation estimation in surveillance video. In: 2012 IEEE Conference on Computer Vision and Pattern Recognition (CVPR), pp. 1544–1551. IEEE (2012)
16. Cristani, M., et al.: Social interaction discovery by statistical analysis of F-formations. In: BMVC (2011)
17. Dehghan, A., Assari, S.M., Shah, M.: GMMCP tracker: globally optimal generalized maximum multi clique problem for multiple object tracking. In: CVPR, vol. 1, p. 2 (2015)
18. Del Pero, L., Guan, J., Brau, E., Schlecht, J., Barnard, K.: Sampling bedrooms. In: CVPR, pp. 2009–2016 (2011)
19. Duffner, S., Garcia, C.: Visual focus of attention estimation with unsupervised incremental learning. IEEE Trans. Circuits Syst. Video Technol. **26**(12), 2264–2272 (2016)
20. Felzenszwalb, P., Girshick, R., McAllester, D., Ramanan, D.: Object detection with discriminatively trained part-based models. In: IEEE PAMI (2009)
21. Gee, A., Cipolla, R.: Determining the gaze of faces in images. Image Vis. Comput. **12**(10), 639–647 (1994)
22. Gu, L., Kanade, T.: 3D alignment of face in a single image. In: 2006 IEEE Computer Society Conference on Computer Vision and Pattern Recognition, vol. 1, pp. 1305–1312. IEEE (2006)
23. Hartley, R., Zisserman, A.: Multiple View Geometry in Computer Vision. Cambridge University Press, New York (2000)

24. Hastie, T., Tibshirani, R., Friedman, J.: The Elements of Statistical Learning; Data Mining, Inference, and Prediction. Springer Series in Statistics. Springer, New York (2001)
25. Horprasert, T., Yacoob, Y., Davis, L.S.: Computing 3d head orientation from a monocular image sequence. In: 25th Annual AIPR Workshop on Emerging Applications of Computer Vision, pp. 244–252. International Society for Optics and Photonics (1997)
26. Huang, J., Shao, X., Wechsler, H.: Face pose discrimination using support vector machines (SVM). In: Proceedings of the Fourteenth International Conference on Pattern Recognition, vol. 1, pp. 154–156. IEEE (1998)
27. Huang, Y., Duan, D., Cui, J., Davoine, F., Wang, L., Zha, H.: Joint estimation of head pose and visual focus of attention. In: 2014 IEEE International Conference on Image Processing (ICIP), pp. 3332–3336. IEEE (2014)
28. Isard, M., MacCormick, J.: BraMBLe: a Bayesian multiple-blob tracker. In: ICCV, pp. 34–41 (2001)
29. Jayagopi, D.B., et al.: The vernissage corpus: a multimodal human-robot-interaction dataset. Technical report (2012)
30. Kitani, K.M., Ziebart, B.D., Bagnell, J.A., Hebert, M.: Activity forecasting. In: Fitzgibbon, A., Lazebnik, S., Perona, P., Sato, Y., Schmid, C. (eds.) ECCV 2012. LNCS, vol. 7575, pp. 201–214. Springer, Heidelberg (2012). https://doi.org/10.1007/978-3-642-33765-9_15
31. Kuo, C., Huang, C., Nevatia, R.: Multi-target tracking by on-line learned discriminative appearance models. In: CVPR, pp. 685–692 (2010)
32. La Cascia, M., Sclaroff, S., Athitsos, V.: Fast, reliable head tracking under varying illumination: an approach based on registration of texture-mapped 3d models. IEEE Trans. Pattern Anal. Mach. Intell. 22(4), 322–336 (2000)
33. Li, Y., Gong, S., Liddell, H.: Support vector regression and classification based multi-view face detection and recognition. In: Proceedings of the Fourth IEEE International Conference on Automatic Face and Gesture Recognition, pp. 300–305. IEEE (2000)
34. Li, Y., Gong, S., Sherrah, J., Liddell, H.: Support vector machine based multi-view face detection and recognition. Image Vis. Comput. 22(5), 413–427 (2004)
35. Liu, C.: Exploring new representations and applications for motion analysis. Ph.D. thesis, M.I.T (2009)
36. Massé, B., Ba, S., Horaud, R.: Simultaneous estimation of gaze direction and visual focus of attention for multi-person-to-robot interaction. In: 2016 IEEE International Conference on Multimedia and Expo (ICME), pp. 1–6. IEEE (2016)
37. Milan, A., Leal-Taixé, L., Schindler, K., Reid, I.: Joint tracking and segmentation of multiple targets. In: Proceedings of the IEEE Conference on Computer Vision and Pattern Recognition, pp. 5397–5406 (2015)
38. Murphy-Chutorian, E., Trivedi, M.M.: Head pose estimation in computer vision: a survey. IEEE Trans. Pattern Anal. Mach. Intell. 31(4), 607–626 (2009)
39. Niyogi, S., Freeman, W.T.: Example-based head tracking. In: Proceedings of the Second International Conference on Automatic Face and Gesture Recognition, pp. 374–378. IEEE (1996)
40. Oh, S.: Bayesian formulation of data association and Markov chain Monte Carlo data association. In: Robotics: Science and Systems Conference (RSS) Workshop Inside Data association (2008)
41. Oh, S., Russell, S., Sastry, S.: Markov chain Monte Carlo data association for general multiple target tracking problems (2004)

42. Otsuka, K., Takemae, Y., Yamato, J.: A probabilistic inference of multiparty-conversation structure based on Markov-switching models of gaze patterns, head directions, and utterances. In: Proceedings of the 7th International Conference on Multimodal Interfaces, pp. 191–198. ACM (2005)

43. Otsuka, K., Yamato, J., Takemae, Y., Murase, H.: Conversation scene analysis with dynamic Bayesian network basedon visual head tracking. In: 2006 IEEE International Conference on Multimedia and Expo, pp. 949–952. IEEE (2006)

44. Pirsiavash, H., Ramanan, D., Fowlkes, C.: Globally-optimal greedy algorithms for tracking a variable number of objects. In: CVPR, pp. 1201–1208 (2011)

45. Sankaranarayanan, K., Chang, M.C., Krahnstoever, N.: Tracking gaze direction from far-field surveillance cameras. In: 2011 IEEE Workshop on Applications of Computer Vision (WACV), pp. 519–526. IEEE (2011)

46. Segal, A.V., Reid, I.: Latent data association: Bayesian model selection for multi-target tracking. In: 2013 IEEE International Conference on Computer Vision (ICCV), pp. 2904–2911. IEEE (2013)

47. Sheikhi, S., Odobez, J.-M.: Recognizing the visual focus of attention for human robot interaction. In: Salah, A.A., Ruiz-del-Solar, J., Meriçli, Ç., Oudeyer, P.-Y. (eds.) HBU 2012. LNCS, vol. 7559, pp. 99–112. Springer, Heidelberg (2012). https://doi.org/10.1007/978-3-642-34014-7_9

48. Smith, K., Ba, S.O., Gatica-Perez, D., Odobez, J.M.: Tracking the multi person wandering visual focus of attention. In: Proceedings of the 8th International Conference on Multimodal Interfaces, pp. 265–272. ACM (2006)

49. Smith, K., Ba, S.O., Odobez, J.M., Gatica-Perez, D.: Tracking the visual focus of attention for a varying number of wandering people. IEEE Trans. Pattern Anal. Mach. Intell. **30**(7), 1212–1229 (2008)

50. Stiefelhagen, R., Bernardin, K., Bowers, R., Garofolo, J., Mostefa, D., Soundararajan, P.: The CLEAR 2006 evaluation. In: Stiefelhagen, R., Garofolo, J. (eds.) CLEAR 2006. LNCS, vol. 4122, pp. 1–44. Springer, Heidelberg (2007). https://doi.org/10.1007/978-3-540-69568-4_1

51. Stiefelhagen, R., Yang, J., Waibel, A.: Modeling focus of attention for meeting indexing. In: Proceedings of the seventh ACM International Conference on Multimedia (Part 1), pp. 3–10. ACM (1999)

52. Stiefelhagen, R., Yang, J., Waibel, A.: Modeling focus of attention for meeting indexing based on multiple cues. IEEE Trans. Neural Netw. **13**(4), 928–938 (2002)

53. Stiefelhagen, R., Zhu, J.: Head orientation and gaze direction in meetings. In: Extended Abstracts on Human Factors in Computing Systems, CHI 2002, pp. 858–859. ACM (2002)

54. Tang, S., Andres, B., Andriluka, M., Schiele, B.: Subgraph decomposition for multi-target tracking. In: Proceedings of the IEEE Conference on Computer Vision and Pattern Recognition, pp. 5033–5041 (2015)

55. Titsias, M.K., Lawrence, N.D., Rattray, M.: Efficient sampling for Gaussian Process inference using control variables. In: Advances in Neural Information Processing Systems, vol. 21, pp. 1681–1688. Curran Associates Inc., Vancouver, British Columbia, Canada (2008)

56. Valenti, R., Sebe, N., Gevers, T.: Combining head pose and eye location information for gaze estimation. IEEE Trans. Image Process. **21**(2), 802–815 (2012)

57. Voit, M., Nickel, K., Stiefelhagen, R.: Head pose estimation in single- and multi-view environments - results on the CLEAR'07 benchmarks. In: Stiefelhagen, R., Bowers, R., Fiscus, J. (eds.) CLEAR/RT -2007. LNCS, vol. 4625, pp. 307–316. Springer, Heidelberg (2008). https://doi.org/10.1007/978-3-540-68585-2_29

58. Voit, M., Stiefelhagen, R.: Deducing the visual focus of attention from head pose estimation in dynamic multi-view meeting scenarios. In: Proceedings of the 10th International Conference on Multimodal Interfaces, pp. 173–180. ACM (2008)

59. Voit, M., Stiefelhagen, R.: 3D user-perspective, voxel-based estimation of visual focus of attention in dynamic meeting scenarios. In: International Conference on Multimodal Interfaces and the Workshop on Machine Learning for Multimodal Interaction, p. 51. ACM (2010)

60. Vondrick, C., Patterson, D., Ramanan, D.: Efficiently scaling up crowdsourced video annotation. Int. J. Comput. Vis. **101**, 1–21 (2013). https://doi.org/10.1007/s11263-012-0564-1

61. Wei, P., Zhao, Y., Zheng, N., Zhu, S.C.: Modeling 4d human-object interactions for joint event segmentation, recognition, and object localization. IEEE Trans Pattern Anal. Mach. Intell. **39**, 1165–1179 (2016)

62. Wu, Y., Toyama, K.: Wide-range, person-and illumination-insensitive head orientation estimation. In: Proceedings of the Fourth IEEE International Conference on Automatic Face and Gesture Recognition, pp. 183–188. IEEE (2000)

63. Xiao, J., Moriyama, T., Kanade, T., Cohn, J.F.: Robust full-motion recovery of head by dynamic templates and re-registration techniques. Int. J. Imaging Syst. Technol. **13**(1), 85–94 (2003)

64. Xie, D., Todorovicy, S., Zhu, S.C.: Inferring "dark matter" and "dark energy" from videos. In: ICCV (2013)

65. Yang, R., Zhang, Z.: Model-based head pose tracking with stereovision. In: Proceedings of the Fifth IEEE International Conference on Automatic Face and Gesture Recognition, pp. 255–260. IEEE (2002)

66. Yi, Y., Xu, H.: Hierarchical data association framework with occlusion handling for multiple targets tracking. IEEE Signal Process. Lett. **21**(3), 288–291 (2014)

67. Yücel, Z., Salah, A.A., Mericli, C., Meriçli, T., Valenti, R., Gevers, T.: Joint attention by gaze interpolation and saliency. IEEE Trans. Cybern. **43**(3), 829–842 (2013)

68. Zen, G., Lepri, B., Ricci, E., Lanz, O.: Space speaks: towards socially and personality aware visual surveillance. In: 1st ACM International Workshop on Multimodal Pervasive Video Analysis, pp. 37–42. ACM, Firenze, Italy (2010)

69. Zhang, L., Li, Y., Nevatia, R.: Global data association for multi-object tracking using network flows. In: IEEE Conference on Computer Vision and Pattern Recognition, CVPR 2008, pp. 1–8. IEEE (2008)

70. Zhao, G., Chen, L., Song, J., Chen, G.: Large head movement tracking using sift-based registration. In: Proceedings of the 15th International Conference on Multimedia, pp. 807–810. ACM (2007)

71. Zhu, X., Ramanan, D.: Face detection, pose estimation, and landmark localization in the wild. In: 2012 IEEE Conference on Computer Vision and Pattern Recognition (CVPR), pp. 2879–2886. IEEE (2012)

Video

Learning-Based Video Motion Magnification

Tae-Hyun Oh[1]([✉]), Ronnachai Jaroensri[1], Changil Kim[1], Mohamed Elgharib[2],
Frédo Durand[1], William T. Freeman[1,3], and Wojciech Matusik[1]

[1] MIT CSAIL, Cambridge, MA, USA
{taehyun,tiam}@csail.mit.edu
[2] HBKU QCRI, Doha, Qatar
[3] Google Research, Cambridge, USA

Abstract. Video motion magnification techniques allow us to see small
motions previously invisible to the naked eyes, such as those of vibrating
airplane wings, or swaying buildings under the influence of the wind.
Because the motion is small, the magnification results are prone to noise
or excessive blurring. The state of the art relies on hand-designed filters
to extract representations that may not be optimal. In this paper, we seek
to learn the filters directly from examples using deep convolutional neural
networks. To make training tractable, we carefully design a synthetic
dataset that captures small motion well, and use two-frame input for
training. We show that the learned filters achieve high-quality results
on real videos, with less ringing artifacts and better noise characteristics
than previous methods. While our model is not trained with temporal
filters, we found that the temporal filters can be used with our extracted
representations up to a moderate magnification, enabling a frequency-
based motion selection. Finally, we analyze the learned filters and show
that they behave similarly to the derivative filters used in previous works.
Our code, trained model, and datasets will be available online.

Keywords: Motion manipulation · Motion magnification
Deep convolutional neural network

1 Introduction

The ability to discern small motions enables important applications such as
understanding a building's structural health [3] and measuring a person's vital
sign [1]. Video motion magnification techniques allow us to perceive such
motions. This is a difficult task, because the motions are so small that they

---

T.-H. Oh and R. Jaroensri—Contributed equally.

Electronic supplementary material The online version of this chapter (https://
doi.org/10.1007/978-3-030-01225-0_39) contains supplementary material, which is
available to authorized users.

© Springer Nature Switzerland AG 2018
V. Ferrari et al. (Eds.): ECCV 2018, LNCS 11208, pp. 663–679, 2018.
https://doi.org/10.1007/978-3-030-01225-0_39

can be indistinguishable from noise. As a result, current video magnification techniques suffer from noisy outputs and excessive blurring, especially when the magnification factor is large [24,25,27,28].

Current video magnification techniques typically decompose video frames into representations that allow them to magnify motion [24,25,27,28].Their decomposition typically relies on hand-designed filters, such as the complex steerable filters [6], which may not be optimal. In this paper, we seek to learn the decomposition filter directly from examples using deep convolutional neural networks (CNN). Because real motion-magnified video pairs are difficult to obtain, we designed a synthetic dataset that realistically simulates small motion. We carefully interpolate pixel values, and we explicitly model quantization, which could round away sub-level values that result from subpixel motions. These careful considerations allow us to train a network that generalizes well in real videos.

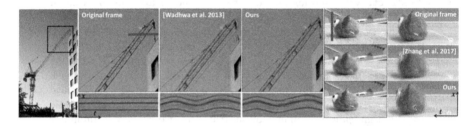

Fig. 1. While our model learns spatial decomposition filters from synthetically generated inputs, it performs well on real videos with results showing less ringing artifacts and noise. (Left) the *crane* sequence magnified 75× with the same temporal filter as Wadhwa *et al.* [24]. (Right) Dynamic mode magnifies difference (velocity) between consecutive frames, allowing us to deal with large motion as did Zhang *et al.* [28]. The red lines indicate the sampled regions for drawing x-t and y-t slice views. (Color figure online)

Motivated by Wadhwa *et al.* [24], we design a network consisting of three main parts: the spatial decomposition filters, the representation manipulator, and the reconstruction filters. To make training tractable, we simplify our training using two-frame input, and the magnified difference as the target instead of fully specifying temporal aspects of motion. Despite training on the simplified two-frames setting and synthetic data, our network achieves better noise performance and has fewer edge artifacts (See Fig. 1). Our result also suggests that the learned representations support linear operations enough to be used with linear temporal filters up to a moderate magnification factor. This enables us to select motion based on frequency bands of interest.

Finally, we visualize the learned filters and the activations to have a better understanding of what the network has learned. While the filter weights themselves show no apparent pattern, a linear approximation of our learned (nonlinear) filters resembles derivative filters, which are the basis for decomposition filters in the prior art [24,27].

The main contributions of this paper are as follows:

- We present the first learning-based approach for the video motion magnification, which achieves high-quality magnification with fewer ringing artifacts, and has better noise characteristics.
- We present a synthetic data generation method that captures small motions, allowing the learned filters to generalize well in real videos.
- We analyze our model, and show that our learned filters exhibit similarity to the previously hand-engineered filters.

We will release the codes, the trained model, and the dataset online.

Table 1. Comparisons of the prior arts.

Method	Liu *et al.* [13]	Wu *et al.* [27]	Wadhwa *et al.* [24]	Wadhwa *et al.* [25]	Zhang *et al.* [28]	Ours
Spatial decomposition	Tracking, optical flow	Laplacian pyramid	Steerable filters	Riesz pyramid	Steerable filters	Deep convolution layers
Motion isolation	-	Temporal bandpass filter	Temporal bandpass filter	Temporal bandpass filter	Temporal bandpass filter (2nd-order derivative)	Subtraction or temporal bandpass filter
Representation denoising	Expectation-Maximization	-	Amplitude weighted Gaussian filtering	Amplitude weighted Gaussian filtering	Amplitude weighted Gaussian filtering	Trainable convolution

2 Related Work

Video Motion Magnification. Motion magnification techniques can be divided into two categories: Lagrangian and Eulerian approaches. The Lagrangian approach explicitly extracts the motion field (optical flow) and uses it to move the pixels directly [13]. The Eulerian approaches [24,25,27], on the other hand, decompose video frames into representations that facilitate manipulation of motions, without requiring explicit tracking. These techniques usually consist of three stages: decomposing frames into an alternative representation, manipulating the representation, and reconstructing the manipulated representation to magnified frames. Wu *et al.* [27] use a spatial decomposition motivated by the first-order Taylor expansion, while Wadhwa *et al.* [24,25] use the complex steerable pyramid [6] to extract a phase-based representation. Current Eulerian techniques are good at revealing subtle motions, but they are hand-designed [24,25,27], and do not take into account many issues such as occlusion. Because of this, they are prone to noise and often suffer from excessive blurring. Our technique belongs to the Eulerian approach, but our decomposition is directly learned from examples, so it has fewer edge artifacts and better noise characteristics.

One key component of the previous motion magnification techniques is the multi-frame temporal filtering over the representations, which helps to isolate motions of interest and to prevent noise from being magnified. Wu *et al.* [27] and Wadhwa *et al.* [24,25] utilize standard frequency bandpass filters.

Their methods achieve high-quality results, but suffer from degraded quality when large motions or drifts occur in the input video. Elgharib *et al.* [4] and Zhang *et al.* [28] address this limitation. Elgharib *et al.* [4] model large motions using affine transformation, while Zhang *et al.* [28] use a different temporal processing equivalent to a second-order derivative (*i.e.*, acceleration). On the other hand, our method achieves comparable quality even without using temporal filtering. The comparisons of our method to the prior arts are summarized in Table 1.

Deep Representation for Video Synthesis. Frame interpolation can be viewed as a complementary problem to the motion magnification problem, where the magnification factor is less than 1. Recent techniques demonstrate high-quality results by explicitly shifting pixels using either optical flow [10,14,26] or pixel-shifting convolution kernels [17,18]. However, these techniques usually require re-training when changing the manipulation factor. Our representation can be directly configured for different magnification factors without re-training. For frame extrapolation, there is a line of recent work [16,22,23] that directly synthesizes RGB pixel values to predict dynamic video frames in the future, but their results are often blurry. Our work focusing on magnifying motion within a video, without concerns about what happens in the future.

3   Learning-Based Motion Magnification

In this section, we introduce the motion magnification problem and our learning setup. Then, we explain how we simplify the learning to make it tractable. Finally, we describe the network architecture and give the full detail of our dataset generation.

3.1   Problem Statement

We follow Wu *et al.*'s and Wadhwa *et al.*'s definition of motion magnification [24,27]. Namely, given an image $I(\mathbf{x}, t) = f(\mathbf{x} + \delta(\mathbf{x}, t))$, where $\delta(\mathbf{x}, t)$ represents the motion field as a function of position $\mathbf{x}$ and time t, the goal of motion magnification is to magnify the motion such that the magnified image $\tilde{I}$ becomes

$$\tilde{I}(\mathbf{x}, t) = f(\mathbf{x} + (1 + \alpha)\delta(\mathbf{x}, t)),\tag{1}$$

where α is the magnification factor. In practice, we only want to magnify certain signal $\tilde{\delta}(\mathbf{x}, t) = \mathcal{T}(\delta(\mathbf{x}, t))$ for a selector $\mathcal{T}(\cdot)$ that selects motion of interest, which is typically a temporal bandpass filter [24,27].

While previous techniques rely on hand-crafted filters [24,27], our goal is to learn a set of filters that extracts and manipulates representations of the motion signal $\delta(\mathbf{x}, t)$ to generate output magnified frames. To simplify our training, we consider a simple two-frames input case. Specifically, we generate two input frames, $\mathbf{X}_a$ and $\mathbf{X}_b$ with a small motion displacement, and an output motion-magnified frame $\mathbf{Y}$ of $\mathbf{X}_b$ with respect to $\mathbf{X}_a$. This reduces parameters characterizing each training pair to just the magnification factor. While this simplified setting loses the temporal aspect of motion, we will show that the network learns a linear enough representation *w.r.t.* the displacement to be compatible with linear temporal filters up to a moderate magnification factor.

3.2 Deep Convolutional Neural Network Architecture

Similar to Wadhwa *et al.* [24], our goal is to design a network that extracts a representation, which we can use to manipulate motion simply by multiplication and to reconstruct a magnified frame. Therefore, our network consists of three parts: the encoder $G_e(\cdot)$, the manipulator $G_m(\cdot)$, and the decoder $G_d(\cdot)$, as illustrated in Fig. 2. The encoder acts as a spatial decomposition filter that extracts a shape representation [9] from a single frame, which we can use to manipulate motion (analogous to the phase of the steerable pyramid and Riesz pyramid [24,25]). The manipulator takes this representation and manipulates it to magnify the motion (by multiplying the difference). Finally, the decoder reconstructs the modified representation into the resulting motion-magnified frames.

Our encoder and decoder are fully convolutional, which enables them to work on any resolution [15]. They use residual blocks to generate high-quality output [21]. To reduce memory footprint and increase the receptive field size, we downsample the activation by 2× at the beginning of the encoder, and upsample it at the end of the decoder. We downsample with the strided convolution [20], and we use nearest-neighbor upsampling followed by a convolution layer to avoid checkerboard artifacts [19]. We experimentally found that three 3 × 3 residual blocks in the encoder and nine in the decoder generally yield good results.

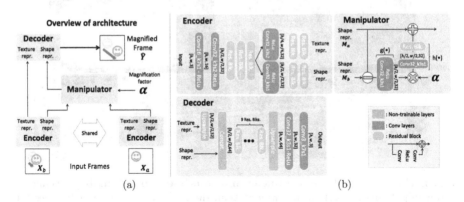

Fig. 2. Our network architecture. (a) Overview of the architecture. Our network consists of 3 main parts: the encoder, the manipulator, and the decoder. During training, the inputs to the network are two video frames, $(\mathbf{X}_a, \mathbf{X}_b)$, with a magnification factor α, and the output is the magnified frame $\hat{\mathbf{Y}}$. (b) Detailed diagram for each part. $\texttt{Conv}\langle c\rangle\_\texttt{k}\langle k\rangle\_\texttt{s}\langle s\rangle$ denotes a convolutional layer of c channels, $k \times k$ kernel size, and stride s.

While Eq. (1) suggests no intensity change (constant $f(\cdot)$), this is not true in general. This causes our network to also magnify intensity changes. To cope with this, we introduce another output from the encoder that represents intensity information ("texture representation" [9]) similar to the amplitude of the steerable pyramid decomposition. This representation reduces undesired intensity magnification as well as noise in the final output. We downsample the representation 2× further because it helps reduce noise. We denote the texture and shape representation outputs of the encoder as $\mathbf{V} = G_{e,texture}(\mathbf{X})$ and $\mathbf{M} = G_{e,shape}(\mathbf{X})$, respectively. During training, we add a regularization loss to separate these two representations, which we will discuss in more detail later.

We want to learn a shape representation $\mathbf{M}$ that is linear with respect to $\delta(\mathbf{x}, t)$. So, our manipulator works by taking the difference between shape representations of two given frames, and directly multiplying a magnification factor to it. That is,

$$G_m(\mathbf{M}_a, \mathbf{M}_b, \alpha) = \mathbf{M}_a + \alpha(\mathbf{M}_b - \mathbf{M}_a). \tag{2}$$

In practice, we found that some non-linearity in the manipulator improves the quality of the result (See Fig. 3). Namely,

$$G_m(\mathbf{M}_a, \mathbf{M}_b, \alpha) = \mathbf{M}_a + h\left(\alpha \cdot g(\mathbf{M}_b - \mathbf{M}_a)\right), \tag{3}$$

where $g(\cdot)$ is represented by a 3×3 convolution followed by ReLU, and $h(\cdot)$ is a 3×3 convolution followed by a 3×3 residual block.

Linear   Non-Linear

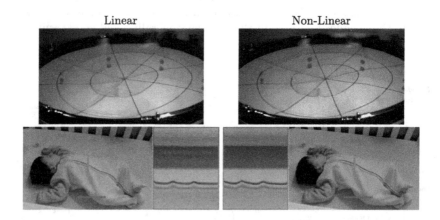

Fig. 3. Comparison between linear and non-linear manipulators. While the two manipulators are able to magnify motion, the linear manipulator (left) does blur strong edges (top) sometimes, and is more prone to noise (bottom). Non-linearity in the manipulator reduces this problem (right).

Loss Function. We train the whole network in an end-to-end manner. We use l_1-loss between the network output $\hat{\mathbf{Y}}$ and the ground-truth magnified frame $\mathbf{Y}$. We found no noticeable difference in quality when using more advanced losses, such as the perceptual [8] or the adversarial losses [7]. In order to drive the separation of the texture and the shape representations, we perturbed the intensity of some frames, and expect the texture representations of perturbed frames to be the same, while their shape representation remain unchanged. Specifically, we create perturbed frames $\mathbf{X}'_b$ and $\mathbf{Y}'$, where the prime symbol indicates color perturbation. Then, we impose loses between $\mathbf{V}'_b$ and $\mathbf{V}'_Y$ (perturbed frames), $\mathbf{V}_a$ and $\mathbf{V}_b$ (un-perturbed frames), and $\mathbf{M}'_b$ and $\mathbf{M}_b$ (shape of perturbed frames should remain unchanged). We used l_1-loss for all regularizations. Therefore, we train the whole network G by minimizing the final loss function $\mathcal{L}_1(\mathbf{Y}, \hat{\mathbf{Y}}) + \lambda(\mathcal{L}_1(\mathbf{V}_a, \mathbf{V}_b) + \mathcal{L}_1(\mathbf{V}'_b, \mathbf{V}'_Y) + \mathcal{L}_1(\mathbf{M}_b, \mathbf{M}'_b))$, where λ is the regularization weight (set to 0.1).

Training. We use ADAM [11] with $\beta_1 = 0.9$ and $\beta_2 = 0.999$ to minimize the loss with the batch size 4. We set the learning rate to 10^{-4} with no weight decay. In order to improve robustness to noise, we add Poisson noise with random strengths whose standard deviation is up to 3 on a $0-255$ scale for a mid-gray pixel.

Applying 2-Frames Setting to Videos. Since there was no temporal concept during training, our network can be applied as long as the input has two frames. We consider two different modes where we use different frames as a reference. The Static mode uses the 1st frame as an anchor, and the Dynamic uses the previous frames as a reference, *i.e.* we consider $(\mathbf{X}_{t-1}, \mathbf{X}_t)$ as inputs in the Dynamic mode.

Intuitively, the Static mode follows the classical definition of motion magnification as defined in Eq. (1), while the Dynamic mode magnifies the difference (*velocity*) between consecutive frames. Note that the magnification factor in each case has different meanings, because we are magnifying the motion against a fixed reference, and the velocity respectively. Because there is no temporal filter, undesired motion and noise quickly becomes a problem as the magnification factor increases, and achieving high-quality result is more challenging.

Temporal Operation. Even though our network has been trained in the 2-frame setting only, we find that the shape representation is linear enough *w.r.t.* the displacement to be compatible with linear temporal filters. Given the shape representation $\mathbf{M}(t)$ of a video (extracted frame-wise), we replace the difference operation with a pixel-wise temporal filter $\mathcal{T}(\cdot)$ across the temporal axis in the manipulator $G_m(\cdot)$. That is, the temporal filtering version of the manipulator, $G_{m,temporal}(\cdot)$, is given by,

$$G_{m,temporal}(\mathbf{M}(t), \alpha) = \mathbf{M}(t) + \alpha \mathcal{T}(\mathbf{M}(t)). \tag{4}$$

The decoder takes the temporally-filtered shape representation and the texture representation of the current frame, and generates temporally filtered motion magnified frames.

3.3   Synthetic Training Dataset

Obtaining real motion magnified video pairs is challenging. Therefore, we utilize synthetic data which can be generated in large quantity. However, simulating small motions involves several considerations because any small error will be relatively large. Our dataset is carefully designed and we will later show that the network trained on this data generalizes well to real videos. In this section, we describe considerations we make in generating our dataset.

Foreground Objects and Background Images. We utilize real image datasets for their realistic texture. We use $200,000$ images from MS COCO dataset [12] for background, and we use $7,000$ segmented objects the PAS-CAL VOC dataset [5] for the foreground. As the motion is magnified, filling the occluded area becomes important, so we paste our foreground objects directly onto the background to simulate occlusion effect. Each training sample contains 7 to 15 foreground objects, randomly scaled from its original size. We limit the scaling factor at 2 to avoid blurry texture. The amount and direction of motions of background and each object are also randomized to ensure that the network learns local motions.

Low Contrast Texture, Global Motion, and Static Scenes. The training examples described in the previous paragraphs are full of sharp and strong edges where the foreground and background meet. This causes the network to generalize poorly on low contrast textures. To improve generalization in these cases, we add two types of examples: where (1) the background is blurred, and (2) there is only a moving background in the scene to mimic a large object. These improve the performance on large and low contrast objects in real videos.

Small motion can be indistinguishable from noise. We find that including static scenes in the dataset helps the network learn changes that are due to noise only. We add additional two subsets where (1) the scene is completely static, and (2) the background is not moving, but the foreground is moving. With these, our dataset contains a total of 5 parts, each with $20,000$ samples of 384×384 images. The examples of our dataset can be found in the supplementary material.

Input Motion and Amplification Factor. Motion magnification techniques are designed to magnify small motions at high magnifications. The task becomes even harder when the magnified motion is large (*e.g.* >30 pixels). To ensure the learnability of the task, we carefully parameterize each training example to make sure it is within a defined range. Specifically, we limit the magnification factor α up to 100 and sample the input motion (up to 10 pixels), so that the magnified motion does not exceed 30 pixels.

Subpixel Motion Generation. How subpixel motion manifests depends on demosaicking algorithm and camera sensor pattern. Fortunately, even though our raw images are already demosaicked, they have high enough resolution that they can be downsampled to avoid artifacts from demosaicking. To ensure proper resampling, we reconstruct our image in the continuous domain before applying translation or resizing. We find that our results are not sensitive to the interpolation method used, so we chose bicubic interpolation for the reconstruction. To reduce error that results from translating by a small amount, we first generate our dataset at a higher resolution (where the motion appears larger), then downsample each frame to the desired size. We reduce aliasing when downsampling by applying a Gaussian filter whose kernel is 1 pixel in the destination domain.

Subpixel motion appears as small intensity changes that are often below the 8-bit quantization level. These changes are often rounded away especially for low contrast region. To cope with this, we add uniform quantization noise before quantizing the image. This way, each pixel has a chance of rounding up proportional to its rounding residual (*e.g.*, if a pixel value is 102.3, it will have 30% chance of rounding up).

4   Results and Evaluations

In this section, we demonstrate the effectiveness of our proposed network and analyze its intermediate representation to shed light on what it does. We compare qualitatively and quantitatively with the state-of-the-art [24] and show that our network performs better in many aspects. Finally, we discuss limitations of our work. The comparison videos are available in our supplementary material.

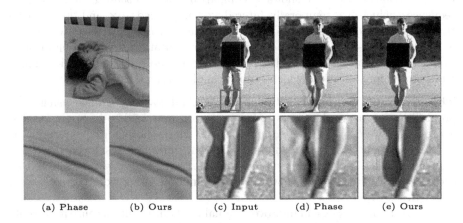

(a) Phase   (b) Ours   (c) Input   (d) Phase   (e) Ours

Fig. 4. Qualitative comparison. (a, b) *Baby* sequence (20×). (c, d, e) *Balance* sequence (8×). The phase-based method shows more ringing artifacts and blurring than ours near edges (left) and occlusion boundaries (right).

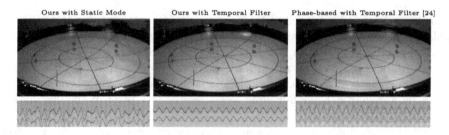

Fig. 5. Temporal filter reduces artifacts. Our method benefits from applying temporal filters (middle); blurring artifacts are reduced. Nonetheless, even without temporal filters (left), our method still preserves edges better than the phase-based method (right), which shows severe ringing artifacts.

4.1   Comparison with the State-of-the-Art

In this section, we compare our method with the state of the art. Because the Riesz pyramid [25] gives similar results as the steerable pyramids [24], we focus our comparison on the steerable pyramid. We perform both qualitative and quantitative evaluation as follows. All results in this section were processed with temporal filters unless otherwise noted.

Qualitative Comparison. Our method preserves edges well, and has fewer ringing artifacts. Figure 4 shows a comparison of the *balance* and the *baby* sequences, which are temporally filtered and magnified 10× and 20× respectively. The phase-based method shows significant ringing artifact, while ours is nearly artifact-free. This is because our representation is trained end-to-end from example motion, whereas the phase-based method relies on hand-designed multi-scale representation, which cannot handle strong edges well.

The Effect of Temporal Filters. Our method was not trained using temporal filters, so using the filters to select motion may lead to incorrect results. To test this, we consider the *guitar* sequence, which shows strings vibrating at different frequencies. Figure 7 shows the 25× magnification results on the *guitar* sequence using different temporal filters. The strings were correctly selected by each temporal filter, which shows that the temporal filters work correctly with our representation.

Temporal processing can improve the quality of our result, because it prevents our network from magnifying unwanted motion. Figure 5 shows a comparison on the *drum* sequence. The temporal filter reduces blurring artifacts present when we magnify using two frames (`static` mode). However, even without the use of the temporal filter, our method still preserves edges well, and show no ringing artifacts. In contrast, the phase-based method shows significant ringing artifacts even when the temporal filter is applied.

Two-Frames Setting Results. Applying our network with two-frames input corresponds best to its training. We consider magnifying consecutive frames using our network (`dynamic` mode), and compare the result with Zhang *et al.* [28].

Figure 6 shows the result of *gun* sequence, where we apply our network in the dynamic mode without a temporal filter. As before, our result is nearly artifact free, while Zhang *et al.* suffers from ringing artifacts and excessive blurring, because their method is also based on the complex steerable pyramid [24]. Note that our magnification factor in the dynamic mode may have a different meaning to that of Zhang *et al.*, but we found that for this particular sequence, using the same magnification factor (8×) produces a magnified motion which has roughly the same size.

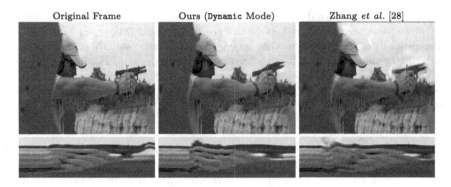

Fig. 6. Applying our network in 2-frame settings. We compare our network applied in dynamic mode to acceleration magnification [28]. Because [28] is based on the complex steerable pyramid, their result suffers from ringing artifacts and blurring.

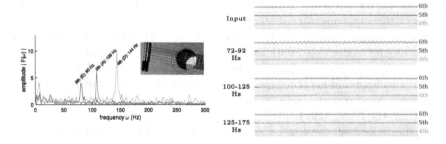

Fig. 7. Temporal filtering at different frequency bands. (Left) Intensity signal over the pixel on each string. (Right) y-t plot of the result using different temporal filters. Our representation is linear enough to be compatible with temporal filters. The strings from top to bottom correspond to the 6-th to 4-th strings. Each string vibrates at different frequencies, which are correctly selected by corresponding temporal filters. For visualization purpose, we invert the color of the $y - t$ slices.

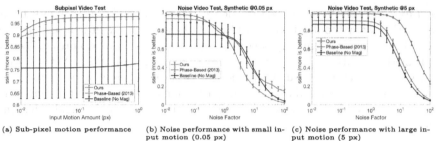

(a) Sub-pixel motion performance

(b) Noise performance with small input motion (0.05 px)

(c) Noise performance with large input motion (5 px)

Fig. 8. Quantitative analysis. (a) Subpixel test, our network performs well down to 0.01 pixels, and is consistently better than the phase-based [24]. (b, c) Noise tests at different levels of input motion. Our network's performance stays high and is consistently better than the phase-based whose performance drops to the baseline level as the noise factor exceeds 1. Our performance in (b) is worse than (c) because the motion is smaller, which is expected because a smaller motion is harder to be distinguished from noise.

Quantitative Analysis. The strength of motion magnification techniques lies in its ability to visualize sub-pixel motion at high magnification factors, while being resilient to noise. To quantify these strengths and understand the limit of our method, we quantitatively evaluate our method and compare it with the phase-based method on various factors. We want to focus on comparing the representation and not temporal processing, so we generate synthetic examples whose motion is a single-frequency sinusoid and use a temporal filter that has wide passband.[1] Because our network was trained without the temporal filter, we test our method without the temporal filter, but we use temporal filters with the phase-based method. We summarize the results in Fig. 8 and its parameter ranges in the supplementary material.

For the subpixel motion test, we generate synthetic data having foreground input motion ranging from 0.01 to 1 pixel. We vary the magnification factor α such that the magnified motion is 10 pixels. No noise was added. Additionally, we move the background for the same amount of motion but in a different direction to all foreground objects. This ensures that no method could do well by simply replicating the background.

In the noise test, we fixed the amount of input motion and magnification factor and added noise to the input frames. We do not move background in this case. To simulate photon noise, we create a noise image whose variance equals the value of each pixel in the original image. A multiplicative noise factor controls the final strength of noise image to be added.

---

[1] Our motion is 3 Hz at 30 fps, and the temporal filter used is a 30-tap FIR with a passband between 0.5–7.5 Hz.

Because the magnified motion is not very large (10 pixels), the input and the output magnified frames could be largely similar. We also calculate the SSIM between the input and output frames as a baseline reference in addition to the phase-based method.

In all tests, our method performs better than the phase-based method. As Fig. 8(a) shows, our sub-pixel performance remains high all the way down to 0.01 pixels, and it exceeds 1 standard deviation of the phase-based performance as the motion increase above 0.02 pixels. Interestingly, despite being trained only up to 100× magnification, the network performs considerably well at the smallest input motion (0.01), where magnification factor reaches 1,000×. This suggests that our network are more limited by the amount of output motion it needs to generate, rather than the magnification factors it was given.

Figure 8(b, c) show the test results under noisy conditions with different amounts of input motion. In all cases, the performance of our method is consistently higher than that of the phase-based method, which quickly drops to the level of the baseline as the noise factor increase above 1.0. Comparing across different input motion, our performance degrades faster as the input motion becomes smaller (See Fig. 8(b, c)). This is expected because when the motion is small, it becomes harder to distinguish actual motion from noise. Some video outputs from these tests are included in the supplementary material.

4.2   Physical Accuracy of Our Method

In nearly all of our *real* test videos, the resulting motions produced by our method have similar magnitude as, and are in phase with, the motions produced by [24] (see Fig. 1, and the supplementary videos). This shows that our method is at least as physically accurate as the phase-based method, while exhibiting fewer artifacts.

We also obtained the hammer sequence from the authors of [24], where accelerometer measurement was available. We integrated twice the accelerometer signal and used a zero-phase high-pass filter to remove drifts. As Fig. 10 shows, the resulting signal (blue line) matches up well with our 10× magnified (without temporal filter) result, suggesting that our method is physically accurate.

4.3   Visualizing Network Activation

Deep neural networks achieve high performance in a wide variety of vision tasks, but their inner working is still largely unknown [2]. In this section, we analyze our network to understand what it does, and show that it extracts relevant information to the task. We analyze the response of the encoder, by approximating it as a linear system. We pass several test images through the encoder, and calculate the average impulse responses across the images. Figure 9 shows the samples of the linear kernel approximation of the encoder's shape response. Many of these responses resemble Gabor filters and Laplacian filters, which suggests that our network learns to extract similar information as done by the complex steerable filters [24]. By contrast, the texture kernel responses show many blurring kernels.

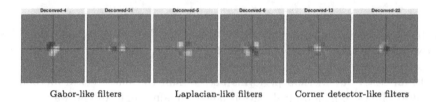

| Gabor-like filters | Laplacian-like filters | Corner detector-like filters |

Fig. 9. Approximate shape encoder kernel. We approximate our (non-linear) spatial encoder as linear convolution kernels and show top-8 by approximation error. These kernels resemble directional edge detector (left), Laplacian operator (middle), and corner detector-like (right).

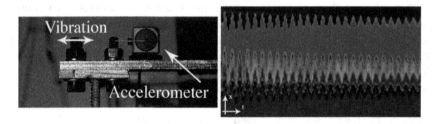

Fig. 10. Physical accuracy of our method Comparison between our magnified output and the twice-integrated accelerometer measurement (blue line). Our result and the accelerometer signal match closely. (Color figure online)

4.4   Limitations

While our network performs well in the 2-frame setting, its performance degrades with temporal filters when the magnification factor is high and motion is small. Figure 11 shows an example frame of temporally-filtered magnified synthetic videos with increasing the magnification factor. As the magnification factor increases, blurring becomes prominent, and strong color artifacts appear as the magnification factor exceeds what the network was trained on.

In some real videos, our method with temporal filter appears to be blind to very small motions. This results in patchy magnification where some patches get occasionally magnified when their motions are large enough for the network to see. Figure 12 shows our magnification results of the *eye* sequence compared to that of the phase-based method [24]. Our magnification result shows little motion, except on a few occasions, while the phase-based method reveals a richer motion of the iris. We expect to see some artifact on our network running with temporal filters, because it was not what it was trained on. However, this limits its usefulness in cases where the temporal filter is essential to selecting small motion of interest. Improving compatibility with the temporal filter will be an important direction for future work.

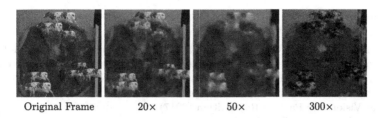

Original Frame   20×   50×   300×

Fig. 11. Temporal filtered result at high magnification. Our technique works well with temporal filter only at lower magnification factors. The quality degrades as the magnification factor increases beyond 20×.

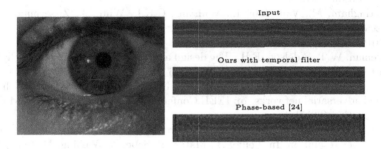

Fig. 12. One of our failure cases. Our method is not fully compatible with the temporal filter. This *eye* sequence has a small motion that requires a temporal filter to extract. Our method is blind to this motion and produces a relatively still motion, while the phase-based method is able to reveal it.

5   Conclusion

Current motion magnification techniques are based on hand-designed filters, and are prone to noise and excessive blurring. We present a new learning-based motion magnification method that seeks to learn the filters directly from data. We simplify training by using the two-frames input setting to make it tractable. We generate a set of carefully designed synthetic data that captures aspects of small motion well. Despite these simplifications, we show that our network performs well, and has less edge artifact and better noise characteristics than the state of the arts. Our method is compatible with temporal filters, and yielded good results up to a moderate magnification factor. Improving compatibility with temporal filters so that it works at higher magnification is an important direction for future work.

Acknowledgment. The authors would like to thank Qatar Computing Research Institute, Toyota Research Institute, and Shell Research for their generous support of this project. Changil Kim was supported by a Swiss National Science Foundation fellowship P2EZP2 168785.

References

1. Balakrishnan, G., Durand, F., Guttag, J.: Detecting pulse from head motions in video. In: IEEE Conference on Computer Vision and Pattern Recognition (2013)
2. Bau, D., Zhou, B., Khosla, A., Oliva, A., Torralba, A.: Network dissection: quantifying interpretability of deep visual representations. In: IEEE Conference on Computer Vision and Pattern Recognition (2017)
3. Cha, Y.J., Chen, J., Büyüköztürk, O.: Output-only computer vision based damage detection using phase-based optical flow and unscented Kalman filters. Eng. Struct. **132**, 300–313 (2017)
4. Elgharib, M.A., Hefeeda, M., Durand, F., Freeman, W.T.: Video magnification in presence of large motions. In: IEEE Conference on Computer Vision and Pattern Recognition (2015)
5. Everingham, M., Van Gool, L., Williams, C.K.I., Winn, J., Zisserman, A.: The pascal visual object classes (VOC) challenge. Int. J. Comput. Vis. **88**(2), 303–338 (2010)
6. Freeman, W.T., Adelson, E.H.: The design and use of steerable filters. IEEE Trans. Pattern Anal. Mach. Intell. **13**(9), 891–906 (1991)
7. Isola, P., Zhu, J.Y., Zhou, T., Efros, A.A.: Image-to-image translation with conditional adversarial networks. In: IEEE Conference on Computer Vision and Pattern Recognition (2017)
8. Johnson, J., Alahi, A., Fei-Fei, L.: Perceptual losses for real-time style transfer and super-resolution. In: Leibe, B., Matas, J., Sebe, N., Welling, M. (eds.) ECCV 2016. LNCS, vol. 9906, pp. 694–711. Springer, Cham (2016). https://doi.org/10.1007/978-3-319-46475-6_43
9. Jones, M.J., Poggio, T.: Multidimensional morphable models: a framework for representing and matching object classes. Int. J. Comput. Vis. **29**(2), 107–131 (1998)
10. Kalantari, N.K., Wang, T.C., Ramamoorthi, R.: Learning-based view synthesis for light field cameras. ACM Trans. Graph. (SIGGRAPH Asia) **35**(6), 193–10 (2016)
11. Kingma, D.P., Ba, J.: Adam: a method for stochastic optimization. arXiv preprint arXiv:1412.6980 (2014)
12. Lin, T.-Y., et al.: Microsoft COCO: common objects in context. In: Fleet, D., Pajdla, T., Schiele, B., Tuytelaars, T. (eds.) ECCV 2014. LNCS, vol. 8693, pp. 740–755. Springer, Cham (2014). https://doi.org/10.1007/978-3-319-10602-1_48
13. Liu, C., Torralba, A., Freeman, W.T., Durand, F., Adelson, E.H.: Motion magnification. ACM Trans. Graph. (SIGGRAPH) **24**(3), 519–526 (2005)
14. Liu, Z., Yeh, R.A., Tang, X., Liu, Y., Agarwala, A.: Video frame synthesis using deep voxel flow. In: IEEE International Conference on Computer Vision (2017)
15. Long, J., Shelhamer, E., Darrell, T.: Fully convolutional networks for semantic segmentation. In: IEEE Conference on Computer Vision and Pattern Recognition (2015)
16. Mathieu, M., Couprie, C., LeCun, Y.: Deep multi-scale video prediction beyond mean square error. In: International Conference on Learning Representations (2016)
17. Niklaus, S., Mai, L., Liu, F.: Video frame interpolation via adaptive convolution. In: IEEE Conference on Computer Vision and Pattern Recognition (2017)
18. Niklaus, S., Mai, L., Liu, F.: Video frame interpolation via adaptive separable convolution. In: IEEE International Conference on Computer Vision (2017)

19. Odena, A., Dumoulin, V., Olah, C.: Deconvolution and checkerboard artifacts. Distill **1**(10), e3 (2016)
20. Radford, A., Metz, L., Chintala, S.: Unsupervised representation learning with deep convolutional generative adversarial networks. arXiv preprint arXiv:1511.06434 (2015)
21. Sajjadi, M.S., Schölkopf, B., Hirsch, M.: EnhanceNet: single image super-resolution through automated texture synthesis. In: IEEE International Conference on Computer Vision (2017)
22. Srivastava, N., Mansimov, E., Salakhudinov, R.: Unsupervised learning of video representations using LSTMs. In: International Conference on Machine Learning (2015)
23. Villegas, R., Yang, J., Hong, S., Lin, X., Lee, H.: Decomposing motion and content for natural video sequence prediction. In: International Conference on Learning Representations (2017)
24. Wadhwa, N., Rubinstein, M., Durand, F., Freeman, W.T.: Phase-based video motion processing. ACM Trans. Graph. (SIGGRAPH) **32**(4), 80 (2013)
25. Wadhwa, N., Rubinstein, M., Durand, F., Freeman, W.T.: Riesz pyramids for fast phase-based video magnification. In: IEEE International Conference on Computational Photography (2014)
26. Wang, T., Zhu, J., Kalantari, N.K., Efros, A.A., Ramamoorthi, R.: Light field video capture using a learning-based hybrid imaging system. ACM Trans. Graph. (SIGGRAPH) **36**(4), 133:1–133:13 (2017)
27. Wu, H.Y., Rubinstein, M., Shih, E., Guttag, J., Durand, F., Freeman, W.: Eulerian video magnification for revealing subtle changes in the world. ACM Trans. Graph. (SIGGRAPH) **31**(4), 65–8 (2012)
28. Zhang, Y., Pintea, S.L., van Gemert, J.C.: Video acceleration magnification. In: IEEE Conference on Computer Vision and Pattern Recognition (2017)

Massively Parallel Video Networks

João Carreira[1], Viorica Pătrăucean[1(✉)], Laurent Mazare[1],
Andrew Zisserman[1,2], and Simon Osindero[1]

[1] DeepMind, London, UK
joaoluis@google.com, viorica@google.com, laurent.mazare@gmail.com,
zisserman@google.com, osindero@google.com
[2] Department of Engineering Science, University of Oxford, Oxford, UK

Abstract. We introduce a class of causal video understanding models that aims to improve efficiency of video processing by maximising throughput, minimising latency, and reducing the number of clock cycles. Leveraging operation pipelining and multi-rate clocks, these models perform a minimal amount of computation (e.g. as few as four convolutional layers) for each frame per timestep to produce an output. The models are still very deep, with dozens of such operations being performed but in a pipelined fashion that enables depth-parallel computation. We illustrate the proposed principles by applying them to existing image architectures and analyse their behaviour on two video tasks: action recognition and human keypoint localisation. The results show that a significant degree of parallelism, and implicitly speedup, can be achieved with little loss in performance.

Keywords: Video processing · Pipelining · Depth-parallelism

1 Introduction

There is a rich structure in videos that is neglected when treating them as a set of still images. Perhaps the most explored benefit of videos is the ability to improve performance by aggregating information over multiple frames [1–3], which enforces temporal smoothness and reduces the uncertainty in tasks that are temporal by nature, e.g., change detection [4], computing optical flow [5], resolving action ambiguities (standing up/sitting down) [6] etc. An underexplored direction, however, is the ability to improve the processing efficiency. In this paper, we focus on this aspect in the context of the causal, frame-by-frame operation mode that is relevant for real-time applications, and show how to transform slow models to ones that can run at frame rate with negligible loss of accuracy.

J. Carreira and V. Pătrăucean—Shared first authors

Electronic supplementary material The online version of this chapter (https://doi.org/10.1007/978-3-030-01225-0_40) contains supplementary material, which is available to authorized users.

Most existing state-of-the-art computer vision systems, such as object detectors [7–9], process video frames independently: each new frame goes through up to one hundred convolutional layers before the output is known and another frame can be processed. This sequential operation in both depth and time can pose several problems: it can limit the rate at which predictions can be made, it can increase the minimum latency with which good predictions are available, and it can also lead to under-utilisation of hardware resources.

General-purpose computer processors encounter the same challenge when executing sequences of program instructions and address it with efficient pipelining strategies, that enable parallel computations. This also resembles the operation mode of biological neurons, which are not tremendously fast, but come in large numbers and operate in a massively parallel fashion [10].

Our proposed design employs similar pipelining strategies, and we make four contributions: first, we propose pipelining schemes tailored to sequence models (we call this *predictive depth-parallelism*); second, we show how such architectures can be augmented using *multi-rate clocks* and how they benefit from skip connections. These designs can be incorporated into any deep image architecture, to increase their throughput (frame rate) by a large factor (up to 10x in our experiments) when applied on videos. However they may also negatively impact accuracy. To reduce this impact, and as a third contribution, we show that it is possible to get better parallel models by *distilling* them from sequential ones and, as a final contribution, we explore other wiring patterns – *temporal filters and feedback* – that improve the expressivity of the resulting models. Collectively, this results in video networks with the ability to make accurate predictions at very high frame rates.

We will discuss related work in the next section. Then, we will move on to describe predictive depth-parallelism, multi-rate clocks and our other technical contributions in Sect. 3. In Sect. 4 we present our main experiments on two types of prediction tasks with different latency requirements: human keypoint localisation (which requires predicting a dense heatmap for each frame in a video); and action recognition (where a single label is predicted for an entire video clip), before the paper concludes.

2   Related Work

The majority of existing video models rely on image models [11–13] executed frame-by-frame, the main challenge being to speed up the image models to process sequentially 25 frames per second. This can be achieved by simplifying the models, either by identifying accurate architectures with fewer parameters [14], by pruning them post-training [15], or by using low-bit representation formats [16]. All of these can be combined with our approach.

A different type of model incorporates recurrent connections [17–19] for propagating information between time steps [18,19]. One simple propagation scheme, used by Zhu et al. [20] proposed periodically warping old activations given fresh external optical flow as input, rather than recomputing them. Our pipelining strategy has the advantage that it does not require external inputs nor special warping modules. Instead, it places the burden on learning.

There are also models that consider the video as a volume by stacking the frames and applying 3D convolutions to extract spatio-temporal features [6,21]. These models scale well and can be trained on large-scale datasets [22–24] due to the use of larger temporal convolution strides at deeper layers. Although they achieve state-of-the-art performance on tasks such as action recognition, these methods still use purely sequential processing in depth (all layers must execute before proceeding to a next input). Moreover, they are not causal – the 3D convolutional kernels extract features from future frames, which makes it challenging to use these models in real-time.

In the causal category, a number of hierarchical architectures have been proposed around the notion of *clocks*, attaching to each module a possibly different clock rate, yielding temporally multi-scale models that scale better to long sequences [25]. The clock rates can be hard-coded [26] or learnt from data [27]. Some recent models [28,29] activate different modules of the network based on the temporal and spatial variance of the inputs, respectively, yielding adaptive clocks. There is also a group of time-budget methods that focuses on reducing latency. If the available time runs out before the data has traversed the entire network, then emergency exits are used to output whatever predictions have been computed thus far [30,31]. This differs from our approach which aims for constant low-latency output.

Ideas related to pipelining were discussed in [28]; a recent paper also proposed pipelining strategies for speeding up backpropagation for faster training in distributed systems [32–34]. Instead, we focus on pipelining at inference time, to reduce latency and maximise frame rate.

3   Efficient Online Video Models

Consider the directed graph obtained by unrolling a video model with n layers over time (see Fig. 1), where the layers of the network are represented by the nodes and the activations transferred between layers are represented by the edges of the graph. All the parameters are shared across time steps. Edges create dependencies in the computational graph and require sequential processing. Video processing can be efficiently parallelised in the offline case, by processing different frames in different computing cores, but not in the online case.

Depth-Parallel Networks. In basic depth-sequential video models, the input to each layer is the output of the previous layer at the same time step, and the network outputs a prediction only after all the layers have processed in sequence the current frame; see Fig. 1(a). In the proposed design, every layer in the network processes its input, passes the activations to the next layer, and immediately starts processing the next input available, without waiting for the whole network to finish computation for the current frame; Fig. 1(b). This is achieved by substituting in the unrolled graph the vertical edges by diagonal ones, so the input to each layer is still the output from the previous layer,

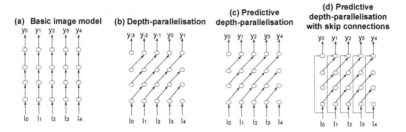

Fig. 1. Illustration of a standard sequential video model that processes frames independently, and depth-parallel versions. The horizontal direction represents the time and the vertical direction represents the depth of the network. The throughput of the basic image model depicted in (**a**) can be increased for real-time video processing using depth-parallelisation, shown in (**b**). This makes it possible to, given a new frame, process all layers in parallel, increasing throughput if parallel resources are available. But this also introduces a delay of a few frames – in this example, the output at time t corresponds to the input at time $t - 3$. It is possible to train the network to anticipate the correct output in order to reduce the latency (**c**). This task can be made easier if the model has skip-connections, as illustrated in (**d**) – this way the model has access to some fresh features (albeit these fresh features have limited computational depth).

as usual, but *from the previous time step*. This makes it possible to process all layers at one time step in parallel, given enough computing cores, since there are no dependencies between them.

Latency and Throughput. We define *computational latency*, or just latency, as the time delay between the moment when a frame is fed to the network and the moment when the network outputs a prediction for that frame. It is the sum of the execution times of all layers for processing a frame. We consider *throughput* as the output rate of a network, i.e. for how many frames does the network output predictions for in a time unit. For the sequential model, throughput is roughly the inverse of the computational latency, hence the deeper the model, the higher the computational latency and the lower the throughput. Here resides a quality of the proposed depth-parallel models: irrespective of the depth, the model can now make predictions at the rate of its slowest layer.

It is useful to also consider the concepts of *information latency* as the number of frames it takes before the input signal reaches the output layer along the network's shortest path. For example, in Fig. 1, the information latency for the video model illustrated in (a) is 0, and for the model in (b) it is equal to 3. We define *prediction latency* as the displacement measured in frames between the moment when a network receives a frame and the moment when the network tries to emit the corresponding output. The prediction latency is a training choice and can have any value. Whenever the prediction latency is smaller than the information latency, the network must make a prediction for an input that it did not process yet completely.

For most of our experiments with depth-parallel models we used a prediction latency of zero based on the assumption that videos may be predictable over short horizons and we train the network to compensate for the delay in its inputs and operate in a predictive fashion; see Fig. 1(c). But the higher the information latency, the more challenging it is to operate with prediction latency of zero. We employ temporal skip connections to minimise the information latency of the different layers in the network, as illustrated in Fig. 1(d). This provides fresher (but shallower) inputs to deeper layers. We term this overall paradigm *predictive depth-parallelism*. We experimented thoroughly with the setting where prediction latency is zero and also report results with slightly higher values (e.g. 2 frames).

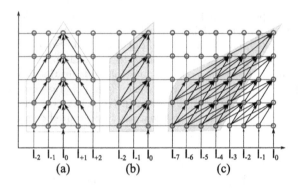

Fig. 2. Temporal receptive fields of: **(a)** standard; **(b)** causal; and **(c)** pipelined models.

Pipelined Operations and Temporal Receptive Field. Depth-parallelism has implications regarding the temporal receptive field of the network. In any standard neural network, by design, the temporal receptive field of a layer, i.e. the frames its input data comes from, is always a subset of the temporal receptive field of the next deeper layer in the network, resulting in a symmetric triangular shape; see Fig. 2(a). Stacked temporal convolutions and pooling layers are used for increasing the temporal visual field for deeper layers. In causal models the temporal receptive field is a right-angled triangle – no layer in the network has access to future frames; see Fig. 2(b). In the proposed design, the temporal receptive field along the depth of the network has a skewed triangular shape, the shallower layers having access to frames that the deeper layers cannot yet see (information latency). For example in Fig. 2(c), the latest frame that the deepest layer can see at time $t = 0$ is the frame I_{-4}, assuming a temporal kernel of 3, which, since we define a prediction latency of zero, means it must predict the output 4 frames in advance. Adding temporal skip connections reduces the information latency; at the extreme the receptive field becomes similar to the causal one, bringing it to zero.

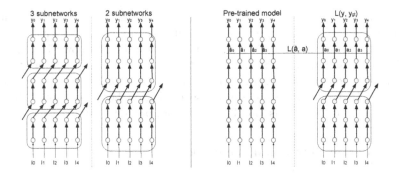

Fig. 3. Left: neural networks with three parallel subnetworks of two layers and two parallel subnetworks of three layers. **Right**: sequential-to-parallel distillation, the additional loss $L(\hat{a}, a)$ leverages intermediate activations of the pre-trained sequential model.

Levels of Parallelism. For simplicity, the proposed design ideas were illustrated in Fig. 1 using the "extreme" models, i.e.: (a) which is fully-sequential (with only vertical edges); and (b–c): which are fully parallel (lacking any vertical edge). However, there is a whole space of semi-parallel models in between, which makes it possible to trade off accuracy and efficiency.

A simple strategy to transform an image model with a linear-chain layer-architecture into a semi-parallel video model is to traverse the network starting from the first layer, and group together contiguous layers into sequential blocks of k layers that we will call *parallel subnetworks* and which can execute independently – see the two diagrams on the right side of Fig. 3, left; basic pseudocode is given in the supp. material.

3.1 Multi-rate Clocks

Features extracted deeper in a neural network tend to be more abstract and to vary less over time [28], obeying the so-called *slowness principle* [35] – fast varying observations can be explained by slow varying latent factors. For example, when tracking a non-rigid moving object, the contours, which are shallow features, change rapidly, but the identity of the object typically does not change at all. Since not all features change at the same rate as the input rate, it is then possible to reduce computation by reusing, and not recomputing, the deeper, more abstract, features. This can be implemented by having multi-rate clocks: whenever the clock of a layer does not tick, that layer does not compute activations, instead it reuses the existing ones. 3D ConvNets implement this principle by using temporal strides but does not keep state and hence cannot efficiently operate frame-by-frame. In our recurrent setting, multi-rate clocks can be implemented by removing nodes from the unrolled graph and preserving an internal state to cache outputs until the next slower-ticking layer can consume them. We used a set of fixed rates in our models, typically reducing clock rates by a factor of two whenever spatial resolution is halved. Instead of just using identity to create the internal state as we did, one could use any spatial recurrent module (conv. versions of vanilla RNNs or LSTMs). This design is shown in Fig. 4(d).

For pixelwise prediction tasks, the state tensors from the last layer of a given spatial resolution are also passed through skip connections, bilinearly upsampled and concatenated as input to the dense prediction head, similar to the skip connections in FCN models [36], but arise from previous time steps[1].

3.2   Temporal Filters and Feedback

The success of depth-parallelism and multi-rate clocks depends on the network being able to learn to compensate for otherwise delayed, possibly stale inputs, which may be feasible since videos are quite redundant and scene dynamics are predictable over short temporal horizons. One way to make learning easier would seem to be by using units with temporal filters. These have shown their worth in a variety of video models [6,21,38]. We illustrate the use of temporal filters in Fig. 4(b) as *temporalisation*. Interestingly, depth-paralellisation by itself also induces temporalisation in models with skip connections.

For dense predictions tasks, we experimented with adding a feedback connection – the outputs of the previous frame are fed as inputs to the early layers of the network (e.g. stacking them with the output of the first conv. layer). The idea is that previous outputs provide a simple starting solution with rich semantics which can be refined in few layers – similar to several recent papers [39–43]. This design is shown in Fig. 4(c).

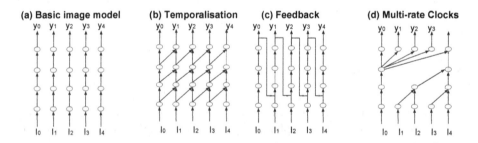

Fig. 4. Basic image models (left) can be extended along the temporal domain using different patterns of connectivity. Temporalisation adds additional inputs to the different computation nodes, increasing their temporal receptive field. Feedback re-injects past high-level activations to the bottom of the network. Both connectivity patterns aim to improve the expressivity of the models. For increasing throughput, having multi-rate clocks avoids always computing deeper activations (here shown for a temporal model), and instead past activations are copied periodically.

---

[1] More sophisticated trainable decoders, such as those in U-Nets [37], could also be used in a similar pipelined fashion as the encoder.

3.3   Sequential-to-Parallel "Distillation"

The proposed parallel models reduce latency, but their computational depth for the current frame at the moment where they produce an output is also reduced compared to their fully sequential counterparts; additionally they are designed to re-use features from previous states through the multi-rate clocks mechanism. These properties typically make learning more difficult. In order to improve the accuracy of our parallel models, we adopt a strategy similar to distillation [44], or to Ladder networks [45], wherein a *teacher* network is privileged relative to a *student* network, either due to having a greater capacity or (in the case of Ladder networks) access to greater amounts of information.

In our case, we consider the sequential model as the teacher, since all of its layers always have access to fresh features extracted from the current frame. We first train a causal fully-sequential model with the same overall architecture as the parallel model. Then we modify the loss of the parallel model to encourage its activations to match those of the sequential model for some given layers, while still minimising the original classification error, such that it predicts how the abstract features would have looked, had the information from the current frame been available. This is illustrated for one layer on the right side of Fig. 3. In our experiment we used the average of this new loss over $m = 3$ layers. The overall loss L_d with distillation is:

$$L_d = L(y, y_{gt}) + \lambda \sum_{i=1}^{m} \frac{1}{n_i} \left\| \hat{a}^{(i)} - a^{(i)} \right\|^2$$

where $L(y, y_{gt})$ is the initial cross-entropy loss between the predictions of the parallel network y and the ground truth y_{gt}, and the second term is the normalised Euclidean distance between the activations of the pre-trained sequential model $\hat{a}^{(i)}$ for layer i and the activation of the parallel model $a^{(i)}$ for the same layer; n_i denotes the number of feature channels of layer i. A parameter λ is used to weight the two components of the new loss. We set $\lambda = 1$ for the dense keypoint prediction and $\lambda = 100$ for action recognition.

4   Experiments

We applied the proposed principles starting from two popular image classification models: a 54 layer DenseNet [12] and Inception [11], which has 22 conv. layers. We chose these models due to their differences in connectivity. Inception has some built-in parallelism due to the parallel branches in the Inception blocks. DenseNet has no parallelism and instead has dense skip connections within blocks, which helps reduce information latency when parallelised. Full details on the architectures are provided in the supp. material.

We instantiated a number of model variations using the principles set in the previous section. In all cases we are interested in the online, causal setting (i.e. no peeking into the future), where efficiency matters the most. In the majority of the experiments we trained models with 0 prediction latency (e.g. the output at time t should correspond to the input at time t), the most challenging setting. We name pipelined DenseNet models as Par-DenseNet and Inception-based models as Par-Inception.

For evaluation, we considered two tasks having different latency and throughput requirements: (1) action classification, where the network must output only one label prediction for the entire video sequence, and (2) human keypoint localisation, where the network must output dense per-frame predictions for the locations of human joints – in our case spatial heatmaps for the keypoints of interest (see Fig. 5).

Table 1. Test accuracy as percentage for action recognition on the miniKinetics dataset [46], using networks with multi-rate clocks and temporal filters. The number of parallel subnetworks is shown in the second column. For the semi-parallel case, Par-Inception uses 5 parallel subnetworks and Par-DenseNet 7. The non-causal, single subnetwork Par-Inception in the first row is equivalent to the I3D model [6].

Model	#Par. Subnets	Par-Inception Top-1	Par-Dense. Top-1
Non-causal	1	71.8	-
Sequential causal	1	71.4	67.6
Semi-parallel causal	5 (7)	66.0	61.3
Parallel causal	10 (14)	54.5	54.0

The dataset for training and evaluation in all cases was miniKinetics [46], which has 80k training videos and 5k test videos. MiniKinetics is a subset of the larger Kinetics [24], but more pratical when studying many factors of variation. For heatmap estimation we populated miniKinetics automatically with poses from a state-of-the-art 2D pose estimation method [47] – that we will call *baseline* from now on – and used those as ground truth. This resulted in a total of 20 million training frames[2].

4.1   Action Recognition

For this task we experimented with three levels of depth-parallelism for both architectures: fully sequential, 5, and 10 parallel subnetworks for Par-Inception models and fully sequential, 7, and 14 parallel subnetworks for Par-DenseNet models. Table 1 presents the results in terms of Top-1 accuracy on miniKinetics. The accuracy of the original I3D model [6] on miniKinetics is 78.3%, as reported in [46]. This model is non-causal, but otherwise equivalent to the fully sequential version of our Par-Inception[3].

---

[2] This is far higher than the largest 2D pose video dataset, PoseTrack [48], which has just 20k annotated frames, hardly sufficient for training large video models from scratch (although cleanly annotated instead of automatically).

[3] Note that this was pre-trained using ImageNet, hence it has a significant advantage over all our models that are trained from scratch.

There is a progressive degradation in performance as more depth-parallelism is added, i.e. as the models become faster and faster, illustrating the trade-off between speedup and accuracy. One possible explanation is the narrowing of the temporal receptive field, shown in Fig. 2. The activations of the last frames in each training clip do not get to be processed by the last classifier layer, which is equivalent to training on shorter sequences – a factor known to impact negatively the classification accuracy. We intend to increase the length of the clips in future work to explore this further. Promisingly, the loss in accuracy can be reduced partially by just using distillation; see Subsect. 4.3.

4.2   Human Keypoint Localisation

For this task we experimented with 5 different levels of depth-parallelism for Par-DenseNet: fully sequential and 2, 4, 7 and 14 parallel subnetworks. For Par-Inception, we used three different depth-parallelism levels: fully sequential, 5, and 10 parallel subnetworks. We employed a weighted sigmoid cross-entropy loss. Since the heatmaps contain mostly background (no-joint) pixels, we found it essential to weight the importance of the keypoint pixels in the loss – we used a factor of 10. For evaluation, we report results on the miniKinetics test set in terms of weighted sigmoid cross-entropy loss.

Results using the pipelining connectivity with multi-rate clock models are shown in Fig. 6, left. For both models, it can be observed that the performance improves as more layers are allowed to execute in sequence. Par-Inception has slightly better performance for higher degrees of parallelism, perhaps due to its built-in parallelism; Par-DenseNet models become better as less parallelism is used.

Since Par-DenseNet offers more possibilities for parallelisation, we used it to investigate more designs, i.e.: with/without multi-rate clocks, temporal filters and feedback. The results are shown in Fig. 6, right. Versions with temporal filters do better than without except for the most parallel models – these have intrinsically temporal receptive fields because of the skip connections in time, without needing explicit temporal filters. Feedback helps slightly. Clocks degrade accuracy a little but provide big speedups (see Subsect. 4.6). We show predictions for two test videos in Fig. 5.

4.3   Sequential to Parallel Distillation

As mentioned in Sect. 3, we investigated training first a sequential model, then fitting the parallel model to a subset of its activations in addition to the original loss function. This led to significant improvements for both models. The parallel causal Par-Inception model obtains a relative improvement in accuracy of about 12%, from 54.5% to 61.2% for action recognition. The improvement for multi-rate Par-DenseNet model on the keypoint localisation task is shown in Fig. 7.

4.4 Training Specifically for Depth-Parallelism

Is it important to train a model specifically for operating in parallel mode or can we rewire a pretrained sequential model and it will work just as well at inference time? We ran an experiment where we initialiased Par-DenseNet models with different levels of parallelism with the weights from the DenseNet fully sequential model and ran inference on the miniKinetics test set. The results are shown in Fig. 8, left, and indicate the importance of training with depth-parallelism enabled, so the network learns to behave predictively. We similarly evaluated the test loss of Par-DenseNet models with different levels of parallelism when initialised from a fully-parallel trained model. As expected, in this case the behaviour does not change much.

Par-DenseNet models with 14 parallel subnetworks, without clocks

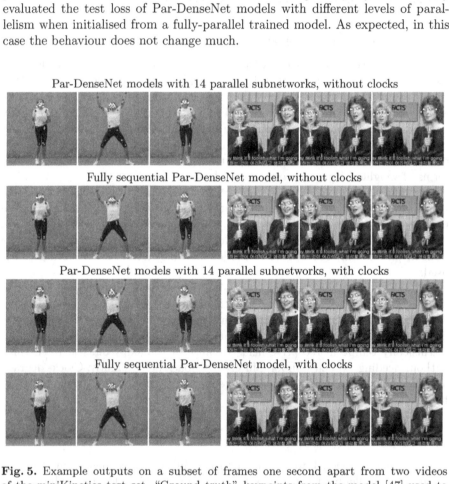

Fully sequential Par-DenseNet model, without clocks

Par-DenseNet models with 14 parallel subnetworks, with clocks

Fully sequential Par-DenseNet model, with clocks

Fig. 5. Example outputs on a subset of frames one second apart from two videos of the miniKinetics test set. "Ground truth" keypoints from the model [47] used to automatically annotate the dataset are shown as triangles, our models predictions are shown as circles. Note that the parallel models exhibit some lag when the legs move quickly on the video on the left. Best seen zoomed on a computer screen in color. (Color figure online)

4.5   Effect of Higher Prediction Latency

All the results above were obtained when training for 0 frames of prediction latency. However, if a parallel model is several times faster than a sequential one, we can afford to introduce a prediction latency greater than zero frames. Figure 8, right, shows results for Par-DenseNet models in this setting. As expected, the test loss decreases as the prediction latency increases, since more layers get to process the input frame before a prediction needs to be made. Strikingly, by using a predictive delay of 2 frames, models with up to 4 depth-parallel subnetworks are as accurate as fully sequential models with 0 frame predictive latency.

4.6   Efficiency Measurements

In this section, we present the efficiency improvements achieved by the proposed models, comparing the cases with and without multi-rate clocks and with different numbers of parallel subnetworks. Our parallel models improve efficiency under the assumption that parallel computation resources are available. We benchmark our models on CPUs and GPUs by running inference on a CPU with 48 cores and on hosts with 2, 4, and 8 k40 GPUs, respectively. The GPUs were on the same machine to avoid network latency. For benchmarking, each model is run on 3000 frames and we average the time used to process each frame. Results are presented in Table 2. A figure illustrating the loss in accuracy as the throughput is increased can be found in the supp. material.

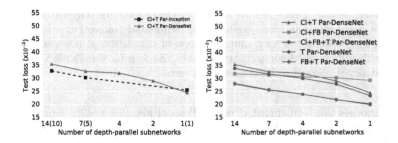

Fig. 6. Weighted sigmoid cross-entropy (lower is better) for human keypoint localisation on miniKinetics test set for zero prediction latency. "Cl" denotes models with multi-rate clocks, "T" – models with temporal filters, "FB" – models with feedback. **Left**: Comparison between Par-Inception and Par-DenseNet for different levels of parallelism. Note that in terms of number of sequential convolutions, 14 subnetworks for Par-DenseNet are equivalent to 10 subnetworks for Par-Inception, and similar for 7(5). **Right**: Variations of Par-DenseNet. In the absence of parallelisation (1 subnetwork), the accuracy of the best models with multi-rate clocks is just slightly worse to that of a much slower sequential model. Parallelisation penalises the accuracy of models with clocks more. The basic Par-DenseNet can have up to 4 parallel subnetworks with modest drop of accuracy.

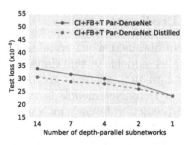

Fig. 7. Comparison between the weighted sigmoid cross-entropy (lower is better) of models with different levels of parallelism and the same models distilled from sequential for human keypoint localisation on miniKinetics test set for zero prediction latency. Results presented for a DenseNet model with multi-rate clocks ("Cl"), temporal filters ("T"), and feedback ("FB"). See text for details.

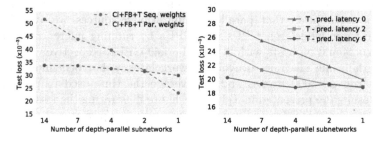

Fig. 8. **Left**: Seq. weights - Behaviour of Par-DenseNet with different levels of parallelism at inference time when trained with sequential connectivity. Par. weights - behaviour of Par-DenseNet with different levels of parallelism at inference time when trained with fully-parallel connectivity. **Right**: Test loss for Par-DenseNet when prediction latency is allowed to be greater than zero.

Our models are implemented using TensorFlow (TF) [49], hence: (1) when running on a multi-core CPU, we can run multiple operations in parallel and to parallelise a single operation, e.g., for conv layers. This means that the sequential model becomes faster with more cores, but only up to a certain point, when the overhead cancels out the gain from parallelism. The proposed parallel models benefit far more from having many CPU cores. (2) Multiple operations cannot run in parallel on the same GPU, hence there is little benefit in running our models on a single GPU. (3) A single operation cannot be split between GPUs. This explains why the sequential image model performance does not improve with more GPUs.

Par-DenseNet. Our Par-DenseNet architecture has a total of $4 + 8 + 8 + 6 = 26$ miniblocks so when using 14 parallel subnetworks, each parallel subnetwork is made of at most 2 miniblocks. When not using multi-rate clocks, 26 miniblocks are executed for each frame resulting in 416 miniblocks executions for a sequence of 16 frames. However when using multi-rate clocks, only 86 miniblocks are executed for such a sequence, which theoretically results in a speedup of 4.8×. We observe some smaller speedup but this is likely to be explained by the miniblocks having different sizes.

Par-Inception. Our models have 9 inception blocks. The most parallel version uses 10 parallel subnetworks: one for the initial convolutions and one for each inception block. For the sequential version, roughly a third of the time is spent on these initial convolutions. This explains why we do not observe speedups greater than 3 for the models without clocks when using more GPUs and we do not see much difference between using 4 and 8 GPU. More details together with execution timelines are included in the supp. material.

Table 2. Throughput improvement factors for Par-DenseNet and Par-Inception models relative to a sequential network without multi-rate clocks. For Par-DenseNet the fastest model processes 7x more frames per second, whereas the fastest Par-Inception model processes 5x more frames per second; see supp. material for absolute numbers in frames per second.

Model	# Par. subnets	48 cores	2 GPUs	4 GPUs	8 GPUs
Par-DenseNet without multi-rate clocks					
Sequential	1	1.0	1.0	1.0	1.0
Semi-parallel	2	1.3	1.6	1.7	1.7
Semi-parallel	4	1.8	1.7	2.5	2.9
Semi-parallel	7	2.2	1.6	2.6	3.7
parallel	14	2.6	1.7	2.7	3.8
Par-DenseNet with multi-rate clocks					
Sequential	1	2.6	3.4	3.4	3.4
Semi-parallel	2	3.0	3.9	4.0	4.0
Semi-parallel	4	3.6	4.5	5.1	5.2
Semi-parallel	7	4.6	4.5	5.6	6.1
Parallel	14	5.1	5.0	6.2	7.4
Par-Inception without multi-rate clocks					
Sequential	1	1.0	1.0	1.0	1.0
Semi-parallel	5	1.3	1.8	2.7	2.7
Parallel	10	1.3	1.8	2.6	2.6
Par-Inception with multi-rate clocks					
Sequential	1	2.4	2.6	2.6	2.6
Semi-parallel	5	3.0	3.4	5.0	5.0
Parallel	10	3.0	3.4	4.9	5.0

5 Conclusion

We introduced the paradigm of processing video sequences using networks that are constrained in the amount of sequential processing they can perform, with the goal of improving their efficiency. As a first exploration of this problem, we proposed a family of models where the number of sequential layers per frame is a design parameter and we evaluated how performance degrades as the allowed number of sequential layers is reduced. We have also shown that more accurate parallel models can be learned by distilling their sequential versions. We benchmarked the performance of these models considering different amounts of available parallel resources together with multi-rate clocks, and analysed the trade-off between accuracy and speedup. Interestingly, we found that the proposed design patterns can bring a speedup of up to 3× to 4× over a basic model that processes frames independently, without significant loss in performance in human action recognition and human keypoint localisation tasks. These are also general techniques – applicable to any state-of-the-art model in order to process video more efficiently. As future work we plan to investigate further the space of possible wirings using automated strategies.

Acknowledgements. We thank Carl Doersch, Relja Arandjelovic, Evan Shelhamer, and Dominic Grewe for valuable discussions and feedback on this work, and Tom Runia for finding typos in our architecture specification.

References

1. Jampani, V., Gadde, R., Gehler, P.V.: Video propagation networks. In: 2017 IEEE Conference on Computer Vision and Pattern Recognition, CVPR 2017, Honolulu, HI, USA, 21–26 July 2017, pp. 3154–3164. IEEE Computer Society (2017)
2. Pfister, T., Charles, J., Zisserman, A.: Flowing convnets for human pose estimation in videos. In: 2015 IEEE International Conference on Computer Vision, ICCV 2015, Santiago, Chile, 7–13 December 2015, pp. 1913–1921. IEEE Computer Society (2015)
3. Zhu, X., Wang, Y., Dai, J., Yuan, L., Wei, Y.: Flow-guided feature aggregation for video object detection. In: IEEE International Conference on Computer Vision, ICCV 2017, Venice, Italy, 22–29 October 2017, pp. pp. 408–417. IEEE Computer Society (2017)
4. Alcantarilla, P.F., Stent, S., Ros, G., Arroyo, R., Gherardi, R.: Street-view change detection with deconvolutional networks. In: Hsu, D., Amato, N.M., Berman, S., Jacobs, S.A. (eds.) Robotics: Science and Systems XII, University of Michigan, Ann Arbor, Michigan, USA, 18–22 June 2016 (2016)
5. Ilg, E., Mayer, N., Saikia, T., Keuper, M., Dosovitskiy, A., Brox, T.: FlowNet 2.0: evolution of optical flow estimation with deep networks. In: 2017 IEEE Conference on Computer Vision and Pattern Recognition, CVPR 2017, Honolulu, HI, USA, 21–26 July 2017, pp. 1647–1655. IEEE Computer Society (2017)
6. Carreira, J., Zisserman, A.: Quo Vadis, action recognition? A new model and the kinetics dataset. In: 2017 IEEE Conference on Computer Vision and Pattern Recognition, CVPR 2017, Honolulu, HI, USA, 21–26 July 2017, pp. 4724–4733. IEEE Computer Society (2017)

7. Ren, S., He, K., Girshick, R., Sun, J.: Faster R-CNN: towards real-time object detection with region proposal networks. In Cortes, C., Lawrence, N.D., Lee, D.D., Sugiyama, M., Garnett, R. (eds.) Advances in Neural Information Processing Systems, vol. 28, pp. 91–99. Curran Associates, Inc. (2015)
8. Redmon, J., Farhadi, A.: YOLO9000: better, faster, stronger. In: 2017 IEEE Conference on Computer Vision and Pattern Recognition, CVPR 2017, Honolulu, HI, USA, 21–26 July 2017, pp. pp. 6517–6525. IEEE Computer Society (2017)
9. He, K., Gkioxari, G., Dollár, P., Girshick, R.B.: Mask R-CNN. In: IEEE International Conference on Computer Vision, ICCV 2017, Venice, Italy, 22–29 October 2017, pp. 2980–2988. IEEE Computer Society (2017)
10. Zeki, S.: A massively asynchronous, parallel brain. Philos. Trans. R. Soc. Lond. B Biol. Sci. **370**(1668), 103–116 (2015)
11. Szegedy, C., et al.: Going deeper with convolutions. In: IEEE Conference on Computer Vision and Pattern Recognition, CVPR 2015, Boston, MA, USA, 7–12 June 2015, pp. 1–9. IEEE Computer Society (2015)
12. Huang, G., Liu, Z., van der Maaten, L., Weinberger, K.Q.: Densely connected convolutional networks. In: 2017 IEEE Conference on Computer Vision and Pattern Recognition, CVPR 2017, Honolulu, HI, USA, 21–26 July 2017, pp. 2261–2269. IEEE Computer Society (2017)
13. Simonyan, K., Zisserman, A.: Very deep convolutional networks for large-scale image recognition. CoRR abs/1409.1556 (2014)
14. Howard, A.G., et al.: MobileNets: efficient convolutional neural networks for mobile vision applications. CoRR abs/1704.04861 (2017)
15. Chen, W., Wilson, J.T., Tyree, S., Weinberger, K.Q., Chen, Y.: Compressing neural networks with the hashing trick. In: Proceedings of the 32nd International Conference on International Conference on Machine Learning, ICML 2015, vol. 37, pp. 2285–2294. JMLR.org (2015)
16. Courbariaux, M., Hubara, I., Soudry, D., El-Yaniv, R., Bengio, Y.: Binarized neural networks: training deep neural networks with weights and activations constrained to +1 or −1. arXiv e-prints abs/1602.02830, February 2016
17. Srivastava, N., Mansimov, E., Salakhutdinov, R.: Unsupervised learning of video representations using LSTMs. In: Bach, F.R., Blei, D.M. (eds.) Proceedings of the 32nd International Conference on Machine Learning, ICML 2015, Lille, France, 6–11 July 2015. JMLR Workshop and Conference Proceedings, vol. 37, pp. 843–852. JMLR.org (2015)
18. Pătrăucean, V., Handa, A., Cipolla, R.: Spatio-temporal video autoencoder with differentiable memory. In: International Conference on Learning Representations (ICLR) Workshop (2016)
19. Tokmakov, P., Alahari, K., Schmid, C.: Learning video object segmentation with visual memory. In: IEEE International Conference on Computer Vision, ICCV 2017, Venice, Italy, 22–29 October 2017, pp. 4491–4500. IEEE Computer Society (2017)
20. Zhu, X., Xiong, Y., Dai, J., Yuan, L., Wei, Y.: Deep feature flow for video recognition. In: 2017 IEEE Conference on Computer Vision and Pattern Recognition, CVPR 2017, Honolulu, HI, USA, 21–26 July 2017, pp. 4141–4150. IEEE Computer Society (2017)
21. Tran, D., Bourdev, L.D., Fergus, R., Torresani, L., Paluri, M.: Learning spatiotemporal features with 3d convolutional networks. In: 2015 IEEE International Conference on Computer Vision, ICCV 2015, Santiago, Chile, 7–13 December 2015, pp. 4489–4497. IEEE Computer Society (2015)

22. Heilbron, F.C., Escorcia, V., Ghanem, B., Niebles, J.C.: Activitynet: a large-scale video benchmark for human activity understanding. In: IEEE Conference on Computer Vision and Pattern Recognition, CVPR 2015, Boston, MA, USA, 7–12 June 2015, pp. 961–970. IEEE Computer Society (2015)
23. Gu, C., et al.: AVA: a video dataset of spatio-temporally localized atomic visual actions. CoRR abs/1705.08421 (2017)
24. Kay, W., et al.: The kinetics human action video dataset. CoRR abs/1705.06950 (2017)
25. Koutník, J., Greff, K., Gomez, F.J., Schmidhuber, J.: A clockwork RNN. In: Proceedings of the 31th International Conference on Machine Learning, ICML 2014, Beijing, China, 21–26 June 2014. JMLR Workshop and Conference Proceedings, vol. 32, pp. 1863–1871. JMLR.org (2014)
26. Vezhnevets, A.S., et al.: Feudal networks for hierarchical reinforcement learning. In: Precup, D., Teh, Y.W. (eds.) Proceedings of the 34th International Conference on Machine Learning, ICML 2017, Sydney, NSW, Australia, 6–11 August 2017. Proceedings of Machine Learning Research, PMLR, vol. 70, pp. 3540–3549 (2017)
27. Neil, D., Pfeiffer, M., Liu, S.: Phased LSTM: accelerating recurrent network training for long or event-based sequences. In: Lee, D.D., Sugiyama, M., von Luxburg, U., Guyon, I., Garnett, R. (eds.) Advances in Neural Information Processing Systems 29: Annual Conference on Neural Information Processing Systems 2016, 5–10 December 2016, Barcelona, Spain, pp. 3882–3890 (2016)
28. Shelhamer, E., Rakelly, K., Hoffman, J., Darrell, T.: Clockwork convnets for video semantic segmentation. In: Hua, G., Jégou, H. (eds.) ECCV 2016. LNCS, vol. 9915, pp. 852–868. Springer, Cham (2016). https://doi.org/10.1007/978-3-319-49409-8_69
29. Figurnov, M., et al.: Spatially adaptive computation time for residual networks. In: 2017 IEEE Conference on Computer Vision and Pattern Recognition, CVPR 2017, Honolulu, HI, USA, 21–26 July 2017, pp. 1790–1799. IEEE Computer Society (2017)
30. Karayev, S., Fritz, M., Darrell, T.: Anytime recognition of objects and scenes. In: 2014 IEEE Conference on Computer Vision and Pattern Recognition, CVPR 2014, Columbus, OH, USA, 23–28 June 2014, pp. 572–579. IEEE Computer Society (2014)
31. Mathe, S., Pirinen, A., Sminchisescu, C.: Reinforcement learning for visual object detection. In: 2016 IEEE Conference on Computer Vision and Pattern Recognition, CVPR 2016, Las Vegas, NV, USA, 27–30 June 2016, pp. 2894–2902. IEEE Computer Society (2016)
32. Petrowski, A., Dreyfus, G., Girault, C.: Performance analysis of a pipelined back-propagation parallel algorithm. Trans. Neural Netw. 4(6), 970–981 (1993)
33. Chen, X., Eversole, A., Li, G., Yu, D., Seide, F.: Pipelined back-propagation for context-dependent deep neural networks. In: INTERSPEECH 2012, 13th Annual Conference of the International Speech Communication Association, Portland, Oregon, USA, 9–13 September 2012, pp. 26–29. ISCA (2012)
34. Jaderberg, M., et al.: Decoupled neural interfaces using synthetic gradients. In: Precup, D., Teh, Y.W. (eds.) Proceedings of the 34th International Conference on Machine Learning, ICML 2017, Sydney, NSW, Australia, 6–11 August 2017. Proceedings of Machine Learning Research, PMLR, vol. 70, pp. 1627–1635 (2017)
35. Wiskott, L., Sejnowski, T.J.: Slow feature analysis: unsupervised learning of invariances. Neural Comput. 14(4), 715–770 (2002)
36. Shelhamer, E., Long, J., Darrell, T.: Fully convolutional networks for semantic segmentation. IEEE Trans. Pattern Anal. Mach. Intell. 39(4), 640–651 (2017)

37. Ronneberger, O., Fischer, P., Brox, T.: U-Net: convolutional networks for biomedical image segmentation. In: Navab, N., Hornegger, J., Wells, W.M., Frangi, A.F. (eds.) MICCAI 2015. LNCS, vol. 9351, pp. 234–241. Springer, Cham (2015). https://doi.org/10.1007/978-3-319-24574-4_28

38. Simonyan, K., Zisserman, A.: Two-stream convolutional networks for action recognition in videos. In: Ghahramani, Z., Welling, M., Cortes, C., Lawrence, N.D., Weinberger, K.Q. (eds.) Advances in Neural Information Processing Systems 27: Annual Conference on Neural Information Processing Systems 2014, 8–13 December 2014, Montreal, Quebec, Canada, pp. 568–576 (2014)

39. Carreira, J., Agrawal, P., Fragkiadaki, K., Malik, J.: Human pose estimation with iterative error feedback. In: 2016 IEEE Conference on Computer Vision and Pattern Recognition, CVPR 2016, Las Vegas, NV, USA, 27–30 June 2016, pp. 4733–4742. IEEE Computer Society (2016)

40. Belagiannis, V., Zisserman, A.: Recurrent human pose estimation. In: 12th IEEE International Conference on Automatic Face & Gesture Recognition, FG 2017, Washington, DC, USA, 30 May–3 June 2017, pp. 468–475. IEEE Computer Society (2017)

41. Li, K., Hariharan, B., Malik, J.: Iterative instance segmentation. In: 2016 IEEE Conference on Computer Vision and Pattern Recognition, CVPR 2016, Las Vegas, NV, USA, 27–30 June 2016, pp. 3659–3667. IEEE Computer Society (2016)

42. Stollenga, M.F., Masci, J., Gomez, F.J., Schmidhuber, J.: Deep networks with internal selective attention through feedback connections. In: Ghahramani, Z., Welling, M., Cortes, C., Lawrence, N.D., Weinberger, K.Q. (eds.) Advances in Neural Information Processing Systems 27: Annual Conference on Neural Information Processing Systems 2014, 8–13 December 2014, Montreal, Quebec, Canada, pp. 3545–3553 (2014)

43. Zamir, A.R., Wu, T., Sun, L., Shen, W.B., Shi, B.E., Malik, J., Savarese, S.: Feedback networks. In: 2017 IEEE Conference on Computer Vision and Pattern Recognition, CVPR 2017, Honolulu, HI, USA, 21–26 July 2017, pp. 1808–1817. IEEE Computer Society (2017)

44. Hinton, G.E., Vinyals, O., Dean, J.: Distilling the knowledge in a neural network. CoRR abs/1503.02531 (2015)

45. Rasmus, A., Valpola, H., Honkala, M., Berglund, M., Raiko, T.: Semi-supervised learning with ladder networks. In: Proceedings of the 28th International Conference on Neural Information Processing Systems, NIPS 2015, Cambridge, MA, USA, vol. 2, pp. 3546–3554. MIT Press (2015)

46. Xie, S., Sun, C., Huang, J., Tu, Z., Murphy, K.: Rethinking spatiotemporal feature learning for video understanding. CoRR abs/1712.04851 (2017)

47. Papandreou, G., et al.: Towards accurate multi-person pose estimation in the wild. In: IEEE Conference on Computer Vision and Pattern Recognition (2017)

48. Iqbal, U., Milan, A., Andriluka, M., Ensafutdinov, E., Pishchulin, L., Gall, J., Schiele, B.: PoseTrack: a benchmark for human pose estimation and tracking. arXiv:1710.10000 [cs] (2017)

49. Abadi, M., et al.: TensorFlow: large-scale machine learning on heterogeneous systems (2015). Software available from tensorflow.org

DeepWrinkles: Accurate and Realistic Clothing Modeling

Zorah Lähner[1,2] , Daniel Cremers[2] , and Tony Tung[1(✉)]

[1] Facebook Reality Labs, Sausalito, CA, USA
tony.tung@fb.com
[2] Technical University Munich, Munich, Germany
{laehner,cremers}@in.tum.de

Abstract. We present a novel method to generate accurate and realistic clothing deformation from real data capture. Previous methods for realistic cloth modeling mainly rely on intensive computation of physics-based simulation (with numerous heuristic parameters), while models reconstructed from visual observations typically suffer from lack of geometric details. Here, we propose an original framework consisting of two modules that work jointly to represent global shape deformation as well as surface details with high fidelity. Global shape deformations are recovered from a subspace model learned from 3D data of clothed people in motion, while high frequency details are added to normal maps created using a conditional Generative Adversarial Network whose architecture is designed to enforce realism and temporal consistency. This leads to unprecedented high-quality rendering of clothing deformation sequences, where fine wrinkles from (real) high resolution observations can be recovered. In addition, as the model is learned independently from body shape and pose, the framework is suitable for applications that require retargeting (e.g., body animation). Our experiments show original high quality results with a flexible model. We claim an entirely data-driven approach to realistic cloth wrinkle generation is possible.

Keywords: 3D surface deformation modeling · Cloth simulation
Normal maps · Deep neural networks

1 Introduction

Realistic garment reconstruction is notoriously a complex problem and its importance is undeniable in many research work and applications, such as accurate body shape and pose estimation in the wild (i.e., from observations of clothed humans), realistic AR/VR experience, movies, video games, virtual try-on, etc.

For the past decades, physics-based simulations have been setting the standard in movie and video game industries, even though they require hours of

Electronic supplementary material The online version of this chapter (https://doi.org/10.1007/978-3-030-01225-0_41) contains supplementary material, which is available to authorized users.

© Springer Nature Switzerland AG 2018
V. Ferrari et al. (Eds.): ECCV 2018, LNCS 11208, pp. 698–715, 2018.
https://doi.org/10.1007/978-3-030-01225-0_41

labor by experts. More recently methods for full clothing reconstruction using multi-view videos or 3D scan systems have also been proposed [38]. Global deformations can be reconstructed with high fidelity semi-automatically. Nevertheless, accurately recovering geometric details such as fine cloth wrinkles has remained a challenge.

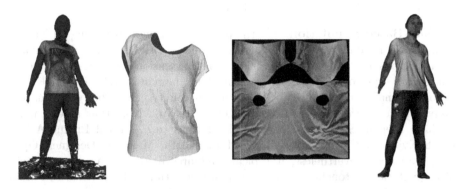

Fig. 1. Accurate and realistic clothing modeling with DeepWrinkles, our entirely data-driven framework. (Left) 4D data capture. (Middle Left) Reconstruction from subspace model. (Middle Right) Fine wrinkles in normal map generated by our adversarial neural network. (Right) 3D rendering and animation on virtual human.

In this paper, we present DeepWrinkles (see Fig. 1), a novel framework to generate accurate and realistic clothing deformation from real data capture. It consists of two complementary modules: (1) A statistical model is learned from 3D scans of clothed people in motion, from which clothing templates are precisely non-rigidly aligned. Clothing shape deformations are therefore modeled using a linear subspace model, where human body shape and pose are factored out, hence enabling body retargeting. (2) Fine geometric details are added to normal maps generated using a conditional adversarial network whose architecture is designed to enforce realism and temporal consistency.

To our knowledge, this is the first method that tackles 3D surface geometry refinement using deep neural network on normal maps. With DeepWrinkles, we obtain unprecedented high-quality rendering of clothing deformation, where global shape as well as fine wrinkles from (real) high resolution observations can be recovered, using an entirely data-driven approach. Figure 2 gives an overview of our framework with a T-shirt as example. Additional materials contain videos of results. We show how the model can be applied to virtual human animation, with body shape and pose retargeting.

2   Related Work

Cloth modeling and garment simulation have a long history that dates back to the mid 80s. A general overview of fundamental methods is given in [51]. There are two mostly opposing approaches to this problem. One is using physics-based simulations to generate realistic wrinkles, and the other captures and reconstructs details from real-world data.

Physics-Based Simulation. For the past decades, models relying on Newtonian physics have been widely applied to simulate cloth behavior. They usually model various material properties such as stretch (tension), stiffness, and weight. For certain types of applications (e.g., involving human body) additional models or external forces have to be taken into account such as body kinematics, body surface friction, interpenetration, etc [4,8,9,16]. Note that several models have been integrated in commercial solutions (e.g., Unreal Engine APEX Cloth/Nvidia NvCloth, Unity Cloth, Maya nCloth, MarvelousDesigner, OptiTex, etc.) [32]. Nevertheless, it typically requires hours or days if not weeks of computation, retouching work, and parameter tuning by experts to obtain realistic cloth deformation effects.

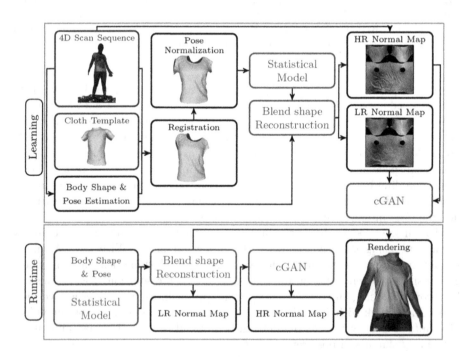

Fig. 2. Outline of DeepWrinkles. During Learning, we learn to reconstruct global shape deformations using a Statistical Model and a mapping from pose parameters to Blend shape parameters using real-world data. We also train a neural network (cGAN) to generate fine details on normal maps from lower resolution ones. During runtime, the learned models reconstruct shape and geometric details given a priori body shape and pose. Inputs are in violet, learned models are in cyan. (Color figure online)

3D Capture and Reconstruction. Vision-based approaches have explored ways to capture cloth surface deformation under stress, and estimate material properties through visual observations for simulation purpose [29,33,34,53]. As well, several methods directly reconstruct whole object surface from real-world measurements. [54] uses texture patterns to track and reconstruct garment from a video, while 3D reconstruction can also be obtained from multi-view videos without markers [7,29,33,41,48,49]. However without sufficient prior, reconstructed geometry can be quite crude. When the target is known (e.g., clothing type), templates can improve the reconstruction quality [3]. Also, more details can be recovered by applying super-resolution techniques on input images [7,17,45,47], or using photometric stereo and information about lighting [22,50]. Naturally, depth information can lead to further improvement [14,36].

In recent work [38], cloth reconstruction is obtained by clothing segmentation and template registration from 4D scan data. Captured garments can be retargeted to different body shapes. However the method has limitations regarding fine wrinkles.

Coarse-to-Fine Approaches. To reconstruct fine details, and consequently handle the bump in resolution at runtime (i.e., higher resolution meshes or more particles for simulation), methods based on dimension reduction (e.g., linear subspace models) [2,21] or coarse-to-fine strategies are commonly applied [25, 35,52]. DRAPE [19] automates the process of learning linear subspaces from simulated data and applying them to different subjects. The model factors out body shape and pose to produce a global cloth shape and then applies the wrinkles of seen garments. However, deformations are applied per triangle as in [42], which is not optimal for online applications. Additionally, for all these methods, simulated data is tedious to generate, and accuracy and realism are limited.

Learning Methods. Previously mentioned methods focus on efficients simulation and representation of previously seen data. Going a step further, several methods have attempted to generalize this knowledge to unseen cases. [46] learns bags of dynamical systems to represent and recognize repeating patterns in wrinkle deformations. In DeepGarment [13] the global shape and low frequency details are reconstructed from a single segmented image using a CNN but no retargeting is possible.

Only sparse work has been done on learning to add realistic details to 3D surfaces with neural networks but several methods to enrich facial scans with texture exist [37,40]. In particular, Generative Adversarial Networks (GANs) [18] are suitable to enhance low dimensional information with details. In [27] it is used create realistic images of clothed people given a (possibly random) pose.

Outside of clothing, SR-GAN [28] solves the super-resolution problem of recovering photo-realistic textures from heavily downsampled images on public benchmark. The task has similarities to ours in generating high frequency details for coarse inputs but we use a content loss motivated by perceptual similarity instead of similarity in pixel space. [10] uses a data-driven approach with a CNN to simulate highly detailed smoke flows. Instead, pix2pix [24] proposes a conditional GAN that creates realistic images from sketches or annotated regions or vice versa. This design suits our problem better as we aim at learning and transferring underlying image structure.

In order to represent the highest possible level of detail at runtime, we propose to revisit the traditional rendering pipeline of 3D engine with computer vision. Our contributions take advantage of the normal mapping technique [11,12,26]. Note that displacement maps have been used to create wrinkle maps using texture information [5,15]. However, while results are visually good on faces, they still require high resolution mesh, and no temporal consistency is guaranteed across time. (Also, faces are arguably less difficult to track than clothing which are prone to occlusions and more loose.)

In this work, we claim the first entirely data-driven method that uses a deep neural network on normal maps to leverage 3D geometry of clothing.

3   Deformation Subspace Model

We model cloth deformations by learning a linear subspace model that factors out body pose and shape, as in [19]. However, our model is learned from real data, and deformations are applied per vertex for speed and flexibility regarding graphics pipelines [31]. Our strategy ensures deformations are represented compactly and with high realism. First, we compute robust template-based non-rigid registrations from a 4D scan sequence (Sect. 3.1), then a clothing deformation statistical model is derived (Sect. 3.2) and finally, a regression model is learned for pose retargeting (Sect. 3.3).

3.1   Data Preparation

Data Capture. For each type of clothing, we capture 4D scan sequences at 60 fps (e.g., 10.8k frames for 3 min) of a subject in motion, and dressed in a full-body suit with one piece of clothing with colored boundaries on top. Each frame contists of a 3D surface mesh with around 200k vertices yielding very detailed folds on the surface but partially corrupted by holes and noise (see Fig. 1a). This setup allows a simple color-based 3D clothing extraction. In addition, capturing only one garment prevents occlusions where clothing normally overlaps (e.g., waistbands) and clothings can be freely combined with each other.

Body Tracking. 3D body pose is estimated at each frame using a method in the spirit of [44]. We define a skeleton with j joints described by p_j parameters representing transformation and bone length. Joint parameters are also adjusted to body shape, which is estimated using [31,55]. Posed human body is obtained using a linear blend skinning function $S : \mathbb{R}^{3 \times v} \times \mathbb{R}^{p_j} \rightarrow \mathbb{R}^{3 \times v}$ that transforms (any subset of) v vertices of a 3D deformable human template in normalized pose (e.g., T-pose) to a pose defined by j skeleton joints.

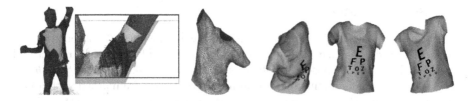

Fig. 3. (Left) Before registration, a template is aligned to clothing scans by skinning. Boundaries are misplaced. (Right) Examples of registrations with different shirts on different people. Texture stability across sequence shows the method is robust to drift.

Registration. We define a template of clothing $\bar{T}$ by choosing a subset of the human template with consistent topology. $\bar{T}$ should contain enough vertices to model deformations (e.g., 5k vertices for a T-shirt), as shown in Fig. 3. The clothing template is then registered to the 4D scan sequence using a variant of non-rigid ICP based on grid deformation [20,30]. The following objective function $\mathcal{E}_{reg}$, which aims at optimizing affine transformations of grid nodes, is iteratively minimized using Gauss-Newton method:

$$\mathcal{E}_{reg} = \mathcal{E}_{data} + \omega_r \cdot \mathcal{E}_{rigid} + \omega_s \cdot \mathcal{E}_{smooth} + \omega_b \cdot \mathcal{E}_{bound}, \tag{1}$$

where the data term $\mathcal{E}_{data}$ aligns template vertices with their nearest neighbors on the target scans, $\mathcal{E}_{rigid}$ encourages each triangle deformation to be as rigid as possible, and $\mathcal{E}_{smooth}$ penalizes inconsistent deformation of neighboring triangles. In addition, we introduce the energy term $\mathcal{E}_{bound}$ to ensure alignment of boundary vertices, which is unlikely to occur otherwise (see below for details). We set $\omega_r = 500$, $\omega_s = 500$, and $\omega_b = 10$ by experiments. One template registration takes around 15s (using CPU only).

Boundary Alignment. During data capture the boundaries of the clothing are marked in a distinguishable color and corresponding points are assigned to the set $\mathcal{B}_S$. We call the set of boundary points on the template $\mathcal{B}_T$. Matching point pairs in $\mathcal{B}_S \times \mathcal{B}_T$ should be distributed equally among the scan and template, and ideally capture all details in the folds. As this is not the case if each point in $\mathcal{B}_T$ is simply paired with the closest scan boundary point (see Fig. 4), we select instead a match $s_t \in \mathcal{B}_S$ for each point $t \in \mathcal{B}_T$ via the following formula:

$$s_t = \max_{s \in \mathcal{C}} \|t - s\| \quad \text{with} \quad \mathcal{C} = \left\{ s' \in \mathcal{B}_S \mid \arg\min_{t' \in \mathcal{B}_T} \|s' - t'\| = t \right\}. \tag{2}$$

Notice that $\mathcal{C}$ might be empty. This ensures consistency along the boundary and better captures high frequency details (which are potentially further away).

3.2 Statistical Model

The statistical model is computed using linear subspace decomposition by PCA [31]. Poses $\{\theta_1, ..., \theta_n\}$ of all n registered meshes $\{\mathcal{R}_1, ..., \mathcal{R}_n\}$ are factored out from the model by pose-normalization using inverse skinning: $S^{-1}(\mathcal{R}_i, \theta_i) = \bar{\mathcal{R}}_i \in \mathbb{R}^{3 \times v}$. In what remains, meshes in normalized pose are marked with a bar. Each registration $\bar{\mathcal{R}}_i$ can be represented by a mean shape $\bar{\mathcal{M}}$ and vertex offsets o_i, such that $\bar{\mathcal{R}}_i = \bar{\mathcal{M}} + o_i$, where the mean shape $\bar{\mathcal{M}} \in \mathbb{R}^{3 \times v}$ is obtained by averaging vertex positions: $\bar{\mathcal{M}} = \sum_{i=1}^{n} \frac{\bar{\mathcal{R}}_i}{n}$. The n principal directions of the matrix $O = [o_1 \ ... \ o_n]$ are obtained by singular value decomposition: $O = U \Sigma V^{\top}$. Ordered by the largest singular values, the corresponding singular vectors contain information about the most dominant deformations.

Finally, each $\mathcal{R}_i$ can be compactly represented by $k \leq n$ parameters $\{\lambda_1^i, ..., \lambda_k^i\} \in \mathbb{R}^k$ (instead of its $3 \times v$ vertex coordinates), with the linear blend shape function B, given a pose θ_i:

$$B(\{\lambda_1^i, ..., \lambda_k^i\}, \theta_i) = S\left(\bar{\mathcal{M}} + \sum_{l=0}^{k} \lambda_l^i \cdot V_l, \theta_i\right) \approx \mathcal{R}_i \in \mathbb{R}^{3 \times v}, \qquad (3)$$

where V_l is the l-th singular vector. For a given registration, $\lambda_l^i = V_l^{\top} \bar{\mathcal{R}}_i$ holds. In practice, choosing $k = 500$ is sufficient to represent all registrations with a negligible error (less than 5 mm).

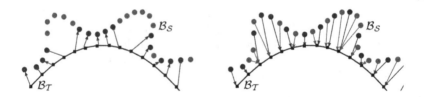

Fig. 4. Strategies for Boundary Alignment. Template boundary points $\mathcal{B}_T$ are denoted in black, scan boundary points $\mathcal{B}_S$ (with significant more points than the template) are in red and blue. Points that are paired with a template point are in blue. (Left) Pairing to the closest neighbor of the template points leads to ignorance of distant details. (Right) Each template point in $\mathcal{B}_T$ is paired with the furthest point (marked in blue) in a set containing its closest points in $\mathcal{B}_S$. (Color figure online)

3.3 Pose-to-Shape Prediction

We now learn a predictive model f, that takes as inputs j joint poses, and outputs a set of k shape parameters Λ. This allows powerful applications where deformations are induced by pose. To take into account deformation dynamics that occur during human motion, the model is also trained with pose velocity, acceleration, and shape parameter history. These inputs are concatenated in the control vector Θ, and f can be obtained using autoregressive models [2,31,39].

In our experiments with clothing, we solved for f in a straightforward way by linear regression: $F = \Lambda \cdot \Theta^\dagger$, where F is the matrix representation of f, and $\dagger$ indicates the Moore-Penrose inverse. While this allows for (limited) pose retargeting, we observed loss in reconstruction details. One reason is that under motion, the same pose can give rise to various configurations of folds depending on the direction of movement, speed and previous fold configurations.

To obtain non-linear mapping, we consider the components of Θ and Λ as multivariate time series, and train a deep multi-layer recurrent neural network (RNN) [43]. A sequence-to-sequence encoder-decoder architecture with Long Short-term Memory (LSTM) units is well suited as it allows continuous predictions, while being easier to train than RNNs and outperforming shallow LSTMs. We compose Θ with j joint parameter poses, plus velocity and acceleration of the joint root. MSE compared to linear regression are reported in Sect. 5.3.

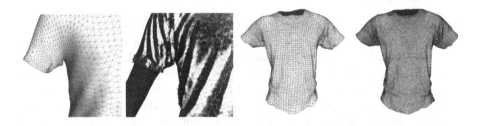

Fig. 5. Limits of registration and subspace model. (Left) Global shape is well recovered, but many visible (high frequency) details are missing. (Right) Increasing the resolution of the template mesh is still not sufficient. Note that [38] suffers from the same limitations.

4   Fine Wrinkle Generation

Our goal is to recover all observable geometric details. As previously mentioned, template-based methods [38] and subspace-based methods [19,21] cannot recover every detail such as fine cloth wrinkles due to resolution and data scaling limitations, as illustrated in Fig. 5.

Assuming the finest details are captured at sensor image pixel resolution, and are reconstructed in 3D (e.g., using a 4D scanner as in [6,38]), all existing geometric details can then be encoded in a normal map of the 3D scan surface at lower resolution (see Fig. 6). To automatically add fine details *on the fly* to reconstructed clothing, we propose to leverage normal maps using a generative adversarial network [18]. See Fig. 8 for the architecture. In particular, our network induces temporal consistency on the normal maps to increase realism in animation applications.

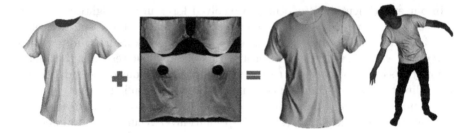

Fig. 6. All visible details from an accurate 3D scan are generated in our normal map for incredible realism. Here, a virtual shirt is seamlessly added on top of an animated virtual human (e.g., scanned subject).

4.1   Data Preparation

We take as inputs a 4D scan sequence, and a sequence of corresponding reconstructed garments. The latter can be either obtained by registration, reconstruction using blend shape or regression, as detailed in Sect. 3. Clothing template meshes $\bar{T}$ are equipped with UV maps which are used to project any pixel from an image to a point on a mesh surface, hence assigning a property encoded in a pixel to each point. Therefore, normal coordinates can be normalized and stored as pixel colors in normal maps. Our training dataset then consists of pairs of normal maps (see Fig. 7): *low resolution* (LR) normal maps obtained by blend shape reconstruction, and *high resolution* (HR) normal maps obtained from the scans. For LR normal maps, the normal at surface point (lying in a face) is linearly interpolated from vertex normals. For HR normal maps, per-pixel normals are obtained by projection of the high resolution observations (i.e., 4D scan) onto triangles of the corresponding low resolution reconstruction, and then the

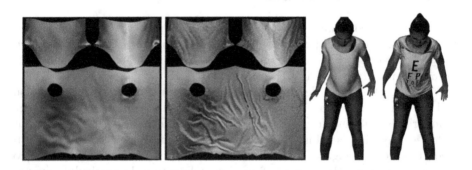

Fig. 7. Examples of our dataset. (Left) Low resolution input normal map, (Middle) High resolution target normal map from scan. Details, and noise, visible on the scan are reproduced in the image. Gray areas indicate no normal information was available on the scan. (Right) T-Shirt on a human model rendered without and with normal map.

normal information is transferred using the UV map of $\bar{\mathcal{T}}$. Note that normal maps cannot be directly calculated from scans because neither is the exact area of the garment defined, nor are they equipped with UV map. Also, our normals are represented in global coordinates, as opposed to tangent space coordinates as is standard for normal maps. The reason is that LR normal maps contain no additional information to the geometry and are therefore constant in tangent space. This makes them unfitting for conditioning our adversarial neural network.

4.2 Network Architecture

Due to the nature of our problem it is natural to explore network architectures designed to enhance images (i.e., super-resolution applications). From our experiments, we observed that models trained on natural images, including those containing a perceptual loss term fail (e.g., SR-GAN [28]). On the other hand, cloth deformations exhibit smooth patterns (wrinkles, creases, folds) that deform continuously in time. In addition, at a finer level, materials and fabric texture also contain high frequency details.

Our proposed network is based on a conditional Generative Adversarial Network (cGAN) inspired from image transfer [24]. We also use a convolution-batchnorm-ReLu structure [23] and a U-Net in the generative network since we want latent information to be transfered across the network layers and the overall structure of the image to be preserved. This happens thanks to the skip connections. The discriminator only penalizes structure at the scale of patches, and works as a texture loss. Our network is conditioned by low-resolution normal map images (size: 256×256) which will be enhanced with fine details learned from our real data normal maps. See Fig. 8 for the complete architecture.

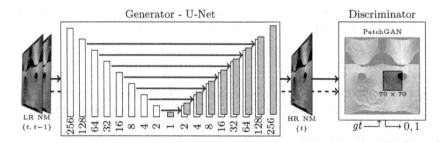

Fig. 8. cGAN for realistic HR normal map generation from LR normal maps as input. Layer sizes are squared. Skip connections (red) in U-Net preserve underlying image structure across network layers. PatchGAN enforces wrinkle pattern consistency. (Color figure online)

Temporal consistency is achieved by extending the $L1$ network loss term. For compelling animations, it is not only important that each frame looks realistic, but also no sudden jumps in the rendering should occur. To ensure smooth transition between consecutively generated images across time, we introduce an additional loss $\mathcal{L}_{loss}$ to the GAN objective that penalizes discrepancies between generated images at t and expected images (from training dataset) at $t-1$:

$$\mathcal{L}_{loss} = \underbrace{\|\mathcal{I}_{gen}^t - \mathcal{I}_{gt}^t\|_1}_{\mathcal{L}_{data}} + \underbrace{|\sum_{i,j}(\mathcal{I}_{gen}^t - \mathcal{I}_{gt}^{t-1})_{i,j}|}_{\mathcal{L}_{temp}}, \qquad (4)$$

where $\mathcal{L}_{data}$ helps to generate images near to ground truth in an L_1 sense (for less blurring). The temporal consistency term $\mathcal{L}_{temp}$ is meant to capture global fold movements over the surface. If something appears somewhere, most of the time, it should have disappeared close-by and vice versa. Our term does not take spatial proximity into account though. We also tried temporal consistency based on the L_1- and L_2-norm, and report the results in Table 1. See Fig. 9 for a comparison of results with and without the temporal consistency term.

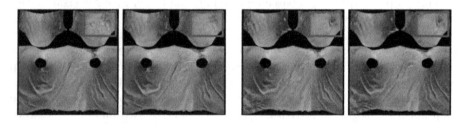

Fig. 9. Examples trained on only 2000 training samples reinforce the effect of the additional loss $\mathcal{L}_{temp}$. The pairs show twice the same consecutive frames: (left) *without* temporal consistency term geometric noise appears or disappears instantly, and (right) *with* temporal consistency term preserves geometric continuity.

5   Experiments

This section evaluates the results of our reconstruction. 4D scan sequences were captured using a temporal-3dMD system (4D) [1]. Sequences are captured at 60fps. Each frame consists of a colored mesh with 200 K vertices. Here, we show results on two different shirts (for female and male). We trained the cGAN network on a dataset of 9213 consecutive frames. The first 8000 images compose the training data set, the next 1000 images the test data set and the remaining 213 images the validation set. Test and validation sets contain poses and movements not seen in the training set. The U-Net auto-encoder is constructed with 2×8 layers, and 64 filters in each of the first convolutional layers. The discriminator uses patches of size 70×70. $\mathcal{L}_{data}$ weight is set to 100, $\mathcal{L}_{temp}$ weight is 50, while GAN weight is 1. The images have a resolution of 256×256, although our early experiments also showed promising results on 512×512.

5.1 Comparison of Approaches

We compare our results to different approaches (see Fig. 10). A physics-based simulation done by a 3D artist using MarvelousDesigner [32] returns a mesh imitating similar material properties as our scan and with a comparable amount of folds but containing 53, 518 vertices (i.e., an order of magnitude more). A linear subspace reconstruction with 50 coefficients derived from the registrations (Sect. 3) produces a mostly flat surface, while the registration itself shows smooth approximations of the major folds in the scan. Our method, DeepWrinkles, adds all high frequency details seen in the scan to the reconstructed surface. These three methods use a mesh with 5, 048 vertices. DeepWrinkles is shown with a 256 × 256 normal map image.

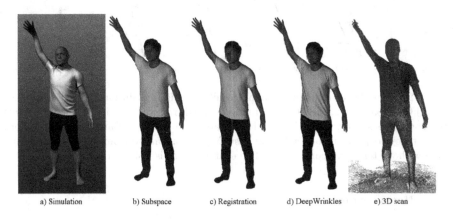

a) Simulation   b) Subspace   c) Registration   d) DeepWrinkles   e) 3D scan

Fig. 10. Comparison of approaches. (a) Physics-based simulation [32], (b) Subspace (50 coefficients) [19], (c) Registration [38], (d) DeepWrinkles (ours), (e) 3D scan (ground truth).

5.2 Importance of Reconstruction Details in Input

Our initial experiments showed promising results reconstructing details from the original registration normal maps. To show the efficacy of the method it is not only necessary to reconstruct details from registration, but also from blend shapes, and after regression. We replaced the input images in the training set by normal maps constructed from the blend shapes with 500, 200 and 100 basis functions and one set from the regression reconstruction. The goal is to determine the amount of detail that is necessary in the input to obtain realistic detailed wrinkles. Table 1 shows the error rates in each experiment. 500 basis functions seem sufficient for a reasonable amount of detail in the result. Probably due to the fact that the reconstruction from regression is more noisy and bumpy, the neural network is not capable of reconstructing long defined folds and instead produces a lot of higher frequency wrinkles (see Fig. 11). This is an indicator that the structures of the inputs are only redefined by the net and important folds have to be visible in the input.

Table 1. Comparison of pixel-wise error values of the neural network for different training types. Data and Temporal are as defined in Eq. 4. (Left) Different temporal consistency terms. $L1$ and $L2$ take the respective distance between the output and target at time $t - 1$. (Right) Different reconstruction methods to produce the input normal map. Registr. refers to registration, BS to the blend shape with a certain number of basis functions and Regre. to regression.

	$L1$ temp	$L2$ temp	Eq. 4	no temp	Registr.	BS 500	BS 200	Regre.
Data	4.63	5.16	3.72	5.06	3.72	6.86	6.40	7.6
Temporal	5.11	4.2	4.2	5.52	4.2	7.05	6.52	7.65

a) No Normal Map   b) Ground-Truth   c) Reg. with temporal   d) 200 with temporal   e) 500 with temporal   f) Reg. no temporal

Fig. 11. Examples of different training results for high resolution normal maps. Left to right: Global shape, target normal map, learned from registration normal map with temporal consistency, learned from blend shape with 200 basis functions and temporal consistency, as previous but with 500 basis functions, learned from registration normal map without temporal consistency. The example pose is not seen in the training set.

5.3   Retargeting

The final goal is to be able to scan one piece of clothing in one or several sequences and then transferring it on new persons with new movements on the go.

Poses. We experimented with various combinations of control vectors Θ, including pose, shape, joint root velocity and acceleration history. It turns out most formulations in the literature are difficult to train or unstable [2,31,39]. We restrict the joint parameters to those directly related to each piece of clothing to reduce the dimensionality. In the case of shirts, this leaves the parameters related to the upper body. In general, linear regression generalized best but smoothed out a lot of overall geometric details, even in the training set. We evaluated on 9213 frames for 500 and 1000 blend shapes: $MSE_{500} = 2.902$ and $MSE_{1000} = 3.114$.

On the other hand, we trained an encoder-decoder with LSTM units (4 layers with dimension 256), using inputs and outputs equally of length 3 (see Sect. 3.3). We obtained promising results: $MSE_{rnn} = 1.892$. Supplemental materials show visually good reconstructed sequences.

Shapes. In 3.2 we represented clothing with folds as offsets of a mean shape. The same can be done with a human template for persons with different body shapes. Each person $\bar{\mathcal{P}}_i$ in normalized pose can be represented as an average template plus a vertex-wise offset $\bar{\mathcal{P}}_i = \bar{T}' + o_i'$. Given the fact that the clothing mean shape $\bar{\mathcal{M}} = \bar{T}'_{|\mathcal{M}} + o'_{|\mathcal{M}}$ contains a subset of vertices of the human template, it can be adjusted to any deformation of the template by taking $\bar{\mathcal{M}}_{o'} = \bar{\mathcal{M}} + o'_{i|\mathcal{M}}$. $|\mathcal{M}$ restricts vertices of the human template to those used for clothing. Then the mean in the blend shape can simply be replaced by $\bar{\mathcal{M}}_{o'}$. Equation 3 becomes:

$$B(\{\lambda_1^i, ..., \lambda_k^i\}, \theta_i) = S\left(\bar{\mathcal{M}}_{o'} + \sum_{l=0}^{k} \lambda_l^i \cdot V_l, \theta_i\right) \approx \mathcal{P}_{i|\mathcal{M}}, \tag{5}$$

Replacing the mean shape affects surface normals. Hence, it is necessary to use normal maps in tangent space at rendering time. This makes them applicable to any body shape (see Fig. 12).

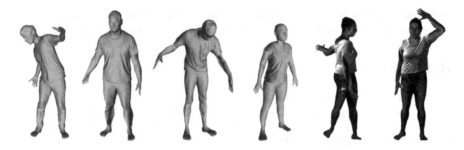

Fig. 12. Body shape retargeting. The first and fourth entry are shirts on the original models, the following two are retargeted to new body shapes.

6   Conclusion

We present DeepWrinkles, a entirely data-driven framework to capture and reconstruct clothing in motion out from 4D scan sequences. Our evaluations show that high frequency details can be added to low resolution normal maps using a conditional adversarial neural network. We introduce an additional temporal loss to the GAN objective that preserves geometric consistency across time, and show qualitative and quantitative evaluations on different datasets. We also give details on how to create low resolution normal maps from registered data, as it turns out registration fidelity is crucial for the cGAN training. The two presented modules are complementary to achieve accurate and realistic rendering of global shape and details of clothing. To the best of our knowledge, our methods exceeds the level of detail of the current state of the art in both physics-based simulation and data-driven approaches by far. Additionally, the space requirement of a normal map is negligible in comparison to increasing the resolution of clothing mesh, which makes our pipeline suitable to standard 3D engines.

Limitations. High resolution normal maps can have missing information in areas not seen by cameras, such as armpit areas. Hence, visually disruptive artifacts can occur although the clothing template can fix most of the issues (e.g., by doing a pass of smoothing). At the moment pose retargeting works best when new poses are similar to ones included in the training dataset. Although the neural network is able to generalize to some unseen poses, reconstructing the global shape from a new joint parameter sequence can be challenging. This should be fixed by scaling the dataset.

Future Work. Scanning setup can be extended to reconstruct all body parts with sufficient details without occlusions, and apply our method to more diverse types of clothing and accessories like coats, scarfs. Normal maps could also be used to add fine details like buttons which are hard to capture in 3D.

Acknowledgements. We would like to thank the FRL teams for their support, and Vignesh Ganapathi-Subramanian for preliminary work on the subspace model.

References

1. Temporal-3dMD systems (4d) (2018). www.3dmd.com
2. de Aguiar, E., Sigal, L., Treuille, A., Hodgins, J.: Stable spaces for real-time clothing. In: Hart, J.C. (ed.) ACM Transactions for Graphics. Association for Computing Machinery (ACM) (2010)
3. de Aguiar, E., Stoll, C., Theobalt, C., Ahmed, N., Seidel, H., Thrun, S.: Performance capture from sparse multi-view video. In: Hart, J.C. (ed.) ACM Transactions for Graphics, vol. 27, pp. 98:1–98:10. Association for Computing Machinery (ACM) (2008)
4. Baraff, D., Witkin, A., Kass, M.: Untangling cloth. In: Hart, J.C. (ed.) ACM Transactions on Graphics, vol. 22, pp. 862–870. Association for Computing Machinery (ACM), New York, NY, USA, July 2003
5. Beeler, T., et al.: High-quality passive facial performance capture using anchor frames. In: Alexa, M. (ed.) ACM Transactions for Graphics, vol. 30, pp. 75:1–75:10. Association for Computing Machinery (ACM), New York, NY, USA, August 2011
6. Bogo, F., Romero, J., Pons-Moll, G., Black, M.J.: Dynamic FAUST: registering human bodies in motion. In: IEEE Conference on Computer Vision and Pattern Recognition (CVPR). IEEE, July 2017
7. Bradley, D., Popa, T., Sheffer, A., Heidrich, W., Boubekeur, T.: Markerless garment capture. In: Hart, J.C. (ed.) ACM Transactions for Graphics, vol. 27, pp. 99:1–99:9. Association for Computing Machinery (ACM), New York, NY, USA, August 2008
8. Bridson, R., Marino, S., Fedkiw, R.: Simulation of clothing with folds and wrinkles. In: Proceedings of the ACM SIGGRAPH/Eurographics Symposium on Computer Animation, pp. 28–36. Eurographics Association, San Diego, CA, USA, July 2003
9. Choi, K.J., Ko, H.S.: Stable but responsive cloth. In: Proceedings of the 29th Annual Conference on Computer Graphics and Interactive Techniques, SIGGRAPH, pp. 604–611. ACM, New York, NY, USA (2002)
10. Chu, M., Thuerey, N.: Data-driven synthesis of smoke flows with CNN-based feature descriptors. In: Alexa, M. (ed.) ACM Transactions for Graphics, vol. 36, pp. 69:1–69:14. Association for Computing Machinery (ACM), New York, NY, USA, July 2017

11. Cignoni, P., Montani, C., Scopigno, R., Rocchini, C.: A general method for preserving attribute values on simplified meshes. In: Proceedings of IEEE Conference on Visualization, pp. 59–66. IEEE (1998)
12. Cohen, J.D., Olano, M., Manocha, D.: Appearance-preserving simplification. In: Proceedings of the 25th Annual Conference on Computer Graphics and Interactive Techniques, SIGGRAPH, pp. 115–122. ACM, Orlando, FL, USA, July 1998
13. Danerek, R., Dibra, E., Öztireli, C., Ziegler, R., Gross, M.: Deepgarment : 3d garment shape estimation from a single image. In: Chen, M., Zhang, R. (eds.) Computer Graphics Forum, vol. 36, pp. 269–280. Eurographics Association (2017)
14. Dou, M., et al.: Fusion4d: real-time performance capture of challenging scenes. In: Alexa, M. (ed.) ACM Transactions for Graphics, vol. 35, pp. 114:1–114:13. Association for Computing Machinery (ACM), New York, NY, USA, July 2016
15. Fyffe, G., et al.: Multi-view stereo on consistent face topology. Comput. Graph. Forum 36(2), 295–309 (2017)
16. Goldenthal, R., Harmon, D., Fattal, R., Bercovier, M., Grinspun, E.: Efficient simulation of inextensible cloth. In: Hart, J.C. (ed.) ACM Transactions for Graphics, vol. 26, p. 49. Association for Computing Machinery (ACM) (2007)
17. Goldlücke, B., Cremers, D.: Superresolution texture maps for multiview reconstruction. In: IEEE 12th International Conference on Computer Vision, ICCV, pp. 1677–1684. IEEE Computer Society, September 2009
18. Goodfellow, I.J., et al.: Generative adversarial nets. In: Ghahramani, Z., Welling, M., Cortes, C., Lawrence, N., Weinberger., K. (eds.) Advances in Neural Information Processing Systems 27: Annual Conference on Neural Information Processing Systems (NIPS), pp. 2672–2680. Curran Associates Inc, Montreal, Quebec, Canada, December 2014
19. Guan, P., Reiss, L., Hirshberg, D.A., Weiss, A., Black, M.J.: DRAPE: dressing any person. ACM Trans. Graph. 31(4), 35:1–35:10 (2012)
20. Guo, K., Xu, F., Wang, Y., Liu, Y., Dai, Q.: Robust non-rigid motion tracking and surface reconstruction using l0 regularization, pp. 3083–3091. IEEE Computer Society (2015)
21. Hahn, F., et al.: Subspace clothing simulation using adaptive bases. In: Alexa, M. (ed.) ACM Transactions for Graphics, vol. 33, pp. 105:1–105:9. Association for Computing Machinery (ACM) (2014)
22. Hernández, C., Vogiatzis, G., Brostow, G.J., Stenger, B.,Cipolla, R.: Non-rigid photometric stereo with colored lights. In: IEEE 11th International Conference on Computer Vision, ICCV, pp. 1–8. IEEE Computer Society, Rio de Janeiro, Brazil, October 2007
23. Ioffe, S., Szegedy, C.: Batch normalization: accelerating deep network training by reducing internal covariate shift. In: Proceedings of the 32nd International Conference on Machine Learning, ICML, vol. 37, pp. 448–456. ACM (2015)
24. Isola, P., Zhu, J., Zhou, T., Efros, A.A.: Image-to-imagetranslation with conditional adversarial networks. In: 2017 IEEE Conference on Computer Vision and Pattern Recognition, CVPR, pp. 5967–5976. IEEE Computer Society, Honolulu, HI, USA, July 2017
25. Kavan, L., Gerszewski, D., Bargteil, A.W., Sloan, P.P.: Physics-inspired upsampling for cloth simulation in games. In: Hart, J.C. (ed.) ACM Transactions for Graphics, vol. 30, pp. 93:1–93:10. Association for Computing Machinery (ACM), New York, NY, USA, July 2011
26. Krishnamurthy, V., Levoy, M.: Fitting smooth surfaces to dense polygon meshes. In: Proceedings of the 23rd Annual Conference on Computer Graphics and Interactive Techniques, SIGGRAPH, New Orleans, LA, USA, August 1996

27. Lassner, C., Pons-Moll, G., Gehler, P.V.: A generative model of people in clothing. In: IEEE International Conference on Computer Vision, ICCV, pp. 853–862. IEEE Computer Society, Venice, Italy, October 2017

28. Ledig, C., et al.: Photo-realistic single image super-resolution using a generative adversarial network. In: IEEE Conference on Computer Vision and Pattern Recognition, CVPR, pp. 105–114. IEEE Computer Society, Honolulu, HI, USA, July 2017

29. Leroy, V., Franco, J., Boyer, E.: Multi-view dynamic shape refinement using local temporal integration. In: IEEE International Conference on Computer Vision, ICCV, pp. 3113–3122, Venice, Italy (2017)

30. Li, H., Adams, B., Guibas, L.J., Pauly, M.: Robust single-view geometry and motion reconstruction. In: Hart, J.C. (ed.) ACM Transactions for Graphics, vol. 28, pp. 175:1–175:10. Association for Computing Machinery (ACM), New York, NY, USA, December 2009

31. Loper, M., Mahmood, N., Romero, J., Pons-Moll, G., Black, M.J.: SMPL: a skinned multi-person linear model. In: Alexa, M. (ed.) ACM Transactions for Graphics, vol. 34, pp. 248:1–248:16. Association for Computing Machinery (ACM) (2015)

32. MarvelousDesigner (2018). www.marvelousdesigner.com

33. Matsuyama, T., Nobuhara, S., Takai, T., Tung, T.: 3D Video and Its Applications. Springer, London (2012). https://doi.org/10.1007/978-1-4471-4120-4

34. Miguel, E., et al.: Data-driven estimation of cloth simulation models. Comput. Graph. Forum **31**(2), 519–528 (2012)

35. Müller, M., Chentanez, N.: Wrinkle meshes. In: Proceedings of the 2010 ACM SIGGRAPH/Eurographics Symposium on Computer Animation, SCA 2010, pp. 85–92. Eurographics Association, Aire-la-Ville, Switzerland, Switzerland (2010)

36. Newcombe, R.A., Fox, D., Seitz, S.M.: Dynamicfusion: Reconstruction and tracking of non-rigid scenes in real-time. In: IEEE Conference on Computer Vision and Pattern Recognition, CVPR, pp. 343–352. IEEE Computer Society, Boston, MA, USA, June 2015

37. Olszewski, K., et al.: Realistic dynamic facial textures from a single image using GANs. In: IEEE International Conference on Computer Vision, ICCV, pp. 5439–5448. IEEE Computer Society, Venice, Italy, October 2017

38. Pons-Moll, G., Pujades, S., Hu, S., Black, M.: ClothCap: seamless 4d clothing capture and retargeting. ACM Trans. Graph. (Proc. SIGGRAPH) **36**(4), 73 (2017)

39. Pons-Moll, G., Romero, J., Mahmood, N., Black, M.J.: Dyna: a model of dynamic human shape in motion. In: Alexa, M. (ed.) ACM Transactions for Graphics, vol. 34, pp. 120:1–120:14. Association for Computing Machinery (ACM), August 2015

40. Saito, S., Wei, L., Hu, L., Nagano, K., Li, H.: Photorealistic facial texture inference using deep neural networks. IEEE Conference on Computer Vision and Pattern Recognition, CVPR pp. 2326–2335 (Jul 2017)

41. Starck, J., Hilton, A.: Surface capture for performance-based animation. IEEE Comput. Graph. Appl. **27**(3), 21–31 (2007)

42. Sumner, R.W., Popović, J.: Deformation transfer for triangle meshes. In: Hart, J.C. (ed.) ACM Transactions for Graphics, vol. 23, pp. 399–405. Association for Computing Machinery (ACM), New York, NY, USA, August 2004

43. Sutskever, I., Vinyals, O., Le, Q.V.: Sequence to sequence learning with neural networks. In: Ghahramani, Z., Welling, M., Cortes, C.,Lawrence, N., Weinberger, K. (eds.) Advances in Neural Information Processing Systems 27: Annual Conference on Neural Information Processing Systems (NIPS), pp. 3104–3112. Curran Associates, Inc., Montreal, Quebec, Canada, December 2014

44. Taylor, J., Shotton, J., Sharp, T., Fitzgibbon, A.: The vitruvian manifold: Inferring dense correspondences for one-shot human pose estimation. In: Computer Vision and Pattern Recognition (CVPR), pp. 103–110. IEEE Computer Society, July 2012
45. Tsiminaki, V., Franco, J., Boyer, E.: High resolution 3d shape texture from multiple videos. In: IEEE Conference on Computer Vision and Pattern Recognition, CVPR, pp. 1502–1509. IEEE Computer Society, Columbus, OH, USA, June 2014
46. Tung, T., Matsuyama, T.: Intrinsic characterization of dynamic surfaces. In: IEEE Conference on Computer Vision and Pattern Recognition (CVPR), pp. 233–240. IEEE Computer Society, Portland, OR, USA, June 2013
47. Tung, T., Nobuhara, S., Matsuyama, T.: Simultaneous super-resolution and 3d video using graph-cuts. In: IEEE Computer Society Conference on Computer Vision and Pattern Recognition (CVPR). IEEE Computer Society, Anchorage, Alaska, USA, June 2008
48. Tung, T., Nobuhara, S., Matsuyama, T.: Complete multi-view reconstruction of dynamic scenes from probabilistic fusion of narrow and wide baseline stereo. In: IEEE 12th International Conference on Computer Vision, ICCV, pp. 1709–1716. IEEE Computer Society, Kyoto, Japan, September 2009
49. Vlasic, D., Baran, I., Matusik, W., Popović, J.: Articulated mesh animation from multi-view silhouettes. In: Hart, J.C. (ed.) ACM Transactions for Graphics, pp. 97:1–97:9. Association for Computing Machinery (ACM), New York, NY, USA (2008)
50. Vlasic, D., et al.: Dynamic shape capture using multi-view photometric stereo. In: Proceedings of ACM SIGGRAPH Asia, pp. 174:1–174:11. ACM, New York, NY, USA (2009)
51. Volino, P., Magnenat-Thalmann, N.: Virtual Clothing - Theory and Practice. Springer, Heidelberg (2000). https://doi.org/10.1007/978-3-642-57278-4
52. Wang, H., Hecht, F., Ramamoorthi, R., O'Brien, J.F.: Example-based wrinkle synthesis for clothing animation. In: Alexa, M. (ed.) ACM Transactions for Graphics, vol. 29, Article no. 107:1–107:8. Association for Computing Machinery (ACM), Los Angles, CA, July 2010
53. Wang, H., Ramamoorthi, R., O'Brien, J.F.: Data-driven elastic models for cloth: Modeling and measurement. In: Alexa, M. (ed.) ACM Transactions for Graphics, vol. 30, pp. 71:1–71:11. Association for Computing Machinery (ACM), Vancouver, BC Canada, July 2011
54. White, R., Crane, K., Forsyth, D.A.: Capturing and animating occluded cloth. In: Hart, J.C. (ed.) ACM Transactions for Graphics, vol. 26, p. 34. Association for Computing Machinery (ACM) (2007)
55. Zhang, C., Pujades, S., Black, M.J., Pons-Moll, G.: Detailed, accurate, human shape estimation from clothed 3d scan sequences. In: IEEE Conference on Computer Vision and Pattern Recognition (CVPR), pp. 5484–5493. IEEE Computer Society, Honolulu, HI, USA, July 2017

Learning Discriminative Video Representations Using Adversarial Perturbations

Jue Wang[1]([⊠]) [iD] and Anoop Cherian[2] [iD]

[1] Data61/CSIRO, ANU, Canberra, Australia
jue.wang@anu.edu.au
[2] MERL Cambridge, Cambridge, MA, USA
cherian@merl.com

Abstract. Adversarial perturbations are noise-like patterns that can subtly change the data, while failing an otherwise accurate classifier. In this paper, we propose to use such perturbations for improving the robustness of video representations. To this end, given a well-trained deep model for per-frame video recognition, we first generate adversarial noise adapted to this model. Using the original data features from the full video sequence and their perturbed counterparts, as two separate bags, we develop a binary classification problem that learns a set of discriminative hyperplanes – as a subspace – that will separate the two bags from each other. This subspace is then used as a descriptor for the video, dubbed *discriminative subspace pooling*. As the perturbed features belong to data classes that are likely to be confused with the original features, the discriminative subspace will characterize parts of the feature space that are more representative of the original data, and thus may provide robust video representations. To learn such descriptors, we formulate a subspace learning objective on the Stiefel manifold and resort to Riemannian optimization methods for solving it efficiently. We provide experiments on several video datasets and demonstrate state-of-the-art results.

1 Introduction

Deep learning has enabled significant advancements in several areas of computer vision; however, the sub-area of video-based recognition continues to be elusive. In comparison to image data, the volumetric nature of video data makes it significantly more difficult to design models that can remain within the limitations of existing hardware and the available training datasets. Typical ways to adapt image-based deep models to videos are to resort to recurrent deep architectures

---

J. Wang—Work done while interning at MERL.

Electronic supplementary material The online version of this chapter (https://doi.org/10.1007/978-3-030-01225-0_42) contains supplementary material, which is available to authorized users.

© Springer Nature Switzerland AG 2018
V. Ferrari et al. (Eds.): ECCV 2018, LNCS 11208, pp. 716–733, 2018.
https://doi.org/10.1007/978-3-030-01225-0_42

or use three-dimensional spatio-temporal convolutional filters [8,42,50]. Due to hardware limitations, the 3D filters cannot be arbitrarily long. As a result, they usually have fixed temporal receptive fields (of a few frames) [50]. While recurrent networks, such as LSTM and GRU, have shown promising results on video tasks [3,33,60], training them is often difficult, and so far their performance has been inferior to models that look at parts of the video followed by a late fusion [8,41].

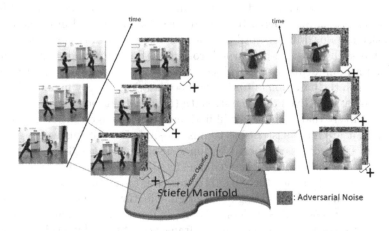

Fig. 1. A graphical illustration of our discriminative subspace pooling with adversarial noise. For every video sequence (as CNN features), our scheme generates a positive bag (with these features) and a negative bag by adding adversarial perturbations to the features. Next, we learn discriminative temporally-ordered hyperplanes that separate the two bags. We use orthogonality constraints on these hyperplanes and use them as representations for the video. As such representations belong to a Stiefel manifold, we use a classifier on this manifold for video recognition.

While, better CNN architectures, such as the recent I3D framework [8], is essential for pushing the state-of-the-art on video tasks, it is also important to have efficient representation learning schemes that can capture the long-term temporal video dynamics from predictions generated by a temporally local model. Recent efforts in this direction, such as rank pooling, temporal segment networks and temporal relation networks [5,10,18,21,22,45,55], aim to incorporate temporal dynamics over clip-level features. However, such models often ignore the noise in the videos, and use representations that adhere to a plausible criteria. For example, in the rank pooling scheme [5,10,20–22], it is assumed that the features from each frame are temporally-ordered, and learns a representation that preserves such order – however without accounting for whether the learned representation fits to data foreground or background.

In this paper, we present a novel pooling framework for temporally-ordered feature summarization. In contrast to prior works, we assume that per-frame video features consist of noisy parts that could confuse a classifier in a downstream task, such as for example, action recognition. A robust representation, in this setting, will be one that could avoid the classifier from using these vulnerable features for making predictions. However, finding these features is challenging as well. To this end, we resort to some intuitions made in a few works recently in the area of adversarial perturbations [34–36,56]. Such perturbations are noise-like patterns that, when added to data, can fail an otherwise well-trained highly accurate classifier. Such perturbations are usually subtle, and in image recognition tasks, are quasi-imperceptible to a human. It was shown in several recent works that such noise can be learned from data. Specifically, by taking gradient ascent on a minimizing learning objective, one can produce such perturbations that will push the data points to the class boundaries, thereby making the classifier to mis-classify. Given that the strength (norm) of this noise is often bounded, it is highly likely that such noise will find minimum strength patterns that select features that are most susceptible to mis-classification. To this end, we use the recent universal adversarial perturbation generation scheme [35].

Once the perturbations are learned (and fixed) for the dataset, we use it to learn robust representations for the video. To this end, for features from every frame, we make two bags, one consisting of the original features, while the other one consisting of features perturbed by noise. Next, we learn a discriminative hyperplane that separates the bags in a max-margin framework. Such a hyperplane, which in our case is produced by a primal support vector machine (SVM), finds decision boundaries that could well-separate the bags; the resulting hyperplane is a single vector and is a weighted combination of all the data points in the bags. Given that the data features are non-linear, and given that a kernelized SVM might not scale well with sequence lengths, we propose to instead use multiple hyperplanes for the classification task, by stacking several such hyperplanes into a column matrix. We propose to use this matrix as our data representation for the video sequence.

However, there is a practical problem with our descriptor; each such descriptor is local to its respective sequences and thus may not be comparable between videos. To this end, we make additional restrictions on the hyperplanes – regularizing them to be orthogonal, resulting in our representation being subspaces. Such subspaces mathematically belong to the so-called Stiefel manifold [6]. We formulate a novel objective on this manifold for learning such subspaces on video features. Further, as each feature is not independent of the previous ones, we make additional temporal constraints. We provide efficient Riemannian optimization algorithms for solving our objective, specifically using the Riemannian conjugate gradient scheme that has been used in several other recent works [10,25,28]. Our overall pipeline is graphically illustrated in Fig. 1.

We present experiments on three video recognition tasks, namely (i) action recognition, (ii) dynamic texture recognition, and (iii) 3D skeleton based action recognition. On all the experiments, we show that our scheme leads to state-of-the-art results, often improving the accuracy between 3–14%.

Before moving on, we summarize the main contributions of this work:

- We introduce adversarial perturbations into the video recognition setting for learning robust video representations.
- We formulate a binary classification problem to learn temporally-ordered discriminative subspaces that separate the data features from their perturbed counterparts.
- We provide efficient Riemannian optimization schemes for solving our objective on the Stiefel manifold.
- Our experiments on three datasets demonstrate state-of-the-art results.

2 Related Work

Traditional video learning methods use hand-crafted features (from a few frames) – such as dense trajectories, HOG, HOF, etc. [52] – to capture the appearance and the video dynamics, and summarize them using a bag-of-words representation or more elegantly using Fisher vectors [38]. With the success of deep learning methods, feeding video data as RGB frames, optical flow subsequences, RGB differences, or 3D skeleton data directly into CNNs is preferred. One successful such approach is the two-stream model (and its variants) [17,18,27,42] that use video segments (of a few frames) to train deep models, the predictions from the segments are fused via average pooling to generate a video level prediction. There are also extensions of this approach that directly learn models in an end-to-end manner [17]. While, such models are appealing to capture the video dynamics, it demands memory for storing the intermediate feature maps of the entire sequence, which may be impractical for long sequences. Recurrent models [2,13,14,31,46,57] have been explored for solving this issue, that can learn to filter useful information while streaming the videos through them, but they are often found difficult to train [37]; perhaps due to the need to back-propagate over time. Using 3D convolutional kernels [8,50] is another idea that proves to be promising, but bring along more parameters. The above architectures are usually trained for improving the classification accuracy, however, do not consider the robustness of their internal representations – accounting for which may improve their generalizability to unseen test data. To this end, we explore the vulnerable factors in a model (via generating adversarial perturbations [35]), and learn representations that are resilient to such factors in a network-agnostic manner.

Our main inspiration comes from the recent work of Moosavi et al. [35] that show the existence of quasi-imperceptible image perturbations that can fool a well-trained CNN model. They provide a systematic procedure to learn such perturbations in an image-agnostic way. In Xie et al. [56], such perturbations are used to improve the robustness of an object detection system. Similar ideas have been explored in [34,36,58]. In Sun et al. [48], a latent model is used to explicitly localize discriminative video segments. In Chang et al. [9], a semantic pooling scheme is introduced for localizing events in untrimmed videos. While these schemes share similar motivation as ours, the problem setup and formulations are entirely different.

On the representation learning front of our contribution, there are a few prior pooling schemes that are similar in the sense that they also use the parameters of an optimization functional as a representation. The most related work is rank-pooling and its variants [4,11,20–22,47,53] that use a rank-SVM for capturing the video temporal evolution. Similar to ours, Cherian et al. [10] propose to use a subspace to represent video sequences. However, none of these methods ensure if the temporal-ordering constraints capture useful video content or capture some temporally-varying noise. To overcome this issue, Wang et al [54] proposes a representation using the decision boundaries of a support vector machine classifier that separates data features from independently sampled noise. In this paper, we revisit this problem in the setting of data dependent noise generation via an adversarial noise design and learns a non-linear decision boundary using Riemannian optimization; our learned representations per sequence are more expressive and leads to significant performance benefits.

3   Proposed Method

Let us assume $X = \langle x_1, x_2, ..., x_n \rangle$ be a sequence of video features, where $x_i \in \mathbb{R}^d$ represents the feature from the i-th frame. We use 'frame' in a loose sense; it could mean a single RGB frame or a sequence of a few RGB or optical flow frames (as in the two stream [43] or the I3D architectures [8]) or a 3D skeleton. The feature representation x_i could be the outputs from intermediate layers of a CNN. As alluded to in the introduction, our key idea is the following. We look forward to an effective representation of X that is (i) compact, (ii) preserves characteristics that are beneficial for the downstream task (such as video dynamics), and (iii) efficient to compute. Recent methods such as generalized rank pooling [10] have similar motivations and propose a formulation that learns compact temporal descriptors that are closer to the original data in ℓ_2 norm. However, such a reconstructive objective may also capture noise, thus leading to sub-optimal performance. Instead, we take a different approach. Specifically, we assume to have access to some noise features $Z = \{z_1, z_2, ..., z_m\}$, each $z_i \in \mathbb{R}^d$. Let us call X the positive bag, with a label $y = +1$ and Z the negative bag with label $y = -1$. Our main goal is to find a discriminative hyperplane that separates the two bags; these hyperplanes can then be used as the representation for the bags.

An obvious question is how such a hyperplane can be a good data representation? To answer this, let us consider the following standard SVM formulation with a single discriminator $w \in \mathbb{R}^d$:

$$\min_{w, \xi \geq 0} \frac{1}{2} \|w\|^2 + \sum_{\theta \in X \cup Z} \left[\max(0, 1 - y(\theta)w^\top \theta + \xi_\theta) + C\xi_\theta \right], \quad (1)$$

Input: Feature points x_{ij}, Network weighting W, fooling rate ψ, cross entropy
loss with softmax funtion $f(.)$, normalization operator $N(.)$.
Output: Adversarial noise vector ϵ.
Initialization: $\epsilon \leftarrow 0$.
repeat
$\quad \Delta\epsilon \leftarrow \arg\min_{r} \|r\|_2 - \sum_{ij} f(W^\top(x_{ij}), W^\top(x_{ij} + \epsilon + r));$
$\quad \epsilon \leftarrow N(\epsilon + \Delta\epsilon);$
until $Accuracy \leq 1 - \psi;$
return v

Algorithm 1: Optimization step for solving adversarial noise.

where with a slight abuse of notation, we assume $y(\theta) \in \{+1, -1\}$ is the label of θ, ξ are the slack variables, and C is a regularization constant on the slacks. Given the positive and negative bags, the above objective learns a linear classification boundary that could separate the two bags with a classification accuracy of say γ. If the two bags are easily separable, then the number of support vectors used to construct the separating hyperplane might be a few and thus may not capture a weighted combination of a majority of the points in the bags - as a result, the learned hyperplane would not be representative of the bags. However, if the negative bag Z is suitably selected and we demand a high γ, we may turn (1) into a difficult optimization problem and would demand the solver to overfit the decision boundary to the bags; this overfitting creates a significantly better summarized representation, as it may need to span a larger portion of the bags to satisfy the γ accuracy.[1] This overfitting of the hyperplane is our key idea, that allows to avoid using data features that are susceptible to perturbations, while summarizing the rest.

There are two key challenges to be addressed in developing such a representation, namely (i) an appropriate noise distribution for the negative bag, and (ii) a formulation to learn the separating hyperplanes. We explore and address these challenges below.

3.1 Finding Noise Patterns

As alluded to above, having good noise distributions that help us identify the vulnerable parts of the feature space is important for our scheme to perform well. To this end, we resort to the recent idea of universal adversarial perturbations (UAP) [35]. This scheme is dataset-agnostic and provides a systematic and mathematically grounded formulation for generating adversarial noise that when added to the original features is highly-likely to mis-classify a pre-trained classifier. Further, this scheme is computationally efficient and requires less data for building relatively generalizable universal perturbations.

---

[1] Here regularization parameter C is mainly assumed to help avoid outliers.

Precisely, suppose $\mathcal{X}$ denotes our dataset, let h be a CNN trained on $\mathcal{X}$ such that $h(x)$ for $x \in \mathcal{X}$ is a class label predicted by h. Universal perturbations are noise vectors ϵ found by solving the following objective:

$$\min_{\epsilon} \|\epsilon\| \text{ s.t. } h(x + \epsilon) \neq h(x), \forall x \in \mathcal{X}, \tag{2}$$

where $\|\epsilon\|$ is a suitable normalization on ϵ such that its magnitude remains small, and thus will not change x significantly. In [35], it is argued that this norm-bound restricts the optimization problem in (2) to look for the minimal perturbation ϵ that will move the data points towards the class boundaries; i.e., selecting features that are most vulnerable – which is precisely the type of noise we need in our representation learning framework.

To this end, we extend the scheme described in [35], to our setting. Differently to their work, we aim to learn a UAP on high-level CNN features as detailed in Algorithm 1 above, where the x_{ij} refers to the ith frame in the jth video. We use the classification accuracy before and after adding the noise as our optimization criteria as captured by maximizing the cross-entropy loss.

3.2   Discriminative Subspace Pooling

Once a "challenging" noise distribution is chosen, the next step is to find a summarization technique for the given video features. While one could use a simple discriminative classifier, such as described in (1) to achieve this, such a linear classifier might not be sufficiently powerful to separate the potentially non-linear CNN features and their adversarial perturbations. An alternative is to resort to non-linear decision boundaries using a kernelized SVM; however that may make our approach less scalable and poses challenges for end-to-end learning. Thus, we look forward to a representation within the span of data features, while having more capacity for separating non-linear features.

Our main idea is to use a subspace of discriminative directions (as against a single one as in (1)) for separating the two bags such that every feature x_i is classified by at least one of the hyperplanes to the correct class label. Such a scheme can be looked upon as an approximation to a non-linear decision boundary by a set of linear ones, each one separating portions of the data. Mathematically, suppose $W \in \mathbb{R}^{d \times p}$ is a matrix with each hyperplane as its columns, then we seek to optimize:

$$\min_{W, \xi} \Omega(W) + \sum_{\theta \in X \cup Z} \left[\max\left(0, 1 - \max\left(\mathbf{y}(\theta) \odot \mathbf{W}^{\top}\theta\right) - \xi_{\theta}\right) + C\xi_{\theta} \right], \tag{3}$$

where $\mathbf{y}$ is a vector with the label y repeated p times along its rows. The quantity Ω is a suitable regularization for W, of which one possibility is to use $\Omega(W) = W^{\top}W = \mathbf{I}_p$, in which case W spans a p dimensional subspace of $\mathbb{R}^d$. Enforcing such subspace constraints (orthonormality) on these hyperplanes are often empirically seen to demonstrate better performance as is also observed in [10]. The operator $\odot$ is the element-wise multiplication and the quantity

$\max(\mathbf{y}(\theta) \odot \mathbf{W}^\top \theta)$ captures the maximum value of the element-wise multiplication, signifying that if at least one hyperplane classifies θ correctly, then the hinge-loss will be zero.

Recall that we work with video data, and thus there are temporal characteristics of this data modality that may need to be captured by our representation. In fact, recent works show that such temporal ordering constraints indeed results in better performance, e.g., in action recognition [4,5,10,21]. However, one well-known issue with such ordered pooling techniques is that they impose a global temporal order on all frames jointly. Such holistic ordering ignores the repetitive nature of human actions, for example, in actions such as clapping or hand-waving. As a result, it may lead the pooled descriptor to overfit to non-repetitive features in the video data, which might be corresponding to noise/background. Usually a slack variable is introduced in the optimization to handle such repetitions, however its effectiveness is questionable. To this end, we propose a simple temporal segmentation based ordering constraints, where we first segment a video sequence into multiple non-overlapping temporal segments $\mathcal{T}_0, \mathcal{T}_1, \dots \mathcal{T}_{\lfloor n/\delta \rfloor}$, and then enforce ordering constraints only within the segments. We find the segment length δ as the minimum number of consecutive frames that do not result in a repeat in the action features.

With the subspace constraints on W and introducing temporal segment-based ordering constraints on the video features, our complete **order-constrained discriminative subspace pooling optimization** can be written as:

$$\min_{\substack{W^\top W = \mathbf{I}_p, \\ \xi, \zeta \geq 0}} \sum_{\theta \in X \cup Z} [\max(0, 1 - \max(\mathbf{y}(\theta) \odot \mathbf{W}^\top \theta) - \xi_\theta)] + C_1 \sum_{\theta \in X \cup Z} \xi_\theta + C_2 \sum_{i<j} \zeta_{ij}, \quad (4)$$

$$\left\| W^\top x_i \right\|^2 + 1 \leq \left\| W^\top x_j \right\|^2 + \zeta_{ij}, \quad i < j, \forall (i,j) \in \mathcal{T}_k, \text{where} \quad (5)$$

$$\mathcal{T}_k = \{k\delta + 1, k\delta + 2, \dots, \min(n, (k+1)\delta)\}, \forall k \in \{0, 1, \dots, \lfloor n/\delta \rfloor\} \quad (6)$$

$$\delta = b^* - a^*, \text{ where } (a^*, b^*) = \arg\min_{a,b>a} \|x_a - x_b\|, \quad (7)$$

where (5) captures the temporal order, while the last two equations define the temporal segments, and computes the appropriate segment length δ, respectively. Note that, the temporal segmentation part could be done offline, by using all videos in the dataset, and selecting a δ which is the mean. In the next section, we present a scheme for optimizing W by solving the objective in (4) and (5).

Once each video sequence is encoded by a subspace descriptor, we use a classifier on the Stiefel manifold for recognition. Specifically, we use the standard exponential projection metric kernel [10,26] to capture the similarity between two such representations, which are then classified using a kernelized SVM.

3.3   Efficient Optimization

The orthogonality constraints on W results in a non-convex optimization problem that may seem difficult to solve at first glance. However, note that such subspaces belong to well-studied objects in differential geometry. Specifically, they are elements of the Stiefel manifold $\mathcal{S}(d,p)$ (p subspaces in $\mathbb{R}^d$), which are a type of Riemannian manifolds with positive curvature [6]. There exists several well-known optimization techniques for solving objectives defined on this manifold [1], one efficient scheme is Riemannian conjugate gradient (RCG) [44]. This method is similar to the conjugate gradient scheme in Euclidean spaces, except that in the case of curved-manifold-valued objects, the gradients should adhere to the geometry (curvature) of the manifold (such as orthogonal columns in our case), which can be achieved via suitable projection operations (called exponential maps). However, such projections may be costly. Fortunately, there are well-known approximate projection methods, termed *retractions* that could achieve these projections efficiently without losing on the accuracy. Thus, tying up all together, for using RCG on our problem, the only part that we need to derive is the Euclidean gradient of our objective with respect to W. To this end, rewriting (5) as a hinge loss on (4), our objective on W and its gradient are:

$$\min_{W \in \mathcal{S}(d,p)} g(W) := \sum_{\theta \in X \cup Z} \left[\max\left(0, 1 - \max\left(\mathbf{y}(\theta) \odot \mathbf{W}^\top \theta \right) - \xi_\theta \right) \right]$$

$$+ \frac{1}{n(n-1)} \sum_{i<j} \max(0, 1 + \left\| W^\top x_i \right\|^2 - \left\| W^\top x_j \right\|^2 - \zeta_{ij}), \quad (8)$$

$$\frac{\partial g}{\partial W} = \sum_{\theta \in X \cup Z} A(W; \theta, y(\theta)) + \frac{1}{n(n-1)} \sum_{i<j} B(W; x_i, x_j), \text{ where} \quad (9)$$

$$A(W; \theta, y(\theta)) = \begin{cases} 0, & \text{if } \max(y(\theta) \odot W^\top \theta - \xi_\theta) \geq 1 \\ -\left[\mathbf{0}_{d \times r-1} \; y(\theta)\theta \; \mathbf{0}_{d \times p-r} \right], & r = \arg\max_q y(\theta) \odot W_q^\top \theta, \text{ else} \end{cases} \quad (10)$$

$$B(W; x_i, x_j) = \begin{cases} 0, & \text{if } \left\| W^\top x_j \right\|^2 \geq 1 + \left\| W^\top x_i \right\|^2 - \zeta_{ij} \\ 2(x_i x_i^\top - x_j x_j^\top)W, & \text{else.} \end{cases} \quad (11)$$

In the definition of $A(W)$, we use $W_q^\top$ to denote the q-th column of W. To reduce clutter in the derivations, we have avoided including the terms using T. Assuming the matrices of the form xx^T can be computed offline, on careful scrutiny we see that the cost of gradient computations on each data pair is only $O(d^2p)$ for $B(W)$ and $O(dp)$ for the discriminative part $A(W)$. If we include temporal segmentation with k segments, the complexity for $B(W)$ is $O(d^2p/k)$.

End-to-End Learning: The proposed scheme can be used in an end-to-end CNN learning setup where the representations can be learned jointly with the CNN weights. In this case, CNN backpropogation would need gradients with respect to the solutions of an argmin problem defined in (4), which may seem difficult. However, there exist well-founded techniques [12,15] [Chap. 5] to address such problems, specifically in the CNN setting [23] and such techniques can be directly applied to our setup. However, since gradient derivations using these techniques will require review of some well-known theoretical results that could be a digression from the course of this paper, we provide them in the supplementary materials.

4   Experiments

In this section, we demonstrate the utility of our discriminative subspace pooling (DSP) on several standard vision tasks (including action recognition, skeleton-based video classification, and dynamic video understanding), and on diverse CNN architectures such as ResNet-152, Temporal Convolutional Network (TCN), and Inception-ResNet-v2. We implement our pooling scheme using the ManOpt Matlab package [7] and use the RCG optimizer with the Hestenes-Stiefel's [24] update rule. We found that the optimization produces useful representations in about 50 iterations and takes about 5 ms per frame on a single core 2.6 GHz CPU. We set the slack regularization constant $C = 1$. As for the CNN features, we used public code for the respective architectures to extract the features. Generating the adversarial perturbation plays a key role in our algorithm, as it is used to generate our negative bag for learning the discriminative hyperplanes. We follow the experimental setting in [35] to generate UAP noise for each model by solving the energy function as depicted in Algorithm 1. Differently from [35], we generate the perturbation in the shape of the high level CNN feature instead of an RGB image. We review below our the datasets, their evaluation protocols, the CNN features next.

4.1   Datasets, CNN Architectures, and Feature Extraction

HMDB-51 [29]: is a popular video benchmark for human action recognition, consisting of 6766 Internet videos over 51 classes; each video is about 20–1000 frames. The standard evaluation protocol reports average classification accuracy on three-folds. To extract features, we train a two-stream ResNet-152 model (as in [42]) taking as input RGB frames (in the spatial stream) and a stack of optical flow frames (in the temporal stream). We use features from the pool5 layer of each stream as input to DSP, which are sequences of 2048D vectors.

NTU-RGBD [39]: is by far the largest 3D skeleton-based video action recognition dataset. It has 56,880 video sequences across 60 classes, 40 subjects, and 80 views. The videos have on average 70 frames and consist of people performing various actions; each frame annotated for 25 3D human skeletal keypoints (some videos have multiple people). According to different subjects and camera views, two evaluation protocols are used, namely cross-view and cross-subject evaluation [39]. We use the scheme in Shahroudy et al. [39] as our baseline in which a temporal CNN (with residual units) is applied on the raw skeleton data. We use the 256D features from the bottleneck layer (before their global average pooling layer) as input to our scheme.

YUP++ Dataset [18]: is a recent dataset for dynamic video-texture understanding. It has 20 scene classes with 60 videos in each class. Importantly, half of the sequences in each class are collected by a static camera and the rest are recorded by a moving camera. The latter is divided into two sub-datasets, YUP++ stationary and YUP++ moving. As described in the [18], we apply the same 1/9 train-test ratio for evaluation. There are about 100–150 frames per sequence. We train an Inception-ResNet-v2 on the respective training set to generate the features and fine-tune a network that was pre-trained on the ImageNet dataset. In detail, we apply the 1/9 train-test ratio and follow the standard supervised training procedure of image-based tasks; following which we extract frame-level features (1536D) from the second-last fully-connected layer.

4.2   Parameter Analysis

Evaluating the Choice of Noise: As is clear by now, the noise patterns should be properly chosen, as it will affect how well the discriminative hyperplanes characterize useful video features. To investigate the quality of UAP features, we compare it with the baseline of choosing noise from a Gaussian distribution with the data mean and standard deviation computed on the respective video dataset (as done in the work of Wang et al. [54]). We repeat this experiment 10-times on the HMDB-51 split-1 features. In Fig. 2(a), we plot the average classification accuracy after our pooling operation against an increasing number of hyperplanes in the subspaces. As is clear, using UAP significantly improves the performance against the alternative, substantiating our intuition. Further, we also find that using more hyperplanes is beneficial, suggesting that adding UAP to the features leads to a non-linear problem requiring more than a single discriminator to capture the informative content.

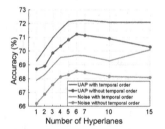 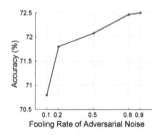

Fig. 2. Analysis of the hyper parameters used in our scheme. All experiments use ResNet-152 features on HMDB-51 split-1 with a fooling rate of 0.8 in (a) and 6 hyperplanes in (b). See text for details.

Evaluating Temporal Constraints: Next, we evaluate the merit of including temporal-ordering constraints in the DSP objective, viz. (4). In Fig. 2(a), we plot the accuracy with and without such temporal order, using the same settings as in the above experiment. As is clear, embedding temporal constraint will help the discriminative subspace capture representations that are related to the video dynamics, thereby showing better accuracy. In terms of the number of hyperplanes, the accuracy increases about 3% from one hyperplane to when using six hyperplanes, and drops around 0.5% from 6 hyperplanes to 15 hyperplanes, suggesting that the number of hyperplanes (6 in this case) is sufficient for representing most sequences.

Table 1. The accuracy comparison between our Discriminative subspace pooling (DSP) with standard Average pooling (AP) and Max pooling (MP).

	HMDB-51			NTU-RGBD		YUP++	
	Spatial	Temporal	Two-stream	Cross-subject	Cross-view	Stationary	Moving
AP	46.7% [19]	60.0% [19]	63.8% [19]	74.3% [45]	83.1% [45]	85.1%	76.5%
MP	45.1%	58.5%	60.6%	65.4%	78.5%	81.8%	72.4%
DSP	**58.5%**	**67.0%**	**72.5%**	**81.6%**	**88.7%**	**95.1%**	**88.3%**

Table 2. Comparisons to the state-of-the-art on each dataset following their respective official evaluation protocols. We used three splits for HMDB-51. 'TS' refers to 'Two-Stream'.

HMDB-51		NTU-RGBD		
Method	Accuracy	Method	Cross-Subject	Cross-View
Temporal Seg. n/w [55]	69.4%	VA-LSTM [59]	79.4%	87.6%
TS I3D [8]	80.9%	TS-LSTM [30]	74.6%	81.3%
ST-ResNet [16]	66.4%	ST-LSTM+Trust Gate [32]	69.2%	77.7%
ST-ResNet+IDT [16]	70.3%	SVMP [54]	78.5%	86.4%
STM Network [17]	68.9%	GRP [10]	76.0%	85.1%
STM Network+IDT [17]	72.2%	Res-TCN [45]	74.3%	83.1%
ShuttleNet+MIFS [40]	71.7%	Ours	**81.6%**	**88.7%**
GRP [10]	70.9%	YUP++		
SVMP [54]	71.0%	Method	Stationary	Moving
L^2STM [49]	66.2%	TRN [18]	92.4%	81.5%
Ours(TS ResNet)	**72.4%**	SVMP [54]	92.5%	83.1%
Ours(TS ResNet+IDT)	**74.3%**	GRP [10]	92.9%	83.6%
Ours(TS I3D)	**81.5%**	Ours	**95.1%**	**88.3%**

UAP Fooling Rate: In Fig. 2(b), we analyze the fooling rate of UAP that controls the quality of the adversary to confuse the trained classifier. The higher the fooling rate is, the more it will mix the information of the feature in different classes. As would be expected, we see that increasing the fooling rate from 0.1 to 0.9 increases the performance of our pooling scheme as well. Interestingly, our algorithm could perform relatively well without requiring a very high value of the fooling rate. From [35], a lower fooling rate would reduce the amount of data needed for generating the adversarial noise, making their algorithm computationally cheaper. Further, comparing Figs. 2(a) and (b), we see that incorporating a UAP noise that has a fooling rate of even 10% does show substantial improvements in DSP performance against using Gaussian random noise (70.8% in Fig. 2(b) against 69.8% in Fig. 2(a)).

Experimental Settings: Going by our observations in the above analysis, for all the experiments in the sequel, we use six subspaces in our pooling scheme, use temporal ordering constraints in our objective, and use a fooling rate of 0.8 in UAP. Further, as mentioned earlier, we use an exponential projection metric kernel [11] for the final classification of the subspace descriptors using a kernel SVM. Results using end-to-end learning are provided in the supplementary materials.

4.3   Experimental Results

Compared with Standard Pooling: In Table 1, we show the performance of DSP on the three datasets and compare to standard pooling methods such as average pooling and max pooling. As is clear, we outperform the baseline results by a large margin. Specifically, we achieve 9% improvement on the HMDB-51 dataset split-1 and 5%–8% improvement on the NTU-RGBD dataset. On these two datasets, we simply apply our pooling method on the CNN features extracted from the pre-trained model. We achieve a substantial boost (of up to 12%) after applying our scheme.

Comparisons to the State of the Art: In Table 2, we compare DSP to the state-of-the-art results on each dataset. On the HMDB-51 dataset, we also report accuracy when DSP is combined hand-crafted features (computed using dense trajectories [51] and summarized as Fisher vectors (IDT-FV)). As the results show, our scheme achieves significant improvements over the state of the art. For example, without IDT-FV, our scheme is 3% better than the next best scheme [55] (69.4% vs. 72.4% ours). Incorporating IDT-FV improves this to 74.3% which is again better than other schemes. We note that the I3D architecture [8] was introduced recently that is pre-trained on the larger Kinectics dataset and when fine-tuned on the HMDB-51 leads to about 80.9% accuracy. To understand the advantages of DSP on pooling I3D model generated features, we applied our scheme to their bottleneck features (extracted using the public code provided by the authors) from the fine-tuned model. We find that our scheme further improves I3D by about 0.6% showing that there is still room for improvement for this model. On the other two datasets, NTU-RGBD and YUP++, we find that our scheme leads to about 5–7% and 3–6% improvements respectively, and outperforms prior schemes based on recurrent networks and temporal relation models, suggesting that our pooling scheme captures spatio-temporal cues much better than recurrent models.

Run Time Analysis: In Fig. 3, we compare the run time of DSP with similar methods such as rank pooling, dynamic images, and GRP. We used the Matlab implementations of other schemes and used the same hardware platform (2.6 GHz Intel CPU single core) for our comparisons. To be fair, we used a single hyperplane in DSP. As the plot shows, our scheme is similar in computations to rank pooling and GRP.

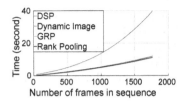

Fig. 3. Run time analysis of DSP against GRP [10], RP [21], and Dynamic Images [5].

Table 3. Comparison of I3D performance on sequences of increasing lengths in HMDB-51 split-1.

#frames	1	80	100	140	160	180	260
#classes	51	49	34	27	23	21	12
AP [8]	**80.8**	81.8	86.1	84.1	82.3	78.0	**77.3**
DSP (ours)	**81.6**	82.8	88.5	88.0	86.1	83.3	**82.6**

Analysis of Results on I3D Features: To understand why the improvement of DSP on I3D (80.9% against our 81.5%) is not significant (on HMDB-51) in comparison to our results on other datasets, we further explored the reasons. Apparently, the I3D scheme uses chunks of 64 frames as input to generate one feature output. However, to obtain DSP representations, we need a sufficient number of features per video sequence to solve the underlying Riemannian optimization problem adequately, which may be unavailable for shorter video clips. To this end, we re-categorized HMDB-51 into subsets of sequences according to their lengths. In Table 3, we show the performance on these subsets and the number of action classes for sequences in these subsets. As our results show, while the difference between average pool (AP) (as is done in [8]) and DSP is less significant when the sequences are smaller (<80 frames), it becomes significant (>5%) when the videos are longer (>260 frames). This clearly shows that DSP on I3D is significantly better than AP on I3D.

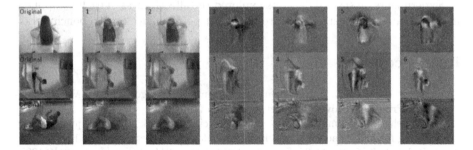

Fig. 4. Visualizations of our DSP descriptor (when applied on raw RGB frames) on an HMDB-51 video sequences. First column shows a sample frame from the video, second-to-seventh columns show the six hyperplanes produced by DSP. Interestingly, we find that each hyperplane captures different aspects of the sequences–first two mostly capture spatial, while the rest capture the temporal dynamics at increasing granularities.

Qualitative Results: In Fig. 4, we visualize the hyperplanes that our scheme produces when applied to raw RGB frames from HMDB-51 videos – i.e., instead of CNN features, we directly feed the raw RGB frames into our DSP, with adversarial noise generated as suggested in [35]. We find that the subspaces capture spatial and temporal properties of the data separately; e.g., the first two hyperplanes seem to capture mostly the spatial cues in the video (such as the objects, background, etc.) while the rest capture mostly the temporal dynamics at greater granularities. Note that we do not provide any specific criteria to achieve this behavior, instead the scheme automatically seem to learn such hyperplanes corresponding to various levels of discriminative information. In the supplementary materials, we provide comparisons of this visualization against those generated by PCA and generalized rank pooling [10].

5 Conclusions

In this paper, we investigated the problem of representation learning for video sequences. Our main innovation is to generate and use synthetic noise, in the form of adversarial perturbations, for producing our representation. Assuming the video frames are encoded as CNN features, such perturbations are often seen to affect vulnerable parts of the features. Using such generated perturbations to our benefit, we propose a discriminative classifier, in a max-margin setup, via learning a set of hyperplanes as a subspace, that could separate our synthetic noise from data. As such hyperplanes need to fit to useful parts of the features for achieving good performance, it is reasonable to assume they capture data parts that are robust. We provided a non-linear objective for learning our subspace representation and explored efficient optimization schemes for computing it. Experiments on several datasets explored the effectiveness of each component in our scheme, demonstrating state-of-the-art performance on the benchmarks.

References

1. Absil, P.A., Mahony, R., Sepulchre, R.: Optimization Algorithms on Matrix Manifolds. Princeton University Press, Princeton (2009)
2. Baccouche, M., Mamalet, F., Wolf, C., Garcia, C., Baskurt, A.: Sequential deep learning for human action recognition. In: Salah, A.A., Lepri, B. (eds.) HBU 2011. LNCS, vol. 7065, pp. 29–39. Springer, Heidelberg (2011). https://doi.org/10.1007/978-3-642-25446-8_4
3. Ballas, N., Yao, L., Pal, C., Courville, A.: Delving deeper into convolutional networks for learning video representations. In: ICLR (2016)
4. Bilen, H., Fernando, B., Gavves, E., Vedaldi, A.: Action recognition with dynamic image networks. PAMI (2017)
5. Bilen, H., Fernando, B., Gavves, E., Vedaldi, A., Gould, S.: Dynamic image networks for action recognition. In: CVPR (2016)
6. Boothby, W.M.: An Introduction to Differentiable Manifolds and Riemannian Geometry, vol. 120. Academic press, Orlando (1986)

7. Boumal, N., Mishra, B., Absil, P.A., Sepulchre, R.: Manopt, a matlab toolbox for optimization on manifolds. JMLR **15**(1), 1455–1459 (2014)
8. Carreira, J., Zisserman, A.: Quo vadis, action recognition? A new model and the kinetics dataset. In: CVPR, July 2017
9. Chang, X., Yu, Y.L., Yang, Y., Xing, E.P.: Semantic pooling for complex event analysis in untrimmed videos. PAMI **39**(8), 1617–1632 (2017)
10. Cherian, A., Fernando, B., Harandi, M., Gould, S.: Generalized rank pooling for activity recognition. In: CVPR (2017)
11. Cherian, A., Sra, S., Gould, S., Hartley, R.: Non-linear temporal subspace representations for activity recognition. In: CVPR (2018)
12. Chiang, A.C.: Fundamental Methods of Mathematical Economics. McGraw-Hill, New York (1984)
13. Donahue, J., et al.: Long-term recurrent convolutional networks for visual recognition and description. In: CVPR (2015)
14. Du, Y., Wang, W., Wang, L.: Hierarchical recurrent neural network for skeleton based action recognition. In: CVPR (2015)
15. Faugeras, O.: Three-Dimensional Computer Vision: A Geometric Viewpoint. MIT press, Cambridge (1993)
16. Feichtenhofer, C., Pinz, A., Wildes, R.: Spatiotemporal residual networks for video action recognition. In: NIPS (2016)
17. Feichtenhofer, C., Pinz, A., Wildes, R.P.: Spatiotemporal multiplier networks for video action recognition. In: CVPR (2017)
18. Feichtenhofer, C., Pinz, A., Wildes, R.P.: Temporal residual networks for dynamic scene recognition. In: CVPR (2017)
19. Feichtenhofer, C., Pinz, A., Zisserman, A.: Convolutional two-stream network fusion for video action recognition. In: CVPR (2016)
20. Fernando, B., Anderson, P., Hutter, M., Gould, S.: Discriminative hierarchical rank pooling for activity recognition. In: CVPR (2016)
21. Fernando, B., Gavves, E., Oramas, J.M., Ghodrati, A., Tuytelaars, T.: Modeling video evolution for action recognition. In: CVPR (2015)
22. Fernando, B., Gould, S.: Learning end-to-end video classification with rank-pooling. In: ICML (2016)
23. Gould, S., Fernando, B., Cherian, A., Anderson, P., Cruz, R.S., Guo, E.: On differentiating parameterized argmin and argmax problems with application to bi-level optimization. arXiv preprint arXiv:1607.05447 (2016)
24. Hager, W.W., Zhang, H.: A new conjugate gradient method with guaranteed descent and an efficient line search. SIAM J. Optim. **16**(1), 170–192 (2005)
25. Harandi, M.T., Salzmann, M., Hartley, R.: From manifold to manifold: geometry-aware dimensionality reduction for SPD matrices. In: Fleet, D., Pajdla, T., Schiele, B., Tuytelaars, T. (eds.) ECCV 2014. LNCS, vol. 8690, pp. 17–32. Springer, Cham (2014). https://doi.org/10.1007/978-3-319-10605-2_2
26. Harandi, M.T., Salzmann, M., Jayasumana, S., Hartley, R., Li, H.: Expanding the family of grassmannian kernels: an embedding perspective. In: Fleet, D., Pajdla, T., Schiele, B., Tuytelaars, T. (eds.) ECCV 2014. LNCS, vol. 8695, pp. 408–423. Springer, Cham (2014). https://doi.org/10.1007/978-3-319-10584-0_27
27. Hayat, M., Bennamoun, M., An, S.: Deep reconstruction models for image set classification. PAMI **37**(4), 713–727 (2015)
28. Huang, Z., Wang, R., Shan, S., Chen, X.: Projection metric learning on GDrassmann manifold with application to video based face recognition. In: CVPR (2015)
29. Kuehne, H., Jhuang, H., Garrote, E., Poggio, T., Serre, T.: HMDB: a large video database for human motion recognition. In: ICCV (2011)

30. Lee, I., Kim, D., Kang, S., Lee, S.: Ensemble deep learning for skeleton-based action recognition using temporal sliding LSTM networks. In: ICCV (2017)
31. Li, Q., Qiu, Z., Yao, T., Mei, T., Rui, Y., Luo, J.: Action recognition by learning deep multi-granular spatio-temporal video representation. In: ICMR (2016)
32. Liu, J., Shahroudy, A., Xu, D., Kot, A.C., Wang, G.: Skeleton-based action recognition using spatio-temporal LSTM network with trust gates. arXiv preprint arXiv:1706.08276 (2017)
33. Liu, J., Shahroudy, A., Xu, D., Wang, G.: Spatio-temporal LSTM with trust gates for 3D human action recognition. In: Leibe, B., Matas, J., Sebe, N., Welling, M. (eds.) ECCV 2016. LNCS, vol. 9907, pp. 816–833. Springer, Cham (2016). https://doi.org/10.1007/978-3-319-46487-9_50
34. Lu, J., Issaranon, T., Forsyth, D.: SafetyNet: detecting and rejecting adversarial examples robustly. In: ICCV (2017)
35. Moosavi-Dezfooli, S.M., Fawzi, A., Fawzi, O., Frossard, P.: Universal adversarial perturbations (2017)
36. Oh, S.J., Fritz, M., Schiele, B.: Adversarial image perturbation for privacy protection-a game theory perspective. In: ICCV (2017)
37. Pascanu, R., Mikolov, T., Bengio, Y.: On the difficulty of training recurrent neural networks. In: ICML (2013)
38. Sadanand, S., Corso, J.J.: Action bank: a high-level representation of activity in video. In: CVPR (2012)
39. Shahroudy, A., Liu, J., Ng, T.T., Wang, G.: NTU RGB+ D: a large scale dataset for 3d human activity analysis. In: CVPR (2016)
40. Shi, Y., Tian, Y., Wang, Y., Zeng, W., Huang, T.: Learning long-term dependencies for action recognition with a biologically-inspired deep network. In: ICCV (2017)
41. Simonyan, K., Vedaldi, A., Zisserman, A.: Deep inside convolutional networks: Visualising image classification models and saliency maps. arXiv preprint arXiv:1312.6034 (2013)
42. Simonyan, K., Zisserman, A.: Two-stream convolutional networks for action recognition in videos. In: NIPS (2014)
43. Simonyan, K., Zisserman, A.: Very deep convolutional networks for large-scale image recognition. arXiv preprint arXiv:1409.1556 (2014)
44. Smith, S.T.: Optimization techniques on riemannian manifolds. Fields Inst. Commun. **3**(3), 113–135 (1994)
45. Soo Kim, T., Reiter, A.: Interpretable 3d human action analysis with temporal convolutional networks. In: CVPR Workshops (2017)
46. Srivastava, N., Mansimov, E., Salakhutdinov, R.: Unsupervised learning of video representations using LSTMs. In: ICML (2015)
47. Su, B., Zhou, J., Ding, X., Wang, H., Wu, Y.: Hierarchical dynamic parsing and encoding for action recognition. In: Leibe, B., Matas, J., Sebe, N., Welling, M. (eds.) ECCV 2016. LNCS, vol. 9908, pp. 202–217. Springer, Cham (2016). https://doi.org/10.1007/978-3-319-46493-0_13
48. Sun, C., Nevatia, R.: Discover: discovering important segments for classification of video events and recounting. In: CVPR (2014)
49. Sun, L., Jia, K., Chen, K., Yeung, D.Y., Shi, B.E., Savarese, S.: Lattice long short-term memory for human action recognition. In: ICCV (2017)
50. Tran, D., Bourdev, L., Fergus, R., Torresani, L., Paluri, M.: Learning spatiotemporal features with 3d convolutional networks. In: ICCV (2015)
51. Wang, H., Kläser, A., Schmid, C., Liu, C.L.: Dense trajectories and motion boundary descriptors for action recognition. IJCV **103**(1), 60–79 (2013)

52. Wang, H., Schmid, C.: Action recognition with improved trajectories. In: ICCV (2013)
53. Wang, J., Cherian, A., Porikli, F.: Ordered pooling of optical flow sequences for action recognition. In: WACV. IEEE (2017)
54. Wang, J., Cherian, A., Porikli, F., Gould, S.: Video representation learning using discriminative pooling. In: CVPR (2018)
55. Wang, L., et al.: Temporal segment networks: towards good practices for deep action recognition. In: Leibe, B., Matas, J., Sebe, N., Welling, M. (eds.) ECCV 2016. LNCS, vol. 9912, pp. 20–36. Springer, Cham (2016). https://doi.org/10.1007/978-3-319-46484-8_2
56. Xie, C., Wang, J., Zhang, Z., Zhou, Y., Xie, L., Yuille, A.: Adversarial examples for semantic segmentation and object detection. In: ICCV (2017)
57. Yue-Hei Ng, J., Hausknecht, M., Vijayanarasimhan, S., Vinyals, O., Monga, R., Toderici, G.: Beyond short snippets: deep networks for video classification. In: CVPR (2015)
58. Zhang, J., Zhang, T., Dai, Y., Harandi, M., Hartley, R.: Deep unsupervised saliency detection: a multiple noisy labeling perspective. In: CVPR (2018)
59. Zhang, P., Lan, C., Xing, J., Zeng, W., Xue, J., Zheng, N.: View adaptive recurrent neural networks for high performance human action recognition from skeleton data. In: ICCV (2017)
60. Zhu, W., et al.: Co-occurrence feature learning for skeleton based action recognition using regularized deep LSTM networks. In: AAAI (2016)

End-to-End Joint Semantic Segmentation of Actors and Actions in Video

Jingwei Ji[1]([envelope]), Shyamal Buch[1], Alvaro Soto[2], and Juan Carlos Niebles[1]

[1] Stanford Vision and Learning Lab, Stanford, USA
{jingweij,shyamal,jniebles}@cs.stanford.edu
[2] Pontificia Universidad Católica de Chile, Santiago, Chile
asoto@ing.puc.cl

Abstract. Traditional video understanding tasks include human action recognition and actor/object semantic segmentation. However, the combined task of providing semantic segmentation for different actor classes simultaneously with their action class remains a challenging but necessary task for many applications. In this work, we propose a new end-to-end architecture for tackling this task in videos. Our model effectively leverages multiple input modalities, contextual information, and multi-task learning in the video to directly output semantic segmentations in a single unified framework. We train and benchmark our model on the Actor-Action Dataset (A2D) for joint actor-action semantic segmentation, and demonstrate state-of-the-art performance for both segmentation and detection. We also perform experiments verifying our approach improves performance for zero-shot recognition, indicating generalizability of our jointly learned feature space.

Keywords: Semantic segmentation · Actor · Action · Video End-to-End · Zero-shot

1 Introduction

Action understanding is one of the key tasks in the field of video analysis. Recent progress has been primarily focused on obtaining a relatively coarse understanding of human-centric actions in video [10,12]. However, a more comprehensive understanding of actions requires to identify fine-grained details from a video sequence, such as what actors are involved in an action, how are they interacting, and where are their precise spatial locations. Such pixel-level joint understanding of actors and actions can open a series of new exciting applications, such as activity-aware robots able to accurately localize potential users, understand their needs, and interact with them to assist. Furthermore, expanding action understanding to non-human actors is essential for autonomous vehicles.

More fundamentally, delving deeper into the synergies between action recognition and object segmentation can be mutually beneficial, and improve overall video understanding. As an example, an accurate and fine grained spatial identification of the main actors involved in an action may increase the robustness

© Springer Nature Switzerland AG 2018
V. Ferrari et al. (Eds.): ECCV 2018, LNCS 11208, pp. 734–749, 2018.
https://doi.org/10.1007/978-3-030-01225-0_43

of action recognition. Similarly, the correct recognition of the underlying action in a video sequence can facilitate the identification of relevant finer details, such as precise actor locations. Building a working model that takes advantage of these insights requires careful architecture design, incorporating two design components in a synergistic manner. First, this would require integrating a finer localization of the main actors executing the action within the action recognition pipeline. Second, the model must also have a strong understanding of the activities occurring within the video, a task that is more traditionally context-dependent. With the above observation and philosophy, we tackle the problem of **joint actor-action semantic segmentation**, which asks the perception algorithm to predict actor and action class labels at the pixel level in the input video clip.

This task of actor-action semantic segmentation is inherently challenging. First, we desire actor and action knowledge to be learned jointly to benefit each other's prediction. At the same time, the learned representations should be decoupled well enough to prevent an explosion of joint classes in the actor-action cross product space. Second, although the problem can be addressed by a multistage refinement approach – where actor detection, semantic segmentation, and action recognition are separate – a direct end-to-end design can reduce multistage engineering. Third, in contrast with pixelwise segmentation on a static image, contextual information from other frames may need to be considered to predict accurate action labels.

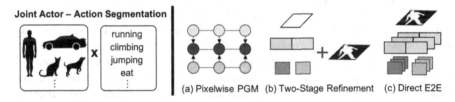

Fig. 1. We tackle the problem of joint actor-action semantic segmentation in videos, which requires simultaneous pixelwise recognition of different actor and action classes. Prior work have proposed (a) pixelwise probabilistic graphical model (PGM) approaches [27,28] and (b) two-stage refinement approaches [11]. (c) In this work, we propose a new direct end-to-end architecture that combines video action recognition and actor segmentation in a single unified model.

A few prior works [11,27–29] have examined the challenging joint task of actor-action semantic segmentation, as illustrated in Fig. 1. For example, Xu et al. [27] proposed a graphical model that adaptively groups spatial and temporal information from supervoxels in videos. Kalogeiton et al. [11] proposed a joint actor-action detector on single frames and then perform segmentation. While all of these methods made important progress towards the actor-action semantic segmentation problem, they either do not decouple the actor and action label spaces, rely on two-stage refinement, or do not effectively leverage contextual information. In our work, we address all of these challenges simultaneously. Thus, our **contributions** can be summarized as follows:

- We propose a new *end-to-end* architecture for actor-action semantic segmentation in video that effectively leverages multiple input modalities, contextual information from video, and joint multitask learning.
- We observe that our approach significantly outperforms prior state-of-the-art methods on both actor-action segmentation and detection in videos.
- Finally, we demonstrate the generalization capabilities of our network for stronger zero-shot detection of actor-action pairs over previous work.

2 Related Work

In this section, we discuss related work in instance segmentation from single images, recent advances on convolutional networks for video analysis and actor-action semantic segmentation.

2.1 Instance Segmentation

The instance segmentation problem for images has been widely studied with significant recent advances [4,5,8,16,17,21]. Recent progress in this field includes DeepMask [16] and its following works [4,5,17] resort to only instance segmentation without semantic labels, or predicting semantic labels as a second stage. Another approach is predicting masks and semantic labels in parallel, as in Mask R-CNN [8], which is more flexible and straightforward. Although these approaches focus on static images, they provide a gateway to perform per-frame semantic segmentation in videos.

Another line of work directly tackles the problem of video object segmentation [2,13,24]. These algorithms generally require access to ground truth mask annotation in the first frame of test video. In practice, such detailed annotation is not present in real-world applications at inference time. Furthermore, these approaches attempt to build object-agnostic algorithms that do not have access to the object class during training time, and are not capable of predicting object labels during test time. In this paper, we are interested in performing actor-action segmentation when no annotations are available at inference time, and in generating pixel-wise label inference of foreground actors and background pixels.

2.2 3D ConvNets for Action Recognition

A significant amount of research [3,10,12,18,22,23,26] has considered the problem of action classification in video clips. In that setting, the input is a short video sequence, and the goal is to provide a single action label for the full clip, typically focused on human actions. Recent work [3,18,23,26] has focused on leveraging 3D convolutional networks as the core of the action recognition framework. Recently, Carreira *et al.* [3] proposed the I3D architecture, which considers a two-stream network configuration [12,22] and performs late fusion of the outputs of individual networks trained on RGB and optical flow input, trained separately. Other recent works [18, 26] have proposed similar 3D architectures for recognition, focusing on improving performance while reducing computation cost. In this work, while we aim to tackle a more fine-grained and spatially-oriented action understanding problem, we draw inspiration from these frameworks in our model design. We elaborate on some of the key architectural advances for our stronger joint action-actor performance in Sect. 3.2.

2.3 Actor-Action Semantic Segmentation

The actor-action semantic segmentation problem is first raised by Xu et al. [28], where they collected the dataset A2D to study the problem and introduced a tri-layer model as a first approach to solve this problem. Following [28], Xu et al. [27] proposed a Grouping Process Model (GPM) which adaptively groups segments during inference, and Yan et al. [29] proposed a weakly supervised method with only video-level tags being used in training. These methods depend on Conditional Random Fields (CRF) [21] for pixel-level segmentation, and can be classified as probabilistic graphical model (PGM) approaches. With the recent success of object detection and instance segmentation using deep neural networks, Kalogeiton et al. [11] proposed an actor-action detection network on single frames in video, then applied SharpMask [17] to generate actor-action semantic segmentation. This approach is one of two-stage refinement, whereby the main model provides detection boxes which are used in tandem with output segmentation masks from another method to provide refined outputs.

Our work advances the state-of-the-art in actor-action semantic segmentation. To the best of our knowledge, our method is the first end-to-end deep model for this task. In particular, we propose a unified framework to jointly consider temporal context, actor classification, action recognition, bounding box detection and pixel level segmentation.

3 Proposed Model

Our goal task is to provide semantic segmentation across the joint actor-action class space in input video data. To meet the challenges described in Sect. 1, we hold the following model design philosophy: (1) To be able to decouple actor and action learning, actor and action classification heads should be separated and have their own set of parameters. (2) The network should be end-to-end with knowledge sharing between actor and action understanding, thus we have actor and action sharing the backbone structure for frame feature extraction. (3) The temporal context should be utilized for better action recognition, thus we leverage the short-term and contextual motion cues by 3D convolution layers and flow input.

We propose to tackle this with an end-to-end deep architecture, as illustrated in Fig. 2. Our approach takes both RGB and flow video clips as input streams, leveraging information from both appearance and motion in the video.

Our network simultaneously outputs mask segmentation, and classification for actors in the branch of pixel-level actor localization, which will be elaborated in Sect. 3.1. With the actor localization provided, 3D feature maps from RGB and flow streams are jointly employed to perform action recognition. Details for action recognition will be found in Sect. 3.2. We share the appearance backbone parameters and activations between actor and action branches so that they benefit from each other's knowledge, and the parameters are jointly optimized through the end-to-end joint learning of our architecture (Sect. 3.3).

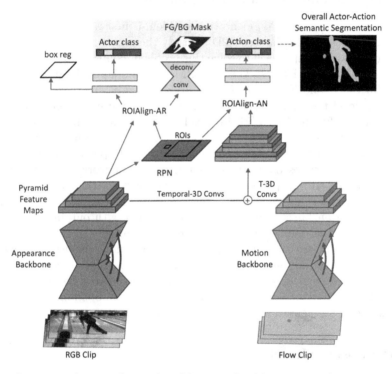

Fig. 2. Overview of our end-to-end architecture for joint actor-action segmentation. The model takes as input a context window of both RGB and optical flow frames, and outputs the semantic segmentation for all actor classes of interest jointly with their actions. Note that in the above example both the bowling ball and the adult are segmented in the same forward pass - we visualize the FG/BG mask for the adult only for clarity. See Sect. 3 for more model details.

3.1   Pixel-Level Actor Localization

For the sub-task of actor localization, we build upon recent successful architectures for 2D object detection and semantic segmentation, such as Faster R-CNN [19] and Mask R-CNN [8]. In particular, we adopt a structure similar to that of Mask R-CNN to achieve pixel-level actor localization.

Appearance Backbone. Given a RGB input clip, each frame would go through the appearance backbone first to generate feature maps that will be used for next steps. On the one hand, the generated feature maps should be of high-level abstraction such that they capture the essential concepts of actor, on the other hand they also maintain the pixel-wise information to be leveraged for segmentation prediction. Therefore, we choose to use Feature Pyramid Network (FPN) [14] backbone feature extractor. Here the FPN is composed of a vanilla ResNet-101 [9] and a top-down architecture with skip connections between activations of the same resolution. The ResNet-101 is powerful at extracting high-level features, while the skip connections avoid low-level information being lost. Note that FPN is fully convolutional, which preserves the spatial correspondence between the output feature maps and input frames. Rather than outputting a single feature map for every single frame, the appearance backbone outputs a pyramid of feature maps, which is composed of feature maps from different resolution. In our network, we utilize feature maps from 4 different resolutions. Denote the height and width of input frame as H and W, the resolutions are (H, W) devided by 4, 8, 16, 32, respectively. Considering that we are working on a variety of 'actors' from *baby* and *adult* to *bird* and *ball*, the pyramid feature maps help detecting actors of different scales.

Region Proposal Network. As in Mask R-CNN, the next step of actor localization is done by Region Proposal Network (RPN) [19]. Given the pyramid feature maps, the RPN generates Region of Interests (RoIs) in the form of bounding boxes. Feature maps of different resolution will go through the same RPN to generate a bunch of RoIs, and the final RoIs are the concatenation of all of them. Note that different from [11], we only use the feature maps output by appearance model to generate RoIs, while they also use features from motion model. We found in experiment that RoIs from appearance models are of much higher quality than those from motion model, thus we stick with RoIs from appearance model only.

Multitask Heads. With the RoIs generated by RPN, and the pyramid feature maps of each video frame, an RoIAlign operation [8] is executed to crop and resize feature map according to RoI bounding boxes. Different from the RoI pooling operation in [19], RoIAlign fixes the misalignment and unnecessary quantization in spatial dimensions, and has shown better performance in [8]. An important fact is that RoIAlign finds the matching resolution of feature map from the pyramid according to the size of RoI, which enables the network to capture small actors such as *ball* and *bird*. To distinguish with the RoIAlign operation in action part, we name them RoIAlign-AR and RoIAlign-AN respectively.

The cropped and resized feature patch output by RoIAlign-AR will be fed into multiple heads to fulfill different sub-tasks. This is in line with the similar setup in Mask R-CNN. In total, there are three parallel sub-tasks in the pixel-level actor localization: (1) bounding box regression, (2) actor classification, and (3) foreground/background segmentation. The bounding box regressor and actor classifier is composed of fully connected layers operated on flattened feature patch, while the segmentation head is fully convolutional (conv and deconv layers).

3.2   Two-Stream Action Recognition with Temporal Aggregation

Backbones. For action recognition, different from actor branch, two backbones are used. On the one hand, the same backbone from appearance model is shared such that appearance features of the actors also contribute in action understanding. Besides information from appearance, as shown in [22], motion patterns are also valuable in action recognition. Therefore we build a mirrored motion backbone with a separate set of parameters, which takes in flow clips, and extracts motion patterns from them. These two backbones formulate the two-stream attributes of our model. Following [3,7,22], the input of the flow branch is a tensor of three channels with the x and y coordinates and the magnitude of flow.

Temporal Aggregation. As we discussed in Sect. 1, one challenge in the actor-action semantic segmentation in video is how to leverage the temporal context information for better action recognition. Here we resort to 3D CNN as the ingredient to achieve temporal aggregation. We apply separate 3D convolutional layers on the top of the pyramid feature maps output by each backbone to aggregate the temporal context. The pyramid feature maps from two backbones are then concatenated at the corresponding resolution, which will be further employed for action recognition. Specifically, $3 \times 1 \times 1$ conv layers [18] are applied to feature maps of every spatial scale, so the information of neighboring frames are aggregated into 3D pyramid feature maps. We note that we adopt an efficient "top-heavy" design [26], focusing 3D temporal convolutions on the upper portion of the network. We demonstrate in Sect. 4.3 that such aggregation of temporal context is helpful for improved performance.

After temporal 3D conv layers, the 3D pyramid feature maps from each backbone are concatenated on the corresponding resolution level. As suggested by [11] for 2D architecture, and corroborated by our own experiments, late fusion in standard action recognition approaches [3,7,22] does *not* work well when considering the joint task of actor/action recognition and semantic segmentation. Therefore we choose to fuse appearance and motion in the mid-level.

Action Classification. With the RoIs provided by actor localization branch, fused 3D pyramid feature maps go through another RoIAlign-AN layer. The cropped and resized 3D feature map output by RoIAlign-AN incorporate information not only from the local actor, but also temporal context via temporal layers, and spatial context with proper receptive fields. The rich spatial and temporal contexts provide sufficient information for pixelwise action recognition over localized regions.

3.3 Joint Learning of Actors and Actions

Our end-to-end network enables joint learning for actor and action classification and segmentation. Joint learning all subtasks force the backbone features to contain necessary information for actor detection, actor classification, action recognition and actor-action segmentation. We use a multitask loss for parameter optimization:

$$L = \lambda_1 L_{RoI-cls} + \lambda_2 L_{box-reg} + \lambda_3 L_{actor-cls} + \lambda_4 L_{action-cls} + \lambda_5 L_{mask} \quad (1)$$

where $L_{RoI-cls}$ and $L_{box-reg}$ are as defined in [6], and λ's are hyperparameters. Actor and action classification losses are the negative log likelihood of the ground truth class. Denote the set of actor classes as X, the set of action classes as Y, the ground truth actor class as x, action class as y, we have:

$$L_{actor-cls} = -\log p_X(x), L_{action-cls} = -\log p_Y(y). \quad (2)$$

The mask head generates $|X|$ masks corresponding to every possible actor. Assuming the ground truth actor class is k, then L_{mask} will only be computed on the k-th mask. As in [8], L_{mask} is defined as the average binary cross-entropy loss.

Note that the losses are computed respect to frames rather than the whole video. Together with the temporal layers, our network design and learning setup are able to train even when some of the context frames have missing annotations, while still leveraging temporal context to obtain better spatial action recognition for the joint task.

4 Experiments

Dataset Details. We train and evaluate our model on the Actor-Action (A2D) dataset [28] for joint actor/action semantic segmentation To the best of our knowledge, A2D is the largest dataset that covers multiple actor and action classes and provides pixel-level semantic labels, and is the only joint action-actor segmentation benchmark for video reported in prior work [11,27,28]. This dataset comprises of 3782 YouTube videos, with sparse pixel-level joint semantic segmentation annotations and instance bounding boxes over 3–5 frames for each video. A2D covers 7 actor classes: *adult, baby, ball, bird, car, cat, dog*, and 9 action classes: *climb, crawl, eat, fly, jump, roll, run, walk, none* (no action). We note that some of the joint classes in the cross products are invalid, e.g. *car-eating*, and we exclude them in training and inference, as per prior work.

Implementation Details. We implement our end-to-end architecture in TensorFlow [1]. For the spatial dimensions of our 3D network, we initialize the model by leveraging pre-trained weights from Mask R-CNN [8] on MS-COCO [15]. The ResNet-101 backbone in the optical flow input branch is separately initialized with pre-trained weights on ImageNet [20], as per prior work [11,25]. The weights for the temporal convolutions do not leverage pre-trained weights and are randomly initialized. We use SGD optimizer with learning rate of 2e-4. Additional details and code are provided in our supplementary.

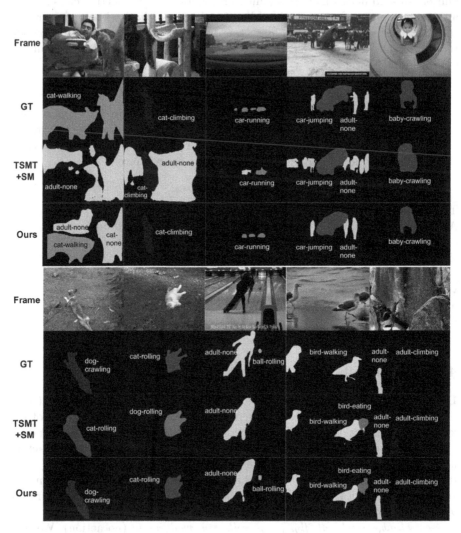

Fig. 3. Qualitative results. We visualize the input key frame and groundtruth (GT) semantic segmentation masks. The TSMT model + SharpMask (SM) outputs are provided by the authors of [11]. We qualitatively observe improved actor-action semantic segmentation performance of our end-to-end model in many cases over the prior work. Interestingly, we note that in some cases our method provides even more accurate predictions than the original groundtruth annotations, such as in the top left example with the adult and cats. See Sect. 4.1 for details and supplementary for video visualizations.

Table 1. Joint Actor-Action Semantic Segmentation Quantitative Results. We observe our end-to-end model significantly improved performance over prior state-of-the-art approaches using pixelwise PGMs or two-stage refinement architectures [11,27,28] for actor, action, and joint actor-action (A,A) semantic segmentation in videos. We provide additional discussion in Sect. 4.1, and detailed ablation analysis in Sect. 4.3.

Approach	Actor			Action			Joint (A,A)		
	ave	glo	mIoU	ave	glo	mIoU	ave	glo	mIoU
Trilayer [28]	45.7	74.6	-	47.0	74.6	-	25.4	76.2	-
GPM+TSP [27]	58.3	85.2	33.4	60.5	85.3	32.0	43.3	84.2	19.9
GPM+GBH [27]	59.4	84.8	33.3	61.2	84.9	31.9	43.9	83.8	19.9
TSMT [11] + GBH	72.9	85.8	42.7	61.4	84.6	35.5	48.0	83.9	24.9
TSMT [11] + SM	73.7	90.6	49.5	60.5	89.3	42.2	47.5	88.7	29.7
Ours	**79.1**	**94.5**	**66.4**	**62.9**	**92.6**	**46.3**	**51.4**	**92.5**	**36.9**

4.1 Joint Actor-Action Semantic Segmentation

Table 1 shows a comparison of our joint method against prior state-of-the-art methods. We note that these prior methods leverage external techniques to generate initial semantic segmentation masks, such as GBH [27] and SharpMask (SM) [17], before refining them. However, our approach is trained end-to-end to directly output pixelwise segmentation for both actors and actions.

We report three different types of metrics following [11]: (1) ave - the average per-class accuracy, (2) glo - the global pixel accuracy, and (3) mIoU - mean pixel Intersection-over-Union. Pixel accuracy is the percentage of pixels whose labels are being correctly predicted. ave first computes pixel accuracy for each class and then average over classes, while glo is computed over all pixels. As noted in [11], mIoU is the most representative metric on this dataset since it's not biased towards background pixels, though we demonstrate consistent improved performance across the board. We report the comparison on evaluation with prior works in Table 1, where we measure all three metrics on actor label, action label, and actor-action pair label (Joint(A,A)) settings, as described in [11]. Since a correct labeling for actor-action pair requires both actor and action labels to be correct, the corresponding numbers in Joint(A,A) are in general lower than actor and action alone. Note that these metrics are not only indicating foreground/background segmentation quality, but also actor classification and action recognition performance at the pixel level.

Figure 3 shows qualitative results from our experiment. We observe qualitative improvement across many actor and action classes over prior work [11]. Interestingly, we observe that model predictions can pick up on new instances not labeled in the groundtruth annotations, and in some cases even provides more accurate joint class labels than the groundtruth. We note that these qualitative observations further highlight the importance of mIoU as a metric over ave and glo going forward for joint actor-action semantic segmentation. We also include qualitative results on video in our supplementary.

Table 2. Joint Spatial Detection of Actors and Actions (mAP). Since our end-to-end model outputs detection bounding boxes as an auxiliary task, we can also benchmark our approach against prior work [11] - we observe significant improvement in performance for actor, action, and joint actor/action (A,A) spatial detection.

Method	Actors	Actions	Joint Actor-Action (A,A)
TSCT [11]	67.2	60.2	49.2
TSHR [11]	67.9	59.6	49.6
TSMT [11]	68.3	60.0	48.9
Ours (Current)	**77.2**	**62.4**	**55.5**

4.2 Joint Spatial Detection of Actors and Actions

Our joint model predicts bounding boxes as an auxiliary task for the segmentation in the same forward pass. Thus, we also verify that our joint end-to-end approach for actor-action segmentation results in improved spatial detection of actors and actions for spatial *detection* as well, to compare against prior work [11]. Once again, we evaluate our method for actor and action spatial detection performance separately, as well as the overall performance on the joint task. Our experimental results are summarized in Table 2. We demonstrate that our method also outperforms the state-of-the-art over all three metrics, which is natural since we aim at finer level problem and have boosted the performance on that, hence the performance of coarser level problem is also improved.

4.3 Ablation Analysis

In this section, we examine critical components in our architecture to verify that each of them play an important role in contributing to the overall performance.

Mask R-CNN Baseline. Due to the recent success of Mask R-CNN on instance-wise semantic segmentation, we first perform a baseline experiment where we evaluate the power of Mask R-CNN as a direct input to achieve actor-action semantic segmentation. Consequently, this baseline considers only a single semantic label. Similar as the setup in [27,28], we use the cross-product of the actor and action labels in A2D as single semantic labels, e.g. *baby-crawling*. With number of actor classes $|X| = 7$, number of action classes $|Y| = 9$, there are 63 cross-product labels, out of which 43 are valid. Invalid labels include *adult-flying*, etc, and are not considered during training and testing. The baseline experiment is performed only on single frame and single stream, with no temporal information or flow input. The parameters are initialized with pretrained weights on MS-COCO [15].

Comparing the first two rows in Table 3, we can observe the significant performance gap between our full model and Mask R-CNN baseline. Tackling actor-action segmentation problem directly using Mask R-CNN has the following weaknesses: (1) The number of cross-product classes is $O(|X||Y|)$, which makes it hard to scale up with more classes of actor and action to be considered in future works. (2) Mask R-CNN aims at segmentation on single RGB frame, while in video, especially when action recognition is involved, temporal context and motion patterns should be leveraged in the model. (3) Actor and action classification are treated symmetrically, which does not reflect the intuition that actor is more defined spatially while action is also relying on the motion and temporal cues. Considering all these weaknesses, we design our network to decouple the actor and action classification heads, include temporal architecture, take in flow information, and use actor spatial localization to guide action recognition on feature maps aggregating temporal context.

Table 3. Ablation Analysis: Actor-Action Segmentation Results. We verify the contribution of each component of our network over baselines such as Mask R-CNN [8] and a Two-Stage Refinement variant of our method (Ours w/o Mask + SM), based on [11] and also leveraging SharpMask (SM) [17]. Please see Sect. 4.3 for more details.

Approach	Actor			Action			Joint (A,A)		
	ave	glo	mIoU	ave	glo	mIoU	ave	glo	mIoU
Ours (Full)	*79.1*	**94.5**	*66.4*	**62.9**	**92.6**	**46.3**	**51.4**	**92.5**	**36.9**
Mask R-CNN [8] Baseline	62.8	84.2	33.7	59.6	84.0	30.3	41.7	82.5	19.1
Ours w/o Mask + SM [17]	76.6	92.2	60.3	60.7	90.3	42.9	49.0	89.8	32.4
Ours w/o Temp Context	79.0	94.1	66.1	61.8	92.0	45.5	50.3	90.2	35.3
Ours w/o Flow Stream	**79.5**	93.7	**66.5**	60.4	86.3	36.8	46.2	87.8	29.4
Ours w/o Joint Training	77.7	93.2	63.2	62.1	91.3	45.2	50.9	90.1	33.6

Ours w/o Mask (Two-Stage Refinement Baseline). As in [11], one approach to achieve actor-action segmentation is based on a two-stage scheme: first perform actor-action detection at bounding box level, then as a post-processing step, perform foreground/background segmentation within the bounding box limits using a standard segmentation method. This approach is not an end-to-end solution for actor-action segmentation, and the knowledge learned in segmentation part can not benefit the action recognition during training. To show the effect of having mask head in the end-to-end network, we perform an ablation experiment with mask head chopped off, only predicting actor-action bounding boxes, and using SharpMask [17] as the segmentation method following [11]. With better actor-action spatial detection as shown in Sect. 4.2, this two-stage method outperforms the similar experiment setup in [11]. Still, the two-stage method is not as good as the full model on any metrics listed in Table 3, which shows the necessity to include the mask head in the end-to-end architecture.

Ours w/o Temporal Context. To demonstrate the impact of temporal layers, we perform an experiment where we remove these layers. The removal of temporal layers turns the network into a single frame model, which does not take the neighboring frames into account when predicting action label for each RoI. As shown in the fourth row in Table 3, although the actor segmentation is not much affected, the action segmentation performs worse without temporal layers aggregating information from its temporal context for each frame. Our exploration in leveraging temporal context on this task is partly limited by the fact that labels in A2D are temporally sparse, which may also be a limiting factor with regards to its relative impact on the performance improvement of our overall approach. We expect more future works on this task with focus on temporal context.

Ours w/o Flow Stream. As shown in related work [3,22], information about motion patterns contained in optical flow is crucial for many action tasks. When the flow modality is absent, the actor performance is almost untouched, since the actor localization is not using optical flow directly in our model. Comparing between 'Ours (Full)' and 'Ours - Flow' in Table 3, motion cues significantly contributes to action recognition and thus actor-action segmentation.

Ours w/o Joint Learning. In our end-to-end network, we can choose from two training procedures: jointly learn all sub-tasks at the same time, or separately learn them one-by-one. To compare with our main joint learning approach, we perform a separate learning experiment whereby the actor branch is first trained until convergence, and then we train the layers related to action recognition. Note that actor and action branches share the same backbone feature extractor, so when separately trained, the final network can be biased to the actor localization subtask or action recognition subtask. By comparing the first and last row in Table 3, we can conclude that joint learning is helpful to avoid such subtask biases and achieves best benchmark performance.

4.4 Zero-Shot Learning of Actions

A successful actor-action semantic segmentation model should not only infer the actor-action cross-product labels seen during training, but also be capable of generalizing to unseen actor-action pairs. This requires our model to maintain ability to *decouple* actor and action understanding while jointly learning them.

To verify the decoupling ability of our network, we follow the zero-shot learning experiment setup from [11] on A2D. We train the network 7 times, where each time one actor class x' is excluded for training its action labels. Note that we still train the actor classification for x', so during inference, the network can still localize and segment this actor. Formally, $L_{actor-cls}$ maintains the same, while action classification loss becomes $L_{action-cls} = -\mathbb{1}\{x' \neq x\} \log p_Y(y)$.

In order to maintain consistency on evaluation with respect to [11], we report the metric of AP as shown in Fig. 4. Each actor's AP is averaged over all valid actions of that actor. It shows that our method outperforms [11] on all actors on the AP metric. We can observe that actors like *ball* and *car* has less commonalities on actions with other features. A problem of AP is that, this metric can be interpreted as benefited from the overall learning capability of the network, or just the effect of decoupling ability.

We also analyze the zero-shot learning performance using the following metric for zero-shot learning of actions:

$$r_{zs} = \frac{AP_{zero-shot}}{AP_{full}}. \tag{3}$$

The performance ratio (r_{zs}) reflects the relative performance of zero-shot learning compared to normal learning setup where all actors are seen in the training. This metric removes the impact of the overall performance of the full model, and only examines the network's ability to decouple actor and action understanding. We compare r_{zs} on [11] and ours method in Fig. 4, where we can observe that our method matches with or outperforms [11] on all actors, demonstrating superior capability to capture commonalities of an action performed by various actors.

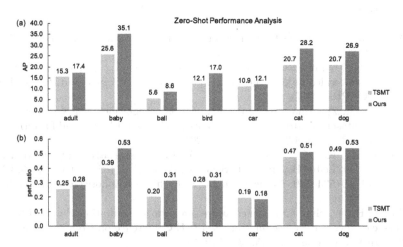

Fig. 4. Analysis of the generalizability and decoupling of the jointly learned embedding space for zero-shot detection of actor-action pairs. (a) We report *average precision* (AP) for each of the seven models, and observe stronger zero-shot performance compared with TSMT [11]. (b) We also observe a smaller *performance ratio* (r_{zs}) between zero-shot and full supervision inference. See Sect. 4.4 for more details.

5 Conclusion

We present a new end-to-end model able to jointly perform pixel-level actor-action segmentation and recognition. Our overall results and ablation study provide empirical support for the link between detailed spatial semantic segmentation in the joint pixelwise actor and action recognition pipeline. In particular, we demonstrate that the resulting model outperforms by a significant margin a model scheme based on a coarser bounding box actor-action localization, as well as other prior state-of-the-art work. We also show that it outperforms a model scheme based on a joint actor-action classification method that does not decouple actor and action classes at all. Consequently, our improved performance for the full joint task indicates that our overall end-to-end approach supports similar further directions for multitask research in video action understanding. Similarly, the stronger improvement in zero shot generalizability in terms of both raw performance and overall performance ratio indicates this approach shows strong promise for video representation learning directions as well.

Acknowledgments. Toyota Research Institute ("TRI") provided funds to assist the authors with their research but this article solely reflects the opinions and conclusions of its authors and not TRI or any other Toyota entity. This work is also partially funded by the Millennium Institute for Foundational Research on Data. We also thank NVIDIA for their DGX-1 donation.

References

1. Abadi, M., et al.: TensorFlow: a system for large-scale machine learning. OSDI **16**, 265–283 (2016)
2. Caelles, S., Maninis, K.K., Pont-Tuset, J., Leal-Taixé, L., Cremers, D., Van Gool, L.: One-shot video object segmentation. In: Computer Vision and Pattern Recognition (CVPR) (2017)
3. Carreira, J., Zisserman, A.: Quo vadis, action recognition? a new model and the kinetics dataset. In: 2017 IEEE Conference on Computer Vision and Pattern Recognition (CVPR), pp. 4724–4733. IEEE (2017)
4. Dai, J., He, K., Li, Y., Ren, S., Sun, J.: Instance-sensitive fully convolutional networks. In: Leibe, B., Matas, J., Sebe, N., Welling, M. (eds.) ECCV 2016. LNCS, vol. 9910, pp. 534–549. Springer, Cham (2016). https://doi.org/10.1007/978-3-319-46466-4_32
5. Dai, J., He, K., Sun, J.: Instance-aware semantic segmentation via multi-task network cascades. In: Proceedings of the IEEE Conference on Computer Vision and Pattern Recognition, pp. 3150–3158 (2016)
6. Girshick, R.: Fast R-CNN. In: International Conference on Computer Vision (ICCV) (2015)
7. Gkioxari, G., Malik, J.: Finding action tubes. In: IEEE Conference on Computer Vision and Pattern Recognition, CVPR, pp. 759–768 (2015)
8. He, K., Gkioxari, G., Dollár, P., Girshick, R.: Mask R-CNN. In: 2017 IEEE International Conference on Computer Vision (ICCV), pp. 2980–2988. IEEE (2017)
9. He, K., Zhang, X., Ren, S., Sun, J.: Deep residual learning for image recognition. In: Proceedings of the IEEE Conference on Computer Vision and Pattern Recognition, pp. 770–778 (2016)
10. Herath, S., Harandi, M., Porikli, F.: Going deeper into action recognition: a survey. arXiv preprint arXiv:1605.04988 (2016)
11. Kalogeiton, V., Weinzaepfel, P., Ferrari, V., Schmid, C.: Joint learning of object and action detectors. In: The IEEE International Conference on Computer Vision (ICCV), October 2017
12. Karpathy, A., et al.: Large-scale video classification with convolutional neural networks. In: CVPR (2014)

13. Li, X., et al.: Video object segmentation with re-identification. arXiv preprint arXiv:1708.00197 (2017)

14. Lin, T.Y., Dollár, P., Girshick, R., He, K., Hariharan, B., Belongie, S.: Feature pyramid networks for object detection. In: CVPR, vol. 1, p. 4 (2017)

15. Lin, T.-Y., et al.: Microsoft COCO: common objects in context. In: Fleet, D., Pajdla, T., Schiele, B., Tuytelaars, T. (eds.) ECCV 2014. LNCS, vol. 8693, pp. 740–755. Springer, Cham (2014). https://doi.org/10.1007/978-3-319-10602-1_48

16. Pinheiro, P.O., Collobert, R., Dollár, P.: Learning to segment object candidates. In: Advances in Neural Information Processing Systems, pp. 1990–1998 (2015)

17. Pinheiro, P.O., Lin, T.-Y., Collobert, R., Dollár, P.: Learning to refine object segments. In: Leibe, B., Matas, J., Sebe, N., Welling, M. (eds.) ECCV 2016. LNCS, vol. 9905, pp. 75–91. Springer, Cham (2016). https://doi.org/10.1007/978-3-319-46448-0_5

18. Qiu, Z., Yao, T., Mei, T.: Learning spatio-temporal representation with pseudo-3D residual networks. In: 2017 IEEE International Conference on Computer Vision (ICCV), pp. 5534–5542. IEEE (2017)

19. Ren, S., He, K., Girshick, R., Sun, J.: Faster R-CNN: towards real-time object detection with region proposal networks. In: Advances in Neural Information Processing Systems, pp. 91–99 (2015)

20. Russakovsky, O., et al.: ImageNet large scale visual recognition challenge. Int. J. Comput. Vis. (IJCV) **115**(3), 211–252 (2015). https://doi.org/10.1007/s11263-015-0816-y

21. Russell, C., Kohli, P., Torr, P.H., et al.: Associative hierarchical CRFs for object class image segmentation. In: IEEE 12th International Conference on Computer Vision, pp. 739–746. IEEE (2009)

22. Simonyan, K., Zisserman, A.: Very deep convolutional networks for large-scale image recognition. In: NIPS (2014)

23. Tran, D., Bourdev, L., Fergus, R., Torresani, L., Paluri, M.: Learning spatiotemporal features with 3D convolutional networks. In: 2015 IEEE International Conference on Computer Vision (ICCV), pp. 4489–4497. IEEE (2015)

24. Voigtlaender, P., Leibe, B.: Online adaptation of convolutional neural networks for video object segmentation. In: BMVC (2017)

25. Wang, L., et al.: Temporal segment networks: towards good practices for deep action recognition. In: Leibe, B., Matas, J., Sebe, N., Welling, M. (eds.) ECCV 2016. LNCS, vol. 9912, pp. 20–36. Springer, Cham (2016). https://doi.org/10.1007/978-3-319-46484-8_2

26. Xie, S., Sun, C., Huang, J., Tu, Z., Murphy, K.: Rethinking spatiotemporal feature learning for video understanding. arXiv preprint arXiv:1712.04851 (2017)

27. Xu, C., Corso, J.J.: Actor-action semantic segmentation with grouping process models. In: 2016 IEEE Conference on Computer Vision and Pattern Recognition (CVPR), pp. 3083–3092, June 2016. https://doi.org/10.1109/CVPR.2016.336

28. Xu, C., Hsieh, S.H., Xiong, C., Corso, J.J.: Can humans fly? Action understanding with multiple classes of actors. In: Proceedings of IEEE Conference on Computer Vision and Pattern Recognition (2015). http://web.eecs.umich.edu/~jjcorso/pubs/xu_corso_CVPR2015_A2D.pdf

29. Yan, Y., Xu, C., Cai, D., Corso, J.J.: Weakly supervised actor-action segmentation via robust multi-task ranking. In: The IEEE Conference on Computer Vision and Pattern Recognition (CVPR), July 2017

Humans Analysis

Scaling Egocentric Vision:
The EPIC-KITCHENS Dataset

Dima Damen[1]([⊠]) [iD], Hazel Doughty[1], Giovanni Maria Farinella[2], Sanja Fidler[3],
Antonino Furnari[2], Evangelos Kazakos[1], Davide Moltisanti[1],
Jonathan Munro[1], Toby Perrett[1], Will Price[1], and Michael Wray[1]

[1] University of Bristol, Bristol, UK
`dima.damen@bristol.ac.uk`
[2] University of Catania, Catania, Italy
[3] University of Toronto, Toronto, Canada

Abstract. First-person vision is gaining interest as it offers a unique
viewpoint on people's interaction with objects, their attention, and even
intention. However, progress in this challenging domain has been relatively slow due to the lack of sufficiently large datasets. In this paper, we
introduce EPIC-KITCHENS, a large-scale egocentric video benchmark
recorded by 32 participants in their native kitchen environments. Our
videos depict **non-scripted** daily activities: we simply asked each participant to start recording every time they entered their kitchen. Recording took place in 4 cities (in North America and Europe) by participants belonging to 10 different nationalities, resulting in highly diverse
cooking styles. Our dataset features 55h of video consisting of 11.5M
frames, which we densely labelled for a total of 39.6K action segments
and 454.3K object bounding boxes. Our annotation is unique in that
we had the participants narrate their own videos (after recording), thus
reflecting true intention, and we crowd-sourced ground-truths based on
these. We describe our object, action and anticipation challenges, and
evaluate several baselines over two test splits, *seen* and *unseen* kitchens.

Keywords: Egocentric vision · Dataset · Benchmarks
First-person vision · Egocentric object detection
Action recognition and anticipation

1 Introduction

In recent years, we have seen significant progress in many domains such
as image classification [19], object detection [37], captioning [26] and visual
question-answering [3]. This success has in large part been due to advances
in deep learning [27] as well as the availability of large-scale image benchmarks [9,11,30,55]. While gaining attention, work in video understanding has

Electronic supplementary material The online version of this chapter (https://
doi.org/10.1007/978-3-030-01225-0_44) contains supplementary material, which is
available to authorized users.

© Springer Nature Switzerland AG 2018
V. Ferrari et al. (Eds.): ECCV 2018, LNCS 11208, pp. 753–771, 2018.
https://doi.org/10.1007/978-3-030-01225-0_44

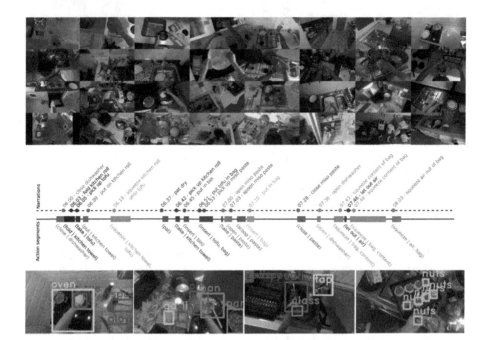

Fig. 1. From top: Frames from the 32 environments; Narrations by participants used to annotate action segments; Active object bounding box annotations

been more scarce, mainly due to the lack of annotated datasets. This has been changing recently, with the release of the action classification benchmarks such as [1,14,18,38,46,54]. With the exception of [46], most of these datasets contain videos that are very short in duration, i.e., only a few seconds long, focusing on a single action. Charades [42] makes a step towards activity recognition by collecting 10 K videos of humans performing various tasks in their home. While this dataset is a nice attempt to collect daily actions, the videos have been recorded in a scripted way, by asking AMT workers to act out a script in front of the camera. This makes the videos look oftentimes less natural, and they also lack the progression and multi-tasking of actions that occur in real life.

Here we focus on first-person vision, which offers a unique viewpoint on people's daily activities. This data is rich as it reflects our goals and motivation, ability to multi-task, and the many different ways to perform a variety of important, but mundane, everyday tasks (such as cleaning the dishes). Egocentric data has also recently been proven valuable for human-to-robot imitation learning [34,53], and has a direct impact on HCI applications. However, datasets to evaluate first-person vision algorithms [6,8,13,16,36,41] have been significantly smaller in size than their third-person counterparts, often captured in a single environment [6,8,13,16]. Daily interactions from wearable cameras are also scarcely available online, making this a largely unavailable source of information.

In this paper, we introduce EPIC-KITCHENS, a large-scale egocentric dataset. Our data was collected by 32 participants, belonging to 10 nationalities, in their native kitchens (Fig. 1). The participants were asked to capture all their daily kitchen activities, and record sequences regardless of their duration. The recordings, which include both video and sound, not only feature the typical interactions with one's own kitchenware and appliances, but importantly show the natural multi-tasking that one performs, like washing a few dishes amidst cooking. Such parallel-goal interactions have not been captured in existing datasets, making this both a more realistic as well as a more challenging set of recordings. A video introduction to the recordings is available at: http://youtu.be/Dj6Y3H0ubDw.

Altogether, EPIC-KITCHENS has 55 h of recording, densely annotated with start/end times for each action/interaction, as well as bounding boxes around objects subject to interaction. We describe our object, action and anticipation challenges, and report baselines in two scenarios, i.e., *seen* and *unseen* kitchens. The dataset and leaderboards to track the community's progress on all challenges, with held out test ground-truth are at: http://epic-kitchens.github.io.

Table 1. Comparative overview of relevant datasets *action classes with >50 samples

Dataset	Ego?	Non-Scripted?	Native Env?	Year	Frames	Sequ-ences	Action Segments	Action Classes	Object BBs	Object Classes	Partici-pants	No. Env.s
EPIC-KITCHENS	✓	✓	✓	2018	11.5M	432	39,596	149*	454,255	323	32	32
EGTEA Gaze+ [16]	✓	✗	✗	2018	2.4M	86	10,325	106	0	0	32	1
Charades-ego [41]	70% ✓	✗	✓	2018	2.3M	2,751	30,516	157	0	38	71	N/A
BEOID [6]	✓	✗	✗	2014	0.1M	58	742	34	0	0	5	1
GTEA Gaze+ [13]	✓	✗	✗	2012	0.4M	35	3,371	42	0	0	13	1
ADL [36]	✓	✗	✓	2012	1.0M	20	436	32	137,780	42	20	20
CMU [8]	✓	✗	✗	2009	0.2M	16	516	31	0	0	16	1
YouCook2 [56]	✗	✓	✓	2018 @30fps	15.8M	2,000	13,829	89	0	0	2K	N/A
VLOG [14]	✗	✓	✓	2017	37.2M	114K	0	0	0	0	10.7K	N/A
Charades [42]	✗	✗	✓	2016	7.4M	9,848	67,000	157	0	0	N/A	267
Breakfast [28]	✗	✓	✓	2014	3.0M	433	3078	50	0	0	52	18
50 Salads [44]	✗	✗	✗	2013	0.6M	50	2967	52	0	0	25	1
MPII Cooking 2 [39]	✗	✗	✗	2012	2.9M	273	14,105	88	0	0	30	1

2 Related Datasets

We compare EPIC-KITCHENS to four commonly-used [6,8,13,36] and two recent [16,41] egocentric datasets in Table 1, as well as six third-person activity-recognition datasets [14,28,39,42,44,56] that focus on object-interaction activities. We exclude egocentric datasets that focus on inter-person interactions [2, 12,40], as these target a different research question.

A few datasets aim at capturing activities in native environments, most of which are recorded in third-person [14,18,28,41,42]. [28] focuses on cooking dishes based on a list of breakfast recipes. In [14], short segments linked to interactions with 30 daily objects are collected by querying YouTube, while [18,41,42] are scripted – subjects are requested to enact a crowd-sourced storyline [41,42] or a given action [18], which oftentimes results in less natural looking actions. All egocentric datasets similarly use scripted activities, i.e. people are told what actions to perform. When following instructions, participants perform steps in a sequential order, as opposed to the more natural real-life scenarios addressed in our work, which involve multi-tasking, searching for an item, thinking what to do next, changing one's mind or even unexpected surprises. EPIC-KITCHENS is most closely related to the ADL dataset [36] which also provides egocentric recordings in native environments. However, our dataset is substantially larger: it has 11.5M frames vs 1M in ADL, 90x more annotated action segments, and 4x more object bounding boxes, making it the largest first-person dataset to date.

3   The EPIC-KITCHENS Dataset

In this section, we describe our data collection and annotation pipeline. We also present various statistics, showcasing different aspects of our collected data.

Use any word you prefer. Feel free to vary your words or stick to a few.
Use present tense verbs (e.g. cut/open/close).
Use verb-object pairs (e.g. wash carrot).
You may (if you prefer) skip articles and pronouns (e.g. "cut kiwi" rather than "I cut the kiwi").
Use propositions when needed (e.g. "pour water into kettle").
Use 'and' when actions are co-occurring (e.g. "hold mug and pour water").
If an action is taking long, you can narrate again (e.g. "still stirring soup").

Fig. 2. Instructions used to collect video narrations from our participants

3.1   Data Collection

The dataset was recorded by 32 individuals in 4 cities in different countries (in North America and Europe): 15 in Bristol/UK, 8 in Toronto/Canada, 8 in Catania/Italy and 1 in Seattle/USA between May and Nov 2017. Participants were asked to capture all kitchen visits *for three consecutive days*, with the recording starting immediately before entering the kitchen, and only stopped before leaving the kitchen. They recorded the dataset voluntarily and were not financially rewarded. The participants were asked to be in the kitchen alone for all the recordings, thus capturing only one-person activities. We also asked them to remove all items that would disclose their identity such as portraits or mirrors. Data was captured using a head-mounted GoPro with an adjustable mounting to control the viewpoint for different environments and participants' heights. Before each recording, the participants checked the battery life and viewpoint, using the GoPro Capture app, so that their stretched hands were approximately located at the middle of the camera frame. The camera was set to linear field of view, 59.94 *fps* and Full HD resolution of 1920×1080, however some subjects made minor changes like wide or ultra-wide FOV or resolution, as they recorded multiple sequences in their homes, and thus were switching the device off and on over several days. Specifically, 1% of the videos were recorded at 1280 × 720 and 0.5% at 1920 × 1440. Also, 1% at 30 *fps*, 1% at 48 *fps* and 0.2% at 90 *fps*.

The recording lengths varied depending on the participant's kitchen engagement. On average, people recorded for 1.7 h, with the maximum being 4.6 h. Cooking a single meal can span multiple sequences, depending on whether one stays in the kitchen, or leaves and returns later. On average, each participant recorded 13.6 sequences. Figure 3 presents statistics on time of day using the local time of the recording, high-level goals and sequence durations.

Since crowd-sourcing annotations for such long videos is very challenging, we had our original participants do a coarse first annotation. Each participant was asked to watch their videos, after completing all recordings, and narrate the actions carried out, using a hand-held recording device. We opted for a sound recording rather than written captions as this is arguably much faster for the participants, who were thus more willing to provide these annotations. These are analogous to a *live commentary* of the video. The general instructions for narrations are listed in Fig. 2. The participant narrated in English if sufficiently fluent or in their native language. In total, 5 languages were used: 17 narrated in English, 7 in Italian, 6 in Spanish, 1 in Greek and 1 in Chinese. Figure 3 shows wordles of the most frequent words in each language.

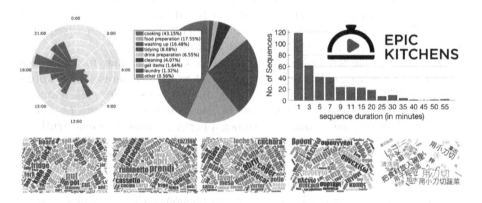

Fig. 3. Top (left to right): time of day of the recording, pie chart of high-level goals, histogram of sequence durations and dataset logo; **Bottom:** Wordles of narrations in native languages (English, Italian, Spanish, Greek and Chinese)

Our decision to collect narrations from the participants themselves is because they are the most qualified to label the activity compared to an independent observer, as they were the ones performing the actions. We opted for a post-recording narration such that the participant performs her/his daily activities undisturbed, without being concerned about labelling.

Table 2. Extracts from 6 transcription files in .sbv format

0:14:44.190,0:14:45.310	0:00:02.780,0:00:04.640	0:04:37.880,0:04:39.620	0:06:40.669,0:06:41.669	0:12:28.000,0:12:28.000	0:00:03.280,0:00:06.000
pour tofu onto pan	open the bin	Take onion	pick up spatula	pour pasta into container	open fridge
0:14:45.310,0:14:49.540	0:00:04.640,0:00:06.100	0:04:39.620,0:04:48.160	0:06:41.669,0:06:45.250	0:12:33.000,0:12:33.000	0:00:06.000,0:00:09.349
put down tofu container	pick up the bag	Cut onion	stir potatoes	take jar of pesto	take milk
0:14:49.540,0:15:02.690	0:00:06.100,0:00:09.530	0:04:48.160,0:04:49.160	0:06:45.250,0:06:46.250	0 :12:39.000,0:12:39.000	0:00:09.349,0:00:10.910
stir vegetables and tofu	tie the bag	Peel onion	put down spatula	take teaspoon	put milk
0:15:02.690,0:15:06.260	0:00:09.530,0:00:10.610	0:04:49.160,0:04:51.290	0:06:46.250,0:06:50.830	0:12:41.000,0:12:41.000	0:00:10.910,0:00:12.690
put down spatula	tie the bag again	Peel onion	turn down hob	pour pesto in container	open cupboard
0:15:06.260,0:15:07.820	0:00:10.610,0:00:14.309	0:04:51.290,0:05:06.350	0:06:50.830,0:06:55.819	0:12:55.000,0:12:55.000	0:00:12.690,0:00:15.089
take tofu container	pick up bag	Put peel in bin	pick up pan	place pesto bottle on table	take bowl
0:15:07.820,0:15:10.040	0:00:14.309,0:00:17.520	0:05:06.350,0:05:15.200	0:06:55.819,0:06:57.170	0:12:58.000,0:12:58.000	0:00:15.089,0:00:18.080
throw something into the bin	put bag down	Put peel in bin	tip out paneer	take wooden spoon	open drawer

We tested several automatic audio-to-text APIs [5,17,23], which failed to produce accurate transcriptions as these expect a relevant corpus and complete sentences for context. We thus collected manual transcriptions via Amazon Mechanical Turk (AMT), and used the YouTube's automatic closed caption alignment tool to produce accurate timings. For non-English narrations, we also asked AMT workers to translate the sentences. To make the job more suitable for AMT, narration audio files are split by removing silence below a pre-specified decibel threshold (after compression and normalisation). Speech chunks are then combined into HITs with a duration of around 30 s each. To ensure consistency, we submit the same HIT three times and select the ones with an edit distance of 0 to at least one other HIT. We manually corrected cases when there was no agreement. Examples of transcribed and timed narrations are provided in Table 2. The participants were also asked to provide one sentence per sequence describing the overall goal or activity that took place.

In total, we collected 39,596 action narrations, corresponding to a narration every 4.9 s in the video. The average number of words per phrase is 2.8 words. These narrations give us an initial labelling of all actions with rough temporal alignment, obtained from the timestamp of the audio narration with respect to the video. However, narrations are also not a perfect source of ground-truth:

- The narrations can be incomplete, i.e., the participants were selective in which actions they chose to narrate. We noticed that they labelled the 'open' actions more than their counter-action 'close', as the narrator's attention has already moved to the next goal. We consider this phenomena in our evaluation, by only evaluating actions that have been narrated.
- Temporally, the narrations are belated, after the action takes place. This is adjusted using ground-truth action segments (see Sect. 3.2).
- Participants use their own vocabulary and free language. While this is a challenging issue, we believe it is important to push the community to go beyond the pre-selected list of labels (also argued in [55]). We here resolve this issue by grouping verbs and nouns into minimally overlapping classes (see Sect. 3.4).

3.2   Action Segment Annotations

For each narrated sentence, we adjust the start and end times of the action using AMT. To ensure the annotators are trained to perform temporal localisation, we use a clip from our previous work's understanding [33] that explains temporal bounds of actions. Each HIT is composed of a maximum of 10 consecutive narrated phrases p_i, where annotators label $A_i = [t_{s_i}, t_{e_i}]$ as the start and end times of the ith action. Two constraints were added to decrease the amount of noisy annotations: (1) action has to be at least 0.5 s in length; (2) action cannot start before the preceding action's start time. Note that consecutive actions are allowed to overlap. Moreover, the annotators could indicate that the action does not appear in the video. This handles occluded, impossible to distinguish or out-of-bounds cases.

To ensure consistency, we ask $\mathcal{K}_a = 4$ annotators to annotate each HIT. Given one annotation $A_i(j)$ (i is the action and j indexes the annotator), we calculate the agreement as follows: $\alpha_i(j) = \frac{1}{K_a} \sum_{k=1}^{\mathcal{K}_a} \mathrm{IoU}(A_i(j), A_i(k))$. We first find the annotator with the maximum agreement $\hat{j} = \arg\max_j \alpha_i(j)$, and find $\hat{k} = \arg\max_k \mathrm{IoU}(A_i(\hat{j}), A_i(k))$. The ground-truth action segment A_i is then defined as:

$$A_i = \begin{cases} \mathrm{Union}(A_i(\hat{j}), A_i(\hat{k})), & \text{if } \mathrm{IoU}(A_i(\hat{j}), A_i(\hat{k})) > 0.5 \\ A_i(\hat{j}), & \text{otherwise} \end{cases} \tag{1}$$

We thus combine two annotations when they have a strong agreement, since in some cases the single (best) annotation results in a too tight of a segment. Figure 4 shows examples of combining annotations.

Fig. 4. An example of annotated action segments for 2 consecutive actions

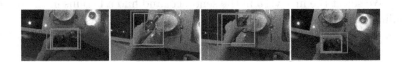

Fig. 5. Object annotation from three AMT workers (orange, blue and green). The green participant's annotations are selected as the final annotations (Color figure online)

In total, we collected such labels for $39,564$ action segments (lengths: $\mu = 3.7s$, $\sigma = 5.6\,s$). These represent 99.9% of narrated segments. The missed annotations were those labelled as "not visible" by the annotators, though mentioned in narrations.

3.3   Active Object Bounding Box Annotations

The narrated *nouns* correspond to objects relevant to the action [6,29]. Assume $\mathcal{O}_i$ is the set of one or more nouns in the phrase p_i associated with the action segment $A_i = [t_{s_i}, t_{e_i}]$. We consider each frame f within $[t_{s_i} - 2s, t_{e_i} + 2s]$ as a potential frame to annotate the bounding box(es), for each object in $\mathcal{O}_i$. We build on the interface from [49] for annotating bounding boxes on AMT. Each HIT aims to get an annotation for one object, for the maximum duration of 25 s, which corresponds to 50 consecutive frames at $2\,fps$. The annotator can also note that the object does not exist in f. We particularly ask the same annotator to annotate consecutive frames to avoid subjective decisions on the extents of objects. We also assess annotators' quality by ensuring that the annotators obtain an IoU ≥ 0.7 on two golden annotations at the start of every HIT. We request $\mathcal{K}_o = 3$ workers per HIT, and select the one with maximum agreement β:

$$\beta(q) = \sum_f \max_{j \neq q}^{\mathcal{K}_o} \max_{k,l} \mathrm{IoU}(\mathrm{BB}(j, f, k), \mathrm{BB}(q, f, l)) \qquad (2)$$

where $\mathrm{BB}(q, f, k)$ is the kth bounding box annotation by annotator q in frame f. Ties are broken by selecting the worker who provides the tighter bounding boxes. Figure 5 shows multiple annotations for four keyframes in a sequence.

Overall, 77% of requested annotations resulted in at least one bounding box. In total, we collected 454,255 bounding boxes ($\mu = 1.64$ boxes/frame, $\sigma = 0.92$). Sample action segments and object bounding boxes are shown in Fig. 6.

3.4   Verb and Noun Classes

Since our participants annotated using free text in multiple languages, a variety of verbs and nouns have been collected. We group these into classes with minimal semantic overlap, to accommodate the more typical approaches to multiclass detection and recognition where each example is believed to belong to one class only. We estimate Part-of-Speech (POS), using SpaCy's English core web model. We select the first verb in the sentence, and find all nouns in the sentence excluding any that match the chosen verb. When a noun is absent or replaced by a pronoun (*e.g.* '*it*'), we use the noun from the directly preceding narration (e.g. p_i: 'rinse cup', p_{i+1}: 'place it to dry').

We refer to the set of minimally-overlapping verb classes as C_V, and similarly C_N for nouns. We attempted to automate the clustering of verbs and nouns using combinations of WordNet [32], Word2Vec [31], and Lesk algorithm [4], however, due to limited context there were too many meaningless clusters. We thus elected to manually cluster the verbs and semi-automatically cluster the nouns. We preprocessed the compound nouns *e.g.* 'pizza cutter' as a subset of the second noun *e.g.* 'cutter'. We then manually adjusted the clustering, merging the variety of names used for the same object, *e.g.* 'cup' and 'mug', as well as splitting some base nouns, *e.g.* 'washing machine' vs 'coffee machine'.

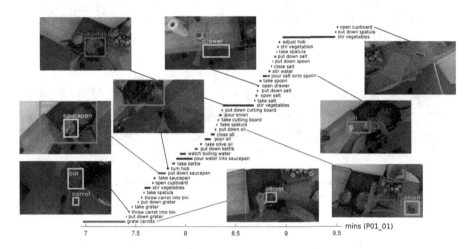

Fig. 6. Sample consecutive action segments with keyframe object annotations

In total, we have 125 C_V classes and 331 C_N classes. Table 3 shows a sample of grouped verbs and nouns into classes. These classes are used in all three defined challenges. In Fig. 7, we show C_V ordered by frequency of occurrence in action segments, as well as C_N ordered by number of annotated bounding boxes. These are grouped into 19 super categories, of which 9 are food and drinks, with the rest containing kitchen essentials from appliances to cutlery. Co-occurring classes are presented in Fig. 8.

3.5 Annotation Quality Assurance

To analyse the quality of annotations, we choose 300 random samples, and manually assess correctness. We report:

- **Action Segment Boundaries** (A_i): We check that the start/end times fully enclose the action boundaries, with any additional frames not part of other actions - error: *5.7%*.
- **Object Bounding Boxes** $(\mathcal{O}_i)$: We check that the bounding box encapsulates the object or its parts, with minimal overlap with other objects, and that all instances of the class in the frame have been labelled – error: *6.3%*.
- **Verb classes** (C_V): We check that the verb class is correct – error: *3.3%*.
- **Noun classes** (C_N): We check that the noun class is correct – error: *6.0%*.

These error rates are comparable to recently published datasets [54].

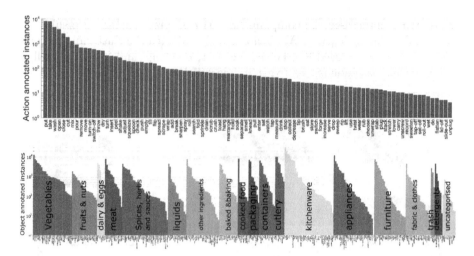

Fig. 7. Top: Frequency of verb classes in action segments; **Bottom**: Frequency of noun clusters in bounding box annotations, by category

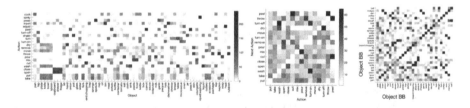

Fig. 8. Left: Frequently co-occurring verb/nouns in action segments [e.g. (open/close, cupboard/drawer/fridge), (peel, carrot/onion/potato/peach), (adjust, heat)]; **Middle**: Next-action excluding repetitive instances of the same action [e.g. peel → cut, turn-on → wash, pour → mix].; **Right**: Co-occurring bounding boxes in one frame [e.g. (pot, coffee), (knife, chopping board), (tap, sponge)]

4   Benchmarks and Baseline Results

EPIC-KITCHENS offers a variety of potential challenges from routine understanding, to activity recognition and object detection. As a start, we define three challenges for which we provide baseline results, and avail online leaderboards. For the evaluation protocols, we hold out ground truth annotations for 27% of the data (Table 4). We particularly aim to assess the generalizability to novel environments, and we thus structured our test set to have a collection of *seen* and previously *unseen* kitchens:

Seen Kitchens (S1): In this split, each kitchen is seen in both training and testing, where roughly 80% of sequences are in training and 20% in testing. We do not split sequences, thus each sequence is in either training or testing.

Unseen Kitchens (S2): This divides the participants/kitchens so all sequences of the same kitchen are either in training or testing. We hold out the complete sequences for 4 participants for this testing protocol. The test set of S2 is only 7% of the dataset in terms of frame count, but the challenges remain considerable.

Table 3. Sample verb and noun classes

	ClassNo (Key)	Clustered Words
VERB	0 (take)	Take, grab, pick, get, fetch, pick-up, ...
	3 (close)	Close, close-off, shut
	12 (turn-on)	Turn-on, start, begin, ignite, switch-on, activate, restart, light, ...
NOUN	1 (pan)	Pan, frying pan, saucepan, wok, ...
	8 (cupboard)	Cupboard, cabinet, locker, flap, cabinet door, cupboard door, closet, ...
	51 (cheese)	Cheese slice, mozzarella, paneer, parmesan, ...
	78 (top)	Top, counter, counter top, surface, kitchen counter, kitchen top, tiles, ...

Table 4. Statistics of test splits: seen (S1) and unseen (S2) kitchens

	#Subjects	#Sequences	Duration (s)	%	Narrated Segments	Action Segments	Bounding Boxes
Train/Val	28	272	141731		28,587	28,561	326,388
S1 Test	28	106	39084	20%	8,069	8,064	97,872
S2 Test	4	54	13231	7%	2,939	2,939	29,995

We now evaluate several existing methods on our benchmarks, to gain an understanding of how challenging our dataset is.

4.1 Object Detection Benchmark

Challenge: This challenge focuses on object detection for all of our C_N classes. Note that our annotations only capture the 'active' objects pre-, during- and post- interaction. We thus restrict the images evaluated per class to those where the object has been annotated. We particularly aim to break the performance down into multi-shot and few-shot class groups, so as to analyse the capabilities of the approaches to quickly learn novel objects (with only a few examples). Our challenge leaderboard reflects the methods' abilities on both sets of classes.

Method: We evaluate object detection using Faster R-CNN [37] due to its state-of-the-art performance. Faster R-CNN uses a region proposal network (RPN) to first generate class agnostic object proposals, and then classifies these and outputs refined bounding box predictions. We use the implementation from [21, 22] with a base architecture of ResNet-101 [19] pre-trained on MS-COCO [30].

Table 5. Baseline results for the Object Detection challenge

mAP		15 Most Frequent Object Classes														Totals		
	pan	plate	bowl	onion	tap	pot	knife	spoon	meat	food	potato	cup	pasta	cupboard	lid	few-shot	many-shot	all
S1 IoU > 0.05	78.40	74.34	66.86	65.40	86.40	68.32	49.96	45.79	39.59	48.31	58.59	61.85	77.65	52.17	62.46	31.59	51.60	47.84
IoU > 0.5	70.63	68.21	61.93	41.92	73.04	62.90	33.77	26.96	27.69	38.10	50.07	51.71	69.74	36.00	58.64	20.72	38.81	35.41
IoU > 0.75	22.26	46.34	36.98	3.50	26.59	20.47	4.13	2.48	5.53	9.39	13.21	11.25	22.61	7.37	30.53	2.70	10.07	8.69
S2 IoU > 0.05	80.35	88.38	66.79	47.65	83.40	71.17	63.24	46.36	71.87	29.91	N/A	55.36	78.02	55.17	61.55	23.19	49.30	46.64
IoU > 0.5	67.42	85.62	62.75	26.27	65.90	59.22	44.14	30.30	56.28	24.31	N/A	47.00	73.82	39.49	51.56	16.95	34.95	33.11
IoU > 0.75	18.41	60.43	33.32	2.21	6.41	14.55	4.65	1.77	12.80	7.40	N/A	7.54	36.94	9.45	22.1	2.46	8.68	8.05

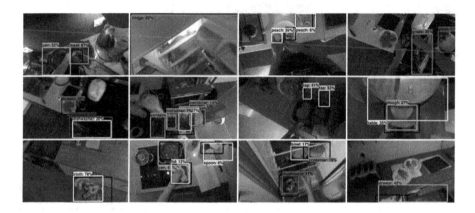

Fig. 9. Qualitative results for the object detection challenge

Implementation Details: Learning rate is initialised to 0.0003 decaying by a factor of 10 after 90 K and stopped after 120 K iterations. We use a mini-batch size of 4 on 8 Nvidia P100 GPUs on a single compute node (Nvidia DGX-1) with distributed training and parameter synchronisation – i.e. overall mini-batch size of 32. As in [37], images are rescaled such that their shortest side is 600 pixels and the aspect ratio is maintained. We use a stride of 16 on the last convolution layer for feature extraction and for anchors we use 4 scales of 0.25, 0.5, 1.0 and 2.0; and aspect ratios of 1:1, 1:2 and 2:1. To reduce redundancy, NMS is used with an IoU threshold of 0.7. In training and testing we use 300 RPN proposals.

Evaluation Metrics: For each class, we only report results on $I^{c_n \in C_N}$, these are all images where class c_n has been annotated. We use the mean average precision (mAP) metric from PASCAL VOC [11], using IoU thresholds of 0.05, 0.5 and 0.75 similar to [30].

Results: We report results in Table 5 for many-shot classes (those with ≥ 100 bounding boxes in training) and few shot classes (with ≥ 10 and < 100 bounding boxes in training), alongside AP for the 15 most frequent classes. There are a total of 202 many-shot classes and 88 few-shot classes. One can see that our objects are generally harder to detect than in most existing datasets, with performance at the standard IoU > 0.5 below 40%. Even at a very small IoU threshold, the performance is relatively low. The more challenging classes are "meat", "knife", and "spoon", despite being some of the most frequent ones. Notice that the performance for the low-shot regime is substantially lower than in the many-shot regime. This points to interesting challenges for the future. However, performances for the *Seen* and *Unseen* splits in object detection are comparable, thus showing generalization capability across environments.

Figure 9 shows qualitative results with detections shown in colour and ground truth shown in black. The examples in the right-hand column are failure cases.

4.2   Action Recognition Benchmark

Challenge: Given an action segment $A_i = [t_{s_i}, t_{e_i}]$, we aim to classify the segment into its action class, where classes are defined as $C_a = \{(c_v \in C_V, c_n \in C_N)\}$, and c_n is the first noun in the narration when multiple nouns are present. Note that our dataset supports more complex action-level challenges, such as action localisation in the videos of full duration. We decided to focus on the classification challenge first (the segment is provided) since most existing works tackle this challenge.

Table 6. Baseline results for the action recognition challenge

	Top-1 Accuracy			Top-5 Accuracy			Avg Class Precision			Avg Class Recall		
	VERB	NOUN	ACTION	VERB	NOUN	ACTION	VERB	NOUN	ACTION	VERB	NOUN	ACTION
Chance/Random	12.62	1.73	00.22	43.39	08.12	03.68	03.67	01.15	00.08	03.67	01.15	00.05
Largest Class	22.41	04.50	01.59	70.20	18.89	14.90	00.86	00.06	00.00	03.84	01.40	00.12
S1 2SCNN (FUSION)	42.16	29.14	13.23	80.58	53.70	30.36	29.39	30.73	5.35	14.83	21.10	04.46
TSN (RGB)	45.68	**36.80**	19.86	**85.56**	**64.19**	**41.89**	**61.64**	34.32	09.96	**23.81**	**31.62**	08.81
TSN (FLOW)	42.75	17.40	09.02	79.52	39.43	21.92	21.42	13.75	02.33	15.58	09.51	02.06
TSN (FUSION)	**48.23**	36.71	**20.54**	84.09	62.32	39.79	47.26	**35.42**	**10.46**	22.33	30.53	**08.83**
Chance/Random	10.71	01.89	00.22	38.98	09.31	03.81	03.56	01.08	00.08	03.56	01.08	00.05
Largest Class	22.26	04.80	00.10	63.76	19.44	17.17	00.85	00.06	00.00	03.84	01.40	00.12
S2 2SCNN (FUSION)	36.16	18.03	07.31	71.97	38.41	19.49	18.11	15.31	02.86	10.52	12.55	02.69
TSN (RGB)	34.89	21.82	10.11	**74.56**	45.34	**25.33**	19.48	14.67	04.77	11.22	17.24	05.67
TSN (FLOW)	**40.08**	14.51	06.73	73.40	33.77	18.64	19.98	09.48	02.08	**13.81**	08.58	02.27
TSN (FUSION)	39.40	**22.70**	**10.89**	74.29	**45.72**	25.26	**22.54**	**15.33**	**05.60**	13.06	**17.52**	**05.81**

Table 7. Sample baseline action recognition per-class metrics (using TSN fusion)

		15 Most Frequent (in Train Set) Verb Classes													
		put	take	wash	open	close	cut	mix	pour	move	turn-on	remove	turn-off	throw	dry	peel
S1	RECALL	67.51	48.27	83.19	63.32	25.45	77.64	50.20	26.32	00.00	08.28	05.11	05.45	24.18	36.49	30.43
S1	PRECISION	36.29	43.21	63.01	69.74	75.50	68.71	68.51	60.98	-	46.15	53.85	66.67	75.86	81.82	51.85
S2	RECALL	74.23	34.05	83.67	43.64	18.40	33.90	35.85	13.13	00.00	00.00	00.00	00.00	00.00	2.70	00.00
S2	PRECISION	29.60	30.68	67.06	56.28	66.67	88.89	70.37	76.47	-	-	00.00	-	-	100.0	00.00

Network Architecture: We train the Temporal Segment Network (TSN) [48] as a state-of-the-art architecture in action recognition, but adjust the output layer to predict both verb and noun classes jointly, with independent losses, as in [25]. We use the PyTorch implementation [51] with the Inception architecture [45], batch normalization [24] and pre-trained on ImageNet [9].

Implementation Details: We train both spatial and temporal streams, the latter on dense optical flow at $30\,fps$ extracted using the TV-L$_1$ algorithm [52] between RGB frames using the formulation TV-L$_1(I_{2t}, I_{2t+3})$ to eliminate optical flicker, and released the computed flow as part of the dataset. We do not perform stratification or weighted sampling, allowing the dataset class imbalance to propagate into the mini-batch. We train each model on 8 Nvidia P100 GPUs on a single compute node (Nvidia DGX-1) for 80 epochs with a mini-batch size of 512. We set learning rate to 0.01 for spatial and 0.001 for temporal streams decreasing it by a factor of 10 after epochs 20 and 40. After averaging the 25 samples within the action segment each with 10 spatial croppings as in [48], we fuse both streams by averaging class predictions with equal weights. All unspecified parameters use the same values as [48].

Evaluation Metrics: We report two sets of metrics: aggregate and per-class, which are equivalent to the class-agnostic and class-aware metrics in [54]. For aggregate metrics, we compute top-1 and top-5 accuracy for correct predictions of c_v, c_n and their combination (c_v, c_n) – we refer to these as 'verb', 'noun' and 'action'. Accuracy is reported on the full test set. For per-class metrics, we compute precision and recall, for classes with more than 100 samples in training, then average the metrics across classes - these are 26 verb classes, 71 noun classes, and 819 action classes. Per-class metrics for smaller classes are ≈ 0 as TSN is better suited for classes with sufficient training data.

Results: We report results in Table 6 for aggregate metrics and per-class metrics. We compare TSN (3 segments) to 2SCNN [43] (1 segment), chance and largest class baselines. Fused results perform best or are comparable to the best stream (spatial/temporal). The challenge of getting both verb and noun labels correct remains significant for both *seen* (top-1 accuracy 20.5%) and *unseen* (top-1 accuracy 10.9%) environments. This implies that for many examples, we only get one of the two labels (verb/noun) right. Results also show that generalising to *unseen* environments is a harder challenge for actions than it is for objects. We give a breakdown per-class metrics for the 15 largest verb classes in Table 7.

Fig. 10. Qualitative results for the action recognition and anticipation challenges

Figure 10 reports qualitative results, with success highlighted in green, and failures in red. In the first column both the verb and the noun are correctly predicted, in the second column one of them is correctly predicted, while in the third column both are incorrect. Challenging cases like distinguishing 'adjust heat' from turning it on, or pouring soy sauce vs oil are shown.

4.3 Action Anticipation Benchmark

Challenge: Anticipating the next action is a well-mastered skill by humans, and automating it has direct implications in assertive living. Given any of the upcoming wearable system (e.g. Microsoft Hololens or Google Glass), anticipating the wearer's next action, from a first-person view, could trigger smart home appliances, providing a seamless achievement of the wearer's goals. Previous works have investigated different anticipation tasks from an egocentric perspective, e.g. predicting future localisation [35] or next-active object [15]. We here consider the task of forecasting an action before it happens. Let τ_a be the 'anticipation time', how far in advance to recognise the action, and τ_o be the 'observation time', the length of the observed video segment preceding the action. Given an action segment $A_i = [t_{s_i}, t_{e_i}]$, we predict the action class C_a by observing the video segment *preceding* the action start time t_{s_i} by τ_a, that is $[t_{s_i} - (\tau_a + \tau_o), t_{s_i} - \tau_a]$.

Network Architecture: As in Sect. 4.2, we train TSN [48] to provide baseline action anticipation results and compare with 2SCNN [43]. We feed the model with the video segments preceding annotated actions and train it to predict verb and noun classes jointly as in [25]. Similarly to [47], we set $\tau_a = 1$ s. We report results with $\tau_o = 1$ s, and note that performance drops with longer segments.

Implementation Details: Models for both spatial and temporal modalities are trained using a single Nvidia Titan X with a batch size of 64, for 80 epochs, setting the initial learning rate to 0.001 and dropping it by a factor of 10 after 30 and 60 epochs. Fusion weights spatial and temporal streams with 0.6 and 0.4 respectively. All other parameters use the values specified in [48].

Evaluation Metrics: We use the same evaluation metrics as in Sect. 4.2.

Results: Table 8 reports baseline results for the action anticipation challenge. As expected, this is a harder challenge than action recognition, and thus we note a drop in performance throughout. Unlike the case of action recognition, the flow stream and fusion do not generally improve performances. TSN often offers small, but consistent improvements over 2SCNN.

Figure 10 reports qualitative results. Success examples are highlighted in green, and failure cases in red. As the qualitative figure shows, the method over-predicts 'put' as the next action. Once an object is picked up, the learned model has a tendency to believe it will be put down next. Methods that focus on long-term understanding of the goal, as well as multi-scale history would be needed to circumvent such a tendency.

Table 8. Baseline results for the action anticipation challenge

	Top-1 Accuracy			Top-5 Accuracy			Avg Class Precision			Avg Class Recall		
	VERB	NOUN	ACTION	VERB	NOUN	ACTION	VERB	NOUN	ACTION	VERB	NOUN	ACTION
2SCNN (RGB)	29.76	15.15	04.32	76.03	38.56	15.21	13.76	17.19	02.48	07.32	10.72	01.81
TSN (RGB)	**31.81**	**16.22**	**06.00**	**76.56**	**42.15**	**18.21**	**23.91**	19.13	**03.13**	**09.33**	11.93	**02.39**
S1 TSN (FLOW)	29.64	10.30	02.93	73.70	30.09	10.92	18.34	10.70	01.41	06.99	05.48	01.00
TSN (FUSION)	30.66	14.86	04.62	75.32	40.11	16.01	08.84	**21.85**	02.25	06.76	09.15	01.55
2SCNN (RGB)	25.23	09.97	02.29	**68.66**	27.38	09.35	16.37	06.98	00.85	05.80	06.37	**01.14**
TSN (RGB)	25.30	**10.41**	**02.39**	68.32	**29.50**	**09.63**	07.63	**08.79**	00.80	06.06	**06.74**	01.07
S2 TSN (FLOW)	**25.61**	08.40	01.78	67.57	24.62	08.19	10.80	04.99	01.02	**06.34**	04.72	00.84
TSN (FUSION)	25.37	09.76	01.74	68.25	27.24	09.05	**13.03**	05.13	00.90	05.65	05.58	00.79

Discussion: The three defined challenges form the base for higher-level understanding of the wearer's goals. We have shown that existing methods are still far from tackling these tasks with high precision, pointing to exciting future directions. Our dataset lends itself naturally to a variety of less explored tasks. We are planning to provide a wider set of challenges, including action localisation [50], video parsing [42], visual dialogue [7], goal completion [20] and skill determination [10] (e.g. how good are you at making your eggs for breakfast?). Since real-time performance is crucial in this domain, our leaderboard will reflect this, pressing the community to come up with efficient and effective solutions.

5   Conclusion and Future Work

We present the largest and most varied dataset in egocentric vision to date, EPIC-KITCHENS, captured in participants' native environments. We collect 55 hours of video data recorded on a head-mounted GoPro, and annotate it with narrations, action segments and object annotations using a pipeline that starts with live commentary of recorded videos by the participants themselves. Baseline results on object detection, action recognition and anticipation challenges show the great potential of the dataset for pushing approaches that target fine-grained video understanding to new frontiers. Dataset and online leaderboard for the three challenges are available from http://epic-kitchens.github.io.

Acknowledgement. Annotations sponsored by a charitable donation from Nokia Technologies and UoB's Jean Golding Institute. Research supported by EPSRC DTP, EPSRC GLANCE (EP/N013964/1), EPSRC LOCATE (EP/N033779/1) and Piano della Ricerca 2016–2018 linea di Intervento 2 of DMI. The object detection baseline helped by code from, and discussions with, Davide Acuña.

References

1. Abu-El-Haija, S., et al.: YouTube-8M: a large-scale video classification benchmark. In: CoRR (2016)
2. Alletto, S., Serra, G., Calderara, S., Cucchiara, R.: Understanding social relationships in egocentric vision. Pattern Recogn. (2015)
3. Antol, S., et al.: VQA: visual question answering. In: ICCV (2015)

4. Banerjee, S., Pedersen, T.: An adapted lesk algorithm for word sense disambiguation using wordnet. In: CICLing (2002)
5. Carnegie Mellon University: CMU sphinx. https://cmusphinx.github.io/
6. Damen, D., Leelasawassuk, T., Haines, O., Calway, A., Mayol-Cuevas, W.: You-do, I-learn: discovering task relevant objects and their modes of interaction from multi-user egocentric video. In: BMVC (2014)
7. Das, A., et al.: Visual Dialog. In: CVPR (2017)
8. De La Torre, F., et al.: Guide to the carnegie mellon university multimodal activity (CMU-MMAC) database. In: Robotics Institute (2008)
9. Deng, J., Dong, W., Socher, R., Li, L.J., Li, K., Fei-Fei, L.: ImageNet: a large-scale hierarchical image database. In: CVPR (2009)
10. Doughty, H., Damen, D., Mayol-Cuevas, W.: Who's better? who's best? Pairwise deep ranking for skill determination. In: CVPR (2018)
11. Everingham, M., Van Gool, L., Williams, C.K.I., Winn, J., Zisserman, A.: The PASCAL visual object classes (VOC) challenge. IJCV (2010)
12. Fathi, A., Hodgins, J., Rehg, J.: Social interactions: a first-person perspective. In: CVPR (2012)
13. Fathi, A., Li, Y., Rehg, J.M.: Learning to recognize daily actions using gaze. In: Fitzgibbon, A., Lazebnik, S., Perona, P., Sato, Y., Schmid, C. (eds.) ECCV 2012. LNCS, vol. 7572, pp. 314–327. Springer, Heidelberg (2012). https://doi.org/10.1007/978-3-642-33718-5_23
14. Fouhey, D.F., Kuo, W.c., Efros, A.A., Malik, J.: From lifestyle vlogs to everyday interactions. arXiv preprint arXiv:1712.02310 (2017)
15. Furnari, A., Battiato, S., Grauman, K., Farinella, G.M.: Next-active-object prediction from egocentric videos. JVCIR (2017)
16. Georgia Tech: Extended GTEA Gaze+ (2018). http://webshare.ipat.gatech.edu/coc-rim-wall-lab/web/yli440/egtea_gp
17. Google: Google cloud speech api. https://cloud.google.com/speech
18. Goyal, R., et al.: The "something something" video database for learning and evaluating visual common sense. In: ICCV (2017)
19. He, K., Zhang, X., Ren, S., Sun, J.: Deep residual learning for image recognition. In: CVPR (2016)
20. Heidarivincheh, F., Mirmehdi, M., Damen, D.: Action completion: a temporal model for moment detection. In: BMVC (2018)
21. Huang, J., et al.: Tensorflow Object Detection API. https://github.com/tensorflow/models/tree/master/research/object_detection
22. Huang, J., et al.: Speed/accuracy trade-offs for modern convolutional object detectors. In: CVPR (2017)
23. IBM: IBM watson speech to text. https://www.ibm.com/watson/services/speech-to-text
24. Ioffe, S., Szegedy, C.: Batch normalization: Accelerating deep network training by reducing internal covariate shift. In: ICML (2015)
25. Kalogeiton, V., Weinzaepfel, P., Ferrari, V., Schmid, C.: Joint learning of object and action detectors. In: ICCV (2017)
26. Karpathy, A., Fei-Fei, L.: Deep visual-semantic alignments for generating image descriptions. In: CVPR (2015)
27. Krizhevsky, A., Sutskever, I., Hinton, G.E.: Imagenet classification with deep convolutional neural networks. In: NIPS (2012)
28. Kuehne, H., Arslan, A., Serre, T.: The language of actions: recovering the syntax and semantics of goal-directed human activities. In: CVPR (2014)

29. Lee, Y., Ghosh, J., Grauman, K.: Discovering important people and objects for egocentric video summarization. In: CVPR (2012)
30. Lin, T.-Y., et al.: Microsoft COCO: common objects in context. In: Fleet, D., Pajdla, T., Schiele, B., Tuytelaars, T. (eds.) ECCV 2014. LNCS, vol. 8693, pp. 740–755. Springer, Cham (2014). https://doi.org/10.1007/978-3-319-10602-1_48
31. Mikolov, T., Chen, K., Corrado, G., Dean, J.: Efficient estimation of word representations in vector space. arXiv preprint arXiv:1301.3781 (2013)
32. Miller, G.: WordNet: a lexical database for English. In: CACM (1995)
33. Moltisanti, D., Wray, M., Mayol-Cuevas, W., Damen, D.: Trespassing the boundaries: Labeling temporal bounds for object interactions in egocentric video. In: ICCV (2017)
34. Nair, A., et al.: Combining self-supervised learning and imitation for vision-based rope manipulation. In: ICRA (2017)
35. Park, H.S., Hwang, J.J., Niu, Y., Shi, J.: Egocentric future localization. In: CVPR (2016)
36. Pirsiavash, H., Ramanan, D.: Detecting activities of daily living in first-person camera views. In: CVPR (2012)
37. Ren, S., He, K., Girshick, R., Sun, J.: Faster R-CNN: towards real-time object detection with region proposal networks. In: NIPS (2015)
38. Rohrbach, A., Rohrbach, M., Tandon, N., Schiele, B.: A dataset for movie description. In: CVPR (2015)
39. Rohrbach, M., Amin, S., Andriluka, M., Schiele, B.: A database for fine grained activity detection of cooking activities. In: CVPR (2012)
40. Ryoo, M.S., Matthies, L.: First-person activity recognition: what are they doing to me? In: CVPR (2013)
41. Sigurdsson, G.A., Gupta, A., Schmid, C., Farhadi, A., Alahari, K.: Charades-ego: a large-scale dataset of paired third and first person videos. In: ArXiv (2018)
42. Sigurdsson, G.A., Varol, G., Wang, X., Farhadi, A., Laptev, I., Gupta, A.: Hollywood in homes: crowdsourcing data collection for activity understanding. In: Leibe, B., Matas, J., Sebe, N., Welling, M. (eds.) ECCV 2016. LNCS, vol. 9905, pp. 510–526. Springer, Cham (2016). https://doi.org/10.1007/978-3-319-46448-0_31
43. Simonyan, K., Zisserman, A.: Two-stream convolutional networks for action recognition in videos. In: Advances in Neural Information Processing Systems, pp. 568–576 (2014)
44. Stein, S., McKenna, S.: Combining embedded accelerometers with computer vision for recognizing food preparation activities. In: UbiComp (2013)
45. Szegedy, C., et al.: Going deeper with convolutions. In: CVPR (2015)
46. Tapaswi, M., Zhu, Y., Stiefelhagen, R., Torralba, A., Urtasun, R., Fidler, S.: MovieQA: understanding stories in movies through question-answering. In: CVPR (2016)
47. Vondrick, C., Pirsiavash, H., Torralba, A.: Anticipating visual representations from unlabeled video. In: CVPR (2016)
48. Wang, L., et al.: Temporal segment networks: towards good practices for deep action recognition. In: Leibe, B., Matas, J., Sebe, N., Welling, M. (eds.) ECCV 2016. LNCS, vol. 9912, pp. 20–36. Springer, Cham (2016). https://doi.org/10.1007/978-3-319-46484-8_2
49. Yamaguchi, K.: Bbox-annotator. https://github.com/kyamagu/bbox-annotator
50. Yeung, S., Russakovsky, O., Jin, N., Andriluka, M., Mori, G., Fei-Fei, L.: Every moment counts: dense detailed labeling of actions in complex videos. IJCV (2018)
51. Yuanjun, X.: PyTorch Temporal Segment Network (2017). https://github.com/yjxiong/tsn-pytorch

52. Zach, C., Pock, T., Bischof, H.: A duality based approach for realtime TV-L1 optical flow. Pattern Recogn. (2007)
53. Zhang, T., McCarthy, Z., Jow, O., Lee, D., Goldberg, K., Abbeel, P.: Deep imitation learning for complex manipulation tasks from virtual reality teleoperation. In: ICRA (2018)
54. Zhao, H., Yan, Z., Wang, H., Torresani, L., Torralba, A.: SLAC: a sparsely labeled dataset for action classification and localization. arXiv preprint arXiv:1712.09374 (2017)
55. Zhou, B., Zhao, H., Puig, X., Fidler, S., Barriuso, A., Torralba, A.: Scene parsing through ADE20K dataset. In: CVPR (2017)
56. Zhou, L., Xu, C., Corso, J.J.: Towards automatic learning of procedures from web instructional videos. arXiv preprint arXiv:1703.09788 (2017)

Unsupervised Person Re-identification by Deep Learning Tracklet Association

Minxian Li[1,2(✉)], Xiatian Zhu[3], and Shaogang Gong[2]

[1] Nanjing University of Science and Technology, Nanjing, China
minxianli@njust.edu.cn
[2] Queen Mary University of London, London, UK
s.gong@qmul.ac.uk
[3] Vision Semantics Limited, London, UK
eddy@visionsemantics.com

Abstract. Most existing person re-identification (re-id) methods rely on *supervised* model learning on per-camera-pair *manually* labelled pairwise training data. This leads to poor scalability in practical re-id deployment due to the lack of exhaustive identity labelling of image positive and negative pairs for every camera pair. In this work, we address this problem by proposing an unsupervised re-id deep learning approach capable of incrementally discovering and exploiting the underlying re-id discriminative information from *automatically* generated person tracklet data from videos in an end-to-end model optimisation. We formulate a *Tracklet Association Unsupervised Deep Learning* (TAUDL) framework characterised by jointly learning per-camera (within-camera) tracklet association (labelling) and cross-camera tracklet correlation by maximising the discovery of most likely tracklet relationships across camera views. Extensive experiments demonstrate the superiority of the proposed TAUDL model over the state-of-the-art unsupervised and domain adaptation re-id methods using six person re-id benchmarking datasets.

Keywords: Person re-identification · Unsupervised learning
Tracklet · Surveillance video

1 Introduction

Person re-identification (re-id) aims to match the underlying identities of person bounding box images detected from non-overlapping camera views [15]. In recent years, extensive research attention has been attracted [1,7,10,11,14,18,29–31,43,45,52,57] to address the re-id problem. Most existing re-id methods, in particular deep learning models, adopt the *supervised* learning approach. These supervised deep models assume the availability of a large number of *manually* labelled *cross-view identity (ID) matching image pairs* for each camera pair in order to induce a feature representation or a distance metric function optimised

© Springer Nature Switzerland AG 2018
V. Ferrari et al. (Eds.): ECCV 2018, LNCS 11208, pp. 772–788, 2018.
https://doi.org/10.1007/978-3-030-01225-0_45

just for that camera pair. This assumption is inherently limited for generalising a re-id model to many different camera networks therefore cannot scale in practical deployments[1].

It is no surprise then that person re-id by *unsupervised* learning has become a focus in recent research where per-camera pairwise ID labelled training data is not required in model learning [22,24,25,32,35,37,46,48,54,58]. However, all these classical unsupervised learning models are significantly weaker in re-id performance than the supervised models. This is because the lack of cross-view pairwise ID labelled data deprives a model's ability to learn from strong context-aware ID discriminative information in order to cope with significant visual appearance change between every camera pair, as defined by a triplet verification loss function. An alternative approach is to leverage jointly (1) unlabelled data from a target domain which is freely available, e.g. videos of thousands of people travelling through a camera view everyday in a public scene; and (2) pairwise ID labelled datasets from independent source domains [13,38,42,49,55]. The main idea is to first learn a "view-invariant" representation from ID labelled source data, then adapt the model to a target domain by using only unlabelled target data. This approach makes an implicit assumption that the source and target domains share some common cross-view characteristics and a view-invariant representation can be estimated, which is not always true.

In this work, we consider a *pure* unsupervised person re-id deep learning problem. That is, no ID labelled training data is assumed, neither cross-view nor within-view ID labelling. Although this learning objective is similar to two domain transfer models [13,49], both those models do require *suitable*, i.e. visually similar to the target domain, person identity labelled source domain training data. Specifically, we consider unsupervised re-id model learning by jointly optimising unlabelled person tracklet data *within-camera* view to be more discriminative and *cross-camera* view to be more associative in an end-to-end manner.

Our **contributions** are: We formulate a novel unsupervised person re-id deep learning method using person tracklets without the need for camera pairwise ID labelled training data, i.e. *unsupervised tracklet re-id discriminative learning*. Specifically, we propose a **Tracklet Association Unsupervised Deep Learning** (TAUDL) model with two key innovations: (1) *Per-Camera Tracklet Discrimination Learning* that optimises "local" within-camera tracklet label discrimination for facilitating cross-camera tracklet association given per-camera independently created tracklet label spaces. (2) *Cross-Camera Tracklet Association Learning* that maximises "global" cross-camera tracklet label association. This is formulated as to maximise jointly cross-camera tracklet similarity and within-camera tracklet dissimilarity in an end-to-end deep learning framework.

Comparative experiments show the advantages of TAUDL over the state-of-the-art unsupervised and domain adaptation person re-id models using six benchmarks including three multi-shot image based and three video based re-

---

[1] Exhaustive manual ID labelling of person image pairs for every camera-pair is prohibitively expensive as there are a quadratic number of camera pairs in a network.

id datasets: CUHK03 [29], Market-1501 [60], DukeMTMC [41], iLIDS-VID [50], PRID2011 [19], and MARS [59].

2   Related Work

Most existing re-id models are built by *supervised* model learning on a separate set of per-camera-pair ID labelled training data [1,7–11,18,20,29–31,43,45,47, 51,52,57,62]. Hence, their scalability and usability is poor for real-world re-id deployments where no such large training sets are available for every camera pair. Classical unsupervised learning methods based on hand-crafted features offer poor re-id performance [14,22,24,25,32,35,37,46,48,54,58] when compared to the supervised learning based re-id models. While a balancing trade-off between model scalability and re-id accuracy can be achieved by semi-supervised learning [33,48], these models still assume sufficiently large sized cross-view pairwise labelled data for model training. More recently, there are some attempts on unsupervised learning of domain adaptation models [13,38,42,49,55]. The main idea is to explore knowledge from pairwise labelled data in "related" source domains with model adaptation on unlabelled target domain data. Whilst these domain adaptation models perform better than the classical unsupervised learning methods (Tables 2 and 3), they requires implicitly similar data distributions and viewing conditions between the labelled source domain and the unlabelled target domains. This restricts their scalability to arbitrarily diverse (and unknown) target domains.

In contrast to all these existing unsupervised learning re-id methods, the proposed tracklet association based method enables unsupervised re-id deep end-to-end learning from scratch without any assumption on either the scene characteristic similarity between source and target domains, or the complexity of handling identity label space (or lack of) knowledge transfer in model optimisation. Instead, our method directly learns to discover the re-id discriminative knowledge from *unsupervised* tracklet label data automatically generated and annotated from the video data using a common deep learning network architecture. Moreover, this method does not assume any overlap of person ID classes across camera views, therefore scalable to any camera networks without any knowledge about camera space-time topology and/or time-profiling on people cross-view appearing patterns [36]. Compared to classical unsupervised methods relying on extra hand-crafted features, our method learns tracklet based re-id discriminative features from an end-to-end deep learning process. To our best knowledge, this is the *first* attempt at unsupervised tracklet association based person re-id deep learning model without relying on any ID labelled training data (either videos or images).

3   Unsupervised Deep Learning Tracklet Association

To overcome the limitation of *supervised re-id model training*, we propose a novel **Tracklet Association Unsupervised Deep Learning** (TAUDL) approach to

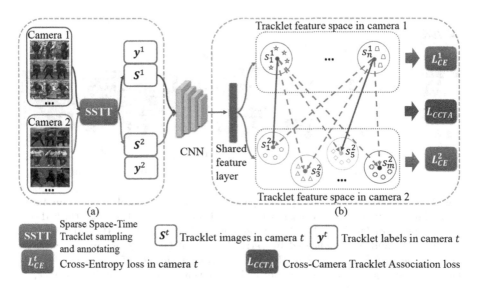

Fig. 1. An overview of Tracklet Association Unsupervised Deep Learning (TAUDL) re-id model: (a) Per-camera unsupervised tracklet sampling and label assignment; (b) Joint learning of both within-camera tracklet discrimination and cross-camera tracklet association in an end-to-end global deep learning on tracklets from all the cameras.

person re-id in video (or multi-shot images in general) by uniquely exploiting person *tracklet labelling* obtained by an *unsupervised* tracklet formation (sampling) mechanism[2] *without* any ID labelling of the training data (either cross-view or within-view). The TAUDL trains a person re-id model in an end-to-end manner in order to benefit from the inherent overall model optimisation advantages from deep learning. In the following, we first present a data sampling mechanism for unsupervised within-camera tracklet labelling (Sect. 3.1) and then describe our model design for cross-camera tracklet association by joint unsupervised deep learning (Sect. 3.2).

3.1 Unsupervised Within-View Tracklet Labelling

Given a large quantity of video data from multiple disjoint cameras, we can readily deploy existing pedestrian detection and tracking models [26,41,56,61], to extract person tracklets. In general, the space-time trajectory of a person in a single-camera view from a public scene is likely to be fragmented into an arbitrary number of short tracklets due to imperfect tracking and background clutter. Given a large number of person tracklets per camera, we want to annotate them for deep re-id model learning in an *unsupervised* manner without any manual

---

[2] Although object tracklets can be generated by any independent single-camera-view multi-object tracking (MOT) models widely available today, a conventional MOT model is *not* end-to-end optimised for cross-camera tracklet association.

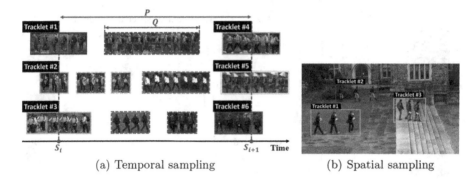

(a) Temporal sampling   (b) Spatial sampling

Fig. 2. An illustration of the Sparse Space-Time Tracklet sampling and annotating method for unsupervised tracklet labelling. Solid box: Sampled tracklets; Dashed box: Non-sampled tracklets; Each colour represents a distinct person ID. (a) Two time instances (S_i and S_{i+1} indicated by vertical lines) of temporal sampling are shown with a time gap P greater than the common transit time Q of a camera view. (b) Three spatially sparse tracklets are formed at a given temporal sampling instance.

identity verification on tracklets. To this end, we need an automatic tracklet labelling method to minimise the person ID duplication (i.e. multiple tracklet labels corresponding the same person ID label) rate among these labelled tracklets. To this end, we propose a **Sparse Space-Time Tracklet** (SSTT) sampling and label assignment method.

Our SSTT method is built on three observations typical in surveillance videos: **(1)** For most people, re-appearing in a camera view is rare during a short time period. As such, the dominant factor for causing person tracklet duplication (of the same ID) in auto-generated person tracklets is trajectory fragmentation, and if we assign every tracklet with a distinct label. To address this problem, we perform sparse temporal sampling of tracklets (Fig. 2(a)) as follows: (i) At the i-th temporal sampling instance corresponding to a time point S_i, we retrieve all tracklets at time S_i and annotate each tracklet with a distinct label. This is based on the factor that **(2)** people co-occurring at the same time in a single-view but at different spatial locations should have distinct ID labels. (ii) Given a time gap P, the next $((i+1)$-th) temporal sampling and label assignment is repeated, where P controls the sparsity of the temporal sampling rate. Based on observation **(3)** that most people in a public scene travel through a single camera view in a common time period $Q < P$, it is expected that at most one tracklet per person can be sampled at such a sparse temporal sampling rate (assuming no re-appearing once out of the same camera view). Consequently, we can significantly reduce the ID duplication even in highly crowded scenes with greater degrees of trajectory fragmentation.

To further mitigate the negative effect of inaccurate person detection and tracking at each temporal sampling instance, we further impose a sparse spatial sampling constraint – only selecting the co-occurring tracklets distantly distributed over the scene space (Fig. 2(b)). In doing so, the tracklet labels are more likely to be of independent person identities with minimum ID duplications in each i-th temporal sampling instance.

By deploying this SSTT tracklet labelling method in each camera view, we can obtain an independent set of labelled tracklets $\{S_i, y_i\}$ per-camera in a camera network, where each tracklet contains a varying number of person bounding boxes as $S = \{I_1, I_2, \cdots\}$. Our objective is to use these SSTT labelled tracklets for optimising a cross-view person re-id deep learning model without any cross-view ID labelled pairwise training data.

3.2 Unsupervised Tracklet Association

Given per-camera independently-labelled tracklets $\{S_i, y_i\}$ generated by SSTT, we perform *tracklet label re-id discriminative learning* without person ID labels in a conventional classification deep learning framework. To that end, we formulate a **Tracklet Association Unsupervised Deep Learning** (TAUDL) model. The overall design of our TAUDL architecture is shown in Fig. 1. The TAUDL contains two model components: **(I)** *Per-Camera Tracklet Discrimination Learning* with the aim to optimise "local" (within-camera) tracklet label discrimination for facilitating cross-camera tracklet association given independently created tracklet label spaces in different camera views. **(II)** *Cross-Camera Tracklet Association Learning* with the aim to maximise "global" (cross-camera) tracklet label association. The two components integrate as a whole in a single deep learning network architecture, learn jointly and mutually benefit each other in an incremental end-to-end manner.

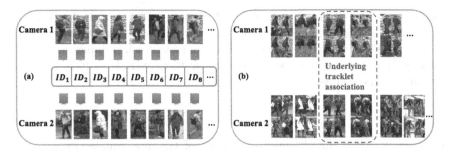

Fig. 3. Comparing (a) Fine-grained *explicit instance-level* cross-view ID labelled image pairs for supervised person re-id model learning and (b) Coarse-grained *latent group-level* cross-view tracklet (a multi-shot group) label correlation for ID label-free (unsupervised) person re-id learning using TAUDL.

(I) Per-Camera Tracklet Discrimination Learning. For accurate cross-camera tracklet association, it is important to formulate a robust image feature representation for describing the person appearance of each tracklet that helps cross-view person re-id association. However, it is sub-optimal to achieve "local" per-camera tracklet discriminative learning using only per-camera independent tracklet labels without "global" cross-camera tracklet correlations. We wish to optimise jointly both local tracklet within-view discrimination and global tracklet cross-view association. To that end, we design a Per-Camera Tracklet Discrimination (PCTD) learning algorithm. Our key idea is that, instead of relying on the conventional fine-grained *explicit instance-level* cross-view ID pairwise supervised learning (Fig. 3(a)), we learn to maximise coarse-grained *latent group-level* cross-camera tracklet association by set correlation (Fig. 3(b)).

Specifically, we treat each individual camera view separately by optimising per-camera labelled tracklet discrimination as a classification task against the tracklet labels per-camera (not person ID labels). Therefore, we have a total of T different tracklet classification tasks each corresponding to a specific camera view. Importantly, we further formulate these T classification tasks in a multi-branch architecture design where every task shares the *same* feature representation whilst enjoys an individual classification branch (Fig. 1(b)). Conceptually, this model design is in a spirit of the multi-task learning principle [2,12].

Formally, given unsupervised training data $\{I, y\}$ extracted from a camera view $t \in \{1, \cdots, T\}$, where I specifies a tracklet frame and $y \in \{1, \cdots, M_t\}$ the tracklet label (obtained as in Sect. 3.1) with a total of M_t different labels, we adopt the softmax Cross-Entropy (CE) loss function to optimise the corresponding classification task (the t-th branch). The CE loss on a training image sample (I, y) is computed as:

$$\mathcal{L}_{\text{ce}} = -\log\Big(\frac{\exp(W_y^\top x)}{\sum_{k=1}^{M_t} \exp(W_k^\top x)}\Big), \tag{1}$$

where x specifies the feature vector of I extracted by the task-shared feature representation component and W_y the y-th class prediction function parameters. Given a mini-batch, we compute the CE loss for each such training sample w.r.t. the respective tracklet label space and utilise their average to form the model learning supervision as:

$$\mathcal{L}_{\text{pctd}} = \frac{1}{N_{\text{bs}}} \sum_{t=1}^{T} \mathcal{L}_{\text{ce}}^t, \tag{2}$$

where $\mathcal{L}_{\text{ce}}^t$ denotes the CE loss summation of training samples from the t-th camera among a total of T and N_{bs} the batch size.

Discussion: In PCTD, the deep learning objective loss function (Eq. (1)) aims to optimise by supervised learning person tracklet discrimination *within* each camera view without any knowledge on *cross-camera* tracklet association. However, when jointly learning all the per-camera tracklet discrimination tasks together, the learned representation model is somewhat *implicitly* and *collectively* cross-view tracklet discriminative in a latent manner, due to the existence of cross-camera tracklet correlation. In other words, the shared feature representation is optimised *concurrently* to be discriminative for tracklet discrimination in multiple camera views, therefore propagating model discriminative learning from per-camera to cross-camera. We will evaluate the effect of this model design in our experiments (Table 4).

(II) Cross-Camera Tracklet Association Learning. While the PCTD algorithm described above achieves somewhat global (all the camera views) tracklet discrimination implicitly, the learned model representation remains sub-optimal due to the lack of *explicitly* optimising cross-camera tracklet association at the fine-grained instance level. It is significantly harder to impose cross-view person re-id discriminative model learning without camera pairwise ID labels. To address this problem, we introduce a Cross-Camera Tracklet Association (CCTA) loss function. The CCTA loss is formulated based on the idea of *batch-wise incrementally aligning cross-view per tracklet feature distribution* in the shared multi-task learning feature space. Critically, CCTA integrates seamlessly with PCTD to jointly optimise model learning on discovering cross-camera tracklet association for person re-id in a single end-to-end batch-wise learning process.

Formally, given a mini-batch including a subset of tracklets $\{(\boldsymbol{S}_i^t, y_i^t)\}$ where $\boldsymbol{S}_i^t$ specifies the i-th tracklet from t-th camera view with the label y_i^t where tracklets in a mini-batch come from all the camera views, we want to establish for each in-batch tracklet a discriminative association with other tracklets from different camera views. In absence of person identity pairwise labelling as a learning constraint, we propose to align *similar* and *dissimilar* tracklets in each mini-batch given the up-to-date shared multi-task (multi-camera) feature representation from optimising PCTD. More specifically, for each tracklet $\boldsymbol{S}_i^t$, we first retrieve K cross-view nearest tracklets $\mathcal{N}_i^t$ in the feature space, with the remaining $\tilde{\mathcal{N}}_i^t$ considered as dissimilar ones. We then impose a soft discriminative structure constraint by encouraging the model to pull $\mathcal{N}_i^t$ close to $\boldsymbol{S}_i^t$ whilst to push away $\tilde{\mathcal{N}}_i^t$ from $\boldsymbol{S}_i^t$. Conceptually, this is a per-tracklet cross-view data structure distribution alignment. To achieve this, we formulate a CCTA deep learning objective loss for each tracklet $\boldsymbol{S}_i^t$ in a training mini-batch as:

$$\mathcal{L}_{\text{ccta}} = -\log \frac{\sum_{z_k \in \mathcal{N}_i^t} \exp(-\frac{1}{2\sigma^2} \parallel \boldsymbol{s}_i^t - \boldsymbol{z}_k \parallel_2)}{\sum_{t'=1}^{T} \sum_{j=1}^{n_j} \exp(-\frac{1}{2\sigma^2} \parallel \boldsymbol{s}_i^t - \boldsymbol{s}_j^{t'} \parallel_2)}, \tag{3}$$

where n_j denotes the number of in-batch tracklets from j-th camera view, T the camera view number, σ a scaling parameter, $\boldsymbol{s}_i^t$ the up-to-date feature representation of the tracklet $\boldsymbol{S}_i^t$. Given the incremental iterative deep learning nature, we represent a tracklet $\boldsymbol{S}$ by the average of its in-batch frames' feature vectors on-the-fly. Hence, the tracklet representation is kept up-to-date without the need for maintaining external per-tracklet feature representations.

Discussion: The proposed CCTA loss formulation is conceptually similar to the Histogram Loss [44] in terms of distribution alignment. However, the Histogram Loss is a *supervised* loss that requires supervised label training data, whilst the CCTA is purely *unsupervised* and derived directly from feature similarity measures. CCTA is also related to the surrogate (artificially built) class based unsupervised deep learning loss formulations [4,5], by not requiring groundtruth class-labelled data in model training. Unlike CCTA without the need for creating surrogate classes, the surrogate based models not only require additional global data clustering, but also are sensitive to the clustering quality and initial feature selection. Moreover, they do not consider the label distribution alignment across cameras and label spaces for which the CCTA loss is designed.

Joint Loss Function. After merging the CCTA and PCTD learning constraints, we obtain the final model objective function as:

$$\mathcal{L}_{\text{taudl}} = (1 - \lambda)\mathcal{L}_{\text{pctd}} + \lambda\mathcal{L}_{\text{ccta}}, \tag{4}$$

where λ is a weighting parameter estimated by cross-validation. Note that $\mathcal{L}_{\text{pctd}}$ is an average loss term at the tracklet individual image level whilst $\mathcal{L}_{\text{ccta}}$ at the tracklet group (set) level, both derived from the same training batch concurrently. As such, the overall TAUDL method naturally enables end-to-end deep model learning using the Stochastic Gradient Descent optimisation algorithm.

4   Experiments

Datasets. To evaluate the proposed TAUDL model, we tested both video (MARS [59], iLIDS-Video [50], PRID2011 [19]) and image (CUHK03 [29], Market-1501 [60], DukeMTMC [41,61]) based person re-id benchmarking datasets. In previous studies, these datasets were mostly evaluated separately. We consider since recent large sized image based re-id datasets were typically constructed by sampling person bounding boxes from video, these image datasets share similar characteristics of those video based datasets. We adopted the standard person re-id setting on training/test ID split and the test protocols (Table 1).

Fig. 4. Example cross-view matched image/tracklet pairs from (a) CUHK03, (b) Market-1501, (c) DukeMTMC, (d) PRID2011, (e) iLIDS-VID, (f) MARS.

Tracklet Label Assignment. For all six datasets, we cannot perform real SSTT tracklet sampling and label assignment due to no information available on spatial and temporal location w.r.t. the original video data. In our experiment, we instead conducted simulated SSTT to obtain the per-camera tracklet/image

Table 1. Dataset statistics and evaluation setting.

Dataset	# ID	# Train	# Test	# Images	# Tracklet
iLIDS-VID [50]	300	150	150	43,800	600
PRID2011 [19]	178	89	89	38,466	354
MARS [59]	1,261	625	636	1,191,003	20,478
CUHK03 [29]	1,467	767	700	14,097	0
Market-1501 [60]	1,501	751	750	32,668	0
DukeMTMC [41]	1,812	702	1,110	36,411	0

labels. For all datasets, we assume no re-appearing subjects per camera (very rare in these datasets) and sparse spatial sampling. As both iLIDS-VID and PRID2011 provide only one tracklet per ID per camera (i.e. no fragmentation), it is impossible to have per-camera ID duplication. Therefore, each tracklet is assigned a unique label. The MARS gives multiple tracklets per ID per camera. Based on SSTT, at most only one tracklet can be sampled for each ID per camera (see Sect. 3.1). Therefore, a MARS tracklet per ID per camera was randomly selected and assigned a label. For all image based datasets, we assume all images per ID per camera were drawn from a single tracklet, same as in iLIDS-VID and PRID2011. The same tracklet label assignment procedure was adopted as above.

Performance Metrics. We use the common cumulative matching characteristic (CMC) and mean Average Precision (mAP) metrics [60].

Implementation Details. We adopted an ImageNet pre-trained ResNet-50 [17] as the backbone in evaluating the proposed TAUDL method. We set the feature dimension of the camera-shared representation space derived on top of ResNet-50 to 2,048. Each camera-specific branch contains one FC classification layer. Person images are resized to 256 × 128 for all datasets. To ensure that each batch has the capacity of containing person images from all cameras, we set the batch size to 384 for all datasets. For balancing the model learning speed over different cameras, we randomly selected the same number of training frame images per camera when sampling each mini-batch. We adopted the Adam optimiser [23] with the initial learning rate of 3.5×10^{-4}. We empirically set $\lambda = 0.7$ for Eq. (4), $\sigma = 2$ for Eq. (3), and $K = T/2$ (T is the number of cameras) for cross-view nearest tracklets $\mathcal{N}_i^t$ in Eq. (3) for all the experiments.

4.1 Comparisons to State-of-the-Arts

We compared two different sets of state-of-the-art methods on image and video re-id datasets, due to the independent studies on them in the literature.

Unsupervised Person Re-ID on Image Datasets. Table 2 shows the unsupervised re-id performance of the proposed TAUDL and 10 state-of-the-art methods including 3 hand-crafted feature based methods (Dic [25], ISR [32], RKSL [48])

Table 2. Unsupervised re-id on image datasets. 1st/2nd best results are in red/blue.

Dataset	CUHK03 [29]		Market-1501 [60]		DukeMTMC [61]	
Metric (%)	Rank-1	mAP	Rank-1	mAP	Rank-1	mAP
Dic [25]	36.5	-	50.2	22.7	-	-
ISR [32]	38.5	-	40.3	14.3	-	-
RKSL [48]	34.8	-	34.0	11.0	-	-
SAE [27]	30.5	-	42.4	16.2	-	-
JSTL [52]	33.2	-	44.7	18.4	-	-
AML [53]	31.4	-	44.7	18.4	-	-
UsNCA [40]	29.6	-	45.2	18.9	-	-
CAMEL [55]	**39.4**	-	54.5	26.3	-	-
PUL [13]	-	-	44.7	20.1	30.4	16.4
TJ-AIDL [49]	-	-	**58.2**	**26.5**	**44.3**	**23.0**
TAUDL	44.7	31.2	63.7	41.2	61.7	43.5
GCS [6](*Supervised*)	88.8	97.2	93.5	81.6	84.9	69.5

and 7 auxiliary knowledge (identity/attribute) transfer based models (AE [27], AML [53], UsNCA [40], CAMEL [55], JSTL [52], PUL [13], TJ-AIDL [49]). These results show: (1) Among existing methods, the knowledge transfer based method is superior, e.g. on CUHK03, Rank-1 39.4% by CAMEL vs. 36.5% by Dic; On Market-1501, 58.2% by TJ-AIDL vs. 50.2% by Dic. To that end, CAMEL benefits from learning on 7 different person re-id datasets of diverse domains (CUHK03 [29], CUHK01 [28], PRID [19], VIPeR [16], 3DPeS [3], i-LIDS [39], Shinpuhkan [21]) including a total of 44,685 images and 3,791 identities; TJ-AIDL utilises labelled Market-1501 (750 IDs and 27 attribute classes) or DukeMTMC (702 IDs and 23 attribute classes) as source training data. (2) Our new model TAUDL outperforms all competitors with significant margins. For example, the Rank-1 margin by TAUDL over TJ-AIDL is 5.5% (63.7–58.2) on Market-1501 and 17.4% (61.7–44.3) on DukeMTMC. Moreover, it is worth pointing out that TAUDL dose not benefit from any additional labelled source domain training data as compared to TJ-AIDL. TAUDL is potentially more scalable due to no need to consider source and target domains similarities. (3) Our TAUDL is simpler to train with a simple end-to-end model learning, as compared to the alternated deep CNN training and clustering required by PUL and a two-stage model training of TJ-AIDL. These results show both the performance advantage and model design superiority of the proposed TAUDL model over a wide variety of state-of-the-art re-id models.

Unsupervised Person Re-ID on Video Datasets. We compared the proposed TAUDL with six state-of-the-art unsupervised video person re-id models. Unlike TAUDL, all these existing models are not end-to-end deep learning methods with either hand-crafted or separately trained deep features as model input. Table 3 shows that TAUDL outperforms all existing video-based person re-id

Table 3. Unsupervised re-id on video datasets. $1^{st}/2^{nd}$ best results are in red/blue.

Dataset	PRID2011 [19]			iLIDS-VID [50]			MARS [59]			
Metric (%)	R1	R5	R20	R1	R5	R20	R1	R5	R20	mAP
DTW [37]	41.7	67.1	90.1	31.5	62.1	82.4	-	-	-	-
GRDL [24]	41.6	76.4	89.9	25.7	49.9	77.6	19.3	33.2	46.5	9.56
UnKISS [22]	58.1	81.9	96.0	35.9	**63.3**	83.4	22.3	37.4	53.6	10.6
SMP [35]	80.9	95.6	99.4	41.7	66.3	80.7	23.9	35.8	44.9	10.5
DGM+MLAPG [54]	**73.1**	**92.5**	**99.0**	**37.1**	61.3	82.0	24.6	42.6	57.2	11.8
DGM+IDE [54]	56.4	81.3	96.4	36.2	62.8	**82.7**	**36.8**	**54.0**	**68.5**	**21.3**
TAUDL	49.4	78.7	98.9	26.7	51.3	82.0	43.8	59.9	72.8	29.1
QAN [34](*Supervised*)	90.3	98.2	100.0	68.0	86.8	97.4	73.7	84.9	91.6	51.7

models on the large scale video dataset MARS, e.g. by a Rank-1 margin of 7.0% (43.8–36.8) over the best competitor DGM+IDE (which additionally using the ID label information of one camera view for model initialisation). However, TAUDL is inferior than some of the existing models on the two small benchmarks iLIDS-VID (300 training tracklets) and PRID2011 (178 training tracklets), in comparison to its performance on the MARS benchmark (8,298 training tracklets). This shows that TAUDL does need sufficient tracklet data from larger video datasets in order to have its performance advantage. As the tracklet data required are not manually labelled, this requirement is not a hindrance to its scalability to large scale data. Quite the contrary, TAUDL works the best when large scale unlabelled video data is available. A model would benefit particularly from pre-training using TAUDL on large auxiliary unlabelled video data from similar camera viewing conditions.

4.2 Component Analysis and Discussions

Effectiveness of Per-Camera Tracklet Discrimination. The PCTD component was evaluated by comparing a baseline that treats all cameras together by concatenating per-camera tracklet label sets and deploying the Cross-Entropy loss to learn a unified classification task. We call this baseline Joint-Camera Classification (JCC). In this analysis, we do not consider the cross-camera tracklet association component for a clear evaluation. Table 4 shows that our PCTD design is significantly superior over the JCC learning algorithm, e.g. achieving Rank-1 gain of 4.0%, 34.6%, 36.3%, and 19.9% on CUHK03, Market-1501, DukeMTMC, and MARS respectively. This verifies the modelling advantages of the proposed per-camera tracklet discrimination learning scheme on the unsupervised tracklet labels in inducing cross-view re-id discriminative feature learning.

Effectiveness of Cross-Camera Tracklet Association. The CCTA learning component was evaluated by testing the performance drop after eliminating it. Table 5 shows a significant performance benefit from this model component, e.g. a Rank-1 boost of 10.9%, 11.6%, 10.5%, and 5.8% on CUHK03, Market-1501, DukeMTMC, and MARS respectively. This validates the importance of modelling the correlation across cameras in discriminative optimisation and the effectiveness of our CCTA deep learning objective loss formulation in an end-to-end manner. Additionally, this also suggests the effectiveness of the PCTD model component in facilitating the cross-view identity discrimination learning by providing re-id sensitive features in a joint incremental learning manner.

Table 4. Effect of Per-Camera Tracklet Discrimination (PCTD) learning.

Dataset	CUHK03 [29]		Market-1501 [60]		DukeMTMC [41]		MARS [59]	
Metric(%)	R1	mAP	R1	mAP	R1	mAP	R1	mAP
JCC	29.8	12.5	17.5	7.9	14.9	3.5	18.1	13.1
PCTD	**33.8**	**18.9**	**52.1**	**26.6**	**51.2**	**32.9**	**38.0**	**23.9**

Table 5. Effect of Cross-Camera Tracklet Association (CCTA)

Dataset	CUHK03 [29]		Market-1501 [60]		DukeMTMC [61]		MARS [59]	
CCTA	R1	mAP	R1	mAP	R1	mAP	R1	mAP
✗	33.8	18.9	52.1	26.6	51.2	32.9	38.0	23.9
✓	**44.7**	**31.2**	**63.7**	**41.2**	**61.7**	**43.5**	**43.8**	**29.1**

Model Robustness Analysis. Finally, we performed an analysis on model robustness against person ID duplication rates in tracklet labelling. We conducted a controlled evaluation on MARS where multiple tracklets per ID per camera are available for setting simulation. Recall that the ID duplication may mainly come with imperfect temporal sampling due to trajectory fragmentation and when some people stay in the same camera view for a longer time period than the temporal sampling gap. To simulate such a situation, we assume a varying percentage (10%~50%) of IDs per camera have two random tracklets sampled and annotated with different tracklet labels. More tracklets per ID per camera are likely to be sampled, which can make this analysis more complex due to the interference from the number of duplicated person IDs. Table 6 shows that our TAUDL model is robust against the ID duplication rate, e.g. with only a Rank-1 drop of 3.1% given as high as 50% per-camera ID duplication rate. In reality, it is not too hard to minimise ID duplication rate among tracklets (Sect. 3.1), e.g. conducting very sparse sampling over time and space. Note, we do not care about exhaustive sampling of all the tracklets from video in a given time period. The model learning benefits from very sparse and diverse tracklet sampling from a large pool of unlabelled video data.

The robustness of our TAUDL comes with two model components: **(1)** The model learning optimisation is not only subject to a single per-camera tracklet label constraint, but also concurrently to the constraints of all cameras. This facilitates optimising cross-camera tracklet association globally across all cameras in a common space, due to the Per-Camera Tracklet Discrimination learning mechanism (Eq. (2)). This provides model learning tolerance against per-camera tracklet label duplication errors. **(2)** The cross-camera tracklet association learning is designed as a feature similarity based "soft" objective learning constraint (Eq. (3)), without a direct dependence on the tracklet ID labels. Therefore, the ID duplication rate has little effect on this objective loss constraint.

Table 6. Model robustness analysis on varying ID duplication rates on MARS [59].

ID duplication rate (%)	Rank-1	Rank-5	Rank-10	Rank-20	mAP
0	**43.8**	**59.9**	**66.0**	**72.8**	**29.1**
10	42.8	59.7	65.5	71.6	28.3
20	42.2	58.8	64.7	70.6	27.4
30	41.6	57.9	64.5	69.7	26.7
50	40.7	57.0	63.4	69.6	25.6

5 Conclusions

In this work, we presented a novel *Tracklet Association Unsupervised Deep Learning* (TAUDL) model for unsupervised person re-identification using unsupervised person tracklet data extracted from videos, therefore eliminating the tedious and exhaustive manual labelling required by all supervised learning based re-id model learning. This enables TAUDL to be much more scalable to real-world re-id deployment at large scale video data. In contrast to most existing re-id methods that either require exhaustively pairwise labelled training data for every camera pair or assume the availability of additional labelled source domain training data for target domain adaptation, the proposed TAUDL model is capable of end-to-end deep learning a discriminative person re-id model from scratch on totally unlabelled tracklet data. This is achieved by optimising jointly both the Per-Camera Tracklet Discrimination loss function and the Cross-Camera Tracklet Association loss function in a single end-to-end deep learning framework. To our knowledge, this is the first completely unsupervised learning based re-id model without any identity labels for model learning, neither pairwise cross-view image pair labelling nor single-view image identity class labelling. Extensive comparative evaluations were conducted on six image and video based re-id benchmarks to validate the advantages of the proposed TAUDL model over a wide range of state-of-the-art unsupervised and domain adaptation re-id methods. We also conducted in-depth TAUDL model component evaluation and robustness test to give insights on model performance advantage and model learning stability.

Acknowledgments. This work is partially supported by the China Scholarship Council, Vision Semantics Limited, National Natural Science Foundation of China (Project No. 61401212), the Key Technology Research and Development Program of Jiangsu Province (Project No. BE2015162), the Science and Technology Support Project of Jiangsu Province (Project No. BE2014714), Royal Society Newton Advanced Fellowship Programme (NA150459), and Innovate UK Industrial Challenge Project on Developing and Commercialising Intelligent Video Analytics Solutions for Public Safety (98111-571149).

References

1. Ahmed, E., Jones, M., Marks, T.K.: An improved deep learning architecture for person re-identification. In: CVPR (2015)
2. Ando, R.K., Zhang, T.: A framework for learning predictive structures from multiple tasks and unlabeled data. JMLR **6**, 1817–1853 (2005)
3. Baltieri, D., Vezzani, R., Cucchiara, R.: 3DPeS: 3D people dataset for surveillance and forensics. In: J-HGBU (2011)
4. Bautista, M.A., Sanakoyeu, A., Ommer, B.: Deep unsupervised similarity learning using partially ordered sets. In: CVPR (2017)
5. Bautista, M.A., Sanakoyeu, A., Tikhoncheva, E., Ommer, B.: CliqueCNN: deep unsupervised exemplar learning. In: NIPS (2016)
6. Chen, D., Xu, D., Li, H., Sebe, N., Wang, X.: Group consistent similarity learning via deep CRF for person re-identification. In: CVPR (2018)
7. Chen, W., Chen, X., Zhang, J., Huang, K.: Beyond triplet loss: a deep quadruplet network for person re-identification. In: CVPR (2017)
8. Chen, Y., Zhu, X., Gong, S.: Person re-identification by deep learning multi-scale representations. In: ICCV Workshop (2017)
9. Chen, Y.C., Zhu, X., Zheng, W.S., Lai, J.H.: Person re-identification by camera correlation aware feature augmentation. IEEE TPAMI **40**(2), 392–408 (2018)
10. Cheng, D., Gong, Y., Zhou, S., Wang, J., Zheng, N.: Person re-identification by multi-channel parts-based cnn with improved triplet loss function. In: CVPR (2016)
11. Cho, Y.J., Yoon, K.J.: Improving person re-identification via pose-aware multi-shot matching. In: CVPR (2016)
12. Evgeniou, T., Pontil, M.: Regularized multi-task learning. In: SIGKDD (2004)
13. Fan, H., Zheng, L., Yang, Y.: Unsupervised person re-identification: clustering and fine-tuning. arXiv preprint arXiv:1705.10444 (2017)
14. Farenzena, M., Bazzani, L., Perina, A., Murino, V., Cristani, M.: Person re-identification by symmetry-driven accumulation of local features. In: CVPR (2010)
15. Gong, S., Cristani, M., Yan, S., Loy, C.C.: Person Re-identification. Springer, London (2014). https://doi.org/10.1007/978-1-4471-6296-4
16. Gray, D., Tao, H.: Viewpoint invariant pedestrian recognition with an ensemble of localized features. In: Forsyth, D., Torr, P., Zisserman, A. (eds.) ECCV 2008. LNCS, vol. 5302, pp. 262–275. Springer, Heidelberg (2008). https://doi.org/10.1007/978-3-540-88682-2_21
17. He, K., Zhang, X., Ren, S., Sun, J.: Deep residual learning for image recognition. In: CVPR (2016)
18. Hermans, A., Beyer, L., Leibe, B.: In defense of the triplet loss for person re-identification. arXiv preprint arXiv:1703.07737 (2017)

19. Hirzer, M., Beleznai, C., Roth, P.M., Bischof, H.: Person re-identification by descriptive and discriminative classification. In: Heyden, A., Kahl, F. (eds.) SCIA 2011. LNCS, vol. 6688, pp. 91–102. Springer, Heidelberg (2011). https://doi.org/10.1007/978-3-642-21227-7_9

20. Jiao, J., Zheng, W.S., Wu, A., Zhu, X., Gong, S.: Deep low-resolution person re-identification. In: AAAI (2018)

21. Kawanishi, Y., Wu, Y., Mukunoki, M., Minoh, M.: Shinpuhkan 2014: A multi-camera pedestrian dataset for tracking people across multiple cameras. In: FCV (2014)

22. Khan, F.M., Bremond, F.: Unsupervised data association for metric learning in the context of multi-shot person re-identification. In: AVSS (2016)

23. Kingma, D.P., Ba, J.: Adam: a method for stochastic optimization. arXiv preprint arXiv:1412.6980 (2014)

24. Kodirov, E., Xiang, T., Fu, Z., Gong, S.: Person re-identification by unsupervised l_1 graph learning. In: ECCV (2016)

25. Kodirov, E., Xiang, T., Gong, S.: Dictionary learning with iterative Laplacian regularisation for unsupervised person re-identification. In: BMVC (2015)

26. Leal-Taixé, L., Milan, A., Reid, I., Roth, S., Schindler, K.: Motchallenge 2015: towards a benchmark for multi-target tracking. arXiv preprint arXiv:1504.01942 (2015)

27. Lee, H., Ekanadham, C., Ng, A.Y.: Sparse deep belief net model for visual area v2. In: NIPS (2008)

28. Li, W., Zhao, R., Wang, X.: Human reidentification with transferred metric learning. In: Lee, K.M., Matsushita, Y., Rehg, J.M., Hu, Z. (eds.) ACCV 2012. LNCS, vol. 7724, pp. 31–44. Springer, Heidelberg (2013). https://doi.org/10.1007/978-3-642-37331-2_3

29. Li, W., Zhao, R., Xiao, T., Wang, X.: DeepReID: deep filter pairing neural network for person re-identification. In: CVPR (2014)

30. Li, W., Zhu, X., Gong, S.: Person re-identification by deep joint learning of multi-loss classification. In: IJCAI (2017)

31. Li, W., Zhu, X., Gong, S.: Harmonious attention network for person re-identification. In: CVPR (2018)

32. Lisanti, G., Masi, I., Bagdanov, A.D., Del Bimbo, A.: Person re-identification by iterative re-weighted sparse ranking. IEEE TPAMI **37**(8), 1629–1642 (2015)

33. Liu, X., Song, M., Tao, D., Zhou, X., Chen, C., Bu, J.: Semi-supervised coupled dictionary learning for person re-identification. In: CVPR (2014)

34. Liu, Y., Yan, J., Ouyang, W.: Quality aware network for set to set recognition. In: CVPR (2017)

35. Liu, Z., Wang, D., Lu, H.: Stepwise metric promotion for unsupervised video person re-identification. In: ICCV (2017)

36. Loy, C., Xiang, T., Gong, S.: Time-delayed correlation analysis for multi-camera activity understanding. IJCV **90**(1), 106–129 (2010)

37. Ma, X., Zhu, X., Gong, S., Xie, X., Hu, J., Lam, K.M., Zhong, Y.: Person re-identification by unsupervised video matching. Pattern Recogn. **65**, 197–210 (2017)

38. Peng, P., Xiang, T., Wang, Y., Pontil, M., Gong, S., Huang, T., Tian, Y.: Unsupervised cross-dataset transfer learning for person re-identification. In: CVPR (2016)

39. Prosser, B.J., Zheng, W.S., Gong, S., Xiang, T.: Person re-identification by support vector ranking. In: BMVC (2010)

40. Qin, C., Song, S., Huang, G., Zhu, L.: Unsupervised neighborhood component analysis for clustering. Neurocomputing **168**, 609–617 (2015)

41. Ristani, E., Solera, F., Zou, R., Cucchiara, R., Tomasi, C.: Performance measures and a data set for multi-target, multi-camera tracking. In: ECCV Workshop (2016)
42. Su, C., Zhang, S., Xing, J., Gao, W., Tian, Q.: Deep attributes driven multi-camera person re-identification. In: Leibe, B., Matas, J., Sebe, N., Welling, M. (eds.) ECCV 2016. LNCS, vol. 9906, pp. 475–491. Springer, Cham (2016). https://doi.org/10.1007/978-3-319-46475-6_30
43. Subramaniam, A., Chatterjee, M., Mittal, A: Deep neural networks with inexact matching for person re-identification. In: NIPS (2016)
44. Ustinova, E., Lempitsky, V.: Learning deep embeddings with histogram loss. In: NIPS (2016)
45. Wang, F., Zuo, W., Lin, L., Zhang, D., Zhang, L.: Joint learning of single-image and cross-image representations for person re-identification. In: CVPR (2016)
46. Wang, H., Gong, S., Xiang, T.: Unsupervised learning of generative topic saliency for person re-identification. In: BMVC (2014)
47. Wang, H., Zhu, X., Gong, S., Xiang, T.: Person re-identification in identity regression space. IJCV (2018)
48. Wang, H., Zhu, X., Xiang, T., Gong, S.: Towards unsupervised open-set person re-identification. In: ICIP (2016)
49. Wang, J., Zhu, X., Gong, S., Li, W.: Transferable joint attribute-identity deep learning for unsupervised person re-identification. In: CVPR (2018)
50. Wang, T., Gong, S., Zhu, X., Wang, S.: Person re-identification by video ranking. In: ECCV (2014)
51. Wang, T., Gong, S., Zhu, X., Wang, S.: Person re-identification by discriminative selection in video ranking. IEEE TPAMI 38(12), 2501–2514 (2016)
52. Xiao, T., Li, H., Ouyang, W., Wang, X.: Learning deep feature representations with domain guided dropout for person re-identification. In: CVPR (2016)
53. Ye, J., Zhao, Z., Liu, H.: Adaptive distance metric learning for clustering. In: CVPR (2007)
54. Ye, M., Ma, A.J., Zheng, L., Li, J., Yuen, P.C.: Dynamic label graph matching for unsupervised video re-identification. In: ICCV (2017)
55. Yu, H.X., Wu, A., Zheng, W.S.: Cross-view asymmetric metric learning for unsupervised person re-identification. In: ICCV (2017)
56. Zhang, S., Benenson, R., Omran, M., Hosang, J., Schiele, B.: How far are we from solving pedestrian detection? In: CVPR (2016)
57. Zhang, Y., Xiang, T., Hospedales, T.M., Lu, H.: Deep mutual learning. In: CVPR (2018)
58. Zhao, R., Oyang, W., Wang, X.: Person re-identification by saliency learning. IEEE TPAMI 39(2), 356–370 (2017)
59. Zheng, L., et al.: Mars: a video benchmark for large-scale person re-identification. In: ECCV (2016)
60. Zheng, L., Shen, L., Tian, L., Wang, S., Wang, J., Tian, Q.: Scalable person re-identification: a benchmark. In: CVPR (2015)
61. Zheng, Z., Zheng, L., Yang, Y.: Unlabeled samples generated by GAN improve the person re-identification baseline in vitro. In: ICCV (2017)
62. Zhu, X., Wu, B., Huang, D., Zheng, W.S.: Fast openworld person re-identification. In: IEEE TIP, pp. 2286–2300 (2017)

Predicting Gaze in Egocentric Video by Learning Task-Dependent Attention Transition

Yifei Huang[1], Minjie Cai[1,2(✉)], Zhenqiang Li[1], and Yoichi Sato[1]

[1] The University of Tokyo, Tokyo, Japan
{hyf,cai-mj,lzq,ysato}@iis.u-tokyo.ac.jp
[2] Hunan University, Changsha, China

Abstract. We present a new computational model for gaze prediction in egocentric videos by exploring patterns in temporal shift of gaze fixations (attention transition) that are dependent on egocentric manipulation tasks. Our assumption is that the high-level context of how a task is completed in a certain way has a strong influence on attention transition and should be modeled for gaze prediction in natural dynamic scenes. Specifically, we propose a hybrid model based on deep neural networks which integrates task-dependent attention transition with bottom-up saliency prediction. In particular, the task-dependent attention transition is learned with a recurrent neural network to exploit the temporal context of gaze fixations, *e.g.* looking at a cup after moving gaze away from a grasped bottle. Experiments on public egocentric activity datasets show that our model significantly outperforms state-of-the-art gaze prediction methods and is able to learn meaningful transition of human attention.

Keywords: Gaze prediction · Egocentric video · Attention transition

1 Introduction

With the increasing popularity of wearable or action cameras in recording our life experience, egocentric vision [1], which aims at automatic analysis of videos captured from a first-person perspective [4,6,21], has become an emerging field in computer vision. In particular, as the camera wearer's point-of-gaze in egocentric video contains important information about interacted objects and the camera wearer's intent [17], gaze prediction can be used to infer important regions in images and videos to reduce the amount of computation needed in learning and inference of various analysis tasks [5,7,11,36].

This paper aims to develop a computational model for predicting the camera wearer's point-of-gaze from an egocentric video. Most previous methods have formulated gaze prediction as the problem of saliency detection, and computational models of visual saliency have been studied to the find image regions that are likely to attract human attention. The saliency-based paradigm is reasonable because it is known that highly salient regions are strongly correlated with actual

© Springer Nature Switzerland AG 2018
V. Ferrari et al. (Eds.): ECCV 2018, LNCS 11208, pp. 789–804, 2018.
https://doi.org/10.1007/978-3-030-01225-0_46

gaze locations [27]. However, the saliency model-based gaze prediction becomes much more difficult in natural dynamic scenes, *e.g.* cooking in a kitchen, where high-level knowledge of the task has a strong influence on human attention.

In a natural dynamic scene, a person perceives the surrounding environment with a series of gaze fixations which point to the objects/regions related to the person's interactions with the environment. It has been observed that the attention transition is deeply related to the task carried out by the person. Especially in object manipulation tasks, the high-level knowledge of an undergoing task determines a stream of objects or places to be attended successively and thus influences the transition of human attention. For example, to pour water from a bottle to a cup, a person always first looks at the bottle before grasping it and then change the fixation onto the cup during the action of pouring. Therefore, we argue that it is necessary to explore the task-dependent patterns in attention transition in order to achieve accurate gaze prediction.

In this paper, we propose a hybrid gaze prediction model that combines bottom-up visual saliency with task-dependent attention transition learned from successively attended image regions in training data. The proposed model is mainly composed of three modules. The first module generates saliency maps directly from video frames. It is based on a two-stream Convolutional Neural Network (CNN) which is similar to traditional bottom-up saliency prediction models. The second module is based on a recurrent neural network and a fixation state predictor which generates an attention map for each frame based on previously fixated regions and head motion. It is built based on two assumptions. Firstly, a person's gaze tends to be located on the same object during each fixation, and a large gaze shift almost always occurs along with large head motion [23]. Secondly, patterns in the temporal shift between regions of attention are dependent on the performed task and can be learned from data. The last module is based on a fully convolutional network which fuses the saliency map and the attention map from the first two modules and generates a final gaze map, from which the final prediction of 2D gaze position is made.

Main contributions of this work are summarized as follows:

- We propose a new hybrid model for gaze prediction that leverages both bottom-up visual saliency and task-dependent attention transition.
- We propose a novel model for task-dependent attention transition that explores the patterns in the temporal shift of gaze fixations and can be used to predict the region of attention based on previous fixations.
- The proposed approach achieves state-of-the-art gaze prediction performance on public egocentric activity datasets.

2   Related Works

Visual Saliency Prediction. Visual saliency is a way to measure image regions that are likely to attract human attention and thus gaze fixation [2]. Traditional saliency models are based on the feature integration theory [35] telling that an image region with high saliency contains distinct visual features such as color, intensity and contrast compared to other regions. After Itti *et al.*'s primary work [19] on a computational saliency model, various bottom-up computational models of visual saliency have been proposed such as a graph-based model [13] and a spectral clustering-based model [15]. Recent saliency models [16,25,26] leveraged a deep Convolutional Neural Network (CNN) to improve their performance. More recently, high-level context has been considered in deep learning-based saliency models. In [8,31], class labels were used to compute the partial derivatives of CNN response with respect to input image regions to obtain a class-specific saliency map. In [40], a salient object is detected by combining global context of the whole image and local context of each image superpixel. In [29], region-to-word mapping in a neural saliency model was learned by using image captions as high-level input.

However, none of the previous methods explored the patterns in the transition of human attention inherent in a complex task. In this work, we propose to learn the task-dependent attention transition on how gaze shifts between different objects/regions to better model human attention in natural dynamic scenes.

Egocentric Gaze Prediction. Egocentric vision is an emerging research domain in computer vision which focuses on automatic analysis of egocentric videos recorded with wearable cameras. Egocentric gaze is a key component in egocentric vision which benefits various egocentric applications such as action recognition [11] and video summarization [36]. Although there is correlation between visually salient image regions and gaze fixation locations [27], it has been found that traditional bottom-up models for visual saliency is insufficient to model and predict human gaze in egocentric video [37]. Yamada *et al.* [38] presented a gaze prediction model by exploring the correlation between gaze and head motion. In their model, bottom-up saliency map is integrated with an attention map obtained based on camera rotation and translation to infer final egocentric gaze position. Li *et al.* [24] explored different egocentric cues like global camera motion, hand motion and hand positions to model egocentric gaze in hand manipulation activities. They built a graphical model and further combined the dynamic behaviour of gaze as latent variables to improve the gaze prediction. However, their model is dependent on predefined egocentric cues and may not generalize well to other activities where hands are not always involved. Recently, Zhang *et al.* [39] proposed the gaze anticipation problem in egocentric videos. In their work, a Generative Adversarial Network (GAN) based model is proposed to generate future frames from a current video frame, and gaze positions are predicted on the generated future frames based on a 3D-CNN based saliency prediction model.

In this paper, we propose a new hybrid model to predict gaze in egocentric videos, which combines bottom-up visual saliency with task-dependent attention transition. To the best of our knowledge, this is the first work to explore the patterns in attention transition for egocentric gaze prediction.

3   Gaze Prediction Model

In this section, we first give overview of the network architecture of the proposed gaze prediction model, and then explain the details of each component. The details of training the model are provided in the end.

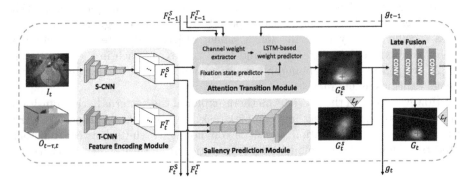

Fig. 1. The architecture of our proposed gaze prediction model. The red crosses in the figure indicate ground truth gaze positions. (Color figure online)

3.1   Model Architecture

Given consecutive video frames as input, we aim to predict a gaze position in each frame. To leverage both bottom-up visual saliency and task-dependent attention transition, we propose a hybrid model that (1) predicts a saliency map from each video frame, (2) predicts an attention map by exploiting temporal context of gaze fixations, and (3) fuses the saliency map and the attention map to output a final gaze map.

The model architecture is shown in Fig. 1. The feature encoding module is composed by a spatial Convolutional Neural Network (S-CNN) and a temporal Convolutional Neural Network (T-CNN), which extract latent representations from a single RGB image and stacked optical flow images respectively. The saliency prediction module generates a saliency map based on the extracted latent representation. The attention transition module generates an attention map based on previous gaze fixations and head motion. The late fusion module combines the results of saliency prediction and attention transition to generate a final gaze map. The details of each module will be given in the following part.

3.2   Feature Encoding

At time t, the current video frame I_t and stacked optical flow $O_{t-\tau,t}$ are fed into S-CNN and T-CNN to extract latent representations $F_t^S = h^S(I_t)$ from the current RGB frame, and $F_t^T = h^T(O_{t-\tau,t})$ from the stacked optical flow images for later use. Here τ is fixed as 10 following [32].

The feature encoding network of S-CNN and T-CNN follows the base architecture of the first five convolutional blocks in Two Stream CNN [32], while omitting the final max pooling layer. We choose to use the output feature map of the last convolution layer from the 5-th convolutional group, i.e., *conv5_3*. Further analysis of different choices of deep feature maps from other layers is described in Sect. 4.4.

3.3 Saliency Prediction Module

Biologically, human tends to gaze at an image region with high saliency, i.e., a region containing unique and distinctive visual features [34]. In the saliency prediction module of our gaze prediction model, we learn to generate a visual saliency map which reflects image regions that are likely to attract human gaze. We fuse the latent representations F_t^S and F_t^T as an input to a saliency prediction decoder (denoted as S) to obtain the initial gaze prediction map G_t^s (Eq. 1). We use the "3dconv + pooling" method of [12] to fuse the two input feature streams. Since our task is different from [12], we modify the kernel sizes of the fusion part, which can be seen in detail in Sect. 3.7. The decoder outputs a visual saliency map with each pixel value within the range of $[0, 1]$. Details of the architecture of the decoder is described in Sect. 3.7. The equation for generating the visual saliency map is:

$$G_t^s = S(F_t^S, F_t^T) \tag{1}$$

However, a saliency map alone does not predict accurately where people actually look [37], especially in egocentric videos of natural dynamic scenes where the knowledge of a task has a strong influence on human gaze. To achieve better gaze prediction, high-level knowledge about a task, such as which object is to be looked at and manipulated next, has to be considered.

3.4 Attention Transition Module

During the procedure of performing a task, the task knowledge strongly influences the temporal transition of human gaze fixations on a series of objects. Therefore, given previous gaze fixations, it is possible to anticipate the image region where next attention occurs. However, direct modeling the object transition explicitly such as using object categories is problematic since a reliable and generic object detector is needed. Motivated by the fact that different channels of a feature map in top convolutional layers correspond well to spatial responses of different high-level semantics such as different object categories [9,41], we represent the region that is likely to attract human attention by weighting each channel of the feature map differently. We train a Long Short Term Memory (LSTM) model [14] to predict a vector of channel weights which is used to predict the region of attention at next fixation. Figure 2 depicts the framework of the proposed attention transition module. The module is composed of a channel weight extractor (C), a fixation state predictor (P), and a LSTM-based weight predictor (L).

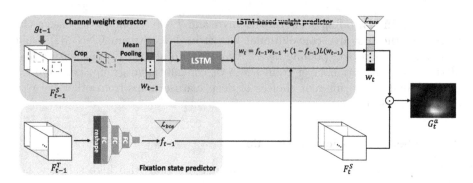

Fig. 2. The architecture of the attention transition module.

The channel weight extractor takes as input the latent representation F_{t-1}^S and the predicted gaze point g_{t-1} from the previous frame. F_{t-1}^S is in fact a stack of feature maps with spatial resolution 14×14 and 512 channels. From each channel, we project the predicted gaze position g_{t-1} onto the 14×14 feature map, and crop a fixed size area with height H_c and width W_c centered at the projected gaze position. We then average the value of the cropped feature map at each channel, obtaining a 512-dimensional vector of channel weight w_{t-1}:

$$w_{t-1} = C(F_{t-1}^S, g_{t-1}) \tag{2}$$

where $C(\cdot)$ indicates the cropping and averaging operation, w_{t-1} is used as feature representation of the region of attention around the gaze point at frame $t-1$.

The fixation state predictor takes the latent representation of F_{t-1}^T as input and outputs a probabilistic score of fixation state $f_{t-1}^p = P(F_{t-1}^T) \in [0, 1]$. Basically, the score tells how likely fixation is occurring in the frame $t - 1$. The fixation state predictor is composed by three fully connected layers followed by a final softmax layer to output a probabilistic score for gaze fixation state.

We use a LSTM to learn the attention transition by learning the transition of channel weights. The LSTM is trained based on a sequence of channel weight vectors extracted from images *at the boundaries of* all gaze fixation periods with ground-truth gaze points, *i.e.* we only extract one channel weight vector for each fixation to learn its transition between fixations. During testing, given a channel weight vector w_{t-1}, the trained LSTM outputs a channel weight vector $L(w_{t-1})$ that represents the region of attention at next gaze fixation. We also consider the dynamic behavior of gaze and its influence on attention transition. Intuitively speaking, during a period of fixation, the region of attention tends to remain unchanged, and the attended region changes only when saccade happens.

Therefore, we compute the region of attention at current frame w_t as a linear combination of previous region of attention w_{t-1} and the anticipated region of attention at next fixation $L(w_{t-1})$, weighted by the predicted fixation probability f_{t-1}^p:

$$w_t = f_{t-1}^p \cdot w_{t-1} + (1 - f_{t-1}^p) \cdot L(w_{t-1}) \tag{3}$$

Finally, an attention map G_t^a is computed as the weighted sum of the latent representation F_t^S at frame t by using the resulting channel weight vector w_t:

$$G_t^a = \sum_{c=1}^{n} w_t[c] \cdot F_t^S[c] \tag{4}$$

where $[c]$ denotes the c-th dimension/channel of w_t/F_t^S respectively.

3.5 Late Fusion

We build the late fusion module (LF) on top of the saliency prediction module and the attention transition module, which takes G_t^s and G_t^a as input and outputs the predicted gaze map G_t.

$$G_t = LF(G_t^s, G_t^a) \tag{5}$$

Finally, a predicted 2D gaze position g_t is given as the spatial coordinate of maximum value of G_t.

3.6 Training

For training gaze prediction in saliency prediction module and late fusion module, the ground truth gaze map $\hat{G}$ is given by convolving an isotropic Gaussian over the measured gaze position in the image. Previous work used either Binary Cross-Entropy loss [22], or KL divergence loss [39] between the predicted gaze map and the ground truth gaze map for training neural networks. However, these loss functions do not work well with noisy gaze measurement. A measured gaze position is not static but continuously quivers in a small spatial range, even during fixation, and conventional loss functions are sensitive to small fluctuations of gaze. This observation motivates us to propose a new loss function, where the loss of pixels within small distance from the measured gaze position is down-weighted. More concretely, we modify the Binary Cross-Entropy loss function ($\mathcal{L}_{bce}$) across all the N pixels with the weighting term $1 + d_i$ as:

$$\mathcal{L}_f(G, \hat{G}) = -\frac{1}{N} \sum_{i=1}^{N} (1 + d_i)\{\hat{G}[i] \cdot log(G[i]) + (1 - \hat{G}[i]) \cdot log(1 - G[i])\} \tag{6}$$

where d_i is the euclidean distance between ground truth gaze position and the pixel i, normalized by the image width.

For training the fixation state predictor in the attention transition module, we treat the fixation prediction of each frame as a binary classification problem.

Thus, we use the Binary Cross-Entropy loss function for training the fixation state predictor. For training the LSTM-based weight predictor in the attention transition module, we use the mean squared error loss function across all the n channels:

$$\mathcal{L}_{mse}(w_t, \hat{w}_t) = \frac{1}{n} \sum_{i=1}^{n} (w_t[i] - \hat{w}_t[i])^2 \tag{7}$$

where $w_t[i]$ denotes the i-th element of w_t.

3.7 Implementation Details

We describe the network structure and training details in this section. Our implementation is based on the PyTorch [28] library. The feature encoding module follows the base architecture of the first five convolutional blocks (*conv1* ∼ *conv5*) of VGG16 [33] network. We remove the last max-pooling layer in the 5-th convolutional block. We initialize these convolutional layers using pre-trained weights on ImageNet [10]. Following [32], since the input channels of T-CNN is changed to 20, we average the weights of the first convolution layer of T-CNN part. The saliency prediction module is a set of 5 convolution layer groups following the inverse order of VGG16 while changing all max pooling layers into upsampling layers. We change the last layer to output 1 channel and add sigmoid activation on top. Since the input of the saliency prediction module contains latent representations from both S-CNN and T-CNN, we use a 3d convolution layer (with a kernel size of $1 \times 3 \times 3$) and a 3d pooling layer (with a kernel size of $2 \times 1 \times 1$) to fuse the inputs. Thus, the input and output sizes are all 224×224. The fixation state predictor is a set of fully connected (FC) layers, whose output sizes are 4096,1024,2 sequentially. The LSTM is a 3-layer LSTM whose input and output sizes are both 512. The late fusion module consists of 4 convolution layers followed by sigmoid activation. The first three layers have a kernel size of 3×3, 1 zero padding, and output channels 32,32,8 respectively, and the last convolution layer has a kernel size of 1 with a single output channel. We empirically set both the height H_c and width W_c for cropping the latent representations to be 3.

The whole model is trained using Adam optimizer [20] with its default settings. We fix the learning rate as 1e−7 and first train the saliency prediction module for 5 epochs for the module to converge. We then fix the saliency prediction module and train the LSTM-based weight predictor and the fixation state predictor in the attention transition module. Learning rates for other modules in our framework are all fixed as 1e−4. After training the attention transition module, we fix the saliency prediction and the attention transition module to train the late fusion module in the end.

4   Experiments

We first evaluate our gaze prediction model on two public egocentric activity datasets (**GTEA Gaze** and **GTEA Gaze Plus**). We compare the proposed model with other state-of-the-art methods and provide detailed analysis of our model through ablation study and visualization of outputs of different modules. Furthermore, to examine our model's ability in learning attention transition, we visualize output of the attention transition module on a newly collected test set from GTEA Gaze Plus dataset (denoted as **GTEA-sub**).

4.1 Datasets

We introduce the datasets used for gaze prediction and attention transition.

GTEA Gaze contains 17 video sequences of kitchen tasks performed by 14 subjects. Each video clip lasts for about 4 min with the frame rate of 15 fps and an image resolution of 480×640. We use videos 1, 4, 6–22 as a training set and the rest as a test set as in Yin *et al.* [24].

GTEA Gaze Plus contains 37 videos with the frame rate of 24 fps and an image resolution of 960×1280. In this dataset each of the 5 subjects performs 7 meal preparation activities in a more natural environment. Each video clip is 10 to 15 min long on average. Similarly to [24], gaze prediction accuracy is evaluated with 5-fold cross validation across all 5 subjects.

GTEA-sub contains 227 video frames selected from the sampled frames of GTEA Gaze Plus dataset. Each selected frame is not only under a gaze fixation, but also contains the object (or region) that is to be attended at the next fixation. We manually draw bounding boxes on those regions by inspecting future frames. The dataset is used to examine whether or not our model trained on GTEA Gaze Plus (excluding GTEA-sub) has successfully learned the task-dependent attention transition.

4.2 Evaluation Metrics

We use two standard evaluation metrics for gaze prediction in egocentric videos: Area Under the Curve (AUC) [3] and Average Angular Error (AAE) [30]. **AUC** is the area under a curve of true positive rate versus false positive rate for different thresholds on the predicted gaze map. It is a commonly used evaluation metric in saliency prediction. **AAE** is the average angular distance between the predicted and the ground truth gaze positions.

4.3 Results on Gaze Prediction

Baselines. We use the following baselines for gaze prediction:

- *Saliency prediction algorithms*: We compare our method with several representative saliency prediction methods. More specifically, we used Itti's model [18], Graph Based Visual Saliency (GBVS [13]), and a deep neural network based saliency model as the current state of the art (SALICON [16]).
- *Center bias*: Since egocentric gaze data is observed to have a strong center bias, we use the image center as the predicted gaze position as in [24].

– *Gaze prediction algorithms*: We also compare our method with two state-of-the-art gaze prediction methods: the egocentric cue-based method (Yin *et al.* [24]), and the GAN-based method (DFG [39]). Note that although the goal of [39] is gaze anticipation in future frames, it also reported gaze prediction in the current frame.

Performance Comparison. The quantitative results of different methods on two datasets are given in Table 1. Our method significantly outperforms all baselines on both datasets, particularly on the AAE score. Although there is only a small improvement on the AUC score, it can be seen that previous method of DFG [39] has already achieved quite high score and the space of improvement is limited. Besides, we have observed from experiments that high AUC score does not necessarily mean high performance of gaze prediction. The overall performance on GTEA Gaze is lower than that on GTEA Gaze Plus. The reason might be that the number of training samples in GTEA Gaze is smaller and over 25% of ground truth gaze measurements are missing. It is also interesting to see that the center bias outperforms all saliency-based methods and works only slightly worse than Yin *et al.* [24] on GTEA Gaze Plus, which demonstrates the strong spatial bias of gaze in egocentric videos.

Table 1. Performance comparison of different methods for gaze prediction on two public datasets. Higher AUC (or lower AAE) means higher performance.

Metrics	GTEA Gaze Plus		GTEA Gaze	
	AAE (deg)	AUC	AAE (deg)	AUC
Itti *et al.* [18]	19.9	0.753	18.4	0.747
GBVS [13]	14.7	0.803	15.3	0.769
SALICON [16]	15.6	0.818	16.5	0.761
Center bias	8.6	0.819	10.2	0.789
Yin *et al.* [24]	7.9	0.867	8.4	0.878
DFG [39]	6.6	0.952	10.5	0.883
Our full model	**4.0**	**0.957**	**7.6**	**0.898**

Ablation Study. To study the effect of each module of our model, and the effectiveness of our modified binary cross entropy loss (Eq. 6), we conduct an ablation study and test each component on both GTEA Gaze Plus and GTEA Gaze datasets. Our baselines include: (1) single-stream saliency prediction with binary cross entropy loss (**S-CNN bce** and **T-CNN bce**), (2) single-stream saliency prediction with our modified bce loss (**S-CNN** and **T-CNN**), (3) two-stream saliency prediction with bce loss (**SP bce**), (4) two-stream input saliency prediction with our modified bce loss (**SP**), (5) the attention transition module (**AT**), and our full model.

Table 2 shows the results of the ablation study. The comparison of the same framework with different loss functions shows that our modified bce loss function is more suitable for the training of gaze prediction in egocentric video. The SP module performs better than either of the single-stream saliency prediction (S-CNN and T-CNN), indicating that both spatial and temporal information are needed for accurate gaze prediction. It is important to see that the AT module performs competitively or better than the SP module. This validates our claim that learning task-dependent attention transition is important in egocentric gaze prediction. More importantly, our full model outperforms all separate components by a large margin, which confirms that the bottom-up visual saliency and high-level task-dependent attention are complementary cues to each other and should be considered together in modeling human attention.

Table 2. Results of ablation study

Metrics	GTEA Gaze plus		GTEA Gaze	
	AAE (deg)	AUC	AAE (deg)	AUC
S-CNN (bce)	5.61	0.893	9.90	0.854
T-CNN (bce)	6.15	0.906	10.08	0.854
S-CNN	5.57	0.905	9.72	0.857
T-CNN	6.07	0.906	9.6	0.859
SP (bce)	5.63	0.918	9.53	0.860
SP	5.52	0.928	9.43	0.861
AT	5.02	0.940	9.51	0.857
Our full model	**4.05**	**0.957**	**7.58**	**0.898**

Visualization. Figure 3 shows qualitative results of our model. Group (1a, 1b) shows a typical gaze shift: the camera wearer shifts his attention to the pan after turning on the oven. SP fails to find the correct gaze position in (1b) only from visual features of the current frame. Since AT exploits the high-level temporal context of gaze fixations, it successfully predicts the region to be on the pan. Group (2a, 2b) demonstrates a "put" action: the camera wearer first looks at the target location, then puts the can to that location. It is interesting that AT has learned the camera wearer's intention, and predicts the region at the target location rather than the more salient hand region in (2a). In group (3a, 3b), the camera wearer searches for a spatula after looking at the pan. Again, AT has learned this context which leads to more accurate gaze prediction than SP. Finally, group (4a, 4b) shows that SP and AT are complementary to each other. While AT performs better in (4a), and SP performs better in (4b), the full model combines the merits of both AT and SP to make better prediction. Overall, these results demonstrate that the attention transition plays an important role in improving gaze prediction accuracy.

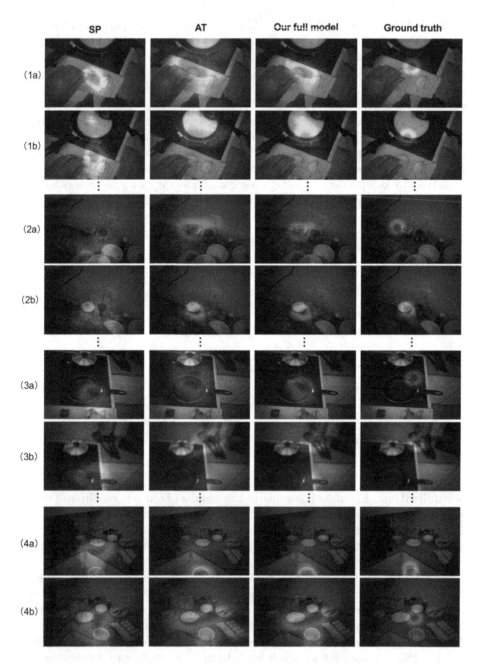

Fig. 3. Visualization of predicted gaze maps from our model. Each group contains two images from two consecutive fixations, where a happens before b. We show the output heatmap from the saliency prediction module (**SP**) and the attention transition module (**AT**) as well as our full model. The ground truth gaze map (the rightmost column) is obtained by convolving an isotropic Gaussian on the measured gaze point.

Cross Task Validation. To examine how the task-dependent attention transition learned in our model can generalize to different tasks under same (kitchen) scene, we perform a cross validation across the 7 different meal preparation tasks on GTEA Gaze Plus dataset. We consider the following experiment settings:

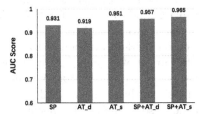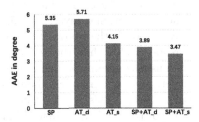

Fig. 4. AUC and AAE scores of cross task validation. Five different experiment settings (explained in the text below) are compared to study the differences of attention transition in different tasks.

- **SP**: The saliency prediction module is treated as a generic component and trained on a separate subset of the dataset. We also use it as a baseline for studying the performance variation of different settings.
- **AT_d**: The attention transition module is trained and validated under different tasks. Average performance of 7-fold cross validation is reported.
- **AT_s**: The attention transition module is trained and validated on two splits of the same task. Average performance of 7 tasks is reported.
- **SP+AT_d**: The late fusion on top of **SP** and **AT_d**.
- **SP+AT_s**: The late fusion on top of **SP** and **AT_s**.

Quantitative results of different settings are shown in Fig. 4. Both AUC and AAE scores show the same performance trend with different settings. AT_d works worse than SP, while AT_s outperforms SP. This is probably due to the differences of gaze behavior contained in different tasks. However, SP+AT_d with the late fusion module can still improve the performance compared with SP and AT_s, even with the context learned from different tasks.

4.4   Examination of the Attention Transition Module

We further demonstrate that our attention transition module is able to learn meaningful transition between adjacent gaze fixations. This ability has important applications in computer-aided AR system, such as implying a person where to look next in performing a complex task. We conduct a new experiment on the GTEA-sub dataset (as introduced in Sect. 4.1) to test the attention transition module of our model. Since here we focus on the module's ability of attention transition, we omit the fixation state predictor in the module and assume the output of the fixation state predictor as $f_t = 0$ in the test frame. The module takes w_t calculated from the region of current fixation as input and outputs an attention map on the same frame which represents the predicted region of the next fixation. We extract a 2D position from the maximum value of the predicted heatmap and calculate its rate of falling within the annotated bounding box as the transition accuracy.

We conduct experiments based on different latent representations extracted from the convolutional layer: *conv5_1*, *conv5_2*, and *conv5_3* of S-CNN. The accuracy based on the above three convolutional layers are 71.7%, 83.0%, and 86.8% respectively, while the accuracy based on random position is 10.7%. We also tried using random channel weight as the output of channel weight predictor to compute attention map based on the latent representation of *conv5_3*, and the accuracy is 9.4%. This verifies that our model can learn meaningful attention transition of the performed task. Figure 5 shows some qualitative results of the attention transition module learned based on layer *conv5_3*. It can be seen that the attention transition module can successfully predict the image region of next fixation.

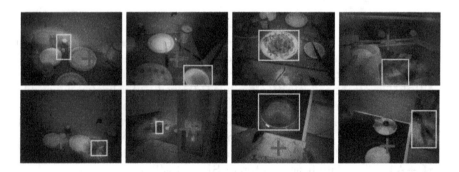

Fig. 5. Qualitative results of attention transition. We visualize the predicted heatmap on the current frame, together with the current gaze position (red cross) and ground truth bounding box of the object/region of the next fixation (yellow box). (Color figure online)

5   Conclusion and Future Work

This paper presents a hybrid model for gaze prediction in egocentric videos. Task-dependent attention transition is learned to predict human attention from previous fixations by exploiting the temporal context of gaze fixations. The task-dependent attention transition is further integrated with a CNN-based saliency model to leverage the cues from both bottom-up visual saliency and high-level attention transition. The proposed model achieves state-of-the-art performance in two public egocentric datasets.

As for our future work, we plan to explore the task-dependent gaze behavior in a broader scale, *i.e.* tasks in an office or in a manufacturing factory, and to study the generalizability of our model in different task domains.

Acknowledgments. This work was supported by JST CREST Grant Number JPMJCR14E1, Japan.

References

1. Betancourt, A., Morerio, P., Regazzoni, C.S., Rauterberg, M.: The evolution of first person vision methods: a survey. IEEE Trans. Circ. Syst. Video Technol. **25**(5), 744–760 (2015)
2. Borji, A., Itti, L.: State-of-the-art in visual attention modeling. IEEE Trans. Pattern Anal. Mach. Intell. **35**(1), 185–207 (2013)
3. Borji, A., Tavakoli, H.R., Sihite, D.N., Itti, L.: Analysis of scores, datasets, and models in visual saliency prediction. In: ICCV (2013)
4. Cai, M., Kitani, K.M., Sato, Y.: A scalable approach for understanding the visual structures of hand grasps. In: ICRA (2015)
5. Cai, M., Kitani, K.M., Sato, Y.: Understanding hand-object manipulation with grasp types and object attributes. In: Robotics: Science and Systems (2016)
6. Cai, M., Kitani, K.M., Sato, Y.: An ego-vision system for hand grasp analysis. IEEE Trans. Hum. Mach. Syst. **47**(4), 524–535 (2017)
7. Cai, M., Lu, F., Gao, Y.: Desktop action recognition from first-person point-of-view. IEEE Trans. Cybern. **PP**(99), 1–13 (2018)
8. Cao, C., et al.: Look and think twice: capturing top-down visual attention with feedback convolutional neural networks. In: ICCV (2015)
9. Chen, L., et al.: SCA-CNN: spatial and channel-wise attention in convolutional networks for image captioning. In: CVPR (2017)
10. Deng, J., Dong, W., Socher, R., Li, L.J., Li, K., Fei-Fei, L.: Imagenet: a large-scale hierarchical image database. In: CVPR (2009)
11. Fathi, A., Li, Y., Rehg, J.M.: Learning to recognize daily actions using gaze. In: Fitzgibbon, A., Lazebnik, S., Perona, P., Sato, Y., Schmid, C. (eds.) ECCV 2012. LNCS, vol. 7572, pp. 314–327. Springer, Heidelberg (2012). https://doi.org/10.1007/978-3-642-33718-5_23
12. Feichtenhofer, C., Pinz, A., Zisserman, A.: Convolutional two-stream network fusion for video action recognition. In: CVPR (2016)
13. Harel, J., Koch, C., Perona, P.: Graph-based visual saliency. In: NIPS (2007)
14. Hochreiter, S., Schmidhuber, J.: Long short-term memory. Neural Comput. **9**(8), 1735–1780 (1997)
15. Hou, X., Harel, J., Koch, C.: Image signature: highlighting sparse salient regions. IEEE Trans. Pattern Anal. Mach. Intell. **34**(1), 194–201 (2012)
16. Huang, X., Shen, C., Boix, X., Zhao, Q.: SALICON: reducing the semantic gap in saliency prediction by adapting deep neural networks. In: ICCV (2015)
17. Huang, Y., Cai, M., Kera, H., Yonetani, R., Higuchi, K., Sato, Y.: Temporal localization and spatial segmentation of joint attention in multiple first-person videos. In: ICCV Workshop (2017)
18. Itti, L., Koch, C.: A saliency-based search mechanism for overt and covert shifts of visual attention. Vis. Res. **40**(10–12), 1489–1506 (2000)
19. Itti, L., Koch, C., Niebur, E.: A model of saliency-based visual attention for rapid scene analysis. IEEE Trans. Pattern Anal. Mach. Intell. **20**(11), 1254–1259 (1998)
20. Kingma, D.P., Ba, J.: Adam: a method for stochastic optimization. arXiv preprint arXiv:1412.6980 (2014)
21. Kitani, K.M., Okabe, T., Sato, Y., Sugimoto, A.: Fast unsupervised ego-action learning for first-person sports videos. In: CVPR (2011)

22. Kuen, J., Wang, Z., Wang, G.: Recurrent attentional networks for saliency detection. In: CVPR (2016)
23. Land, M.F.: The coordination of rotations of the eyes, head and trunk in saccadic turns produced in natural situations. Exp. Brain Res. **159**(2), 151–160 (2004)
24. Li, Y., Fathi, A., Rehg, J.M.: Learning to predict gaze in egocentric video. In: ICCV (2013)
25. Lin, Y., Kong, S., Wang, D., Zhuang, Y.: Saliency detection within a deep convolutional architecture. In: AAAI Workshops (2014)
26. Pan, J., Sayrol, E., Giro-i Nieto, X., McGuinness, K., O'Connor, N.E.: Shallow and deep convolutional networks for saliency prediction. In: CVPR (2016)
27. Parkhurst, D., Law, K., Niebur, E.: Modeling the role of salience in the allocation of overt visual attention. Vis. Res. **42**(1), 107–123 (2002)
28. Paszke, A., et al.: Automatic differentiation in PyTorch (2017)
29. Ramanishka, V., Das, A., Zhang, J., Saenko, K.: Top-down visual saliency guided by captions. In: CVPR (2017)
30. Riche, N., Duvinage, M., Mancas, M., Gosselin, B., Dutoit, T.: Saliency and human fixations: state-of-the-art and study of comparison metrics. In: ICCV (2013)
31. Simonyan, K., Vedaldi, A., Zisserman, A.: Deep inside convolutional networks: visualising image classification models and saliency maps. arXiv preprint arXiv:1312.6034 (2013)
32. Simonyan, K., Zisserman, A.: Two-stream convolutional networks for action recognition in videos. In: NIPS (2014)
33. Simonyan, K., Zisserman, A.: Very deep convolutional networks for large-scale image recognition. arXiv preprint arXiv:1409.1556 (2014)
34. Sugano, Y., Matsushita, Y., Sato, Y.: Appearance-based gaze estimation using visual saliency. IEEE Trans. Pattern Anal. Mach. Intell. **35**(2), 329–341 (2013)
35. Treisman, A.M., Gelade, G.: A feature-integration theory of attention. Cogn. Psychol. **12**(1), 97–136 (1980)
36. Xu, J., Mukherjee, L., Li, Y., Warner, J., Rehg, J.M., Singh, V.: Gaze-enabled egocentric video summarization via constrained submodular maximization. In: CVPR (2015)
37. Yamada, K., Sugano, Y., Okabe, T., Sato, Y., Sugimoto, A., Hiraki, K.: Can saliency map models predict human egocentric visual attention? In: Koch, R., Huang, F. (eds.) ACCV 2010. LNCS, vol. 6468, pp. 420–429. Springer, Heidelberg (2011). https://doi.org/10.1007/978-3-642-22822-3_42
38. Yamada, K., Sugano, Y., Okabe, T., Sato, Y., Sugimoto, A., Hiraki, K.: Attention prediction in egocentric video using motion and visual saliency. In: Ho, Y.-S. (ed.) PSIVT 2011. LNCS, vol. 7087, pp. 277–288. Springer, Heidelberg (2011). https://doi.org/10.1007/978-3-642-25367-6_25
39. Zhang, M., Teck Ma, K., Hwee Lim, J., Zhao, Q., Feng, J.: Deep future gaze: gaze anticipation on egocentric videos using adversarial networks. In: CVPR (2017)
40. Zhao, R., Ouyang, W., Li, H., Wang, X.: Saliency detection by multi-context deep learning. In: CVPR (2015)
41. Zhou, B., Khosla, A., Lapedriza, A., Oliva, A., Torralba, A.: Learning deep features for discriminative localization. In: CVPR (2016)

Instance-Level Human Parsing via Part Grouping Network

Ke Gong[1], Xiaodan Liang[1(✉)], Yicheng Li[1], Yimin Chen[2], Ming Yang[3], and Liang Lin[1,2]

[1] Sun Yat-sen University, Guangzhou, China
gongk3@mail2.sysu.edu.cn, xdliang328@gmail.com, liyicheng199506@gmail.com,
linlng@mail.sysu.edu.cn
[2] SenseTime Group (Limited), Beijing, China
chenyimin@sensetime.com
[3] CVTE Research, Guangzhou, China
yangming@cvte.com

Abstract. Instance-level human parsing towards real-world human analysis scenarios is still under-explored due to the absence of sufficient data resources and technical difficulty in parsing multiple instances in a single pass. Several related works all follow the "parsing-by-detection" pipeline that heavily relies on separately trained detection models to localize instances and then performs human parsing for each instance sequentially. Nonetheless, two discrepant optimization targets of detection and parsing lead to suboptimal representation learning and error accumulation for final results. In this work, we make the first attempt to explore a detection-free Part Grouping Network (PGN) for efficiently parsing multiple people in an image in a single pass. Our PGN reformulates instance-level human parsing as two twinned sub-tasks that can be jointly learned and mutually refined via a unified network: (1) semantic part segmentation for assigning each pixel as a human part (e.g., face, arms); (2) instance-aware edge detection to group semantic parts into distinct person instances. Thus the shared intermediate representation would be endowed with capabilities in both characterizing fine-grained parts and inferring instance belongings of each part. Finally, a simple instance partition process is employed to get final results during inference. We conducted experiments on PASCAL-Person-Part dataset and our PGN outperforms all state-of-the-art methods. Furthermore, we show its superiority on a newly collected multi-person parsing dataset (CIHP) including 38,280 diverse images, which is the largest dataset so far and can facilitate more advanced human analysis. The CIHP benchmark and our source code are available at http://sysu-hcp.net/lip/.

Keywords: Instance-level human parsing · Semantic part segmentation · Part grouping network

Electronic supplementary material The online version of this chapter (https://doi.org/10.1007/978-3-030-01225-0_47) contains supplementary material, which is available to authorized users.

© Springer Nature Switzerland AG 2018
V. Ferrari et al. (Eds.): ECCV 2018, LNCS 11208, pp. 805–822, 2018.
https://doi.org/10.1007/978-3-030-01225-0_47

1   Introduction

Human parsing for recognizing each semantic part (*e.g.*, arms, legs) is one of the most fundamental and critical tasks in analyzing human in the wild and plays an important role in higher level application domains, such as video surveillance [38], human behavior analysis [10,22].

Driven by the advance of fully convolutional networks (FCNs) [29], human parsing, or semantic part segmentation has recently witnessed great progress thanks to deeply learned features [14,37], large-scale annotations [11,24], and advanced reasoning over graphical models [3,45]. However, previous approaches only focus on the single-person parsing task in the simplified and limited conditions, such as fashion pictures [6,8,18,23,41] with upright poses and diverse daily images [11], and disregard more real-world cases where multiple person instances appear in one image. Such ill-posed single-person parsing task severely prohibits the potential applications of human analysis towards more challenging scenarios (*e.g.*, group behavior prediction).

In this work, we aim at resolving the more challenging instance-level human parsing task, which needs to not only segment various body parts or clothes but also associate each part with one instance, as shown in Fig. 1. Besides the difficulties shared with single-person parsing (*e.g.*, various appearance/viewpoints, self-occlusions), instance-level human parsing is posed as a more challenging task since the number of person instances in an image varies immensely, which cannot be conventionally addressed using traditional single-person parsing pipelines with fixed prediction space that categorizes a fixed number of part labels.

Fig. 1. Examples of our large-scale "Crowd Instance-level Human Parsing (CIHP)" dataset, which contains 38,280 multi-person images with elaborate annotations and high appearance variability as well as complexity. The images are presented in the first row. The annotations of semantic part segmentation and instance-level human parsing are shown in the second and third row respectively. Best viewed in color.

The very recent work [16] explored this task following the "parsing-by-detection" pipeline [7,12,13,21,31] that firstly localizes bounding boxes of instances and then performs fine-grained semantic parsing for each box. However, such complex pipelines are trained using several independent targets and stages for the detection and segmentation, which may lead to inconsistent results for coarse localization and pixel-wise part segmentation. For example, segmentation models may predict semantic part regions outside the detected boxes by detection models since their intermediate representations are dragged into different directions.

In this work, we reformulate the instance-level human parsing from a new perspective, that is, tackling two coherent segment grouping goals via a unified network, including the part-level pixel-grouping and instance-level part-grouping. First, part-level pixel-grouping can be addressed by the semantic part segmentation task that assigns each pixel as one part label, which learns the categorization property. Second, given a set of independent semantic parts, instance-level part-grouping can determine the instance belongings of all parts according to the predicted instance-aware edges, where parts that are separated by instance edges will be grouped into distinct person instances. We call this detection-free unified network that jointly optimizes semantic part segmentation and instance-aware edge detection as Part Grouping Network (PGN) illustrated in Fig. 4.

Moreover, unlike other proposal-free methods [15,22,25] that break the task of instance object segmentation into several sub-tasks by a few separate networks and resort to complex post-processing, our PGN seamlessly integrates part segmentation and edge detection under a unified network that first learns shared representation and then appends two parallel branches with respect to semantic part segmentation and instance-aware edge detection. As two targets are highly correlated with each other by sharing coherent grouping goals, PGN further incorporates a refinement branch to make two targets mutually benefit from each other by exploiting complementary contextual information. This integrated refinement scheme is especially advantageous for challenging cases by seamlessly remedying the errors from each target. As shown in Fig. 2, a small person may fail to be localized by segmentation branch but successfully detected by edge branch or the mistakenly labeled background edges from instance boundaries could be corrected with our refinement algorithm. Given semantic part segmentation and instance edges, an efficient cutting inference can be used to generate instance-level human parsing results using a breadth-first search over line segments obtained by jointly scanning the segmentation and edges maps.

Furthermore, to our best knowledge, there is no available large-scale dataset for instance-level human parsing research, until our work fills this gap. We introduce a new large-scale dataset, named as Crowd Instance-level Human Parsing (CIHP), including 38,280 multi-person images with pixel-wise annotations of 19 semantic parts in instance-level. The dataset is elaborately annotated focusing on the semantic understanding of multiple people in the wild, as shown in Fig. 1. With the new dataset, we also propose a public server benchmark for automatically reporting evaluation results for fair comparison on this topic.

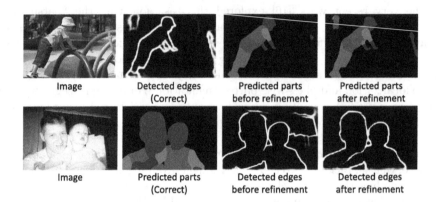

| Image | Detected edges (Correct) | Predicted parts before refinement | Predicted parts after refinement |

| Image | Predicted parts (Correct) | Detected edges before refinement | Detected edges after refinement |

Fig. 2. Two examples show that the errors of parts and edges of challenging cases can be seamlessly remedied by the refinement scheme in our PGN. In the first row, segmentation branch fails to locate the small objects (*e.g.*, the person at the left-top corner and the hand at the right-bottom corner) but edge branch detects them successfully. In the second row, the background edges are mistakenly labeled. However, these incorrect results are rectified by the refinement branch in our PGN.

Our contributions are summarized in the following aspects. (1) We investigate a more challenging instance-level human parsing, which pushes the research boundary of human parsing to match real-world scenarios much better. (2) A novel Part Grouping Network (PGN) is proposed to solve multi-person human parsing in a unified network at once by reformulating it as two twinned grouping tasks that can be mutually refined: semantic part segmentation and instance-aware edge detection. (3) We build a new large-scale benchmark for instance-level human parsing and present a detailed dataset analysis. (4) PGN surpasses previous methods for both semantic part segmentation and edge detection tasks, and achieves state-of-the-art performance for instance-level human parsing on both the existing PASCAL-Person-Part [6] and our new CIHP dataset.

2   Related Work

Human Parsing. Recently, many research efforts have been devoted to human parsing [5,11,23,26,35,39,41,42] for advancing human-centric analysis research. For example, Liang *et al.* [23] proposed a novel Co-CNN architecture that integrates multiple levels of image contexts into a unified network. Gong *et al.* [11] designed a structure-sensitive learning to enforce the produced parsing results semantically consistent with the human joint structures. However, all these prior works only focus on the relatively simple single-person human parsing without considering the common multiple instance cases in the real world.

As for current data resources, we summarized the publicly available datasets for human parsing in Table 1. Previous datasets only include very few person instances and categories in one image, and require prior works only evaluate pure part segmentation performance while disregarding their instance belongings. On the contrary, containing 38,280 images, the proposed CIHP dataset is the first and also the most comprehensive dataset for instance-level human parsing to date. Although there exist a few datasets in the vision community that were dedicated to other tasks, *e.g.*, clothes recognition, retrieval [28,30] and fashion modeling [36], our CIHP that mainly focuses on instance-level human parsing is the largest one and provides more elaborate dense annotations for diverse images. A standard server benchmark for our CIHP can facilitate the human analysis research by enabling fair comparison among current approaches.

Table 1. Comparison among the publicly available datasets for human parsing. For each dataset, we report the number of person instances per image, the total number of images, the separate number of images in training, validation, and test sets as well as the number of part labels including the background.

Dataset	# Instances/image	# Total	# Train	# Validation	# Test	Categories
Fashionista [42]	1	685	456	-	229	56
PASCAL-Person-Part [6]	2.2	3,533	1,716	-	1,817	7
ATR [23]	1	17,700	16,000	700	1,000	18
LIP [11]	1	50,462	30,462	10,000	10,000	20
CIHP	3.4	38,280	28,280	5,000	5,000	20

Instance-Level Object Segmentation. Our target is also very relevant to instance-level object segmentation task that aims to predict a whole mask for each object in an image. Most of the prior works [7,12,13,21,31,31] addressed this task by sequentially performance optimizing object detection and foreground/background segmentation. Dai *et al.* [7] proposed a multiple-stage cascade to unify bounding box proposal generation, segment proposal generation, and classification. In [1,16], a CRF is used to assign each pixel to an object detection box by exploiting semantic segmentation maps. More recently, Mask R-CNN [13] extended the Faster R-CNN detection framework [33] by adding a branch for predicting segmentation masks of each region-of-interest. However, these proposal-based methods may fail to model the interactions among different instances, which is critical for performing more fine-grained segmentation for each instance in our instance-level human parsing.

Nonetheless, some approaches [2,15,22,25,32,34] are also proposed to bypass the object proposal step for instance-level segmentation. In PFN [22], the number of instances and per-pixel bounding boxes are predicted for clustering to produce instance segmentation. In [15], semantic segmentation and object boundary prediction were exploited to separate instances by a complicated image partitioning formulation. Similarly, SGN [25] proposed to predict object breakpoints for creating line segments, which are then grouped into connected components for generating object regions. Despite their similar intuition with ours in grouping regions to generate an instance, these two pipelines separately learn several sub-networks and thus obtain final results relying on a few independent steps.

Here, we emphasize this work investigates a more challenging fine-grained instance-level human parsing task that integrates the current semantic part segmentation and instance-level object segmentation tasks. From the technical perspective, we present a novel detection-free Part Grouping Network that unifies and mutually refines two twinned grouping tasks in an end-to-end way: semantic part segmentation and instance-aware edge detection. Without the expensive CRF refinement used in [16], the final results can then be effortlessly obtained by a simple instance partition process.

3   Crowd Instance-Level Human Parsing Dataset

To benchmark the more challenging multi-person human parsing task, we build a large-scale dataset called Crowd Instance-level Human Parsing (CIHP) Dataset, which has several appealing properties. First, with 38,280 diverse human images, it is the largest multi-person human parsing dataset to date. Second, CIHP is annotated with rich information of person items. The images in this dataset are labeled with pixel-wise annotations on 20 categories and instance-level identification. Third, the images collected from the real-world scenarios contain people appearing with challenging poses and viewpoints, heavy occlusions, various appearances and in a wide range of resolutions. Some examples are shown in Fig. 1. With the CIHP dataset, we propose a new benchmark for instance-level human parsing together with a standard evaluation server where the test set will be kept secret to avoid overfitting.

3.1   Image Annotation

The images in the CIHP are collected from unconstrained resources like Google and Bing. We manually specify several keywords (*e.g.*, family, couple, party, meeting, *etc.*) to gain a great diversity of multi-person images. The crawled images are elaborately annotated by a professional labeling organization with well quality control. We supervise the whole annotation process and conduct a second-round check for each annotated image. We remove the unusable images that are of low resolution, image quality, or contain one or no person instance.

In total, 38,280 images are kept to construct the CIHP dataset. Following random selection, we arrive at a unique split that consists of 28,280 training and 5,000 validation images with publicly available annotations, as well as 5,000 test images with annotations withheld for benchmarking purposes.

3.2   Dataset Statistics

We now introduce the images and categories in the CIHP dataset with more statistical details. Superior to the previous attempts [6,11,23] with average one or two person instances in an image, all images of the CIHP dataset contain two or more instances with an average of 3.4. The distribution of the number of persons per image is illustrated in Fig. 3 (Left). Generally, we follow LIP [11] to define and annotate the semantic part labels. However, we find that the Jumpsuit label defined in LIP [11] is infrequent compared to other labels. To parse the human more completely and precisely, we use a more common body part label (Tosor-skin) instead. The 19 semantic part labels in the CIHP are Hat, Hair, Sunglasses, Upper-clothes, Dress, Coat, Socks, Pants, Gloves, Scarf, Skirt, Torso-skin, Face, Right/Left arm, Right/Left leg, and Right/Left shoe. The numbers of images for each semantic part label are presented in Fig. 3 (Right).

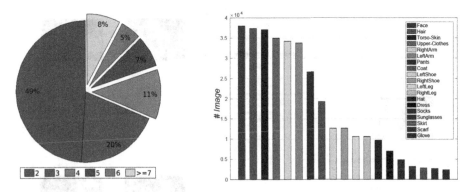

Fig. 3. Left: Statistics on the number of persons in one image. Right: The data distribution on 19 semantic part labels in the CIHP dataset.

4   Part Grouping Network

In this section, we begin by presenting a general pipeline of our approach (see Fig. 4) and then describe each component in detail. The proposed Part Grouping Network (PGN) jointly train and refine the semantic part segmentation and instance-aware edge detection in a unified network. Technically, these two sub-tasks are both pixel-wise classification problem, on which Fully Convolutional Networks (FCNs) [29] perform well. Our PGN is thus constructed based on FCNs structure, which first learns common representation using shared intermediate layers and then appends two parallel branches with respect to semantic part segmentation and edge detection. To explore and take advantage of the semantic correlation of these two tasks, a refinement branch is further incorporated to make two targets mutually beneficial for each other by exploiting complementary contextual information. Finally, an efficient partition process with a heuristic grouping algorithm can be used to generate instance-level human parsing results using a breadth-first search over line segments obtained by jointly scanning the generated semantic part segmentation maps and instance-aware edge maps.

4.1   PGN Architecture

Backbone Sub-network. Basically, we use a repurposed ResNet-101 network, Deeplab-v2 [3] as our human feature encoder, because of its high performance demonstrated in dense prediction tasks. It employs convolution with upsampled filters, or ?atrous convolution?, which effectively enlarges the field of view of filters to incorporate larger context without increasing the number of parameters or the amount of computation. The coupled problems of semantic segmentation and edge detection share several key properties that can be efficiently learned by a few shared convolutional layers. Intuitively, they both desire satisfying dense recognition according to low-level contextual cues from nearby pixels and high-level semantic information for better localization. In this way, instead of training two separate networks to handle these two tasks, we perform a single backbone network that allows weight sharing for learning common feature representation.

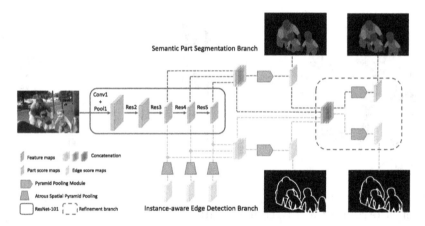

Fig. 4. Illustration of our Part Grouping Network (PGN). Given an input image, we use ResNet-101 to extract the shared feature maps. Then, two branches are appended to capture part context and human boundary context while simultaneously generating part score maps and edge score maps. Finally, a refinement branch is performed to refine both predicted segmentation maps and edge maps by integrating part segmentation and human boundary contexts.

However, in the original Deeplab-v2 architecture [3], an input image is downsampled by two different ratios (0.75 and 0.5) to produce multi-scale inputs at three different resolutions, which are independently processed by ResNet-101 using shared weights. The output feature maps are then upsampled and combined by taking the element-wise maximum. This multi-scale scheme requires enormous memory and is time-consuming. Alternatively, we use single scale input and employ two more efficient and powerful coarse-to-fine schemes. Firstly, inspired by skip architecture [29] that combines semantic information from a deep, coarse layer with appearance information from a shallow, fine layer to produce accurate and detailed segmentation, we concatenate the activations of the final three blocks of ResNet-101 as the final extracted feature maps. Thanks to the atrous convolution, this information combination allows the network to make local predictions instructed by global structure without upscale operation. Secondly, following PSPNet [44] which exploits the capability of global context information by different region-based context aggregation, we use the pyramid pooling module on top of the extracted feature maps before the final classification layers. The extracted feature maps are average-pooled with four different kernel sizes, giving us four feature maps with spatial resolutions 1×1, 2×2, 3×3, and 6×6 respectively. Each feature map undergoes convolution and upsampling, before being concatenated together with each other. Benefiting from these two coarse-to-fine schemes, the backbone sub-network is able to capture contextual information with different scales and varying among different sub-regions.

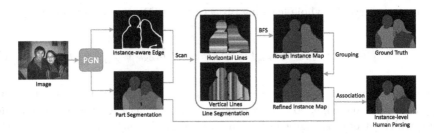

Fig. 5. The whole pipeline of our approach to tackle instance-level human parsing. Generated from the PGN, the part segmentation maps and edge maps are scanned simultaneously to create horizontal and vertical segmented lines. Just like a connected graph problem, the breadth-first search can be applied to group segmented lines into regions. Furthermore, the small regions near the instance boundary are merged into their neighbor regions that cover larger areas and several part labels. Associating the instance maps and part segmentation maps, the pipeline finally outputs a well-predicted instance-level human parsing result without any proposals from object detection.

Semantic Part Segmentation Branch. The common technique [3,5] for semantic segmentation is to predict the image at several different scales with shared network weights and then combine predictions together with learned attention weights. To reinforce the efficiency and generalization of our unified network, discarding the multi-scale input, we apply another context aggregation pattern with various average-pooling kernel sizes, which is introduced in [44]. We append one side branch to perform pixel-wise recognition for assigning each pixel with one semantic part label. The 1×1 convolutional classifiers output K channels, corresponding to the number of target part labels including a background class.

Instance-Aware Edge Detection Branch. Following [40], we attach side outputs for edge detection to the final three blocks of ResNet-101. Deep supervision is imposed at each side-output layer to learn rich hierarchical representations towards edge predictions. Particularly, we use atrous spatial pyramid pooling

(ASPP) [3] for the three edge side output layers to robustly detect boundaries at multiple scales. The ASPP we used consists of one 1×1 convolution and four 3×3 atrous convolutions with dilation rates of 2, 4, 8, and 16. In the final classification layers for edge detection, we use pyramid pooling module to collect more global information for better reasoning. We apply 1×1 convolutional layers with one channel for all edge outputs to generate edge score maps.

Refinement Branch. We design a simple yet efficient refinement branch for jointly refining segmentation and edge predictions. As shown in Fig. 4, the refinement branch integrates the segmentation and edge predictions back into the feature space by mapping them to a larger number of channels with an additional 1×1 convolution. The remapped feature maps are combined with the extracted feature maps from both the segmentation branch and edge branch, which are finally fed into another two pyramid pooling modules to mutually boost segmentation and edges results.

In summary, the whole learning objective of PGN can be written as:

$$L = \alpha \cdot (L_{\text{seg}} + L'_{\text{seg}}) + \beta \cdot (L_{\text{edge}} + L'_{\text{edge}} + \sum_{n=1}^{N} L_{\text{side}}^n). \tag{1}$$

The resolution of the output score maps is $m \times m$, which is the same for both segmentation and edge. So the segmentation branch has a Km^2-dimensional output, which encodes K segmentation maps of resolution $m \times m$, one for each of the K classes. During training, we apply a per-pixel softmax and define L_{seg} as the multinomial cross-entropy loss. L'_{seg} is the same but for the refined segmentation results. For each m^2-dimensional edge output, we use a per-pixel sigmoid binary cross-entropy loss. L_{edge}, L'_{edge}, and L_{side}^n denote the loss of the first predicted edge, refined edge and the side-output edge respectively. In our network, the number of edge side output, N is 3. α and β are the balance weights.

We use the batch normalization parameters provided by [3], which are fixed during our training process. Our added modules (including ASPP and pyramid pooling module) on top of ResNet eliminate batch normalization because the whole network is trained end-to-end with a small batch size due to the limitation of physical memory on GPU cards. The ReLU activation function is applied following each convolutional layer except the final classification layers.

4.2   Instance Partition Process

Since the couple tasks of semantic part segmentation and instance-aware edge detection are able to incorporate all required information for depicting instance-level human parsing, we thus employ a simple instance partition process to get final results during inference, which groups human parts into instances based on edge guidance. The whole process is illustrated in Fig. 5.

First, inspired by the line decoding process in [25], we simultaneously scan part segmentation maps and edge maps thinned by non-maximal suppression [40] to create horizontal and vertical line segments. To create horizontal lines, we slide from left to right along each row. The background positions of segmentation maps are directly skipped and a new line starts when we hit a foreground label of segmentation. The lines are terminated when we hit an edge point and a new line should start at the next position. We label each new line with an individual number, so the edge points can cut off the lines and produce a boundary between two different instances. We perform similar operations but slide from top to bottom to create vertical lines.

The next step is to aggregate these two kinds of lines to create instances. We can treat the horizontal lines and vertical lines jointly as a connected graph. The points in the same lines can be thought as connected since they have the same labeled number. We traverse the connected graph by the breadth-first search to find connected components. In detail, when visiting a point, we search its connected neighbors horizontally and vertically and then push them into the queue that stores the points belonging to the same regions. As a result, the lines of the same instance are grouped and different instance regions are separated.

This simple process inevitably introduces errors if there are false edge points inside instances, resulting in many small regions at the area around instance boundaries. We further design a grouping algorithm to handle this issue. Rethinking of the separated regions, if a region contains several semantic part labels and covers a large area, it must be a person instance. On the contrary, if a region is small and only contains one part segmentation labels, we can certainly judge it as an erroneously separated region and then merge it to its neighbor instance region. We treat a region as a person instance if it contains at least two part labels and covers an area over 30 pixels, which works best in our experiments.

Following this instance partition process, person instance maps could be generated directly from semantic part segmentation and instance-aware edge maps.

Table 2. Comparison of semantic part segmentation performance with the state-of-the-art methods on the PASCAL-Person-Part [6].

Method	Head	Torso	u-arms	l-arms	u-legs	l-legs	Bkg	Avg
HAZN [39]	80.79	59.11	43.05	42.76	38.99	34.46	93.59	56.11
Attention [5]	81.47	59.06	44.15	42.50	38.28	35.62	93.65	56.39
LG-LSTM [20]	82.72	60.99	45.40	47.76	42.33	37.96	88.63	57.97
LIP [11]	83.26	62.40	47.80	45.58	42.32	39.48	94.68	59.36
Graph LSTM [19]	82.69	62.68	46.88	47.71	45.66	40.93	94.59	60.16
Structure-evolving LSTM [17]	82.89	67.15	51.42	48.72	51.72	**45.91**	**97.18**	63.57
DeepLab v2 [3]	-	-	-	-	-	-	-	64.94
Holistic [16]	-	-	-	-	-	-	-	66.3
PGN (segmentation)	89.98	73.70	54.75	60.26	50.58	39.16	95.09	66.22
PGN (w/o refinement)	90.11	72.93	54.01	59.47	54.57	42.03	95.12	66.91
PGN	**90.89**	**75.12**	**55.83**	**64.61**	**55.42**	41.57	95.33	**68.40**

5 Experiments

5.1 Experimental Settings

Training Details: We use the basic structure and network settings provided by Deeplab-v2 [3]. The 512×512 inputs are randomly cropped from the images during training. The size of the output scope maps, m equals to 64 with the downsampling scale of $1/8$. The number of category K is 7 for PASCAL-Person-part dataset [6] and 20 for our CIHP dataset.

The initial learning rate is 0.0001, the parsing loss weight α is 1 and the edge loss weight β is 0.01. Following [4], we employ a 'poly' learning rate policy where the initial learning rate is multiplied by $(1 - \frac{iter}{max\_iter})^{power}$ with power = 0.9. We train all models with a batch size of 4 images and momentum of 0.9.

We apply data augmentation, including randomly scaling the input images (from 0.5 to 2.0), randomly cropping and randomly left-right flipping during training for all datasets. As reported in [16], the baseline methods, Holistic [16] and MNC [7] are pre-trained on Pascal VOC Dataset [9]. For fair comparisons, we train the PGN at the same settings for roughly 80 epochs.

Our method is implemented by extending the TensorFlow framework. All networks are trained on four NVIDIA GeForce GTX 1080 GPUs.

Inference: During testing, the resolution of every input is consistent with the original image. We average the predictions produced by the part segmentation branch and the refinement branch as the final results for part segmentation. For edge detection, we only use the results of the refinement branch. To stabilize the predictions, we perform inference by combining results of multi-scale inputs and left-right flipped images. In particular, the scale is 0.5 to 1.75 in increments of 0.25 for segmentation and from 1.0 to 1.75 for edge detection. In partition process, we break the lines when the activation of edge point is larger than 0.2.

Table 3. Comparison of instance-aware edge detection performance on the PASCAL-Person-Part dataset [6].

Method	ODS	OIS
RCF [27]	38.2	39.8
CEDN [43]	38.9	40.1
HED [40]	39.6	41.3
PGN (edge)	41.8	43.0
PGN (w/o refinement)	42.1	43.5
PGN	**42.5**	**43.9**

Evaluation Metric: The standard intersection over union (IoU) criterion is adopted for evaluation on semantic part segmentation, following [6]. To evaluate instance-aware edge detection performance, we use the same measures for traditional edge detection [27]: fixed contour threshold (ODS) and per-image best threshold (OIS). In terms of instance-level human parsing, we define metrics drawing inspirations from the evaluation of instance-level semantic segmentation. Specifically, we adopt mean Average Precision, referred to as AP^r [12]. We also compare the mean of the AP^r score for overlap thresholds varying from 0.1 to 0.9 in increments of 0.1, noted as AP^r_{vol} [16].

5.2 PASCAL-Person-Part Dataset

We first evaluate the performance of our PGN on the PASCAL-Person-part dataset [6] with 1,716 images for training and 1,817 for testing. Following [5,39], the annotations are merged to include six person part classes and one background class which are Head, Torse, Upper/Lower arms and Upper/Lower legs.

Table 4. Comparison of AP^r at various IoU thresholds for instance-level human parsing on the PASCAL-Person-Part dataset [6].

Method	IoU threshold			AP^r_{vol}
	0.5	0.6	0.7	
MNC [7]	38.8	28.1	19.3	36.7
Holistic [16]	**40.6**	**30.4**	19.1	38.4
PGN (edge + segmentation)	36.2	25.9	16.3	35.6
PGN (w/o refinement)	39.1	29.3	19.5	37.8
PGN (w/o grouping)	37.1	28.2	19.3	38.2
PGN (large-area grouping)	37.6	28.7	19.7	38.6
PGN	39.6	29.9	**20.0**	**39.2**

Comparison on Semantic Part Segmentation. We report the semantic part segmentation results compared with the state-of-the-art methods in Table 2. The proposed PGN substantially outperforms all baselines in terms of most of the categories. Particularly, our best model achieves 2.1% improvements in average IoU compared with the closest competitor. This superior performance confirms the effectiveness of our unified network on semantic part segmentation, which incorporates the information of object boundaries into the pixel-wise prediction.

Comparison on Instance-Aware Edge Detection. We report the statistic comparison of our PGN and state-of-the-art methods on instance-aware edge detection in Table 3. Our PGN gives a huge boost in terms of ODS and OIS. This large improvement demonstrates that edge detection can benefit from semantic part segmentation in our unified network.

Comparison on Instance-Level Human Parsing. Table 4 shows the comparison results of instance-level human parsing with two baseline methods [7,16], which rely on object detection framework to generate a large number of proposals for separating instances. Our PGN method achieves state-of-the-art performance, especially in terms of high IoU threshold, thanks to the more smooth boundaries of segmentation refined by edge context. It verifies the rationality of our PGN based on the assumption that semantic part segmentation and edge detection together can directly depict the key characteristics to achieve good capability in instance-level human parsing. The joint feature learning scheme in PGN also makes the part-level grouping by semantic part segmentation and instance-level grouping by instance-aware edge detection mutually benefit from each other by seamlessly incorporating multi-level contextual information.

Table 5. Performance comparison of edges (Left), part segmentation (Middle) and instance-level human parsing (Right) from different components of PGN on the CIHP.

Method	ODS	OIS	Mean IoU	IoU threshold			AP^r_{vol}
				0.5	0.6	0.7	
PGN (edge) + PGN (segmentation)	44.8	44.9	50.7	28.5	22.9	16.4	27.8
PGN (w/o refinement)	45.3	45.6	54.1	33.3	26.3	18.5	31.4
PGN (w/o grouping)	-	-	-	34.7	27.8	20.1	32.9
PGN (large-area grouping)	-	-	-	35.1	28.2	20.4	33.4
PGN	**45.5**	**46.0**	**55.8**	**35.8**	**28.6**	**20.5**	**33.6**

5.3 CIHP Dataset

As there are no available codes of baseline methods [16], we extensively evaluate each component of our PGN architecture on the CIHP test set, as shown in Table 5. For part segmentation and instance-level human parsing, the performance on CIHP is worse than those on PASCAL-Person-Part [6], because the CIHP dataset contains more instances with more diverse poses, appearance patterns and occlusions, which is more consistent with real-world scenarios, as shown in Fig. 6. However, the images in CIHP are high-quality with higher resolutions, which makes the results of edge detection become better.

5.4 Ablation Studies

We further evaluate the effect of the main components of our PGN.

The Unified Network. We train two independent networks, PGN (segmentation) and PGN(edge), with only a segmentation branch or an edge branch, as reported in Tables 2, 3, 4 and 5. From the comparisons, we can learn that our unified network incorporating information from part context and boundaries context can predict a better result than using a single task network. Moreover, the joint training can also improve the final instance-level human parsing results.

The Refinement Branch. The comparisons between PGN and PGN (w/o refinement) show that our refinement branch helps part segmentation and instance edges benefit each other by exploiting complementary contextual information, which is an implicit joint optimization just like graphical models. With the well-predicted segmentation and edges, our partition algorithm can generate instance-level results more efficiently than other complex decoding processes [1,16,25].

The Grouping Algorithm. Finally, we prove that the grouping algorithm in the instance partition process is an effective way to refine results of instance-level human parsing, by inspecting the performance of PGN (w/o grouping) in Tables 4 and 5. Additionally, PGN (large-area grouping) represents that in the grouping algorithm, whether a region is a person instance only depends on if it covers a large area. The results indicate that our proposed framework including the heuristic grouping algorithm can be generalized and works as well in the case of standard instance segmentation where the part labels are not predicted.

5.5 Qualitative Results

The qualitative results on the PASCAL-Person-Part dataset [6] and the CIHP dataset are visualized in Fig. 6. Compared to Holistic [16], our part segmentation and instance-level human parsing results are more precise because the predicted edges can eliminate the interference from the background, such as the flag in group (a) and the dog in group (b). Overall, our PGN outputs very semantically meaningful predictions, thanks to the mutual refinement between edge detection and semantic part segmentation.

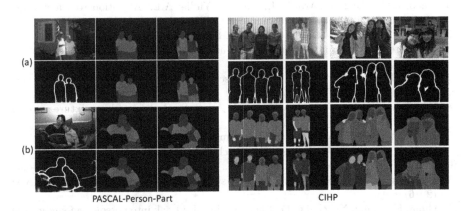

PASCAL-Person-Part   CIHP

Fig. 6. Left: Visualized results on the PASCAL-Person-Part dataset [6]. In each group, the first line shows the input image, segmentation and instance results of Holistic [16] (provided by the authors), and the results of our PGN are presented in the second line. Right: The images and the predicted results of edges, segmentation and instance-level human parsing by our PGN on the CIHP dataset are presented vertically.

6   Conclusion

In this paper, we presented a novel detection-free Part Grouping Network to investigate instance-level human parsing, which is a more pioneering and challenging work in analyzing human in the wild. Our approach jointly optimizes semantic part segmentation and instance-aware edge detection in an end-to-end way and makes these two correlated tasks mutually refine each other. To push the research boundary of human parsing to match real-world scenarios much better, we further introduce a new large-scale benchmark for instance-level human parsing task, including 38,280 images with pixel-wise annotations on 19 semantic part labels. Experimental results on PASCAL-Person-Part [6] and our CIHP dataset demonstrate the superiority of our proposed approach, which surpasses previous methods for both semantic part segmentation and edge detection tasks, and achieves state-of-the-art performance for instance-level human parsing.

References

1. Arnab, A., Torr, P.H.S.: Pixelwise instance segmentation with a dynamically instantiated network. In: CVPR (2017)
2. Bai, M., Urtasun, R.: Deep watershed transform for instance segmentation. In: CVPR (2017)
3. Chen, L.C., Papandreou, G., Kokkinos, I., Murphy, K., Yuille, A.L.: DeepLab: semantic image segmentation with deep convolutional nets, atrous convolution, and fully connected CRFs. arXiv preprint arXiv:1606.00915 (2016)
4. Chen, L.C., Papandreou, G., Schroff, F., Adam, H.: Rethinking atrous convolution for semantic image segmentation. arXiv preprint arXiv:1706.05587 (2017)
5. Chen, L.C., Yang, Y., Wang, J., Xu, W., Yuille, A.L.: Attention to scale: scale-aware semantic image segmentation. In: CVPR (2016)
6. Chen, X., Mottaghi, R., Liu, X., Fidler, S., Urtasun, R., et al.: Detect what you can: detecting and representing objects using holistic models and body parts. In: CVPR (2014)
7. Dai, J., He, K., Sun, J.: Instance-aware semantic segmentation via multi-task network cascades. In: CVPR (2016)
8. Dong, J., Chen, Q., Xia, W., Huang, Z., Yan, S.: A deformable mixture parsing model with parselets. In: ICCV (2013)
9. Everingham, M., Van Gool, L., Williams, C.K., Winn, J., Zisserman, A.: The PASCAL Visual Object Classes (VOC) challenge. IJCV (2010)
10. Gan, C., Lin, M., Yang, Y., de Melo, G., Hauptmann, A.G.: Concepts not alone: exploring pairwise relationships for zero-shot video activity recognition. In: AAAI (2016)
11. Gong, K., Liang, X., Zhang, D., Shen, X., Lin, L.: Look into person: self-supervised structure-sensitive learning and a new benchmark for human parsing. In: CVPR (2017)
12. Hariharan, B., Arbeláez, P., Girshick, R., Malik, J.: Simultaneous detection and segmentation. In: Fleet, D., Pajdla, T., Schiele, B., Tuytelaars, T. (eds.) ECCV 2014. LNCS, vol. 8695, pp. 297–312. Springer, Cham (2014). https://doi.org/10. 1007/978-3-319-10584-0_20
13. He, K., Gkioxari, G., Dollar, P., Girshick, R.: Mask R-CNN. In: ICCV (2017)

14. He, K., Zhang, X., Ren, S., Sun, J.: Deep residual learning for image recognition. In: CVPR (2016)
15. Kirillov, A., Levinkov, E., Andres, B., Savchynskyy, B., Rother, C.: InstanceCut: from Edges to Instances with MultiCut. In: CVPR (2017)
16. Li, Q., Arnab, A., Torr, P.H.: Holistic, instance-level human parsing. arXiv preprint arXiv:1709.03612 (2017)
17. Liang, X., Lin, L., Shen, X., Feng, J., Yan, S., Xing, E.P.: Interpretable structure-evolving LSTM. In: CVPR (2017)
18. Liang, X., et al.: Deep human parsing with active template regression. In: TPAMI (2015)
19. Liang, X., Shen, X., Feng, J., Lin, L., Yan, S.: Semantic object parsing with graph LSTM. In: ECCV (2016)
20. Liang, X., Shen, X., Xiang, D., Feng, J., Lin, L., Yan, S.: Semantic object parsing with local-global long short-term memory. In: CVPR (2016)
21. Liang, X., et al.: Reversible recursive instance-level object segmentation. In: CVPR (2016)
22. Liang, X., Wei, Y., Shen, X., Yang, J., Lin, L., Yan, S.: Proposal-free network for instance-level object segmentation. arXiv preprint arXiv:1509.02636 (2015)
23. Liang, X., et al.: Human parsing with contextualized convolutional neural network. In: ICCV (2015)
24. Lin, T.-Y., et al.: Microsoft COCO: Common Objects in Context. In: Fleet, D., Pajdla, T., Schiele, B., Tuytelaars, T. (eds.) ECCV 2014. LNCS, vol. 8693, pp. 740–755. Springer, Cham (2014). https://doi.org/10.1007/978-3-319-10602-1_48
25. Liu, S., Jia, J., Fidler, S., Urtasun, R.: SGN: sequential grouping networks for instance segmentation. In: ICCV (2017)
26. Liu, S., et al.: Matching-CNN meets KNN: quasi-parametric human parsing. In: CVPR (2015)
27. Liu, Y., Cheng, M.M., Hu, X., Wang, K., Bai, X.: Richer convolutional features for edge detection. In: CVPR (2017)
28. Liu, Z., Luo, P., Qiu, S., Wang, X., Tang, X.: DeepFashion: powering robust clothes recognition and retrieval with rich annotations. In: CVPR (2016)
29. Long, J., Shelhamer, E., Darrell, T.: Fully convolutional networks for semantic segmentation. In: CVPR (2015)
30. Hadi Kiapour, M., Han, X., Lazebnik, S., Berg, A.C., Berg, T.L.: Where to buy it: matching street clothing photos in online shops. In: ICCV (2015)
31. Pinheiro, P.O., Collobert, R., Dollár, P.: Learning to segment object candidates. In: NIPS (2015)
32. Ren, M., Zemel, R.S.: End-to-end instance segmentation with recurrent attention. In: CVPR (2017)
33. Ren, S., He, K., Girshick, R., Sun, J.: Faster R-CNN: towards real-time object detection with region proposal networks. In: NIPS (2015)
34. Romera-Paredes, B., Torr, P.H.S.: Recurrent instance segmentation. In: ECCV (2016)
35. Simo-Serra, E., Fidler, S., Moreno-Noguer, F., Urtasun, R.: A high performance CRF model for clothes parsing. In: ACCV (2014)
36. Simo-Serra, E., Fidler, S., Moreno-Noguer, F., Urtasun, R.: Neuroaesthetics in fashion: modeling the perception of fashionability. In: CVPR (2015)
37. Simonyan, K., Zisserman, A.: Very deep convolutional networks for large-scale image recognition. arXiv preprint arXiv:1409.1556 (2014)
38. Wang, L., Ji, X., Deng, Q., Jia, M.: Deformable part model based multiple pedestrian detection for video surveillance in crowded scenes. In: VISAPP (2014)

39. Xia, F., Wang, P., Chen, L.C., Yuille, A.L.: Zoom better to see clearer: Human part segmentation with auto zoom net. In: ECCV (2016)
40. Xie, S., Tu, Z.: Holistically-nested edge detection. In: ICCV (2015)
41. Yamaguchi, K., Kiapour, M., Berg, T.: Paper doll parsing: Retrieving similar styles to parse clothing items. In: ICCV (2013)
42. Yamaguchi, K., Kiapour, M., Ortiz, L., Berg, T.: Parsing clothing in fashion photographs. In: CVPR (2012)
43. Yang, J., Price, B., Cohen, S., Lee, H., Yang, M.H.: Object contour detection with a fully convolutional encoder-decoder network. In: CVPR (2016)
44. Zhao, H., Shi, J., Qi, X., Wang, X., Jia, J.: Pyramid scene parsing network. In: CVPR (2017)
45. Zheng, S., et al.: Conditional random fields as recurrent neural networks. In: ICCV (2015)

Adversarial Geometry-Aware Human Motion Prediction

Liang-Yan Gui$^{(\boxtimes)}$, Yu-Xiong Wang, Xiaodan Liang, and José M. F. Moura

Carnegie Mellon University, Pittsburgh, USA
{lgui,yuxiongw,xiaodan1,moura}@andrew.cmu.edu

Abstract. We explore an approach to forecasting human motion in a few milliseconds given an input 3D skeleton sequence based on a recurrent encoder-decoder framework. Current approaches suffer from the problem of prediction discontinuities and may fail to predict human-like motion in longer time horizons due to error accumulation. We address these critical issues by incorporating local geometric structure constraints and regularizing predictions with plausible temporal smoothness and continuity from a global perspective. Specifically, rather than using the conventional Euclidean loss, we propose a novel *frame-wise geodesic loss* as a geometrically meaningful, more precise distance measurement. Moreover, inspired by the adversarial training mechanism, we present a new learning procedure to simultaneously validate the sequence-level plausibility of the prediction and its coherence with the input sequence by introducing *two global recurrent discriminators*. An unconditional, fidelity discriminator and a conditional, continuity discriminator are jointly trained along with the predictor in an adversarial manner. Our resulting *adversarial geometry-aware encoder-decoder (AGED)* model significantly outperforms state-of-the-art deep learning based approaches on the heavily benchmarked H3.6M dataset in both short-term and long-term predictions.

Keywords: Human motion prediction · Adversarial learning
Geodesic loss

1 Introduction

Consider the following scenario: a robot is working in our everyday lives and interacting with humans, for example shaking hands during socialization or delivering tools to a surgeon when assisting a surgery. In a seamless interaction, the robot is supposed to not only recognize but also anticipate human actions, such as accurately predicting limbs' pose and position, so that it can respond appropriately and expeditiously [17,25]. Such an ability of forecasting how a human moves or acts in the near future conditioning on a series of historical movements is typically addressed in human motion prediction [4,8,12,13,16,17,24,31]. In addition

---

L.-Y. Gui and Y.-X. Wang—Equal contributions.

© Springer Nature Switzerland AG 2018
V. Ferrari et al. (Eds.): ECCV 2018, LNCS 11208, pp. 823–842, 2018.
https://doi.org/10.1007/978-3-030-01225-0_48

to the above scenario of human-robot interaction and collaboration [28], human motion prediction also has great application potential in various tasks in computer vision and robotic vision, such as action anticipation [20,27], motion generation for computer graphics [29], and proactive decision-making in autonomous driving systems [35].

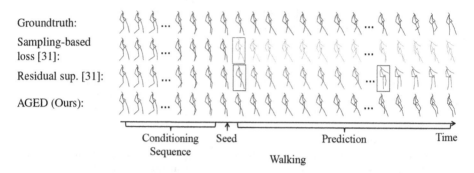

Fig. 1. Human motion prediction task. Top: the conditioning sequence and the groundtruth of the predicted sequence. Middle two: state-of-the-art prediction results (sampling-based loss and residual sup. [31]). Bottom: our prediction. The groundtruth and the input sequences are shown in black. Given the black seed motion frame in the middle, predictions are shown in color. As highlighted in the rectangles, a severe discontinuity exists between the seed motion frame and the first predicted frame for sampling-based loss (2nd row); the prediction is further away from the groundtruth than ours (3rd row, left) and error accumulates in long time horizons (3rd row, right) for residual sup. Our *single* model consistently outperforms the baselines and produces low-error, smooth, and human-like prediction. **Best viewed in color with zoom.** (Color figure online)

Modeling Motion Dynamics: Predicting human motion for diverse actions is challenging yet under-explored, because of the uncertainty of human conscious movements and the difficulty of modeling long-term motion dynamics. State-of-the-art deep learning based approaches typically formulate the task as a sequence-to-sequence problem, and solve it by using recurrent neural networks (RNNs) to capture the underlying temporal dependencies in the sequential data [31]. Despite their extensive efforts on exploring different types of encoder-decoder architectures (*e.g.*, encoder-recurrent-decoder (ERD) [12] and residual [31] architectures), they can only predict periodic actions well (*e.g.*, walking) and show unsatisfactory performance on longer-term aperiodic actions (*e.g.*, discussion), due to error accumulation and severe motion jump between the predicted and input sequences, as shown in Fig. 1. One of the main reasons is that the previous work only considers the frame-wise correctness based on a Euclidean metric at each recurrent training step, while ignoring the critical geometric structure of motion frames and the sequence-level motion fidelity and continuity from a global perspective.

Human-Like Motion Prediction: In this work, we aim to address human-like motion prediction so that the predicted sequences are more plausible and temporally coherent with past sequences. By leveraging the local frame-wise geometric structure and addressing the global sequence-level fidelity and continuity, we propose a novel model that significantly improves the performance of short-term 3D human motion prediction as well as generates realistic periodic and aperiodic long-term motion.

Geometric Structure Aware Loss Function at the Frame Level: Although the motion frames are represented as 3D rotations between joint angles, the standard Euclidean distance is commonly used as the loss function when regressing the predicted frames to the groundtruth during encoder-decoder training. The Euclidean loss fails to exploit the intrinsic geometric structure of 3D rotations, making the prediction inaccurate and even frozen to some mean pose for long-term prediction [24,32]. *Our key insight* is that the matrix representation of 3D rotations belongs to Special Orthogonal Group $SO(3)$ [43], an algebraic group with a Riemannian manifold structure. This manifold structure allows us to define a geodesic distance that is the shortest path between two rotations. We thus introduce a novel geodesic loss between the predicted motion and the groundtruth motion to replace the Euclidean loss. This geometrically more meaningful loss leads to more precise distance measurement and is computationally inexpensive.

Adversarial Training at the Sequence Level: To achieve human-like motion prediction, the model is supposed to be able to validate its entire generated sequence. Unfortunately, such a mechanism is missing in the current prediction framework. In the spirit of generative adversarial networks (GANs) [14], we introduce two global discriminators to validate the prediction while casting our predictor as a generator, and we jointly train them in an adversarial manner. To deal with sequential data, we design our discriminators as *recurrent networks*. The first *unconditional, fidelity discriminator* distinguishes the predicted sequence from the groundtruth sequence. The second *conditional, continuity discriminator* distinguishes between the long sequences that are concatenated from the input sequence and the predicted or groundtruth sequence. *Intuitively*, the fidelity discriminator aims to examine whether the generated motion sequence is human-like and plausible overall, and the continuity discriminator is responsible for checking whether the predicted motion sequence is coherent with the input sequence without a noticeable discontinuity between them.

Our contributions are three-fold. (1) We address human-like motion prediction by modeling both the frame-level geometric structure and the sequence-level fidelity and continuity. (2) We propose a novel geodesic loss and demonstrate that it is more suitable to evaluate 3D motion as the regression loss and is computationally inexpensive. (3) We introduce two complementary recurrent discriminators tailored for the motion prediction task, which are jointly trained along with the geometry-aware encoder-decoder predictor in an adversarial manner. Our full model, which we call *adversarial geometry-aware* *encoder-decoder (AGED)*, significantly surpasses the state-of-the-art deep learning based approaches when evaluated on the heavily benchmarked, large-scale motion capture (mocap) H3.6M dataset [22]. Our approach is also general and can be potentially incorporated into any encoder-decoder based prediction framework.

2 Related Work

Human Motion Prediction: Human motion prediction is typically addressed by state-space models. Traditional approaches focus on bilinear spatio-temporal basis models [1], hidden Markov models [7], Gaussian process latent variable models [50,53], linear dynamic models [38], and restricted Boltzmann machines [45,47–49]. More recently, driven by the advances of deep learning architectures and large-scale public datasets, various deep learning based approaches have been proposed [4,8,12,13,16,24,31], which significantly improve the prediction performance on a variety of actions.

RNNs for Motion Prediction: In addition to their success in machine translation [26], image caption [58], and time-series prediction [52,57], RNNs [44,54,55] have become the widely used framework for human motion prediction. Fragkiadaki *et al.* [12] propose a 3-layer long short-term memory (LSTM-3LR) network and an encoder-recurrent-decoder (ERD) model that use curriculum learning to jointly learn a representation of pose data and temporal dynamics. Jain *et al.* [24] introduce high-level semantics of human dynamics into RNNs by modeling human activity with a spatio-temporal graph. These two approaches design action-specific models and restrict the training process on subsets of the mocap dataset. Some recent work explores motion prediction for general action classes. Ghosh *et al.* [13] propose a DAE-LSTM model that combines an LSTM-3LR with a dropout autoencoder to model temporal and spatial structures. Martinez *et al.* [31] develop a simple residual encoder-decoder and multi-action architecture by using one-hot vectors to incorporate the action class information. The residual connection exploits first-order motion derivatives to decrease the motion jump between the predicted and input sequences, but its effect is still unsatisfactory. Moreover, error accumulation has been observed in the predicted sequence, since RNNs cannot recover from their own mistake [5]. Some work [12,24] alleviates this problem via a noise scheduling scheme [6] by adding noise to the input during training; nevertheless, this scheme makes the prediction discontinuous and makes the hyper-parameters difficult to tune. While our approach is developed in deterministic motion prediction, it can be potentially extended to probabilistic prediction [4,38,53].

Loss Functions in Prediction Tasks: The commonly used Euclidean loss (*i.e.,* the ℓ_2 loss, and to a lesser extent ℓ_1 loss) [24,31] in prediction tasks can cause the model to average between two possible futures [32] and thus result in blurred video prediction [34] or unrealistic mean motion prediction [24], increasingly worse when predicting further in the future. An image gradient difference loss is proposed to address this issue for pixel-level video prediction [32], which is not applicable in our task. Here, by taking into the account the intrinsic geometric structure of the motion frames, we adopt a more effective geodesic metric [18,21] to measure 3D rotation errors.

GANs: GANs [2,14] have shown impressive performance in various generation tasks [10,30,32,40,41,51,56,60]. Rather than exploring different objectives in GANs, we investigate how to improve human motion prediction by leveraging the adversarial training mechanism. Our model is different from standard GANs in three ways. (1) Architecture: the discriminators in GANs are mainly convolutional or fully-connected networks [4,23,32,59]; by contrast, our generator and discriminators are both with RNN structures so as to deal with sequences. (2) Training procedure: two discriminators are used at the same time to address the fidelity and continuity challenges, respectively. (3) Loss function: we combine a geodesic (regression) loss with GAN adversarial losses to benefit from both of them. From a broader perspective, our approach can be viewed as imposing (and yet not explicitly enforcing) certain regularizations on the predicted motion, which is loosely related to the classical smoothing, filtering, and prediction techniques [11] but is more trainable and adaptable to real human motion statistics.

3   Adversarial Geometry-Aware Encoder-Decoder Model

Figure 2 illustrates the framework of our adversarial geometry-aware encoder-decoder (AGED) model for human motion prediction. The encoder and decoder constitute the *predictor*, which is trained to minimize the distance between the predicted future sequence and the groundtruth sequence. The standard Euclidean distance is commonly used as the regression loss function. However, it makes the predicted skeleton non-smooth and discontinuous for short-term prediction and frozen to some mean pose for long-term prediction. To deal with such limitations, we introduce an adversarial training process and new loss functions at the global sequence and local frame levels, respectively.

Problem Formulation: We represent human motion as sequential data. Given a motion sequence, we predict possible short-term and long-term motion in the future. That is, we aim to find a mapping $\mathcal{P}$ from an input sequence to an output sequence. The input sequence of length n is denoted as $\mathbf{X} = \{\mathbf{x}_1, \mathbf{x}_2, ..., \mathbf{x}_n\}$, where $\mathbf{x}_i \in \mathbb{R}^K$ ($i \in [1, n]$) is a mocap vector that consists of a set of 3D body joint angles with their exponential map representations [33] and K is the number of joint angles. Consistent with [12,31,48], we standardize the inputs and focus on relative rotations between joints, since they contain information of the actions. We predict the future motion sequence in the next m timesteps as the output, denoted as $\widehat{\mathbf{X}} = \{\widehat{\mathbf{x}}_{n+1}, \widehat{\mathbf{x}}_{n+2}, ..., \widehat{\mathbf{x}}_{n+m}\}$, where $\widehat{\mathbf{x}}_j \in \mathbb{R}^K$ ($j \in [n+1, n+m]$) is the predicted mocap vector at the j-th timestep. The groundtruth of the m timesteps is given as $\mathbf{X}_{\mathrm{gt}} = \{\mathbf{x}_{n+1}, \mathbf{x}_{n+2}, ..., \mathbf{x}_{n+m}\}$.

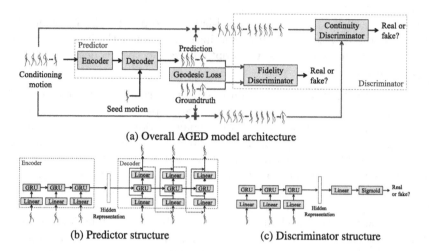

(a) Overall AGED model architecture

(b) Predictor structure   (c) Discriminator structure

Fig. 2. An overview of our adversarial geometry-aware encoder-decoder (AGED) model. Blue-red skeletons represent the input sequence and groundtruth, and green-purple skeletons represent the prediction. An input sequence is fed into a sequence-to-sequence encoder-decoder network to produce the output sequence (b). We propose a *frame-wise geodesic loss* as a more precise distance measurement to regress the predicted sequence to the groundtruth (a). We further introduce *two global recurrent discriminators* (an unconditional, fidelity discriminator and a conditional, continuity discriminator) to validate the sequence-level plausibility of the prediction and its coherence with the input sequence (c). By jointly optimizing the geometry-aware predictor and the two discriminators in an adversarial manner, we generate the final prediction. (Color figure online)

3.1   Geometry-Aware Encoder-Decoder Predictor

Learning the predictor, *i.e.*, the mapping $\mathcal{P}$ from the input to output sequences, is cast as solving a sequence-to-sequence problem based on an encoder-decoder network architecture [31,46]. The encoder learns a hidden representation from the input sequence. The hidden representation and a seed motion frame are then fed into the decoder to produce the output sequence. Other modifications such as attention mechanisms [3] and bi-directional encoders [42] could be also incorporated into this general architecture.

We use a similar network architecture as in [31] for our predictor $\mathcal{P}$, which has achieved the state-of-the-art performance on motion prediction. The encoder and decoder consist of gated recurrent unit (GRU) [9] cells instead of LSTM [19] or other RNN variants. We use a residual connection to model the motion velocities rather than operating with absolute angles, given that the residual connection has been shown to improve prediction smoothness [31]. Each frame of the input sequence, concatenated with a one-hot vector which indicates the action class of the current input, is fed into the encoder. The decoder takes the output of itself as the next timestep input.

Geodesic Loss: At the local frame level, we introduce a geodesic loss to regress the predicted sequence to the groundtruth sequence frame by frame. Given that the motion frame is represented as 3D rotations of all joint angles, we are interested in measuring the distance between two 3D rotations. The widespread measurement is the Euclidean distance [12,24,31]. However, the crucial geometric structure of 3D rotations is ignored, leading to inaccurate prediction [24,32].

To address such an issue, we introduce a more precise distance measurement and define the new loss accordingly. For a rotation with its Euler angles $\theta = (\alpha, \beta, \gamma)$ about rotation axis $u = (u_1, u_2, u_3)^T$, the corresponding rotation matrix is defined as $\mathbf{R} = [\theta \cdot u]_\times$, where $\cdot$ and $\times$ denote the inner and outer products, respectively. Such 3D rotation matrices form Special Orthogonal Group $SO(3)$ of orthogonal matrices with determinant 1 [43]. $SO(3)$ is a Lie Group, an algebraic group with a Riemannian manifold structure. It is natural to introduce the geodesic distance to quantify the similarity between two rotations, which is the shortest path between them on the manifold. The geodesic distance in $SO(3)$ can be defined with the angle between two rotation matrices.

Specifically, given two rotation matrices $\widehat{\mathbf{R}}$ and $\mathbf{R}$, the product $\widehat{\mathbf{R}}\mathbf{R}^T$ is the rotation matrix of the difference angle between $\widehat{\mathbf{R}}$ and $\mathbf{R}$. The angle can be calculated using the logarithm map in $SO(3)$ [43] as

$$\log \widehat{\mathbf{R}}\mathbf{R}^T = A \frac{\arcsin\left(\|A\|_2\right)}{\|A\|_2}, \tag{1}$$

where $A = (a_1, a_2, a_3)^T$ and is computed from

$$\frac{\left(\widehat{\mathbf{R}}\mathbf{R}^T - \mathbf{R}\widehat{\mathbf{R}}^T\right)}{2} = \begin{bmatrix} 0 & -a_3 & a_2 \\ a_3 & 0 & -a_1 \\ -a_2 & a_1 & 0 \end{bmatrix}. \tag{2}$$

The geodesic distance between $\widehat{\mathbf{R}}$ and $\mathbf{R}$ is defined as

$$d_G\left(\widehat{\mathbf{R}}, \mathbf{R}\right) = \left\|\log\left(\widehat{\mathbf{R}}\mathbf{R}^T\right)\right\|_2. \tag{3}$$

Based on this geodesic distance, we now define a geodesic loss $\mathcal{L}_{\text{geo}}$ between the prediction $\widehat{\mathbf{X}}$ and the groundtruth $\mathbf{X}_{\text{gt}}$. We first revert the exponential map representations $\widehat{\mathbf{x}}_j^k$, $\mathbf{x}_j^k$ of the k-th joint in the j-th frame to the Euler format $\widehat{\theta}_j^k$, θ_j^k [43], respectively, and calculate their corresponding rotation matrices $\widehat{\mathbf{R}}_j^k$, $\mathbf{R}_j^k$, where $k \in [1, K/3]$, $K/3$ is the number of joints (since each joint has 3D joint angles), and $j \in [n+1, n+m]$. By summing up the geodesic distances between the predicted frames and the groundtruth frames, we obtain the geodesic loss in the form of

$$\mathcal{L}_{\text{geo}}(\mathcal{P}) = \sum_{j=n+1}^{j=n+m} \sum_{k=1}^{k=K/3} d_G^2\left(\widehat{\mathbf{R}}_j^k, \mathbf{R}_j^k\right). \tag{4}$$

The gradient of Eq. (4) can be computed using automatic gradient computations implemented in the software package such as PyTorch [36] given the forward function. Note that there are other distance metrics that can be defined in $SO(3)$ as well, including the one using quaternion representations [18,21]. Regarding *computing distances*, the quaternion based metric is *functionally equivalent* to our metric [18,21]. Regarding *optimization and computing gradient* as in our case, our current experimental observations indicated that the quaternion based metric led to worse results, possibly due to the need for renormalization of quaternions during optimization [15,39].

3.2 Fidelity and Continuity Discriminators

The sequence-to-sequence predictor architecture explores the temporal information of human motion and produces coarsely plausible motion. However, as shown in Fig. 1, we have observed that there exist some discontinuities between the last frames of the input sequences and the first predicted frames. For long-term prediction, the predicted motion tends to be less realistic due to error accumulation. Such phenomena were also observed in [31]. This is partially because using a frame-wise regression loss solely cannot check the fidelity of the entire predicted sequence from a global perspective. Inspired by the *adversarial training mechanism* in GANs [2,14], we address this issue by introducing *two sequence-level discriminators*.

A standard GAN framework consists of (1) a generator that captures the data distribution, and (2) a discriminator that estimates the probability of a sample being real or generated. The generator is trained to generate samples to fool the discriminator and the discriminator is trained to distinguish the generation from the real samples.

Accordingly, in our model we view the encoder-decoder predictor as a generator, and introduce two discriminators. An unconditional, fidelity discriminator $\mathcal{D}_f$ distinguishes between "short" sequences $\widehat{\mathbf{X}}$ and $\mathbf{X}_{\text{gt}}$. A conditional, continuity discriminator $\mathcal{D}_c$ distinguishes between "long" sequences $\{\mathbf{X}, \widehat{\mathbf{X}}\}$ and $\{\mathbf{X}, \mathbf{X}_{\text{gt}}\}$. Their outputs are the probabilities of their inputs to be "real" rather than "fake". Intuitively, the fidelity discriminator evaluates how smooth and human-like the predicted sequence is and the continuity discriminator checks whether the motion of the predicted sequence is coherent with the input sequence. The quality of the predictor $\mathcal{P}$ is then judged by evaluating how well $\widehat{\mathbf{X}}$ fools $\mathcal{D}_f$ and how well the concatenated sequence $\{\mathbf{X}, \widehat{\mathbf{X}}\}$ fools $\mathcal{D}_c$. More formally, following [14], we solve the minimax optimization problem:

$$\arg\min_{\mathcal{P}} \max_{\mathcal{D}_f, \mathcal{D}_c} \mathcal{L}_{\text{adv}}^f \left(\mathcal{P}, \mathcal{D}_f\right) + \mathcal{L}_{\text{adv}}^c \left(\mathcal{P}, \mathcal{D}_c\right), \tag{5}$$

where

$$\mathcal{L}_{\text{adv}}^f \left(\mathcal{P}, \mathcal{D}_f\right) = \mathbb{E}_{\mathbf{X}_{gt}} \left[\log\left(\mathcal{D}_f(\mathbf{X}_{\text{gt}})\right)\right] + \mathbb{E}_{\mathbf{X}} \left[\log\left(1 - \mathcal{D}_f(\mathcal{P}\left(\mathbf{X}\right))\right)\right], \tag{6}$$

$$\mathcal{L}_{\text{adv}}^c \left(\mathcal{P}, \mathcal{D}_c\right) = \mathbb{E}_{\{\mathbf{X}, \mathbf{X}_{gt}\}} \left[\log\left(\mathcal{D}_c(\{\mathbf{X}, \mathbf{X}_{\text{gt}}\})\right)\right] + \mathbb{E}_{\mathbf{X}} \left[\log\left(1 - \mathcal{D}_c(\{\mathbf{X}, \mathcal{P}(\mathbf{X})\})\right)\right], \tag{7}$$

and the distributions $\mathbb{E}(\cdot)$ are over the training motion sequences. Unlike the previous work [4,32,59], we design our discriminators as *recurrent networks* to deal with sequential data. Each of the discriminators consists of GRU cells to extract a hidden representation of its input sequence. A fully-connected layer with sigmoid activation is followed to output the probability that the input sequence is real.

Our entire model thus consists of a *single predictor* and *two discriminators*, extending the generator and discriminator in GANs with recurrent structures. Note that our "generator" is actually a predictor, which is the RNN encoder-decoder *without any noise inputs*. In this sense, the GAN generator maps from noise space to data space, whereas our predictor maps from past sequences to future sequences. During training, the two discriminators are learned jointly.

3.3   Joint Loss Function and Adversarial Training

We integrate the geodesic (regression) loss and the two adversarial losses, and obtain the optimal predictor by jointly optimizing the following minimax objective function:

$$\mathcal{P}^* = \arg\min_{\mathcal{P}} \max_{\mathcal{D}_f, \mathcal{D}_c} \lambda \left(\mathcal{L}_{\text{adv}}^f (\mathcal{P}, \mathcal{D}_f) + \mathcal{L}_{\text{adv}}^c (\mathcal{P}, \mathcal{D}_c) \right) + \mathcal{L}_{\text{geo}} (\mathcal{P}), \qquad (8)$$

where λ is the trade-off hyper-parameter that balances the two types of losses. The predictor $\mathcal{P}$ tries to minimize the objective against the adversarial discriminators $\mathcal{D}_f$ and $\mathcal{D}_c$ that aim to maximize it.

Consistent with the recent work [23,37], our combination of a regression loss and GAN adversarial losses provides some complementary benefits. On the one hand, GAN tends to learn a better representation and tries to make prediction look real, which is difficult to achieve using standard hand-crafted metrics. On the other hand, GAN is well known to be hard to train, and easily gets stuck into local minimum (*i.e.*, not learning the distribution). By contrast, the regression loss is responsible for capturing the overall motion geometric structure and explicitly aligning the prediction with the groundtruth.

Implementation Details: We use a similar predictor architecture as in [31] for its state-of-the-art performance. The encoder and decoder consist of a single GRU cell [9] with hidden size 1,024, respectively. Consistent with [31], we found that GRUs are computationally less expensive and a single GRU cell outperforms multiple GRU cells. In addition, it is easier to train and avoids over-fitting compared with the deeper models in [12,24]. We use linear mappings between the K-dim input/output joint angles and the 1,024-dim GRU hidden state. Our two discriminators have the same architectures. For each of them, we also use a single GRU cell. Note that the frames of the sequence being evaluated are fed into the corresponding discriminator sequentially, making its number of parameters unaffected by the sequence length. Our entire model has the same inference time as the baseline model with the plain predictor [31]. The hyper-parameter λ in Eq. (8) is set as 0.6 by cross-validation. We found that the performance is generally robust with its value ranging from 0.45 to 0.75. We use a learning rate 0.005 and a batch size 16, and we clip the gradient to a maximum ℓ_2-norm of 5. We use PyTorch [36] to train our model and run 50 epochs. It takes 35ms for forward processing and back-propagation per iteration on an NVIDIA Titan GPU.

4   Experiments

In this section, we explore the use of our adversarial geometry-aware encoder-decoder (AGED) model for human motion prediction on the heavily bench-marked motion capture (mocap) dataset [22]. Consistent with the recent work [31], we mainly focus on short-term prediction (<500 ms). We begin with descriptions of the dataset, baselines, and evaluation protocols. Through extensive evaluation, we show that our approach achieves the state-of-the-art short-term prediction performance both quantitatively and qualitatively. We then provide ablation studies, verifying that different losses and modules are complementary with each other for temporal coherent and smooth prediction. Finally, we investigate our approach in long-term prediction (>500 ms) and demonstrate its more human-like prediction results compared with baselines.

Dataset: We focus on the Human 3.6M (H3.6M) dataset [22], a large-scale publicly available dataset including 3.6 million 3D mocap data. This is an important and widely used benchmark in human motion analysis. H3.6M includes seven actors performing 15 varied activities, such as walking, smoking, engaging in a discussion, and taking pictures. We follow the standard experimental setup in [12,24,31]: we down-sample H3.6M by two, train on six subjects, and test on subject five. For short-term prediction, we are given 50 mocap frames (2 seconds in total) and forecast the future 10 frames (400 ms in total). For long-term prediction, we are given the same 50 mocap frames and forecast the future 25 frames (1 second in total) or even more (4 seconds in total).

Baselines: We compare against recent deep RNNs based approaches: (1) LSTM-3LR and ERD [12], (2) SRNN [24], (3) DAE-LSTM [13], and (4) residual sup. and sampling-based loss [31]. Following [31], we also consider a zero-velocity baseline that constantly predicts the last observed frame. As shown in [31], this is a simple but strong baseline: none of these learning based approaches quantitatively outperformed zero-velocity consistently, especially in short-term prediction scenarios.

Evaluation Protocols: We evaluate our approach under three metrics and show both quantitative and qualitative comparisons:

- (Quantitative mean angle error) For a fair comparison, we evaluate the performance using the same error measurement on subject five as in [12,24,31], which is the mean error between the predicted frames and the groundtruth frames in the angle space. Following the preprocessing in [31,48], we exclude the translation and rotation of the whole body.

Table 1. Quantitative comparisons of mean angle error between our AGED model and state-of-the-art approaches for short-term motion prediction on 4 representative activities of the H3.6M dataset. Our model variants include AGED with only the geodesic loss, AGED with two discriminators (the adversarial losses and the conventional Euclidean loss), and full AGED. Our AGED consistently outperforms the existing deep learning based approaches. While the zero-velocity baseline has slightly better performance on smoking at 80 ms prediction, ours outperforms it in all the other cases

	Walking				Eating				Smoking				Discussion			
milliseconds	80	160	320	400	80	160	320	400	80	160	320	400	80	160	320	400
Zero-velocity [31]	0.39	0.68	0.99	1.15	0.27	0.48	0.73	0.86	**0.26**	0.48	0.97	0.95	0.31	0.67	0.94	1.04
ERD [12]	1.30	1.56	1.84	-	1.66	1.93	2.28	-	2.34	2.74	3.73	-	2.67	2.97	3.23	-
LSTM-3LR [12]	1.18	1.50	1.67	-	1.36	1.79	2.29	-	2.05	2.34	3.10	-	2.25	2.33	2.45	-
SRNN [31]	1.08	1.34	1.60	-	1.35	1.71	2.12	-	1.90	2.30	2.90	-	1.67	2.03	2.20	-
DAE-LSTM [13]	1.00	1.11	1.39	-	1.31	1.49	1.86	-	0.92	1.03	1.15	-	1.11	1.20	1.38	-
Sampling-based loss [31]	0.92	0.98	1.02	1.20	0.98	0.99	1.18	1.31	1.38	1.39	1.56	1.65	1.78	1.80	1.83	1.90
Residual sup. [31]	0.28	0.49	0.72	0.81	0.23	0.39	0.62	0.76	0.33	0.61	1.05	1.15	0.31	0.68	1.01	1.09
AGED w/ geo (Ours)	0.28	0.42	0.66	0.73	0.22	0.35	0.61	0.74	0.30	0.55	0.98	0.99	0.30	0.63	0.97	1.06
AGED w/ adv+euc (Ours)	0.27	0.42	0.62	0.71	0.22	0.32	0.53	0.67	0.28	0.47	0.90	0.86	0.28	0.60	0.78	0.87
AGED w/ adv+geo (Ours)	**0.22**	**0.36**	**0.55**	**0.67**	**0.17**	**0.28**	**0.51**	**0.64**	0.27	**0.43**	**0.82**	**0.84**	**0.27**	**0.56**	**0.76**	**0.83**

- (Human evaluation) We also ran double-blind user studies to gauge the plausibility of the prediction as a response to the user. We randomly sample two input sequences from each of the 15 activities on H3.6M, leading to 30 input sequences. We use our model as well as sampling-based loss and residual sup. [31] (which are the top performing baselines as shown below) to generate both short-term and long-term predictions. We thus have 120 short-term motion videos and 120 long-term videos in total, including the short-term and long-term groundtruth videos. We design pairwise evaluations and 25 judges are asked to watch randomly chosen pairs of videos and then choose the one that is considered to be more realistic and reasonable.
- (Qualitative visualization) Following [12,13,24,31], we visualize some representative predictions frame by frame.

For short-term prediction in which the motion is more certain, we evaluate using all the three metrics. For long-term prediction which are more difficult to evaluate quantitatively and might not be unique [31], *we mainly focus on the user studies and visualizations*, and show some quantitative comparisons for reference.

4.1 Short-Term Motion Prediction

Prediction for less than 500 ms is typically considered as short-term prediction. Within this time range, motion is more certain and constrained by physics, and we thus focus on measuring the prediction error with respect to the groundtruth, following [12,24,31]. In these experiments, the network is trained to minimize the loss over 400 ms.

Table 2. Quantitative comparisons of mean angle error between our AGED model and top performing baselines for short-term motion prediction on the remaining 11 activities of the H3.6M dataset. Our AGED model consistently outperforms these baselines in almost all the scenarios

milliseconds	Directions				Greeting				Phoning				Posing				Purchases				Sitting			
	80	160	320	400	80	160	320	400	80	160	320	400	80	160	320	400	80	160	320	400	80	160	320	400
Zero-velocity [31]	0.39	0.59	0.79	0.89	0.54	0.89	1.30	1.49	0.64	1.21	1.65	1.83	0.28	0.57	1.13	1.37	0.62	0.88	1.19	1.27	0.40	1.63	1.02	1.18
Residual sup. [31]	0.26	0.47	0.72	0.84	0.75	1.17	1.74	1.83	0.23	0.43	0.69	0.82	0.36	0.71	1.22	1.48	0.51	0.97	1.07	1.16	0.41	1.05	1.49	1.63
AGED w/ geo (Ours)	0.26	0.46	0.71	0.81	0.61	0.95	1.44	1.61	0.23	0.42	0.61	0.79	0.34	0.70	1.19	1.40	0.46	0.89	1.06	1.11	0.46	0.87	1.23	1.51
AGED w/ adv+euc (Ours)	0.26	0.42	0.66	0.73	0.58	0.88	1.31	1.49	0.21	0.37	0.51	0.69	0.34	0.62	1.15	1.39	0.49	0.83	1.05	1.12	0.44	0.77	1.08	1.21
AGED w/ adv+geo (Ours)	0.23	0.39	0.63	0.69	0.56	0.81	1.30	1.46	0.19	0.34	0.50	0.68	0.31	0.58	1.12	1.34	0.46	0.78	1.01	1.07	0.41	0.76	1.05	1.19

milliseconds	Sitting Down				Taking Photo				Waiting				Walking Dog				Walking Together				Average			
	80	160	320	400	80	160	320	400	80	160	320	400	80	160	320	400	80	160	320	400	80	160	320	400
Zero-velocity [31]	0.39	0.74	1.07	1.19	0.25	0.51	0.79	0.92	0.34	0.67	1.22	1.47	0.60	0.98	1.36	1.50	0.33	0.66	0.94	0.99	0.40	0.71	1.07	1.21
Residual sup. [31]	0.39	0.81	1.40	1.62	0.24	0.51	0.90	1.05	0.28	0.53	1.02	1.14	0.56	0.91	1.26	1.40	0.31	0.58	0.87	0.91	0.36	0.67	1.02	1.15
AGED w/ geo (Ours)	0.38	0.77	1.18	1.41	0.24	0.52	0.92	1.01	0.31	0.64	1.08	1.12	0.51	0.87	1.21	1.33	0.29	0.51	0.72	0.75	0.32	0.62	0.96	1.07
AGED w/ adv+euc (Ours)	0.34	0.67	1.01	1.11	0.24	0.49	0.84	0.97	0.26	0.54	1.05	1.28	0.55	0.84	1.16	1.30	0.24	0.44	0.60	0.64	0.33	0.58	0.88	1.00
AGED w/ adv+geo (Ours)	0.33	0.62	0.98	1.10	0.23	0.48	0.81	0.95	0.24	0.50	1.02	1.13	0.50	0.81	1.15	1.27	0.23	0.41	0.56	0.62	0.31	0.54	0.85	0.97

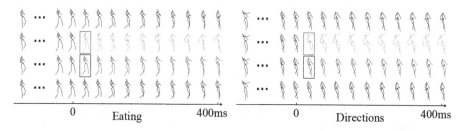

| 0 | Eating | 400ms | | 0 | Directions | 400ms |

Fig. 3. Short-term motion prediction visualizations. From top to bottom: groundtruth, sampling-based loss [31], residual sup. [31], and our AGED. As highlighted in the rectangles, discontinuities exit between the inputs and the first predicted frames (2nd rows); the predictions are further away from the groundtruth than ours (3rd rows). Our AGED produces lower-error, less-jump, and smoother predictions. **Best viewed in color with zoom.** (Color figure online)

Comparisons with State-of-the-Art Deep Learning Baselines: Table 1 shows the quantitative comparisons with the full set of deep learning baselines on 4 representative activities, including walking, smoking, eating, and discussion. Table 2 compares our approach with the best performing residual sup. baseline on the remaining 11 activities. Compared with residual sup. that uses a similar predictor network but a Euclidean loss, our geodesic loss generates more precise prediction. Our discriminators further greatly boost the performance, validating that the high-level fidelity examination of the entire predicted sequence is essential for smooth and coherent motion prediction. Their combination achieves the best performance and makes our AGED model consistently outperform the existing deep learning based approaches *in all the scenarios.*

Comparisons with the Zero-Velocity Baseline: Tables 1 and 2 also summarize the comparisons with the zero-velocity approach. Although zero-velocity does not produce interesting motion, it is difficult for the existing deep learning based approaches to outperform it quantitatively in short-term prediction, mainly on complicated actions (*e.g.*, smoking) and highly aperiodic actions (*e.g.*, sitting), which is consistent with the observations in [31]. Our AGED model shows some promising progress. (1) For *complicated motion prediction*, zero-velocity outperforms the other baselines, whereas our AGED outperforms zero-velocity, due to our adversarial discriminators. This type of action consists of small movements in upper-body, which is difficult to model as the learning based baselines only verify frame-wise predictions and ignore their temporal dependencies. By contrast, our AGED, equipped with a fidelity discriminator and a continuity discriminator, is able to check globally how smooth and human-like the entire generated sequence is, leading to significant performance improvement. (2) For *highly aperiodic motion prediction*, because these actions are very difficult to model, zero-velocity outperforms all the learning methods.

Qualitative Visualizations: Figure 3 visualizes the motion prediction results. We compare with residual sup., the best performing baseline as shown in Tables 1 and 2. Both our AGED model and residual sup. predict realistic short-term motion. One noticeable difference between them is the degree of jump (*i.e.*, discontinuity) between the last input frame and the first predicted frame. The jump in our AGED is relatively small, which is consistent with its lower prediction error and due to the introduced continuity discriminator. We also include sampling-based loss, a variant of residual sup., which shows superior qualitative visualization in long-term prediction. We observe severe discontinuities in sampling-based loss. More comparisons are shown in Fig. 1.

User Studies: Our model again outperforms the baselines by a large margin under human evaluation, as shown in Table 3. The first row summarizes the success rates of our AGED against the groundtruth and baselines. For short-term prediction, we observe that (1) our AGED has a success rate of 53.3% against the groundtruth, showing that our predictions are *on par with the groundtruth*; and (2) our AGED has a success rate of 98.6% against sampling-based loss and of 69.6% against residual sup., showing that the judges notice the jump and discontinuities between the baseline predictions and the input sequences. As a reference, the second row summarizes the success rates of the groundtruth against all the models, which have similar trends as our rates and are slightly better. These observations thus validate that users favor more realistic and plausible motion and our predictions are judged qualitatively realistic by humans.

4.2 More Ablation Studies

In addition to the comparisons between the geodesic loss and the adversarial losses in Tables 1 and 2, we conduct more thorough ablations in Table 4 to understand the impact of each loss component and their combinations. We can see that our geodesic loss is superior to the conventional Euclidean loss. This observation empirically verifies that the geodesic distance is a geometrically more meaningful and more precise measurement for 3D rotations, as also supported by the theoretical analysis in [18, 21, 43]. Moreover, our full model consistently outperforms its variants in short-term prediction, showing the effectiveness and complementarity of each component.

Table 3. Human voting results of short-term and long-term prediction videos. Each number represents the percentage that our prediction or the groundtruth is chosen from a pair of predictions as being more realistic and reasonable. The first row shows the percentages that our predictions are chosen against the groundtruth and baseline predictions. As a reference, the second row shows the percentages for the groundtruth. Our AGED predictions are on par with the groundtruth and significantly outperform baseline models

Model pair	Short-term				Long-term			
	Ours	Groundtruth	sampling-based loss [31]	residual sup. [31]	Ours	Groundtruth	sampling-based loss [31]	residual sup. [31]
Ours vs.	n/a	53.3%	98.6%	69.6%	n/a	48.7%	83.5%	93.1%
Groundtruth vs.	46.7%	n/a	99.7%	75.7%	51.3%	n/a	83.7%	94.9%

Table 4. Ablation analysis for short-term prediction. Some of the results are included from Table 1 for completeness. We compare our geodesic loss with the conventional Euclidean loss as the predictor regression loss and evaluate the impact of different discriminators and their combinations. Our full AGED model achieves the best performance, showing that the different components complement each other

milliseconds			Walking				Eating				Smoking				Discussion			
reg loss	fid dis	con dis	80	160	320	400	80	160	320	400	80	160	320	400	80	160	320	400
n/a	✓	✓	1.35	1.33	1.31	1.55	1.29	1.22	1.38	1.41	1.39	1.51	1.53	1.69	1.37	1.22	1.15	1.51
euc			0.28	0.49	0.72	0.81	0.23	0.39	0.62	0.76	0.33	0.61	1.05	1.15	0.31	0.68	1.01	1.09
euc	✓		0.27	0.43	0.66	0.74	0.23	0.35	0.58	0.71	0.28	0.52	0.94	0.90	0.42	0.62	0.87	0.93
euc		✓	0.26	0.42	0.63	0.71	0.22	0.34	0.54	0.68	0.28	0.48	0.92	0.91	0.39	0.63	0.86	0.96
euc	✓	✓	0.27	0.42	0.62	0.71	0.22	0.32	0.53	0.67	0.28	0.47	0.90	0.86	0.28	0.60	0.78	0.87
geo			0.28	0.42	0.66	0.73	0.22	0.35	0.61	0.74	0.30	0.55	0.98	0.99	0.30	0.63	0.97	1.06
geo	✓		0.24	0.39	0.62	0.71	0.22	0.32	0.56	0.68	0.27	0.46	0.89	0.87	0.33	0.59	0.80	0.91
geo		✓	0.24	0.39	0.58	0.68	0.21	0.30	0.52	0.66	0.27	0.45	0.84	0.86	0.34	0.57	0.81	0.90
geo	✓	✓	**0.22**	**0.36**	**0.55**	**0.67**	**0.17**	**0.28**	**0.51**	**0.64**	**0.27**	**0.43**	**0.82**	**0.84**	**0.27**	**0.56**	**0.76**	**0.83**

4.3   Long-Term Motion Prediction

Long-term prediction (>500 ms) is more challenging than short-term prediction due to error accumulation and the uncertainty of human motion. Given that long-term prediction is difficult to evaluate quantitatively [31], we mainly focus on the qualitative comparisons in Fig. 4 and the user studies in Table 4. For completeness, we provide representative quantitative evaluation in Table 5. Here the network is trained to minimize the loss over 1 second. While residual sup. [31] achieves the best performance among the baselines in short-term prediction, it is shown that sampling-based loss [31], a variant of residual sup. without residual connections and one-hot vector inputs, qualitatively outperforms it in long-term prediction. We show that our AGED model *consistently* outperforms these two baselines in both short-term and long-term predictions.

Table 5. Representative quantitative comparisons of mean angle error between our AGED model and state-of-the-art approaches for long-term motion prediction on 4 activities of the H3.6M dataset. Our AGED model consistently achieves the best performance

milliseconds	Walking		Eating		Smoking		Discussion	
	560	1000	560	1000	560	1000	560	1000
Zero-velocity [31]	1.35	1.32	1.04	1.38	1.02	1.69	1.41	1.96
ERD [12]	2.00	2.38	2.36	2.41	3.68	3.82	3.47	2.92
LSTM-3LR [12]	1.81	2.20	2.49	2.82	3.24	3.42	2.48	2.93
SRNN [31]	1.90	2.13	2.28	2.58	3.21	3.23	2.39	2.43
DAE-LSTM [13]	1.55	1.39	1.76	2.01	1.38	1.77	1.53	1.73
Sampling-based loss [31]	1.36	1.59	1.48	1.55	1.78	2.31	1.77	1.61
Residual sup. [31]	0.93	1.03	0.95	1.08	1.25	1.50	1.43	1.69
AGED w/ geo (Ours)	0.89	1.02	0.92	1.01	1.15	1.43	1.33	1.56
AGED w/ adv+euc (Ours)	0.87	0.99	0.87	0.96	1.16	1.38	1.31	1.39
AGED w/ adv+geo (Ours)	**0.78**	**0.91**	**0.86**	**0.93**	**1.06**	**1.21**	**1.25**	**1.30**

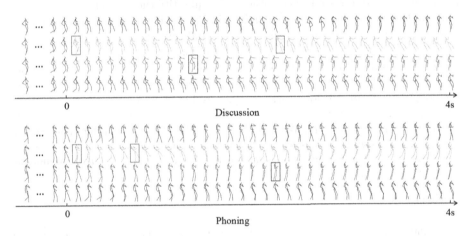

Fig. 4. Long-term motion prediction visualizations. From top to bottom for each activity: groundtruth, sampling-based loss [31], residual sup. [31], and our AGED. As highlighted in the rectangles, discontinuities exit between the inputs and the first predicted frames (2nd rows, left) and predictions drift away to unrealistic motions (2nd rows, right); predictions converge to mean poses (3rd rows). Our AGED produces more realistic, continuous, and human-like predictions. **Best viewed in color with zoom.** (Color figure online)

Qualitative Visualizations: Figure 4 shows some representative comparisons on discussion and phoning activities, which are challenging aperiodic actions. We observe that the generated predictions by residual sup. converge to mean poses and the predictions of sampling-based loss often drift away from the input sequences, making them unrealistic anymore. Our model, however, produces more plausible, continuous, and human-like prediction in long time horizons (4 seconds).

User Studies: As shown in Table 3, our model significantly improves long-term prediction based on human evaluation. Our AGED has a success rate of 48.7% against the groundtruth, showing that our predictions are still *comparable with the groundtruth*. Moreover, our AGED has success rates of 83.5% and 93.1% against sampling-based loss and residual sup., respectively, which are much larger margins of improvement compared with the corresponding rates in short-term prediction. These results demonstrate that the judges consider that our predictions are more realistic and plausible.

5   Conclusions

We present a novel adversarial geometry-aware encoder-decoder model to address the challenges in human-like motion prediction: how to make the predicted sequences temporally coherent with past sequences and more realistic. At the frame level, we propose a new geodesic loss to quantify the difference between the predicted 3D rotations and the groundtruth. We further introduce two recurrent discriminators, a fidelity discriminator and a continuity discriminator, to validate the predicted motion sequence from a global perspective. Training integrates the two objectives and is conducted in an adversarial manner. Extensive experiments on the heavily benchmarked H3.6M dataset show the effectiveness of our model for both short-term and long-term motion predictions.

Acknowledgments. We thank Richard Newcombe, Hauke Strasdat, and Steven Lovegrove for insightful discussions at Facebook Reality Labs where L.-Y. Gui was a research intern. We also thank Deva Ramanan and Hongdong Li for valuable comments.

References

1. Akhter, I., Simon, T., Khan, S., Matthews, I., Sheikh, Y.: Bilinear spatiotemporal basis models. ACM Trans. Graph. (TOG) **31**(2), 17:1–17:12 (2012)
2. Arjovsky, M., Chintala, S., Bottou, L.: Wasserstein GAN, January 2017. arXiv preprint arXiv:1701.07875
3. Bahdanau, D., Cho, K., Bengio, Y.: Neural machine translation by jointly learning to align and translate. In: International Conference on Learning Representations (ICLR), San Diego, CA, USA, May 2015
4. Barsoum, E., Kender, J., Liu, Z.: HP-GAN: probabilistic 3D human motion prediction via GAN, November 2017. arXiv preprint arXiv:1711.09561
5. Bengio, S., Vinyals, O., Jaitly, N., Shazeer, N.: Scheduled sampling for sequence prediction with recurrent neural networks. In: Advances in Neural Information Processing Systems (NIPS), Montréal, Canada, pp. 1171–1179, December 2015
6. Bengio, Y., Louradour, J., Collobert, R., Weston, J.: Curriculum learning. In: International Conference on Machine Learning (ICML), Montréal, Canada, pp. 41–48, June 2009
7. Brand, M., Hertzmann, A.: Style machines. In: ACM International Conference on Computer Graphics and Interactive Techniques (SIGGRAPH), New Orleans, LA, USA, pp. 183–192, July 2000

8. Bütepage, J., Black, M.J., Kragic, D., Kjellström, H.: Deep representation learning for human motion prediction and classification. In: IEEE Conference on Computer Vision and Pattern Recognition (CVPR), Honolulu, HI, USA, pp. 1591–1599, July 2017

9. Cho, K., Van Merriënboer, B., Bahdanau, D., Bengio, Y.: On the properties of neural machine translation: encoder-decoder approaches. In: Workshop on Syntax, Semantics and Structure in Statistical Translation (SSST), Doha, Qatar, pp. 103–111, October 2014

10. Denton, E.L., Chintala, S., Fergus, R.: Deep generative image models using a Laplacian pyramid of adversarial networks. In: Advances in Neural Information Processing Systems (NIPS), Montréal, Canada, pp. 1486–1494, December 2015

11. Einicke, G.A.: Smoothing, filtering and prediction: estimating the past, present and future. InTech, February 2012

12. Fragkiadaki, K., Levine, S., Felsen, P., Malik, J.: Recurrent network models for human dynamics. In: IEEE International Conference on Computer Vision (ICCV), Las Condes, Chile, pp. 4346–4354, December 2015

13. Ghosh, P., Song, J., Aksan, E., Hilliges, O.: Learning human motion models for long-term predictions. In: International Conference on 3D Vision (3DV), Qingdao, China, pp. 458–466, October 2017

14. Goodfellow, I., et al.: Generative adversarial nets. In: Advances in Neural Information Processing Systems (NIPS), Montréal, Canada, pp. 2672–2680, December 2014

15. Grassia, F.S.: Practical parameterization of rotations using the exponential map. J. Graph. Tools 3(3), 29–48 (1998)

16. Gui, L.Y., Wang, Y.X., Ramanan, D., Moura, J.M.F.: Few-shot human motion prediction via meta-learning. In: European Conference on Computer Vision (ECCV), Munich, Germany, September 2018

17. Gui, L.Y., Zhang, K., Wang, Y.X., Liang, X., Moura, J.M.F., Veloso, M.M.: Teaching robots to predict human motion. In: IEEE/RSJ International Conference on Intelligent Robots (IROS), Madrid, Spain, October 2018

18. Hartley, R., Trumpf, J., Dai, Y., Li, H.: Rotation averaging. Int. J. Comput. Vis. (IJCV) 103(3), 267–305 (2013)

19. Hochreiter, S., Schmidhuber, J.: Long short-term memory. Neural Comput. 9(8), 1735–1780 (1997)

20. Huang, D.-A., Kitani, K.M.: Action-reaction: forecasting the dynamics of human interaction. In: Fleet, D., Pajdla, T., Schiele, B., Tuytelaars, T. (eds.) ECCV 2014. LNCS, vol. 8695, pp. 489–504. Springer, Cham (2014). https://doi.org/10.1007/978-3-319-10584-0_32

21. Huynh, D.Q.: Metrics for 3D rotations: comparison and analysis. J. Math. Imaging Vis. 35(2), 155–164 (2009)

22. Ionescu, C., Papava, D., Olaru, V., Sminchisescu, C.: Human3.6M: large scale datasets and predictive methods for 3D human sensing in natural environments. IEEE Trans. Pattern Anal. Mach. Intell. (TPAMI) 36(7), 1325–1339 (2014)

23. Isola, P., Zhu, J.Y., Zhou, T., Efros, A.A.: Image-to-image translation with conditional adversarial networks. In: IEEE Conference on Computer Vision and Pattern Recognition (CVPR), Honolulu, HI, USA, pp. 5967–5976, July 2017

24. Jain, A., Zamir, A.R., Savarese, S., Saxena, A.: Structural-RNN: deep learning on spatio-temporal graphs. In: IEEE Conference on Computer Vision and Pattern Recognition (CVPR), Las Vegas, NV, USA, pp. 5308–5317, June–July 2016

25. Jong, M.D., et al.: Towards a robust interactive and learning social robot. In: International Conference on Autonomous Agents and Multiagent Systems (AAMAS 2018), Stockholm, Sweden, July 2018
26. Kiros, R., et al.: Skip-thought vectors. In: Advances in Neural Information Processing Systems (NIPS), Montréal, Canada, pp. 3294–3302, December 2015
27. Koppula, H., Saxena, A.: Learning spatio-temporal structure from RGB-D videos for human activity detection and anticipation. In: International Conference on Machine Learning (ICML), Atlanta, GA, USA, pp. 792–800, June 2013
28. Koppula, H.S., Saxena, A.: Anticipating human activities using object affordances for reactive robotic response. IEEE Trans. Pattern Anal. Mach. Intell. (TPAMI) **38**(1), 14–29 (2016)
29. Kovar, L., Gleicher, M., Pighin, F.: Motion graphs. In: ACM International Conference on Computer Graphics and Interactive Techniques (SIGGRAPH), San Antonio, TX, USA, pp. 473–482, July 2002
30. Liang, X., Lee, L., Dai, W., Xing, E.P.: Dual motion GAN for future-flow embedded video prediction. In: IEEE International Conference on Computer Vision (ICCV), Venice, Italy, pp. 1762–1770, October 2017
31. Martinez, J., Black, M.J., Romero, J.: On human motion prediction using recurrent neural networks. In: IEEE Conference on Computer Vision and Pattern Recognition (CVPR), Honolulu, HI, USA, pp. 4674–4683, July 2017
32. Mathieu, M., Couprie, C., LeCun, Y.: Deep multi-scale video prediction beyond mean square error. In: International Conference on Learning Representations (ICLR), San Juan, PR, USA, May 2016
33. Murray, R.M., Li, Z., Sastry, S.S., Sastry, S.S.: A Mathematical Introduction to Robotic Manipulation, 1st edn. CRC Press, Boca Raton (1994)
34. Oh, J., Guo, X., Lee, H., Lewis, R.L., Singh, S.: Action-conditional video prediction using deep networks in Atari games. In: Advances in Neural Information Processing Systems (NIPS), Montréal, Canada, pp. 2863–2871, December 2015
35. Paden, B., Čáp, M., Yong, S.Z., Yershov, D., Frazzoli, E.: A survey of motion planning and control techniques for self-driving urban vehicles. IEEE Trans. Intell. Veh. (T-IV) **1**(1), 33–55 (2016)
36. Paszke, A., et al.: Automatic differentiation in PyTorch. In: Advances in Neural Information Processing Systems (NIPS) Workshops, Long Beach, CA, USA, December 2017
37. Pathak, D., Krähenbühl, P., Donahue, J., Darrell, T., Efros, A.: Context encoders: feature learning by inpainting. In: IEEE Conference on Computer Vision and Pattern Recognition (CVPR), Las Vegas, LV, USA, pp. 2536–2544, June–July 2016
38. Pavlovic, V., Rehg, J.M., MacCormick, J.: Learning switching linear models of human motion. In: Advances in Neural Information Processing Systems (NIPS), Vancouver, Canada, pp. 981–987, December 2001
39. Pennec, X., Thirion, J.P.: A framework for uncertainty and validation of 3-D registration methods based on points and frames. Int. J. Comput. Vis. (IJCV) **25**(3), 203–229 (1997)
40. Radford, A., Metz, L., Chintala, S.: Unsupervised representation learning with deep convolutional generative adversarial networks. In: International Conference on Learning Representations (ICLR), San Juan, PR, USA, May 2016
41. Reed, S., Akata, Z., Yan, X., Logeswaran, L., Schiele, B., Lee, H.: Generative adversarial text to image synthesis. In: International Conference on Machine Learning (ICML), New York, USA, pp. 1060–1069, June 2016

42. Ren, M., Kiros, R., Zemel, R.: Exploring models and data for image question answering. In: Advances in Neural Information Processing Systems (NIPS), Montréal, Canada, pp. 2953–2961, December 2015
43. Rossmann, W.: Lie Groups: An Introduction Through Linear Groups, vol. 5. Oxford University Press, Oxford (2002)
44. Rumelhart, D.E., Hinton, G.E., Williams, R.J.: Learning representations by back-propagating errors. Nature **323**(6088), 533–536 (1986)
45. Sutskever, I., Hinton, G.E., Taylor, G.W.: The recurrent temporal restricted Boltzmann machine. In: Advances in Neural Information Processing Systems (NIPS), Vancouver, Canada, pp. 1601–1608, December 2009
46. Sutskever, I., Vinyals, O., Le, Q.V.: Sequence to sequence learning with neural networks. In: Advances in Neural Information Processing Systems (NIPS), Montréal, Canada, pp. 3104–3112, December 2014
47. Taylor, G.W., Hinton, G.E.: Factored conditional restricted Boltzmann machines for modeling motion style. In: International Conference on Machine Learning (ICML), Montréal, Canada, pp. 1025–1032, June 2009
48. Taylor, G.W., Hinton, G.E., Roweis, S.T.: Modeling human motion using binary latent variables. In: Advances in Neural Information Processing Systems (NIPS), Vancouver, Canada, pp. 1345–1352, December 2007
49. Taylor, G.W., Sigal, L., Fleet, D.J., Hinton, G.E.: Dynamical binary latent variable models for 3D human pose tracking. In: IEEE Conference on Computer Vision and Pattern Recognition (CVPR), San Francisco, CA, USA, pp. 631–638, June 2010
50. Urtasun, R., Fleet, D.J., Geiger, A., Popović, J., Darrell, T.J., Lawrence, N.D.: Topologically-constrained latent variable models. In: International Conference on Machine Learning (ICML), Helsinki, Finland, pp. 1080–1087, July 2008
51. Vondrick, C., Pirsiavash, H., Torralba, A.: Generating videos with scene dynamics. In: Advances in Neural Information Processing Systems (NIPS), Barcelona, Spain, pp. 613–621, December 2016
52. Walker, J., Marino, K., Gupta, A., Hebert, M.: The pose knows: video forecasting by generating pose futures. In: IEEE International Conference on Computer Vision (ICCV), Venice, Italy, pp. 3352–3361, October 2017
53. Wang, J.M., Fleet, D.J., Hertzmann, A.: Gaussian process dynamical models for human motion. IEEE Trans. Pattern Anal. Mach. Intell. (TPAMI) **30**(2), 283–298 (2008)
54. Werbos, P.J.: Backpropagation through time: what it does and how to do it. Proc. IEEE **78**(10), 1550–1560 (1990)
55. Williams, R.J., Zipser, D.: A learning algorithm for continually running fully recurrent neural networks. Neural Comput. **1**(2), 270–280 (1989)
56. Wu, J., Zhang, C., Xue, T., Freeman, B., Tenenbaum, J.: Learning a probabilistic latent space of object shapes via 3D generative-adversarial modeling. In: Advances in Neural Information Processing Systems (NIPS), Barcelona, Spain, pp. 82–90, December 2016
57. Xue, T., Wu, J., Bouman, K., Freeman, B.: Visual dynamics: probabilistic future frame synthesis via cross convolutional networks. In: Advances in Neural Information Processing Systems (NIPS), Barcelona, Spain, pp. 91–99, December 2016

58. Yang, Z., Yuan, Y., Wu, Y., Cohen, W.W., Salakhutdinov, R.R.: Review networks for caption generation. In: Advances in Neural Information Processing Systems (NIPS), Barcelona, Spain, pp. 2361–2369, December 2016

59. Zhou, Y., Berg, T.L.: Learning temporal transformations from time-lapse videos. In: Leibe, B., Matas, J., Sebe, N., Welling, M. (eds.) ECCV 2016. LNCS, vol. 9912, pp. 262–277. Springer, Cham (2016). https://doi.org/10.1007/978-3-319-46484-8_16

60. Zhu, J.Y., Park, T., Isola, P., Efros, A.A.: Unpaired image-to-image translation using cycle-consistent adversarial networks. In: IEEE International Conference on Computer Vision (ICCV), Venice, Italy, pp. 2223–2232, October 2017

Author Index